Sexual Assault and Child Sexual Abuse

A National Directory of Victim/Survivor Services and Prevention Programs

Sexual Assault and Child Sexual Abuse

A National Directory of Victim/Survivor Services and Prevention Programs

Compiled and Edited by Linda Webster

ORYX PRESS
1989

The rare Arabian Oryx is believed to have inspired the myth of the unicorn. This desert antelope became virtually extinct in the early 1960s. At that time several groups of international conservationists arranged to have 9 animals sent to the Phoenix Zoo to be the nucleus of a captive breeding herd. Today the Oryx population is nearly 800, and over 400 have been returned to reserves in the Middle East.

Copyright © 1989 by
The Oryx Press
2214 North Central at Encanto
Phoenix, Arizona 85004-1483

Published simultaneously in Canada

All rights reserved
No part of this publication may be reproduced or transmitted in any form or by any means, electronic or mechanical, including photocopying, recording, or by any information storage and retrieval system, without permission in writing from The Oryx Press.

Printed and Bound in the United States of America

Library of Congress Cataloging-in-Publication Data

Webster, Linda, 1947–
  Sexual assault and child sexual abuse.

  Includes indexes.
  1. Adult child sexual abuse victims—
Services for—United States—Directories. 2. Rape victims—Services for—United States—Directories.
I. Title.
RC569.5.A28W43   362.88′3   89-8549
ISBN 0-89774-445-4

For Cynthia Medina, who taught me about courage and daring, and had confidence in me while I learned.
For my daughter Karen, my son Ben, and for all of us, that we may be joyous and free.

> We walked straight through our fears
> We formed the circle
> We danced
> We spoke the truth
> We dared to live it

Excerpt from *Truth or Dare* by Starhawk. Copyright ©1987 by Miriam Simos. Reprinted by permission of Harper & Row, Publishers, Inc.

CONTENTS

Foreword ix
Introduction xiii
Basic Services xix
Acknowledgments xxiii
List of Abbreviations xxv
Main Entry Section—Agency Profiles 1
Appendix A—State Agencies 303
Appendix B—National Organizations and Resources 318
Alphabetical List of Facilities in Agency Profiles 327
Index to Specialized Services and Clientele in Agency Profiles 342

FOREWORD

by Nancy Fride Biele

When I was asked to write a Foreword to *Sexual Assault and Child Sexual Abuse: A National Directory of Victim/Survivor Services and Prevention Programs* that discussed some of the historical perspective on sexual assault services and some of my thoughts on the future, I was somewhat overwhelmed by the idea of doing that in a short space. Fifteen years ago I began working in the anti-sexual assault movement, first as a founding mother, advocate and board member of the Program on Aid to Victims of Sexual Assault in Duluth, Minnesota. I have held varying roles with Twin Cities Women for Take Back the Night, the Minnesota Coalition of Sexual Assault Services and the National Coalition Against Sexual Assault. We have as a movement learned so much. There are so many more resources; so much research has been done; there is even some money available to provide services. Still, it has taken years for sexual assault to be seen as a public issue rather than personal trouble.

STATISTICS ABOUT SEXUAL ASSAULT

One of the questions I'm asked most often is just how much sexual assault actually occurs? People want exact, national figures. They make assumptions that sexual assault gets reported now, and police statistics are correct. I must explain over and over again that women and children and men are not reporting sexual abuse to the police that much more than they were a few years ago. Rape is still the most underreported of felonies. Individual states have different laws so that what is a crime in one state may not be in another. Degrees of criminality differ. At the rape centers, our definitions are probably the broadest and most comprehensive of all because we are less concerned about the ability to prosecute than we are the victim/survivor's perception and healing. Another problem with statistics is the seeming inability of the community to mobilize unless there are huge numbers. One victim of sexual assault is too many.

Nevertheless, there are a number of studies and statistics to provide in the "numbers game:"

- Diana Russell's landmark study (1984) showed 28% of females being sexually victimized by age 14, 38% by age 18. In the same study, one in every seven women who had been married had either an attempted or completed rape by the husband.
- A report by the Center for the Prevention of Domestic and Sexual Violence (1985) indicates one in seven boys are victims by age 18.
- The American Humane Society reported 100,000 cases of child sexual abuse in 1984, a 35% increase over 1983.
- Regarding acquaintance rape, Mary Koss' 1985 study shows that 38 women per 1,000 had been victims of rape or attempted rape in the six months preceding the survey. Twenty-five percent of women in that study had been victims of rape or attempted rape.
- A study done at Auburn University found that out of 600 victims of acquaintance rape, four had reported to the police.
- Sexual harassment costs the average major firm 6.7 million dollars in related costs. According to Chapman and Chapman (1984) approximately 20 million women in the U.S. labor force are victims of sexual harassment annually.
- Sexual abuse of the elderly accounted for 13% of the 1046 substantiated cases under the Vulnerable Adults Act in Minnesota in 1985. Some of the assaults, such as sexual exploitation by counselors and ritualistic abuse are harder to document, but our numbers of reports are increasing.

There is no evidence to show that sexual assault is decreasing.

Nancy Fride Biele is executive director of the Sexual Violence Center in Minneapolis, Minnesota.

THE HISTORY OF RAPE

I would like for a moment to delve far back into the history of rape. That rape has a history is important to those of us who would like to deny it a future. It need not be a part of the human condition or a piece of the natural order as was so long believed. So, perhaps it is helpful for us to understand where we come from. Unfortunately, most of what we have to study from ancient time was derived from law, and law has been written by men of property to protect men of property. We have few stories of how the women felt, or what they really experienced.

Early history is full of references to rape. Mythology and early law are full of misunderstanding of and rationalizations for rape. Victims were blamed instead of rapists. Rape was seen as a property crime against the man who "owned" the woman; thus, damages were paid to the victim's father or husband. Rape was a regulated part of conquest among warring tribes and countries. Bride capture, an often calculated attempt of acquiring property or higher social standing, has been common in many cultures. Sexual contact, whether forced or willing, was a sign of permanent possession. There was also a belief that victims were defiled or dirty; under some laws the husband of a raped woman was legally compelled to divorce her lest he also become tainted. There was also the suspicion in both tradition and law that rape is really a matter of sexual consent; women could always have avoided the act. In more recent eras, rape began to be quietly discussed under the guise of "unspeakable things" happening to women. There was a characteristic view of women as pure and chaste and men as base and lustful. Therefore, women needed constant protection. Always, class, culture and race were important factors in how a rape was viewed and dealt with; the social norms and laws were often used as tools of social control by the dominant culture.

So where are we now? We would like to believe we have come a long way. However, each of the pieces of "tradition" from ancient history still affects our work. There are vestiges left in our laws, in our systems and certainly in the community's attitudes. But in the last 20 years, we have begun talking. When the anti-rape movement began, the naming began. First, stranger rape was what was disclosed most often; then women began to talk about prior victimization, about child sexual abuse and incest. As our knowledge grew, acquaintance rape, sexual harassment and marital rape were recognized. As we move into the second decade, we are dealing with sexual exploitation by counselors, therapists and clergy as well as with ritualistic abuse. Pornography and prostitution have emerged as victim issues. Naming the sources of the violence was an important piece of the anti-rape work—naming the oppressions of racism, of sexism, of class inequality, of the dominant culture's efforts to remain in power. The earliest anti-rape movement had as its goal the elimination of sexual assault in our society and, in the meantime, to aid survivors.

RAPE CRISIS CENTERS

Rape crisis centers were born out of the most recent phase of the women's movement in the late 1960s which derived some of its direction from the civil rights movement of the early 1960s. Community, grass-roots organizing against social ills flourished. Political organizations formed for and about women. And women began to speak about their experiences with sexual assault. First in small groups and then in larger speakouts, women began to share the histories and the pain and the rage that would form into a new social movement to end violence against women. Some of the history of that first surge of energy is sketchy. The first community-based rape crisis center seems to be (and there is some dispute as to who was the very first) Bay Area Women Against Rape in Berkeley in late 1969. About six or seven additional rape crisis centers were founded in other cities within the next year or two. In 1973, the National Organization for Women established a National Task Force on Rape and initiated task forces in local communities; by 1974 there were 136 NOW-affiliated anti-rape projects in 39 states. By that same year there were 61 rape crisis centers identified in 27 states. There was an accepted definition of a rape crisis center offering a hotline or other services, some specific training (sporadic at first) and some standardized protocol for victims. The National Center for the Prevention and Control of Rape was established in 1976 to sponsor research and training. Over the years, rape centers have helped to materially improve the lives of survivors, have given women a sense of power and strength enabling them to build structures for further change, educated women politically thereby enhancing the ability to criticize and challenge systems in the future, and aided in weakening the patriarchal control of society's institutions and enabling women to gain control.

NETWORKING AND COOPERATION

Throughout all of the growth process in providing services and educating the public and professionals, one of the most important aspects of this movement has been the networking, the sharing of information that has formed our belief system. For too long, isolation reigned. Survivors believed that they were the only ones that sexual violence had happened to; no one else talked about it. Then a few groups started taking action in their communities; they had neither the time nor the money to begin connecting with others. As people began to recognize the value of connecting with other survivors and others in the anti-sexual assault movement, statewide coalitions and national organizations have formed (and are still forming!). We have realized that we don't have to reinvent the wheel on every issue and service. We are also an increasingly mobile society and cross-country referrals and trainings are common. This underscores the importance of resource directories such as this one. Collective energy found in sharing resources is a fundamental need if the anti-sexual assault movement is going to realize its goals of providing safe places for survivors to heal and take action and to change the society that permits the oppression of women and children and the sexual violence against them.

INTRODUCTION

VICTIM TO SURVIVOR

Sexual assault and child sexual abuse continue to impact the lives of many girls and boys, women and men. Consider the following statistics. One in three girls and one in six boys will be sexually abused before the age of 18. In about half of these cases, the perpetrator is in a family-type relationship with the child (1). Twenty-five percent of women in college have been victims of rape or attempted rape. Eighty-four percent of these women knew their assailants; fifty-seven percent of the rapes happened on dates. At the same time, one in twelve male students admit committing acts that met the legal definitions of rape or attempted rape, yet virtually none of these men identify themselves as rapists (2). Nearly four out of ten women report having been raped; one in seven women report having been raped by their husbands (3). One in eleven men is sexually assaulted (4). As a result of the assault/abuse, victims experience feelings of fear, guilt, shame, grief, despair, loss of self-confidence, stress-related illness, betrayal and loss of trust. And the impact of the assault/abuse extends to all areas of the individual's life and to all their relationships—home, work, school.

Sexual assault can include several kinds of crimes: rape, sexual harassment, child molestation, marital rape, exposure and voyeurism (5). Child sexual abuse is defined as "a sexual act imposed on a child who cannot reasonably choose to consent or refuse because of age, understanding or relationship to the offender. Sexual abuse can include touching and nontouching acts, sexual exploitation and permitting a child to participate in prostitution" (6). Contact can take many forms: fondling of the breasts or genitals; oral, vaginal or anal intercourse (penetration by genitals or by an object); or exposing sexual parts of the body. When sexual contact occurs within a family, the sexual abuse is called incest (7).

Recovery from sexual assault and abuse takes time. It requires that the abuse be stopped and that the victim be protected from further abuse/assault. It may involve the victim in the investigation and prosecution of the crime. It also involves opportunities for the victim/survivor to talk with others about the crime, to get support for the immediate after-shock of the crisis, and to participate in longer-term counseling, support groups, and healing experiences with other survivors.

While the magnitude of the crime of sexual assault/abuse is staggering, in recent years many new agencies and new services have developed to assist victim/survivors and their families. *Sexual Assault and Child Sexual Abuse: A National Directory of Victim/Survivor Services and Prevention Programs* is designed to assist victims/survivors, their families and friends, to find the help they need.

This directory includes rape crisis centers, domestic violence shelters, victim assistance programs, and counseling and mental health centers with services for child victims of sexual abuse and their families. The directory also includes programs and support groups for adult survivors of childhood sexual abuse. In addition, there are child sexual abuse prevention programs, date rape and dating violence prevention programs, and self-defense classes for women and children. Offender treatment programs are also included. For more information on the basic services provided by the most common agencies dealing with sexual assault, see the next section on Basic Services.

Underlying the diversity of programs and services in this directory is the basic commitment to assist individuals as they move from victims to survivors. Marie Fortune describes "victim" as "one who has been made powerless by the actions of another and thus is harmed in some way." A "survivor" is "a former victim who is no longer being harmed by an abusive situation but who carries that as part of her/his history. . . . 'Survivor' also connotes a condition of healing and empowerment and frequently a pro-active stance of choosing to no longer be victimized by the memory of an abusive . . . experience" (8).

CONTENT OF THE DIRECTORY

Sexual Assault and Child Sexual Abuse: A National Directory of Victim/Survivor Services and Prevention Programs includes approximately 2,700 local agencies, 268 state agencies/organizations, and 100 national organizations in the United States that are concerned with sexual assault and child sexual abuse. Included are agencies that responded to questionnaire or telephone inquiries and whose focus is on services for sexual assault and child sexual abuse victims/survivors. No attempt was made to judge the quality of services provided. Inclusion in this directory does not constitute recommendation. Descriptions of programs and services were provided by the agencies profiled.

Many additional community agencies provide general crisis and counseling services that can include victims/survivors of sexual assault and abuse but are not necessarily geared to their special needs. For example, community crisis hotlines, local women's commissions, and women's centers often provide information and referral services. Many local agencies come in contact with victims/survivors in the course of providing other services; for instance, legal aid programs, campus mental health centers, runaway youth shelters, and substance abuse programs. Individual counselors and therapists in private practice have clients who are victims/survivors. Local child protective agencies and law enforcement agencies investigate reports of child abuse, including sexual abuse, and sexual assault. This directory is not intended to be a comprehensive resource for these types of services.

USERS OF THE DIRECTORY

Victims/survivors and their families can use the directory to find local services. Service providers can use the directory for referrals when clients move or need additional services. Those interested in offender treatment programs or prevention programs can find resources here. Hotlines, women's centers, human services agencies, state/national referral centers, and libraries can use this information to augment their existing referral files. Finally, this directory describes an array of expertise and resources that can be used for regional and national networking.

HOW THE DIRECTORY IS ORGANIZED

There are five sections in this directory. The main section, Agency Profiles, includes local listings, which are organized by state and then alphabetically by city. Within each city, agencies and organizations are arranged alphabetically by name.

Each entry includes agency name, address, crisis and information telephone numbers, when available, and contact name. The type of agency is indicated, as are the clients/services. The entry indicates geographic areas served by the agency; the names given are most often counties, but some cities and regional areas are also listed. Additional information includes years in operation, accessibility for individuals with disabilities, and the percentage of agency cases involving sexual assault. Many listings do not include a description of basic services. Instead, consult the section following this one, Basic Services, for descriptions of typical services provided by the most prevalent types of agencies. Some listings include requirements for services and a description of special programs/services.

The amount of information in the local entries varies based on the amount of information submitted by the agencies. Respondents were given the option of completing a short form of the questionnaire as well as the opportunity to send additional information about their programs. Some agencies contacted by phone are included with brief information only.

The second section, Appendix A, includes state listings, which are organized by state and then alphabetically by the name of the agency or organization. Included here are the state coalitions against sexual assault and the state agencies that administer state and federal funds for rape crisis centers. State agencies responsible for child protective services are in this section, as well as descriptions of child abuse reporting procedures. Also included are state committees to prevent child abuse. Some states have additional listings, based on responses to questionnaires.

The third section, Appendix B, includes national listings, which are grouped by subject categories and then arranged alphabetically by the name of the organization. Included in this section are national associations for service providers, information clearinghouses, research centers, and publishers. There are also nationwide prevention and self-help programs with local chapters. Some of these national organizations provide referrals to local services. These have been marked with an asterisk.

There are two indexes to the local agencies listed in Agency Profiles. First is an alphabetical listing of the agencies. The geographic location is listed in the index, rather than the page number, for locating the agency listing in the directory.

The second index lists the specialized services and clientele that many agencies deal with, since this directory often provides information on specially developed programs for clientele such as lesbians, minority groups and the elderly. Directory listings also indicate special programs providing opportunities for healing from sexual assault. These include art, writing, dance, music, and wilderness therapy. In addition, the directory also identifies the availability of publications or nonprint media from local agencies. To locate these special features, consult the Index of Specialized Services and Clientele in Agency Profiles.

State and national organizations are not included in the indexes.

HOW TO LOCATE ADDITIONAL SERVICES

If a particular town is not listed in this directory or if needed services are not listed in a specific city, here are a number of suggestions:

1. Check the telephone book or directory assistance. A new program may have been started since the directory was published.
2. Call an agency in this directory and ask for referrals. Rape crisis centers are equipped to provide referrals to a variety of community services, including individual therapists in private practice.
3. Locate agencies in this directory from neighboring communities. Check in the Agency Profile listings under "Areas Served," since many agencies cover a multicounty area.
4. If there is a nearby college or university, contact the campus mental health center or student services office. Sometimes campus services are available to community residents on a short-term basis or for a modest fee. Campus counselors may also be able to provide referrals.
5. Contact state organizations or governmental agencies for referrals to local services. For example, the state coalition against sexual assault can provide a referral to the nearest rape crisis center. The state agency funding victim assistance programs can identify a nearby victim assistance program. (See Appendix A, State Agencies, of this directory for phone numbers and contact names.)
6. Some national organizations provide referrals to local services. In Appendix B, National Organizations and Resources, refer to those marked with an asterisk for phone numbers and contact names.

HOW THE DIRECTORY WAS COMPILED

This directory traces its ancestry to the National Directory: Rape Prevention and Treatment Resources, published in 1981 by the National Center for the Prevention and Control of Rape. In compiling the directory, I consulted the following publications:

Child Welfare League of America. *CWLA Directory 1986-87*. Washington, D.C.: Child Welfare League of America, 1986.

Directory of Child Sexual Abuse Treatment Programs. Denver, Colo.: Denver Research Institute, 1986. Prepared for National Center on Child Abuse and Neglect.

Family Service America. *1988 Directory*. Milwaukee, Wis.: FSA, 1988.

National Coalition Against Domestic Violence. *1986 National Directory of Domestic Violence Programs*. Washington, D.C.: NCADV, 1986

National Coalition Against Sexual Assault. *NCASA Directory 1988*. Washington, D.C.: NCASA, 1988.

National Directory of Children & Youth Services 1988-89. 5th ed. Longmont, Colo.: National Directory, 1987.

National Organization of Victim Assistance. *Directory*. Washington, D.C.: NOVA, 1986?

Pennsylvania Coalition Against Rape. *Sexual Assault Services: A National Directory*. Harrisburg, Pa.: PCAR, 1986-87.

RAVEN. *The Ending Men's Violence National Referral Directory. 1st ed. and supplement*. St. Louis, Mo.: RAVEN, 1986.

The Self-Help Sourcebook. 2nd ed. Denville, N.J.: Saint Clares-Riverside Medical Center, Self-Help Clearinghouse, 1988.

Survivor's Network Directory, 1988. Tarzana, Calif.: Survivors Network, 1988.

Warrior, Betsy. *Battered Women's Directory*. Richmond, Ind.: Earlham College, 1985.

In addition, the National Victims Center (Fort Worth, Texas) and the National Women's Mailing List (Jenner, California) provided printouts of their databases. Lists of rape crisis centers, domestic violence shelters, and victim assistance programs were sent by state agencies and state coalitions. I did three mailings to approximately 10,000 agencies from July 1988 through January 1989. I received additional referrals from people who responded to the questionnaire.

UPDATING THE DIRECTORY

To be included in the next edition, send your name and the name and address of the agency to: Linda Webster, 2202-A Pompton Dr., Austin, TX 78758. I also welcome comments and suggestions.

REFERENCES

1. Wisconsin Coalition Against Sexual Assault, "Child Sexual Abuse/Incest Facts," *Connections* 3 (March 1989).

2. Robin Warshaw. *I Never Called It Rape: The Ms. Report on Recognizing, Fighting, and Surviving Date and Acquaintance Rape*. New York: Harper & Row, 1988.

3. Diana Russell. *Sexual Exploitation*. Beverly Hills, Calif.: Sage Publications, 1984.

4. Center for the Prevention of Domestic and Sexual Violence. Seattle, 1985.

5. National Coalition Against Sexual Assault. "Information about Rape and Sexual Assault" (National Coalition Against Sexual Assault, 1987).

6. Wisconsin Coalition Against Sexual Assault. "Child Sexual Abuse/Incest Facts," *Connections* 3 (March 1989).

7. National Coalition Against Sexual Assault, "Information about Child Sexual Abuse" (National Coalition Against Sexual Assault, 1987).

8. Marie Fortune. "Making Justice: Sources of Healing for Incest Survivors," *Woman of Power* 5 (Winter 1987), pp. 34-35.

FOR MORE INFORMATION

ADULT SURVIVORS OF CHILD SEXUAL ABUSE

Bass, Ellen and Laura Davis. *The Courage to Heal: A Guide for Women Survivors of Child Sexual Abuse.* New York: Harper & Row, 1988.

Bear, Euan and Peter T. Dimock. *Adults Molested as Children: A Survivor's Manual for Women & Men.* Orwell, Vt.: The Safer Society Press, 1988.

Cleveland, Dianne. *Incest: The Story of Three Women.* Lexington, Mass.: Lexington Books, 1986.

Daugherty, Lynn B. *Why Me? Help for Victims of Child Sexual Abuse (Even If They Are Adults Now).* Racine, Wis.: Mother Courage Press, 1984.

Evert, Kathy and Inie Bijkerk. *When You're Ready: A Woman's Healing from Childhood Physical and Sexual Abuse by Her Mother.* Walnut Creek, Calif.: Launch Press, 1987.

Gil, Eliana. *Outgrowing the Pain: A Book for and about Adults Abused as Children.* San Francisco, Calif.: Launch Press, 1983.

Lew, Mike. *Victims No Longer: Men Recovering from Incest and Other Sexual Child Abuse.* New York: Nevraumont Publishing Co., 1988.

Maltz, Wendy and Beverly Holman. *Incest and Sexuality: A Guide to Understanding and Healing.* Lexington, Mass.: Lexington Books, 1987.

CHILD SEXUAL ABUSE AND INCEST

Butler, Sandra. *Conspiracy of Silence: The Trauma of Incest.* Rev. ed. San Francisco: Volcano Press, 1985.

Finkelhor, David. *Sexually Victimized Children.* New York: Free Press, 1979.

Finkelhor, David and Associates. *A Sourcebook on Child Sexual Abuse.* Newbury Park, Calif.: Sage, 1986.

Rush, Florence. *The Best Kept Secret: Sexual Abuse of Children.* New York: McGraw-Hill Book Company, 1980.

Russell, Diana E. H. *The Secret Trauma: Incest in the Lives of Girls and Women.* New York: Basic Books, 1986.

Satullo, Jane A., Roberta Russell and Pat A. Bradway. *It Happens to Boys Too.* Pittsfield, Mass.: Rape Crisis Center of the Berkshires Press, 1987.

Ward, Elizabeth. *Father-Daughter Rape.* New York: Grove Press, 1985.

FOR PARENTS AND TEACHERS

Adams, Caren, Jennifer Fay and Jan Loreen-Martin. *NO Is Not Enough: Helping Teenagers Avoid Sexual Assault.* San Luis Obispo, Calif.: Impact Publishers, 1984.

Adams, Caren and Jennifer Fay. *Protecting Your Child from Sexual Assault.* San Luis Obispo, Calif.: Impact Publishers, 1981.

Bateman, Py and Gayle Stringer. *Where Do I Start? A Parents' Guide for Talking to Teens About Acquaintance Rape.* Dubuque, Ia.: Kendall/Hunt Publishing Company, 1984.

Byerly, Carolyn M. *The Mother's Book: How to Survive the Incest of Your Child.* Dubuque, Ia.: Kendall/Hunt Publishing Company, 1985.

Colao, Flora and Tamar Hosansky. *Your Children Should Know.* New York: Harper & Row, 1987.

"He Told Me Not to Tell: A Parent's Guide for Talking to Your Child about Sexual Assault." Renton, Wash.: King County Rape Relief, 1979.

Nelson, Mary and Kay Clark, eds. *The Educator's Guide to Preventing Child Sexual Abuse.* Santa Cruz, Calif.: Network Publications, 1986.

Sanford, Linda T. *Silent Children: A Parent's Guide to the Prevention of Child Sexual Abuse.* New York: McGraw-Hill, 1980.

OFFENDERS

Freeman-Longo, Robert E. and Laren Bays. *Who Am I and Why Am I in Treatment? A Guided Workbook for Clients in Evaluation and Beginning Treatment.* Orwell, Vt.: The Safer Society Press, 1988. S.O.S. (Sex-Offenders' Studies) Series, no. 1.

Gil, Eliana. *Children Who Molest: A Guide for Parents of Young Sex Offenders.* Walnut Creek, Calif.: Launch Press, 1987.

Groth, A. Nicholas, with H. Jean Birnbaum. *Men Who Rape: The Psychology of the Offender.* New York: Plenum Press, 1979.

Knopp, Fay Honey. *Female Sexual Abusers.* Orwell, Vt.: The Safer Society Press, 1987.

Knopp, Fay Honey. *Retraining Adult Sex Offenders: Methods & Models.* Orwell, Vt.: The Safer Society Press, 1984.

Salter, Anna C. *Treating Child Sex Offenders and Victims: A Practical Guide.* Newbury Park, Calif.: Sage, 1988.

Sonkin, Daniel Jay and Michael Durphy. *Learning to Live Without Violence: A Handbook for Men.* Rev. ed. San Francisco: Volcano Press, 1985.

SELF-DEFENSE AND RAPE PREVENTION

Bart, Pauline B. and Patricia H. O'Brien. *Stopping Rape: Successful Survival Strategies.* Pergamon Press, 1985.

Bateman, Py. *Fear into Anger: A Manual of Self-Defense for Women.* Chicago: Nelson-Hall, 1978.

Caignon, Denise and Gail Groves. *Her Wits About Her: Self-Defense Success Stories by Women.* New York: Harper & Row, 1987.

Los Angeles Commission on Assaults Against Women. *Women's Self-Defense: A Complete Guide to Assault Prevention.* Los Angeles: Los Angeles Commission on Assaults Against Women, 1987.

Smith, Susan E. *Fear or Freedom: A Woman's Options in Social Survival and Physical Defense.* Racine, Wis.: Mother Courage Press, 1986.

SEXUAL ASSAULT

Beneke, Timothy. *Men on Rape: What They Have to Say About Sexual Violence.* New York: St. Martin's Press, 1982.

Burgess, Ann Wolbert, ed. *Rape and Sexual Assault Research Handbooks.* Volumes 1 & 2. New York: Garland Publishing, 1983, 1987.

Ehrhart, Julie K. and Bernice R. Sandler. *Campus Gang Rape: Party Games?* Washington, D.C.: Association of American Colleges, 1985.

Estrich, Susan. *Real Rape.* Cambridge, Mass.: Harvard University Press, 1987.

Fay, Jennifer J. and Billie Joe Flerchinger. *Top Secret: Sexual Assault Information for Teenagers Only.* Renton, Wash.: King County Rape Relief, 1982. (Also available: *Top Secret: A Discussion Guide.* Santa Cruz, Calif.: Network Publications, 1985.)

Fortune, Marie. *Sexual Violence: The Unmentionable Sin: An Ethical and Pastoral Perspective.* New York: The Pilgrim Press, 1983.

Gordon, Margaret T. and Stephanie Riger. *The Female Fear.* New York: Free Press, 1989.

Grossman, Rochel and Joan Sutherland. *Surviving Sexual Assault.* Prepared for the Los Angeles Commission on Assaults Against Women. New York: Congdon & Weed, 1983.

Hughes, Jean O'Gorman and Bernice R. Sandler. "'Friends' Raping Friends: Could It Happen to You?" Washington, D.C.: Association of American Colleges, 1987.

Katz, Judy H. *No Fairy Godmothers, No Magic Wands: The Healing Process after Rape.* Saratoga, Calif.: R & E Publishers, 1984.

Ledray, Linda E. *Recovering from Rape.* New York: Henry Holt and Company, 1988.

Russell, Diana E. H. *Rape in Marriage.* New York: Collier Books, 1982.

"Stopping Sexual Assault in Marriage: A Guide for Women, Counselors and Advocates." New York: The Center for Constitutional Rights, 1986.

Stringer, Gayle M. and Deanna Rants-Rodriguez. *So What's It to Me? Sexual Assault Information for Guys.* Renton, Wash.: King County Rape Relief, 1987.

Warshaw, Robin. *I Never Called It Rape: The Ms. Report on Recognizing, Fighting and Surviving Date and Acquaintance Rape.* New York: Harper & Row, 1988.

SEXUAL HARASSMENT AND SEXUAL EXPLOITATION

Bates, Carolyn M. and Annette Brodsky. *Sex in the Therapy Hour: A Case of Professional Incest.* New York: Guilford Press, 1989.

Burgess, Ann W. and Carol R. Hartman, eds. *Sexual Exploitation of Patients by Health Professionals.* New York: Praeger, 1986.

Deane, Nancy H., ed. *Sexual Harassment Issues and Answers: A Guide for Education, Business, Industry.* Washington, D.C.: College and University Personnel Association, 1986.

Gutek, Barbara A. *Sex and the Workplace: The Impact of Sexual Behavior and Harassment on Women, Men and Organizations.* San Francisco: Jossey-Bass, 1985.

"It's Never O.K.: A Handbook for Victims and Victim Advocates on Sexual Exploitation by Counselors and Therapists." St. Paul, Minn.: Minnesota Dept. of Corrections, Minnesota Program for Victims of Sexual Assault, 1988.

SURVIVORS' WRITINGS

Bass, Ellen and Louise Thornton, eds. *I Never Told Anyone: Writings by Women Survivors of Child Sexual Abuse.* New York: Harper & Row, 1983.

Bryant, Marcella. *Ancient Child: Poetry About Incest.* Austin, Tex.: Plain View Press, 1989.

Fraser, Sylvia. *My Father's House: A Memoir of Incest and Healing.* New York: Ticknor & Fields, 1988.

Gallagher, Sister Vera with William F. Dodds. *Speaking Out, Fighting Back: Personal Experiences of Women Who Survived Childhood Sexual Abuse in the Home.* Seattle, Wash.: Madrona Publishers, 1985.

Hill, Eleanore. *The Family Secret: A Personal Account of Incest.* New York: Laurel, 1985.

Janssen, Martha. *Silent Scream.* Philadelphia: Fortress Press, 1983.

Kushner, Leah Pesa. *Dragonchild: One Lesbian's Journey of Survival Through a Childhood of Battering and Sexual Abuse.* Iowa City, Ia.: Iowa City Women's Press, 1984.

McNaron, Toni A. H. and Yarrow Morgan, eds. *Voices in the Night: Women Speaking About Incest.* Pittsburgh, Pa.: Cleis Press, 1982.

Portwood, Pamela, Michele Gorcey and Peggy Sanders. *Rebirth of Power: Overcoming the Effects of Sexual Abuse Through the Experiences of Others.* Racine, Wis.: Mother Courage Press, 1987.

Randall, Margaret. *This Is About Incest.* Ithaca, N.Y.: Firebrand Books, 1987.

Sisk, Sheila and Charlotte Foster Hoffman. *Inside Scars: Incest Recovery as Told by a Survivor and Her Therapist.* Gainesville, Fla.: Pandora Press, 1987.

Wisechild, Louise M. *The Obsidian Mirror: An Adult Healing from Incest.* Seattle, Wash.: The Seal Press, 1988.

Wood, Wendy Ann and Leslie Ann Hatton. *Triumph Over Darkness: Understanding and Healing the Trauma of Childhood Sexual Abuse.* Hillsboro, Ore.: Beyond Words Publishing, 1988.

BASIC SERVICES

This section describes the basic services usually provided by the most common/prevalent types of agencies. These general services have not been repeated in the directory listings. Instead, use these descriptions of services to supplement the information in the directory. Other types of agencies included in the Agency Profiles are child abuse services, child abuse prevention programs, child sexual abuse services, child sexual abuse prevention programs, acquaintance/date rape prevention programs, women's centers, child advocacy programs, shelters, adolescent programs, college/university-based services, hospital/medical centers, legal services agencies, correctional facilities, public school systems, residential treatment facilities, training/research programs, and interagency networks.

RAPE CRISIS CENTERS

Setting. Rape crisis centers are usually community-based organizations with paid staff and trained volunteers. Rape crisis services may also be provided through special programs in hospitals, community mental health centers, or campus women's centers. Crisis services are free, confidential and available to female and male victims.

Requirements. Most rape crisis centers provide short-term crisis services to victims of all ages, but in some states, sexually abused children must be referred immediately to child protective services. A few rape crisis centers refer male victims to other community agencies after the initial crisis contact.

Services. General services usually include a 24-hour crisis hotline and support/counseling for victims and families and friends of victims/survivors. Volunteers or staff members are available to accompany victims to the hospital, law enforcement agency, prosecuting attorney's office and court. Referrals are provided to other community agencies.

Counseling services include short-term counseling for victims/survivors with referrals for long-term counseling, if not available through the rape crisis center. Most have support groups for rape victims/survivors and for adult survivors of childhood sexual abuse. Some rape crisis centers also provide counseling for sexually abused children.

Community Education. Public awareness and community education are important components of the total rape crisis program. Prevention programs on rape avoidance, personal safety and self-defense strategies are available to community residents. Child/adolescent sexual abuse prevention programs are usually available for children, teenagers, teachers and parents. Sometimes these programs are available through the public school system and day care centers, sometimes through parent and teacher education.

Rape crisis centers also provide training programs for other professionals in the community, such as police, hospital staff, teachers, mental health professionals, and the clergy. Rape crisis centers are often a part of interagency sexual assault teams and interagency child sexual abuse teams in the community.

DOMESTIC VIOLENCE PROGRAMS

Setting. Domestic violence programs in this directory are of three types: shelters, safehomes and counseling programs. Domestic violence shelters provide emergency housing for battered women and their children in a specially designated shelter in the community, while safehomes are homes of community residents. To guarantee safety, the location of the shelter or the safehomes is kept confidential. Domestic violence counseling programs provide crisis counseling and referrals but no emergency housing. Services are free and confidential.

Domestic violence programs are included in this directory for a number of reasons. In some communities, services for victims/survivors of domestic and sexual violence are provided by the same agency. Domestic violence sometimes includes marital rape. Many battered women are also adult survivors of child sexual abuse and/or sexual assault. Sometimes their children are victims of physical/sexual abuse.

Requirements. Requirements for services vary. Most shelters have a maximum length of stay (for example, 30 days). Shelters usually require that the women must be adults (16 or 18 years of age or older) or emancipated minors and that children are sheltered only if accompanied by their mother. Usually there is an age limit for boys (sometimes no older than 12).

Services. Services usually include a 24-hour crisis hotline, safe emergency housing, individual and group counseling for battered women, and children's services. In addition, legal advocacy, court accompaniment, social service advocacy, peer support groups and referrals are provided. Some domestic violence shelters offer services for battered women in the community as well as those in the shelter.

Domestic violence programs work closely with local rape crisis centers and child protective services to locate counseling and support groups for battered women who are also dealing with issues of sexual abuse, for themselves and their children. Some domestic violence programs have support groups for mothers of sexually abused children. Some domestic violence shelters provide short-term shelter for rape victims whose homes are not safe due to the rape.

Offenders. Many domestic violence programs provide individual and group counseling for batterers in a location separate from the shelter.

Community Education. Community education and in-service training for professionals are provided by the staff of the domestic violence program. Some shelters are involved in developing programs on dating violence prevention.

VICTIM ASSISTANCE PROGRAMS

Setting. Victim assistance programs provide services for all victims of violent crime, including sexual assault, domestic violence and child sexual abuse. These programs can be administered through the prosecuting attorney's office, a law enforcement agency, or a community mental health center. They can also be established as an independent agency in the community. Services are free of charge.

Requirements. Some victim assistance programs have no requirements for services. Programs based in a prosecuting attorney's office or a law enforcement agency may require that the victim file charges to receive the full range of services. (For example, some programs provide crisis services to all victims of crime, but state law requires that the victim file charges to be eligible for victim compensation.) In addition, there can be geographic requirements pertaining to where the crime was committed and/or where the victim lives or works.

Services. Services may include a 24-hour hotline and victim advocacy/support at the hospital and police station. Staff provide orientation to the criminal justice system, court preparation and accompaniment, assistance in filing for crime victims compensation (if eligible), and information about the status and disposition of cases. Victims and family members receive short-term counseling and emotional support, as well as referrals to community resources for additional help. Sometimes victim assistance programs have support groups for victims.

COUNSELING/MENTAL HEALTH SERVICES

Services. Community mental health centers, family service agencies and therapists in group private practice provide short- and long-term individual and group counseling for survivors of sexual assault and adult survivors of child sexual abuse (both female and male). They often have a child sexual abuse treatment program that provides individual, group and family therapy for sexually abused children and their families, including the offending parent. Mental health centers often provide treatment for batterers, child sexual abuse/incest offenders, rapists and adolescent sex offenders.

Some mental health centers sponsor chapters of Parents United/Daughters & Sons United, self-help groups for incestuous families, as well as Adults Molested as Children United, self-help groups for adult survivors of child sexual abuse. They may also sponsor Parents Anonymous groups, a self-help program for parents who abuse or are at risk of abusing their children. (For additional information about these programs, see the section on national organizations.) Some mental health centers and family-based counseling centers offer special parenting services to assist families at risk for child abuse.

Requirements. Most community mental health centers have sliding scale fees. Some have geographic requirements for specially funded services or requirements for sliding scale fees eligibility.

PREVENTION PROGRAMS

Services. Community education and prevention programs are conducted by many of the agencies in this directory as they carry out their long-term commitment to end sexual violence and abuse. Community education programs generally provide information about sex role stereotypes and myths that underpin sexual assault and abuse. Some programs provide guidance for parents in talking with their children about sexual abuse. Other programs teach personal safety strategies and self-defense tactics. Special programs have been developed for adolescents concerning acquaintance/date rape awareness and dating violence prevention. There are also prevention programs for older adults, people with physical disabilities, and those who are mentally retarded and developmentally disabled.

Child sexual/physical abuse prevention programs are available for children from preschool through high school. Programs may be conducted by rape crisis centers, prevention organizations, and family service agencies. Training is also provided to teachers and parents.

Prevention programs for children emphasize the "touch continuum" (comfortable-uncomfortable touch) and the child's right to say "no" to unwanted touch from people they know, as well as strangers. Prevention programs encourage the child to get help by telling an adult. Children have the opportunity to think through strategies for troubling situations in an atmosphere that will not frighten them.

The shift in emphasis from "stranger-danger" to saying "no" to people the child knows and trusts is important, since studies indicate that approximately 85% of sexually abused children have been abused by someone they know (1).

OFFENDER TREATMENT

Setting. Adult and adolescent sex offender treatment programs are provided by community mental health centers, by private therapists in group practice, and in correctional facilities for incarcerated sex offenders. Some programs focus on young sex offenders (between 10 and 15) who have experienced sexual abuse themselves.

Requirements. Programs sometimes require that offenders be court-mandated into treatment. Others accept offenders with a contract for treatment for a specified time period. Some family-based programs require that the offender pay for the child's therapy.

Services. Offender treatment can be a combination of individual, group, couple and family therapy, as appropriate. Treatment may include behavioral and cognitive restructuring approaches, reading and writing exercises, training in communications and assertiveness skills, information on sexuality, and support groups as well as therapy.

A. Nicholas Groth identifies four issues in recovery for offenders: understanding the nature of sexual assault; being able to empathize with the victim; acknowledging their own history of victimization (about 80% of sex offenders are adult survivors of child sexual/physical abuse); and taking the initiative for restitution or atonement (2).

REFERENCES

1. Jennifer Fay. "Guidelines for Selecting Prevention Education Resources," in *Preventing Child Sexual Abuse*, edited by Mary Nelson and Kay Clark (Network Publications, 1986), p. 98.

2. A. Nicholas Groth, Workshop on Sex Offender Treatment, sponsored by Parents Anonymous of Texas (Austin, Texas, November 18, 1988).

ACKNOWLEDGMENTS

Many websters have been working during the past ten years, weaving connections between victims/survivors and those who have resources to help them heal. I acknowledge the work that has been done before me, including the directories of the National Coalition Against Sexual Assault, the National Coalition Against Domestic Violence, the national directory compiled by the Pennsylvania Coalition Against Rape, Warrior's *Battered Women's Directory*, and RAVEN's *The Ending Men's Violence National Referral Directory*.

My special thanks to the National Victims Center in Fort Worth, Texas, and to the National Women's Mailing List in Jenner, California, for providing me with printouts of their extensive databases; to Parents United for its list of chapters; to the Self-Help Clearinghouse, St. Clares-Riverside Medical Center, in Denville, New Jersey, for permission to use its list of state self-help centers; and to the National Committee for Prevention of Child Abuse for permission to print its list of state chapters. I also received assistance from the staff of state agencies and organizations in every state, who sent me information about rape crisis centers, domestic violence shelters and victim assistance programs and who answered innumerable questions by phone.

I thank all of you who responded to the questionnaire, taking time to share the important work you are doing. Many of you had words of encouragement that helped me remember that my work would one day be of use of others.

I thank Nancy Biehl for her enthusiastic "yes" to writing a Foreword for the directory.

Many Austin women have shared my vision for this directory and have helped make it real: Jennifer Carloye, Alana Cash, Karen Croneis, Bobbie Erb, Jeanie Forsyth, Marion Magarick, Alison Tartt, Barbara Weeks and J. Cole White. The Women's Spirituality Group of the First Unitarian Church of Austin and my Sunday women's group have held me lovingly in their circles and have believed in me and my work.

My son Ben Webster, Carol Lackey, and Suzanne Abreu helped with organization of the questionnaires, a painstaking task which they accomplished with careful attention.

Sue Frankewicz, Lacey Sloan, Roxanne McKimmey, Cynthia Medina, and Rosemarie Penzerro have each made a significant difference to victims/survivors through their work at the Hays County Women's Center in San Marcos, Texas. They are sources of inspiration to me as staunch advocates for women and children.

I think back to a time, three long years ago, when Jim Thomas first talked to me about undertaking a national directory of rape crisis centers. I thank him for offering me this opportunity. Cynthia Medina challenged me to think about including not just rape crisis centers but also services for marital rape victims and sexually abused children. She helped me broaden my vision to make this a more comprehensive directory.

At Oryx Press there are many people to thank. Sam Mongeau and Gene Price gave this project a good start. Susan Johnson, my editor, helped clarify the content and organization of the directory, kept me and the directory on schedule with a light hand, worked with me to develop the subject index, and listened with care to my ideas and concerns. Mary Blackwell and Rhonda Shapiro accomplished data input and proofing with incredible accuracy and consistency. Susan Sims' suggestions and assistance with typesetting and page design were invaluable in developing this directory. And I thank Oryx Press for its commitment to this project.

Finally, I honor all the women and men who are working to end sexual assault and abuse. This directory is a testimony to their commitment and hope.

LIST OF ABBREVIATIONS

Admin	Administration, Administrative, Administrator
AMAC	Adults Molested as Children
Assoc	Associate
Asst	Assistant
Atty	Attorney
CAPP	Child Assault Prevention Project
Casewkr	Caseworker
Comm	Commission, Community
Coord	Coordinator
Couns	Counselor
Ctr	Center
CYF	Children, youth, and families
Dir	Director
Educ	Education, Educator
Exec	Executive
Lic	licensed
Mgr	Manager
MH	Mental health
NCASA	National Coalition Against Sexual Assault
NCPCA	National Committee for Prevention of Child Abuse
Ofc	Office, Officer
PA	Parents Anonymous
Pres	President
Prev	Prevention
Prog	Program
Proj	Project
PU	Parents United
Res	Residence, Resident, Residential
Soc	Social
Spec	Specialist
Supt	Superintendent
Supv	Supervisor
Svc(s)	Service(s)
TAPP	Teen Assault Prevention Project
VOCA	Victims of Crime Act
Vol	Volunteer
V/W	Victim/witness
Wkr	Worker

Sexual Assault and Child Sexual Abuse

A National Directory
of Victim/Survivor Services
and Prevention Programs

ALABAMA

ANNISTON

DISTRICT ATTORNEY'S OFFICE
PO Box 2131, Anniston, AL 36202
Information: (205) 238-8516 8am-4:30pm
Contact: Jean Ayers Reid, Victim Svc Off
TYPE OF AGENCY: Victim/witness assistance program
AREAS SERVED: Calhoun, Cleburne
YEARS IN OPERATION: 3
ACCESSIBILITY: Wheelchair accessible
CASES SEXUAL ASSAULT/ABUSE (%): 15
CLIENTS/SERVICES: Sexual assault survivors; Child victims of sexual abuse
REQUIREMENTS: Client must file charges

BIRMINGHAM

THE PRESCOTT HOUSE
1730 14th Ave S, Birmingham, AL 35205
Information: (205) 325-5065 8am-5pm
Contact: Francis L Sartain, Dir
TYPE OF AGENCY: Victim/witness assistance program; Child sexual abuse services; Child advocacy
AREAS SERVED: Jefferson
YEARS IN OPERATION: 2
CASES SEXUAL ASSAULT/ABUSE (%): 100
DESCRIPTION: Children's advocacy center designed to interview the child victim in a non-threatening environment with emphasis on prosecution of the offender. Closely associated with the county district attorney
CLIENTS/SERVICES: Child victims of sexual abuse; Adolescent survivors of sexual abuse
REQUIREMENTS: Victim must be under 18 years of age

RAPE RESPONSE
3600 8th Ave S, Ste 501, Birmingham, AL 35222
Crisis hotline: **(205) 323-7273 24 hrs**
Information: (205) 323-7782 8am-4:30pm
Contact: Patti Dunne, Prog Coord
TYPE OF AGENCY: Rape crisis center
SPONSORING ORGANIZATION: Crisis Center, Inc
AREAS SERVED: Jefferson, Shelby, St Clair, Blount, Walker
YEARS IN OPERATION: 12
ACCESSIBILITY: Wheelchair accessible
CASES SEXUAL ASSAULT/ABUSE (%): 100
CLIENTS/SERVICES: Sexual assault survivors; Marital rape/sexual abuse survivors; Child victims of sexual abuse; Adult survivors of child sexual abuse; Prevention program; Community education; Adolescent survivors of sexual abuse; Male survivors of sexual abuse
SPECIAL PROGRAMS/SERVICES: In addition to counselors for sexual assault victims, Rape Response provides male support volunteers who have been specially trained to counsel men who are close to victims of rape

DOTHAN

THE HOUSE OF RUTH
PO Box 968, Dothan, AL 36302
Crisis hotline: **(205) 793-2232 24 hrs**
Information: (205) 793-5214 8am-4:30pm (Mon-Fri)
Contact: Beverly S Youse, LSW, MS, Exec Dir
TYPE OF AGENCY: Domestic violence program
AREAS SERVED: Barbour, Bullock, Coffee, Dale, Geneva, Henry, Houston, Pike
YEARS IN OPERATION: 6½
ACCESSIBILITY: Wheelchair accessible; Signers for the hearing impaired (by arrangement)
CLIENTS/SERVICES: Marital rape/sexual abuse survivors; Community education

EUFAULA

DISTRICT ATTORNEY'S OFFICE—VICTIM/WITNESS PROGRAM
PO Box 61, Eufaula, AL 36027
Information: (205) 687-7638 8am-5pm
Contact: Judith Brown, Victim Svc Officer
TYPE OF AGENCY: Victim/witness assistance program
AREAS SERVED: Barbour, Bullock
ACCESSIBILITY: Telecommunications for the hearing impaired (TTY, TDY, etc.); Signers for the hearing impaired
CLIENTS/SERVICES: Sexual assault survivors; Marital rape/sexual abuse survivors; Child victims of sexual abuse; Incest victims/survivors

FLORENCE

SAFEPLACE, INC
PO Box 1456, Florence, AL 35630
Crisis hotline: **(205) 767-6210 24 hrs**
Information: (205) 767-3076, 767-5952 8am-5pm (Mon-Fri)
Contact: Arneda Heath, Exec Dir
TYPE OF AGENCY: Domestic violence program; Child sexual abuse prevention program
AREAS SERVED: Colbert, Lauderdale, Lawrence, Franklin, Marion, Winston
YEARS IN OPERATION: 7½
ACCESSIBILITY: Wheelchair accessible
CASES SEXUAL ASSAULT/ABUSE (%): 30
DESCRIPTION: Provides multipurpose family violence program, with a transitional home for battered women in addition to the shelter program
CLIENTS/SERVICES: Sexual assault survivors; Marital rape/sexual abuse survivors; Child victims of sexual abuse; Adult survivors of child sexual abuse; Incest victims/survivors; Prevention program; Community education

GADSDEN

CHRISTIAN COUNSELING CENTER
310 S 3rd St, Gadsden, AL 35901
Information: (205) 547-5219 24 hrs
Contact: Laetitia Hutchinson, Exec Dir
TYPE OF AGENCY: Counseling/mental health services; Child sexual abuse prevention program
AREAS SERVED: Northern Alabama
YEARS IN OPERATION: 10
ACCESSIBILITY: Wheelchair accessible
CASES SEXUAL ASSAULT/ABUSE (%): 30
DESCRIPTION: Therapy for survivors, child sexual abuse/incest offenders, and batterers provided by professionally trained Christian counselors
CLIENTS/SERVICES: Sexual assault survivors; Marital rape/sexual abuse survivors; Child victims of sexual abuse; Adult survivors of child sexual abuse; Incest victims/survivors; Prevention program; Community education; Offender treatment program; Adolescent survivors of sexual abuse; Male survivors of sexual abuse
REQUIREMENTS: Sliding scale fee
SPECIAL PROGRAMS/SERVICES: Summer programs for children ages 6-11 teach personal safety through the use of role play, videos, puppet shows, and group discussions

THE SHELTER, INC
PO Box 1548, Gadsden, AL 35902
Crisis hotline: **(205) 543-3059 24 hrs**
Information: (205) 543-2408 24 hrs
Contact: Gayla W Sauls, Exec Dir
TYPE OF AGENCY: Domestic violence program
AREAS SERVED: Etowah, Cherokee, DeKalb, Marshall, Calhoun, Blount, St Claire
YEARS IN OPERATION: 3
LANGUAGES: Spanish
CASES SEXUAL ASSAULT/ABUSE (%): 50
CLIENTS/SERVICES: Sexual assault survivors; Marital rape/sexual abuse survivors; Child victims of sexual abuse; Prevention program; Community education

VICTIM SERVICE OFFICE
800 Forrest Ave, Etowah County Courthouse, Gadsden, AL 35999
Crisis hotline: **(205) 546-9310 8am-5pm**
Information: (205) 546-2821, ext 291 8am-5pm
Contact: Margie Wetzel, Victim Svcs Officer
TYPE OF AGENCY: Victim/witness assistance program
SPONSORING ORGANIZATION: 16th Judicial Circuit, District Attorney's Office
AREAS SERVED: Etowah
YEARS IN OPERATION: 2
CASES SEXUAL ASSAULT/ABUSE (%): 15-20
CLIENTS/SERVICES: Sexual assault survivors; Marital rape/sexual abuse survivors; Child victims of sexual abuse; Adult survivors of child sexual abuse; Incest victims/survivors; Com-

VICTIM SERVICE OFFICE *(continued)*

munity education; Adolescent survivors of sexual abuse; Male survivors of sexual abuse

HUNTSVILLE

FAMILY SERVICES CENTER
2003 Harvard Rd, Huntsville, AL 35801
Crisis hotline: **(205) 539-1000 as needed for clients**
Information: (205) 539-5717 8:30am-5:30pm (Mon, Wed, Fri); 8:30am-9pm (Tue, Thu)
Contact: Martha B Mantler, Admin Asst
TYPE OF AGENCY: Counseling/mental health services
AREAS SERVED: North AL, South Central TN
YEARS IN OPERATION: 25
LANGUAGES: Translators available
ACCESSIBILITY: Wheelchair accessible; Signers for the hearing impaired (by arrangement)
CASES SEXUAL ASSAULT/ABUSE (%): 20
DESCRIPTION: Therapy for victims/survivors, including group therapy for females and males. Treatment for rapists, child sexual abuse/incest offenders, and batterers
CLIENTS/SERVICES: Sexual assault survivors; Marital rape/sexual abuse survivors; Child victims of sexual abuse; Adult survivors of child sexual abuse; Incest victims/survivors; Community education; Offender treatment program; Adolescent survivors of sexual abuse; Male survivors of sexual abuse
REQUIREMENTS: Exclusions: Psychotic or otherwise so severely disturbed and/or depressed to be in need of inpatient treatment or protective custody

HOPE PLACE, INC
PO Box 687, Huntsville, AL 35804
Crisis hotline: **(205) 539-1000 24 hrs**
Information: (205) 534-4052 8am-5pm (Mon-Fri)
Contact: Norma Harwood, Exec Dir
TYPE OF AGENCY: Domestic violence program
AREAS SERVED: Madison, Morgan, Marshall, Limestone, Jackson
YEARS IN OPERATION: 5½
CASES SEXUAL ASSAULT/ABUSE (%): 70
CLIENTS/SERVICES: Marital rape/sexual abuse survivors

NATIONAL CHILDREN'S ADVOCACY CENTER
106 Lincoln St, Huntsville, AL 35801
Information: (205) 533-5437 8:30am-5pm (pager for emergencies 24 hrs)
Contact: R E Cramer, Board of Dir Pres
TYPE OF AGENCY: Child sexual abuse services
AREAS SERVED: Madison
YEARS IN OPERATION: 3
CASES SEXUAL ASSAULT/ABUSE (%): 100
CLIENTS/SERVICES: Child victims of sexual abuse; Adult survivors of child sexual abuse; Incest victims/survivors; Community education; Adolescent survivors of sexual abuse
REQUIREMENTS: Offense must be reported to CPS or law enforcement agency as sexual abuse or serious physical abuse

RAPE RESPONSE PROGRAM
PO Box 92, Huntsville, AL 35804
Crisis hotline: **(205) 539-6161 24 hrs daily**
Information: (205) 534-1779 8am-5pm
Contact: Judy Ray, Coord
TYPE OF AGENCY: Rape crisis center
SPONSORING ORGANIZATION: HELPline
AREAS SERVED: Madison
YEARS IN OPERATION: 2½
CASES SEXUAL ASSAULT/ABUSE (%): 100
CLIENTS/SERVICES: Sexual assault survivors; Marital rape/sexual abuse survivors; Adult survivors of child sexual abuse; Prevention program; Community education; Adolescent survivors of sexual abuse; Male survivors of sexual abuse

JASPER

FAMILY RESOURCE CENTER OF NORTHWEST ALABAMA—DAYBREAK
PO Box 3429, Jasper, AL 35502
Crisis hotline: **(205) 387-1157 24 hrs**
Information: (205) 387-1157 24 hrs
Contact: Jan Ingle, Prog Dir; Leah Martin, Coord
TYPE OF AGENCY: Domestic violence program
AREAS SERVED: Primarily Walker, also Winston, Marion
YEARS IN OPERATION: 2½
ACCESSIBILITY: Wheelchair accessible
CASES SEXUAL ASSAULT/ABUSE (%): 2-3
CLIENTS/SERVICES: Marital rape/sexual abuse survivors; Child victims of sexual abuse
REQUIREMENTS: Spouse/child abuse (physical and mental) survivors seeking a secure, safe shelter

MOBILE

CATHOLIC SOCIAL SERVICES
PO Box 759, Mobile, AL 36601
Information: (205) 438-1603 8:30am-4:30pm; evenings and weekends by arrangement
Contact: Sarah Phillips, Clinical Svcs Dir
TYPE OF AGENCY: Counseling/mental health services
AREAS SERVED: Mobile, Baldwin
YEARS IN OPERATION: 52
ACCESSIBILITY: Wheelchair accessible
CASES SEXUAL ASSAULT/ABUSE (%): 30-40
CLIENTS/SERVICES: Sexual assault survivors; Marital rape/sexual abuse survivors; Child victims of sexual abuse; Adult survivors of child sexual abuse; Incest victims/survivors; Prevention program; Adolescent survivors of sexual abuse; Male survivors of sexual abuse

CHILD ADVOCACY CENTER
1351 Springhill Ave, Mobile, AL 36604
Information: (205) 432-1101 8am-5pm
Contact: Patrick Guyton, Dir
TYPE OF AGENCY: Child sexual abuse services; Child sexual abuse prevention program; Child abuse services; Child advocacy
AREAS SERVED: Mobile
YEARS IN OPERATION: 1
ACCESSIBILITY: Wheelchair accessible
CASES SEXUAL ASSAULT/ABUSE (%): 95
DESCRIPTION: A homelike facility where victims of child abuse are brought to be interviewed by a specially trained team of law enforcement representatives, social workers from the Department of Human Resources, and assistant district attorneys. Has a full-time assistant district attorney on staff who provides vertical prosecution in child abuse cases. Also has criminal investigators from the Mobile Police Department and County Sheriff's office. Offers referrals for counseling services.
CLIENTS/SERVICES: Child victims of sexual abuse; Incest victims/survivors; Prevention program; Community education; Adolescent survivors of sexual abuse
REQUIREMENTS: Referrals from law enforcement agencies and the Department of Human Resources.
SPECIAL PROGRAMS/SERVICES: Once each week a multidisciplinary team meets at the center to review all of the cases of the past week to determine if there is a need for prosecution, referral for counseling, further investigation, medical exams, etc. The team is made up of representatives of the District Attorney's office, victim advocate, mental health care providers, medical health care providers, law enforcement, and the Department of Human Resources. The agency recently became one of the first child advocacy centers in the United States to complete and get signed a comprehensive interagency agreement which details the duties and responsibilities of all the agencies cooperating with the center in the attack on child abuse.

MONTGOMERY

COUNCIL AGAINST RAPE
830 S Court St, Montgomery, AL 36104
Crisis hotline: **(205) 264-RAPE 24 hrs**
Information: (205) 263-4481 9am-5pm
Contact: Tamara Martin
TYPE OF AGENCY: Rape crisis center; Counseling/mental health services
SPONSORING ORGANIZATION: Lighthouse Counseling Center
CLIENTS/SERVICES: Sexual assault survivors; Marital rape/sexual abuse survivors; Child victims of sexual abuse; Adult survivors of child sexual abuse; Incest victims/survivors

DISTRICT ATTORNEY VICTIM/WITNESS PROGRAM
PO Box 1667, Montgomery, AL 36192-2501
Information: (205) 832-2550 8am-5pm
Contact: Laura Culberson, Victim Svc Officer
TYPE OF AGENCY: Victim/witness assistance program
AREAS SERVED: Montgomery
CLIENTS/SERVICES: Sexual assault survivors; Child victims of sexual abuse

MONTGOMERY AREA FAMILY VIOLENCE PROGRAM (MAFVP)
802 Forest Ave, Montgomery, AL 36106
Crisis hotline: **(205) 263-0063 24 hrs**
Information: (205) 263-2300 9am-5pm (Mon-Fri)
Contact: Karen Sellers, Exec Dir
TYPE OF AGENCY: Domestic violence program; Child sexual abuse services; Child sexual abuse prevention program
AREAS SERVED: Montgomery, Elmore, Lowdnes, Autauga
YEARS IN OPERATION: 7
CLIENTS/SERVICES: Sexual assault survivors; Marital rape/sexual abuse survivors; Child victims of sexual abuse; Adult survivors of child sexual abuse; Incest victims/survivors; Prevention program; Community education; Offender treatment program; Adolescent survivors of sexual abuse; Male survivors of sexual abuse
SPECIAL PROGRAMS/SERVICES: ABC program designed to educate children in the prevention of sexual and physical abuse.

MONTGOMERY COUNSELING CENTER
2900 McGehee Rd, Montgomery, AL 36111
Information: (205) 284-4787 9am-6pm
Contact: William Mitchell, Dir
TYPE OF AGENCY: Private practice
YEARS IN OPERATION: 5
ACCESSIBILITY: Wheelchair accessible
CASES SEXUAL ASSAULT/ABUSE (%): 15
DESCRIPTION: Treatment for adolescent sexual offenders, adult offenders, and victims
CLIENTS/SERVICES: Marital rape/sexual abuse survivors; Offender treatment program

SAFE PLACE
880 S Lawrence St, Montgomery, AL 36104
Crisis hotline: **(205) 265-2652 24 hrs**
Information: (205) 262-2953 9am-4pm (Mon-Fri)
Contact: Martha Nachman, Prog Dir
TYPE OF AGENCY: Child sexual abuse services; Child abuse services; Shelter
SPONSORING ORGANIZATION: Group Homes for Children
AREAS SERVED: Montgomery, Autauga
YEARS IN OPERATION: 2½
ACCESSIBILITY: Wheelchair accessible
CASES SEXUAL ASSAULT/ABUSE (%): 10
CLIENTS/SERVICES: Sexual assault survivors; Child victims of sexual abuse; Prevention program; Community education; Adolescent survivors of sexual abuse

SAFE PLACE *(continued)*
REQUIREMENTS: In runaway shelter, ages 11-18; In neglect shelter, referred by Department of Human Resources, all ages up to 18

SUNSHINE CENTER
802 Forest Ave, Montgomery, AL 36106
Crisis hotline: **(205) 263-0218 24 hrs**
Information: (205) 263-2300 9am-5pm (Mon-Fri)
Contact: Carol Nelson, Counselor Coord
TYPE OF AGENCY: Domestic violence program; Child sexual abuse services; Child sexual abuse prevention program
SPONSORING ORGANIZATION: Montgomery Area Family Violence Program
AREAS SERVED: Montgomery, Elmore, Autauga, Lowndes
YEARS IN OPERATION: 7
LANGUAGES: Interpreters available
ACCESSIBILITY: Signers for the hearing impaired
CASES SEXUAL ASSAULT/ABUSE (%): 50
CLIENTS/SERVICES: Marital rape/sexual abuse survivors; Child victims of sexual abuse; Adult survivors of child sexual abuse; Incest victims/survivors; Prevention program; Community education; Adolescent survivors of sexual abuse; Male survivors of sexual abuse

MOULTON

DISTRICT ATTORNEY'S OFFICE
PO Box 625, Moulton, AL 35650
Information: (205) 974-2446 8am-5pm
Contact: Freda Sutton, Victim Svc Off
TYPE OF AGENCY: Victim/witness assistance program
AREAS SERVED: Lawrence
ACCESSIBILITY: Wheelchair accessible
CASES SEXUAL ASSAULT/ABUSE (%): 5
CLIENTS/SERVICES: Sexual assault survivors; Marital rape/sexual abuse survivors; Child victims of sexual abuse; Incest victims/survivors; Adolescent survivors of sexual abuse

TUSCALOOSA

FAMILY COUNSELING SERVICES
600 12th St, Tuscaloosa, AL 35401
Crisis hotline: **(205) 752-2504 8:30am-5pm**
Information: (205) 752-2504 8:30am-5pm
Contact: Freda Coleman-Reed, Personal Growth and Enrichment Prog Coord
TYPE OF AGENCY: Counseling/mental health services; Acquaintance/date rape prevention program
AREAS SERVED: Tuscaloosa and surrounding area
YEARS IN OPERATION: 20
ACCESSIBILITY: Wheelchair accessible
CASES SEXUAL ASSAULT/ABUSE (%): 10
DESCRIPTION: Provides counseling and therapy for individuals, families, couples, and groups. Operates adolescent survivors of incest group
CLIENTS/SERVICES: Child victims of sexual abuse; Adult survivors of child sexual abuse; Incest victims/survivors; Prevention program; Community education; Adolescent survivors of sexual abuse
SPECIAL PROGRAMS/SERVICES: The In-Touch program is a local school-based child abuse prevention project for adolescents grades 8-12. Education is presented in the areas of date/acquaintance rape, cycle of violence, four types of abuse/neglect, and available community resources.

RAPE AWARENESS PROGRAM (RAP)
Box 1391, Women Studies, Tuscaloosa, AL 35486
Crisis hotline: **(205) 345-1600 24 hrs**
Information: (205) 348-5782 8am-5pm (Mon-Fri)
Contact: Ute Winston, Asst Dir
TYPE OF AGENCY: College/university-based services; Rape prevention program
SPONSORING ORGANIZATION: University of Alabama—Women Studies
AREAS SERVED: Tuscaloosa, county and campus
YEARS IN OPERATION: 3
ACCESSIBILITY: Wheelchair accessible
DESCRIPTION: Provides rape prevention and awareness programs; Feminist martial arts/self defense program; Sponsors Take Back the Night March
CLIENTS/SERVICES: Sexual assault survivors; Prevention program; Community education; Publications/media
SPECIAL PROGRAMS/SERVICES: Media program: Take Back The Night

SPOUSE ABUSE NETWORK
PO Box 1165, Tuscaloosa, AL 35403
Crisis hotline: **(205) 553-2016 24 hrs**
Information: (205) 553-2016 8am-5pm (Mon-Fri)
Contact: Denise Mosely, Victim Case Mgr
TYPE OF AGENCY: Domestic violence program
AREAS SERVED: Tuscaloosa, Bibb, Fayette, Greene, Hale, Lamar, Marengo, Pickens, Perry, Sumter
YEARS IN OPERATION: 8
CLIENTS/SERVICES: Marital rape/sexual abuse survivors

THE TUSCALOOSA CHILDREN'S CENTER, INC
PO Box 2072, Tuscaloosa, AL 35401
Information: (205) 349-1252 8:30am-5pm
Contact: Amy L Walker, Victim Svc Officer
TYPE OF AGENCY: Victim/witness assistance program; Child sexual abuse services
AREAS SERVED: Tuscaloosa
YEARS IN OPERATION: 2
ACCESSIBILITY: Wheelchair accessible
DESCRIPTION: Home-like interview facility for sexually/physically abused children
CLIENTS/SERVICES: Sexual assault survivors; Child victims of sexual abuse; Adult survivors of child sexual abuse; Incest victims/survivors; Adolescent survivors of sexual abuse

UNIVERSITY

RUSSELL STUDENT HEALTH CENTER—MENTAL HEALTH SECTION
PO Box Y, University, AL 35486
Crisis hotline: **(205) 348-6262 Nights/weekends**
Information: (205) 348-3863 8am-5pm (Crisis calls also accepted during these hrs)
Contact: Dr Marianne Rosenzweig, Senior Clinical Psychologist
TYPE OF AGENCY: College/university-based services
SPONSORING ORGANIZATION: University of Alabama
YEARS IN OPERATION: 20
ACCESSIBILITY: Wheelchair accessible
DESCRIPTION: Crisis intervention/short-term individual psychotherapy for university students, including date rape victims
CLIENTS/SERVICES: Sexual assault survivors; Marital rape/sexual abuse survivors; Adult survivors of child sexual abuse; Incest victims/survivors; Prevention program; Community education; Adolescent survivors of sexual abuse; Male survivors of sexual abuse
REQUIREMENTS: Clients must be currently enrolled University of Alabama students, or must meet specific fee-for-service requirements.

ALASKA

ANCHORAGE

ANCHORAGE CENTER FOR FAMILIES
3745 Community Park Loop, Ste 102, Anchorage, AK 99508
Crisis hotline: **(907) 276-8511 24 hrs**
Information: (907) 276-4994 8:30am-8pm (Mon-Thu); 8:30am-6pm (Fri)
Contact: Milli Andreini, Clinical Prog Dir
TYPE OF AGENCY: Counseling/mental health services; Child sexual abuse services; Child abuse services
AREAS SERVED: Municipality of Anchorage
YEARS IN OPERATION: 16
ACCESSIBILITY: Wheelchair accessible
CASES SEXUAL ASSAULT/ABUSE (%): 35
DESCRIPTION: Prevention and treatment (child abuse and family distress); Treatment services for victims of child sexual abuse
CLIENTS/SERVICES: Child victims of sexual abuse; Adult survivors of child sexual abuse; Incest victims/survivors; Community education; Adolescent survivors of sexual abuse; Male survivors of sexual abuse
REQUIREMENTS: Services are provided for families with children ages birth to 18 years.
SPECIAL PROGRAMS/SERVICES: INTERMISSION is a residential child care center which assists families during times of stress or crisis by providing them with temporary relief from child care responsibilities. The Parent Aid Program involves trained volunteers who provide home-based support for parents under stress. Friendly Visitors are volunteers who provide in-home support for high-risk families

CHILD ADVOCACY NETWORK
PO Box 196650, Anchorage, AK 99519-6650
Crisis hotline: **(907) 276-7279 24 hrs 7 days**
Information: (907) 348-4876, TTY 276-7282 or 274-6882 8am-5pm
Contact: Lauren Ewing, Coord
TYPE OF AGENCY: Child sexual abuse services; Child abuse services; Interagency network
SPONSORING ORGANIZATION: Municipality of Anchorage
AREAS SERVED: Anchorage
YEARS IN OPERATION: 10
ACCESSIBILITY: Wheelchair accessible; Telecommunications for the hearing impaired (TTY, TDY, etc.); Signers for the hearing impaired
CASES SEXUAL ASSAULT/ABUSE (%): 15
DESCRIPTION: Coordination of all child abuse/neglect services, including specialized sexual assault, child protective services, offender treatment, etc
CLIENTS/SERVICES: Child victims of sexual abuse; Adult survivors of child sexual abuse; Incest victims/survivors; Prevention program; Community education; Adolescent survivors of sexual abuse; Male survivors of sexual abuse

LANGDON PSYCHIATRIC CLINIC
4001 Dale, Ste 101, Anchorage, AK 99508
Crisis hotline: **(907) 561-1361 24 hrs**
Information: (907) 561-1361 8:30am-6:30pm
Contact: Bruce N Smith, Sex Offender Prog Dir; Jackie Joday and Helen Craig, Clinical Soc Wkrs
TYPE OF AGENCY: Private practice; Offender treatment
AREAS SERVED: Anchorage and surrounding areas including Wasilla, Eagle River, Kenai, Soldotna
ACCESSIBILITY: Signers for the hearing impaired
CASES SEXUAL ASSAULT/ABUSE (%): 35
DESCRIPTION: Provides psychotherapy services for children and adults who are victims of sexual assault/abuse. On a contractual basis, manages a sex offender program for the state—rapists, child sexual abuse/incest offenders, batterers, and offenders in correctional settings. Sex offender treatment for both male and female offenders and educable mentally retarded offenders
CLIENTS/SERVICES: Sexual assault survivors; Marital rape/sexual abuse survivors; Child victims of sexual abuse; Adult survivors of child sexual abuse; Incest victims/survivors; Offender treatment program; Adolescent survivors of sexual abuse; Male survivors of sexual abuse; Developmentally disabled; Prisoners
REQUIREMENTS: Ability to pay charges; accepts Medicaid

MOVE (MEN OVERCOMING VIOLENT EXPRESSION)
549 W International Airport Rd, B-11, Anchorage, AK 99518
Information: (907) 562-1242 12pm-8pm (Mon-Sat)
Contact: Bruce Bibee, Prog Mgr
TYPE OF AGENCY: Domestic violence program
SPONSORING ORGANIZATION: Anchorage Transpersonal Training Network
YEARS IN OPERATION: 2
DESCRIPTION: Individual and group therapy for batterers, based on transpersonal psychology and involving spiritual healing
CLIENTS/SERVICES: Offender treatment program
SPECIAL PROGRAMS/SERVICES: MOVE workshop, a 2-½ day session on how to set up and run a spouse abuse treatment program for men who have used emotional, physical, sexual abuse in their primary relationships

STANDING TOGETHER AGAINST RAPE (STAR)
3925 Reka Dr, Anchorage, AK 99508
Crisis hotline: **(907) 276-7273, 276-7827 24 hrs**
Information: (907) 276-7279 8:30am-5:30pm (Mon-Fri)
Contact: Mona Maehara, Exec Dir
TYPE OF AGENCY: Rape crisis center; Child sexual abuse services; Child sexual abuse prevention program
YEARS IN OPERATION: 10
LANGUAGES: Translators available
ACCESSIBILITY: Wheelchair accessible; Telecommunications for the hearing impaired (TTY, TDY, etc.)
CASES SEXUAL ASSAULT/ABUSE (%): 100
DESCRIPTION: Provides direct services for sexual assault victims and significant others, prevention workshops for all groups, safe touch sexual abuse curriculum for preschoolers, and feminist martial arts/self-defense
CLIENTS/SERVICES: Sexual assault survivors; Marital rape/sexual abuse survivors; Child victims of sexual abuse; Adult survivors of child sexual abuse; Incest victims/survivors; Prevention program; Community education; Adolescent survivors of sexual abuse; Male survivors of sexual abuse
REQUIREMENTS: Incident must be reported in order for minors to receive in-house counseling
SPECIAL PROGRAMS/SERVICES: *Safe Touch: A Sexual Abuse Prevention Curriculum for Preschoolers.* This is a complete kit which teaches child care providers, parents, and teachers the same child sexual abuse prevention skills that STAR uses in its prevention workshops (Cost $325)

BARROW

ARCTIC WOMEN IN CRISIS (AWIC)
PO Box 69, Barrow, AK 99723
Crisis hotline: **(907) 852-4357 (HELP) 24 hrs**
Information: (907) 852-2942 24 hrs
Contact: Cheryl Fraley, Coord; Jeanne Cross, Counselor
TYPE OF AGENCY: Rape crisis center; Domestic violence program; Child sexual abuse services; Child sexual abuse prevention program
SPONSORING ORGANIZATION: State of Alaska/North Slope Borough
AREAS SERVED: North Slope Borough Villages; clients out of area
YEARS IN OPERATION: 9
LANGUAGES: Inupiak, Tagalik
CLIENTS/SERVICES: Sexual assault survivors; Marital rape/sexual abuse survivors; Child victims of sexual abuse; Adult survivors of child sexual abuse; Incest victims/survivors; Prevention program; Community education; Adolescent survivors of sexual abuse; Male survivors of sexual abuse

BETHEL

SOUTHWESTERN ALASKA COUNCIL FOR PREVENTION OF CHILD SEXUAL ABUSE
PO Box 1948, Bethel, AK 99559
Information: (907) 543-3994, 543-3995 8am-5pm
Contact: Hollis Brettschneider, Dir; Lynn Quackenbush, Dir
TYPE OF AGENCY: Child sexual abuse services; Child sexual abuse prevention program
AREAS SERVED: City of Bethel and 56 surrounding villages
YEARS IN OPERATION: 6
LANGUAGES: Yup'ik
CASES SEXUAL ASSAULT/ABUSE (%): 100
CLIENTS/SERVICES: Child victims of sexual abuse; Incest victims/survivors; Prevention program; Community education; Adolescent survivors of sexual abuse; Male survivors of sexual abuse; Publications/media
SPECIAL PROGRAMS/SERVICES: Publications: *Child Sexual Assault Prevention Information*; *The Right Touch: A Sexual Abuse Prevention Story Based in Rural Alaska*. *The Right Touch* was written to help parents and teachers talk to young children (ages 3 to 9) about sexual abuse. The setting of this story is rural Alaska. The main characters are a Yup'ik Eskimo father and his son. The story emphasizes that children can say no and can tell their parents right away if a family friend or a family member tries to molest them. The story affirms a child's natural instinct for sensing danger and will help a child feel strong and loved.

DILLINGHAM

DISTRICT ATTORNEY'S OFFICE—VICTIM/WITNESS ASSISTANCE PROGRAM
PO Box 470, Dillingham, AK 99576
Information: (907) 842-2482 8am-4:30pm
Contact: Susan Kaltenbacher, Paralegal and Victim/Witness Coord
TYPE OF AGENCY: Victim/witness assistance program
SPONSORING ORGANIZATION: 3rd Judicial District, Dept of Law
AREAS SERVED: 3rd Judicial District-Bristol Bay Region
YEARS IN OPERATION: 4
LANGUAGES: Yup'ik, Aleut
CASES SEXUAL ASSAULT/ABUSE (%): 25
CLIENTS/SERVICES: Sexual assault survivors; Child victims of sexual abuse; Incest victims/survivors; Male survivors of sexual abuse
REQUIREMENTS: Charges must be filed.

SAFE AND FEAR FREE ENVIRONMENT (SAFE)
PO Box 94, Dillingham, AK 99576
Crisis hotline: **(907) 842-2316 24 hrs**
Information: (907) 842-2320 8:30am-5pm
Contact: Beverly Fletcher, Exec Dir
TYPE OF AGENCY: Rape crisis center; Domestic violence program
AREAS SERVED: Bristol Bay Region (Dillingham and 32 villages)
YEARS IN OPERATION: 6
LANGUAGES: Yup'ik Eskimo
CASES SEXUAL ASSAULT/ABUSE (%): 25
CLIENTS/SERVICES: Sexual assault survivors; Marital rape/sexual abuse survivors; Child victims of sexual abuse; Adult survivors of child sexual abuse; Incest victims/survivors; Prevention program; Community education; Adolescent survivors of sexual abuse; Male survivors of sexual abuse

FAIRBANKS

FAIRBANKS CHILD SEXUAL ABUSE TASK FORCE
1550 Gillam Way, Fairbanks, AK 99701
Crisis hotline: **(907) 452-1844 (CPS) 24 hrs**
Information: (907) 456-2866 9am-5pm
Contact: Theresa Tanoury, Coord
TYPE OF AGENCY: Child sexual abuse services; Interagency network
SPONSORING ORGANIZATION: Resource Center for Parents and Children
AREAS SERVED: Fairbanks North Star Borough
YEARS IN OPERATION: 6
CASES SEXUAL ASSAULT/ABUSE (%): 100
DESCRIPTION: Interagency coordination and consultation for all nonprofit organizations concerned about child sexual abuse, including interagency case staffing, data collection, and resource and referral services
CLIENTS/SERVICES: Child victims of sexual abuse; Adolescent survivors of sexual abuse; Male survivors of sexual abuse

WOMEN IN CRISIS—COUNSELING AND ASSISTANCE (WICCA)
702 10th Ave, Fairbanks, AK 99701
Crisis hotline: **(907) 452-RAPE 24 hrs**
Information: (907) 452-2293 9am-5pm (Mon-Fri)
Contact: Ruth Lister, Exec Dir
TYPE OF AGENCY: Rape crisis center; Domestic violence program; Child sexual abuse services; Child sexual abuse prevention program
AREAS SERVED: Interior Alaska
YEARS IN OPERATION: 11
LANGUAGES: Translators available, Yup'ik, Kutchin
ACCESSIBILITY: Wheelchair accessible; Telecommunications for the hearing impaired (TTY, TDY, etc.)
CASES SEXUAL ASSAULT/ABUSE (%): 15
CLIENTS/SERVICES: Sexual assault survivors; Marital rape/sexual abuse survivors; Child victims of sexual abuse; Adult survivors of child sexual abuse; Incest victims/survivors; Prevention program; Community education; Adolescent survivors of sexual abuse; Male survivors of sexual abuse; Healing; Publications/media
SPECIAL PROGRAMS/SERVICES: *Aware Children, Safe Children* ($12.50) is a curriculum for child sexual abuse prevention specifically addressing rural communities. Healing through wilderness therapy available for adult survivors of child sexual abuse.

HOMER

SOUTH PENINSULA WOMEN'S SERVICES, INC
PO Box 2328, Homer, AK 99603
Crisis hotline: **(907) 235-8101 5pm-8:30am (Mon-Fri); 24 hrs (Sat, Sun, and holidays)**
Information: (907) 235-8101, 235-7712 8:30am-5pm (Mon-Fri)
Contact: Jayne Andreen, Exec Dir
TYPE OF AGENCY: Rape crisis center; Domestic violence program; Child sexual abuse services
AREAS SERVED: Homer, Anchor Point, Seldovia, Ninilchik, English Bay, Port Graham, and Nikolysk
YEARS IN OPERATION: 7
CASES SEXUAL ASSAULT/ABUSE (%): 15
DESCRIPTION: Services for survivors of sexual assault and domestic violence; Treatment for batterers using group therapy
CLIENTS/SERVICES: Sexual assault survivors; Marital rape/sexual abuse survivors; Child victims of sexual abuse; Adult survivors of child sexual abuse; Incest victims/survivors; Community education; Adolescent survivors of sexual abuse; Male survivors of sexual abuse

JUNEAU

AIDING WOMEN FROM ABUSE AND RAPE EMERGENCIES (AWARE)
PO Box 020809, Juneau, AK 99802
Crisis hotline: **(907) 586-1090 24 hrs**
Information: (907) 586-6623 8am-5pm
Contact: Marsha Kaighan, Exec Dir
TYPE OF AGENCY: Rape crisis center; Domestic violence program; Child sexual abuse services; Child sexual abuse prevention program
YEARS IN OPERATION: 10
LANGUAGES: Filipino
CASES SEXUAL ASSAULT/ABUSE (%): 23
DESCRIPTION: Provides shelter, advocacy, and education for victims (and their children) of domestic violence and sexual assault; Elder abuse advocates available
CLIENTS/SERVICES: Sexual assault survivors; Marital rape/sexual abuse survivors; Child victims of sexual abuse; Adult survivors of child sexual abuse; Incest victims/survivors; Prevention program; Community education; Adolescent survivors of sexual abuse; Male survivors of sexual abuse; Elderly

MEN, INC
222 Seward St, Ste 202, Juneau, AK 99801
Crisis hotline: **(907) 586-3585 24 hrs**
Information: (907) 586-3585 8:30am-5pm
Contact: Sharon Brogan, Exec Dir
TYPE OF AGENCY: Offender treatment
AREAS SERVED: Borough of Juneau
YEARS IN OPERATION: 8
CASES SEXUAL ASSAULT/ABUSE (%): 70
DESCRIPTION: Counseling services for perpetrators of domestic violence and sexual assault.
CLIENTS/SERVICES: Offender treatment program
REQUIREMENTS: Middle school age or older.

KENAI

DISTRICT ATTORNEY'S OFFICE—VICTIM/WITNESS ASSISTANCE PROGRAM
145 Main St Loop, Rm 201, Kenai, AK 99611
Information: (907) 283-3131 8am-5pm
Contact: Bonnie Graveley, DA's Ofc
TYPE OF AGENCY: Victim/witness assistance program
CLIENTS/SERVICES: Sexual assault survivors; Child victims of sexual abuse

WOMEN'S RESOURCE AND CRISIS CENTER/LEESHORE
325 S Spruce St, Kenai, AK 99611
Crisis hotline: **(907) 283-7257 24 hrs**
Information: (907) 283-9479 9am-5pm
Contact: Joanne Lopez, Exec Dir
TYPE OF AGENCY: Rape crisis center; Domestic violence program
AREAS SERVED: Kenai Peninsula Borough
YEARS IN OPERATION: 11
ACCESSIBILITY: Wheelchair accessible; Signers for the hearing impaired
CASES SEXUAL ASSAULT/ABUSE (%): 10
DESCRIPTION: Services for survivors of sexual assault and domestic violence; Treatment for batterers using group therapy
CLIENTS/SERVICES: Sexual assault survivors; Marital rape/sexual abuse survivors; Child victims of sexual abuse; Adult survivors of child sexual abuse; Incest victims/survivors; Prevention program; Community education; Offender treatment program; Adolescent survivors of sexual abuse; Male survivors of sexual abuse

KETCHIKAN

DISTRICT ATTORNEY'S OFFICE—VICTIM/WITNESS ASSISTANCE
415 Main St, Rm 304, Ketchikan, AK 99901
Information: (907) 225-6128 8am-4:30pm (Mon-Fri)
Contact: Judy Beatty, Paralegal Asst

DISTRICT ATTORNEY'S OFFICE—VICTIM/WITNESS ASSISTANCE *(continued)*

TYPE OF AGENCY: Victim/witness assistance program
AREAS SERVED: Ketchikan Gateway Borough, Petersburg, Kake, Prince of Wales Island
YEARS IN OPERATION: 6
CLIENTS/SERVICES: Sexual assault survivors; Child victims of sexual abuse
REQUIREMENTS: Case must be prosecuted or considered for prosecution

WOMEN IN SAFE HOMES (WISH)
PO Box 6552, Ketchikan, AK 99901
Crisis hotline: **(907) 225-9474 24 hrs**
Information: (907) 225-9474, (800) 478-9474 24 hrs
Contact: Vicky Armstrong, Admin Asst
TYPE OF AGENCY: Rape crisis center; Domestic violence program; Child sexual abuse services; Child sexual abuse prevention program
AREAS SERVED: Ketchikan, Prince of Wales Island, Wrangell Petersburg, Metlakatla
YEARS IN OPERATION: 10
ACCESSIBILITY: Wheelchair accessible
CASES SEXUAL ASSAULT/ABUSE (%): 10-20
CLIENTS/SERVICES: Sexual assault survivors; Marital rape/sexual abuse survivors; Child victims of sexual abuse; Adult survivors of child sexual abuse; Incest victims/survivors; Prevention program; Community education; Adolescent survivors of sexual abuse; Male survivors of sexual abuse; Publications/media
SPECIAL PROGRAMS/SERVICES: The following publications are for sale: *My Body Belongs to Me Book*, a personal safety coloring book ($3.00); *Hitting Hurts, Ask the Bears*, a domestic violence coloring book ($3.00); *The Woman Inside*, an incest survivor's workbook ($15.00).

KODIAK

KODIAK WOMEN'S RESOURCE AND CRISIS CENTER
PO Box 2122, Kodiak, AK 99615
Crisis hotline: **(907) 486-3625 24 hrs**
Information: (907) 486-6171 7:30am-11pm
Contact: Letitia Raub, Exec Dir
TYPE OF AGENCY: Domestic violence program
AREAS SERVED: Kodiak Island
YEARS IN OPERATION: 10
ACCESSIBILITY: Wheelchair accessible
CASES SEXUAL ASSAULT/ABUSE (%): 6
CLIENTS/SERVICES: Sexual assault survivors; Marital rape/sexual abuse survivors; Child victims of sexual abuse; Adult survivors of child sexual abuse; Incest victims/survivors; Prevention program; Community education; Adolescent survivors of sexual abuse; Male survivors of sexual abuse

KOTZEBUE

MANIILAQ REGIONAL WOMEN'S CRISIS PROJECT
PO Box 256, Kotzebue, AK 99752
Crisis hotline: **(907) 442-3969 24 hrs**
Information: (907) 442-3311, ext 123 8am-5pm (Mon-Fri)
Contact: Aurora Kramer, Prog Mgr
TYPE OF AGENCY: Domestic violence program
AREAS SERVED: Nana region
YEARS IN OPERATION: 8
LANGUAGES: Inupiak
ACCESSIBILITY: Wheelchair accessible
DESCRIPTION: Services for survivors of sexual and domestic violence; Treatment for batterers using men's anger control group
CLIENTS/SERVICES: Sexual assault survivors; Marital rape/sexual abuse survivors; Child victims of sexual abuse; Incest victims/survivors; Prevention program; Community education; Offender treatment program; Adolescent survivors of sexual abuse

NOME

BERING SEA WOMEN'S GROUP
Box 1596, Nome, AK 99762
Crisis hotline: **(907) 443-5444 24 hrs**
Information: (907) 443-5941 8am-5pm
Contact: Cathryn J Weber, Children's Svcs Coord
TYPE OF AGENCY: Rape crisis center; Domestic violence program; Child sexual abuse services; Child sexual abuse prevention program
AREAS SERVED: Bering Straits, Norton Sound region (Nome and 15 villages)
YEARS IN OPERATION: 10
LANGUAGES: Siberian, Yup'ik, Inupiat
DESCRIPTION: Services for sexual assault and domestic violence survivors; Treatment for rapists, batterers, and child sexual abuse offenders in local correctional center
CLIENTS/SERVICES: Sexual assault survivors; Marital rape/sexual abuse survivors; Child victims of sexual abuse; Adult survivors of child sexual abuse; Incest victims/survivors; Prevention program; Community education; Offender treatment program; Adolescent survivors of sexual abuse; Male survivors of sexual abuse; Publications/media
SPECIAL PROGRAMS/SERVICES: Media program: *Village to Village* produced in Alaskan rural villages

PALMER

DISTRICT ATTORNEY'S OFFICE—VICTIM/WITNESS ASSISTANCE PROGRAM
809 S Chugach, Ste 3, Palmer, AK 99645
Information: (907) 745-5027 8am-5pm
Contact: Cindy A Belcher, Paralegal Asst; Kathryn M Dawkins, Paralegal Asst
TYPE OF AGENCY: Victim/witness assistance program
AREAS SERVED: Matanuska-Susitna Borough
ACCESSIBILITY: Wheelchair accessible
CLIENTS/SERVICES: Sexual assault survivors; Child victims of sexual abuse
REQUIREMENTS: The victim must report to law enforcement; District Attorney files charges as appropriate.

VALDEZ

ADVOCATES FOR VICTIMS OF VIOLENCE (AVV)
PO Box 524, Valdez, AK 99686
Crisis hotline: **(907) 835-2999 24 hrs**
Information: (907) 835-2980 8:30am-5pm
Contact: Evie Smith, Exec Dir
TYPE OF AGENCY: Rape crisis center; Domestic violence program
AREAS SERVED: Copper Basin area, Cordova, Tatitlek
YEARS IN OPERATION: 8
LANGUAGES: Interpreters available
ACCESSIBILITY: Signers for the hearing impaired
CLIENTS/SERVICES: Sexual assault survivors; Marital rape/sexual abuse survivors; Child victims of sexual abuse; Adult survivors of child sexual abuse; Incest victims/survivors; Prevention program; Community education; Adolescent survivors of sexual abuse; Male survivors of sexual abuse

ARIZONA

CASA GRANDE

BEHAVIORAL HEALTH AGENCY OF CENTRAL ARIZONA
102 W Main St, Casa Grande, AZ 85222
Crisis hotline: **(602) 836-2880, 723-3027, (800) 822-3046 24 hrs**
Information: (602) 836-1688 8am-5pm; Evening hrs available, as arranged with therapists
Contact: Tino DeAnda, Exec Dir; Anne Marie Cardinal, Family Svcs Coord
TYPE OF AGENCY: Counseling/mental health services; Child sexual abuse services
AREAS SERVED: Pinal
LANGUAGES: Spanish, Sign, Papago
ACCESSIBILITY: Wheelchair accessible; Signers for the hearing impaired
CASES SEXUAL ASSAULT/ABUSE (%): 20
CLIENTS/SERVICES: Sexual assault survivors; Marital rape/sexual abuse survivors; Child victims of sexual abuse; Adult survivors of child sexual abuse; Incest victims/survivors; Community education; Adolescent survivors of sexual abuse; Male survivors of sexual abuse
REQUIREMENTS: Sliding scale fee
SPECIAL PROGRAMS/SERVICES: The agency is planning a support group for mothers of victims of sexual abuse that incorporates a Native American "talking circle"

FLAGSTAFF

CENTER AGAINST DOMESTIC VIOLENCE, INC
2501 N 4th St, Ste 18, Flagstaff, AZ 86004
Crisis hotline: **(602) 774-7353 24 hrs**
Information: (602) 774-4503 8am-5pm (Mon-Fri); Evenings and weekends
Contact: Dottie Deerwester, Exec Dir
TYPE OF AGENCY: Domestic violence program
AREAS SERVED: Coconino, Mohave, Yavapai, Navajo, Apache, and Indian Reservations
YEARS IN OPERATION: 9
LANGUAGES: Spanish, Navajo, Hopi
ACCESSIBILITY: Wheelchair accessible; Telecommunications for the hearing impaired (TTY, TDY, etc.); Signers for the hearing impaired
CASES SEXUAL ASSAULT/ABUSE (%): 30
DESCRIPTION: Services for domestic violence survivors; Treatment for batterers using individual and group therapy
CLIENTS/SERVICES: Sexual assault survivors; Marital rape/sexual abuse survivors; Child victims of sexual abuse; Adult survivors of child sexual abuse; Incest victims/survivors; Prevention program; Community education; Offender treatment program; Adolescent survivors of sexual abuse; Male survivors of sexual abuse; Ethnic minorities
REQUIREMENTS: Sliding fee scale.

VICTIM/WITNESS SERVICES FOR COCONINO COUNTY
13 N San Francisco, Ste 102, Flagstaff, AZ 86001
Crisis hotline: **(602) 774-1411 24 hrs**
Information: (602) 779-6163 8:30am-4:30pm
Contact: Colleen Hendricks, Exec Dir
TYPE OF AGENCY: Victim/witness assistance program
AREAS SERVED: Coconino
YEARS IN OPERATION: 4
CASES SEXUAL ASSAULT/ABUSE (%): 6
CLIENTS/SERVICES: Sexual assault survivors; Marital rape/sexual abuse survivors; Child victims of sexual abuse; Adult survivors of child sexual abuse; Incest victims/survivors; Prevention program; Community education; Adolescent survivors of sexual abuse; Male survivors of sexual abuse
SPECIAL PROGRAMS/SERVICES: This agency has presented a public forum for parents of children who have been sexually assaulted.

GLENDALE

GLENDALE VICTIM ASSISTANCE
5850 W Glendale Ave, Glendale, AZ 85301
Crisis hotline: **(602) 931-5500 (through police after hours) 24 hrs**
Information: (602) 435-4063 9am-5:30pm (Mon-Fri)
Contact: Terrence Neary, Caseworker Coord
TYPE OF AGENCY: Victim/witness assistance program
SPONSORING ORGANIZATION: City of Glendale
AREAS SERVED: City of Glendale
YEARS IN OPERATION: 13
LANGUAGES: Spanish
ACCESSIBILITY: Wheelchair accessible; Telecommunications for the hearing impaired (TTY, TDY, etc.) (can be arranged); Signers for the hearing impaired (can be arranged)
CASES SEXUAL ASSAULT/ABUSE (%): 24
CLIENTS/SERVICES: Sexual assault survivors; Child victims of sexual abuse; Adolescent survivors of sexual abuse; Male survivors of sexual abuse

WEST VALLEY CHILD CRISIS CENTER, INC
PO Box 844, Glendale, AZ 85311-0844
Information: (602) 848-8863 24 hrs daily
Contact: Renea Gentry, Exec Dir
TYPE OF AGENCY: Child sexual abuse services; Residential treatment facility; Child abuse services; Shelter
AREAS SERVED: Maricopa
YEARS IN OPERATION: ½
LANGUAGES: Spanish translators available
ACCESSIBILITY: Wheelchair accessible; Signers for the hearing impaired
DESCRIPTION: Provides shelter for victims of child abuse and neglect, including sexual abuse, from infancy to 8 years of age
CLIENTS/SERVICES: Child victims of sexual abuse; Preschoolers
REQUIREMENTS: Children from infancy to 8 years of age are brought to center by CPS or law enforcement agencies

MESA

FAMILY SERVICE AGENCY
623 W Southern, No 5, Mesa, AZ 85210
Information: (602) 834-9290
Contact: William Rose, DSW
TYPE OF AGENCY: Counseling/mental health services
AREAS SERVED: Maricopa, Pinal
YEARS IN OPERATION: 14
ACCESSIBILITY: Wheelchair accessible
CASES SEXUAL ASSAULT/ABUSE (%): 30
DESCRIPTION: Counseling services for individuals, couples and families. Counselors have specialized training for working with adults molested as children
CLIENTS/SERVICES: Sexual assault survivors; Marital rape/sexual abuse survivors; Adult survivors of child sexual abuse; Incest victims/survivors
REQUIREMENTS: Sliding scale fee

PREHAB'S AUTUMN HOUSE
PO Drawer 5860, Mesa, AZ 85211-5860
Crisis hotline: **(602) 835-5555 24 hrs**
Information: (602) 835-5782 24 hrs
Contact: Mellisa Womack, Dir
TYPE OF AGENCY: Domestic violence program
SPONSORING ORGANIZATION: Prehab of Arizona
AREAS SERVED: East Valley, Maricopa County
YEARS IN OPERATION: 5
CASES SEXUAL ASSAULT/ABUSE (%): 15
CLIENTS/SERVICES: Sexual assault survivors; Marital rape/sexual abuse survivors; Child victims of sexual abuse; Adult survivors of child sexual abuse; Incest victims/survivors; Prevention program; Community education; Adolescent survivors of sexual abuse

VALLEY EAST COUNSELING
628 N Center, No 203, Mesa, AZ 85201
Information: (602) 827-9064 9am-6pm
Contact: Adele Mayer, PhD
TYPE OF AGENCY: Private practice
AREAS SERVED: Maricopa, Pinal
YEARS IN OPERATION: 4½
CASES SEXUAL ASSAULT/ABUSE (%): 100
DESCRIPTION: Specialist in sex abuse; Author of 3 books on sex abuse; contract with victim witness, juvenile probation, Dept of Economic Security; have volunteer paraprofessionals assisting
CLIENTS/SERVICES: Sexual assault survivors; Marital rape/sexual abuse survivors; Child victims of sexual abuse; Adult survivors of child

VALLEY EAST COUNSELING (continued)

sexual abuse; Incest victims/survivors; Community education

PAGE

PAGE WOMEN'S RESOURCE CENTER
PO Box 3049, Page, AZ 86040
Crisis hotline: **(602) 645-8843 24 hrs**
Information: (602) 645-8843 24 hrs
Contact: Cherlyn Leach, Supv
TYPE OF AGENCY: Rape crisis center; Domestic violence program
SPONSORING ORGANIZATION: Coconino Community Guidance Center
AREAS SERVED: Coconino
YEARS IN OPERATION: 6
CASES SEXUAL ASSAULT/ABUSE (%): 40
DESCRIPTION: Services for sexual assault and domestic violence survivors; Individual therapy for incest offenders and batterers
CLIENTS/SERVICES: Sexual assault survivors; Marital rape/sexual abuse survivors; Child victims of sexual abuse; Adult survivors of child sexual abuse; Incest victims/survivors; Prevention program; Community education; Adolescent survivors of sexual abuse

PHOENIX

CENTER AGAINST SEXUAL ASSAULT
2211 E Highland, No 100, Phoenix, AZ 85016
Crisis hotline: **(602) 257-8095 24 hrs**
Information: (602) 956-1163 8am-5pm
Contact: Stephanie Orr, Exec Dir
TYPE OF AGENCY: Rape crisis center; Child sexual abuse services; Child sexual abuse prevention program; Acquaintance/date rape prevention program
AREAS SERVED: Maricopa
YEARS IN OPERATION: 16
LANGUAGES: Spanish
CASES SEXUAL ASSAULT/ABUSE (%): 100
DESCRIPTION: Comprehensive rape crisis services; Individual therapy for adolescent offenders
CLIENTS/SERVICES: Sexual assault survivors; Marital rape/sexual abuse survivors; Child victims of sexual abuse; Adult survivors of child sexual abuse; Incest victims/survivors; Prevention program; Community education; Offender treatment program; Adolescent survivors of sexual abuse; Male survivors of sexual abuse; Publications/media
SPECIAL PROGRAMS/SERVICES: Offers media program on date rape

CENTER FOR LIVING
4545 N 36th St, Ste 215, Phoenix, AZ 85018
Crisis hotline: **(602) 955-9757 evenings**
Information: (602) 955-9757 8am-6pm
Contact: Ken Olson, EdD, Clinical Psychologist/ Lutheran Pastor
TYPE OF AGENCY: Counseling/mental health services
AREAS SERVED: Maricopa
YEARS IN OPERATION: 7
CASES SEXUAL ASSAULT/ABUSE (%): 10
DESCRIPTION: This center provides a special ministry of healing the whole person, emotional, mental, spiritual, and physical, according to the teachings of Jesus Christ. Service is provided through individual, marital, and family therapy.
CLIENTS/SERVICES: Sexual assault survivors; Marital rape/sexual abuse survivors; Child victims of sexual abuse; Adult survivors of child sexual abuse; Incest victims/survivors; Prevention program; Community education; Offender treatment program; Adolescent survivors of sexual abuse; Male survivors of sexual abuse; Healing
SPECIAL PROGRAMS/SERVICES: Laying on of hands for healing wounded emotions and memories

CRIME VICTIM FOUNDATION
101 W Jefferson, 4th Fl, Phoenix, AZ 85003
Information: (602) 262-3653 8am-5pm
Contact: Carol Hebert, Exec Dir
TYPE OF AGENCY: Victim/witness assistance program
AREAS SERVED: Maricopa
YEARS IN OPERATION: 4
LANGUAGES: Spanish
ACCESSIBILITY: Wheelchair accessible
DESCRIPTION: Financial compensation and assistance for victims of violent crime. Money for victim compensation comes almost entirely from the community
CLIENTS/SERVICES: Sexual assault survivors; Marital rape/sexual abuse survivors; Child victims of sexual abuse; Adult survivors of child sexual abuse; Incest victims/survivors; Community education; Adolescent survivors of sexual abuse; Male survivors of sexual abuse
REQUIREMENTS: Must file a police report within 72 hours of occurrence; Claim must be filed with the foundation within 1 year of occurrence, except on child molestation cases

JEWISH FAMILY AND CHILDREN'S SERVICE
2033 N 7th St, Phoenix, AZ 85006
Information: (602) 257-1904 8am-8pm (Mon, Tue); 8am-5pm (Wed, Thu); 8am-3:30pm (Fri)
Contact: Adrien Shalowitz, Dir
TYPE OF AGENCY: Counseling/mental health services
AREAS SERVED: Maricopa
YEARS IN OPERATION: 33
LANGUAGES: Spanish
ACCESSIBILITY: Wheelchair accessible
CASES SEXUAL ASSAULT/ABUSE (%): 10
CLIENTS/SERVICES: Sexual assault survivors; Marital rape/sexual abuse survivors; Child victims of sexual abuse; Adult survivors of child sexual abuse; Incest victims/survivors; Offender treatment program; Adolescent survivors of sexual abuse; Male survivors of sexual abuse

MARICOPA COUNTY ATTORNEY'S OFFICE—VICTIM WITNESS PROGRAM
101 W Jefferson Ave, 4th Fl, Phoenix, AZ 85003
Information: (602) 262-8522 7:30am-5pm (Mon-Fri)
Contact: Carol McFadden, MSW, Dir
TYPE OF AGENCY: Victim/witness assistance program
AREAS SERVED: Maricopa
YEARS IN OPERATION: 10
LANGUAGES: Spanish
ACCESSIBILITY: Wheelchair accessible
CASES SEXUAL ASSAULT/ABUSE (%): 10
CLIENTS/SERVICES: Sexual assault survivors; Marital rape/sexual abuse survivors; Child victims of sexual abuse; Incest victims/survivors

SOJOURNER CENTER
PO Box 2649, 361 N 4th Ave, Phoenix, AZ 85003
Crisis hotline: **(602) 258-5344 24 hrs**
Information: (602) 258-5344 8am-5pm
Contact: Carol Minon, Clinical Dir
TYPE OF AGENCY: Domestic violence program
AREAS SERVED: Maricopa
YEARS IN OPERATION: 10
LANGUAGES: Interpreters available
ACCESSIBILITY: Wheelchair accessible
CASES SEXUAL ASSAULT/ABUSE (%): 10
DESCRIPTION: Services for survivors of sexual assault and domestic violence; Batterers treatment using individual and group therapy
CLIENTS/SERVICES: Sexual assault survivors; Marital rape/sexual abuse survivors; Child victims of sexual abuse; Adult survivors of child sexual abuse; Incest victims/survivors; Prevention program; Community education; Adolescent survivors of sexual abuse; Male survivors of sexual abuse

PRESCOTT

ARIZONA CENTER FOR PSYCHOTHERAPY
1680 Iron Springs Rd, Prescott, AZ 86301
Information: (602) 445-3136 24 hr answering machine
Contact: Dr Mitchell Gelber
TYPE OF AGENCY: Private practice
AREAS SERVED: Yavapai
YEARS IN OPERATION: 2½
ACCESSIBILITY: Wheelchair accessible
CASES SEXUAL ASSAULT/ABUSE (%): 30-50
DESCRIPTION: Counseling for survivors; Support groups for female and male survivors of sexual abuse/assault; Treatment for child sexual abuse/incest offenders and batterers
CLIENTS/SERVICES: Sexual assault survivors; Marital rape/sexual abuse survivors; Child victims of sexual abuse; Adult survivors of child sexual abuse; Incest victims/survivors; Community education; Offender treatment program; Adolescent survivors of sexual abuse; Male survivors of sexual abuse
REQUIREMENTS: Does not serve the mentally retarded
SPECIAL PROGRAMS/SERVICES: Second location at 402 N Mt Vernon, Prescott, AZ 86301, (602) 445-3435, Contact: Karen Sullivan

FAITH HOUSE, INC
1535 Private Rd, Prescott, AZ 86301
Crisis hotline: **(602) 445-4673 24 hrs**
Information: (602) 445-4705 24 hrs
Contact: Robin Burke, Dir
TYPE OF AGENCY: Rape crisis center; Domestic violence program; Child sexual abuse services; Child sexual abuse prevention program
AREAS SERVED: Northern AZ
YEARS IN OPERATION: 9
ACCESSIBILITY: Wheelchair accessible
CASES SEXUAL ASSAULT/ABUSE (%): 97
CLIENTS/SERVICES: Sexual assault survivors; Marital rape/sexual abuse survivors; Child victims of sexual abuse; Adult survivors of child sexual abuse; Incest victims/survivors; Prevention program; Community education; Offender treatment program; Adolescent survivors of sexual abuse; Male survivors of sexual abuse

WEST YAVAPAI VICTIM ASSISTANCE PROGRAM
505 S Cortez St, Prescott, AZ 86303
Crisis hotline: **(602) 445-7730 24 hrs**
Information: (602) 445-7730 8am-5pm (Mon, Wed, Fri); 8am-9pm (Tue, Thu)
Contact: Katherine Vlasic Seal, Prog Coord
TYPE OF AGENCY: Victim/witness assistance program; Counseling/mental health services; Child sexual abuse services; Residential treatment facility
SPONSORING ORGANIZATION: West Yavapai Guidance Clinic
AREAS SERVED: Western half of Yavapai
YEARS IN OPERATION: Victim Svcs 1; Clinic 22
LANGUAGES: Spanish
ACCESSIBILITY: Wheelchair accessible
CASES SEXUAL ASSAULT/ABUSE (%): 80
DESCRIPTION: Counseling and victim advocacy for survivors; Individual therapy for rapists, child sexual abuse offenders, incest offenders, and batterers
CLIENTS/SERVICES: Sexual assault survivors; Marital rape/sexual abuse survivors; Child victims of sexual abuse; Adult survivors of child sexual abuse; Incest victims/survivors; Community education; Adolescent survivors of sexual abuse; Male survivors of sexual abuse

SAFFORD

GRAHAM COUNTY ATTORNEY'S VICTIM WITNESS ASSISTANCE
523 10th Ave, Safford, AZ 85546
Crisis hotline: **(602) 428-3141 24 hrs**
Information: (602) 428-4678, 428-4787 8am-5pm
Contact: Ricci Vergara, Dir
TYPE OF AGENCY: Victim/witness assistance program
AREAS SERVED: Graham
YEARS IN OPERATION: 1
ACCESSIBILITY: Wheelchair accessible
CLIENTS/SERVICES: Sexual assault survivors; Marital rape/sexual abuse survivors; Child victims of sexual abuse; Adolescent survivors of sexual abuse; Male survivors of sexual abuse
REQUIREMENTS: Crime must be reported to a law enforcement/criminal justice agency.

SCOTTSDALE

CHILD SEXUAL ABUSE AWARENESS
7412 E Indian School Rd, Scottsdale, AZ 85251
Information: (602) 949-0631 8am-6pm (Mon-Thu)
Contact: LuAnn Richardson, Prog Coord
TYPE OF AGENCY: Child sexual abuse prevention program
SPONSORING ORGANIZATION: Coalition of City of Scottsdale, Scottsdale School District, and the Junior League of Phoenix
AREAS SERVED: Maricopa
YEARS IN OPERATION: 1½
CLIENTS/SERVICES: Prevention program; Community education

SIERRA VISTA

FORGACH HOUSE DOMESTIC CRISIS SHELTER
PO Box 1961, Sierra Vista, AZ 85636
Crisis hotline: **(602) 458-9096 24 hrs**
Information: (602) 458-9096 24 hrs
Contact: Tonianne Goebel, Dir
TYPE OF AGENCY: Domestic violence program
SPONSORING ORGANIZATION: Catholic Community Services
AREAS SERVED: Cochise
YEARS IN OPERATION: 5
LANGUAGES: Spanish
ACCESSIBILITY: Wheelchair accessible
CASES SEXUAL ASSAULT/ABUSE (%): 40
CLIENTS/SERVICES: Sexual assault survivors; Marital rape/sexual abuse survivors; Child victims of sexual abuse; Adult survivors of sexual abuse; Incest victims/survivors; Prevention program; Community education; Adolescent survivors of sexual abuse; Publications/media
REQUIREMENTS: Clients under the age of 18 must be accompanied by their mothers.
SPECIAL PROGRAMS/SERVICES: Media program: *Strong Kids, Safe Kids*

TEMPE

CHILD SEXUAL ABUSE TREATMENT CENTER
4653 S Lakeshore Dr, Ste 2, Tempe, AZ 85282
Information: (602) 820-2208 9am-5pm
Contact: Lee Fischler, Dir
TYPE OF AGENCY: Child sexual abuse services
AREAS SERVED: Maricopa
YEARS IN OPERATION: 4
CASES SEXUAL ASSAULT/ABUSE (%): 100
DESCRIPTION: Treatment for incestuous families and adults molested as children; Parents United Chapter; Individual and group therapy for child sexual abuse offenders and incest offenders
CLIENTS/SERVICES: Sexual assault survivors; Marital rape/sexual abuse survivors; Child victims of sexual abuse; Adult survivors of sexual abuse; Incest victims/survivors; Offender treatment program; Adolescent survivors of sexual abuse; Male survivors of sexual abuse

SOUTHWEST INSTITUTE FOR RESEARCH AND TREATMENT IN HUMAN SEXUALITY, LTD
5005 S Ash Ave, Ste 18, Tempe, AZ 85282
Information: (602) 831-5708 9am-10pm, 24-hr answering service
Contact: Lee L Fischler, Psychotherapist
TYPE OF AGENCY: Child sexual abuse services; Child sexual abuse prevention program; Private practice
AREAS SERVED: Statewide
YEARS IN OPERATION: 5
CASES SEXUAL ASSAULT/ABUSE (%): 100
DESCRIPTION: Treatment of victims, perpetrators, and spouses, including groups for female and male survivors and therapy for rapists, child sexual abuse/incest offenders, and batterers. Also provides therapy for sexual dysfunction
CLIENTS/SERVICES: Sexual assault survivors; Marital rape/sexual abuse survivors; Child victims of sexual abuse; Adult survivors of child sexual abuse; Incest victims/survivors; Prevention program; Community education; Offender treatment program; Adolescent survivors of sexual abuse; Male survivors of sexual abuse

TUCSON

ASSOCIATES IN PSYCHOTHERAPY
1647 N Alvernon, Ste 1, Tucson, AZ 85712
Crisis hotline: **(602) 326-3365 8:30am-4:30pm, 24-hr answering service**
Information: (602) 326-3365 8:30am-4:30pm, 24-hr answering service
Contact: Cindi Noshay, ACSW, Psychotherapist
TYPE OF AGENCY: Private practice
AREAS SERVED: Pima
YEARS IN OPERATION: 9
ACCESSIBILITY: Wheelchair accessible
CASES SEXUAL ASSAULT/ABUSE (%): 50
CLIENTS/SERVICES: Sexual assault survivors; Marital rape/sexual abuse survivors; Adult survivors of child sexual abuse; Incest victims/survivors; Community education; Male survivors of sexual abuse
REQUIREMENTS: Legal adult age and from abusive home

CASA DE LOS NINOS
347 E Speedway Blvd, Tucson, AZ 85715
Information: (602) 624-5600 24 hrs
Contact: Jeanne Landdeck-Sisco, Exec Dir
TYPE OF AGENCY: Hospital/medical center; Child sexual abuse services; Child sexual abuse prevention program; Child abuse services; Child abuse prevention program; Shelter
AREAS SERVED: Pima county and surrounding communities
YEARS IN OPERATION: 15
LANGUAGES: Spanish
CASES SEXUAL ASSAULT/ABUSE (%): 42
DESCRIPTION: Provides temporary residential care for abused and neglected infants and children from birth through age eleven
CLIENTS/SERVICES: Child victims of sexual abuse; Prevention program; Community education; Preschoolers
REQUIREMENTS: Children from infancy through age eleven

LA FRONTERA CENTER, INC
502 W 29th St, Tucson, AZ 85713
Information: (602) 884-9920 8am-6:30pm (Mon); 8am-8pm (Tue-Thu); 8am-5pm (Fri)
Contact: Nelba Chavez, PhD, Exec Dir
TYPE OF AGENCY: Counseling/mental health services; Child sexual abuse prevention program
AREAS SERVED: Pima
YEARS IN OPERATION: 20
LANGUAGES: Spanish
ACCESSIBILITY: Wheelchair accessible
CASES SEXUAL ASSAULT/ABUSE (%): 9.3
DESCRIPTION: Counseling for survivors; Individual and group therapy for rapists, child sexual abuse offenders, incest offenders, and batterers
CLIENTS/SERVICES: Sexual assault survivors; Marital rape/sexual abuse survivors; Child victims of sexual abuse; Adult survivors of child sexual abuse; Incest victims/survivors; Prevention program; Community education; Adolescent survivors of sexual abuse; Male survivors of sexual abuse
SPECIAL PROGRAMS/SERVICES: Volunteers work with staff in presenting a sex abuse prevention workshop for parents and children ages 5-10 years.

LAS FAMILIAS
3618 E Pima, Tucson, AZ 85716
Crisis hotline: **(602) 327-7122 8am-5pm (Mon-Fri)**
Information: (602) 327-7122
Contact: Donnah Colbert, Exec Dir
TYPE OF AGENCY: Counseling/mental health services; Child sexual abuse services
AREAS SERVED: Pima
YEARS IN OPERATION: 8
ACCESSIBILITY: Wheelchair accessible
CASES SEXUAL ASSAULT/ABUSE (%): 100
CLIENTS/SERVICES: Child victims of sexual abuse; Adult survivors of child sexual abuse; Offender treatment program; Adolescent survivors of sexual abuse; Male survivors of sexual abuse

MENTAL HEALTH ASSOCIATION OF GREATER TUCSON
121 S Olsen Ave, Tucson, AZ 85719
Information: (602) 623-7506 8:30am-4:30pm
Contact: Kathie Giarnieri, Ofc Mgr
TYPE OF AGENCY: Information center
AREAS SERVED: Pima
YEARS IN OPERATION: 30
DESCRIPTION: Resource center of films, videotapes, filmstrips, and books on topics pertaining to children and youth, including child sexual abuse
CLIENTS/SERVICES: Community education; Publications/media

OUR TOWN FAMILY CENTER
423 N Tucson Blvd, Tucson, AZ 85716
Crisis hotline: **(602) 323-1706 24 hrs 7 days**
Information: (602) 323-1708 9am-10pm
Contact: Joe Sadowsky, Prog Mgr
TYPE OF AGENCY: Counseling/mental health services; Child sexual abuse services; Child sexual abuse prevention program; Acquaintance/date rape prevention program; Adolescent program
AREAS SERVED: Pima
YEARS IN OPERATION: 10
LANGUAGES: Spanish, Yaqui
ACCESSIBILITY: Wheelchair accessible
CASES SEXUAL ASSAULT/ABUSE (%): 20
CLIENTS/SERVICES: Child victims of sexual abuse; Incest victims/survivors; Prevention program; Community education; Adolescent survivors of sexual abuse; Publications/media
REQUIREMENTS: Crisis counseling: Identified client must be under 18, but entire family will be seen. Extended counseling: Identified client must be under 18 and meet financial requirements for free services, sliding scale fee, EAP programs
SPECIAL PROGRAMS/SERVICES: Uses an interactive teen theatre model (role plays and discussion) to present the Date Rape and Teen Relationship Violence Prevention programs. Each school's drama department provides the actors who present to students, teachers, and parents in that school. OTFC staff trains school counselor to facilitate the program with the assistance of OTFC. Brochures, manual (including scripts, discussion guide, follow-up activities and program information) and videotapes are offered to schools. Also sponsors Child Assault Prevention Program (CAPP)

PSYCHOLOGICAL AND CONSULTING SERVICES
123 S Stone, No 2, Tucson, AZ 85704
Information: (602) 622-8887 8am-9pm
Contact: Steven Gray, Psychologist/Dir
TYPE OF AGENCY: Private practice; Offender treatment
AREAS SERVED: Pima
YEARS IN OPERATION: 2
CASES SEXUAL ASSAULT/ABUSE (%): 100
DESCRIPTION: Primarily provides assessment and treatment for perpetrators and victims of sexual assault and their families. Most work is with juveniles and adults under supervision of the department of corrections: rapists, child sexual abuse/incest offenders, and batterers
CLIENTS/SERVICES: Sexual assault survivors; Marital rape/sexual abuse survivors; Child victims of sexual abuse; Adult survivors of child sexual abuse; Incest victims/survivors; Offender treatment program; Adolescent survivors of sexual abuse; Male survivors of sexual abuse

SOUTHERN ARIZONA CENTER AGAINST SEXUAL ASSAULT (SACASA)
PO Box 40306, Tucson, AZ 85717
Crisis hotline: **(602) 623-7273 24 hrs**
Information: (602) 624-7273 9am-5pm
Contact: Gertha Brown-Hurd, Exec Dir
TYPE OF AGENCY: Rape crisis center
CLIENTS/SERVICES: Sexual assault survivors; Marital rape/sexual abuse survivors; Child victims of sexual abuse; Adult survivors of child sexual abuse; Incest victims/survivors; Community education; Adolescent survivors of sexual abuse
REQUIREMENTS: Children ages 8 and older, and adults

TUCSON CENTERS FOR WOMEN AND CHILDREN
PO Box 2632, Tucson, AZ 85702
Crisis hotline: **(602) 792-1929, 792-0285 24 hrs**
Information: (602) 795-4266 9am-5pm (Mon-Fri)
Contact: Amanda Phillips, Exec Dir
TYPE OF AGENCY: Domestic violence program
AREAS SERVED: Pima
YEARS IN OPERATION: 13
LANGUAGES: Spanish
CASES SEXUAL ASSAULT/ABUSE (%): 66
DESCRIPTION: Services for survivors of domestic violence; Can shelter rape victims and mothers of sexually abused children; Group therapy for batterers
CLIENTS/SERVICES: Sexual assault survivors; Marital rape/sexual abuse survivors; Child victims of sexual abuse; Adult survivors of child sexual abuse; Incest victims/survivors; Community education

YUMA

CASA DE YUMA
PO Box 4201, Yuma, AZ 85364
Crisis hotline: **(602) 782-7273 24 hrs**
Information: (602) 783-1860 8am-Noon
Contact: Kathy Jung Bierl
TYPE OF AGENCY: Rape crisis center; Domestic violence program; Child sexual abuse prevention program; Private practice
AREAS SERVED: Yuma
YEARS IN OPERATION: 10
LANGUAGES: Spanish
CASES SEXUAL ASSAULT/ABUSE (%): 99
CLIENTS/SERVICES: Sexual assault survivors; Marital rape/sexual abuse survivors; Child victims of sexual abuse; Adult survivors of child sexual abuse; Incest victims/survivors; Prevention program; Community education

ARKANSAS

ARKADELPHIA

RAPE CRISIS INTERVENTION
PO Box 924, Arkadelphia, AR 71923
Crisis hotline: **(501) 246-2587 24 hrs**
Information: (501) 246-3122 9am-5pm
Contact: Janye Bell, Exec Dir
TYPE OF AGENCY: Rape crisis center; Domestic violence program; Child sexual abuse services; Child sexual abuse prevention program; Shelter
SPONSORING ORGANIZATION: Abused Women and Children, Inc
AREAS SERVED: Clark, Dallas, Pike
YEARS IN OPERATION: 2
ACCESSIBILITY: Wheelchair accessible
CLIENTS/SERVICES: Sexual assault survivors; Marital rape/sexual abuse survivors; Child victims of sexual abuse; Adult survivors of child sexual abuse; Incest victims/survivors; Prevention program; Community education; Adolescent survivors of sexual abuse; Male survivors of sexual abuse

CONWAY

HAVEN
PO Box 1528, Conway, AR 72032
Crisis hotline: **(501) 327-1701 24 hrs**
Information: (501) 327-7706 8am-5pm
Contact: Lou Green, Prog Coord
TYPE OF AGENCY: Child sexual abuse services; Child sexual abuse prevention program; Residential treatment facility; Child abuse services; Shelter
SPONSORING ORGANIZATION: Counseling Associates
AREAS SERVED: Statewide
YEARS IN OPERATION: 2
ACCESSIBILITY: Signers for the hearing impaired
CASES SEXUAL ASSAULT/ABUSE (%): 50
DESCRIPTION: 24-hour emergency shelter for abused children
CLIENTS/SERVICES: Child victims of sexual abuse; Adult survivors of child sexual abuse; Prevention program; Community education; Adolescent survivors of sexual abuse
REQUIREMENTS: Must be 18 or younger; Non-abusing parent may accompany

FAYETTEVILLE

NORTHWEST ARKANSAS RAPE CRISIS, INC
PO Box 1824, Fayetteville, AR 72702
Crisis hotline: **(501) 443-2000 24 hrs**
Information: (501) 442-3833 8am-5pm
Contact: Kim Sampson, Dir
TYPE OF AGENCY: Rape crisis center
AREAS SERVED: Washington, Benton, Madison, Carroll
YEARS IN OPERATION: 10
LANGUAGES: Spanish
CASES SEXUAL ASSAULT/ABUSE (%): 100
CLIENTS/SERVICES: Sexual assault survivors; Marital rape/sexual abuse survivors; Child victims of sexual abuse; Adult survivors of child sexual abuse; Incest victims/survivors; Prevention program; Community education; Adolescent survivors of sexual abuse; Publications/media
SPECIAL PROGRAMS/SERVICES: Media program: 15-minute video describing services and plight of the victims

PROJECT FOR VICTIMS OF FAMILY VIOLENCE
PO Box 2915, Fayetteville, AR 72702
Crisis hotline: **(501) 442-9811 24 hrs**
Information: (501) 442-9811 24 hrs
TYPE OF AGENCY: Domestic violence program
AREAS SERVED: Washington, Benton, Madison, Carroll
YEARS IN OPERATION: 12
ACCESSIBILITY: Wheelchair accessible
CASES SEXUAL ASSAULT/ABUSE (%): 38
CLIENTS/SERVICES: Marital rape/sexual abuse survivors; Child victims of sexual abuse; Adult survivors of child sexual abuse; Incest victims/survivors; Community education; Offender treatment program; Adolescent survivors of sexual abuse; Publications/media
SPECIAL PROGRAMS/SERVICES: Publications: program manuals on working with battered women and their children, children's services in shelters, and outreach to rural battered women

WASHINGTON COUNTY PROSECUTING ATTORNEY'S OFFICE—VICTIM ADVOCACY PROGRAM
Courthouse Annex, Fayetteville, AR 72701
Information: (501) 521-8400, ext 462 8am-4:30pm
Contact: Kim Sampson, Victim Advocate
TYPE OF AGENCY: Victim/witness assistance program
AREAS SERVED: Washington
YEARS IN OPERATION: 2
ACCESSIBILITY: Wheelchair accessible
CASES SEXUAL ASSAULT/ABUSE (%): 75
CLIENTS/SERVICES: Sexual assault survivors; Marital rape/sexual abuse survivors; Child victims of sexual abuse; Incest victims/survivors; Community education

FORT SMITH

PROSECUTING ATTORNEY'S OFFICE
Sebastian County Courthouse, Fort Smith, AR 72901
Information: (501) 783-8976 8am-5pm
Contact: Rose Marie Riggs, Victim/Witness Coord
TYPE OF AGENCY: Victim/witness assistance program
AREAS SERVED: Sebastian, Crawford
YEARS IN OPERATION: 6
ACCESSIBILITY: Wheelchair accessible
CASES SEXUAL ASSAULT/ABUSE (%): 10-15
CLIENTS/SERVICES: Sexual assault survivors; Child victims of sexual abuse

RAPE CRISIS SERVICE
PO Box 2887, Station A, Fort Smith, AR 72913
Crisis hotline: **(501) 452-6650 24 hrs**
Information: (501) 452-6650 24 hrs
Contact: Jennifer A Johnson, Volunteer Coord
TYPE OF AGENCY: Rape crisis center; Counseling/mental health services
SPONSORING ORGANIZATION: Western Arkansas Counseling and Guidance Center
AREAS SERVED: Sebastian, Crawford
YEARS IN OPERATION: 10
CASES SEXUAL ASSAULT/ABUSE (%): 100
CLIENTS/SERVICES: Sexual assault survivors; Marital rape/sexual abuse survivors; Child victims of sexual abuse; Prevention program; Community education; Adolescent survivors of sexual abuse; Male survivors of sexual abuse

HARRISON

SANCTUARY, INC
PO Box 762, Harrison, AR 72601
Crisis hotline: **(501) 741-2121 24 hrs**
Information: (501) 741-2121 24 hrs
Contact: Neva Hacker, Coord
TYPE OF AGENCY: Rape crisis center; Domestic violence program; Victim/witness assistance program; Child sexual abuse prevention program
AREAS SERVED: 17 counties of northern Arkansas
YEARS IN OPERATION: 7
CASES SEXUAL ASSAULT/ABUSE (%): 43
CLIENTS/SERVICES: Sexual assault survivors; Marital rape/sexual abuse survivors; Child victims of sexual abuse; Adult survivors of child sexual abuse; Prevention program; Community education

HOT SPRINGS

COMMUNITY COUNSELING SERVICES, INC
PO Box 6399, Hot Springs, AR 71902
Crisis hotline: **(501) 624-7111 24 hrs**
Information: (501) 624-7111 9am-5pm (Mon-Fri)
Contact: Betty Harrison, RN, Clinical Dir and CEP Svc Dir
TYPE OF AGENCY: Counseling/mental health services
AREAS SERVED: Garland, Montgomery, Pike, Clark, Hot Spring
YEARS IN OPERATION: 19
ACCESSIBILITY: Wheelchair accessible; Signers for the hearing impaired
CASES SEXUAL ASSAULT/ABUSE (%): 10-12

COMMUNITY COUNSELING SERVICES, INC (continued)

CLIENTS/SERVICES: Sexual assault survivors; Marital rape/sexual abuse survivors; Child victims of sexual abuse; Adult survivors of child sexual abuse; Incest victims/survivors; Prevention program; Community education; Adolescent survivors of sexual abuse; Male survivors of sexual abuse
SPECIAL PROGRAMS/SERVICES: Classes in assertiveness, rape crisis, family effectiveness

GARLAND COUNTY RAPE TASK FORCE
705 Malvern Ave, Hot Springs, AR 71901
Crisis hotline: **(501) 623-4048 24 hrs**
Information: (501) 623-4048 8am-5pm
Contact: Jane Kuykendall, Pres
TYPE OF AGENCY: Rape crisis center
AREAS SERVED: Garland
YEARS IN OPERATION: 6
CASES SEXUAL ASSAULT/ABUSE (%): 100
CLIENTS/SERVICES: Sexual assault survivors; Marital rape/sexual abuse survivors; Child victims of sexual abuse; Incest victims/survivors; Prevention program; Community education

LITTLE ROCK

ARKANSAS CHILDREN'S HOSPITAL/ DEPARTMENT OF PEDIATRICS PROGRAM FOR CHILDREN AT RISK
800 Marshall St, Little Rock, AR 72202-3591
Crisis hotline: **(501) 370-1100 24 hrs**
Information: (501) 370-1013 8am-4:30pm
Contact: Jerry G Jones, MD, Prog Dir
TYPE OF AGENCY: Hospital/medical center; Child sexual abuse services; Child abuse services
SPONSORING ORGANIZATION: University of Arkansas for Medical Sciences
AREAS SERVED: Statewide
YEARS IN OPERATION: 8
ACCESSIBILITY: Wheelchair accessible
CASES SEXUAL ASSAULT/ABUSE (%): 70
DESCRIPTION: Child sexual abuse initial and follow-up evaluations and treatment for victims and their families; Training in conducting sexual abuse examinations for health professionals; Coordinates case management with community social services and legal agencies
CLIENTS/SERVICES: Child victims of sexual abuse; Adult survivors of child sexual abuse; Incest victims/survivors; Community education; Adolescent survivors of sexual abuse; Male survivors of sexual abuse
REQUIREMENTS: Post-menarchal female patients are referred outside the program
SPECIAL PROGRAMS/SERVICES: Support for sexually abused children during physical evaluation; preparation for and support during the examination provided for both the child and his/her non-perpetrating parent with protocol designed to emphasize the difference between the abuse and the examination. In the process of developing a videotape on physicians' evaluation and management of sexually abused children

SCAN VOLUNTEER SERVICE, INC
PO Box 7445, 2500 N Tyler, Little Rock, AR 72217
Information: (501) 661-1474
Contact: Norma Smothers, Training Dir
TYPE OF AGENCY: Child sexual abuse services; Child abuse services
DESCRIPTION: Conducts investigations and provides treatment or access to treatment for families experiencing a problem with child abuse, including child sexual abuse
CLIENTS/SERVICES: Child victims of sexual abuse; Adult survivors of child sexual abuse; Incest victims/survivors; Community education

PINE BLUFF

VOLUNTEERS IN COURTS RAPE CRISIS COUNSELING PROGRAM
509 National Bldg, Pine Bluff, AR 71601
Crisis hotline: **(501) 535-6770, 541-7100 24 hrs**
Information: (501) 535-6770 9am-5pm
Contact: Jackie Lowe, Counseling Coord
TYPE OF AGENCY: Rape crisis center
SPONSORING ORGANIZATION: Volunteers in Courts
AREAS SERVED: Jefferson, Lincoln, Desha, Cleveland
YEARS IN OPERATION: 3
CASES SEXUAL ASSAULT/ABUSE (%): 100
CLIENTS/SERVICES: Sexual assault survivors; Marital rape/sexual abuse survivors; Adult survivors of child sexual abuse; Prevention program; Community education; Adolescent survivors of sexual abuse; Male survivors of sexual abuse
REQUIREMENTS: Does not handle current incest cases on minors. (Those cases are referred to Department of Human Services)

CALIFORNIA

ALBANY

WESTCOAST CHILDREN'S CENTER
1501 Washington Ave, Albany, CA 94707
Information: (415) 527-7249 9am-5pm (Mon-Fri); 24-hr answering service
Contact: Margaret Kokka, Exec Dir
TYPE OF AGENCY: Counseling/mental health services; Child sexual abuse services
AREAS SERVED: Alameda, Contra Costa
YEARS IN OPERATION: 10
LANGUAGES: Spanish
CASES SEXUAL ASSAULT/ABUSE (%): 20
DESCRIPTION: Provision of psychotherapy for children and their families, including services for child and adolescent survivors of sexual abuse
CLIENTS/SERVICES: Child victims of sexual abuse; Incest victims/survivors; Adolescent survivors of sexual abuse; Male survivors of sexual abuse
REQUIREMENTS: Ages 2-18 and family members. Sliding scale fees

ANAHEIM

ORANGE COUNTY CENTER FOR HEALTH, INC
503 N Anaheim Blvd, Anaheim, CA 92805
Crisis hotline: **(714) 956-1900 9:30am-9:30pm (Mon-Thu); 9:30am-4pm (Fri)**
Information: (714) 956-1900 9:30am-9:30pm (Mon-Thu); 9:30am-4pm (Fri)
Contact: Richard Weber, PhD, Psychological Svcs Dir; Marcia Lyn Vickery, Exec Dir
TYPE OF AGENCY: Hospital/medical center; Counseling/mental health services
SPONSORING ORGANIZATION: United Way
AREAS SERVED: Orange
YEARS IN OPERATION: 20
LANGUAGES: Spanish, Vietnamese, Sign
ACCESSIBILITY: Wheelchair accessible; Signers for the hearing impaired
CASES SEXUAL ASSAULT/ABUSE (%): 2-5
DESCRIPTION: Offers comprehensive affordable medical services to all ages. The counseling program serves those seeking emotional support for the following: anxiety, phobias, child abuse, incest, sexual abuse, depression, domestic violence, death and dying, subustance abuse and suicide
CLIENTS/SERVICES: Sexual assault survivors; Marital rape/sexual abuse survivors; Child victims of sexual abuse; Adult survivors of child sexual abuse; Incest victims/survivors; Community education; Offender treatment program; Adolescent survivors of sexual abuse; Male survivors of sexual abuse
REQUIREMENTS: Payment of subsidized fee schedule charges, but no one is turned away because of an inability to afford payments

APTOS

CABRILLO COLLEGE RAPE PREVENTION PROGRAM
6500 Soquel Dr, Aptos, CA 95003
Information: (408) 479-6249 10am-5pm (Mon-Thu)
Contact: Melyssa Jo, Prog Coord
TYPE OF AGENCY: College/university-based services; Rape prevention program
SPONSORING ORGANIZATION: Cabrillo Women's Center
AREAS SERVED: Santa Cruz
YEARS IN OPERATION: 1
LANGUAGES: Spanish
ACCESSIBILITY: Wheelchair accessible; Telecommunications for the hearing impaired (TTY, TDY, etc.); Signers for the hearing impaired
DESCRIPTION: Education programs including women's self defense, confrontation training, classroom presentations, films and videos relating to all forms of violence against women
CLIENTS/SERVICES: Sexual assault survivors; Marital rape/sexual abuse survivors; Child victims of sexual abuse; Adult survivors of child sexual abuse; Incest victims/survivors; Prevention program; Community education; Adolescent survivors of sexual abuse; Sexual harassment
SPECIAL PROGRAMS/SERVICES: Confrontation training workshops teach women ways to confront harassment in work, school, street, and social situations. The program utilizes assertiveness and self defense training, using teachers, discussion, exercises and role-playing.

ATASCADERO

SEX OFFENDER TREATMENT AND EVALUATION PROJECT
Box 7001, Atascadero, CA 93423
Information: (805) 461-2497 8am-4pm
Contact: Craig Nelson, PhD, Treatment Dir
TYPE OF AGENCY: Correctional facility; Training/research; Offender treatment
SPONSORING ORGANIZATION: California Department of Mental Health
AREAS SERVED: Statewide
YEARS IN OPERATION: 3
CASES SEXUAL ASSAULT/ABUSE (%): 100
DESCRIPTION: Six-year clinical research study examining the effectiveness of treatment in reducing recidivism rates among child molesters and rapists
CLIENTS/SERVICES: Offender treatment program
REQUIREMENTS: Clients must be inmates of California Department of Corrections; between ages of 18-60; IQ above 80; speak English; not severely mentally ill; admit committing the offense; have between 18-30 months left on their sentence; and volunteer for treatment
SPECIAL PROGRAMS/SERVICES: The Project has a number of published and unpublished articles and manuals describing relapse prevention treatment with sex offenders. The project will share this material with other offender treatment programs

ATWATER

NORTHSIDE COMMUNITY COUNSELING CENTER
1510 Winton Way, Atwater, CA 95301
Crisis hotline: **(209) 723-8861 24 hrs**
Information: (209) 357-2333
TYPE OF AGENCY: Counseling/mental health services; Child sexual abuse services
CLIENTS/SERVICES: Sexual assault survivors; Child victims of sexual abuse; Adult survivors of child sexual abuse; Incest victims/survivors; Offender treatment program; Adolescent survivors of sexual abuse; Male survivors of sexual abuse

AUBURN

DISTRICT ATTORNEY'S OFFICE—VICTIM/WITNESS PROGRAM
11562 B St, Dewitt Center, Auburn, CA 95603
Information: (916) 823-4759 7:30am-5:30pm
Contact: Dechantal A Hughes, Prog Coord
TYPE OF AGENCY: Victim/witness assistance program
AREAS SERVED: Placer
YEARS IN OPERATION: 7
LANGUAGES: Spanish
ACCESSIBILITY: Wheelchair accessible; Signers for the hearing impaired
CASES SEXUAL ASSAULT/ABUSE (%): 45
CLIENTS/SERVICES: Sexual assault survivors; Marital rape/sexual abuse survivors; Child victims of sexual abuse
REQUIREMENTS: Must file report within one year of incident and be cooperative with law enforcement agencies and/or prosecution

PLACER COUNTY CHILD SEXUAL ABUSE TREATMENT PROGRAM
11427 D Ave, Auburn, CA 95603
Crisis hotline: **(916) 889-7240 24 hrs**
Information: (916) 889-7310 8am-5pm
Contact: Linda H Farley, MFCC, Dir
TYPE OF AGENCY: Counseling/mental health services; Child sexual abuse services; Child sexual abuse prevention program
SPONSORING ORGANIZATION: Placer County Mental Health
AREAS SERVED: Placer
YEARS IN OPERATION: 8
ACCESSIBILITY: Wheelchair accessible
CASES SEXUAL ASSAULT/ABUSE (%): 100

PLACER COUNTY CHILD SEXUAL ABUSE TREATMENT PROGRAM *(continued)*
CLIENTS/SERVICES: Child victims of sexual abuse; Incest victims/survivors; Prevention program; Community education; Offender treatment program; Adolescent survivors of sexual abuse
REQUIREMENTS: Victims between birth to 18 and members of their family are served

PLACER WOMEN'S CENTER
PO Box 5462, Auburn, CA 95604
Crisis hotline: **(916) 652-6558 24 hrs daily**
Information: (916) 885-0441 8am-5pm (Mon-Fri)
Contact: E Di Russo, Exec Dir
TYPE OF AGENCY: Domestic violence program
YEARS IN OPERATION: 12
LANGUAGES: Spanish
ACCESSIBILITY: Wheelchair accessible
CASES SEXUAL ASSAULT/ABUSE (%): 35
CLIENTS/SERVICES: Sexual assault survivors; Marital rape/sexual abuse survivors; Child victims of sexual abuse; Adult survivors of child sexual abuse; Incest victims/survivors; Prevention program; Community education

BAKERSFIELD

ALLIANCE ON FAMILY VIOLENCE
PO Box 2054, Bakersfield, CA 93303
Crisis hotline: **(800) 423-7337 24 hrs 7 days**
Information: (805) 322-0931 9am-5pm (Mon-Fri)
Contact: Millie Gilson, Dir
TYPE OF AGENCY: Rape crisis center; Domestic violence program
AREAS SERVED: Kern
YEARS IN OPERATION: 10
LANGUAGES: Spanish
ACCESSIBILITY: Wheelchair accessible
CASES SEXUAL ASSAULT/ABUSE (%): 10
DESCRIPTION: Provides a shelter for battered women; Outreach counseling; Community education; Men's support service program; Treatment for batterers; Feminist martial arts/self-defense
CLIENTS/SERVICES: Sexual assault survivors; Marital rape/sexual abuse survivors; Child victims of sexual abuse; Adult survivors of child sexual abuse; Incest victims/survivors; Prevention program; Community education; Adolescent survivors of sexual abuse; Male survivors of sexual abuse

COMMUNITY COUNSELING AND PSYCHOLOGICAL SERVICES
4800 Easton Dr, Ste 109, Bakersfield, CA 93309
Information: (805) 326-8167 24 hrs
Contact: Jack Byrom, PhD, Clinical Dir
TYPE OF AGENCY: Private practice; Community agency counseling service
AREAS SERVED: Kern
YEARS IN OPERATION: 10
ACCESSIBILITY: Wheelchair accessible
CASES SEXUAL ASSAULT/ABUSE (%): 50
DESCRIPTION: Community agency providing individual, conjoint, family counseling. Services provided by staff composed of psychiatrist, psychologist, MFCC therapists and psychiatric interns. Provides psychiatric assessment for legal defense
CLIENTS/SERVICES: Sexual assault survivors; Marital rape/sexual abuse survivors; Child victims of sexual abuse; Adult survivors of child sexual abuse; Incest victims/survivors; Adolescent survivors of sexual abuse; Male survivors of sexual abuse
REQUIREMENTS: Sliding scale fee

KERN COUNTY MENTAL HEALTH
2151 College Ave, Bakersfield, CA 93307
Crisis hotline: **(805) 395-0690 24 hrs**
Information: (805) 861-2251 8am-5pm
TYPE OF AGENCY: Counseling/mental health services
AREAS SERVED: Kern
LANGUAGES: Spanish
ACCESSIBILITY: Wheelchair accessible
CASES SEXUAL ASSAULT/ABUSE (%): 100
DESCRIPTION: Provides counseling for both victims/survivors and rapists and child sexual abuse/incest offenders; Sponsors chapters of Parents United for offenders and their families, AMAC groups for adults who were molested as children, and Daughters and Sons United for children (6-18) who have been molested
CLIENTS/SERVICES: Sexual assault survivors; Child victims of sexual abuse; Adult survivors of child sexual abuse; Incest victims/survivors; Community education; Offender treatment program; Adolescent survivors of sexual abuse; Male survivors of sexual abuse

HENRIETTA WEILL MEMORIAL CHILD GUIDANCE CLINIC
3628 Stockdale Hwy, Bakersfield, CA 93309
Information: (805) 322-1021 8am-5pm, answering service after 5pm
Contact: Barbara Reifel, Child Abuse Prog Mgr
TYPE OF AGENCY: Counseling/mental health services; Child sexual abuse services; Child sexual abuse prevention program
AREAS SERVED: Kern
YEARS IN OPERATION: 43
LANGUAGES: Spanish
ACCESSIBILITY: Wheelchair accessible
CASES SEXUAL ASSAULT/ABUSE (%): 20
DESCRIPTION: Mental health clinic for children includes a child abuse prevention program, a sexual abuse treatment program, treatment for juvenile sex offenders. Clinic staff also helps co-lead some Parents United groups sponsored by Kern County Mental Health
CLIENTS/SERVICES: Child victims of sexual abuse; Prevention program; Offender treatment program; Adolescent survivors of sexual abuse
REQUIREMENTS: Must be under 18

BANNING

MID-STEP MID-COUNTY INTERAGENCY SEXUAL ABUSE TREATMENT PROGRAM
PO Box 1024, Banning, CA 92220
Information: (714) 849-1725 24 hrs
Contact: Tim Bynum, MS, Coord
TYPE OF AGENCY: Child sexual abuse services
AREAS SERVED: Riverside
YEARS IN OPERATION: 2
CASES SEXUAL ASSAULT/ABUSE (%): 100
DESCRIPTION: Group treatment of incest with chapters of Parents United, Daughters and Sons United, Adults Molested As Children United
CLIENTS/SERVICES: Child victims of sexual abuse; Adult survivors of child sexual abuse; Incest victims/survivors; Community education; Offender treatment program; Adolescent survivors of sexual abuse; Male survivors of sexual abuse
SPECIAL PROGRAMS/SERVICES: Interagency coordination of treatment for incest families

BARSTOW

BARSTOW VICTIM/WITNESS CENTER
235 E Mountain View, Barstow, CA 92311
Information: (619) 256-4810 8am-5pm
Contact: Jesse R Fulbright, Victim/Witness Advocate
TYPE OF AGENCY: Victim/witness assistance program
SPONSORING ORGANIZATION: San Bernardino District Attorney's Office
AREAS SERVED: San Bernardino
YEARS IN OPERATION: 6
LANGUAGES: Spanish
ACCESSIBILITY: Wheelchair accessible
CASES SEXUAL ASSAULT/ABUSE (%): 50
CLIENTS/SERVICES: Sexual assault survivors; Marital rape/sexual abuse survivors; Child victims of sexual abuse; Incest victims/survivors; Community education; Male survivors of sexual abuse
REQUIREMENTS: For victim of violent crime funds, client must file charges

BAYSIDE

SURVIVORS OF INCEST ANONYMOUS
PO Box 358, Bayside, CA 95524
Information: (707) 826-1334, 442-3466
Contact: Diana, Sec; Debra, Group Representative
TYPE OF AGENCY: Adult survivors services
DESCRIPTION: 12-step recovery program for adults who were sexually abused as children. Planning for "Child Within" party
CLIENTS/SERVICES: Adult survivors of child sexual abuse; Incest victims/survivors; Healing

BERKELEY

FAMILY VIOLENCE LAW CENTER
PO Box 209, Berkeley, CA 94701
Crisis hotline: **(415) 540-5354 24 hrs answering service**
Information: (415) 549-2628 10am-5pm
Contact: Elaine Lee, Exec Dir
TYPE OF AGENCY: Domestic violence program; Legal services agency
AREAS SERVED: Northern Alameda
YEARS IN OPERATION: 10
LANGUAGES: Spanish
ACCESSIBILITY: Wheelchair accessible
CASES SEXUAL ASSAULT/ABUSE (%): 30-40
DESCRIPTION: Assists victims of domestic violence and sexual assault by securing a restraining order to keep the abuser away from the client and her children. The restraining order can also order the abuser to move out of the home; Provides child custody, visitation and support orders
CLIENTS/SERVICES: Marital rape/sexual abuse survivors; Community education

UNIVERSITY OF CALIFORNIA AT BERKELEY—RAPE PREVENTION EDUCATION PROGRAM
Cowell Memorial Hospital, Univ of CA, Rm 381, Berkeley, CA 94720
Information: (415) 642-7202 8am-5pm (Mon-Fri)
Contact: Roberta Friedman, Coord
TYPE OF AGENCY: College/university-based services; Rape prevention program
AREAS SERVED: Alameda
YEARS IN OPERATION: 12
ACCESSIBILITY: Wheelchair accessible
DESCRIPTION: Offers educational workshops for campus and community on acquaintance and stranger rape and prevention; Self-defense classes for women; Support and therapy groups for incest survivors, sexual assault survivors, battered women; Crisis counseling; Advocacy for victims and significant others; Information and referrals on ritual abuse
CLIENTS/SERVICES: Sexual assault survivors; Marital rape/sexual abuse survivors; Adult survivors of child sexual abuse; Incest victims/survivors; Prevention program; Community education; Male survivors of sexual abuse
REQUIREMENTS: Campus affiliates take priority
SPECIAL PROGRAMS/SERVICES: Conferences on ritual and satanic abuse, women molested by mothers, incest, and other topics. Has resource list for service providers who address the issue of ritual abuse

BIG BEAR LAKE

DOVES OF BIG BEAR VALLEY, INC
PO Box 3646, Big Bear Lake, CA 92315
Crisis hotline: **(714) 866-5723 24 hrs**
Information: (714) 585-0388 8am-4:30pm (Mon-Fri)
Contact: Kathy Parmenter, Prog Dir
TYPE OF AGENCY: Domestic violence program
AREAS SERVED: San Bernardino, Riverside, Los Angeles, Orange
YEARS IN OPERATION: 5
CASES SEXUAL ASSAULT/ABUSE (%): 10
DESCRIPTION: Domestic violence program, including group therapy for batterers
CLIENTS/SERVICES: Sexual assault survivors; Marital rape/sexual abuse survivors; Adult survivors of child sexual abuse; Incest victims/survivors; Community education; Adolescent survivors of sexual abuse

BISHOP

WILD IRIS WOMEN'S SERVICES
PO Box 57, Bishop, CA 93514
Crisis hotline: **(619) 873-7384 24 hrs**
Information: (619) 873-6601 10am-2pm (Mon-Fri)
Contact: Carla Scheidlinger, Exec Dir
TYPE OF AGENCY: Rape crisis center; Child sexual abuse prevention program
AREAS SERVED: Inyo, Mono
YEARS IN OPERATION: 7
LANGUAGES: Spanish
ACCESSIBILITY: Wheelchair accessible; Telecommunications for the hearing impaired (TTY, TDY, etc.)
CASES SEXUAL ASSAULT/ABUSE (%): 14
DESCRIPTION: Rape crisis center offering a complete child assault prevention program in schools for grades K-12; Rape prevention-self protection program; Services to women and children in crisis regarding issues of domestic violence, sexual assault, child abuse, and other social crises
CLIENTS/SERVICES: Sexual assault survivors; Marital rape/sexual abuse survivors; Child victims of sexual abuse; Adult survivors of child sexual abuse; Incest victims/survivors; Prevention program; Community education; Adolescent survivors of sexual abuse

BURLINGAME

FAMILY STRESS SERVICE
1811 Trousdale Dr, Burlingame, CA 94010
Crisis hotline: **(415) 697-2111 24 hrs daily**
Information: (415) 692-6662 8:30am-5pm
Contact: Yolanda Kohnert, Family Stress Svcs Dir
TYPE OF AGENCY: Counseling/mental health services
AREAS SERVED: San Mateo
YEARS IN OPERATION: 6
ACCESSIBILITY: Telecommunications for the hearing impaired (TTY, TDY, etc.)
DESCRIPTION: Counseling, support groups, and family therapy for survivors and their families; Group therapy for batterers
CLIENTS/SERVICES: Child victims of sexual abuse; Incest victims/survivors; Offender treatment program; Adolescent survivors of sexual abuse; Male survivors of sexual abuse
REQUIREMENTS: All clients must have an assessment session with therapist at agency. Sliding fee scales

PARENTS UNITED/CHILDREN UNITED
1870 El Camino Real, Burlingame, CA 94010
Crisis hotline: **(415) 697-2111 24 hrs daily**
Information: (415) 692-0555 9am-9pm (Mon-Thu); 9am-5pm (Fri, Sat)
Contact: Kassandra Dills, Prog Supv
TYPE OF AGENCY: Counseling/mental health services; Child sexual abuse services
SPONSORING ORGANIZATION: Family Service Agency
AREAS SERVED: San Mateo
YEARS IN OPERATION: 10
LANGUAGES: Spanish
CASES SEXUAL ASSAULT/ABUSE (%): 100
DESCRIPTION: Treats child victims of sexual abuse (both familial and nonfamilial), offenders, and nonoffending spouses referred by Children's Protective Services. Provides crisis counseling and outreach, individual and group therapies. Group for adults molested as children; Spanish-speaking Parents United Group
CLIENTS/SERVICES: Child victims of sexual abuse; Adult survivors of child sexual abuse; Incest victims/survivors; Offender treatment program; Adolescent survivors of sexual abuse
REQUIREMENTS: Child victims must be 5-17 years of age

RAPE CRISIS SERVICE OF SAN MATEO COUNTY
1811 Trousdale Dr, Burlingame, CA 94010
Crisis hotline: **(415) 692-7273 24 hrs daily**
Information: (415) 692-6662 8:30am-5pm
Contact: Dodi Lazarow, Rape Crisis Svc Dir
TYPE OF AGENCY: Rape crisis center
SPONSORING ORGANIZATION: Suicide Prevention and Crisis Center of San Mateo County
AREAS SERVED: San Mateo
YEARS IN OPERATION: 9
LANGUAGES: Spanish
ACCESSIBILITY: Telecommunications for the hearing impaired (TTY, TDY, etc.)
CASES SEXUAL ASSAULT/ABUSE (%): 99
CLIENTS/SERVICES: Sexual assault survivors; Marital rape/sexual abuse survivors; Adult survivors of child sexual abuse; Prevention program; Community education; Adolescent survivors of sexual abuse; Male survivors of sexual abuse

CAMARILLO

INTERFACE: CHILDREN, FAMILY SERVICES—CHILD ABUSE INTERVENTION AND PREVENTION SERVICES
1305 Del Norte Rd, No 130, Camarillo, CA 93010-8436
Crisis hotline: **(805) 647-7855 24 hrs**
Information: (805) 487-3945 9am-5pm
Contact: Francois Kirby, Coord
TYPE OF AGENCY: Child sexual abuse services; Child sexual abuse prevention program; Private practice; Child abuse services; Child abuse prevention program
AREAS SERVED: Ventura
YEARS IN OPERATION: 7
LANGUAGES: Spanish, French
CASES SEXUAL ASSAULT/ABUSE (%): 70
DESCRIPTION: Provides child abuse intervention and prevention services, therapy and parent training to high risk families and victims.
CLIENTS/SERVICES: Marital rape/sexual abuse survivors; Child victims of sexual abuse; Incest victims/survivors; Prevention program; Community education; Adolescent survivors of sexual abuse; Male survivors of sexual abuse
REQUIREMENTS: Must be referred by PSSA or CPS

RAPE AND SEXUAL ABUSE CENTER OF VENTURA COUNTY
80 Wood Rd, Ste 304, Camarillo, CA 93010
Crisis hotline: **(805) 987-0428 24 hrs 7 days**
Information: (805) 987-0429 7:30am-6pm
Contact: Dr Barbara Farber, Clinical Dir
TYPE OF AGENCY: Rape crisis center; Acquaintance/date rape prevention program; Adolescent program
AREAS SERVED: Ventura, parts of Los Angeles and Santa Barbara
YEARS IN OPERATION: 15
LANGUAGES: Spanish
ACCESSIBILITY: Wheelchair accessible
CASES SEXUAL ASSAULT/ABUSE (%): 100
DESCRIPTION: Comprehensive services for sexual assault survivors, including martial arts/self-defense program
CLIENTS/SERVICES: Sexual assault survivors; Marital rape/sexual abuse survivors; Child victims of sexual abuse; Adult survivors of child sexual abuse; Incest victims/survivors; Prevention program; Community education; Adolescent survivors of sexual abuse; Male survivors of sexual abuse; Publications/media
SPECIAL PROGRAMS/SERVICES: Offers 8-week therapy groups for adult survivors of incest, male victims, and rape survivors. Each group has a separate protocol. The groups are structured with a specific issue being addressed each week. Included is a session for significant others. Developing protocols for foster parents/adoptive parents who are having sexually abused children placed in their homes, as well as group for mothers of molested children. Videos for classroom use on male assault and date rape. High Risk Adolescent Abuse Program (HRAAP) specializes in child abuse prevention and education for teenagers who are considered particularly vulnerable to either being victimized or perpetrators of abuse. Through discussions on domestic violence, parenting, child maltreatment, self-esteem, anger management, and sexual abuse. Facilitates teenager's ability to problem solve, make appropriate decisions and deal with others in positive ways

CANOGA PARK

FAMILIES OF CRIMES OF SILENCE
PO Box 2338, Canoga Park, CA 91306
Information: (818) 718-1576
Contact: Doreen Kenney, Pres
TYPE OF AGENCY: Child sexual abuse services
YEARS IN OPERATION: 3
DESCRIPTION: Support groups for families of abused children; Recreational and social activities for groups of sexually abused children
CLIENTS/SERVICES: Child victims of sexual abuse; Adult survivors of child sexual abuse

CHICO

CATALYST WOMEN'S ADVOCATES
PO Box 4184, Chico, CA 95927
Crisis hotline: **(916) 895-8476 24 hrs**
Information: (916) 343-7711 9am-5pm (Mon-Fri); answering machine after hrs
Contact: Lois Hooker, Prog Dir
TYPE OF AGENCY: Domestic violence program; Child sexual abuse prevention program
AREAS SERVED: Butte
YEARS IN OPERATION: 10
LANGUAGES: Spanish
ACCESSIBILITY: Wheelchair accessible
CASES SEXUAL ASSAULT/ABUSE (%): 75
DESCRIPTION: Provides counseling, information, shelter for physically and sexually abused women and children
CLIENTS/SERVICES: Marital rape/sexual abuse survivors; Child victims of sexual abuse; Adult survivors of child sexual abuse; Prevention program; Adolescent survivors of sexual abuse

EDUCATION AND SUPPORT PROGRAMS FOR WOMEN
Women's Resource Center, California State University, Chico, CA 95929-0750
Information: (916) 895-5724 9am-3pm (Mon-Fri)
Contact: Cynthia Peterson, Dir
TYPE OF AGENCY: College/university-based services; Information and referral
AREAS SERVED: Butte
YEARS IN OPERATION: 12
ACCESSIBILITY: Wheelchair accessible
DESCRIPTION: Provides referrals
CLIENTS/SERVICES: Sexual assault survivors; Community education

FAMILY SERVICE ASSOCIATION OF BUTTE AND GLENN COUNTIES
853 Manzanita Ct, Chico, CA 95926
Information: (916) 891-1731 8am-5pm; by appointment evenings and Sat
Contact: Richard Cahoon, Exec Dir
TYPE OF AGENCY: Counseling/mental health services
AREAS SERVED: Butte, Glenn
YEARS IN OPERATION: 30
ACCESSIBILITY: Wheelchair accessible
CASES SEXUAL ASSAULT/ABUSE (%): 35
CLIENTS/SERVICES: Sexual assault survivors; Marital rape/sexual abuse survivors; Child victims of sexual abuse; Adult survivors of child sexual abuse; Incest victims/survivors; Adolescent survivors of sexual abuse; Male survivors of sexual abuse
REQUIREMENTS: Sliding scale fee; Referrals from Child Protective Services are free
SPECIAL PROGRAMS/SERVICES: Children's self-esteem enhancement groups; Psychodrama

RAPE CRISIS INTERVENTION
PO Box 423, Chico, CA 95927
Crisis hotline: **(916) 342-7273 24 hrs**
Information: (916) 891-1331 9am-5pm
Contact: Coleen Jarvis, Exec Dir
TYPE OF AGENCY: Rape crisis center; Child sexual abuse prevention program
AREAS SERVED: Butte, Glenn, Tehama
ACCESSIBILITY: Wheelchair accessible
DESCRIPTION: Comprehensive rape crisis services; Primary prevention program for preschool through high school; Feminist martial arts/self-defense program
CLIENTS/SERVICES: Sexual assault survivors; Marital rape/sexual abuse survivors; Adult survivors of child sexual abuse; Incest victims/survivors; Prevention program; Community education; Adolescent survivors of sexual abuse; Male survivors of sexual abuse
REQUIREMENTS: Primarily works with teenage and adult survivors; children are referred to other agencies/services

STEP II PSYCHOLOGICAL SERVICES
366 Rio Lindo Ave, Chico, CA 95926
Crisis hotline: **(916) 532-9242 (CLASP Program) 8am-11pm**
Information: (916) 891-0674 9am-6pm
Contact: Dr Emmett Anderson, Sexual Assault Svcs Dir
TYPE OF AGENCY: Private practice
AREAS SERVED: Butte, Glenn, Plumas, Nevada, Tehama, Yuba, Sutter
YEARS IN OPERATION: 8
ACCESSIBILITY: Wheelchair accessible; Signers for the hearing impaired
CASES SEXUAL ASSAULT/ABUSE (%): 40
DESCRIPTION: Counseling for survivors; Individual and group therapy for offenders—rapists, batterers, and child sexual abuse/incest offenders
CLIENTS/SERVICES: Sexual assault survivors; Marital rape/sexual abuse survivors; Child victims of sexual abuse; Adult survivors of child sexual abuse; Incest victims/survivors; Community education; Offender treatment program; Adolescent survivors of sexual abuse; Male survivors of sexual abuse

CHULA VISTA

FAMILY STRESS CENTER
571 3rd Ave, Chula Vista, CA 92010
Crisis hotline: **(619) 691-1331 8:30am-5pm (Mon-Fri)**
Information: (619) 691-1331 8:30am-5pm (Mon-Fri)
Contact: Gail Edwards, Dir
TYPE OF AGENCY: Child sexual abuse services; Child sexual abuse prevention program; Child abuse services
SPONSORING ORGANIZATION: YMCA of San Diego County
AREAS SERVED: San Diego
YEARS IN OPERATION: 14
LANGUAGES: Spanish
ACCESSIBILITY: Wheelchair accessible
CASES SEXUAL ASSAULT/ABUSE (%): 80
DESCRIPTION: Individual, family, and group counseling for child and adult survivors of sexual/physical abuse; Prevention programs for K-12th grade students on self-protection skills; Treatment for child sexual abuse/incest offenders and batterers; Sponsorship of Parents United and Daughters/Sons United groups in English and Spanish
CLIENTS/SERVICES: Sexual assault survivors; Child victims of sexual abuse; Adult survivors of child sexual abuse; Incest victims/survivors; Prevention program; Community education; Offender treatment program; Adolescent survivors of sexual abuse; Male survivors of sexual abuse
SPECIAL PROGRAMS/SERVICES: Weekend marathons for sexual offenders

CLAREMONT

HOUSE OF RUTH
PO Box 457, Claremont, CA 91711
Crisis hotline: **(714) 988-5559 24 hrs daily**
Information: (714) 623-4364 8:30am-5pm (Mon-Fri)
Contact: Sue Crumpton, Exec Dir
TYPE OF AGENCY: Domestic violence program
AREAS SERVED: Los Angeles, San Bernardino
YEARS IN OPERATION: 10
LANGUAGES: Spanish
CASES SEXUAL ASSAULT/ABUSE (%): 100
CLIENTS/SERVICES: Marital rape/sexual abuse survivors; Child victims of sexual abuse; Adult survivors of child sexual abuse; Community education; Elderly; Healing
SPECIAL PROGRAMS/SERVICES: Provides training manual and training sessions on elder abuse; Journal workshop for adult survivors of child sexual abuse

PROJECT SISTER SEXUAL ASSAULT CRISIS SERVICES
PO Box 621, Claremont, CA 91711
Crisis hotline: **(714) 626-4357 24 hrs**
Information: (714) 623-1619 8am-5pm (Mon-Fri)
Contact: Kay Loraine, Interim Exec Dir
TYPE OF AGENCY: Rape crisis center
AREAS SERVED: San Bernardino, Los Angeles
YEARS IN OPERATION: 16
LANGUAGES: Spanish
ACCESSIBILITY: Wheelchair accessible
CASES SEXUAL ASSAULT/ABUSE (%): 100
DESCRIPTION: Comprehensive rape crisis services; Rape survivors support group; Referrals for long-term counseling and information; Feminist martial arts/self-defense program
CLIENTS/SERVICES: Sexual assault survivors; Marital rape/sexual abuse survivors; Child victims of sexual abuse; Adult survivors of child sexual abuse; Incest victims/survivors; Prevention program; Community education; Adolescent survivors of sexual abuse; Male survivors of sexual abuse

COMPTON

COMPTON YWCA SEXUAL ASSAULT CRISIS PROGRAM
509 E Compton Blvd, Compton, CA 90221
Crisis hotline: **(213) 979-NEED 24 hrs**
Information: (213) 636-1429 9am-5:30pm
Contact: Monica Taylor-Williams, Proj Dir
TYPE OF AGENCY: Rape crisis center
SPONSORING ORGANIZATION: YWCA of Los Angeles, Compton Center
AREAS SERVED: Los Angeles
YEARS IN OPERATION: 3½
LANGUAGES: Spanish
ACCESSIBILITY: Wheelchair accessible
CASES SEXUAL ASSAULT/ABUSE (%): 95
DESCRIPTION: Offers support for rape survivors, family, and friends; Sensitizes community to the emotional and physical needs of sexual assault survivors; Support groups for both female and male survivors; Feminist martial arts/self-defense program
CLIENTS/SERVICES: Sexual assault survivors; Marital rape/sexual abuse survivors; Child victims of sexual abuse; Adult survivors of child sexual abuse; Incest victims/survivors; Prevention program; Community education; Adolescent survivors of sexual abuse; Male survivors of sexual abuse; Healing
SPECIAL PROGRAMS/SERVICES: Offers arts and crafts, self-defense, and self-esteem workshops to promote the healing process for survivors. Program outreach messages are carried by local cable channel

CONCORD

BATTERED WOMEN'S ALTERNATIVES
PO Box 6406, Concord, CA 94524
Crisis hotline: **(415) 930-8300 24 hrs**
Information: (415) 676-2845 9am-5pm (Mon-Fri)
Contact: Deedee Jenson, Community Educ Dir; Rollie Mullen, Exec Dir
TYPE OF AGENCY: Domestic violence program; Acquaintance/date rape prevention program; Adolescent program
AREAS SERVED: Contra Costa
YEARS IN OPERATION: 12
LANGUAGES: Spanish
ACCESSIBILITY: Wheelchair accessible; Telecommunications for the hearing impaired (TTY, TDY, etc.)
DESCRIPTION: Provides battered women and their children with emergency shelter and safehome network; Treatment for batterers
CLIENTS/SERVICES: Marital rape/sexual abuse survivors; Prevention program; Community education; Publications/media
SPECIAL PROGRAMS/SERVICES: *My Girl*, a one-hour video on violence in teen relationships for ages 14 and older. Accompanied by curriculum guide to facilitate the discussion of physical, emotional, and sexual abuse raised by video (purchase $225; rental $35)

CHILD ASSAULT PREVENTION OF CONTRA COSTA COUNTY, INC
3020 Grant St, Concord, CA 94520
Information: (415) 827-3891 9am-5pm (Mon-Fri)
Contact: Cynthia Bacon, MSW, Exec Dir
TYPE OF AGENCY: Child sexual abuse prevention program; Acquaintance/date rape prevention program
AREAS SERVED: Contra Costa
YEARS IN OPERATION: 5
LANGUAGES: Spanish
ACCESSIBILITY: Wheelchair accessible
CASES SEXUAL ASSAULT/ABUSE (%): 70
CLIENTS/SERVICES: Prevention program; Community education
SPECIAL PROGRAMS/SERVICES: Programs with other violence prevention organizations to present a comprehensive view of the interrelatedness of violence. The youth violence prevention project works with crisis and suicide, conflict resolution, battered women's alternatives, as well as CAPP to combat all forms of violence. CAPP's segment on date rape brings about many questions between boys and girls vital to ending violence

GIL AND ASSOCIATES
2827 Concord Blvd, Concord, CA 94519
Information: (415) 685-9670 9am-5pm
Contact: Teresa Davi, Prog Mgr
TYPE OF AGENCY: Child sexual abuse services; Private practice
AREAS SERVED: Alameda, Contra Costa, Solano, Santa Clara, and surrounding areas
YEARS IN OPERATION: 4

GIL AND ASSOCIATES (continued)
ACCESSIBILITY: Wheelchair accessible
CASES SEXUAL ASSAULT/ABUSE (%): 90
DESCRIPTION: Therapy for victim/survivors, including support groups for female and male survivors; Treatment for child sexual abuse/incest offenders and adolescent sex offenders
CLIENTS/SERVICES: Sexual assault survivors; Marital rape/sexual abuse survivors; Child victims of sexual abuse; Adult survivors of child sexual abuse; Incest victims/survivors; Offender treatment program; Adolescent survivors of sexual abuse; Male survivors of sexual abuse

RAPE CRISIS OF CENTRAL CONTRA COSTA COUNTY
1760 Clayton Rd, Concord, CA 94520
Crisis hotline: **(415) 798-7273 24 hrs**
Information: (415) 676-6178
Contact: Inge Hoogerhuis, Intervention Coord
TYPE OF AGENCY: Rape crisis center; Child sexual abuse prevention program; Child assault prevention (CAP) project; Acquaintance/date rape prevention program
SPONSORING ORGANIZATION: Rape Crisis of West Contra Costa County
AREAS SERVED: Contra Costa
CASES SEXUAL ASSAULT/ABUSE (%): 100
DESCRIPTION: Provides comprehensive rape crisis services and support groups; Child Assault Prevention (CAP) Project and TAPP for teens; Assertiveness and self-defense class for young women ages 12-17
CLIENTS/SERVICES: Sexual assault survivors; Child victims of sexual abuse; Adult survivors of child sexual abuse; Incest victims/survivors; Prevention program; Community education; Adolescent survivors of sexual abuse

VICTIM/WITNESS PROGRAM
2525 Stanwell Dr, Ste 300, Concord, CA 94520
Information: (415) 646-5401 (Central County); 374-3272 (West County); (800) 648-0600 Toll Free 8am-12pm, 1pm-5pm (machine recorder when office closed)
Contact: Gemma Pasto, Prog Coord
TYPE OF AGENCY: Victim/witness assistance program
SPONSORING ORGANIZATION: Contra Costa County Probation Department
AREAS SERVED: Contra Costa
YEARS IN OPERATION: 2
LANGUAGES: Spanish (by appointment)
ACCESSIBILITY: Wheelchair accessible
CLIENTS/SERVICES: Sexual assault survivors; Marital rape/sexual abuse survivors; Child victims of sexual abuse; Adult survivors of child sexual abuse; Incest victims/survivors; Prevention program
REQUIREMENTS: Information/referral services to any crime victim or witness. For eligibility for state victims' restitution fund, victim must cooperate with law enforcement including prosecution if authorities choose to proceed; Must not have contributed to occurrence of crime; Must be victim of violent crime

COSTA MESA

SEXUAL ASSAULT VICTIM SERVICES/PREVENTION PROGRAM
2803 Royal Palm Dr, Costa Mesa, CA 92626
Crisis hotline: **(714) 957-2737 24 hrs daily**
Information: (714) 834-4317 8am-5pm (Mon-Fri)
Contact: Barbara J Phillips, Dir; Janice Hansen, Supv
TYPE OF AGENCY: Rape crisis center; Victim/witness assistance program; Child sexual abuse services; Child sexual abuse prevention program
AREAS SERVED: Orange
YEARS IN OPERATION: 7
LANGUAGES: Spanish, Vietnamese, Japanese
ACCESSIBILITY: Wheelchair accessible; Signers for the hearing impaired
CASES SEXUAL ASSAULT/ABUSE (%): 100
CLIENTS/SERVICES: Sexual assault survivors; Child victims of sexual abuse; Incest victims/survivors; Prevention program; Adolescent survivors of sexual abuse; Male survivors of sexual abuse
SPECIAL PROGRAMS/SERVICES: Orange County Victim/Witness Assistance Program and Child Abuse Prevention Program are also components of CSP, Inc. Services are coordinated between all components of the agency to ensure that each client is afforded quality service and support

CUPERTINO

SOCIAL ADVOCATES FOR YOUTH
20432 Silverado, Ste 214, Cupertino, CA 95014
Information: (408) 253-3540 24 hrs
Contact: J William Visher, PhD, Clinical Coord
TYPE OF AGENCY: Counseling/mental health services; Child sexual abuse services
AREAS SERVED: Santa Clara
YEARS IN OPERATION: 5
CASES SEXUAL ASSAULT/ABUSE (%): 20
CLIENTS/SERVICES: Sexual assault survivors; Marital rape/sexual abuse survivors; Child victims of sexual abuse; Adult survivors of child sexual abuse; Incest victims/survivors; Adolescent survivors of sexual abuse; Male survivors of sexual abuse
REQUIREMENTS: Sliding scale fee structure

DAVIS

RAPE PREVENTION EDUCATION PROGRAM
University of California, Davis, Police Dept, Davis, CA 95616
Information: (916) 752-3299 8am-5pm (Mon-Fri)
Contact: Brittany Burch, Coord
TYPE OF AGENCY: Rape crisis center; College/university-based services; Rape prevention program
SPONSORING ORGANIZATION: University of California, Davis
AREAS SERVED: Yolo
YEARS IN OPERATION: 10
ACCESSIBILITY: Wheelchair accessible
CASES SEXUAL ASSAULT/ABUSE (%): 100
DESCRIPTION: Educational outreach to university and community, including feminist martial arts/self defense and programs in fraternities and sororities; Short-term counseling and support group for survivors
CLIENTS/SERVICES: Sexual assault survivors; Adult survivors of child sexual abuse; Prevention program; Community education; Adolescent survivors of sexual abuse; Male survivors of sexual abuse
REQUIREMENTS: Services are primarily offered to the university community

EL CENTRO

IMPERIAL COUNTY VICTIM/WITNESS
217 S 10th, Bldg B, El Centro, CA 92243
Information: (619) 339-4357 8am-5pm (Mon-Fri)
Contact: Pamela Littrell, Proj Coord
TYPE OF AGENCY: Victim/witness assistance program
SPONSORING ORGANIZATION: Imperial County Probation
AREAS SERVED: Imperial
YEARS IN OPERATION: 2
LANGUAGES: Spanish
ACCESSIBILITY: Wheelchair accessible; Telecommunications for the hearing impaired (TTY, TDY, etc.) (by arrangement); Signers for the hearing impaired (by arrangement)
CASES SEXUAL ASSAULT/ABUSE (%): 35-40
DESCRIPTION: Provides support and services for victims of all types of crime. For child abuse: court preparation; arranges counseling and meetings with DA. For sexual assault: court support; compensation application for counseling; home visits; works with rape crisis hotline. Sponsors victim/witness advisory committee, an interagency group
CLIENTS/SERVICES: Sexual assault survivors; Child victims of sexual abuse; Incest victims/survivors; Community education

PEOPLE AGAINST RAPE
120 N 6th St, El Centro, CA 92243
Crisis hotline: **(619) 352-7273 24 hrs 7 days**
Information: (619) 352-7273 8am-5pm (Mon-Fri)
Contact: E Loretta Pipkin, Dir
TYPE OF AGENCY: Rape crisis center; Child sexual abuse prevention program
AREAS SERVED: Imperial and outlying areas
YEARS IN OPERATION: 11
LANGUAGES: Spanish and other translators available
ACCESSIBILITY: Wheelchair accessible; Signers for the hearing impaired
CLIENTS/SERVICES: Sexual assault survivors; Marital rape/sexual abuse survivors; Child victims of sexual abuse; Adult survivors of child sexual abuse; Incest victims/survivors; Prevention program; Community education; Adolescent survivors of sexual abuse; Male survivors of sexual abuse
REQUIREMENTS: Clients under 18 must be reported

EL CERRITO

THE WOMEN'S THERAPY CENTER
501 Kearney St, El Cerrito, CA 94530
Information: (415) 524-8288 24-hr answering machine
Contact: Susan Straley, Dir
TYPE OF AGENCY: Counseling/mental health services
AREAS SERVED: Alameda, Contra Costa
YEARS IN OPERATION: 10
ACCESSIBILITY: Wheelchair accessible
CASES SEXUAL ASSAULT/ABUSE (%): 90
DESCRIPTION: 2-year training program for women accruing their supervised hours toward California licenses (MFCC, LCSW, and PhD). As part of their training, the 16 interns see clients in this low-fee clinic. Offers individual long-term psychodynamic psychotherapy to women.
CLIENTS/SERVICES: Sexual assault survivors; Marital rape/sexual abuse survivors; Adult survivors of child sexual abuse; Incest victims/survivors
REQUIREMENTS: Does not serve actively addicted women who are not in a recovery program of some kind; women with a psychiatric hospitalization within the last year; women on psychiatric medication not under the supervision of a psychiatrist; actively homicidal or suicidal women; or clients whose main intent is to obtain a psychological evaluation for SSI, SDI, or other court-ordered action

ESCONDIDO

ESCONDIDO YOUTH ENCOUNTER
165 E Lincoln, Escondido, CA 92026
Crisis hotline: **(619) 747-6281 24 hrs**
Information: (619) 747-6281, 744-3117 8am-5pm
Contact: Jonathan Siegel, PhD, Treatment Svcs Dir
TYPE OF AGENCY: Counseling/mental health services; Child sexual abuse services; Child sexual abuse prevention program; Shelter
AREAS SERVED: San Diego
YEARS IN OPERATION: 20
LANGUAGES: Spanish
ACCESSIBILITY: Wheelchair accessible
CASES SEXUAL ASSAULT/ABUSE (%): 50
DESCRIPTION: Counseling for survivors and offenders—child sexual abuse/incest offenders, batterers and adolescent sex offenders. Spon-

ESCONDIDO YOUTH ENCOUNTER
(continued)

sors Daughters and Sons United Chapter; Hidden Valley House, an emergency shelter for women and children in crisis; Personal safety program for grades K-12
CLIENTS/SERVICES: Sexual assault survivors; Marital rape/sexual abuse survivors; Child victims of sexual abuse; Adult survivors of child sexual abuse; Incest victims/survivors; Prevention program; Community education; Offender treatment program; Adolescent survivors of sexual abuse; Male survivors of sexual abuse

EUREKA

CHILD SEXUAL ABUSE THERAPY PROGRAM/PARENTS UNITED
2841 E St, Eureka, CA 95501
Information: (707) 443-7358 9am-5pm
Contact: Karen A Jandebeur, Prog Dir
TYPE OF AGENCY: Child sexual abuse services; Private practice
SPONSORING ORGANIZATION: Humboldt Family Service Center
AREAS SERVED: Humboldt
YEARS IN OPERATION: 3
CASES SEXUAL ASSAULT/ABUSE (%): 100
DESCRIPTION: Coordination of treatment for children suffering post-traumatic stress disorders; Coordination of treatment for families of those children (non-offending parent, offending parent, siblings).
CLIENTS/SERVICES: Sexual assault survivors; Child victims of sexual abuse; Adult survivors of child sexual abuse; Incest victims/survivors; Community education; Offender treatment program; Adolescent survivors of sexual abuse; Male survivors of sexual abuse

DELSON-KOKISH ASSOCIATES
305 O St, Eureka, CA 95501
Information: (707) 442-8912 8:30am-7:30pm
Contact: Niki Delson, LCSW; Ron Kokish, MFCC
TYPE OF AGENCY: Private practice; Offender treatment
AREAS SERVED: Humboldt
YEARS IN OPERATION: 3
LANGUAGES: German
CASES SEXUAL ASSAULT/ABUSE (%): 85
DESCRIPTION: Offers a complete range of services (group, individual, and family) for victims and offenders—rapists, child sexual abuse/incest offenders, and batterers. Therapy for those who are developmentally delayed, both adult survivors and offenders. Group for non-offending parents; group for cognitive restructuring for anti-social thinkers
CLIENTS/SERVICES: Sexual assault survivors; Child victims of sexual abuse; Adult survivors of child sexual abuse; Incest victims/survivors; Community education; Offender treatment program; Male survivors of sexual abuse; Developmentally disabled
REQUIREMENTS: Ability to pay fee or reimbursement through victim of crime program—fee reductions possible for victims/survivors

HUMBOLDT COUNTY DISTRICT ATTORNEY'S VICTIM-WITNESS PROGRAM
825 5th St, Eureka, CA 95501
Information: (707) 445-7417 8:30am-12pm, 1pm-5pm
Contact: Kate Green, Victim-Witness Prog
TYPE OF AGENCY: Victim/witness assistance program
AREAS SERVED: Humboldt
YEARS IN OPERATION: 7
ACCESSIBILITY: Signers for the hearing impaired (available)
CLIENTS/SERVICES: Crime victims

SPECIAL PROGRAMS/SERVICES: Special court orientation program for children utilizing videotape of puppets in the courtroom. Program also gives bears to children going to court and a certificate from District Attorney's Victim Witness that they "told the truth"

HUMBOLDT COUNTY RAPE CRISIS TEAM
PO Box 543, Eureka, CA 95502
Crisis hotline: **(707) 445-2881 24 hrs**
Information: (707) 443-2737 9am-4pm (Mon-Fri)
Contact: Diana Livingston, Prog Dir
TYPE OF AGENCY: Rape crisis center; Child sexual abuse prevention program; Acquaintance/date rape prevention program
AREAS SERVED: Humboldt, Del Norte
YEARS IN OPERATION: 10
CASES SEXUAL ASSAULT/ABUSE (%): 100
CLIENTS/SERVICES: Sexual assault survivors; Marital rape/sexual abuse survivors; Child victims of sexual abuse; Prevention program; Community education; Adolescent survivors of sexual abuse; Male survivors of sexual abuse
SPECIAL PROGRAMS/SERVICES: Provides Child Assault Prevention Project in schools

HUMBOLDT WOMEN FOR SHELTER
PO Box 969, Eureka, CA 95502
Crisis hotline: **(707) 443-6042 24 hrs**
Information: (707) 444-9255 9am-5pm (Mon-Fri)
Contact: Sheri Johnson, Prog Dir
TYPE OF AGENCY: Domestic violence program
AREAS SERVED: Humboldt
YEARS IN OPERATION: 12
LANGUAGES: Spanish; Translator referrals available for other languages
ACCESSIBILITY: Wheelchair accessible
CASES SEXUAL ASSAULT/ABUSE (%): 50
CLIENTS/SERVICES: Marital rape/sexual abuse survivors

FAIRFIELD

DISTRICT ATTORNEY'S OFFICE—VICTIM/WITNESS ASSISTANCE PROGRAM
600 Union Ave, Hall of Justice, Fairfield, CA 94533
Information: (707) 429-6451 7:30am-6pm
Contact: Janis Robinson, Asst Spec/Temp Coord
TYPE OF AGENCY: Victim/witness assistance program
AREAS SERVED: Solano
YEARS IN OPERATION: 8
LANGUAGES: Spanish translators available
ACCESSIBILITY: Wheelchair accessible
CASES SEXUAL ASSAULT/ABUSE (%): 90
CLIENTS/SERVICES: Sexual assault survivors; Marital rape/sexual abuse survivors; Child victims of sexual abuse; Adult survivors of child sexual abuse; Incest victims/survivors; Prevention program; Community education
REQUIREMENTS: Crime must be reported to law enforcement agency; Victim must cooperate in the investigation and prosecution of any known suspects

PARENTS UNITED
PO Box 2223, Fairfield, CA 94533
Crisis hotline: **(707) 425-9400 24 hrs**
Information: (707) 425-9414 9am-5pm (Mon-Fri)
Contact: Karen DeLeew, Exec Dir
TYPE OF AGENCY: Child sexual abuse services
SPONSORING ORGANIZATION: Community Treatment Center
AREAS SERVED: Solano
LANGUAGES: Spanish, Farsi
CASES SEXUAL ASSAULT/ABUSE (%): 100
DESCRIPTION: Sponsors Parents United, Daughters and Sons United, and Adults Molested as Children for child and adult survivors and their families, including offending and non-offending parents; Treatment program for juvenile sex offenders and their families

CLIENTS/SERVICES: Child victims of sexual abuse; Adult survivors of child sexual abuse; Incest victims/survivors; Offender treatment program; Adolescent survivors of sexual abuse

FORT BRAGG

CAARE PROJECT, INC
461 N Franklin St, Fort Bragg, CA 95437
Crisis hotline: **(707) 964-HELP 24 hrs daily**
Information: (707) 964-4055 9am-5pm (Mon-Fri)
Contact: Sallie Werson, Sexual Assault Counseling Svcs Coord
TYPE OF AGENCY: Rape crisis center; Domestic violence program; Child sexual abuse prevention program
AREAS SERVED: Mendocino
YEARS IN OPERATION: 11
LANGUAGES: Spanish
ACCESSIBILITY: Wheelchair accessible
CASES SEXUAL ASSAULT/ABUSE (%): 90
DESCRIPTION: Offers crisis intervention for sexual assault, child sexual assault and abuse, and domestic violence; feminist martial arts/self-defense program; CAPP program and employment training for battered women. In addition, offers individual and group therapy for rapists, child sexual abuse offenders, incest offenders, and batterers
CLIENTS/SERVICES: Sexual assault survivors; Marital rape/sexual abuse survivors; Child victims of sexual abuse; Adult survivors of child sexual abuse; Incest victims/survivors; Prevention program; Community education; Offender treatment program; Adolescent survivors of sexual abuse; Male survivors of sexual abuse
SPECIAL PROGRAMS/SERVICES: Offers writing workshops for incest survivors and sexual assault survivors

FREMONT

BAY AREA WOMEN AGAINST RAPE
2140 Peralta, No 111, Fremont, CA 94536
Crisis hotline: **(415) 845-7273, 796-8838 24 hrs**
Information: (415) 465-3890, 796-7273 Fremont 9am-5pm (Mon-Fri), Oakland 10am-3pm (Mon-Fri)
Contact: C Barber, Youth Svcs Dir
TYPE OF AGENCY: Rape crisis center; Child sexual abuse prevention program
AREAS SERVED: Alameda
YEARS IN OPERATION: 17
LANGUAGES: Spanish
ACCESSIBILITY: Wheelchair accessible; Telecommunications for the hearing impaired (TTY, TDY, etc.)
CASES SEXUAL ASSAULT/ABUSE (%): 100
DESCRIPTION: Comprehensive rape crisis services; Treatment program for rapists. Feminist martial arts/self-defense program available
CLIENTS/SERVICES: Sexual assault survivors; Marital rape/sexual abuse survivors; Adult survivors of child sexual abuse; Incest victims/survivors; Prevention program; Community education; Offender treatment program; Adolescent survivors of sexual abuse; Male survivors of sexual abuse
SPECIAL PROGRAMS/SERVICES: School-based prevention programs include Child Assault Prevention (CAP) Project and the Teen Assault Awareness Program

CHILD SEXUAL ABUSE TREATMENT PROGRAM
4519 Eggers Dr, Fremont, CA 94536
Crisis hotline: **(415) 790-3800 24 hrs**
Information: (415) 790-3803 9am-9pm (Mon-Fri)
Contact: Karin E Wandrei, LCSW, Prog Mgr
TYPE OF AGENCY: Child sexual abuse services
SPONSORING ORGANIZATION: Parental Stress Service, Inc
AREAS SERVED: Southern Alameda
YEARS IN OPERATION: 5
LANGUAGES: Spanish

CHILD SEXUAL ABUSE TREATMENT PROGRAM (continued)
ACCESSIBILITY: Wheelchair accessible
CASES SEXUAL ASSAULT/ABUSE (%): 100
DESCRIPTION: Provides therapy services for sexually abused children and their families in or out of the home (individual, play, family and group therapy). Has a specialized offender treatment program for offenders who are not denying. Parental Stress Service provides parent education classes, respite care, and general counseling on parenting issues. Also has feminist martial arts/self-defense programs
CLIENTS/SERVICES: Child victims of sexual abuse; Incest victims/survivors; Community education; Offender treatment program; Adolescent survivors of sexual abuse; Male survivors of sexual abuse

COMMUNITY COUNSELING AND EDUCATION CENTER
39355 California St, Ste 100, Fremont, CA 94539
Information: (415) 792-4964 9am-9pm (Mon-Thu); 9am-4pm (Fri)
Contact: D Rodriguez, Clinic Dir
TYPE OF AGENCY: Counseling/mental health services
AREAS SERVED: Alameda, Santa Clara, San Mateo
YEARS IN OPERATION: 19
ACCESSIBILITY: Wheelchair accessible
CASES SEXUAL ASSAULT/ABUSE (%): 10
CLIENTS/SERVICES: Sexual assault survivors; Marital rape/sexual abuse survivors; Child victims of sexual abuse; Adult survivors of child sexual abuse; Incest victims/survivors; Adolescent survivors of sexual abuse; Male survivors of sexual abuse

FAMILY SERVICE OF THE EAST BAY
4537 Mattos Dr, Fremont, CA 94536
Information: (415) 791-3322 24-hr answering service
Contact: Helen Motroni, Clinical Supv
TYPE OF AGENCY: Counseling/mental health services
AREAS SERVED: Alameda
YEARS IN OPERATION: 100
CASES SEXUAL ASSAULT/ABUSE (%): 45
DESCRIPTION: Counseling for individuals, couples, families and children
CLIENTS/SERVICES: Sexual assault survivors; Marital rape/sexual abuse survivors; Child victims of sexual abuse; Adult survivors of child sexual abuse; Incest victims/survivors; Adolescent survivors of sexual abuse; Male survivors of sexual abuse

SHELTER AGAINST VIOLENT ENVIRONMENT (SAVE)
PO Box 8283, Fremont, CA 94537
Crisis hotline: **(415) 794-6055 24 hrs**
Information: (415) 794-6056 8:30am-5pm (Mon-Fri)
TYPE OF AGENCY: Domestic violence program
AREAS SERVED: Alameda
YEARS IN OPERATION: 11
ACCESSIBILITY: Wheelchair accessible
CLIENTS/SERVICES: Marital rape/sexual abuse survivors

VICTIM SERVICES PROJECT
39710 Civic Center Dr, Fremont, CA 94537
Information: (415) 790-6847 8am-6pm
Contact: Priscilla Kremer, Community Svcs Officer
TYPE OF AGENCY: Victim/witness assistance program
SPONSORING ORGANIZATION: Fremont Police Dept
ACCESSIBILITY: Wheelchair accessible; Telecommunications for the hearing impaired (TTY, TDY, etc.); Signers for the hearing impaired
DESCRIPTION: Provides referrals to other community agencies and sexual assault training to police
CLIENTS/SERVICES: Sexual assault survivors; Child victims of sexual abuse
REQUIREMENTS: Report and complaint must be filed if suspect is known

FRESNO

COMPREHENSIVE SEXUAL AWARENESS AND TREATMENT TEAM (CSATT)
4753 E Olive, Ste 103, Fresno, CA 93702
Information: (209) 251-7558 8am-6pm (Mon-Fri)
Contact: Patricia Shea, Exec Dir
TYPE OF AGENCY: Counseling/mental health services; Child sexual abuse services; Child sexual abuse prevention program; Adolescent program
SPONSORING ORGANIZATION: ACT (Associated Center for Therapy)
AREAS SERVED: Fresno, Madera, Tulare, Kings
YEARS IN OPERATION: 4
ACCESSIBILITY: Wheelchair accessible
CASES SEXUAL ASSAULT/ABUSE (%): 100
DESCRIPTION: Provides comprehensive sexual abuse treatment and prevention services for minors and their families who have come in contact with the juvenile justice system. Two populations are targeted: adjudicated adolescent sex offenders and delinquent youth who have previously been sexually abused
CLIENTS/SERVICES: Sexual assault survivors; Child victims of sexual abuse; Incest victims/survivors; Prevention program; Community education; Offender treatment program; Adolescent survivors of sexual abuse; Male survivors of sexual abuse
REQUIREMENTS: Adolescent offenders must be adjudicated of sex offense in Fresno County. Victims must be identified through the juvenile justice system

FRESNO COUNTY VICTIM/WITNESS ASSISTANCE CENTER
PO Box 453, Fresno, CA 93709
Crisis hotline: **(209) 488-3425 8am-6pm, evenings and weekends by arrangement**
Information: (209) 488-3425 8am-6pm, evenings and weekends by arrangement
Contact: Rose Marie Gibbs, Proj Coord
TYPE OF AGENCY: Victim/witness assistance program
SPONSORING ORGANIZATION: Fresno County Probation Department
AREAS SERVED: Fresno
YEARS IN OPERATION: 13
LANGUAGES: Spanish
ACCESSIBILITY: Wheelchair accessible
CASES SEXUAL ASSAULT/ABUSE (%): 20-25
DESCRIPTION: Comprehensive services including crisis intervention, counseling, referral, court assistance, and 24-hour crime scene response
CLIENTS/SERVICES: Sexual assault survivors; Marital rape/sexual abuse survivors; Child victims of sexual abuse; Adult survivors of child sexual abuse; Incest victims/survivors; Community education; Adolescent survivors of sexual abuse; Male survivors of sexual abuse
REQUIREMENTS: Report to law enforcement

MARJAREE MASON CENTER/YWCA
1600 M St, Fresno, CA 93721
Crisis hotline: **(209) 237-4701 24 hrs**
Information: (209) 237-4706 24 hrs
Contact: Janet Samuelian, Prog Dir
TYPE OF AGENCY: Domestic violence program
SPONSORING ORGANIZATION: YWCA
AREAS SERVED: Fresno
YEARS IN OPERATION: 10
LANGUAGES: Spanish, Hmong, Laotian
ACCESSIBILITY: Wheelchair accessible
CASES SEXUAL ASSAULT/ABUSE (%): 25-50
CLIENTS/SERVICES: Marital rape/sexual abuse survivors; Child victims of sexual abuse; Prevention program; Community education; Offender treatment program; Adolescent survivors of sexual abuse; Male survivors of sexual abuse
SPECIAL PROGRAMS/SERVICES: Counseling Alternatives to Physical Abuse and Anger for batterers. The children's therapy program involves many creative activities, including music, art, and play therapies. Prevention programs on domestic violence, dating violence and child abuse

RAPE COUNSELING SERVICE
1347 Bulldog Ln, Fresno, CA 93710
Crisis hotline: **(209) 222-7273 24 hrs**
Information: (209) 227-1800 8am-5pm; late night appointments by arrangement
Contact: Nancy Brenneman, Crisis Intervention and Comm Svc Mgr
TYPE OF AGENCY: Rape crisis center; Child sexual abuse prevention program
AREAS SERVED: Fresno, Tulare, Kings
YEARS IN OPERATION: 15
LANGUAGES: Interpreters available
CLIENTS/SERVICES: Sexual assault survivors; Marital rape/sexual abuse survivors; Child victims of sexual abuse; Adult survivors of child sexual abuse; Incest victims/survivors; Prevention program; Community education; Adolescent survivors of sexual abuse; Male survivors of sexual abuse

FULLERTON

CSP SEXUAL ASSAULT VICTIM SERVICES/ PREVENTION PROGRAM
1275 N Berkeley Ave, Fullerton, CA 92635
Crisis hotline: **(714) 957-2737 24 hrs**
Information: (714) 773-4575 8am-5pm (Mon-Fri)
TYPE OF AGENCY: Victim/witness assistance program; Child sexual abuse services; Child sexual abuse prevention program; Referral program
SPONSORING ORGANIZATION: North County Municipal Court
AREAS SERVED: Orange
YEARS IN OPERATION: 7
LANGUAGES: Spanish, Vietnamese, Japanese
ACCESSIBILITY: Wheelchair accessible; Signers for the hearing impaired
CASES SEXUAL ASSAULT/ABUSE (%): 100
DESCRIPTION: Provides comprehensive services for victims and witnesses and encourages their cooperation in the investigation of the case and prosecution of the offender
CLIENTS/SERVICES: Sexual assault survivors; Marital rape/sexual abuse survivors; Child victims of sexual abuse; Adult survivors of child sexual abuse; Incest victims/survivors; Prevention program; Community education; Adolescent survivors of sexual abuse; Male survivors of sexual abuse
SPECIAL PROGRAMS/SERVICES: The Orange County Victim/Witness Assistance Program and Child Abuse Prevention Program are also components of CSP, Inc. Services are coordinated between all components of the agency to ensure that each client is afforded quality service and support

GARDEN GROVE

GAY AND LESBIAN COMMUNITY CENTER OF ORANGE COUNTY
12832 Garden Grove Blvd, Ste A, Garden Grove, CA 92643
Information: (714) 534-0862 12pm-10pm
Contact: Randolph Ferrell, PhD, Counseling Dir
TYPE OF AGENCY: Counseling/mental health services
AREAS SERVED: Orange
YEARS IN OPERATION: 10
LANGUAGES: Spanish

GAY AND LESBIAN COMMUNITY CENTER OF ORANGE COUNTY *(continued)*
ACCESSIBILITY: Wheelchair accessible; Telecommunications for the hearing impaired (TTY, TDY, etc.); Signers for the hearing impaired
CASES SEXUAL ASSAULT/ABUSE (%): 20
DESCRIPTION: Provides counseling for gays and lesbians and their families and significant others. Many have experienced incest or abuse as children and some are victims of sexual assault.
CLIENTS/SERVICES: Sexual assault survivors; Marital rape/sexual abuse survivors; Adult survivors of child sexual abuse; Incest victims/survivors; Offender treatment program; Adolescent survivors of sexual abuse; Male survivors of sexual abuse; Lesbians; Gay men

TURNING POINT FAMILY SERVICES PROGRAM, INC
12912 Brookhurst St, Ste 150, Garden Grove, CA 92640
Information: (714) 636-3823 9am-8pm (Mon-Thu); 9am-5pm (Fri)
Contact: Ed Surman, MFCC, Prog Dir
TYPE OF AGENCY: Counseling/mental health services; Child sexual abuse services; Child sexual abuse prevention program; Child abuse services; Child abuse prevention program
AREAS SERVED: Orange and surrounding areas
YEARS IN OPERATION: 14
LANGUAGES: Spanish
ACCESSIBILITY: Wheelchair accessible
CASES SEXUAL ASSAULT/ABUSE (%): 30
DESCRIPTION: Serves youth and their families involved with or at risk of child abuse/neglect and substance abuse; Conjoint family therapy for sexually abused children; Family reunification therapy for child sexual abuse/incest offenders
CLIENTS/SERVICES: Child victims of sexual abuse; Incest victims/survivors; Community education; Offender treatment program; Adolescent survivors of sexual abuse; Male survivors of sexual abuse
REQUIREMENTS: Primary client (victim) must be under 18 years of age; Sliding scale fee
SPECIAL PROGRAMS/SERVICES: STARS group: Female survivors of sexual molest; ages 12/13-17/18 meets once weekly 1½ hours for at least 10 sessions. RAP group: Adolescent sex offenders; ages 14-18; meets once weekly; 1½ hours; client must be adjudicated and must have probation officer. Commitment of at least 1 year. In future, will include parents group

GILROY

THE BRIDGE CHILDREN AND FAMILY SERVICES
8315-A Monterey Rd, Gilroy, CA 95020
Crisis hotline: **(408) 779-2113 24 hrs**
Information: (408) 847-3388 9am-5pm (Mon-Fri)
Contact: Rosalinda B Lopez, MS, Child Abuse Svcs Supv
TYPE OF AGENCY: Counseling/mental health services; Child sexual abuse services; Child sexual abuse prevention program
SPONSORING ORGANIZATION: The Bridge Counseling Center Inc, PO Box 546, 16430 S Monterey, Morgan Hill, CA 95037
AREAS SERVED: Santa Clara, San Benito
YEARS IN OPERATION: 15
LANGUAGES: Spanish
CASES SEXUAL ASSAULT/ABUSE (%): 70-80
CLIENTS/SERVICES: Sexual assault survivors; Child victims of sexual abuse; Incest victims/survivors; Prevention program; Community education; Offender treatment program; Adolescent survivors of sexual abuse; Male survivors of sexual abuse
REQUIREMENTS: Victims of sexual, physical abuse or neglect or at risk of becoming victims and their families. Adult perpetrators must submit crime report for screening purposes

GAVILAN COMMUNITY COLLEGE RE-ENTRY PROGRAM
5055 Santa Teresa Blvd, Gilroy, CA 95020
Information: (408) 848-4831 8am-5pm daily
Contact: Terri Arballo, Prog Asst; Sharon Madhvani, Re-Entry Couns
TYPE OF AGENCY: College/university-based services
AREAS SERVED: Santa Clara, San Benito
YEARS IN OPERATION: 15
LANGUAGES: Spanish
ACCESSIBILITY: Wheelchair accessible; Telecommunications for the hearing impaired (TTY, TDY, etc.); Signers for the hearing impaired
DESCRIPTION: Provides personal counseling for all students who request it, including survivors of sexual assault
CLIENTS/SERVICES: Sexual assault survivors; Adult survivors of child sexual abuse
REQUIREMENTS: Must be an enrolled student

GRASS VALLEY

DOMESTIC VIOLENCE COALITION
PO Box 484, Grass Valley, CA 95945
Crisis hotline: **(916) 272-3467 24 hrs**
Information: (916) 272-2046 9am-5pm
Contact: W Joy Bennallack, Exec Dir
TYPE OF AGENCY: Rape crisis center; Domestic violence program
AREAS SERVED: Nevada
YEARS IN OPERATION: 9
DESCRIPTION: Provides shelter, counseling, and referrals for survivors of domestic violence, marital rape/sexual abuse; Treatment for batterers
CLIENTS/SERVICES: Sexual assault survivors; Marital rape/sexual abuse survivors; Prevention program; Community education

HANFORD

KINGS COMMUNITY ACTION ORGANIZATION
1222 W Lacey Blvd, Hanford, CA 93230
Information: (209) 582-4386 8am-5pm
Contact: Joan Bryant, Asst Dept Prog Dir
TYPE OF AGENCY: Child sexual abuse prevention program
AREAS SERVED: Kings
LANGUAGES: Spanish
ACCESSIBILITY: Wheelchair accessible
CLIENTS/SERVICES: Prevention program; Community education

HAWTHORNE

RICHSTONE FAMILY CENTER
13620 Cordory Ave, Hawthorne, CA 90250
Information: (213) 970-1921 8:30am-7pm
Contact: Elaine Struhl, MA MFCC, Clinical Dir
TYPE OF AGENCY: Counseling/mental health services; Child sexual abuse services; Child sexual abuse prevention program; Child abuse services
AREAS SERVED: Los Angeles
YEARS IN OPERATION: 11
LANGUAGES: Spanish
ACCESSIBILITY: Wheelchair accessible
CASES SEXUAL ASSAULT/ABUSE (%): 50
DESCRIPTION: Outpatient counseling for child victims of sexual/physical abuse and the non-offending parent
CLIENTS/SERVICES: Child victims of sexual abuse; Prevention program; Community education; Adolescent survivors of sexual abuse

HAYWARD

CHILD SEXUAL ABUSE TREATMENT PROGRAM
24301 Southland Dr, Ste B-8, Hayward, CA 94545
Crisis hotline: **(415) 790-3800 24 hrs**
Information: (415) 786-0145 9am-9pm (Mon-Fri)
Contact: Karin E Wandrei, LCSW, Prog Mgr
TYPE OF AGENCY: Child sexual abuse services
SPONSORING ORGANIZATION: Parental Stress Service, Inc
AREAS SERVED: Southern Alameda
YEARS IN OPERATION: 5
LANGUAGES: Spanish
ACCESSIBILITY: Wheelchair accessible
CASES SEXUAL ASSAULT/ABUSE (%): 100
DESCRIPTION: Provides therapy services for sexually abused children and their families (individual, play, family and group therapy). Has a specialized offender treatment program for offenders who are not denying. Parental Stress Service provides parent education classes, respite care, and general counseling on parenting issues. Also has feminist martial arts/self-defense program
CLIENTS/SERVICES: Child victims of sexual abuse; Incest victims/survivors; Community education; Offender treatment program; Adolescent survivors of sexual abuse; Male survivors of sexual abuse

LA FAMILIA COUNSELING SERVICE
26081 Mocine Ave, Hayward, CA 94544
Information: (415) 881-5921 9am-5pm
Contact: Alfredo Gomez, Counselor
TYPE OF AGENCY: Counseling/mental health services; Adolescent program
AREAS SERVED: Southern Alameda
YEARS IN OPERATION: 13
LANGUAGES: Spanish
ACCESSIBILITY: Wheelchair accessible
CASES SEXUAL ASSAULT/ABUSE (%): 15
DESCRIPTION: Bilingual/bicultural counseling for individuals and families. Las Piramides day treatment program for children and Hijos del Sol outreach services for adolescents. Also provides treatment for rapists, batterers, and child sexual abuse/incest offenders
CLIENTS/SERVICES: Sexual assault survivors; Marital rape/sexual abuse survivors; Child victims of sexual abuse; Adult survivors of child sexual abuse; Incest victims/survivors; Community education; Offender treatment program; Adolescent survivors of sexual abuse; Male survivors of sexual abuse; Ethnic minorities

HEMET

HEMET/SAN JACINTO CENTER AGAINST SEXUAL ASSAULT
PO Box 2564, Hemet, CA 92343-0481
Crisis hotline: **(714) 652-8300 24 hrs**
Information: (714) 652-8300 8am-10am (Mon-Fri)
Contact: Sheila Hughes, Svcs Coord
TYPE OF AGENCY: Rape crisis center
AREAS SERVED: Riverside mid-county area
YEARS IN OPERATION: 3
LANGUAGES: Spanish available
CASES SEXUAL ASSAULT/ABUSE (%): 100
CLIENTS/SERVICES: Sexual assault survivors; Marital rape/sexual abuse survivors; Child victims of sexual abuse; Adult survivors of child sexual abuse; Incest victims/survivors; Community education; Adolescent survivors of sexual abuse; Male survivors of sexual abuse
SPECIAL PROGRAMS/SERVICES: The local sexual assault response team, an interagency effort, was launched in May 1988 to return victims to local hospitals for exam and treatment. Offers "filling-the-gaps" education programs in local schools

HOLLYWOOD

CHILDREN OF THE NIGHT
1800 N Highland, No 128, Hollywood, CA 90028-4520
Crisis hotline: **(213) 550-7188 6pm-9am (Mon-Fri); 24 hrs weekends**
Information: (213) 461-3160 9am-6pm (Mon-Fri)
Contact: Vikki Balet, Prog Dir
TYPE OF AGENCY: Adolescent program
AREAS SERVED: Los Angeles, Orange, San Diego
YEARS IN OPERATION: 9
LANGUAGES: Spanish
ACCESSIBILITY: Wheelchair accessible; Telecommunications for the hearing impaired (TTY, TDY, etc.)
CASES SEXUAL ASSAULT/ABUSE (%): 80
DESCRIPTION: Services for teen prostitutes and children involved in pornography
CLIENTS/SERVICES: Sexual assault survivors; Child victims of sexual abuse; Adult survivors of child sexual abuse; Incest victims/survivors; Community education; Pornography; Adolescent survivors of sexual abuse; Male survivors of sexual abuse; Prostitutes
REQUIREMENTS: Clients ages 10-17; Older clients served in special circumstances
SPECIAL PROGRAMS/SERVICES: On-The-Street Outreach in prostitution areas of southern California to let children and teens know of assistance available

INDIO

FAMILY SERVICE OF COACHELLA VALLEY
45-701 Monroe St, Ste A, Indio, CA 92201
Information: (619) 345-5166, 347-2397 8am-5pm
Contact: Gladys Martin, Clinical Dir
TYPE OF AGENCY: Counseling/mental health services
AREAS SERVED: Riverside
YEARS IN OPERATION: 29
LANGUAGES: Spanish
ACCESSIBILITY: Wheelchair accessible
CASES SEXUAL ASSAULT/ABUSE (%): 15
DESCRIPTION: Provides individual and family therapy for survivors of sexual assault
CLIENTS/SERVICES: Sexual assault survivors; Child victims of sexual abuse; Adult survivors of child sexual abuse; Incest victims/survivors; Adolescent survivors of sexual abuse; Male survivors of sexual abuse
REQUIREMENTS: Sliding scale fee

SEXUAL ASSAULT SERVICES
82-380 Miles Ave, Ste 109, Indio, CA 92201
Crisis hotline: **(619) 568-9071 24 hrs**
Information: (619) 347-8440 8am-5pm (Mon-Fri)
Contact: Mary Franklin, Sexual Assault Svcs Coord
TYPE OF AGENCY: Rape crisis center
SPONSORING ORGANIZATION: Harvest of Wellness Foundation
AREAS SERVED: Eastern Riverside
YEARS IN OPERATION: 12
LANGUAGES: Spanish, Italian
ACCESSIBILITY: Wheelchair accessible
CASES SEXUAL ASSAULT/ABUSE (%): 100
DESCRIPTION: Full service rape crisis center. Deals primarily with adults, but also works with adolescents who are raped, and with children when it is an out-of-home, stranger-type of molestation
CLIENTS/SERVICES: Sexual assault survivors; Marital rape/sexual abuse survivors; Child victims of sexual abuse; Adult survivors of child sexual abuse; Community education; Adolescent survivors of sexual abuse; Male survivors of sexual abuse

IONE

OAK SPECIALIZED COUNSELING PROGRAM
201 Waterman Rd, Ione, CA 95640
Information: (209) 274-4771 8am-4:30pm
Contact: Gary Lowe, Prog Mgr
TYPE OF AGENCY: Correctional facility; Residential treatment facility
SPONSORING ORGANIZATION: California Youth Authority
AREAS SERVED: Statewide
YEARS IN OPERATION: 16
LANGUAGES: Spanish
CASES SEXUAL ASSAULT/ABUSE (%): 90
DESCRIPTION: Program provides intensive counseling for adolescent sex offenders who have been victims of sexual abuse
CLIENTS/SERVICES: Offender treatment program; Adolescent survivors of sexual abuse; Male survivors of sexual abuse
REQUIREMENTS: All clients are adjudicated male offenders 14-24 years of age

IRVINE

RAPE PREVENTION EDUCATION PROGRAM, WOMEN'S RESOURCE CENTER
100 Gateway Commons, University of California, Irvine, CA 92717
Crisis hotline: **(714) 856-7273 24 hrs**
Information: (714) 856-7273 8am-5pm (Mon-Fri)
Contact: Christine M Leon, MSW, Coord
TYPE OF AGENCY: College/university-based services; Rape prevention program; Acquaintance/date rape prevention program
SPONSORING ORGANIZATION: University of California-Irvine
YEARS IN OPERATION: 10
LANGUAGES: Spanish
ACCESSIBILITY: Wheelchair accessible
CASES SEXUAL ASSAULT/ABUSE (%): 100
DESCRIPTION: Prevention education topics, such as sexual assault and date rape, pornography, partying without regrets, and skills for violence-free relationships, are offered to women and men via lectures, workshops, films, and training seminars. Also offers short-term crisis counseling and referrals for long-term counseling; Free self-defense training "for women only" offered at least quarterly by certified instructors
CLIENTS/SERVICES: Sexual assault survivors; Marital rape/sexual abuse survivors; Adult survivors of child sexual abuse; Incest victims/survivors; Prevention program; Community education; Adolescent survivors of sexual abuse; Male survivors of sexual abuse
REQUIREMENTS: Member of UC Irvine community (student, staff, or significant others) and those outside the UC Irvine community, e.g. training and prevention education to local law enforcement, high school students, etc

JACKSON

VICTIM/WITNESS PROGRAM
108 Court St, Jackson, CA 95642
Information: (209) 223-6474 8am-5pm
Contact: Mark MacCaffrey, Coord
TYPE OF AGENCY: Victim/witness assistance program
AREAS SERVED: Amador, Alpine, Calaveras
YEARS IN OPERATION: 5
ACCESSIBILITY: Signers for the hearing impaired
CASES SEXUAL ASSAULT/ABUSE (%): 30-40
CLIENTS/SERVICES: Sexual assault survivors; Marital rape/sexual abuse survivors; Child victims of sexual abuse; Adult survivors of child sexual abuse; Incest victims/survivors; Adolescent survivors of sexual abuse; Male survivors of sexual abuse

LA VERNE

UNIVERSITY OF LA VERNE COUNSELING CENTER
1950 3rd St, La Verne, CA 91750
Information: (714) 593-3511, ext 4325 8am-4:30pm (Mon-Thu)
Contact: Dr Valerie Jordan, Dir
TYPE OF AGENCY: College/university-based services
AREAS SERVED: Los Angeles, San Bernardino
YEARS IN OPERATION: 5
CASES SEXUAL ASSAULT/ABUSE (%): 25
CLIENTS/SERVICES: Sexual assault survivors; Adult survivors of child sexual abuse; Incest victims/survivors; Prevention program; Male survivors of sexual abuse
REQUIREMENTS: Must be a student or staff member

LAGUNA NIGUEL

CSP SEXUAL ASSAULT VICTIM SERVICES/PREVENTION PROGRAM
30143 Crown Valley Pkwy, Laguna Niguel, CA 92677
Crisis hotline: **(714) 957-2737 24 hrs**
Information: (714) 249-5037 8am-5pm (Mon-Fri)
TYPE OF AGENCY: Victim/witness assistance program; Child sexual abuse services; Child sexual abuse prevention program; Referral program
SPONSORING ORGANIZATION: South County Municipal Court
AREAS SERVED: Orange
YEARS IN OPERATION: 7
LANGUAGES: Spanish, Vietnamese, Japanese
ACCESSIBILITY: Wheelchair accessible; Signers for the hearing impaired
CASES SEXUAL ASSAULT/ABUSE (%): 100
DESCRIPTION: Provides comprehensive services for victims and witnesses and encourages their cooperation in the investigation of the case and prosecution of the offender
CLIENTS/SERVICES: Sexual assault survivors; Marital rape/sexual abuse survivors; Child victims of sexual abuse; Adult survivors of child sexual abuse; Incest victims/survivors; Prevention program; Community education; Adolescent survivors of sexual abuse; Male survivors of sexual abuse
SPECIAL PROGRAMS/SERVICES: The Orange County Victim/Witness Assistance Program and Child Abuse Prevention Program are also components of CSP, Inc. Services are coordinated between all components of the agency to ensure that each client is afforded quality service and support

LAKE VIEW TERRACE

HILLVIEW MENTAL HEALTH CENTER, INC
11500 Eldridge Ave, Ste 206, Lake View Terrace, CA 91342
Information: (818) 896-1161, ext 207 9am-5:30pm (Mon-Fri)
Contact: Cathy Costa, LCSW, Clinical Dir
TYPE OF AGENCY: Counseling/mental health services
AREAS SERVED: Los Angeles
YEARS IN OPERATION: 23
LANGUAGES: Spanish, Yiddish
ACCESSIBILITY: Wheelchair accessible
DESCRIPTION: Specializes in services for the severely and chronically mentally ill and mentally ill offenders (those with a major diagnosis of schizophrenia, bipolar/manic-depression, major depression or affective disorders). Many of the center's clients have been victims of sexual abuse/assault or have been sex offenders
CLIENTS/SERVICES: Sexual assault survivors; Marital rape/sexual abuse survivors; Adult survivors of child sexual abuse; Incest victims/survivors; Prevention program; Community

HILLVIEW MENTAL HEALTH CENTER, INC *(continued)*
education; Offender treatment program; Male survivors of sexual abuse
REQUIREMENTS: Adults 18 years old and older

LAKEPORT

LAKE COUNTY OFFICE OF THE DISTRICT ATTORNEY—VICTIM/WITNESS ASSISTANCE CENTER
255 N Forbes St, Lakeport, CA 95453
Information: (707) 263-2255, 263-2254 8am-5pm (Mon-Fri)
Contact: Sheryl Lynch, Proj Coord
TYPE OF AGENCY: Victim/witness assistance program
AREAS SERVED: Lake
YEARS IN OPERATION: 4
ACCESSIBILITY: Wheelchair accessible
CASES SEXUAL ASSAULT/ABUSE (%): 45
DESCRIPTION: Provides comprehensive services for victims and witnesses of all types of crimes, specifically sexual assault/sexual abuse crimes because there is no rape crisis center in Lake county. Provides criminal justice process orientation, compensation application assistance, referrals for long-term counseling
CLIENTS/SERVICES: Sexual assault survivors; Marital rape/sexual abuse survivors; Child victims of sexual abuse; Adult survivors of child sexual abuse; Incest victims/survivors; Community education; Adolescent survivors of sexual abuse; Male survivors of sexual abuse

LANCASTER

SEXUAL ASSAULT RESPONSE SERVICE
1600 W Ave J, Annex, Rm 32, Lancaster, CA 93534
Crisis hotline: **(805) 945-3933 24 hrs**
Information: (805) 949-5566 9am-5pm
Contact: Sandy Darrington, Coord
TYPE OF AGENCY: Rape crisis center; Hospital/medical center
SPONSORING ORGANIZATION: Antelope Valley Hospital Medical Center
AREAS SERVED: Los Angeles, Kern, Orange, Riverside, San Bernardino
YEARS IN OPERATION: 10
LANGUAGES: Translators available
ACCESSIBILITY: Wheelchair accessible; Signers for the hearing impaired
CASES SEXUAL ASSAULT/ABUSE (%): 100
DESCRIPTION: Emergency room based program focusing on meeting the individual needs of rape, incest, child molestation (adolescents 14-17) survivors, adults molested as children, and their significant others
CLIENTS/SERVICES: Sexual assault survivors; Marital rape/sexual abuse survivors; Adult survivors of child sexual abuse; Incest victims/survivors; Community education; Adolescent survivors of sexual abuse; Male survivors of sexual abuse
REQUIREMENTS: Ages 14 and older

VALLEY OASIS
PO Box 4226, Lancaster, CA 93539
Crisis hotline: **(805) 945-6736 24 hrs**
Information: (805) 945-5509 9am-5pm
Contact: Dee Summers, Counselor
TYPE OF AGENCY: Domestic violence program
SPONSORING ORGANIZATION: Antelope Valley Domestic Violence Council
AREAS SERVED: Los Angeles, other southern California counties
YEARS IN OPERATION: 8
CASES SEXUAL ASSAULT/ABUSE (%): 85-95
DESCRIPTION: Shelter and counseling for battered women and their children; Support groups; Feminist martial arts/self-defense
CLIENTS/SERVICES: Sexual assault survivors; Marital rape/sexual abuse survivors; Adult survivors of child sexual abuse; Incest victims/survivors; Prevention program; Community education

LIVERMORE

TRI-VALLEY HAVEN
PO Box 2190, Livermore, CA 94550
Crisis hotline: **(415) 449-5842 24 hrs daily**
Information: (415) 449-5845 8am-6pm (Mon-Fri)
Contact: Pat Crumpley, Sexual Assault Svcs Mgr
TYPE OF AGENCY: Rape crisis center; Domestic violence program
AREAS SERVED: Alameda
YEARS IN OPERATION: 8
LANGUAGES: Spanish
ACCESSIBILITY: Wheelchair accessible; Signers for the hearing impaired
CASES SEXUAL ASSAULT/ABUSE (%): 50
CLIENTS/SERVICES: Sexual assault survivors; Marital rape/sexual abuse survivors; Child victims of sexual abuse; Adult survivors of child sexual abuse; Incest victims/survivors; Prevention program; Community education; Adolescent survivors of sexual abuse; Male survivors of sexual abuse

LOMITA

INSTITUTE FOR HUMAN PROGRESS
25601 Narbonne Ave, No 8, Lomita, CA 90717
Information: (213) 530-5654
Contact: Richard Baska, Dir-MFCC
TYPE OF AGENCY: Counseling/mental health services; Private practice
AREAS SERVED: Los Angeles
YEARS IN OPERATION: 12
CASES SEXUAL ASSAULT/ABUSE (%): 35
CLIENTS/SERVICES: Offender treatment program; Male survivors of sexual abuse

LOMPOC

CRISIS CENTER OF LOMPOC—RAPE CRISIS/FOR KIDS SAKE
PO Box 148, Lompoc, CA 93438
Crisis hotline: **(805) 736-7273 24 hrs**
Information: (805) 736-8913 9am-5pm (Mon-Fri)
Contact: Shannon Rose Chavez, Exec Dir; Denise Goodwin, Rape Crisis Coord
TYPE OF AGENCY: Rape crisis center; Child sexual abuse prevention program
AREAS SERVED: Northern Santa Barbara
YEARS IN OPERATION: 15
LANGUAGES: Spanish
ACCESSIBILITY: Wheelchair accessible
CASES SEXUAL ASSAULT/ABUSE (%): 50
DESCRIPTION: Provides intervention and direct services for victims of sexual assault and child abuse (including support groups for male survivors); Provides education and prevention services; Feminist martial arts/self-defense available
CLIENTS/SERVICES: Sexual assault survivors; Marital rape/sexual abuse survivors; Child victims of sexual abuse; Adult survivors of child sexual abuse; Incest victims/survivors; Prevention program; Community education; Adolescent survivors of sexual abuse; Male survivors of sexual abuse
SPECIAL PROGRAMS/SERVICES: Participation in SART (Sexual Assault Response Team) planning/implementation for northern Santa Barbara county; Development of hospital/law enforcement protocol for sexual assault survivors; Development of nursing in-service for CEU (Continuing education credit)

LONG BEACH

SARAH CENTER
2632 Pacific Ave, Long Beach, CA 90806
Information: (213) 427-7671 8:30am-5pm (Mon-Fri)
Contact: Beverly Fancher, Exec Dir
TYPE OF AGENCY: Child sexual abuse services
AREAS SERVED: Long Beach
YEARS IN OPERATION: 4½
CASES SEXUAL ASSAULT/ABUSE (%): 100
CLIENTS/SERVICES: Child victims of sexual abuse; Adult survivors of child sexual abuse; Preschoolers
REQUIREMENTS: Ages 2 to 8

SEXUAL ASSAULT CRISIS AGENCY
PO Box 14377, Long Beach, CA 90803
Crisis hotline: **(213) 597-2002 24 hrs**
Information: (213) 433-1337 9am-5pm (Mon-Fri)
Contact: Kimberly Meek, Exec Dir
TYPE OF AGENCY: Rape crisis center
AREAS SERVED: Los Angeles
YEARS IN OPERATION: 14
LANGUAGES: Spanish
ACCESSIBILITY: Wheelchair accessible
CASES SEXUAL ASSAULT/ABUSE (%): 95
DESCRIPTION: Comprehensive rape crisis services, including self-defense workshops
CLIENTS/SERVICES: Sexual assault survivors; Marital rape/sexual abuse survivors; Child victims of sexual abuse; Adult survivors of child sexual abuse; Incest victims/survivors; Prevention program; Community education; Adolescent survivors of sexual abuse; Male survivors of sexual abuse
REQUIREMENTS: Must report victims under the age of 18 if phone number, address, or last name are known

LOS ANGELES

ALCOHOLISM CENTER FOR WOMEN—PREVENTION SERVICES
1147 S Alvarado St, Los Angeles, CA 90006
Information: (213) 381-7805 9am-5pm
Contact: Clarissa Chandler, Prevention and Comm Svcs Dir
TYPE OF AGENCY: Counseling/mental health services; Substance abuse treatment/counseling
AREAS SERVED: Los Angeles
YEARS IN OPERATION: 13
LANGUAGES: Spanish, Sign
ACCESSIBILITY: Telecommunications for the hearing impaired (TTY, TDY, etc.); Signers for the hearing impaired (by arrangement)
DESCRIPTION: Offers direct services for recovering alcoholic women and women at high risk for alcohol-related problems, including incest survivors, battering survivors, adult daughters of alcoholics, and lesbians
CLIENTS/SERVICES: Adult survivors of child sexual abuse; Incest victims/survivors; Alcoholic women; Lesbians
REQUIREMENTS: Must be adult with 24 hours of sobriety for the recovery program. Recovering alcoholic or addict must be clean and sober for one year to participate in prevention workshops

CENTER FOR THE PACIFIC-ASIAN FAMILY, INC
543 N Fairfax, No 100, Los Angeles, CA 90036
Crisis hotline: **(213) 653-4042 24 hrs**
Information: (213) 653-4045 9am-5pm
Contact: N Rimonte, Exec Dir
TYPE OF AGENCY: Rape crisis center; Domestic violence program
AREAS SERVED: Los Angeles, southern California
YEARS IN OPERATION: 11
LANGUAGES: Filipino, Thai, Lao, Bengali, Hindi, Gujerati, Vietnamese, Chinese, Korean, Japanese
CASES SEXUAL ASSAULT/ABUSE (%): 7-10

CENTER FOR THE PACIFIC-ASIAN FAMILY, INC (continued)

DESCRIPTION: Serves Pacific-Asian community; Provides intervention and prevention services for victims of sexual assault, domestic violence, child abuse and their families; Offers Women Entrepreneurs, a self-employment and business development program
CLIENTS/SERVICES: Sexual assault survivors; Marital rape/sexual abuse survivors; Child victims of sexual abuse; Adult survivors of child sexual abuse; Incest victims/survivors; Prevention program; Community education; Adolescent survivors of sexual abuse; Ethnic minorities
REQUIREMENTS: Focus on Pacific Asians who can't use other services because of culture and language

CHILD SEXUAL ABUSE PROGRAM
5427 Whittier Blvd, Los Angeles, CA 90022
Information: (213) 727-4080 8:30am-5pm
Contact: Carol Walker, MFCC, Supervising Childrens Svcs Wkr
TYPE OF AGENCY: Child sexual abuse services; Child sexual abuse prevention program
SPONSORING ORGANIZATION: Los Angeles County Department of Children's Services
AREAS SERVED: Los Angeles
YEARS IN OPERATION: 12
LANGUAGES: Spanish
ACCESSIBILITY: Wheelchair accessible
CASES SEXUAL ASSAULT/ABUSE (%): 100
CLIENTS/SERVICES: Sexual assault survivors; Child victims of sexual abuse; Adult survivors of child sexual abuse; Incest victims/survivors; Community education; Offender treatment program; Adolescent survivors of sexual abuse
REQUIREMENTS: Intrafamilial sexual offenses must be reported to Child Protective Services

CHILDREN'S INSTITUTE INTERNATIONAL—FAMILY CARE CENTER
711 S New Hampshire Ave, Los Angeles, CA 90005
Crisis hotline: **(213) 385-5100 24 hrs**
Information: (213) 385-5100
Contact: Esther Gillies, Family Care Ctr Dir
TYPE OF AGENCY: Child sexual abuse services; Training/research
DESCRIPTION: Treatment for sexually abused children and adolescents and non-offending family members; Treatment for abuse reactive victim/perpetrators aged 13 and younger; Provides training and seminars in the area of child sexual abuse
CLIENTS/SERVICES: Child victims of sexual abuse; Community education; Offender treatment program; Adolescent survivors of sexual abuse; Male survivors of sexual abuse
REQUIREMENTS: Children under the age of 18

CITY ATTORNEY'S OFFICE—DOMESTIC VIOLENCE UNIT
200 N Main St, Los Angeles, CA 90012
Information: (213) 485-5474 8:30am-5pm
Contact: Alana Bowman, Dep City Atty Unit Coord
TYPE OF AGENCY: Victim/witness assistance program
AREAS SERVED: City of Los Angeles
YEARS IN OPERATION: 2
LANGUAGES: Spanish
ACCESSIBILITY: Wheelchair accessible; Telecommunications for the hearing impaired (TTY, TDY, etc.); Signers for the hearing impaired
DESCRIPTION: Domestic violence unit includes sexual batteries and spousal rape; Victim advocates (many are formerly battered women) are available for survivors
CLIENTS/SERVICES: Sexual assault survivors; Marital rape/sexual abuse survivors; Child victims of sexual abuse; Community education
REQUIREMENTS: Victim must file a police report

CRIME VICTIM CENTER
4311 Wilshire Blvd, Ste 510, Los Angeles, CA 90010
Crisis hotline: **(213) 937-7753, Latino hotline only 24 hrs**
Information: (213) 857-5855 9am-5pm (Mon-Fri)
Contact: Brenda Ingram, LLSW, Clinical Coord
TYPE OF AGENCY: Victim/witness assistance program
AREAS SERVED: Los Angeles, San Bernardino, Orange
YEARS IN OPERATION: 4½
LANGUAGES: Spanish
ACCESSIBILITY: Wheelchair accessible
CASES SEXUAL ASSAULT/ABUSE (%): 25
CLIENTS/SERVICES: Sexual assault survivors; Marital rape/sexual abuse survivors; Child victims of sexual abuse; Community education; Adolescent survivors of sexual abuse; Male survivors of sexual abuse

EAST LOS ANGELES RAPE HOTLINE, INC
PO Box 63245, Los Angeles, CA 90063
Crisis hotline: **(213) 262-0944 24 hrs**
Information: (213) 726-2201 8am-5pm (Mon-Fri)
Contact: Elena Alvarado, Exec Dir
TYPE OF AGENCY: Rape crisis center; Child abuse prevention program; Acquaintance/date rape prevention program; Adolescent program
AREAS SERVED: Los Angeles
YEARS IN OPERATION: 14
LANGUAGES: Spanish
ACCESSIBILITY: Wheelchair accessible
CASES SEXUAL ASSAULT/ABUSE (%): 100
DESCRIPTION: Provides crisis intervention, escort services, counseling and advocacy for survivors of sexual assault. Prevention programs, including feminist martial arts/self-defense and Community Teatro presentations.
CLIENTS/SERVICES: Sexual assault survivors; Marital rape/sexual abuse survivors; Child victims of sexual abuse; Incest victims/survivors; Prevention program; Community education; Adolescent survivors of sexual abuse; Male survivors of sexual abuse
SPECIAL PROGRAMS/SERVICES: Provides community educational programs on sexual assault, child abuse and AIDS. Programs range from TEEN Teatro on Rape Awareness to video presentations on Child Abuse Prevention

EL CENTRO HUMAN SERVICES CORPORATION
972 S Goodrich Blvd, Los Angeles, CA 90022
Crisis hotline: **(213) 725-1337 24 hrs**
Information: (213) 725-1337 8am-9pm (Mon-Fri)
Contact: Beatriz Garcia-De La Rocha, Family Unit Clinical Supv
TYPE OF AGENCY: Counseling/mental health services; Child sexual abuse services; Child sexual abuse prevention program; Residential treatment facility
AREAS SERVED: East Los Angeles, city of Commerce, Montebello
YEARS IN OPERATION: 19
LANGUAGES: Spanish
ACCESSIBILITY: Wheelchair accessible
DESCRIPTION: Team approach to treatment of intrafamilial sexual abuse; Treatment for batterers and child sexual abuse/incest offenders; Bilingual/bicultural staff for Hispanic population
CLIENTS/SERVICES: Sexual assault survivors; Marital rape/sexual abuse survivors; Child victims of sexual abuse; Adult survivors of child sexual abuse; Incest victims/survivors; Prevention program; Community education; Offender treatment program; Adolescent survivors of sexual abuse; Male survivors of sexual abuse; Ethnic minorities
SPECIAL PROGRAMS/SERVICES: Bilingual (Spanish/English) brochure; Hispanic Foster Parent Training Project offers training in Spanish or English to foster parents of sexually abused children

LOS ANGELES CITY ATTORNEY—VICTIM ASSISTANCE PROGRAM
808 N Spring St, 4th Fl, Los Angeles, CA 90012
Crisis hotline: **(213) 485-6976 8am-5pm (Mon-Fri)**
Information: (213) 485-6976 8am-5pm (Mon-Fri)
Contact: Alex V Vargas, Prog Admin
TYPE OF AGENCY: Victim/witness assistance program
AREAS SERVED: Statewide
YEARS IN OPERATION: 8
LANGUAGES: Spanish
ACCESSIBILITY: Wheelchair accessible
CASES SEXUAL ASSAULT/ABUSE (%): 5
CLIENTS/SERVICES: Sexual assault survivors; Marital rape/sexual abuse survivors; Child victims of sexual abuse; Adult survivors of child sexual abuse; Incest victims/survivors; Community education; Adolescent survivors of sexual abuse; Male survivors of sexual abuse

LOS ANGELES COMMISSION ON ASSAULTS AGAINST WOMEN
543 N Fairfax Ave, Los Angeles, CA 90036
Crisis hotline: **(213) 392-8381, 626-3393 24 hrs; TDD Hotline (213) 651-4610 24 hrs**
Information: (213) 655-4235 9am-5pm
Contact: Patricia Giggans, Exec Dir
TYPE OF AGENCY: Rape crisis center; Child sexual abuse prevention program
AREAS SERVED: Los Angeles
YEARS IN OPERATION: 17
LANGUAGES: Spanish, Sign, Farsi, Arabic, Hebrew
ACCESSIBILITY: Telecommunications for the hearing impaired (TTY, TDY, etc.); Signers for the hearing impaired
CASES SEXUAL ASSAULT/ABUSE (%): 100
DESCRIPTION: Comprehensive rape crisis intervention and prevention program, including feminist martial arts/self defense and domestic violence prevention program
CLIENTS/SERVICES: Sexual assault survivors; Marital rape/sexual abuse survivors; Adult survivors of child sexual abuse; Incest victims/survivors; Prevention program; Community education; Adolescent survivors of sexual abuse; Male survivors of sexual abuse
SPECIAL PROGRAMS/SERVICES: Kids self-defense and safety program serving K-12; Deaf services program providing self-defense instruction, education, crisis counseling, and advocacy by deaf volunteers; Self-defense for women; Personal safety and awareness training program for businesses; Domestic violence prevention education program (radio/TV PSAs, training of law enforcement and criminal justice personnel, community education); Men's caucus: a group of concerned men who work with male groups of all ages, examining the role and responsibility of men in the task of eliminating violence against women. Publications: *Survivor*, booklet in various languages, Braille and large print, as well as special edition for developmentally disabled survivors; *Self defense: Women Teaching Women* (2 hour videotape/manual for instructors); *Women's Self-Defense—A Complete Guide to Assault Prevention* (workbook)

LOS ANGELES COUNTY DEPARTMENT OF CHILDREN'S SERVICES
1125 W 6th St, Los Angeles, CA 90017
Crisis hotline: **Child abuse hotline: Zenith 2-1234 24 hrs**
Information: (213) 482-2767 8:30am-5pm
Contact: Emery Bontrager, Exec Asst
TYPE OF AGENCY: Child sexual abuse services; Child abuse services
AREAS SERVED: Los Angeles
YEARS IN OPERATION: 4½
LANGUAGES: Most locally used languages
CASES SEXUAL ASSAULT/ABUSE (%): 17
DESCRIPTION: Children's Protective Services agency, providing short-term crisis counseling for sexually abused children and support

LOS ANGELES COUNTY DEPARTMENT OF CHILDREN'S SERVICES (continued)

groups for adolescent survivors and adult survivors of child sexual abuse
CLIENTS/SERVICES: Child victims of sexual abuse; Adult survivors of child sexual abuse; Prevention program; Community education; Adolescent survivors of sexual abuse

LOS ANGELES WOMEN'S THERAPY CENTER
728 S La Brea, Los Angeles, CA 90036
Information: (213) 931-5445
Contact: Dr Lynn Steinberg, Psychotherapist
TYPE OF AGENCY: Counseling/mental health services; Child sexual abuse services; Private practice
AREAS SERVED: Los Angeles and surrounding area
YEARS IN OPERATION: 11
CASES SEXUAL ASSAULT/ABUSE (%): 90
DESCRIPTION: Individual counseling and groups dealing with women's issues which include child sexual abuse. Ongoing groups include abuse survivors group, abuse survivor couples groups (lesbian, gay men, heterosexual), adult children of alcoholics/addicts, healing and spirituality group. Treatment available for rapists, batterers, and child sexual abuse/incest offenders
CLIENTS/SERVICES: Sexual assault survivors; Marital rape/sexual abuse survivors; Child victims of sexual abuse; Adult survivors of child sexual abuse; Incest victims/survivors; Prevention program; Community education; Offender treatment program; Adolescent survivors of sexual abuse; Male survivors of sexual abuse; Lesbians; Gay men; Healing

MEN'S CAUCUS
543 Fairfax Ave, Los Angeles, CA 90036
Information: (213) 655-4235 Evenings, weekends, and daytime with notice
Contact: Joseph Megel, Dir
TYPE OF AGENCY: Rape crisis center; Men's program
SPONSORING ORGANIZATION: Los Angeles Commission on Assaults Against Women
AREAS SERVED: Los Angeles
YEARS IN OPERATION: 4
DESCRIPTION: To prevent violence against women by educating and working with men of all ages on issues of violence, sexual assault, date/acquaintance rape, sexism, male sexuality, and other prevention issues
CLIENTS/SERVICES: Prevention program; Community education

ROSA PARKS SEXUAL ASSAULT CRISIS CENTER
4182 S Western Ave, Los Angeles, CA 90062
Crisis hotline: **(213) 295-HOPE**
Information: (213) 295-1999
Contact: Joan Crear
TYPE OF AGENCY: Rape crisis center
CLIENTS/SERVICES: Sexual assault survivors

RESPONSE PROGRAM
8730 Alden Dr, Rm C301, Los Angeles, CA 90048
Crisis hotline: **(213) 855-3506 24 hrs 7 days**
Information: (213) 855-3530 9am-9pm (Mon-Fri)
Contact: Sherry Anderson, Coord
TYPE OF AGENCY: Rape crisis center; Counseling/mental health services
SPONSORING ORGANIZATION: Cedars-Sinai Medical Center
AREAS SERVED: Los Angeles and surrounding areas
YEARS IN OPERATION: 12
LANGUAGES: Spanish
ACCESSIBILITY: Wheelchair accessible; Signers for the hearing impaired (by arrangement)
CASES SEXUAL ASSAULT/ABUSE (%): 95
DESCRIPTION: Short-term crisis intervention for victims of violent crimes, primarily rape, but also battering, child sexual abuse, and mugging. Bilingual counselors available, and clients can state preference for a male or female counselor
CLIENTS/SERVICES: Sexual assault survivors; Marital rape/sexual abuse survivors; Child victims of sexual abuse; Adult survivors of child sexual abuse; Incest victims/survivors; Prevention program; Community education; Adolescent survivors of sexual abuse; Male survivors of sexual abuse

SPEAKS (SURVIVORS OF PHYSICAL AND EMOTIONAL ABUSE AS KIDS)
7120 Franklin Ave, Los Angeles, CA 90046
Information: (213) 876-0933
Contact: Linda Levinson, MSW, LCSW, Prog Dir
TYPE OF AGENCY: Adult survivors services
SPONSORING ORGANIZATION: Parents Anonymous of California
DESCRIPTION: Weekly support groups, facilitated by mental health professionals, for adults who survived physical, emotional, sexual abuse as children; sponsored by Parents Anonymous
CLIENTS/SERVICES: Adult survivors of child sexual abuse

UNIVERSITY OF CALIFORNIA LOS ANGELES—PSYCHOLOGY CLINIC
2191 Franz Hall, Dept of Psychology, University of California, Los Angeles, Los Angeles, CA 90024-1563
Information: (213) 825-2305 by appointment (Mon-Fri)
Contact: Pam Marks, Intake Sec; Jill Waterman, PhD, Asst Clinic Coord
TYPE OF AGENCY: College/university-based services; Child sexual abuse services; Training/research
AREAS SERVED: Los Angeles
YEARS IN OPERATION: 40
LANGUAGES: Spanish
ACCESSIBILITY: Wheelchair accessible
CASES SEXUAL ASSAULT/ABUSE (%): 15-25
DESCRIPTION: The UCLA psychology clinic is the training clinic for the UCLA PhD program in clinical psychology, specializing in treating sexual abuse victims and male survivors of childhood sexual abuse. Support groups available for female and male survivors
CLIENTS/SERVICES: Sexual assault survivors; Marital rape/sexual abuse survivors; Child victims of sexual abuse; Adult survivors of child sexual abuse; Incest victims/survivors; Adolescent survivors of sexual abuse; Male survivors of sexual abuse
REQUIREMENTS: Must not require hospitalization

MANHATTAN BEACH

COUNSELING AND HEALTH ASSOCIATES
920 Manhattan Beach Blvd, No 2, Manhattan Beach, CA 90266
Information: (213) 545-8802 8am-9pm
Contact: Wendy Deaton, MFCC
TYPE OF AGENCY: Private practice
AREAS SERVED: Los Angeles
YEARS IN OPERATION: 3
CASES SEXUAL ASSAULT/ABUSE (%): 10-25
CLIENTS/SERVICES: Sexual assault survivors; Marital rape/sexual abuse survivors; Child victims of sexual abuse; Adult survivors of child sexual abuse; Incest victims/survivors; Community education
REQUIREMENTS: Fee for service

SOUTH BAY CENTER FOR COUNSELING
2617 Bell Ave, Manhattan Beach, CA 90266
Crisis hotline: **(213) 545-6575 24 hrs**
Information: (213) 545-6575 9am-8pm
Contact: Barney Bartelle, Clinical Soc Wkr
TYPE OF AGENCY: Counseling/mental health services; Child sexual abuse services
AREAS SERVED: Los Angeles
YEARS IN OPERATION: 15
LANGUAGES: Spanish
ACCESSIBILITY: Wheelchair accessible
DESCRIPTION: Specializing in child sexual abuse and ritualistic abuse; Provides evaluation and treatment of all types of child abuse through play, individual, group, and family therapy
CLIENTS/SERVICES: Sexual assault survivors; Marital rape/sexual abuse survivors; Child victims of sexual abuse; Adult survivors of child sexual abuse; Incest victims/survivors; Adolescent survivors of sexual abuse; Male survivors of sexual abuse; Ritualistic abuse victims/survivors

MARTINEZ

CHILD AND FAMILY THERAPY CENTER
1210 Alhambra Ave, Martinez, CA 94553
Information: (415) 229-4090 9am-5pm (Mon-Fri)
Contact: Mary Krentz, PhD, Prog Dir
TYPE OF AGENCY: Child sexual abuse services
AREAS SERVED: Contra Costa
YEARS IN OPERATION: 10
LANGUAGES: Spanish, French, German
ACCESSIBILITY: Wheelchair accessible
CASES SEXUAL ASSAULT/ABUSE (%): 100
DESCRIPTION: Provides diagnostic evaluation and treatment for intrafamilial sexually abused children and their families
CLIENTS/SERVICES: Child victims of sexual abuse; Adult survivors of child sexual abuse; Incest victims/survivors; Community education; Offender treatment program; Adolescent survivors of sexual abuse
REQUIREMENTS: Sliding scale fee; Children ages birth to 18

MERCED

MERCED COUNTY MENTAL HEALTH
480 E 13th St, Merced, CA 95340
Crisis hotline: **(209) 723-8861 24 hrs**
Information: (209) 723-8861 8am-5pm
Contact: Liz Freitas, Sex Abuse Svcs Coord
TYPE OF AGENCY: Counseling/mental health services
AREAS SERVED: Merced
LANGUAGES: Spanish, Hmong
ACCESSIBILITY: Wheelchair accessible
CLIENTS/SERVICES: Sexual assault survivors; Marital rape/sexual abuse survivors; Child victims of sexual abuse; Adult survivors of child sexual abuse; Incest victims/survivors; Offender treatment program; Adolescent survivors of sexual abuse; Male survivors of sexual abuse
SPECIAL PROGRAMS/SERVICES: HOPES (Helping Other People Ease Sorrow): 4-week multifamily group for victims, siblings, and non-offending parents; STARS (Specialized Treatment and Rehabilitation Services): individual, group, and family treatment for young male victims

MODESTO

PARENTS UNITED OF STANISLAUS COUNTY/STANISLAUS COUNTY CHILD ABUSE TREATMENT TEAM
346 Burney St, Modesto, CA 95354
Crisis hotline: **(209) 529-6767 24 hrs 7 days**
Information: (209) 525-7454 8am-5pm (Mon-Fri)
Contact: Debra Johnsen, Coord
TYPE OF AGENCY: Counseling/mental health services; Child sexual abuse services
SPONSORING ORGANIZATION: Stanislaus County Mental Health
AREAS SERVED: Stanislaus
YEARS IN OPERATION: 9
LANGUAGES: Spanish
ACCESSIBILITY: Wheelchair accessible
CASES SEXUAL ASSAULT/ABUSE (%): 100

PARENTS UNITED OF STANISLAUS COUNTY/STANISLAUS COUNTY CHILD ABUSE TREATMENT TEAM *(continued)*
DESCRIPTION: Self-help and mutual support groups for parents, children, and former victims concerned with child sexual abuse; Support groups for child sexual abuse/incest offenders. Provides case monitoring for "convicted deniers" and pedophiles, with group treatment focus
CLIENTS/SERVICES: Marital rape/sexual abuse survivors; Child victims of sexual abuse; Adult survivors of child sexual abuse; Incest victims/survivors; Prevention program; Community education; Offender treatment program; Adolescent survivors of sexual abuse; Male survivors of sexual abuse
SPECIAL PROGRAMS/SERVICES: Media program entitled *From Tears to Laughter* focusing on adult survivors (19 minutes)

STANISLAUS COUNTY DISTRICT ATTORNEY'S OFFICE—VICTIM/WITNESS PROGRAM
PO Box 442, Modesto, CA 95353
Information: (209) 525-5550 8am-5pm
Contact: Margaret Speed, Prog Supv
TYPE OF AGENCY: Victim/witness assistance program
AREAS SERVED: Stanislaus
YEARS IN OPERATION: 7
LANGUAGES: Spanish
ACCESSIBILITY: Wheelchair accessible; Signers for the hearing impaired
CASES SEXUAL ASSAULT/ABUSE (%): 25
CLIENTS/SERVICES: Sexual assault survivors; Marital rape/sexual abuse survivors; Child victims of sexual abuse; Incest victims/survivors; Community education
REQUIREMENTS: Cooperate with law enforcement agencies; Report the crime; Must not have participated in crime or events leading to crime

STANISLAUS RAPE CRISIS CENTER
1024 J St, No 316, Modesto, CA 95354
Crisis hotline: **(209) 527-5558 24 hrs**
Information: (209) 577-4344 8am-4pm
Contact: Melba W Mathias, Proj Dir
TYPE OF AGENCY: Rape crisis center
AREAS SERVED: Stanislaus
YEARS IN OPERATION: 15
LANGUAGES: Spanish
ACCESSIBILITY: Wheelchair accessible
CASES SEXUAL ASSAULT/ABUSE (%): 100
CLIENTS/SERVICES: Sexual assault survivors; Marital rape/sexual abuse survivors; Adult survivors of child sexual abuse; Incest victims/survivors; Prevention program; Community education; Adolescent survivors of sexual abuse; Male survivors of sexual abuse

MONTEREY

DISTRICT ATTORNEY VICTIM/WITNESS PROGRAM
PO Box 1070, Monterey, CA 93940
Information: (408) 647-7770 8am-5pm (Mon-Fri)
Contact: Martha Gleason or Terri Dorman, Victim/Witness Coords
TYPE OF AGENCY: Victim/witness assistance program
AREAS SERVED: Monterey
YEARS IN OPERATION: 23
LANGUAGES: Spanish
ACCESSIBILITY: Wheelchair accessible
CASES SEXUAL ASSAULT/ABUSE (%): 50
CLIENTS/SERVICES: Sexual assault survivors; Child victims of sexual abuse
REQUIREMENTS: Police report must be filed and victim must be willing to cooperate with all law enforcement agencies; Victim must not have contributed to the crime.

MONTEREY RAPE CRISIS CENTER
PO Box 2630, Monterey, CA 93950
Crisis hotline: **(408) 375-4357, 633-5900 24 hrs**
Information: (408) 373-3955 9am-5pm
Contact: Karen Stafford, Client Svcs Dir; Clare Mounteer, Exec Dir
TYPE OF AGENCY: Rape crisis center; Child sexual abuse prevention program
AREAS SERVED: Monterey Peninsula, North Monterey
YEARS IN OPERATION: 15
LANGUAGES: Spanish
CASES SEXUAL ASSAULT/ABUSE (%): 99
CLIENTS/SERVICES: Sexual assault survivors; Marital rape/sexual abuse survivors; Adult survivors of child sexual abuse; Incest victims/survivors; Prevention program; Community education; Adolescent survivors of sexual abuse; Male survivors of sexual abuse
REQUIREMENTS: Minors referred to Family Resource Center
SPECIAL PROGRAMS/SERVICES: *It's OK to Say No* is a child abuse primary prevention program delivered to children in preschool through 10th grade

MOUNTAIN VIEW

MID-PENINSULA SUPPORT NETWORK FOR BATTERED WOMEN
448 E Middlefield Rd, Mountain View, CA 94043
Crisis hotline: **(415) 964-2266 24 hrs daily**
Information: (415) 964-6503 9am-5pm (Mon-Fri)
Contact: Sylvia Inman, Client Svcs Dir
TYPE OF AGENCY: Domestic violence program
AREAS SERVED: Santa Clara, parts of San Mateo
YEARS IN OPERATION: 10
LANGUAGES: Spanish, Vietnamese, French
ACCESSIBILITY: Wheelchair accessible
CASES SEXUAL ASSAULT/ABUSE (%): 20 reported
DESCRIPTION: Provides services and prevention work to eliminate domestic violence; Male counseling program for batterers
CLIENTS/SERVICES: Marital rape/sexual abuse survivors; Prevention program; Community education

NAPA

SEXUAL ASSAULT VICTIMS SERVICES
1700 2nd St, Ste 308, Napa, CA 94559
Crisis hotline: **(707) 258-8000 24 hrs**
Information: (707) 252-6222
Contact: Christina Cunningham, Exec Dir
TYPE OF AGENCY: Rape crisis center; Child sexual abuse prevention program
SPONSORING ORGANIZATION: Volunteer Center of Napa County, Inc
CLIENTS/SERVICES: Sexual assault survivors; Child victims of sexual abuse; Adult survivors of child sexual abuse; Incest victims/survivors; Prevention program; Community education; Adolescent survivors of sexual abuse; Male survivors of sexual abuse

NEVADA CITY

NEVADA COUNTY VICTIM/WITNESS ASSISTANCE CENTER
Courthouse, 2nd Fl, Nevada City, CA 95959
Crisis hotline: **(916) 265-1730 24 hrs**
Information: (916) 265-1200 8am-5pm
Contact: Jean Carli, Proj Coord
TYPE OF AGENCY: Victim/witness assistance program
SPONSORING ORGANIZATION: Nevada County Probation Department
AREAS SERVED: Nevada, Sierra
YEARS IN OPERATION: 4
LANGUAGES: Spanish
CASES SEXUAL ASSAULT/ABUSE (%): 70-75
CLIENTS/SERVICES: Sexual assault survivors; Marital rape/sexual abuse survivors; Child victims of sexual abuse; Adult survivors of child sexual abuse; Incest victims/survivors; Prevention program; Community education; Adolescent survivors of sexual abuse; Male survivors of sexual abuse
REQUIREMENTS: Victims must cooperate with law enforcement

NEWPORT BEACH

VICTIM/WITNESS ASSISTANCE PROGRAM
4601 Jamboree Blvd, Ste 103, Newport Beach, CA 92660
Crisis hotline: **(714) 957-2737 24 hrs**
Information: (714) 476-4855 8am-5pm
Contact: Cleo Victa, Supv
TYPE OF AGENCY: Victim/witness assistance program
SPONSORING ORGANIZATION: Community Service Agency
AREAS SERVED: Orange
YEARS IN OPERATION: 10
LANGUAGES: Spanish, Vietnamese
CASES SEXUAL ASSAULT/ABUSE (%): 40
CLIENTS/SERVICES: Sexual assault survivors; Marital rape/sexual abuse survivors; Child victims of sexual abuse; Adult survivors of child sexual abuse; Incest victims/survivors; Adolescent survivors of sexual abuse; Male survivors of sexual abuse
REQUIREMENTS: Client must file charges and be cooperative with the prosecution of the defendant.

NORTHRIDGE

ALTERNATIVES FOR PEOPLE
9010 Reseda Blvd, Ste 212, Northridge, CA 91324
Information: (818) 349-7554 7am-9pm (Mon-Fri)
Contact: Gail J Chase, LCSW, Lic Clinical Soc Wkr
TYPE OF AGENCY: Counseling/mental health services; Private practice
AREAS SERVED: Primarily Los Angeles, Ventura
YEARS IN OPERATION: 9
DESCRIPTION: Individual therapy, work with couples, and have experience with incest/molestation survivors
CLIENTS/SERVICES: Sexual assault survivors; Marital rape/sexual abuse survivors; Adult survivors of child sexual abuse; Incest victims/survivors; Adolescent survivors of sexual abuse; Male survivors of sexual abuse
REQUIREMENTS: Age 15 or older
SPECIAL PROGRAMS/SERVICES: Self-esteem groups for women

FAMILY CRISIS SERVICE
9650 Zelzah Ave, Northridge, CA 91325
Crisis hotline: **(818) 993-9311 24 hrs**
Information: (818) 993-9311 8:30am-5pm (Mon, Fri); 8:30am-9pm (Tue, Wed, Thu)
Contact: Joan Mandell, Co-Coord
TYPE OF AGENCY: Child sexual abuse services; Child sexual abuse prevention program; Child abuse services; Child abuse prevention program
SPONSORING ORGANIZATION: San Fernando Valley Child Guidance Clinic
AREAS SERVED: Los Angeles Districts 3 and 5
YEARS IN OPERATION: 6
LANGUAGES: Spanish
ACCESSIBILITY: Wheelchair accessible
CASES SEXUAL ASSAULT/ABUSE (%): 90
DESCRIPTION: Evaluation and treatment for child victims who have been or are at risk of sexual or physical abuse and neglect and their families; Treatment for adolescent sex offenders
CLIENTS/SERVICES: Child victims of sexual abuse; Incest victims/survivors; Prevention program; Community education; Offender treatment program; Adolescent survivors of sexual abuse
REQUIREMENTS: Ages 7-14

OAKLAND

ALAMEDA COUNTY DISTRICT ATTORNEY—VICTIM WITNESS ASSISTANCE DIVISION
1401 Lakeside Dr, Ste 802, Oakland, CA 94612
Information: (415) 272-6180 8am-5pm (Mon-Fri)
Contact: Harold O Boscovich, Dir
TYPE OF AGENCY: Victim/witness assistance program
AREAS SERVED: Alameda
YEARS IN OPERATION: 14
LANGUAGES: Spanish
ACCESSIBILITY: Wheelchair accessible; Signers for the hearing impaired (with prior notice)
CLIENTS/SERVICES: Sexual assault survivors; Marital rape/sexual abuse survivors; Child victims of sexual abuse; Adult survivors of child sexual abuse; Incest victims/survivors; Community education; Adolescent survivors of sexual abuse; Male survivors of sexual abuse
SPECIAL PROGRAMS/SERVICES: A mobile crisis intervention team works seven days per week including holidays from 5pm-1:30am patrolling the city of Oakland in a county vehicle (police radio equipped) responding to calls for crisis intervention by Oakland Police Dispatcher

ASIAN COMMUNITY MENTAL HEALTH SERVICES
310 8th St, Ste 201, Oakland, CA 94607
Crisis hotline: **(415) 548-0412 (Oakland Consortium on Sexual Assault) 24 hrs**
Information: (415) 451-6729 9am-5pm (Mon-Fri)
Contact: Tomoko Ishii, MA, Psychotherapist
TYPE OF AGENCY: Counseling/mental health services; Child sexual abuse prevention program
AREAS SERVED: Alameda
YEARS IN OPERATION: 14
LANGUAGES: Chinese, Japanese, Korean, Tagalog, Cambodian, Lao, Mien, Vietnamese, Afghani
ACCESSIBILITY: Wheelchair accessible
DESCRIPTION: Counseling for Asian-American community; Individual and couple therapy for child sexual abuse offenders and incest offenders
CLIENTS/SERVICES: Sexual assault survivors; Child victims of sexual abuse; Adult survivors of child sexual abuse; Incest victims/survivors; Prevention program; Community education; Offender treatment program; Adolescent survivors of sexual abuse; Male survivors of sexual abuse; Ethnic minorities; Publications/media
REQUIREMENTS: Client must be a resident of Alameda County
SPECIAL PROGRAMS/SERVICES: Videotapes on prevention in 9 languages

ASIAN PROGRAM
285 17th St, Oakland, CA 94612
Information: (415) 271-4360 8:30am-5pm
Contact: Loretta Huahn, Prog Dir
TYPE OF AGENCY: Counseling/mental health services
SPONSORING ORGANIZATION: Central Oakland Community Mental Health Center
AREAS SERVED: Alameda
YEARS IN OPERATION: 12
LANGUAGES: Chinese, Vietnamese
ACCESSIBILITY: Wheelchair accessible
CASES SEXUAL ASSAULT/ABUSE (%): 5
CLIENTS/SERVICES: Sexual assault survivors; Marital rape/sexual abuse survivors; Adult survivors of child sexual abuse; Incest victims/survivors; Male survivors of sexual abuse; Ethnic minorities
REQUIREMENTS: 18 and older; Sliding scale fees; Medi-Cal and Medicare accepted

BANANAS, CHILD CARE RESOURCE AND REFERRAL AND PARENT SUPPORT
6501 Telegraph Ave, Oakland, CA 94609
Crisis hotline: **(415) 658-6046 9:30am-4:30pm (Mon-Fri)**
Information: (415) 658-7101 9:30am-4:30pm (Mon-Fri)
Contact: Judy Calder, Health Svcs Coord; Betty Cohen, Soc Svcs Coord
TYPE OF AGENCY: Child sexual abuse prevention program; Information and referral; Child abuse prevention program
AREAS SERVED: Northern Alameda
YEARS IN OPERATION: 16
LANGUAGES: Spanish, Chinese, Vietnamese
ACCESSIBILITY: Wheelchair accessible; Telecommunications for the hearing impaired (TTY, TDY, etc.)
CASES SEXUAL ASSAULT/ABUSE (%): 10
DESCRIPTION: Prevention services include payment of child care services for the provision of respite or for services referred by Child Protective Services. Provides warmline, a pre-crisis health and development counseling line. Parent and child care workers education includes information and referral, classes, seminars, workshops
CLIENTS/SERVICES: Prevention program; Community education; Child care providers; Preschoolers; Publications/media
SPECIAL PROGRAMS/SERVICES: Publications: *Making a Difference: A Handbook for Child Care Providers* includes information on preventing child abuse and neglect, such as warning signs, how to work with abused children and their families, child sexual abuse, responsibilities for reporting abuse, and positive child guidance and discipline. (72 pages; Spanish and English editions available)

BAY AREA WOMEN AGAINST RAPE
1515 Webster, Oakland, CA 94612
Crisis hotline: **(415) 845-7273, 796-8838 24 hrs**
Information: (415) 465-3890, 796-7273 Fremont 9am-5pm (Mon-Fri), Oakland 10am-3pm (Mon-Fri)
Contact: C Barber, Youth Svcs Dir
TYPE OF AGENCY: Rape crisis center; Child sexual abuse prevention program
AREAS SERVED: Alameda
YEARS IN OPERATION: 17
LANGUAGES: Spanish
ACCESSIBILITY: Wheelchair accessible; Telecommunications for the hearing impaired (TTY, TDY, etc.)
CASES SEXUAL ASSAULT/ABUSE (%): 100
DESCRIPTION: Comprehensive services for sexual assault survivors; Treatment program for rapists. Feminist martial arts/self-defense program available
CLIENTS/SERVICES: Sexual assault survivors; Marital rape/sexual abuse survivors; Adult survivors of child sexual abuse; Incest victims/survivors; Prevention program; Community education; Offender treatment program; Adolescent survivors of sexual abuse; Male survivors of sexual abuse
SPECIAL PROGRAMS/SERVICES: School-based prevention programs include Child Assault Prevention (CAP) Project and the Teen Assault Awareness Program

CHILD ASSAULT PREVENTION TRAINING CENTER OF NORTHERN CALIFORNIA
1727 Martin Luther King Jr Way, No 108, Oakland, CA 94612
Information: (415) 893-0413 9am-5pm (Mon-Fri)
Contact: Tom Bolan, Regional Dir
TYPE OF AGENCY: Child sexual abuse prevention program; Consultation; Training/research
AREAS SERVED: Northern California
YEARS IN OPERATION: 8
DESCRIPTION: Local program: Provides prevention education for children in classrooms from preschool through high school, as well as for parents and school staff. Regional program: Provides technical assistance and training for child abuse primary prevention education programs
CLIENTS/SERVICES: Prevention program; Community education
SPECIAL PROGRAMS/SERVICES: *The CAP Preschool Program* a training manual

FAMILY SERVICE OF THE EAST BAY
445 30th St, Oakland, CA 94609
Information: (415) 834-5433 9am-5pm
Contact: Marjorie Schwartz, Clinical Supv
TYPE OF AGENCY: Counseling/mental health services; Child sexual abuse services
AREAS SERVED: Alameda
YEARS IN OPERATION: 100
LANGUAGES: Spanish
CASES SEXUAL ASSAULT/ABUSE (%): 25
DESCRIPTION: Individual and group counseling for child and adult survivors of sexual assault/abuse; Self-help groups for women survivors of incest and child sexual abuse
CLIENTS/SERVICES: Sexual assault survivors; Marital rape/sexual abuse survivors; Child victims of sexual abuse; Adult survivors of child sexual abuse; Incest victims/survivors; Community education; Adolescent survivors of sexual abuse; Male survivors of sexual abuse

HIGHLAND SEXUAL ASSAULT CENTER
1411 E 31st St, Oakland, CA 94602
Crisis hotline: **(415) 548-0412 24 hrs daily**
Information: (415) 437-4688, 437-4574 24 hrs
Contact: Alice Washington, Proj Coord
TYPE OF AGENCY: Rape crisis center; Hospital/medical center; Child sexual abuse services; Child sexual abuse prevention program
AREAS SERVED: Alameda
YEARS IN OPERATION: 4
LANGUAGES: Translators available
ACCESSIBILITY: Wheelchair accessible; Telecommunications for the hearing impaired (TTY, TDY, etc.); Signers for the hearing impaired
CASES SEXUAL ASSAULT/ABUSE (%): 100
DESCRIPTION: Multiethnic, multidisciplined, multicultural organization providing 24-hour crisis intervention services, advocacy, and follow-up counseling for survivors of sexual assault; Support groups for both female and male survivors
CLIENTS/SERVICES: Sexual assault survivors; Marital rape/sexual abuse survivors; Child victims of sexual abuse; Adult survivors of child sexual abuse; Incest victims/survivors; Prevention program; Community education; Adolescent survivors of sexual abuse; Male survivors of sexual abuse
REQUIREMENTS: Survivors 14 and younger are referred to Children's Hospital of Oakland

LA CLINICA DE LA RAZA—FRUITVALE HEALTH PROJECT, INC
1515 Fruitvale Ave, Oakland, CA 94601
Information: (415) 534-0078 9am-5:30pm
Contact: Ana O'Connor, Contracts/Svcs Admin
TYPE OF AGENCY: Hospital/medical center; Counseling/mental health services; Child sexual abuse services
AREAS SERVED: Alameda
YEARS IN OPERATION: 15
LANGUAGES: Spanish
ACCESSIBILITY: Wheelchair accessible
CASES SEXUAL ASSAULT/ABUSE (%): 25
CLIENTS/SERVICES: Sexual assault survivors; Marital rape/sexual abuse survivors; Child victims of sexual abuse; Adult survivors of child sexual abuse; Incest victims/survivors; Community education; Adolescent survivors of sexual abuse; Male survivors of sexual abuse; Ethnic minorities

PIEDMONT CENTER FOR COUNSELING AND PSYCHOTHERAPY
4442 Piedmont Ave, Ste C, Oakland, CA 94611
Information: (415) 841-6100 By appointment
Contact: Maggie Phillips, PhD, Psychologist
TYPE OF AGENCY: Private practice
AREAS SERVED: Alameda
YEARS IN OPERATION: 8
CASES SEXUAL ASSAULT/ABUSE (%): 20

PIEDMONT CENTER FOR COUNSELING AND PSYCHOTHERAPY *(continued)*
CLIENTS/SERVICES: Sexual assault survivors; Marital rape/sexual abuse survivors; Adult survivors of child sexual abuse; Incest victims/survivors; Adolescent survivors of sexual abuse

RAINBOW PSYCHOTHERAPY ASSOCIATES
1727 Martin Luther King Jr Way, Oakland, CA 94612
Contact: Susan Borows, Therapist
TYPE OF AGENCY: Private practice
AREAS SERVED: Contra Costa, Alameda
YEARS IN OPERATION: 4
ACCESSIBILITY: Wheelchair accessible
DESCRIPTION: All of the associates worked in a treatment program concerned with abuse at the Oakland Children's Hospital Child Trauma Center. Individual and group therapy for survivors and their families; Individual therapy for child sexual abuse/incest offenders and batterers
CLIENTS/SERVICES: Sexual assault survivors; Marital rape/sexual abuse survivors; Child victims of sexual abuse; Adult survivors of child sexual abuse; Incest victims/survivors; Community education; Offender treatment program; Adolescent survivors of sexual abuse; Male survivors of sexual abuse

A SAFE PLACE
PO Box 275, Oakland, CA 94604
Crisis hotline: **(415) 536-7233 24 hrs**
Information: (415) 444-7255 9am-5pm
Contact: Carolyn Russell, Exec Dir
TYPE OF AGENCY: Domestic violence program
AREAS SERVED: Alameda
YEARS IN OPERATION: 10
LANGUAGES: Spanish
ACCESSIBILITY: Wheelchair accessible
CLIENTS/SERVICES: Marital rape/sexual abuse survivors; Child victims of sexual abuse; Adult survivors of child sexual abuse; Community education; Adolescent survivors of sexual abuse

THERAPY NETWORK
5848 Chabot Rd, Oakland, CA 94618
Information: (415) 769-3812
Contact: Shelly Fields, Coord Committee Member
TYPE OF AGENCY: Information and referral
AREAS SERVED: Alameda, Marin, San Francisco
YEARS IN OPERATION: 7
DESCRIPTION: Provides referrals to therapists who specialize in survivor issues
CLIENTS/SERVICES: Sexual assault survivors; Adult survivors of child sexual abuse; Incest victims/survivors

WEST OAKLAND MENTAL HEALTH CENTER—MENTAL HEALTH DEPARTMENT
2730 Adeline St, Oakland, CA 94607
Information: (415) 465-1800, ext 311 8am-7pm
Contact: Derethia DuVal, Sexual Assault Therapist
TYPE OF AGENCY: Hospital/medical center; Counseling/mental health services; Child sexual abuse services
AREAS SERVED: Alameda
YEARS IN OPERATION: 3
ACCESSIBILITY: Wheelchair accessible
CASES SEXUAL ASSAULT/ABUSE (%): 50
DESCRIPTION: Provides brief and long-term therapy for survivors of sexual assault, referral from the hospital-based program (Highland Hospital) and general community referrals
CLIENTS/SERVICES: Sexual assault survivors; Marital rape/sexual abuse survivors; Child victims of sexual abuse; Adult survivors of child sexual abuse; Incest victims/survivors; Offender treatment program; Adolescent survivors of sexual abuse; Male survivors of sexual abuse

SPECIAL PROGRAMS/SERVICES: Specialist in working with women of color, low-income women, and women who experience multiple traumatic issues impacting on their lives over a long period of time

WOMEN'S CHOICE CLINIC
2930 McClure St, Oakland, CA 94609
Crisis hotline: **(415) 444-5676 24 hrs**
Information: (415) 444-5676 9am-6pm (Mon-Fri)
Contact: Debbie Gregg, Dir
TYPE OF AGENCY: Hospital/medical center
AREAS SERVED: Primarily Alameda, Contra Costa
YEARS IN OPERATION: 15
LANGUAGES: Spanish
CASES SEXUAL ASSAULT/ABUSE (%): 5
DESCRIPTION: Provides reproductive health services for women and men, sexually transmitted disease screening and pregnancy screening services for rape survivors; Incest Survivors Anonymous groups meet on site
CLIENTS/SERVICES: Sexual assault survivors; Marital rape/sexual abuse survivors; Adult survivors of child sexual abuse; Incest victims/survivors

ORANGE

COUNTY OF ORANGE SOCIAL SERVICES AGENCY—CHILDREN'S SERVICES
PO Box 6685, Orange, CA 92613-6685
Crisis hotline: **(714) 834-5353 24 hrs**
Information: (714) 834-5353 8am-6pm
Contact: Nathan Nishimoto, Prog Mgr
TYPE OF AGENCY: Child sexual abuse services
AREAS SERVED: Orange
YEARS IN OPERATION: 20
LANGUAGES: Spanish, Vietnamese
ACCESSIBILITY: Wheelchair accessible
CASES SEXUAL ASSAULT/ABUSE (%): 25
DESCRIPTION: Provides mandated child protective services which include assessment and investigation, foster care, permanent planning and adoption services
CLIENTS/SERVICES: Community education; 24-hour reporting line; Adolescent survivors of sexual abuse
REQUIREMENTS: Minors up to 18 years old who are residing in Orange County
SPECIAL PROGRAMS/SERVICES: Part of the Child Abuse Services Team (CAST), a multidisciplinary center whose purpose is to reduce the number of interviews a child must endure once a disclosure has been made. Participants of CAST include district attorney, police, social services workers, medical practitioners, therapist and volunteers

ORANGE COUNTY SEXUAL ASSAULT NETWORK (OCSAN)
PO Box 5663, Orange, CA 92613-5663
Crisis hotline: **(714) 831-9110 24 hrs**
Information: (714) 538-7878 9am-5pm
Contact: Cheryl A Bode, Exec Dir
TYPE OF AGENCY: Rape crisis center; Acquaintance/date rape prevention program
AREAS SERVED: Orange
YEARS IN OPERATION: 4
LANGUAGES: Spanish
ACCESSIBILITY: Wheelchair accessible
CASES SEXUAL ASSAULT/ABUSE (%): 100
DESCRIPTION: Provides full range of rape crisis services, support groups, and self-defense workshops
CLIENTS/SERVICES: Sexual assault survivors; Marital rape/sexual abuse survivors; Child victims of sexual abuse; Adult survivors of child sexual abuse; Incest victims/survivors; Prevention program; Community education; Adolescent survivors of sexual abuse; Male survivors of sexual abuse; Publications/media
SPECIAL PROGRAMS/SERVICES: Date rape prevention program for senior high school and freshman college students, with a ½-hour video on date rape; 16-page date rape booklet for high school students; Booklet for college students. Working with other county agencies in forming a sexual assault response team for medical exams

SEXUAL ASSAULT VICTIM SERVICES/ PREVENTION PROGRAM
301 The City Dr S, Orange, CA 92668
Crisis hotline: **(714) 957-2737 24 hrs**
Information: (714) 834-7074 8am-5pm (Mon-Fri)
TYPE OF AGENCY: Victim/witness assistance program; Child sexual abuse services; Child sexual abuse prevention program
SPONSORING ORGANIZATION: Juvenile Court
AREAS SERVED: Orange
YEARS IN OPERATION: 7
LANGUAGES: Spanish, Vietnamese, Japanese
ACCESSIBILITY: Wheelchair accessible; Signers for the hearing impaired
CASES SEXUAL ASSAULT/ABUSE (%): 100
DESCRIPTION: Provides comprehensive services for victims and witnesses and encourages their cooperation in the investigation of the case and prosecution of the offender
CLIENTS/SERVICES: Sexual assault survivors; Marital rape/sexual abuse survivors; Child victims of sexual abuse; Adult survivors of child sexual abuse; Incest victims/survivors; Prevention program; Community education; Adolescent survivors of sexual abuse; Male survivors of sexual abuse
SPECIAL PROGRAMS/SERVICES: The Orange County Victim/Witness Assistance Program and Child Abuse Prevention Program are also components of CSP, Inc. Services are coordinated between all components of the agency to ensure that each client is afforded quality service and support

WOMEN'S TRANSITIONAL LIVING CENTER
PO Box 6103, Orange, CA 92667
Crisis hotline: **(714) 992-1931 24 hrs 7 days**
Information: (714) 992-1939 8am-5:30pm
Contact: Barbara Clippinger, Prog Dir
TYPE OF AGENCY: Domestic violence program; Child sexual abuse services
AREAS SERVED: Orange
YEARS IN OPERATION: 12
LANGUAGES: Spanish
ACCESSIBILITY: Wheelchair accessible; Signers for the hearing impaired
CLIENTS/SERVICES: Sexual assault survivors; Marital rape/sexual abuse survivors; Child victims of sexual abuse; Adult survivors of child sexual abuse; Incest victims/survivors; Prevention program; Community education; Adolescent survivors of sexual abuse; Male survivors of sexual abuse

OROVILLE

BUTTE COUNTY VICTIM WITNESS PROGRAM
2279 Del Oro, Ste C, Oroville, CA 95965
Crisis hotline: **(916) 538-7340 8am-5pm (Mon-Fri)**
Information: (916) 538-7340 8am-5pm (Mon-Fri)
Contact: John M Wardell, Prog Coord/Supervising Probation Off
TYPE OF AGENCY: Victim/witness assistance program
AREAS SERVED: Butte
YEARS IN OPERATION: 10
ACCESSIBILITY: Wheelchair accessible
CASES SEXUAL ASSAULT/ABUSE (%): 20-25
CLIENTS/SERVICES: Sexual assault survivors; Marital rape/sexual abuse survivors; Child victims of sexual abuse; Adult survivors of child sexual abuse; Incest victims/survivors; Adolescent survivors of sexual abuse
REQUIREMENTS: Victim of a violent crime; Aid in prosecution; Noncontributor to the crime

PARENTS UNITED/DAUGHTERS AND SONS UNITED
PO Box 1649, 3 County Center Dr, Oroville, CA 95965
Crisis hotline: **(800) 824-0902 24 hrs**
Information: (916) 538-7026 8am-5pm
Contact: Dwayne Elam, Agency Coord
TYPE OF AGENCY: Child sexual abuse services
SPONSORING ORGANIZATION: Butte County Child Protective Agency
AREAS SERVED: Butte
YEARS IN OPERATION: 3
ACCESSIBILITY: Wheelchair accessible; Signers for the hearing impaired (by request)
CASES SEXUAL ASSAULT/ABUSE (%): 100
DESCRIPTION: Treatment groups for child and adolescent victims, adults molested as children, spouses of offenders, sex offenders (molest and incest) groups held weekly
CLIENTS/SERVICES: Child victims of sexual abuse; Adult survivors of child sexual abuse; Incest victims/survivors; Prevention program; Community education; Offender treatment program; Adolescent survivors of sexual abuse; Male survivors of sexual abuse; Healing
REQUIREMENTS: Victim or offender referred by Butte County Child Protective Services

OXNARD

OXNARD POLICE DEPARTMENT—VICTIM SERVICES UNIT
251 S "C" St, Oxnard, CA 93033
Crisis hotline: **(805) 486-4311 (Police office) 24 hrs**
Information: (805) 984-4675 8am-5pm
Contact: Robert Owens, Chief of Police
TYPE OF AGENCY: Victim/witness assistance program
AREAS SERVED: City of Oxnard
LANGUAGES: Spanish
CASES SEXUAL ASSAULT/ABUSE (%): 80
CLIENTS/SERVICES: Sexual assault survivors; Marital rape/sexual abuse survivors; Child victims of sexual abuse
REQUIREMENTS: Majority of clients are reported crime victims but services are provided for those victims who do not wish to file charges

PALO ALTO

CHILD ADVOCACY COUNCIL
460 California Ave, Ste 13, Palo Alto, CA 94306
Information: (415) 327-8120 8am-5pm (Mon-Fri)
TYPE OF AGENCY: Child sexual abuse prevention program; Child abuse prevention program; Adolescent program
AREAS SERVED: San Mateo, Santa Clara
YEARS IN OPERATION: 10
LANGUAGES: Spanish
ACCESSIBILITY: Wheelchair accessible
DESCRIPTION: Prevention programs include Children's Personal Safety Program and Adolescent Awareness
CLIENTS/SERVICES: Prevention program; Community education

MID-PENINSULA YWCA RAPE CRISIS CENTER
4161 Alma St, Palo Alto, CA 94306
Crisis hotline: **(415) 493-7273 24 hrs**
Information: (415) 494-0993 9am-5pm
Contact: Teresa Rodriguez, Dir
TYPE OF AGENCY: Rape crisis center; Child sexual abuse prevention program; Acquaintance/date rape prevention program
AREAS SERVED: Northern Santa Clara
YEARS IN OPERATION: 15
LANGUAGES: Spanish, French
ACCESSIBILITY: Wheelchair accessible
CASES SEXUAL ASSAULT/ABUSE (%): 100
DESCRIPTION: Comprehensive rape crisis services and prevention program including feminist martial arts/self-defense
CLIENTS/SERVICES: Sexual assault survivors; Marital rape/sexual abuse survivors; Child victims of sexual abuse; Adult survivors of child sexual abuse; Incest victims/survivors; Prevention program; Community education; Male survivors of sexual abuse
SPECIAL PROGRAMS/SERVICES: Child Assault Prevention Project and Teen Assault Prevention Project presents programs in the classroom from preschool to high school. The goals of the programs are to focus on children's rights and help children recognize actions which violate their rights, as well as acquaintance rape prevention. Prevention and assertiveness techniques are demonstrated through age-appropriate role plays

PASADENA

FOOTHILL FAMILY SERVICE AGENCY
118 S Oak Knoll Ave, Pasadena, CA 91101
Crisis hotline: **(818) 795-6907 24 hrs**
Information: (818) 795-6907
TYPE OF AGENCY: Child sexual abuse services; Counseling/mental health services
DESCRIPTION: Special program for sexually abused children ages 5-13; Victim/young offender program for abuse reactive young perpetrators ages 5-13
CLIENTS/SERVICES: Sexual assault survivors; Child victims of sexual abuse; Adult survivors of child sexual abuse; Incest victims/survivors; Offender treatment program; Adolescent survivors of sexual abuse; Male survivors of sexual abuse

HAVEN HOUSE, INC
PO Box 50007, Pasadena, CA 91105-0007
Crisis hotline: **(213) 681-2626 24 hrs**
Information: (213) 681-5044 8:30am-5:30pm
Contact: Cindy Friedman, Exec Dir
TYPE OF AGENCY: Domestic violence program
YEARS IN OPERATION: 23
LANGUAGES: Spanish
ACCESSIBILITY: Wheelchair accessible; Telecommunications for the hearing impaired (TTY, TDY, etc.) (TDD); Signers for the hearing impaired
CASES SEXUAL ASSAULT/ABUSE (%): 15
DESCRIPTION: Provides shelter and counseling for battered women and their children and to families of alcoholics. Some of the women have experienced sexual abuse; some are adult survivors of incest
CLIENTS/SERVICES: Marital rape/sexual abuse survivors; Child victims of sexual abuse; Adult survivors of child sexual abuse; Incest victims/survivors; Prevention program; Community education; Adolescent survivors of sexual abuse

PACIFIC CLINICS
66 Hurlbut St, Pasadena, CA 91105
Information: (818) 795-8471 8am-8pm (Mon-Thu); 8am-5pm (Fri)
TYPE OF AGENCY: Counseling/mental health services
AREAS SERVED: Los Angeles
YEARS IN OPERATION: 62
LANGUAGES: Spanish
ACCESSIBILITY: Wheelchair accessible
CASES SEXUAL ASSAULT/ABUSE (%): 35
DESCRIPTION: Outpatient services include family, group, and individual therapies for victims of abuse, family violence, rape, or sexual molestation; Treatment for incest offenders
CLIENTS/SERVICES: Sexual assault survivors; Marital rape/sexual abuse survivors; Child victims of sexual abuse; Adult survivors of child sexual abuse; Incest victims/survivors; Prevention program; Offender treatment program; Adolescent survivors of sexual abuse
REQUIREMENTS: Priority is given to MediCal and low-income clients

PASADENA YWCA RAPE CRISIS CENTER
78 N Marengo Ave, Pasadena, CA 91001
Crisis hotline: **(818) 793-3385 24 hrs**
Information: (818) 793-5171 9am-5pm (Mon-Fri)
Contact: Liza Culick, Asst Dir/Hot Line Supv
TYPE OF AGENCY: Rape crisis center
AREAS SERVED: West San Gabriel Valley in Los Angeles County
YEARS IN OPERATION: 14
LANGUAGES: Spanish by request
CASES SEXUAL ASSAULT/ABUSE (%): 100
DESCRIPTION: Provides comprehensive services for sexual assault/abuse survivors and their families/significant others. Feminist martial arts/self-defense program also available
CLIENTS/SERVICES: Sexual assault survivors; Marital rape/sexual abuse survivors; Adult survivors of child sexual abuse; Incest victims/survivors; Prevention program; Community education; Adolescent survivors of sexual abuse; Male survivors of sexual abuse

PLACERVILLE

VICTIM WITNESS PROGRAM
295 Fair Ln, Placerville, CA 95667
Information: (916) 621-5640
Contact: Lynda Parker, Victim Witness Prog Coord
TYPE OF AGENCY: Victim/witness assistance program
SPONSORING ORGANIZATION: El Dorado County Probation Department
AREAS SERVED: El Dorado
YEARS IN OPERATION: 15
ACCESSIBILITY: Wheelchair accessible
CASES SEXUAL ASSAULT/ABUSE (%): 80
CLIENTS/SERVICES: Crime victims
REQUIREMENTS: Must report crime and cooperate with prosecution if applicable.

PLEASANT HILL

CHILD ABUSE PREVENTION COUNCIL OF CONTRA COSTA COUNTY, INC
3313 Vincent Rd, Ste 206, Pleasant Hill, CA 94523
Information: (415) 946-9961 9am-Noon, 1pm-5pm (Mon-Fri)
Contact: Carol Bryant, PhD, Exec Dir
TYPE OF AGENCY: Child sexual abuse prevention program; Child abuse prevention program
AREAS SERVED: Contra Costa
YEARS IN OPERATION: 10
LANGUAGES: Spanish
CLIENTS/SERVICES: Prevention program; Community education

RANCHO CUCAMONGA

RANCHO VICTIM/WITNESS ASSISTANCE PROGRAM
8303 Haven Ave, Rancho Cucamonga, CA 91730
Information: (714) 945-4233, 945-4235 8am-5pm
Contact: Carol B Anderson, Victim Advocate
TYPE OF AGENCY: Victim/witness assistance program
SPONSORING ORGANIZATION: San Bernardino County District Attorney's Office
AREAS SERVED: San Bernardino
YEARS IN OPERATION: 24
LANGUAGES: Spanish
ACCESSIBILITY: Wheelchair accessible
CASES SEXUAL ASSAULT/ABUSE (%): 50
CLIENTS/SERVICES: Sexual assault survivors; Marital rape/sexual abuse survivors; Child victims of sexual abuse; Incest victims/survivors; Community education; Male survivors of sexual abuse
REQUIREMENTS: Cannot contribute to crime; Must assist with the investigation and prosecution of crime; For violent crime funds, client must file charges

RANCHO MIRAGE

BARBARA SINATRA CHILDREN'S CENTER
39000 Bob Hope Dr, Rancho Mirage, CA 92270
Crisis hotline: **(619) 340-2200 24 hrs**
Information: (619) 340-2336 8am-5pm
Contact: Bonnie Shields, Child Abuse Prog Dir
TYPE OF AGENCY: Counseling/mental health services; Child sexual abuse services; Child sexual abuse prevention program
AREAS SERVED: Riverside
YEARS IN OPERATION: 2
LANGUAGES: Spanish
ACCESSIBILITY: Wheelchair accessible
CASES SEXUAL ASSAULT/ABUSE (%): 95
DESCRIPTION: Counseling and support groups for victims/survivors of child sexual abuse and child sexual abuse/incest offenders. Provides medical exams for sexually abused children
CLIENTS/SERVICES: Child victims of sexual abuse; Adult survivors of child sexual abuse; Incest victims/survivors; Community education; Offender treatment program; Adolescent survivors of sexual abuse; Male survivors of sexual abuse

REDDING

PSYCHOTHERAPY SERVICES
1240 Pine St, Redding, CA 96001
Crisis hotline: **(916) 244-9088 24 hrs**
Information: (916) 244-9088 24 hrs
Contact: Marilyn Wooley, PhD, Clinical Psychologist
TYPE OF AGENCY: Private practice
AREAS SERVED: Shasta, Tehama, Trinity, Butte, Humboldt
YEARS IN OPERATION: 8
ACCESSIBILITY: Wheelchair accessible
CASES SEXUAL ASSAULT/ABUSE (%): 40-50
DESCRIPTION: Therapy for survivors, including group therapy for female and male survivors and art therapy for child and adult survivors. Treatment for offenders—rapists, child sexual abuse/incest offenders and batterers
CLIENTS/SERVICES: Sexual assault survivors; Marital rape/sexual abuse survivors; Child victims of sexual abuse; Adult survivors of child sexual abuse; Incest victims/survivors; Community education; Offender treatment program; Adolescent survivors of sexual abuse; Male survivors of sexual abuse; Healing

SHASTA COUNTY CHILD SEXUAL ABUSE TREATMENT PROGRAM
611 Iris, Redding, CA 96002
Crisis hotline: **(916) 222-5777 7am-9pm**
Information: (916) 222-5777 7am-9pm
Contact: Christine Doud, Coord
TYPE OF AGENCY: Child sexual abuse services
AREAS SERVED: Shasta, Trinity, Modoc, Butte, Glenn, Tehama
YEARS IN OPERATION: 6
CASES SEXUAL ASSAULT/ABUSE (%): 95
DESCRIPTION: Parents United and Adults Molested as Children groups
CLIENTS/SERVICES: Child victims of sexual abuse; Adult survivors of child sexual abuse; Incest victims/survivors; Offender treatment program; Adolescent survivors of sexual abuse; Male survivors of sexual abuse

SHASTA COUNTY MENTAL HEALTH SERVICES—OUTPATIENT CHILDREN'S PROGRAM
2750 Eureka Way, Redding, CA 96001
Crisis hotline: **(916) 225-5200 8am-5pm**
Information: (916) 225-5200 8am-5pm
Contact: Terrence Nunn, PhD, Prog Mgr
TYPE OF AGENCY: Counseling/mental health services; Child sexual abuse services
AREAS SERVED: Shasta
YEARS IN OPERATION: 3
LANGUAGES: Spanish
ACCESSIBILITY: Wheelchair accessible; Signers for the hearing impaired
CASES SEXUAL ASSAULT/ABUSE (%): 10-20
DESCRIPTION: County outpatient clinic providing a variety of therapeutic services including individual, family, and group therapy for sexually abused children
CLIENTS/SERVICES: Child victims of sexual abuse; Offender treatment program; Adolescent survivors of sexual abuse
REQUIREMENTS: Must be under 18

SHASTA COUNTY WOMEN'S REFUGE
PO Box 4211, Redding, CA 96099
Crisis hotline: **(916) 244-0117 24 hrs**
Information: (916) 244-0117 8am-5pm (Mon-Fri)
Contact: Shirley P Thompson, Interim Exec Dir
TYPE OF AGENCY: Rape crisis center; Domestic violence program
AREAS SERVED: Shasta
YEARS IN OPERATION: 10
ACCESSIBILITY: Wheelchair accessible
CASES SEXUAL ASSAULT/ABUSE (%): 12
DESCRIPTION: Provides a facility for battered and/or sexually assaulted women, Assists abusive men to deal with their anger and fear in a non-violent manner
CLIENTS/SERVICES: Sexual assault survivors; Marital rape/sexual abuse survivors; Adult survivors of child sexual abuse; Community education

REDONDO BEACH

PENINSULA COUNSELING
324 Pacific Coast Hwy, No 201, Redondo Beach, CA 90277
Crisis hotline: **(213) 540-5864 24 hrs**
Information: (213) 540-5864 24 hrs
Contact: Johann Hampton-Wagener, MS
TYPE OF AGENCY: Counseling/mental health services; Private practice
AREAS SERVED: Los Angeles
YEARS IN OPERATION: 4
CASES SEXUAL ASSAULT/ABUSE (%): 10-15
DESCRIPTION: Individual short- and long-term counseling for survivors and individual counseling for incest offenders and batterers
CLIENTS/SERVICES: Sexual assault survivors; Child victims of sexual abuse; Adult survivors of child sexual abuse; Incest victims/survivors; Offender treatment program; Adolescent survivors of sexual abuse; Male survivors of sexual abuse

REDWOOD CITY

VICTIM CENTER OF SAN MATEO COUNTY
2317 Broadway, Ste 140, Redwood City, CA 94063
Information: (415) 363-4010 8am-5pm
Contact: Chuck Coggeshall, Prog Mgr
TYPE OF AGENCY: Victim/witness assistance program
SPONSORING ORGANIZATION: San Mateo County Probation Department
AREAS SERVED: San Mateo
YEARS IN OPERATION: 13
LANGUAGES: Translators available
ACCESSIBILITY: Wheelchair accessible; Signers for the hearing impaired
CASES SEXUAL ASSAULT/ABUSE (%): 25
CLIENTS/SERVICES: Sexual assault survivors; Marital rape/sexual abuse survivors; Child victims of sexual abuse; Adult survivors of child sexual abuse; Incest victims/survivors; Community education; Adolescent survivors of sexual abuse; Male survivors of sexual abuse

RIDGECREST

WOMEN'S SHELTER NETWORK
PO Box 1657, Ridgecrest, CA 93555
Crisis hotline: **(619) 375-7525 24 hrs**
Information: (619) 446-7491 24 hrs
Contact: Judy Banks, Dir
TYPE OF AGENCY: Domestic violence program
AREAS SERVED: Kern
YEARS IN OPERATION: 5
ACCESSIBILITY: Signers for the hearing impaired
CASES SEXUAL ASSAULT/ABUSE (%): 100
CLIENTS/SERVICES: Marital rape/sexual abuse survivors; Adult survivors of child sexual abuse; Prevention program; Community education

RIVERSIDE

FAMILY SERVICE ASSOCIATION OF RIVERSIDE
6927 Brockton Ave, Ste 1A, Riverside, CA 92507
Crisis hotline: **(714) 686-3706 24 hrs**
Information: (714) 686-3706 8am-9pm
Contact: Ray Liles, DSW, Clinical Coord
TYPE OF AGENCY: Counseling/mental health services; Child sexual abuse services
AREAS SERVED: Riverside
ACCESSIBILITY: Wheelchair accessible
CASES SEXUAL ASSAULT/ABUSE (%): 50
DESCRIPTION: Individual, marital, family, and group therapy; Family anger management program; Child abuse intervention
CLIENTS/SERVICES: Sexual assault survivors; Marital rape/sexual abuse survivors; Child victims of sexual abuse; Adult survivors of child sexual abuse; Incest victims/survivors; Adolescent survivors of sexual abuse; Male survivors of sexual abuse
REQUIREMENTS: Sliding scale fee

RAPE PREVENTION EDUCATION PROGRAM
Women's Resource Center, Riverside, CA 92521
Information: (714) 787-5000 8am-5pm (Mon-Fri)
Contact: Zipora Golenberg, Coord
TYPE OF AGENCY: College/university-based services; Rape prevention program; Acquaintance/date rape prevention program
SPONSORING ORGANIZATION: University of California Riverside
YEARS IN OPERATION: 10
ACCESSIBILITY: Wheelchair accessible
DESCRIPTION: Student service program to reduce individual vulnerability to rape, and to mitigate the trauma of sexual assault victims; Offers prevention and awareness programs (including acquaintance rape prevention), self-defense classes, short-term counseling, advocacy for sexual harassment cases, referrals; Small collection of books and articles is available for reference on sexual assault
CLIENTS/SERVICES: Sexual assault survivors; Marital rape/sexual abuse survivors; Adult survivors of child sexual abuse; Incest victims/survivors; Prevention program; Community education; Sexual harassment

RIVERSIDE AREA RAPE CRISIS CENTER
2060 University Ave, Ste 101, Riverside, CA 92507
Crisis hotline: **(714) 686-7273 24 hrs**
Information: (714) 686-7273 8am-5pm
Contact: Mary Beth Wadding, Exec Dir
TYPE OF AGENCY: Rape crisis center; Child sexual abuse prevention program
AREAS SERVED: Western Riverside
YEARS IN OPERATION: 15
LANGUAGES: Spanish
ACCESSIBILITY: Wheelchair accessible
CASES SEXUAL ASSAULT/ABUSE (%): 100
DESCRIPTION: Crisis counseling, advocacy, support for sexual assault survivors of all ages; Support groups for sexual assault survivors and for adult survivors of child sexual abuse; Feminist martial arts/self-defense program

RIVERSIDE AREA RAPE CRISIS CENTER
(continued)
CLIENTS/SERVICES: Sexual assault survivors; Marital rape/sexual abuse survivors; Child victims of sexual abuse; Adult survivors of child sexual abuse; Incest victims/survivors; Prevention program; Community education; Adolescent survivors of sexual abuse; Male survivors of sexual abuse
SPECIAL PROGRAMS/SERVICES: *Senior Outreach Against Rape* brochure

SACRAMENTO

AFTER/PARENTS UNITED OF SACRAMENTO
4811 Chippendale Dr, Ste 208, Sacramento, CA 95841
Information: (916) 344-0249 8am-5pm
Contact: Marsha Nohl, Co-Dir
TYPE OF AGENCY: Counseling/mental health services; Child sexual abuse services
AREAS SERVED: El Dorado, Sacramento, Yolo
YEARS IN OPERATION: 3
ACCESSIBILITY: Wheelchair accessible
CASES SEXUAL ASSAULT/ABUSE (%): 100
DESCRIPTION: Treatment of families and individuals affected by molest trauma
CLIENTS/SERVICES: Child victims of sexual abuse; Adult survivors of child sexual abuse; Incest victims/survivors; Community education; Offender treatment program; Adolescent survivors of sexual abuse; Male survivors of sexual abuse
REQUIREMENTS: All clients who attend group therapy must also be in individual therapy

CHILD ABUSE COUNCIL OF SACRAMENTO, INC
2335 American River Dr, Ste 400, Sacramento, CA 95825
Information: (916) 920-1765 8am-5pm (Mon-Fri)
Contact: Marie Marsh, Exec Dir
TYPE OF AGENCY: Child sexual abuse prevention program; Child abuse prevention program; Interagency network
AREAS SERVED: Sacramento
YEARS IN OPERATION: 10
LANGUAGES: Cantonese
ACCESSIBILITY: Wheelchair accessible
DESCRIPTION: Major coordinating body in the county, for the entire child protection system. Efforts include: Community education; Services coordination; Training and technical assistance; Major provider of the Primary Prevention Program which offers workshops to children on how to prevent child abuse
CLIENTS/SERVICES: Prevention program; Community education

CHILD AND FAMILY INSTITUTE
4545 9th Ave, Sacramento, CA 95820
Crisis hotline: **(916) 736-1720 9am-5pm, answering machine after hours**
Information: (916) 736-0828 9am-5pm
Contact: James Chambers, PhD, Asst Dir
TYPE OF AGENCY: Child sexual abuse services; Child sexual abuse prevention program; Adolescent program
AREAS SERVED: Sacramento, Placer, Yolo, El Dorado, San Joaquin
YEARS IN OPERATION: 10
ACCESSIBILITY: Wheelchair accessible
CASES SEXUAL ASSAULT/ABUSE (%): 100
DESCRIPTION: Sacramento Child Sexual Abuse Treatment Program for sexually abused children and their families. Clients participate in weekly treatment groups, individual and family counseling sessions. Voluntary Treatment and Play Therapy Program for child sexual abuse victims, ages 3-18 and their non-offending parents. Juvenile Victim/Offender Treatment Program serves boys and girls ages 6-19, who have a history of child abuse and are beginning to act out sexually. Supervised Visitation for court-referred parents and children involved in custody disputes
CLIENTS/SERVICES: Child victims of sexual abuse; Incest victims/survivors; Prevention program; Offender treatment program; Adolescent survivors of sexual abuse; Male survivors of sexual abuse
REQUIREMENTS: Offenders must bereferred by criminal justice system
SPECIAL PROGRAMS/SERVICES: Educational programs and curriculum providing current information on boy victims of sexual abuse and their treatment needs, including: factors unique in the sexual abuse experiences of boy victims; misinformation surrounding male sexual victimization; societal attitudes and beliefs that promote and perpetuate this victimization; long-term psychological and behavioral effects of sexual abuse for boys; how professionals/parents can sensitively deal with boy victims; treatment goals and objectives; characteristics of offenders who molest boys; and preventing the sexual abuse of boys by teaching specific skills and providing information to boys and their families

SACRAMENTO COUNTY DISTRICT ATTORNEY'S OFFICE—VICTIM AND WITNESS ASSISTANCE PROGRAM
PO Box 749, Sacramento, CA 95812-0749
Information: (916) 440-5701 8am-5pm
Contact: Kerry Martin, Prog Coord
TYPE OF AGENCY: Victim/witness assistance program
AREAS SERVED: Sacramento
YEARS IN OPERATION: 11
LANGUAGES: Spanish
ACCESSIBILITY: Wheelchair accessible
CASES SEXUAL ASSAULT/ABUSE (%): 40
DESCRIPTION: Provides services for victims of violent crimes such as crisis counseling, referrals, resource counseling, court support, advocacy, assistance in filing for reimbursement from state victims program
CLIENTS/SERVICES: Sexual assault survivors; Marital rape/sexual abuse survivors; Child victims of sexual abuse; Community education
REQUIREMENTS: Client usually must make police report except in cases where domestic violence victims obtain restraining orders

SACRAMENTO RAPE CRISIS CENTER
1831 I St, Sacramento, CA 95814
Crisis hotline: **(916) 447-RAPE 24 hrs**
Information: (916) 447-3223 9am-6pm (Mon-Fri)
Contact: Ellen Yin, Exec Dir
TYPE OF AGENCY: Rape crisis center
SPONSORING ORGANIZATION: Sacramento Center for Abuse Prevention and Advocacy
AREAS SERVED: 2 ½
YEARS IN OPERATION: Spanish, Chinese, Serbo-Croatian
CASES SEXUAL ASSAULT/ABUSE (%): 100
CLIENTS/SERVICES: Sexual assault survivors; Marital rape/sexual abuse survivors; Adult survivors of child sexual abuse; Incest victims/survivors; Community education; Adolescent survivors of sexual abuse; Male survivors of sexual abuse

SACRAMENTO YOUTH AND FAMILY SERVICES CENTER
9099 Tuolumne Dr, Sacramento, CA 95826
Crisis hotline: **(916) 363-0063 24 hrs daily**
Information: (916) 363-9943 9am-5pm (Mon-Fri)
Contact: Lyn Cottingham, Assoc Dir
TYPE OF AGENCY: Shelter; Adolescent program
SPONSORING ORGANIZATION: Diogenes Youth Services, Inc
AREAS SERVED: Sacramento
YEARS IN OPERATION: 12
ACCESSIBILITY: Wheelchair accessible
CASES SEXUAL ASSAULT/ABUSE (%): 65
DESCRIPTION: Provides individual, group and family counseling; Temporary shelter for runaways and other troubled youth, including protective custody for abused youth; Weekly family support groups; Adolescent abuse groups
CLIENTS/SERVICES: Sexual assault survivors; Child victims of sexual abuse; Incest victims/survivors; Prevention program; Community education; Adolescent survivors of sexual abuse; Male survivors of sexual abuse
REQUIREMENTS: Focus on ages 12 to 17

WEAVE, INC
PO Box 161356, Sacramento, CA 95816
Crisis hotline: **(916) 920-2952 24 hrs**
Information: (916) 448-2321 9am-9pm (Mon-Thu); 9am-6pm (Fri)
Contact: Gail Jones, Exec Dir
TYPE OF AGENCY: Rape crisis center; Domestic violence program
AREAS SERVED: Sacramento
YEARS IN OPERATION: 10
LANGUAGES: Spanish
ACCESSIBILITY: Wheelchair accessible
CASES SEXUAL ASSAULT/ABUSE (%): 100
DESCRIPTION: Comprehensive services for survivors of both rape and domestic violence and treatment for batterers
CLIENTS/SERVICES: Sexual assault survivors; Marital rape/sexual abuse survivors; Prevention program; Community education; Male survivors of sexual abuse

WOMEN'S RESOURCE CENTER—RAPE PREVENTION EDUCATION PROGRAM
6000 J St, Sacramento, CA 95819
Information: (916) 278-7388, 278-4444 8am-5pm
Contact: Ashley Sinclaire, Dir
TYPE OF AGENCY: College/university-based services; Rape prevention program; Acquaintance/date rape prevention program
SPONSORING ORGANIZATION: California State University-Sacramento
AREAS SERVED: Sacramento
YEARS IN OPERATION: 8
LANGUAGES: Spanish
ACCESSIBILITY: Wheelchair accessible; Signers for the hearing impaired
DESCRIPTION: Survivor support services and advocacy for members of the campus community; Workshops and presentations on rape awareness, self-defense, and acquaintance rape
CLIENTS/SERVICES: Sexual assault survivors; Adult survivors of child sexual abuse; Incest victims/survivors; Prevention program; Community education; Adolescent survivors of sexual abuse; Male survivors of sexual abuse

SALINAS

DOMESTIC CRISIS SERVICES OF MONTEREY COUNTY
PO Box 3584, Salinas, CA 93912
Crisis hotline: **(408) 422-2201 24 hrs**
Information: (408) 758-5769 8am-5pm
Contact: Joan C Tregenza, Exec Dir
TYPE OF AGENCY: Domestic violence program
AREAS SERVED: Monterey
YEARS IN OPERATION: 11
LANGUAGES: Spanish
ACCESSIBILITY: Wheelchair accessible
CASES SEXUAL ASSAULT/ABUSE (%): 20
CLIENTS/SERVICES: Sexual assault survivors; Marital rape/sexual abuse survivors; Child victims of sexual abuse

FAMILY RESOURCE CENTER
328 Cayuga St, Salinas, CA 93901
Information: (408) 757-7915 9am-5pm
Contact: Jean Costello, Treatment Coord
TYPE OF AGENCY: Victim/witness assistance program; Child sexual abuse services; Child abuse services; Child abuse prevention program
AREAS SERVED: Monterey
CASES SEXUAL ASSAULT/ABUSE (%): 90

FAMILY RESOURCE CENTER *(continued)*
DESCRIPTION: Individual and family therapy for sexually and physically abused clients as well as support groups for children, adolescents, and adult women who were sexually abused as children. Also offers parent education
CLIENTS/SERVICES: Sexual assault survivors; Child victims of sexual abuse; Adult survivors of child sexual abuse; Incest victims/survivors; Prevention program; Community education; Adolescent survivors of sexual abuse; Male survivors of sexual abuse

WOMEN'S CRISIS CENTER OF SALINAS VALLEY
109 Central Ave, Salinas, CA 93901
Crisis hotline: **(408) 757-1002 24 hrs daily**
Information: (408) 757-1001 9am-5pm
Contact: Michelle Sgarlato, Sexual Assault Unit Coord
TYPE OF AGENCY: Rape crisis center; Child sexual abuse prevention program; Acquaintance/date rape prevention program
AREAS SERVED: Monterey
YEARS IN OPERATION: 14
LANGUAGES: Spanish, other interpreters by arrangement
CASES SEXUAL ASSAULT/ABUSE (%): 33
DESCRIPTION: Comprehensive services for sexual assault and domestic violence, support groups, and feminist martial arts/self defense
CLIENTS/SERVICES: Sexual assault survivors; Marital rape/sexual abuse survivors; Child victims of sexual abuse; Adult survivors of child sexual abuse; Incest victims/survivors; Prevention program; Community education; Offender treatment program; Adolescent survivors of sexual abuse; Male survivors of sexual abuse; Prisoners
SPECIAL PROGRAMS/SERVICES: Women's Empowerment Program, a 5-week structured program for all women, 18 or older, helps women enhance the positive and change the negative aspects of their lives. 500 women have participated in this program and have given positive feedback regarding their experience. Date rape prevention program in grades 6-12. Child Assault Prevention Program (CAPP). Works with Soledad Prison in developing an offender/survivor program

SAN BERNARDINO

FAMILY SERVICE AGENCY CHILD ABUSE TREATMENT
1661 N "E" St, San Bernardino, CA 92405
Information: (714) 881-2691 8am-5pm
Contact: Jennie Smith, Prog Coord
TYPE OF AGENCY: Counseling/mental health services; Child sexual abuse services; Child sexual abuse prevention program
AREAS SERVED: San Bernardino
YEARS IN OPERATION: 8
ACCESSIBILITY: Wheelchair accessible
CASES SEXUAL ASSAULT/ABUSE (%): 100
DESCRIPTION: Parents United chapter in San Bernardino and Ontario treats incest victims and perpetrators through group therapy. Provides education program in public and private schools
CLIENTS/SERVICES: Child victims of sexual abuse; Incest victims/survivors; Prevention program; Community education; Offender treatment program; Adolescent survivors of sexual abuse

SAN BERNARDINO DISTRICT ATTORNEY'S OFFICE—VICTIM/WITNESS CENTER
316 N Mountain View Ave, San Bernardino, CA 92415
Information: (714) 387-6583 8am-5pm
Contact: Mike Stevens, Victim/Witness Advocate; Jo Ann Nunez, Prog Coord
TYPE OF AGENCY: Victim/witness assistance program
AREAS SERVED: San Bernardino
YEARS IN OPERATION: 10
LANGUAGES: Spanish
ACCESSIBILITY: Wheelchair accessible
CASES SEXUAL ASSAULT/ABUSE (%): 50
CLIENTS/SERVICES: Sexual assault survivors; Marital rape/sexual abuse survivors; Child victims of sexual abuse; Adult survivors of child sexual abuse; Incest victims/survivors; Prevention program; Community education; Male survivors of sexual abuse
REQUIREMENTS: For victim of violent crime funds, client must file charges

SAN BERNARDINO SEXUAL ASSAULT SERVICE
1875 N "D" St, San Bernardino, CA 92404
Crisis hotline: **(800) 222-RAPE 24 hrs**
Information: (714) 883-8689, 825-1033 9am-5pm
Contact: Kay Hannan, Exec Dir
TYPE OF AGENCY: Rape crisis center
AREAS SERVED: San Bernardino
YEARS IN OPERATION: 10
LANGUAGES: Spanish, Moroccan Arabic
ACCESSIBILITY: Signers for the hearing impaired
CASES SEXUAL ASSAULT/ABUSE (%): 100
CLIENTS/SERVICES: Sexual assault survivors; Marital rape/sexual abuse survivors; Adult survivors of child sexual abuse; Prevention program; Community education; Adolescent survivors of sexual abuse; Male survivors of sexual abuse
REQUIREMENTS: Must be 14 or older; Referrals for younger than 14

SAN DIEGO

CENTER FOR TREATMENT OF SEXUAL ABUSE
9455 Ridgehaven Ct, Ste 250, San Diego, CA 92123
Information: (619) 569-2055 10am-6pm
Contact: Lewis Ribner, PhD, Lic Psychologist
TYPE OF AGENCY: Child sexual abuse services; Private practice
SPONSORING ORGANIZATION: Kearny Mesa Psychological Services
AREAS SERVED: San Diego
YEARS IN OPERATION: 5½
CASES SEXUAL ASSAULT/ABUSE (%): 85
DESCRIPTION: Provides individual, marital, family therapy to people in need of treatment for sexual abuse issues. Works with sexually abused children and their families, adults who were molested as children, rape victims, and adults involved in sexually abusive situations. Provides individual therapy for batterers and child sexual abuse/incest offenders
CLIENTS/SERVICES: Sexual assault survivors; Marital rape/sexual abuse survivors; Child victims of sexual abuse; Adult survivors of child sexual abuse; Incest victims/survivors; Community education; Offender treatment program; Adolescent survivors of sexual abuse; Male survivors of sexual abuse
REQUIREMENTS: Some ability to pay for services

CLINIC FOR THE SEXUALITIES
591 Camino De La Reina, Ste 533, San Diego, CA 92108
Crisis hotline: **(619) 293-3330 24 hrs 7 days**
Information: (619) 293-3330 24 hrs 7 days
Contact: Dr L C Miccio-Fonseca, Clinic Dir, Clinical Psychologist
TYPE OF AGENCY: Child sexual abuse services; Private practice
AREAS SERVED: San Diego
YEARS IN OPERATION: 3
LANGUAGES: Spanish
ACCESSIBILITY: Wheelchair accessible
CASES SEXUAL ASSAULT/ABUSE (%): 100
CLIENTS/SERVICES: Sexual assault survivors; Marital rape/sexual abuse survivors; Child victims of sexual abuse; Adult survivors of child sexual abuse; Incest victims/survivors; Community education; Offender treatment program; Adolescent survivors of sexual abuse; Male survivors of sexual abuse

DISTRICT ATTORNEY'S VICTIM-WITNESS ASSISTANCE PROGRAM
PO Box X-1011, San Diego, CA 92112
Information: (616) 531-4287 8am-5pm (Mon-Fri)
Contact: Dee Fuller, Prog Dir
TYPE OF AGENCY: Victim/witness assistance program
AREAS SERVED: San Diego
YEARS IN OPERATION: 8
LANGUAGES: Spanish
ACCESSIBILITY: Wheelchair accessible
DESCRIPTION: Crisis intervention; Referrals; Assistance with victim compensation claims; Court information and support
CLIENTS/SERVICES: Sexual assault survivors; Child victims of sexual abuse; Incest victims/survivors

FAMILY SERVICE ASSOCIATION OF SAN DIEGO COUNTY
7645 Family Cir, San Diego, CA 92111
Information: (619) 279-0400 8am-9pm (Mon-Fri)
Contact: Fred Ihler, Intake Supv
TYPE OF AGENCY: Counseling/mental health services
AREAS SERVED: San Diego
YEARS IN OPERATION: 100
LANGUAGES: Spanish
ACCESSIBILITY: Wheelchair accessible
CASES SEXUAL ASSAULT/ABUSE (%): 10
DESCRIPTION: Individual, couple, family, and group counseling
CLIENTS/SERVICES: Sexual assault survivors; Marital rape/sexual abuse survivors; Child victims of sexual abuse; Adult survivors of child sexual abuse; Incest victims/survivors; Adolescent survivors of sexual abuse; Male survivors of sexual abuse
REQUIREMENTS: No age requirements, but children need parental permission to receive services after the first session

HOME START, INC
3251 Adams Ave, San Diego, CA 92116
Information: (619) 283-6152 8:30am-5pm (Mon-Fri)
Contact: Laura Spiegel, Exec Dir
TYPE OF AGENCY: Counseling/mental health services; Child sexual abuse services; Child abuse services
AREAS SERVED: San Diego
YEARS IN OPERATION: 17
LANGUAGES: Tagalog, Spanish
CASES SEXUAL ASSAULT/ABUSE (%): 40
DESCRIPTION: In-home counseling and therapeutic services for families with actual or potential child abuse/neglect
CLIENTS/SERVICES: Child victims of sexual abuse; Adult survivors of child sexual abuse; Incest victims/survivors; Adolescent survivors of sexual abuse
REQUIREMENTS: Families at risk of or already experiencing a child abuse/neglect problem

NLP (NEURO-LINGUISTIC PROGRAMMING) INSTITUTE OF SAN DIEGO
2264 5th Ave, San Diego, CA 92101
Information: (619) 696-7666 8am-9pm
Contact: Marilyn J Blank, LCSW, Co-Dir
TYPE OF AGENCY: Counseling/mental health services; Private practice; Training/research
AREAS SERVED: San Diego
YEARS IN OPERATION: 5
ACCESSIBILITY: Wheelchair accessible; Signers for the hearing impaired
CASES SEXUAL ASSAULT/ABUSE (%): 50-60
DESCRIPTION: Provides psychotherapy using the Neuro-Linguistic Programming; uses the re-unification model for mother and child, as well as for the child within the adult survivor who was victimized. Also provides Imperative

NLP (NEURO-LINGUISTIC PROGRAMMING) INSTITUTE OF SAN DIEGO
(continued)

Self therapy to identify and change the core patterns of personality.
CLIENTS/SERVICES: Sexual assault survivors; Marital rape/sexual abuse survivors; Child victims of sexual abuse; Adult survivors of child sexual abuse; Incest victims/survivors; Community education

THE RAPE CRISIS CENTER
2467 E St, San Diego, CA 92102
Information: (619) 233-8984
Contact: Laurie MacKenize, Rape Crisis Ctr Coord
TYPE OF AGENCY: Rape crisis center; Child sexual abuse prevention program
SPONSORING ORGANIZATION: Center for Women's Studies and Services
DESCRIPTION: Feminist organization that provides crisis intervention counseling for rape and domestic violence victims on the 24-hour hotline; Hospital accompaniment; Individual and group counseling; Feminist martial arts/self-defense training
CLIENTS/SERVICES: Sexual assault survivors; Marital rape/sexual abuse survivors; Child victims of sexual abuse; Incest victims/survivors; Adult survivors of child sexual abuse; Prevention program; Community education
SPECIAL PROGRAMS/SERVICES: Currently starting a database to keep track of hotline calls; has developed one for domestic violence clients

SAN DIEGO COUNTY CHILD SEXUAL ABUSE TREATMENT PROGRAM
6950 Levant St, San Diego, CA 92111
Crisis hotline: **(800) 422-4453 24 hrs daily**
Information: (619) 694-5285 8am-5pm (Mon-Fri)
Contact: Gerald A Vernon, PhD, Dir
TYPE OF AGENCY: Counseling/mental health services; Child sexual abuse services; Adolescent program
SPONSORING ORGANIZATION: Department of Social Services
AREAS SERVED: San Diego
YEARS IN OPERATION: 12
LANGUAGES: Spanish
ACCESSIBILITY: Wheelchair accessible
CASES SEXUAL ASSAULT/ABUSE (%): 100
DESCRIPTION: Provides counseling services, self-help groups, and professional referrals for families which have incest or intrafamilial child molestation problems; Treatment programs for incest offenders and adolescent sex offenders; Community training, educational presentations, and consultation on child sexual abuse; Training program for graduate-level students and practicing professionals; Sponsors chapter of Parents United and Daughters and Sons United
CLIENTS/SERVICES: Child victims of sexual abuse; Adult survivors of child sexual abuse; Incest victims/survivors; Community education; Offender treatment program; Adolescent survivors of sexual abuse; Male survivors of sexual abuse
REQUIREMENTS: Ages 3 to 17 for victims; Must be incest or intrafamilial child sexual abuse
SPECIAL PROGRAMS/SERVICES: Sexually reactive adolescents program for adolescent incest or intrafamilial child sexual abuse offenders and families based on psychoeducational and AA 12-step program

SAN DIEGO YOUTH AND COMMUNITY SERVICES
3878 Old Town Ave, Ste 200B, San Diego, CA 92110
Crisis hotline: **(619) 280-6150, 579-8761 24 hrs 7 days**
Information: (619) 297-9310 9am-5pm
Contact: Liz Shear, Exec Dir
TYPE OF AGENCY: Counseling/mental health services; Shelter; Adolescent program
AREAS SERVED: San Diego
YEARS IN OPERATION: 19
ACCESSIBILITY: Wheelchair accessible
DESCRIPTION: Multi-service agency: Youth shelters; Foster care; Community-based counseling clinics; Dispute-resolution services; Emergency services for the homeless
CLIENTS/SERVICES: Child victims of sexual abuse; Adult survivors of child sexual abuse; Prevention program; Community education; Adolescent survivors of sexual abuse

YWCA/BATTERED WOMEN'S SERVICES
PO Box 4007, San Diego, CA 92104
Crisis hotline: **(619) 234-3164 24 hrs**
Information: (619) 239-2342 8:30am-5pm
Contact: Gretchen Alspach, Spec Proj Coord
TYPE OF AGENCY: Domestic violence program
SPONSORING ORGANIZATION: YWCA
AREAS SERVED: San Diego
YEARS IN OPERATION: 10
LANGUAGES: Spanish
ACCESSIBILITY: Wheelchair accessible; Telecommunications for the hearing impaired (TTY, TDY, etc.); Signers for the hearing impaired (as needed)
CASES SEXUAL ASSAULT/ABUSE (%): 50-80
DESCRIPTION: Assists survivors of domestic violence, many of whom have been sexually abused as adults or children; Therapy for batterers
CLIENTS/SERVICES: Sexual assault survivors; Marital rape/sexual abuse survivors; Child victims of sexual abuse; Adult survivors of child sexual abuse; Incest victims/survivors; Community education; Adolescent survivors of sexual abuse

SAN FRANCISCO

BAY AREA SEXUAL HARASSMENT CLINIC
1370 Mission St, 3rd Fl, San Francisco, CA 94103
Information: (415) 621-7938
TYPE OF AGENCY: Legal services agency
DESCRIPTION: Services available by phone; Drop-in clinic open on Wednesday evenings, 6:30pm-8:30pm
CLIENTS/SERVICES: Sexual harassment

CENTER FOR SPECIAL PROBLEMS
1700 Jackson St, San Francisco, CA 94109
Crisis hotline: **(415) 558-4801 9pm-midnight, 2pm-4pm**
Information: (415) 558-4801 8am-5pm (Tue, Wed, Fri); 8am-9pm (Mon, Thu)
Contact: Mary Tam Ma, LCSW, Victim Svcs Coord
TYPE OF AGENCY: Counseling/mental health services
AREAS SERVED: San Francisco
YEARS IN OPERATION: 25
LANGUAGES: Spanish, Cantonese, Swatownese
ACCESSIBILITY: Wheelchair accessible
CASES SEXUAL ASSAULT/ABUSE (%): 20
DESCRIPTION: Outpatient forensic mental health center for adults, serving both the victims/survivors and the offenders. Individual and group therapy for men and women who are survivors of rape, incest, and physical abuse, both within and outside their families. Treatment for rapists, batterers, and child sexual abuse/incest offenders
CLIENTS/SERVICES: Sexual assault survivors; Marital rape/sexual abuse survivors; Adult survivors of child sexual abuse; Incest victims/survivors; Community education; Offender treatment program; Adolescent survivors of sexual abuse; Male survivors of sexual abuse; Lesbians; Gay men; Bisexuals; Ethnic minorities
REQUIREMENTS: Ages 16 and older

CHILD AND ADOLESCENT SEXUAL ABUSE RESOURCE CENTER
995 Potrero Ave, Bldg 80, WD, No 83, San Francisco, CA 94404
Crisis hotline: **(415) 821-8386 24 hrs**
Information: (415) 554-2850 24 hrs
Contact: Francis Smith, Act Dir; Naomi C Schwartz, Clin Supv
TYPE OF AGENCY: Hospital/medical center; Child sexual abuse services; Adolescent program
SPONSORING ORGANIZATION: San Francisco General Hospital
AREAS SERVED: San Francisco City and County
YEARS IN OPERATION: 12
LANGUAGES: Spanish
ACCESSIBILITY: Wheelchair accessible; Telecommunications for the hearing impaired (TTY, TDY, etc.)
CASES SEXUAL ASSAULT/ABUSE (%): 100
DESCRIPTION: 24-hour crisis center for child victims of sexual abuse and their families; Immediate crisis counseling and medical treatment; Short-term therapy for victim and family; Court accompaniment and advocacy; Long-term survivor groups; Groups for parents of sexually abused children
CLIENTS/SERVICES: Sexual assault survivors; Child victims of sexual abuse; Incest victims/survivors; Community education; Adolescent survivors of sexual abuse
REQUIREMENTS: Ages 0-17 and family

CHILD SEXUAL ABUSE TREATMENT PROGRAM
1010 Gough St, San Francisco, CA 94109
Crisis hotline: **(415) 441-KIDS 24 hrs**
Information: (415) 474-7310 by appointment (Mon-Fri)
Contact: Claudia Kruse, MFCC, Prog Coord
TYPE OF AGENCY: Child sexual abuse services
SPONSORING ORGANIZATION: Family Service Agency of San Francisco
AREAS SERVED: San Francisco, San Mateo, Marin
YEARS IN OPERATION: 3
LANGUAGES: Spanish
ACCESSIBILITY: Wheelchair accessible
CASES SEXUAL ASSAULT/ABUSE (%): 100
DESCRIPTION: Joint project linking staff from the FSA with a hospital-based crisis program at San Francisco General Hospital (CASARC-Child and Adolescent Sexual Abuse Resource Center); Works at SFGH with children who need assessment and short-term treatment and at FSA with children who need longer term psychotherapy and case management services
CLIENTS/SERVICES: Sexual assault survivors; Child victims of sexual abuse; Incest victims/survivors
REQUIREMENTS: Child victims 13 years of age or younger and their families, mostly with non-offending parents

CHILDREN'S SELF-HELP PROJECT
170 Fell St, Rm 34, San Francisco, CA 94102
Information: (415) 552-8304 9am-5pm
Contact: Pnina Tobin, Exec Dir
TYPE OF AGENCY: Child sexual abuse prevention program; Acquaintance/date rape prevention program; Adolescent program
AREAS SERVED: San Francisco
YEARS IN OPERATION: 7
LANGUAGES: Spanish, Tagalog
ACCESSIBILITY: Wheelchair accessible; Signers for the hearing impaired
DESCRIPTION: Provides classroom workshops for parents, teachers, and abused children
CLIENTS/SERVICES: Child victims of sexual abuse; Prevention program; Community education; Preschoolers
REQUIREMENTS: Attend SF Unified School District or state-funded preschools
SPECIAL PROGRAMS/SERVICES: Programs offered for: preschool, using songs, puppets, and skits; elementary school, for K-3rd grades, using skits and songs; middle school, using age-appropriate information and decision-making

CHILDREN'S SELF-HELP PROJECT
(continued)

skills; high school, a peer education program (pep) trains teens to provide abuse prevention workshop for peers. Also offers "For Girls Only," an abuse and pregnancy prevention program for teenaged girls which provides seven sessions in self-esteem building, assertiveness, and decision-making skills, information on sex-role conditioning, and problem solving

COMMUNITY UNITED AGAINST VIOLENCE
514 Castro St, San Francisco, CA 94114
Crisis hotline: **(415) 864-7233 24 hrs**
Information: (415) 864-3112 10am-6pm (Mon-Fri)
Contact: Lester Olmstead-Rose, Community Organizer; Randy Schell, Sr Client Advocate
TYPE OF AGENCY: Domestic violence program; Men's program; Crisis intervention program
AREAS SERVED: San Francisco Bay area
YEARS IN OPERATION: 10
CASES SEXUAL ASSAULT/ABUSE (%): 10
DESCRIPTION: Serving victims of anti-gay/anti-lesbian violence (a certain percent of such violence is sexual abuse); Gay men's domestic violence counseling and groups; Crisis counseling; Criminal justice advocacy; Community education; Deals with sexual abuse, usually against gay men (e.g. rape of gay men or sexual attacks)
CLIENTS/SERVICES: Sexual assault survivors; Marital rape/sexual abuse survivors; Adult survivors of child sexual abuse; Incest victims/survivors; Prevention program; Community education; Male survivors of sexual abuse; Lesbians; Gay men
SPECIAL PROGRAMS/SERVICES: Gay men's domestic violence project is a one-of-its-kind, offering crisis counseling. Pioneered models for police cooperation with community groups, including monitor training for community events; Strong community education programs; Self-defense programs are being developed; Consortiums with minority groups on the issue of hate crimes

HOSPITALITY HOUSE
146 Leavenworth, San Francisco, CA 94102
Information: (415) 776-2102 9am-5pm
Contact: Ann O'Halleran, Youth Dept Dir
TYPE OF AGENCY: Shelter; Adolescent program
AREAS SERVED: San Francisco
YEARS IN OPERATION: 21
LANGUAGES: Spanish
CASES SEXUAL ASSAULT/ABUSE (%): 20
DESCRIPTION: Independent living program for runaway, throwaway, and homeless youth; Special focus on juvenile prostitutes, providing shelter, food, vocational training, individual and group counseling
CLIENTS/SERVICES: Sexual assault survivors; Child victims of sexual abuse; Incest victims/survivors; Community education; Adolescent survivors of sexual abuse; Male survivors of sexual abuse; Prostitutes
REQUIREMENTS: Clients must be between the ages of 15 and 21; Voluntary program
SPECIAL PROGRAMS/SERVICES: Many of the runaway homeless youthful clients have been victims of sexual abuse, and once on the streets, the cycle perpetuates itself when they become victims of sexual exploitation

LA CASA DE LAS MADRES
965 Mission, No 218, San Francisco, CA 94103
Crisis hotline: **(415) 333-1515 24 hrs**
Information: (415) 777-1808 9am-6pm
Contact: Ellen Fisher, Exec Dir
TYPE OF AGENCY: Domestic violence program
AREAS SERVED: San Francisco, Alameda, Contra Costa, San Mateo
YEARS IN OPERATION: 13
LANGUAGES: Spanish
ACCESSIBILITY: Wheelchair accessible
CASES SEXUAL ASSAULT/ABUSE (%): 80
CLIENTS/SERVICES: Marital rape/sexual abuse survivors; Child victims of sexual abuse; Adult survivors of child sexual abuse; Incest victims/survivors; Community education; Adolescent survivors of sexual abuse

LEGAL SERVICES FOR CHILDREN, INC
1254 Market St, 3rd Fl, San Francisco, CA 94102
Information: (415) 863-3762 8:30am-5:30pm (Mon-Fri) Answering service during other hrs
Contact: Carole Brill, Dir
TYPE OF AGENCY: Legal services agency; Child sexual abuse services; Adolescent program
AREAS SERVED: San Francisco and other San Francisco Bay areas
YEARS IN OPERATION: 13
LANGUAGES: Spanish, Interpreters for other languages by arrangement
ACCESSIBILITY: Wheelchair accessible; Signers for the hearing impaired (by arrangement)
CASES SEXUAL ASSAULT/ABUSE (%): 15-25
CLIENTS/SERVICES: Child victims of sexual abuse; Adolescent survivors of sexual abuse
REQUIREMENTS: Client must be a minor.
SPECIAL PROGRAMS/SERVICES: This is the nation's first free and comprehensive law firm just for children and youth, ranging in age from infancy to 17. It provides independent legal assistance, representation and support services for child-victims of sexual assault including: Explaining how the legal system works; Assistance with reporting sexual abuse and in arranging the kinds of interviews which follow; Advocacy for legal and in-court protection; Accompaniment and support when they testify; Legal representation for youngsters in juvenile court sexual abuse cases, family court custody disputes, and other related legal proceedings; Preparing procedural and protective orders such as restraining orders against molesters and other civil actions to enforce the child-victim's rights; Preparing victim compensation claims with follow-up to pay for related medical services and counseling; Referrals to professionals who have expertise in child sexual abuse.

LYON-MARTIN WOMEN'S HEALTH SERVICES
2480 Mission St, No 214, San Francisco, CA 94110
Information: (415) 641-0220 9am-8pm (Mon, Tue); 9am-5pm (Wed, Thu, Fri); Answering machine after hrs
Contact: Fran Miller, Exec Dir
TYPE OF AGENCY: Hospital/medical center
AREAS SERVED: Greater San Francisco Bay area
YEARS IN OPERATION: 10
LANGUAGES: Spanish
ACCESSIBILITY: Wheelchair accessible
DESCRIPTION: General medical care for women with emphasis on lesbian health care; Chinese medicine (Acupuncture and herbs); Lesbian/gay parenting project; AIDS education and safe sex kits for women
CLIENTS/SERVICES: Sexual assault survivors; Adult survivors of child sexual abuse; Incest victims/survivors; Community education; Lesbians; Gay men

OFFICE OF DISTRICT ATTORNEY—VICTIM WITNESS ASSISTANCE CENTER
850 Bryant St, Rm 320, San Francisco, CA 94103
Information: (415) 553-9044 8am-5pm
Contact: Jean Hassett, Victim Witness Spec
TYPE OF AGENCY: Victim/witness assistance program
AREAS SERVED: San Francisco
YEARS IN OPERATION: 10
LANGUAGES: Spanish, Cantonese, Mandarin
ACCESSIBILITY: Wheelchair accessible; Telecommunications for the hearing impaired (TTY, TDY, etc.) (through family violence project)
CASES SEXUAL ASSAULT/ABUSE (%): 5
CLIENTS/SERVICES: Sexual assault survivors; Marital rape/sexual abuse survivors; Child victims of sexual abuse; Adult survivors of child sexual abuse; Incest victims/survivors; Community education
REQUIREMENTS: If filing for victim compensation, victim must file police report and press charges if suspect is apprehended; Other forms of assistance vis-a-vis social services can be provided for victims without having to file a report

SAN FRANCISCO RAPE TREATMENT CENTER
San Francisco General Hospital, 995 Potrero Ave, Ward 87, San Francisco, CA 94110
Crisis hotline: **(415) 821-3222 24 hrs**
Information: (415) 821-3222 8:30am-5pm, and by appointment
Contact: Lynda M Frattaroli, Health Prog Coord
TYPE OF AGENCY: Rape crisis center; Hospital/medical center
SPONSORING ORGANIZATION: San Francisco Department of Public Health
AREAS SERVED: San Francisco
YEARS IN OPERATION: 12
LANGUAGES: Spanish, Signers available, interpreters available for Tagalog, Chinese, Vietnamese, Cambodian
ACCESSIBILITY: Wheelchair accessible; Telecommunications for the hearing impaired (TTY, TDY, etc.); Signers for the hearing impaired (by arrangement)
CASES SEXUAL ASSAULT/ABUSE (%): 100
DESCRIPTION: Provides hospital-based, 24-hour emergency medical care, crisis counseling, and legal evidence collection for women and men who have been recent victims of sexual violence. Follow-up counseling available
CLIENTS/SERVICES: Sexual assault survivors; Marital rape/sexual abuse survivors; Adult survivors of child sexual abuse; Prevention program; Community education; Male survivors of sexual abuse
REQUIREMENTS: Client must be 18 or older

SAN FRANCISCO WOMEN AGAINST RAPE
3543 18th St, Box 7, San Francisco, CA 94110
Crisis hotline: **(415) 647-RAPE 24 hrs**
Information: (415) 861-2024 9am-5pm
Contact: Dana Cayce, Svcs Coord
TYPE OF AGENCY: Rape crisis center
AREAS SERVED: San Francisco area
YEARS IN OPERATION: 15
LANGUAGES: Spanish by request
ACCESSIBILITY: Wheelchair accessible
CASES SEXUAL ASSAULT/ABUSE (%): 100
CLIENTS/SERVICES: Sexual assault survivors; Marital rape/sexual abuse survivors; Adult survivors of child sexual abuse; Prevention program; Community education; Male survivors of sexual abuse
REQUIREMENTS: Counsels both men and women on crisis line (24-hours) but only sees women in-person. Women must be 18 or older.
SPECIAL PROGRAMS/SERVICES: Bilingual (Spanish/English) brochure

SAN FRANCISCO WOMEN'S CENTER/THE WOMEN'S BUILDING
3543 18th St, San Francisco, CA 94110
Information: (415) 431-1180 9am-5pm (Mon-Fri)
Contact: Janice Rothstein, Info and Referral Coord
TYPE OF AGENCY: Women's center
AREAS SERVED: San Francisco
YEARS IN OPERATION: 10
LANGUAGES: Spanish
ACCESSIBILITY: Wheelchair accessible
CLIENTS/SERVICES: Information and referral

UCSF RAPE PREVENTION EDUCATION PROGRAM
1308 3rd Ave, San Francisco, CA 94143
Information: (415) 476-5222 9am-5pm (Mon-Fri)
Contact: Leslie Simon, Prog Coord
TYPE OF AGENCY: College/university-based services; Rape prevention program; Acquaintance/date rape prevention program
AREAS SERVED: San Francisco
YEARS IN OPERATION: 9
LANGUAGES: Spanish translation available via phone
CASES SEXUAL ASSAULT/ABUSE (%): 75
DESCRIPTION: Offers educational workshops for the campus and community on rape prevention; In-service training for sexual assault service providers; Resource/referrals for victim/survivors; Short-term crisis counseling; Support groups for survivors; Self-defense classes for children and adolescents; Resource library
CLIENTS/SERVICES: Sexual assault survivors; Prevention program; Community education; Sexual harassment; Publications/media
SPECIAL PROGRAMS/SERVICES: Resources Against Sexual Assault: *Prevention Through Empowerment* informational booklet for men and women; *Prevention Through Empowerment* bookmarks on acquaintance rape, harmful stereotypes of rape, race and class, lesbian survivors, and sexual harassment. *Give It All You've Got*, a 16-minute film documentary of five women who have taken a self-defense class and then used the physical and verbal techniques to successfully deter an assault. The film documents these true stories and then flashes back to the class to illustrate the skills. (rental: $20; purchase price: $125 for 16mm, $27 for video)

WOMAN, INC
2940 16th St, San Francisco, CA 94103
Crisis hotline: **(415) 864-4722 24 hrs**
Information: (415) 864-4777 9am-6pm (Mon-Fri)
Contact: Jeanie Morrow, Crisis Svcs Dir
TYPE OF AGENCY: Domestic violence program
AREAS SERVED: Bay area
YEARS IN OPERATION: 10
LANGUAGES: Spanish, Asian
ACCESSIBILITY: Wheelchair accessible
CASES SEXUAL ASSAULT/ABUSE (%): 30-65
DESCRIPTION: Provides a 24-hour hotline, counseling, groups, restraining order clinic, and referrals for battered women, including battered lesbians
CLIENTS/SERVICES: Marital rape/sexual abuse survivors; Community education; Adolescent survivors of sexual abuse; Male survivors of sexual abuse; Lesbians
SPECIAL PROGRAMS/SERVICES: This is one of the few lesbian service programs specifically designed for lesbians in abusive situations. Provides services for lesbian batterers on the crisis hotline and offers referrals, but does not see them in person

YOUTH LINE
3940 Geary Blvd, San Francisco, CA 94118
Crisis hotline: **(415) 752-2000 5pm-11pm (Wed); 7pm-2am (Fri, Sat)**
Information: (415) 752-4866 9am-5pm (Mon-Fri)
Contact: Margeaux Brochtrup, Youth Line Coord
TYPE OF AGENCY: Counseling/mental health services; Telephone crisis hotline; Information and referral
SPONSORING ORGANIZATION: San Francisco Suicide Prevention
AREAS SERVED: San Francisco
YEARS IN OPERATION: 1
CASES SEXUAL ASSAULT/ABUSE (%): 20
DESCRIPTION: Peer-run telephone counseling service with trained high school and college student volunteers. Provides emotional support, information, referrals, and crisis intervention
CLIENTS/SERVICES: Sexual assault survivors; Child victims of sexual abuse; Adolescent survivors of sexual abuse

REQUIREMENTS: Ages 13 to 24

SAN JOSE

INSTITUTE FOR THE COMMUNITY AS EXTENDED FAMILY
PO Box 952, San Jose, CA 95108
Crisis hotline: **(408) 280-5055 8:30am-5:30pm**
Information: (408) 280-5055 8:30am-5:30pm
Contact: Susie Ruggels, CATP Admin
TYPE OF AGENCY: Child sexual abuse services; Parents United; CAP training
AREAS SERVED: Santa Clara, edges of San Mateo and Alameda
YEARS IN OPERATION: 17
ACCESSIBILITY: Wheelchair accessible
CASES SEXUAL ASSAULT/ABUSE (%): 99
DESCRIPTION: Treats child sexual abuse by treating the entire family, including the offender; Uses individual and group therapy, plus peer support and self-help of Parents United. Also is a training institute. The treatment model has been replicated 150 times in this country and abroad
CLIENTS/SERVICES: Child victims of sexual abuse; Adult survivors of child sexual abuse; Incest victims/survivors; Community education; Offender treatment program; Publications; Media programs; Adolescent survivors of sexual abuse; Male survivors of sexual abuse
REQUIREMENTS: Child must be 3 years old; Offender must be an incest offender; Clients must be nonpsychotic and currently free of substance abuse
SPECIAL PROGRAMS/SERVICES: Publications: *Integrated Treatment of Child Sexual Abuse* by Hank Giarretto ($27) and literature on specific aspects of treatment for sexually abused children and adolescents and adult offenders ($1-$7); booklets written by Daughters and Sons United members and Adults Molested as Children members ($1-$5). Videotapes on treatment issues pertaining to sexually abused children, adult survivors, adolescent and adult offenders, and family therapy ($75 each). Some videotapes feature Hank Giarretto

PERSONAL AND FAMILY DEVELOPMENT CENTER
696 E Santa Clara St, San Jose, CA 95112
Crisis hotline: **(408) 287-4090**
Information: (408) 287-2333
Contact: Shirley Fuller, Dir
TYPE OF AGENCY: Hospital/medical center; Counseling/mental health services; Child sexual abuse services
SPONSORING ORGANIZATION: Women's Community Clinic, Inc
AREAS SERVED: Santa Clara
YEARS IN OPERATION: 10
LANGUAGES: Spanish
ACCESSIBILITY: Wheelchair accessible
CLIENTS/SERVICES: Sexual assault survivors; Marital rape/sexual abuse survivors; Child victims of sexual abuse; Adult survivors of child sexual abuse; Incest victims/survivors; Adolescent survivors of sexual abuse; Male survivors of sexual abuse

SANTA CLARA COUNTY VICTIM WITNESS ASSISTANCE CENTER
777 N 1st St, San Jose, CA 95112
Crisis hotline: **(408) 295-2656 24 hrs**
Information: (408) 295-2656 8am-5pm
Contact: Joe Yomtov, Victim Ctr Dir
TYPE OF AGENCY: Victim/witness assistance program
SPONSORING ORGANIZATION: National Conference of Christians and Jews, Inc
AREAS SERVED: Santa Clara
YEARS IN OPERATION: 12
LANGUAGES: Spanish, Vietnamese, Arabic
ACCESSIBILITY: Signers for the hearing impaired
CASES SEXUAL ASSAULT/ABUSE (%): 40

CLIENTS/SERVICES: Sexual assault survivors; Marital rape/sexual abuse survivors; Child victims of sexual abuse; Adult survivors of child sexual abuse; Incest victims/survivors; Community education
SPECIAL PROGRAMS/SERVICES: Victim Support Network for Santa Clara County is an effective local association which joins all non-profit service providers and sponsors an annual conference

SOUTH BAY COMMUNITY COUNSELING CENTER
1101 S Winchester Blvd, Bldg 0, Ste 284, San Jose, CA 95128
Crisis hotline: **(408) 947-6282 24 hrs for message; Calls returned 8am-10pm**
Information: (408) 947-6282 24 hrs
Contact: Rhona Kastle, MFCC, Marriage, Family and Child Counselor
TYPE OF AGENCY: Counseling/mental health services
AREAS SERVED: Santa Clara
YEARS IN OPERATION: 14
ACCESSIBILITY: Wheelchair accessible
CASES SEXUAL ASSAULT/ABUSE (%): 30-40
DESCRIPTION: Counseling for survivors; Individual counseling for rapists, child sexual abuse offenders, incest offenders, and batterers
CLIENTS/SERVICES: Sexual assault survivors; Marital rape/sexual abuse survivors; Child victims of sexual abuse; Adult survivors of child sexual abuse; Incest victims/survivors; Community education; Adolescent survivors of sexual abuse; Male survivors of sexual abuse

WOMA (THE WOMAN'S ALLIANCE)
160 E Virginia St, No 230, San Jose, CA 95112
Crisis hotline: **(408) 279-2962 24 hrs**
Information: (408) 298-3505 8am-5pm (Mon-Fri)
Contact: Maricela Martinez, Community Educ Coord
TYPE OF AGENCY: Domestic violence program
AREAS SERVED: Santa Clara
YEARS IN OPERATION: 14
LANGUAGES: Spanish
CASES SEXUAL ASSAULT/ABUSE (%): 80
DESCRIPTION: Provides legal services, 24-hour hotline, counseling, support groups, a children's school and public education; Treatment for batterers available
CLIENTS/SERVICES: Sexual assault survivors; Marital rape/sexual abuse survivors; Child victims of sexual abuse; Adult survivors of child sexual abuse; Incest victims/survivors; Community education

YWCA ASSAULT PREVENTION AND INTERVENTION SERVICES
375 S 3rd St, San Jose, CA 95112
Crisis hotline: **(408) 287-3000 24 hrs**
Information: (408) 295-4011 9am-5pm
Contact: Jacky E McClure, VRCC Prog Dir; Anita Montero, CAP Prog Dir
TYPE OF AGENCY: Rape crisis center; Child sexual abuse prevention program; Acquaintance/date rape prevention program
AREAS SERVED: Santa Clara
YEARS IN OPERATION: 17
LANGUAGES: Spanish, Vietnamese, Mandarin, Cantonese, Sign
ACCESSIBILITY: Wheelchair accessible; Signers for the hearing impaired
CASES SEXUAL ASSAULT/ABUSE (%): 100
DESCRIPTION: Comprehensive rape crisis services and prevention programs, including Child Assault Prevention (CAP) Project, Prevention of Assault on Teens (PAT), and feminist martial arts/self-defense
CLIENTS/SERVICES: Sexual assault survivors; Marital rape/sexual abuse survivors; Child victims of sexual abuse; Adult survivors of child sexual abuse; Incest victims/survivors; Prevention program; Community education; Adolescent survivors of sexual abuse; Male survivors of sexual abuse

YWCA VALLEY RAPE CRISIS CENTER (VRCC)/YWCA CHILD ASSAULT PREVENTION (CAP) SERVICES
375 S 3rd St, San Jose, CA 95112
Crisis hotline: **(408) 287-3000 24 hrs**
Information: (408) 295-4011 9am-5pm
Contact: Jacky E McClure, VRCC Prog Dir; Anita Montero, CAP Prog Dir
TYPE OF AGENCY: Rape crisis center; Child sexual abuse services; Acquaintance/date rape prevention program
AREAS SERVED: Santa Clara
YEARS IN OPERATION: 17
LANGUAGES: Spanish, Vietnamese, Mandarin, Cantonese, Sign
ACCESSIBILITY: Wheelchair accessible; Signers for the hearing impaired
CASES SEXUAL ASSAULT/ABUSE (%): 100
DESCRIPTION: Comprehensive rape crisis services and prevention programs, including Child Assault Prevention (CAP) Project, Prevention of Assault on Teens (PAT), and feminist martial arts/self-defense
CLIENTS/SERVICES: Sexual assault survivors; Adult survivors of child sexual abuse; Prevention program; Community education; Adolescent survivors of sexual abuse; Male survivors of sexual abuse

SAN LEANDRO

FAMILY ABUSE PROJECT
15400 Foothill Blvd, San Leandro, CA 94578
Information: (415) 667-7544 8:30am-5pm
Contact: Fernando Cristancho, Clinical Psychologist
TYPE OF AGENCY: Counseling/mental health services; Child sexual abuse services
SPONSORING ORGANIZATION: Eden Mental Health Center
AREAS SERVED: Alameda
YEARS IN OPERATION: 2
LANGUAGES: Spanish
ACCESSIBILITY: Wheelchair accessible; Telecommunications for the hearing impaired (TTY, TDY, etc.); Signers for the hearing impaired
CASES SEXUAL ASSAULT/ABUSE (%): 100
CLIENTS/SERVICES: Child victims of sexual abuse; Adult survivors of child sexual abuse; Incest victims/survivors; Prevention program; Community education; Offender treatment program; Adolescent survivors of sexual abuse; Male survivors of sexual abuse

PATHWAYS COUNSELING CENTER
2450 Washington Ave, Ste 240, San Leandro, CA 94577
Information: (415) 357-5515 9am-9pm (Mon, Thu); 9am-5pm (Tue, Wed, Fri)
Contact: Rebecca Cannon, Clinical Dir
TYPE OF AGENCY: Counseling/mental health services; Child sexual abuse services; Child sexual abuse prevention program
SPONSORING ORGANIZATION: San Leandro Girls Club
AREAS SERVED: Alameda
YEARS IN OPERATION: 12
LANGUAGES: Spanish
ACCESSIBILITY: Wheelchair accessible
CASES SEXUAL ASSAULT/ABUSE (%): 70
CLIENTS/SERVICES: Sexual assault survivors; Marital rape/sexual abuse survivors; Child victims of sexual abuse; Adult survivors of child sexual abuse; Incest victims/survivors; Prevention program; Community education; Adolescent survivors of sexual abuse; Male survivors of sexual abuse

SAN LEANDRO COMMUNITY COUNSELING
296 Broadmoor Blvd, San Leandro, CA 94577
Information: (415) 638-6603 9am-5pm, 5pm-9pm by appointment (Mon-Thu)
Contact: Dr Elsa Johnson, Clinical Dir
TYPE OF AGENCY: Counseling/mental health services; Child sexual abuse services
AREAS SERVED: Alameda, Contra Costa
YEARS IN OPERATION: 14
LANGUAGES: Spanish
ACCESSIBILITY: Wheelchair accessible; Signers for the hearing impaired
CASES SEXUAL ASSAULT/ABUSE (%): 10
CLIENTS/SERVICES: Sexual assault survivors; Marital rape/sexual abuse survivors; Child victims of sexual abuse; Adult survivors of child sexual abuse; Incest victims/survivors; Adolescent survivors of sexual abuse; Male survivors of sexual abuse
REQUIREMENTS: 11 years to adulthood; younger children accepted in family therapy

SAN LUIS OBISPO

SAN LUIS OBISPO COUNTY RAPE CRISIS CENTER
PO Box 52, San Luis Obispo, CA 93406
Crisis hotline: **(805) 543-7273 24 hrs**
Information: (805) 549-5798 8am-5pm
Contact: Cindy Phipps, Exec Dir
TYPE OF AGENCY: Rape crisis center; Child sexual abuse prevention program
AREAS SERVED: San Luis Obispo
YEARS IN OPERATION: 12
LANGUAGES: Spanish
ACCESSIBILITY: Wheelchair accessible; Signers for the hearing impaired
CASES SEXUAL ASSAULT/ABUSE (%): 100
DESCRIPTION: Comprehensive rape crisis services; Support groups available for female and male survivors
CLIENTS/SERVICES: Sexual assault survivors; Marital rape/sexual abuse survivors; Child victims of sexual abuse; Adult survivors of child sexual abuse; Incest victims/survivors; Prevention program; Community education; Adolescent survivors of sexual abuse; Male survivors of sexual abuse

SAN LUIS OBISPO COUNTY VICTIM/ WITNESS ASSISTANCE CENTER
County Government Center, Rm 121, San Luis Obispo, CA 93408
Crisis hotline: **(805) 544-6163 24 hrs**
Information: (805) 549-5821 8am-5pm (Mon-Fri)
Contact: Cindy Marie Absey, Supv
TYPE OF AGENCY: Victim/witness assistance program
SPONSORING ORGANIZATION: Office of the District Attorney
AREAS SERVED: San Luis Obispo
YEARS IN OPERATION: 12
LANGUAGES: Spanish, German
ACCESSIBILITY: Wheelchair accessible
CASES SEXUAL ASSAULT/ABUSE (%): 10
CLIENTS/SERVICES: Sexual assault survivors; Marital rape/sexual abuse survivors; Child victims of sexual abuse; Adult survivors of child sexual abuse; Incest victims/survivors; Community education; Adolescent survivors of sexual abuse; Male survivors of sexual abuse
SPECIAL PROGRAMS/SERVICES: An interagency Sexual Assault Response Team (SART) is comprised of law enforcement, medical personnel, rape crisis, victim/witness, child protective services. Sexual assault unit (child molest vertical prosecution) in DA's office includes 3 sexual assault attorneys, 1 sexual assault investigator, 2 victim/witness sexual assault case coordinators. A special interview room is available for child victims

WOMEN'S SHELTER PROGRAM OF SAN LUIS OBISPO
PO Box 125, San Luis Obispo, CA 93406
Crisis hotline: **(805) 544-6163 24 hrs**
Information: (805) 544-2321 24 hrs
Contact: Marianne Kennedy, Exec Dir
TYPE OF AGENCY: Domestic violence program
AREAS SERVED: San Luis Obispo
YEARS IN OPERATION: 12
CLIENTS/SERVICES: Sexual assault survivors; Marital rape/sexual abuse survivors; Child victims of sexual abuse; Adult survivors of child sexual abuse; Incest victims/survivors; Community education

SAN LUIS REY

PARENTS/DAUGHTERS/SONS UNITED
PO Box 438, San Luis Rey, CA 92068
Crisis hotline: **(619) 721-2167 24 hrs**
Information: (619) 757-1200 24 hrs
Contact: Patricia Roche, MFCC, Family Svcs Dir
TYPE OF AGENCY: Child sexual abuse services
SPONSORING ORGANIZATION: Child Sexual Abuse Treatment Program of Casa de Amparo
AREAS SERVED: San Diego
YEARS IN OPERATION: 11
CASES SEXUAL ASSAULT/ABUSE (%): 100
DESCRIPTION: Weekly group therapy with a self-help component for all members of a family, including offenders, where incest has occurred. Children's groups from age 6. Also treats batterers
CLIENTS/SERVICES: Child victims of sexual abuse; Adult survivors of child sexual abuse; Incest victims/survivors; Community education; Offender treatment program; Adolescent survivors of sexual abuse; Male survivors of sexual abuse

WOMEN'S RESOURCE CENTER
PO Box 499, 4070 Mission Ave, San Luis Rey, CA 92068
Crisis hotline: **(619) 757-3500 24 hrs**
Information: (619) 757-3500 8am-5pm (Mon-Fri)
Contact: Brenda Balmer
TYPE OF AGENCY: Rape crisis center; Domestic violence program; Child sexual abuse prevention program
AREAS SERVED: San Diego
YEARS IN OPERATION: 14
LANGUAGES: Spanish
CASES SEXUAL ASSAULT/ABUSE (%): 14
DESCRIPTION: Crisis services and counseling for victims/survivors of sexual assault and domestic violence; Self-defense program; Prevention programs for children and adolescents; Counseling for batterers
CLIENTS/SERVICES: Sexual assault survivors; Marital rape/sexual abuse survivors; Child victims of sexual abuse; Adult survivors of child sexual abuse; Incest victims/survivors; Community education; Adolescent survivors of sexual abuse; Male survivors of sexual abuse; Publications/media
SPECIAL PROGRAMS/SERVICES: Publications: *You Need to Know About Child Sexual Abuse* (1983)

SAN MARTIN

PARENTS UNITED, SOUTH SANTA CLARA CHAPTER
PO Box 668, San Martin, CA 95046
Information: (408) 683-2344 8am-5pm (Mon-Fri)
Contact: Lewis Pollard, Health Svcs Supv
TYPE OF AGENCY: Counseling/mental health services
SPONSORING ORGANIZATION: South County Mental Health Center
AREAS SERVED: Santa Clara
YEARS IN OPERATION: 4
LANGUAGES: Spanish
ACCESSIBILITY: Wheelchair accessible
CASES SEXUAL ASSAULT/ABUSE (%): 20
CLIENTS/SERVICES: Child victims of sexual abuse; Adult survivors of child sexual abuse; Incest victims/survivors; Offender treatment program; Adolescent survivors of sexual abuse; Male survivors of sexual abuse

SAN MATEO

SAFE 'N' STRONG
225 Tilton Ave, San Mateo, CA 94401
Information: (415) 343-3377 8:30am-5pm
Contact: Annette Passalacqua, Prog Dir
TYPE OF AGENCY: Counseling/mental health services; Child sexual abuse prevention program; Child abuse prevention program
SPONSORING ORGANIZATION: Center for Abuse Prevention
AREAS SERVED: San Mateo
YEARS IN OPERATION: 4
LANGUAGES: Spanish
DESCRIPTION: Provides abuse prevention education in the areas of child physical/sexual abuse, battering in dating and marriage relationships, and elder abuse. Crisis counseling and information and referral. Feminist martial arts/self-defense. Specializes in working with the religious community to increase their effectiveness in prevention and as a resource for survivors.
CLIENTS/SERVICES: Sexual assault survivors; Marital rape/sexual abuse survivors; Child victims of sexual abuse; Adult survivors of child sexual abuse; Incest victims/survivors; Prevention program; Community education; Adolescent survivors of sexual abuse; Male survivors of sexual abuse
SPECIAL PROGRAMS/SERVICES: Offers the only training program for black parents in Northern California. Offers both full-time direct training services and specialized work with the religious community.

SAN MATEO WOMEN'S SHELTER
PO Box 652, San Mateo, CA 94401
Crisis hotline: **(415) 342-0850 24 hrs**
Information: (415) 342-0850
Contact: Roberta Lee-Siegmann, Exec Dir
TYPE OF AGENCY: Domestic violence program
AREAS SERVED: San Mateo
YEARS IN OPERATION: 10
LANGUAGES: Spanish
CASES SEXUAL ASSAULT/ABUSE (%): 50
CLIENTS/SERVICES: Marital rape/sexual abuse survivors; Adult survivors of child sexual abuse; Incest victims/survivors; Community education

SEXUAL ASSAULT CARE CENTER
222 W 39th Ave, San Mateo, CA 94403
Crisis hotline: **(415) 573-2671 24 hrs 7 days**
Information: (415) 573-2671
Contact: S Petterson, RN BSN, Day Charge Nurse/Sexual Assault Coord
TYPE OF AGENCY: Hospital/medical center; Child sexual abuse services
SPONSORING ORGANIZATION: Chope Hospital Emergency Department
AREAS SERVED: San Mateo
YEARS IN OPERATION: 5
LANGUAGES: Spanish
ACCESSIBILITY: Wheelchair accessible; Telecommunications for the hearing impaired (TTY, TDY, etc.); Signers for the hearing impaired
CLIENTS/SERVICES: Sexual assault survivors; Marital rape/sexual abuse survivors; Child victims of sexual abuse; Incest victims/survivors

SAN PABLO

RAPE CRISIS CENTER OF WEST CONTRA COSTA
Brookside Hospital, 2000 Vale Rd, San Pablo, CA 94806
Crisis hotline: **(415) 236-7273 24 hrs**
Information: (415) 237-0113 9am-4:30pm
Contact: Gloria Sandoval, Exec Dir
TYPE OF AGENCY: Rape crisis center; Hospital/medical center; Child sexual abuse services; Child sexual abuse prevention program; Training/research
AREAS SERVED: Central/west Contra Costa, Marin
YEARS IN OPERATION: 14
LANGUAGES: Spanish
ACCESSIBILITY: Wheelchair accessible
CASES SEXUAL ASSAULT/ABUSE (%): 100
DESCRIPTION: Advocacy, intervention, prevention, treatment services for adult and child victims of sexual assault; Feminist martial arts/self-defense program available
CLIENTS/SERVICES: Sexual assault survivors; Marital rape/sexual abuse survivors; Child victims of sexual abuse; Adult survivors of child sexual abuse; Incest victims/survivors; Prevention program; Community education; Adolescent survivors of sexual abuse; Male survivors of sexual abuse; Disabled; Publications/media
SPECIAL PROGRAMS/SERVICES: Internship program which trains MFCC therapists in feminist therapy applied to survivors of sexual assault/abuse; Developed *Strong and Able* an in-school assault prevention program modeled on CAPP for children with disabilities (*Strong and Able* manual for $20); Videotape of five adults with disabilities talking about the vulnerability of disabled children to sexual assault and their own experiences as children

SAN PEDRO

RAINBOW SERVICES LTD
PO Box 1925, San Pedro, CA 90733
Crisis hotline: **(213) 547-9343 24 hrs**
Information: (213) 548-5450 9am-5pm
Contact: Blanca Malpartida, Exec Dir
TYPE OF AGENCY: Domestic violence program
AREAS SERVED: Los Angeles, Orange, Ventura
YEARS IN OPERATION: 11
CASES SEXUAL ASSAULT/ABUSE (%): 20
CLIENTS/SERVICES: Sexual assault survivors; Marital rape/sexual abuse survivors; Child victims of sexual abuse; Adult survivors of child sexual abuse; Incest victims/survivors; Prevention program; Adolescent survivors of sexual abuse

SAN RAFAEL

CHILD SEXUAL ABUSE TREATMENT TEAM
39 Trellis Dr, Ste 2B, San Rafael, CA 94903
Information: (415) 499-8490 9am-5pm
Contact: Judith Wachs, Parents United Coord; Michael Grogan, Clinical Dir
TYPE OF AGENCY: Child sexual abuse services
SPONSORING ORGANIZATION: Family Service Agency
AREAS SERVED: Marin
YEARS IN OPERATION: 10
LANGUAGES: Spanish
ACCESSIBILITY: Wheelchair accessible; Signers for the hearing impaired
CASES SEXUAL ASSAULT/ABUSE (%): 100
DESCRIPTION: Supports parents whose children have been sexually abused and provides treatment services for child and family, including incest offenders, and juvenile offenders. Groups include Parents United, Adults Molested as Children, children's groups for different ages and separate groups for boys and girls, nonoffending parents, mother/daughter group, anger group, human sexuality group and family education group
CLIENTS/SERVICES: Child victims of sexual abuse; Adult survivors of child sexual abuse; Incest victims/survivors; Community education; Offender treatment program; Adolescent survivors of sexual abuse; Male survivors of sexual abuse

MARIN ABUSED WOMEN'S SERVICES
1717 5th Ave, San Rafael, CA 94901
Crisis hotline: **(415) 924-6616 24 hrs**
Information: (415) 457-2464 8:30am-5pm (Mon-Fri)
Contact: Pat Kuta, Community Educ and Development Dir
TYPE OF AGENCY: Domestic violence program; Adolescent program
AREAS SERVED: Marin
YEARS IN OPERATION: 12
LANGUAGES: Spanish
ACCESSIBILITY: Wheelchair accessible
CASES SEXUAL ASSAULT/ABUSE (%): 15-25
CLIENTS/SERVICES: Marital rape/sexual abuse survivors; Child victims of sexual abuse; Prevention program; Community education; Publications/media
SPECIAL PROGRAMS/SERVICES: Publications and media: *When Love Hurts*, a 17-minute video on teen dating violence, including physical, sexual and emotional abuse ($75 for domestic violence programs, $225 institutional rate), and accompanying manual *RAPP (Relationship Abuse Prevention Project)* ($12.50). Audio cassettes ($15 each) on *Asian Women and Abuse, Latinas Maltratadas, Black Battered Women, Lesbian Battering*, and *Emily: Portrait of a Battered Woman*.

MARIN COUNTY DISTRICT ATTORNEY'S VICTIM WITNESS SERVICE
Hall of Justice-Civic Center, Rm 183, San Rafael, CA 94903
Information: (415) 499-6482 8am-5pm (Mon-Fri)
Contact: Michele Boyer, Prog Coord
TYPE OF AGENCY: Victim/witness assistance program
AREAS SERVED: Marin
YEARS IN OPERATION: 10
LANGUAGES: Spanish
ACCESSIBILITY: Wheelchair accessible
CASES SEXUAL ASSAULT/ABUSE (%): 15
CLIENTS/SERVICES: Sexual assault survivors; Child victims of sexual abuse; Adult survivors of child sexual abuse; Incest victims/survivors; Community education; Adolescent survivors of sexual abuse; Male survivors of sexual abuse

PARENTS UNITED OF MARIN
PO Box 4013, San Rafael, CA 94913
Crisis hotline: **(415) 479-STOP 9am-5pm (or tape)**
Information: (415) 499-8490 9am-5pm (Mon-Fri)
Contact: Judy Wachs, Coord
TYPE OF AGENCY: Counseling/mental health services; Child sexual abuse services
SPONSORING ORGANIZATION: Family Service Agency
AREAS SERVED: Marin, San Francisco
YEARS IN OPERATION: 10
LANGUAGES: Spanish
ACCESSIBILITY: Wheelchair accessible; Signers for the hearing impaired
CASES SEXUAL ASSAULT/ABUSE (%): 100
DESCRIPTION: Self-help program composed of adults molested as children, spouses and perpetrators who explore the effects of abuse on themselves and other family members.
CLIENTS/SERVICES: Sexual assault survivors; Child victims of sexual abuse; Adult survivors of child sexual abuse; Incest victims/survivors; Prevention program; Community education; Offender treatment program; Adolescent survivors of sexual abuse; Male survivors of sexual abuse
REQUIREMENTS: For adult group, must be 18 or older; For Daughters/Sons United group, must be 3 and older. All offenders must be screened by therapeutic team; children and teens must be interviewed for appropriate placement

RAPE CRISIS CENTER OF MARIN
24 H St, San Rafael, CA 94901
Crisis hotline: **(415) 924-2100 24 hrs**
Information: (415) 454-3263 9am-4:30pm (Mon-Fri)
Contact: Gloria Sandoval, Exec Dir
TYPE OF AGENCY: Rape crisis center
SPONSORING ORGANIZATION: Rape Crisis Center of West Contra Costa

RAPE CRISIS CENTER OF MARIN
(continued)
AREAS SERVED: Marin
YEARS IN OPERATION: 1
CASES SEXUAL ASSAULT/ABUSE (%): 100
DESCRIPTION: Provides crisis intervention through the 24-hour crisis line and court and medical advocacy; Treatment through group and individual therapy; Feminist martial arts/self-defense program
CLIENTS/SERVICES: Sexual assault survivors; Marital rape/sexual abuse survivors; Adult survivors of child sexual abuse; Incest victims/survivors; Community education

SANTA ANA

CSP SEXUAL ASSAULT VICTIM SERVICES/PREVENTION PROGRAM
PO Box 1994, Superior Court, Santa Ana, CA 92702
Crisis hotline: **(714) 957-2737 24 hrs daily**
Information: (714) 834-4317 8am-5pm (Mon-Fri)
Contact: Barbara J Phillips, Dir; Janice Hansen, Supv
TYPE OF AGENCY: Victim/witness assistance program; Child sexual abuse services; Child sexual abuse prevention program
AREAS SERVED: Orange
YEARS IN OPERATION: 7
LANGUAGES: Spanish, Vietnamese, Japanese
ACCESSIBILITY: Wheelchair accessible; Signers for the hearing impaired
CASES SEXUAL ASSAULT/ABUSE (%): 100
DESCRIPTION: Provides comprehensive services for victims and witnesses and encourages their cooperation in the investigation of the case and prosecution of the offender
CLIENTS/SERVICES: Sexual assault survivors; Marital rape/sexual abuse survivors; Child victims of sexual abuse; Adult survivors of child sexual abuse; Incest victims/survivors; Prevention program; Community education; Adolescent survivors of sexual abuse; Male survivors of sexual abuse
SPECIAL PROGRAMS/SERVICES: The Orange County Victim/Witness Assistance Program and Child Abuse Prevention Program are also components of CSP, Inc. Services are coordinated between all components of the agency to ensure that each client is afforded quality service and support

LAO FAMILY COMMUNITY, INC
531 N Fairview, Santa Ana, CA 92703
Information: (714) 541-8236 8am-5pm (Mon-Fri)
Contact: David A Glavas, Child Abuse and Intervention and Counseling Prog Coord
TYPE OF AGENCY: Counseling/mental health services; Child sexual abuse services
AREAS SERVED: Orange
YEARS IN OPERATION: 11
LANGUAGES: Vietnamese, Lao, Hmong, Thai, Chinese, French, Spanish
DESCRIPTION: Provides intervention and counseling services for Southeast Asian (Vietnamese and Laotian) children and their families
CLIENTS/SERVICES: Sexual assault survivors; Child victims of sexual abuse; Community education; Ethnic minorities
REQUIREMENTS: A child aged birth to 18 must be involved

SEXUAL ASSAULT VICTIM SERVICES/PREVENTION PROGRAM
PO Box 1994, Superior Court, Santa Ana, CA 92720
Crisis hotline: **(714) 957-2737 24 hrs**
Information: (714) 834-4317 8am-5pm
Contact: Janice Hansen, Supv
TYPE OF AGENCY: Counseling/mental health services; Child sexual abuse prevention program; Victim assistance program
SPONSORING ORGANIZATION: Community Services Programs, Inc
AREAS SERVED: Orange
YEARS IN OPERATION: 7
LANGUAGES: Spanish
ACCESSIBILITY: Wheelchair accessible
CASES SEXUAL ASSAULT/ABUSE (%): 100
DESCRIPTION: Works with victims from initial contact in the hospital or police department through the court system
CLIENTS/SERVICES: Sexual assault survivors; Marital rape/sexual abuse survivors; Child victims of sexual abuse; Adult survivors of child sexual abuse; Incest victims/survivors; Prevention program; Community education; Adolescent survivors of sexual abuse; Male survivors of sexual abuse

SANTA BARBARA

CALM (CHILD ABUSE LISTENING AND MEDICATION)
PO Box 90754, Santa Barbara, CA 93190-0754
Crisis hotline: **(805) 569-2255 24 hrs**
Information: (805) 965-2376
Contact: Michelle M Brown, Office Mgr
TYPE OF AGENCY: Child sexual abuse services; Parenting programs; Child abuse services; Child abuse prevention program
LANGUAGES: Spanish
DESCRIPTION: Provides prevention and intervention programs for child abuse victims, "at-risk" families, the family of the victim, and adult and adolescent sex offenders. Sponsors Parents United and Daughters and Sons United groups; Parent education groups (The Nurturing Program and a Parents Network Group), and bilingual parents' and children's groups
CLIENTS/SERVICES: Child victims of sexual abuse; Adult survivors of child sexual abuse; Incest victims/survivors; Prevention program; Community education; Offender treatment program; Ethnic minorities

CHILD GUIDANCE CLINIC OF THE FAMILY SERVICE AGENCY
123 W Gutierrez St, Santa Barbara, CA 93101
Information: (805) 965-1001 8am-5pm (Mon, Fri); 8am-7pm (Tue, Wed, Thu); 8am-noon (Sat)
Contact: Dr Carolyn Dennis, Child Guidance Clinic Dir
TYPE OF AGENCY: Counseling/mental health services; Child sexual abuse services; Child sexual abuse prevention program; Child abuse services
AREAS SERVED: Santa Barbara
YEARS IN OPERATION: 90
LANGUAGES: Spanish
ACCESSIBILITY: Wheelchair accessible
CASES SEXUAL ASSAULT/ABUSE (%): 30
DESCRIPTION: Serves the mental health needs of children and families, including sexually abused children and adult survivors. Child abuse prevention curricula are presented by staff to all K-4th grade students in local school districts. In addition, yearly teacher in-service on child abuse and parent workshops on prevention are included
CLIENTS/SERVICES: Child victims of sexual abuse; Adult survivors of child sexual abuse; Prevention program; Community education; Preschoolers; Publications/media
REQUIREMENTS: Children from birth to age 12 and their families
SPECIAL PROGRAMS/SERVICES: Publications: *Together We're Safe*, a child-parent handbook on stranger safety, good discipline and touching safety for parents to use at home with their kindergartners. Workbook format gives children a chance to draw, color and respond in many ways to the information. Publication for fourth-graders also available

SANTA BARBARA COUNTY DISTRICT ATTORNEY'S VICTIM/WITNESS ASSISTANCE PROGRAM
118 E Figueroa St, Santa Barbara, CA 93101
Information: (805) 568-2400 8am-5pm (Mon-Fri)
Contact: Karin Roser, Coord
TYPE OF AGENCY: Victim/witness assistance program
AREAS SERVED: Santa Barbara
YEARS IN OPERATION: 9
LANGUAGES: Spanish
ACCESSIBILITY: Wheelchair accessible
CASES SEXUAL ASSAULT/ABUSE (%): 25
CLIENTS/SERVICES: Sexual assault survivors; Marital rape/sexual abuse survivors; Child victims of sexual abuse; Community education

SANTA BARBARA RAPE CRISIS CENTER
700 N Milpas St, Santa Barbara, CA 93103
Crisis hotline: **(805) 569-CALL 24 hrs**
Information: (805) 963-6832 10am-5pm (Mon-Fri)
Contact: Barbara K Webber, Exec Dir
TYPE OF AGENCY: Rape crisis center; Counseling/mental health services; Acquaintance/date rape prevention program; Adolescent program
AREAS SERVED: Santa Barbara South
YEARS IN OPERATION: 15
LANGUAGES: Spanish, French
ACCESSIBILITY: Wheelchair accessible; Telecommunications for the hearing impaired (TTY, TDY, etc.)
CASES SEXUAL ASSAULT/ABUSE (%): 98
DESCRIPTION: Provides crisis services and advocacy for survivors of sexual assault and their families and friends
CLIENTS/SERVICES: Sexual assault survivors; Marital rape/sexual abuse survivors; Adult survivors of child sexual abuse; Incest victims/survivors; Prevention program; Community education; Adolescent survivors of sexual abuse; Male survivors of sexual abuse; Sexual harassment; Publications/media
SPECIAL PROGRAMS/SERVICES: SBRCC has a non-crisis sexual assault counseling program especially designed for survivors in the later stages of rape trauma syndrome. The program is set up as a radical feminist counseling collective and currently comprised of 12 members. Has produced a 150-page adolescent sexual assault prevention (ASAP) curriculum for a five-day, male/female team taught program ($50). Working at county level to implement a sexual assault response team for medical/legal exams using nurse practitioners. Locally produced media program on older women as survivors

SEXUAL ASSAULT RESPONSE TEAM (SART)
300 San Antonio Rd, Santa Barbara, CA 93110
Crisis hotline: **(805) 569-2255 9am-5pm (Mon-Fri)**
Information: (805) 681-5460 8am-5pm; 24 hrs on call
Contact: Pam Dohrman, RN, MS, Coord
TYPE OF AGENCY: Hospital/medical center; Child sexual abuse services
SPONSORING ORGANIZATION: Santa Barbara County Public Health Department
AREAS SERVED: Santa Maria, Lompoc, Santa Barbara
YEARS IN OPERATION: 1½
ACCESSIBILITY: Wheelchair accessible
CASES SEXUAL ASSAULT/ABUSE (%): 100
DESCRIPTION: SART exam, a medical-legal exam to be used if the case goes to court
CLIENTS/SERVICES: Sexual assault survivors; Child victims of sexual abuse; Incest victims/survivors; Community education
REQUIREMENTS: Referral by Child Protective Service or law enforcement agency

SHELTER SERVICES FOR WOMEN, INC
PO Box 1536, Santa Barbara, CA 93102
Crisis hotline: **(805) 964-5245, 925-2160, 736-0965 24 hrs daily**

SHELTER SERVICES FOR WOMEN, INC
(continued)

Information: (805) 963-4458 9am-5pm (Mon-Fri)
Contact: Carolyn Contreras, Exec Dir
TYPE OF AGENCY: Domestic violence program
AREAS SERVED: Santa Barbara
YEARS IN OPERATION: 10
LANGUAGES: Spanish
ACCESSIBILITY: Wheelchair accessible
CASES SEXUAL ASSAULT/ABUSE (%): 5
CLIENTS/SERVICES: Sexual assault survivors; Marital rape/sexual abuse survivors; Community education

WOMEN'S CENTER AND POLICE DEPARTMENT'S RAPE PREVENTION EDUCATION PROGRAM
University of California, Santa Barbara, CA 93106
Information: (805) 961-3778 8am-5pm (Mon-Fri)
Contact: Cheri Gurse, RPEP Coord
TYPE OF AGENCY: College/university-based services; Rape prevention program; Acquaintance/date rape prevention program
AREAS SERVED: Santa Barbara
YEARS IN OPERATION: 10
LANGUAGES: Spanish
ACCESSIBILITY: Wheelchair accessible; Telecommunications for the hearing impaired (TTY, TDY, etc.)
CASES SEXUAL ASSAULT/ABUSE (%): 100
DESCRIPTION: Date rape awareness; Coordinates help for sexual abuse survivors; Rape-responsiveness via academic and student life services
CLIENTS/SERVICES: Sexual assault survivors; Marital rape/sexual abuse survivors; Adult survivors of child sexual abuse; Incest victims/survivors; Prevention program; Community education; Adolescent survivors of sexual abuse; Male survivors of sexual abuse
SPECIAL PROGRAMS/SERVICES: 1½ hour program on sex, dating, communicating and date rape; Responsive to the language, attitudes and values of 18-22 year olds; Address heterosexism, racism, and sexism

SANTA CRUZ

PACIFIC TREATMENT ASSOCIATES
313 Soquel Ave, Ste B, Santa Cruz, CA 95062
Information: (408) 423-3303 9am-8pm (Mon-Thu); 10am-2pm (Fri)
Contact: Vee Duvall, Co-Dir
TYPE OF AGENCY: Counseling/mental health services; Offender treatment
AREAS SERVED: Santa Cruz, Monterey
YEARS IN OPERATION: 3 months
LANGUAGES: Spanish
ACCESSIBILITY: Signers for the hearing impaired
CASES SEXUAL ASSAULT/ABUSE (%): 95
DESCRIPTION: Structured long-term treatment program for offenders with the specific goal of preventing reoffense; Work with wives and families also
CLIENTS/SERVICES: Marital rape/sexual abuse survivors; Community education; Offender treatment program; Male survivors of sexual abuse
REQUIREMENTS: Client must be adult, admit offense, be non-violent, and amenable to treatment.

PARENTS CENTER
530 Soquel Ave, Santa Cruz, CA 95062
Crisis hotline: **(408) 426-7322 24 hrs**
Information: (408) 426-7322 by appointment
Contact: Arline Ganzler, Asst Dir
TYPE OF AGENCY: Child sexual abuse services; Child sexual abuse prevention program; Child abuse services; Child abuse prevention program
AREAS SERVED: Santa Cruz, Monterey
YEARS IN OPERATION: 13
LANGUAGES: Spanish
ACCESSIBILITY: Wheelchair accessible

CASES SEXUAL ASSAULT/ABUSE (%): 33
DESCRIPTION: Provides counseling and support groups for families experiencing child physical and/or sexual abuse; Prevention programs; Parenting classes
CLIENTS/SERVICES: Child victims of sexual abuse; Prevention program; Adolescent survivors of sexual abuse
REQUIREMENTS: Sliding scale fee

SANTA CRUZ MEN'S ALTERNATIVES TO VIOLENCE
PO Box 2126, Santa Cruz, CA 95063-2126
Crisis hotline: **(408) 425-5248 24 hrs**
Information: (408) 425-5248 1pm-8pm
Contact: Glen Fitch, Exec Dir
TYPE OF AGENCY: Men's program
AREAS SERVED: Santa Cruz
YEARS IN OPERATION: 13
LANGUAGES: Spanish
CASES SEXUAL ASSAULT/ABUSE (%): 5
DESCRIPTION: Works with men in crisis who often turn to violence to resolve conflicts; Works with men close to women who survive rape, and male survivors of sexual assault
CLIENTS/SERVICES: Sexual assault survivors; Marital rape/sexual abuse survivors; Child victims of sexual abuse; Adult survivors of child sexual abuse; Incest victims/survivors; Prevention program; Community education; Adolescent survivors of sexual abuse; Male survivors of sexual abuse; Publications/media
SPECIAL PROGRAMS/SERVICES: *Men: What happens when the crime no one thinks can happen...happens?* $2.00

SANTA CRUZ VICTIM/WITNESS CENTER
701 Ocean St, No 200-C, Santa Cruz, CA 95060
Information: (408) 425-2610 8am-5pm (Mon-Fri)
Contact: Judith Osborn, V/W Coord
TYPE OF AGENCY: Hospital/medical center; Victim/witness assistance program
SPONSORING ORGANIZATION: Santa Cruz District Attorney's Office
AREAS SERVED: Santa Cruz
YEARS IN OPERATION: 7
LANGUAGES: Spanish
ACCESSIBILITY: Wheelchair accessible
CASES SEXUAL ASSAULT/ABUSE (%): 20
DESCRIPTION: Victim emergency response team/sexual assault response team available at hospitals for crime victims and rape victims (RNs used for rape exam). Provides crisis intervention, emergency assistance, follow-up counseling, referral, orientation to justice system, court escort, aid in state victim claims
CLIENTS/SERVICES: Sexual assault survivors; Marital rape/sexual abuse survivors; Child victims of sexual abuse; Incest victims/survivors; Male survivors of sexual abuse

SEXUAL ASSAULT RESPONSE TEAM/SEXUAL ASSAULT NURSE EXAMINER PROGRAM
1555 Soquel Dr, Dominican Hospital, Santa Cruz, CA 95065
Information: (408) 462-7744 8am-5pm (Mon-Fri)
Contact: Sherry Arndt, RN, Coord
TYPE OF AGENCY: Hospital/medical center; Training/research
AREAS SERVED: Santa Cruz
YEARS IN OPERATION: 2
LANGUAGES: Spanish, other languages by arrangement
ACCESSIBILITY: Wheelchair accessible; Telecommunications for the hearing impaired (TTY, TDY, etc.); Signers for the hearing impaired
CASES SEXUAL ASSAULT/ABUSE (%): 100
DESCRIPTION: Coordinates the county's emergency response to sexual assault reports; provides law enforcement officer, advocate, and sexual assault nurse examiner to all hospitals in county. Specialized pediatricians are also part of the team for clients 13 and younger. Hospitals provide separate, private, specialized exam rooms for clients

CLIENTS/SERVICES: Sexual assault survivors; Marital rape/sexual abuse survivors; Child victims of sexual abuse; Adult survivors of child sexual abuse; Incest victims/survivors; Community education; Adolescent survivors of sexual abuse; Male survivors of sexual abuse
REQUIREMENTS: Exams must be authorized by law enforcement officials to be paid for at public expense
SPECIAL PROGRAMS/SERVICES: SART Certification Institute is the only program of its kind in California for training registered nurses, law enforcement officers, and advocates wanting to participate in the Sexual Assault Response Team. This is also the only county in California to use nurse examiners.

SURVIVORS HEALING CENTER
423 Bellevue St, Santa Cruz, CA 95060
Information: (408) 423-2609 5pm-10pm (Mon-Fri), answering machine after hrs
Contact: Amy Pine, LMFCC, VPres
TYPE OF AGENCY: Private practice; Retreat center; Adult survivors services
YEARS IN OPERATION: Workshops 5, Other services 2
ACCESSIBILITY: Wheelchair accessible
CASES SEXUAL ASSAULT/ABUSE (%): 100
DESCRIPTION: Provides opportunities for healing from childhood sexual abuse through education, workshops, and ongoing groups for survivors and their partners; National referrals; Training seminars for professionals and public lectures
CLIENTS/SERVICES: Adult survivors of child sexual abuse; Incest victims/survivors; Community education; Adolescent survivors of sexual abuse; Healing
REQUIREMENTS: Clean and sober attendance; Participants must register only themselves; Phone screening; Additional screening if under age, suicidal, or using prescribed medication
SPECIAL PROGRAMS/SERVICES: *I Never Told Anyone* weekend workshops for adult women survivors of child sexual abuse, facilitated by Ellen Bass and Amy Pine. Ellen Bass is co-author of *I Never Told Anyone: Writings by Women Survivors of Child Abuse* (Harper and Row, 1983) and *The Courage to Heal: A Guide for Survivors of Child Sexual Abuse* (Harper and Row, 1988)

UC SANTA CRUZ RAPE PREVENTION EDUCATION PROGRAM
Cowell Health Center-UC Santa Cruz, Santa Cruz, CA 95064
Information: (408) 429-2721
Contact: Gillian Greensite
TYPE OF AGENCY: College/university-based services; Rape prevention program; Date/acquaintance rape prevention program
CLIENTS/SERVICES: Prevention program; Community education

WOMEN'S CRISIS SUPPORT
1025 Center St, Santa Cruz, CA 95060
Crisis hotline: **(408) 429-1478 24 hrs**
Information: (408) 425-5525 9am-5pm (Mon-Fri)
Contact: Kathy Robinson, Client Svcs Coord
TYPE OF AGENCY: Rape crisis center; Domestic violence program; Counseling/mental health services; Substance abuse treatment/counseling
AREAS SERVED: Santa Cruz
YEARS IN OPERATION: 11
LANGUAGES: Spanish
ACCESSIBILITY: Wheelchair accessible (office)
CASES SEXUAL ASSAULT/ABUSE (%): 25
CLIENTS/SERVICES: Sexual assault survivors; Marital rape/sexual abuse survivors; Adult survivors of child sexual abuse; Incest victims/survivors; Prevention program; Community education; Adolescent survivors of sexual abuse

SANTA MARIA

SANTA MARIA VALLEY YOUTH AND FAMILY CENTER
225 E Mill, Santa Maria, CA 93454
Information: (805) 928-1707 8:30am-6pm
Contact: William Rogers, Dir
TYPE OF AGENCY: Counseling/mental health services; Child sexual abuse services; Child sexual abuse prevention program; Adolescent program
AREAS SERVED: Santa Barbara
YEARS IN OPERATION: 15
LANGUAGES: Spanish, Tagalog
ACCESSIBILITY: Signers for the hearing impaired
CASES SEXUAL ASSAULT/ABUSE (%): 20
CLIENTS/SERVICES: Child victims of sexual abuse; Adult survivors of child sexual abuse; Incest victims/survivors; Prevention program; Community education; Adolescent survivors of sexual abuse; Male survivors of sexual abuse
REQUIREMENTS: Youth 3-18 years and their families

SANTA MONICA

RAPE TREATMENT CENTER
1225 15th St, Santa Monica, CA 90404
Crisis hotline: **(213) 319-4000 24 hrs**
Information: (213) 319-4000 8am-5pm
Contact: Gail Abarbanel, Dir
TYPE OF AGENCY: Rape crisis center; Hospital/medical center; Child sexual abuse services; Acquaintance/date rape prevention program
SPONSORING ORGANIZATION: Santa Monica Hospital
AREAS SERVED: Los Angeles
YEARS IN OPERATION: 14
LANGUAGES: Spanish
ACCESSIBILITY: Wheelchair accessible
CASES SEXUAL ASSAULT/ABUSE (%): 100
DESCRIPTION: Provides emergency medical care, medicolegal evidence collection, crisis intervention, advocacy and accompaniment services, legal assistance, and ongoing counseling for child and adult survivors and their families, with special culturally appropriate outreach to Hispanic community. Extensive community-based prevention program and training for medical personnel, criminal justice and law enforcement personnel, and educators
CLIENTS/SERVICES: Sexual assault survivors; Marital rape/sexual abuse survivors; Child victims of sexual abuse; Adult survivors of child sexual abuse; Incest victims/survivors; Prevention program; Community education; Adolescent survivors of sexual abuse; Male survivors of sexual abuse; Ethnic minorities
SPECIAL PROGRAMS/SERVICES: Senderos, a program with bilingual/bicultural staff providing outreach, education, treatment, and advocacy for Latinos. National Institute of Mental Health produced educational film onsite about the Rape Treatment Center's model of survivor care, which is used for training (along with a companion booklet) in hospitals, medical and nursing schools. Prevention media include a video training program to educate teachers and school counselors about ways to help child and adolescent rape victims. Publications include: *How It Happens: Understanding Sexual Abuse and Date Rape* (for teenagers); *Taking Action: What to Do if You Are Raped*; *Being Safe: Protecting Yourself, Your Family, and Your Home*; *Sexual Assault On Campus: What Colleges Can Do*

SOJOURN SERVICES FOR BATTERED WOMEN AND THEIR CHILDREN
237 Hill St, Santa Monica, CA 90405
Crisis hotline: **(213) 392-9896 24 hrs**
Information: (213) 399-9239 9am-5pm (Mon-Fri)
Contact: Linda Wineland, Dir; Gaile Price, Children's Prog Coord
TYPE OF AGENCY: Domestic violence program
SPONSORING ORGANIZATION: Ocean Park Community Center
AREAS SERVED: Los Angeles
YEARS IN OPERATION: 11
LANGUAGES: Spanish
CASES SEXUAL ASSAULT/ABUSE (%): 85
CLIENTS/SERVICES: Sexual assault survivors; Marital rape/sexual abuse survivors; Child victims of sexual abuse; Adult survivors of child sexual abuse; Incest victims/survivors; Adolescent survivors of sexual abuse

SANTA ROSA

CHRYSALIS COUNSELING SERVICES FOR WOMEN, INC
2635 Cleveland Ave, No 8, Santa Rosa, CA 95403
Information: (707) 545-1670 8am-8pm (Mon-Fri)
Contact: Lisa Mathiesen, Admin Coord
TYPE OF AGENCY: Counseling/mental health services
AREAS SERVED: Sonoma, Marin, Napa, Mendocino
YEARS IN OPERATION: 7
ACCESSIBILITY: Wheelchair accessible
CASES SEXUAL ASSAULT/ABUSE (%): 50-75
DESCRIPTION: A feminist counseling agency that provides low-fee counseling to low income women, their partners, and families. Counseling includes short-term, long-term, individual and group
CLIENTS/SERVICES: Sexual assault survivors; Marital rape/sexual abuse survivors; Adult survivors of child sexual abuse; Incest victims/survivors
REQUIREMENTS: Individual client income may not exceed $1,000.00 (net). This can vary if client has dependents or shares income with another person

SONOMA COUNTY CHILD ABUSE COUNCIL
1212 College Ave, Santa Rosa, CA 95404
Information: (707) 544-3077 9am-5pm (Mon-Fri)
Contact: Marianne Schwarz-Kesling, Prog Mgr
TYPE OF AGENCY: Child sexual abuse prevention program; Child abuse prevention program; Interagency network
SPONSORING ORGANIZATION: Community Child Care Council of Sonoma County (4CS)
AREAS SERVED: Sonoma
YEARS IN OPERATION: 8
LANGUAGES: Spanish
CASES SEXUAL ASSAULT/ABUSE (%): 30
CLIENTS/SERVICES: Child victims of sexual abuse; Adult survivors of child sexual abuse; Incest victims/survivors; Prevention program; Community education
SPECIAL PROGRAMS/SERVICES: Respite child care for children at risk; Publications: *Child Protection Handbook* in Spanish and English

SONOMA COUNTY VICTIM WITNESS PROJECT
2230 Professional Dr, Santa Rosa, CA 95403
Information: (707) 527-2002 8am-5pm
Contact: J Ingenito, Prog Coord
TYPE OF AGENCY: Victim/witness assistance program
SPONSORING ORGANIZATION: Sonoma County Probation Department
AREAS SERVED: Sonoma
YEARS IN OPERATION: 8
CASES SEXUAL ASSAULT/ABUSE (%): 50-65
CLIENTS/SERVICES: Sexual assault survivors; Marital rape/sexual abuse survivors; Child victims of sexual abuse; Incest victims/survivors; Community education
REQUIREMENTS: Client must cooperate with law enforcement

SONOMA COUNTY WOMEN AGAINST RAPE
PO Box 1426, Santa Rosa, CA 95402
Crisis hotline: **(707) 545-7273 24 hrs**
Information: (707) 545-7270 9am-5pm
Contact: Deborah Evind, Coord
TYPE OF AGENCY: Rape crisis center; Child sexual abuse prevention program; Acquaintance/date rape prevention program; Adolescent program
AREAS SERVED: Sonoma
YEARS IN OPERATION: 14
LANGUAGES: Spanish
ACCESSIBILITY: Wheelchair accessible
CASES SEXUAL ASSAULT/ABUSE (%): 100
DESCRIPTION: Intervention services for rape survivors and their significant others; Feminist martial arts/self-defense program; Child Assault Prevention (CAP) Project; Teen Assault Prevention Project (TAPP)
CLIENTS/SERVICES: Sexual assault survivors; Marital rape/sexual abuse survivors; Adult survivors of child sexual abuse; Incest victims/survivors; Prevention program; Community education; Adolescent survivors of sexual abuse; Male survivors of sexual abuse
SPECIAL PROGRAMS/SERVICES: Child Assault Prevention (CAP) Program and Teen Assault Prevention Program (TAPP) for junior and senior high students geared toward prevention of sexual assault and physical and emotional abuse. Brochures concerning prevention programs in Spanish and English

SEASIDE

FAMILY RESOURCE CENTER
500 Hilby Ave, Seaside, CA 93955
Information: (408) 394-4622 9am-5pm
Contact: Judy Masliyah, Treatment Coord
TYPE OF AGENCY: Victim/witness assistance program; Child sexual abuse services; Child abuse prevention program
AREAS SERVED: Monterey
CASES SEXUAL ASSAULT/ABUSE (%): 90
DESCRIPTION: Individual and family therapy for sexually and physically abused clients as well as support groups for children, adolescents, and adult women who were sexually abused as children. Also offers parent education
CLIENTS/SERVICES: Sexual assault survivors; Child victims of sexual abuse; Adult survivors of child sexual abuse; Incest victims/survivors; Prevention program; Community education; Adolescent survivors of sexual abuse; Male survivors of sexual abuse

SONORA

MOTHER LODE WOMEN'S CENTER
PO Box 663, Sonora, CA 95383
Crisis hotline: **(209) 532-4707 24 hrs**
Information: (209) 532-4746 9am-5pm (Mon-Fri)
Contact: Pat Cervelli, Sexual Assault Svcs Prog Coord
TYPE OF AGENCY: Rape crisis center; Domestic violence program; Child sexual abuse prevention program
AREAS SERVED: Tuolumne
YEARS IN OPERATION: 13
LANGUAGES: Spanish
CLIENTS/SERVICES: Sexual assault survivors; Marital rape/sexual abuse survivors; Adult survivors of child sexual abuse; Incest victims/survivors; Prevention program; Community education; Adolescent survivors of sexual abuse; Male survivors of sexual abuse

SOUTH LAKE TAHOE

WOMENSPACE UNLIMITED
PO Box 13111, South Lake Tahoe, CA 95702
Crisis hotline: **(916) 544-4444 24 hrs**
Information: (916) 544-2118 8am-5pm (Mon-Fri)
Contact: Kathy Bottini, Prog Coord

WOMENSPACE UNLIMITED *(continued)*
TYPE OF AGENCY: Rape crisis center; Domestic violence program; Child sexual abuse services; Child sexual abuse prevention program
AREAS SERVED: El Dorado
YEARS IN OPERATION: 11
LANGUAGES: Spanish
CASES SEXUAL ASSAULT/ABUSE (%): 15
DESCRIPTION: Provides comprehensive services for sexual assault survivors and groups for adult survivors of incest; Professional counseling for sexually abused children and their families; Services for domestic violence survivors. Presents the Child Assault Prevention (CAP) Program for children; Sponsors social skills and non-aggressive play group (SSNAP) for children 3-5 years old; Anger management groups for men
CLIENTS/SERVICES: Sexual assault survivors; Marital rape/sexual abuse survivors; Child victims of sexual abuse; Adult survivors of child sexual abuse; Incest victims/survivors; Prevention program; Community education; Preschoolers

SOUTH SAN FRANCISCO

VICTIM CENTER OF SAN MATEO COUNTY
1024 Mission Rd, South San Francisco, CA 94080
Information: (415) 877-5494 8am-5pm
Contact: Chuck Coggeshall, Prog Mgr
TYPE OF AGENCY: Victim/witness assistance program
SPONSORING ORGANIZATION: San Mateo County Probation Department
AREAS SERVED: San Mateo
YEARS IN OPERATION: 13
LANGUAGES: Translators available
ACCESSIBILITY: Wheelchair accessible; Signers for the hearing impaired
CASES SEXUAL ASSAULT/ABUSE (%): 25
CLIENTS/SERVICES: Sexual assault survivors; Marital rape/sexual abuse survivors; Child victims of sexual abuse; Adult survivors of child sexual abuse; Incest victims/survivors; Community education; Adolescent survivors of sexual abuse; Male survivors of sexual abuse

STANFORD

THE BRIDGE
640 Campus Dr, Stanford, CA 94305
Crisis hotline: **(415) 723-3392 24 hrs**
Information: (415) 723-3393 24 hrs
Contact: Stephanie Kondik, Live-in
TYPE OF AGENCY: College/university-based services; Counseling/mental health services; Peer counseling
SPONSORING ORGANIZATION: SOS-Stanford University
AREAS SERVED: Santa Clara, San Mateo
YEARS IN OPERATION: 17
ACCESSIBILITY: Wheelchair accessible
CASES SEXUAL ASSAULT/ABUSE (%): 20
DESCRIPTION: Group of Stanford University students offering free and confidential peer counseling for anyone on any issue. Overeaters Anonymous, Alcoholics Anonymous, and Gay and Lesbian Coming Out Group
CLIENTS/SERVICES: Sexual assault survivors; Marital rape/sexual abuse survivors; Adult survivors of child sexual abuse; Incest victims/survivors; Community education

STOCKTON

SEXUAL ASSAULT CENTER
930 N Commerce St, Stockton, CA 95202
Crisis hotline: **(209) 465-4997 24 hrs daily**
Information: (209) 941-2611 8:30am-5pm (Mon-Fri)
Contact: Barbara E Webster, Dir
TYPE OF AGENCY: Rape crisis center; Domestic violence program; Child sexual abuse services; Child sexual abuse prevention program; Women's center
SPONSORING ORGANIZATION: Women's Center of San Joaquin County
AREAS SERVED: San Joaquin
YEARS IN OPERATION: 12
LANGUAGES: Spanish, Cambodian, Laotian, Vietnamese interpreters available
ACCESSIBILITY: Wheelchair accessible
CASES SEXUAL ASSAULT/ABUSE (%): 100
CLIENTS/SERVICES: Sexual assault survivors; Marital rape/sexual abuse survivors; Child victims of sexual abuse; Adult survivors of child sexual abuse; Incest victims/survivors; Prevention program; Community education; Adolescent survivors of sexual abuse; Male survivors of sexual abuse

VALLEY COMMUNITY COUNSELING SERVICES, INC
1335 N Hunter St, Stockton, CA 95202
Information: (209) 464-2825 9am-6pm
Contact: David D Love, MFCC, Exec Dir
TYPE OF AGENCY: Counseling/mental health services; Child sexual abuse services; Child sexual abuse prevention program
AREAS SERVED: San Joaquin, Tuolumne
YEARS IN OPERATION: 14
LANGUAGES: Spanish
ACCESSIBILITY: Wheelchair accessible
CASES SEXUAL ASSAULT/ABUSE (%): 25
CLIENTS/SERVICES: Sexual assault survivors; Marital rape/sexual abuse survivors; Child victims of sexual abuse; Adult survivors of child sexual abuse; Incest victims/survivors; Prevention program; Community education; Offender treatment program; Adolescent survivors of sexual abuse; Male survivors of sexual abuse

TORRANCE

LOS ANGELES COUNTY CHILD SEXUAL ABUSE CRISIS CENTER
1000 W Carson St, A-7, Torrance, CA 90509
Information: (213) 533-3567
TYPE OF AGENCY: Hospital/medical center; Child sexual abuse services
SPONSORING ORGANIZATION: Harbor-UCLA Medical Center
DESCRIPTION: Provides comprehensive psychosocial assessment of child and parent and medical evaluation of child. Evaluations for sexually reactive children (victims/young offenders).
CLIENTS/SERVICES: Child victims of sexual abuse; Offender treatment program; Adolescent survivors of sexual abuse; Male survivors of sexual abuse
REQUIREMENTS: Ages 0-18

TULARE

TULARE COUNTY CHILD SEXUAL ABUSE TREATMENT PROGRAM
PO Box 202, Tulare, CA 93274
Crisis hotline: **(209) 688-2043 8am-5pm (Mon, Fri); 8am-8pm (Tue, Wed, Thu)**
Information: (209) 688-2043 8am-5pm (Mon, Fri); 8am-8pm (Tue, Wed, Thu)
Contact: Edward Martin, Clinic Dir
TYPE OF AGENCY: Counseling/mental health services; Child sexual abuse services
SPONSORING ORGANIZATION: Tulare Youth Service Bureau
AREAS SERVED: Tulare
YEARS IN OPERATION: 9
LANGUAGES: Spanish
ACCESSIBILITY: Wheelchair accessible; Signers for the hearing impaired
CASES SEXUAL ASSAULT/ABUSE (%): 30
CLIENTS/SERVICES: Child victims of sexual abuse; Adult survivors of child sexual abuse; Incest victims/survivors; Community education; Offender treatment program; Adolescent survivors of sexual abuse; Male survivors of sexual abuse
REQUIREMENTS: Must be a victim of incest; Perpetrators must be non-violent and not pedophiles

TUSTIN

CHILD SEXUAL ABUSE TREATMENT PROGRAM (CSATP)
17421 Irvine Blvd, Tustin, CA 92680
Information: (714) 838-7395 (Mon-Sat)
Contact: Tom Bell, Prog Dir
TYPE OF AGENCY: Counseling/mental health services; Child sexual abuse services
SPONSORING ORGANIZATION: Family Service Association of Orange County (FSAOC)
AREAS SERVED: Orange
YEARS IN OPERATION: 6½
LANGUAGES: Spanish
ACCESSIBILITY: Wheelchair accessible
CASES SEXUAL ASSAULT/ABUSE (%): 100
CLIENTS/SERVICES: Child victims of sexual abuse; Adult survivors of child sexual abuse; Incest victims/survivors; Community education; Offender treatment program; Adolescent survivors of sexual abuse; Male survivors of sexual abuse
REQUIREMENTS: Must be an incest case, ages 5 or older

VOICES OF CALIFORNIA, INC
PO Box 1722, Tustin, CA 92681-1722
Information: (714) 567-3183 24 hrs
Contact: Mary Cangelosi, Exec Dir
TYPE OF AGENCY: Counseling/mental health services
AREAS SERVED: Orange, Riverside, Los Angeles, San Bernardino
YEARS IN OPERATION: 5
ACCESSIBILITY: Wheelchair accessible
CASES SEXUAL ASSAULT/ABUSE (%): 100
DESCRIPTION: Group therapy with licensed therapists; Informational meetings; Seminars and a speakers' bureau; Peer-led support groups; Referrals to professionals for individual therapy; Support groups for male incest survivors
CLIENTS/SERVICES: Adult survivors of child sexual abuse; Incest victims/survivors; Community education; Male survivors of sexual abuse
REQUIREMENTS: Must be 18 or older or an emancipated minor

UKIAH

MENDOCINO COUNTY CHILD SEXUAL ABUSE TREATMENT PROJECT
202 S State St, Ukiah, CA 95482
Crisis hotline: **(707) 463-HELP 24 hrs**
Information: (707) 463-4915 8am-5pm
Contact: Mimine Govatoes, Proj Coord
TYPE OF AGENCY: Child sexual abuse services
SPONSORING ORGANIZATION: Mendocino Youth Project
AREAS SERVED: Mendocino
YEARS IN OPERATION: 9
CASES SEXUAL ASSAULT/ABUSE (%): 100
DESCRIPTION: Provides groups, family and individual counseling for sexually abused children and their families, including offenders in cases of incest
CLIENTS/SERVICES: Child victims of sexual abuse; Adult survivors of child sexual abuse; Incest victims/survivors; Community education; Adolescent survivors of sexual abuse; Male survivors of sexual abuse

MENDOCINO COUNTY DISTRICT ATTORNEY'S VICTIM WITNESS ASSISTANCE
PO Box 144, Ukiah, CA 95482
Information: (707) 463-4218 8am-5pm
Contact: Sheelagh Jaquay, Coord II; Polly Palecek, Coord I

MENDOCINO COUNTY DISTRICT ATTORNEY'S VICTIM WITNESS ASSISTANCE *(continued)*
TYPE OF AGENCY: Victim/witness assistance program
AREAS SERVED: Mendocino
YEARS IN OPERATION: 8
ACCESSIBILITY: Wheelchair accessible
CASES SEXUAL ASSAULT/ABUSE (%): 50-75
CLIENTS/SERVICES: Sexual assault survivors; Marital rape/sexual abuse survivors; Child victims of sexual abuse; Adult survivors of child sexual abuse; Incest victims/survivors; Community education; Adolescent survivors of sexual abuse; Male survivors of sexual abuse
REQUIREMENTS: Must be a reported violent crime; Victim must cooperate with prosecution

PROJECT SANCTUARY
PO Box 995, Ukiah, CA 95482
Crisis hotline: **(707) 462-7988, 463-HELP 24 hrs**
Information: (707) 462-9196 8:30am-4:30pm
Contact: Judy Albert, Sexual Assault Crisis Svcs Dir
TYPE OF AGENCY: Rape crisis center; Domestic violence program; Child sexual abuse prevention program
AREAS SERVED: Mendocino
YEARS IN OPERATION: 12
LANGUAGES: Spanish
ACCESSIBILITY: Wheelchair accessible
DESCRIPTION: Provides a 24-hour crisis line, shelter, support groups, and education for survivors of sexual assault and domestic violence. Child Assault Prevention (CAP) Program
CLIENTS/SERVICES: Sexual assault survivors; Marital rape/sexual abuse survivors; Adult survivors of child sexual abuse; Incest victims/survivors; Prevention program; Community education; Adolescent survivors of sexual abuse

VAN NUYS

FAMILY VIOLENCE PROJECT
6851 Lennox Ave, Van Nuys, CA 91405
Information: (818) 908-5007 8:30am-5pm (Mon-Thu); 8:30am-3:30pm (Fri)
Contact: Ellen Ledley, Proj Dir
TYPE OF AGENCY: Domestic violence program
SPONSORING ORGANIZATION: Jewish Family Service
AREAS SERVED: Los Angeles
YEARS IN OPERATION: 5
ACCESSIBILITY: Wheelchair accessible
DESCRIPTION: Provides shelter, financial assistance, and counseling for survivors of domestic violence/sexual abuse; Treatment program for batterers; Prevention programs concerning teen dating violence and rape and self-defense
CLIENTS/SERVICES: Marital rape/sexual abuse survivors; Adult survivors of child sexual abuse; Incest victims/survivors; Prevention program; Community education

FORTE FOUNDATION
7543 Woodley Ave, Ste 200, Van Nuys, CA 91406
Information: (818) 788-6800, 788-6809 24 hrs 7 days
Contact: Elaine Gethard, MA, Exec Dir; Thomas Glennon, PhD, Clinical Dir
TYPE OF AGENCY: Counseling/mental health services; Child sexual abuse services; Child abuse services
AREAS SERVED: Los Angeles
YEARS IN OPERATION: 12
ACCESSIBILITY: Wheelchair accessible
CASES SEXUAL ASSAULT/ABUSE (%): 30-40
DESCRIPTION: State-licensed community mental health clinic treating victims of sexual and physical abuse, their families, and the perpetrators of abuse. Treatment includes individual and family therapy, parenting and batterers groups.
CLIENTS/SERVICES: Sexual assault survivors; Marital rape/sexual abuse survivors; Child victims of sexual abuse; Adult survivors of child sexual abuse; Incest victims/survivors; Community education; Offender treatment program; Adolescent survivors of sexual abuse; Male survivors of sexual abuse
REQUIREMENTS: Fees are based on a sliding scale.

SAN FERNANDO VALLEY CHILD GUIDANCE CLINIC
7347 Van Nuys Blvd, Van Nuys, CA 91405
Crisis hotline: **(818) 993-9311 24 hrs**
Information: (818) 989-5975 8:30am-7pm (Mon-Thu); 8:30am-5pm (Fri)
TYPE OF AGENCY: Child sexual abuse services; Child abuse services
SPONSORING ORGANIZATION: Family Stress Center, Family Crisis Services
AREAS SERVED: Los Angeles
YEARS IN OPERATION: 30
LANGUAGES: Spanish
ACCESSIBILITY: Wheelchair accessible
CASES SEXUAL ASSAULT/ABUSE (%): 98
DESCRIPTION: Individual, family, and group treatment for child sexual abuse victims; Group treatment for physically/sexually abused toddlers and their caretakers; Counseling for parents who are adult survivors of child sexual abuse
CLIENTS/SERVICES: Child victims of sexual abuse; Adult survivors of child sexual abuse; Prevention program; Community education; Male survivors of sexual abuse; Preschoolers; Publications/media
REQUIREMENTS: Children ages 1-17
SPECIAL PROGRAMS/SERVICES: *Hugs 'N Kids* parent education video

VENTURA

PARENTS UNITED, VENTURA COUNTY CHAPTER
300 Hillmont Ave, Ventura, CA 93003
Crisis hotline: **(805) 652-6727 24 hrs**
Information: (805) 652-6759 9am-6pm
Contact: Herman Kagan, PhD, Coord
TYPE OF AGENCY: Child sexual abuse services
SPONSORING ORGANIZATION: Ventura County Mental Health
AREAS SERVED: Ventura
YEARS IN OPERATION: 10
ACCESSIBILITY: Wheelchair accessible
CASES SEXUAL ASSAULT/ABUSE (%): 100
CLIENTS/SERVICES: Child victims of sexual abuse; Adult survivors of child sexual abuse; Incest victims/survivors; Community education; Offender treatment program; Adolescent survivors of sexual abuse; Male survivors of sexual abuse

VICTIM/WITNESS ASSISTANCE
800 S Victoria Ave, Rm 311, Ventura, CA 93009
Information: (805) 654-3622 8am-5pm
Contact: Ellie Liston, Victim Advocate III; Deanna Cox, Victim Advocate II
TYPE OF AGENCY: Victim/witness assistance program
SPONSORING ORGANIZATION: District Attorney's Office, Ventura County
AREAS SERVED: Ventura
YEARS IN OPERATION: 8
LANGUAGES: Spanish
ACCESSIBILITY: Wheelchair accessible
CASES SEXUAL ASSAULT/ABUSE (%): 50
CLIENTS/SERVICES: Sexual assault survivors; Marital rape/sexual abuse survivors; Child victims of sexual abuse; Adult survivors of child sexual abuse; Incest victims/survivors; Community education; Adolescent survivors of sexual abuse; Male survivors of sexual abuse

VICTORVILLE

CHILD ABUSE PREVENTION INTERVENTION EDUCATION PROGRAM
14972 Circle Dr, Victorville, CA 92392
Information: (619) 243-1868 8:30am-5:30pm
Contact: Karen Stilwell, Service Area Coord
TYPE OF AGENCY: Counseling/mental health services; Child sexual abuse prevention program; Child abuse prevention program
SPONSORING ORGANIZATION: Family Service Agency of San Bernardino
AREAS SERVED: San Bernardino
YEARS IN OPERATION: 4
LANGUAGES: Spanish
ACCESSIBILITY: Wheelchair accessible
CLIENTS/SERVICES: Prevention program
REQUIREMENTS: Enrolled or associated with public school system

DISTRICT ATTORNEY'S OFFICE—VICTIM/WITNESS ASSISTANCE PROGRAM
14455 Civic Dr, Victorville, CA 92392
Information: (619) 243-8619, 243-8620 8am-5pm (Mon-Fri)
Contact: Marta Woodfield, Victim/Witness Advocate II
TYPE OF AGENCY: Victim/witness assistance program
SPONSORING ORGANIZATION: State of California, San Bernardino District Attorney
AREAS SERVED: San Bernardino
YEARS IN OPERATION: 6
LANGUAGES: Spanish
ACCESSIBILITY: Wheelchair accessible
CASES SEXUAL ASSAULT/ABUSE (%): 75
CLIENTS/SERVICES: Sexual assault survivors; Marital rape/sexual abuse survivors; Child victims of sexual abuse; Adult survivors of child sexual abuse; Incest victims/survivors; Prevention program; Community education; Adolescent survivors of sexual abuse; Male survivors of sexual abuse
REQUIREMENTS: To apply for violent crime funds, clients must file charges

VISALIA

FAMILY SERVICES OF TULARE COUNTY
PO Box 510, Visalia, CA 93279
Crisis hotline: **(209) 732-5941 24 hrs**
Information: (209) 732-2514 7:30am-5pm
Contact: Dr Jacque Smith, Exec Dir
TYPE OF AGENCY: Domestic violence program
AREAS SERVED: Tulare, Kings
YEARS IN OPERATION: 5
LANGUAGES: Spanish
ACCESSIBILITY: Wheelchair accessible
DESCRIPTION: Comprehensive services for survivors of domestic violence; Treatment for batterers
CLIENTS/SERVICES: Marital rape/sexual abuse survivors; Child victims of sexual abuse; Adult survivors of child sexual abuse; Community education; Adolescent survivors of sexual abuse

WALNUT CREEK

CONTRA COSTA CRISIS AND SUICIDE INTERVENTION SERVICE
PO Box 4852, Walnut Creek, CA 94596
Crisis hotline: **Central Co (415) 939-3232; West Co (toll free) (415) 620-0174; East Co (toll free) (415) 754-7080 24 hrs daily**
Information: (415) 939-1916 9am-5pm (Mon-Fri)
Contact: Joan W Stern, Hotline Coord
TYPE OF AGENCY: Counseling/mental health services; Telephone crisis hotline
AREAS SERVED: Contra Costa, Alameda
YEARS IN OPERATION: 25
ACCESSIBILITY: Wheelchair accessible
CASES SEXUAL ASSAULT/ABUSE (%): 20

CONTRA COSTA CRISIS AND SUICIDE INTERVENTION SERVICE *(continued)*

DESCRIPTION: Provides telephone crisis and suicide intervention services 24 hours/day. Many callers have issues relating to physical or sexual abuse. Also receives calls from suicidal children and adults who have been abused
CLIENTS/SERVICES: Sexual assault survivors; Child victims of sexual abuse; Adult survivors of child sexual abuse; Incest victims/survivors; Male survivors of sexual abuse

WEAVERVILLE

HUMAN RESPONSE NETWORK/FAMILY CARE PROJECT
PO Box 2370, Weaverville, CA 96093
Crisis hotline: **(916) 623-HELP 24 hrs**
Information: (916) 623-2024 8am-5pm (Mon-Fri)
Contact: Linda Dickerson, Proj Dir
TYPE OF AGENCY: Domestic violence program; Counseling/mental health services; Child sexual abuse prevention program; Rape crisis program
SPONSORING ORGANIZATION: Family Crisis Line Project
AREAS SERVED: Trinity
YEARS IN OPERATION: 8
LANGUAGES: Interpreters available
ACCESSIBILITY: Wheelchair accessible; Signers for the hearing impaired
DESCRIPTION: Human Response Network provides peer counseling, support groups, and legal advocacy for victims of spouse abuse, child abuse, and rape, as well as group therapy for batterers. The Family Care Project provides support, advocacy, and counseling through home visits by paraprofessionals for families with children ages 0-14 and experiencing stress
CLIENTS/SERVICES: Sexual assault survivors; Marital rape/sexual abuse survivors; Child victims of sexual abuse; Adult survivors of child sexual abuse; Incest victims/survivors; Prevention program; Community education; Lesbians

WEST HILLS

THURSDAY'S CHILD—TEEN OUTREACH PROGRAM
24100 Hartland St, West Hills, CA 91307
Crisis hotline: **(818) 710-1181 24 hrs**
Information: (818) 712-0159 9am-5pm
Contact: Don Austen, Exec Dir
TYPE OF AGENCY: Counseling/mental health services; Telephone crisis hotline; Adolescent program
AREAS SERVED: Los Angeles, Ventura, Orange, Riverside
YEARS IN OPERATION: 6
CASES SEXUAL ASSAULT/ABUSE (%): 10
DESCRIPTION: Teen crisis services for runaways, potential runaways, and child prostitutes
CLIENTS/SERVICES: Sexual assault survivors; Child victims of sexual abuse; Incest victims/survivors; Prevention program; Runaways; Adolescent survivors of sexual abuse; Prostitutes
REQUIREMENTS: Up to 18 years of age

WESTLAKE VILLAGE

WESTOAKS PERSONAL GROWTH CENTER
2239 Townsgate Rd, Ste 107, Westlake Village, CA 91361
Information: (805) 496-3800 24-hr answering machine
Contact: Dr Barbara Farber, Dir
TYPE OF AGENCY: Private practice
AREAS SERVED: Los Angeles, Ventura
YEARS IN OPERATION: 10
LANGUAGES: Spanish
ACCESSIBILITY: Wheelchair accessible
CASES SEXUAL ASSAULT/ABUSE (%): 98
DESCRIPTION: Specializes in the treatment of sexual assault, domestic violence and the resultant post-traumatic stress symptomatology. The treatment of dissociative disorders is also provided
CLIENTS/SERVICES: Sexual assault survivors; Marital rape/sexual abuse survivors; Child victims of sexual abuse; Adult survivors of child sexual abuse; Incest victims/survivors; Community education; Adolescent survivors of sexual abuse; Male survivors of sexual abuse
REQUIREMENTS: Ability to pay for private therapy. Victim witness cases are accepted as is private insurance

WESTMINSTER

CSP SEXUAL ASSAULT VICTIM SERVICES/ PREVENTION PROGRAM
8141 13th St, Westminster, CA 92683
Crisis hotline: **(714) 957-2737 24 hrs**
Information: (714) 896-7188 8am-5pm (Mon-Fri)
TYPE OF AGENCY: Victim/witness assistance program; Child sexual abuse services; Child sexual abuse prevention program; Referral program
SPONSORING ORGANIZATION: West County Municipal Court
AREAS SERVED: Orange
YEARS IN OPERATION: 7
LANGUAGES: Spanish, Vietnamese, Japanese
ACCESSIBILITY: Wheelchair accessible; Signers for the hearing impaired
CASES SEXUAL ASSAULT/ABUSE (%): 100
CLIENTS/SERVICES: Sexual assault survivors; Marital rape/sexual abuse survivors; Child victims of sexual abuse; Adult survivors of child sexual abuse; Incest victims/survivors; Prevention program; Community education; Adolescent survivors of sexual abuse; Male survivors of sexual abuse
SPECIAL PROGRAMS/SERVICES: The Orange County Victim/Witness Assistance Program and Child Abuse Prevention Program are also components of CSP, Inc. Services are coordinated between all components of the agency to ensure that each client is afforded quality service and support

WOODLAND

CHILD SEXUAL ABUSE TREATMENT CENTER OF YOLO COUNTY
451 1st St, Woodland, CA 95695
Information: (916) 662-0943 8:30am-5pm, answering machine
Contact: Wendy Walsh, Exec Dir
TYPE OF AGENCY: Child sexual abuse services; Child sexual abuse prevention program
AREAS SERVED: Yolo
YEARS IN OPERATION: 5
LANGUAGES: Spanish
ACCESSIBILITY: Wheelchair accessible
CASES SEXUAL ASSAULT/ABUSE (%): 100
DESCRIPTION: Provides services for child victims of sexual abuse and their families, incorporating a family systems philosophy into weekly group therapy and family counseling. Individual and group therapy for child sexual abuse/incest offenders and juvenile offenders. Also provides foster parent group
CLIENTS/SERVICES: Child victims of sexual abuse; Adult survivors of child sexual abuse; Incest victims/survivors; Community education; Offender treatment program; Adolescent survivors of sexual abuse; Male survivors of sexual abuse
REQUIREMENTS: Services are provided for victims of intrafamilial child sexual abuse ages 3-18, as well as non-offending parents and selected adult and juvenile offenders. Filing charges is not a requirement for the program

YOLO COUNTY DISTRICT ATTORNEY'S OFFICE—VICTIM/WITNESS ASSISTANCE PROGRAM
PO Box 1247, Woodland, CA 95695
Information: (916) 666-8180 8am-Noon, 1pm-5pm (Mon-Fri)
Contact: Barbara Soby, Prog Coord
TYPE OF AGENCY: Victim/witness assistance program
AREAS SERVED: Yolo
YEARS IN OPERATION: 9
LANGUAGES: Spanish; translator available for Southeast Asian languages
ACCESSIBILITY: Wheelchair accessible
CASES SEXUAL ASSAULT/ABUSE (%): 50
CLIENTS/SERVICES: Sexual assault survivors; Marital rape/sexual abuse survivors; Child victims of sexual abuse; Adult survivors of child sexual abuse; Incest victims/survivors; Community education; Adolescent survivors of sexual abuse; Male survivors of sexual abuse
REQUIREMENTS: Client must make police report or be referred by word of mouth

YOLO COUNTY SEXUAL ASSAULT AND DOMESTIC VIOLENCE CENTER
933 Court St, Woodland, CA 95695
Crisis hotline: **East Yolo (916) 371-1907, Davis (916) 758-8400, Woodland (916) 662-1133 24 hrs**
Information: (916) 661-6336 9am-5pm (Mon-Fri)
Contact: Allison Alcalay, Exec Dir
TYPE OF AGENCY: Rape crisis center; Domestic violence program; Child sexual abuse prevention program
AREAS SERVED: Yolo
YEARS IN OPERATION: 11
LANGUAGES: Spanish
ACCESSIBILITY: Wheelchair accessible
CASES SEXUAL ASSAULT/ABUSE (%): 30
DESCRIPTION: Provides assistance for victims of sexual assault and domestic violence; The child/youth assault prevention program targets youth from 4 to 18 years of age; Group therapy for batterers available
CLIENTS/SERVICES: Sexual assault survivors; Marital rape/sexual abuse survivors; Child victims of sexual abuse; Adult survivors of child sexual abuse; Incest victims/survivors; Prevention program; Community education; Adolescent survivors of sexual abuse; Male survivors of sexual abuse; Ethnic minorities; Publications/media
SPECIAL PROGRAMS/SERVICES: Latina Outreach Project provides assistance for Latina women who are experiencing the related problems of alcohol and physical abuse. Counseling and support services are available in Spanish. Locally produced media program on Latina outreach

YREKA

SISKIYOU SEXUAL ASSAULT
PO Box 1679, 618 4th St, No 8, Yreka, CA 96097
Crisis hotline: **(916) 842-4068 24 hrs**
Information: (916) 842-6629 11am-4pm
Contact: Candy Janssen, Prog Dir
TYPE OF AGENCY: Rape crisis center; Domestic violence program
SPONSORING ORGANIZATION: Siskiyou Domestic Violence Program
AREAS SERVED: Siskiyou
YEARS IN OPERATION: 5
LANGUAGES: Translators available
ACCESSIBILITY: Wheelchair accessible
DESCRIPTION: Crisis counseling, support groups, legal, medical, social welfare advocacy; Shelter (safe home) for victims; Group therapy for batterers

SISKIYOU SEXUAL ASSAULT *(continued)*

CLIENTS/SERVICES: Sexual assault survivors; Marital rape/sexual abuse survivors; Prevention program; Community education; Offender treatment program; Adolescent survivors of sexual abuse

COLORADO

ARVADA

ASSOCIATES FOR SEXUAL ABUSE TREATMENT
7850 Vance, Ste 183, Arvada, CO 80003
Information: (303) 467-1616 Answering machine
Contact: John Dean, MSW, LSW II
TYPE OF AGENCY: Private practice
YEARS IN OPERATION: 8
ACCESSIBILITY: Wheelchair accessible
CASES SEXUAL ASSAULT/ABUSE (%): 100
CLIENTS/SERVICES: Sexual assault survivors; Marital rape/sexual abuse survivors; Adult survivors of child sexual abuse; Incest victims/survivors; Offender treatment program; Male survivors of sexual abuse

WOMEN IN CRISIS
PO Box 1586, Arvada, CO 80001
Crisis hotline: **(303) 420-6752 24 hrs**
Information: (303) 420-6752 24 hrs
Contact: Rita Smith, Prog Dir
TYPE OF AGENCY: Domestic violence program
SPONSORING ORGANIZATION: Family Tree, Inc
AREAS SERVED: Primarily Jefferson
YEARS IN OPERATION: 11
LANGUAGES: Spanish
ACCESSIBILITY: Wheelchair accessible; Signers for the hearing impaired (obtained as needed)
CLIENTS/SERVICES: Marital rape/sexual abuse survivors; Prevention program; Community education

ASPEN

RESPONSE
Box 1340, Aspen, CO 81612
Crisis hotline: **(303) 920-5555 24 hrs**
Information: (303) 920-5357 hrs vary
Contact: Peg McGavock, Exec Dir
TYPE OF AGENCY: Rape crisis center; Domestic violence program
AREAS SERVED: Pitkin, Eagle
YEARS IN OPERATION: 6
CASES SEXUAL ASSAULT/ABUSE (%): 1
CLIENTS/SERVICES: Sexual assault survivors; Marital rape/sexual abuse survivors; Adult survivors of child sexual abuse; Prevention program; Community education; Male survivors of sexual abuse

AURORA

AURORA COMMUNITY MENTAL HEALTH CENTER
14301 E Hampden Ave, Aurora, CO 80014
Crisis hotline: **(303) 693-9500 24 hrs**
Information: (303) 693-9500 8am-5pm
TYPE OF AGENCY: Victim/witness assistance program; Counseling/mental health services; Child sexual abuse services; Residential treatment facility
AREAS SERVED: Adams, Arapahoe, and East Aurora city limits
YEARS IN OPERATION: 13
ACCESSIBILITY: Wheelchair accessible; Telecommunications for the hearing impaired (TTY, TDY, etc.)
CLIENTS/SERVICES: Sexual assault survivors; Marital rape/sexual abuse survivors; Child victims of sexual abuse; Adult survivors of child sexual abuse; Incest victims/survivors; Adolescent survivors of sexual abuse; Male survivors of sexual abuse

FAMILIES FIRST
PO Box 14190, 2760-R S Havana Station, Aurora, CO 80014
Information: (303) 745-0327 24 hrs
TYPE OF AGENCY: Child sexual abuse services; Child sexual abuse prevention program; Child abuse services; Child abuse prevention program; Shelter
AREAS SERVED: Denver metro area
YEARS IN OPERATION: 3
LANGUAGES: Spanish
CASES SEXUAL ASSAULT/ABUSE (%): 50
DESCRIPTION: 24-hour crisis shelter. Children (ages 3-12) are admitted through the county departments of social services. Shelter provides short-term (60 days) family treatment with goal of reuniting the families if possible
CLIENTS/SERVICES: Child victims of sexual abuse; Prevention program; Community education; Preschoolers
REQUIREMENTS: Children ages 3-12; Will not admit children who are runaways, drug or alcohol involved, psychotic, assaultive, etc

BOULDER

BOULDER COUNTY RAPE CRISIS TEAM
1333 Iris Ave, Boulder, CO 80302
Crisis hotline: **(303) 443-7300 24 hrs**
Information: (303) 443-8500 9am-5pm
Contact: Vanessa Kelly, Dir
TYPE OF AGENCY: Rape crisis center
SPONSORING ORGANIZATION: Boulder County Mental Health Center
AREAS SERVED: Boulder
YEARS IN OPERATION: 16
LANGUAGES: Spanish (by arrangement)
ACCESSIBILITY: Wheelchair accessible; Signers for the hearing impaired (available by arrangement)
CASES SEXUAL ASSAULT/ABUSE (%): 100
DESCRIPTION: Comprehensive rape crisis and prevention services, including support groups for male and female survivors; Male counselors available for male survivors; Feminist martial arts/self-defense
CLIENTS/SERVICES: Sexual assault survivors; Marital rape/sexual abuse survivors; Child victims of sexual abuse; Adult survivors of child sexual abuse; Incest victims/survivors; Prevention program; Community education; Adolescent survivors of sexual abuse; Male survivors of sexual abuse; Prisoners; Healing; Publications/media
SPECIAL PROGRAMS/SERVICES: Participates in the Acquaintance Rape Task Force, which is a community effort to educate and impact prosecution of acquaintance rape. The task force includes DA's office, other victim advocates, local police departments throughout the county, school officials (junior high through university level), fraternities, sororities, among other groups. Media program: *From Victim to Survivor,* video on the healing process. Healing for adult survivors includes self-defense training and work with Outward Bound for wilderness therapy

BOULDER COUNTY SAFEHOUSE
PO Box 4157, Boulder, CO 80306
Crisis hotline: **(303) 449-8623 24 hrs**
Information: (303) 449-6190 9am-5pm (Mon-Fri)
Contact: Barbara Paradiso, Exec Dir
TYPE OF AGENCY: Domestic violence program; Adolescent program
AREAS SERVED: Boulder
YEARS IN OPERATION: 9
LANGUAGES: Spanish
ACCESSIBILITY: Wheelchair accessible; Signers for the hearing impaired
CASES SEXUAL ASSAULT/ABUSE (%): 24
CLIENTS/SERVICES: Marital rape/sexual abuse survivors; Adult survivors of child sexual abuse; Prevention program; Community education; Adolescent survivors of sexual abuse
SPECIAL PROGRAMS/SERVICES: Date violence prevention curriculum

BOULDER COUNTY SEXUAL ABUSE TEAM
3400 Broadway, Boulder, CO 80302
Crisis hotline: **(303) 441-1249 24 hrs**
Information: (303) 441-1102 8am-4:30pm
Contact: Holly Smith, Supv
TYPE OF AGENCY: Counseling/mental health services; Child sexual abuse services
AREAS SERVED: Boulder
YEARS IN OPERATION: 10
LANGUAGES: Spanish
ACCESSIBILITY: Wheelchair accessible
CASES SEXUAL ASSAULT/ABUSE (%): 100
DESCRIPTION: Provides investigation and treatment of sex abuse (intrafamily) cases; Parents United and Daughters United groups; WMAC groups; Victim-offenders program for adolescent sex offenders; Individual, group, and family therapy for child sexual abuse offenders and incest offenders

BOULDER COUNTY SEXUAL ABUSE TEAM *(continued)*

CLIENTS/SERVICES: Sexual assault survivors; Child victims of sexual abuse; Adult survivors of child sexual abuse; Incest victims/survivors; Community education; Offender treatment program; Adolescent survivors of sexual abuse; Male survivors of sexual abuse
REQUIREMENTS: Case must be open to department of social services; Admission of offense by perpetrator is required for group therapy.

BOULDER DISTRICT ATTORNEY'S OFFICE—VICTIM/WITNESS ASSISTANCE PROGRAM

PO Box 471, Boulder, CO 80303
Information: (303) 441-3730 8am-5pm (Mon-Fri)
Contact: Barbara Kendall, Dir
TYPE OF AGENCY: Victim/witness assistance program
AREAS SERVED: Boulder
YEARS IN OPERATION: 11½
LANGUAGES: Spanish
CASES SEXUAL ASSAULT/ABUSE (%): 10
CLIENTS/SERVICES: Sexual assault survivors; Marital rape/sexual abuse survivors; Child victims of sexual abuse; Incest victims/survivors; Community education; Adolescent survivors of sexual abuse
REQUIREMENTS: Victim must report to law enforcement agency.

BRIGHTON

DISTRICT ATTORNEY'S OFFICE—VICTIM WITNESS ASSISTANCE UNIT

450 S 4th Ave, Brighton, CO 80601
Information: Administration (303) 659-7720, Courthouse 659-7735 8am-5pm (Mon-Fri)
Contact: Kate Murphy, Victim Witness Coord
TYPE OF AGENCY: Victim/witness assistance program
SPONSORING ORGANIZATION: 17th Judicial District
AREAS SERVED: Adams
YEARS IN OPERATION: 10
LANGUAGES: Spanish
ACCESSIBILITY: Wheelchair accessible; Signers for the hearing impaired
CASES SEXUAL ASSAULT/ABUSE (%): Child 8, adult 2
CLIENTS/SERVICES: Sexual assault survivors; Marital rape/sexual abuse survivors; Child victims of sexual abuse; Community education
REQUIREMENTS: Criminal charges must be filed with and accepted by the District Attorney's office; For assistance with victim compensation, an offense report filed with an Adam's County law enforcement agency is required.

BUENA VISTA

COLORADO DEPARTMENT OF CORRECTIONS

Box R, Buena Vista, CO 81211
Contact: Peggy Herl, MSW, Dir
TYPE OF AGENCY: Correctional facility; Offender treatment
YEARS IN OPERATION: 6
CASES SEXUAL ASSAULT/ABUSE (%): 100
CLIENTS/SERVICES: Adult survivors of child sexual abuse; Offender treatment program; Male survivors of sexual abuse
REQUIREMENTS: Each member must admit committing a sexual offense; Member must feel offense indicates a problem in his life

CANON CITY

FAMILY CRISIS SERVICES

PO Box 308, Canon City, CO 81212
Crisis hotline: **(719) 275-2429 24 hrs**
Information: (719) 275-2429 9am-5pm (Mon-Fri)
Contact: Theodora Barychewsky, Dir
TYPE OF AGENCY: Rape crisis center; Domestic violence program; Child sexual abuse services; Child sexual abuse prevention program
AREAS SERVED: Fremont and Custer
YEARS IN OPERATION: 7
CASES SEXUAL ASSAULT/ABUSE (%): 50
CLIENTS/SERVICES: Sexual assault survivors; Marital rape/sexual abuse survivors; Child victims of sexual abuse; Adult survivors of child sexual abuse; Incest victims/survivors; Prevention program; Community education; Adolescent survivors of sexual abuse; Male survivors of sexual abuse

CASTLE ROCK

DOUGLAS COUNTY SHERIFF VICTIM ASSISTANCE

355 S Wilcox St, Castle Rock, CO 80104
Crisis hotline: **Dispatch (303) 660-7500 24 hrs**
Information: (303) 660-7538 8am-4:30pm (Mon-Fri)
Contact: Patty Moschner, Victim Assistance Coord
TYPE OF AGENCY: Victim/witness assistance program
AREAS SERVED: Douglas, Elbert
YEARS IN OPERATION: 5
CASES SEXUAL ASSAULT/ABUSE (%): 9
CLIENTS/SERVICES: Sexual assault survivors; Marital rape/sexual abuse survivors; Child victims of sexual abuse; Incest victims/survivors; Prevention program; Community education
REQUIREMENTS: Must make report of crime

COLORADO SPRINGS

ASSOCIATES FOR PSYCHOTHERAPY AND EDUCATION

928 N Weber, Colorado Springs, CO 80903
Information: (719) 630-1182 9am-6pm
Contact: Beth Brown Walker, Psychotherapist
TYPE OF AGENCY: Child sexual abuse services; Private practice
AREAS SERVED: El Paso, Pueblo, Fremont
YEARS IN OPERATION: 15
LANGUAGES: Spanish
ACCESSIBILITY: Wheelchair accessible
CASES SEXUAL ASSAULT/ABUSE (%): 10-15
DESCRIPTION: Counseling for victims/survivors, as well as child sexual abuse/incest offenders and batterers
CLIENTS/SERVICES: Sexual assault survivors; Marital rape/sexual abuse survivors; Child victims of sexual abuse; Adult survivors of child sexual abuse; Incest victims/survivors; Adolescent survivors of sexual abuse; Male survivors of sexual abuse; Healing; Publications/media
REQUIREMENTS: Ability to pay for services
SPECIAL PROGRAMS/SERVICES: Media program: slide presentation on sexual abuse which includes statistics, research, symptoms, treatment and recovery criteria. Art therapy in work with adult survivors of sexual assault and child sexual abuse

DISTRICT ATTORNEY'S OFFICE—CHILDREN'S ADVOCACY CENTER

326 S Tejon St, Colorado Springs, CO 80903
Crisis hotline: **(719) 520-6168 8am-5pm (Mon-Fri)**
Information: (719) 520-6168 8am-5pm (Mon-Fri)
Contact: Rebecca Stocker, DA Office Mgr; Cheryl Mustian, Adm Asst
TYPE OF AGENCY: Victim/witness assistance program; Child sexual abuse services; Child abuse services
SPONSORING ORGANIZATION: 4th Judicial District
AREAS SERVED: El Paso and Teller
YEARS IN OPERATION: ½
LANGUAGES: Spanish
ACCESSIBILITY: Signers for the hearing impaired (on request)
CASES SEXUAL ASSAULT/ABUSE (%): 100
DESCRIPTION: Child-oriented facility set up to centralize the investigative function in child sexual abuse cases. There are two interview rooms with one-way mirrors and video tape equipment, as well as play room. By centralizing the initial joint interview between the Department of Social Services and law enforcement, multiple interviews are decreased and trauma to the victim lessened.
CLIENTS/SERVICES: Child victims of sexual abuse; Incest victims/survivors; Community education
REQUIREMENTS: Any child reported to have been sexually or physically abused is eligible to be interviewed at the Advocacy Center.

DOMESTIC VIOLENCE PREVENTION CENTER

PO Box 2662, Colorado Springs, CO 80901
Crisis hotline: **(719) 633-3819 24 hrs daily**
Information: (719) 633-1462 8:30am-5pm (Mon-Fri)
Contact: Pat Kreuser, Act Dir
TYPE OF AGENCY: Domestic violence program
AREAS SERVED: El Paso, Teller
YEARS IN OPERATION: 11
LANGUAGES: Spanish
ACCESSIBILITY: Wheelchair accessible
CASES SEXUAL ASSAULT/ABUSE (%): 30
DESCRIPTION: Provides crisis intervention, temporary emergency shelter, and individual and support group counseling for battered women and their children; MOVE (Men Overcoming Violent Encounters) provides educational and counseling services and support groups to help men deal with violent behavior
CLIENTS/SERVICES: Marital rape/sexual abuse survivors; Child victims of sexual abuse; Adult survivors of child sexual abuse; Prevention program; Community education

THE LEARNING AND COUNSELING CENTER

825 N Weber, Colorado Springs, CO 80903
Crisis hotline: **(719) 471-7837 24 hrs**
Information: (719) 471-7837 8am-6pm
Contact: Stephen Witty, PhD, Dir
TYPE OF AGENCY: Child sexual abuse services; Private practice; Offender treatment
AREAS SERVED: El Paso, Teller
YEARS IN OPERATION: 6
ACCESSIBILITY: Wheelchair accessible
CASES SEXUAL ASSAULT/ABUSE (%): 40
DESCRIPTION: Counseling and psychological services, specializing in treatment of victims/survivors and adolescent sex offenders and child sexual abuse/incest offenders
CLIENTS/SERVICES: Sexual assault survivors; Child victims of sexual abuse; Adult survivors of child sexual abuse; Incest victims/survivors; Offender treatment program; Adolescent survivors of sexual abuse; Male survivors of sexual abuse
REQUIREMENTS: For perpetrators: full admission; evaluated as treatable

MARRIAGE AND FAMILY TREATMENT CENTER

322 N Tejon, Ste 204, Colorado Springs, CO 80903
Crisis hotline: **(719) 520-1711 24 hrs**
Information: (719) 520-1711 24 hrs
Contact: Bob Williams, PhD, Managing Partner
TYPE OF AGENCY: Child sexual abuse services; Private practice
AREAS SERVED: Statewide
YEARS IN OPERATION: 6
CASES SEXUAL ASSAULT/ABUSE (%): 75
DESCRIPTION: Counseling for survivors; Co-dependency and co-addiction issues; Sexual addiction counseling; Individual and group ther-

MARRIAGE AND FAMILY TREATMENT CENTER *(continued)*

apy for child sexual abuse offenders, incest offenders, and batterers
CLIENTS/SERVICES: Marital rape/sexual abuse survivors; Child victims of sexual abuse; Adult survivors of child sexual abuse; Incest victims/survivors; Prevention program; Community education; Offender treatment program; Adolescent survivors of sexual abuse; Male survivors of sexual abuse

YOUTH/VICTIM SERVICES
105 E Vermijo, Colorado Springs, CO 80910
Crisis hotline: **(719) 632-6611 24 hrs**
Information: (719) 578-6704 8am-5pm (Mon-Fri)
Contact: Patricia Wyka, Dir
TYPE OF AGENCY: Victim/witness assistance program; Child sexual abuse services; Adolescent program
SPONSORING ORGANIZATION: Colorado Springs Police Department
AREAS SERVED: El Paso, limited to Teller
YEARS IN OPERATION: 13
LANGUAGES: Interpreters available
ACCESSIBILITY: Wheelchair accessible; Signers for the hearing impaired
CASES SEXUAL ASSAULT/ABUSE (%): 95
CLIENTS/SERVICES: Sexual assault survivors; Marital rape/sexual abuse survivors; Child victims of sexual abuse; Adult survivors of child sexual abuse; Incest victims/survivors; Prevention program; Community education; Adolescent survivors of sexual abuse; Male survivors of sexual abuse
SPECIAL PROGRAMS/SERVICES: The programs include STOP Incest Treatment Program monitored by an interagency team; Juvenile Sex Offenders Program (same model as adult program, but not limited to incest); and Children's Advocacy Center with videotaping. Staff members have mental health backgrounds and are a part of the front-line, immediate response to all sexual assault victims. Contact is maintained throughout the criminal justice process, from initial report through court disposition. This organization also trains all CSPD officers in the area of sexual assault, both child and adult.

CORTEZ

DISTRICT ATTORNEY'S OFFICE—VICTIM/WITNESS ASSISTANCE UNIT
PO Box 912, Cortez, CO 81321
Information: (303) 565-1147 8am-12pm (Mon-Fri)
Contact: Lu Millican, Coord
TYPE OF AGENCY: Victim/witness assistance program
SPONSORING ORGANIZATION: 22nd Judicial District
AREAS SERVED: Montezuma and Dolores
YEARS IN OPERATION: 3
ACCESSIBILITY: Wheelchair accessible
CASES SEXUAL ASSAULT/ABUSE (%): 25
CLIENTS/SERVICES: Sexual assault survivors; Marital rape/sexual abuse survivors; Child victims of sexual abuse; Adolescent survivors of sexual abuse

CRAIG

ABUSED AND BATTERED HUMANS, INC
PO Box 1050, Craig, CO 81626
Crisis hotline: **(303) 824-2400 24 hrs**
Information: (303) 824-9709 9am-2pm (Mon-Thu)
Contact: Sue Pickering, Office Mgr
TYPE OF AGENCY: Rape crisis center; Domestic violence program
AREAS SERVED: Moffat
YEARS IN OPERATION: 8
CLIENTS/SERVICES: Sexual assault survivors; Community education

DENVER

COLORADO OUTWARD BOUND SCHOOL
945 Pennsylvania St, Denver, CO 80203
Information: (303) 837-0880 8:30am-5pm
Contact: Penny Brodeur, Prog Dir
TYPE OF AGENCY: Counseling/mental health services; Wilderness program
AREAS SERVED: National
YEARS IN OPERATION: 25
CASES SEXUAL ASSAULT/ABUSE (%): 20
DESCRIPTION: Through the health services program at COBS, victims of sexual assault, incest, and domestic violence participate in a therapeutic wilderness program. Therapy time may be reduced by up to 6 months by participating in this 3-day experience. Wilderness therapy also provided for batterers
CLIENTS/SERVICES: Sexual assault survivors; Marital rape/sexual abuse survivors; Child victims of sexual abuse; Adult survivors of child sexual abuse; Incest victims/survivors; Offender treatment program; Adolescent survivors of sexual abuse; Male survivors of sexual abuse
REQUIREMENTS: Participants must either be in ongoing therapy or have completed their therapy for the victimization.
SPECIAL PROGRAMS/SERVICES: The Victims of Violence Recovery Program, under the auspices of the Health Services Program at COBS, provides wilderness therapy programs for victims of sexual assault, incest and domestic violence. Clients may participate either through their ongoing support/therapy agency or the Empowerment Program for Women. The Empowerment Program is a 4-day course for women who are transitioning out of therapy. Professional development seminars for victim service professionals is offered twice a year. This is a 3-day wilderness experience which focuses on issues of team building, communication, support, and networking. Four times a year an empowerment course for any woman, survivor or not, interested in a 4-day course emphasizing issues of empowerment, ie power, trust, and support

DENVER DISTRICT ATTORNEY—DOMESTIC VIOLENCE UNIT
303 W Colfax, No 1200, Denver, CO 80204
Information: (303) 575-5822 8:30am-5pm
Contact: Christine Agosta, Victim Advocate
TYPE OF AGENCY: Domestic violence program; Victim/witness assistance program; Child abuse services
AREAS SERVED: Denver
LANGUAGES: Spanish
ACCESSIBILITY: Wheelchair accessible
CASES SEXUAL ASSAULT/ABUSE (%): 20
DESCRIPTION: This unit works with all filed child or spousal abuse cases in Denver.
CLIENTS/SERVICES: Sexual assault survivors; Child victims of sexual abuse; Adult survivors of child sexual abuse; Incest victims/survivors
REQUIREMENTS: The case must be accepted by the District Attorney's office.

DENVER GENERAL HOSPITAL—SEXUAL ASSAULT VICTIM ADVOCATE PROGRAM
777 Bannock St, Denver, CO 80204
Information: (303) 893-6000 8am-4pm (Mon-Fri)
Contact: Linda Lenander, Clinical Soc Wkr
TYPE OF AGENCY: Hospital/medical center
AREAS SERVED: Denver
YEARS IN OPERATION: 14
ACCESSIBILITY: Wheelchair accessible; Telecommunications for the hearing impaired (TTY, TDY, etc.); Signers for the hearing impaired
DESCRIPTION: Provides medical treatment, collection of evidence and crisis counseling for victims of sexual assault on a 24-hour basis
CLIENTS/SERVICES: Sexual assault survivors; Marital rape/sexual abuse survivors; Child victims of sexual abuse; Incest victims/survivors; Community education; Adolescent survivors of sexual abuse; Male survivors of sexual abuse

ENDING VIOLENCE EFFECTIVELY
PO Box 18212, Denver, CO 80218
Information: (303) 322-7010 Noon-4pm, 24-hr answering service
Contact: Tamara Guyton and Mary Lewis, Office Assts
TYPE OF AGENCY: Private practice
AREAS SERVED: Statewide
YEARS IN OPERATION: 8
ACCESSIBILITY: Telecommunications for the hearing impaired (TTY, TDY, etc.)
CASES SEXUAL ASSAULT/ABUSE (%): 99
DESCRIPTION: Provides individual, group, couples, family therapy for survivors of sexual assault and their families; Support groups for male survivors of child sexual abuse; Long-term counseling for male survivors of rape; Parenting classes
CLIENTS/SERVICES: Sexual assault survivors; Marital rape/sexual abuse survivors; Child victims of sexual abuse; Adult survivors of child sexual abuse; Incest victims/survivors; Prevention program; Community education; Adolescent survivors of sexual abuse; Male survivors of sexual abuse; Healing
SPECIAL PROGRAMS/SERVICES: Wilderness therapy; Self-defense classes; Some ritual and body work

FAMILY FOCUS, INC.
1649 Downing St, Denver, CO 80218
Information: (303) 860-0023 8am-4:30pm (Mon-Fri)
Contact: Linda S Puckett, Deputy Dir
TYPE OF AGENCY: Counseling/mental health services; Child advocacy
AREAS SERVED: Denver, Arapahoe, Adams, Jefferson
YEARS IN OPERATION: 13
CASES SEXUAL ASSAULT/ABUSE (%): 90
DESCRIPTION: Provides prevention, treatment, advocacy services for families at risk of physical abuse/neglect, emotional abuse/neglect, and sexual abuse; Provides home-based parent-aide and child-aide services; Court appointed special advocates program monitors cases of children involved in the juvenile legal system
CLIENTS/SERVICES: Marital rape/sexual abuse survivors; Child victims of sexual abuse; Adult survivors of child sexual abuse; Incest victims/survivors; Community education; Developmentally disabled; Prostitutes; Publications/media
REQUIREMENTS: Families with children ages birth to 12 who are at risk of, or have experienced, physical abuse/neglect, emotional abuse/neglect, or sexual abuse.
SPECIAL PROGRAMS/SERVICES: Publications: *Training Volunteers in the Field of Child Abuse and Neglect* ($25) and *Managing Volunteers in the Field of Child Abuse and Neglect* ($25)

GAY AND LESBIAN COMMUNITY CENTER OF COLORADO, INC
PO Drawer E, Denver, CO 80218
Crisis hotline: **(303) 837-1598 10am-10pm**
Information: (303) 831-6268 10am-10pm
Contact: Sue Ware, Exec Dir
TYPE OF AGENCY: Counseling/mental health services; Information and referral; Telephone crisis hotline
AREAS SERVED: Denver, Arapahoe, Jefferson, Elbert, Douglas, Adams
YEARS IN OPERATION: 10
LANGUAGES: Spanish

GAY AND LESBIAN COMMUNITY CENTER OF COLORADO, INC *(continued)*
CLIENTS/SERVICES: Sexual assault survivors; Adult survivors of child sexual abuse; Incest victims/survivors; Prevention program; Community education; Adolescent survivors of sexual abuse; Male survivors of sexual abuse; Lesbians; Gay men; Healing
SPECIAL PROGRAMS/SERVICES: Groups on crystal healing, alternatives to traditional medical practice, self-defense, support groups, speaker's bureau, and involvement with volunteers through training on crisis lines and suicide prevention

PEOPLE RESEARCH
3035 Quitman, Denver, CO 80212-1416
Information: (303) 433-6130 8am-6pm, evening appointments
Contact: Jami Powell, MA, Counseling and Psychology
TYPE OF AGENCY: Private practice
YEARS IN OPERATION: 2
CASES SEXUAL ASSAULT/ABUSE (%): 100
CLIENTS/SERVICES: Adult survivors of child sexual abuse; Incest victims/survivors; Publications/media
REQUIREMENTS: Sliding scale fee
SPECIAL PROGRAMS/SERVICES: *Women Recovering From Incestuous Assault*, 60-minute video focuses on four women who speak with strength and simplicity about their adult experiences of denying, then facing and recovering from incestuous assault, ($35)

PROJECT PROMOTING ALTERNATIVES TO VIOLENCE THROUGH EDUCATION (PAVE), INC
1245 E Colfax, Ste 312, Denver, CO 80218
Crisis hotline: **(303) 832-5228 9am-6pm; answering machine after hrs**
Information: (303) 832-5228 9am-6pm (Mon-Fri)
Contact: Linda Fischer, Prog and Svcs Dir
TYPE OF AGENCY: Child sexual abuse services; Child sexual abuse prevention program; Acquaintance/date rape prevention program; Adolescent program
AREAS SERVED: Denver, Arapahoe, Jefferson, Adams
YEARS IN OPERATION: 3½
ACCESSIBILITY: Wheelchair accessible; Signers for the hearing impaired
CASES SEXUAL ASSAULT/ABUSE (%): 85
DESCRIPTION: Educational programs on relationship violence, including teen dating violence, incest, and date rape; Individual and group counseling for victims of physical or sexual relationship violence; Adolescent sex offender and parents programs
CLIENTS/SERVICES: Sexual assault survivors; Child victims of sexual abuse; Incest victims/survivors; Prevention program; Community education; Offender treatment program; Adolescent survivors of sexual abuse; Male survivors of sexual abuse
REQUIREMENTS: Victims between the ages of 11-19; Offenders between the ages of 11-21
SPECIAL PROGRAMS/SERVICES: Community-based education and counseling programs for schools, group homes, juvenile detention centers, medical centers, etc. Provides "big brother," "big sister" and advocate/friend programs for youth. The youth who successfully complete the program are asked to "adopt" younger youth to provide them with support and mentoring. The youth, especially offenders, are asked to participate in community education programs against violence with other youth and adults. They speak out, make videos, sit on panels, provide peer counseling for groups, etc.

RAPE ASSISTANCE AND AWARENESS PROGRAM
Box 112, 640 Broadway, Denver, CO 80203
Information: (303) 329-9922
Contact: Anne Byrne, Dir
TYPE OF AGENCY: Rape crisis center
CLIENTS/SERVICES: Sexual assault survivors

SERVICIOS DE LA RAZA, INC
4055 Tejon St, Denver, CO 80211
Information: (303) 458-5851 8am-5pm
Contact: Jose Mondragon, Exec Dir
TYPE OF AGENCY: Victim/witness assistance program; Counseling/mental health services; Child sexual abuse services
AREAS SERVED: Denver
LANGUAGES: Spanish
CASES SEXUAL ASSAULT/ABUSE (%): 9
DESCRIPTION: Specialty clinic for the Hispanic community of Denver; Culturally relevant services are provided by bilingual bicultural staff using holistic approach. A child/family therapist of the mental health component deals with child sexual abuse cases
CLIENTS/SERVICES: Child victims of sexual abuse; Adult survivors of child sexual abuse; Incest victims/survivors; Community education; Adolescent survivors of sexual abuse; Male survivors of sexual abuse
REQUIREMENTS: Child and adolescent (0-17) victims of sexual abuse and their families; Perpetrators must plead guilty and accept responsibility for his/her crime

DURANGO

RAPE INTERVENTION TEAM, INC
PO Box 2723, Durango, CO 81302
Crisis hotline: **(303) 247-5400 24 hrs 7 days**
Information: (303) 247-4311, ext 257 8am-5pm (Mon-Fri)
Contact: Clare Graham, Coord
TYPE OF AGENCY: Rape crisis center; Hospital/medical center
SPONSORING ORGANIZATION: Mercy Medical Center
AREAS SERVED: La Plata, Archuleta, San Juan, Montezuma
YEARS IN OPERATION: 10
LANGUAGES: Spanish
ACCESSIBILITY: Wheelchair accessible
CASES SEXUAL ASSAULT/ABUSE (%): 99
CLIENTS/SERVICES: Sexual assault survivors; Marital rape/sexual abuse survivors; Adult survivors of child sexual abuse; Incest victims/survivors; Prevention program; Community education

ENGLEWOOD

DISTRICT ATTORNEY'S OFFICE—VICTIM/WITNESS ASSISTANCE
7325 S Potomac St, Ste 241, Englewood, CO 80112
Information: (303) 799-1310 8am-5pm (Mon-Fri)
Contact: Shar Halford, Victim Witness Coord
TYPE OF AGENCY: Victim/witness assistance program
SPONSORING ORGANIZATION: 18th Judicial District
AREAS SERVED: Arapahoe, Douglas, Lincoln, Elbert
YEARS IN OPERATION: 10
LANGUAGES: Interpreter services arranged as needed
ACCESSIBILITY: Wheelchair accessible; Signers for the hearing impaired
CLIENTS/SERVICES: Sexual assault survivors; Marital rape/sexual abuse survivors; Child victims of sexual abuse; Adult survivors of child sexual abuse; Incest victims/survivors; Community education; Adolescent survivors of sexual abuse
REQUIREMENTS: Victim must report to police agency in order to be eligible for victim compensation funds; Most services are provided in cases in which charges are accepted for filing by the District Attorney.

EVERGREEN

VICTIM OUTREACH INFORMATION
PO Box 20245, Evergreen, CO 80439
Crisis hotline: **(303) 674-9769 24 hrs**
Information: (303) 674-9769 24 hrs
Contact: Maryellen Jagel, Exec Dir
TYPE OF AGENCY: Victim/witness assistance program
AREAS SERVED: Jefferson
YEARS IN OPERATION: 2
LANGUAGES: Interpreters available as needed
CASES SEXUAL ASSAULT/ABUSE (%): 20
CLIENTS/SERVICES: Sexual assault survivors; Marital rape/sexual abuse survivors; Child victims of sexual abuse; Adult survivors of child sexual abuse; Incest victims/survivors; Community education

FORT COLLINS

CHILD SAFE
1006 Robertson, Ste 101A, Fort Collins, CO 80524
Information: (303) 221-2582 answering machine
Contact: Michael Kehl, Dir
TYPE OF AGENCY: Child sexual abuse services; Private practice
AREAS SERVED: Larimer and surrounding
YEARS IN OPERATION: 4
ACCESSIBILITY: Wheelchair accessible
CASES SEXUAL ASSAULT/ABUSE (%): 95
DESCRIPTION: Services include: Child Sexual Abuse Treatment Program for child or adolescent incest victims, family members, and the abusive parent; Adult Victims of Child Sexual Abuse Program; Sexual Offense Specific Rehabilitation Program for adults who have sexually molested a child; Project for Healthy Adolescent Sexual Expression (PHASE) for sexually inappropriate and abusive adolescents
CLIENTS/SERVICES: Child victims of sexual abuse; Adult survivors of child sexual abuse; Incest victims/survivors; Community education; Offender treatment program; Adolescent survivors of sexual abuse; Male survivors of sexual abuse

CROSSROADS SAFEHOUSE FOR BATTERED WOMEN AND THEIR CHILDREN
PO Box 993, Fort Collins, CO 80522
Crisis hotline: **(303) 493-3888 24 hrs**
Information: (303) 482-3502 9am-5pm
Contact: Barbara Chase, Dir
TYPE OF AGENCY: Domestic violence program
AREAS SERVED: Larimer
YEARS IN OPERATION: 9
ACCESSIBILITY: Wheelchair accessible
CASES SEXUAL ASSAULT/ABUSE (%): 20
CLIENTS/SERVICES: Sexual assault survivors; Marital rape/sexual abuse survivors; Child victims of sexual abuse; Adult survivors of child sexual abuse; Incest victims/survivors; Prevention program; Community education

THE JACOB CENTER, INC
420 S Howes, Ste 101, Fort Collins, CO 80521
Information: (303) 484-8427 9am-5pm (Mon-Fri); 24-hr emergency answering service
Contact: Ardith Ervin, Soc Wkr
TYPE OF AGENCY: Counseling/mental health services; Adolescent program; Offender treatment
AREAS SERVED: Larimer
YEARS IN OPERATION: 1
ACCESSIBILITY: Wheelchair accessible
CASES SEXUAL ASSAULT/ABUSE (%): 20
DESCRIPTION: Private youth and family treatment center using individual, group, and family treatment modalities and specializing in

THE JACOB CENTER, INC (continued)
adolescent services. PHASE (Project for Healthy Adolescent Sexual Expression) is a treatment program for adolescent sexual abuse victim-perpetrators (those with a history of victimization who in turn have become perpetrators). Also sponsors sexuality groups for adolescents who have been sexually victimized
CLIENTS/SERVICES: Marital rape/sexual abuse survivors; Child victims of sexual abuse; Adult survivors of child sexual abuse; Incest victims/survivors; Offender treatment program; Adolescent survivors of sexual abuse; Male survivors of sexual abuse

LARIMER COUNTY ADVOCATES FOR VICTIMS OF SEXUAL ASSAULT
PO Box 1190, Fort Collins, CO 80524
Crisis hotline: **(303) 221-7141 24 hrs**
Information: (303) 221-7610 8am-5pm
Contact: Joan Hopkins, Coord
TYPE OF AGENCY: Rape crisis center; Child sexual abuse services; Child sexual abuse prevention program
SPONSORING ORGANIZATION: Larimer County Mental Health
AREAS SERVED: Larimer
YEARS IN OPERATION: 10
LANGUAGES: Spanish
ACCESSIBILITY: Wheelchair accessible; Signers for the hearing impaired
CASES SEXUAL ASSAULT/ABUSE (%): 100
DESCRIPTION: Provides crisis intervention and ongoing therapy; Free medical screening for VD and AIDS; Individual and group therapy for rapists, child sexual abuse offenders, incest offenders, and batterers
CLIENTS/SERVICES: Sexual assault survivors; Marital rape/sexual abuse survivors; Child victims of sexual abuse; Adult survivors of child sexual abuse; Incest victims/survivors; Prevention program; Community education; Offender treatment program; Adolescent survivors of sexual abuse

LARIMER COUNTY CHILD SEXUAL ABUSE TREATMENT PROGRAM
1006 Robertson, Fort Collins, CO 80524
Information: Mike Kehl, MSW, (303) 221-2582; Kandy Moore, MS, (303) 493-8006 24 hr answering service
Contact: Mike Kehl, MSW, Offender Treatment Coord; Kandy C Moore, MS, Victim Treatment Coord
TYPE OF AGENCY: Child sexual abuse services; Child sexual abuse prevention program; Private practice
AREAS SERVED: Larimer
YEARS IN OPERATION: 3
CASES SEXUAL ASSAULT/ABUSE (%): 90
DESCRIPTION: Counseling for sexually abused children and their families; Individual and group therapy for child sexual abuse offenders and incest offenders; Support groups for female and male survivors of sexual abuse/assault
CLIENTS/SERVICES: Child victims of sexual abuse; Adult survivors of child sexual abuse; Incest victims/survivors; Prevention program; Community education; Offender treatment program; Adolescent survivors of sexual abuse; Male survivors of sexual abuse
REQUIREMENTS: Offenders must admit to the offense.

ROADHOUSE CRISIS AND INFORMATION
Colorado State University, Fort Collins, CO 80523
Crisis hotline: **(303) 491-5744 5pm-8am**
Information: (303) 491-5744 5pm-8am
Contact: Lisa Drees, Management Para-pro
TYPE OF AGENCY: College/university-based services; Counseling/mental health services; Telephone crisis hotline; Information and referrals
AREAS SERVED: Larimer
YEARS IN OPERATION: 17
CASES SEXUAL ASSAULT/ABUSE (%): 1
DESCRIPTION: Crisis information line on CSU campus, run by students. Handles all calls, some of which may be about sexual assault
CLIENTS/SERVICES: Sexual assault survivors; Marital rape/sexual abuse survivors; Adult survivors of child sexual abuse; Incest victims/survivors

VICTIM ASSISTANCE TEAM
112 Student Services Building, Fort Collins, CO 80526
Crisis hotline: **(303) 491-7111 24 hrs**
Information: (303) 491-6384
Contact: Karen J Wedge, Dir
TYPE OF AGENCY: College/university-based services
SPONSORING ORGANIZATION: Colorado State University—Office of Women's Programs and Studies
AREAS SERVED: The campus community
YEARS IN OPERATION: 10
LANGUAGES: Spanish
ACCESSIBILITY: Wheelchair accessible; Telecommunications for the hearing impaired (TTY, TDY, etc.); Signers for the hearing impaired
CLIENTS/SERVICES: Sexual assault survivors; Marital rape/sexual abuse survivors; Child victims of sexual abuse; Adult survivors of child sexual abuse; Incest victims/survivors; Prevention program; Community education
REQUIREMENTS: Client must be a student, faculty or staff member, or a visitor.

FORT MORGAN

VICTIMS COMPENSATION COORDINATOR
PO Box 1337, Fort Morgan, CO 80701
Information: (303) 867-9413 9am-4:30pm
Contact: Paula D Bragg, Victims Comp Coord
TYPE OF AGENCY: Victim/witness assistance program
SPONSORING ORGANIZATION: District Attorney's Office
AREAS SERVED: Morgan, Washington, Yuma, Kit Carson, Logan, Sedgewick, Phillips
YEARS IN OPERATION: 7
ACCESSIBILITY: Wheelchair accessible
CASES SEXUAL ASSAULT/ABUSE (%): 70
CLIENTS/SERVICES: Sexual assault survivors; Marital rape/sexual abuse survivors; Child victims of sexual abuse; Adult survivors of child sexual abuse; Incest victims/survivors; Community education
REQUIREMENTS: The perpetrator cannot remain in the home if spouse or guardian.

FRISCO

ADVOCATES FOR VICTIMS OF ASSAULT
PO Box 1859, Frisco, CO 80443
Crisis hotline: **(303) 668-3906 24 hrs**
Information: (303) 668-3906 8am-5pm (Mon-Fri)
Contact: Susan Manganiello, Dir
TYPE OF AGENCY: Rape crisis center; Domestic violence program
AREAS SERVED: Summit
YEARS IN OPERATION: 10
ACCESSIBILITY: Wheelchair accessible
DESCRIPTION: Services for victims/survivors of sexual assault and domestic violence; Provides batterers group
CLIENTS/SERVICES: Sexual assault survivors; Marital rape/sexual abuse survivors; Child victims of sexual abuse; Adult survivors of child sexual abuse; Incest victims/survivors; Prevention program; Community education; Adolescent survivors of sexual abuse; Male survivors of sexual abuse

GLENWOOD SPRINGS

CHILD AND FAMILY COUNSELING CENTER
410 20th St, Ste 104, Glenwood Springs, CO 81601
Information: (303) 945-9841 9am-6pm
Contact: Debbie McKenna, Child Development Svcs; Mary Williams, Psychiatric Nurse; Susan Maisch, MSW
TYPE OF AGENCY: Private practice
AREAS SERVED: Garfield, Eagle, Pitkin
YEARS IN OPERATION: 8
ACCESSIBILITY: Wheelchair accessible
CASES SEXUAL ASSAULT/ABUSE (%): 30
DESCRIPTION: Offers psychological evaluations and individual and group therapy for adults, families, and children. Many clients are adults molested as children or children who have been sexually molested
CLIENTS/SERVICES: Sexual assault survivors; Marital rape/sexual abuse survivors; Child victims of sexual abuse; Adult survivors of child sexual abuse; Incest victims/survivors; Community education; Adolescent survivors of sexual abuse; Male survivors of sexual abuse

SOPRIS MENTAL HEALTH CLINIC
PO Box 955, Glenwood Springs, CO 81602
Crisis hotline: **(303) 945-2583 24 hrs**
Information: (303) 945-2583 9am-5pm (Mon-Fri)
Contact: Carol Kramer, Prog Dir
TYPE OF AGENCY: Counseling/mental health services; Child sexual abuse services
SPONSORING ORGANIZATION: Colorado West Regional Mental Health Center
AREAS SERVED: Garfield
YEARS IN OPERATION: 13
ACCESSIBILITY: Wheelchair accessible
CLIENTS/SERVICES: Sexual assault survivors; Marital rape/sexual abuse survivors; Child victims of sexual abuse; Adult survivors of child sexual abuse; Incest victims/survivors; Prevention program; Community education; Offender treatment program; Adolescent survivors of sexual abuse; Male survivors of sexual abuse
REQUIREMENTS: Sliding scale fee

GOLDEN

DISTRICT ATTORNEY'S OFFICE—VICTIM/WITNESS ASSISTANCE
1726 Cole Blvd, No 300, Golden, CO 80401
Information: (303) 278-6840 8am-5pm (Mon-Fri)
Contact: Kim Slaughter, Vict/Wit Asst Unit Dir
TYPE OF AGENCY: Victim/witness assistance program
SPONSORING ORGANIZATION: First Judicial District
AREAS SERVED: Jefferson, Gilpin
ACCESSIBILITY: Wheelchair accessible
CASES SEXUAL ASSAULT/ABUSE (%): 50
CLIENTS/SERVICES: Sexual assault survivors; Marital rape/sexual abuse survivors; Child victims of sexual abuse; Adult survivors of child sexual abuse; Community education; Offender treatment program; Adolescent survivors of sexual abuse; Male survivors of sexual abuse
REQUIREMENTS: Clients must file charges and cooperate with law enforcement agencies

GRAND JUNCTION

COUNSELING ASSOCIATES
960 Belford, Ste B, Grand Junction, CO 81501
Information: (303) 245-6818 by appointment
Contact: Sue Polan, Associate
TYPE OF AGENCY: Child sexual abuse services; Private practice
AREAS SERVED: Mesa, Garfield
YEARS IN OPERATION: 1
CASES SEXUAL ASSAULT/ABUSE (%): 75
CLIENTS/SERVICES: Sexual assault survivors; Child victims of sexual abuse; Adult survivors of child sexual abuse; Incest victims/survivors;

COUNSELING ASSOCIATES (continued)
Prevention program; Community education; Adolescent survivors of sexual abuse

DISTRICT ATTORNEY VICTIM/WITNESS ASSISTANCE PROGRAM
PO Box 20,000-5031, Grand Junction, CO 81502
Information: (303) 244-1632 8am-5pm
Contact: Mary Sommerfeld, Victim/Witness Coord
TYPE OF AGENCY: Victim/witness assistance program
SPONSORING ORGANIZATION: 21st Judicial District
AREAS SERVED: Mesa
YEARS IN OPERATION: 3
ACCESSIBILITY: Wheelchair accessible; Signers for the hearing impaired
CLIENTS/SERVICES: Sexual assault survivors; Marital rape/sexual abuse survivors; Child victims of sexual abuse; Incest victims/survivors
REQUIREMENTS: For victim/witness services, there must be an open court case. For victim compensation, the crime must be reported to a law enforcement agency within 72 hours.
SPECIAL PROGRAMS/SERVICES: Agencies may apply through victim assistance and law enforcement board for grants to do training independently or in conjunction with this program

INDIVIDUAL AND FAMILY COUNSELING/CRISIS LINE
1425 N 5th St, Grand Junction, CO 81501
Information: (303) 243-4414 9am-5pm
Contact: Phillip Shayne, Dir
TYPE OF AGENCY: Counseling/mental health services; Child sexual abuse services
AREAS SERVED: Primarily Mesa
YEARS IN OPERATION: 16
LANGUAGES: Spanish
ACCESSIBILITY: Wheelchair accessible
CASES SEXUAL ASSAULT/ABUSE (%): 15
CLIENTS/SERVICES: Sexual assault survivors; Marital rape/sexual abuse survivors; Child victims of sexual abuse; Adult survivors of child sexual abuse; Incest victims/survivors; Offender treatment program; Adolescent survivors of sexual abuse; Male survivors of sexual abuse
REQUIREMENTS: Children 4 years and older; Must be able to pay fee on sliding scale with $10.00 minimum.

SEXUAL ASSAULT SUPPORT
1129 Colorado Ave, Grand Junction, CO 81501
Crisis hotline: **(303) 243-0190 24 hrs**
Information: (303) 243-0190 8am-5pm
Contact: Carmen Gram, Counselor/Educator
TYPE OF AGENCY: Rape crisis center; Counseling/mental health services
SPONSORING ORGANIZATION: The Resource Center, Inc
AREAS SERVED: Mesa County
YEARS IN OPERATION: 13
ACCESSIBILITY: Wheelchair accessible
CLIENTS/SERVICES: Sexual assault survivors; Marital rape/sexual abuse survivors; Adult survivors of child sexual abuse; Incest victims/survivors; Prevention program; Community education; Male survivors of sexual abuse

GREELEY

CHILD ADVOCACY RESOURCE AND EDUCATION, INC
PO Box 945, 1001 9th Ave, Greeley, CO 80631
Crisis hotline: **(303) 356-6751**
Information: (303) 356-6751
Contact: Kathy Luker, Exec Dir
TYPE OF AGENCY: Child sexual abuse prevention program; Child abuse prevention program
AREAS SERVED: Weld
YEARS IN OPERATION: 12
CASES SEXUAL ASSAULT/ABUSE (%): 50-80
DESCRIPTION: Parenting classes (4 levels); Children's groups on personal body safety and intervention around sexual abuse to break victimization cycle; Prevention programs on child abuse for children ages 3-18
CLIENTS/SERVICES: Prevention program; Community education

WELD COUNTY DISTRICT ATTORNEY'S OFFICE—VICTIM/WITNESS PROGRAM
PO Box 1167, Greeley, CO 80632
Crisis hotline: **(303) 356-4000 24 hrs**
Information: (303) 356-4000, ext 4748 8am-5pm
Contact: Carol Poole, Vic Comp Coord; Jennifer Walker, Vic Asst Coun
TYPE OF AGENCY: Victim/witness assistance program
AREAS SERVED: Weld
YEARS IN OPERATION: 2
LANGUAGES: Spanish
ACCESSIBILITY: Wheelchair accessible; Signers for the hearing impaired
CASES SEXUAL ASSAULT/ABUSE (%): 19
CLIENTS/SERVICES: Sexual assault survivors; Marital rape/sexual abuse survivors; Child victims of sexual abuse; Incest victims/survivors; Community education; Male survivors of sexual abuse; Publications/media
SPECIAL PROGRAMS/SERVICES: This program has utilized the video *The Clinical Interview* (Kee McFarlane) to train law enforcement officers. Also has a film about agency services

WELD SEXUAL ASSAULT SUPPORT TEAM
PO Box 240, Greeley, CO 80632
Crisis hotline: **(303) 352-7273 24 hrs**
Information: (303) 352-7273
Contact: Linda Matthews, Dir
TYPE OF AGENCY: Rape crisis center
AREAS SERVED: Weld
YEARS IN OPERATION: 14
LANGUAGES: Spanish
CLIENTS/SERVICES: Sexual assault survivors; Child victims of sexual abuse; Adult survivors of child sexual abuse; Incest victims/survivors; Prevention program; Community education; Adolescent survivors of sexual abuse; Male survivors of sexual abuse

HOT SULPHUR SPRINGS

DISTRICT ATTORNEY'S OFFICE—VICTIM/WITNESS ASSISTANCE
PO Box 168, Hot Sulphur Springs, CO 80451
Information: (303) 725-3371 8am-5pm (Mon-Fri)
Contact: L Diane Brueske, Victim/Witness Coord
TYPE OF AGENCY: Victim/witness assistance program
SPONSORING ORGANIZATION: 14th Judicial District
AREAS SERVED: Grand
YEARS IN OPERATION: 7
ACCESSIBILITY: Wheelchair accessible
CASES SEXUAL ASSAULT/ABUSE (%): 15
CLIENTS/SERVICES: Sexual assault survivors; Marital rape/sexual abuse survivors; Child victims of sexual abuse; Incest victims/survivors
REQUIREMENTS: The crime must be reported; but it is not necessary that charges be filed.

LAKEWOOD

CLLB PSYCHOTHERAPY
720 Kipling, Ste 113, Lakewood, CO 80215
Information: (303) 740-8695 By appointment
Contact: Carolyn L Davis, LCSW, Pres; Beverly Wilson, LCSW
TYPE OF AGENCY: Private practice
AREAS SERVED: Metropolitan Denver and Boulder
YEARS IN OPERATION: 9
LANGUAGES: Spanish
CASES SEXUAL ASSAULT/ABUSE (%): 75
CLIENTS/SERVICES: Sexual assault survivors; Marital rape/sexual abuse survivors; Child victims of sexual abuse; Adult survivors of child sexual abuse; Incest victims/survivors; Community education; Offender treatment program; Adolescent survivors of sexual abuse; Male survivors of sexual abuse; Healing
REQUIREMENTS: Offenders treated only if court-ordered for therapy
SPECIAL PROGRAMS/SERVICES: Healing experiences through hypnosis and several structured group exercises focus on healing (grief letters, empty chair technique, effigy work)

RSA, INC (REDIRECTING SEXUAL AGGRESSION)
1420 Vance St, No 202, Lakewood, CO 80215
Information: (303) 232-5749 10am-7pm (Mon-Fri); answering machine aft hrs 7 days
Contact: Connie Isaac, Exec Dir
TYPE OF AGENCY: Private practice; Consultation; Training/research; Offender treatment
AREAS SERVED: Jefferson, Denver, Adams, Arapahoe, Boulder
YEARS IN OPERATION: 5
CASES SEXUAL ASSAULT/ABUSE (%): 100
DESCRIPTION: Provides specific treatment intervention for sexual perpetrators: rapists, child sexual abuse/incest offenders, and batterers. Provides individual and group psychoeducational, cognitive, restructuring and behavioral components
CLIENTS/SERVICES: Community education; Offender treatment program
REQUIREMENTS: Client age range 7-75 years, male and female. Must acknowledge involvement in the sexually abusive/aggressive behavior
SPECIAL PROGRAMS/SERVICES: Provides therapy programs for young (7-9 years) male victims who have begun to act out in a sexually inappropriate manner; Support groups, parent groups, spouse groups for significant others of both adolescent and adult perpetrators; Victim/perpetrator therapeutic dyads

LEADVILLE

ADVOCATES OF LAKE COUNTY, INC
PO Box 325, Leadville, CO 80461
Crisis hotline: **(719) 486-3530, 486-1249 24 hrs 7 days**
Information: (719) 486-3530 9am-12am, 1pm-3pm (Mon-Thu)
Contact: Karla Duran, Office Mgr
TYPE OF AGENCY: Domestic violence program
AREAS SERVED: Lake
YEARS IN OPERATION: 8
LANGUAGES: Spanish
CASES SEXUAL ASSAULT/ABUSE (%): 20
CLIENTS/SERVICES: Sexual assault survivors; Marital rape/sexual abuse survivors; Child victims of sexual abuse; Adult survivors of child sexual abuse; Incest victims/survivors; Community education; Adolescent survivors of sexual abuse; Male survivors of sexual abuse

DISTRICT ATTORNEY'S OFFICE—VICTIM/WITNESS ASSISTANCE
Box 965, Leadville, CO 80461
Information: (719) 486-1186 8am-5pm
Contact: Linda Coxen, Admin
TYPE OF AGENCY: Victim/witness assistance program
AREAS SERVED: Lake, Summit, Eagle, Clear Creek
YEARS IN OPERATION: 3
ACCESSIBILITY: Wheelchair accessible
CASES SEXUAL ASSAULT/ABUSE (%): 40
CLIENTS/SERVICES: Sexual assault survivors; Marital rape/sexual abuse survivors; Child victims of sexual abuse; Adult survivors of child sexual abuse; Incest victims/survivors

DISTRICT ATTORNEY'S OFFICE—VICTIM/WITNESS ASSISTANCE
(continued)

REQUIREMENTS: Police report must be filed within 48 hours; Victim must agree to cooperate with the District Attorney's Office

LOVELAND

ALTERNATIVES FOR BATTERED WOMEN, INC
320 N Cleveland, Loveland, CO 80537
Crisis hotline: **(303) 669-5150 24 hrs**
Information: (303) 669-5150 8:30am-4:30pm (Mon-Fri)
Contact: Pat Linson, Dir
TYPE OF AGENCY: Rape crisis center; Domestic violence program
AREAS SERVED: Southern Larimer
YEARS IN OPERATION: 7
LANGUAGES: Spanish by arrangement
ACCESSIBILITY: Wheelchair accessible
CLIENTS/SERVICES: Sexual assault survivors; Marital rape/sexual abuse survivors; Adult survivors of child sexual abuse; Incest victims/survivors; Community education

WOMEN AGAINST RAPE (WAR)
PO Box 0546, Loveland, CO 80539
Crisis hotline: **(303) 663-6443 24 hrs**
Information: (303) 663-6443 24 hrs
Contact: Karen Vaughn-Jamison, Founder
TYPE OF AGENCY: Rape crisis center
AREAS SERVED: Larimer
YEARS IN OPERATION: 2
CASES SEXUAL ASSAULT/ABUSE (%): 100
DESCRIPTION: Works to change current sexual assault laws; Assists victims with information on referrals, court proceedings, etc
CLIENTS/SERVICES: Sexual assault survivors; Marital rape/sexual abuse survivors; Incest victims/survivors; Prevention program; Community education; Adolescent survivors of sexual abuse; Male survivors of sexual abuse

MONTROSE

MONTROSE COUNTY INCEST GROUP TREATMENT PROGRAM
PO Box 216, Montrose, CO 81402
Information: (303) 249-3401 8am-5pm
Contact: Jody Anderson, Case Wkr IV; Babs Schmerler, LSW II, Midwestern Mental Health Center
TYPE OF AGENCY: Counseling/mental health services; Child sexual abuse services
SPONSORING ORGANIZATION: Montrose County Department of Social Services
AREAS SERVED: Montrose
YEARS IN OPERATION: 4½
CASES SEXUAL ASSAULT/ABUSE (%): 100
DESCRIPTION: This is a joint effort between the Midwestern Colorado Mental Health Center and the Department of Social Services. Programs include group sessions for teenaged females who are victims/survivors of all forms of sexual assault and for perpetrators of incest and their spouses. Opportunity to confront perpetrator
CLIENTS/SERVICES: Child victims of sexual abuse; Adult survivors of child sexual abuse; Incest victims/survivors; Offender treatment program; Adolescent survivors of sexual abuse; Male survivors of sexual abuse
REQUIREMENTS: For the victim/survivor group females must be 12-14 years old. No third-party treatment unless also involved in incest.
SPECIAL PROGRAMS/SERVICES: The spouse's and perpetrator's group is basically composed of couples, although perpetrators and mothers without spouses are included. There are also multifamily groups that meet about every six weeks. Approximately six times a year, these multifamily groups engage in planned social events for the purpose of decreasing social isolation.

WOMEN'S RESOURCE CENTER OF MONTROSE
307 Main St, Ste 1, Montrose, CO 81401
Crisis hotline: **(303) 249-2486 24 hrs**
Information: (303) 249-2486 9am-1pm
Contact: Sarah Hillary, Dir
TYPE OF AGENCY: Domestic violence program
AREAS SERVED: Ouray, San Miguel, Montrose
YEARS IN OPERATION: 8
CLIENTS/SERVICES: Sexual assault survivors

PUEBLO

ASSOCIATES FOR PSYCHOTHERAPY AND EDUCATION
229 W 12th St, Pueblo, CO 81003
Information: (719) 546-0396 9am-6pm
Contact: Beth Brown Walker, Psychotherapist
TYPE OF AGENCY: Child sexual abuse services; Private practice
AREAS SERVED: El Paso, Pueblo, Fremont
YEARS IN OPERATION: 15
LANGUAGES: Spanish
ACCESSIBILITY: Wheelchair accessible
CASES SEXUAL ASSAULT/ABUSE (%): 10-15
DESCRIPTION: Counseling for victims/survivors, as well as child sexual abuse/incest offenders and batterers
CLIENTS/SERVICES: Sexual assault survivors; Marital rape/sexual abuse survivors; Child victims of sexual abuse; Adult survivors of child sexual abuse; Incest victims/survivors; Male survivors of sexual abuse; Healing; Publications/media
REQUIREMENTS: Ability to pay for services
SPECIAL PROGRAMS/SERVICES: Media program: slide presentation on sexual abuse which includes statistics, research, symptoms, treatment and recovery criteria. Art therapy in work with adult survivors of sexual assault and child sexual abuse

PUEBLO YWCA RAPE CRISIS CENTER
801 N Santa Fe Ave, Pueblo, CO 81003
Crisis hotline: **(719) 544-7007 24 hrs**
Information: (719) 543-7112 9am-2pm (Mon-Wed-Thu)
Contact: Janet McCain, Debbie Daffey, Co-Coords
TYPE OF AGENCY: Rape crisis center
AREAS SERVED: Pueblo County
YEARS IN OPERATION: 5
LANGUAGES: Spanish
ACCESSIBILITY: Wheelchair accessible
CASES SEXUAL ASSAULT/ABUSE (%): 100
DESCRIPTION: Comprehensive rape crisis services, including feminist martial arts/self defense; Wilderness therapy for sexual assault survivors
CLIENTS/SERVICES: Sexual assault survivors; Marital rape/sexual abuse survivors; Child victims of sexual abuse; Adult survivors of child sexual abuse; Incest victims/survivors; Community education; Adolescent survivors of sexual abuse; Male survivors of sexual abuse; Healing

YWCA STEPPING STONES TEEN PROGRAM
2109 Chautard, Pueblo, CO 81005
Crisis hotline: **(719) 561-0521 24 hrs**
Information: (719) 561-0521 24 hrs
Contact: Debra Santos, Prog Dir
TYPE OF AGENCY: Counseling/mental health services; Adolescent program
AREAS SERVED: Colorado
YEARS IN OPERATION: 5½
CASES SEXUAL ASSAULT/ABUSE (%): 35
CLIENTS/SERVICES: Child victims of sexual abuse; Incest victims/survivors; Adolescent survivors of sexual abuse

RIFLE

PARENTS UNITED
140 E 3rd St, Rifle, CO 81650
Information: (303) 625-1425 8am-5pm
Contact: Steve Dempsy, MSW, Dir
TYPE OF AGENCY: Child sexual abuse services
SPONSORING ORGANIZATION: Family Resource Center
AREAS SERVED: Garfield, Pitkin, Moffett, Rio Blanco
YEARS IN OPERATION: 5
CASES SEXUAL ASSAULT/ABUSE (%): 100
CLIENTS/SERVICES: Child victims of sexual abuse; Adult survivors of child sexual abuse; Incest victims/survivors; Prevention program; Community education; Offender treatment program; Adolescent survivors of sexual abuse
REQUIREMENTS: Only for in-treatment clients who have been certified by their therapists as ready for a self-help program. Must have co-operated with law enforcement and social service systems

STERLING

HELP FOR ABUSED PARTNERS
PO Box 1286, Sterling, CO 80751
Crisis hotline: **(303) 522-2844 24 hrs daily**
Information: (303) 522-2307 8:30am-3pm
Contact: Troy Stasenka, Dir
TYPE OF AGENCY: Domestic violence program
AREAS SERVED: Logan
YEARS IN OPERATION: 8
CASES SEXUAL ASSAULT/ABUSE (%): 5
CLIENTS/SERVICES: Sexual assault survivors; Marital rape/sexual abuse survivors; Child victims of sexual abuse; Adult survivors of child sexual abuse; Incest victims/survivors; Adolescent survivors of sexual abuse; Male survivors of sexual abuse

TRINIDAD

ADVOCATES AGAINST DOMESTIC ASSAULT
PO Box 696, Trinidad, CO 81082
Crisis hotline: **(719) 846-HELP 24 hrs**
Information: (719) 846-6665 8am-11:30pm, 12:30pm-4pm
Contact: Vicki Rienks, Crisis Intervention Wkr
TYPE OF AGENCY: Domestic violence program
AREAS SERVED: Las Animas
YEARS IN OPERATION: 4
LANGUAGES: Spanish
DESCRIPTION: Deals primarily with battered women but occasionally works with rape survivors
CLIENTS/SERVICES: Sexual assault survivors; Marital rape/sexual abuse survivors; Child victims of sexual abuse; Adult survivors of child sexual abuse; Community education

VAIL

WOMEN'S RESOURCE CENTER OF EAGLE COUNTY
PO Box 3414, Vail, CO 81658
Crisis hotline: **(303) 476-7384 24 hrs**
Information: (303) 476-7384, 476-3569 hrs vary
Contact: Cheryl L Paller, Dir
TYPE OF AGENCY: Domestic violence program
AREAS SERVED: Eagle
YEARS IN OPERATION: 5
LANGUAGES: French, Spanish
CASES SEXUAL ASSAULT/ABUSE (%): 25
CLIENTS/SERVICES: Marital rape/sexual abuse survivors; Child victims of sexual abuse; Adult survivors of child sexual abuse; Community education; Male survivors of sexual abuse

WESTMINSTER

COUNSELORS FOR PERSONAL GROWTH
1400 W 122nd Ave, Ste 200, Westminster, CO 80234
Information: (303) 451-0144 24 hrs
Contact: Karyl McBride, MA, Eds, Psychotherapist/Owner
TYPE OF AGENCY: Child sexual abuse services; Private practice
AREAS SERVED: Adams, Jefferson, Gilpin
YEARS IN OPERATION: 8
CASES SEXUAL ASSAULT/ABUSE (%): 40
DESCRIPTION: Provides counseling for all ages, marriage and family counseling, women's support groups and counseling for issues of sexual abuse; Works with three county victim compensation programs
CLIENTS/SERVICES: Sexual assault survivors; Marital rape/sexual abuse survivors; Child victims of sexual abuse; Adult survivors of child sexual abuse; Incest victims/survivors; Prevention program; Adolescent survivors of sexual abuse; Male survivors of sexual abuse

WOMEN'S CENTER
3645 W 112th Ave, Westminster, CO 80030
Information: (303) 466-8811, ext 253 8am-7pm (Mon-Thu); 8am-4pm (Fri)
TYPE OF AGENCY: College/university-based services
SPONSORING ORGANIZATION: Front Range Community College
AREAS SERVED: Adams, Boulder, Denver, Jefferson, part of Weld
YEARS IN OPERATION: 3
ACCESSIBILITY: Wheelchair accessible; Telecommunications for the hearing impaired (TTY, TDY, etc.); Signers for the hearing impaired
CASES SEXUAL ASSAULT/ABUSE (%): 5-10
DESCRIPTION: Counseling and crisis intervention services, support groups, and workshops/seminars on violence against women
CLIENTS/SERVICES: Sexual assault survivors; Marital rape/sexual abuse survivors; Adult survivors of child sexual abuse; Incest victims/survivors; Community education; Adolescent survivors of sexual abuse

WHEAT RIDGE

ASSAULT SURVIVORS ASSISTANCE PROGRAM
8300 W 38th Ave, Wheat Ridge, CO 80033
Information: (303) 425-2727 Appointments Mon-Sat; Messages 24 hrs
Contact: Lea Ann Farlow, Prog Dir
TYPE OF AGENCY: Hospital/medical center
SPONSORING ORGANIZATION: Lutheran Medical Center
AREAS SERVED: Jefferson, Gilpin
YEARS IN OPERATION: 2
LANGUAGES: Interpreters available as needed
ACCESSIBILITY: Wheelchair accessible
CASES SEXUAL ASSAULT/ABUSE (%): 80
CLIENTS/SERVICES: Sexual assault survivors; Marital rape/sexual abuse survivors; Adult survivors of child sexual abuse; Incest victims/survivors; Prevention program; Community education; Adolescent survivors of sexual abuse; Male survivors of sexual abuse
REQUIREMENTS: Clients must be ages 14 and older; Priority is given to residents of Jefferson and Gilpin counties.

CONNECTICUT

BRISTOL

LIFEGUIDES COUNSELING SERVICES
160 Farmington Ave, Bristol, CT 06010
Information: (203) 223-9291, 583-9225 9am-5pm; Wednesday evenings by appointment
Contact: Robert L Covey, ACSW, LifeGuides Counseling Svcs Dir
TYPE OF AGENCY: Counseling/mental health services
SPONSORING ORGANIZATION: Family Service, Inc
YEARS IN OPERATION: 99
CASES SEXUAL ASSAULT/ABUSE (%): 20-30
CLIENTS/SERVICES: Sexual assault survivors; Marital rape/sexual abuse survivors; Adult survivors of child sexual abuse; Incest victims/survivors; Adolescent survivors of sexual abuse; Male survivors of sexual abuse
REQUIREMENTS: Sliding scale fee; Able to develop commitment to treatment

DANBURY

RAPE CRISIS SERVICES
256 Main St, Danbury, CT 06810
Crisis hotline: **(203) 743-9463 24 hrs**
Information: (203) 790-7267 9am-5pm
Contact: Terry Hogan, Dir
TYPE OF AGENCY: Rape crisis center; Child sexual abuse services; Child sexual abuse prevention program
SPONSORING ORGANIZATION: Women's Center of Greater Danbury
AREAS SERVED: Litchfield, Fairfield
YEARS IN OPERATION: 13
LANGUAGES: French, Spanish, Korean
ACCESSIBILITY: Wheelchair accessible
CASES SEXUAL ASSAULT/ABUSE (%): 100
DESCRIPTION: Comprehensive rape crisis services; Support groups for female and male survivors of sexual assault/abuse
CLIENTS/SERVICES: Sexual assault survivors; Marital rape/sexual abuse survivors; Child victims of sexual abuse; Adult survivors of child sexual abuse; Incest victims/survivors; Community education; Adolescent survivors of sexual abuse; Male survivors of sexual abuse

DAYVILLE

DOMESTIC VIOLENCE PROGRAM
PO Box 251, 1007 N Main St, Dayville, CT 06241
Crisis hotline: **(203) 774-8648 24 hrs**
Information: (203) 774-2020, 456-2261 9am-9pm (Mon-Fri); 24-hr emergency on-call
Contact: Virginia Sazama, Domestic Violence Dir
TYPE OF AGENCY: Counseling/mental health services; Child sexual abuse services; Child sexual abuse prevention program
SPONSORING ORGANIZATION: United Social and Mental Health Services, Inc
AREAS SERVED: Windham, part of Tolland
YEARS IN OPERATION: 24
LANGUAGES: Spanish
ACCESSIBILITY: Wheelchair accessible; Telecommunications for the hearing impaired (TTY, TDY, etc.); Signers for the hearing impaired
CASES SEXUAL ASSAULT/ABUSE (%): 25
CLIENTS/SERVICES: Sexual assault survivors; Marital rape/sexual abuse survivors; Child victims of sexual abuse; Adult survivors of child sexual abuse; Incest victims/survivors; Prevention program; Community education; Offender treatment program

ENFIELD

CATHOLIC FAMILY SERVICES
109 Elm St, Enfield, CT 06082
Information: (203) 745-1727 9am-5pm (Mon, Wed, Thu, Fri); 12pm-8pm (Tue); 24-hr answering service
Contact: Hal March, Dir
TYPE OF AGENCY: Counseling/mental health services
AREAS SERVED: Enfield, Windsor, East Granby
YEARS IN OPERATION: 5
CASES SEXUAL ASSAULT/ABUSE (%): 20
CLIENTS/SERVICES: Sexual assault survivors; Child victims of sexual abuse; Adult survivors of child sexual abuse; Adolescent survivors of sexual abuse; Male survivors of sexual abuse

GREENWICH

THE FAMILY CENTER, INC
40 Arch St, Greenwich, CT 06850
Crisis hotline: **(203) 324-1010 (Infoline) 24 hrs**
Information: (203) 869-4848 9am-8pm (Mon-Thu); 9am-5pm (Fri)
Contact: Joanne Peyser, Professional Svcs Dir
TYPE OF AGENCY: Counseling/mental health services
AREAS SERVED: City of Greenwich and surrounding area
YEARS IN OPERATION: 82
LANGUAGES: Spanish
DESCRIPTION: Family service agency and mental health clinic providing a range of clinical services (individual, group, marital and family counseling). Issues of sexual assault and child sexual abuse are among the issues handled
CLIENTS/SERVICES: Sexual assault survivors; Marital rape/sexual abuse survivors; Child victims of sexual abuse; Adult survivors of child sexual abuse; Incest victims/survivors; Adolescent survivors of sexual abuse; Male survivors of sexual abuse
REQUIREMENTS: People who live or work in Greenwich are eligible for financial assistance if necessary; others seen at full fee

HARTFORD

DR ISAIAH CLARK FAMILY AND YOUTH CLINIC
1229 Albany Ave, Hartford, CT 06112
Information: (203) 241-0888 8:30am-6pm (Thu); 8:30am-4:30pm (Mon, Wed); 8:30am-Noon (Fri)
Contact: Nelly R Schwan, Svc Dir
TYPE OF AGENCY: Counseling/mental health services; Child sexual abuse services
SPONSORING ORGANIZATION: Child and Family Services, Inc
AREAS SERVED: Hartford north end
YEARS IN OPERATION: 6
LANGUAGES: Spanish
ACCESSIBILITY: Wheelchair accessible
DESCRIPTION: Psychotherapeutic services for children, adolescents, and their families; Specialized treatment for victims of sexual abuse; Group therapy
CLIENTS/SERVICES: Child victims of sexual abuse; Adolescent survivors of sexual abuse
REQUIREMENTS: Services for children; Parent participation is required
SPECIAL PROGRAMS/SERVICES: Spanish-language brochure

HARTFORD POLICE CRISIS INTERVENTION UNIT
150 Sisson Ave, Hartford, CT 06105
Crisis hotline: **(203) 236-6071 8:30am-11pm (Mon-Fri)**
Information: (203) 236-6071 8:30am-11pm (Mon-Fri)
Contact: Roland Chasse, Casework Supv
TYPE OF AGENCY: Victim/witness assistance program
AREAS SERVED: City of Hartford only
YEARS IN OPERATION: 9
LANGUAGES: Spanish
CASES SEXUAL ASSAULT/ABUSE (%): 40
CLIENTS/SERVICES: Sexual assault survivors; Marital rape/sexual abuse survivors; Child victims of sexual abuse; Incest victims/survivors
REQUIREMENTS: Client must have been involved with police for this unit to intervene.

HARTFORD REGION YWCA SEXUAL ASSAULT CRISIS SERVICE
135 Broad St, Hartford, CT 06105
Crisis hotline: **(203) 522-6666 24 hrs**
Information: (203) 525-1163 9am-5pm
Contact: Ilia Castro, Dir
TYPE OF AGENCY: Rape crisis center; Child sexual abuse services; Child sexual abuse prevention program
AREAS SERVED: Hartford region, 22 towns
YEARS IN OPERATION: 14
LANGUAGES: Spanish
CASES SEXUAL ASSAULT/ABUSE (%): 100

HARTFORD REGION YWCA SEXUAL ASSAULT CRISIS SERVICE (continued)

CLIENTS/SERVICES: Sexual assault survivors; Marital rape/sexual abuse survivors; Child victims of sexual abuse; Adult survivors of child sexual abuse; Incest victims/survivors; Prevention program; Community education; Adolescent survivors of sexual abuse; Male survivors of sexual abuse
SPECIAL PROGRAMS/SERVICES: This agency provides 44-hour spring and fall training for volunteer-counselors which includes counseling issues of black, hispanic, and lesbian women and personal exploration of racism. Publication: "Las Victimas," (bilingual) photonovella

MANCHESTER

THE SEXUAL ABUSE TREATMENT PROGRAM
317 N Main St, Manchester, CT 06040
Information: (203) 643-2101 24 hrs
Contact: Barry W Baker, Sexual Abuse Treatment Team Coord
TYPE OF AGENCY: Counseling/mental health services; Child sexual abuse services
SPONSORING ORGANIZATION: Community Child Guidance Clinic
AREAS SERVED: Hartford, Tolland
YEARS IN OPERATION: 10
ACCESSIBILITY: Wheelchair accessible
CASES SEXUAL ASSAULT/ABUSE (%): 100
DESCRIPTION: The SATT Program, part of a regional mental health center, involves 11 clinicians (psychiatrists, psychologists, and psychiatric social workers) dealing primarily with intra- and extra-familial sexual abuse of children. Provides individual, family, couple, and group therapy, and crisis intervention. Treats child sexual abuse/incest offenders in relation to child's treatment
CLIENTS/SERVICES: Marital rape/sexual abuse survivors; Child victims of sexual abuse; Prevention program; Community education; Offender treatment program; Adolescent survivors of sexual abuse; Male survivors of sexual abuse

MERIDEN

MERIDEN/WALLINGFORD CHRYSALIS
PO Box 663, Meriden, CT 06450
Crisis hotline: **(203) 238-1501 24 hrs**
Information: (203) 237-3713 9am-4pm
Contact: Diane Shearer, Res Coord
TYPE OF AGENCY: Domestic violence program
SPONSORING ORGANIZATION: Meriden/Wallingford Battered Women's Shelter
AREAS SERVED: Meriden, Wallingford
YEARS IN OPERATION: 10
LANGUAGES: Spanish
CLIENTS/SERVICES: Marital rape/sexual abuse survivors; Child victims of sexual abuse; Adult survivors of child sexual abuse; Incest victims/survivors

SEXUAL ABUSE TREATMENT PROGRAM/ VICTIM AND OFFENDER SERVICES
195 Cook Ave, Meriden, CT 06450
Information: (203) 238-8200, ext 3260 24 hrs
Contact: Dennis Gibeau, PhD, Dir
TYPE OF AGENCY: Hospital/medical center; Child sexual abuse services
SPONSORING ORGANIZATION: Meriden-Wallingford Hospital and Child Guidance Clinic
AREAS SERVED: Statewide
YEARS IN OPERATION: 8
LANGUAGES: Spanish
ACCESSIBILITY: Wheelchair accessible
CASES SEXUAL ASSAULT/ABUSE (%): 100
DESCRIPTION: Individual, family and group therapies for victims/survivors and rapists, child sexual abuse/incest offenders and batterers
CLIENTS/SERVICES: Sexual assault survivors; Marital rape/sexual abuse survivors; Child victims of sexual abuse; Adult survivors of child sexual abuse; Incest victims/survivors; Prevention program; Community education; Offender treatment program; Adolescent survivors of sexual abuse; Male survivors of sexual abuse

SEXUAL ASSAULT CRISIS SERVICE
169 Colony St, Meriden, CT 06450
Crisis hotline: **(203) 235-4444 24 hrs**
Information: (203) 235-9297 9am-5pm (Mon-Fri)
Contact: Sheila Greenstein, Prog Coord
TYPE OF AGENCY: Rape crisis center; Child sexual abuse services; Child sexual abuse prevention program
SPONSORING ORGANIZATION: YWCA of Meriden, CT
AREAS SERVED: In New Haven: Meriden, Wallingford, Cheshire
YEARS IN OPERATION: 4
LANGUAGES: Spanish, Italian, Russian
ACCESSIBILITY: Signers for the hearing impaired
CASES SEXUAL ASSAULT/ABUSE (%): 100
DESCRIPTION: Comprehensive rape crisis program, including prevention programs for camp and daycare facilities
CLIENTS/SERVICES: Sexual assault survivors; Marital rape/sexual abuse survivors; Child victims of sexual abuse; Adult survivors of child sexual abuse; Incest victims/survivors; Prevention program; Community education; Adolescent survivors of sexual abuse; Male survivors of sexual abuse
SPECIAL PROGRAMS/SERVICES: Brochure in Spanish

MIDDLETOWN

SEXUAL ASSAULT CRISIS SERVICE OF MIDDLESEX COUNTY, INC
PO Box 1514, Middletown, CT 06457
Crisis hotline: **(203) 346-7233 24 hrs 7 days**
Information: (203) 346-7233 9am-4:30pm
Contact: Marea Downes, Exec Dir
TYPE OF AGENCY: Rape crisis center; Child sexual abuse services; Child sexual abuse prevention program
AREAS SERVED: Middlesex
YEARS IN OPERATION: 10
LANGUAGES: Spanish
ACCESSIBILITY: Wheelchair accessible
CASES SEXUAL ASSAULT/ABUSE (%): 100
DESCRIPTION: Comprehensive rape crisis services; Parents of Sexually Abused Children Support Group, a weekly support group for parents to share their guilt, anger, frustration, how to deal with sexually abused child
CLIENTS/SERVICES: Sexual assault survivors; Marital rape/sexual abuse survivors; Child victims of sexual abuse; Adult survivors of child sexual abuse; Incest victims/survivors; Prevention program; Community education; Adolescent survivors of sexual abuse; Male survivors of sexual abuse

MILFORD

RAPE CRISIS CENTER OF MILFORD, INC
PO Box 521, 70 W River St, Milford, CT 06460
Crisis hotline: **(203) 878-1212 24 hrs**
Information: (203) 874-8712 8am-5pm
Contact: Nancy Vinci, Dir
TYPE OF AGENCY: Rape crisis center
AREAS SERVED: New Haven
YEARS IN OPERATION: 13
ACCESSIBILITY: Wheelchair accessible
CASES SEXUAL ASSAULT/ABUSE (%): 100
CLIENTS/SERVICES: Sexual assault survivors; Marital rape/sexual abuse survivors; Child victims of sexual abuse; Adult survivors of child sexual abuse; Incest victims/survivors; Prevention program; Community education; Adolescent survivors of sexual abuse; Male survivors of sexual abuse

NEW BRITAIN

LIFEGUIDES COUNSELING SERVICES
92 Vine St, New Britain, CT 06052
Information: (203) 223-9291, 583-9225 9am-5pm; Wednesday evenings by appointment
Contact: Robert L Covey, ACSW, LifeGuides Counseling Svcs Dir
TYPE OF AGENCY: Counseling/mental health services
SPONSORING ORGANIZATION: Family Service, Inc
YEARS IN OPERATION: 99
CASES SEXUAL ASSAULT/ABUSE (%): 20-30
CLIENTS/SERVICES: Sexual assault survivors; Marital rape/sexual abuse survivors; Adult survivors of child sexual abuse; Incest victims/survivors; Adolescent survivors of sexual abuse; Male survivors of sexual abuse
REQUIREMENTS: Sliding scale fee; Able to develop commitment to treatment

YWCA RAPE CRISIS SERVICE
22 Glen St, New Britain, CT 06051
Crisis hotline: **(203) 223-1787 24 hrs 7 days**
Information: (203) 225-4681 9am-5pm (Mon-Fri)
Contact: Susan E Hyde, Rape Crisis Svc Dir
TYPE OF AGENCY: Rape crisis center
AREAS SERVED: New Britain, Berlin, Bristol, Burlington, Plymouth, Plainville, Southington
YEARS IN OPERATION: 5
LANGUAGES: Spanish, Polish, Sign
ACCESSIBILITY: Wheelchair accessible; Telecommunications for the hearing impaired (TTY, TDY, etc.); Signers for the hearing impaired
CASES SEXUAL ASSAULT/ABUSE (%): 100
CLIENTS/SERVICES: Sexual assault survivors; Marital rape/sexual abuse survivors; Child victims of sexual abuse; Adult survivors of child sexual abuse; Incest victims/survivors; Prevention program; Community education; Adolescent survivors of sexual abuse; Male survivors of sexual abuse
SPECIAL PROGRAMS/SERVICES: This association provides self-defense programs for women and children. The programs teach safety through increasing awareness, assertive behavior training, providing practical tips on safety in the home and in public, as well as actual self-defense techniques that will quickly incapacitate an attacker. These techniques are easily learned and used. The course for children can be adapted for a child of any age.

NEW HAVEN

FAMILY COUNSELING OF GREATER NEW HAVEN, INC
1 State St, New Haven, CT 06511
Crisis hotline: **(203) 865-1125 24-hr answering service**
Information: (203) 865-1125 9am-8pm (Mon-Thu); 9am-5pm (Fri)
Contact: William F Mecca, ACSW, CADC, Exec Dir
TYPE OF AGENCY: Counseling/mental health services
AREAS SERVED: New Haven, Middlesex
YEARS IN OPERATION: 110
LANGUAGES: Spanish
ACCESSIBILITY: Wheelchair accessible
CASES SEXUAL ASSAULT/ABUSE (%): 20
DESCRIPTION: Outpatient psychiatric facility licensed by the State of Connecticut Department of Health Services, provides family, marriage, group and individual therapy for a variety of problems, including treatment for adults and children who are victims of sexual abuse and domestic violence
CLIENTS/SERVICES: Sexual assault survivors; Marital rape/sexual abuse survivors; Child victims of sexual abuse; Adult survivors of child sexual abuse; Incest victims/survivors; Community education; Offender treatment pro-

FAMILY COUNSELING OF GREATER NEW HAVEN, INC (continued)

gram; Adolescent survivors of sexual abuse; Male survivors of sexual abuse
REQUIREMENTS: Sliding scale fee

NEW HAVEN PROJECT FOR BATTERED WOMEN
PO Box 1329, New Haven, CT 06505
Crisis hotline: **(203) 789-8104 24 hrs**
Information: (203) 865-1957 9am-5pm (Mon-Fri)
Contact: Pat Johansen, Asst Dir
TYPE OF AGENCY: Domestic violence program
AREAS SERVED: New Haven
YEARS IN OPERATION: 10
LANGUAGES: Spanish
ACCESSIBILITY: Wheelchair accessible
CLIENTS/SERVICES: Sexual assault survivors; Marital rape/sexual abuse survivors; Child victims of sexual abuse; Adult survivors of child sexual abuse; Incest victims/survivors; Community education

NEW HAVEN SEXUAL HARASSMENT SUPPORT GROUP
614 Orange St, New Haven, CT 06511
Crisis hotline: **(203) 937-8665 24 hrs**
Information: (203) 937-8665 24 hrs
Contact: Margaret Caisholm, Organizer
TYPE OF AGENCY: Women's center
SPONSORING ORGANIZATION: New Haven Women's Liberation Center
AREAS SERVED: New Haven, Fairfield, Hartford
YEARS IN OPERATION: 4 months
LANGUAGES: Spanish
CASES SEXUAL ASSAULT/ABUSE (%): 100
DESCRIPTION: Exploration of the ways in which sexual harassment (in the workplace, in schools, and in rental housing) affects lives and relationships. Sexual harassment is defined as sexual abuse, i.e. a misuse of power that employs sex as an instrument.
CLIENTS/SERVICES: Male survivors of sexual abuse; Sexual harassment
SPECIAL PROGRAMS/SERVICES: Healing program is based on the theory that sexual harassment, like rape or incest, takes away someone's power by inflicting shame and control in a sexual context. Therefore, the program addresses post-traumatic stress disorders, relying on theories and methods developed by Alice Miller *The Drama of the Gifted Child*, by International Torture-debriefing Centers and by incest survivors *The Courage to Heal*. This is not a drop-in group; members are screened by phone, in advance. Each member is asked to make a six-week commitment, so that a measure of trust and confidentiality can be established within the group. Meetings are held once a week. Support and information provided for individuals who wish to start their own groups.

YALE NEW HAVEN HOSPITAL
20 York St, New Haven, CT 06511
Crisis hotline: **(203) 785-2222 24 hrs 7 days**
Information: (203) 785-4790 8:30am-5pm (Mon-Fri)
Contact: Julie Hamilton, MSSW/ACSW CISW, Chief Soc Wkr
TYPE OF AGENCY: Hospital/medical center; Child sexual abuse services
SPONSORING ORGANIZATION: Social Work and Pediatric Medical Departments
AREAS SERVED: New Haven and surrounding towns
YEARS IN OPERATION: 20
LANGUAGES: Spanish
ACCESSIBILITY: Wheelchair accessible; Telecommunications for the hearing impaired (TTY, TDY, etc.); Signers for the hearing impaired
DESCRIPTION: Counseling and medical/psychosocial evaluations for victims/survivors; Group therapy for child sexual abuse/incest offenders and batterers
CLIENTS/SERVICES: Child victims of sexual abuse; Adult survivors of child sexual abuse; Incest victims/survivors; Prevention program; Community education; Offender treatment program; Adolescent survivors of sexual abuse; Male survivors of sexual abuse

YWCA OF GREATER NEW HAVEN—RAPE CRISIS SERVICES
48 Howe St, New Haven, CT 06511
Crisis hotline: **(203) 624-2273 24 hrs**
Information: (203) 789-1425 11am-7pm (Mon-Fri)
Contact: B Moynihan, Dir
TYPE OF AGENCY: Rape crisis center; College/university-based services; Child sexual abuse services; Child sexual abuse prevention program; Interagency network
AREAS SERVED: New Haven
YEARS IN OPERATION: 5
LANGUAGES: Spanish
ACCESSIBILITY: Wheelchair accessible; Telecommunications for the hearing impaired (TTY, TDY, etc.); Signers for the hearing impaired
CASES SEXUAL ASSAULT/ABUSE (%): 100
DESCRIPTION: Comprehensive rape crisis services, including support groups for female and male survivors of sexual assault/abuse
CLIENTS/SERVICES: Sexual assault survivors; Marital rape/sexual abuse survivors; Child victims of sexual abuse; Adult survivors of child sexual abuse; Incest victims/survivors; Prevention program; Community education; Adolescent survivors of sexual abuse; Male survivors of sexual abuse
SPECIAL PROGRAMS/SERVICES: The College Consortium on Sexual Assault involves the community rape crisis center and representatives of colleges and universities in the New Haven area to increase awareness about sexual assault and quality initial intervention for assault victims on campus.

NEW LONDON

FORENSIC MENTAL HEALTH SERVICES OF CONNECTICUT, INC
190 Governor Winthrop Blvd, New London, CT 06320
Information: (203) 447-1128 9am-4pm (Mon-Thu); 9am-1pm (Fri)
Contact: Maxine L Varanko, Exec Dir
TYPE OF AGENCY: Child sexual abuse services; Offender treatment
YEARS IN OPERATION: 6
ACCESSIBILITY: Wheelchair accessible
CASES SEXUAL ASSAULT/ABUSE (%): 100
DESCRIPTION: Provides treatment for adult and juvenile sex offenders and victims of sexual abuse. Offender treatment includes rapists, child sexual abuse/incest offenders, and batterers
CLIENTS/SERVICES: Sexual assault survivors; Marital rape/sexual abuse survivors; Child victims of sexual abuse; Adult survivors of child sexual abuse; Incest victims/survivors; Offender treatment program; Adolescent survivors of sexual abuse; Male survivors of sexual abuse
REQUIREMENTS: Juvenile and adult sex offenders must be involved with police/court process

THE WOMEN'S CENTER OF SOUTHEASTERN CONNECTICUT, INC
Box 572, 120 Broad St, New London, CT 06320
Crisis hotline: **(203) 442-HELP 24 hrs**
Information: (203) 447-0366 9am-5pm
Contact: Marian Chatfield-Taylor, Community Educ Dir; Patricia Finnegan, Exec Dir
TYPE OF AGENCY: Rape crisis center; Domestic violence program; Child sexual abuse prevention program
AREAS SERVED: New London
YEARS IN OPERATION: 12
LANGUAGES: Spanish
CLIENTS/SERVICES: Sexual assault survivors; Marital rape/sexual abuse survivors; Child victims of sexual abuse; Adult survivors of child sexual abuse; Incest victims/survivors; Prevention program; Community education; Adolescent survivors of sexual abuse; Male survivors of sexual abuse

NORWALK

COALITION FOR CHILDREN AND YOUTH, INC
PO Box 2151, Belden Station, Norwalk, CT 06852
Information: (203) 846-0388 8:30am-4pm; 24-hr answering service
Contact: Pat Blumenthal, Dir
TYPE OF AGENCY: Counseling/mental health services; Child sexual abuse services; Interagency network
YEARS IN OPERATION: 11
LANGUAGES: Spoken as needed
DESCRIPTION: This organization sponsors the 17-member Sexual Abuse Response Group, which provides coordinated services for victims of child sexual abuse and their families. The organization also provides a weekly support group for adults caring for children who have been sexually abused.
CLIENTS/SERVICES: Child victims of sexual abuse

SEXUAL ABUSE TREATMENT TEAM
74 Newtown Ave, Norwalk, CT 06851
Crisis hotline: **(203) 853-2525 24 hrs**
Information: (203) 847-3891 9am-5pm (Mon and Fri) 9am-9pm (Tue, Wed, Thu)
Contact: Hildy Koltenuk, ACSW, Proj Dir
TYPE OF AGENCY: Counseling/mental health services
SPONSORING ORGANIZATION: Mid-Fairfield Child Guidance Center
AREAS SERVED: Fairfield
YEARS IN OPERATION: 1½
LANGUAGES: Spanish
CASES SEXUAL ASSAULT/ABUSE (%): 100
CLIENTS/SERVICES: Child victims of sexual abuse; Incest victims/survivors; Community education; Adolescent survivors of sexual abuse
REQUIREMENTS: Services are provided for children up to age 18 and their families.
SPECIAL PROGRAMS/SERVICES: The interdisciplinary treatment team is composed of two clinical social workers, a bilingual masters level therapist, a psychologist, and a psychiatrist. Ongoing staff training uses individual and group supervision, as well as one-way mirror observation. The project director is a member of both county and state committees on child sexual abuse.

PLAINVILLE

LIFEGUIDES COUNSELING SERVICES
130 W Main St, Plainville, CT 06062
Information: (203) 223-9291, 583-9225 9am-5pm; Wednesday evenings by appointment
Contact: Robert L Covey, ACSW, LifeGuides Counseling Svcs Dir
TYPE OF AGENCY: Counseling/mental health services
SPONSORING ORGANIZATION: Family Service, Inc
YEARS IN OPERATION: 99
ACCESSIBILITY: Wheelchair accessible
CASES SEXUAL ASSAULT/ABUSE (%): 20-30
CLIENTS/SERVICES: Sexual assault survivors; Marital rape/sexual abuse survivors; Adult survivors of child sexual abuse; Incest victims/survivors; Adolescent survivors of sexual abuse; Male survivors of sexual abuse
REQUIREMENTS: Sliding scale fee; Able to develop commitment to treatment

SOMERS

SEX OFFENDER PROGRAM
PO Box 100, Somers, CT 06071
Information: (203) 749-8391, ext 5424 8am-4pm
Contact: William F Hobson, Prog Dir
TYPE OF AGENCY: Correctional facility; Offender treatment
SPONSORING ORGANIZATION: Connecticut Correctional Institution-Somers
YEARS IN OPERATION: 11
LANGUAGES: Spanish
CASES SEXUAL ASSAULT/ABUSE (%): 100
DESCRIPTION: Treatment services for convicted adult male sex offenders incarcerated within a three-institution complex
CLIENTS/SERVICES: Offender treatment program
REQUIREMENTS: Clients must be over the age of 18, convicted, and sentenced to prison.

SOUTH NORWALK

WOMEN'S CRISIS CENTER
PO Box 1375, South Norwalk, CT 06854
Crisis hotline: **(203) 853-2525 24 hrs**
Information: (203) 852-1980 8am-10am
TYPE OF AGENCY: Domestic violence program
AREAS SERVED: Fairfield, greater Norwalk area
YEARS IN OPERATION: 8
LANGUAGES: Spanish
CASES SEXUAL ASSAULT/ABUSE (%): 20
CLIENTS/SERVICES: Marital rape/sexual abuse survivors; Community education

STAMFORD

COMMISSION ON VICTIM SERVICES
c/o State Attorney's Office, 115 Hoyt St, Stamford, CT 06905
Information: (203) 965-5215; (800) 822-VICT (information and referral) 9am-5pm (Mon-Fri)
Contact: Chyai Mulberg, Victim Advocate
TYPE OF AGENCY: Victim/witness assistance program
AREAS SERVED: Stamford/Norwalk Judicial District
YEARS IN OPERATION: 2
LANGUAGES: Spanish interpreter available; Others accommodated as needed through state interpreters
CLIENTS/SERVICES: Sexual assault survivors; Marital rape/sexual abuse survivors; Child victims of sexual abuse; Community education; Adolescent survivors of sexual abuse; Male survivors of sexual abuse

RAPE AND SEXUAL ABUSE CRISIS CENTER, INC
Stamford Hospital, Shellburne Rd, Stamford, CT 06902
Crisis hotline: **(203) 329-2929 24 hrs**
Information: (203) 348-9346 9am-4pm
Contact: Catha Abrahams, Dir
TYPE OF AGENCY: Rape crisis center
AREAS SERVED: Southern Fairfield County
YEARS IN OPERATION: 11
LANGUAGES: Spanish, French
CASES SEXUAL ASSAULT/ABUSE (%): 100
DESCRIPTION: Comprehensive rape crisis services, including support groups for female and male survivors of sexual assault/abuse
CLIENTS/SERVICES: Sexual assault survivors; Marital rape/sexual abuse survivors; Child victims of sexual abuse; Adult survivors of child sexual abuse; Incest victims/survivors; Prevention program; Community education; Adolescent survivors of sexual abuse; Male survivors of sexual abuse

TERRYVILLE

LIFEGUIDES COUNSELING SERVICES
25 Allen St, Terryville, CT 06786
Information: (203) 223-9291, 583-9225 9am-5pm; Wednesday evenings by appointment
Contact: Robert L Covey, ACSW, LifeGuides Counseling Svcs Dir
TYPE OF AGENCY: Counseling/mental health services
SPONSORING ORGANIZATION: Family Service, Inc
YEARS IN OPERATION: 99
CASES SEXUAL ASSAULT/ABUSE (%): 20-30
CLIENTS/SERVICES: Sexual assault survivors; Marital rape/sexual abuse survivors; Adult survivors of child sexual abuse; Incest victims/survivors; Adolescent survivors of sexual abuse; Male survivors of sexual abuse
REQUIREMENTS: Sliding scale fee; Able to develop commitment to treatment

TORRINGTON

THE SUSAN B ANTHONY PROJECT, INC
PO Box 846, 367 Goshen Rd, Torrington, CT 06790
Crisis hotline: **(203) 482-7133 24 hrs**
Information: (203) 489-3798 8:30am-4:30pm (Mon-Fri)
Contact: Claudette Baril, Exec Dir
TYPE OF AGENCY: Rape crisis center; Domestic violence program; Child sexual abuse prevention program; Acquaintance/date rape prevention program
AREAS SERVED: Litchfield
YEARS IN OPERATION: 5
CASES SEXUAL ASSAULT/ABUSE (%): 40
DESCRIPTION: Comprehensive services for survivors of sexual assault; SAFE KIDS and date rape presentations in area schools
CLIENTS/SERVICES: Sexual assault survivors; Marital rape/sexual abuse survivors; Child victims of sexual abuse; Adult survivors of child sexual abuse; Incest victims/survivors; Prevention program; Community education; Adolescent survivors of sexual abuse; Male survivors of sexual abuse
SPECIAL PROGRAMS/SERVICES: This project has a shelter-based sexual assault crisis counselor who works with shelter clients of domestic violence on identifying and/or responding to issues of marital rape. It is currently the only center in Connecticut to use this model. Local access cable TV presentations

WATERBURY

FAMILY SERVICE ASSOCIATION OF WATERBURY
34 Murray St, Waterbury, CT 06710
Crisis hotline: **(203) 753-0171 24 hr phone coverage**
Information: (203) 756-8317 9am-5pm (Mon-Fri); some evenings and Saturdays by appointment
Contact: Marcia Borenstein, Family Violence Coord
TYPE OF AGENCY: Counseling/mental health services; Child sexual abuse services; Child abuse services
AREAS SERVED: Greater Waterbury area
YEARS IN OPERATION: 10
ACCESSIBILITY: Wheelchair accessible
CASES SEXUAL ASSAULT/ABUSE (%): 15
DESCRIPTION: The Family Violence Project provides counseling for all victims and survivors of sexual abuse; The crisis nursery provides day care for children of abuse
CLIENTS/SERVICES: Sexual assault survivors; Marital rape/sexual abuse survivors; Child victims of sexual abuse; Adult survivors of child sexual abuse; Incest victims/survivors; Preschoolers

SEXUAL ASSAULT CRISIS SERVICE
80 Prospect St, Waterbury, CT 06702
Crisis hotline: **(203) 753-3613 24 hrs**
Information: (203) 753-3613 8am-4:30pm (Mon-Fri)
Contact: Susan V Thomas, Dir
TYPE OF AGENCY: Rape crisis center; Child sexual abuse services; Child sexual abuse prevention program
SPONSORING ORGANIZATION: YWCA of Greater Waterbury, Inc
AREAS SERVED: Central Naugatuck Valley
YEARS IN OPERATION: 10
LANGUAGES: Spanish
ACCESSIBILITY: Wheelchair accessible
CASES SEXUAL ASSAULT/ABUSE (%): 100
CLIENTS/SERVICES: Sexual assault survivors; Marital rape/sexual abuse survivors; Child victims of sexual abuse; Adult survivors of child sexual abuse; Incest victims/survivors; Prevention program; Community education; Adolescent survivors of sexual abuse; Male survivors of sexual abuse

WEST HARTFORD

CREATIVE COUNSELING SERVICES
PO Box 408, West Hartford, CT 06107
Information: (203) 233-6962 24 hr answering machine
Contact: Mallory Crawford, MA, Psychotherapist/Owner
TYPE OF AGENCY: Private practice
AREAS SERVED: Statewide
YEARS IN OPERATION: 8
LANGUAGES: Spanish
ACCESSIBILITY: Wheelchair accessible
CASES SEXUAL ASSAULT/ABUSE (%): 25
DESCRIPTION: Private practice appealing in particular to progressive, feminist women, men, couples, and adolescents. Experienced in working with runaways, lesbian couples who are dealing with past child sexual abuse of one or both women, clients with multiple personality, and clients involved in s/m sexual practices. Two clients successfully filed charges against sexually abusive doctors. Feminist martial arts program (akido); Individual and couple therapy for rapists, child sexual abuse offenders, incest offenders, and batterers; Couple counseling, siblings, parent/child counseling for males who have been sexually assaulted/abused
CLIENTS/SERVICES: Sexual assault survivors; Marital rape/sexual abuse survivors; Adult survivors of child sexual abuse; Incest victims/survivors; Community education; Offender treatment program; Adolescent survivors of sexual abuse; Male survivors of sexual abuse; Lesbians; Sexual harassment
REQUIREMENTS: Client must be an adolescent or older
SPECIAL PROGRAMS/SERVICES: Healing through art, storytelling, psychodrama, movement, music, ritual, writing, role playing

NEW ENGLAND CLINICAL ASSOCIATES
970 Farmington Ave, Ste 209, West Hartford, CT 06107
Information: (203) 561-3980 9am-8pm (Mon, Tue); 9am-7pm (Wed, Thu); 9am-5pm (Fri)
Contact: Suzanne M Sgroi, MD, Exec Dir
TYPE OF AGENCY: Child sexual abuse services
YEARS IN OPERATION: 4
ACCESSIBILITY: Wheelchair accessible
CASES SEXUAL ASSAULT/ABUSE (%): 100
DESCRIPTION: Peer group therapy for male and female adolescent and adult survivors. Also treats child sexual abuse/incest offenders
CLIENTS/SERVICES: Child victims of sexual abuse; Adult survivors of child sexual abuse; Incest victims/survivors; Offender treatment program; Adolescent survivors of sexual abuse; Male survivors of sexual abuse; Developmentally disabled

NEW ENGLAND CLINICAL ASSOCIATES
(continued)

REQUIREMENTS: Private pay. All current cases must be reported to child protective services. Will not treat if offender is living with victim

WILLAMANTIC

NORTHEASTERN CONNECTICUT SEXUAL ASSAULT CRISIS SERVICES, INC
c/o Windham Community Memorial Hospital, 96 Mansfield Ave, Willamantic, CT 06226
Crisis hotline: **(203) 423-9201, ext 2515 24 hrs**
Information: (203) 423-9201, exts 3222, 2577 9am-5pm and some evenings
Contact: Linda L Johnston, Dir
TYPE OF AGENCY: Rape crisis center; Child sexual abuse services; Child sexual abuse prevention program
AREAS SERVED: Windham, Tolland, New London
YEARS IN OPERATION: 13
LANGUAGES: Spanish
ACCESSIBILITY: Wheelchair accessible (by arrangement); Telecommunications for the hearing impaired (TTY, TDY, etc.) (by arrangement); Signers for the hearing impaired (by arrangement)
CASES SEXUAL ASSAULT/ABUSE (%): 100
DESCRIPTION: Crisis services and support for all victims of sexual assault, including support groups for males and females, and male counselors for male victims
CLIENTS/SERVICES: Sexual assault survivors; Marital rape/sexual abuse survivors; Child victims of sexual abuse; Adult survivors of child sexual abuse; Incest victims/survivors; Prevention program; Community education; Adolescent survivors of sexual abuse; Male survivors of sexual abuse

DELAWARE

DOVER

DELAWARE STATE POLICE—VICTIM ASSISTANCE UNIT
PO Box 431, Dover, DE 19903
Information: (302) 736-3711 8am-4pm
Contact: Cpl Gary R Melvin, Coord
TYPE OF AGENCY: Victim/witness assistance program; Child sexual abuse prevention program
AREAS SERVED: New Castle, Kent, Sussex
YEARS IN OPERATION: 1
DESCRIPTION: A referral agency which contacts victims and refers them to services that help them through the traumatic event. Provides no counseling
CLIENTS/SERVICES: Sexual assault survivors; Marital rape/sexual abuse survivors; Child victims of sexual abuse; Incest victims/survivors; Prevention program; Community education
REQUIREMENTS: Victim or survivor of violent crime or incident, (e.g. rape, homicide, suicide, fatal accidents); any victim over the age of 60 years of any crime

MILFORD

FAMILIES IN TRANSITION CENTER
219 S Walnut St, Milford, DE 19963
Crisis hotline: **(302) 422-8058, 856-4919 24 hrs**
Information: (302) 422-8058, 856-4919 24 hrs
Contact: Cindy Boehmer, Prog Dir
TYPE OF AGENCY: Domestic violence program
AREAS SERVED: Kent, Sussex
YEARS IN OPERATION: 11
ACCESSIBILITY: Signers for the hearing impaired
CASES SEXUAL ASSAULT/ABUSE (%): 85
CLIENTS/SERVICES: Marital rape/sexual abuse survivors; Child victims of sexual abuse

RAPE CRISIS—CONTACT
PO Box 61, Milford, DE 19963
Crisis hotline: **(800) 262-9800 24 hrs daily**
Information: (302) 422-2078 9am-5pm (Mon-Fri)
Contact: Betty Metzler, Prog Dir
TYPE OF AGENCY: Rape crisis center
SPONSORING ORGANIZATION: CONTACT-Delaware, Inc
AREAS SERVED: Kent, Sussex
YEARS IN OPERATION: 2
CASES SEXUAL ASSAULT/ABUSE (%): 100
CLIENTS/SERVICES: Sexual assault survivors; Marital rape/sexual abuse survivors; Adult survivors of child sexual abuse; Incest victims/survivors; Prevention program; Community education; Adolescent survivors of sexual abuse; Male survivors of sexual abuse

SEAFORD

TURNABOUT COUNSELING CENTER
PO Box 729, Seaford, DE 19973
Crisis hotline: **(800) 345-6785 24 hrs**
Information: (302) 856-5757 8am-5pm
Contact: Carol R Baker, PhD, Exec Dir
TYPE OF AGENCY: Counseling/mental health services
SPONSORING ORGANIZATION: Seaford Action Committee, Inc
AREAS SERVED: Sussex and portions of Kent
YEARS IN OPERATION: 14
LANGUAGES: Spanish, French, German, Haitian
ACCESSIBILITY: Wheelchair accessible
DESCRIPTION: Counseling for survivors; Support groups for female and male survivors of sexual assault/abuse; Individual and group therapy for child sexual abuse offenders, incest offenders, and batterers
CLIENTS/SERVICES: Sexual assault survivors; Marital rape/sexual abuse survivors; Child victims of sexual abuse; Adult survivors of child sexual abuse; Incest victims/survivors; Prevention program; Community education; Offender treatment program; Adolescent survivors of sexual abuse; Male survivors of sexual abuse

WILMINGTON

CHILDREN'S BUREAU OF DELAWARE
2005 Baynard Blvd, Wilmington, DE 19802
Information: (302) 658-5177 9am-5pm
Contact: Russell Widder, LCSW, Clinical Soc Wkr
TYPE OF AGENCY: Counseling/mental health services; Child sexual abuse services
AREAS SERVED: New Castle
LANGUAGES: Spanish
DESCRIPTION: Individual, marital, family, and group therapies
CLIENTS/SERVICES: Child victims of sexual abuse; Incest victims/survivors; Offender treatment program; Adolescent survivors of sexual abuse

RAPE CRISIS CONTACT
PO Box 2939, Wilmington, DE 19805
Crisis hotline: **(302) 575-1112 24 hrs**
Information: (302) 656-6222 8:30am-4:30pm
Contact: Pat Tedford, Exec Dir; Betty Metzler, Prog Dir
TYPE OF AGENCY: Rape crisis center
SPONSORING ORGANIZATION: Contact Delaware
AREAS SERVED: New Castle, Kent, Sussex
YEARS IN OPERATION: 3
CASES SEXUAL ASSAULT/ABUSE (%): 99
CLIENTS/SERVICES: Sexual assault survivors; Marital rape/sexual abuse survivors; Adult survivors of child sexual abuse; Incest victims/survivors; Prevention program; Community education; Adolescent survivors of sexual abuse; Male survivors of sexual abuse

DISTRICT OF COLUMBIA

WASHINGTON

DC HOTLINE, INC
PO Box 57194, Washington, DC 20037
Crisis hotline: **(202) 223-CALL 1pm-1am (Mon-Fri); 9am-1am (Sat-Sun)**
Information: (202) 223-0020 9:30-5:30
Contact: Julie Nathanson, Vol Svcs Dir
TYPE OF AGENCY: Counseling/mental health services; Telephone crisis hotline; Information and referral
AREAS SERVED: DC Metro Area
YEARS IN OPERATION: 13
ACCESSIBILITY: Wheelchair accessible
CASES SEXUAL ASSAULT/ABUSE (%): 5
DESCRIPTION: This is primarily a telephone service which provides information and referrals and crisis intervention to DC residents. It works closely with DC Rape Crisis Center in cross-training both groups of volunteers.
CLIENTS/SERVICES: Sexual assault survivors; Marital rape/sexual abuse survivors; Child victims of sexual abuse; Adult survivors of child sexual abuse; Incest victims/survivors; Community education; Male survivors of sexual abuse

DC NOW TASK FORCE AGAINST CHILD SEXUAL ABUSE
3104 18th St NW, Washington, DC 20010
Contact: Paula McKenzie, Chair
TYPE OF AGENCY: Child advocacy
SPONSORING ORGANIZATION: National Orgainization for Women
YEARS IN OPERATION: 1
DESCRIPTION: Raises public awareness; Reviews and works to revise current laws concerning child sexual abuse to better protect children and their parents
CLIENTS/SERVICES: Community education

DEPARTMENT OF EMPLOYMENT SERVICES
1200 Upshur St NW, Washington, DC 20011
Information: (202) 576-7706 8:30am-5pm
Contact: Delores Hollingsworth, Div of Disability and Crime Compensation Chief
TYPE OF AGENCY: Victim compensation program
YEARS IN OPERATION: 6
ACCESSIBILITY: Wheelchair accessible; Signers for the hearing impaired
CASES SEXUAL ASSAULT/ABUSE (%): 15
DESCRIPTION: The DC Crime Victims Compensation Program provides compensation benefits up to $25,000 for eligible innocent victims of violent crime for medical expense, lost wages, funeral expense, loss of support, loss of services and rehabilitation
CLIENTS/SERVICES: Sexual assault survivors; Marital rape/sexual abuse survivors; Male survivors of sexual abuse
REQUIREMENTS: Crime of rape/sexual assault must have occurred in the District of Columbia and be reported to the police within 7 days of its occurrence. Parents or guardians of minor sexual assault victims may apply

FACT HOTLINE—FAMILIES AND CHILDREN IN TROUBLE/TOGETHER
1400 20th St NW, Ste G-100, Washington, DC 20036
Crisis hotline: **(202) 628-FACT 24 hrs**
Information: (202) 965-1900 9am-5pm (Mon-Fri)
Contact: Joan Cox Danzansky, Agency Exec Dir
TYPE OF AGENCY: Counseling/mental health services; Child sexual abuse prevention program; Information center; Child abuse prevention program
SPONSORING ORGANIZATION: Family Stress Services of DC; DC Chapter, National Committee for Prevention of Child Abuse
AREAS SERVED: Washington, DC and metropolitan area
YEARS IN OPERATION: 13
CASES SEXUAL ASSAULT/ABUSE (%): 20
CLIENTS/SERVICES: Prevention program; Community education; Publications/media
SPECIAL PROGRAMS/SERVICES: This organization operates a public education/community awareness program focused on the prevention of child abuse and neglect. The agency develops, publishes and distributes a variety of materials and bibliographies on child sexual abuse, child abuse and parenting skills; has an extensive resource and information library; and can refer persons to a large network of other organizations, programs, and publishers, where appropriate. The program activities include researching information requests, mailing materials to fulfill requests, and provision of speakers and/or films for community groups.

HOUSE OF IMAGENE
214 P St NW, Washington, DC 20001
Information: (202) 797-7460 Evening only
Contact: Reverend Imagene Stewart, Founder
TYPE OF AGENCY: Domestic violence program; Shelter
YEARS IN OPERATION: 12
ACCESSIBILITY: Wheelchair accessible
CASES SEXUAL ASSAULT/ABUSE (%): 1
DESCRIPTION: Shelter for battered and homeless women
CLIENTS/SERVICES: Sexual assault survivors; Marital rape/sexual abuse survivors; Child victims of sexual abuse; Adult survivors of child sexual abuse; Adolescent survivors of sexual abuse; Male survivors of sexual abuse

MALCOMB GROW USAF MEDICAL CENTER/FAMILY ADVOCACY PROGRAM
MGMC/SGHA, Andrews AFB, Washington, DC 20331-5300
Crisis hotline: **(301) 981-2158 (emergency room) 5pm-8am**
Information: (301) 981-7253, 981-7650 8am-5pm
Contact: Capt Marilyn David-Topperman, Family Advocacy Officer
TYPE OF AGENCY: Hospital/medical center; Military services; Domestic violence program; Child abuse services
YEARS IN OPERATION: 14
LANGUAGES: Spanish, German
ACCESSIBILITY: Wheelchair accessible
CASES SEXUAL ASSAULT/ABUSE (%): 30-50
DESCRIPTION: Provides identification, assessment, treatment, and prevention of child abuse/neglect and spouse abuse including marital sexual assault and child sexual abuse. Non-marital sexual assault cases are handled through the outpatient mental health clinic and emergency room
CLIENTS/SERVICES: Marital rape/sexual abuse survivors; Child victims of sexual abuse; Adult survivors of child sexual abuse; Incest victims/survivors; Community education; Adolescent survivors of sexual abuse; Male survivors of sexual abuse
REQUIREMENTS: Client must be eligible for military health benefits-i.e., must be active duty, retired or dependents thereof

SARAH HOUSE
1329 N St NW, Washington, DC 61701
Information: (202) 232-6167 24 hrs
Contact: Vivian E Hauser, Act Dir
TYPE OF AGENCY: Shelter
SPONSORING ORGANIZATION: Luther Place Memorial Church
YEARS IN OPERATION: 8
CASES SEXUAL ASSAULT/ABUSE (%): 10
DESCRIPTION: Transitional shelter for women, many of whom have been abused
CLIENTS/SERVICES: Marital rape/sexual abuse survivors; Adult survivors of child sexual abuse
REQUIREMENTS: Client must be female, over the age of 18, able to participate in cooperative household. Referrals are preferred.

UNITED STATES ATTORNEY'S OFFICE— VICTIM/WITNESS ASSISTANCE UNIT
555 4th St NW, Ste 3633, Washington, DC 20001
Information: (202) 272-9164
Contact: Anita B Boles, Victim/Witness Assistance Unit Chief
TYPE OF AGENCY: Victim/witness assistance program
CLIENTS/SERVICES: Sexual assault survivors; Child victims of sexual abuse

WOMEN'S GROWTH AND THERAPY CENTER
3000 Connecticut Ave NW, Washington, DC 20008
Information: (202) 483-9376 9am-5pm
Contact: Rosalie Mandelbaum, Dir
TYPE OF AGENCY: Counseling/mental health services; Private practice
YEARS IN OPERATION: 11
CASES SEXUAL ASSAULT/ABUSE (%): 25
CLIENTS/SERVICES: Sexual assault survivors; Marital rape/sexual abuse survivors; Adult survivors of child sexual abuse; Incest victims/survivors
REQUIREMENTS: Women must be 18 years or older; Minimum fees.

FLORIDA

BARTOW

POLK COUNTY SHERIFF'S OFFICE—CRIME PREVENTION SECTION
455 N Broadway, Bartow, FL 33830
Crisis hotline: **(813) 533-3141 24 hrs**
Information: (813) 533-0344 24 hrs
Contact: Lt Mary N Campbell
TYPE OF AGENCY: Victim/witness assistance program
AREAS SERVED: Polk
ACCESSIBILITY: Wheelchair accessible; Telecommunications for the hearing impaired (TTY, TDY, etc.)
CASES SEXUAL ASSAULT/ABUSE (%): 30
CLIENTS/SERVICES: Sexual assault survivors; Marital rape/sexual abuse survivors; Child victims of sexual abuse; Adult survivors of child sexual abuse; Incest victims/survivors; Prevention program; Community education
REQUIREMENTS: Complaint must be submitted to the Sheriff's Office or other county agency

BONIFAY

LIFE MANAGEMENT CENTER OF NORTHWEST FLORIDA, INC
801 S Weeks St, Bonifay, FL 32425
Crisis hotline: **(904) 547-2472 24 hrs**
Information: (904) 547-2472 8am-5pm
Contact: Laura Hohnecker, Area Dir
TYPE OF AGENCY: Counseling/mental health services
AREAS SERVED: Holmes, Washington
YEARS IN OPERATION: 12
ACCESSIBILITY: Wheelchair accessible; Signers for the hearing impaired
CASES SEXUAL ASSAULT/ABUSE (%): 5
DESCRIPTION: Counseling for survivors and child sexual abuse/incest offenders as part of a comprehensive mental health program
CLIENTS/SERVICES: Sexual assault survivors; Marital rape/sexual abuse survivors; Child victims of sexual abuse; Adult survivors of child sexual abuse; Incest victims/survivors; Offender treatment program; Adolescent survivors of sexual abuse; Male survivors of sexual abuse

BRADENTON

CHILD PROTECTION TEAM
4301 32nd St W, Ste E-7, Bradenton, FL 34205
Crisis hotline: **(813) 756-1765 8:30am-5pm**
Information: (813) 756-1765 8:30am-5pm
Contact: Olga O'Neill, Supv Case Coord
TYPE OF AGENCY: Child sexual abuse services
SPONSORING ORGANIZATION: Children's Medical Services
AREAS SERVED: Manatee
YEARS IN OPERATION: 4
CASES SEXUAL ASSAULT/ABUSE (%): 90
DESCRIPTION: This organization assists Health and Rehabilitative Services and law enforcement in familial sexual assault investigations by providing a medical exam for the child, interviewing child on videotape, providing a case staffing when needed, referring child for counseling, and gathering a social history of the family when needed.
CLIENTS/SERVICES: Child victims of sexual abuse
REQUIREMENTS: Familial sexual abuse cases reported to Health and Rehabilitative Services.

HOPE OF MANATEE, INC
PO Box 1624, Bradenton, FL 34206
Crisis hotline: **(813) 755-6805 24 hrs**
Information: (813) 747-7790 9am-5pm (Mon-Fri)
Contact: Ashley Leonard, Exec Dir
TYPE OF AGENCY: Domestic violence program
AREAS SERVED: Manatee
YEARS IN OPERATION: 10
LANGUAGES: Spanish translators available
DESCRIPTION: Comprehensive domestic violence services, including batterers group
CLIENTS/SERVICES: Marital rape/sexual abuse survivors

MANATEE RAPE CRISIS
PO Box 9478, Bradenton, FL 34206
Crisis hotline: **(813) 748-8585 24 hrs daily**
Information: (813) 747-8648 8:30am-5pm
Contact: Marge Stoklosa, Rape Crisis Supv
TYPE OF AGENCY: Rape crisis center
SPONSORING ORGANIZATION: Manatee Glens Corp
AREAS SERVED: Manatee
YEARS IN OPERATION: 8
ACCESSIBILITY: Wheelchair accessible
CASES SEXUAL ASSAULT/ABUSE (%): 100
CLIENTS/SERVICES: Sexual assault survivors; Marital rape/sexual abuse survivors; Child victims of sexual abuse; Community education; Adolescent survivors of sexual abuse; Male survivors of sexual abuse
REQUIREMENTS: No therapy for children below age 14

BROOKSVILLE

CHILD SEX ABUSE TREATMENT PROGRAM
11331 Ponce De Leon Blvd, Brooksville, FL 34601
Crisis hotline: **(904) 796-9497 24 hrs**
Information: (904) 688-0701 9am-5pm (Mon-Thu)
Contact: Alfred S Arvay, PhD, Coord
TYPE OF AGENCY: Counseling/mental health services; Child sexual abuse services
SPONSORING ORGANIZATION: Hernando County Mental Health Center, Springfield, FL
AREAS SERVED: Hernando
YEARS IN OPERATION: 2
CASES SEXUAL ASSAULT/ABUSE (%): 100
DESCRIPTION: Counseling for child survivors of incest and their families; Individual, group, and family counseling for incest offenders and juvenile offenders
CLIENTS/SERVICES: Child victims of sexual abuse; Adult survivors of child sexual abuse; Incest victims/survivors; Prevention program; Community education; Offender treatment program; Adolescent survivors of sexual abuse; Male survivors of sexual abuse
REQUIREMENTS: Cases involving incest only; Offenders must admit responsibility for the abuse in order to enter or remain in the program.

HERNANDO COUNTY CHILD ABUSE PREVENTION PROJECT
19353 Oliver St, Brooksville, FL 34601
Crisis hotline: **(800) 342-9152 24 hrs**
Information: (904) 796-2292 9am-5pm
Contact: Noreen Trowell, Svc Coord
TYPE OF AGENCY: Child sexual abuse prevention program; Child abuse prevention program
SPONSORING ORGANIZATION: University of Florida Pediatrics Department
AREAS SERVED: Hernando
YEARS IN OPERATION: 5
LANGUAGES: Interpreters available
CLIENTS/SERVICES: Prevention program; Community education

HERNANDO COUNTY RAPE CRISIS/SPOUSE ABUSE CENTER
201 E Liberty St, Brooksville, FL 34601
Crisis hotline: **(904) 799-0657 24 hrs**
Information: (904) 796-4358 by appointment
Contact: Noreen Trowell, Ctr Coord
TYPE OF AGENCY: Rape crisis center; Domestic violence program
SPONSORING ORGANIZATION: Creative Services, Inc
AREAS SERVED: Hernando
YEARS IN OPERATION: 3
CASES SEXUAL ASSAULT/ABUSE (%): 43
CLIENTS/SERVICES: Sexual assault survivors; Marital rape/sexual abuse survivors; Child victims of sexual abuse; Adult survivors of child sexual abuse; Incest victims/survivors; Community education; Adolescent survivors of sexual abuse; Male survivors of sexual abuse

CLEARWATER

CLEARWATER POLICE DEPARTMENT—VICTIM ASSISTANCE PROGRAM
644 Pierce St, Clearwater, FL 34616
Crisis hotline: **(813) 462-6262 24 hrs**
Information: (813) 462-6950 9am-5pm
Contact: Penny Goatcher, Victim Asst
TYPE OF AGENCY: Victim/witness assistance program
AREAS SERVED: City of Clearwater

CLEARWATER POLICE DEPARTMENT—VICTIM ASSISTANCE PROGRAM *(continued)*
YEARS IN OPERATION: 11
ACCESSIBILITY: Wheelchair accessible; Telecommunications for the hearing impaired (TTY, TDY, etc.) (arranged); Signers for the hearing impaired (arranged)
CASES SEXUAL ASSAULT/ABUSE (%): 8
CLIENTS/SERVICES: Sexual assault survivors; Marital rape/sexual abuse survivors; Child victims of sexual abuse; Adult survivors of child sexual abuse; Incest victims/survivors; Prevention program; Community education; Adolescent survivors of sexual abuse; Male survivors of sexual abuse

SEXUAL ASSAULT AND FAMILY EMERGENCY (SAFE) CENTER
2960 Roosevelt Blvd, Clearwater, FL 34620
Crisis hotline: **(813) 526-5351 24 hrs**
Information: (813) 535-9811 8:30am-4:30pm
Contact: Joan T McCluney, Prog Dir
TYPE OF AGENCY: Rape crisis center; Child sexual abuse services; Child sexual abuse prevention program
SPONSORING ORGANIZATION: Family Service Centers of Pinellas County, Inc
AREAS SERVED: Pinellas
ACCESSIBILITY: Wheelchair accessible
CASES SEXUAL ASSAULT/ABUSE (%): 100
DESCRIPTION: Counseling for survivors of sexual assault and child sexual abuse; Group therapy for child sexual abuse offenders, incest offenders, batterers, and juvenile sex offenders
CLIENTS/SERVICES: Sexual assault survivors; Marital rape/sexual abuse survivors; Child victims of sexual abuse; Adult survivors of child sexual abuse; Incest victims/survivors; Prevention program; Community education; Offender treatment program; Adolescent survivors of sexual abuse; Male survivors of sexual abuse; Healing
SPECIAL PROGRAMS/SERVICES: Art therapy for sexual assault survivors

COCOA

CHILD/TEEN ABUSE PREVENTION PROGRAM
1519 Clearlake Rd, U121, Cocoa, FL 32780
Information: (407) 632-1111, ext 5526 8am-5pm
Contact: Joan Richardson, Child Abuse Prevention Coord
TYPE OF AGENCY: Child sexual abuse prevention program; Acquaintance/date rape prevention program; Adolescent program
SPONSORING ORGANIZATION: Brevard Community College
AREAS SERVED: Brevard
YEARS IN OPERATION: 5
ACCESSIBILITY: Wheelchair accessible
CASES SEXUAL ASSAULT/ABUSE (%): 50
DESCRIPTION: Personal safety from sexual abuse prevention programs available to children, teens, and parents; Speaker/trainer; Resource material (film, videos); Educational materials available to professionals and community
CLIENTS/SERVICES: Prevention program; Community education; Publications/media
SPECIAL PROGRAMS/SERVICES: Publication: *A Parent's Guide for Talking to a Child About Sexual Abuse* (13-page booklet)

DAVIE

REACH
4801 S University Dr, Ste 305, Davie, FL 33328
Information: (305) 434-2207 5:30pm-9:15pm
Contact: Seth Krieger, PhD, Dir
TYPE OF AGENCY: Private practice; Offender treatment
SPONSORING ORGANIZATION: Pines Psychological Associates
AREAS SERVED: Broward, Dade, Palm Beach
YEARS IN OPERATION: 11
ACCESSIBILITY: Wheelchair accessible
CASES SEXUAL ASSAULT/ABUSE (%): 100
DESCRIPTION: Outpatient sex offender program for rapists, child sexual abuse/incest offenders, and batterers
CLIENTS/SERVICES: Offender treatment program
REQUIREMENTS: Not psychotic; 18 years or older; Not intellectually impaired

DAYTONA BEACH

CHILD PROTECTION TEAM/CHILD CRISIS PREVENTION PROGRAM/SEXUAL ASSAULT TREATMENT PROGRAM
PO Box 1990, Halifax Medical Center, Daytona Beach, FL 32015
Crisis hotline: **(800) 96-ABUSE 24 hrs**
Information: (904) 254-4038 8am-5pm
Contact: Anita Parker, MSW, Team Coord; Charles Fanning, PhD; Robert Crimmins
TYPE OF AGENCY: Hospital/medical center; Child sexual abuse services; Child abuse services
SPONSORING ORGANIZATION: Children's Crisis Team of Volusia and Flagler Counties, Inc.—HRS
AREAS SERVED: Volusia, Flagler
YEARS IN OPERATION: 10
LANGUAGES: Spanish
ACCESSIBILITY: Wheelchair accessible
CASES SEXUAL ASSAULT/ABUSE (%): 70
DESCRIPTION: Provides psychosocial assessments, medical examinations, interviews the abused client, and provides psychological treatment in cases of intrafamilial abuse
CLIENTS/SERVICES: Child victims of sexual abuse; Incest victims/survivors; Community education; Adolescent survivors of sexual abuse
REQUIREMENTS: Intrafamilial abuse

INDEPENDENT CHILD ABUSE RELIEF ENTERPRISE (I-CARE)
304 N Frederick Ave, Daytona Beach, FL 32014
Crisis hotline: **(800) 96-ABUSE 24 hrs**
Information: (904) 258-0250 8:30am-5pm
Contact: Judith S Wilhelm, Exec Dir
TYPE OF AGENCY: Counseling/mental health services; Child sexual abuse services; Child sexual abuse prevention program; Child abuse services; Child abuse prevention program
AREAS SERVED: Volusia
YEARS IN OPERATION: 8
ACCESSIBILITY: Wheelchair accessible
CASES SEXUAL ASSAULT/ABUSE (%): 100
DESCRIPTION: Provides counseling treatment/prevention programs for victims of child abuse
CLIENTS/SERVICES: Sexual assault survivors; Child victims of sexual abuse; Prevention program; Community education; Adolescent survivors of sexual abuse
REQUIREMENTS: Services are open to all child victims, ages 3-17 years; Fees are based on family's ability to pay.
SPECIAL PROGRAMS/SERVICES: The child abuse prevention program includes a Parents Anonymous group, a self-help group for parents at risk of physical and emotional abuse; Parent Resource Program for education and counseling; AUNT CAREE volunteers, who are matched with the family as support persons; Personal Safety Awareness (No, Go, Tell message) program, which is a film and discussion series for schools, day care centers, churches, preschool through high school; and parent resource "warmline", a telephone listening ear offering reassurance, nonmedical advice, and referral to community resources.

RAPE CRISIS CENTER OF VOLUSIA COUNTY, INC
PO Box 63, Daytona Beach, FL 32015
Crisis hotline: **(904) 258-7273 24 hrs**
Information: (904) 254-4106 8am-4:30pm
Contact: Kathy Wilkes, Exec Dir
TYPE OF AGENCY: Rape crisis center
AREAS SERVED: Volusia
YEARS IN OPERATION: 2½
ACCESSIBILITY: Wheelchair accessible
CASES SEXUAL ASSAULT/ABUSE (%): 100
CLIENTS/SERVICES: Sexual assault survivors; Marital rape/sexual abuse survivors; Adult survivors of child sexual abuse; Incest victims/survivors; Prevention program; Community education; Adolescent survivors of sexual abuse; Male survivors of sexual abuse

DEFUNIAK SPRINGS

CHAUTAUQUA OFFICES OF PSYCHOTHERAPY AND EVALUATION (COPE)
PO Box 607, DeFuniak Springs, FL 32433
Crisis hotline: **(904) 892-4357 24 hrs daily**
Information: (904) 892-2167 8am-5pm
Contact: Neda Jackson, Counselor, Sexual Abuse Treatment Team
TYPE OF AGENCY: Counseling/mental health services
AREAS SERVED: Walton, Okaloosa
YEARS IN OPERATION: 15
LANGUAGES: Spanish
ACCESSIBILITY: Wheelchair accessible
CASES SEXUAL ASSAULT/ABUSE (%): 3
CLIENTS/SERVICES: Sexual assault survivors; Marital rape/sexual abuse survivors; Child victims of sexual abuse; Adult survivors of child sexual abuse; Incest victims/survivors; Prevention program; Community education; Offender treatment program
REQUIREMENTS: Offender must admit guilt or be willing to participate in counseling and must not be exclusively pedophiliac

EUSTIS

LAKE SUMTER RAPE CRISIS CENTER
129 N Grove St, Eustis, FL 32726
Crisis hotline: **(904) 483-2700 24 hrs**
Information: (904) 483-2700 9am-3pm (Mon, Wed, Fri)
Contact: Connie Croak, Counselor/Coord
TYPE OF AGENCY: Rape crisis center
SPONSORING ORGANIZATION: Creative Services
AREAS SERVED: Lake, Sumter
YEARS IN OPERATION: 4
LANGUAGES: Spanish
ACCESSIBILITY: Wheelchair accessible; Signers for the hearing impaired
CASES SEXUAL ASSAULT/ABUSE (%): 100
CLIENTS/SERVICES: Sexual assault survivors; Marital rape/sexual abuse survivors; Child victims of sexual abuse; Adult survivors of child sexual abuse; Incest victims/survivors; Prevention program; Community education; Adolescent survivors of sexual abuse; Male survivors of sexual abuse

FORT LAUDERDALE

BROWARD COUNTY SEXUAL ASSAULT TREATMENT CENTER
400 NE 4th St, Fort Lauderdale, FL 33301
Crisis hotline: **(305) 761-7273 24 hrs**
Information: (305) 765-4124 24 hrs
Contact: Joanne G Richter, Dir
TYPE OF AGENCY: Rape crisis center; Child sexual abuse services
SPONSORING ORGANIZATION: Broward County Board of County Commissioners
AREAS SERVED: Broward
YEARS IN OPERATION: 11
LANGUAGES: Spanish, Creole; interpreters on call
ACCESSIBILITY: Wheelchair accessible; Signers for the hearing impaired (on call)
CASES SEXUAL ASSAULT/ABUSE (%): 100
DESCRIPTION: Comprehensive rape crisis services; Support groups for female and male survivors of sexual assault/abuse; Individual

BROWARD COUNTY SEXUAL ASSAULT TREATMENT CENTER (continued)
and group therapy for incest offenders; Medical exams on-site
CLIENTS/SERVICES: Sexual assault survivors; Marital rape/sexual abuse survivors; Child victims of sexual abuse; Adult survivors of child sexual abuse; Incest victims/survivors; Prevention program; Community education; Offender treatment program; Adolescent survivors of sexual abuse; Male survivors of sexual abuse

CHILD PROTECTION TEAM OF BROWARD COUNTY, INC
255 SE 14th St, Fort Lauderdale, FL 33316
Crisis hotline: **(305) 779-1430 24 hrs daily**
Information: (305) 779-1430 24 hrs daily
Contact: Sandra Huff, MSW, Clinical Supv
TYPE OF AGENCY: Counseling/mental health services; Child sexual abuse services
AREAS SERVED: Broward
YEARS IN OPERATION: 7
LANGUAGES: Spanish
ACCESSIBILITY: Wheelchair accessible; Signers for the hearing impaired
CASES SEXUAL ASSAULT/ABUSE (%): 15
CLIENTS/SERVICES: Child victims of sexual abuse; Incest victims/survivors; Community education

KIDS IN DISTRESS, INC
727 NE 3rd Ave, Fort Lauderdale, FL 33304
Crisis hotline: **(305) 565-2211 24 hrs**
Information: (305) 765-1022 8am-5pm
Contact: Jeanne Miley, Exec Dir
TYPE OF AGENCY: Counseling/mental health services; Child sexual abuse services; Residential treatment facility; Child abuse services
AREAS SERVED: Broward
YEARS IN OPERATION: 9
LANGUAGES: Spanish
ACCESSIBILITY: Wheelchair accessible; Signers for the hearing impaired
CASES SEXUAL ASSAULT/ABUSE (%): 55
DESCRIPTION: Provides treatment services for young victims of physical and sexual abuse and their families, including a crisis home for children 11 and under and a therapeutic preschool
CLIENTS/SERVICES: Child victims of sexual abuse; Incest victims/survivors; Community education; Preschoolers
REQUIREMENTS: Referred by Child Protection Services; Children under age 11 for crisis home; Children under age 6 for therapeutic preschool

VICTIM ADVOCATE OFFICE
1300 W Broward Blvd, Fort Lauderdale, FL 33312
Information: (305) 761-5632 10am-6pm
Contact: Mozell Battle, Victim Advocate
TYPE OF AGENCY: Victim/witness assistance program
SPONSORING ORGANIZATION: Fort Lauderdale Police Dept, Programs for Sexual Assault Victims
AREAS SERVED: Broward
YEARS IN OPERATION: 14
CLIENTS/SERVICES: Sexual assault survivors; Child victims of sexual abuse; Incest victims/survivors; Prevention program; Community education

WOMEN IN DISTRESS OF BROWARD COUNTY, INC
PO Box 676, Fort Lauderdale, FL 33302
Crisis hotline: **(305) 761-1133 24 hrs, 7 days**
Information: (305) 760-9800 9am-5pm (Mon-Fri)
Contact: Bonnie M Flynn, Exec Dir
TYPE OF AGENCY: Domestic violence program
AREAS SERVED: Primarily Broward
YEARS IN OPERATION: 14
LANGUAGES: Spanish
ACCESSIBILITY: Wheelchair accessible; Telecommunications for the hearing impaired (TTY, TDY, etc.)
CASES SEXUAL ASSAULT/ABUSE (%): 75
DESCRIPTION: Provides services for domestic violence survivors; Group counseling for abusive males.
CLIENTS/SERVICES: Sexual assault survivors; Marital rape/sexual abuse survivors; Adult survivors of child sexual abuse; Incest victims/survivors; Prevention program; Community education; Offender treatment program

FORT MYERS

ABUSE COUNSELING AND TREATMENT, INC (ACT)
PO Box 06401, Fort Myers, FL 33906
Crisis hotline: **(813) 939-3112 24 hrs**
Information: (813) 939-3112 8am-5pm (Mon-Fri)
Contact: Sherree Houston, Exec Dir
TYPE OF AGENCY: Rape crisis center; Domestic violence program
AREAS SERVED: Lee, Collier, Hendry, Glades
YEARS IN OPERATION: 10
LANGUAGES: Spanish
ACCESSIBILITY: Wheelchair accessible
CASES SEXUAL ASSAULT/ABUSE (%): 20
CLIENTS/SERVICES: Sexual assault survivors; Marital rape/sexual abuse survivors; Child victims of sexual abuse; Prevention program; Community education; Adolescent survivors of sexual abuse; Male survivors of sexual abuse
REQUIREMENTS: Child victims must be 13 years or older.

CHILD PROTECTION TEAM
1940 Ricardo Ave, Fort Myers, FL 33901
Crisis hotline: **(813) 939-2808 24 hrs**
Information: (813) 939-2808 8am-5pm
Contact: Jill Turner, Team Coord
TYPE OF AGENCY: Counseling/mental health services
SPONSORING ORGANIZATION: Children's Centre
AREAS SERVED: Lee, Charlotte, Hendry, Glades
YEARS IN OPERATION: 7
ACCESSIBILITY: Wheelchair accessible
CASES SEXUAL ASSAULT/ABUSE (%): 50-60
CLIENTS/SERVICES: Child victims of sexual abuse; Incest victims/survivors; Community education; Adolescent survivors of sexual abuse
REQUIREMENTS: Must be 18 years or younger and suspected of being sexually abused.

LEE COUNTY WITNESS MANAGEMENT/VICTIM ASSISTANCE
Lee County Justice Center, 1700 Monroe St, Fort Myers, FL 33901
Information: (813) 335-2626 7:30am-5pm
Contact: Betty Sarkis, Prog Spec II
TYPE OF AGENCY: Victim/witness assistance program
AREAS SERVED: Lee
YEARS IN OPERATION: 9
LANGUAGES: Spanish
ACCESSIBILITY: Wheelchair accessible
CLIENTS/SERVICES: Sexual assault survivors; Marital rape/sexual abuse survivors; Child victims of sexual abuse; Adult survivors of child sexual abuse; Incest victims/survivors

SEXUAL ABUSE TREATMENT PROGRAM
3614 Evans Ave, Fort Myers, FL 33901
Information: (813) 275-4566 8:30am-5:30pm
Contact: Mary Robinson, Exec Dir
TYPE OF AGENCY: Child sexual abuse services; Child sexual abuse prevention program
SPONSORING ORGANIZATION: Concerned Citizens for Sexually Abused Children of Lee County, Inc
AREAS SERVED: Lee, Collier
YEARS IN OPERATION: 5
ACCESSIBILITY: Wheelchair accessible
CASES SEXUAL ASSAULT/ABUSE (%): 100
DESCRIPTION: Provides individual, family, and group therapy for victims of sexual abuse and their families; Incest offender treatment program
CLIENTS/SERVICES: Child victims of sexual abuse; Adult survivors of child sexual abuse; Incest victims/survivors; Prevention program; Offender treatment program; Adolescent survivors of sexual abuse
REQUIREMENTS: Offenders must be court-ordered to participate

STATE OF FLORIDA GUARDIAN AD LITEM PROGRAM—20TH JUDICIAL CIRCUIT
1700 Monroe St, Lee County Justice Center, Fort Myers, FL 33901
Information: (813) 335-2146 8:30am-5pm
Contact: Marcia L Soden, Dir
TYPE OF AGENCY: Child advocacy
AREAS SERVED: Lee, Charlotte, Collier, Hendry, Glades
YEARS IN OPERATION: 7
ACCESSIBILITY: Wheelchair accessible
DESCRIPTION: Court-appointed volunteers represent the best interest of children involved in the judicial system. Volunteers investigate, report to the court, act as monitors, protectors and spokespersons for the child/children
CLIENTS/SERVICES: Child victims of sexual abuse; Community education; Adolescent survivors of sexual abuse
REQUIREMENTS: Any child involved in dependency, dissolution/custody or criminal proceedings

FORT PIERCE

STATE ATTORNEY'S OFFICE—SEXUAL ASSAULT ASSISTANCE PROGRAM
PO Drawer 4401, Fort Pierce, FL 33448
Crisis hotline: **(407) 569-0209 (Indian River); (407) 286-5773 (Martin); (407) 465-1814 (St Lucie) 24 hrs**
Information: (407) 465-3000 8:30am-5pm (Mon-Fri)
Contact: Harriette E Rowe, Dir
TYPE OF AGENCY: Victim/witness assistance program
AREAS SERVED: Martin, St Lucie, Indian River
YEARS IN OPERATION: 8
ACCESSIBILITY: Wheelchair accessible; Signers for the hearing impaired
CASES SEXUAL ASSAULT/ABUSE (%): 100
CLIENTS/SERVICES: Sexual assault survivors; Marital rape/sexual abuse survivors; Child victims of sexual abuse; Adult survivors of child sexual abuse; Incest victims/survivors; Prevention program; Community education; Adolescent survivors of sexual abuse; Male survivors of sexual abuse

FORT WALTON BEACH

RAPE VICTIM ADVOCATE PROGRAM
205 Shell Ave SE, Fort Walton Beach, FL 32548
Crisis hotline: **(904) 244-9191 24 hrs**
Information: (904) 244-9191 10am-4pm
Contact: DeAnna Hickenbotham, MA, Dir
TYPE OF AGENCY: Rape crisis center
SPONSORING ORGANIZATION: Okaloosa Guidance Clinic Crisis Line
AREAS SERVED: Okaloosa
YEARS IN OPERATION: 10
CASES SEXUAL ASSAULT/ABUSE (%): 100
CLIENTS/SERVICES: Sexual assault survivors; Marital rape/sexual abuse survivors; Child victims of sexual abuse; Adult survivors of child sexual abuse; Incest victims/survivors; Prevention program; Community education; Adolescent survivors of sexual abuse; Male survivors of sexual abuse

GAINESVILLE

ALACHUA COUNTY RAPE AND CRIME VICTIM ADVOCATE PROGRAM
730 N Waldo Rd, Ste 100, Gainesville, FL 32601
Crisis hotline: **(904) 377-7273 24 hrs**
Information: (904) 377-7273 8:30am-5pm
Contact: Liz Jones, Dir
TYPE OF AGENCY: Rape crisis center; Victim/witness assistance program
AREAS SERVED: Alachua
YEARS IN OPERATION: 10
ACCESSIBILITY: Wheelchair accessible
CASES SEXUAL ASSAULT/ABUSE (%): 100
CLIENTS/SERVICES: Sexual assault survivors; Marital rape/sexual abuse survivors; Child victims of sexual abuse; Adult survivors of child sexual abuse; Incest victims/survivors; Community education; Adolescent survivors of sexual abuse; Male survivors of sexual abuse

CHILD SEXUAL ABUSE TREATMENT PROGRAM/PARENTS UNITED—MENTAL HEALTH SERVICES, INC
4300 SW 13th St, Gainesville, FL 32608
Information: (904) 374-5640 8:30am-5pm (Mon-Fri)
Contact: Williams J Peterson, Parents United Coord; Sandra Sullivan, PhD, Prog Dir
TYPE OF AGENCY: Counseling/mental health services; Child sexual abuse services
AREAS SERVED: Alachua
YEARS IN OPERATION: 4 (CSATP)
ACCESSIBILITY: Wheelchair accessible
CASES SEXUAL ASSAULT/ABUSE (%): 100
DESCRIPTION: Family and group therapy for survivors and families; Individual, group, and family therapy for incest offenders and juvenile offenders
CLIENTS/SERVICES: Child victims of sexual abuse; Adult survivors of child sexual abuse; Incest victims/survivors; Offender treatment program; Adolescent survivors of sexual abuse
REQUIREMENTS: Offenders must acknowledge problem; pedophiles not admitted.

COMMUNITY BEHAVIORAL SERVICES
1212 NW 12th Ave, Gainesville, FL 32601
Crisis hotline: **(904) 372-6645 24 hr answering service**
Information: (904) 372-6645 8am-8pm
Contact: Dr Harry Krop, Lic Psychologist Dir
TYPE OF AGENCY: Child sexual abuse services; Private practice
AREAS SERVED: Alachua, Marion, Bradford, Columbia, Putnam, Clay, Duval, Sawannee
YEARS IN OPERATION: 14
LANGUAGES: Sign
ACCESSIBILITY: Wheelchair accessible; Signers for the hearing impaired
CASES SEXUAL ASSAULT/ABUSE (%): 30-40
DESCRIPTION: Comprehensive incest treatment program with services for the victim, the mother, and the offender; Adult survivor groups; Treatment for rapists, batterers, adult and adolescent sex offenders
CLIENTS/SERVICES: Child victims of sexual abuse; Adult survivors of child sexual abuse; Incest victims/survivors; Prevention program; Community education; Offender treatment program; Adolescent survivors of sexual abuse; Male survivors of sexual abuse
SPECIAL PROGRAMS/SERVICES: Incest family graduation team assists new incest families

DISTRICT III—CHILD PROTECTION TEAM
5700 SW 34th St, Ste 1310, Gainesville, FL 32608
Crisis hotline: **(904) 392-5960 24 hrs**
Information: (904) 392-5960 24 hrs
Contact: James G Spencer, MSW, Project Coord
TYPE OF AGENCY: Child sexual abuse services; Child abuse services
SPONSORING ORGANIZATION: HRS/Children's Medical Services
AREAS SERVED: Alachua, Bradford, Columbia, Dixie, Gilchrist, Hernando, Lafayette, Lake, Levy, Marion, Putnam, Suwannee, Union, Citrus, Sumter, Hamilton
YEARS IN OPERATION: 7
ACCESSIBILITY: Wheelchair accessible
CASES SEXUAL ASSAULT/ABUSE (%): 80
DESCRIPTION: A multidisciplinary team providing diagnosis, assessment, and case management assistance to HRS and other agencies in the more complex cases of child abuse and neglect.
CLIENTS/SERVICES: Child victims of sexual abuse; Incest victims/survivors; Community education
REQUIREMENTS: Child (less than 18 years of age) and family must first be referred to Health and Rehabilitative Services

SEXUAL AND PHYSICAL ABUSE RESOURCE CENTER (SPARC)
PO Box 12367, Gainesville, FL 32604
Crisis hotline: **(904) 377-8255 24 hrs**
Information: (904) 378-1762 8:30am-5:30pm (Mon-Fri)
Contact: Linda Osmundson, Exec Dir
TYPE OF AGENCY: Domestic violence program
AREAS SERVED: Alachua, Bradford, Columbia, Dixie, Gilchrist, Lafayette, Levy, Hamilton, Suwannee, Union, Putnam
YEARS IN OPERATION: 10
DESCRIPTION: Comprehensive domestic violence services; Individual and group therapy for batterers
CLIENTS/SERVICES: Marital rape/sexual abuse survivors; Community education; Offender treatment program

SEXUAL ASSAULT RECOVERY SERVICE
University of Florida, Gainesville, FL 32611
Information: (904) 392-1161 8am-5pm (Mon-Fri)
Contact: Claire P Walsh, Dir
TYPE OF AGENCY: College/university-based services; Rape prevention program; Acquaintance/date rape prevention program
SPONSORING ORGANIZATION: Student Health Services
YEARS IN OPERATION: 8
ACCESSIBILITY: Wheelchair accessible
CASES SEXUAL ASSAULT/ABUSE (%): 100
DESCRIPTION: Crisis intervention and long-term counseling for sexual assault and sexual harassment survivors; Support groups for female and male survivors of sexual abuse/assault
CLIENTS/SERVICES: Sexual assault survivors; Marital rape/sexual abuse survivors; Child victims of sexual abuse; Adult survivors of child sexual abuse; Incest victims/survivors; Prevention program; Community education; Male survivors of sexual abuse; Sexual harassment; Publications/media
REQUIREMENTS: Affiliation with U of F as student or student's sponse. Family and significant others are also seen when appropriate to the recovery of clients.
SPECIAL PROGRAMS/SERVICES: COAR (Campus Organized Against Rape) is governed by female and male students whose goal is to decrease sexual victimization through educational activities, such as designing and preparing displays, and brochures and slide presentations that raise awareness about the problem of rape and describe services available to students; Preparing on- and off-campus educational programs and events on rape prevention, date-acquaintance rape and sexual harassment; Resource library on sexual assault and date rape. Training student volunteers to be part of a speakers' bureau on sexual assault; Sponsoring a bimonthly public lecture series on issues related to sex role socialization, community patterns between males and females, and cultural influences on sexual victimization. COAR has developed a 17-minute film on acquaintance rape called *Casting Shadows*. The unique feature of this film is that it depicts positive male role models as well as positive female role models. During the fall of 1983, the first class for credit on contemporary sex role victimization was taught in the College of Education. Myth of the Month bookmarks are produced ("The urge for a man to rape is inherent and uncontrollable.") Publication: *Dealing With Sexual Exploitation*

SEXUAL BATTERY COMMITTEE OF THE GAINESVILLE COMMISSION ON THE STATUS OF WOMEN
PO Box 490, Gainesville, FL 32602
Information: (904) 338-0397
Contact: Gilda S Josephson, PhD, Chairperson
TYPE OF AGENCY: Women's commission
SPONSORING ORGANIZATION: City of Gainesville
DESCRIPTION: Monthly meetings provide an opportunity for representatives from law enforcement, social services, criminal justice, advocacy groups, prevention and treatment groups to network; Goal is to raise awareness in the community about sexual battery/abuse/exploitation of women and children
CLIENTS/SERVICES: Sexual assault survivors; Marital rape/sexual abuse survivors; Child victims of sexual abuse; Incest victims/survivors; Adult survivors of child sexual abuse; Prevention program; Community education; Sexual harassment; Publications/media
SPECIAL PROGRAMS/SERVICES: Annual conference in May for local and statewide community held for the past 7 years. Some titles: *Family Violence and Substance Abuse-The Intimate Connection, Social Issues and Sexual Abuse, Impact of Violence on Women and Children*. National keynote speakers of local professionals present workshops for 350-400 individuals each year

HOLLYWOOD

DR GERALDINE BOOZER REHABILITATION PROGRAM FOR SEX OFFENDERS
1000 SW 84th Ave, Hollywood, FL 33025-1499
Crisis hotline: **(305) 963-6040 24 hrs**
Information: (305) 983-4321, ext 2321 8am-4:30pm (Mon-Fri)
Contact: Norma Wagner, Dir
TYPE OF AGENCY: Residential treatment facility; Offender treatment
SPONSORING ORGANIZATION: South Florida State Hospital
AREAS SERVED: Statewide
YEARS IN OPERATION: 16
CASES SEXUAL ASSAULT/ABUSE (%): 100
DESCRIPTION: Alters the sex offender's irresponsible, antisocial, and deviant behaviors into a responsible pattern of living. Treatment for rapists, child sexual abuse/incest offenders, and batterers
CLIENTS/SERVICES: Community education; Offender treatment program; Relatives Support Group
REQUIREMENTS: Must be convicted as an adult of a sex offense, currently incarcerated in the Florida Department of Corrections, non-psychotic, not retarded and considered to be amenable to treatment, and voluntary participant

HOMESTEAD

ADVOCATES FOR VICTIMS PROGRAM/ADVOCATES FOR SEXUALLY ABUSED CHILDREN
49 W Mowry St, Homestead, FL 33030
Crisis hotline: **(305) 247-4249 24 hrs**
Information: (305) 247-4249 24 hrs
TYPE OF AGENCY: Domestic violence program; Child sexual abuse services; Child sexual abuse prevention program
SPONSORING ORGANIZATION: South Dade Victims' Center
AREAS SERVED: Dade

ADVOCATES FOR VICTIMS PROGRAM/ ADVOCATES FOR SEXUALLY ABUSED CHILDREN (continued)

YEARS IN OPERATION: 14
LANGUAGES: Spanish, Creole
ACCESSIBILITY: Wheelchair accessible
CLIENTS/SERVICES: Sexual assault survivors; Marital rape/sexual abuse survivors; Child victims of sexual abuse; Incest victims/survivors; Community education; Adolescent survivors of sexual abuse; Male survivors of sexual abuse

INVERNESS

CITRUS COUNTY ABUSE SHELTER ASSOCIATION
PO Box 205, Inverness, FL 32651
Crisis hotline: **(904) 344-8111 24 hrs**
Information: (904) 344-8112 8:30am-5pm
Contact: Mary Hendrickson, Exec Dir
TYPE OF AGENCY: Rape crisis center; Domestic violence program; Child sexual abuse services; Child sexual abuse prevention program
AREAS SERVED: Citrus
YEARS IN OPERATION: 5
LANGUAGES: Spanish
ACCESSIBILITY: Wheelchair accessible; Signers for the hearing impaired
CASES SEXUAL ASSAULT/ABUSE (%): 10
CLIENTS/SERVICES: Sexual assault survivors; Marital rape/sexual abuse survivors; Child victims of sexual abuse; Incest victims/survivors; Prevention program; Community education

JACKSONVILLE

THE ARLINGTON PSYCHOLOGICAL CENTER
8049 Arlington Expressway, Ste 12, Jacksonville, FL 32211
Crisis hotline: **(904) 724-2405 8am-12pm**
Information: (904) 724-2405 8am-5pm
Contact: James Vallely, PhD; Nan Jobson, MSW
TYPE OF AGENCY: Child sexual abuse services; Private practice; Training/research; Offender treatment
AREAS SERVED: Duval, Nassau, St Johns
YEARS IN OPERATION: 4
ACCESSIBILITY: Wheelchair accessible
CASES SEXUAL ASSAULT/ABUSE (%): 75-80
DESCRIPTION: Specializes in all aspects of child sexual abuse, including family therapy, groups for adult female and male and child victims and adult and adolescent offenders. Evaluation services
CLIENTS/SERVICES: Sexual assault survivors; Child victims of sexual abuse; Adult survivors of child sexual abuse; Incest victims/survivors; Community education; Offender treatment program; Adolescent survivors of sexual abuse; Male survivors of sexual abuse
REQUIREMENTS: Offender must meet financial responsibility, admit abuse by 2nd month, demonstrate motivation
SPECIAL PROGRAMS/SERVICES: Uses voice stress analyzer lie detection for alleged offenders. Provides pre- and post-evaluations of offenders in therapy. Offender subjected to lie detector testing and psychometrics before release from therapy

CHILD PROTECTION TEAM
PO Box 40729, 655 W 8th St, Jacksonville, FL 32203
Crisis hotline: **(904) 350-6666 24 hrs**
Information: (904) 350-6666 9am-5pm
Contact: Jim Hutcheson, Team Coord
TYPE OF AGENCY: Hospital/medical center; Child sexual abuse services; Child abuse services
SPONSORING ORGANIZATION: Children's Crisis Center, Inc
AREAS SERVED: Duval, Nassau, Baker, Clay, St Johns
YEARS IN OPERATION: 10
ACCESSIBILITY: Wheelchair accessible; Signers for the hearing impaired
CASES SEXUAL ASSAULT/ABUSE (%): 60
CLIENTS/SERVICES: Child victims of sexual abuse; Incest victims/survivors

DEVEREUX AND ASSOCIATES
454 University Blvd N, Jacksonville, FL 32211
Information: (904) 721-3806 By appointment
Contact: William Devereux, PhD; Nancy J Thomas, PhD, Lic Psychologists
TYPE OF AGENCY: Private practice
AREAS SERVED: Duval, St Johns, Clay
YEARS IN OPERATION: 2
ACCESSIBILITY: Wheelchair accessible
CASES SEXUAL ASSAULT/ABUSE (%): 50
CLIENTS/SERVICES: Sexual assault survivors; Marital rape/sexual abuse survivors; Child victims of sexual abuse; Adult survivors of child sexual abuse; Incest victims/survivors; Adolescent survivors of sexual abuse; Male survivors of sexual abuse
REQUIREMENTS: Insurance/Champus accepted

HUBBARD HOUSE, INC
PO Box 4909, Jacksonville, FL 32201
Crisis hotline: **(904) 354-3114 24 hrs**
Information: (904) 354-3122 8am-4:30pm
Contact: Rita K DeYoung, Exec Dir
TYPE OF AGENCY: Domestic violence program
AREAS SERVED: Duval, Nassau, St Johns, Baker, Clay
YEARS IN OPERATION: 12
CLIENTS/SERVICES: Marital rape/sexual abuse survivors; Child victims of sexual abuse; Prevention program; Community education

SEXUAL ASSAULT CENTER
PO Box 40279, 655 W 8th St, Jacksonville, FL 32203-0279
Crisis hotline: **(904) 355-RAPE 24 hrs**
Information: (904) 350-6808 8am-5pm (Mon-Fri)
Contact: Deborah Thomas, Coord
TYPE OF AGENCY: Rape crisis center; Hospital/medical center; Child sexual abuse services
SPONSORING ORGANIZATION: Children's Crisis Center, Inc
AREAS SERVED: Duval, Nassau, Baker, Clay, St Johns
YEARS IN OPERATION: 6
LANGUAGES: Translators available
ACCESSIBILITY: Wheelchair accessible; Signers for the hearing impaired
CASES SEXUAL ASSAULT/ABUSE (%): 100
CLIENTS/SERVICES: Sexual assault survivors; Marital rape/sexual abuse survivors; Child victims of sexual abuse; Incest victims/survivors; Prevention program; Community education; Adolescent survivors of sexual abuse; Male survivors of sexual abuse; Publications/media
REQUIREMENTS: Medical/forensic exam only in reported cases; Crisis intervention in all cases.
SPECIAL PROGRAMS/SERVICES: Member of Greater Jacksonville Network for Victims (monthly meeting of sexual assault services providers to plan goals and assess needs) and Victim Assistance Advisory Council to the Mayor (forum of victim services providers to assist victims, create community awareness and make recommendations to the mayor). Media program sponsored by Chamber of Commerce: Rape Awareness and Prevention geared to businesses and organizations

VICTIM SERVICES DIVISION
134 E Church St, Jacksonville, FL 32202
Information: (904) 630-6300 8am-5pm
Contact: Jerry Flakus, Chief
TYPE OF AGENCY: Victim/witness assistance program; Counseling/mental health services
SPONSORING ORGANIZATION: Jacksonville Human Services
AREAS SERVED: Duval
YEARS IN OPERATION: 3
ACCESSIBILITY: Wheelchair accessible
CASES SEXUAL ASSAULT/ABUSE (%): 30
CLIENTS/SERVICES: Sexual assault survivors; Marital rape/sexual abuse survivors; Child victims of sexual abuse; Adult survivors of child sexual abuse; Incest victims/survivors; Community education; Adolescent survivors of sexual abuse

JACKSONVILLE BEACH

LAW FIRM OF ANDERSON AND HOWELL
2029 N 3rd St, Jacksonville Beach, FL 32250
Information: (904) 247-1972 9am-6pm
Contact: Jay Howell, Attorney
TYPE OF AGENCY: Legal services agency
YEARS IN OPERATION: 2
CASES SEXUAL ASSAULT/ABUSE (%): 90
DESCRIPTION: Legal representation in civil litigation on behalf of victims of sexual assault and child sexual and physical abuse
CLIENTS/SERVICES: Sexual assault survivors; Child victims of sexual abuse

KEY WEST

OFFICE OF THE STATE ATTORNEY—VICTIM/WITNESS ASSISTANCE PROGRAM
PO Box 1086, 302 Fleming St, Key West, FL 33041-1086
Information: (305) 294-5165 8:30am-5pm
Contact: Kathy M Peters, Victim Witness Counselor III
TYPE OF AGENCY: Victim/witness assistance program
AREAS SERVED: Monroe
LANGUAGES: Spanish
ACCESSIBILITY: Wheelchair accessible
DESCRIPTION: Assist crime victims through the criminal justice system with recent expansion to provide outreach services in cases which cannot be prosecuted.
CLIENTS/SERVICES: Sexual assault survivors; Marital rape/sexual abuse survivors; Child victims of sexual abuse; Incest victims/survivors; Community education; Male survivors of sexual abuse
SPECIAL PROGRAMS/SERVICES: Created a victim outreach program called *Operation Victim*. This program reviews all law enforcement agency reports to obtain victim contact information. In this manner assistance is provided when most critical-immediately following the crime, not 7-10 days later when the case reaches the state attorneys office; or, in some cases when no assistance is offered if that case cannot be prosecuted.

LAKELAND

DISTRICT VI B—CHILD PROTECTION TEAM
1129 US Hwy 98 S, Ste A, Lakeland, FL 33801
Information: (813) 687-7166 8am-5pm (On call 24 hrs)
Contact: Dickie McGowan, Team Coord
TYPE OF AGENCY: Child sexual abuse services
SPONSORING ORGANIZATION: Health and Rehabilitative Services
AREAS SERVED: Polk, Highlands, Hardee
YEARS IN OPERATION: 7
ACCESSIBILITY: Wheelchair accessible
CASES SEXUAL ASSAULT/ABUSE (%): 64
DESCRIPTION: Medical exams of victims of sexual and physical abuse
CLIENTS/SERVICES: Child victims of sexual abuse; Community education

PEACE RIVER CENTER—RAPE CRISIS PROGRAM
1835 N Gilmore Ave, Lakeland, FL 33805
Crisis hotline: **(813) 533-4323 24 hrs**
Information: (813) 683-5701 8:30am-4:30pm
Contact: Laura Fitzgerald, Vol Coord

PEACE RIVER CENTER—RAPE CRISIS PROGRAM (continued)
TYPE OF AGENCY: Rape crisis center; Domestic violence program; Child sexual abuse services; Counseling/mental health services; Child sexual abuse prevention program
AREAS SERVED: Polk, Highlands, Hardee
YEARS IN OPERATION: 6
LANGUAGES: Spanish through interpreter
ACCESSIBILITY: Wheelchair accessible
CASES SEXUAL ASSAULT/ABUSE (%): 100
DESCRIPTION: Comprehensive rape crisis services, including support groups for female and male survivors; Individual and group therapy for incest offenders and batterers
CLIENTS/SERVICES: Sexual assault survivors; Marital rape/sexual abuse survivors; Child victims of sexual abuse; Adult survivors of child sexual abuse; Incest victims/survivors; Prevention program; Community education; Adolescent survivors of sexual abuse; Male survivors of sexual abuse

LIVE OAK

VICTIM/WITNESS SERVICES
PO Box 1546, Live Oak, FL 32060
Information: (904) 362-2320 8:30am-5pm
Contact: Lois Hipp, Victim/Witness Coord
TYPE OF AGENCY: Victim/witness assistance program
SPONSORING ORGANIZATION: State Attorney's Office, Third Judicial Circuit
AREAS SERVED: Columbia, Suwannee
YEARS IN OPERATION: 1
ACCESSIBILITY: Wheelchair accessible
CLIENTS/SERVICES: Sexual assault survivors; Marital rape/sexual abuse survivors; Child victims of sexual abuse; Community education; Adolescent survivors of sexual abuse; Male survivors of sexual abuse
REQUIREMENTS: Client must file a police report

MANGONIA PARK

CHILD PROTECTION TEAM, INC/FAMILY SEXUAL ABUSE TREATMENT PROGRAM
1720 E Tiffany Dr, No 101, Mangonia Park, FL 33407
Crisis hotline: **(407) 863-1611 8am-5pm, or by appointment**
Information: (407) 863-1611 8am-5pm, or by appointment
Contact: Bunny M Berman, ACSW, Treatment Coord
TYPE OF AGENCY: Counseling/mental health services; Child sexual abuse services; Child sexual abuse prevention program
AREAS SERVED: Palm Beach
YEARS IN OPERATION: 7
LANGUAGES: Spanish
ACCESSIBILITY: Wheelchair accessible
CASES SEXUAL ASSAULT/ABUSE (%): 100
DESCRIPTION: Comprehensive treatment program for incest families: group, family, marital, dyad, and individual therapies; Parents United model for intervention. Treatment for adolescent sex offenders.
CLIENTS/SERVICES: Child victims of sexual abuse; Adult survivors of child sexual abuse; Incest victims/survivors; Prevention program; Community education; Offender treatment program; Adolescent survivors of sexual abuse; Male survivors of sexual abuse
REQUIREMENTS: Victims ages 3-18; Families must have been reported to state agency and investigated—most cases are admitted prior to treatment
SPECIAL PROGRAMS/SERVICES: Videotape on investigation of child sexual abuse cases

MARATHON

DOMESTIC ABUSE SHELTER, INC
PO Box 1145, Marathon, FL 33050-1145
Crisis hotline: **(305) 743-4440 24 hrs**
Information: (305) 743-9465 9am-5pm (Mon-Fri)
Contact: Claudia Ewald, Shelter Coord
TYPE OF AGENCY: Domestic violence program
AREAS SERVED: Monroe
YEARS IN OPERATION: 4
DESCRIPTION: Services for domestic violence survivors; Groups for batterers
CLIENTS/SERVICES: Marital rape/sexual abuse survivors

MELBOURNE

SOUTH BREVARD WOMEN'S CENTER
901 E New Haven Ave, Ste 2, Melbourne, FL 32901
Crisis hotline: **(407) 631-8944**
Information: (407) 727-2200 9am-7pm (Mon), 9am-4pm (Tue-Fri), 9am-12pm (Sat)
Contact: M Fronk, Co-Dir
TYPE OF AGENCY: Women's center
AREAS SERVED: Brevard
YEARS IN OPERATION: 13
LANGUAGES: Spanish
DESCRIPTION: Family support; Parenting education; Spouse abuse/child abuse prevention programs; Community information and referral; Health education; Support groups for women, including incest survivors
CLIENTS/SERVICES: Incest victims/survivors; Community education

MERRITT ISLAND

YOUTH SERVICES CENTER, INC
PO Box 540625, Merritt Island, FL 32937
Crisis hotline: **(407) 452-0800 24 hrs**
Information: (407) 452-8988, 452-8933 9am-5pm
Contact: Susan Jennings, Exec Dir
TYPE OF AGENCY: Counseling/mental health services; Child sexual abuse services; Child sexual abuse prevention program; Shelter; Adolescent program
AREAS SERVED: Brevard
YEARS IN OPERATION: 12
LANGUAGES: Spanish
ACCESSIBILITY: Wheelchair accessible; Signers for the hearing impaired
CASES SEXUAL ASSAULT/ABUSE (%): 60
DESCRIPTION: Provides crisis intervention, prevention, and outreach services for adolescents and their families; short-term residential shelter for runaways, abused and neglected youth.
CLIENTS/SERVICES: Sexual assault survivors; Child victims of sexual abuse; Prevention program; Community education; Adolescent survivors of sexual abuse; Male survivors of sexual abuse
REQUIREMENTS: Residential services are for males and females ages 12 through 17.
SPECIAL PROGRAMS/SERVICES: Any distressed teenager may seek the refuge of a Safe Place. There are over 120 public and/or business locations throughout Brevard County that are part of its network. Trained site employees and volunteers are coordinated so that a troubled youth can receive guidance at any Safe Place. Many are open 24 hours a day, or if not, a central phone number to call is posted on the front door.

MIAMI

ADVOCATES FOR VICTIMS PROGRAM/ ADVOCATES FOR SEXUALLY ABUSED CHILDREN
7831 NE Miami Ct, Miami, FL 33138
Crisis hotline: **(305) 758-2546 24 hrs**
Information: (305) 758-2546 24 hrs
Contact: Sarah M Lenett, Asst Dir
TYPE OF AGENCY: Domestic violence program; Child sexual abuse services; Child sexual abuse prevention program
SPONSORING ORGANIZATION: North Dade Victims' Center
AREAS SERVED: Dade
YEARS IN OPERATION: 14
LANGUAGES: Spanish, Creole
ACCESSIBILITY: Wheelchair accessible
CASES SEXUAL ASSAULT/ABUSE (%): 50
CLIENTS/SERVICES: Sexual assault survivors; Marital rape/sexual abuse survivors; Child victims of sexual abuse; Incest victims/survivors; Community education; Adolescent survivors of sexual abuse; Male survivors of sexual abuse

CHILD ABUSE TREATMENT PROGRAM
2742 SW 8th St, Rm 10-A, Miami, FL 33141
Crisis hotline: **(305) 634-4074, (800) 342-9152 24 hrs**
Information: (305) 643-7540 8am-5pm
Contact: Ines Sanchez-Ferreira, Sr CYF Counselor
TYPE OF AGENCY: Child sexual abuse services; Child abuse services
SPONSORING ORGANIZATION: FL Health and Rehabilitative Services
AREAS SERVED: Dade
YEARS IN OPERATION: 12
LANGUAGES: Spanish
ACCESSIBILITY: Wheelchair accessible
CASES SEXUAL ASSAULT/ABUSE (%): 50
DESCRIPTION: Individual, group, and family therapy for sexually abused children and abusive parents, child sexual abuse offenders, and incest offenders
CLIENTS/SERVICES: Child victims of sexual abuse; Incest victims/survivors; Prevention program; Community education; Offender treatment program; Adolescent survivors of sexual abuse

CHILDREN'S CENTER
1350 NW 12th Ave, Miami, FL 33136
Information: (305) 545-4407 8am-5pm
Contact: Teresa Pooler, Dir
TYPE OF AGENCY: Victim/witness assistance program; Child sexual abuse services
SPONSORING ORGANIZATION: Dade County State Attorney's Office
AREAS SERVED: Dade
YEARS IN OPERATION: 2
LANGUAGES: Creole, Spanish
ACCESSIBILITY: Wheelchair accessible; Signers for the hearing impaired
CASES SEXUAL ASSAULT/ABUSE (%): 75
DESCRIPTION: Investigation and prosecution of child sexual abuse; videotaping for court testimony; groups for sexually abused children
CLIENTS/SERVICES: Child victims of sexual abuse
REQUIREMENTS: Clients must be under 18 years of age.

CMS CHILD PROTECTION TEAM
PO Box 016820 (D-820), 1150 NW 14th St, Ste 212, Miami, FL 33136
Crisis hotline: **(305) 547-6916 24 hrs**
Information: (305) 547-6916 8:30am-5pm (Mon-Fri)
Contact: Johnathan Cloud, Team Coord
TYPE OF AGENCY: College/university-based services; Child sexual abuse services
SPONSORING ORGANIZATION: University of Miami School of Medicine
AREAS SERVED: Dade
YEARS IN OPERATION: 9
LANGUAGES: Spanish
ACCESSIBILITY: Wheelchair accessible
DESCRIPTION: Supports HRS and provides medical and psychological evaluations of victims and family members, and a primarily investigative family needs assessment
CLIENTS/SERVICES: Child victims of sexual abuse
REQUIREMENTS: Victims must be under 18 years of age

FAMILY SERVICES PROGRAM
1515 NW 7th St, Ste 220, Miami, FL 33125
Crisis hotline: **(305) 547-5482 9am-6pm**
Information: (305) 547-5482 9am-6pm
Contact: Marcy Prince, Clinical Soc Wkr Lead
TYPE OF AGENCY: Child sexual abuse services
SPONSORING ORGANIZATION: Metro-Dade Department of Justice Assistance
AREAS SERVED: Dade
YEARS IN OPERATION: 4
LANGUAGES: Spanish
ACCESSIBILITY: Wheelchair accessible
CASES SEXUAL ASSAULT/ABUSE (%): 100
DESCRIPTION: Provides long-term treatment for child victims of sexual assault, offenders of intrafamilial sexual abuse, and for their families; Individual, group, and family therapy
CLIENTS/SERVICES: Child victims of sexual abuse; Community education; Offender treatment program; Adolescent survivors of sexual abuse
REQUIREMENTS: Offenders are generally court-ordered into treatment
SPECIAL PROGRAMS/SERVICES: Has an arrangement with the local state attorney's office whereby an offender may be court-ordered into treatment on a "diversionary" basis, as an alternative to prosecution. If offender does not comply with the requirements of the program, his case is returned to the court for disposition.

JEWISH FAMILY SERVICE OF GREATER MIAMI
1790 SW 27th Ave, Miami, FL 33145
Crisis hotline: **(305) 445-0555 24 hrs**
Information: (305) 445-0555 9am-5pm
Contact: Daniel Shaw, PhD, Prevention Dept Dir
TYPE OF AGENCY: Counseling/mental health services; Training/research
AREAS SERVED: Dade
YEARS IN OPERATION: 65
LANGUAGES: Spanish
ACCESSIBILITY: Wheelchair accessible; Telecommunications for the hearing impaired (TTY, TDY, etc.); Signers for the hearing impaired
CASES SEXUAL ASSAULT/ABUSE (%): 5
DESCRIPTION: Advanced professional seminars; Counseling for family and child abuse victims and treatment for child sexual abuse/incest offenders and batterers. Sponsors advanced professional seminars for experienced human services practitioners
CLIENTS/SERVICES: Sexual assault survivors; Marital rape/sexual abuse survivors; Child victims of sexual abuse; Adult survivors of child sexual abuse; Incest victims/survivors; Prevention program; Community education; Offender treatment program; Adolescent survivors of sexual abuse; Male survivors of sexual abuse

RAPE TREATMENT CENTER
1611 NW 12th Ave, Miami, FL 33136
Crisis hotline: **(305) 549-RAPE 24 hrs**
Information: (305) 549-6949 24 hrs
Contact: Laurie Forbes, LCSW, Prog Admin
TYPE OF AGENCY: Rape crisis center; Hospital/medical center
SPONSORING ORGANIZATION: Jackson Memorial Hospital
AREAS SERVED: Dade
YEARS IN OPERATION: 14
LANGUAGES: Spanish
ACCESSIBILITY: Wheelchair accessible
CASES SEXUAL ASSAULT/ABUSE (%): 100
CLIENTS/SERVICES: Sexual assault survivors; Marital rape/sexual abuse survivors; Child victims of sexual abuse; Adult survivors of child sexual abuse; Incest victims/survivors; Community education; Adolescent survivors of sexual abuse; Male survivors of sexual abuse

STOP SEXUAL ADDICTIONS AND DISORDERS TREATMENT PROGRAM
7241 SW 63 Ave, Miami, FL 33143
Crisis hotline: **(305) 667-6600 8am-5pm**
Information: (305) 667-6600 8am-8pm
Contact: Josefina Perez-Castro, Clinical Dir
TYPE OF AGENCY: Hospital/medical center; Counseling/mental health services; Training/research; Offender treatment
SPONSORING ORGANIZATION: A and A Professional Associates
AREAS SERVED: Dade, Broward, Monroe, and SE USA
YEARS IN OPERATION: 7
LANGUAGES: Spanish
ACCESSIBILITY: Wheelchair accessible
CASES SEXUAL ASSAULT/ABUSE (%): 100
DESCRIPTION: Treatment for survivors of sexual assault and abuse, incest families, and rapists, child sexual abuse/incest offenders, and batterers
CLIENTS/SERVICES: Sexual assault survivors; Marital rape/sexual abuse survivors; Child victims of sexual abuse; Adult survivors of child sexual abuse; Incest victims/survivors; Prevention program; Community education; Offender treatment program; Adolescent survivors of sexual abuse; Male survivors of sexual abuse
REQUIREMENTS: Not mentally retarded, and ability to pay for services
SPECIAL PROGRAMS/SERVICES: Has inpatient hospital based programs for adults and adolescents—for offenders and for victims (depression, suicidal, multiple personality). Sponsorship of Sexual Abuse Training Program, a series of monthly workshops for mental health professionals during 1989.

MILTON

THE AVALON CENTER, INC
PO Box 769, Milton, FL 32572
Crisis hotline: **(904) 623-6363 5pm-8am**
Information: (904) 623-9434 8am-5pm
TYPE OF AGENCY: Counseling/mental health services
AREAS SERVED: Santa Rosa
YEARS IN OPERATION: 14
ACCESSIBILITY: Wheelchair accessible
DESCRIPTION: Community mental health, alcohol, and drug abuse treatment agency; Provides crisis intervention and screening, referrals, as well as limited follow-up therapy for victims of sexual assault and child abuse
CLIENTS/SERVICES: Sexual assault survivors; Child victims of sexual abuse; Adult survivors of child sexual abuse; Incest victims/survivors; Prevention program; Community education; Adolescent survivors of sexual abuse; Male survivors of sexual abuse

NAPLES

CHILD PROTECTION TEAM OF COLLIER COUNTY
2500 Airport Rd S, Ste 308, Naples, FL 33962
Crisis hotline: **(813) 793-3939 24 hrs**
Information: (813) 793-3939 8am-5pm
Contact: Sandra Glover, Team Coord
TYPE OF AGENCY: Child sexual abuse services; Child abuse services
SPONSORING ORGANIZATION: Collier County Child Advocacy Council and Department of Health and Rehabilitative Services, Children's Medical Services
AREAS SERVED: Collier
YEARS IN OPERATION: 7
LANGUAGES: Spanish
ACCESSIBILITY: Wheelchair accessible; Telecommunications for the hearing impaired (TTY, TDY, etc.); Signers for the hearing impaired (arranged)
CASES SEXUAL ASSAULT/ABUSE (%): 55-60
DESCRIPTION: Provides videotaped interviewing of child victim in conjunction with Child Protective Services and law enforcement; Crisis counseling for the child and their family; Medical evaluations for the diagnosis of child abuse and neglect; Psychosocial assessments of family dynamics; Multidisciplinary case staffings, and court testimony for juvenile and criminal court
CLIENTS/SERVICES: Child victims of sexual abuse; Community education
REQUIREMENTS: Suspected sexual abuse of a child age 0-18 by a family member, guardian or caretaker.
SPECIAL PROGRAMS/SERVICES: The 15-week Nurturing Treatment Program for parents and their children is geared toward increasing the parenting and nurturing skills of parents and their children who are experiencing interaction problems.

PROJECT HELP, INC
PO Box 7804, Naples, FL 33940
Crisis hotline: **(813) 262-7227 24 hrs**
Information: (813) 649-1404 10am-6pm
Contact: Beth Knake, Exec Dir
TYPE OF AGENCY: Victim/witness assistance program; Counseling/mental health services; Telephone crisis hotline; Acquaintance/date rape prevention program
AREAS SERVED: Collier
YEARS IN OPERATION: 2½
LANGUAGES: Spanish interpreter available
DESCRIPTION: Suicide/crisis intervention; Telephone hotline counseling; Rape crisis services; Support for crime victims
CLIENTS/SERVICES: Sexual assault survivors; Marital rape/sexual abuse survivors; Child victims of sexual abuse; Adult survivors of child sexual abuse; Prevention program; Community education; Adolescent survivors of sexual abuse
REQUIREMENTS: Primarily deals with those 14 years and older.
SPECIAL PROGRAMS/SERVICES: Teaches date rape prevention/precaution in schools

NEW PORT RICHEY

FLORIDA VISITING FAMILY THERAPY ASSOCIATES, INC
7602 Congress St, New Port Richey, FL 34653
Crisis hotline: **(813) 848-5555 24 hrs daily**
Information: (813) 842-5151 24 hrs daily
Contact: Greg Kaufman, Lic Psychotherapist
TYPE OF AGENCY: Private practice
AREAS SERVED: Pasco
YEARS IN OPERATION: 2
ACCESSIBILITY: Wheelchair accessible
CASES SEXUAL ASSAULT/ABUSE (%): 50
DESCRIPTION: Provides short- and long-term counseling and support groups for victims and treatment for child sexual abuse/incest offenders; Contracts with SAVE Program to do training with volunteers
CLIENTS/SERVICES: Sexual assault survivors; Marital rape/sexual abuse survivors; Child victims of sexual abuse; Adult survivors of child sexual abuse; Incest victims/survivors; Community education; Offender treatment program; Adolescent survivors of sexual abuse; Male survivors of sexual abuse
REQUIREMENTS: Client must file charges to be eligible for VOCA or SAVE victim services

HUMAN DEVELOPMENT CENTER OF PASCO
250 School Rd, New Port Richey, FL 34657
Crisis hotline: **(813) 848-5322 24 hrs**
Information: (813) 847-4700 8am-5pm (Mon-Fri)
Contact: Juanita Lowman, Children Svcs Prog Admin
TYPE OF AGENCY: Counseling/mental health services
AREAS SERVED: Pasco

HUMAN DEVELOPMENT CENTER OF PASCO *(continued)*
YEARS IN OPERATION: 10+
LANGUAGES: Spanish
ACCESSIBILITY: Wheelchair accessible; Telecommunications for the hearing impaired (TTY, TDY, etc.); Signers for the hearing impaired (provided by another agency)
CASES SEXUAL ASSAULT/ABUSE (%): 35
DESCRIPTION: Counseling for survivors; Individual and group therapy for rapists, child sexual abuse offenders, incest offenders, and batterers
CLIENTS/SERVICES: Sexual assault survivors; Marital rape/sexual abuse survivors; Child victims of sexual abuse; Adult survivors of child sexual abuse; Incest victims/survivors; Offender treatment program; Adolescent survivors of sexual abuse; Male survivors of sexual abuse

PASCO COUNTY SAVE (SEXUAL ABUSE VICTIM EXAMINATION) PROGRAM
530 Sunset Rd, Rm 104, New Port Richey, FL 34652
Crisis hotline: **(813) 845-4444 24 hrs**
Information: (813) 847-2411, ext 8255 8am-5pm
Contact: Carole A Daniels, Coord
TYPE OF AGENCY: Hospital/medical center; Child sexual abuse services
AREAS SERVED: Pasco County
YEARS IN OPERATION: 2
CASES SEXUAL ASSAULT/ABUSE (%): 100
DESCRIPTION: Medical exam and counseling for victims of sexual assault and child sexual abuse
CLIENTS/SERVICES: Sexual assault survivors; Marital rape/sexual abuse survivors; Child victims of sexual abuse; Adult survivors of child sexual abuse; Incest victims/survivors; Community education; Adolescent survivors of sexual abuse; Male survivors of sexual abuse
REQUIREMENTS: Victims who report the crime to law enforcement receive a medical exam and counseling services free of charge. Victims who do not report have access to counseling services on a sliding scale basis.

OCALA

RAPE CRISIS/SPOUSE ABUSE CENTER
PO Box 2193, Ocala, FL 32678
Crisis hotline: **(904) 622-8495 24 hrs**
Information: (904) 622-5919 8am-5pm (Mon-Fri)
Contact: Dr Judy Wilson, Exec Dir
TYPE OF AGENCY: Rape crisis center; Domestic violence program; Child sexual abuse services; Child sexual abuse prevention program
AREAS SERVED: Marion, Lake, Hernando
YEARS IN OPERATION: 14
LANGUAGES: Spanish, Sign
ACCESSIBILITY: Wheelchair accessible; Signers for the hearing impaired
CLIENTS/SERVICES: Sexual assault survivors; Marital rape/sexual abuse survivors; Child victims of sexual abuse; Adult survivors of child sexual abuse; Incest victims/survivors; Prevention program; Community education; Adolescent survivors of sexual abuse; Male survivors of sexual abuse

STATE ATTORNEY'S OFFICE—VICTIM/WITNESS ASSISTANCE PROGRAM
19 NW Pine Ave, Ocala, FL 32670
Information: (904) 622-0352 8am-5pm
Contact: Deborah D Beville, Exec Dir
TYPE OF AGENCY: Victim/witness assistance program
SPONSORING ORGANIZATION: Fifth Judicial Circuit
AREAS SERVED: Marion, Lake, Sumter, Citrus, Hernando
YEARS IN OPERATION: 3
ACCESSIBILITY: Wheelchair accessible

DESCRIPTION: Full-service victim/witness program, special sexual assault unit, child deposition rooms; Domestic violence deferred prosecution program for batterers
CLIENTS/SERVICES: Sexual assault survivors; Child victims of sexual abuse; Community education
SPECIAL PROGRAMS/SERVICES: *My Day in Court* coloring book for children

ORANGE PARK

CENTER FOR PSYCHOLOGICAL SERVICES
PO Box 1556, Orange Park, FL 32067
Crisis hotline: **(904) 269-6677 8am-10pm, 24-hr on call**
Information: (904) 269-6677 8am-10pm, 24-hr on call
Contact: Dr Keith R D'amato, Dir
TYPE OF AGENCY: Private practice
AREAS SERVED: Duval, Clay, Nausau, Baker, St Johns
YEARS IN OPERATION: 1
ACCESSIBILITY: Wheelchair accessible; Signers for the hearing impaired
CASES SEXUAL ASSAULT/ABUSE (%): 50
CLIENTS/SERVICES: Sexual assault survivors; Marital rape/sexual abuse survivors; Child victims of sexual abuse; Adult survivors of child sexual abuse; Incest victims/survivors; Prevention program; Community education; Offender treatment program; Adolescent survivors of sexual abuse; Male survivors of sexual abuse

COMMUNITY BEHAVIORAL SERVICES
1409 Kingsley Ave, Orange Park, FL 32073
Information: (904) 269-3324 8am-8pm
Contact: Dr Harry Krop, Lic Psychologist, Dir
TYPE OF AGENCY: Child sexual abuse services
AREAS SERVED: Alachua, Marion, Bradford, Columbia, Putnam, Clay, Duval, Sawannee
YEARS IN OPERATION: 14
LANGUAGES: Sign
ACCESSIBILITY: Wheelchair accessible; Signers for the hearing impaired
CASES SEXUAL ASSAULT/ABUSE (%): 30-40
CLIENTS/SERVICES: Child victims of sexual abuse; Incest victims/survivors

JUSTICE FOR ABUSED CHILDREN, INC
3659 Red Oak Cir W, Orange Park, FL 32073
Crisis hotline: **(800) 346-6184, 346-6185, 346-6186 24 hrs**
Information: (904) 269-8021 24 hrs
Contact: Beverly Chapman, Pres
TYPE OF AGENCY: Child sexual abuse services; Child sexual abuse prevention program
AREAS SERVED: Duval, Clay, Baker, Nassau, St Johns
YEARS IN OPERATION: 1
CASES SEXUAL ASSAULT/ABUSE (%): 100
DESCRIPTION: Support groups for survivors; Prevention programs, including feminist martial arts/self-defense program
CLIENTS/SERVICES: Child victims of sexual abuse; Adult survivors of child sexual abuse; Incest victims/survivors; Prevention program; Community education; Adolescent survivors of sexual abuse; Male survivors of sexual abuse
SPECIAL PROGRAMS/SERVICES: Video: Henry Winkler's *Good Touch, Bad Touch*.

ORLANDO

CENTER FOR LIFE MANAGEMENT
1414 S Kuhl Ave, Orlando, FL 32806
Information: (407) 841-5171 8am-8pm
Contact: Carol P Sevlie, RN
TYPE OF AGENCY: Hospital/medical center; Counseling/mental health services
AREAS SERVED: Orlando area
YEARS IN OPERATION: 20
LANGUAGES: Spanish
ACCESSIBILITY: Wheelchair accessible

CLIENTS/SERVICES: Child victims of sexual abuse; Adult survivors of child sexual abuse; Incest victims/survivors; Adolescent survivors of sexual abuse; Male survivors of sexual abuse
REQUIREMENTS: Southeast Orange County catchment area residents are charged sliding scale fees; other clients are charged full fee. Insurance and Medicaid/Medicare are accepted

ORANGE COUNTY SHERIFF'S OFFICE—VICTIM ASSISTANCE PROGRAM
2400 W 33rd St, Orlando, FL 32809
Crisis hotline: **(407) 648-3028 24 hrs**
Information: (407) 648-3020 8am-5pm
Contact: Pam Brooks, Victim Advocate
TYPE OF AGENCY: Victim/witness assistance program
AREAS SERVED: Orange
YEARS IN OPERATION: 10
ACCESSIBILITY: Wheelchair accessible
CASES SEXUAL ASSAULT/ABUSE (%): 90
CLIENTS/SERVICES: Sexual assault survivors; Marital rape/sexual abuse survivors; Community education
REQUIREMENTS: Client does not have to file charges

RAPERESPONSE PROGRAM
1510 E Colonial, Ste 301, Orlando, FL 32803
Crisis hotline: **(407) 740-5408 24 hrs**
Information: (407) 898-4228 8:30am-5pm
Contact: Vicky R Remus, RapeResponse Prog Dir
TYPE OF AGENCY: Rape crisis center
SPONSORING ORGANIZATION: Women's Resource Center
AREAS SERVED: Orange, Osceola, Seminole
YEARS IN OPERATION: 2
ACCESSIBILITY: Wheelchair accessible
CASES SEXUAL ASSAULT/ABUSE (%): 75
CLIENTS/SERVICES: Sexual assault survivors; Marital rape/sexual abuse survivors; Adult survivors of child sexual abuse; Incest victims/survivors; Prevention program; Community education; Adolescent survivors of sexual abuse; Male survivors of sexual abuse
REQUIREMENTS: Ages 13 or older

SPOUSE ABUSE, INC
PO Box 536276, Orlando, FL 32853-6276
Crisis hotline: **(407) 886-2856 24 hrs 7 days**
Information: (407) 886-2856 9am-4:30pm
Contact: Margaret Anglin, Exec Dir
TYPE OF AGENCY: Domestic violence program
AREAS SERVED: Orange, Seminole, and Osceola
YEARS IN OPERATION: 11
LANGUAGES: Spanish
ACCESSIBILITY: Wheelchair accessible; Telecommunications for the hearing impaired (TTY, TDY, etc.)
CASES SEXUAL ASSAULT/ABUSE (%): 70
CLIENTS/SERVICES: Marital rape/sexual abuse survivors; Incest victims/survivors; Community education

PANAMA CITY

BAY FAMILY AND CHILD CENTER
1008 Jenks Ave, Panama City, FL 32401
Crisis hotline: **(904) 785-3739 24 hrs**
Information: (904) 785-3739 8:30am-5:30pm
Contact: Carol Wartenberg, PhD, Psychologist
TYPE OF AGENCY: Child sexual abuse services; Private practice
AREAS SERVED: Bay, Holmes, Washington, Walton, Okaloosa, Gulf
YEARS IN OPERATION: 2
ACCESSIBILITY: Wheelchair accessible
DESCRIPTION: Counseling for victims/survivors, including support groups for female and male survivors
CLIENTS/SERVICES: Sexual assault survivors; Marital rape/sexual abuse survivors; Child victims of sexual abuse; Adult survivors of child sexual abuse; Incest victims/survivors; Adoles-

BAY FAMILY AND CHILD CENTER
(continued)
cent survivors of sexual abuse; Male survivors of sexual abuse
REQUIREMENTS: Fee for service; Will obtain and file insurance information for clients

LIFE MANAGEMENT CENTER
525 E 15th St, Panama City, FL 32405
Crisis hotline: **(904) 769-9481 24 hrs**
Information: (904) 769-9481 8am-5pm
Contact: Lorretta Glass, MA, Sexual Abuse Treatment Prog Dir
TYPE OF AGENCY: Counseling/mental health services
AREAS SERVED: Bay, Washington, Holmes
YEARS IN OPERATION: 25+
ACCESSIBILITY: Wheelchair accessible
CASES SEXUAL ASSAULT/ABUSE (%): 5
CLIENTS/SERVICES: Marital rape/sexual abuse survivors; Child victims of sexual abuse; Adult survivors of child sexual abuse; Incest victims/survivors; Offender treatment program; Adolescent survivors of sexual abuse
REQUIREMENTS: Private or agency referral; Fees charged

PENSACOLA

NORTHWEST FLORIDA COMPREHENSIVE SERVICES FOR CHILDREN, INC—IMPACT
3902 N 9th Ave, Ste 4, Pensacola, FL 32503
Information: (904) 434-0850 24 hrs
Contact: Sally Putters, RN, Proj Coord; Mimi Chappuis, Coord
TYPE OF AGENCY: Child sexual abuse services; Child sexual abuse prevention program; Private practice; Child abuse services; Child abuse prevention program
SPONSORING ORGANIZATION: Child Protection Team
AREAS SERVED: Escambia, Santa Rosa, Okaloosa, Walton
YEARS IN OPERATION: 8
ACCESSIBILITY: Wheelchair accessible
CASES SEXUAL ASSAULT/ABUSE (%): 50
DESCRIPTION: Multidisciplinary Child Protection Team for diagnosis, crisis intervention, and evaluation of child physical and sexual abuse; Comprehensive treatment for incest families, including group therapy for incest offenders; Educational component and relapse prevention model with offenders; CAN prevention project for child physical and sexual abuse
CLIENTS/SERVICES: Child victims of sexual abuse; Adult survivors of child sexual abuse; Incest victims/survivors; Prevention program; Community education; Offender treatment program; Adolescent survivors of sexual abuse
REQUIREMENTS: Offender outpatient treatability by evaluation; Child to 18 (with some exceptions) for Impact treatment. Private practice- Adult survivors of sexual abuse

RAPE CRISIS CENTER OF NORTHWEST FLORIDA
1221 W Lakeview Ave, Pensacola, FL 32501
Crisis hotline: **(904) 433-RAPE 24 hrs**
Information: (904) 432-1222, ext 336 8am-5pm (Mon-Fri)
Contact: Jeanne Halpern, Dir
TYPE OF AGENCY: Rape crisis center
SPONSORING ORGANIZATION: Lakeview Center
AREAS SERVED: Escambia, Santa Rosa on request
YEARS IN OPERATION: 11
ACCESSIBILITY: Wheelchair accessible
CASES SEXUAL ASSAULT/ABUSE (%): 100
CLIENTS/SERVICES: Sexual assault survivors; Marital rape/sexual abuse survivors; Child victims of sexual abuse; Adult survivors of child sexual abuse; Incest victims/survivors; Prevention program; Community education; Adolescent survivors of sexual abuse; Male survivors of sexual abuse; Healing
SPECIAL PROGRAMS/SERVICES: Nationally certified art therapist on staff

PINELLAS PARK

PINELLAS PARK POLICE DEPARTMENT
7700 59th St N, Pinellas Park, FL 34665
Crisis hotline: **(813) 541-3564 24 hrs**
Information: (813) 546-3015 8am-5pm (Mon-Fri)
Contact: Lisa Jones, Victim Advocate
TYPE OF AGENCY: Victim/witness assistance program
AREAS SERVED: Pinellas (City of Pinellas Park)
YEARS IN OPERATION: 6
ACCESSIBILITY: Wheelchair accessible
CASES SEXUAL ASSAULT/ABUSE (%): 25
CLIENTS/SERVICES: Sexual assault survivors; Marital rape/sexual abuse survivors; Child victims of sexual abuse; Adult survivors of child sexual abuse; Incest victims/survivors; Prevention program; Community education; Adolescent survivors of sexual abuse; Male survivors of sexual abuse
REQUIREMENTS: Police officer referral preferred. Incident must be reported and have occurred within the jurisdiction of Pinellas Park

PUNTA GORDA

CENTER FOR ABUSE AND RAPE EMERGENCIES, INC
PO Box 234, Punta Gorda, FL 33951-0234
Crisis hotline: **(813) 627-6000 24 hrs**
Information: (813) 639-5499 8am-5pm
Contact: Nancy L Lisby, Exec Dir
TYPE OF AGENCY: Rape crisis center; Domestic violence program
AREAS SERVED: Charlotte
YEARS IN OPERATION: 6
LANGUAGES: Spanish, French
ACCESSIBILITY: Wheelchair accessible; Signers for the hearing impaired
CASES SEXUAL ASSAULT/ABUSE (%): 10
DESCRIPTION: Comprehensive services for sexual assault and domestic violence survivors; Provides batterers group
CLIENTS/SERVICES: Sexual assault survivors; Marital rape/sexual abuse survivors; Child victims of sexual abuse; Adult survivors of child sexual abuse; Incest victims/survivors; Prevention program; Community education; Adolescent survivors of sexual abuse

ROCKLEDGE

BREVARD COUNTY COMMISSION AGAINST SEXUAL ASSAULT
1018-A S Florida Ave, Rockledge, FL 32955
Crisis hotline: **(407) 784-HELP 24 hrs**
Information: (407) 631-3444 8am-5pm (Mon-Fri)
Contact: Ginger Conley, Prog Supv
TYPE OF AGENCY: Rape crisis center
YEARS IN OPERATION: 10
LANGUAGES: Foreign language assistance available
ACCESSIBILITY: Wheelchair accessible
CASES SEXUAL ASSAULT/ABUSE (%): 100
CLIENTS/SERVICES: Sexual assault survivors; Marital rape/sexual abuse survivors; Child victims of sexual abuse; Adult survivors of child sexual abuse; Incest victims/survivors; Prevention program; Community education; Offender treatment program

CHILD PROTECTION TEAM OF BREVARD COUNTY
1260 S US Hwy, No 1, Ste 203, Rockledge, FL 32955
Information: (407) 632-7107, 8am-4:30pm after hours (407) 636-3066 8am-4:30pm
Contact: Joie Nace-Goldsmith, Team Coord
TYPE OF AGENCY: Child sexual abuse services
AREAS SERVED: Brevard
YEARS IN OPERATION: 8
ACCESSIBILITY: Wheelchair accessible
CASES SEXUAL ASSAULT/ABUSE (%): 56
CLIENTS/SERVICES: Child victims of sexual abuse; Incest victims/survivors; Community education; Preschoolers
REQUIREMENTS: Clients must be under the age of 18
SPECIAL PROGRAMS/SERVICES: The sexual abuse task force provides free group support programs for victims of child sexual abuse and their families. SATF is a community-based program with members representing Health and Rehabilitative Services, Child Protection Team, the guardian ad litem program, local mental health agencies and private therapists. The following groups are available free of charge: mother's group (10 weeks); children's group, for survivors aged 7-12 (10 weeks); preschool group, for survivors aged 2-5, using play therapy to help children deal with their sexual abuse experiences; adolescent sexual offender group (16 weeks). Parents' groups accompany the preschool and adolescent sexual offender groups.

SAINT AUGUSTINE

PSYCHOLOGICAL SERVICES OF ST AUGUSTINE
236 Southpark Cir E, Saint Augustine, FL 32086
Information: (904) 824-7733 9am-5pm
Contact: Karen Selig, MA, Clinical Coord
TYPE OF AGENCY: Child sexual abuse services; Private practice
AREAS SERVED: St Johns
YEARS IN OPERATION: 6
ACCESSIBILITY: Wheelchair accessible
CASES SEXUAL ASSAULT/ABUSE (%): 20
DESCRIPTION: Multidisciplinary team of therapists use systems orientation to deal with children and families. Dept of Human Resources and the Child Protection Team refer to child sex abuse/incest program
CLIENTS/SERVICES: Sexual assault survivors; Marital rape/sexual abuse survivors; Child victims of sexual abuse; Adult survivors of child sexual abuse; Incest victims/survivors; Prevention program; Community education; Offender treatment program; Adolescent survivors of sexual abuse; Male survivors of sexual abuse
REQUIREMENTS: Sex abuse program free to the victim and her/his family. Offenders must pay for treatment

SAINT PETERSBURG

PINELLAS COUNTY SAVE (SEXUAL ASSAULT VICTIM EXAMINATION)
PO Box 13549, Saint Petersburg, FL 33733
Crisis hotline: **(813) 823-8967 24 hrs**
Information: (813) 823-0401, ext 294 8am-5pm (Mon-Fri)
Contact: Rita Hall, Nursing Prog Spec
TYPE OF AGENCY: Hospital/medical center; Child sexual abuse services
SPONSORING ORGANIZATION: Pinellas County Health Dept
AREAS SERVED: Pinellas
YEARS IN OPERATION: 3
LANGUAGES: Interpreters available
ACCESSIBILITY: Wheelchair accessible; Signers for the hearing impaired
CASES SEXUAL ASSAULT/ABUSE (%): 100
DESCRIPTION: Collects medical evidence for prosecution of sexual assault cases; Provides medical care and counseling for survivors, whether or not they report the crime to a law enforcement agency.
CLIENTS/SERVICES: Sexual assault survivors; Marital rape/sexual abuse survivors; Child victims of sexual abuse; Adult survivors of child sexual abuse; Incest victims/survivors; Community education; Adolescent survivors of sexual abuse; Male survivors of sexual abuse

SARASOTA

FAMILY COUNSELING CENTER
3205 Southgate Cir, Sarasota, FL 34239
Crisis hotline: **(813) 955-7017 8am-8pm (Mon-Fri)**
Information: (813) 955-7017 8am-8pm (Mon-Fri)
Contact: Claire Linzel, Clinical Supv
TYPE OF AGENCY: Counseling/mental health services
AREAS SERVED: Sarasota
YEARS IN OPERATION: 25
ACCESSIBILITY: Wheelchair accessible
CASES SEXUAL ASSAULT/ABUSE (%): 8
CLIENTS/SERVICES: Sexual assault survivors; Marital rape/sexual abuse survivors; Child victims of sexual abuse; Adult survivors of child sexual abuse; Incest victims/survivors; Community education; Offender treatment program

SAFE PLACE AND RAPE CRISIS CENTER (SPARCC)
PO Box 1675, Sarasota, FL 34230-1675
Crisis hotline: **(813) 365-1976 24 hrs**
Information: (813) 365-0208 9am-5pm (Mon-Fri)
Contact: Jean Gay, Exec Dir
TYPE OF AGENCY: Rape crisis center; Domestic violence program; Acquaintance/date rape prevention program
AREAS SERVED: Sarasota
YEARS IN OPERATION: 9
LANGUAGES: Spanish translator available
ACCESSIBILITY: Wheelchair accessible
CASES SEXUAL ASSAULT/ABUSE (%): 10
DESCRIPTION: Comprehensive services for survivors of domestic violence and sexual assault; High school prevention program for acquaintance rape
CLIENTS/SERVICES: Sexual assault survivors; Marital rape/sexual abuse survivors; Adult survivors of child sexual abuse; Prevention program; Community education
REQUIREMENTS: Client must be over 18 or have parental (guardian) consent.

SEXUAL ABUSE TREATMENT PROGRAM OF SARASOTA
2075 Main St, Ste 2, Sarasota, FL 34237
Crisis hotline: **(813) 365-1277 24 hrs**
Information: (813) 365-1277 9am-5pm
Contact: Herb Glover, Exec Dir
TYPE OF AGENCY: Child sexual abuse services; Child sexual abuse prevention program; Child abuse services; Child abuse prevention program
SPONSORING ORGANIZATION: Community Coalition for Families, Inc
AREAS SERVED: Sarasota
YEARS IN OPERATION: 3
ACCESSIBILITY: Wheelchair accessible
CASES SEXUAL ASSAULT/ABUSE (%): 100
DESCRIPTION: To provide individual, family, and group treatment for sexually abused children, siblings, non-offending parents, and adolescent offenders
CLIENTS/SERVICES: Sexual assault survivors; Marital rape/sexual abuse survivors; Child victims of sexual abuse; Adult survivors of child sexual abuse; Incest victims/survivors; Prevention program; Community education

WOMEN EMPOWERED, INC
6332 Glencoe Ave, Sarasota, FL 34231
Information: (813) 922-5242 8am-6pm
Contact: K Zahn, Pres
TYPE OF AGENCY: Rape prevention program
AREAS SERVED: Sarasota
YEARS IN OPERATION: 1
DESCRIPTION: Teaches personal safety and basic self-defense skills to women and children
CLIENTS/SERVICES: Sexual assault survivors; Marital rape/sexual abuse survivors; Child victims of sexual abuse; Adult survivors of child sexual abuse; Incest victims/survivors; Prevention program; Community education
REQUIREMENTS: Women's basic course is offered to any female over the age of 12; Children's personal safety program is offered to girls and boys between the ages of 3 and 12

SPRING HILL

SEXUAL ABUSE TREATMENT PROGRAM (SATP)
7496 Forest Oaks Blvd, Spring Hill, FL 34606
Crisis hotline: **(904) 688-0700 8am-5pm (Mon-Fri)**
Information: (904) 688-0700
Contact: Colleen Lowe, MA, Sexual Abuse Treatment Prog Coord
TYPE OF AGENCY: Counseling/mental health services; Child sexual abuse services
SPONSORING ORGANIZATION: Hernando County Mental Health, Inc
AREAS SERVED: Hernando
YEARS IN OPERATION: 3
CASES SEXUAL ASSAULT/ABUSE (%): 100
DESCRIPTION: Family treatment program for intrafamilial sexual abuse victims and their families, including offenders
CLIENTS/SERVICES: Child victims of sexual abuse; Adult survivors of child sexual abuse; Incest victims/survivors; Community education; Offender treatment program; Adolescent survivors of sexual abuse
REQUIREMENTS: Offender must admit responsibility for offense

TALLAHASSEE

CHILD PROTECTION TEAM
1126-B Lee Ave, Tallahassee, FL 32303
Crisis hotline: **(904) 487-2838 24 hrs for crisis and medical services**
Information: (904) 487-2838 8am-5pm (Mon-Fri)
Contact: Elizabeth Jackson, Team Coord
TYPE OF AGENCY: Child sexual abuse services
SPONSORING ORGANIZATION: Tallahassee Pediatric Foundation
AREAS SERVED: Leon, Wakulla, Gadsden, Taylor, Jefferson, Madison
YEARS IN OPERATION: 7
ACCESSIBILITY: Wheelchair accessible; Telecommunications for the hearing impaired (TTY, TDY, etc.); Signers for the hearing impaired
CASES SEXUAL ASSAULT/ABUSE (%): 60
DESCRIPTION: Multidisciplinary team that provides comprehensive services for sexually abused children, their families and incest offenders
CLIENTS/SERVICES: Child victims of sexual abuse; Incest victims/survivors; Community education; Offender treatment program; Adolescent survivors of sexual abuse
REQUIREMENTS: Child under age 18 who has been abused or suspected of being abused. If the abuser is a parent or caretaker, a referral to HRS abuse registry must be made. If the abuser is of a non-custodial type, then a referral to law enforcement will be made.

THE FAMILY LIVING CENTER
565 E Tennessee St, Tallahassee, FL 32302
Information: (904) 487-2930 9am-8pm (Mon-Thu); 1pm-5pm (Fri)
Contact: JoAnn Womack, Counselor
TYPE OF AGENCY: Counseling/mental health services
SPONSORING ORGANIZATION: Apalachee Center for Human Services
AREAS SERVED: Franklin, Gadsden, Jefferson, Leon, Liberty, Madison, Taylor, Wakulla
YEARS IN OPERATION: 16
ACCESSIBILITY: Wheelchair accessible
CASES SEXUAL ASSAULT/ABUSE (%): 30
CLIENTS/SERVICES: Sexual assault survivors; Marital rape/sexual abuse survivors; Child victims of sexual abuse; Adult survivors of child sexual abuse; Incest victims/survivors; Adolescent survivors of sexual abuse; Male survivors of sexual abuse; Preschoolers
REQUIREMENTS: Must be 18 and under or parents/guardians of child.
SPECIAL PROGRAMS/SERVICES: Group therapy for preschool-age children

REFUGE HOUSE/RAPE CRISIS CENTER
PO Box 4356, Tallahassee, FL 32315
Crisis hotline: **(904) 681-2111 24 hrs**
Information: (904) 681-2111 24 hrs
Contact: Kim Harris, Exec Dir
TYPE OF AGENCY: Rape crisis center; Domestic violence program
AREAS SERVED: Leon, Madison, Taylor, Gadsden, Jefferson, Liberty, Calhoun, Wakulla
YEARS IN OPERATION: 10
CASES SEXUAL ASSAULT/ABUSE (%): Approx 20
CLIENTS/SERVICES: Sexual assault survivors; Marital rape/sexual abuse survivors; Community education; Adolescent survivors of sexual abuse; Male survivors of sexual abuse

STATE ATTORNEY'S OFFICE—VICTIM/WITNESS UNIT
301 S Monroe, Leon County Courthouse, 4th Fl, Tallahassee, FL 32301
Information: (904) 488-6701
Contact: Kay Rifken, Victim/Witness Coord
TYPE OF AGENCY: Victim/witness assistance program
DESCRIPTION: Assists victims of violent crimes through the judicial process; Works closely with the Child Protection Team in the area of child sexual abuse
CLIENTS/SERVICES: Sexual assault survivors; Marital rape/sexual abuse survivors; Child victims of sexual abuse; Prevention program; Community education; Male survivors of sexual abuse

US ATTORNEY'S OFFICE, NORTHERN DISTRICT OF FLORIDA—VICTIM-WITNESS PROGRAM
227 N Bronough St, Ste 4014, Tallahassee, FL 32303
Information: (904) 681-7360 8am-5pm
Contact: Gail London, Victim-Witness/Law Enforcement Svcs Dir
TYPE OF AGENCY: Victim/witness assistance program
AREAS SERVED: Northwest Florida
YEARS IN OPERATION: 2½
ACCESSIBILITY: Wheelchair accessible
CASES SEXUAL ASSAULT/ABUSE (%): 1
DESCRIPTION: Prosecutes all federal offenses occurring in this district and child abuse and sexual assault offenses occurring on military bases. Primarily information and referral services; Provides direct services on more difficult cases
CLIENTS/SERVICES: Sexual assault survivors; Child victims of sexual abuse; Community education
REQUIREMENTS: Must be a federal crime or state crime occurring on federal property

TAMPA

CHILDREN'S MEDICAL CARE
4 Columbia Dr, Ste 815, Tampa, FL 33606
Information: (813) 253-2787 8am-5pm, 24-hr emergency, answering machine after hrs
Contact: Bonnie C Sklaren, Advanced RN Practitioner
TYPE OF AGENCY: Hospital/medical center; Child sexual abuse services
SPONSORING ORGANIZATION: TEAM
AREAS SERVED: Hillsborough
YEARS IN OPERATION: 2
ACCESSIBILITY: Wheelchair accessible; Signers for the hearing impaired (on call)
CASES SEXUAL ASSAULT/ABUSE (%): 100
DESCRIPTION: Provides medical evaluations for the juvenile sex crime victim; Referral to counseling services; Coordination of services with all agencies involved

CHILDREN'S MEDICAL CARE *(continued)*

CLIENTS/SERVICES: Child victims of sexual abuse; Community education
REQUIREMENTS: Juvenile victims only 18 or younger; Law enforcement report required

HILLSBOROUGH COUNTY CRISIS CENTER, INC/SEXUAL ABUSE TREATMENT CENTER
2214 E Henry Ave, Tampa, FL 33610
Crisis hotline: **(813) 238-7273, 238-8821 24 hrs**
Information: (813) 238-8411 8am-5pm (Mon-Fri)
Contact: Lerea Goldthwaite, Client Svcs Mgr; Mary Ruth Austin, Community Education Coord
TYPE OF AGENCY: Rape crisis center; Hospital/medical center; Counseling/mental health services; Child sexual abuse services; Child sexual abuse prevention program
AREAS SERVED: Hillsborough
YEARS IN OPERATION: 14
LANGUAGES: Spanish
ACCESSIBILITY: Wheelchair accessible; Telecommunications for the hearing impaired (TTY, TDY, etc.); Signers for the hearing impaired
CASES SEXUAL ASSAULT/ABUSE (%): 50
DESCRIPTION: Comprehensive rape crisis services; Support groups for female and male survivors of sexual assault/abuse; Group therapy for child abuse offenders and incest offenders
CLIENTS/SERVICES: Sexual assault survivors; Marital rape/sexual abuse survivors; Child victims of sexual abuse; Adult survivors of child sexual abuse; Incest victims/survivors; Prevention program; Community education; Offender treatment program; Adolescent survivors of sexual abuse; Male survivors of sexual abuse
REQUIREMENTS: Ages 5 and older
SPECIAL PROGRAMS/SERVICES: Nurse examiner program provides 24-hour medical examinations for female sexual assault victims ages 18 years and older. Expert testimony is given by nurse examiners in court-related procedures. This crisis center was the pilot program in FL and has helped establish similar nurse examiner programs at several other sites in FL and throughout the U.S.

UNIVERSITY OF SOUTH FLORIDA—EVERYWOMAN'S CENTER
University of Flordia, CTR 2438, Tampa, FL 33620
Information: (813) 974-3332 hrs vary
Contact: Beth Hahamovitch, Coord
TYPE OF AGENCY: College/university-based services
SPONSORING ORGANIZATION: Student Organization
AREAS SERVED: Hillsborough
YEARS IN OPERATION: 15
LANGUAGES: French, Spanish
ACCESSIBILITY: Wheelchair accessible
DESCRIPTION: Informational and educational services, support groups, and feminist martial arts/self defense
CLIENTS/SERVICES: Sexual assault survivors; Marital rape/sexual abuse survivors; Child victims of sexual abuse; Adult survivors of child sexual abuse; Incest victims/survivors; Community education

VICTIM ASSISTANCE PROGRAM
902 N Florida Ave, Tampa, FL 33602
Information: (813) 272-6472 (Victim assistance), 272-6423 (Domestic violence intervention program) 8am-5pm (counselors); 24 hrs daily (advocates)
Contact: Marie Apsey, Victim Assist Coord
TYPE OF AGENCY: Domestic violence program; Victim/witness assistance program
SPONSORING ORGANIZATION: State Attorney's Office
AREAS SERVED: Hillsborough
YEARS IN OPERATION: 4
LANGUAGES: Spanish

ACCESSIBILITY: Wheelchair accessible; Telecommunications for the hearing impaired (TTY, TDY, etc.) (by arrangement); Signers for the hearing impaired (by arrangement)
CASES SEXUAL ASSAULT/ABUSE (%): 20
CLIENTS/SERVICES: Sexual assault survivors; Marital rape/sexual abuse survivors; Community education
REQUIREMENTS: Must report to law enforcement; Must be willing to testify; Must be 18 or older

TRENTON

MENTAL HEALTH SERVICES, INC (TRI-COUNTY)
PO Box 667, Trenton, FL 32693
Crisis hotline: **(904) 376-4444 24 hrs daily**
Information: (904) 463-7303 8:30am-5pm
Contact: Cheryl Smith, Area Dir
TYPE OF AGENCY: Counseling/mental health services; Child sexual abuse services
AREAS SERVED: Levy, Gilchrist, Dixie
YEARS IN OPERATION: 15
ACCESSIBILITY: Wheelchair accessible
CASES SEXUAL ASSAULT/ABUSE (%): 10-15
DESCRIPTION: Outpatient mental health and addictions services with special contract for child sexual abuse treatment with victim, family, perpetrator
CLIENTS/SERVICES: Child victims of sexual abuse; Incest victims/survivors; Community education; Offender treatment program; Adolescent survivors of sexual abuse; Male survivors of sexual abuse

VERO BEACH

SAFE SPACE DOMESTIC VIOLENCE PROGRAM
PO Box 2822, Vero Beach, FL 32961
Crisis hotline: **(407) 569-7233 (Indian River); (407) 464-4555 (St Lucie); (407) 288-7023 (Martin) 24 hrs, all crisis numbers**
Information: (407) 562-3374 8:30am-5pm
Contact: Leslie Kesy, Exec Dir
TYPE OF AGENCY: Domestic violence program
AREAS SERVED: Indian River, St Lucie, Martin and Okeechobee
YEARS IN OPERATION: 9
LANGUAGES: Spanish
ACCESSIBILITY: Wheelchair accessible
CASES SEXUAL ASSAULT/ABUSE (%): 60
CLIENTS/SERVICES: Marital rape/sexual abuse survivors; Child victims of sexual abuse

WEST PALM BEACH

PALM BEACH COUNTY SEXUAL ASSAULT PROGRAM
307 N Dixie Hwy, Ste 407, West Palm Beach, FL 33401
Crisis hotline: **(407) 833-7273 24 hrs**
Information: (407) 355-2073 8:30am-5pm
Contact: Kris Karna, Coord
TYPE OF AGENCY: Rape crisis center; Child sexual abuse services; Child sexual abuse prevention program
AREAS SERVED: Palm Beach
YEARS IN OPERATION: 13
LANGUAGES: Spanish, Creole, Finnish, French
ACCESSIBILITY: Wheelchair accessible
CASES SEXUAL ASSAULT/ABUSE (%): 100
CLIENTS/SERVICES: Sexual assault survivors; Marital rape/sexual abuse survivors; Child victims of sexual abuse; Adult survivors of child sexual abuse; Incest victims/survivors; Prevention program; Community education; Adolescent survivors of sexual abuse; Male survivors of sexual abuse

YWCA DOMESTIC ASSAULT SHELTER
901 S Olive Ave, West Palm Beach, FL 33401
Crisis hotline: **(407) 655-6106 24 hrs 7 days**
Information: (407) 655-6106 24 hrs 7 days
Contact: Shandra Dawkins, Dir
TYPE OF AGENCY: Domestic violence program
AREAS SERVED: Palm Beach and surrounding counties
YEARS IN OPERATION: 10
CASES SEXUAL ASSAULT/ABUSE (%): 35
CLIENTS/SERVICES: Marital rape/sexual abuse survivors; Prevention program; Community education

WINTER HAVEN

FAMILY LEARNING CENTER—COMMUNITY MENTAL HEALTH CENTER
Ave F NE, 200, Winter Haven, FL 33881
Crisis hotline: **(813) 299-5858; (800) 282-7631 24 hrs; 24 hrs**
Information: (813) 293-1121, ext 1478; 299-4744 8am-5pm (Mon, Wed, Thu, Fri); 8am-7pm (Tue)
Contact: Marabeth Plowman, Prog Dir
TYPE OF AGENCY: Counseling/mental health services
SPONSORING ORGANIZATION: Winter Haven Hospital
AREAS SERVED: Polk, Highlands
ACCESSIBILITY: Wheelchair accessible
CASES SEXUAL ASSAULT/ABUSE (%): 60
DESCRIPTION: Team approach to coordinate longer-term individual, family, and group therapy for each family member. Group therapy available for child sex abuse victims, nonoffending parents, and adult and juvenile offenders. Parents United chapter
CLIENTS/SERVICES: Child victims of sexual abuse; Adult survivors of child sexual abuse; Incest victims/survivors; Prevention program; Community education; Offender treatment program
REQUIREMENTS: Children ages 0-18 and their families

SEXUAL ABUSE TREATMENT PROGRAM/SAFE (SAFETY AWARENESS FOR EVERYONE)
200 Ave F NE, Winter Haven, FL 33881
Information: (813) 965-1817 (SAFE), (813) 293-1121, ext 1478 (treatment) 8am-4pm
Contact: Kathy Hayes, Child/Adolescent Svcs Dir
TYPE OF AGENCY: Counseling/mental health services; Child sexual abuse services; Child sexual abuse prevention program
SPONSORING ORGANIZATION: Winter Haven Hospital Community Mental Health Center
AREAS SERVED: Polk for treatment; Polk, Highlands, Hardee for SAFE
YEARS IN OPERATION: 4
DESCRIPTION: The Sexual Abuse Treatment Program approaches intrafamilial sexual abuse. SAFE is a child sexual abuse prevention program offered through the schools
CLIENTS/SERVICES: Sexual assault survivors; Child victims of sexual abuse; Adult survivors of child sexual abuse; Incest victims/survivors; Prevention program; Community education; Offender treatment program; Adolescent survivors of sexual abuse; Male survivors of sexual abuse
REQUIREMENTS: Victims are referred primarily through the county child protection team. Those who come in referred from another source are routed back through that team

WINTER PARK

HELP END ABUSE TODAY (HEAT)
PO Box 546, Winter Park, FL 32790-0546
Crisis hotline: **(800) 342-9152 9am-3pm**
Information: (407) 850-HEAT 9am-3pm
Contact: Diana M Healy, Exec Dir

HELP END ABUSE TODAY (HEAT)
(continued)

TYPE OF AGENCY: Child sexual abuse prevention program; Child abuse prevention program
AREAS SERVED: Orange, Seminole, Polk
YEARS IN OPERATION: 2
DESCRIPTION: Active in areas of education and legislation concerning issues of child abuse/neglect.
CLIENTS/SERVICES: Child victims of sexual abuse; Community education
SPECIAL PROGRAMS/SERVICES: Keep Kids Safe program for middle schools and high schools

GEORGIA

ALBANY

RAPE CRISIS
PO Box 1828, Albany, GA 31703
Crisis hotline: **(912) 432-7273 24 hrs**
Information: (912) 432-7273 24 hrs
Contact: Ginger Goodyear, Coord
TYPE OF AGENCY: Rape crisis center; Hospital/medical center
SPONSORING ORGANIZATION: Phoebe Putney Memorial Hospital
YEARS IN OPERATION: 4
ACCESSIBILITY: Wheelchair accessible
CASES SEXUAL ASSAULT/ABUSE (%): 100
CLIENTS/SERVICES: Sexual assault survivors; Marital rape/sexual abuse survivors; Adult survivors of child sexual abuse; Incest victims/survivors; Prevention program; Community education; Male survivors of sexual abuse
REQUIREMENTS: Sexual assault victim age 15 or older

ATHENS

ATHENS RAPE CRISIS LINE
1247 Prince, Athens, GA 30606
Crisis hotline: **(404) 353-1912 5pm-8am**
TYPE OF AGENCY: Rape crisis center
SPONSORING ORGANIZATION: NE GA Mental Health
AREAS SERVED: Clarke, Barrow, Jackson, Madison, Oconee, Statham, Morgan, Oglethorpe, Walton
YEARS IN OPERATION: 14
CASES SEXUAL ASSAULT/ABUSE (%): 50
CLIENTS/SERVICES: Sexual assault survivors; Community education

ATLANTA

THE HIGHLAND INSTITUTE FOR BEHAVIORAL CHANGE, INC
3785 Presidential Pkwy, Ste 118, Atlanta, GA 30340
Information: (404) 455-0835 7am-10pm
Contact: Deloris T Roys, Dir
TYPE OF AGENCY: Offender treatment
AREAS SERVED: Fulton, Dekalb, Rockdale, Forsyth, Cobb, Gwinett, Douglas, Henry, Clayton, Coweta
YEARS IN OPERATION: 1
ACCESSIBILITY: Wheelchair accessible
CASES SEXUAL ASSAULT/ABUSE (%): 100
DESCRIPTION: Sexual offender treatment center (child sexual abuse/incest offenders, voyeurs, exhibitionists), modeled on the cognitive/behavioral restructuring type treatments available in other parts of the country. Family work, but main focus is the offender
CLIENTS/SERVICES: Community education; Offender treatment program
REQUIREMENTS: No rapists, no persons who have used weapons in the commission of their offense, no persons with organicity or psychoses. No one accepted with drug or alcohol problems unless they are under control

RAPE CRISIS CENTER
80 Butler St SE, Atlanta, GA 30335
Crisis hotline: **(404) 659-7273 24 hrs**
Information: (404) 589-4861 8:30am-5pm (Mon-Fri)
Contact: Dr Peg Ziegler, Dir
TYPE OF AGENCY: Rape crisis center
SPONSORING ORGANIZATION: Grady Memorial Hospital
AREAS SERVED: Fulton, Dekalb
YEARS IN OPERATION: 14
LANGUAGES: All available
ACCESSIBILITY: Wheelchair accessible; Signers for the hearing impaired
CASES SEXUAL ASSAULT/ABUSE (%): 100
CLIENTS/SERVICES: Sexual assault survivors; Marital rape/sexual abuse survivors; Child victims of sexual abuse; Adult survivors of child sexual abuse; Incest victims/survivors; Prevention program; Community education; Adolescent survivors of sexual abuse; Male survivors of sexual abuse

AUGUSTA

RAPE CRISIS AND SEXUAL ASSAULT SERVICES
1350 Walton Way, Augusta, GA 30910-3599
Crisis hotline: **(404) 724-5200 24 hrs**
Information: (404) 724-5200, 722-9011, ext 2740 8:30am-5pm
Contact: Anne Ealick Henry, Rape Crisis and Sexual Assault Svcs Coord
TYPE OF AGENCY: Rape crisis center; Hospital/medical center; Child sexual abuse services; Child sexual abuse prevention program
SPONSORING ORGANIZATION: University Health Services, Inc
AREAS SERVED: Richmond, Columbia, Burke, Screven, Jenkins, GA; Aiken, SC
YEARS IN OPERATION: 14
LANGUAGES: Spanish, German, French, Vietnamese, Laotian
ACCESSIBILITY: Wheelchair accessible; Telecommunications for the hearing impaired (TTY, TDY, etc.); Signers for the hearing impaired
CASES SEXUAL ASSAULT/ABUSE (%): 100
CLIENTS/SERVICES: Sexual assault survivors; Marital rape/sexual abuse survivors; Child victims of sexual abuse; Adult survivors of child sexual abuse; Incest victims/survivors; Prevention program; Community education; Adolescent survivors of sexual abuse; Male survivors of sexual abuse

COLUMBUS

COLUMBUS RAPE CRISIS, INC
1314 Munro Ave, Columbus, GA 31906
Crisis hotline: **(404) 571-6010 24 hrs 7 days**
Information: (404) 323-5010
Contact: Marcia D Wolfe, Dir
TYPE OF AGENCY: Rape crisis center
AREAS SERVED: Muscogee (Consolidated City and County)
YEARS IN OPERATION: 6
ACCESSIBILITY: Signers for the hearing impaired
CASES SEXUAL ASSAULT/ABUSE (%): 100
CLIENTS/SERVICES: Sexual assault survivors; Marital rape/sexual abuse survivors; Child victims of sexual abuse; Adult survivors of child sexual abuse; Incest victims/survivors; Prevention program; Community education; Adolescent survivors of sexual abuse; Male survivors of sexual abuse

DALTON

GEORGIA HIGHLANDS CENTER FOR MENTAL HEALTH
1407 Burleyson Dr, Dalton, GA 30720
Crisis hotline: **(404) 272-2305 24 hrs**
Information: (404) 272-2305 8:30am-5pm
Contact: Rhonda Whitfield, Women's Group Therapist MEd
TYPE OF AGENCY: Counseling/mental health services
AREAS SERVED: Whitfield, Murray, Pickens, Fannin, Gilmer, Cherokee
YEARS IN OPERATION: 40
LANGUAGES: Spanish
ACCESSIBILITY: Wheelchair accessible; Signers for the hearing impaired
CASES SEXUAL ASSAULT/ABUSE (%): 10
DESCRIPTION: Counseling for victims/survivors and rapists and child sexual abuse/incest offenders
CLIENTS/SERVICES: Sexual assault survivors; Marital rape/sexual abuse survivors; Child victims of sexual abuse; Adult survivors of child sexual abuse; Incest victims/survivors; Community education; Offender treatment program; Adolescent survivors of sexual abuse; Male survivors of sexual abuse

FORT MCPHERSON

ARMY FAMILY ADVOCACY PROGRAM
Bldg 65, Rm 30, Fort McPherson, GA 30330-5000
Information: (404) 752-2439, 752-2536 7:30am-4:30pm
Contact: Brenda Watson, Family Advocacy Prog Mgr
TYPE OF AGENCY: Counseling/mental health services; Military services

ARMY FAMILY ADVOCACY PROGRAM
(continued)

SPONSORING ORGANIZATION: Army Community Service
AREAS SERVED: 44 North Georgia counties—installation located at Atlanta
YEARS IN OPERATION: 10
LANGUAGES: Access to a language bank
CLIENTS/SERVICES: Prevention program; Community education
REQUIREMENTS: Clients must be members of the uniformed services, active or retired, or their family members, or others entitled to care in military medical treatment facilities.

GAINESVILLE

RAPE RESPONSE, INC
PO Box 2883, Gainesville, GA 30503
Crisis hotline: **(404) 535-8962 24 hrs**
Information: (404) 535-8962 8am-6pm
Contact: Elaine Gerke, Coord
TYPE OF AGENCY: Rape crisis center
AREAS SERVED: Hall and Habersham
YEARS IN OPERATION: 2½ years
ACCESSIBILITY: Wheelchair accessible
CASES SEXUAL ASSAULT/ABUSE (%): 100
CLIENTS/SERVICES: Sexual assault survivors; Marital rape/sexual abuse survivors; Adult survivors of child sexual abuse; Prevention program; Community education; Male survivors of sexual abuse
REQUIREMENTS: Rape survivor must be 14 years or older. Rape or attempted rape must have been committed by a non-family member.

HINESVILLE

COASTAL AREA COMMUNITY MENTAL HEALTH
PO Box 1489, Hinesville, GA 31313
Crisis hotline: **(912) 368-HELP 24 hrs**
Information: (912) 368-3344 8am-5pm (Mon-Fri)
Contact: Jackie Itzkovitz, MSW
TYPE OF AGENCY: Counseling/mental health services
AREAS SERVED: Liberty, Long, Bryan
YEARS IN OPERATION: 1
ACCESSIBILITY: Wheelchair accessible
CLIENTS/SERVICES: Sexual assault survivors; Marital rape/sexual abuse survivors; Child victims of sexual abuse; Adult survivors of child sexual abuse; Incest victims/survivors; Prevention program; Community education

MACON

MACON RESCUE MISSION
PO Box 749, Macon, GA 31202
Crisis hotline: **(912) 746-5684, 743-5445 8am-7pm**
Information: (912) 935-8626 9am-5pm
Contact: Wayne Bevill, Exec Dir; Janna Malchow, Coord
TYPE OF AGENCY: Domestic violence program; Child sexual abuse services; Shelter
AREAS SERVED: Statewide
YEARS IN OPERATION: 9
CASES SEXUAL ASSAULT/ABUSE (%): 90
DESCRIPTION: Videotaped interviews of sexually abused children for the Department of Family and Children's Services; Follow-up; Battered women's shelter; Homeless shelter
CLIENTS/SERVICES: Marital rape/sexual abuse survivors; Child victims of sexual abuse; Adult survivors of child sexual abuse; Incest victims/survivors; Prevention program; Community education; Offender treatment program; Adolescent survivors of sexual abuse; Male survivors of sexual abuse
REQUIREMENTS: Must be referred by Dept of Family and Children's Services for sexual abuse; Children and teens ages 1-17
SPECIAL PROGRAMS/SERVICES: Animal farm for children teaches them to love, nurture and have responsibility

MEDICAL CENTER OF CENTRAL GEORGIA
PO Box 6000, No 151, 777 Hemlock St, Macon, GA 31208
Information: (912) 744-1467 8am-5pm
Contact: Montez Carr, LMSW, Ob/Gyn Soc Wkr
TYPE OF AGENCY: Hospital/medical center
AREAS SERVED: Monroe, Jones, Peach, Twiggs, Baldwin
YEARS IN OPERATION: 7½
ACCESSIBILITY: Wheelchair accessible
DESCRIPTION: Specially trained assault team nurses work with survivors in emergency room. Member of community-wide interagency sexual assault team
CLIENTS/SERVICES: Sexual assault survivors; Marital rape/sexual abuse survivors; Child victims of sexual abuse; Adult survivors of child sexual abuse; Incest victims/survivors; Community education; Adolescent survivors of sexual abuse; Male survivors of sexual abuse

RAPE CRISIS TEAM
PO Box 56, Mercer Station, Macon, GA 31201
Crisis hotline: **(912) 745-9292 24 hrs**
Information: (912) 745-9293 9am-5pm
Contact: Lynn Sasby, Coord
TYPE OF AGENCY: Rape crisis center
SPONSORING ORGANIZATION: Crisis Line of Macon and Bibb County
AREAS SERVED: Middle Georgia area
YEARS IN OPERATION: 7
LANGUAGES: Spanish
ACCESSIBILITY: Wheelchair accessible
CASES SEXUAL ASSAULT/ABUSE (%): 100
CLIENTS/SERVICES: Sexual assault survivors; Marital rape/sexual abuse survivors; Child victims of sexual abuse; Community education; Adolescent survivors of sexual abuse; Male survivors of sexual abuse

MARIETTA

YWCA RAPE CRISIS CENTER OF COBB COUNTY
48 Henderson St, Marietta, GA 30364
Crisis hotline: **(404) 428-2666 24 hrs**
Information: (404) 427-3492 9am-5pm
TYPE OF AGENCY: Rape crisis center; Child sexual abuse prevention program
SPONSORING ORGANIZATION: YWCA and United Way
AREAS SERVED: Cobb, metropolitan Atlanta and surrounding areas
YEARS IN OPERATION: 10
LANGUAGES: Spanish
ACCESSIBILITY: Wheelchair accessible; Signers for the hearing impaired
CASES SEXUAL ASSAULT/ABUSE (%): 100
DESCRIPTION: Crisis services and support groups for sexual assault survivors; School-based personal safety program for children; Acquaintance/date rape prevention program for adolescents and university students
CLIENTS/SERVICES: Sexual assault survivors; Marital rape/sexual abuse survivors; Adult survivors of child sexual abuse; Incest victims/survivors; Prevention program; Community education; Male survivors of sexual abuse

ROME

DISTRICT ATTORNEY'S OFFICE—VICTIM/WITNESS ASSISTANCE PROGRAM
Floyd County Courthouse, 12 E 4th Ave, Rome, GA 30161
Information: (404) 291-5210 8:30am-5pm
Contact: Janet Carver, Victim/Witness Dir
TYPE OF AGENCY: Victim/witness assistance program
AREAS SERVED: Floyd
YEARS IN OPERATION: 3
ACCESSIBILITY: Wheelchair accessible; Signers for the hearing impaired (by arrangement)
CASES SEXUAL ASSAULT/ABUSE (%): 75
CLIENTS/SERVICES: Sexual assault survivors; Child victims of sexual abuse; Community education
REQUIREMENTS: The program most often becomes involved after an arrest has been made.

HOSPITALITY HOUSE FOR WOMEN, INC
PO Box 6163, Rome, GA 30161
Crisis hotline: **(404) 235-4673 24 hrs**
Information: (404) 235-4608 8am-5pm
Contact: Lynn McLeod, Dir
TYPE OF AGENCY: Domestic violence program; Shelter
AREAS SERVED: Rome, Bartow, Polk, Chattooga, Gordon
YEARS IN OPERATION: 10
CASES SEXUAL ASSAULT/ABUSE (%): 75
CLIENTS/SERVICES: Sexual assault survivors; Child victims of sexual abuse; Community education

SAVANNAH

THE FAMILY COUNSELING CENTER
21 E Broad St, Savannah, GA 31401
Information: (912) 238-2777 9am-9pm (Mon-Thu); 9am-5pm (Fri)
Contact: Stephen R Fishack, Prog Dir
TYPE OF AGENCY: Counseling/mental health services
SPONSORING ORGANIZATION: Parent and Child Development Services, Inc
AREAS SERVED: Chatham, Bryan, Effingham
YEARS IN OPERATION: 78
ACCESSIBILITY: Wheelchair accessible
CASES SEXUAL ASSAULT/ABUSE (%): 10
DESCRIPTION: Individual, couple, and family counseling
CLIENTS/SERVICES: Sexual assault survivors; Child victims of sexual abuse; Adult survivors of child sexual abuse; Incest victims/survivors; Offender treatment program

RAPE CRISIS CENTER OF THE COASTAL EMPIRE, INC
PO Box 8492, Savannah, GA 31412
Crisis hotline: **(912) 233-7273 24 hrs**
Information: (912) 354-6742 8am-5pm
Contact: Mary Hannaford, Exec Dir
TYPE OF AGENCY: Rape crisis center
AREAS SERVED: Chatham, Effingham, Bryan
YEARS IN OPERATION: 13
ACCESSIBILITY: Wheelchair accessible; Signers for the hearing impaired
CASES SEXUAL ASSAULT/ABUSE (%): 100
DESCRIPTION: Comprehensive rape crisis services; Support groups for female and male survivors of sexual assault/abuse; Group therapy for child sexual abuse offenders
CLIENTS/SERVICES: Sexual assault survivors; Marital rape/sexual abuse survivors; Child victims of sexual abuse; Adult survivors of child sexual abuse; Incest victims/survivors; Prevention program; Community education; Offender treatment program; Adolescent survivors of sexual abuse; Male survivors of sexual abuse

VALDOSTA

FAMILY AND CHILDREN EVALUATION SERVICES (FACES)
3018 N Patterson St, Valdosta, GA 31602
Information: (912) 244-6444 8am-7pm
Contact: Pat Hastings, MS, Prog Dir; C Rick Hastings, MEd, Intake Coord
TYPE OF AGENCY: Counseling/mental health services; Child sexual abuse services; Child sexual abuse prevention program
AREAS SERVED: Lowndes, Brooks, Cook, Berrien, Lanier, Tift, Echols
YEARS IN OPERATION: 4
LANGUAGES: Spanish

FAMILY AND CHILDREN EVALUATION SERVICES (FACES) *(continued)*
ACCESSIBILITY: Wheelchair accessible
CASES SEXUAL ASSAULT/ABUSE (%): 70
CLIENTS/SERVICES: Sexual assault survivors; Marital rape/sexual abuse survivors; Child victims of sexual abuse; Adult survivors of child sexual abuse; Incest victims/survivors; Prevention program; Community education; Offender treatment program; Adolescent survivors of sexual abuse; Male survivors of sexual abuse
REQUIREMENTS: Offender must acknowledge responsibility for behavior.

WARNER ROBINS

HOUSTON DRUG ACTION COUNCIL (HODAC)—RAPE CRISIS PROGRAM
PO Box 1004, Warner Robins, GA 31099
Crisis hotline: **(912) 922-4144 24 hrs 7 days**
Information: (912) 922-4144 8:30am-5:30pm (Mon-Fri)
Contact: Deborah Chan-Friday, Rape Crisis Prog Coord
TYPE OF AGENCY: Rape crisis center; Counseling/mental health services; Child sexual abuse services; Child sexual abuse prevention program
AREAS SERVED: Houston and Peach
ACCESSIBILITY: Wheelchair accessible
CASES SEXUAL ASSAULT/ABUSE (%): 80
DESCRIPTION: Rape advocacy services for rape victims at emergency facilities; Short- and long-term counseling for sexual assault/abuse victims; Trains educators to facilitate child sexual abuse prevention program; Intervention curriculum in junior high and high schools in Houston County
CLIENTS/SERVICES: Sexual assault survivors; Marital rape/sexual abuse survivors; Child victims of sexual abuse; Adult survivors of child sexual abuse; Incest victims/survivors; Prevention program; Community education; Adolescent survivors of sexual abuse; Male survivors of sexual abuse
SPECIAL PROGRAMS/SERVICES: Provides *Good Touch, Bad Touch*, prevention program for grades K through 6

WAYCROSS

SATILLA COMMUNITY MENTAL HEALTH CLINIC
PO Box 1397, Waycross, GA 31501
Crisis hotline: **(800) 342-8168 24 hrs**
Information: (912) 285-6142 8am-5pm (Mon-Fri)
Contact: Julie Currie, Admin Clinical Dir
TYPE OF AGENCY: Counseling/mental health services
AREAS SERVED: Atkinson, Bacon, Brantley, Charlton, Clinch, Coffee, Pierce, Ware
ACCESSIBILITY: Wheelchair accessible
CASES SEXUAL ASSAULT/ABUSE (%): 20
CLIENTS/SERVICES: Sexual assault survivors; Marital rape/sexual abuse survivors; Child victims of sexual abuse; Adult survivors of child sexual abuse; Incest victims/survivors; Prevention program; Community education; Adolescent survivors of sexual abuse; Male survivors of sexual abuse

WAYCROSS AREA SHELTER FOR THE ABUSED, INC
1204½ Blackshear Ave, Waycross, GA 31501
Crisis hotline: **(912) 285-5850 24 hrs**
Information: (912) 285-5850
Contact: Donna Elbrink, Dir
TYPE OF AGENCY: Domestic violence program
AREAS SERVED: Atkinson, Bacon, Brantley, Charlton, Clinch, Coffee, Pierce, Ware
YEARS IN OPERATION: 8½
LANGUAGES: Spanish, Haitian, German interpreters available
ACCESSIBILITY: Wheelchair accessible
CASES SEXUAL ASSAULT/ABUSE (%): 60-75
CLIENTS/SERVICES: Sexual assault survivors; Marital rape/sexual abuse survivors; Child victims of sexual abuse; Adult survivors of child sexual abuse; Incest victims/survivors; Adolescent survivors of sexual abuse; Male survivors of sexual abuse

WOODSTOCK

CHEROKEE COUNSELING AND PSYCHOLOGICAL ASSOCIATION
110 S Main St, Ste 301, Woodstock, GA 30188
Information: (404) 924-1818 9am-8pm (Mon-Fri)
Contact: Anna Crawford, PhD, Therapist
TYPE OF AGENCY: Private practice
AREAS SERVED: Cherokee, Cobb, Fulton, Forsyth, Bartow, Gordon, Gwinnett, DeKalb
YEARS IN OPERATION: 5
LANGUAGES: Spanish
ACCESSIBILITY: Signers for the hearing impaired (by arrangement)
CASES SEXUAL ASSAULT/ABUSE (%): 50
DESCRIPTION: Multi-purpose counseling facility, with special emphasis and training in domestic violence, sexual abuse and family therapy. Provides counseling for survivors and treatment for child sexual abuse/incest offenders and batterers
CLIENTS/SERVICES: Sexual assault survivors; Marital rape/sexual abuse survivors; Child victims of sexual abuse; Adult survivors of child sexual abuse; Incest victims/survivors; Prevention program; Community education; Offender treatment program; Adolescent survivors of sexual abuse; Male survivors of sexual abuse
REQUIREMENTS: All fees are due at time of service. Client must file insurance

HAWAII

HILO

HAWAII ISLAND YWCA—SEXUAL ASSAULT SUPPORT SERVICE
145 Ululani St, Hilo, HI 96720
Crisis hotline: **(808) 935-0677 24 hrs**
Information: (808) 935-7141 8am-4:30pm
Contact: Cynthia Wells, Prog Dir
TYPE OF AGENCY: Rape crisis center; Child sexual abuse services; Child sexual abuse prevention program
AREAS SERVED: Hawaii
YEARS IN OPERATION: 10
LANGUAGES: Illacano
ACCESSIBILITY: Wheelchair accessible; Telecommunications for the hearing impaired (TTY, TDY, etc.); Signers for the hearing impaired
CASES SEXUAL ASSAULT/ABUSE (%): 100
CLIENTS/SERVICES: Sexual assault survivors; Marital rape/sexual abuse survivors; Child victims of sexual abuse; Adult survivors of child sexual abuse; Incest victims/survivors; Prevention program; Community education; Adolescent survivors of sexual abuse

PROSECUTOR'S OFFICE—VICTIM/WITNESS ASSISTANCE PROGRAM
34 Rainbow Dr, Hilo, HI 96720
Information: (808) 961-0466 7:45am-4:30pm (Mon-Fri)
Contact: Phyllis Shinno, Coord
TYPE OF AGENCY: Victim/witness assistance program
AREAS SERVED: Hawaii (Island of Hawaii)
YEARS IN OPERATION: 10
ACCESSIBILITY: Wheelchair accessible
CASES SEXUAL ASSAULT/ABUSE (%): 5-10
CLIENTS/SERVICES: Sexual assault survivors; Child victims of sexual abuse; Incest victims/survivors; Community education; Adolescent survivors of sexual abuse; Male survivors of sexual abuse
REQUIREMENTS: Clients must make a police report to engage the full range of services; otherwise, counseling and referrals to other agencies are provided.

HONOLULU

ALTERNATIVES FOR WOMEN
550 Makapuu Ave, Honolulu, HI 96816
Information: (808) 735-5452 7:45am-4:30pm
Contact: Isabel Orloff, Act Dir
TYPE OF AGENCY: Counseling/mental health services
SPONSORING ORGANIZATION: Diamond Health Mental Health Services Branch
AREAS SERVED: Honolulu
ACCESSIBILITY: Wheelchair accessible; Signers for the hearing impaired
CASES SEXUAL ASSAULT/ABUSE (%): 10
DESCRIPTION: Provides women with individual and couples therapy, support group; Older women's support group; Workshops in the areas of self-esteem, assertiveness training and relationships, stress management
CLIENTS/SERVICES: Sexual assault survivors; Marital rape/sexual abuse survivors; Adult survivors of child sexual abuse; Incest victims/survivors
REQUIREMENTS: Client must be female.

CHILD SEX ABUSE TREATMENT PROGRAM
745 Fort St, Ste 610, Honolulu, HI 96815
Information: (808) 536-1831 8:15am-4:30pm
Contact: Lynn Adams, Prog Dir
TYPE OF AGENCY: Child sexual abuse services
SPONSORING ORGANIZATION: Catholic Services to Families
AREAS SERVED: Oahu
YEARS IN OPERATION: 8
ACCESSIBILITY: Wheelchair accessible
CASES SEXUAL ASSAULT/ABUSE (%): 100
DESCRIPTION: Long-term intrafamilial sex abuse treatment program; Also treats juvenile sex offenders in cases of nonfamilial abuse. In both cases, all family members are treated
CLIENTS/SERVICES: Child victims of sexual abuse; Offender treatment program; Adolescent survivors of sexual abuse; Male survivors of sexual abuse
REQUIREMENTS: CPS or family court referrals only

HAWAII STATE JUDICIARY—CHILDREN'S ADVOCACY CENTER
3019 Pali Hwy, Honolulu, HI 96817
Information: (808) 548-6021 7:45am-4:30pm
Contact: Judy Lind, Dir
TYPE OF AGENCY: Child sexual abuse services
AREAS SERVED: Island of Oahu, City and County of Honolulu
YEARS IN OPERATION: ½
LANGUAGES: Interpreters available as needed
CASES SEXUAL ASSAULT/ABUSE (%): 100
DESCRIPTION: Provides a supportive, homelike environment for child victims of sexual abuse to be interviewed. The interviews are conducted by specially trained teams of social workers and law enforcement officers in three interview rooms with adjacent observation rooms designed for different-aged children
CLIENTS/SERVICES: Child victims of sexual abuse; Adolescent survivors of sexual abuse
REQUIREMENTS: 2-17 years of age

MILITARY FAMILY ABUSE SHELTER
PO Box 2218, Honolulu, HI 96804
Crisis hotline: **(808) 533-7125 24 hrs**
Information: (808) 836-0772 8:30am-4:30pm
Contact: Carol Lee, Dir
TYPE OF AGENCY: Domestic violence program; Military services
SPONSORING ORGANIZATION: Armed Services YMCA
AREAS SERVED: Oahu
YEARS IN OPERATION: 6
LANGUAGES: Interpreters available for Asian/Oriental
CLIENTS/SERVICES: Marital rape/sexual abuse survivors; Community education
REQUIREMENTS: Active duty, retired, or military dependent.

PACIFIC CENTER FOR SEXUAL HEALTH
1314 S King, 1st Interstate Bldg, Ste 953, Honolulu, HI 96814
Crisis hotline: **(808) 599-5902 24 hrs**
Information: (808) 599-5942
Contact: Joseph Giorannoni, MS, MA, RN, CS
TYPE OF AGENCY: Child sexual abuse services; Child sexual abuse prevention program; Private practice
AREAS SERVED: Honolulu
YEARS IN OPERATION: 2
CASES SEXUAL ASSAULT/ABUSE (%): 80
DESCRIPTION: Therapy for victims/survivors and rapists, child sexual abuse/incest offenders, and batterers. Assessment of offenders includes penile plethysmograph
CLIENTS/SERVICES: Sexual assault survivors; Marital rape/sexual abuse survivors; Child victims of sexual abuse; Adult survivors of child sexual abuse; Incest victims/survivors; Community education; Offender treatment program; Adolescent survivors of sexual abuse; Male survivors of sexual abuse

SEX ABUSE TREATMENT CENTER
1415 Kalakaua Ave, Ste 201, Honolulu, HI 96826
Crisis hotline: **(808) 524-7273 24 hrs**
Information: (808) 947-8337 8am-4:30pm (Mon-Fri)
Contact: Adriana Ramelli, MSW, Dir
TYPE OF AGENCY: Rape crisis center; Hospital/medical center
AREAS SERVED: Island of Oahu and referrals from outer islands
YEARS IN OPERATION: 12
ACCESSIBILITY: Wheelchair accessible; Telecommunications for the hearing impaired (TTY, TDY, etc.); Signers for the hearing impaired
CASES SEXUAL ASSAULT/ABUSE (%): 98
CLIENTS/SERVICES: Sexual assault survivors; Child victims of sexual abuse; Adult survivors of child sexual abuse; Prevention program; Community education

WOMEN'S COUNSELING CLINIC
1314 S King St, Ste 1553, Honolulu, HI 96814
Information: (808) 536-9976 24 hrs
Contact: Hilarie Cash, MA, Assoc
TYPE OF AGENCY: Counseling/mental health services
YEARS IN OPERATION: 20

WOMEN'S COUNSELING CLINIC
(continued)

LANGUAGES: French, Spanish, Sign
ACCESSIBILITY: Wheelchair accessible; Signers for the hearing impaired
CLIENTS/SERVICES: Sexual assault survivors; Child victims of sexual abuse; Adult survivors of child sexual abuse; Incest victims/survivors; Adolescent survivors of sexual abuse; Prevention program; Healing
REQUIREMENTS: Fees are charged
SPECIAL PROGRAMS/SERVICES: The clinic is part of a national organization called North American Riding for the Handicapped (NARHA). For several years it has worked with adults and children in a program which uses horses and the riding experience as therapeutic tools

LIHUE

KAUAI VICTIM WITNESS PROGRAM
4193 Hardy St, Unit 4, Lihue, HI 96766
Information: (808) 245-5388 24 hrs
Contact: Michael Iwai, Prog Coord
TYPE OF AGENCY: Victim/witness assistance program
AREAS SERVED: Kauai
YEARS IN OPERATION: 7
ACCESSIBILITY: Wheelchair accessible
CASES SEXUAL ASSAULT/ABUSE (%): 5
CLIENTS/SERVICES: Sexual assault survivors; Marital rape/sexual abuse survivors; Child victims of sexual abuse; Adult survivors of child sexual abuse; Incest victims/survivors; Community education; Adolescent survivors of sexual abuse; Male survivors of sexual abuse

SEX ABUSE TREATMENT PROGRAM
3094 Elua St, Lihue, HI 96766
Crisis hotline: **(808) 245-4144 24 hrs**
Information: (808) 245-5959 8am-5pm
Contact: Susan McIntyre-King, Dir
TYPE OF AGENCY: Rape crisis center; Child sexual abuse services; Child sexual abuse prevention program
SPONSORING ORGANIZATION: YWCA
AREAS SERVED: Kauai
YEARS IN OPERATION: 7
CASES SEXUAL ASSAULT/ABUSE (%): 100
DESCRIPTION: Provides hotline, support groups, individual and group therapy, and escort services for victims of sexual abuse/assault. Also offers individual and group therapy for rapists, child sexual abuse offenders, and incest offenders
CLIENTS/SERVICES: Sexual assault survivors; Marital rape/sexual abuse survivors; Child victims of sexual abuse; Adult survivors of child sexual abuse; Incest victims/survivors; Prevention program; Community education; Offender treatment program; Adolescent survivors of sexual abuse; Male survivors of sexual abuse

WAILUKU

DEPARTMENT OF THE PROSECUTING ATTORNEY—VICTIM/WITNESS ASSISTANCE PROGRAM
200 S High St, Wailuku, HI 96793
Information: (808) 244-7799 7:45am-4:30pm (Mon-Fri)
Contact: Dr Brian Ogawa, Coord
TYPE OF AGENCY: Victim/witness assistance program
AREAS SERVED: Maui
YEARS IN OPERATION: 6
ACCESSIBILITY: Wheelchair accessible
CASES SEXUAL ASSAULT/ABUSE (%): 50
CLIENTS/SERVICES: Sexual assault survivors; Marital rape/sexual abuse survivors; Child victims of sexual abuse; Community education

SEX ABUSE INTERVENTIONS, INC
PO Box 1278, Wailuku, HI 96793
Crisis hotline: **(808) 242-4357 24 hrs**
Information: (808) 242-4335 9am-5pm
Contact: Christine Moschetti, Exec Dir
TYPE OF AGENCY: Rape crisis center; Child sexual abuse services; Child sexual abuse prevention program
SPONSORING ORGANIZATION: Sexual Assault Crisis Center—Maui Family Resource Center
AREAS SERVED: Maui (Maui, Molokai, Lanai)
YEARS IN OPERATION: 6½
ACCESSIBILITY: Wheelchair accessible; Telecommunications for the hearing impaired (TTY, TDY, etc.); Signers for the hearing impaired (by arrangement)
CASES SEXUAL ASSAULT/ABUSE (%): 100
DESCRIPTION: Comprehensive rape crisis services; Counseling for incest families; Feminist martial arts/self-defense program; Individual and group counseling for child sexual abuse offenders and incest offender, as well as family and couple counseling, assessment and plethysmograph
CLIENTS/SERVICES: Sexual assault survivors; Marital rape/sexual abuse survivors; Child victims of sexual abuse; Adult survivors of child sexual abuse; Incest victims/survivors; Prevention program; Community education; Offender treatment program; Adolescent survivors of sexual abuse; Male survivors of sexual abuse

IDAHO

BLACKFOOT

BINGHAM CRISIS CENTER
PO Box 714, Blackfoot, ID 83221
Crisis hotline: **(208) 785-4181 24 hrs**
Information: (208) 785-1200, ext 264 8am-12pm
TYPE OF AGENCY: Rape crisis center; Domestic violence program
AREAS SERVED: Bingham
YEARS IN OPERATION: 9
CASES SEXUAL ASSAULT/ABUSE (%): 5
CLIENTS/SERVICES: Marital rape/sexual abuse survivors; Community education

BOISE

ADA COUNTY SHERIFF'S DEPARTMENT— VICTIM-WITNESS UNIT
7200 Barrister Dr, Boise, ID 83704
Information: (208) 377-6735 8am-4pm, person on call 24 hrs
Contact: Michelle Macaw, Victim-Witness Coord
TYPE OF AGENCY: Victim/witness assistance program
AREAS SERVED: Ada
YEARS IN OPERATION: 4
ACCESSIBILITY: Wheelchair accessible; Signers for the hearing impaired
CASES SEXUAL ASSAULT/ABUSE (%): 70
DESCRIPTION: Works with victims/witnesses of felony crimes from the investigation through the court process. Many cases involve sexual assault/child sexual abuse
CLIENTS/SERVICES: Sexual assault survivors; Marital rape/sexual abuse survivors; Child victims of sexual abuse; Incest victims/survivors; Prevention program; Community education
REQUIREMENTS: Victims must file charges with the Sheriff's Department and cooperate with law enforcement agencies

ADA COUNTY VICTIM/WITNESS ASSISTANCE UNIT
Ada County Courthouse, Rm 103, Boise, ID 83702
Crisis hotline: **(208) 338-4827 24 hrs**
Information: (208) 383-1237 8am-5pm
Contact: Laurie Gillis, Admin
TYPE OF AGENCY: Victim/witness assistance program
SPONSORING ORGANIZATION: Ada County Prosecutor's Office
AREAS SERVED: Ada
YEARS IN OPERATION: 2½
CASES SEXUAL ASSAULT/ABUSE (%): 90
CLIENTS/SERVICES: Sexual assault survivors; Marital rape/sexual abuse survivors; Child victims of sexual abuse; Incest victims/survivors; Prevention program; Community education; Adolescent survivors of sexual abuse; Male survivors of sexual abuse

BOISE HOTLINE
PO Box 235, Boise, ID 83701
Crisis hotline: **(208) 322-5811 3pm-11pm**
Information: (208) 322-7093 3pm-11pm
Contact: Ann Patterson, Consultant/Dir
TYPE OF AGENCY: Counseling/mental health services; Crisis telephone hotline
AREAS SERVED: Ada
YEARS IN OPERATION: 17
CASES SEXUAL ASSAULT/ABUSE (%): 20
CLIENTS/SERVICES: Sexual assault survivors

BOISE VALLEY CHAPTER OF PARENTS UNITED
State of ID, Dept H and W Region IV Office
Statehouse Mail, Boise, ID 83720
Crisis hotline: **(208) 334-6800 (Child Protection) 24 hrs**
Information: (208) 334-6800 8am-5pm (Mon-Fri)
Contact: Susan Allen, Parents United Coord
TYPE OF AGENCY: Child sexual abuse services; Child sexual abuse prevention program
SPONSORING ORGANIZATION: Department of Health and Welfare Region IV Famil and Childrens Services
AREAS SERVED: Ada
YEARS IN OPERATION: 6
ACCESSIBILITY: Wheelchair accessible
CASES SEXUAL ASSAULT/ABUSE (%): 100
DESCRIPTION: Dedicated to the identification, prevention, and humanistic treatment of child sexual abuse. Provides group therapy for family members where incest has occurred; Groups for adults molested as children, non-offending parents, teen and young children offenders group. Utilizes a self-help model including prevention activities, speakers bureaus, fundraising, social events, and community education for professionals and community members
CLIENTS/SERVICES: Sexual assault survivors; Child victims of sexual abuse; Adult survivors of child sexual abuse; Incest victims/survivors; Prevention program; Community education; Offender treatment program; Adolescent survivors of sexual abuse; Male survivors of sexual abuse
SPECIAL PROGRAMS/SERVICES: Video: *Adults Molested as Children-Survivors*, personal testimony from adult survivors about the abuse, family dynamics, secrets, disclosure, recovery process, new beginnings

DEPARTMENT OF SOCIOLOGY, ANTHROPOLOGY, AND CRIMINAL JUSTICE ADMINISTRATION
1910 University Dr, Boise, ID 83725
Information: (208) 385-1011
Contact: Jane Foraker-Thompson, Criminal Justice Assoc Professor
TYPE OF AGENCY: College/university-based services; Rape prevention program
SPONSORING ORGANIZATION: Boise State University
DESCRIPTION: Cosponsors Victims' Rights Week every April and Sexual Assault Awareness week on campus every fall. Involvement of many professionals in the community, criminal justice and mental health/healing organizations and individuals, as well as recovering survivors
CLIENTS/SERVICES: Sexual assault survivors; Community education

EMERGENCY HOUSING SERVICE, INC
PO Box 286, Boise, ID 83701
Crisis hotline: **(208) 342-9719 6pm-9am**
Information: (208) 342-9719
TYPE OF AGENCY: Domestic violence program
AREAS SERVED: Ada, Elmore, Canyon, Payette
YEARS IN OPERATION: 10
CASES SEXUAL ASSAULT/ABUSE (%): 10
CLIENTS/SERVICES: Sexual assault survivors; Marital rape/sexual abuse survivors
REQUIREMENTS: Client must be female.

HAYS SHELTER HOME
1122 Wild Phlox Way, Boise, ID 83709
Crisis hotline: **(208) 322-6686 24 hrs**
Information: (208) 322-6686 24 hrs
Contact: Liz Mills, Prog Mgr
TYPE OF AGENCY: Counseling/mental health services; Child sexual abuse services; Shelter; Adolescent program
AREAS SERVED: Primarily Ada
YEARS IN OPERATION: 16
CASES SEXUAL ASSAULT/ABUSE (%): 30
DESCRIPTION: Emergency, 24-hour shelter for abused, neglected, homeless males and females ages 9-17.
CLIENTS/SERVICES: Child victims of sexual abuse

PLANNED PARENTHOOD ASSOCIATION OF IDAHO
4301 Franklin Rd, Boise, ID 83705
Information: (208) 345-0760 9am-7pm
Contact: Sherry Iverson, Educ Dir
TYPE OF AGENCY: Child sexual abuse prevention program; Acquaintance/date rape prevention program
AREAS SERVED: Ada, Canyon
YEARS IN OPERATION: 17
DESCRIPTION: Provides sexual abuse prevention programs targeted to preschoolers ages 3-6, K-3rd grades, and date rape information and materials for adolescents
CLIENTS/SERVICES: Prevention program; Community education; Preschoolers

SANE (SEXUAL ABUSE NOW ENDED)
1010 N Orchard, Ste 7, Boise, ID 83706
Information: (208) 345-1170 9am-5pm
Contact: Chris Paul Nelson, Admin Dir

SANE (SEXUAL ABUSE NOW ENDED)
(continued)
TYPE OF AGENCY: Child sexual abuse services; Child sexual abuse prevention program
SPONSORING ORGANIZATION: Terry Reilly Health Services
AREAS SERVED: Ada, Canyon
YEARS IN OPERATION: 6
CASES SEXUAL ASSAULT/ABUSE (%): 100
DESCRIPTION: Individual, group, and family treatment for sexually abused children and offenders, including juvenile sex offenders
CLIENTS/SERVICES: Marital rape/sexual abuse survivors; Child victims of sexual abuse; Adult survivors of child sexual abuse; Incest victims/survivors; Prevention program; Community education; Offender treatment program; Adolescent survivors of sexual abuse; Male survivors of sexual abuse

YWCA WOMEN'S CRISIS CENTER—RAPE CRISIS ALLIANCE
720 W Washington St, Boise, ID 83702
Crisis hotline: **(208) 345-RAPE 24 hrs**
Information: (208) 343-3688 8am-5:30pm
Contact: Shay Scrivner, Women's Crisis Ctr Dir
TYPE OF AGENCY: Rape crisis center; Domestic violence program
AREAS SERVED: Ada, Canyon, Elmore
YEARS IN OPERATION: 10
CASES SEXUAL ASSAULT/ABUSE (%): 100
CLIENTS/SERVICES: Sexual assault survivors; Marital rape/sexual abuse survivors; Adult survivors of child sexual abuse; Incest victims/survivors; Prevention program; Community education; Adolescent survivors of sexual abuse

CALDWELL

REGION III MENTAL HEALTH
PO Box 1219, Caldwell, ID 83606
Crisis hotline: **(208) 459-0092 24 hrs**
Information: (208) 459-0092 24 hrs
Contact: Al Sanchez, MH Prog Mgr
TYPE OF AGENCY: Counseling/mental health services
SPONSORING ORGANIZATION: Department of Health and Welfare
AREAS SERVED: Canyon
YEARS IN OPERATION: 20
LANGUAGES: Spanish
ACCESSIBILITY: Wheelchair accessible
CASES SEXUAL ASSAULT/ABUSE (%): 5
DESCRIPTION: Provides psychotherapy for individuals with a broad range of needs, including sexual assault and abuse; counseling for family and friends of survivors
CLIENTS/SERVICES: Sexual assault survivors; Marital rape/sexual abuse survivors; Child victims of sexual abuse; Adult survivors of child sexual abuse; Incest victims/survivors

COEUR D'ALENE

INTERFAITH FAMILY COUNSELING SERVICES, INC
1420 Lincoln Way, No 300, Coeur D'Alene, ID 83814
Information: (208) 667-1261 8am-6pm (Mon-Fri)
Contact: Tom Hearn, ACSW, Lic Clinical Soc Wkr
TYPE OF AGENCY: Counseling/mental health services; Private practice; Christian counseling
AREAS SERVED: North Idaho, Eastern Washington
YEARS IN OPERATION: 14
CASES SEXUAL ASSAULT/ABUSE (%): 40-50
DESCRIPTION: Treatment for child sexual abuse victims, offenders, and adult survivors. Offender treatment based on Seattle model from the Northwest Treatment Associates. Also treats batterers
CLIENTS/SERVICES: Sexual assault survivors; Marital rape/sexual abuse survivors; Child victims of sexual abuse; Adult survivors of child sexual abuse; Incest victims/survivors; Community education; Offender treatment program; Adolescent survivors of sexual abuse; Male survivors of sexual abuse
REQUIREMENTS: Offenders have acknowledged crime and be under some form of legal obligation to attend treatment

IDAHO FALLS

HELP, INC
545 Shoup Ave, Ste 330, Idaho Falls, ID 83402
Crisis hotline: **(208) 525-1502 24 hrs**
Information: (208) 522-5545 9am-4pm (Mon-Thu)
Contact: Marie Gokey, Exec Dir
TYPE OF AGENCY: Victim/witness assistance program; Child sexual abuse services; Child sexual abuse prevention program; Child abuse services; Child abuse prevention program
SPONSORING ORGANIZATION: National Exchange Club Center for the Prevention of Child Abuse
AREAS SERVED: Bonneville, Jefferson, Madison, Bingham (southeastern ID)
YEARS IN OPERATION: 6
ACCESSIBILITY: Wheelchair accessible; Signers for the hearing impaired
CASES SEXUAL ASSAULT/ABUSE (%): 90
DESCRIPTION: Sponsors family support groups for children and teens in different age groups, parents' group, adult children of abuse groups, and women's group. Parent aides are matched with at-risk families
CLIENTS/SERVICES: Sexual assault survivors; Marital rape/sexual abuse survivors; Child victims of sexual abuse; Adult survivors of child sexual abuse; Incest victims/survivors; Prevention program; Community education; Adolescent survivors of sexual abuse; Male survivors of sexual abuse

SEXUAL ASSAULT AND RAPE RELIEF OF BONNEVILLE COUNTY, INC
545 Shoup Ave, Ste 314, Idaho Falls, ID 83402
Crisis hotline: **(208) 525-1831 24 hrs**
Information: (208) 522-7016 24 hrs
Contact: Pat Day Hartwell, Pres
TYPE OF AGENCY: Rape crisis center; Child sexual abuse services; Child sexual abuse prevention program
AREAS SERVED: Bonneville, Bingham, Jefferson, Teton, Madison, Fremont, Clark, Custer
YEARS IN OPERATION: 11
LANGUAGES: Spanish
ACCESSIBILITY: Wheelchair accessible; Signers for the hearing impaired
CASES SEXUAL ASSAULT/ABUSE (%): 100
CLIENTS/SERVICES: Sexual assault survivors; Marital rape/sexual abuse survivors; Child victims of sexual abuse; Adult survivors of child sexual abuse; Incest victims/survivors; Prevention program; Community education; Adolescent survivors of sexual abuse; Male survivors of sexual abuse

KETCHUM

CRISIS HOTLINE
PO Box 939, Ketchum, ID 83340
Crisis hotline: **(208) 726-3596 24 hrs**
Information: (208) 726-3597 8:30am-12:30pm (Mon-Fri)
Contact: Margaret MacDonald-Stewart, Crisis Hotline Dir
TYPE OF AGENCY: Counseling/mental health services; Telephone crisis hotline; Information and referral
AREAS SERVED: Blaine
YEARS IN OPERATION: 2
LANGUAGES: Spanish (by request)
CASES SEXUAL ASSAULT/ABUSE (%): 8
CLIENTS/SERVICES: Sexual assault survivors; Marital rape/sexual abuse survivors; Adult survivors of child sexual abuse; Incest victims/survivors; Adolescent survivors of sexual abuse

LEWISTON

YWCA LEWISTON/CLARKSTON CRISIS SERVICES
300 Main St, Lewiston, ID 83501
Crisis hotline: **(208) 746-9655 24 hrs**
Information: (208) 746-9655 24 hrs
Contact: Florence Giammanco, Emerg Svcs Coord
TYPE OF AGENCY: Rape crisis center; Domestic violence program
AREAS SERVED: Nez Perce, Clearwater, in ID; Asotin, Garfield in WA
YEARS IN OPERATION: 5
CASES SEXUAL ASSAULT/ABUSE (%): 20
CLIENTS/SERVICES: Sexual assault survivors; Marital rape/sexual abuse survivors; Child victims of sexual abuse; Incest victims/survivors; Prevention program; Community education
REQUIREMENTS: Clients must be at least 18 years of age, or be accompanied by a legal guardian, or provide documentation of emancipation.

MOSCOW

ALTERNATIVES TO VIOLENCE OF PALOUSE, INC
PO Box 8517, Moscow, ID 83843
Crisis hotline: **(208) 883-HELP, 332-HELP**
Information: (208) 882-3720
Contact: Kathleen Tobin
TYPE OF AGENCY: Rape crisis center; Domestic violence program
CLIENTS/SERVICES: Sexual assault survivors

WOMEN'S CENTER—UNIVERSITY OF IDAHO
University of Idaho, Moscow, ID 83843
Information: (208) 885-6616 8am-5pm
Contact: Betsy Thomas, Dir
TYPE OF AGENCY: College/university-based services; Acquaintance/date rape prevention program
YEARS IN OPERATION: 16
ACCESSIBILITY: Wheelchair accessible (by arrangement); Signers for the hearing impaired (by arrangement)
CASES SEXUAL ASSAULT/ABUSE (%): 5-10
DESCRIPTION: Serves as the headquarters for the acquaintance sexual assault education program at the University of Idaho. Trains students to give presentations in the dormitories, sororities, and fraternities. A professional from the center always accompanies the student teams at the presentations. Participates in the resident advisor's training and Greek leadership training. Serves as a resource for the residence halls. Also provides crisis intervention for rape victims, and police and court room advocacy; Group for survivors
CLIENTS/SERVICES: Sexual assault survivors; Marital rape/sexual abuse survivors; Adult survivors of child sexual abuse; Incest victims/survivors; Prevention program; Community education; Adolescent survivors of sexual abuse

NAMPA

MERCY HOUSE, INC
PO Box 558, Nampa, ID 83653
Crisis hotline: **(208) 465-5011 24 hrs**
Information: (208) 467-4130 8am-5pm
Contact: Sharon Richardson, Prog Dir
TYPE OF AGENCY: Domestic violence program
AREAS SERVED: Canyon, Owyhee, Adams, Gem, Washington, Payette
YEARS IN OPERATION: 4

MERCY HOUSE, INC *(continued)*
CASES SEXUAL ASSAULT/ABUSE (%): Child cases 25%; adult cases 95%
CLIENTS/SERVICES: Marital rape/sexual abuse survivors; Child victims of sexual abuse; Community education

PAYETTE

QUAD UNIT INTERVENTION AND TREATMENT PROGRAM (QUIT)
PO Box 481, Payette, ID 83661
Crisis hotline: **(208) 642-9041 24 hrs**
Information: (208) 642-9041, 642-4436 24 hrs
Contact: Lois Malpass, Sr Soc Wkr/Therapist
TYPE OF AGENCY: Child sexual abuse services
SPONSORING ORGANIZATION: Western Idaho Community Action
AREAS SERVED: Adams, Washington, Payette, Gem
YEARS IN OPERATION: 5
ACCESSIBILITY: Wheelchair accessible
CASES SEXUAL ASSAULT/ABUSE (%): 100
DESCRIPTION: Treatment program for children who have been sexually abused, nonoffending parents, and offenders through individual and group therapy; Groups for female and male survivors; Treats juvenile sex offenders
CLIENTS/SERVICES: Child victims of sexual abuse; Adult survivors of child sexual abuse; Incest victims/survivors; Offender treatment program; Adolescent survivors of sexual abuse; Male survivors of sexual abuse

POCATELLO

POCATELLO YWCA WOMEN'S ADVOCATES
454 N Garfield, Pocatello, ID 83204
Crisis hotline: **(208) 232-9169 24 hrs**
Information: (208) 232-0799 10am-4pm
Contact: Judi Robinson, Prog Dir
TYPE OF AGENCY: Rape crisis center; Domestic violence program
AREAS SERVED: Bannock
YEARS IN OPERATION: 14
CASES SEXUAL ASSAULT/ABUSE (%): 40
CLIENTS/SERVICES: Sexual assault survivors; Marital rape/sexual abuse survivors; Prevention program; Community education; Adolescent survivors of sexual abuse

SAINT MARIES

CRISIS INTERVENTION CENTER
PO Box 22, Saint Maries, ID 83861
Crisis hotline: **(208) 245-5353 24 hrs daily**
Information: (208) 245-5353
Contact: Lois Tuel, Dir
TYPE OF AGENCY: Rape crisis center; Domestic violence program
AREAS SERVED: Benewah, parts of Shoshone and Kootenai
YEARS IN OPERATION: 4
ACCESSIBILITY: Wheelchair accessible
CLIENTS/SERVICES: Sexual assault survivors; Marital rape/sexual abuse survivors; Male survivors of sexual abuse

SANDPOINT

BONNER COUNTY CRISIS LINE, INC
PO Box 1213, Sandpoint, ID 83864
Crisis hotline: **(208) 263-1241 24 hrs**
Information: (208) 263-1241 24 hrs
Contact: Mary Ziegler, Sexual Assault Prog Dir
TYPE OF AGENCY: Rape crisis center; Domestic violence program
AREAS SERVED: Bonner
YEARS IN OPERATION: 5
LANGUAGES: Spanish, interpreters available
ACCESSIBILITY: Signers for the hearing impaired
CASES SEXUAL ASSAULT/ABUSE (%): 3-10
CLIENTS/SERVICES: Sexual assault survivors; Marital rape/sexual abuse survivors; Adult survivors of child sexual abuse; Community education; Male survivors of sexual abuse

CONTINENTAL CROWN COUNSELING
1327 Superior St, Sandpoint, ID 83864
Information: (208) 263-9640
Contact: Toni L Jones, Primary Therapist Dir
TYPE OF AGENCY: Private practice
AREAS SERVED: Boundary, Bonner, Kootenai
YEARS IN OPERATION: 3
ACCESSIBILITY: Wheelchair accessible; Signers for the hearing impaired
CASES SEXUAL ASSAULT/ABUSE (%): 70
DESCRIPTION: Victim centered treatment that includes all members of the family; Primary focus of offender treatment is to repair the damage to his/her victim
CLIENTS/SERVICES: Sexual assault survivors; Marital rape/sexual abuse survivors; Child victims of sexual abuse; Adult survivors of child sexual abuse; Incest victims/survivors; Prevention program; Community education; Offender treatment program; Adolescent survivors of sexual abuse; Male survivors of sexual abuse
REQUIREMENTS: Offenders must plead guilty or if not charged, admit to abusive behavior

TWIN FALLS

GUARDIAN AD LITEM
PO Box 531, Twin Falls, ID 83303-0531
Information: (208) 733-9351 9am-4pm
Contact: Merelda Okelberry, Prog Sec
TYPE OF AGENCY: Child sexual abuse services; Child advocacy
SPONSORING ORGANIZATION: South Central Community Action Agency
AREAS SERVED: Blaine, Cassia, Camas, Minidoka, Lincoln, Gooding, Jerome, Twin Falls
LANGUAGES: Spanish
ACCESSIBILITY: Wheelchair accessible
CASES SEXUAL ASSAULT/ABUSE (%): 51
DESCRIPTION: Guardians Ad Litem are citizens who volunteer to represent children during the family crisis, at the court proceedings, and after the court disposes of the case.
CLIENTS/SERVICES: Child victims of sexual abuse; Adolescent survivors of sexual abuse

VOLUNTEERS AGAINST VIOLENCE
PO Box 2444, Twin Falls, ID 83301
Crisis hotline: **(208) 733-0100 24 hrs**
Information: (208) 733-5054
Contact: Janace Quinn, Prog Dir
TYPE OF AGENCY: Domestic violence program
AREAS SERVED: Blaine, Camas, Cassia, Lincoln, Gooding, Minidoka, Twin Falls, Jerome
YEARS IN OPERATION: 6
LANGUAGES: Spanish
CASES SEXUAL ASSAULT/ABUSE (%): 10-15
CLIENTS/SERVICES: Marital rape/sexual abuse survivors; Community education

ILLINOIS

ARLINGTON HEIGHTS

ARLINGTON COUNSELING ASSOCIATES
3375 N Arlington Heights Rd, Ste F, Arlington Heights, IL 60004
Information: (312) 577-4530 24 hrs, answering service
Contact: Dave Carlson, ACSW, Arlington Counseling Assoc Pres
TYPE OF AGENCY: Child sexual abuse services; Child sexual abuse prevention program; Private practice
AREAS SERVED: Cook, Lake, McHenry
YEARS IN OPERATION: 7
ACCESSIBILITY: Wheelchair accessible
CASES SEXUAL ASSAULT/ABUSE (%): 50
DESCRIPTION: Dedicated to the promotion of emotional, relational, and spiritual healing and growth. A variety of services are offered within the Judeo-Christian perspective. Because a large percentage of clients have been abused, it is a key issue in treatment
CLIENTS/SERVICES: Sexual assault survivors; Marital rape/sexual abuse survivors; Child victims of sexual abuse; Adult survivors of child sexual abuse; Incest victims/survivors; Prevention program; Community education

AURORA

FAMILY COUNSELING CENTER OF AURORA
122 W Downer Pl, Aurora, IL 60506
Information: (312) 844-2662 8:30am-9pm (Mon-Thu); 8:30am-5pm (Fri); 8:30am-noon (Sat)
Contact: Jeanette C Zweifel, EdD, Counseling Svc Dir
TYPE OF AGENCY: Counseling/mental health services
AREAS SERVED: Southern Kane, Kendall
YEARS IN OPERATION: 62
LANGUAGES: Spanish
ACCESSIBILITY: Wheelchair accessible
CASES SEXUAL ASSAULT/ABUSE (%): 30
CLIENTS/SERVICES: Sexual assault survivors; Marital rape/sexual abuse survivors; Child victims of sexual abuse; Adult survivors of child sexual abuse; Incest victims/survivors; Adolescent survivors of sexual abuse; Male survivors of sexual abuse
REQUIREMENTS: Sliding scale fee for residents of service area. Those outside the service area are eligible for services but pay full fee

FAMILY SUPPORT CENTER
256 W Downer Pl, Aurora, IL 60506
Crisis hotline: **(312) 897-1003 24 hrs**
Information: (312) 897-1003 9am-8pm (Mon-Thu); 9am-3pm (Fri)
Contact: Nancy Schroeder, Clinical Dir
TYPE OF AGENCY: Counseling/mental health services; Child sexual abuse services; Child sexual abuse prevention program
AREAS SERVED: Kane, Kendall, DuPage
YEARS IN OPERATION: 13
CASES SEXUAL ASSAULT/ABUSE (%): 40
DESCRIPTION: Child sexual assault prevention programs in preschool and elementary school classrooms, as well as counseling services
CLIENTS/SERVICES: Child victims of sexual abuse; Prevention program; Community education; Offender treatment program; Adolescent survivors of sexual abuse; Male survivors of sexual abuse
REQUIREMENTS: Self-referring family with children under six; Parents who were abused as children; State referral where abuse has occurred

MUTUAL GROUND, INC
PO Box 843, Aurora, IL 60507
Crisis hotline: **(312) 897-8383 24 hrs**
Information: (312) 897-8989 8am-4pm
Contact: Linda R Healy, Sexual Assault Svcs Coord
TYPE OF AGENCY: Rape crisis center; Domestic violence program
AREAS SERVED: South Kane, Kendall
YEARS IN OPERATION: 10
LANGUAGES: Spanish
ACCESSIBILITY: Wheelchair accessible; Signers for the hearing impaired
CLIENTS/SERVICES: Sexual assault survivors; Marital rape/sexual abuse survivors; Child victims of sexual abuse; Adult survivors of child sexual abuse; Incest victims/survivors; Prevention program; Community education; Adolescent survivors of sexual abuse; Male survivors of sexual abuse

BELLEVILLE

SEXUAL ASSAULT VICTIMS CARE UNIT
9400 Lebanon Rd, Belleville, IL 62203-2214
Crisis hotline: **(618) 397-0975 24 hrs**
Information: (618) 397-0975 24 hrs
Contact: Judy Sledge, Prog Mgr
TYPE OF AGENCY: Rape crisis center
SPONSORING ORGANIZATION: Call for Help
AREAS SERVED: Monroe, St Clair
YEARS IN OPERATION: 7
ACCESSIBILITY: Wheelchair accessible; Telecommunications for the hearing impaired (TTY, TDY, etc.)
CASES SEXUAL ASSAULT/ABUSE (%): 100
DESCRIPTION: Comprehensive rape crisis services; Prevention for children and adolescents; Feminist martial arts/self-defense
CLIENTS/SERVICES: Sexual assault survivors; Marital rape/sexual abuse survivors; Child victims of sexual abuse; Adult survivors of child sexual abuse; Incest victims/survivors; Prevention program; Community education; Adolescent survivors of sexual abuse; Male survivors of sexual abuse
SPECIAL PROGRAMS/SERVICES: Annual retreat for adult survivors, focusing on self-esteem issues and some work with dance as a form of relaxation

BLOOMINGTON

MCLEAN COUNTY STATE ATTORNEY'S OFFICE—VICTIM/WITNESS SERVICE
104 W Front St, Rm 102, Bloomington, IL 61701
Information: (309) 888-5415 8:30am-5pm
Contact: Marjorie Meegan-Jordan, Dir
TYPE OF AGENCY: Victim/witness assistance program
AREAS SERVED: McLean
YEARS IN OPERATION: 8½
ACCESSIBILITY: Wheelchair accessible
CASES SEXUAL ASSAULT/ABUSE (%): 10
CLIENTS/SERVICES: Sexual assault survivors; Marital rape/sexual abuse survivors; Child victims of sexual abuse; Community education

RAPE CRISIS CENTER OF MCLEAN COUNTY
PO Box 995, Bloomington, IL 61702
Crisis hotline: **(309) 827-4005**
Information: (309) 827-4005
TYPE OF AGENCY: Rape crisis center
CLIENTS/SERVICES: Sexual assault survivors

BOLINGBROOK

CHILD SEXUAL ABUSE TREATMENT AND TRAINING CENTER
345 Manor Court, Bolingbrook, IL 60439
Crisis hotline: **(312) 739-0786 24 hrs**
Information: (312) 739-0491 9am-9pm (Mon-Thu); 9am-5pm (Fri)
Contact: Thomas S Ryan, Exec Dir
TYPE OF AGENCY: Counseling/mental health services; Child sexual abuse services; Child sexual abuse prevention program; Parents United; Training/research
SPONSORING ORGANIZATION: Evangelical Health Systems
AREAS SERVED: Primarily Will, DuPage, Cook
YEARS IN OPERATION: 10
ACCESSIBILITY: Wheelchair accessible
CASES SEXUAL ASSAULT/ABUSE (%): 100
DESCRIPTION: Treats victims and intrafamilial child sexual abuse and their families; Chapters of Parents United, Daughters and Sons United, and Adults Molested as Children United. Treatment for rapists, child sexual abuse offenders, and batterers
CLIENTS/SERVICES: Child victims of sexual abuse; Adult survivors of child sexual abuse; Incest victims/survivors; Community education; Of-

CHILD SEXUAL ABUSE TREATMENT AND TRAINING CENTER (continued)
fender treatment program; Adolescent survivors of sexual abuse; Male survivors of sexual abuse
REQUIREMENTS: Court-ordered treatment of molester

CAIRO

CAIRO WOMEN'S SHELTER
PO Box 907, Cairo, IL 62914
Crisis hotline: **(618) 734-4357 24 hrs**
Information: (618) 734-4357 24 hrs
Contact: Dee Dee Huber, Dir
TYPE OF AGENCY: Domestic violence program
SPONSORING ORGANIZATION: Community Health and Emergency Services, Inc
AREAS SERVED: Alexander, Pulaski, Massac
YEARS IN OPERATION: 7
LANGUAGES: Spanish
ACCESSIBILITY: Wheelchair accessible
CASES SEXUAL ASSAULT/ABUSE (%): 10
DESCRIPTION: Provides services for survivors of sexual assault, child sexual abuse, marital rape, and incest; Feminist martial arts/self-defense training
CLIENTS/SERVICES: Sexual assault survivors; Marital rape/sexual abuse survivors; Child victims of sexual abuse; Adult survivors of child sexual abuse; Incest victims/survivors; Prevention program; Community education; Adolescent survivors of sexual abuse

CALUMET CITY

THE CHANGING WOMAN COUNSELING AND EDUCATIONAL CENTER
102 Pulaski Rd, Calumet City, IL 60466
Information: (312) 862-2555 by appointment
Contact: Mary Ideran, Clinical Dir
TYPE OF AGENCY: Counseling/mental health services; Child sexual abuse services; Substance abuse treatment/counseling services; Women's center
YEARS IN OPERATION: 3
CASES SEXUAL ASSAULT/ABUSE (%): 90
DESCRIPTION: Provides individual and group counseling for survivors, parents of sexually abused children, issues dealing with addictions, and other issues pertaining to women's process and life choices. Also offers a variety of seminars, including violence against women and children, self-defense, sexual assault prevention for teens, and women's spirituality
CLIENTS/SERVICES: Sexual assault survivors; Marital rape/sexual abuse survivors; Child victims of sexual abuse; Adult survivors of child sexual abuse; Incest victims/survivors; Prevention program; Community education; Adolescent survivors of sexual abuse
REQUIREMENTS: Offers a sliding scale fee and can collect from insurance

CARBONDALE

THE RAPE ACTION COMMITTEE OF THE WOMEN'S CENTER, INC
PO Box 337, Carbondale, IL 62903
Crisis hotline: **(618) 529-2324 24 hrs**
Information: (618) 529-2324 8am-5pm
TYPE OF AGENCY: Rape crisis center; Domestic violence program; Child sexual abuse prevention program
AREAS SERVED: Jackson, Williamson, Perry, Franklin, Union
YEARS IN OPERATION: 14
LANGUAGES: Spanish
ACCESSIBILITY: Wheelchair accessible; Signers for the hearing impaired
CASES SEXUAL ASSAULT/ABUSE (%): 100
DESCRIPTION: Services for sexual assault and domestic violence survivors; Feminist martial arts/self-defense program; Prevention programs for child sexual abuse
CLIENTS/SERVICES: Sexual assault survivors; Marital rape/sexual abuse survivors; Child victims of sexual abuse; Adult survivors of child sexual abuse; Incest victims/survivors; Prevention program; Community education; Adolescent survivors of sexual abuse; Male survivors of sexual abuse

CENTRALIA

PEOPLE AGAINST VIOLENT ENVIRONMENTS
PO Box 342, Centralia, IL 62801
Crisis hotline: **(618) 533-7233 24 hrs**
Information: (618) 533-7233 8am-5pm
Contact: Robin Mayfield, Exec Dir
TYPE OF AGENCY: Domestic violence program
AREAS SERVED: Marion, Jefferson, Clinton, Washington, Fayette
YEARS IN OPERATION: 10
LANGUAGES: Spanish
ACCESSIBILITY: Signers for the hearing impaired
CASES SEXUAL ASSAULT/ABUSE (%): 25
CLIENTS/SERVICES: Marital rape/sexual abuse survivors; Child victims of sexual abuse; Adult survivors of child sexual abuse; Incest victims/survivors; Community education; Adolescent survivors of sexual abuse

CHAMPAIGN

FAMILY SERVICE OF CHAMPAIGN COUNTY
405 S State St, Champaign, IL 61820
Information: (217) 352-0099 8:30am-5pm (Mon, Thu, Fri); 8:30am-8pm (Tue, Wed)
Contact: Karen Aprill, Prog Mgr
TYPE OF AGENCY: Counseling/mental health services
AREAS SERVED: Champaign
YEARS IN OPERATION: 75
ACCESSIBILITY: Wheelchair accessible
CASES SEXUAL ASSAULT/ABUSE (%): 25
DESCRIPTION: Sexual abuse services include individual, family and group therapy
CLIENTS/SERVICES: Sexual assault survivors; Marital rape/sexual abuse survivors; Child victims of sexual abuse; Adult survivors of child sexual abuse; Incest victims/survivors; Adolescent survivors of sexual abuse; Male survivors of sexual abuse
REQUIREMENTS: If active substance abuser, must be in substance abuse treatment simultaneously or stop using

UNIVERSITY OF ILLINOIS AT URBANA-CHAMPAIGN—OFFICE FOR WOMEN'S RESOURCES AND SERVICES
610 E John St, 346 Student Services Bldg, Champaign, IL 61820
Information: (217) 333-3137 8am-Noon, 1pm-5pm (Mon-Fri)
Contact: Betty Hembrough, Dir/Assoc Dean
TYPE OF AGENCY: College/university-based services; Rape prevention program; Acquaintance/date rape prevention program
AREAS SERVED: Champaign (mainly university student population)
YEARS IN OPERATION: 12
ACCESSIBILITY: Wheelchair accessible
DESCRIPTION: Provides programs and services especially affecting women students; Collects and publishes police statistics for campus area sexual assault categories; Provides educational programs and individual counseling. Membership on the following campus committees: The Rape Awareness and Prevention Committee and the Committee on Acquaintance Rape Education
CLIENTS/SERVICES: Prevention program; Community education
REQUIREMENTS: Usually university students

CHARLESTON

SEXUAL ASSAULT COUNSELING AND INFORMATION SERVICE
2505 Kari Knoll, Charleston, IL 61920
Crisis hotline: **(217) 348-7666, 234-6405 24 hrs**
Information: (217) 348-5033
Contact: Bonnie Buckley, Dir
TYPE OF AGENCY: Rape crisis center; Child sexual abuse prevention program; Acquaintance/date rape prevention program
AREAS SERVED: Primarily Coles; Clark, Cumberland, Shelby, Effingham by request
YEARS IN OPERATION: 11
ACCESSIBILITY: Wheelchair accessible; Signers for the hearing impaired
CASES SEXUAL ASSAULT/ABUSE (%): 100
CLIENTS/SERVICES: Sexual assault survivors; Marital rape/sexual abuse survivors; Child victims of sexual abuse; Adult survivors of child sexual abuse; Incest victims/survivors; Prevention program; Community education; Adolescent survivors of sexual abuse; Male survivors of sexual abuse
SPECIAL PROGRAMS/SERVICES: Provides child sexual abuse prevention programs for K-6th grades, a two-day program for junior high students, and a ten-day program for high school freshmen; Currently developing programs for children with various types of disabilities and their parents, teachers, and support staff

CHICAGO

ASSOCIATION HOUSE OF CHICAGO
1608 N Milwaukee, Chicago, IL 60647
Information: (312) 276-8836 24 hrs
Contact: Carlos F Pozzi, Prog Supv
TYPE OF AGENCY: Child sexual abuse services
AREAS SERVED: Cook
YEARS IN OPERATION: 25
LANGUAGES: Spanish
CASES SEXUAL ASSAULT/ABUSE (%): 15
CLIENTS/SERVICES: Child victims of sexual abuse; Community education; Adolescent survivors of sexual abuse
REQUIREMENTS: Clients must be between the ages of 4 and 17 and live in the west town, Humboldt Park area.

CAUSES (CHILD ABUSE UNIT FOR STUDIES, EDUCATION AND SERVICES)
836 W Wellington Ave, Chicago, IL 60657
Information: (312) 883-7169 24 hrs
Contact: Nahman Greenberg, MD, Exec Dir
TYPE OF AGENCY: Correctional facility; Child sexual abuse services; Child abuse services; Training/research
AREAS SERVED: Cook
YEARS IN OPERATION: 12
LANGUAGES: Spanish
CASES SEXUAL ASSAULT/ABUSE (%): 80
DESCRIPTION: Provides clinical services for abused children, their families and other caretakers. Clinical research to identify at-risk parents and other adults. Education and training for professionals in techniques of assessment and treatment of child abuse
CLIENTS/SERVICES: Child victims of sexual abuse; Adult survivors of child sexual abuse; Incest victims/survivors; Offender treatment program
REQUIREMENTS: No age restrictions; Sliding scale fee; Accepts third party payment

CHICAGO ABUSED WOMEN COALITION—GREENHOUSE SHELTER
PO Box 476608, Chicago, IL 60647-6608
Crisis hotline: **(312) 278-4566 24 hrs**
Information: (312) 278-4110 24 hrs
Contact: C Costa, Act Exec Dir
TYPE OF AGENCY: Domestic violence program
AREAS SERVED: Cook
YEARS IN OPERATION: 10
LANGUAGES: Spanish, Polish, German

CHICAGO ABUSED WOMEN COALITION—GREENHOUSE SHELTER (continued)
ACCESSIBILITY: Wheelchair accessible; Telecommunications for the hearing impaired (TTY, TDY, etc.); Signers for the hearing impaired
CLIENTS/SERVICES: Marital rape/sexual abuse survivors; Child victims of sexual abuse; Adult survivors of child sexual abuse; Incest victims/survivors; Community education
SPECIAL PROGRAMS/SERVICES: Bilingual brochure (Spanish-English)

CHICAGO COMMISSION ON WOMEN—SAFETY AND LEGAL SYSTEM COMMITTEE
500 N Peshtigo Court, Rm 6-B, Chicago, IL 60611
Information: (312) 744-4427
Contact: Peggy A Montes, Exec Dir
TYPE OF AGENCY: Women's commission
DESCRIPTION: Provides ongoing technical assistance to the Chicago Police Department in developing improved victim assistance and case management regarding sexual assault cases
CLIENTS/SERVICES: Sexual assault survivors; Child victims of sexual abuse; Incest victims/survivors; Community education

CHICAGO COUNSELING AND PSYCHOTHERAPY CENTER
5711 S Woodlawn Ave, Chicago, IL 60637
Information: (312) 684-1800 24 hrs daily
TYPE OF AGENCY: Child sexual abuse services; Private practice
AREAS SERVED: Cook
YEARS IN OPERATION: 16
ACCESSIBILITY: Wheelchair accessible
CASES SEXUAL ASSAULT/ABUSE (%): 15
DESCRIPTION: Provides therapy using a person-centered perspective which provides a non-intrusive environment for people to work through issues; Offers incest survivors groups and services for lesbians and gay men
CLIENTS/SERVICES: Sexual assault survivors; Marital rape/sexual abuse survivors; Child victims of sexual abuse; Adult survivors of child sexual abuse; Incest victims/survivors; Adolescent survivors of sexual abuse; Male survivors of sexual abuse; Healing
REQUIREMENTS: Client files own insurance forms; Sliding scale fee
SPECIAL PROGRAMS/SERVICES: Uses focusing to help people learn to deal with feelings that might otherwise be overwhelming. Some therapists use play and art therapy with adults to help them get in touch with experiences that are not able to be communicated verbally. Honors client's process, believing that this is especially important when working with people who have been abused

THE CHICAGO SEXUAL ASSAULT SERVICES NETWORK
2730 W 15th Pl, Rm 663, Chicago, IL 60608
Information: (312) 277-6080 9am-5pm
Contact: Betty Warner, Exec Dir
TYPE OF AGENCY: Interagency network
AREAS SERVED: Cook
YEARS IN OPERATION: 4
LANGUAGES: Spanish
ACCESSIBILITY: Wheelchair accessible
CLIENTS/SERVICES: Prevention program; Community education
SPECIAL PROGRAMS/SERVICES: The Chicago Sexual Assault Services Network is a membership organization made up of agencies across the city who share their concerns and pool their efforts to enhance services in the city for victims of sexual assault. Its Institutional Advocacy Committee works with city officials, the criminal justice system, law enforcement, and the medical system.

COOK COUNTY STATE'S ATTORNEY'S OFFICE—VICTIM/WITNESS ASSISTANCE
2650 S California, Rm 12D42, Chicago, IL 60608
Information: (312) 890-7200 8am-4:30pm
Contact: Eileen J Murphy, Dir
TYPE OF AGENCY: Victim/witness assistance program
AREAS SERVED: Cook
YEARS IN OPERATION: 7
LANGUAGES: Spanish
ACCESSIBILITY: Wheelchair accessible; Telecommunications for the hearing impaired (TTY, TDY, etc.)
CLIENTS/SERVICES: Sexual assault survivors; Child victims of sexual abuse
SPECIAL PROGRAMS/SERVICES: Special program for children who must testify in court. The purpose of the program is to lessen the fear and trauma most children experience when having to testify in a criminal proceeding. The program is held twice a month. A large cartoon-like character (a hippo) takes the children and their parents into a courtroom to explain what everything is. Other court personnel join the hippo to explain their roles in court (a judge, a court reporter, a sheriff, a court clerk, etc). After the program ends, the children are invited to explore the courtroom in order to allow them to feel comfortable in it.

CRIME VICTIMS ASSISTANCE PROGRAM
911 S Kedzie Ave, Chicago, IL 60612
Crisis hotline: **(312) 638-4111 24 hrs**
Information: (312) 638-2343 9am-5pm
Contact: Linda Baumgart, sexual assault victim advocate (16 and younger); Toylee Green, sexual assault victim advocate (17 and older)
TYPE OF AGENCY: Victim/witness assistance program
SPONSORING ORGANIZATION: Legal Assistance Foundation of Chicago
YEARS IN OPERATION: 2½
ACCESSIBILITY: Signers for the hearing impaired
CASES SEXUAL ASSAULT/ABUSE (%): 50
DESCRIPTION: Court orientation; Escort to court and state's attorney
CLIENTS/SERVICES: Community education; Adolescent survivors of sexual abuse; Male survivors of sexual abuse

ECUMENICAL WOMEN'S CENTER
5253 N Kenmore Ave, Chicago, IL 60640
Information: (312) 728-1850 9am-4:30pm
Contact: Elizabeth Okayama, Coord
TYPE OF AGENCY: Information and referral; Women's organization; Women's center
YEARS IN OPERATION: 16
DESCRIPTION: Referrals for women in crisis; Short-term counseling for sexual assault victims; Provides resources on women's issues in general and works to develop ministries for women in the church and in society
CLIENTS/SERVICES: Sexual assault survivors; Community education; Adolescent survivors of sexual abuse Prisoners
SPECIAL PROGRAMS/SERVICES: Leads workshops on anti-racism for women's service-providing agencies, where staff is heavily white and clients are primarily women of color. Maintains nationwide database of services and resources for women in prison

HARRIS YWCA WOMEN'S SERVICES
6200 S Drexel, Chicago, IL 60637
Crisis hotline: **(312) 955-3100 9am-5pm**
Information: (312) 955-3100 9am-5pm
Contact: Deborah Chalmers, Prog Dir
TYPE OF AGENCY: Rape crisis center
AREAS SERVED: Cook
YEARS IN OPERATION: 4
CASES SEXUAL ASSAULT/ABUSE (%): 100
DESCRIPTION: Services for adult and adolescent victims of sexual assault/sexual abuse through legal advocacy, medical advocacy, individual counseling, group counseling, for female and male survivors, and community education
CLIENTS/SERVICES: Sexual assault survivors; Marital rape/sexual abuse survivors; Adult survivors of child sexual abuse; Incest victims/survivors; Prevention program; Community education; Adolescent survivors of sexual abuse; Male survivors of sexual abuse
REQUIREMENTS: Must be 12 or older
SPECIAL PROGRAMS/SERVICES: Special outreach within the black community

HUMAN EFFECTIVE LIVING PROGRAMS (HELP)
20 E Jackson, Ste 350, Chicago, IL 60604
Information: (312) 939-6633 8:30am-9pm
Contact: Gabriella Cohen, Exec Dir
TYPE OF AGENCY: Child sexual abuse services; Youth program
AREAS SERVED: Cook
YEARS IN OPERATION: 8
CASES SEXUAL ASSAULT/ABUSE (%): 100
DESCRIPTION: Serves child victims of sexual abuse/assault from point of disclosure, including support groups for female and male survivors. Court-ordered evaluation and treatment for child sexual abuse/incest offenders
CLIENTS/SERVICES: Child victims of sexual abuse; Adult survivors of child sexual abuse; Incest victims/survivors; Community education; Offender treatment program; Adolescent survivors of sexual abuse; Male survivors of sexual abuse
REQUIREMENTS: Victims 18 or under or parents or family of child victim; Offenders must be court-ordered into evaluation, plead guilty and be court-ordered into treatment
SPECIAL PROGRAMS/SERVICES: *Project Self-Esteem* for adolescent survivors. Volunteer suburban families take adolescents for weekends monthly

JOURNEYS
30 N Michigan Ave, Ste 1522, Chicago, IL 60602
Information: (312) 784-1126 24 hrs
Contact: Stephen H English, Survivor/Therapist; Sheila D Sheehan, Survivor/Therapist/Clinically Cert Drug Abuse Counselors
TYPE OF AGENCY: Private practice
AREAS SERVED: Cook and neighboring counties
ACCESSIBILITY: Wheelchair accessible
CASES SEXUAL ASSAULT/ABUSE (%): 100
DESCRIPTION: Specializes in male and female childhood sexual abuse. Believes treatment is a process in which we learn to heal our inner-child, mourn childhood losses, gain power and control over our own lives, feel whole, and develop healthy, loving relationships by learning to trust
CLIENTS/SERVICES: Sexual assault survivors; Marital rape/sexual abuse survivors; Child victims of sexual abuse; Adult survivors of child sexual abuse; Incest victims/survivors; Community education; Adolescent survivors of sexual abuse; Male survivors of sexual abuse; Healing
REQUIREMENTS: Sliding scale fee
SPECIAL PROGRAMS/SERVICES: Works with multiple personalities on an outpatient basis and with substance abuse issues, such as drug and alcohol abuse, eating disorders, and other compulsive behaviors resulting from childhood sexual abuse trauma

MIDWEST FAMILY RESOURCE
320 N Michigan Ave, No 1801, Chicago, IL 60601
Crisis hotline: **(312) 424-6000 24 hrs**
Information: (312) 424-6000 8:30am-5pm
Contact: Mary Jo Barrett, Dir; Mack Winn, Asst Dir
TYPE OF AGENCY: Counseling/mental health services; Child sexual abuse services
AREAS SERVED: Will, Cook, DuPage, Lake
YEARS IN OPERATION: 15
LANGUAGES: Spanish

MIDWEST FAMILY RESOURCE
(continued)

ACCESSIBILITY: Wheelchair accessible
CASES SEXUAL ASSAULT/ABUSE (%): 80
DESCRIPTION: Counseling for victims/survivors and offenders—child sexual abuse/incest offenders and batterers
CLIENTS/SERVICES: Sexual assault survivors; Marital rape/sexual abuse survivors; Child victims of sexual abuse; Adult survivors of child sexual abuse; Incest victims/survivors; Community education; Offender treatment program; Adolescent survivors of sexual abuse; Male survivors of sexual abuse

PARENTAL STRESS SERVICES
600 S Federal St, No 205, Chicago, IL 60605
Crisis hotline: **(312) 427-6644 24 hrs**
Information: (312) 427-1161 9am-5pm
Contact: Maureen Sheehy, Sexual Abuse Prevention Proj Coord
TYPE OF AGENCY: Child sexual abuse prevention program; Child abuse prevention program
AREAS SERVED: Cook
YEARS IN OPERATION: 15
DESCRIPTION: Child abuse prevention agency with support groups for parents (Parents Anonymous), and parenting classes; Hot-line for parents; School-based child sexual abuse prevention program
CLIENTS/SERVICES: Prevention program; Community education

PLANNED PARENTHOOD OF CHICAGO
17 N State, Ste 1500, Chicago, IL 60602
Crisis hotline: **(312) 781-9560 9am-5pm (Mon, Wed, Thu, Fri); 9am-8pm (Tue); 9am-3pm (Sat)**
Information: (312) 781-9550 hrs vary
Contact: Julie C Magnus, MSW, Counseling Coord
TYPE OF AGENCY: Counseling/mental health services
AREAS SERVED: Cook, Will, Du Page
YEARS IN OPERATION: 1½
CASES SEXUAL ASSAULT/ABUSE (%): 15
CLIENTS/SERVICES: Sexual assault survivors; Marital rape/sexual abuse survivors; Adult survivors of child sexual abuse; Incest victims/survivors; Prevention program; Community education; Adolescent survivors of sexual abuse; Male survivors of sexual abuse

RAINBOW HOUSE/ARCO IRIS
PO Box 29019, Chicago, IL 60629
Crisis hotline: **(312) 521-4865 24 hrs**
Information: (312) 521-5501 7am-7pm
Contact: Marge Jozsa, Exec Dir
TYPE OF AGENCY: Domestic violence program
AREAS SERVED: No county boundaries
YEARS IN OPERATION: 6
LANGUAGES: Spanish
ACCESSIBILITY: Telecommunications for the hearing impaired (TTY, TDY, etc.); Signers for the hearing impaired
CASES SEXUAL ASSAULT/ABUSE (%): 60
CLIENTS/SERVICES: Sexual assault survivors; Marital rape/sexual abuse survivors; Child victims of sexual abuse; Adult survivors of child sexual abuse; Incest victims/survivors; Prevention program; Community education

RAPE VICTIM ADVOCATES
25 W Chicago Ave, Ste 208, Chicago, IL 60610
Information: (312) 649-1855 9am-5pm (Mon-Fri)
Contact: Sarah Howells, Inter Dir
TYPE OF AGENCY: Rape crisis center; Hospital/medical center
AREAS SERVED: Cook
YEARS IN OPERATION: 14
LANGUAGES: Spanish, German
ACCESSIBILITY: Wheelchair accessible; Signers for the hearing impaired
CASES SEXUAL ASSAULT/ABUSE (%): 100
CLIENTS/SERVICES: Sexual assault survivors; Marital rape/sexual abuse survivors; Child victims of sexual abuse; Community education; Male survivors of sexual abuse
REQUIREMENTS: Must be present at one of the 8 member hospitals
SPECIAL PROGRAMS/SERVICES: Video *Why Am I Hiding...?* dealing with the myths of sexual assault and incest

RAPE VICTIM SERVICES PROGRAM
4740 N Clark, Chicago, IL 60640
Information: (312) 769-0205
Contact: Heidi Kon, Rape Victim Svcs Prog Dir
TYPE OF AGENCY: Rape crisis center
SPONSORING ORGANIZATION: Edgewater Uptown Community Mental Health Center
DESCRIPTION: Provides comprehensive, culturally appropriate services for victims of sexual assault and their significant others, including individual and group counseling, court advocacy, public education and training and institutional advocacy
CLIENTS/SERVICES: Sexual assault survivors; Marital rape/sexual abuse survivors; Male survivors of sexual abuse; Child victims of sexual abuse; Incest victims/survivors; Adult survivors of child sexual abuse; Prevention program; Community education

RAVENSWOOD HOSPITAL COMMUNITY MENTAL HEALTH CENTER
4550 N Winchester Ave, Chicago, IL 60640
Crisis hotline: **(312) 769-6200 24 hrs**
Information: (312) 878-4300, ext 1400 or 1455 9am-5pm
Contact: Carroll Cradock, PhD, CandA Dir
TYPE OF AGENCY: Hospital/medical center; Counseling/mental health services; Child sexual abuse services; Child sexual abuse prevention program
AREAS SERVED: Cook
YEARS IN OPERATION: 18
LANGUAGES: Spanish, Sign
ACCESSIBILITY: Wheelchair accessible; Telecommunications for the hearing impaired (TTY, TDY, etc.); Signers for the hearing impaired
CASES SEXUAL ASSAULT/ABUSE (%): 20-30
DESCRIPTION: Provides comprehensive mental health services including individual, family and group therapy for adults, children, and adolescents; Provides individual therapy for batterers; Self-help groups for adult survivors of child sexual abuse, groups for partners/spouses of survivors; Groups for male survivors of abuse and groups for victims of rape. Also provides educational program on ritualistic abuse
CLIENTS/SERVICES: Sexual assault survivors; Marital rape/sexual abuse survivors; Child victims of sexual abuse; Adult survivors of child sexual abuse; Incest victims/survivors; Prevention program; Community education; Adolescent survivors of sexual abuse; Male survivors of sexual abuse; Ritualistic abuse victims/survivors
REQUIREMENTS: Sliding scale fee; Agency must report child abuse to the state agency
SPECIAL PROGRAMS/SERVICES: The Consultation-Education Services train survivors of child sexual abuse to lead the support self-help groups for adult survivors (both men and women) and for partners/spouses of survivors. This department also does training in the Chicago public school system with teachers, providing them instruction to teach children sexual abuse prevention as part of the family life education curriculum

ISAAC RAY CENTER, INC
1720 W Polk St, Chicago, IL 60612
Information: (312) 942-4462 9am-5pm
Contact: Susanne Liles, Coord
TYPE OF AGENCY: Private practice
SPONSORING ORGANIZATION: Sexual Behaviors Clinic
YEARS IN OPERATION: 11
ACCESSIBILITY: Wheelchair accessible
CASES SEXUAL ASSAULT/ABUSE (%): 100
CLIENTS/SERVICES: Offender treatment program
REQUIREMENTS: Fee for services

RUSH—PRESBYTERIAN—ST LUKE'S MEDICAL CENTER FAMILY VIOLENCE PROGRAM
1653 W Congress Pkwy, Chicago, IL 60612
Crisis hotline: **(312) 94-ABUSE 24 hrs**
Information: (312) 94-ABUSE 24 hrs
Contact: Daniel Sheridan, MS, RN, Family Violence Prog Coord
TYPE OF AGENCY: Domestic violence program; Hospital/medical center; Child sexual abuse services; Child abuse services
AREAS SERVED: Primarily Cook
YEARS IN OPERATION: 2
LANGUAGES: Spanish, Polish
ACCESSIBILITY: Wheelchair accessible
CASES SEXUAL ASSAULT/ABUSE (%): 20
DESCRIPTION: Comprehensive hospital-based program for survivors of child abuse/neglect, child sexual abuse, battered women, elder abuse, other forms of adult family violence and adult sexual assault; Provides crisis counseling, systems advocacy, referrals to hospitals or community-based follow-up services
CLIENTS/SERVICES: Sexual assault survivors; Marital rape/sexual abuse survivors; Child victims of sexual abuse; Adult survivors of child sexual abuse; Incest victims/survivors; Community education; Offender treatment program; Adolescent survivors of sexual abuse

SALVATION ARMY FAMILY SERVICE DIVISION
4800 N Marine Dr, Chicago, IL 60640
Information: (312) 275-6233 8:30am-5pm; evenings by appointment
Contact: Janet Wilson, Prog Coord
TYPE OF AGENCY: Counseling/mental health services
AREAS SERVED: Cook
YEARS IN OPERATION: 52
LANGUAGES: Spanish
ACCESSIBILITY: Wheelchair accessible
CLIENTS/SERVICES: Sexual assault survivors; Marital rape/sexual abuse survivors; Child victims of sexual abuse; Adult survivors of child sexual abuse; Incest victims/survivors; Offender treatment program; Adolescent survivors of sexual abuse; Male survivors of sexual abuse

SEX AND MARITAL THERAPY CLINIC
5841 S Maryland Ave, Chicago, IL 60637
Information: (312) 702-9703 8am-6pm (Mon-Fri)
Contact: Richard Carroll, PhD, Sex and Marital Therapy Clinic Dir
TYPE OF AGENCY: Hospital/medical center; Counseling/mental health services
SPONSORING ORGANIZATION: Department of Psychiatry University of Chicago Hospitals
AREAS SERVED: Cook, DuPage, Chicago metro area; NW IN
YEARS IN OPERATION: 10
ACCESSIBILITY: Wheelchair accessible
CASES SEXUAL ASSAULT/ABUSE (%): 25
DESCRIPTION: Outpatient assessment and treatment of adult victims; Individual and behavior therapy for rapists, child sexual abuse/incest offenders, and batterers
CLIENTS/SERVICES: Sexual assault survivors; Marital rape/sexual abuse survivors; Adult survivors of child sexual abuse; Incest victims/survivors; Offender treatment program; Male survivors of sexual abuse

SOUTHWEST WOMEN WORKING TOGETHER
3201 W 63rd St, Chicago, IL 60629
Information: (312) 436-0550 9am-5pm (Mon-Fri)
Contact: Joan Cmar, Counseling Dir

SOUTHWEST WOMEN WORKING TOGETHER *(continued)*
TYPE OF AGENCY: Domestic violence program; Counseling/mental health services; Child sexual abuse services
AREAS SERVED: Cook
YEARS IN OPERATION: 14
LANGUAGES: Sign
ACCESSIBILITY: Signers for the hearing impaired
CASES SEXUAL ASSAULT/ABUSE (%): 25
CLIENTS/SERVICES: Sexual assault survivors; Marital rape/sexual abuse survivors; Child victims of sexual abuse; Adult survivors of child sexual abuse; Incest victims/survivors; Community education; Adolescent survivors of sexual abuse
REQUIREMENTS: No adult males served

SPIN (SPECIAL PEOPLE IN NEED)
431 S Dearborn, Ste 502, Chicago, IL 60605
Crisis hotline: **(312) 733-2546 24 hrs**
Information: (312) 699-1906 9am-9pm (Mon-Sat)
Contact: Tom Johnson, Dir
TYPE OF AGENCY: Child sexual abuse services; Offender treatment
AREAS SERVED: Cook, Lake, DuPage, Will, McHenry
YEARS IN OPERATION: 6
LANGUAGES: Spanish, Italian, Swedish, German
ACCESSIBILITY: Wheelchair accessible
CASES SEXUAL ASSAULT/ABUSE (%): 100
DESCRIPTION: Specializes in the treatment of sexual abuse. Provides groups for adult female and male survivors, adolescent female and male survivors, and children, as well as individual therapy for all ages. Treatment for rapists, child sexual abuse/incest offenders and batterers
CLIENTS/SERVICES: Sexual assault survivors; Marital rape/sexual abuse survivors; Child victims of sexual abuse; Adult survivors of child sexual abuse; Incest victims/survivors; Community education; Offender treatment program; Adolescent survivors of sexual abuse; Male survivors of sexual abuse

HARRIET TUBMAN SHELTER FOR BATTERED WOMEN
417 S Dearborn, Chicago, IL 60605
Crisis hotline: **(312) 924-3151 24 hrs**
Information: (312) 924-3151 24 hrs
Contact: Valerie Sims-Rucker, Prog Dir
TYPE OF AGENCY: Domestic violence program; Child sexual abuse services
SPONSORING ORGANIZATION: Human Resources Development Institute, Inc
AREAS SERVED: Cook and surrounding suburbs
YEARS IN OPERATION: 4
CASES SEXUAL ASSAULT/ABUSE (%): 10
CLIENTS/SERVICES: Sexual assault survivors; Marital rape/sexual abuse survivors; Child victims of sexual abuse; Adult survivors of child sexual abuse; Incest victims/survivors; Prevention program; Community education; Adolescent survivors of sexual abuse

VICTIM SERVICES PROGRAM
8704 S Constance, Chicago, IL 60617
Crisis hotline: **(312) 734-4033 24 hrs**
Information: (312) 734-4033 9am-5pm (Wed, Fri); 9am-9pm (Mon, Tue, Thu)
Contact: Bambade Shakoor, Coord
TYPE OF AGENCY: Victim/witness assistance program; Counseling/mental health services; Child sexual abuse services
SPONSORING ORGANIZATION: Community Mental Health Council, Inc
AREAS SERVED: Cook
YEARS IN OPERATION: 4
ACCESSIBILITY: Wheelchair accessible
CASES SEXUAL ASSAULT/ABUSE (%): 50
DESCRIPTION: Crisis intervention and court advocacy for sexual assault/abuse survivors; Groups for preschool children; Separate children's (7-11 years) and adolescents' (12-17 years) groups for males and females; Groups for mothers of victims, adult survivors of incest, and sexual assault victims. Treatment for rapists and child sexual abuse/incest offenders.
CLIENTS/SERVICES: Sexual assault survivors; Child victims of sexual abuse; Adult survivors of child sexual abuse; Incest victims/survivors; Prevention program; Community education; Offender treatment program; Adolescent survivors of sexual abuse; Male survivors of sexual abuse; Preschoolers; Healing
SPECIAL PROGRAMS/SERVICES: Dance therapy for adult survivors of child sexual abuse

THE WOMEN'S GYM FITNESS CENTER
1212 W Belmont Ave, Chicago, IL 60657
Information: (312) 549-0700 2:30pm-9:30pm
Contact: Nancy Lanoue, Prog Dir
TYPE OF AGENCY: Rape prevention program
YEARS IN OPERATION: 3½
DESCRIPTION: Offers an ongoing women's karate program (all women instructors) and short-term practical self-defense/rape prevention courses for women and girls
CLIENTS/SERVICES: Sexual assault survivors; Prevention program
REQUIREMENTS: Open to women and girls (12 years and older)

WOMEN'S HEALTH RESOURCES
904 W Oakdale, Chicago, IL 60657
Information: (312) 883-7052, 262-7331 7am-9pm (Mon-Sat)
Contact: Margie Schaps, Dir
TYPE OF AGENCY: Hospital/medical center
SPONSORING ORGANIZATION: Illinois Masonic Medical Center
AREAS SERVED: Cook, Lake
YEARS IN OPERATION: 6
CASES SEXUAL ASSAULT/ABUSE (%): 10
DESCRIPTION: Provides medical and psychological services for adult women through individual therapy and support groups; Psychotherapy group for survivors of incest; Educational lectures; Information; Referrals; Feminist martial arts/self-defense
CLIENTS/SERVICES: Sexual assault survivors; Marital rape/sexual abuse survivors; Adult survivors of child sexual abuse; Incest victims/survivors; Community education
REQUIREMENTS: Must be 18 or older

YWCA WOMEN'S SERVICES/LOOP
180 N Wabash, Chicago, IL 60601
Information: (312) 372-6600 9am-5pm (Mon-Fri)
Contact: Mary Scott Boria, Dir
TYPE OF AGENCY: Rape crisis center
AREAS SERVED: Metropolitan Chicago
YEARS IN OPERATION: 10
LANGUAGES: Spanish
ACCESSIBILITY: Wheelchair accessible
CASES SEXUAL ASSAULT/ABUSE (%): 75
CLIENTS/SERVICES: Sexual assault survivors; Marital rape/sexual abuse survivors; Child victims of sexual abuse; Adult survivors of child sexual abuse; Incest victims/survivors; Prevention program; Community education; Adolescent survivors of sexual abuse; Male survivors of sexual abuse

COLLINSVILLE

FAMILY LIFE CONSULTANTS
PO Box 1001, No 3C Meadow Heights Professional Pk, Collinsville, IL 62234
Information: (618) 345-9536 8:30am-5pm (Mon-Sat)
Contact: Sandra Becker-Warden, Dir
TYPE OF AGENCY: Child sexual abuse services; Child sexual abuse prevention program; Private practice
AREAS SERVED: Madison, St Clair, Bond, Green, Jersey
YEARS IN OPERATION: 3½
CASES SEXUAL ASSAULT/ABUSE (%): 35
DESCRIPTION: Psychiatric, psychological and social work approaches; marital, family and individual treatment. Intensive short-term sexual abuse treatment program (1 year) includes offenders, group, spouses group, victims group, family, individual, and marital therapy; Treatment for batterers
CLIENTS/SERVICES: Sexual assault survivors; Child victims of sexual abuse; Adult survivors of child sexual abuse; Incest victims/survivors; Prevention program; Offender treatment program; Adolescent survivors of sexual abuse; Male survivors of sexual abuse

DANVILLE

SEXUAL ASSAULT CRISIS SERVICES
201 N Hazel St, Danville, IL 61832
Crisis hotline: **(217) 443-5566**
Information: (217) 446-1217
Contact: Peggy Johnson
TYPE OF AGENCY: Rape crisis center; Domestic violence program
SPONSORING ORGANIZATION: YWCA
CLIENTS/SERVICES: Sexual assault survivors

VERMILION COUNTY STATE'S ATTORNEY—VICTIM ASSISTANCE PROGRAM
7 N Vermilion, Danville, IL 61832
Crisis hotline: **(217) 431-2674 8:30am-4:30pm**
Information: (217) 431-2672 8:30am-4:30pm
Contact: Barbara Thornton, Victim Assistance Coord
TYPE OF AGENCY: Victim/witness assistance program
AREAS SERVED: Vermilion
YEARS IN OPERATION: 2
ACCESSIBILITY: Wheelchair accessible; Telecommunications for the hearing impaired (TTY, TDY, etc.); Signers for the hearing impaired
DESCRIPTION: Court assistance; Safe waiting area; Crime victim compensation assistance; Primary focus is on child sexual abuse, with a contract for counseling services with Catholic Social Services; Instrumental in beginning the Child Sexual Abuse Task Force
CLIENTS/SERVICES: Sexual assault survivors; Marital rape/sexual abuse survivors; Child victims of sexual abuse; Adult survivors of child sexual abuse; Incest victims/survivors; Prevention program; Community education; Adolescent survivors of sexual abuse; Male survivors of sexual abuse

DECATUR

DOVE DOMESTIC VIOLENCE PROGRAM
788 E Clay, Decatur, IL 62521
Crisis hotline: **(217) 423-2238 24 hrs**
Information: (217) 423-0950 8am-5pm (Mon-Fri)
Contact: Lois Bond, Client Svcs Coord
TYPE OF AGENCY: Domestic violence program
SPONSORING ORGANIZATION: Dove, Inc
AREAS SERVED: Macon, Shelby, Moultrie, Piatt, De Witt
YEARS IN OPERATION: 9
ACCESSIBILITY: Wheelchair accessible
CASES SEXUAL ASSAULT/ABUSE (%): 40-50
CLIENTS/SERVICES: Sexual assault survivors; Marital rape/sexual abuse survivors; Child victims of sexual abuse; Adult survivors of child sexual abuse; Incest victims/survivors; Community education

GROWING STRONG SEXUAL ASSAULT CENTER
PO Box 45, Decatur, IL 62525
Crisis hotline: **(217) 428-0770 24 hrs**
Information: (217) 428-0770 8:30am-4pm
Contact: Beverly J Harris, Dir
TYPE OF AGENCY: Rape crisis center; Child sexual abuse services; Child sexual abuse prevention program

GROWING STRONG SEXUAL ASSAULT CENTER *(continued)*
AREAS SERVED: Macon, Moultrie, Shelby, Piatt, DeWitt
YEARS IN OPERATION: 3
ACCESSIBILITY: Wheelchair accessible
CASES SEXUAL ASSAULT/ABUSE (%): 100
CLIENTS/SERVICES: Sexual assault survivors; Marital rape/sexual abuse survivors; Child victims of sexual abuse; Adult survivors of child sexual abuse; Incest victims/survivors; Prevention program; Community education; Adolescent survivors of sexual abuse; Male survivors of sexual abuse

DEKALB

SAFE PASSAGE, INC
PO Box 621, DeKalb, IL 60115
Crisis hotline: **(815) 756-2228 24 hrs**
Information: (815) 756-5228
Contact: Sue Breneman, Exec Dir
TYPE OF AGENCY: Domestic violence program
AREAS SERVED: DeKalb
YEARS IN OPERATION: 7
CLIENTS/SERVICES: Marital rape/sexual abuse survivors; Incest victims/survivors

DES PLAINES

BRESLER AND DUGO, LTD
2644 Dempster, Ste 215, Des Plaines, IL 60016
Crisis hotline: **(312) 299-3628 24 hrs daily**
Information: (312) 299-3628 24 hrs daily
Contact: Dr M Bresler, Registered Psychologist Diplomate (ABPP)
TYPE OF AGENCY: Private practice
AREAS SERVED: Cook
YEARS IN OPERATION: 12
CASES SEXUAL ASSAULT/ABUSE (%): 20
DESCRIPTION: Extensive practice with children, adolescents, and families, including work in a hospital setting. Consultation with courts and agencies that handle abuse, and drug counseling. Support groups for female and male survivors of sexual abuse and treatment for batterers
CLIENTS/SERVICES: Sexual assault survivors; Marital rape/sexual abuse survivors; Child victims of sexual abuse; Adult survivors of child sexual abuse; Incest victims/survivors; Prevention program; Adolescent survivors of sexual abuse; Male survivors of sexual abuse

LIFE SPAN
Box 445, Des Plaines, IL 60016
Crisis hotline: **(312) 824-4454 24 hrs**
Information: (312) 824-0382 9am-5pm
Contact: Joan Cmar, Clinical Sup Proj Coord
TYPE OF AGENCY: Domestic violence program
AREAS SERVED: Cook
YEARS IN OPERATION: 10
ACCESSIBILITY: Wheelchair accessible; Telecommunications for the hearing impaired (TTY, TDY, etc.); Signers for the hearing impaired
CASES SEXUAL ASSAULT/ABUSE (%): 10
CLIENTS/SERVICES: Sexual assault survivors; Marital rape/sexual abuse survivors; Child victims of sexual abuse; Adult survivors of child sexual abuse; Incest victims/survivors; Community education; Adolescent survivors of sexual abuse

DIXON

VICTIM COORDINATOR SERVICES
PO Box 462, Dixon, IL 61021
Information: (815) 284-5245 8am-4pm (Mon-Fri)
Contact: Barb McCaskey, Victim/Witness Coord
TYPE OF AGENCY: Victim/witness assistance program
SPONSORING ORGANIZATION: Lee County State's Attorney's Office
AREAS SERVED: Lee
YEARS IN OPERATION: 2
CASES SEXUAL ASSAULT/ABUSE (%): 10
CLIENTS/SERVICES: Sexual assault survivors; Marital rape/sexual abuse survivors; Child victims of sexual abuse

EAST SAINT LOUIS

VOLUNTEERS OF AMERICA OF ILLINOIS
4700 State St, Ste 2, East Saint Louis, IL 62205
Information: (618) 271-9833
Contact: Fern Ferguson, Dir
TYPE OF AGENCY: Rape crisis center; Child sexual abuse services
CLIENTS/SERVICES: Sexual assault survivors; Child victims of sexual abuse; Community education; Adolescent survivors of sexual abuse; Male survivors of sexual abuse

EDGEMONT

CHILDREN'S CENTER FOR BEHAVIORAL DEVELOPMENT
353 N 88th St, Edgemont, IL 62203
Crisis hotline: **(618) 397-0963 24 hrs**
Information: (618) 398-1152 8am-4pm (Mon-Fri)
Contact: Donya L Adkerson, Outpatient Svcs Coord
TYPE OF AGENCY: Counseling/mental health services; Child sexual abuse services; Offender treatment
AREAS SERVED: Madison, Monroe, St Clair, IL; St Louis City and County, MO
YEARS IN OPERATION: 2½
ACCESSIBILITY: Wheelchair accessible
CASES SEXUAL ASSAULT/ABUSE (%): 100
DESCRIPTION: Program for Reshaping Adolescent Sexual Expression (PRASE) provides specialized treatment for teenaged (11-17) male and female sexual abuse perpetrators using individual, group, and family therapy; Perpetrator Intervention and Prevention (PIP) is for male victims (6-12) who are at risk of becoming perpetrators; Organization also provides individual and family therapy for other types of victims
CLIENTS/SERVICES: Child victims of sexual abuse; Incest victims/survivors; Community education; Offender treatment program; Adolescent survivors of sexual abuse; Male survivors of sexual abuse
REQUIREMENTS: PRASE ages 11-17; PIP male sexual abuse victims ages 6-12

SEXUAL ASSAULT VICTIMS CARE UNIT
9400 Lebanon Rd, Edgemont, IL 62203
Crisis hotline: **(618) 397-0975 24 hrs**
Information: (618) 397-0975 24 hrs
Contact: Judy Sledge, Prog Mgr
TYPE OF AGENCY: Rape crisis center; Child sexual abuse services; Child sexual abuse prevention program; Acquaintance/date rape prevention program
SPONSORING ORGANIZATION: Call For Help
AREAS SERVED: St Clair, Monroe
YEARS IN OPERATION: 5
LANGUAGES: Spanish
ACCESSIBILITY: Wheelchair accessible
CASES SEXUAL ASSAULT/ABUSE (%): 100
DESCRIPTION: Crisis intervention; Advocacy; Victim assistance; Individual and group counseling; Date rape prevention program; Limited treatment program for offenders who have also been victims
CLIENTS/SERVICES: Sexual assault survivors; Marital rape/sexual abuse survivors; Child victims of sexual abuse; Adult survivors of child sexual abuse; Incest victims/survivors; Prevention program; Community education; Offender treatment program; Adolescent survivors of sexual abuse; Male survivors of sexual abuse
SPECIAL PROGRAMS/SERVICES: Art therapy for sexual assault survivors

EDWARDSVILLE

RAPE AND SEXUAL ABUSE CARE CENTER
Box 1154, Edwardsville, IL 62026-1154
Crisis hotline: **(618) 692-2197 24 hrs**
Information: (618) 692-2197 8am-4:30pm
Contact: Rebecca K Carr, Dir
TYPE OF AGENCY: Rape crisis center; Child sexual abuse services
SPONSORING ORGANIZATION: Southern Illinois University at Edwardsville
AREAS SERVED: Calhoun, Greene, Jersey, Macoupin, Montgomery, Madison, Bond, Clinton, Washington, Marion, Randolph, Monroe, St Clair, Fayette
YEARS IN OPERATION: 10
ACCESSIBILITY: Wheelchair accessible
CASES SEXUAL ASSAULT/ABUSE (%): 100
CLIENTS/SERVICES: Sexual assault survivors; Marital rape/sexual abuse survivors; Child victims of sexual abuse; Adult survivors of child sexual abuse; Incest victims/survivors; Prevention program; Community education; Adolescent survivors of sexual abuse; Male survivors of sexual abuse

ELGIN

CENTRAL BAPTIST FAMILY SERVICES
676 Prospect, Elgin, IL 60120
Information: (312) 741-7140 9am-5pm
Contact: Mary Langerohl, Supv
TYPE OF AGENCY: Counseling/mental health services; Child sexual abuse services
AREAS SERVED: Kane
YEARS IN OPERATION: 4
CASES SEXUAL ASSAULT/ABUSE (%): 40-45
DESCRIPTION: Provides sexual abuse treatment program on a contractual basis with the Illinois Department of Children and Family Services
CLIENTS/SERVICES: Child victims of sexual abuse

COMMUNITY CRISIS CENTER
PO Box 1390, Elgin, IL 60121
Crisis hotline: **(312) 697-2380 24 hrs daily**
Information: (312) 697-2380 24 hrs daily
Contact: Danise Habun-Schaefer, Advocacy and Sexual Assault Svcs Coord
TYPE OF AGENCY: Rape crisis center; Domestic violence program; Shelter
AREAS SERVED: Kane, Cook, McHenry
YEARS IN OPERATION: 13
ACCESSIBILITY: Wheelchair accessible
CASES SEXUAL ASSAULT/ABUSE (%): 25
CLIENTS/SERVICES: Sexual assault survivors; Marital rape/sexual abuse survivors; Child victims of sexual abuse; Adult survivors of child sexual abuse; Incest victims/survivors; Prevention program; Community education; Adolescent survivors of sexual abuse; Male survivors of sexual abuse

EVANSTON

EARLY CHILDHOOD DEVELOPMENT CENTER
826 Ridge Ave, Evanston, IL 60202
Information: (312) 866-8880, 318-6040 9am-5pm; evenings and Sat by appointment
Contact: Dr Goodson, Dir
TYPE OF AGENCY: Counseling/mental health services; Child sexual abuse services
AREAS SERVED: Cook
YEARS IN OPERATION: 20
LANGUAGES: Spanish
CASES SEXUAL ASSAULT/ABUSE (%): 10-15
DESCRIPTION: Early intervention, prevention, treatment (psychotherapy) of existing disturbance in children 0-10 and their parents
CLIENTS/SERVICES: Child victims of sexual abuse; Prevention program
REQUIREMENTS: Children 0-10 with emotional disturbances and their parents

FAMILY COUNSELING SERVICE OF EVANSTON AND SKOKIE VALLEY
1114 Church St, Evanston, IL 60201
Information: (312) 328-2404 9am-5pm (Mon, Wed, Fri, Sat); 9am-9pm (Tue, Thu)
Contact: Tana Paul, ACSW, Supv
TYPE OF AGENCY: Counseling/mental health services; Child sexual abuse services; Child sexual abuse prevention program; Child abuse services
AREAS SERVED: Evanston, Skokie, Niles, Morton, Grove, Golf communities
YEARS IN OPERATION: 78
LANGUAGES: Spanish
ACCESSIBILITY: Wheelchair accessible
CASES SEXUAL ASSAULT/ABUSE (%): 35
DESCRIPTION: Child and Family Advocates (CAFA) is the child abuse treatment and prevention program. It involves a coalition of four agencies that provide counseling
CLIENTS/SERVICES: Sexual assault survivors; Marital rape/sexual abuse survivors; Child victims of sexual abuse; Adult survivors of child sexual abuse; Incest victims/survivors; Prevention program; Community education; Offender treatment program
REQUIREMENTS: Service free of charge for most clients; sliding scale fee for others

ROBERT KEARNEY AND ASSOCIATES
813 Dempster St, Evanston, IL 60201
Crisis hotline: **(312) 864-1353 24 hrs**
Information: (312) 864-1353 8:30am-10pm (Mon-Sat)
TYPE OF AGENCY: Private practice
AREAS SERVED: Cook County, Chicago area
YEARS IN OPERATION: 14
CASES SEXUAL ASSAULT/ABUSE (%): 75
CLIENTS/SERVICES: Sexual assault survivors; Marital rape/sexual abuse survivors; Child victims of sexual abuse; Adult survivors of child sexual abuse; Incest victims/survivors; Community education; Offender treatment program; Adolescent survivors of sexual abuse; Male survivors of sexual abuse
REQUIREMENTS: Insurance or ability to pay
SPECIAL PROGRAMS/SERVICES: Forensic services: collaboration with attorneys regarding preparation and management of cases involved in criminal, domestic relations, and juvenile court. Forensic evaluations of abuse allegation and mediation re: custody and visitation

NORTHWESTERN UNIVERSITY—WOMEN'S CENTER
2000 Sheridan Rd, Evanston, IL 60208
Information: (312) 491-7360 9am-5pm (Mon-Fri)
Contact: June C Terpstra, Dir
TYPE OF AGENCY: College/university-based services; Private practice; Rape prevention program; Acquaintance/date rape prevention program
AREAS SERVED: University only
YEARS IN OPERATION: 2
LANGUAGES: Spanish
CASES SEXUAL ASSAULT/ABUSE (%): 30
DESCRIPTION: Provides counseling services for victims/survivors; Feminist martial arts/self-defense program; Sexual Assault Education Program (firesides and films about issues surrounding sexual assault, acquaintance rape, and campus safety)
CLIENTS/SERVICES: Sexual assault survivors; Marital rape/sexual abuse survivors; Adult survivors of child sexual abuse; Incest victims/survivors; Prevention program; Community education; Male survivors of sexual abuse
REQUIREMENTS: Free to women faculty, staff, and students
SPECIAL PROGRAMS/SERVICES: The Campus Climate Project: Sexism and Racism Examined portrays the experiences of women and minorities through the medium of theater

SAINT FRANCIS HOSPITAL EMERGENCY DEPARTMENT
355 Ridge, Evanston, IL 60202
Crisis hotline: **(312) 492-2440 24 hrs**
Contact: Carole Kenneally, RN, Patient Care Dir
TYPE OF AGENCY: Hospital/medical center
AREAS SERVED: Northern Cook
ACCESSIBILITY: Wheelchair accessible; Telecommunications for the hearing impaired (TTY, TDY, etc.)
DESCRIPTION: Post-assault care, including physical exam and evidence collection. Rape victim advocate called for each patient
CLIENTS/SERVICES: Sexual assault survivors; Marital rape/sexual abuse survivors; Child victims of sexual abuse

EVERGREEN PARK

MIDWEST FAMILY RESOURCE
9730 S Western Ave, No 326, Evergreen Park, IL 60202
Crisis hotline: **(312) 424-6000 for clients 24 hrs**
Information: (312) 424-6000 9am-9pm (Mon-Fri)
Contact: Mary Jo Barrett, Dir; Mack Winn, Asst Dir
TYPE OF AGENCY: Counseling/mental health services; Child sexual abuse services; Child abuse services
AREAS SERVED: Cook, Lake, DuPage
YEARS IN OPERATION: 15
LANGUAGES: Spanish
ACCESSIBILITY: Wheelchair accessible
CASES SEXUAL ASSAULT/ABUSE (%): 75
DESCRIPTION: Provides services for the abusive family, both offenders and victims; Treats both intrafamilial and extrafamilial physical, emotional, and sexual abuse with a combination of individual, family, and group treatment; Support groups for female and male survivors; Treatment for rapists, child sexual abuse/incest offenders, and batterers
CLIENTS/SERVICES: Marital rape/sexual abuse survivors; Child victims of sexual abuse; Adult survivors of child sexual abuse; Incest victims/survivors; Community education; Offender treatment program; Adolescent survivors of sexual abuse; Male survivors of sexual abuse

FOREST PARK

FOREST PARK CENTER FOR COUNSELING
7208 Dixon St, Forest Park, IL 60130
Information: (312) 366-6680 12pm-9pm (Mon-Fri); answering machine other times
Contact: Cleo Enockson Hagen, Dir
TYPE OF AGENCY: Counseling/mental health services; Private practice; Substance abuse treatment/counseling
AREAS SERVED: Cook, DuPage
YEARS IN OPERATION: 3½
CASES SEXUAL ASSAULT/ABUSE (%): 25
DESCRIPTION: Provides individual, family, marital and group therapy, with staff specialization in working with sexually abused children and adult survivors of child sexual abuse, as well as working with addictions
CLIENTS/SERVICES: Sexual assault survivors; Marital rape/sexual abuse survivors; Child victims of sexual abuse; Adult survivors of child sexual abuse; Incest victims/survivors; Community education; Adolescent survivors of sexual abuse; Male survivors of sexual abuse
REQUIREMENTS: Fee for services
SPECIAL PROGRAMS/SERVICES: Because two of the staff members are addictions counselors as well, can provide addictions counseling for those victims who are also substance abusers; Will provide group treatment when client load demands it

FREEPORT

YWCA DOMESTIC VIOLENCE PROGRAM
641 W Stephenson St, Freeport, IL 61032
Crisis hotline: **(815) 232-1641 24 hrs**
Information: (815) 232-1681 8am-12pm, 1pm-5pm (Mon-Fri)
Contact: Vicki C Sauer, Prog Dir
TYPE OF AGENCY: Domestic violence program
AREAS SERVED: Stephenson, Ogle, Winnebago, Jo Davies, Carroll
YEARS IN OPERATION: 7
LANGUAGES: Spanish
ACCESSIBILITY: Wheelchair accessible
CASES SEXUAL ASSAULT/ABUSE (%): 90
CLIENTS/SERVICES: Sexual assault survivors; Marital rape/sexual abuse survivors; Child victims of sexual abuse; Adult survivors of child sexual abuse; Incest victims/survivors; Prevention program; Community education; Adolescent survivors of sexual abuse

GLEN ELLYN

DUPAGE WOMEN AGAINST RAPE
739 Roosevelt Rd, Bldg 8, Ste 210, Glen Ellyn, IL 60137
Crisis hotline: **(312) 790-6600 24 hrs**
Information: (312) 629-0170 9am-5pm
Contact: Nancy Carlson, Sex Assault Svcs Dir
TYPE OF AGENCY: Rape crisis center
SPONSORING ORGANIZATION: YWCA West Suburban District
AREAS SERVED: DuPage
YEARS IN OPERATION: 16
ACCESSIBILITY: Wheelchair accessible
CASES SEXUAL ASSAULT/ABUSE (%): 100
CLIENTS/SERVICES: Sexual assault survivors; Marital rape/sexual abuse survivors; Child victims of sexual abuse; Adult survivors of child sexual abuse; Incest victims/survivors; Prevention program; Community education; Adolescent survivors of sexual abuse; Male survivors of sexual abuse

DUPAGE YWCA COUNSELING SERVICES
739 Roosevelt Rd, Bldg 8, Ste 210, Glen Ellyn, IL 60137
Crisis hotline: **(312) 790-6600 24 hrs**
Information: (312) 629-0170 9am-8:30pm (Mon, Tue, Wed, Thu); 9am-5pm (Fri)
Contact: Ellen Shaeffer, Counseling Svcs Dir
TYPE OF AGENCY: Rape crisis center; Child sexual abuse services; Child sexual abuse prevention program
SPONSORING ORGANIZATION: YWCA of Metropolitan Chicago
AREAS SERVED: DuPage
YEARS IN OPERATION: 22
ACCESSIBILITY: Wheelchair accessible
CASES SEXUAL ASSAULT/ABUSE (%): 75
DESCRIPTION: Provides counseling for victims of sexual assault and their significant others; Prevention programs for children and adolescents; Feminist martial arts/self-defense
CLIENTS/SERVICES: Sexual assault survivors; Marital rape/sexual abuse survivors; Child victims of sexual abuse; Adult survivors of child sexual abuse; Incest victims/survivors; Prevention program; Community education; Adolescent survivors of sexual abuse; Male survivors of sexual abuse

GRANITE CITY

CATHOLIC CHARITIES
2012 Delmar, Granite City, IL 62040
Information: (618) 877-1184 8:30am-4:30pm (Mon-Fri)
Contact: David A Daly, MS, Therapist
TYPE OF AGENCY: Counseling/mental health services
AREAS SERVED: Madison
YEARS IN OPERATION: 35
ACCESSIBILITY: Wheelchair accessible

CATHOLIC CHARITIES (continued)
CASES SEXUAL ASSAULT/ABUSE (%): 55
CLIENTS/SERVICES: Marital rape/sexual abuse survivors; Child victims of sexual abuse; Adult survivors of child sexual abuse; Incest victims/survivors; Adolescent survivors of sexual abuse; Male survivors of sexual abuse

ST ELIZABETH MEDICAL CENTER
2100 Madison Ave, Granite City, IL 62040
Crisis hotline: **(618) 798-3000 24 hrs**
Information: (618) 798-3000 24 hrs
Contact: Ralpha J Hausmann, Soc Wrk Dir
TYPE OF AGENCY: Hospital/medical center
AREAS SERVED: Madison
ACCESSIBILITY: Wheelchair accessible; Telecommunications for the hearing impaired (TTY, TDY, etc.); Signers for the hearing impaired
CLIENTS/SERVICES: Sexual assault survivors; Marital rape/sexual abuse survivors; Child victims of sexual abuse; Adult survivors of child sexual abuse; Incest victims/survivors; Adolescent survivors of sexual abuse; Male survivors of sexual abuse

GREAT LAKES

AMERICAN RED CROSS FAMILY VIOLENCE TEAM, GREAT LAKES SERVICE CENTER
Bldg 76 NTC, Great Lakes, IL 60088
Crisis hotline: **(312) 440-2000 24 hrs**
Information: (312) 688-5676 8am-8pm
Contact: Shirley Robinson, ACSW, Coord
TYPE OF AGENCY: Counseling/mental health services; Military services
SPONSORING ORGANIZATION: American Red Cross, Mid-America Chapter
AREAS SERVED: Lake (Military installations)
YEARS IN OPERATION: 4
CASES SEXUAL ASSAULT/ABUSE (%): 25
CLIENTS/SERVICES: Sexual assault survivors; Marital rape/sexual abuse survivors; Child victims of sexual abuse; Adult survivors of child sexual abuse; Incest victims/survivors; Offender treatment program; Adolescent survivors of sexual abuse; Male survivors of sexual abuse
REQUIREMENTS: Military personnel and their families

HARRISBURG

ANNA BIXBY WOMEN'S CENTER
202 S Granger, Harrisburg, IL 62982
Crisis hotline: **(618) 252-8389 24 hrs**
Information: (618) 252-8380 8am-4pm (Mon-Fri)
Contact: Barbara Wingo, Dir
TYPE OF AGENCY: Domestic violence program; Child sexual abuse prevention program
AREAS SERVED: Saline, Pope, Hardin, Hamilton, Gallatin, White, Johnson
YEARS IN OPERATION: 10
LANGUAGES: Spanish, French interpreters available
ACCESSIBILITY: Wheelchair accessible; Signers for the hearing impaired
CASES SEXUAL ASSAULT/ABUSE (%): 70
CLIENTS/SERVICES: Marital rape/sexual abuse survivors; Child victims of sexual abuse; Incest victims/survivors; Prevention program; Community education; Adolescent survivors of sexual abuse

HERRIN

ASSOCIATED PSYCHOTHERAPISTS
120 W Walnut, Herrin, IL 62948
Crisis hotline: **(618) 988-1757 24 hrs**
Information: (618) 988-1757 24 hrs
Contact: David Matthews, ACSW
TYPE OF AGENCY: Child sexual abuse services; Private practice
YEARS IN OPERATION: 3
CASES SEXUAL ASSAULT/ABUSE (%): 30-40
CLIENTS/SERVICES: Sexual assault survivors; Marital rape/sexual abuse survivors; Child victims of sexual abuse; Adult survivors of child sexual abuse; Incest victims/survivors; Community education; Offender treatment program; Adolescent survivors of sexual abuse; Male survivors of sexual abuse
REQUIREMENTS: Must follow state reporting laws

JOLIET

CRISIS LINE OF WILL COUNTY
PO Box 2354, Joliet, IL 60434-9998
Crisis hotline: **Joliet (815) 722-3344; Frankfort (815) 469-6166; Wilmington (815) 476-6969; Grundy County (815) 942-6611; Mokena (312) 479-1399; Peotone (312) 258-3333; Bolingbrook (312) 759-4555 24 hrs 7 days**
Information: (815) 744-5280 9am-5pm
Contact: Sr Mary Frances Seeley, Exec Dir
TYPE OF AGENCY: Counseling/mental health services; Telephone crisis hotline; Information and referral
AREAS SERVED: Will, Grundy
YEARS IN OPERATION: 12
ACCESSIBILITY: Telecommunications for the hearing impaired (TTY, TDY, etc.)
CASES SEXUAL ASSAULT/ABUSE (%): 2
DESCRIPTION: Comprehensive hotline system providing counseling, information, and referral; Answers and screens all calls for the local shelter for abused women and children; Answers calls for the Parents United group; Provides phone counseling for rape victims
CLIENTS/SERVICES: Sexual assault survivors; Marital rape/sexual abuse survivors; Child victims of sexual abuse; Adult survivors of child sexual abuse; Incest victims/survivors; Community education

KANKAKEE

KANKAKEE COUNTY COALITION AGAINST DOMESTIC VIOLENCE, INC—HARBOR HOUSE
PO Box 1824, Kankakee, IL 60901
Crisis hotline: **(815) 932-5800 24 hrs**
Information: (815) 932-5814 8:30am-5pm
Contact: Lois Brakebill, Exec Dir
TYPE OF AGENCY: Domestic violence program
AREAS SERVED: Kankakee, Iroquois
YEARS IN OPERATION: 5
ACCESSIBILITY: Wheelchair accessible
CASES SEXUAL ASSAULT/ABUSE (%): 66-75
CLIENTS/SERVICES: Sexual assault survivors; Marital rape/sexual abuse survivors; Child victims of sexual abuse; Adult survivors of child sexual abuse; Incest victims/survivors; Community education; Adolescent survivors of sexual abuse
REQUIREMENTS: Residential clients need to make a police report (not file charges)

YW CASA
1086 E Court St, Kankakee, IL 60901
Crisis hotline: **(815) 937-0384 24 hrs**
Information: (815) 937-0384
Contact: John Tate, YWCASA Pres
TYPE OF AGENCY: Rape crisis center
SPONSORING ORGANIZATION: YWCA
CLIENTS/SERVICES: Sexual assault survivors; Marital rape/sexual abuse survivors; Male survivors of sexual abuse; Child victims of sexual abuse; Incest victims/survivors; Adult survivors of child sexual abuse; Community education; Adolescent survivors of sexual abuse

LIBERTYVILLE

FAMILY STRESS CLINIC LTD
1641 N Milwaukee, No 7, Libertyville, IL 60048
Crisis hotline: **(312) 362-6919 24 hr answering machine, 6 days**
Information: (312) 362-6919
Contact: Nan Claassen, MSW, Michelle Redman, MSW, Deanna Lulofs, Associates
TYPE OF AGENCY: Private practice
AREAS SERVED: Lake, Cook, McHenry
YEARS IN OPERATION: 5
ACCESSIBILITY: Wheelchair accessible
CASES SEXUAL ASSAULT/ABUSE (%): 60
DESCRIPTION: Specializes in working with child victims under the age of 6; Provides individual and family psychotherapy for victims of domestic violence and sexual assault/abuse
CLIENTS/SERVICES: Sexual assault survivors; Marital rape/sexual abuse survivors; Child victims of sexual abuse; Adult survivors of child sexual abuse; Incest victims/survivors; Offender treatment program; Adolescent survivors of sexual abuse; Male survivors of sexual abuse; Preschoolers

LOMBARD

YWCA—WEST SUBURBAN
26 W St Charles Rd, Lombard, IL 60148
Crisis hotline: **(312) 971-3927 24 hrs**
Information: (312) 629-0170 9am-5pm
Contact: Ellen Sheaffer, Counseling Svcs Dir
TYPE OF AGENCY: Rape crisis center; Child sexual abuse prevention program; Acquaintance/date rape prevention program
SPONSORING ORGANIZATION: YWCA of Metropolitan Chicago
AREAS SERVED: DuPage
YEARS IN OPERATION: 23
ACCESSIBILITY: Wheelchair accessible
CASES SEXUAL ASSAULT/ABUSE (%): 60
DESCRIPTION: Provides rape crisis hotline, short-term individual counseling, hospital and court advocacy; Prevention programs include CAP (Child Assault Prevention) for preschool and elementary school students, acquaintance rape prevention for teens presented in schools; Self-defense courses
CLIENTS/SERVICES: Sexual assault survivors; Marital rape/sexual abuse survivors; Child victims of sexual abuse; Adult survivors of child sexual abuse; Incest victims/survivors; Prevention program; Community education; Adolescent survivors of sexual abuse

MACOMB

MCDONOUGH COUNTY STATE'S ATTORNEY—VICTIM/WITNESS ASSISTANCE PROGRAM
McDonough County Courthouse, Macomb, IL 61455
Information: (309) 837-2309 8am-Noon, 1pm-4pm (Mon-Fri)
Contact: Jennifer Heinz, Coord
TYPE OF AGENCY: Victim/witness assistance program
AREAS SERVED: McDonough
YEARS IN OPERATION: 1½
ACCESSIBILITY: Wheelchair accessible
CLIENTS/SERVICES: Sexual assault survivors; Marital rape/sexual abuse survivors; Child victims of sexual abuse; Adult survivors of child sexual abuse; Incest victims/survivors; Adolescent survivors of sexual abuse; Male survivors of sexual abuse

QUAD COUNTY COALITION AGAINST DOMESTIC VIOLENCE
Box 157, Macomb, IL 61455
Crisis hotline: **(309) 837-5555 24 hrs**
Information: (309) 837-6622 8am-4pm (Mon-Fri)
Contact: Lucy Raizman, Prog Coord
TYPE OF AGENCY: Domestic violence program
SPONSORING ORGANIZATION: Western Illinois Regional Council—Community Action Agency
AREAS SERVED: Hancock, Henderson, McDonough, Warren
YEARS IN OPERATION: 2½
ACCESSIBILITY: Wheelchair accessible

QUAD COUNTY COALITION AGAINST DOMESTIC VIOLENCE *(continued)*

CLIENTS/SERVICES: Marital rape/sexual abuse survivors; Community education

MARION

DEPARTMENT OF CHILDREN AND FAMILY SERVICES
2309 W Main, Marion, IL 62812
Crisis hotline: **(800) 252-2873 24 hrs**
Information: (618) 997-4371 8:30am-5pm
Contact: Beverly Chaplain, Child Welfare Spec, Sexual Abuse Treatment Prog Site Coord
TYPE OF AGENCY: Counseling/mental health services
AREAS SERVED: Franklin, Williamson
YEARS IN OPERATION: 5
ACCESSIBILITY: Wheelchair accessible
CASES SEXUAL ASSAULT/ABUSE (%): 33
DESCRIPTION: Provides treatment for sexually abusive families and family members, as well as child sexual abuse/incest offenders
CLIENTS/SERVICES: Child victims of sexual abuse; Incest victims/survivors; Prevention program; Community education; Offender treatment program; Adolescent survivors of sexual abuse
REQUIREMENTS: Family must have a child victim of abuse under the age of 18, or be the family of an offender of child sexual abuse

MATTOON

COLES COUNTY MENTAL HEALTH CENTER
PO Box 907, 213 S 17th St, Mattoon, IL 61938
Crisis hotline: **(217) 234-6405, 348-7666 24 hrs**
Information: (217) 234-6405, 348-7666 9am-5pm
Contact: Martha Carter, Sexual Abuse Treatment Coord
TYPE OF AGENCY: Counseling/mental health services; Child sexual abuse services
AREAS SERVED: Coles
ACCESSIBILITY: Wheelchair accessible
CASES SEXUAL ASSAULT/ABUSE (%): 30
CLIENTS/SERVICES: Sexual assault survivors; Marital rape/sexual abuse survivors; Child victims of sexual abuse; Adult survivors of child sexual abuse; Incest victims/survivors; Community education; Offender treatment program; Adolescent survivors of sexual abuse; Male survivors of sexual abuse
REQUIREMENTS: Residents of Coles County are given priority; Treatment for offenders must be court-ordered

MOLINE

SEXUAL ABUSE TREATMENT PROGRAM
525 16th St, Moline, IL 61265
Crisis hotline: **(309) 757-8555 Parent Helpline 24 hrs**
Information: (309) 764-4733 SATP, 764-7017 CCR 8:30am-5pm (Mon-Fri)
Contact: Marcia Rexroat, Sue Gallagher, Therapists
TYPE OF AGENCY: Child sexual abuse services; Child sexual abuse prevention program; Child abuse services; Child abuse prevention program
SPONSORING ORGANIZATION: Council on Children At Risk
AREAS SERVED: Rock Island, Henry, Mercer, IL; Scott, Muscatine, Clinton, Johnson, DeWitt, IA
YEARS IN OPERATION: 10
ACCESSIBILITY: Wheelchair accessible; Telecommunications for the hearing impaired (TTY, TDY, etc.) (by arrangement); Signers for the hearing impaired (by arrangement)
CASES SEXUAL ASSAULT/ABUSE (%): 100
DESCRIPTION: Council on Children at Risk assists the community to respond effectively to the problems of child abuse/neglect. The Sexual Abuse Treatment Program is designed to provide therapy for families in which incest and sexual abuse has occurred
CLIENTS/SERVICES: Child victims of sexual abuse; Adult survivors of child sexual abuse; Incest victims/survivors; Prevention program; Community education; Offender treatment program; Adolescent survivors of sexual abuse
REQUIREMENTS: Open case and referral by the Illinois Department of Children and Family Services or the Iowa Department of Human Services; Victims are under age of 18; Perpetrator must be related to, or caretaker of, victim

MOUNT VERNON

PARENTS UNITED OF JEFFERSON AREA
3405 Broadway, Mount Vernon, IL 62864
Crisis hotline: **To report statewide abuse/neglect (800) 25A-BUSE 24 hrs 7 days**
Information: (618) 242-6556 8:30am-5pm (Mon-Fri)
Contact: Larry Johnson, ACSW, Prog Coord; Diane Curry Johnson, Chld Welf Spec, SAT Coord
TYPE OF AGENCY: Counseling/mental health services; Child sexual abuse services
SPONSORING ORGANIZATION: Department of Children and Family Services
AREAS SERVED: Jefferson, Wayne, Hamilton
YEARS IN OPERATION: 5
ACCESSIBILITY: Wheelchair accessible
CASES SEXUAL ASSAULT/ABUSE (%): 100
DESCRIPTION: Support groups for sexually abused children, family members and incest offenders in cases of intrafamilial sexual abuse
CLIENTS/SERVICES: Child victims of sexual abuse; Incest victims/survivors; Offender treatment program; Adolescent survivors of sexual abuse; Male survivors of sexual abuse
REQUIREMENTS: Family must have a child under the age of 18 who has an indicated report of child sexual abuse by a perpetrator in that child's immediate family.

MURPHYSBORO

JACKSON COUNTY STATE'S ATTORNEY'S OFFICE—VICTIM/WITNESS PROGRAM
Courthouse, Murphysboro, IL 62966
Information: (618) 684-2155 8am-4pm (Mon-Fri)
Contact: Bonnie Reisin, Victim Advocate
TYPE OF AGENCY: Victim/witness assistance program
AREAS SERVED: Jackson
YEARS IN OPERATION: 8
LANGUAGES: Spanish
ACCESSIBILITY: Wheelchair accessible; Signers for the hearing impaired
CLIENTS/SERVICES: Sexual assault survivors; Marital rape/sexual abuse survivors; Child victims of sexual abuse
REQUIREMENTS: Services are provided to all victims of crime whether or not charges are filed

OLNEY

SWAN (STOPPING WOMEN ABUSE NOW)
PO Box 176, 1114 S West St, Olney, IL 62450
Crisis hotline: **(618) 392-3556 24 hrs**
Information: (618) 392-2769, Mt Carmel (618) 262-5583, Robinson (618) 546-5461, Flora (618) 662-7216, Fairfield (618) 842-2611 24 hrs
Contact: Linda Bookwalter, Dir
TYPE OF AGENCY: Domestic violence program; Child sexual abuse services
AREAS SERVED: Clay, Crawford, Edwards, Effingham, Jasper, Lawrence, Richland, Wabash, Wayne
YEARS IN OPERATION: 7
ACCESSIBILITY: Wheelchair accessible
CASES SEXUAL ASSAULT/ABUSE (%): 40
DESCRIPTION: Shelter for victims of domestic violence/sexual assault and for the homeless
CLIENTS/SERVICES: Sexual assault survivors; Marital rape/sexual abuse survivors; Child victims of sexual abuse; Adult survivors of child sexual abuse; Incest victims/survivors; Community education; Adolescent survivors of sexual abuse
SPECIAL PROGRAMS/SERVICES: Provides elder abuse hotline and crisis team

OLYMPIA FIELDS

YW CARES (COMMITTEE AGAINST RAPE EMERGENCY/EDUCATIONAL SERVICES)
3612 W Lincoln Hwy, Olympia Fields, IL 60461
Crisis hotline: **(312) 748-5672 24 hrs**
Information: (312) 748-6600 9am-5pm (Mon-Fri); Answering machine 24 hrs
Contact: Barbara L Davis, MS, Women's Svcs Dir
TYPE OF AGENCY: Rape crisis center; Child sexual abuse services; Child sexual abuse prevention program; Acquaintance/date rape prevention program
SPONSORING ORGANIZATION: YWCA of Metropolitan Chicago, South Suburban Area
ACCESSIBILITY: Signers for the hearing impaired
CASES SEXUAL ASSAULT/ABUSE (%): 100
DESCRIPTION: Sexual assault is primary focus; Provides comprehensive services for victim/survivors, including long-term therapy, institutional advocacy, public education, and prevention programs; Feminist martial arts/self-defense
CLIENTS/SERVICES: Sexual assault survivors; Marital rape/sexual abuse survivors; Child victims of sexual abuse; Adult survivors of child sexual abuse; Incest victims/survivors; Prevention program; Community education; Adolescent survivors of sexual abuse; Male survivors of sexual abuse
REQUIREMENTS: Ages 3 to adult
SPECIAL PROGRAMS/SERVICES: Prevention services include: a play for children (*Little Bear*); Acquaintance Rape Prevention program for teens. Yearly professional training is provided as well as 40-hour volunteer training sessions

OTTAWA

LASALLE COUNTY YOUTH SERVICES BUREAU, INC
827 Columbus St, Ottawa, IL 61350
Crisis hotline: **(815) 433-3953 24 hrs**
Information: (815) 433-3953 9am-5pm (Mon-Fri)
Contact: Liz Davis, Sexual Abuse Svcs Supv
TYPE OF AGENCY: Counseling/mental health services; Child sexual abuse services; Child sexual abuse prevention program
AREAS SERVED: LaSalle
YEARS IN OPERATION: 13
LANGUAGES: Spanish
DESCRIPTION: Provides services ranging from information and referral to long-term counseling for victims of sexual abuse and their families
CLIENTS/SERVICES: Child victims of sexual abuse; Incest victims/survivors; Prevention program; Offender treatment program

MENTAL HEALTH CENTER OF LASALLE COUNTY
1000 E Norris Dr, Ottawa, IL 61350
Crisis hotline: **(815) 434-4727 24 hrs**
Information: (815) 434-4727 9am-5pm
Contact: Gene Smith, Therapist
TYPE OF AGENCY: Counseling/mental health services
SPONSORING ORGANIZATION: Youth Service Bureau of LaSalle County
AREAS SERVED: LaSalle
YEARS IN OPERATION: 5
ACCESSIBILITY: Wheelchair accessible
CLIENTS/SERVICES: Sexual assault survivors; Child victims of sexual abuse; Adult survivors of child sexual abuse; Incest victims/survivors; Prevention program; Community education;

MENTAL HEALTH CENTER OF LASALLE COUNTY *(continued)*
Adolescent survivors of sexual abuse; Male survivors of sexual abuse

PARK RIDGE

SAIF—SURVIVORS OF ABUSE IN FAMILIES
711 Bldg Devon Ave, Ste 208, Park Ridge, IL 60068
Crisis hotline: **(312) 635-4100 On call**
Information: (312) 518-0028 On call
Contact: Barbara A Ward, CSW, ACSW, Dir
TYPE OF AGENCY: Hospital/medical center; Child sexual abuse services; Child sexual abuse prevention program; Private practice
YEARS IN OPERATION: 10
CASES SEXUAL ASSAULT/ABUSE (%): 95
DESCRIPTION: Evaluation and treatment of survivors and adolescent and adult sex offenders; In-patient treatment and consultation in several Chicago psychiatric hospitals
CLIENTS/SERVICES: Sexual assault survivors; Marital rape/sexual abuse survivors; Child victims of sexual abuse; Adult survivors of child sexual abuse; Incest victims/survivors; Prevention program; Community education; Offender treatment program; Adolescent survivors of sexual abuse; Male survivors of sexual abuse

PEORIA

CENTER AGAINST SEXUAL ASSAULT (CASA)
2508 N Sheridan Rd, Ste 3, Peoria, IL 61604
Information: (309) 685-4711 8:30am-5:50pm
Contact: Pam Greenslate, Dir
TYPE OF AGENCY: Private practice
AREAS SERVED: Central IL
YEARS IN OPERATION: 4
CASES SEXUAL ASSAULT/ABUSE (%): 90-95
DESCRIPTION: Provides individual, marital, family and group therapy for any person who has been the victim of any type of sexual exploitation. Counseling services are also provided for family members and significant others of the victim. In situations of incest, counseling may be offered to offender, as well as non-offending parent, non-abused siblings and victim
CLIENTS/SERVICES: Sexual assault survivors; Marital rape/sexual abuse survivors; Child victims of sexual abuse; Adult survivors of child sexual abuse; Incest victims/survivors; Prevention program; Community education; Offender treatment program; Adolescent survivors of sexual abuse; Male survivors of sexual abuse
REQUIREMENTS: Fee based services

PSYCHOLOGICAL ASSOCIATES
7150 N University, Peoria, IL 61614
Information: (309) 691-0420 8am-8pm (Mon-Fri), 9am-1pm (Sat)
Contact: Lisa Batz, Psychologist/Intake
TYPE OF AGENCY: Counseling/mental health services; Child sexual abuse services
AREAS SERVED: Peoria, Tazwell, Woodford
YEARS IN OPERATION: 10
CASES SEXUAL ASSAULT/ABUSE (%): 40
DESCRIPTION: Mental health services; Support groups for male and female survivors of sexual assault/abuse; Treatment for child sexual abuse/incest offenders
CLIENTS/SERVICES: Sexual assault survivors; Marital rape/sexual abuse survivors; Child victims of sexual abuse; Adult survivors of child sexual abuse; Incest victims/survivors; Community education; Offender treatment program; Adolescent survivors of sexual abuse; Male survivors of sexual abuse

TRI-COUNTY WOMEN STRENGTH
PO Box 3172, Peoria, IL 61614
Crisis hotline: **(309) 691-4111 24 hrs**
Information: (309) 691-0551 9am-5pm
Contact: Edna Palmer, Sexual Assault Coord
TYPE OF AGENCY: Rape crisis center; Domestic violence program; Child sexual abuse prevention program
AREAS SERVED: Peoria, Tazewell, Woodford
YEARS IN OPERATION: 10
ACCESSIBILITY: Wheelchair accessible
CASES SEXUAL ASSAULT/ABUSE (%): 27
DESCRIPTION: Crisis intervention for sexual assault, domestic violence, and elder abuse
CLIENTS/SERVICES: Sexual assault survivors; Marital rape/sexual abuse survivors; Adult survivors of child sexual abuse; Incest victims/survivors; Prevention program; Community education; Adolescent survivors of sexual abuse; Male survivors of sexual abuse; Elderly
REQUIREMENTS: Must be 13 or older
SPECIAL PROGRAMS/SERVICES: *Better Safe Than Sorry*, child sexual abuse prevention programs are conducted during the school year in grade and high schools

PEORIA HEIGHTS

EDMUND L DECKER AND ASSOCIATES
4617 N Prospect Ave, Peoria Heights, IL 61614
Information: (309) 688-1112 Days and evenings by appointment
Contact: E L Decker, MSW, CSW
TYPE OF AGENCY: Private practice
YEARS IN OPERATION: 23
CASES SEXUAL ASSAULT/ABUSE (%): 5%, 60% have experienced sexual assault/abuse in the past
DESCRIPTION: Evaluation and therapy for victims and families of sexual abuse; Individual therapy for child sexual abuse/incest offenders and batterers
CLIENTS/SERVICES: Sexual assault survivors; Marital rape/sexual abuse survivors; Child victims of sexual abuse; Adult survivors of child sexual abuse; Incest victims/survivors; Offender treatment program; Adolescent survivors of sexual abuse; Male survivors of sexual abuse
REQUIREMENTS: Afford fee

PRINCETON

FREEDOM HOUSE SHELTER, INC
PO Box 544, Princeton, IL 61356
Crisis hotline: **(815) 875-8233 24 hrs**
Information: (815) 872-0087 8:30am-3:30pm (Mon-Fri)
Contact: Adina Teska, Dir
TYPE OF AGENCY: Domestic violence program
AREAS SERVED: Bureau, Henry, Stark, Marshall, Putnam
YEARS IN OPERATION: 5
CASES SEXUAL ASSAULT/ABUSE (%): 50
CLIENTS/SERVICES: Marital rape/sexual abuse survivors; Adult survivors of child sexual abuse; Community education

QUAD COUNTY COUNSELING CENTER
530 Park Ave E, Princeton, IL 61356
Crisis hotline: **(815) 875-4458 24 hrs**
Information: (815) 875-4458 9am-5pm
Contact: Robert C Knol, PhD, Exec Dir
TYPE OF AGENCY: Domestic violence program; Counseling/mental health services; Child sexual abuse services
AREAS SERVED: Bureau, Marshall, Putnam, Stark
YEARS IN OPERATION: 16
ACCESSIBILITY: Wheelchair accessible
CASES SEXUAL ASSAULT/ABUSE (%): 1
CLIENTS/SERVICES: Child victims of sexual abuse; Adult survivors of child sexual abuse; Incest victims/survivors; Adolescent survivors of sexual abuse

QUINCY

ADAMS COUNTY STATE'S ATTORNEY—VICTIM WITNESS PROGRAM
521 Vermont St, Quincy, IL 62301
Information: (217) 222-0206 8:30am-4:30pm
Contact: Amy Anderson, Victim Witness Coord
TYPE OF AGENCY: Victim/witness assistance program
AREAS SERVED: Adams
YEARS IN OPERATION: 5
ACCESSIBILITY: Wheelchair accessible; Signers for the hearing impaired
CASES SEXUAL ASSAULT/ABUSE (%): 5
CLIENTS/SERVICES: Sexual assault survivors; Marital rape/sexual abuse survivors; Child victims of sexual abuse; Community education
REQUIREMENTS: Pending charge in State's Attorney's Office

QUANADA
2707 Maine St, Quincy, IL 62301
Crisis hotline: **(217) 22A-BUSE 24 hrs 7 days**
Information: (217) 222-0069 24 hrs 7 days
Contact: Sandra Fenn, Sexual Assault Prog Coord
TYPE OF AGENCY: Rape crisis center; Domestic violence program
AREAS SERVED: Adams, Brown, Pike, Hancock, Schuyler
YEARS IN OPERATION: 4
ACCESSIBILITY: Wheelchair accessible
CASES SEXUAL ASSAULT/ABUSE (%): 30-40
DESCRIPTION: Services for survivors of sexual assault and domestic violence, including support groups for female and male survivors; Feminist martial arts/self-defense program
CLIENTS/SERVICES: Sexual assault survivors; Marital rape/sexual abuse survivors; Child victims of sexual abuse; Adult survivors of child sexual abuse; Incest victims/survivors; Prevention program; Community education; Adolescent survivors of sexual abuse; Male survivors of sexual abuse
REQUIREMENTS: Client must be 18 years of age, or have guardian consent for residence or counseling

ROCK ISLAND

FRANCISCAN MENTAL HEALTH CENTER
2701 17th St, Rock Island, IL 61201
Crisis hotline: **(309) 793-2031, (800) 322-1431 in Illinois 24 hrs daily**
Information: (309) 793-2031 8am-5pm
Contact: Cindy Hamer, MSW, Outpatient Therapist
TYPE OF AGENCY: Counseling/mental health services; Child sexual abuse services; Child sexual abuse prevention program; Residential treatment facility
SPONSORING ORGANIZATION: Franciscan Hospital
YEARS IN OPERATION: 20
LANGUAGES: Spanish
ACCESSIBILITY: Wheelchair accessible; Signers for the hearing impaired
CASES SEXUAL ASSAULT/ABUSE (%): 30
CLIENTS/SERVICES: Sexual assault survivors; Marital rape/sexual abuse survivors; Child victims of sexual abuse; Adult survivors of child sexual abuse; Incest victims/survivors; Prevention program; Community education; Offender treatment program; Adolescent survivors of sexual abuse; Male survivors of sexual abuse

ROCKFORD

FAMILY ADVOCATE
716 N Church St, Rockford, IL 61103
Crisis hotline: **(815) 965-5172 24 hrs**
Information: (815) 965-5172
Contact: Lou Gadow, Dir
TYPE OF AGENCY: Child sexual abuse services; Child sexual abuse prevention program
AREAS SERVED: Winnebago, Ogle, Boone

FAMILY ADVOCATE (continued)
YEARS IN OPERATION: 15
LANGUAGES: Spanish
ACCESSIBILITY: Signers for the hearing impaired
CASES SEXUAL ASSAULT/ABUSE (%): 100
CLIENTS/SERVICES: Child victims of sexual abuse; Adult survivors of child sexual abuse; Incest victims/survivors; Prevention program; Community education; Offender treatment program; Adolescent survivors of sexual abuse; Male survivors of sexual abuse

ROCKFORD SEXUAL ASSAULT COUNSELING, INC
202 W State St, Rockford Trust Bldg, Ste 514, Rockford, IL 61101
Crisis hotline: **(815) 964-2991 24 hrs**
Information: (815) 229-6470 8:30am-5pm (Mon-Fri)
Contact: Millie Zimmerman, Agency Dir
TYPE OF AGENCY: Rape crisis center
AREAS SERVED: Winnebago, Boone
YEARS IN OPERATION: 10
ACCESSIBILITY: Wheelchair accessible
CASES SEXUAL ASSAULT/ABUSE (%): 100
CLIENTS/SERVICES: Sexual assault survivors; Marital rape/sexual abuse survivors; Child victims of sexual abuse; Adult survivors of child sexual abuse; Incest victims/survivors; Prevention program; Community education; Adolescent survivors of sexual abuse; Male survivors of sexual abuse

ROLLING MEADOWS

NORTHWEST ACTION AGAINST RAPE
5005 Newport Dr, No 505, Rolling Meadows, IL 60008
Crisis hotline: **(312) 228-0990 24 hrs**
Information: (312) 253-0220 9am-5pm (Mon-Fri); after hrs by appointment
Contact: Regina Lumpkins, Exec Dir
TYPE OF AGENCY: Rape crisis center; Child sexual abuse prevention program; Acquaintance/date rape prevention program
AREAS SERVED: Cook
YEARS IN OPERATION: 13
LANGUAGES: Spanish
ACCESSIBILITY: Wheelchair accessible
CASES SEXUAL ASSAULT/ABUSE (%): 100
CLIENTS/SERVICES: Sexual assault survivors; Marital rape/sexual abuse survivors; Child victims of sexual abuse; Adult survivors of child sexual abuse; Incest victims/survivors; Prevention program; Community education; Adolescent survivors of sexual abuse; Male survivors of sexual abuse

SKOKIE

AAP (ASSOCIATES IN ADOLESCENT PSYCHIATRY) MENTAL HEALTH RESOURCES
5360 Fargo Ave, Skokie, IL 60077
Crisis hotline: **(312) 675-2161 24 hrs**
Information: (312) 675-2140 24 hrs
Contact: Irene Nelson, Intake Coord
TYPE OF AGENCY: Hospital/medical center; Child sexual abuse services; Private practice; Adolescent program
AREAS SERVED: Cook, Lake, DuPage, Kane, Kendall, Will, Peoria, IL; Northern IN; Southwestern MI
YEARS IN OPERATION: 5
CASES SEXUAL ASSAULT/ABUSE (%): 25
DESCRIPTION: Specialty in the area of sexual abuse
CLIENTS/SERVICES: Sexual assault survivors; Marital rape/sexual abuse survivors; Child victims of sexual abuse; Adult survivors of child sexual abuse; Incest victims/survivors; Community education; Offender treatment program; Adolescent survivors of sexual abuse; Male survivors of sexual abuse

REQUIREMENTS: Any age; Third party payments accepted

SPRINGFIELD

RAPE INFORMATION AND COUNSELING SERVICE
PO Box 2211, Springfield, IL 62705
Crisis hotline: **(217) 753-8081 24 hrs**
Information: (217) 744-2560 9am-5pm
Contact: Susan Chelap-Carr, Exec Dir
TYPE OF AGENCY: Rape crisis center; Child sexual abuse services; Child sexual abuse prevention program
AREAS SERVED: Sangamon, Logan, Mason, Menard, Christian, Macoupin, Montgomery
YEARS IN OPERATION: 14
ACCESSIBILITY: Wheelchair accessible
CLIENTS/SERVICES: Sexual assault survivors; Marital rape/sexual abuse survivors; Child victims of sexual abuse; Adult survivors of child sexual abuse; Incest victims/survivors; Prevention program; Community education; Adolescent survivors of sexual abuse; Male survivors of sexual abuse

SOJOURN WOMEN'S CENTER
PO Box 1052, Springfield, IL 62705
Crisis hotline: **(217) 544-2484 24 hrs**
Information: (217) 544-0203 24 hrs
Contact: Diane DeLeonardo Muncy, Exec Dir
TYPE OF AGENCY: Domestic violence program
AREAS SERVED: Sangamon, Menard, Christian, Logan
YEARS IN OPERATION: 13
ACCESSIBILITY: Wheelchair accessible
CASES SEXUAL ASSAULT/ABUSE (%): 75
DESCRIPTION: Provides shelter for battered women and occasional shelter for rape victims who don't feel safe going home immediately. Many domestic violence survivors are also survivors of marital rape and child sexual abuse
CLIENTS/SERVICES: Marital rape/sexual abuse survivors; Adult survivors of child sexual abuse

STERLING

YWCA/COVE (CITIZENS OPPOSING VIOLENT ENCOUNTERS)
412 1st Ave, Sterling, IL 61081
Crisis hotline: **(815) 626-7277 24 hrs**
Information: (815) 625-0343
Contact: Mary Pat Browne, Sexual Assault Prog Dir
TYPE OF AGENCY: Rape crisis center; Child sexual abuse prevention program
DESCRIPTION: Provides shelter, medical and legal advocacy, emotional support, information about sexual assault, and counseling on a 24-hour basis through the hotline; CAP (Child Assault Prevention) Project in area schools, grades K-6
CLIENTS/SERVICES: Sexual assault survivors; Marital rape/sexual abuse survivors; Child victims of sexual abuse; Adult survivors of child sexual abuse; Incest victims/survivors; Prevention program; Community education; Adolescent survivors of sexual abuse; Male survivors of sexual abuse; Developmentally disabled

SUMMIT

DES PLAINES VALLEY COMMUNITY CENTER—SEXUAL ASSAULT PROGRAM
PO Box 10, Summit, IL 60501
Crisis hotline: **(312) 485-5254 24 hrs**
Information: (312) 458-6920 9am-9pm (Mon-Thu), 9am-6pm (Fri)
Contact: Phyllis Spinal, ACSW, Sexual Assault Prog Dir
TYPE OF AGENCY: Domestic violence program; Counseling/mental health services; Child sexual abuse services; Child sexual abuse prevention program; Rape crisis program

AREAS SERVED: Suburban Cook, Lyons Township
YEARS IN OPERATION: 20, Sexual Assault Program 3
LANGUAGES: Spanish
ACCESSIBILITY: Wheelchair accessible
CASES SEXUAL ASSAULT/ABUSE (%): 50
DESCRIPTION: Comprehensive community-based social service agency with an early education center (Head Start and Day Care) and programs in alcoholism, domestic violence, general mental health, and sexual assault. Sexual assault program provides comprehensive treatment and advocacy services for child and adult victims/survivors. Treatment for incest offenders and batterers
CLIENTS/SERVICES: Sexual assault survivors; Marital rape/sexual abuse survivors; Child victims of sexual abuse; Adult survivors of child sexual abuse; Incest victims/survivors; Prevention program; Community education; Adolescent survivors of sexual abuse; Male survivors of sexual abuse

URBANA

RAPE CRISIS SERVICES
505 W Green St, Urbana, IL 61801
Crisis hotline: **(217) 384-4444 24 hrs daily**
Information: (217) 384-4462 9am-5pm
Contact: Maggie Shannon, Prog Dir
TYPE OF AGENCY: Rape crisis center; Child sexual abuse services; Child sexual abuse prevention program
SPONSORING ORGANIZATION: A Woman's Fund
AREAS SERVED: Primarily Champaign, also Ford, Platt, Douglas
YEARS IN OPERATION: 13
LANGUAGES: Interpreters available
ACCESSIBILITY: Wheelchair accessible
CASES SEXUAL ASSAULT/ABUSE (%): 100
CLIENTS/SERVICES: Sexual assault survivors; Marital rape/sexual abuse survivors; Child victims of sexual abuse; Adult survivors of child sexual abuse; Incest victims/survivors; Prevention program; Community education; Adolescent survivors of sexual abuse; Male survivors of sexual abuse

VANDALIA

SEXUAL ASSAULT AND FAMILY EMERGENCIES
PO Box 192, Vandalia, IL 62471
Crisis hotline: **(618) 283-1414 24 hrs daily**
Information: (618) 283-1414 9am-4pm (Mon-Fri)
Contact: Dorothy Schultz, Coord
TYPE OF AGENCY: Rape crisis center
AREAS SERVED: Fayette
YEARS IN OPERATION: 2
ACCESSIBILITY: Wheelchair accessible
CASES SEXUAL ASSAULT/ABUSE (%): 90
CLIENTS/SERVICES: Sexual assault survivors; Marital rape/sexual abuse survivors; Child victims of sexual abuse; Adult survivors of child sexual abuse; Incest victims/survivors; Prevention program; Community education; Adolescent survivors of sexual abuse; Male survivors of sexual abuse

WAUKEGAN

LAKE COUNTY COUNCIL AGAINST SEXUAL ASSAULT
1105 Greenwood, Waukegan, IL 60085
Crisis hotline: **(312) 872-7799 24 hrs**
Information: (312) 244-1187 9am-5pm
Contact: Toren Flink, Exec Dir
TYPE OF AGENCY: Rape crisis center; Child sexual abuse prevention program
SPONSORING ORGANIZATION: United Way
AREAS SERVED: Lake
YEARS IN OPERATION: 6
LANGUAGES: Spanish
ACCESSIBILITY: Wheelchair accessible
CASES SEXUAL ASSAULT/ABUSE (%): 100

LAKE COUNTY COUNCIL AGAINST SEXUAL ASSAULT *(continued)*
CLIENTS/SERVICES: Sexual assault survivors; Marital rape/sexual abuse survivors; Adult survivors of child sexual abuse; Incest victims/survivors; Prevention program; Community education; Adolescent survivors of sexual abuse; Male survivors of sexual abuse
SPECIAL PROGRAMS/SERVICES: Programs include Child Assault Prevention for grades K-5, and Junior High Prevention for grades 6-8

A SAFE PLACE
PO Box 1067, Waukegan, IL 60079
Crisis hotline: **(312) 249-4450 24 hrs**
Information: (312) 249-5147 9am-5pm
Contact: Barbara Berngard, Exec Dir
TYPE OF AGENCY: Domestic violence program
AREAS SERVED: Lake, McHenry, northern Cook
YEARS IN OPERATION: 9
LANGUAGES: Spanish
ACCESSIBILITY: Wheelchair accessible; Signers for the hearing impaired
CLIENTS/SERVICES: Sexual assault survivors; Marital rape/sexual abuse survivors; Child victims of sexual abuse; Adult survivors of child sexual abuse; Incest victims/survivors

WOODSTOCK

TURNING POINT
PO Box 723, Woodstock, IL 60098
Crisis hotline: **(800) 892-8900 24 hrs**
Information: (815) 338-8081 8:30am-4:30pm (Mon-Fri)
Contact: Lou Ness, Exec Dir
TYPE OF AGENCY: Domestic violence program; Child sexual abuse services
AREAS SERVED: McHenry
YEARS IN OPERATION: 7½
CLIENTS/SERVICES: Marital rape/sexual abuse survivors; Child victims of sexual abuse; Adult survivors of child sexual abuse; Incest victims/survivors; Prevention program; Community education; Adolescent survivors of sexual abuse

WORTH

CRISIS CENTER FOR SOUTH SUBURBIA
PO Box 304, Worth, IL 60482
Crisis hotline: **(312) 974-1791 24 hrs**
Information: (312) 974-1091 24 hrs
Contact: Evie Craig, Exec Dir
TYPE OF AGENCY: Domestic violence program
AREAS SERVED: Southwest Cook
YEARS IN OPERATION: 10
ACCESSIBILITY: Wheelchair accessible
CASES SEXUAL ASSAULT/ABUSE (%): 20-25
CLIENTS/SERVICES: Child victims of sexual abuse; Adult survivors of child sexual abuse; Incest victims/survivors; Community education

FAMILY AND MENTAL HEALTH SERVICES/ SOUTHWEST SEXUAL ASSAULT/ABUSE SERVICES
11220 S Harlem, Worth, IL 60482
Information: (312) 448-5700 9am-5pm (Mon-Fri), day/evening hrs for counseling
Contact: Suzanne Garb, Family Svcs Dir
TYPE OF AGENCY: Counseling/mental health services
AREAS SERVED: Southwest Cook
YEARS IN OPERATION: 22
LANGUAGES: Spanish available
ACCESSIBILITY: Wheelchair accessible
CASES SEXUAL ASSAULT/ABUSE (%): .5
CLIENTS/SERVICES: Sexual assault survivors; Child victims of sexual abuse; Adult survivors of child sexual abuse; Incest victims/survivors; Prevention program; Community education; Offender treatment program

INDIANA

ANDERSON

WOMEN'S ALTERNATIVES, INC
PO Box 1302, Anderson, IN 46015
Crisis hotline: **(317) 643-0200 24 hrs**
Information: (317) 643-0200 8am-5pm (Mon-Fri)
TYPE OF AGENCY: Rape crisis center; Domestic violence program
AREAS SERVED: Madison, Henry, Hancock, and outreach for Hamilton
YEARS IN OPERATION: 11
ACCESSIBILITY: Wheelchair accessible
CLIENTS/SERVICES: Sexual assault survivors; Marital rape/sexual abuse survivors; Child victims of sexual abuse; Adult survivors of child sexual abuse; Incest victims/survivors; Community education; Adolescent survivors of sexual abuse
REQUIREMENTS: Serve survivors of domestic violence or sexual assault who are 18 years of age, emancipated minor or accompanied by a custodial parent

BLOOMINGTON

ALPHA COUNSELING
PO Box 2044, Bloomington, IN 47401
Crisis hotline: **(812) 333-9400 24 hrs**
Information: (812) 333-9400
Contact: Suzanne Pauwels, Couns
TYPE OF AGENCY: Private practice
AREAS SERVED: Monroe, Brown, Greene, Lawrence, Owen, Morgan
YEARS IN OPERATION: 2
CASES SEXUAL ASSAULT/ABUSE (%): 10
DESCRIPTION: Treatment for survivors, as well as individual therapy for rapists, child sexual abuse/incest offenders, and batterers
CLIENTS/SERVICES: Sexual assault survivors; Marital rape/sexual abuse survivors; Child victims of sexual abuse; Adult survivors of child sexual abuse; Incest victims/survivors; Community education; Offender treatment program; Adolescent survivors of sexual abuse; Male survivors of sexual abuse

INDIANA UNIVERSITY OFFICE FOR WOMEN'S AFFAIRS
Memorial Hall East, Rm 123, Indiana University, Bloomington, IN 47405
Information: (812) 855-3849 8am-5pm (Mon-Fri)
Contact: Kathryn Risacher, Victim Asst Couns; Trisha Bracken, Asst to Dean for Women's Affairs
TYPE OF AGENCY: College/university-based services
AREAS SERVED: Monroe (Indiana University Community)
YEARS IN OPERATION: 10
DESCRIPTION: Advocates for women at IU; Work with administration to provide service for victims of sexual assault; Victim assistance counselor in the office
CLIENTS/SERVICES: Sexual assault survivors; Adult survivors of child sexual abuse; Incest victims/survivors; Prevention program; Community education; Adolescent survivors of sexual abuse; Male survivors of sexual abuse; Sexual harassment
REQUIREMENTS: No formal requirement that rape survivor must be student, faculty, or staff.

INDIANA UNIVERSITY SEXUAL ASSAULT CRISIS SERVICE (SACS)
600 N Jordan Ave, Bloomington, IN 47405
Crisis hotline: **(812) 855-8900 24 hrs**
Information: (812) 855-5711 8am-5pm (Mon-Fri)
Contact: Suzanne Pauwels, Counselor
TYPE OF AGENCY: Rape crisis center; College/university-based services; Hospital/medical center
SPONSORING ORGANIZATION: Indiana University
AREAS SERVED: Monroe
YEARS IN OPERATION: ½
ACCESSIBILITY: Wheelchair accessible
CASES SEXUAL ASSAULT/ABUSE (%): 100
DESCRIPTION: Crisis intervention and counseling for survivors of sexual assault; Prevention programs, including feminist martial arts/self-defense; Therapy for rapists, child sexual abuse/incest offenders and batterers
CLIENTS/SERVICES: Sexual assault survivors; Child victims of sexual abuse; Adult survivors of child sexual abuse; Incest victims/survivors; Prevention program; Community education; Offender treatment program; Adolescent survivors of sexual abuse; Male survivors of sexual abuse

MIDDLE WAY HOUSE RAPE CRISIS CENTER
PO Box 95, 404 W 5th St, Bloomington, IN 47402
Crisis hotline: **(812) 336-0846 24 hrs**
Information: (812) 333-7404 9am-6pm
Contact: Toby Strout, Exec Dir
TYPE OF AGENCY: Rape crisis center; Domestic violence program; Child sexual abuse prevention program
AREAS SERVED: Monroe, Morgan, Lawrence, Owen, Greene, Martin
YEARS IN OPERATION: 4 months
LANGUAGES: Spanish, French, Japanese
ACCESSIBILITY: Wheelchair accessible
CASES SEXUAL ASSAULT/ABUSE (%): 100
DESCRIPTION: Rape crisis services, including support groups for female and male survivors of sexual assault/abuse
CLIENTS/SERVICES: Sexual assault survivors; Marital rape/sexual abuse survivors; Child victims of sexual abuse; Adult survivors of child sexual abuse; Incest victims/survivors; Prevention program; Community education; Adolescent survivors of sexual abuse; Male survivors of sexual abuse

COLUMBUS

TURNING POINT
PO Box 103, Columbus, IN 47202
Crisis hotline: **(800) 221-6311 statewide 24 hrs daily**
Information: (812) 379-9844 24 hrs daily
Contact: Ruthanne Rape, Dir
TYPE OF AGENCY: Domestic violence program; Adolescent program
AREAS SERVED: Bartholomew, Brown, Jackson, Jennings, Johnson, Jefferson, Ohio, Ripley, Switzerland, Shelby, Decatur, Dearborn
YEARS IN OPERATION: 7
ACCESSIBILITY: Wheelchair accessible
DESCRIPTION: Provides survivors of domestic violence/sexual abuse with advocacy, crisis intervention, emergency shelter, counseling, information, and referral. Also provides a program for batterers and support groups, individual counseling and crisis counseling for male survivors
CLIENTS/SERVICES: Sexual assault survivors; Marital rape/sexual abuse survivors; Adult survivors of child sexual abuse; Prevention program; Community education; Adolescent survivors of sexual abuse; Male survivors of sexual abuse
SPECIAL PROGRAMS/SERVICES: *When the Good Times Go Bad,* a 25-minute video about teenage dating violence. Video is used in 33 states and comes with manual of domestic violence facts, referral and assistance information, plus a series of exercises for group participants

CONNERSVILLE

FAYETTE COUNTY PROSECUTOR'S OFFICE—SEXUAL ASSAULT SERVICES
326 Central Ave, Connersville, IN 47331
Crisis hotline: **(317) 825-2999 24 hrs**
Information: (317) 825-2999 24 hrs
Contact: Shell Bowne, Dir
TYPE OF AGENCY: Rape crisis center
AREAS SERVED: Fayette
YEARS IN OPERATION: 3
ACCESSIBILITY: Wheelchair accessible
CASES SEXUAL ASSAULT/ABUSE (%): 100
CLIENTS/SERVICES: Sexual assault survivors; Marital rape/sexual abuse survivors; Child victims of sexual abuse; Adult survivors of child sexual abuse; Incest victims/survivors; Adolescent survivors of sexual abuse; Male survivors of sexual abuse

CRAWFORDSVILLE

FAMILY CRISIS SHELTER OF MONTGOMERY COUNTY, INC
PO Box 254, Crawfordsville, IN 47933
Crisis hotline: **(317) 362-2030 24 hrs**
Information: (317) 362-4888 9am-5pm
Contact: Elaine Hatfield, Exec Dir
TYPE OF AGENCY: Domestic violence program
AREAS SERVED: Putnam, Montgomery, Tippecanoe, Fountain
YEARS IN OPERATION: 10
ACCESSIBILITY: Wheelchair accessible; Signers for the hearing impaired
CASES SEXUAL ASSAULT/ABUSE (%): 3
DESCRIPTION: Domestic violence shelter providing emergency services for rape victims, as well as battered women and their children. Also provides batterers group, MEND
CLIENTS/SERVICES: Sexual assault survivors; Marital rape/sexual abuse survivors; Child victims of sexual abuse; Adult survivors of child sexual abuse; Prevention program; Community education

CROWN POINT

SOCIETY'S LEAGUE AGAINST MOLESTATION (SLAM)
PO Box 526, Crown Point, IN 46307
Crisis hotline: **(219) 662-0377 24 hrs**
Contact: Ann Mundis, V Pres
TYPE OF AGENCY: Child sexual abuse services; Child sexual abuse prevention program
AREAS SERVED: Lake (Porter)
YEARS IN OPERATION: 4
CASES SEXUAL ASSAULT/ABUSE (%): 100
DESCRIPTION: Speaking on issues related to child sexual abuse; Monitor courts; Help victims through legal system; Support groups for parents of victims and female and male adolescent and adult survivors
CLIENTS/SERVICES: Child victims of sexual abuse; Incest victims/survivors; Prevention program; Community education; Adolescent survivors of sexual abuse; Male survivors of sexual abuse; Publications/media
SPECIAL PROGRAMS/SERVICES: Purdue-Calumet University did documentary on society support meeting

ELKHART

FAMILY COUNSELING SERVICES OF ELKHART
101 E Hively Ave, Elkhart, IN 46517
Information: (219) 295-6596 8:30am-9pm (Mon, Tue); 8:30am-5pm (Wed, Thu, Fri)
Contact: Ethel Metzler, Clinical Staff Teamleader
TYPE OF AGENCY: Counseling/mental health services
AREAS SERVED: Elkhart, Kosciusko
YEARS IN OPERATION: 40
LANGUAGES: Spanish
ACCESSIBILITY: Wheelchair accessible
CASES SEXUAL ASSAULT/ABUSE (%): 10
CLIENTS/SERVICES: Sexual assault survivors; Child victims of sexual abuse; Adult survivors of child sexual abuse; Incest victims/survivors; Offender treatment program; Adolescent survivors of sexual abuse; Male survivors of sexual abuse

SUPPORT
200 E Jackson Blvd, Elkhart, IN 46516
Crisis hotline: **(219) 293-8671 24 hrs daily**
Information: (219) 295-6915 9am-5pm
Contact: Patricia Schultz, Coord
TYPE OF AGENCY: Rape crisis center; Child sexual abuse services; Child sexual abuse prevention program
SPONSORING ORGANIZATION: YWCA Women's Resource Center
AREAS SERVED: Elkhart
YEARS IN OPERATION: 14
ACCESSIBILITY: Wheelchair accessible
CASES SEXUAL ASSAULT/ABUSE (%): 100
CLIENTS/SERVICES: Sexual assault survivors; Marital rape/sexual abuse survivors; Child victims of sexual abuse; Adult survivors of child sexual abuse; Incest victims/survivors; Prevention program; Community education; Adolescent survivors of sexual abuse; Male survivors of sexual abuse

EVANSVILLE

CITIZENS AGAINST RAPE IN EVANSVILLE
PO Box 2099, Evansville, IN 47714
Crisis hotline: **(812) 424-7273 24 hrs**
Contact: Mary Hooper, Pres
TYPE OF AGENCY: Rape crisis center
YEARS IN OPERATION: 15
ACCESSIBILITY: Signers for the hearing impaired (by arrangement)
CASES SEXUAL ASSAULT/ABUSE (%): 100
CLIENTS/SERVICES: Sexual assault survivors; Adult survivors of child sexual abuse; Incest victims/survivors; Prevention program; Community education; Adolescent survivors of sexual abuse; Male survivors of sexual abuse

SOUTHWESTERN INDIANA MENTAL HEALTH CENTER—RAPE TREATMENT PROGRAM
415 Mulberry St, Evansville, IN 47713
Crisis hotline: **(812) 423-7791 24 hrs**
Information: (812) 423-7791 8am-5pm
Contact: Martha Julian, ACSW, Agency Rape Spec; Judy Reising-Knapp, ACSW, Child Sexual Abuse Coord; Dan DeMuth, ACSW, Perpetrator Spec
TYPE OF AGENCY: Counseling/mental health services; Child sexual abuse services
AREAS SERVED: Gibson, Posey, Warrick, Vanderburgh
YEARS IN OPERATION: 17
ACCESSIBILITY: Wheelchair accessible; Signers for the hearing impaired (arranged)
DESCRIPTION: Counseling for child and adult survivors of sexual assault; Counseling groups for mothers of survivors; Individual and group therapy for rapists, child sexual abuse offenders, incest offenders, batterers, and adolescent offenders
CLIENTS/SERVICES: Sexual assault survivors; Marital rape/sexual abuse survivors; Child victims of sexual abuse; Adult survivors of child sexual abuse; Incest victims/survivors; Prevention program; Community education; Offender treatment program; Adolescent survivors of sexual abuse; Male survivors of sexual abuse
REQUIREMENTS: Consent form for treatment must be signed; Sliding scale fee

WELBORN BAPTIST HOSPITAL— MULBERRY CENTER SEXUAL ABUSE AWARENESS PROGRAM
401 SE 6th St, Evansville, IN 47713
Information: (812) 426-8334 8am-4:30pm
Contact: Janet Raisor, Proj Dir
TYPE OF AGENCY: Hospital/medical center; Child sexual abuse services; Child sexual abuse prevention program; Residential treatment facility; Information center; Training/research
AREAS SERVED: Southern IN, Southeastern IL, KY
YEARS IN OPERATION: 1
ACCESSIBILITY: Wheelchair accessible
DESCRIPTION: Mulberry Center has three mental health units serving patients who may have experienced sexual/physical abuse: pediatric mental health, adolescent mental health, and eating disorders
CLIENTS/SERVICES: Sexual assault survivors; Marital rape/sexual abuse survivors; Child victims of sexual abuse; Adult survivors of child sexual abuse; Incest victims/survivors; Prevention program; Adolescent survivors of sexual abuse; Male survivors of sexual abuse; Publications/media
SPECIAL PROGRAMS/SERVICES: Recently received grant to establish a resource library of publications and videos designed for the continuing education of staff and for patient education in the area of child sexual abuse

YWCA BATTERED WOMEN'S SHELTER
118 Vine St, Evansville, IN 47708
Crisis hotline: **(812) 422-1191 24 hrs**
Information: (812) 422-1191 8am-5pm
Contact: Judy Hughes, Res Dir
TYPE OF AGENCY: Domestic violence program
SPONSORING ORGANIZATION: YWCA of Evansville
AREAS SERVED: Vandenbergh, Posey, Gibson, Warrick, Dubois
YEARS IN OPERATION: 9
CASES SEXUAL ASSAULT/ABUSE (%): 30
CLIENTS/SERVICES: Marital rape/sexual abuse survivors; Community education

FORT WAYNE

FAMILY AND CHILDREN'S SERVICES, INC
2712 S Calhoun St, Fort Wayne, IN 46807
Information: (219) 744-4326 8:30am-7pm (Mon-Fri)
Contact: M Peggy Jones, MSW, Clinical Svcs Dir
TYPE OF AGENCY: Counseling/mental health services; Child sexual abuse services
AREAS SERVED: Primarily Allen
YEARS IN OPERATION: 42
ACCESSIBILITY: Wheelchair accessible
DESCRIPTION: Provides individual therapy, play therapy, and group treatment for survivors; Treatment for child sexual abuse/incest offenders
CLIENTS/SERVICES: Child victims of sexual abuse; Adult survivors of child sexual abuse; Incest victims/survivors; Offender treatment program; Adolescent survivors of sexual abuse; Male survivors of sexual abuse

FORT WAYNE POLICE DEPARTMENT— VICTIM ASSISTANCE PROGRAM
1 Main St, City County Bldg, Fort Wayne, IN 46802
Crisis hotline: **(219) 427-1222 24 hrs**
Information: (219) 427-1205 8am-5pm
Contact: Patricia Smallwood, Dir
TYPE OF AGENCY: Victim/witness assistance program
AREAS SERVED: Allen
YEARS IN OPERATION: 10
LANGUAGES: French
ACCESSIBILITY: Wheelchair accessible
CASES SEXUAL ASSAULT/ABUSE (%): 10
CLIENTS/SERVICES: Sexual assault survivors; Marital rape/sexual abuse survivors; Child victims of sexual abuse; Incest victims/survivors; Community education; Adolescent survivors of sexual abuse; Male survivors of sexual abuse

PARK CENTER
909 E State, Fort Wayne, IN 46805
Crisis hotline: **(219) 482-9111 24 hrs daily**
Information: (219) 482-9111 24 hrs daily
Contact: Jan Tierney, Admis Sec
TYPE OF AGENCY: Counseling/mental health services
AREAS SERVED: Allen, Wells, Adams
YEARS IN OPERATION: 30
LANGUAGES: Spanish
ACCESSIBILITY: Wheelchair accessible; Signers for the hearing impaired
CASES SEXUAL ASSAULT/ABUSE (%): 15
CLIENTS/SERVICES: Sexual assault survivors; Child victims of sexual abuse; Adult survivors of child sexual abuse; Incest victims/survivors; Offender treatment program

Fort Wayne

RAPE AWARENESS PROGRAM
203 W Wayne, Central Bldg, Ste 305, Fort Wayne, IN 46802
Crisis hotline: **(219) 426-7273 (RAPE) 24 hrs**
Information: (219) 424-7977 8am-5pm (Mon-Fri)
Contact: Jeanne Harber Porter, Dir
TYPE OF AGENCY: Rape crisis center; Women's center
SPONSORING ORGANIZATION: Fort Wayne Women's Bureau, Inc
AREAS SERVED: Adams, Allen, DeKalb, Huntington, Noble, LaGrange, Steuben, Wells, Whitley
YEARS IN OPERATION: 12
LANGUAGES: Spanish, French
ACCESSIBILITY: Wheelchair accessible; Signers for the hearing impaired
CASES SEXUAL ASSAULT/ABUSE (%): 100
DESCRIPTION: Comprehensive rape crisis services, including feminist martial arts/self defense program
CLIENTS/SERVICES: Sexual assault survivors; Marital rape/sexual abuse survivors; Child victims of sexual abuse; Adult survivors of child sexual abuse; Incest victims/survivors; Prevention program; Community education; Adolescent survivors of sexual abuse; Male survivors of sexual abuse; Publications/media
SPECIAL PROGRAMS/SERVICES: Common Sense Self-Defense (6-week course) incorporates a co-trainer approach—counselor and instructor—to focus on mental and emotional preparation, verbal and physical self-defense from standing and on-the-ground positions; Media program of self defense class

FRANKLIN

JOHNSON COUNTY PROSECUTOR'S VICTIM ASSISTANCE PROGRAM
Courthouse Annex, Franklin, IN 46131
Crisis hotline: **(317) 736-5155 24 hrs**
Information: (317) 736-3796 9am-4pm (Mon-Wed)
Contact: Debra A Thompson, Prog Coord
TYPE OF AGENCY: Victim/witness assistance program; Child sexual abuse services
AREAS SERVED: Johnson
YEARS IN OPERATION: 3
LANGUAGES: Interpreters available
ACCESSIBILITY: Wheelchair accessible; Signers for the hearing impaired
CASES SEXUAL ASSAULT/ABUSE (%): 30
CLIENTS/SERVICES: Sexual assault survivors; Marital rape/sexual abuse survivors; Child victims of sexual abuse; Adult survivors of child sexual abuse; Incest victims/survivors; Community education; Adolescent survivors of sexual abuse; Male survivors of sexual abuse

GOSHEN

BRIDGEWORK THEATER, INC
113 ½ E Lincoln Ave, Goshen, IN 46526
Information: (219) 534-1085 8:30am-5pm
Contact: Don Yost, Exec Dir/Founder
TYPE OF AGENCY: Child sexual abuse prevention program; Touring theater
AREAS SERVED: States of IN, OH, MI, IL, WS, parts of IA
YEARS IN OPERATION: 9
LANGUAGES: *Little Bear* script available in Spanish
DESCRIPTION: Bridgework Theater is a touring children's theater that performs issue-oriented original plays. *Little Bear* and *Out of the Trap* are designed to help children prevent sexual abuse. The programs consist of three parts: inservice training for teachers, a live play performance, post-performance discussion period. *Little Bear* is for pre- through elementary schoolers and *Out of the Trap* is for upper-elementary and middle school students. *The Parent's Play* is for parents of school-aged children.
CLIENTS/SERVICES: Prevention program; Community education; Publications/media
SPECIAL PROGRAMS/SERVICES: Both *Little Bear* and *Out of the Trap* are available on videotape. Script licenses for agencies who wish to replicate program. *Little Bear* script available in Spanish. Publications: *Preventing Sexual Abuse: Activities and Strategies for Those Working with Children and Adolescents*, by Carol Plummer ($20)

INDIANAPOLIS

ADAPT
1001 W 10th St, Indianapolis, IN 46202
Crisis hotline: **(317) 630-7791 24 hrs**
Information: (317) 630-7606 24 hrs
Contact: Seth Crane, Victims Svcs; Darlene Fishburn, Men's Prog
TYPE OF AGENCY: Rape crisis center; Hospital/medical center
SPONSORING ORGANIZATION: Midtown Mental Health
AREAS SERVED: Marion
YEARS IN OPERATION: 3
LANGUAGES: Spanish, Sign
ACCESSIBILITY: Wheelchair accessible; Telecommunications for the hearing impaired (TTY, TDY, etc.); Signers for the hearing impaired
DESCRIPTION: Emergency room support by clinicians and volunteers for victims; Counseling services; Groups for batterers
CLIENTS/SERVICES: Sexual assault survivors; Marital rape/sexual abuse survivors; Child victims of sexual abuse; Adult survivors of child sexual abuse; Incest victims/survivors; Community education; Offender treatment program; Adolescent survivors of sexual abuse; Male survivors of sexual abuse

ADULT AND CHILD MENTAL HEALTH CENTER, INC
8110 Madison Ave, Winchester Professional Center, Indianapolis, IN 46227
Crisis hotline: **(317) 882-5122 24 hrs**
Information: (317) 882-5122 8am-5pm (Mon-Fri)
Contact: Ben Glancy, ACSW, Clinical Svcs Dir
TYPE OF AGENCY: Counseling/mental health services
AREAS SERVED: Southern Marion, Johnson
YEARS IN OPERATION: 30
DESCRIPTION: Provides diagnostic and treatment services for children, adolescents and their families
CLIENTS/SERVICES: Child victims of sexual abuse; Adolescent survivors of sexual abuse

CRISIS AND SUICIDE INTERVENTION SERVICE
1433 N Meridian St, Rm 202, Indianapolis, IN 46202
Crisis hotline: **(317) 632-7575 24 hrs**
Information: (317) 269-1569 9am-5pm (Mon-Fri)
Contact: Mary Hoffmann, Coord
TYPE OF AGENCY: Counseling/mental health services; Telephone crisis counseling; Information and referral services
SPONSORING ORGANIZATION: Mental Health Association in Marion County
YEARS IN OPERATION: 19
CASES SEXUAL ASSAULT/ABUSE (%): 7
DESCRIPTION: 24-hour telephone referral service; Refers to agencies within an eight county radius; Referrals for shelter, counseling, emergency response, and medical resources
CLIENTS/SERVICES: Sexual assault survivors; Marital rape/sexual abuse survivors; Child victims of sexual abuse; Adult survivors of child sexual abuse; Incest victims/survivors

INDIANAPOLIS POLICE DEPARTMENT— VICTIM ASSISTANCE UNIT
50 N Alabama, Indianapolis, IN 46204
Information: (317) 236-3331 7am-4pm
Contact: Sherri Maxfield, Judy Moore, Supvs
TYPE OF AGENCY: Victim/witness assistance program
YEARS IN OPERATION: 13
ACCESSIBILITY: Wheelchair accessible; Telecommunications for the hearing impaired (TTY, TDY, etc.); Signers for the hearing impaired
CASES SEXUAL ASSAULT/ABUSE (%): 25
CLIENTS/SERVICES: Sexual assault survivors; Marital rape/sexual abuse survivors; Child victims of sexual abuse; Adult survivors of child sexual abuse; Incest victims/survivors; Prevention program; Community education; Adolescent survivors of sexual abuse; Male survivors of sexual abuse

THE JULIAN CENTER, INC
3901 N Meridian St, Ste 10, Indianapolis, IN 46208
Information: (317) 923-9919 9am-5pm (Mon-Fri)
Contact: Naomi Tropp, Exec Dir
TYPE OF AGENCY: Domestic violence program
AREAS SERVED: Central IN
YEARS IN OPERATION: 14
ACCESSIBILITY: Wheelchair accessible
CASES SEXUAL ASSAULT/ABUSE (%): 50
CLIENTS/SERVICES: Sexual assault survivors; Marital rape/sexual abuse survivors; Adult survivors of child sexual abuse; Incest victims/survivors; Community education
REQUIREMENTS: Female and 18 years of age or older

MARION COUNTY PROSECUTOR'S OFFICE—VICTIM/WITNESS PROGRAM
City-County Bldg, Rm W-131, Indianapolis, IN 46204
Information: (317) 236-5103 8am-5pm
Contact: Sallie Wills, Supv
TYPE OF AGENCY: Victim/witness assistance program
AREAS SERVED: Marion
YEARS IN OPERATION: 2
ACCESSIBILITY: Wheelchair accessible
CASES SEXUAL ASSAULT/ABUSE (%): 60-75
CLIENTS/SERVICES: Sexual assault survivors; Marital rape/sexual abuse survivors; Child victims of sexual abuse; Adult survivors of child sexual abuse; Incest victims/survivors; Community education
REQUIREMENTS: Case must be filed and in the legal system

MIDTOWN COMMUNITY MENTAL HEALTH CENTER—FAMILY GROWTH CENTER
964 N Pennsylvania Ave, Indianapolis, IN 46202
Information: (317) 264-6991 8:30am-5pm (Mon-Fri)
Contact: Pat Jordan, Staff Therapist
TYPE OF AGENCY: Counseling/mental health services; Child sexual abuse services
AREAS SERVED: Marion, Johnson
YEARS IN OPERATION: 5
CASES SEXUAL ASSAULT/ABUSE (%): 100
CLIENTS/SERVICES: Child victims of sexual abuse; Incest victims/survivors; Community education; Offender treatment program; Adolescent survivors of sexual abuse
REQUIREMENTS: Referral by county DPW/CPS; Some self-pay, self-referred; Perpetrators pay for own treatment.

THE SALVATION ARMY SOCIAL SERVICE CENTER
540 N Alabama, Indianapolis, IN 46204
Crisis hotline: **(317) 637-5551 24 hrs**
Information: (317) 637-5551 8:30am-4:30pm
Contact: Peggy Burdsall, Family Life Development Coord
TYPE OF AGENCY: Domestic violence program; Counseling/mental health services; Child sexual abuse prevention program
AREAS SERVED: Marion
YEARS IN OPERATION: 25
ACCESSIBILITY: Wheelchair accessible

THE SALVATION ARMY SOCIAL SERVICE CENTER *(continued)*

CLIENTS/SERVICES: Sexual assault survivors; Marital rape/sexual abuse survivors; Child victims of sexual abuse; Adult survivors of child sexual abuse; Incest victims/survivors; Prevention program

SOJOURNER
PO Box 88062, Indianapolis, IN 46208
Crisis hotline: **(317) 632-7575 24 hrs**
Information: (317) 635-4674 24 hrs
Contact: Shelter Dir
TYPE OF AGENCY: Domestic violence program
YEARS IN OPERATION: 6
ACCESSIBILITY: Wheelchair accessible
CASES SEXUAL ASSAULT/ABUSE (%): 40
DESCRIPTION: Shelter for battered women and their children, and for women sexually assaulted by acquaintance or stranger
CLIENTS/SERVICES: Sexual assault survivors; Marital rape/sexual abuse survivors; Community education
REQUIREMENTS: Must be over 18 years

KOKOMO

YWCA—FAMILY INTERVENTION CENTER
406 E Sycamore St, Kokomo, IN 46901
Crisis hotline: **(317) 459-0314, (800) 642-9537 24 hrs**
Information: (317) 457-3293 8am-4pm
Contact: Gail Beaton, YWCA Asst Dir
TYPE OF AGENCY: Rape crisis center; Domestic violence program
AREAS SERVED: Howard, Cass, Miami, Tipton, Wabash
YEARS IN OPERATION: 9
LANGUAGES: Interpreters available
CASES SEXUAL ASSAULT/ABUSE (%): 50
DESCRIPTION: Domestic violence shelter; Counseling for sexual assault victims; Group therapy for batterers available
CLIENTS/SERVICES: Sexual assault survivors; Marital rape/sexual abuse survivors; Child victims of sexual abuse; Adult survivors of child sexual abuse; Incest victims/survivors; Community education; Adolescent survivors of sexual abuse

LA PORTE

VICTIM ADVOCATE DIVISION
Courthouse Sq, 5th Fl, La Porte, IN 46350
Information: (291) 326-6808, ext 373 8:30am-4:30pm
Contact: Diana L Dibkey, Victim Advocate Couns
TYPE OF AGENCY: Victim/witness assistance program
SPONSORING ORGANIZATION: La Porte County Prosecuting Attorney
AREAS SERVED: La Porte
YEARS IN OPERATION: 10
ACCESSIBILITY: Wheelchair accessible
CLIENTS/SERVICES: Sexual assault survivors; Marital rape/sexual abuse survivors; Child victims of sexual abuse; Incest victims/survivors; Community education
REQUIREMENTS: Police report must be filed

LAFAYETTE

FAMILY SERVICES, INC
225 N 4th St, Lafayette, IN 47901
Crisis hotline: **(317) 742-0244 24 hrs**
Information: (317) 423-5361 8am-9pm (Mon-Thu); 8am-5pm (Fri)
Contact: M Kay Hoff, Prog Dir
TYPE OF AGENCY: Counseling/mental health services; Child sexual abuse services; Child sexual abuse prevention program
AREAS SERVED: Tippecanoe and surrounding areas
YEARS IN OPERATION: 25
ACCESSIBILITY: Wheelchair accessible
CASES SEXUAL ASSAULT/ABUSE (%): 40
DESCRIPTION: Individual and family therapy, including therapy for batterers and family members
CLIENTS/SERVICES: Sexual assault survivors; Marital rape/sexual abuse survivors; Child victims of sexual abuse; Adult survivors of child sexual abuse; Incest victims/survivors; Prevention program; Community education; Offender treatment program; Adolescent survivors of sexual abuse; Male survivors of sexual abuse
REQUIREMENTS: Some age restrictions for certain programs; Some income eligibilities for certain services

TECUMSEH AREA PLANNED PARENTHOOD ASSOCIATION, INC
PO Box 1159, Lafayette, IN 47902
Crisis hotline: **(317) 742-9073 answering service after hrs**
Information: (317) 742-7281 9am-5pm
Contact: Jill Strand, RAPE Prog Coord; Patti O'Callaghan, DATE Prog Coord
TYPE OF AGENCY: Rape crisis center; Adolescent survivors services; Acquaintance/date rape prevention program
DESCRIPTION: Rape crisis and prevention services (RAPE Program); DATE program provides crisis intervention for adolescents who have been sexually assaulted and includes a date rape awareness and prevention program for adolescents. Both crisis services and prevention programs are provided by trained high school students who are peer advocates for teens
CLIENTS/SERVICES: Sexual assault survivors; Prevention program; Community education; Adolescent survivors of sexual abuse; Male survivors of sexual abuse
SPECIAL PROGRAMS/SERVICES: Publication: *Date Rape: Awareness and Prevention*, a curriculum guide and resource manual ($19.95)

LAWRENCEBURG

COMMUNITY MENTAL HEALTH CENTER—RAPE CRISIS PROGRAM
285 Bielby Rd, Lawrenceburg, IN 47025
Crisis hotline: **(800) 832-5378 24 hrs**
Information: (812) 537-1302 8:30am-5pm
Contact: Patty Cody, Rape Crisis Coord
TYPE OF AGENCY: Rape crisis center; Child sexual abuse prevention program
AREAS SERVED: Franklin, Ohio, Switzerland, Dearborn, Ripley
YEARS IN OPERATION: 12
ACCESSIBILITY: Wheelchair accessible
CASES SEXUAL ASSAULT/ABUSE (%): 100
CLIENTS/SERVICES: Sexual assault survivors; Prevention program; Community education

MARTINSVILLE

FAMILY SERVICE ASSOCIATION OF INDIANAPOLIS
PO Box 1592, Martinsville, IN 46151
Information: (317) 342-0202 8:30am-5pm (Wed, Fri); 12:30pm-8pm (Tue)
Contact: Mark Smith, Family Therapist
TYPE OF AGENCY: Counseling/mental health services
AREAS SERVED: Morgan
YEARS IN OPERATION: 4
CASES SEXUAL ASSAULT/ABUSE (%): 20
DESCRIPTION: Provides individual, couple, family, and group therapy, and treatment for incest offenders and batterers
CLIENTS/SERVICES: Sexual assault survivors; Marital rape/sexual abuse survivors; Child victims of sexual abuse; Adult survivors of child sexual abuse; Incest victims/survivors; Adolescent survivors of sexual abuse; Male survivors of sexual abuse
REQUIREMENTS: Sliding scale fee
SPECIAL PROGRAMS/SERVICES: Codependency treatment program that includes female and male sexual abuse victims

MISHAWAKA

FAMILY AND CHILDREN'S CENTER
1411 Lincolnway W, Mishawaka, IN 46544
Crisis hotline: **(219) 259-5666**
Information: (219) 259-5666
Contact: Priscilla Metzcus, Sexual Abuse Treatment Prog Supv
TYPE OF AGENCY: Child sexual abuse services; Residential treatment facility
AREAS SERVED: St Joseph, Elkhart, Marshall
YEARS IN OPERATION: 6
LANGUAGES: Spanish
ACCESSIBILITY: Wheelchair accessible
CASES SEXUAL ASSAULT/ABUSE (%): 33
DESCRIPTION: Provides individual, family, marriage, and group counseling for families in which incest has occurred. Services include Parents United and Sons and Daughters United.
CLIENTS/SERVICES: Child victims of sexual abuse; Adult survivors of child sexual abuse; Incest victims/survivors; Community education; Offender treatment program

MUNCIE

ASSOCIATES IN MENTAL HEALTH
420 W Washington, Muncie, IN 47305
Information: (317) 284-0879 8:30am-8pm (Mon-Fri); answering service
Contact: Cynthia Rice, ACSW, Clinical Social Worker
TYPE OF AGENCY: Child sexual abuse services; Private practice; Adult survivors services
AREAS SERVED: Delaware and surrounding counties
YEARS IN OPERATION: 3
LANGUAGES: Sign
ACCESSIBILITY: Wheelchair accessible; Signers for the hearing impaired
CASES SEXUAL ASSAULT/ABUSE (%): 75
DESCRIPTION: Has a well-equipped playroom for play therapy. Specializes in services for both child and adult survivors of sexual abuse. Treatment for child sexual abuse/incest offenders.
CLIENTS/SERVICES: Sexual assault survivors; Marital rape/sexual abuse survivors; Child victims of sexual abuse; Adult survivors of child sexual abuse; Incest victims/survivors; Community education; Offender treatment program; Creative arts therapy; Adolescent survivors of sexual abuse; Male survivors of sexual abuse; Healing
REQUIREMENTS: Take all forms of insurance, no sliding scale fees
SPECIAL PROGRAMS/SERVICES: Women's journal writing group for adult survivors, as well as workshop for women survivors using art, music, visualization, and healing rituals

A BETTER WAY
PO Box 734, Muncie, IN 47308
Crisis hotline: **(317) 747-9107 24 hrs**
Information: (317) 747-9107 24 hrs
Contact: Joyce Houser, Prog Dir
TYPE OF AGENCY: Domestic violence program
SPONSORING ORGANIZATION: Family Services of Delaware County, Inc
AREAS SERVED: Delaware, Blackford, Jay, Randolph, Henry
YEARS IN OPERATION: 10
ACCESSIBILITY: Wheelchair accessible
CLIENTS/SERVICES: Marital rape/sexual abuse survivors

Muncie

COALITION AGAINST RAPE
825 E Washington St, Muncie, IN 47305
Crisis hotline: **(317) 289-0404 24 hrs**
Information: (317) 747-6352 8am-5pm
Contact: Betty Johnson
TYPE OF AGENCY: Rape crisis center
AREAS SERVED: Delaware
YEARS IN OPERATION: 12
DESCRIPTION: Victim assistance/advocacy; Education for the community and the Ball State University campus; Facilitates support groups; Feminist martial arts/self-defense programs available
CLIENTS/SERVICES: Sexual assault survivors; Marital rape/sexual abuse survivors; Child victims of sexual abuse; Adult survivors of child sexual abuse; Incest victims/survivors; Prevention program; Community education; Adolescent survivors of sexual abuse; Male survivors of sexual abuse

PLANNED PARENTHOOD OF EAST CENTRAL INDIANA
110 N Cherry St, Muncie, IN 47305
Information: (317) 282-3546 9am-5:30pm (Mon-Fri)
TYPE OF AGENCY: Counseling/mental health services; Acquaintance/date rape prevention program; Adolescent program
AREAS SERVED: Delaware
YEARS IN OPERATION: 20
ACCESSIBILITY: Wheelchair accessible
DESCRIPTION: Date rape prevention program is included in the family life education program for junior and senior high schools and university students
CLIENTS/SERVICES: Prevention program; Community education
REQUIREMENTS: Teachers or youth service workers must ask for the materials

NOBLESVILLE

PREVAIL, INC
PO Box 755, Noblesville, IN 46060
Crisis hotline: **(317) 773-1282 (sheriffs dept) after hrs, weekends, holidays**
Information: (317) 773-6942 8:30am-5pm (Mon, Wed, Fri); 8:30am-8pm (Tue, Thu)
Contact: Beth Gehlhausen, Exec Dir
TYPE OF AGENCY: Victim/witness assistance program; Acquaintance/date rape prevention program
AREAS SERVED: Hamilton
YEARS IN OPERATION: 2
ACCESSIBILITY: Wheelchair accessible; Signers for the hearing impaired
CASES SEXUAL ASSAULT/ABUSE (%): 19
DESCRIPTION: Victim assistance services with specialized rape response team; Group therapy for batterers
CLIENTS/SERVICES: Sexual assault survivors; Marital rape/sexual abuse survivors; Child victims of sexual abuse; Adult survivors of child sexual abuse; Incest victims/survivors; Prevention program; Community education; Adolescent survivors of sexual abuse; Male survivors of sexual abuse
SPECIAL PROGRAMS/SERVICES: Date rape prevention in junior and senior high schools

SOUTH BEND

SEX OFFENSE SERVICES (SOS)
PO Box 80, 403 E Madison, South Bend, IN 46624
Crisis hotline: **(219) 289-HELP 24 hrs 7 days**
Information: (219) 234-0061 8am-5pm (Mon-Fri)
Contact: Laurel Eslinger, Coord
TYPE OF AGENCY: Rape crisis center; Child sexual abuse services; Child sexual abuse prevention program; Acquaintance/date rape prevention program
SPONSORING ORGANIZATION: Madison Center
AREAS SERVED: St Joseph
YEARS IN OPERATION: 14
LANGUAGES: Spanish
ACCESSIBILITY: Wheelchair accessible
CASES SEXUAL ASSAULT/ABUSE (%): 100
DESCRIPTION: Provides crisis intervention, escort/advocacy services through medical and legal systems and support groups for both female and male survivors. Prevention programs for preschool through elementary and middle school and date rape prevention for high school and college students. Madison Center treats rapists, batterers, and child sexual abuse/incest offenders
CLIENTS/SERVICES: Sexual assault survivors; Marital rape/sexual abuse survivors; Child victims of sexual abuse; Adult survivors of child sexual abuse; Incest victims/survivors; Prevention program; Community education; Adolescent survivors of sexual abuse; Male survivors of sexual abuse
SPECIAL PROGRAMS/SERVICES: Spanish language brochure

YWCA—WOMEN'S SHELTER
802 N Lafayette Blvd, South Bend, IN 46601
Crisis hotline: **(219) 233-9491 24 hrs**
Information: (219) 233-9491 24 hrs
Contact: Myrna Thomas, Domestic Violence Dir; Mona Mathis, Domestic Violence Svcs Dir
TYPE OF AGENCY: Domestic violence program
YEARS IN OPERATION: 7
LANGUAGES: Spanish
ACCESSIBILITY: Wheelchair accessible
CASES SEXUAL ASSAULT/ABUSE (%): 15
DESCRIPTION: Provides safe, temporary housing for victims of physical or emotional abuse and their children; Also serves many child sexual abuse survivors, adult survivors of child abuse, and assault victims where sexual abuse was involved
CLIENTS/SERVICES: Sexual assault survivors; Marital rape/sexual abuse survivors; Child victims of sexual abuse; Adult survivors of child sexual abuse; Incest victims/survivors; Community education; Adolescent survivors of sexual abuse

VALPARAISO

PORTER COUNTY SEXUAL ASSAULT RECOVERY PROJECT
County Courthouse, Rm 409, Valparaiso, IN 46383
Crisis hotline: **(219) 465-3408 8:30am-4:30pm**
Information: (219) 465-3415 8:30am-4:30pm
Contact: Carol Bradley, Proj Dir
TYPE OF AGENCY: Victim/witness assistance program
SPONSORING ORGANIZATION: Prosecutor's Office—Victim Assistance Unit
AREAS SERVED: Porter
YEARS IN OPERATION: 3
ACCESSIBILITY: Wheelchair accessible
CASES SEXUAL ASSAULT/ABUSE (%): 100
CLIENTS/SERVICES: Sexual assault survivors; Marital rape/sexual abuse survivors; Child victims of sexual abuse; Adult survivors of child sexual abuse; Incest victims/survivors; Prevention program; Community education; Adolescent survivors of sexual abuse

VINCENNES

HARBOR HOUSE
PO Box 601, Vincennes, IN 47591
Crisis hotline: **(812) 882-7900 24 hrs**
Information: (812) 882-7900 24 hrs
Contact: Myrna Brown, Exec Dir
TYPE OF AGENCY: Domestic violence program
AREAS SERVED: Knox, Daviess, Pike
YEARS IN OPERATION: 3
CASES SEXUAL ASSAULT/ABUSE (%): 5
CLIENTS/SERVICES: Sexual assault survivors; Marital rape/sexual abuse survivors; Adolescent survivors of sexual abuse

WARSAW

BOWEN CENTER FOR HUMAN SERVICES
850 N Harrison St, Warsaw, IN 46580
Crisis hotline: **(800) 342-5652 24 hrs daily**
Information: (219) 267-7169 8am-5pm (Mon, Wed, Fri); 8am-8pm (Tue, Thu)
Contact: Sandra Jackson, Protective Svcs Dir
TYPE OF AGENCY: Counseling/mental health services; Child sexual abuse services; Child sexual abuse prevention program
AREAS SERVED: Marshall, Kosciusko, Wabash, Huntington, Whitley
ACCESSIBILITY: Wheelchair accessible
DESCRIPTION: Provides individual, family and group counseling for child, adolescent and adult survivors of sexual abuse/assault and their families. Also treats batterers and child sexual abuse/incest offenders
CLIENTS/SERVICES: Sexual assault survivors; Marital rape/sexual abuse survivors; Child victims of sexual abuse; Adult survivors of child sexual abuse; Incest victims/survivors; Prevention program; Community education; Offender treatment program; Adolescent survivors of sexual abuse; Male survivors of sexual abuse
REQUIREMENTS: Offenders are required to attend until completion of program

WHEELER

THE CARING PLACE, INC
PO Box 194, Wheeler, IN 46393
Crisis hotline: **(219) 464-2128 24 hrs**
Information: (219) 464-2128 9am-5pm
Contact: Janet French, Exec Dir
TYPE OF AGENCY: Domestic violence program
AREAS SERVED: Lake, Porter, Starke
YEARS IN OPERATION: 10
ACCESSIBILITY: Wheelchair accessible; Signers for the hearing impaired (through deaf services)
CLIENTS/SERVICES: Sexual assault survivors; Marital rape/sexual abuse survivors; Adult survivors of child sexual abuse; Incest victims/survivors; Community education; Male survivors of sexual abuse

IOWA

AMES

ACCESS (ASSAULT CARE CENTER EXTENDING SHELTER AND SUPPORT)
PO Box 1965, Ames, IA 50010
Crisis hotline: **(515) 232-2303 24 hrs**
Information: (515) 232-5418 9am-5pm (Mon-Fri)
Contact: Laurie Schipper, Dir
TYPE OF AGENCY: Rape crisis center; Domestic violence program
AREAS SERVED: Story, Boone, Marshall, Webster, Greene, Carroll, Hamilton, Hardin
YEARS IN OPERATION: 14
ACCESSIBILITY: Wheelchair accessible
CASES SEXUAL ASSAULT/ABUSE (%): 26
CLIENTS/SERVICES: Sexual assault survivors; Marital rape/sexual abuse survivors; Adult survivors of child sexual abuse; Incest victims/survivors; Community education
REQUIREMENTS: 18 years and over.

CENTRAL IOWA MENTAL HEALTH CENTER
713 S Duff Ave, Ames, IA 50010
Information: (515) 232-5811 8am-6pm
TYPE OF AGENCY: Counseling/mental health services
AREAS SERVED: Boone, Greene, Story
YEARS IN OPERATION: 30
DESCRIPTION: Provides individual counseling for sexual assault survivors and relapse prevention program for sex offenders (rapists and child sexual abuse offenders). Also treats batterers
CLIENTS/SERVICES: Sexual assault survivors; Marital rape/sexual abuse survivors; Adult survivors of child sexual abuse; Incest victims/survivors; Community education; Offender treatment program; Male survivors of sexual abuse

THE CHILD ABUSE PREVENTION AND EDUCATION COUNCIL OF STORY COUNTY
Box 1004, Welch Ave Station, Ames, IA 50010
Information: (515) 292-3123 8am-5pm
Contact: Diane Nethercott, Gen'l Coord
TYPE OF AGENCY: Counseling/mental health services; Child sexual abuse prevention program; Child abuse prevention program
AREAS SERVED: Story
YEARS IN OPERATION: 9
DESCRIPTION: Works in supportive one-to-one relationships with parents to prevent child abuse; Workshops in schools for 3rd graders to prevent sexual abuse, using a creative drama approach
CLIENTS/SERVICES: Prevention program; Community education

CHILDSAFE
713 S Duff, Ste 2200, Ames, IA 50010
Information: (515) 232-3335 10am-5pm (Mon, Tue, Wed)
Contact: Marilyn S Lantz, Exec Dir
TYPE OF AGENCY: Child sexual abuse services
AREAS SERVED: Boone, Story
YEARS IN OPERATION: 3
ACCESSIBILITY: Wheelchair accessible
CASES SEXUAL ASSAULT/ABUSE (%): 100
DESCRIPTION: Counseling for sexually abused children, abusers, and families; Group therapy for incest offenders.
CLIENTS/SERVICES: Child victims of sexual abuse; Adult survivors of child sexual abuse; Incest victims/survivors; Community education; Offender treatment program; Adolescent survivors of sexual abuse
REQUIREMENTS: Survivors: ages 8 through adult. Perpetrators: court-ordered; sex abuse evaluation; must be admitting full responsibility.
SPECIAL PROGRAMS/SERVICES: Story County Intrafamily Sexual Abuse Program Team: made up of representatives from law enforcement, the county attorney's office, the department of human services, child protective investigations, juvenile court, and treatment agencies. Meets monthly to review all reported cases of child sexual abuse in the county, coordinates investigation and prosecution efforts, and makes treatment recommendations. The Child Sexual Abuse Task Force: made up of policymakers from all community agencies which provide services for sexual abuse victims, perpetrators, or family members. Meets to review the continuum of services available in the community, identify needs, and work cooperatively to fill them. Has sponsored training workshops and successfully recommended legislative changes.

OPEN LINE, INC
PO Box 1138, ISU Station, Ames, IA 50010
Crisis hotline: **(515) 292-7000 9am-midnight**
TYPE OF AGENCY: Counseling/mental health services; Telephone crisis hotline; Information and referral
YEARS IN OPERATION: 18
DESCRIPTION: Open Line is a free, confidential, volunteer listener, crisis intervention and information/referral phone service. Listens to people's concerns and helps them find resources to resolve their situation
CLIENTS/SERVICES: Sexual assault survivors

BOONE

YOUTH AND FAMILY COUNSELING CENTER
1015 Union St, Boone, IA 50036
Crisis hotline: **(515) 233-2330 24 hrs**
Information: (515) 432-7983 10am-6pm
Contact: Darla Diederich Jorgensen, Coord
TYPE OF AGENCY: Counseling/mental health services; Child sexual abuse services
SPONSORING ORGANIZATION: Youth and Shelter Services
AREAS SERVED: Boone, Greene
YEARS IN OPERATION: 7
ACCESSIBILITY: Wheelchair accessible
CASES SEXUAL ASSAULT/ABUSE (%): 35
DESCRIPTION: Offers a comprehensive treatment program for victims of child sexual abuse, specifically intrafamilial child sexual abuse. Treatment often includes individual therapy for victims, offender, and nonoffending parent, marital therapy, parent and victim therapy with offending parent, nonoffending parent, victim group therapy
CLIENTS/SERVICES: Child victims of sexual abuse; Incest victims/survivors; Community education; Offender treatment program; Adolescent survivors of sexual abuse; Male survivors of sexual abuse
REQUIREMENTS: Services are available to child victims of sexual abuse, ages 7 through 18, and their family members; Treatment for offenders must be court-ordered; Offense must be intrafamilial; Offender accepted into treatment program only if victim is also referred

BURLINGTON

YOUNG HOUSE FAMILY SERVICES, INC
105 Valley St, Burlington, IA 52601
Crisis hotline: **(319) 752-4000 answering machine**
Information: (319) 752-4000 9am-4pm
Contact: Sally Rodeffer, Family-Centered Svcs Coord
TYPE OF AGENCY: Counseling/mental health services; Child sexual abuse services; Child sexual abuse prevention program; Private practice
AREAS SERVED: Lee, Des Moines, Louisa, Henry
YEARS IN OPERATION: 7
LANGUAGES: Spanish interpreter available
ACCESSIBILITY: Signers for the hearing impaired
CASES SEXUAL ASSAULT/ABUSE (%): 25
DESCRIPTION: Provides family therapy, individual, and group treatment for victims and their families. Victims' groups ages 4-8, 9-12, 13-18 and non-offending spouses
CLIENTS/SERVICES: Child victims of sexual abuse; Adult survivors of child sexual abuse; Incest victims/survivors; Prevention program; Community education; Adolescent survivors of sexual abuse; Male survivors of sexual abuse
REQUIREMENTS: Referred by Dept of Human Services

YWCA SHELTER AND SUBSTANCE ABUSE CENTER
2410 Mt Pleasant, Burlington, IA 52601
Crisis hotline: **(319) 752-4475**
Information: (319) 752-1128
Contact: Sue Birkett
TYPE OF AGENCY: Rape crisis center; Domestic violence program

YWCA SHELTER AND SUBSTANCE ABUSE CENTER *(continued)*

CLIENTS/SERVICES: Sexual assault survivors; Marital rape/sexual abuse survivors; Child victims of sexual abuse; Incest victims/survivors; Adolescent survivors of sexual abuse

CARROLL

SUNRISE COUNSELING AND WELLNESS CENTER
PO Box 314, 322 E 6th St, Carroll, IA 51401
Information: (712) 792-3383 8am-6pm, 24-hr answering machine
Contact: Linda Trudeau, Dir
TYPE OF AGENCY: Private practice
AREAS SERVED: 6 surrounding counties
YEARS IN OPERATION: 1
ACCESSIBILITY: Wheelchair accessible
CASES SEXUAL ASSAULT/ABUSE (%): 10
DESCRIPTION: Individual and group counseling for survivors and their families; Treatment for batterers
CLIENTS/SERVICES: Sexual assault survivors; Marital rape/sexual abuse survivors; Child victims of sexual abuse; Adult survivors of child sexual abuse; Incest victims/survivors; Adolescent survivors of sexual abuse
REQUIREMENTS: If a child, Department of Human Services will be involved and services will be paid for by them under a purchase of services agreement. Adults are all private pay

CEDAR RAPIDS

CHILD PROTECTION CENTER
1026 A Ave NE, Cedar Rapids, IA 52402
Information: (319) 369-7908 24 hrs
Contact: Susan Tesdahl, Coord
TYPE OF AGENCY: Hospital/medical center; Child sexual abuse services; Child sexual abuse prevention program
SPONSORING ORGANIZATION: Saint Lukes Hospital
AREAS SERVED: East and Central Iowa
YEARS IN OPERATION: 2
ACCESSIBILITY: Wheelchair accessible
CASES SEXUAL ASSAULT/ABUSE (%): 94
DESCRIPTION: Provides interviews and physical examinations for children suspected of being sexually abused and counseling for children and non-offending parents
CLIENTS/SERVICES: Child victims of sexual abuse; Incest victims/survivors; Prevention program; Community education; Adolescent survivors of sexual abuse
REQUIREMENTS: Birth to 18 years of age

FAMILY SERVICE AGENCY
1330 1st Ave NE, Cedar Rapids, IA 52317
Information: (319) 398-3574 9am-5pm (Mon, Wed, Fri); 9am-9pm (Tue, Thu)
Contact: Mary E Lester, Marriage and Family Therapist
TYPE OF AGENCY: Counseling/mental health services
AREAS SERVED: Johnson, Linn, Benton
YEARS IN OPERATION: 20
ACCESSIBILITY: Wheelchair accessible
CASES SEXUAL ASSAULT/ABUSE (%): 40
DESCRIPTION: Offers family-oriented treatment, with expertise in domestic violence, child abuse and incest
CLIENTS/SERVICES: Sexual assault survivors; Marital rape/sexual abuse survivors; Child victims of sexual abuse; Adult survivors of child sexual abuse; Incest victims/survivors; Community education; Adolescent survivors of sexual abuse; Male survivors of sexual abuse

SEXUAL ABUSE TREATMENT PROGRAM
2309 C St SW, Cedar Rapids, IA 52404
Crisis hotline: **(319) 365-9164 24 hr pager**
Information: (319) 365-9164 24 hr pager
Contact: Cindy Burke, Coord Supv
TYPE OF AGENCY: Counseling/mental health services; Child sexual abuse services
SPONSORING ORGANIZATION: Children's Home of Cedar Rapids
AREAS SERVED: Linn, Jones, Johnson, Iowa, Benton
YEARS IN OPERATION: 2
ACCESSIBILITY: Wheelchair accessible
DESCRIPTION: Provides individual, family, and group therapy for sexually abused individuals, their families, and offenders in the case of incest. Therapy progresses in sequential fashion over 18-24 months, takes place in the family home, involves therapeutic activities groups for children, and has an evaluation and research component conducted by the University of Iowa School of Social Work
CLIENTS/SERVICES: Sexual assault survivors; Marital rape/sexual abuse survivors; Child victims of sexual abuse; Adult survivors of child sexual abuse; Incest victims/survivors; Community education; Offender treatment program; Adolescent survivors of sexual abuse; Male survivors of sexual abuse

SIXTH DISTRICT DEPARTMENT OF CORRECTIONS, SEX OFFENDERS TREATMENT PROGRAM
221 4th Ave SE, Ste 202, Cedar Rapids, IA 52401
Information: (319) 398-3459 8am-5pm (Mon-Fri)
Contact: Cindy Engler, Parole/ISP/SOTP Supv II
TYPE OF AGENCY: Offender treatment
AREAS SERVED: Linn, Johnson, Jones, Iowa, Tama, Benton
YEARS IN OPERATION: ½
ACCESSIBILITY: Wheelchair accessible; Signers for the hearing impaired
CASES SEXUAL ASSAULT/ABUSE (%): 90
DESCRIPTION: Provides intensive supervision of sex offenders in a community-based program. Treatment through groups, assignments, personal log books, and intensive contact standards for rapists, child sexual abuse/incest offenders, and batterers
CLIENTS/SERVICES: Offender treatment program
REQUIREMENTS: Adult male/female parolee/probationer who meets eligibility guidelines

YWCA SEXUAL ASSAULT INTERVENTION PROGRAM
318 5th St SE, Cedar Rapids, IA 52401
Crisis hotline: **(319) 363-5490 24 hrs**
Information: (319) 365-1458 8am-8pm
Contact: Diane Finnerty, Coord
TYPE OF AGENCY: Rape crisis center; Domestic violence program
AREAS SERVED: Linn, Benton, Cedar, Iowa, Jones
YEARS IN OPERATION: 14
ACCESSIBILITY: Wheelchair accessible; Signers for the hearing impaired
CASES SEXUAL ASSAULT/ABUSE (%): 100
DESCRIPTION: Comprehensive rape crisis services; Personal safety program for the elderly; Groups for batterers
CLIENTS/SERVICES: Sexual assault survivors; Marital rape/sexual abuse survivors; Child victims of sexual abuse; Adult survivors of child sexual abuse; Incest victims/survivors; Prevention program; Community education; Adolescent survivors of sexual abuse; Male survivors of sexual abuse; Elderly

CLINTON

WOMEN'S RESOURCE CENTER
317 7th Ave S, Clinton, IA 52732
Crisis hotline: **(319) 243-7867 24 hrs**
Information: (319) 242-2118 8am-4pm
Contact: Sue Bloch, Dir
TYPE OF AGENCY: Rape crisis center; Domestic violence program
AREAS SERVED: Clinton, Jackson, IA; Whiteside, Carroll, IL
YEARS IN OPERATION: 10
CASES SEXUAL ASSAULT/ABUSE (%): 10
CLIENTS/SERVICES: Sexual assault survivors; Marital rape/sexual abuse survivors; Adult survivors of child sexual abuse; Incest victims/survivors; Prevention program; Community education; Male survivors of sexual abuse

COUNCIL BLUFFS

CATHOLIC SOCIAL SERVICE—DOMESTIC VIOLENCE PROGRAM
315 W Pierce, Council Bluffs, IA 51503
Crisis hotline: **(712) 328-0266 24 hrs**
Information: (712) 328-3087 8:30am-12pm, 1pm-4:30pm (Mon-Fri)
Contact: Stephanie Preusch, Domestic Violence Coord
TYPE OF AGENCY: Rape crisis center; Domestic violence program; Counseling/mental health services; Child sexual abuse services
SPONSORING ORGANIZATION: United Way
AREAS SERVED: Pottawattamie, Mills, Harrison, Shelby, Cass
YEARS IN OPERATION: 9
ACCESSIBILITY: Signers for the hearing impaired
CASES SEXUAL ASSAULT/ABUSE (%): 10
DESCRIPTION: Community-based program designed to work with violence at all levels. Parents United, Daughters and Sons United, Adults Molested as Children programs directly treat offenders, spouses, siblings, and victims of incest and sexual abuse; Individual and group therapy for rapists, child sexual abuse offenders, incest offenders, and batterers
CLIENTS/SERVICES: Sexual assault survivors; Marital rape/sexual abuse survivors; Child victims of sexual abuse; Adult survivors of child sexual abuse; Incest victims/survivors; Community education; Offender treatment program; Non-offending parent; Adolescent survivors of sexual abuse; Male survivors of sexual abuse

SEXUAL ABUSE TREATMENT TEAM/KIDABILITY
Box 779, Council Bluffs, IA 51502
Information: (712) 328-4740 (Mon,Thu)
TYPE OF AGENCY: Child sexual abuse services; Child sexual abuse prevention program
SPONSORING ORGANIZATION: Southwest Iowa Coalition for Families
AREAS SERVED: Pottawattamie
YEARS IN OPERATION: 6
CLIENTS/SERVICES: Child victims of sexual abuse; Prevention program; Offender treatment program

DES MOINES

DES MOINES CHILD AND ADOLESCENT GUIDANCE CENTER, INC
1206 Pleasant St, Des Moines, IA 50309
Information: (515) 244-2267 8:30am-5pm
Contact: Glenn Baughman, ACSW, Chief Soc Wkr
TYPE OF AGENCY: Counseling/mental health services; Child sexual abuse services
AREAS SERVED: Polk, Warren
YEARS IN OPERATION: 52
LANGUAGES: Spanish
ACCESSIBILITY: Wheelchair accessible
CASES SEXUAL ASSAULT/ABUSE (%): 20
DESCRIPTION: Component agency in the Polk County Intrafamily Sexual Abuse Program sponsored by the Polk County Attorney's Office and Department of Human Services, treating sexually abused children and their families and adolescent sex offenders

DES MOINES CHILD AND ADOLESCENT GUIDANCE CENTER, INC
(continued)

CLIENTS/SERVICES: Child victims of sexual abuse; Incest victims/survivors; Offender treatment program; Adolescent survivors of sexual abuse; Male survivors of sexual abuse

POLK COUNTY VICTIM SERVICES—RAPE CARE PROGRAM AND INTRAFAMILY SEXUAL ABUSE PROGRAM
1915 Hickman, Des Moines, IA 50265
Crisis hotline: **(515) 286-3838 24 hrs**
Information: (515) 286-3832 8am-4:30pm
Contact: Marti Anderson, Victim Svcs Dir
TYPE OF AGENCY: Rape crisis center; Counseling/mental health services; Child sexual abuse services
SPONSORING ORGANIZATION: Polk County Department of Social Services
AREAS SERVED: Polk
YEARS IN OPERATION: 15
ACCESSIBILITY: Wheelchair accessible; Signers for the hearing impaired (by arrangement)
CASES SEXUAL ASSAULT/ABUSE (%): 100
CLIENTS/SERVICES: Sexual assault survivors; Marital rape/sexual abuse survivors; Child victims of sexual abuse; Adult survivors of child sexual abuse; Incest victims/survivors; Community education; Adolescent survivors of sexual abuse; Male survivors of sexual abuse; Publications/media
SPECIAL PROGRAMS/SERVICES: Sponsors Take Back the Night, a rally and march protesting violence against women, and Victims Rights Week; Videos on acquaintance rape, child witness and *Why Me?* (Crime victims)

YWCA OF GREATER DES MOINES
717 Grand Ave, Des Moines, IA 50309
Crisis hotline: **(515) 244-8961 24 hrs**
Information: (515) 244-8961 24 hrs
Contact: Bruce Mason, Fac Dir
TYPE OF AGENCY: Domestic violence program
AREAS SERVED: Central Iowa
ACCESSIBILITY: Wheelchair accessible
CASES SEXUAL ASSAULT/ABUSE (%): 1
CLIENTS/SERVICES: Marital rape/sexual abuse survivors

DUBUQUE

RAPE/SEXUAL ASSAULT INTERVENTION PROGRAM
Mercy Dr, Dubuque, IA 52001
Crisis hotline: **(319) 588-4016 24 hrs**
Information: (319) 589-9645 9am-5pm (Mon-Fri)
Contact: Brenna Healy, Psychologist
TYPE OF AGENCY: Counseling/mental health services
SPONSORING ORGANIZATION: Dubuque County Mental Health
AREAS SERVED: Dubuque
YEARS IN OPERATION: 12
ACCESSIBILITY: Wheelchair accessible
CASES SEXUAL ASSAULT/ABUSE (%): 100
DESCRIPTION: Offers group therapy for female adults who are survivors of incest and individual therapy for any survivor of rape or sexual assault. Provides treatment for rapists, child sexual abuse/incest offenders, and batters
CLIENTS/SERVICES: Sexual assault survivors; Marital rape/sexual abuse survivors; Child victims of sexual abuse; Adult survivors of child sexual abuse; Incest victims/survivors; Prevention program; Community education; Adolescent survivors of sexual abuse; Male survivors of sexual abuse

ESTHERVILLE

COUNCIL FOR THE PREVENTION OF DOMESTIC VIOLENCE
PO Box 151, Estherville, IA 51334
Crisis hotline: **(712) 362-4612 24 hrs**
Information: (712) 362-4612 8am-4pm
Contact: Mary Hart, Prog Coord
TYPE OF AGENCY: Rape crisis center; Domestic violence program; Child sexual abuse prevention program
AREAS SERVED: Clay, Dickinson, Emmet, Palo Alto
YEARS IN OPERATION: 4
ACCESSIBILITY: Wheelchair accessible
CASES SEXUAL ASSAULT/ABUSE (%): 50
DESCRIPTION: Provides services for survivors of domestic and sexual assault; Feminist martial arts/self defense program; Treatment program for batterers
CLIENTS/SERVICES: Sexual assault survivors; Marital rape/sexual abuse survivors; Child victims of sexual abuse; Adult survivors of child sexual abuse; Incest victims/survivors; Prevention program; Community education; Adolescent survivors of sexual abuse; Male survivors of sexual abuse

FORT DODGE

RAPE/SEXUAL ASSAULT VICTIM ADVOCATES
S Kenyon Rd, Fort Dodge, IA 50501
Crisis hotline: **(515) 573-8000 24 hrs**
Information: (515) 573-3101, ext 57 9am-3pm (Mon, Tue, Fri)
Contact: Teri Simpson, R/SAVA Coord
TYPE OF AGENCY: Rape crisis center
SPONSORING ORGANIZATION: Trinity Regional Hospital
AREAS SERVED: Webster, Humboldt, Hamilton, Write, Calhoun
YEARS IN OPERATION: 11
CASES SEXUAL ASSAULT/ABUSE (%): 99
CLIENTS/SERVICES: Sexual assault survivors; Child victims of sexual abuse; Incest victims/survivors; Prevention program; Community education; Adolescent survivors of sexual abuse; Male survivors of sexual abuse

IOWA CITY

JOHNSON COUNTY ATTORNEY'S OFFICE—VICTIM/WITNESS ASSISTANCE PROGRAM
PO Box 2450, Iowa City, IA 52244
Information: (319) 339-6100 8am-5pm (Mon-Fri)
Contact: Christie Munson, Coord
TYPE OF AGENCY: Victim/witness assistance program
AREAS SERVED: Johnson
YEARS IN OPERATION: 2
LANGUAGES: Spanish
ACCESSIBILITY: Wheelchair accessible
CLIENTS/SERVICES: Sexual assault survivors; Marital rape/sexual abuse survivors; Child victims of sexual abuse; Community education
REQUIREMENTS: There are no restrictions, however most of the victims served are involved in court process.

RAPE VICTIM ADVOCACY PROGRAM
17 W Prentiss St, Iowa City, IA 52240
Crisis hotline: **(319) 335-6000 24 hrs**
Information: (319) 335-6001 9am-5pm (Mon-Fri)
Contact: Karla S Miller, Dir
TYPE OF AGENCY: Rape crisis center; Child sexual abuse prevention program
AREAS SERVED: Johnson
YEARS IN OPERATION: 16
LANGUAGES: Interpreters available
ACCESSIBILITY: Wheelchair accessible; Signers for the hearing impaired
CASES SEXUAL ASSAULT/ABUSE (%): 100
CLIENTS/SERVICES: Sexual assault survivors; Adult survivors of child sexual abuse; Prevention program; Community education; Adolescent survivors of sexual abuse; Male survivors of sexual abuse; Preschoolers
SPECIAL PROGRAMS/SERVICES: First STEPS (Strategies for Teaching Empowerment, Prevention, and Safety) is a preschool sexual abuse prevention curriculum. Training for daycare/homecare providers on use of the curriculum is offered yearly in Iowa City and in other areas by arrangement

SIXTH JUDICIAL DISTRICT DEPARTMENT OF CORRECTIONAL SERVICES
PO Box 1907, Iowa City, IA 52244
Crisis hotline: **(319) 351-1090 7am-5pm**
Information: (319) 351-1090 7am-5pm
Contact: Rachael Hromidko, Advisor/Co-Facilitator
TYPE OF AGENCY: Correctional facility; Offender treatment
AREAS SERVED: Johnson, Iowa
YEARS IN OPERATION: 1
CASES SEXUAL ASSAULT/ABUSE (%): 100
DESCRIPTION: Group therapy for rapists, child sexual abuse/incest offenders and batterers
CLIENTS/SERVICES: Offender treatment program
REQUIREMENTS: Must have been found guilty of sexual offense and have been referred by the court system

UNITED ACTION FOR YOUTH
410 Iowa Ave, Iowa City, IA 52240
Crisis hotline: **(319) 338-7518 24 hrs daily**
Information: (319) 338-9279 9am-5pm
Contact: Linda Nelson, Prevention Dir
TYPE OF AGENCY: Adolescent program
AREAS SERVED: Johnson
YEARS IN OPERATION: 15
LANGUAGES: Spanish, Filipino
ACCESSIBILITY: Wheelchair accessible; Signers for the hearing impaired (with notice)
CASES SEXUAL ASSAULT/ABUSE (%): 25
DESCRIPTION: Individual and family counseling; Runaway services; Support groups for sexually abused adolescents; Advocacy for youth who are victims of abuse and involved in court process; Parent support services; Workshops for teachers and parents on child sexual abuse prevention and self-defense training for adolescents
CLIENTS/SERVICES: Sexual assault survivors; Child victims of sexual abuse; Incest victims/survivors; Prevention program; Community education; Adolescent survivors of sexual abuse; Male survivors of sexual abuse; Healing; Publications/media
REQUIREMENTS: Ages 12-18
SPECIAL PROGRAMS/SERVICES: Healing for survivors through Synthesis Arts Workshop (music recording studio, television production, 8mm animation, photography, ceramics, electronic music); Publishes *Alternative Shapes of Reality*, a magazine of arts, poetry, prose, photography, and opinions produced by local youth; Sponsors performing drama troupe of high school students which portrays problem situations including sexual abuse and domestic violence faced by children and adolescents

WOMEN'S RESOURCE AND ACTION CENTER
130 N Madison St, Iowa City, IA 52242
Information: (319) 335-1486 9am-7pm (Mon-Thu); 9am-5pm (Fri)
TYPE OF AGENCY: College/university-based services
SPONSORING ORGANIZATION: University of Iowa
AREAS SERVED: Johnson, Linn, Cedar,
YEARS IN OPERATION: 17
LANGUAGES: Spanish
ACCESSIBILITY: Wheelchair accessible; Signers for the hearing impaired
CASES SEXUAL ASSAULT/ABUSE (%): 10

WOMEN'S RESOURCE AND ACTION CENTER (continued)

DESCRIPTION: Feminist agency providing skills, support, information, and advocacy for University of Iowa students, staff, faculty, and women in the surrounding community and throughout the state. Services include counseling and support groups for adult incest survivors.
CLIENTS/SERVICES: Adult survivors of child sexual abuse; Incest victims/survivors
REQUIREMENTS: Services are restricted to women only.

KEOKUK

TRI-STATE COALITION AGAINST FAMILY VIOLENCE
PO Box 494, Keokuk, IA 52632
Crisis hotline: **(319) 524-4445 24 hrs**
Information: (319) 524-4445 24 hrs
Contact: Nancy Jones, Exec Dir
TYPE OF AGENCY: Domestic violence program
AREAS SERVED: Lee, IA; Clark, MS; Hancock, IL
YEARS IN OPERATION: 7
CASES SEXUAL ASSAULT/ABUSE (%): 2
DESCRIPTION: Services for survivors of sexual assault and domestic violence, including support groups for female and male survivors; Group therapy for batterers
CLIENTS/SERVICES: Sexual assault survivors; Marital rape/sexual abuse survivors; Child victims of sexual abuse; Adult survivors of child sexual abuse; Incest victims/survivors; Community education; Adolescent survivors of sexual abuse; Male survivors of sexual abuse

MASON CITY

CRISIS INTERVENTION SERVICE
22 N Georgia, Rm 208, Mason City, IA 50401
Crisis hotline: **(515) 424-9133 24 hrs**
Information: (515) 424-9071 8:30am-5pm (Mon-Fri)
Contact: Jackie Bailey, Proj Coord
TYPE OF AGENCY: Domestic violence program
SPONSORING ORGANIZATION: NIAD Center for Human Development
AREAS SERVED: Cerro Gordo, Floyd, Franklin, Hancock, Kossuth, Mitchell, Winnebago, Worth
YEARS IN OPERATION: 7
LANGUAGES: Spanish
ACCESSIBILITY: Wheelchair accessible; Signers for the hearing impaired
CASES SEXUAL ASSAULT/ABUSE (%): 5
DESCRIPTION: Provides crisis services including a 24-hr crisis line, safe-home shelters, emergency transportation; Feminist martial arts/self defense program
CLIENTS/SERVICES: Marital rape/sexual abuse survivors; Prevention program; Community education; Male survivors of sexual abuse
SPECIAL PROGRAMS/SERVICES: Children's domestic violence *Finding Your Feelings* packet

PARENTS UNITED OF NORTH CENTRAL IOWA, INC
201 Willowbrook Dr, Mason City, IA 50401
Crisis hotline: **(515) 421-1210 24 hrs**
Information: (515) 424-5232 24 hrs
Contact: Delphine Justin, MSW, PU Coord; Patricia Tomson, Asst Coord
TYPE OF AGENCY: Child sexual abuse services; Private practice
SPONSORING ORGANIZATION: Counseling Associates of North Central Iowa, Inc
AREAS SERVED: Cerro Gordo, Winnebago, Worth, Hancock, Franklin, Kassouth, Floyd, Butler, Mitchell
YEARS IN OPERATION: 5
CASES SEXUAL ASSAULT/ABUSE (%): 100
DESCRIPTION: Groups for offenders and survivors of sexual abuse and their families, including Parents United, Adults Molested as Children, spouses of adult survivors, Daughters and Sons United, siblings, adolescent offenders, and Parents United for Non-Incestuous Adults (for parents of children molested outside the family)
CLIENTS/SERVICES: Child victims of sexual abuse; Adult survivors of child sexual abuse; Incest victims/survivors; Prevention program; Community education; Offender treatment program; Adolescent survivors of sexual abuse; Male survivors of sexual abuse
REQUIREMENTS: Offendr must admit to guilt; All family members must be involved if child is involved. If reportable case, it must be reported
SPECIAL PROGRAMS/SERVICES: Annual *Free to Be Me* conference

MOUNT PLEASANT

MOUNT PLEASANT CORRECTIONAL FACILITY
Hwy 218 S, Mount Pleasant, IA 52641
Information: (319) 385-9511 7:30am-4pm (Mon-Fri)
Contact: Dennis Kuster, Unit Mgr
TYPE OF AGENCY: Correctional facility; Offender treatment
SPONSORING ORGANIZATION: Iowa Department of Corrections
AREAS SERVED: Statewide
YEARS IN OPERATION: 5
ACCESSIBILITY: Wheelchair accessible
CASES SEXUAL ASSAULT/ABUSE (%): 100
DESCRIPTION: The sexual offender treatment program is housed in a 600-man medium security prison. Full-treatment therapy program (primarily group therapy) for all types of sex offenders, including rapists, child sexual abuse/incest offenders, and batterers. Since about 50% of offenders were victims themselves, therapy addresses issues for sexual victimization
CLIENTS/SERVICES: Offender treatment program

MUSCATINE

RAPE/ASSAULT CARE SERVICES
Medical Arts Bldg, 119 Sycamore, Ste 200, Muscatine, IA 52761
Crisis hotline: **(319) 263-8080 24 hrs**
Information: (319) 263-8080 24 hrs
Contact: Jeanne Johnson, Prog Coord/Couns
TYPE OF AGENCY: Rape crisis center; Domestic violence program
SPONSORING ORGANIZATION: Family Resources, Inc
AREAS SERVED: Muscatine
YEARS IN OPERATION: 11
ACCESSIBILITY: Wheelchair accessible
CASES SEXUAL ASSAULT/ABUSE (%): 25
CLIENTS/SERVICES: Sexual assault survivors; Marital rape/sexual abuse survivors; Child victims of sexual abuse; Adult survivors of child sexual abuse; Prevention program; Community education; Adolescent survivors of sexual abuse; Male survivors of sexual abuse

NEVADA

STORY COUNTY ATTORNEY'S OFFICE—VICTIM WITNESS ASSISTANCE PROGRAM
Story County Courthouse, Nevada, IA 50201
Information: (515) 382-6581 8am-5pm
Contact: Rhonda Lovell, Victim Witness Coord
TYPE OF AGENCY: Victim/witness assistance program
AREAS SERVED: Story
YEARS IN OPERATION: 2½
LANGUAGES: Spanish
ACCESSIBILITY: Wheelchair accessible
CASES SEXUAL ASSAULT/ABUSE (%): 2-5
CLIENTS/SERVICES: Sexual assault survivors; Marital rape/sexual abuse survivors; Child victims of sexual abuse; Incest victims/survivors; Community education; Adolescent survivors of sexual abuse
REQUIREMENTS: In most cases an offender must be apprehended and charges must be filed

NEW PROVIDENCE

QUAKERDALE HOME
Box 8, New Providence, IA 50206
Crisis hotline: **(515) 497-5295, 497-5296, 497-5297 24 hrs**
Information: (515) 497-5294 8am-5pm (Mon-Fri)
Contact: Elinor Castle, Soc Wkr
TYPE OF AGENCY: Residential treatment facility; Adolescent program
AREAS SERVED: Statewide
YEARS IN OPERATION: 138
ACCESSIBILITY: Wheelchair accessible
CASES SEXUAL ASSAULT/ABUSE (%): 50-60
DESCRIPTION: Residential program for adolescents the court has judged in need of assistance or delinquent; Separate therapy groups for males and females who have been sexually abused; Treatment for adolescent sex offenders
CLIENTS/SERVICES: Sexual assault survivors; Child victims of sexual abuse; Incest victims/survivors; Prevention program; Offender treatment program; Adolescent survivors of sexual abuse; Healing
REQUIREMENTS: Youth ages 12-18; Mandatory reporting of sexual abuse
SPECIAL PROGRAMS/SERVICES: Art therapy and writing, relies heavily on the grief model, since youth have suffered loss of trust, virginity, normal development, normal family roles, and functions

SIOUX CENTER

DOMESTIC VIOLENCE AID CENTER, INC
Professional Bldg, 128 3rd St NW, Sioux Center, IA 51250
Crisis hotline: **(712) 737-3306 24 hrs**
Information: (712) 722-4404 24 hrs
Contact: Phyllis Van Den Hul, Dir
TYPE OF AGENCY: Domestic violence program
AREAS SERVED: Sioux, Lyon, Osceola, O'Brien, Plymouth
YEARS IN OPERATION: 7
ACCESSIBILITY: Wheelchair accessible
DESCRIPTION: Services for domestic violence survivors; Group therapy for batterers
CLIENTS/SERVICES: Marital rape/sexual abuse survivors; Prevention program; Community education

SIOUX CITY

AID CENTER
206 6th St, Sioux City, IA 51101
Crisis hotline: **(712) 258-7233 24 hrs**
Information: (712) 258-7233 24 hrs
Contact: Pat Somsky, Dir
TYPE OF AGENCY: Counseling/mental health services; Information and referral; Telephone crisis hotline
AREAS SERVED: Woodbury
YEARS IN OPERATION: 9
CLIENTS/SERVICES: Sexual assault survivors

BOYS AND GIRLS HOME AND FAMILY SERVICES
2601 Douglas St, Sioux City, IA 51104
Crisis hotline: **(712) 277-4031 24 hrs daily**
Information: (712) 277-4031 8:30am-5pm (Mon, Tue, Thu, Fri); 8:30am-9pm (Wed)
Contact: Dean Williams, ACSW LSW, MH Svcs Dir
TYPE OF AGENCY: Counseling/mental health services; Residential treatment facility
AREAS SERVED: Siouxland area

BOYS AND GIRLS HOME AND FAMILY SERVICES *(continued)*
YEARS IN OPERATION: 94
LANGUAGES: Spanish
CASES SEXUAL ASSAULT/ABUSE (%): 15-20
CLIENTS/SERVICES: Sexual assault survivors; Child victims of sexual abuse; Adult survivors of child sexual abuse; Incest victims/survivors; Offender treatment program; Adolescent survivors of sexual abuse; Male survivors of sexual abuse
REQUIREMENTS: Generally require perpetrators to have charges filed on them

COUNCIL ON SEXUAL ASSAULT AND DOMESTIC VIOLENCE
PO Box 1565, Sioux City, IA 51102
Crisis hotline: **(712) 258-7233 24 hrs**
Information: (712) 258-7233 8am-5pm (Mon-Fri)
Contact: Pat Somsky, Exec Dir
TYPE OF AGENCY: Rape crisis center; Domestic violence program
AREAS SERVED: Woodbury, Plymouth, Crawford, Monona, IA; Union, SD; Dakota, NE
YEARS IN OPERATION: 10
LANGUAGES: Spanish, Vietnamese, interpreters available
ACCESSIBILITY: Wheelchair accessible; Signers for the hearing impaired
CASES SEXUAL ASSAULT/ABUSE (%): 25
DESCRIPTION: Comprehensive services for sexual assault and domestic violence survivors; feminist martial arts/self defense program
CLIENTS/SERVICES: Sexual assault survivors; Marital rape/sexual abuse survivors; Child victims of sexual abuse; Adult survivors of child sexual abuse; Prevention program; Community education; Adolescent survivors of sexual abuse; Male survivors of sexual abuse

PARKVIEW PSYCHOLOGICAL SERVICES
2800 Pierce St, Sioux City, IA 51104
Information: (712) 252-3262 9am-5pm
Contact: Genell Sandberg, PhD, Clinical Psychologist; Carol Wassmuth, RN, MA, Clinical Specialist
TYPE OF AGENCY: Private practice
AREAS SERVED: Woodbury
YEARS IN OPERATION: 1
ACCESSIBILITY: Wheelchair accessible
DESCRIPTION: Individual and group counseling for survivors of interpersonal violence and perpetrators—rapists, child sexual abuse/incest offenders and batterers
CLIENTS/SERVICES: Sexual assault survivors; Marital rape/sexual abuse survivors; Adult survivors of child sexual abuse; Incest victims/survivors; Offender treatment program; Adolescent survivors of sexual abuse; Male survivors of sexual abuse
REQUIREMENTS: Ages 14 and older

SPENCER

NORTHWEST IOWA MENTAL HEALTH CENTER
201 E 11th St, Spencer, IA 51301
Crisis hotline: **(800) 242-5101 24 hrs**
Information: (712) 262-2924 9am-6pm, and Monday evenings
Contact: Patrick Singel, Dir
TYPE OF AGENCY: Counseling/mental health services; Child sexual abuse services
AREAS SERVED: Lyon, Osceola, O'Brien, Clay, Buena Vista, Emmet, Dickinson, Palo Alto, Pocahontas
YEARS IN OPERATION: 30
ACCESSIBILITY: Wheelchair accessible
DESCRIPTION: Has a sexual abuse treatment program with groups for victims, offenders, and mothers; Provides treatment for batterers
CLIENTS/SERVICES: Sexual assault survivors; Marital rape/sexual abuse survivors; Child victims of sexual abuse; Adult survivors of child sexual abuse; Incest victims/survivors; Community education; Offender treatment program; Adolescent survivors of sexual abuse; Male survivors of sexual abuse
REQUIREMENTS: Participants in the intrafamilial sexual abuse treatment program must be court-ordered

WATERLOO

CRISIS SERVICES
2530 University Ave, Waterloo, IA 50701
Crisis hotline: **(319) 233-8484 24 hrs**
Information: (319) 233-8484 7:30am-5:30pm (Mon-Fri)
Contact: Renee Else, Family Violence Interventionist
TYPE OF AGENCY: Rape crisis center; Domestic violence program; Child sexual abuse services; Child sexual abuse prevention program
SPONSORING ORGANIZATION: Family Service League
AREAS SERVED: Blackhawk
YEARS IN OPERATION: 12
ACCESSIBILITY: Wheelchair accessible
DESCRIPTION: Comprehensive rape crisis and domestic violence services, including support groups for female and male survivors of sexual assault/abuse; Group therapy for child sexual abuse offenders and incest offenders
CLIENTS/SERVICES: Sexual assault survivors; Marital rape/sexual abuse survivors; Child victims of sexual abuse; Adult survivors of child sexual abuse; Incest victims/survivors; Prevention program; Community education; Offender treatment program; Adolescent survivors of sexual abuse; Male survivors of sexual abuse

WEST BRANCH

FAMILIES INC
PO Box 130, West Branch, IA 52358
Information: (319) 643-2532 8am-4:30pm
Contact: Barbara Ruppel, LSW, Exec Dir
TYPE OF AGENCY: Counseling/mental health services; Child sexual abuse services; Child sexual abuse prevention program
AREAS SERVED: Eastern IA
YEARS IN OPERATION: 14
CASES SEXUAL ASSAULT/ABUSE (%): 40
CLIENTS/SERVICES: Child victims of sexual abuse; Adult survivors of child sexual abuse; Incest victims/survivors; Adolescent survivors of sexual abuse

KANSAS

EL DORADO

BUTLER COUNTY ASSOCIATION TO COUNTER ABUSE
2365 W Central, El Dorado, KS 67042
Crisis hotline: **(316) 321-7491 24 hrs**
Contact: Connie Phillips, Pres
TYPE OF AGENCY: Rape crisis center; Child sexual abuse prevention program
AREAS SERVED: Butler
YEARS IN OPERATION: 10
CASES SEXUAL ASSAULT/ABUSE (%): 75
CLIENTS/SERVICES: Sexual assault survivors; Marital rape/sexual abuse survivors; Adult survivors of child sexual abuse; Prevention program; Community education; Adolescent survivors of sexual abuse; Male survivors of sexual abuse

EMPORIA

SOS, INC
PO Box 1191, Emporia, KS 66801
Crisis hotline: **(316) 343-2626 5pm-8am and weekends**
Information: (316) 342-0548 8am-5pm (crisis calls accepted during these hrs weekdays)
Contact: Susan Moran, Exec Dir
TYPE OF AGENCY: Rape crisis center; Domestic violence program; Child sexual abuse services; Child sexual abuse prevention program
AREAS SERVED: Lyon, Morris, Marion, Chase, Greenwood, Coffey, Osage, Wabaunsee
YEARS IN OPERATION: 12
LANGUAGES: Spanish, Sign
ACCESSIBILITY: Wheelchair accessible; Signers for the hearing impaired
CASES SEXUAL ASSAULT/ABUSE (%): 10-15
DESCRIPTION: Services for victims of sexual assault and battering; CAP (Child Assault Prevention) Project; Prevention program for Emporia State University students to reduce date/acquaintance rape and dating violence
CLIENTS/SERVICES: Sexual assault survivors; Marital rape/sexual abuse survivors; Child victims of sexual abuse; Adult survivors of child sexual abuse; Incest victims/survivors; Prevention program; Community education; Adolescent survivors of sexual abuse; Male survivors of sexual abuse
SPECIAL PROGRAMS/SERVICES: Sponsors child assault prevention project (CAPP)

GARDEN CITY

FAMILY CRISIS SERVICES, INC
PO Box 1092, Garden City, KS 67846
Crisis hotline: **(316) 275-5911 24 hrs**
Information: (316) 275-2018 9am-5pm
Contact: Lana Christensen, Coord
TYPE OF AGENCY: Rape crisis center; Domestic violence program; Child sexual abuse prevention program
YEARS IN OPERATION: 7
CLIENTS/SERVICES: Sexual assault survivors; Marital rape/sexual abuse survivors; Adult survivors of child sexual abuse; Incest victims/survivors; Prevention program; Community education
SPECIAL PROGRAMS/SERVICES: Brochures in Spanish and Vietnamese; Treatment programs for batterers

GREAT BEND

BARTON COUNTY ATTORNEY'S OFFICE—VICTIM/WITNESS PROGRAM
PO Box 881, 1400 Main, Great Bend, KS 67530
Information: (316) 793-3559 8am-5pm (Mon-Fri)
Contact: Judy Willard, Coord
TYPE OF AGENCY: Victim/witness assistance program
AREAS SERVED: Barton
YEARS IN OPERATION: 3
CASES SEXUAL ASSAULT/ABUSE (%): 30
CLIENTS/SERVICES: Sexual assault survivors; Child victims of sexual abuse
REQUIREMENTS: Victims must file charges

FAMILY CRISIS CENTER
PO Box 1543, Great Bend, KS 67530
Crisis hotline: **(316) 792-1885 24 hrs**
Information: (316) 792-3672 9am-5pm (Mon-Fri)
Contact: Lisa Hoffmann, Dir
TYPE OF AGENCY: Rape crisis center; Domestic violence program
SPONSORING ORGANIZATION: Catholic Social Service
AREAS SERVED: 28 southwest counties of Kansas
YEARS IN OPERATION: 7
LANGUAGES: Spanish
ACCESSIBILITY: Wheelchair accessible
CASES SEXUAL ASSAULT/ABUSE (%): 40
CLIENTS/SERVICES: Sexual assault survivors; Marital rape/sexual abuse survivors; Child victims of sexual abuse; Adult survivors of child sexual abuse; Incest victims/survivors; Adolescent survivors of sexual abuse; Male survivors of sexual abuse

HAYS

HIGH PLAINS MENTAL HEALTH CENTER
208 E 7th St, Hays, KS 67601
Crisis hotline: **(800) 432-0333, (913) 628-2871 24 hrs**
Information: (913) 628-2871 24 hrs
Contact: Ann Young, MS, Children and Youth Svcs Mgr
TYPE OF AGENCY: Counseling/mental health services
AREAS SERVED: Cheyenne, Decatur, Ellis, Gove, Graham, Logan, Ness, Norton, Osborne, Phillips, Rawlins, Rooks, Rush, Russell, Sheridan, Sherman, Smith, Thomas, Trego, Wallace
YEARS IN OPERATION: 29
ACCESSIBILITY: Wheelchair accessible; Telecommunications for the hearing impaired (TTY, TDY, etc.); Signers for the hearing impaired
DESCRIPTION: Comprehensive community mental health center with treatment (individual and family) for sexually abused children. Support group for women survivors, and offenders group for adult males
CLIENTS/SERVICES: Sexual assault survivors; Marital rape/sexual abuse survivors; Child victims of sexual abuse; Adult survivors of child sexual abuse; Incest victims/survivors; Prevention program; Community education; Offender treatment program

NORTHWEST KANSAS FAMILY SHELTER, INC
PO Box 284, Hays, KS 67601
Crisis hotline: **(913) 625-3055, 333-1360 free call 24 hrs**
Information: (913) 625-4202 24 hrs
Contact: Juliene Maska, Prog Dir
TYPE OF AGENCY: Rape crisis center; Domestic violence program
AREAS SERVED: Northwest Kansas
YEARS IN OPERATION: 6
LANGUAGES: Interpreters as needed through the university
ACCESSIBILITY: Wheelchair accessible; Signers for the hearing impaired (as needed)
CASES SEXUAL ASSAULT/ABUSE (%): 20
DESCRIPTION: Provides shelter, crisis line, counseling, advocacy, and referrals for survivors of domestic violence and sexual assault; Program for batterers; Feminist martial arts/self-defense
CLIENTS/SERVICES: Sexual assault survivors; Marital rape/sexual abuse survivors; Child victims of sexual abuse; Adult survivors of child sexual abuse; Incest victims/survivors; Prevention program; Community education; Adolescent survivors of sexual abuse; Male survivors of sexual abuse

HUTCHINSON

HORIZONS MENTAL HEALTH CENTER
1715 E 23rd, Hutchinson, KS 67502
Crisis hotline: **(316) 665-2299, (800) 332-6633 24 hrs**
Information: (316) 665-2240 8am-5pm
Contact: Rich Line, Dept Head; Holly Martin, Sex Abuse Coord
TYPE OF AGENCY: Counseling/mental health services; Child sexual abuse services; Child sexual abuse prevention program
AREAS SERVED: Reno, Barber, Kingman, Harper, Pratt

HORIZONS MENTAL HEALTH CENTER
(continued)
YEARS IN OPERATION: 11
LANGUAGES: Spanish, Sign
ACCESSIBILITY: Wheelchair accessible; Signers for the hearing impaired
CASES SEXUAL ASSAULT/ABUSE (%): 10-20
DESCRIPTION: Counseling for survivors; Assistance for law enforcement in investigative interviews; Personal safety awareness program for 1st, 2nd, 4th, 5th grades. Individual and group therapy for child sexual abuse offenders, incest offenders, and batterers
CLIENTS/SERVICES: Sexual assault survivors; Marital rape/sexual abuse survivors; Child victims of sexual abuse; Adult survivors of child sexual abuse; Incest victims/survivors; Prevention program; Community education; Offender treatment program; Adolescent survivors of sexual abuse; Male survivors of sexual abuse

SEXUAL ASSAULT DOMESTIC VIOLENCE CENTER
PO Box 2856, Hutchinson, KS 67504-2856
Crisis hotline: **(316) 663-2522 24 hrs**
Information: (316) 665-3630 9am-5pm
Contact: Alicia Peppers, Exec Dir
TYPE OF AGENCY: Rape crisis center; Domestic violence program
AREAS SERVED: Reno, Rice, Harvey, McPherson, Stafford
YEARS IN OPERATION: 12
DESCRIPTION: Comprehensive sexual assault crisis services; Feminist martial arts/self defense program; Personal awareness safety program for 1st, 2nd, 4th, and 5th grades
CLIENTS/SERVICES: Sexual assault survivors; Marital rape/sexual abuse survivors; Adult survivors of child sexual abuse; Incest victims/survivors; Community education; Adolescent survivors of sexual abuse; Male survivors of sexual abuse

IOLA

HOPE UNLIMITED, INC
PO Box 12, Iola, KS 66749
Crisis hotline: **(316) 365-3144 24 hrs**
Information: (316) 365-7566 8am-5pm
Contact: Delma Rourk, Exec Dir
TYPE OF AGENCY: Domestic violence program
AREAS SERVED: Allen, Anderson, Neosho, Woodson
YEARS IN OPERATION: 4
ACCESSIBILITY: Wheelchair accessible
DESCRIPTION: Serves battered women and their children; Sexual assault advocates on volunteer roster
CLIENTS/SERVICES: Sexual assault survivors; Community education

JUNCTION CITY

RAPE VICTIM SUPPORT TEAM
1102 St Marys Rd, Junction City, KS 66441
Crisis hotline: **(913) 238-4131 24 hrs**
Information: (913) 238-4131 8am-5pm
Contact: Marty Rombold, Social Wkr
TYPE OF AGENCY: Rape crisis center; Hospital/medical center
SPONSORING ORGANIZATION: Geary Community Hospital
CLIENTS/SERVICES: Sexual assault survivors; Marital rape/sexual abuse survivors; Child victims of sexual abuse; Adolescent survivors of sexual abuse

LAWRENCE

DOUGLAS COUNTY RAPE VICTIM SUPPORT SERVICE
1419 Massachusetts St, Lawrence, KS 66044
Crisis hotline: **(913) 841-2345, 864-3506 24 hrs**
Information: (913) 843-8985 9am-12pm (Mon-Fri)
Contact: Sarah Jane Dillingham, Dir
TYPE OF AGENCY: Rape crisis center
AREAS SERVED: Douglas
YEARS IN OPERATION: 16
ACCESSIBILITY: Signers for the hearing impaired
CASES SEXUAL ASSAULT/ABUSE (%): 80
CLIENTS/SERVICES: Sexual assault survivors; Marital rape/sexual abuse survivors; Child victims of sexual abuse; Prevention program; Community education

WOMEN'S TRANSITIONAL CARE SERVICES, INC
PO Box 633, Lawrence, KS 66044
Crisis hotline: **(913) 841-6887 24 hrs**
Information: (913) 841-6887 8am-6pm
TYPE OF AGENCY: Domestic violence program
AREAS SERVED: Douglas, Jefferson, Franklin, southern Leavenworth, western Johnson
YEARS IN OPERATION: 11
LANGUAGES: Spanish
ACCESSIBILITY: Wheelchair accessible
CLIENTS/SERVICES: Marital rape/sexual abuse survivors; Child victims of sexual abuse; Adult survivors of child sexual abuse; Incest victims/survivors; Community education

LIBERAL

LIBERAL AREA RAPE CRISIS AND DOMESTIC VIOLENCE SERVICE
PO Box 1707, Liberal, KS 67901
Crisis hotline: **(316) 624-8818 24 hrs daily**
Information: (316) 624-8818 8am-5pm (Mon-Fri)
Contact: Debbie Stafford, Coord
TYPE OF AGENCY: Rape crisis center; Domestic violence program
AREAS SERVED: Seward, Stevens
YEARS IN OPERATION: 8
LANGUAGES: Spanish
ACCESSIBILITY: Wheelchair accessible
CASES SEXUAL ASSAULT/ABUSE (%): 10
CLIENTS/SERVICES: Sexual assault survivors; Marital rape/sexual abuse survivors; Child victims of sexual abuse; Adult survivors of child sexual abuse; Incest victims/survivors; Prevention program; Community education; Adolescent survivors of sexual abuse; Male survivors of sexual abuse

MANHATTAN

THE CRISIS CENTER, INC
PO Box 1526 or PO Box 164, Manhattan, KS 66502
Crisis hotline: **(913) 539-2785 24 hrs**
Information: (913) 539-2785 24 hrs
Contact: M J Poehler, Client Svcs Coord
TYPE OF AGENCY: Rape crisis center; Domestic violence program
AREAS SERVED: Riley, Geary, Pottawatomie, Clay, Marshall, Ft Riley
YEARS IN OPERATION: 9½
ACCESSIBILITY: Wheelchair accessible
CASES SEXUAL ASSAULT/ABUSE (%): 10
CLIENTS/SERVICES: Sexual assault survivors; Marital rape/sexual abuse survivors; Adult survivors of child sexual abuse; Incest victims/survivors; Prevention program; Community education; Male survivors of sexual abuse

PAWNEE MENTAL HEALTH SERVICES
2001 Claflin, Manhattan, KS 66502
Crisis hotline: **(913) 539-5337 24 hrs**
Information: (913) 539-5337 8am-5pm (Mon-Wed-Fri); 8am-9pm (Tue-Thu)
Contact: John D Cook, Child Svcs Prog Mgr
TYPE OF AGENCY: Counseling/mental health services
AREAS SERVED: Riley, Pottawatomie, Geary, Marshall, Clay, Cloud, Washington, Republic, Jewell, Mitchell
YEARS IN OPERATION: 20+
ACCESSIBILITY: Wheelchair accessible
CASES SEXUAL ASSAULT/ABUSE (%): 25-30
DESCRIPTION: Counseling for survivors of sexual assault/abuse; Individual and group therapy for rapists, child sexual abuse offenders, incest offenders, and batterers; Anger management for batterers
CLIENTS/SERVICES: Sexual assault survivors; Marital rape/sexual abuse survivors; Child victims of sexual abuse; Adult survivors of child sexual abuse; Incest victims/survivors; Prevention program; Community education; Offender treatment program; Adolescent survivors of sexual abuse; Male survivors of sexual abuse

MCPHERSON

MCPHERSON COUNTY COUNCIL ON VIOLENCE AGAINST PERSONS
PO Box 406, McPherson, KS 67460
Crisis hotline: **(316) 241-6615 24 hrs**
Information: (316) 241-6603, 241-3510 9am-5pm
Contact: Patty Sargent, Battered Persons Team Coord
TYPE OF AGENCY: Domestic violence program
AREAS SERVED: McPherson
YEARS IN OPERATION: 10
CASES SEXUAL ASSAULT/ABUSE (%): 20
CLIENTS/SERVICES: Sexual assault survivors; Marital rape/sexual abuse survivors; Community education

OLATHE

FAMILY SEXUAL ABUSE TREATMENT PROGRAM
15580 S Hwy 169, Olathe, KS 66062
Information: (913) 782-2100 8am-5pm (Mon-Fri)
Contact: Linda Starke, LSCSW, Supv
TYPE OF AGENCY: Counseling/mental health services; Child sexual abuse services
SPONSORING ORGANIZATION: Johnson County Mental Health Center
AREAS SERVED: Johnson
YEARS IN OPERATION: 7
ACCESSIBILITY: Wheelchair accessible; Telecommunications for the hearing impaired (TTY, TDY, etc.); Signers for the hearing impaired
DESCRIPTION: Serves incestuous adult offenders who admit to their behavior, all child sexual abuse victims and their families, all juvenile sexual offenders, and adults molested as children.
CLIENTS/SERVICES: Child victims of sexual abuse; Adult survivors of child sexual abuse; Incest victims/survivors; Offender treatment program; Adolescent survivors of sexual abuse; Male survivors of sexual abuse
REQUIREMENTS: Adult offenders must admit to crime—no restrictions on other services.

JOHNSON COUNTY DISTRICT ATTORNEY'S VICTIM/WITNESS ASSISTANCE PROGRAM
PO Box 728, Olathe, KS 66061
Information: (913) 791-5332 8am-5pm (Mon-Fri); on-call sexual assault medical services, 24 hrs
Contact: Georgia Nesselrode, Dir
TYPE OF AGENCY: Victim/witness assistance program
AREAS SERVED: Johnson
YEARS IN OPERATION: 10
ACCESSIBILITY: Wheelchair accessible; Signers for the hearing impaired (by referral)
CASES SEXUAL ASSAULT/ABUSE (%): 10

JOHNSON COUNTY DISTRICT ATTORNEY'S VICTIM/WITNESS ASSISTANCE PROGRAM *(continued)*

CLIENTS/SERVICES: Sexual assault survivors; Marital rape/sexual abuse survivors; Child victims of sexual abuse; Adult survivors of child sexual abuse; Incest victims/survivors
REQUIREMENTS: Must file charges to receive full range of services.

OVERLAND PARK

SAFEHOME, INC
PO Box 4469, Overland Park, KS 66204
Crisis hotline: **(913) 262-2868 24 hrs**
Information: (913) 262-4559 24 hrs
Contact: Jami McWilliams, Comm Resources Dir
TYPE OF AGENCY: Rape crisis center; Domestic violence program
AREAS SERVED: Primarily Johnson; Other counties in metropolitan area
YEARS IN OPERATION: 4
ACCESSIBILITY: Wheelchair accessible; Telecommunications for the hearing impaired (TTY, TDY, etc.); Signers for the hearing impaired
CLIENTS/SERVICES: Sexual assault survivors; Marital rape/sexual abuse survivors; Child victims of sexual abuse; Adult survivors of child sexual abuse; Incest victims/survivors; Prevention program; Community education
SPECIAL PROGRAMS/SERVICES: Currently working on a city-wide program dealing with date rape for middle and high schools. Will utilize a drama team from a local junior college to portray real life situations.

PITTSBURG

R-VAN (RAPE VICTIMS ASSISTANCE NETWORK)
Box 313, Pittsburg, KS 66762
Crisis hotline: **(316) 231-8251, collect calls accepted 24 hrs daily**
Information: (316) 231-8251, collect calls accepted 24 hrs daily
Contact: Sharon Moray, R-VAN Coord; Dorothy Miller, Dir
TYPE OF AGENCY: Rape crisis center; Domestic violence program; Child sexual abuse services; Child sexual abuse prevention program
SPONSORING ORGANIZATION: Safehouse, Inc
AREAS SERVED: Crawford, Cherokee, Elk, LaBette, Wilson, Woodson, Chataqua, Neosho, Bourbon, Allen, Linn, Montgomery
YEARS IN OPERATION: Program 4; Agency 9
ACCESSIBILITY: Wheelchair accessible
CASES SEXUAL ASSAULT/ABUSE (%): 30
CLIENTS/SERVICES: Sexual assault survivors; Marital rape/sexual abuse survivors; Child victims of sexual abuse; Adult survivors of child sexual abuse; Incest victims/survivors; Prevention program; Community education; Offender treatment program; Adolescent survivors of sexual abuse; Male survivors of sexual abuse
REQUIREMENTS: Must be 18 or older or an emancipated minor

TOPEKA

BATTERED WOMEN'S TASK FORCE
PO Box 1883, Topeka, KS 66601
Crisis hotline: **(913) 233-1730 5pm-9am (Mon-Fri); 24 hrs on weekends**
Information: (913) 354-7927 9am-5pm (Mon-Fri)
Contact: Marilynn Ault, Prog Dir
TYPE OF AGENCY: Rape crisis center; Domestic violence program
SPONSORING ORGANIZATION: Topeka YWCA
AREAS SERVED: Shawnee
YEARS IN OPERATION: 11
ACCESSIBILITY: Wheelchair accessible
CASES SEXUAL ASSAULT/ABUSE (%): 20
DESCRIPTION: Domestic violence crisis services; Individual therapy for batterers
CLIENTS/SERVICES: Marital rape/sexual abuse survivors

MENNINGER FOUNDATION
Box 829, Topeka, KS 66601
Information: (913) 273-7500
Contact: Bonnie J Buchele, PhD, Staff Psychologist and Shawnee County Incest Div Prog Dir
TYPE OF AGENCY: Counseling/mental health services; Child sexual abuse services; Training/research
DESCRIPTION: Provides mental health services, including consultation, diagnostic evaluation, brief psychotherapy, hypnotherapy, biofeedback, pharmacotherapy, individual psychotherapy, group psychotherapy, sex therapy, and family therapy for survivors/victims of rape, incest, spousal abuse, and sexual harassment. Also provides the above services for incest offenders. Provides training for mental health professionals in sexual assault/abuse and sponsors at least one workshop annually concerned with sexual abuse
CLIENTS/SERVICES: Sexual assault survivors; Marital rape/sexual abuse survivors; Child victims of sexual abuse; Adult survivors of child sexual abuse; Incest victims/survivors; Offender treatment program; Adolescent survivors of sexual abuse; Male survivors of sexual abuse; Sexual harassment

RAPE COUNSELING AND PREVENTION
2401 W 6th, Topeka, KS 66606
Crisis hotline: **(913) 233-1730 24 hrs**
Information: (913) 233-1730 8am-5pm
TYPE OF AGENCY: Rape crisis center; Counseling/mental health services
SPONSORING ORGANIZATION: Shawnee Community Mental Health Center
CLIENTS/SERVICES: Sexual assault survivors

WICHITA

SEXUAL ABUSE TREATMENT PROGRAM
1001 S Minnesota, Wichita, KS 67211
Information: (316) 268-7655 8am-5pm (Mon-Fri)
Contact: Larry L Donalson, Prog Coord
TYPE OF AGENCY: Counseling/mental health services; Child sexual abuse services
SPONSORING ORGANIZATION: Sedgwick County Mental Health
AREAS SERVED: Sedgwick
YEARS IN OPERATION: 6
ACCESSIBILITY: Wheelchair accessible
CASES SEXUAL ASSAULT/ABUSE (%): 100
CLIENTS/SERVICES: Child victims of sexual abuse; Incest victims/survivors; Community education; Offender treatment program; Couple and family therapy
REQUIREMENTS: Offender must be 18 years or older, entering therapy via court diversion or probation. Offender must have had relationship to victim prior to abuse, must move out of home during therapy, and must pay for therapy of victim and other family members.

WICHITA AREA SEXUAL ASSAULT CENTER, INC
215 N St Francis, Ste 1, Wichita, KS 67202-2609
Crisis hotline: **(316) 263-3002 24 hrs**
Information: (316) 263-0185 8:30am-5pm
Contact: Kris Wilshusen, Exec Dir
TYPE OF AGENCY: Rape crisis center; Child sexual abuse prevention program
AREAS SERVED: Sedgwick and surrounding counties
YEARS IN OPERATION: 14
ACCESSIBILITY: Wheelchair accessible; Signers for the hearing impaired
CASES SEXUAL ASSAULT/ABUSE (%): 100
DESCRIPTION: Comprehensive rape crisis services, including support groups for female and male survivors of sexual assault/abuse.
CLIENTS/SERVICES: Sexual assault survivors; Marital rape/sexual abuse survivors; Child victims of sexual abuse; Adult survivors of child sexual abuse; Incest victims/survivors; Prevention program; Community education; Adolescent survivors of sexual abuse; Male survivors of sexual abuse
SPECIAL PROGRAMS/SERVICES: Personal Safety Awareness Program for K through 6th grade. Two-week curriculum which involves teachers, police officers, and a speaker from the Sexual Assault Center. Protective Parenting Program is designed to help parents and adults better understand the problems of child sexual abuse and to recognize positive steps to take to reduce children's vulnerability. A group session lasts 1 ½-2 hours.

WICHITA/SEDGWICK COUNTY EXPLOITED AND MISSING CHILD UNIT
1001 S Minnesota, Wichita, KS 67211
Information: (316) 268-7094 8am-5pm (Mon-Fri); On-call teams for emergencies
Contact: Gary Johnson, Operations Dir
TYPE OF AGENCY: Victim/witness assistance program; Counseling/mental health services; Child sexual abuse services; Child sexual abuse prevention program
SPONSORING ORGANIZATION: Wichita Police Department/Sedgwick County Sheriff and District Attorney
AREAS SERVED: Sedgwick
YEARS IN OPERATION: 3½
LANGUAGES: Interpreters available as needed
ACCESSIBILITY: Wheelchair accessible
CASES SEXUAL ASSAULT/ABUSE (%): 100
DESCRIPTION: Law enforcement/social worker teams for investigation of child sexual abuse and crisis intervention
CLIENTS/SERVICES: Child victims of sexual abuse; Adult survivors of child sexual abuse; Incest victims/survivors; Male survivors of sexual abuse
REQUIREMENTS: Client must make a report to the local law enforcement agency, local state rehabilitative service department or directly to this office.

KENTUCKY

ASHLAND

PATHWAYS, INC
PO Box 790, 2162 Greenup Ave, Ashland, KY 41105-0790
Crisis hotline: **(800) 562-8909, (606) 324-1141 24 hrs**
Information: (606) 324-1141 24 hrs
Contact: Debbi Bailey, Rape Crisis Svcs/Women's Prog Dir
TYPE OF AGENCY: Rape crisis center; Domestic violence program; Counseling/mental health services
AREAS SERVED: Bath, Boyd, Carter, Elliott, Rowan, Morgan, Menifee, Greenup, Lawrence, Montgomery
YEARS IN OPERATION: 22
ACCESSIBILITY: Wheelchair accessible
DESCRIPTION: Rape crisis services, including support groups for female and male survivors of sexual abuse/assault
CLIENTS/SERVICES: Sexual assault survivors; Marital rape/sexual abuse survivors; Child victims of sexual abuse; Adult survivors of child sexual abuse; Incest victims/survivors; Prevention program; Community education; Adolescent survivors of sexual abuse; Male survivors of sexual abuse

SAFE HARBOR—SPOUSE ABUSE SHELTER
PO Box 2163, Ashland, KY 41105-2163
Crisis hotline: **(800) 562-8909 (toll-free in KY only), (606) 324-1141 24 hrs**
Information: (800) 562-8909 (toll-free in KY only), (606) 324-1141 8am-5pm
Contact: Hope Lipsitz, Dir
TYPE OF AGENCY: Domestic violence program
AREAS SERVED: Boyd, Greenup, Lawrence, Carter, Elliott, Morgan, Menifee, Montgomery, Bath, Rowan
YEARS IN OPERATION: 6
CASES SEXUAL ASSAULT/ABUSE (%): 20
CLIENTS/SERVICES: Marital rape/sexual abuse survivors

BEATTYVILLE

RESURRECTION HOME, INC—FAMILY ABUSE SHELTER
RR 1, Box 0625, Beattyville, KY 41311
Crisis hotline: **(606) 464-8481 24 hrs**
Information: (606) 464-8481 24 hrs
Contact: Sr Mary K Drouin, OP, Dir
TYPE OF AGENCY: Domestic violence program
AREAS SERVED: Lee
YEARS IN OPERATION: 9½
ACCESSIBILITY: Wheelchair accessible
CASES SEXUAL ASSAULT/ABUSE (%): 50
CLIENTS/SERVICES: Sexual assault survivors; Marital rape/sexual abuse survivors; Child victims of sexual abuse; Adult survivors of child sexual abuse; Incest victims/survivors; Community education

BOWLING GREEN

RAPE CRISIS AND PREVENTION CENTER
PO Box 1865, Bowling Green, KY 42102-1865
Crisis hotline: **(502) 782-1848 24 hrs 7 days**
Information: (502) 782-5014 8am-4pm (Mon-Fri)
Contact: Karen Hurst, Exec Dir
TYPE OF AGENCY: Rape crisis center
AREAS SERVED: Allen, Barren, Butler, Edmonson, Logan, Hart, Simpson, Warren, Metcalfe, Monroe
YEARS IN OPERATION: 3
CASES SEXUAL ASSAULT/ABUSE (%): 100
DESCRIPTION: Rape crisis services; Feminist martial arts/self defense program
CLIENTS/SERVICES: Sexual assault survivors; Marital rape/sexual abuse survivors; Child victims of sexual abuse; Adult survivors of child sexual abuse; Incest victims/survivors; Prevention program; Community education; Adolescent survivors of sexual abuse; Male survivors of sexual abuse

CORBIN

CUMBERLAND RIVER COMPREHENSIVE CARE CENTERS
PO Box 568, Corbin, KY 40701
Crisis hotline: **(606) 864-2104, 573-1624 24 hrs**
Information: Regional Office (606) 528-7010; Harlan 573-1624; Bell 248-4949; Knox 546-3104; Jackson 287-7137; Clay 598-5172; Rock Castle 256-2129; Whitley 549-1440; Laurel 864-2104 8am-4:30pm
Contact: Vivian Zehr, Children's Svcs Dir
TYPE OF AGENCY: Counseling/mental health services
AREAS SERVED: Harlan, Bell, Knox, Jackson, Clay, Rockcastle, Whitley, Laurel
YEARS IN OPERATION: 17
ACCESSIBILITY: Wheelchair accessible; Signers for the hearing impaired (by arrangement)
CASES SEXUAL ASSAULT/ABUSE (%): 4
DESCRIPTION: All mental health, mental retardation, and substance abuse needs are treated, including family violence and child abuse. Also treats rapists, child sexual abuse/incest offenders and batterers
CLIENTS/SERVICES: Sexual assault survivors; Marital rape/sexual abuse survivors; Child victims of sexual abuse; Adult survivors of child sexual abuse; Incest victims/survivors; Prevention program; Community education; Offender treatment program; Adolescent survivors of sexual abuse; Male survivors of sexual abuse

COVINGTON

COMMITTEE FOR KIDS, INC
PO Box 743, Covington, KY 41012
Crisis hotline: **(606) 491-LOVE 24 hrs 7 days**
Information: (606) 491-4905 9am-4pm (Mon-Fri)
Contact: Donna S Saunders, Exec Dir
TYPE OF AGENCY: Counseling/mental health services; Child sexual abuse services; Child sexual abuse prevention program; Child abuse services; Child abuse prevention program
AREAS SERVED: Kenton, Campbell, Boone, Grant
YEARS IN OPERATION: 10
DESCRIPTION: All children and adult services are related to breaking the cycle of child abuse; Sexual abuse groups for children and teen boys; Parents Anonymous chapters; Nurturing/parenting programs; Support groups for children and teens; Saturday respite for children at risk; Hotline
CLIENTS/SERVICES: Child victims of sexual abuse; Incest victims/survivors; Prevention program; Community education; Adolescent survivors of sexual abuse; Male survivors of sexual abuse

DANVILLE

COLLINS, KUBALE, AND MILES COUNSELING OFFICES
PO Box 5, Danville, KY 40422
Crisis hotline: **(606) 236-0853 24 hrs**
Information: (606) 236-0853 24 hrs
Contact: Kathy Miles, Therapist
TYPE OF AGENCY: Rape crisis center; Child sexual abuse services; Child sexual abuse prevention program; Private practice
SPONSORING ORGANIZATION: Lexington Rape Crisis Center
AREAS SERVED: Boyle, Lincoln, Mercer, Garrard
YEARS IN OPERATION: 2½
ACCESSIBILITY: Signers for the hearing impaired (by arrangement)
CASES SEXUAL ASSAULT/ABUSE (%): 10
DESCRIPTION: Sexual abuse and rape treatment, community education, advocacy, and crisis line
CLIENTS/SERVICES: Sexual assault survivors; Marital rape/sexual abuse survivors; Child victims of sexual abuse; Adult survivors of child sexual abuse; Incest victims/survivors; Prevention program; Community education; Adolescent survivors of sexual abuse; Male survivors of sexual abuse

ELIZABETHTOWN

RAPE VICTIMS SERVICES PROGRAM
1311 N Dixie Hwy, Elizabethtown, KY 42701
Crisis hotline: **(502) 769-1304 24 hrs**
Information: (502) 769-1304 8am-5pm (Mon-Fri)
Contact: Collette Gill, Coord

RAPE VICTIMS SERVICES PROGRAM
(continued)

TYPE OF AGENCY: Rape crisis center
SPONSORING ORGANIZATION: Communicare, Inc
AREAS SERVED: Hardin, Larue, Marion, Nelson, Meade, Grayson, Breckinridge, Washington
YEARS IN OPERATION: 1
ACCESSIBILITY: Wheelchair accessible
CASES SEXUAL ASSAULT/ABUSE (%): 100
CLIENTS/SERVICES: Sexual assault survivors; Marital rape/sexual abuse survivors; Child victims of sexual abuse; Adult survivors of child sexual abuse; Incest victims/survivors; Prevention program; Community education; Adolescent survivors of sexual abuse

FORT CAMPBELL

SOCIAL WORK SERVICES
Blanchfield Army Community Hospital, Fort Campbell, KY 42223
Crisis hotline: **(502) 798-8400 24 hrs**
Information: (502) 798-8801 7:30am-4:30pm
Contact: Jon E Harlan, Capt, Med Svc Corp
TYPE OF AGENCY: Hospital/medical center; Military services
SPONSORING ORGANIZATION: US Army Hospital
AREAS SERVED: Fort Campbell (Military)
LANGUAGES: Spanish
ACCESSIBILITY: Wheelchair accessible; Signers for the hearing impaired
CASES SEXUAL ASSAULT/ABUSE (%): 10
CLIENTS/SERVICES: Sexual assault survivors; Marital rape/sexual abuse survivors; Child victims of sexual abuse; Adult survivors of child sexual abuse; Incest victims/survivors; Adolescent survivors of sexual abuse; Male survivors of sexual abuse
REQUIREMENTS: Services are restricted to retired or active military members and their families.

FORT THOMAS

ST LUKE HOSPITAL COMMUNITY PEDIATRIC CLINIC
85 N Grand Ave, Fort Thomas, KY 41075
Information: (606) 572-3207 8:30am-5pm (Mon-Fri)
Contact: Marilyn J Drake, Med Soc Wkr
TYPE OF AGENCY: Hospital/medical center; Child sexual abuse services
AREAS SERVED: Statewide
YEARS IN OPERATION: 2
ACCESSIBILITY: Wheelchair accessible
CASES SEXUAL ASSAULT/ABUSE (%): 100
DESCRIPTION: Provides medical assessment and treatment for sexually abused children, including documentation and expert medical testimony; Short-term counseling and emotional support for child and family
CLIENTS/SERVICES: Child victims of sexual abuse; Male survivors of sexual abuse
REQUIREMENTS: Birth to 18 years; A report is made on each child seen in CPC to protective services and/or police

LEXINGTON

ADOLESCENT, CHILDREN, FAMILY AND GROUP COUNSELING
1025 Dove Run Rd, Ste 106B, Lexington, KY 40502
Information: (606) 269-2548
Contact: Patricia Callahan, Lic Clinical Soc Wkr
TYPE OF AGENCY: Private practice
AREAS SERVED: Central and Eastern KY
YEARS IN OPERATION: 2½
CASES SEXUAL ASSAULT/ABUSE (%): 50
CLIENTS/SERVICES: Sexual assault survivors; Marital rape/sexual abuse survivors; Child victims of sexual abuse; Adult survivors of child sexual abuse; Incest victims/survivors; Offender treatment program; Adolescent survivors of sexual abuse; Male survivors of sexual abuse

REQUIREMENTS: Will only work short-term with perpetrators of child sexual abuse who will claim their responsibility for the impact on the victim

COMPREHENSIVE CARE CENTER/GRAHAM B DIMMICK CHILD GUIDANCE SERVICE
201 Mechanic St, Lexington, KY 40507
Crisis hotline: **(606) 233-0444 24 hrs**
Information: (606) 233-0444 24 hrs
Contact: Nan Riekert, MSW
TYPE OF AGENCY: Counseling/mental health services
AREAS SERVED: Fayette
YEARS IN OPERATION: 54
ACCESSIBILITY: Wheelchair accessible
DESCRIPTION: Group and family therapy for survivors; Court evaluations and psychological assessments of victims and their families, and youthful offenders; Group, individual, and family therapy for child sexual abuse offenders, incest offenders, and juvenile sex offenders
CLIENTS/SERVICES: Sexual assault survivors; Child victims of sexual abuse; Adult survivors of child sexual abuse; Incest victims/survivors; Prevention program; Community education; Offender treatment program; Adolescent survivors of sexual abuse

CRIME VICTIMS ASSISTANCE PROGRAM
116 N Upper St, Ste 300, Lexington, KY 40507
Information: (606) 252-3571 8am-5pm
Contact: Gail A Whitt, Victim Svcs Dir
TYPE OF AGENCY: Victim/witness assistance program
SPONSORING ORGANIZATION: Commonwealth's Attorney's Office
AREAS SERVED: Fayette
YEARS IN OPERATION: 4
ACCESSIBILITY: Wheelchair accessible
CLIENTS/SERVICES: Sexual assault survivors; Child victims of sexual abuse; Adult survivors of child sexual abuse; Incest victims/survivors; Adolescent survivors of sexual abuse; Male survivors of sexual abuse

DEPARTMENT OF FAMILY PRACTICE—FAMILY MEDICAL CENTER
221 John Chambers Bldg (Annex 4), Lexington, KY 40536
Information: (606) 233-5444 9am-5pm
TYPE OF AGENCY: College/university-based services; Child sexual abuse services; Consultation; Child abuse services; Training/research
SPONSORING ORGANIZATION: University of Kentucky College of Medicine
AREAS SERVED: Central Kentucky
YEARS IN OPERATION: ½
ACCESSIBILITY: Wheelchair accessible
DESCRIPTION: Provides medical and psychological evaluation for sexually and physically abused children and adolescents, their families, and child sexual abuse/incest offenders, as well as adult group, marital, and family therapy
CLIENTS/SERVICES: Child victims of sexual abuse; Adult survivors of child sexual abuse; Incest victims/survivors; Community education; Offender treatment program; Adolescent survivors of sexual abuse

LEXINGTON RAPE CRISIS CENTER
PO Box 1603, Lexington, KY 40592
Crisis hotline: **(606) 253-2511 24 hrs**
Information: (606) 253-2615 9am-5pm (Mon-Fri)
Contact: Diane Lawless, Dir
TYPE OF AGENCY: Rape crisis center
AREAS SERVED: Bluegrass area, Fayette
YEARS IN OPERATION: 12
CASES SEXUAL ASSAULT/ABUSE (%): 100
CLIENTS/SERVICES: Sexual assault survivors; Child victims of sexual abuse; Adult survivors of child sexual abuse; Incest victims/survivors; Prevention program; Community education;

Adolescent survivors of sexual abuse; Male survivors of sexual abuse

UNIVERSITY OF KENTUCKY MEDICAL CENTER, DEPARTMENT OF PSYCHIATRY, CHILD ABUSE CLINIC
Department of Psychiatry University of Kentucky Medical Center, Annex 2, Rm 216, Lexington, KY 40536-0080
Information: (606) 233-5444 8:30am-5pm (Mon-Fri)
Contact: Lane Veltkamp, MSW, Dir/Prof
TYPE OF AGENCY: Hospital/medical center; Child sexual abuse services; Training/research
YEARS IN OPERATION: 10
ACCESSIBILITY: Wheelchair accessible
CASES SEXUAL ASSAULT/ABUSE (%): 75
DESCRIPTION: Clinical evaluation; Medical evaluation referrals; Courtroom testimony and written reports; Individual, family, and/or group treatment of child sexual abuse victims, offenders, victims' family members; Treatment of adult survivors of sexual abuse
CLIENTS/SERVICES: Child victims of sexual abuse; Adult survivors of child sexual abuse; Incest victims/survivors; Community education; Offender treatment program; Adolescent survivors of sexual abuse; Male survivors of sexual abuse; Publications/media
REQUIREMENTS: Fees are due when service is delivered.
SPECIAL PROGRAMS/SERVICES: Effective April 1988-April 1991, funding from the KY Cabinet for Human Resources to operate a demonstration project for the interdisciplinary clinical treatment of abusive families in collaboration with the Department of Family Practice. Aspects of this program: (1) To provide clinical and medical evaluations and treatment of abusive families, and (2) To provide state-wide interdisciplinary training regarding how to establish similar treatment programs in regional areas. An interagency, multidisciplinary advisory committee of state and local officials has been established to assist in guiding this program, with particular emphasis on improving interdisciplinary cooperation and collaboration when evaluating and treating abuse victims and their families. 35-minute videotape: *Clinical and Medical Assessment of Child Sexual Abuse* for interdisciplinary professional training

WOMEN'S CENTER OF CENTRAL KENTUCKY, INC
178 N Martin Luther King Blvd, Lexington, KY 40507
Crisis hotline: **(606) 254-9319 8:30am-5pm**
Information: (606) 254-9319 8:30am-5pm
Contact: Alayne L White, Exec Dir
TYPE OF AGENCY: Counseling/mental health services; Substance abuse treatment/counseling; Women's center
AREAS SERVED: Statewide
YEARS IN OPERATION: 15
CLIENTS/SERVICES: Prevention program; Community education

LOUISVILLE

THE FAMILY PLACE: A CHILD ABUSE TREATMENT AGENCY
982 Eastern Pwy, Louisville, KY 40217
Crisis hotline: **(502) 636-2773 7am-11pm**
Information: (502) 636-2801 8:30am-8pm
Contact: Beverly J Bleidt, PhD, Clinical Dir
TYPE OF AGENCY: Child sexual abuse services; Child abuse services
AREAS SERVED: Jefferson, Trimble, Henry, Shelby, Bullitt, Oldham, Spencer, Meade, Hardin Taylor
YEARS IN OPERATION: 10
ACCESSIBILITY: Wheelchair accessible
CASES SEXUAL ASSAULT/ABUSE (%): 60-75

THE FAMILY PLACE: A CHILD ABUSE TREATMENT AGENCY (continued)

DESCRIPTION: Comprehensive treatment to families experiencing the problem of incest, physical or sexual child abuse; Individual, group and family treatment for survivors and child sexual abuse/incest offenders. Day treatment program for preschoolers, crisis care for children and liaison with the legal system. Treatment for incest offenders and juvenile sex offenders
CLIENTS/SERVICES: Child victims of sexual abuse; Adult survivors of child sexual abuse; Incest victims/survivors; Prevention program; Community education; Offender treatment program; Adolescent survivors of sexual abuse; Preschoolers
REQUIREMENTS: Families with children under the age of 18 accepted. Prefer court-ordered treatment although will accept self-referrals. All juvenile perpetrators must have court-ordered treatment (along with their parents).
SPECIAL PROGRAMS/SERVICES: Developed a preschool curriculum for abused children. Curriculum taught in small groups and includes self-esteem building, socialization, sexual abuse prevention, relaxation, impulse control, and foster care. Individual and group treatment in the context of a family in which a child of the adult survivor has been abused

JEFFERSON COUNTY COMMONWEALTH'S ATTORNEY'S OFFICE—VICTIM INFORMATION PROGRAM
514 W Liberty St, Louisville, KY 40202
Information: (502) 588-2340 8:30am-4:30pm
Contact: Susie Evans, Deputy Dir
TYPE OF AGENCY: Victim/witness assistance program
AREAS SERVED: Jefferson
YEARS IN OPERATION: 10
LANGUAGES: Interpreters available
ACCESSIBILITY: Wheelchair accessible; Signers for the hearing impaired
CASES SEXUAL ASSAULT/ABUSE (%): 10
CLIENTS/SERVICES: Sexual assault survivors; Child victims of sexual abuse; Community education; Adolescent survivors of sexual abuse
REQUIREMENTS: Clients must be victims of felony crimes and must file charges.

LEGAL AID SERVICES, INC—SOCIAL SERVICES PROGRAM
425 W Muhammad Ali Blvd, Louisville, KY 40202
Information: (502) 584-1254 8:30am-5pm
Contact: Susan Metcalf, Soc Wkr
TYPE OF AGENCY: Legal services agency
AREAS SERVED: Jefferson
ACCESSIBILITY: Wheelchair accessible; Signers for the hearing impaired
CASES SEXUAL ASSAULT/ABUSE (%): 30
DESCRIPTION: Assessment; Legal representation; Advocacy; Resource development for sexually assaulted and/or abused victims
CLIENTS/SERVICES: Sexual assault survivors; Marital rape/sexual abuse survivors; Child victims of sexual abuse; Adult survivors of child sexual abuse; Incest victims/survivors; Prevention program; Community education; Adolescent survivors of sexual abuse
REQUIREMENTS: Meet eligibility guidelines for income and intake
SPECIAL PROGRAMS/SERVICES: A training program, "Evidence of Child Sexual Abuse," is presented by 3 professionals (social worker, lawyer and doctor) who have 35 years of combined experience in working with victims of sexual abuse and/or assault

PASTORAL COUNSELING AND CONSULTATION CENTER, INC
4007 Kresge Way, Louisville, KY 40207
Crisis hotline: **(502) 589-4313 24 hrs**
Information: (502) 896-5099 8am-8pm (Mon-Fri); 8am-Noon (Sat)
Contact: Susan Smith, Office Mgr
TYPE OF AGENCY: Counseling/mental health services
AREAS SERVED: Statewide and Southern Indiana
YEARS IN OPERATION: 14
ACCESSIBILITY: Wheelchair accessible
CASES SEXUAL ASSAULT/ABUSE (%): 47
DESCRIPTION: Staff is trained in treatment issues, referral network, and court process within the community. Also provides therapy for rapists, child sexual abuse/incest offenders, and batterers
CLIENTS/SERVICES: Sexual assault survivors; Marital rape/sexual abuse survivors; Child victims of sexual abuse; Adult survivors of child sexual abuse; Incest victims/survivors; Offender treatment program; Adolescent survivors of sexual abuse; Male survivors of sexual abuse

YWCA RAPE RELIEF CENTER
226 W Breckridge St, Louisville, KY 40203
Crisis hotline: **(502) 581-7273 24 hrs**
Information: (502) 581-7273 9am-4pm (Mon-Fri)
Contact: Joyce Wilson, Asst Dir
TYPE OF AGENCY: Rape crisis center
AREAS SERVED: Jefferson, Oldham, KY; Clark, Floyd, IN
YEARS IN OPERATION: 15
ACCESSIBILITY: Wheelchair accessible; Signers for the hearing impaired
CASES SEXUAL ASSAULT/ABUSE (%): 95
CLIENTS/SERVICES: Sexual assault survivors; Marital rape/sexual abuse survivors; Child victims of sexual abuse; Adult survivors of child sexual abuse; Incest victims/survivors; Prevention program; Community education; Adolescent survivors of sexual abuse; Male survivors of sexual abuse
SPECIAL PROGRAMS/SERVICES: Victim personalization treatment program for rapists

MAYSVILLE

WOMEN'S CRISIS CENTER
PO Box 484, Maysville, KY 41056
Crisis hotline: **(606) 564-6708 24 hrs**
Information: (606) 564-6708 24 hrs
Contact: Hazel Graham, Counselor/Advocate
TYPE OF AGENCY: Rape crisis center; Domestic violence program; Child sexual abuse services
AREAS SERVED: Mason, Fleming, Bracken, Lewis, Robertson
YEARS IN OPERATION: 4½
ACCESSIBILITY: Wheelchair accessible
CASES SEXUAL ASSAULT/ABUSE (%): 95
CLIENTS/SERVICES: Sexual assault survivors; Marital rape/sexual abuse survivors; Child victims of sexual abuse; Adult survivors of child sexual abuse; Incest victims/survivors; Prevention program; Community education; Adolescent survivors of sexual abuse

NEWPORT

CAMPBELL COUNTY COMMONWEALTH'S ATTORNEY—VICTIM ASSISTANCE PROGRAM
Newport Courthouse, Rm 12, Newport, KY 41071
Information: (606) 292-6490 8:30am-4:30pm
Contact: Sue Dean, Victim Assistance Coord
TYPE OF AGENCY: Victim/witness assistance program
AREAS SERVED: Campbell
YEARS IN OPERATION: 4 months
ACCESSIBILITY: Wheelchair accessible
CLIENTS/SERVICES: Sexual assault survivors; Child victims of sexual abuse

REQUIREMENTS: Any person victimized in Campbell County

WOMEN'S CRISIS CENTER
321 York St, Newport, KY 41071
Crisis hotline: **(606) 491-3335 24 hrs**
Information: (606) 491-3335 8:30am-6pm
Contact: Edwena Walker, Exec Dir
TYPE OF AGENCY: Rape crisis center; Domestic violence program; Child sexual abuse services; Child sexual abuse prevention program
AREAS SERVED: 8 counties of Northern KY; 5 counties of Buffalo Trace District
YEARS IN OPERATION: 12
ACCESSIBILITY: Wheelchair accessible
CASES SEXUAL ASSAULT/ABUSE (%): 30
CLIENTS/SERVICES: Sexual assault survivors; Marital rape/sexual abuse survivors; Child victims of sexual abuse; Adult survivors of child sexual abuse; Incest victims/survivors; Prevention program; Community education; Adolescent survivors of sexual abuse; Male survivors of sexual abuse

OWENSBORO

GREEN RIVER COMPREHENSIVE CARE— CRISIS AND INFORMATION LINE
PO Box 950, Owensboro, KY 42302-0950
Crisis hotline: **(502) 684-9466 24 hrs**
Information: (502) 684-0696 8am-5pm
Contact: Rebecca Hagan, Dir
TYPE OF AGENCY: Counseling/mental health services; Telephone crisis hotline; Information and referral
AREAS SERVED: Daviess, McLean, Hancock, Ohio, Union, Webster, Henderson
YEARS IN OPERATION: 11
ACCESSIBILITY: Wheelchair accessible; Telecommunications for the hearing impaired (TTY, TDY, etc.)
CLIENTS/SERVICES: Sexual assault survivors; Marital rape/sexual abuse survivors; Child victims of sexual abuse; Adult survivors of child sexual abuse; Incest victims/survivors

GREEN RIVER REGIONAL RAPE VICTIM SERVICES, INC
212 E 2nd St, Owensboro, KY 42301
Crisis hotline: **(502) 926-7273 24 hrs**
Information: (502) 926-7273 8am-5pm
Contact: Vicky Shelton, Dir; Janet Jones, Admin Asst
TYPE OF AGENCY: Rape crisis center; Child sexual abuse services; Child sexual abuse prevention program
AREAS SERVED: Daviess, Henderson, Ohio, McLean, Webster, Union, Hancock
YEARS IN OPERATION: 9
ACCESSIBILITY: Wheelchair accessible; Signers for the hearing impaired
CASES SEXUAL ASSAULT/ABUSE (%): 100
CLIENTS/SERVICES: Sexual assault survivors; Marital rape/sexual abuse survivors; Child victims of sexual abuse; Adult survivors of child sexual abuse; Incest victims/survivors; Prevention program; Community education; Adolescent survivors of sexual abuse; Male survivors of sexual abuse
SPECIAL PROGRAMS/SERVICES: Image therapy and art therapy with adult survivors of incest, rescuing the child through images

LEXIE HICKS COUNSELING CENTER
1412 Frederica St, Owensboro, KY 42301
Information: (502) 926-6900 9am-5pm (Tue, Wed, Thu, Fri); 9am-4pm (Mon)
Contact: Lexie Hicks, (AAMFT) Marriage/Family Therapist
TYPE OF AGENCY: Private practice
AREAS SERVED: Western KY; Eastern IN
YEARS IN OPERATION: 10
DESCRIPTION: Provides individual, couples, group, and family therapy with an emphasis on reality therapy and systems theory

LEXIE HICKS COUNSELING CENTER
(continued)
CLIENTS/SERVICES: Sexual assault survivors; Marital rape/sexual abuse survivors; Adult survivors of child sexual abuse; Incest victims/survivors; Community education; Adolescent survivors of sexual abuse; Male survivors of sexual abuse
REQUIREMENTS: Client must be 12 or older; Does strictly psychotherapy with survivors and family

OWINGSVILLE

PATHWAYS, INC
Rte 3, Box 5, Owingsville, KY 40360
Crisis hotline: **(800) 562-8909 24 hrs 7 days**
Contact: Roy E Cox, MA County Supv
TYPE OF AGENCY: Counseling/mental health services
AREAS SERVED: Rowan, Morgan, Menifee, Lawrence, Greenup, Montgomery, Bath, Boyd, Carter, Elliott
YEARS IN OPERATION: 20
ACCESSIBILITY: Wheelchair accessible; Signers for the hearing impaired
CASES SEXUAL ASSAULT/ABUSE (%): 10-15
DESCRIPTION: Counseling, therapy and psychiatric and psychological services available for survivors and perpetrators (rapists, child sexual abuse/incest offenders, and batterers)
CLIENTS/SERVICES: Sexual assault survivors; Marital rape/sexual abuse survivors; Child victims of sexual abuse; Adult survivors of child sexual abuse; Incest victims/survivors; Offender treatment program; Adolescent survivors of sexual abuse; Male survivors of sexual abuse
REQUIREMENTS: Anyone under 18 years old requires written consent from parent or guardian

PADUCAH

PADUCAH MCCRACKEN COUNTY CHILD WATCH, INC
PO Box 1262, Paducah, KY 42002-1262
Crisis hotline: **(502) 443-1440 24 hrs**
Information: (502) 443-1440 9am-3pm
Contact: Sandra Gottschalk, Board of Dir Pres
TYPE OF AGENCY: Child sexual abuse services; Child sexual abuse prevention program; Child abuse prevention program
AREAS SERVED: McCracken, Graves, Ballard, and surrounding counties
YEARS IN OPERATION: 4
CASES SEXUAL ASSAULT/ABUSE (%): 100
DESCRIPTION: Sponsors prevntion programs in the schools from preshcool through high school; Victim's advocacy center provides homelike environment for interviewing child victims and their families, as well as counseling about the legal process
CLIENTS/SERVICES: Child victims of sexual abuse; Prevention program; Community education

WBH/PCM RAPE VICTIM SERVICES
2501 Kentucky Ave, Paducah, KY 42003
Crisis hotline: **(502) 575-2255 24 hrs**
Information: (502) 442-2273 8am-5pm (Mon-Fri)
Contact: Carolyn Smith, Dir
TYPE OF AGENCY: Rape crisis center
SPONSORING ORGANIZATION: Western Baptist Hospital
AREAS SERVED: McCracken, Calkloway, Livingston, Marshall, Graves, Ballard, Hickman, Carlisle, Fulton, KY; Massac, IL
YEARS IN OPERATION: 3
CASES SEXUAL ASSAULT/ABUSE (%): 100
CLIENTS/SERVICES: Sexual assault survivors; Marital rape/sexual abuse survivors; Adult survivors of child sexual abuse; Incest victims/survivors; Prevention program; Community education; Adolescent survivors of sexual abuse; Male survivors of sexual abuse
REQUIREMENTS: Ages 18 and older, rape victims and adult survivors of incest; Ages 13-17, date or stranger rape (no incest).

WESTERN KENTUCKY REGIONAL MENTAL HEALTH/MENTAL RETARDATION BOARD, INC
PO Box 7287, 1530 Lone Oak Rd, Paducah, KY 42002-7287
Crisis hotline: **(800) 592-3980 24 hrs**
Information: (502) 442-7121 8am-5pm (CDT)
Contact: Karen Granger, Reg Children's Svcs Coord
TYPE OF AGENCY: Counseling/mental health services
AREAS SERVED: McCracken, Marshall, Ballard, Carlisle, Livingston, Fulton, Hickman, Calloway, Graves
YEARS IN OPERATION: 22
ACCESSIBILITY: Wheelchair accessible
DESCRIPTION: Counseling for survivors; Support groups for parents of sexually abused children; Individual counseling for child sexual abuse offenders, incest offenders, and batterers
CLIENTS/SERVICES: Sexual assault survivors; Marital rape/sexual abuse survivors; Child victims of sexual abuse; Adult survivors of child sexual abuse; Incest victims/survivors; Community education; Adolescent survivors of sexual abuse; Male survivors of sexual abuse; Healing
SPECIAL PROGRAMS/SERVICES: Use of imagery and ego building techniques in healing of sexual assault survivors. Videotapes: education of public regarding child sexual abuse with local TV station

PRESTONSBURG

RAPE VICTIM SERVICES PROGRAM
18 S Front Ave, Prestonsburg, KY 41653
Crisis hotline: **(800) 422-1060 24 hrs**
Information: (606) 886-8572
Contact: Edna M Ritchie, Dir
TYPE OF AGENCY: Counseling/mental health services
SPONSORING ORGANIZATION: Mountain Comprehensive Care Center
AREAS SERVED: Floyd, Magoffin, Johnson, Martin, Pike
YEARS IN OPERATION: 2
ACCESSIBILITY: Wheelchair accessible
CASES SEXUAL ASSAULT/ABUSE (%): 30
DESCRIPTION: Counseling for survivors; Support groups for female and male survivors of sexual assault/abuse; Individual and group therapy for rapists, child sexual abuse offenders, incest offenders, and batterers
CLIENTS/SERVICES: Sexual assault survivors; Marital rape/sexual abuse survivors; Child victims of sexual abuse; Adult survivors of child sexual abuse; Incest victims/survivors; Prevention program; Community education; Adolescent survivors of sexual abuse; Male survivors of sexual abuse
REQUIREMENTS: Children under the age of 16 must have permission for treatment if clinical services are requested.

SOMERSET

LAKE CUMBERLAND CLINICAL SERVICES
401 Bogle St, Ste 204, Somerset, KY 42501
Crisis hotline: **(800) 633-5599 24 hrs**
Information: (606) 679-7348 8:30am-5pm (Mon-Fri)
Contact: Brenda White, Therapist; Sandra Renfro, Clinic Mgr
TYPE OF AGENCY: Counseling/mental health services; Residential treatment facility
AREAS SERVED: Pulaski, Wayne, McCreary, Green, Taylor, Clinton, Adair, Cumberland
YEARS IN OPERATION: 20
ACCESSIBILITY: Wheelchair accessible
CASES SEXUAL ASSAULT/ABUSE (%): 60
DESCRIPTION: Counseling for survivors; Individual and group therapy for rapists, child sexual abuse offenders, incest offenders, and batterers
CLIENTS/SERVICES: Sexual assault survivors; Marital rape/sexual abuse survivors; Child victims of sexual abuse; Adult survivors of child sexual abuse; Incest victims/survivors; Community education; Adolescent survivors of sexual abuse; Male survivors of sexual abuse
REQUIREMENTS: Sliding scale fees

LOUISIANA

ALEXANDRIA

FAMILY COUNSELING AGENCY, INC—WORK AGAINST RAPE PROGRAM
1404 Murray St, Alexandria, LA 71301
Crisis hotline: **(318) 445-2022 24 hrs**
Information: (318) 448-0284 8am-9pm (Tue, Wed, Thu); 8am-5pm (Mon, Fri)
Contact: Sue Poole, Child Advocate/Coun; Beverly Butler, Work Against Rape Coord
TYPE OF AGENCY: Rape crisis center; Domestic violence program; Counseling/mental health services
AREAS SERVED: Rapides, Grant, La Salle, Catahonla, Avoyelles, Concordia, Vernon, Winn
YEARS IN OPERATION: 75
LANGUAGES: Spanish
ACCESSIBILITY: Wheelchair accessible
DESCRIPTION: Crisis counseling and advocacy for rape and domestic violence survivors; Therapy for sexually abused children; Anger control group for batterers
CLIENTS/SERVICES: Sexual assault survivors; Marital rape/sexual abuse survivors; Child victims of sexual abuse; Adult survivors of child sexual abuse; Incest victims/survivors; Community education; Adolescent survivors of sexual abuse; Male survivors of sexual abuse

BATON ROUGE

DISTRICT ATTORNEY'S STOP RAPE CRISIS CENTER
215 St Louis St, Rm 302, Baton Rouge, LA 70801
Crisis hotline: **(504) 383-7273 24 hrs**
Information: (504) 389-3456 8:30am-4:30pm
Contact: Margaret Griffon, Dir
TYPE OF AGENCY: Rape crisis center; Victim/witness assistance program; Child sexual abuse prevention program
SPONSORING ORGANIZATION: East Baton Rouge Parish District
AREAS SERVED: East Baton Rouge Parish (Escort services and counseling for the surrounding parishes)
YEARS IN OPERATION: 14
ACCESSIBILITY: Wheelchair accessible; Signers for the hearing impaired
DESCRIPTION: Provides escort counselors to the hospital for exam using center's own rape kit and volunteer doctor; Hospital treatment room and testing provided free of charge; Provides escort counselor to court proceedings, crisis and in-house counseling, support groups (sexual assault, teen, incest), and pediatric volunteer doctor
CLIENTS/SERVICES: Sexual assault survivors; Child victims of sexual abuse; Adult survivors of child sexual abuse; Incest victims/survivors; Prevention program; Community education; Adolescent survivors of sexual abuse; Male survivors of sexual abuse
REQUIREMENTS: For hospital and physician services, including hospital escort, the victim must report the incident to a law enforcement agency in East Baton Rouge Parish. The counseling services have no requirements.

LAKE CHARLES

CALCASIEU WOMEN'S SHELTER
PO Box 276, Lake Charles, LA 70602
Crisis hotline: **(800) 223-8066 24 hrs**
Information: (318) 436-4552 24 hrs
Contact: Carol Martin, Children's Coord
TYPE OF AGENCY: Domestic violence program
AREAS SERVED: Calcasieu, Cameron, Vernon, Jefferson Davis, Beauregard, Allen
YEARS IN OPERATION: 10
LANGUAGES: Spanish, French
ACCESSIBILITY: Wheelchair accessible; Signers for the hearing impaired
CASES SEXUAL ASSAULT/ABUSE (%): 14
DESCRIPTION: Domestic violence services; Group counseling for batterers
CLIENTS/SERVICES: Marital rape/sexual abuse survivors; Child victims of sexual abuse; Adult survivors of child sexual abuse; Incest victims/survivors; Prevention program; Community education; Offender treatment program; Adolescent survivors of sexual abuse

ETC
1146 Hodges St, Lake Charles, LA 70601
Information: (318) 433-1062 24 hrs
Contact: Bonnie Hines, Rape Prev Coord
TYPE OF AGENCY: Rape crisis center; Counseling/mental health services; Shelter
ACCESSIBILITY: Wheelchair accessible
CASES SEXUAL ASSAULT/ABUSE (%): 50
DESCRIPTION: Crisis services and counseling for survivors; Emergency shelter for children; Individual and group therapy for rapists, child sexual abuse offenders, incest offenders, and batterers
CLIENTS/SERVICES: Sexual assault survivors; Marital rape/sexual abuse survivors; Child victims of sexual abuse; Adult survivors of child sexual abuse; Incest victims/survivors; Community education; Offender treatment program; Adolescent survivors of sexual abuse; Male survivors of sexual abuse

FAMILY AND YOUTH COUNSELING AGENCY
127 S Ryan St, Lake Charles, LA 70601
Information: (318) 436-9533 8am-7pm (Mon-Fri); 9am-3pm (Sat)
Contact: Cheryl Castille, BCSW, Interim Exec Dir
TYPE OF AGENCY: Counseling/mental health services
AREAS SERVED: Calcasieu, Beauregard, Allen, Jeff Davis, Cameron
YEARS IN OPERATION: 19
ACCESSIBILITY: Wheelchair accessible
CASES SEXUAL ASSAULT/ABUSE (%): 20-30
DESCRIPTION: Services in the sexual assault/child sexual abuse field include individual, group, marital, and family interventions for survivors and rapists, batterers, and child sexual abuse/incest offenders
CLIENTS/SERVICES: Sexual assault survivors; Marital rape/sexual abuse survivors; Child victims of sexual abuse; Adult survivors of child sexual abuse; Incest victims/survivors; Community education; Offender treatment program; Adolescent survivors of sexual abuse; Male survivors of sexual abuse
REQUIREMENTS: Sliding scale fees

METAIRIE

THE SEXUAL TRAUMA INSTITUTE
3901 Houma Blvd, MPIC Plaza No 2, Ste 410, Metairie, LA 70006
Information: (504) 888-2066 8am-5pm
Contact: Chrisa M DeGraeve, Intake Coord
TYPE OF AGENCY: Private practice
SPONSORING ORGANIZATION: Metairie Center for Psychotherapy
YEARS IN OPERATION: 2
ACCESSIBILITY: Wheelchair accessible; Signers for the hearing impaired
CASES SEXUAL ASSAULT/ABUSE (%): 100
DESCRIPTION: Individual and group therapies for victims/survivors, including group for female and male survivors. Treatment for rapists, child sexual abuse/incest offenders, batterers, and juvenile sex offenders
CLIENTS/SERVICES: Sexual assault survivors; Marital rape/sexual abuse survivors; Child victims of sexual abuse; Adult survivors of child sexual abuse; Incest victims/survivors; Community education; Offender treatment program; Adolescent survivors of sexual abuse; Male survivors of sexual abuse

MONROE

FAMILY CONSULTANTS, INC
702 Jackson St, Monroe, LA 71201
Information: (318) 325-9957 8:30am-5pm
Contact: Jane M Brandon, MA, Family Therapist, LPC; DeEtte M Quinn, MA, Family Therapist, LPC
TYPE OF AGENCY: Child sexual abuse services; Child sexual abuse prevention program; Private practice
AREAS SERVED: Ouachita, Lincoln, Morehouse, Franklin, East and West Carrol, Madison
YEARS IN OPERATION: 1
CASES SEXUAL ASSAULT/ABUSE (%): 85

FAMILY CONSULTANTS, INC *(continued)*
DESCRIPTION: Provides families and individuals with necessary life skills through individual, group, and family therapy for victims of sexual abuse and their families; Conducts community awareness and education seminars on the topic of sexual abuse and trains professionals on a statewide level
CLIENTS/SERVICES: Sexual assault survivors; Marital rape/sexual abuse survivors; Child victims of sexual abuse; Adult survivors of child sexual abuse; Incest victims/survivors; Prevention program; Community education; Court advocacy; Adolescent survivors of sexual abuse; Male survivors of sexual abuse
SPECIAL PROGRAMS/SERVICES: Education: KID'S KLINIC child sexual abuse prevention workshops. Training workshop for the community and professionals. Travels to deprived parishes where there are no counseling and services available

OUACHITA PARISH SHERIFF'S DEPARTMENT
PO Box 1803, Monroe, LA 71210
Crisis hotline: **(318) 329-1200 24 hrs**
Information: (318) 329-1200 24 hrs
Contact: Beth Lord, Cpl, Criminal Investigator
TYPE OF AGENCY: Victim/witness assistance program; Child sexual abuse prevention program
AREAS SERVED: Ouachita Parish
YEARS IN OPERATION: 4
LANGUAGES: Interpreters available
ACCESSIBILITY: Wheelchair accessible; Signers for the hearing impaired
CASES SEXUAL ASSAULT/ABUSE (%): 5
CLIENTS/SERVICES: Sexual assault survivors; Marital rape/sexual abuse survivors; Child victims of sexual abuse; Adult survivors of child sexual abuse; Incest victims/survivors; Prevention program; Community education
REQUIREMENTS: Incident must be reported

YWCA
1515 Jackson St, Monroe, LA 71202
Crisis hotline: **(318) 323-1505 (YWCA), 323-9034 (Children's services), 387-HELP (Rape crisis line), 323-1543 24 hrs**
Information: (318) 323-1505 (YWCA), 323-9034 (Children's services), 387-HELP (Rape crisis line) 8:30am-4:30pm
Contact: Jeri Bellan, MA, Rape Crisis Children's Svcs Couns; Margo Rosey, Exec Dir
TYPE OF AGENCY: Rape crisis center; Domestic violence program; Child sexual abuse services
YEARS IN OPERATION: 3
ACCESSIBILITY: Wheelchair accessible
CASES SEXUAL ASSAULT/ABUSE (%): 85-90
DESCRIPTION: Comprehensive rape crisis services, including support groups for female and male survivors of sexual assault/abuse; Services for survivors of sexual assault and domestic violence; Therapy for rapists, child sexual abuse/incest offenders, and batterers
CLIENTS/SERVICES: Sexual assault survivors; Marital rape/sexual abuse survivors; Child victims of sexual abuse; Adult survivors of child sexual abuse; Incest victims/survivors; Prevention program; Community education; Offender treatment program; Adolescent survivors of sexual abuse; Male survivors of sexual abuse
SPECIAL PROGRAMS/SERVICES: Use of rituals and creative arts as part of healing for sexual assault survivors

NATCHITOCHES

NATCHITOCHES SHERIFF'S OFFICE
PO Box 266, Natchitoches, LA 71457
Information: (318) 352-6432 24 hrs
Contact: Sandra Williams, Deputy Sheriff
TYPE OF AGENCY: Victim/witness assistance program
AREAS SERVED: Natchitoches
YEARS IN OPERATION: 8
CLIENTS/SERVICES: Sexual assault survivors; Marital rape/sexual abuse survivors; Child victims of sexual abuse; Incest victims/survivors
REQUIREMENTS: Charges must be filed.

NEW ORLEANS

CHARITY HOSPITAL OF LOUISIANA AT NEW ORLEANS—RAPE CRISIS CENTER
1532 Tulane Ave, New Orleans, LA 70140
Crisis hotline: **(504) 568-3574, 568-3575, 568-8932 24 hrs 7 days**
Information: (504) 568-3574, 568-3575, 568-8932 24 hrs 7 days
Contact: Alice Lowry, Mgr, Emergency Dept Soc Svcs Supv
TYPE OF AGENCY: Hospital/medical center
AREAS SERVED: Orleans and surrounding area
YEARS IN OPERATION: 10
LANGUAGES: Volunteer translators available
ACCESSIBILITY: Wheelchair accessible; Signers for the hearing impaired
CASES SEXUAL ASSAULT/ABUSE (%): 1
DESCRIPTION: Emergency medical treatment and evidence collection; Assessments; Crisis counseling by social workers; Referrals to community services; Follow-up medical care at gyn or other clinic; Member of the Rape Crisis Network, an interagency team
CLIENTS/SERVICES: Sexual assault survivors; Marital rape/sexual abuse survivors; Child victims of sexual abuse; Community education; Adolescent survivors of sexual abuse; Male survivors of sexual abuse

CHILD AND ADOLESCENT MENTAL HEALTH PROGRAM
210 State St, New Orleans, LA 70118
Information: (504) 897-4758 8am-4:30pm
Contact: Nikki Alexander, Clinical Soc Work Spec
TYPE OF AGENCY: Counseling/mental health services; Child sexual abuse services
AREAS SERVED: Orleans, St Bernard, Plaquemines
YEARS IN OPERATION: 15
CASES SEXUAL ASSAULT/ABUSE (%): 10
CLIENTS/SERVICES: Child victims of sexual abuse; Adult survivors of child sexual abuse; Incest victims/survivors; Adolescent survivors of sexual abuse
REQUIREMENTS: Children up to 18 years old and their parents; Client must have symptoms of trauma; Child sexual assault victims who are symptomatic receive priority services

FAMILY SERVICE OF GREATER NEW ORLEANS
2515 Canal St, Ste 201, New Orleans, LA 70119
Information: (504) 822-0800 8am-9pm
Contact: Valerie Wolf, Child Abuse Contract Mgr
TYPE OF AGENCY: Counseling/mental health services; Child sexual abuse services; Child abuse services
AREAS SERVED: Orleans, Jefferson, St Bernard, St Charles, St Tamany, Washington, Plaque Mines
YEARS IN OPERATION: 5
LANGUAGES: Spanish
ACCESSIBILITY: Wheelchair accessible; Signers for the hearing impaired
CASES SEXUAL ASSAULT/ABUSE (%): 40
DESCRIPTION: State grant to provide therapy for children referred by state workers as a result of neglect, physical abuse, or sexual abuse; Multimodel (individual, couple, dyadic, family, and group) treatment; Treatment programs for child sexual abuse/incest offenders and batterers; Family treatment for incest cases
CLIENTS/SERVICES: Sexual assault survivors; Marital rape/sexual abuse survivors; Child victims of sexual abuse; Adult survivors of child sexual abuse; Incest victims/survivors; Prevention program; Community education; Offender treatment program; Adolescent survivors of sexual abuse; Male survivors of sexual abuse
REQUIREMENTS: Client(s) cannot be suicidal or actively psychotic. Some families are seen under state funding, others on sliding fee scale.

SEXUAL TRAUMA INSTITUTE
4460 General Meyer Ave, New Orleans, LA 70131
Crisis hotline: **(504) 367-0707 24 hrs**
Information: (504) 367-0707 24 hrs
Contact: Dr Mark Schwartz, Dir
TYPE OF AGENCY: Hospital/medical center; Child sexual abuse services
SPONSORING ORGANIZATION: Clinics for Marital and Sexual Therapy
AREAS SERVED: Regional
YEARS IN OPERATION: 5
ACCESSIBILITY: Wheelchair accessible
CASES SEXUAL ASSAULT/ABUSE (%): 100
DESCRIPTION: Support groups for female and male survivors of sexual assault/abuse; Individual and group therapy for child sexual abuse offenders, incest offenders, juvenile sex offenders, and batterers
CLIENTS/SERVICES: Sexual assault survivors; Marital rape/sexual abuse survivors; Child victims of sexual abuse; Adult survivors of child sexual abuse; Incest victims/survivors; Offender treatment program; Adolescent survivors of sexual abuse; Male survivors of sexual abuse; Healing
SPECIAL PROGRAMS/SERVICES: Art therapy and ROPES program for survivors

SHERIFF'S OFFICE—VICTIM/WITNESS ASSISTANCE
2800 Gravier St, New Orleans, LA 70119
Information: (504) 822-8000, ext 365 9am-5pm (Mon-Fri)
Contact: April Wilson, Dir
TYPE OF AGENCY: Victim/witness assistance program
AREAS SERVED: Orleans Parish
YEARS IN OPERATION: 5
CLIENTS/SERVICES: Sexual assault survivors; Child victims of sexual abuse

YWCA RAPE CRISIS PROGRAM
601 S Jefferson Davis Pkwy, New Orleans, LA 70119
Crisis hotline: **(504) 483-8888 24 hrs**
Information: (504) 482-9922 9am-5pm
Contact: Gertrude Galloway, Coord
TYPE OF AGENCY: Rape crisis center
AREAS SERVED: Orleans, Jefferson, St Bernard, St Tammany, Plaquemines Parishes
YEARS IN OPERATION: 15
ACCESSIBILITY: Wheelchair accessible; Telecommunications for the hearing impaired (TTY, TDY, etc.)
CASES SEXUAL ASSAULT/ABUSE (%): 100
CLIENTS/SERVICES: Sexual assault survivors; Marital rape/sexual abuse survivors; Child victims of sexual abuse; Adult survivors of child sexual abuse; Incest victims/survivors; Prevention program; Community education; Adolescent survivors of sexual abuse; Male survivors of sexual abuse

RUSTON

RUSTON MAYOR'S COMMISSION FOR WOMEN
Box 576, Ruston, LA 71273-0576
Information: (318) 255-8664
Contact: Dr Marty F Beasley, Exec Dir
TYPE OF AGENCY: Women's commission
DESCRIPTION: Provides volunteers for HELP crisis line, assistance in transporting to safehomes, and sponsorship of public education workshops. Focuses on the prevention of abuse of women and children
CLIENTS/SERVICES: Sexual assault survivors; Child victims of sexual abuse; Community education

SHREVEPORT

YWCA RAPE CRISIS CENTER
710 Travis St, Shreveport, LA 71101
Crisis hotline: **(318) 222-0556 24 hrs**
Information: (318) 222-2116 8am-8pm (Mon-Fri)
Contact: Joyce Segelhorst, Rape Crisis Couns/
  Marriage and Family Therapist
TYPE OF AGENCY: Rape crisis center; Domestic
  violence program
AREAS SERVED: Sabine, Bossier, Caddo, Webster,
  Red River, Natchitoches, DeSoto, Bienville,
  Claiborne
YEARS IN OPERATION: 8
ACCESSIBILITY: Wheelchair accessible; Signers for
  the hearing impaired
CASES SEXUAL ASSAULT/ABUSE (%): 97
DESCRIPTION: Comprehensive sexual assault services; Group therapy for incest offenders and batterers
CLIENTS/SERVICES: Sexual assault survivors; Marital rape/sexual abuse survivors; Child victims of sexual abuse; Adult survivors of child sexual abuse; Incest victims/survivors; Prevention program; Community education; Offender treatment program; Adolescent survivors of sexual abuse; Male survivors of sexual abuse

SLIDELL

YWCA RAPE PREVENTION AND SEXUAL ASSAULT PROGRAMS
769 Robert Rd, Slidell, LA 70458
Crisis hotline: **(504) 483-8888, collect calls accepted 24 hrs**
Information: (504) 643-9922 9am-5pm (Mon-Fri)
Contact: Jamie Sewell, Couns/Commty Educator
TYPE OF AGENCY: Rape crisis center; Child sexual abuse prevention program
AREAS SERVED: New Orleans and surrounding parishes
CASES SEXUAL ASSAULT/ABUSE (%): 80
CLIENTS/SERVICES: Sexual assault survivors; Marital rape/sexual abuse survivors; Adult survivors of child sexual abuse; Incest victims/survivors; Prevention program; Community education; Developmentally disabled
SPECIAL PROGRAMS/SERVICES: Prevention program for developmentally disabled and Child Assault Prevention (CAP) Program

MAINE

ALFRED

DISTRICT ATTORNEY'S OFFICE—VICTIM/WITNESS PROGRAM
York County Courthouse, Alfred, ME 04002
Information: (207) 324-8000 8am-5pm
Contact: Pamela Stewart, Daria Burnes, Victim Advocates
TYPE OF AGENCY: Victim/witness assistance program
AREAS SERVED: York
YEARS IN OPERATION: 3
ACCESSIBILITY: Wheelchair accessible
DESCRIPTION: Assists victims of crime through the criminal justice system; Provides information, support, referrals
CLIENTS/SERVICES: Sexual assault survivors; Child victims of sexual abuse; Male survivors of sexual abuse
REQUIREMENTS: Criminal charges must be brought in most cases
SPECIAL PROGRAMS/SERVICES: Publications: *Going to Court: A Book for Children Who Go to Court in York County, Maine*

AUBURN

ABUSED WOMEN'S ADVOCACY PROJECT
PO Box 713, Auburn, ME 04210
Crisis hotline: **(207) 795-4020 24 hrs**
Information: (207) 784-3995 9am-5pm (Mon-Fri)
Contact: Jeannette Libby, Night Advocate
TYPE OF AGENCY: Domestic violence program
AREAS SERVED: Androscoggin, Oxford, Franklin
YEARS IN OPERATION: 10
LANGUAGES: French
ACCESSIBILITY: Wheelchair accessible; Signers for the hearing impaired
CASES SEXUAL ASSAULT/ABUSE (%): 30-40
CLIENTS/SERVICES: Sexual assault survivors; Marital rape/sexual abuse survivors; Child victims of sexual abuse; Adult survivors of child sexual abuse; Incest victims/survivors; Prevention program; Community education

ADVOCATES FOR CHILDREN
PO Box 3316, Auburn, ME 04210
Information: (207) 783-3990 8am-5pm
Contact: Anne Brennan Belden, Exec Dir
TYPE OF AGENCY: Child sexual abuse prevention program; Child abuse prevention program
AREAS SERVED: Androscoggin
YEARS IN OPERATION: 10
CLIENTS/SERVICES: Prevention program; Community education

SEXUAL ASSAULT CRISIS CENTER
PO Box 6, Auburn, ME 04210
Crisis hotline: **(207) 795-2211 24 hrs**
Information: (207) 784-5272 9am-5pm (Mon-Fri)
Contact: Marty McIntyre, Exec Dir
TYPE OF AGENCY: Rape crisis center
AREAS SERVED: Androscoggin
YEARS IN OPERATION: 4½
LANGUAGES: French, Sign
ACCESSIBILITY: Wheelchair accessible; Signers for the hearing impaired
CASES SEXUAL ASSAULT/ABUSE (%): 100
CLIENTS/SERVICES: Sexual assault survivors; Marital rape/sexual abuse survivors; Child victims of sexual abuse; Adult survivors of child sexual abuse; Incest victims/survivors; Prevention program; Community education; Adolescent survivors of sexual abuse; Male survivors of sexual abuse; Developmentally disabled
SPECIAL PROGRAMS/SERVICES: Pilot program to address the special needs of the mentally retarded population. The program involves sexual assault/abuse awareness training for staff, prevention program for clients, and support groups for clients who have already been victimized

AUGUSTA

AUGUSTA AREA RAPE CRISIS CENTER
33 Winthrop St, Augusta, ME 04330
Crisis hotline: **(207) 626-0660 24 hrs**
Information: (207) 626-3425 8:30am-3pm (Mon-Wed-Thu)
Contact: Laura Fortman, Dir
TYPE OF AGENCY: Rape crisis center; Child sexual abuse services; Child sexual abuse prevention program
AREAS SERVED: South Kennebec, Northern Lincoln
YEARS IN OPERATION: 2
CASES SEXUAL ASSAULT/ABUSE (%): 100
CLIENTS/SERVICES: Sexual assault survivors; Marital rape/sexual abuse survivors; Child victims of sexual abuse; Adult survivors of child sexual abuse; Incest victims/survivors; Prevention program; Community education; Adolescent survivors of sexual abuse; Male survivors of sexual abuse

BANGOR

BEHAVIORAL AND DEVELOPMENTAL PEDIATRICS
417 State St, Bangor, ME 04401
Information: (301) 945-7572, ext 207 8am-5pm (Mon-Fri)
Contact: Elaine Piecuch, LCSW, Group Work Coord
TYPE OF AGENCY: Hospital/medical center; Child sexual abuse services
SPONSORING ORGANIZATION: Eastern Maine Medical Center
YEARS IN OPERATION: 10
ACCESSIBILITY: Wheelchair accessible
CASES SEXUAL ASSAULT/ABUSE (%): 66
CLIENTS/SERVICES: Child victims of sexual abuse; Adolescent survivors of sexual abuse
REQUIREMENTS: Children ages to 18 and their families

FAMILY SUPPORT TEAM
489 State St, Bangor, ME 04401
Crisis hotline: **(301) 945-7000 24 hrs**
Information: (301) 945-7835 8am-5pm
Contact: Patricia W Phillips, MED, Dir
TYPE OF AGENCY: Hospital/medical center
SPONSORING ORGANIZATION: Eastern Maine Medical Center
AREAS SERVED: Penobscot, Piscataquis, Hancock, Waldo, Washington
YEARS IN OPERATION: 5
ACCESSIBILITY: Wheelchair accessible; Signers for the hearing impaired
CASES SEXUAL ASSAULT/ABUSE (%): 50
DESCRIPTION: Early detection/intervention of child sexual abuse; Referrals to appropriate services and follow-up as necessary; Comprehensive, hospital-based child abuse program; Multidisciplinary interagency team
CLIENTS/SERVICES: Child victims of sexual abuse; Prevention program; Community education
REQUIREMENTS: Must be under age 18

SPRUCE RUN ASSOCIATION
PO Box 653, Bangor, ME 04401
Crisis hotline: **(207) 947-0496 24 hrs**
Information: (207) 945-5102, 667-2426 9am-5pm (Mon-Fri); 2426 9am-5pm (Mon)
TYPE OF AGENCY: Domestic violence program
AREAS SERVED: Penobscot, Hancock
YEARS IN OPERATION: 15
LANGUAGES: Spanish, Sign, interpreters for other languages available
ACCESSIBILITY: Signers for the hearing impaired
CASES SEXUAL ASSAULT/ABUSE (%): 35
CLIENTS/SERVICES: Sexual assault survivors; Marital rape/sexual abuse survivors; Child victims of sexual abuse; Adult survivors of child sexual abuse; Incest victims/survivors; Community education; Male survivors of sexual abuse

BELFAST

DISTRICT ATTORNEY'S OFFICE—VICTIM/WITNESS PROGRAM
73 Church St, Belfast, ME 04915
Information: (207) 338-2512 8am-4pm
Contact: Christine Statler, Victim-Witness Advocate
TYPE OF AGENCY: Victim/witness assistance program
AREAS SERVED: Waldo
YEARS IN OPERATION: 9
ACCESSIBILITY: Wheelchair accessible
CASES SEXUAL ASSAULT/ABUSE (%): 25-50
DESCRIPTION: Assists victims and witnesses of crimes that involve sexual assault/abuse through the criminal justice system; Provides

DISTRICT ATTORNEY'S OFFICE—VICTIM/WITNESS PROGRAM *(continued)*

information, support, referrals to other agencies; Coordinates criminal investigations; Coordinates efforts of law enforcement and DHS investigations involving child sexual abuse
CLIENTS/SERVICES: Sexual assault survivors; Child victims of sexual abuse

WALDO COUNTY CHILD AND PARENT COUNCIL
PO Box 224, 10 Market St, Belfast, ME 04915
Information: (207) 338-5446 9am-2pm (Mon-Fri)
Contact: Patrick Walsh, Coord
TYPE OF AGENCY: Counseling/mental health services; Child sexual abuse prevention program; Child abuse prevention program
AREAS SERVED: Waldo
YEARS IN OPERATION: 2
DESCRIPTION: To improve community and professional awareness about child abuse and neglect, and to coordinate local efforts to prevent abuse and neglect. Has a support and educational program for teenaged parents including prenatal classes, individual and group counseling, academic classes, life skills and advocacy
CLIENTS/SERVICES: Prevention program; Community education

BIDDEFORD

YORK COUNTY CHILD ABUSE AND NEGLECT COUNCIL, INC
208 Graham St, Biddeford, ME 04005
Information: (207) 282-6191 8am-5pm
Contact: Marilyn Staples, Dir
TYPE OF AGENCY: Child sexual abuse prevention program; Child abuse prevention program
AREAS SERVED: York
YEARS IN OPERATION: 10
ACCESSIBILITY: Wheelchair accessible
CLIENTS/SERVICES: Prevention program; Community education
SPECIAL PROGRAMS/SERVICES: *I've Got Superpower,* (a musical) child abuse prevention program, preschool through 4th grade

BREWER

CENTER FOR GROWTH AND CHANGE
RFD 1, Box 1373, Brewer, ME 04412
Information: (207) 989-3688 9am-5pm (Mon-Thu)
Contact: Theresa F de Vries, George S Flink, Dirs
TYPE OF AGENCY: Private practice
AREAS SERVED: Statewide
YEARS IN OPERATION: 13
LANGUAGES: Dutch
CASES SEXUAL ASSAULT/ABUSE (%): 50-60
DESCRIPTION: Provides psychotherapy, including marital, family, individual, and group. Ongoing group therapy for female and male survivors and group therapy marathons (weekend-long) twice a year.
CLIENTS/SERVICES: Sexual assault survivors; Marital rape/sexual abuse survivors; Adult survivors of child sexual abuse; Incest victims/survivors; Adolescent survivors of sexual abuse; Male survivors of sexual abuse
REQUIREMENTS: Over 18. Occasionally older teenagers are accepted for therapy

BRUNSWICK

BATH-BRUNSWICK RAPE CRISIS HELPLINE, INC
PO Box 990, Brunswick, ME 04011
Crisis hotline: **(800) 822-5999 24 hrs**
Information: (207) 725-4632 10am-2pm (Mon-Fri)
Contact: Audrey R Alexander, Dir
TYPE OF AGENCY: Rape crisis center
AREAS SERVED: Sagadahoc, Lincoln, eastern Cumberland
YEARS IN OPERATION: 5
CASES SEXUAL ASSAULT/ABUSE (%): 100
CLIENTS/SERVICES: Sexual assault survivors; Marital rape/sexual abuse survivors; Child victims of sexual abuse; Adult survivors of child sexual abuse; Incest victims/survivors; Prevention program; Community education; Adolescent survivors of sexual abuse; Male survivors of sexual abuse

DOVER-FOXCROFT

PISCATAQUIS COUNTY DISTRICT ATTORNEY'S OFFICE—VICTIM/WITNESS SERVICES
59 E Main St, Dover-Foxcroft, ME 04426
Information: (207) 564-2181 8am-4pm (Mon-Fri)
Contact: Gail D'Agostino, Victim-Witness Coord
TYPE OF AGENCY: Victim/witness assistance program
AREAS SERVED: Piscataquis
YEARS IN OPERATION: 3
ACCESSIBILITY: Wheelchair accessible
CASES SEXUAL ASSAULT/ABUSE (%): 10
CLIENTS/SERVICES: Sexual assault survivors; Marital rape/sexual abuse survivors; Child victims of sexual abuse; Adult survivors of child sexual abuse; Incest victims/survivors

WOMANCARE/AEGIS ASSOCIATION
PO Box 192, Dover-Foxcroft, ME 04426
Crisis hotline: **(207) 564-8401 Nights and weekends**
Information: (207) 564-8165 8am-4pm (Mon-Fri)
TYPE OF AGENCY: Domestic violence program
AREAS SERVED: Piscataquis and bordering towns of Somerset and eastern and southwestern Penobscot
YEARS IN OPERATION: 10
CASES SEXUAL ASSAULT/ABUSE (%): 60-80
DESCRIPTION: Comprehensive domestic violence services; Support group for mothers of sexually abused children; Harmony camp, a self-esteem curriculum for 7-10 year olds
CLIENTS/SERVICES: Sexual assault survivors; Marital rape/sexual abuse survivors; Child victims of sexual abuse; Adult survivors of child sexual abuse; Incest victims/survivors; Prevention program; Community education; Adolescent survivors of sexual abuse; Male survivors of sexual abuse
SPECIAL PROGRAMS/SERVICES: Harmony Camp is a mini-day camp (3 days, 3 hours each day) designed for children ages 7 to 10 to promote positive self-concepts and self-images. Through the use of puppets, discussions, art activities and stories, children explore their uniqueness, learn to recognize good qualities in others and develop effective ways of resolving conflict

ELLSWORTH

HANCOCK ADOLESCENT SEX OFFENDER PROGRAM
RFD 1, Box 303, Ellsworth, ME 04605
Information: (207) 667-2358 answering machine after hrs
Contact: Peter Rees, Psychologist
TYPE OF AGENCY: Private practice
AREAS SERVED: Hancock and adjacent counties
YEARS IN OPERATION: 1
CASES SEXUAL ASSAULT/ABUSE (%): 100
DESCRIPTION: Treatment and retraining of juvenile sex offenders who have been adjudicated and are considered suitable for treatment while living in the community
CLIENTS/SERVICES: Offender treatment program
REQUIREMENTS: Juvenile, adjudicated, on probation, judged safe in community

FARMINGTON

SAVES (SEXUAL ASSAULT VICTIMS EMERGENCY SERVICES)
PO Box 349, Farmington, ME 04938
Crisis hotline: **(800) 221-9191 24 hrs**
Information: (207) 778-3856 8:30am-4:30pm (Mon-Fri)
Contact: Janine Winn, Prog Coord
TYPE OF AGENCY: Rape crisis center
AREAS SERVED: Franklin and surrounding towns
YEARS IN OPERATION: 4½
LANGUAGES: Spanish, French
ACCESSIBILITY: Signers for the hearing impaired
CASES SEXUAL ASSAULT/ABUSE (%): 100
CLIENTS/SERVICES: Sexual assault survivors; Marital rape/sexual abuse survivors; Child victims of sexual abuse; Adult survivors of child sexual abuse; Incest victims/survivors; Prevention program; Community education; Adolescent survivors of sexual abuse; Male survivors of sexual abuse
SPECIAL PROGRAMS/SERVICES: University students can get academic credit for volunteer training

HOULTON

NOVA HOUSE
PO Box 986, Houlton, ME 04730
Crisis hotline: **(207) 769-8251 24 hrs**
Information: (207) 532-4004 8:30am-4:30pm
Contact: Donna Baietti, Woman's Advocate
TYPE OF AGENCY: Domestic violence program
SPONSORING ORGANIZATION: Family Support Center
AREAS SERVED: Aroostook
YEARS IN OPERATION: 10
LANGUAGES: French
CASES SEXUAL ASSAULT/ABUSE (%): 100
CLIENTS/SERVICES: Sexual assault survivors; Marital rape/sexual abuse survivors; Child victims of sexual abuse; Adult survivors of child sexual abuse; Incest victims/survivors; Prevention program; Community education

LEWISTON

CHILD AND FAMILY SUPPORT TEAM
73 Pine St, Lewiston, ME 04240
Crisis hotline: **(207) 783-9141 24 hrs**
Information: (207) 783-4661 8:30am-5pm
Contact: Scott Efland, LCSW, Clinical Coord
TYPE OF AGENCY: Counseling/mental health services; Child sexual abuse services
SPONSORING ORGANIZATION: Tri-County Mental Health Services
AREAS SERVED: Androscoggin, Franklin, Oxford
YEARS IN OPERATION: 3
CASES SEXUAL ASSAULT/ABUSE (%): 100
DESCRIPTION: Family-oriented therapy for sexually abused children; Individual, group, family and couple's therapy for child sexual abuse offenders and incest offenders
CLIENTS/SERVICES: Child victims of sexual abuse; Adult survivors of child sexual abuse; Incest victims/survivors; Offender treatment program; Adolescent survivors of sexual abuse; Male survivors of sexual abuse
REQUIREMENTS: Child victim must be adequately protected.

YWCA INTERVENTION PROGRAM
130 East Ave, Lewiston, ME 04240
Information: (207) 795-4054 8:30am-4:30pm (Mon-Fri) and by appointment
Contact: Susan Hall Dreher, Dir
TYPE OF AGENCY: Counseling/mental health services; Adolescent program
AREAS SERVED: Androscoggin and surrounding areas
YEARS IN OPERATION: 14
ACCESSIBILITY: Wheelchair accessible
CASES SEXUAL ASSAULT/ABUSE (%): 60-70

YWCA INTERVENTION PROGRAM
(continued)

DESCRIPTION: Provides sexual abuse treatment groups for both male and female victims ages 11-18
CLIENTS/SERVICES: Sexual assault survivors; Child victims of sexual abuse; Incest victims/survivors; Prevention program; Community education; Adolescent survivors of sexual abuse; Male survivors of sexual abuse
REQUIREMENTS: Clients must be ages 11-18 and must have parental consent; if pregnant or parenting, ages 11-20

LISBON FALLS

HEALING THROUGH PLAY
RFD 2, Box 2740, Lisbon Falls, ME 04252
Information: (207) 353-6323 8am-8pm (Mon-Sun)
Contact: Diana Delach, Healing/Play Consultant
TYPE OF AGENCY: Child sexual abuse services; Private practice
AREAS SERVED: Statewide
YEARS IN OPERATION: 1
LANGUAGES: Spanish, Sign
CASES SEXUAL ASSAULT/ABUSE (%): 50
DESCRIPTION: Gentle interaction, cooperative games to build self-esteem and a play community. Combines play and discussion to tap the inner child's resources—imagination, self-confidence, trust in the universe, and laughter. Personal Milestones Workshops involve creating a celebration to honor an important day/event in person's life—the wisdom of rites of passage. Facilitator is trained in incest work and in ritual/cult abuse
CLIENTS/SERVICES: Sexual assault survivors; Marital rape/sexual abuse survivors; Child victims of sexual abuse; Adult survivors of child sexual abuse; Incest victims/survivors; Community education; Adolescent survivors of sexual abuse; Male survivors of sexual abuse; Ritualistic abuse victims/survivors; Healing
REQUIREMENTS: Must have support system and complete screening questionnaire

MACHIAS

DISTRICT ATTORNEY'S OFFICE—VICTIM/WITNESS ASSISTANCE PROGRAM
PO Box 297, Machias, ME 04654
Information: (207) 255-4425 8am-4pm (Mon-Fri)
Contact: Tess Wright, Victim-Witness Advocate
TYPE OF AGENCY: Victim/witness assistance program
AREAS SERVED: Washington
YEARS IN OPERATION: 2½
ACCESSIBILITY: Wheelchair accessible
CASES SEXUAL ASSAULT/ABUSE (%): 50
CLIENTS/SERVICES: Sexual assault survivors; Marital rape/sexual abuse survivors; Child victims of sexual abuse; Community education; Adolescent survivors of sexual abuse; Male survivors of sexual abuse
REQUIREMENTS: The case must be under investigation by law enforcement.

WOMANKIND, INC
PO Box 493, Machias, ME 04654
Crisis hotline: **(207) 255-4785 24 hrs**
Information: (207) 255-4785; (800) 432-7303 9am-5pm; 5pm-9am
Contact: Eilean Mackenzie, Dir/Prog Coord; Barbara Zawotti, Counselor
TYPE OF AGENCY: Domestic violence program
AREAS SERVED: Washington
YEARS IN OPERATION: 8
CASES SEXUAL ASSAULT/ABUSE (%): 75
CLIENTS/SERVICES: Sexual assault survivors; Marital rape/sexual abuse survivors; Child victims of sexual abuse; Adult survivors of child sexual abuse; Incest victims/survivors; Prevention program; Community education; Adolescent survivors of sexual abuse

NEWCASTLE

NEWCASTLE HOLISTIC CENTER
PO Box 474, Newcastle, ME 04553
Crisis hotline: **(207) 563-1356 answering machine**
Information: (207) 563-1356
Contact: Marjorie J Arber, Counselor
TYPE OF AGENCY: Counseling/mental health services
AREAS SERVED: Statewide
YEARS IN OPERATION: 8
CASES SEXUAL ASSAULT/ABUSE (%): 50
DESCRIPTION: Incest survivor groups dedicated to the healing process; The Fisher-Hoffman Process dedicated to moving through childhood trauma to become one's true self
CLIENTS/SERVICES: Adult survivors of child sexual abuse; Incest victims/survivors; Healing

PORTLAND

COASTAL COUNSELING ASSOCIATION
535 Ocean Ave, Portland, ME 04103
Crisis hotline: **(207) 772-5581 24 hrs**
Information: (207) 772-5581 24 hrs
Contact: Ron Feindech, Dir
TYPE OF AGENCY: Private practice
AREAS SERVED: Cumberland, York
YEARS IN OPERATION: 4
ACCESSIBILITY: Wheelchair accessible; Signers for the hearing impaired
CASES SEXUAL ASSAULT/ABUSE (%): 25
CLIENTS/SERVICES: Sexual assault survivors; Marital rape/sexual abuse survivors; Child victims of sexual abuse; Adult survivors of child sexual abuse; Incest victims/survivors; Offender treatment program

FAIR HARBOR EMERGENCY SHELTER
87 Spring St, Portland, ME 04101
Crisis hotline: **(207) 874-1130, ext 25 24 hrs**
Information: (207) 874-1130, ext 25 24 hrs
TYPE OF AGENCY: Shelter; Adolescent program
SPONSORING ORGANIZATION: YWCA
AREAS SERVED: Primarily Cumberland, York
YEARS IN OPERATION: 14
CASES SEXUAL ASSAULT/ABUSE (%): 80
CLIENTS/SERVICES: Child victims of sexual abuse; Incest victims/survivors; Adolescent survivors of sexual abuse
REQUIREMENTS: Girls ages 7-17. Parents or department of human services must give permission for the girl to stay here. Will not serve youth who are intoxicated, actively violent, actively suicidal, psychotic, or fire-setters

RAPE CRISIS CENTER
PO Box 1371, Portland, ME 04104
Crisis hotline: **(207) 774-3613 24 hrs**
Information: (207) 774-3613
Contact: Susan Cole, Exec Dir
TYPE OF AGENCY: Rape crisis center; Acquaintance/date rape prevention program
AREAS SERVED: York, Cumberland
YEARS IN OPERATION: 12
CASES SEXUAL ASSAULT/ABUSE (%): 100
CLIENTS/SERVICES: Sexual assault survivors; Marital rape/sexual abuse survivors; Child victims of sexual abuse; Adult survivors of child sexual abuse; Incest victims/survivors; Prevention program; Community education; Adolescent survivors of sexual abuse; Male survivors of sexual abuse
SPECIAL PROGRAMS/SERVICES: This center has joined with other local groups to develop a school-based curricula focusing on violence in relationships, including a series of prevention programs which will meet the needs of the school/classroom while delivering very important but not often discussed items. There are a range of options: 1 hour presentations for classrooms; 1 day workshops; teen conferences; teacher and parent training; support groups.

PRESQUE ISLE

FAMILY SUPPORT CENTER
PO Box 22, Presque Isle, ME 04769
Crisis hotline: **(207) 769-8251 24 hrs**
Information: (207) 498-6146 8am-5pm (Mon-Fri)
Contact: Sue Foley, Coord
TYPE OF AGENCY: Domestic violence program
AREAS SERVED: Aroostook
YEARS IN OPERATION: 8
LANGUAGES: French
CASES SEXUAL ASSAULT/ABUSE (%): 95
CLIENTS/SERVICES: Sexual assault survivors; Marital rape/sexual abuse survivors; Child victims of sexual abuse; Adult survivors of child sexual abuse; Incest victims/survivors

SEXUAL ASSAULT HELPLINE/EMERGENCY SERVICES
2 Airport Dr, Presque Isle, ME 04769
Crisis hotline: **(800) 432-7805, (207) 762-4851 24 hrs**
Information: (800) 432-7805, (207) 762-4851 24 hrs
Contact: Margaret Rowland, Emer Svc Coord
TYPE OF AGENCY: Rape crisis center; Counseling/mental health services
SPONSORING ORGANIZATION: Aroostook Mental Health Center
AREAS SERVED: Aroostook
YEARS IN OPERATION: 4
LANGUAGES: French
CASES SEXUAL ASSAULT/ABUSE (%): 100
CLIENTS/SERVICES: Sexual assault survivors; Marital rape/sexual abuse survivors; Adult survivors of child sexual abuse; Incest victims/survivors; Prevention program; Community education; Adolescent survivors of sexual abuse; Male survivors of sexual abuse; Sexual harassment

UNIVERSITY OF MAINE AT PRESQUE ISLE—COUNSELING CENTER
181 Main St, Presque Isle, ME 04769
Crisis hotline: **(207) 762-4851 (Community hotline) 24 hrs**
Information: (207) 764-0311, ext 447 or ext 266
TYPE OF AGENCY: College/university-based services
AREAS SERVED: Central Aroostook
CLIENTS/SERVICES: Sexual assault survivors; Marital rape/sexual abuse survivors; Adult survivors of child sexual abuse; Incest victims/survivors; Community education; Male survivors of sexual abuse
REQUIREMENTS: Students, staff, and faculty

ROCKLAND

NEW HOPE FOR WOMEN
PO Box 642, Rockland, ME 04841
Crisis hotline: **(207) 594-2128 24 hrs**
Information: (207) 594-2128 9am-5pm (Mon-Fri)
Contact: Lisa Pohlmann, Dir
TYPE OF AGENCY: Domestic violence program
AREAS SERVED: Knox, Lincoln, Waldo
YEARS IN OPERATION: 7
CASES SEXUAL ASSAULT/ABUSE (%): 20
CLIENTS/SERVICES: Marital rape/sexual abuse survivors; Adult survivors of child sexual abuse; Incest victims/survivors; Prevention program; Community education
REQUIREMENTS: Adult survivors of child sexual abuse must be older than 16

SANFORD

CARING UNLIMITED
PO Box 1328, Sanford, ME 04073
Crisis hotline: **(207) 324-1802 24 hrs**
Information: (207) 324-1957 9am-5pm (Mon-Fri)
Contact: Laurel Heather, Children's Prog Coord
TYPE OF AGENCY: Domestic violence program
AREAS SERVED: York, Cumberland
YEARS IN OPERATION: 11
LANGUAGES: French
ACCESSIBILITY: Wheelchair accessible
CASES SEXUAL ASSAULT/ABUSE (%): 10
DESCRIPTION: Domestic violence services; Group therapy for batterers
CLIENTS/SERVICES: Marital rape/sexual abuse survivors; Adult survivors of child sexual abuse; Prevention program; Community education; Offender treatment program; Adolescent survivors of sexual abuse
SPECIAL PROGRAMS/SERVICES: Self-esteem group for children ages 5-12 years (8-week sessions) to discuss: feelings, problem solving, family divorce/separation, making friends, trust and risk-taking. Use arts and crafts, story books, and magic circle discussion techniques.

SKOWHEGAN

OFFICE OF DISTRICT ATTORNEY—VICTIM/WITNESS ADVOCATE PROGRAM
Somerset County Courthouse, Skowhegan, ME 04976
Information: (207) 474-2423, 474-5517 8am-5pm
Contact: Wendy Violette, Victim/Witness Advocate
TYPE OF AGENCY: Victim/witness assistance program
AREAS SERVED: Somerset
YEARS IN OPERATION: 9
ACCESSIBILITY: Wheelchair accessible
CASES SEXUAL ASSAULT/ABUSE (%): 90
DESCRIPTION: Provides information about the judicial system and court proceedings, along with emotional support
CLIENTS/SERVICES: Sexual assault survivors; Child victims of sexual abuse
REQUIREMENTS: Must file charges

WATERVILLE

RAPE CRISIS ASSISTANCE
PO Box 924, Waterville, ME 04901
Crisis hotline: **(800) 525-4441 24 hrs**
Information: (207) 872-0601
Contact: Jean Lamond, Dir
TYPE OF AGENCY: Rape crisis center
AREAS SERVED: North Kennebec, Somerset
YEARS IN OPERATION: 4½
LANGUAGES: French
ACCESSIBILITY: Signers for the hearing impaired
CASES SEXUAL ASSAULT/ABUSE (%): 100
CLIENTS/SERVICES: Sexual assault survivors; Marital rape/sexual abuse survivors; Child victims of sexual abuse; Adult survivors of child sexual abuse; Incest victims/survivors; Prevention program; Community education; Adolescent survivors of sexual abuse; Male survivors of sexual abuse

WISCASSET

COUNSELING AND TRAINING ASSOCIATES
PO Box 712, Wiscasset, ME 04578
Information: (207) 442-7264, 882-6526 9am-5pm (Mon-Fri), some evenings
Contact: Helene Grumbach, Loretta Wallace, Co-Founders
TYPE OF AGENCY: Private practice
AREAS SERVED: Sagadahoc, Lincoln
YEARS IN OPERATION: ½
CASES SEXUAL ASSAULT/ABUSE (%): 100
DESCRIPTION: Provides psychotherapy in individual, family, and group settings for victims/survivors and rapists, and child sexual abuse/incest offenders
CLIENTS/SERVICES: Sexual assault survivors; Marital rape/sexual abuse survivors; Child victims of sexual abuse; Adult survivors of child sexual abuse; Incest victims/survivors; Community education; Offender treatment program; Adolescent survivors of sexual abuse; Male survivors of sexual abuse
REQUIREMENTS: Clients must pay for services through self-pay, insurance, probation department funds, or DHS funds

LINCOLN COUNTY DISTRICT ATTORNEY'S OFFICE
Lincoln County Courthouse, High St, Wiscasset, ME 04578
Information: (207) 882-7312
Contact: Shane VerPlanck, Victim-Witness Advocate
TYPE OF AGENCY: Victim/witness assistance program
AREAS SERVED: Lincoln
YEARS IN OPERATION: 7
LANGUAGES: Spanish
ACCESSIBILITY: Wheelchair accessible; Signers for the hearing impaired
CASES SEXUAL ASSAULT/ABUSE (%): 20
CLIENTS/SERVICES: Sexual assault survivors; Marital rape/sexual abuse survivors; Child victims of sexual abuse
REQUIREMENTS: Case must be referred by Dept of Human Services or a community law enforcement agency

MARYLAND

ANNAPOLIS

ANNE ARUNDEL COUNTY SEXUAL ASSAULT CRISIS CENTER
1127 West St, Annapolis, MD 21401
Crisis hotline: **(301) 280-1321 24 hrs**
Information: (301) 280-1321 8:30am-5:30pm
Contact: Karen Goedman Lyon, Exec Dir
TYPE OF AGENCY: Rape crisis center; Child sexual abuse prevention program
SPONSORING ORGANIZATION: Anne Arundel County Executive's Office on Criminal Justice
AREAS SERVED: Anne Arundel County
YEARS IN OPERATION: 10
LANGUAGES: Languages spoken as needed
ACCESSIBILITY: Wheelchair accessible; Signers for the hearing impaired
CASES SEXUAL ASSAULT/ABUSE (%): 100
CLIENTS/SERVICES: Sexual assault survivors; Marital rape/sexual abuse survivors; Child victims of sexual abuse; Adult survivors of child sexual abuse; Incest victims/survivors; Prevention program; Community education; Adolescent survivors of sexual abuse; Male survivors of sexual abuse
SPECIAL PROGRAMS/SERVICES: The center has created a sexual abuse prevention puppet show for preschool and early elementary school children in order to teach them about safety and inappropriate touch. The children are actively involved throughout the puppet show through dramatizations of situations which are both safe and potentially dangerous. Teacher training is provided with each presentation of the puppet show. Teachers are educated regarding the dynamics of sexual abuse and how to intervene when a suspicion of sexual abuse exists, or when a child reveals a sexually abusive situation. Suggested follow-up activities are also presented to teachers. Each school is left with a tape of the "frogs" singing an original prevention song taught during the puppet show.

VICTIM/WITNESS ASSISTANCE CENTER
101 South St, Annapolis, MD 21401
Information: (301) 280-1160
Contact: Maureen Gillmer, Exec Dir
TYPE OF AGENCY: Victim/witness assistance program
SPONSORING ORGANIZATION: State's Attorney's Office
CLIENTS/SERVICES: Sexual assault survivors; Marital rape/sexual abuse survivors; Child victims of sexual abuse; Adult survivors of child sexual abuse; Incest victims/survivors; Community education; Male survivors of sexual abuse

BALTIMORE

HOUSE OF RUTH
2201 Argonne Dr, Baltimore, MD 21218
Crisis hotline: **(301) 889-7884 24 hrs**
Information: (301) 889-0840 9am-5pm (Mon-Fri)
TYPE OF AGENCY: Domestic violence program
YEARS IN OPERATION: 10
ACCESSIBILITY: Wheelchair accessible; Telecommunications for the hearing impaired (TTY, TDY, etc.)
CLIENTS/SERVICES: Marital rape/sexual abuse survivors; Child victims of sexual abuse; Adult survivors of child sexual abuse; Prevention program; Community education; Offender treatment program

SEXUAL ABUSE TREATMENT PROGRAM
312 E Oliver St, Baltimore, MD 21202
Crisis hotline: **(301) 361-2235 24 hrs**
Information: (301) 361-3927 8:30am-4:30pm (Mon-Fri)
Contact: Susan Goldstein, Prog Dir
TYPE OF AGENCY: Counseling/mental health services; Child sexual abuse services
SPONSORING ORGANIZATION: Baltimore City Department of Social Services
AREAS SERVED: Baltimore City
ACCESSIBILITY: Wheelchair accessible; Signers for the hearing impaired
CASES SEXUAL ASSAULT/ABUSE (%): 100
DESCRIPTION: Counseling for sexually abused children and their families, including child sexual abuse/incest offenders
CLIENTS/SERVICES: Child victims of sexual abuse; Offender treatment program; Adolescent survivors of sexual abuse

SEXUAL ASSAULT AND DOMESTIC VIOLENCE CENTER, INC
6229 N Charles St, Baltimore, MD 21212
Crisis hotline: **(301) 828-6390 24 hrs 7 days**
Information: (301) 377-8111 9am-5pm
Contact: Bonnie Ariano, Dir
TYPE OF AGENCY: Rape crisis center; Domestic violence program; Child sexual abuse services; Child sexual abuse prevention program
AREAS SERVED: Primarily Baltimore
YEARS IN OPERATION: 10
LANGUAGES: Spanish
ACCESSIBILITY: Wheelchair accessible; Signers for the hearing impaired
CASES SEXUAL ASSAULT/ABUSE (%): 60
DESCRIPTION: Comprehensive services for sexual assault and domestic violence survivors; Treatment for batterers
CLIENTS/SERVICES: Sexual assault survivors; Marital rape/sexual abuse survivors; Child victims of sexual abuse; Adult survivors of child sexual abuse; Incest victims/survivors; Prevention program; Community education; Treatment for batterers; Adolescent survivors of sexual abuse; Male survivors of sexual abuse
SPECIAL PROGRAMS/SERVICES: Parenting skills classes utilizing "Systematic Training for Effective Parenting." Dance and art therapy for adult survivors of child sexual abuse

SEXUAL ASSAULT RECOVERY CENTER
1010 Saint Paul St, Baltimore, MD 21202
Crisis hotline: **(301) 366-RAPE 24 hrs**
Information: (301) 685-0937 9am-5pm
Contact: Deborah Helfeld, Exec Dir
TYPE OF AGENCY: Rape crisis center; Child sexual abuse services; Child sexual abuse prevention program; Acquaintance/date rape prevention program
YEARS IN OPERATION: 17
ACCESSIBILITY: Wheelchair accessible
CASES SEXUAL ASSAULT/ABUSE (%): 100
CLIENTS/SERVICES: Sexual assault survivors; Marital rape/sexual abuse survivors; Child victims of sexual abuse; Adult survivors of child sexual abuse; Incest victims/survivors; Prevention program; Community education; Adolescent survivors of sexual abuse; Male survivors of sexual abuse
SPECIAL PROGRAMS/SERVICES: Media program: *No Means No*, a video on date rape and date rape prevention

STATE'S ATTORNEY'S OFFICE FOR BALTIMORE CITY—SEX OFFENSE UNIT
111 N Calvert St, Courthouse East, Rm 316, Baltimore, MD 21202
Information: (301) 396-5040 24 hrs
Contact: Wanda Keyes-Robinson, Div Chief
TYPE OF AGENCY: Victim/witness assistance program
AREAS SERVED: Baltimore City
YEARS IN OPERATION: 10
ACCESSIBILITY: Wheelchair accessible
CLIENTS/SERVICES: Prosecution

BEL AIR

SEXUAL ASSAULT/SPOUSE ABUSE RESOURCE CENTER
101 Thomas St, Bel Air, MD 21014
Crisis hotline: **(301) 879-3486, 836-8430 24 hrs 7 days**
Information: (301) 879-3486, 836-8430 8:30am-4:30pm (Mon-Fri)
Contact: Pat Kirby, Joan Parker-Mason, Counselors
TYPE OF AGENCY: Rape crisis center; Domestic violence program
AREAS SERVED: Harford
YEARS IN OPERATION: 10
CASES SEXUAL ASSAULT/ABUSE (%): 50
DESCRIPTION: Provides services for victims of sexual assault and domestic violence; Group education classes for batterers

SEXUAL ASSAULT/SPOUSE ABUSE RESOURCE CENTER *(continued)*
CLIENTS/SERVICES: Sexual assault survivors; Marital rape/sexual abuse survivors; Child victims of sexual abuse; Adult survivors of child sexual abuse; Incest victims/survivors; Community education; Adolescent survivors of sexual abuse; Male survivors of sexual abuse

BETHESDA

SEXOLOGY ASSOCIATES, INC
4835 Del Ray Ave, Bethesda, MD 20814-3013
Information: (301) 652-6448 24 hrs
Contact: Dr Fred Berlin, Clinic Dir
TYPE OF AGENCY: Private practice
AREAS SERVED: Metropolitan Washington, DC
YEARS IN OPERATION: 3
ACCESSIBILITY: Wheelchair accessible; Signers for the hearing impaired
DESCRIPTION: Treatment of adolescent and adult sex offenders (including female offenders): rapists, child sex abuse/incest offenders, and those with other sexual disorders. Group therapy for adults, adolescents, mentally retarded and a support group for family, friends and significant others. Also uses pharmacotherapy
CLIENTS/SERVICES: Sexual assault survivors; Marital rape/sexual abuse survivors; Child victims of sexual abuse; Adult survivors of child sexual abuse; Incest victims/survivors; Offender treatment program; Adolescent survivors of sexual abuse; Male survivors of sexual abuse; Developmentally disabled
SPECIAL PROGRAMS/SERVICES: Annual 2 ½ day seminar on sex offender treatment for legal and medical professionals (third week in February); Weeklong clinical training seminar, and professional consultations

CALIFORNIA

WALDEN/SIERRA, INC
PO Box 224, California, MD 20619
Crisis hotline: **(301) 863-6661, 870-3646 24 hrs daily**
Information: (301) 863-6661, TTY 863-6664 24 hrs
Contact: Kathleen O'Brien, Clinical Coord; Virginia Simpson, SA Prog Coord
TYPE OF AGENCY: Domestic violence program; Counseling/mental health services; Child sexual abuse services; Child sexual abuse prevention program; Residential treatment facility; Adolescent program
AREAS SERVED: St Mary's
YEARS IN OPERATION: 15
ACCESSIBILITY: Wheelchair accessible; Telecommunications for the hearing impaired (TTY, TDY, etc.)
DESCRIPTION: Provides drug abuse treatment and prevention services and general crisis intervention and community mental health services; Residential treatment services for female adolescents; Batterers group and support group for victims of domestic violence; Incest survivors group for women
CLIENTS/SERVICES: Sexual assault survivors; Marital rape/sexual abuse survivors; Child victims of sexual abuse; Adult survivors of child sexual abuse; Incest victims/survivors; Prevention program; Community education; Offender treatment program; Adolescent survivors of sexual abuse; Male survivors of sexual abuse

CHEVERLY

SEXUAL ASSAULT CENTER
3001 Hospital Dr, Cheverly, MD 20785
Crisis hotline: **(301) 341-4942 24 hrs**
Information: (301) 341-2005 24 hrs
Contact: Annette Gilbert-Jackson, Supv
TYPE OF AGENCY: Rape crisis center; Hospital/medical center; Child sexual abuse services; Child sexual abuse prevention program
SPONSORING ORGANIZATION: Prince George's Hospital Center
AREAS SERVED: Prince George's County
YEARS IN OPERATION: 13
LANGUAGES: Languages spoken as needed
ACCESSIBILITY: Wheelchair accessible; Telecommunications for the hearing impaired (TTY, TDY, etc.); Signers for the hearing impaired
CASES SEXUAL ASSAULT/ABUSE (%): 100
DESCRIPTION: Comprehensive sexual assault/abuse services; Individual therapy for child sexual abuse and incest offenders
CLIENTS/SERVICES: Sexual assault survivors; Marital rape/sexual abuse survivors; Child victims of sexual abuse; Adult survivors of child sexual abuse; Incest victims/survivors; Prevention program; Community education; Offender treatment program; Adolescent survivors of sexual abuse; Male survivors of sexual abuse

CLINTON

PSYCHOLOGY AND EDUCATION ASSOCIATES
7700 Old Branch Ave, Ste E203, Clinton, MD 20735
Information: (301) 868-8660 8am-8pm (Mon-Thu); Friday by appointment
Contact: S Peter Resta, LCSW, Psychotherapist; James E Lewis, PhD, Dir
TYPE OF AGENCY: Private practice
AREAS SERVED: Prince George's, Carroll, Calvert, Anne Arundel, Charles, St Mary's
YEARS IN OPERATION: 10
ACCESSIBILITY: Wheelchair accessible
DESCRIPTION: Assessment and therapy for victims/survivors and child sexual abuse/incest offenders
CLIENTS/SERVICES: Sexual assault survivors; Child victims of sexual abuse; Adult survivors of child sexual abuse; Incest victims/survivors; Community education; Offender treatment program; Adolescent survivors of sexual abuse; Male survivors of sexual abuse
REQUIREMENTS: Sliding scale fee available on a case-by-case basis

COLLEGE PARK

MARYLAND INSTITUTE FOR INDIVIDUAL AND FAMILY THERAPY
7307 Baltimore Ave, Ste 208, College Park, MD 20740
Crisis hotline: **(301) 277-3250 24 hrs**
Information: (301) 277-3250 24 hrs
TYPE OF AGENCY: Counseling/mental health services
AREAS SERVED: Prince George's, Montgomery, Anne Arundel, Howard MD; District of Columbia; Alexandria, Fairfax VA
YEARS IN OPERATION: 5
ACCESSIBILITY: Wheelchair accessible
CASES SEXUAL ASSAULT/ABUSE (%): 75
DESCRIPTION: Counseling for survivors and families; Support groups for female and male survivors of sexual abuse/assault; Individual, group, family, and couple therapy for child sexual abuse offenders, incest offenders, and batterers
CLIENTS/SERVICES: Sexual assault survivors; Marital rape/sexual abuse survivors; Child victims of sexual abuse; Adult survivors of child sexual abuse; Incest victims/survivors; Prevention program; Community education; Offender treatment program; Adolescent survivors of sexual abuse; Male survivors of sexual abuse

COLUMBIA

HOWARD COUNTY SEXUAL ASSAULT CENTER
8950 Rte 108, Ste 124, Columbia, MD 21045
Crisis hotline: **(301) 997-3292 24 hrs daily**
Information: (301) 964-0504 9am-4pm
Contact: Lisa Goshen, Exec Dir
TYPE OF AGENCY: Rape crisis center; Child sexual abuse services; Child sexual abuse prevention program
AREAS SERVED: Howard
YEARS IN OPERATION: 14
CASES SEXUAL ASSAULT/ABUSE (%): 100
CLIENTS/SERVICES: Sexual assault survivors; Marital rape/sexual abuse survivors; Child victims of sexual abuse; Adult survivors of child sexual abuse; Incest victims/survivors; Prevention program; Community education; Adolescent survivors of sexual abuse; Male survivors of sexual abuse; Developmentally disabled
SPECIAL PROGRAMS/SERVICES: Publications: *A Parent's Guide to Talking to Your Child About Child Sexual Abuse, Sexual Abuse Prevention An Educational Guide for Parents and Teachers of Children with Special Needs* (developmentally disabled)

CUMBERLAND

FAMILY CRISIS RESOURCE CENTER, INC
59 Prospect Sq, Cumberland, MD 21502
Crisis hotline: **(301) 759-9244 24 hrs**
Information: (301) 759-9246 9am-5pm (Mon-Fri)
Contact: Carolyn P Grahame, Exec Dir
TYPE OF AGENCY: Rape crisis center; Domestic violence program; Child sexual abuse services
AREAS SERVED: Allegany, Garrett
YEARS IN OPERATION: 10½
LANGUAGES: Interpreters available
ACCESSIBILITY: Wheelchair accessible; Signers for the hearing impaired
CASES SEXUAL ASSAULT/ABUSE (%): 30
DESCRIPTION: Individual, group, and couple therapy for batterers
CLIENTS/SERVICES: Sexual assault survivors; Marital rape/sexual abuse survivors; Child victims of sexual abuse; Adult survivors of child sexual abuse; Incest victims/survivors; Community education; Offender treatment program; Adolescent survivors of sexual abuse

ELDERSBURG

THE UNITY GROUP, INC
PO Box 753, Eldersburg, MD 21784
Information: (301) 795-4849 8:30am-9pm
Contact: Angela Lee, Founder
TYPE OF AGENCY: Domestic violence program
AREAS SERVED: Carroll, Baltimore, Howard, Prince Georges, Frederick, Montgomery
YEARS IN OPERATION: 3
LANGUAGES: Spanish, Korean
DESCRIPTION: Advocacy
CLIENTS/SERVICES: Marital rape/sexual abuse survivors; Child victims of sexual abuse; Adult survivors of child sexual abuse; Incest victims/survivors; Community education

FREDERICK

COMMITTEE FOR CHILD ABUSE PREVENTION
33 S Market St, Frederick, MD 21701
Information: (301) 663-0011 9am-4pm
Contact: Emily Daniel, Prevention Prog Coord
TYPE OF AGENCY: Child sexual abuse prevention program; Child abuse prevention program
SPONSORING ORGANIZATION: Mental Health Association of Frederick County
AREAS SERVED: Frederick
YEARS IN OPERATION: 1

COMMITTEE FOR CHILD ABUSE PREVENTION *(continued)*
DESCRIPTION: Provides the *Kids on the Block* puppet show on child sexual and physical abuse to schools and to the community
CLIENTS/SERVICES: Prevention program; Community education
SPECIAL PROGRAMS/SERVICES: Plans to create a group of speakers, including a variety of survivors

FREDERICK PSYCHIATRIC RESOURCES
801 Toll House Ave, Frederick, MD 21701
Information: (301) 695-8390 9am-5pm, 24-hr on-call person
Contact: Barbara DiCocco, Sex Abuse Coord
TYPE OF AGENCY: Private practice
DESCRIPTION: Provides court and social services evaluations in determining sex abuse; Family and individual therapy for survivors, including family work with admitting offender following his involvement in local offender treatment program
CLIENTS/SERVICES: Sexual assault survivors; Child victims of sexual abuse; Adult survivors of child sexual abuse; Incest victims/survivors; Community education; Offender treatment program; Adolescent survivors of sexual abuse; Male survivors of sexual abuse
REQUIREMENTS: Hourly fee for service; Offender must admit and have been involved in individual therapy

HEARTLY HOUSE, INC
PO Box 831, Frederick, MD 21701
Crisis hotline: **(301) 662-8800 24 hrs**
Information: (301) 662-8800 9am-6pm
Contact: Sue Shifflett, Exec Dir
TYPE OF AGENCY: Rape crisis center; Domestic violence program; Child sexual abuse services; Child sexual abuse prevention program
AREAS SERVED: Frederick
YEARS IN OPERATION: 11
ACCESSIBILITY: Wheelchair accessible; Signers for the hearing impaired
DESCRIPTION: Comprehensive services for sexual assault and domestic violence survivors; Group therapy for batterers
CLIENTS/SERVICES: Sexual assault survivors; Marital rape/sexual abuse survivors; Child victims of sexual abuse; Adult survivors of child sexual abuse; Incest victims/survivors; Prevention program; Community education; Adolescent survivors of sexual abuse; Male survivors of sexual abuse

HILLCREST FAMILY CENTER
93 S McCain Dr, Frederick, MD 21701
Crisis hotline: **(301) 663-1111 24 hrs daily**
Information: (301) 662-6892
Contact: Dennis L Hilker, PhD
TYPE OF AGENCY: Private practice; Offender treatment
AREAS SERVED: Frederick, Washington, Montgomery, Eastern VA
YEARS IN OPERATION: 2½
LANGUAGES: Sign
ACCESSIBILITY: Wheelchair accessible
CASES SEXUAL ASSAULT/ABUSE (%): 25
DESCRIPTION: Provides therapy for survivors primarily due to their relationship with the offenders; Group therapy for child sexual abuse/incest offenders; Adolescent sex offender program is family oriented, using concurrent adolescent and parent group therapy. Psychodramatic and behavioral techniques are blended
CLIENTS/SERVICES: Community education; Offender treatment program
REQUIREMENTS: Clients must admit their abusive behavior for acceptance into a treatment program. Prevention program is employed for those who do not admit

HAGERSTOWN

CASA, INC
116 W Baltimore St, Hagerstown, MD 21740
Crisis hotline: **(301) 739-8975**
Information: (301) 739-4990
Contact: Vicki A Sajehvandi
TYPE OF AGENCY: Rape crisis center
CLIENTS/SERVICES: Sexual assault survivors

OFFICE OF THE STATE'S ATTORNEY FOR WASHINGTON COUNTY, MD—VICTIM/WITNESS ASSISTANCE
41 Summit Ave, Hagerstown, MD 21740
Information: (301) 791-3120 8am-4pm
Contact: Joan Ryan Moller, Victim/Witness Assistance
TYPE OF AGENCY: Victim/witness assistance program
AREAS SERVED: Washington
YEARS IN OPERATION: 6
CASES SEXUAL ASSAULT/ABUSE (%): 25
CLIENTS/SERVICES: Sexual assault survivors; Marital rape/sexual abuse survivors; Child victims of sexual abuse; Adult survivors of child sexual abuse; Incest victims/survivors; Community education; Adolescent survivors of sexual abuse
REQUIREMENTS: Case must be in the process of or set for prosecution by this office.

HYATTSVILLE

SEXUAL ABUSE SERVICES UNIT—CHILD PROTECTIVE SERVICES (SASU, CPS)
6111 Ager Rd, Hyattsville, MD 20782
Crisis hotline: **(301) 699-8605 4:30pm-8:30am**
Information: (301) 341-6782 8:30am-4:30pm
Contact: Nainan Thomas, SASU Supv
TYPE OF AGENCY: Child sexual abuse services
SPONSORING ORGANIZATION: Prince George's County Department of Social Services
AREAS SERVED: Prince George's
ACCESSIBILITY: Wheelchair accessible; Telecommunications for the hearing impaired (TTY, TDY, etc.); Signers for the hearing impaired
CASES SEXUAL ASSAULT/ABUSE (%): 100
CLIENTS/SERVICES: Child victims of sexual abuse; Adult survivors of child sexual abuse; Incest victims/survivors; Prevention program; Community education; Offender treatment program; Adolescent survivors of sexual abuse
REQUIREMENTS: Child under 18 years; Sexual abuse indicated
SPECIAL PROGRAMS/SERVICES: SASU received a 3-year federal grant in Oct 1988 for Comprehensive Intrafamilial Child Sexual Abuse Treatment Project. 40 high risk families per year will be served. It will provide treatment for families who would not otherwise be able to afford such treatment (individual, group, family). Purpose is to prevent separation of child from family (foster care) and to reunite children who, as a last resort, do end up in foster care. SASU staff will be trained to lead the groups for victims, non-offending parents, siblings, and offenders.

KENSINGTON

MONTGOMERY COUNTY PROTECTIONLINE
10920 Connecticut Ave, Kensington, MD 20895
Crisis hotline: **(301) 949-6603 24 hrs**
Information: (301) 949-1255 9am-4:30pm
Contact: Ann Reiss, Dir
TYPE OF AGENCY: Counseling/mental health services; Telephone crisis hotline
SPONSORING ORGANIZATION: Mental Health Association
AREAS SERVED: Montgomery
YEARS IN OPERATION: 18
ACCESSIBILITY: Wheelchair accessible
CASES SEXUAL ASSAULT/ABUSE (%): 1

DESCRIPTION: Provides telephone crisis intervention regarding physical and sexual abuse for both children and adults; Works with a local 24-hour crisis center, which provides investigation, case management, advocacy services
CLIENTS/SERVICES: Sexual assault survivors; Child victims of sexual abuse; Adult survivors of child sexual abuse; Incest victims/survivors; Prevention program; Community education

OAKLAND

FAMILY CRISIS RESOURCE CENTER, INC
212 S Third St, Oakland, MD 21550
Information: (301) 334-9701 9am-5pm (Mon-Fri)
Contact: Carolyn P Grahame, Exec Dir
TYPE OF AGENCY: Rape crisis center; Domestic violence program; Child sexual abuse services
AREAS SERVED: Garrett
YEARS IN OPERATION: 10½
LANGUAGES: Interpreters available
ACCESSIBILITY: Wheelchair accessible; Signers for the hearing impaired
CASES SEXUAL ASSAULT/ABUSE (%): 30
DESCRIPTION: Services for survivors of sexual asault and domestic violence, individual, group, and couple therapy for batterers
CLIENTS/SERVICES: Sexual assault survivors; Marital rape/sexual abuse survivors; Child victims of sexual abuse; Adult survivors of child sexual abuse; Incest victims/survivors; Community education; Offender treatment program; Adolescent survivors of sexual abuse

OXON HILL

PSYCHOLOGICAL ASSOCIATES OF OXON HILL
6178 Oxon Hill Rd, Ste 306, Oxon Hill, MD 20745
Information: (301) 567-9297 9am-8:30pm (Mon-Thu)
Contact: Nancy Davis, PhD, Dir; Gail Bethea-Jackson, LCSW
TYPE OF AGENCY: Child sexual abuse services; Private practice
AREAS SERVED: Washington DC metro area
YEARS IN OPERATION: 3
ACCESSIBILITY: Wheelchair accessible
CASES SEXUAL ASSAULT/ABUSE (%): 90
DESCRIPTION: Specializes in treating sexually abused children and in helping children disclose abuse
CLIENTS/SERVICES: Sexual assault survivors; Marital rape/sexual abuse survivors; Child victims of sexual abuse; Adult survivors of child sexual abuse; Incest victims/survivors; Offender treatment program; Adolescent survivors of sexual abuse; Male survivors of sexual abuse; Healing; Publications/media
REQUIREMENTS: Ages 2 and older; CHAMPUS provider; Client must file other insurance
SPECIAL PROGRAMS/SERVICES: Uses visual imagery, hypnosis and therapeutic stories with teenagers and adults. Therapeutic stories also used with children to facilitate disclosure and to heal. Publication: *Therapeutic Stories to Heal Abused Children*, a collection of 70 stories, each with a discussion of the significance of the story ($35)

PRINCE FREDERICK

ABUSED PERSONS PROGRAM
PO Box 980, Prince Frederick, MD 20678
Information: (301) 535-1121
Contact: Patricia Pease, Dir
TYPE OF AGENCY: Rape crisis center; Domestic violence program
AREAS SERVED: Calvert
CLIENTS/SERVICES: Sexual assault survivors; Marital rape/sexual abuse survivors; Child victims of sexual abuse; Adult survivors of child sexual abuse; Incest victims/survivors; Prevention program; Community education

ROCKVILLE

MONTGOMERY COUNTY SEXUAL ASSAULT SERVICES
401 Hungerford Dr, Ste 401, Rockville, MD 20850
Crisis hotline: **(301) 656-9420 24 hrs daily**
Information: (301) 217-1355 9am-5pm (Mon-Fri)
Contact: Marion Burkhalter, Dir
TYPE OF AGENCY: Rape crisis center
SPONSORING ORGANIZATION: Department of Addictions, Victims and Mental Health Services
AREAS SERVED: Montgomery
YEARS IN OPERATION: 10
LANGUAGES: Spanish
ACCESSIBILITY: Wheelchair accessible; Telecommunications for the hearing impaired (TTY, TDY, etc.); Signers for the hearing impaired
CASES SEXUAL ASSAULT/ABUSE (%): 100
DESCRIPTION: Professional services for victims of sexual assault and their families; Support groups for female and male survivors
CLIENTS/SERVICES: Sexual assault survivors; Marital rape/sexual abuse survivors; Child victims of sexual abuse; Adult survivors of child sexual abuse; Incest victims/survivors; Prevention program; Community education; Adolescent survivors of sexual abuse; Male survivors of sexual abuse

STATE'S ATTORNEY FOR MONTGOMERY COUNTY, MD
PO Box 151, 50 Courthouse Sq, Rockville, MD 20850
Information: (301) 217-7300 8:30am-5:30pm
Contact: Suzanne Schneider, Management and Budget Spec
TYPE OF AGENCY: Victim/witness assistance program
AREAS SERVED: Montgomery
LANGUAGES: Spanish, German, Interpreters available for many other languages
ACCESSIBILITY: Wheelchair accessible; Telecommunications for the hearing impaired (TTY, TDY, etc.) (with advanced notice); Signers for the hearing impaired (with advanced notice)
CASES SEXUAL ASSAULT/ABUSE (%): 5
CLIENTS/SERVICES: Sexual assault survivors; Marital rape/sexual abuse survivors; Child victims of sexual abuse

SALISBURY

LIFE CRISIS CENTER, INC
PO Box 387, Salisbury, MD 21801
Crisis hotline: **(301) 749-4357 24 hrs**
Information: (301) 749-0632 8:30am-4:30pm
Contact: Dodie Lazzati, Exec Dir
TYPE OF AGENCY: Rape crisis center; Child sexual abuse services; Child sexual abuse prevention program; Acquaintance/date rape prevention program
AREAS SERVED: Wicomico, Worcester, Somerset
YEARS IN OPERATION: 10
ACCESSIBILITY: Wheelchair accessible; Telecommunications for the hearing impaired (TTY, TDY, etc.)
DESCRIPTION: Rape crisis services; Therapy for batterers; Date rape prevention in middle and high schools; Child sexual abuse prevention program in elementary schools; Task force on violence against children
CLIENTS/SERVICES: Sexual assault survivors; Marital rape/sexual abuse survivors; Child victims of sexual abuse; Adult survivors of child sexual abuse; Incest victims/survivors; Prevention program; Community education; Adolescent survivors of sexual abuse; Male survivors of sexual abuse
REQUIREMENTS: Children under 14 must have consent of parent/guardian prior to treatment

SILVER SPRING

DC SELF DEFENSE KARATE ASSOCIATION AND DC MODEL MUGGING
701 Richmond Ave, Silver Spring, MD 20910
Information: (301) 589-1349 9am-4pm
Contact: Carol Middleton, Dir
TYPE OF AGENCY: Rape prevention program
AREAS SERVED: DC metro area
YEARS IN OPERATION: 13
LANGUAGES: Spanish, Sign, Russian #(by arrangement)#
ACCESSIBILITY: Wheelchair accessible; Telecommunications for the hearing impaired (TTY, TDY, etc.); Signers for the hearing impaired (by arrangement)
CASES SEXUAL ASSAULT/ABUSE (%): 50
DESCRIPTION: Teaches women and children self-defense; Martial arts program to empower women and children. DC Model Mugging: short-term, intensive self-defense (full contact); also works through emotional issues in class, including incest/sexual assault
CLIENTS/SERVICES: Sexual assault survivors; Marital rape/sexual abuse survivors; Child victims of sexual abuse; Adult survivors of child sexual abuse; Incest victims/survivors; Prevention program; Adolescent survivors of sexual abuse; Male survivors of sexual abuse
SPECIAL PROGRAMS/SERVICES: Model Mugging: healing for survivors, allows them to reenact assault but this time with a victorious ending (knock out attacker). Many women say it gives them what years of therapy could not: a way of working through and conquering the fear and experiencing physical and emotional victory

TOWSON

BALTIMORE COUNTY DEPARTMENT OF SOCIAL SERVICES—SEXUAL ABUSE TREATMENT PROGRAM
620 York Rd, Towson, MD 21204
Crisis hotline: **(301) 832-7263 after hrs**
Information: (301) 887-2800 8:30am-4:30pm
Contact: Kristina Debye, Coord
TYPE OF AGENCY: Counseling/mental health services; Child sexual abuse services
AREAS SERVED: Baltimore
ACCESSIBILITY: Wheelchair accessible; Signers for the hearing impaired
CASES SEXUAL ASSAULT/ABUSE (%): 100
DESCRIPTION: Public child protective service agency that also provides treatment for child sexual abuse victims and their families; Also provides treatment for juvenile sex offenders and incest offenders
CLIENTS/SERVICES: Child victims of sexual abuse; Offender treatment program

WESTMINSTER

RAPE CRISIS INTERVENTION SERVICE OF CARROLL COUNTY, INC
PO Box 1563, 98 N Court St, Westminster, MD 21157
Crisis hotline: **(301) 848-2724 24 hrs**
Information: (301) 857-0900 9am-5pm
Contact: Jo Ann Hare, Prog Dir
TYPE OF AGENCY: Rape crisis center
AREAS SERVED: Carroll
YEARS IN OPERATION: 10
CASES SEXUAL ASSAULT/ABUSE (%): 100
CLIENTS/SERVICES: Sexual assault survivors; Marital rape/sexual abuse survivors; Prevention program; Community education; Adolescent survivors of sexual abuse; Male survivors of sexual abuse

SEXUAL ABUSE TREATMENT CENTER
22 N Court St, Westminster, MD 21157
Crisis hotline: **(301) 848-2724 (rape crisis)**, 857-0077 (domestic violence)
Information: (301) 876-1233 8:30am-4:30pm (Mon, Thu, Fri); 8:30am-9pm (Tue, Wed)
Contact: Janice Schwarz-Lantner, Dir
TYPE OF AGENCY: Counseling/mental health services; Child sexual abuse services
SPONSORING ORGANIZATION: Family and Children's Services
AREAS SERVED: Carroll
YEARS IN OPERATION: 3
CASES SEXUAL ASSAULT/ABUSE (%): 100
DESCRIPTION: Provides treatment for child and adolescent victims of sexual abuse/assault and their families, and adult survivors of child sexual abuse; Adult and juvenile offender treatment programs
CLIENTS/SERVICES: Marital rape/sexual abuse survivors; Child victims of sexual abuse; Adult survivors of child sexual abuse; Incest victims/survivors; Community education; Offender treatment program; Adolescent survivors of sexual abuse; Male survivors of sexual abuse
REQUIREMENTS: Sliding scale fee; Offenders must admit offense

MASSACHUSETTS

ACTON

CODE, INC
2 School St, Acton, MA 01720
Crisis hotline: **(508) 263-8777, 486-3130 24 hrs**
Information: (508) 263-3455 9am-5pm (Mon-Fri)
Contact: Betsy Grennan, Act Dir
TYPE OF AGENCY: Counseling/mental health services; Telephone crisis hotline
YEARS IN OPERATION: 18
ACCESSIBILITY: Telecommunications for the hearing impaired (TTY, TDY, etc.)
CASES SEXUAL ASSAULT/ABUSE (%): 5
DESCRIPTION: Crisis intervention hotline; Informs callers of their options and resources
CLIENTS/SERVICES: Sexual assault survivors; Marital rape/sexual abuse survivors; Child victims of sexual abuse; Adult survivors of child sexual abuse; Incest victims/survivors; Adolescent survivors of sexual abuse; Male survivors of sexual abuse

AMHERST

EVERYWOMAN'S CENTER PROGRAMS AGAINST VIOLENCE AGAINST WOMEN
EWC, Wilder Hall, University of Massachusetts, Amherst, MA 01003
Crisis hotline: **(413) 545-0800 24 hrs**
Information: (413) 545-3474 9am-4pm (Mon-Fri)
TYPE OF AGENCY: Rape crisis center; College/university-based services
AREAS SERVED: Hampshire, Franklin
YEARS IN OPERATION: 12
LANGUAGES: Spanish, Chinese, Japanese
ACCESSIBILITY: Telecommunications for the hearing impaired (TTY, TDY, etc.)
DESCRIPTION: Provides services for both community and university women, including reentry programs for nontraditional women students, advocacy and support for women of color, counseling, advocacy for working women and two programs against violence against women
CLIENTS/SERVICES: Sexual assault survivors; Marital rape/sexual abuse survivors; Adult survivors of child sexual abuse; Incest victims/survivors; Prevention program; Community education; Pornography; Adolescent survivors of sexual abuse; Prisoners
REQUIREMENTS: Adolescents and adult women only
SPECIAL PROGRAMS/SERVICES: Discussion groups for women awaiting trial in the local correctional facility concerning domestic violence, sexual assault, legal advocacy. Programs on "Images of Women in Pornography and Advertising"

ARLINGTON

NEW ENGLAND FORENSIC ASSOCIATES
22 Mill St, Ste 208, Arlington, MA 02174
Information: (617) 643-0610 24 hrs
Contact: Carol J Ball, PhD, Theoharis K Seghorn, PhD, Partners
TYPE OF AGENCY: Consultation; Training/research; Offender treatment
AREAS SERVED: Eastern MA, NH, VT, CT
YEARS IN OPERATION: 3
ACCESSIBILITY: Wheelchair accessible
CASES SEXUAL ASSAULT/ABUSE (%): 75
DESCRIPTION: Serves as a resource to the community and mental health and criminal justice professionals in the assessment and comprehensive treatment of sexually aggressive offender. Provides training for other professionals and consultation on program development. Treatment for rapists, child sexual abuse/incest offenders and batterers includes individual and group therapy, behavioral reconditioning, penile plethysmograph, depoprovera therapy, family and couple therapy. Provides support and group therapy for spouses of offenders
CLIENTS/SERVICES: Marital rape/sexual abuse survivors; Adult survivors of child sexual abuse; Incest victims/survivors; Offender treatment program

ATHOL

HUMAN RESOURCE CENTER FOR RURAL COMMUNITIES
100 Main St, Athol, MA 01331
Crisis hotline: **(508) 249-3511 5pm-9am**
Information: (508) 249-9926 9am-5pm
Contact: Sherrill Corian, Clinical Svcs Dir
TYPE OF AGENCY: Counseling/mental health services
AREAS SERVED: Sections of Worcester (Athol and small towns); Sections of Franklin County (Orange and local towns)
YEARS IN OPERATION: 10
ACCESSIBILITY: Wheelchair accessible
CASES SEXUAL ASSAULT/ABUSE (%): 45-50
DESCRIPTION: Counseling for community residents, including sexual assault survivors and rapists and child sexual abuse/incest offenders
CLIENTS/SERVICES: Sexual assault survivors; Marital rape/sexual abuse survivors; Child victims of sexual abuse; Adult survivors of child sexual abuse; Incest victims/survivors; Offender treatment program; Adolescent survivors of sexual abuse; Male survivors of sexual abuse

PEOPLES' BRIDGE ACTION, INC
465 Main St, Athol, MA 01331
Information: (508) 249-2248 9am-5pm
Contact: Richard Baldwin, Prog Coord/ESOT
TYPE OF AGENCY: Counseling/mental health services
AREAS SERVED: Franklin
YEARS IN OPERATION: 14
LANGUAGES: Spanish
CASES SEXUAL ASSAULT/ABUSE (%): 70
CLIENTS/SERVICES: Sexual assault survivors; Marital rape/sexual abuse survivors; Child victims of sexual abuse; Adult survivors of child sexual abuse; Incest victims/survivors; Offender treatment program; Adolescent survivors of sexual abuse; Male survivors of sexual abuse
REQUIREMENTS: Majority of clients must be referred by Dept of Social Services
SPECIAL PROGRAMS/SERVICES: Specializes in providing outreach family and individual therapy in a relatively low income rural area

ATTLEBORO

NEW HOPE, SEXUAL ASSAULT PROGRAM
PO Box 48, Attleboro, MA 02703
Crisis hotline: **(617) 695-2113, 824-4757 24 hrs**
Information: (617) 226-4015 9am-5pm
Contact: Caron Zlotnick, Dir
TYPE OF AGENCY: Rape crisis center; Child sexual abuse prevention program
SPONSORING ORGANIZATION: New Hope, Inc
AREAS SERVED: Southeast Massachusetts
YEARS IN OPERATION: 5
LANGUAGES: Spanish translators available
ACCESSIBILITY: Wheelchair accessible; Telecommunications for the hearing impaired (TTY, TDY, etc.); Signers for the hearing impaired
CASES SEXUAL ASSAULT/ABUSE (%): 100
DESCRIPTION: Provides support, counseling, and escort services for all victim/survivors of sexual assault and significant others. Support groups, prevention workshop for children, feminist martial arts/self-defense program
CLIENTS/SERVICES: Sexual assault survivors; Marital rape/sexual abuse survivors; Child victims of sexual abuse; Adult survivors of child sexual abuse; Incest victims/survivors; Prevention program; Community education; Adolescent survivors of sexual abuse; Male survivors of sexual abuse

BARNSTABLE

DISTRICT ATTORNEY'S VICTIM/WITNESS ASSISTANCE PROGRAM
First District Court House, Barnstable, MA 02630
Information: (508) 362-8103 8:30am-4:30pm
Contact: Patricia Blair, Victim Witness Dir
TYPE OF AGENCY: Victim/witness assistance program
AREAS SERVED: Barnstable, Dukes, Nantucket
YEARS IN OPERATION: 11
LANGUAGES: Portuguese

DISTRICT ATTORNEY'S VICTIM/WITNESS ASSISTANCE PROGRAM
(continued)

ACCESSIBILITY: Wheelchair accessible; Signers for the hearing impaired
CLIENTS/SERVICES: Sexual assault survivors; Marital rape/sexual abuse survivors; Child victims of sexual abuse; Incest victims/survivors
REQUIREMENTS: A criminal complaint must be issued

BEVERLY

NORTH SHORE RAPE CRISIS CENTER
202 Rantoul St, Beverly, MA 01915
Crisis hotline: **(800) 922-8772 24 hrs**
Information: (508) 927-4506 9am-5pm (Mon-Fri)
Contact: Marjorie Scanlon, NSRCC Coord
TYPE OF AGENCY: Rape crisis center
SPONSORING ORGANIZATION: Project RAP
AREAS SERVED: North Shore
YEARS IN OPERATION: 10
LANGUAGES: Spanish
CASES SEXUAL ASSAULT/ABUSE (%): 100
CLIENTS/SERVICES: Sexual assault survivors; Marital rape/sexual abuse survivors; Adult survivors of child sexual abuse; Incest victims/survivors; Community education; Adolescent survivors of sexual abuse
REQUIREMENTS: Over the age of 12

BOSTON

ARADIA COUNSELING FOR WOMEN
520 Commonwealth Ave, Kenmore Square, Boston, MA 02215
Information: (617) 247-4861 by appointment
Contact: Rosalind Gruber or Chippa Martin, Co-Dirs
TYPE OF AGENCY: Counseling/mental health services; Private practice
YEARS IN OPERATION: 11
LANGUAGES: Spanish
ACCESSIBILITY: Wheelchair accessible
CASES SEXUAL ASSAULT/ABUSE (%): 75
CLIENTS/SERVICES: Sexual assault survivors; Marital rape/sexual abuse survivors; Adult survivors of child sexual abuse; Incest victims/survivors

BETH ISRAEL HOSPITAL—RAPE CRISIS INTERVENTION CENTER
330 Brookline Ave, Boston, MA 02115
Crisis hotline: **(617) 735-3338 (emergency room) 24 hrs**
Information: (617) 735-4645 8:30am-5pm (Mon-Fri)
Contact: Veronica Reed Ryback, ACSW, LICSW, Prog Dir
TYPE OF AGENCY: Rape crisis center; Hospital/medical center; Acquaintance/date rape prevention program; Training/research
YEARS IN OPERATION: 15
LANGUAGES: Translators available
CASES SEXUAL ASSAULT/ABUSE (%): 100
DESCRIPTION: Provides medical and psychological services for adult survivors and family members or friends. Those who have been recently raped come through the emergency room, while others come directly into the counseling program. Offers short- and long-term individual and group therapy; Training program for Harvard Medical School; Conducts ongoing education and research in the field of treatment for rape survivors; Prevention program on date rape awareness and prevention
CLIENTS/SERVICES: Sexual assault survivors; Marital rape/sexual abuse survivors; Adult survivors of child sexual abuse; Prevention program; Community education; Adolescent survivors of sexual abuse; Male survivors of sexual abuse
REQUIREMENTS: Age 16 or older; Sliding scale fee with most third party insurance accepted
SPECIAL PROGRAMS/SERVICES: Published guidelines for emergency room procedures for both female and male victims

CASA MYRNA VAZQUEZ, INC
PO Box 18019, Boston, MA 02118
Crisis hotline: **(617) 262-9581 24 hrs**
Information: (617) 262-9581 9am-5pm
Contact: Alba Baerga, Assoc Dir
TYPE OF AGENCY: Domestic violence program
AREAS SERVED: Statewide
YEARS IN OPERATION: 11
LANGUAGES: Spanish
CASES SEXUAL ASSAULT/ABUSE (%): 10
DESCRIPTION: Shelter and support; Safehome network; 24-hour hotline; Counseling; Advocacy
CLIENTS/SERVICES: Marital rape/sexual abuse survivors; Incest victims/survivors; Community education
SPECIAL PROGRAMS/SERVICES: Bilingual (Spanish/English) brochure

CHILDREN'S HOSPITAL—SEXUAL ABUSE TREATMENT TEAM
300 Longwood Ave, Boston, MA 02115
Crisis hotline: **(617) 735-6940 Emergency Room**
Information: (617) 735-6940 9am-5pm
Contact: Susanne Meyer, LICSW, Sexual Abuse Treatment Team Dir
TYPE OF AGENCY: Hospital/medical center; Child sexual abuse services; Training/research
SPONSORING ORGANIZATION: Department of Psychiatry
YEARS IN OPERATION: 10
ACCESSIBILITY: Wheelchair accessible
CASES SEXUAL ASSAULT/ABUSE (%): 100
DESCRIPTION: Follow-up psychological services for young child victims; Community referrals for evaluation and treatment; Training program for psychiatry residents, pre- and postdoctoral psychology and social work fellows
CLIENTS/SERVICES: Child victims of sexual abuse; Adolescent survivors of sexual abuse

FENWAY COMMUNITY HEALTH CENTER: GAY AND LESBIAN VICTIM RECOVERY PROGRAM
93 Massachusetts Ave, Boston, MA 02115
Information: (617) 267-0900 9am-5pm (Mon-Fri)
Contact: Joyce Collier, Victim Recovery Prog Coord
TYPE OF AGENCY: Counseling/mental health services
AREAS SERVED: Massachusetts
YEARS IN OPERATION: 17
LANGUAGES: Spanish
ACCESSIBILITY: Wheelchair accessible
CASES SEXUAL ASSAULT/ABUSE (%): 10
DESCRIPTION: Serves gay and lesbian victims of violence, including those with past histories of abuse and recent sexual assault; Support groups available for men and women; Specializes in services for male rape survivors (both homosexual and heterosexual)
CLIENTS/SERVICES: Sexual assault survivors; Marital rape/sexual abuse survivors; Adult survivors of child sexual abuse; Incest victims/survivors; Prevention program; Community education; Male survivors of sexual abuse; Lesbians; Gay men

MASSACHUSETTS/CAPP
295 Longwood Ave, Boston, MA 02115
Information: (617) 232-8390, ext 5 9am-5pm (Mon-Fri)
Contact: Starr Potts, Dir; Debbie Lewis, Comm Educ Spec
TYPE OF AGENCY: Child sexual abuse prevention program; Consultation; Training/research
SPONSORING ORGANIZATION: Judge Baker Children's Center
AREAS SERVED: Statewide except Fitchburg area
YEARS IN OPERATION: 3
ACCESSIBILITY: Wheelchair accessible; Telecommunications for the hearing impaired (TTY, TDY, etc.) (outgoing calls only)
DESCRIPTION: State-funded training center which offers 3-day training, as well as ongoing technical assistance to communities wanting to implement the Child Assault Prevention curriculum in their schools
CLIENTS/SERVICES: Prevention program
REQUIREMENTS: Training is free of charge for Massachusetts communities. Trainees must have a commitment to working with children and support the concept of children's rights and community/child empowerment. Training is open only to those who will become actively part of a local CAP Project

NEW ENGLAND MEDICAL CENTER— DIVISION OF CHILD PSYCHIATRY
Box 395, 750 Washington St, Boston, MA 02111
Crisis hotline: **(617) 956-5732 24 hrs**
Information: (617) 956-5732
Contact: David Doolittle, PsyD, Sexual Abuse Prog Coord
TYPE OF AGENCY: Hospital/medical center; Child sexual abuse services
CLIENTS/SERVICES: Child victims of sexual abuse; Offender treatment program; Adolescent/juvenile sex offenders; Adolescent survivors of sexual abuse; Male survivors of sexual abuse
REQUIREMENTS: Child and adolescent victims and their families; Adult offenders treated only if victim is in program

SUFFOLK COUNTY DISTRICT ATTORNEY— VICTIM-WITNESS ASSISTANCE
Suffolk County Courthouse, Pemberton Sq, Boston, MA 02108
Information: (617) 725-8600 8:30am-4:30pm
Contact: Julie M Duggan, Victim Witness Prog Chief
TYPE OF AGENCY: Victim/witness assistance program
AREAS SERVED: Suffolk
YEARS IN OPERATION: 10
LANGUAGES: Interpreters requested as needed
ACCESSIBILITY: Wheelchair accessible; Signers for the hearing impaired
CASES SEXUAL ASSAULT/ABUSE (%): 33
CLIENTS/SERVICES: Sexual assault survivors; Marital rape/sexual abuse survivors; Child victims of sexual abuse; Adult survivors of child sexual abuse; Incest victims/survivors; Community education

BRAINTREE

BRAINTREE PSYCHOLOGICAL ASSOCIATES
575 Washington St, Braintree, MA 02184
Information: (617) 848-7745 24 hrs
Contact: Catherine Brennan, LICSW
TYPE OF AGENCY: Private practice
YEARS IN OPERATION: 2
CASES SEXUAL ASSAULT/ABUSE (%): 30
CLIENTS/SERVICES: Sexual assault survivors; Marital rape/sexual abuse survivors; Child victims of sexual abuse; Adult survivors of child sexual abuse; Incest victims/survivors; Community education; Adolescent survivors of sexual abuse; Male survivors of sexual abuse

MASSACHUSETTS SOCIETY FOR THE PREVENTION OF CRUELTY TO CHILDREN
507 Washington St, Braintree, MA 02184
Crisis hotline: **(800) 782-3005 24 hrs**
Information: (617) 848-0110 8:30am-5pm
TYPE OF AGENCY: Child sexual abuse services; Child abuse services
YEARS IN OPERATION: 110
LANGUAGES: Spanish, French
ACCESSIBILITY: Wheelchair accessible

MASSACHUSETTS SOCIETY FOR THE PREVENTION OF CRUELTY TO CHILDREN (continued)

DESCRIPTION: Protects children from the danger of abuse, neglect and exploitation in any of its forms; Provides social services, advocacy and education for children and families. Treatment for child sexual abuse/incest offenders modeled on Parents United

CLIENTS/SERVICES: Child victims of sexual abuse; Adult survivors of child sexual abuse; Incest victims/survivors; Prevention program; Community education; Offender treatment program; Adolescent survivors of sexual abuse; Male survivors of sexual abuse

BROCKTON

MASSACHUSETTS SOCIETY FOR THE PREVENTION OF CRUELTY TO CHILDREN
130 Liberty St, Unit 7, Brockton, MA 02401
Crisis hotline: **Mental Health (800) 442-3035**
Information: (508) 586-2660 9am-5pm (Mon-Fri)
Contact: Albert T Calello, Jr, Regional Admin; Alice Cook, Asst Regional Admin
TYPE OF AGENCY: Counseling/mental health services; Child sexual abuse services; Child sexual abuse prevention program; Child abuse services; Child abuse prevention program
AREAS SERVED: Bristol, Plymouth, Barnstable
YEARS IN OPERATION: 110
LANGUAGES: Spanish, Portuguese
ACCESSIBILITY: Wheelchair accessible
CASES SEXUAL ASSAULT/ABUSE (%): 25
CLIENTS/SERVICES: Sexual assault survivors; Marital rape/sexual abuse survivors; Child victims of sexual abuse; Adult survivors of child sexual abuse; Incest victims/survivors; Prevention program; Community education; Offender treatment program; Adolescent survivors of sexual abuse; Male survivors of sexual abuse; Preschoolers
SPECIAL PROGRAMS/SERVICES: Project Good Start, an early intervention program for at-risk infants under the age of one year, uses volunteers and professionals

PARENTS UNITED; SONS AND DAUGHTERS UNITED; ADULTS MOLESTED AS CHILDREN UNITED; SEX ADDICTS ANONYMOUS
PO Box 579, Brockton, MA 02403
Information: (508) 586-9410 24 hrs
Contact: Mary Devlin, Coord
TYPE OF AGENCY: Child sexual abuse services
YEARS IN OPERATION: 10
ACCESSIBILITY: Wheelchair accessible
CASES SEXUAL ASSAULT/ABUSE (%): 100
DESCRIPTION: Groups for male and female offenders, survivors, children and other family members; Effected on the addiction model
CLIENTS/SERVICES: Sexual assault survivors; Marital rape/sexual abuse survivors; Child victims of sexual abuse; Adult survivors of child sexual abuse; Incest victims/survivors; Community education; Offender treatment program; Adolescent survivors of sexual abuse; Male survivors of sexual abuse

PLYMOUTH COUNTY RAPE CRISIS CENTER
PO Box 4206, Brockton, MA 02403-4206
Crisis hotline: **(508) 588-8255 24 hrs**
Information: (508) 588-8255 9am-5pm (Mon-Fri)
Contact: Noreen Kelly, Prog Coord
TYPE OF AGENCY: Rape crisis center
AREAS SERVED: Plymouth
LANGUAGES: Spanish
ACCESSIBILITY: Wheelchair accessible
CASES SEXUAL ASSAULT/ABUSE (%): 100
CLIENTS/SERVICES: Sexual assault survivors; Marital rape/sexual abuse survivors; Child victims of sexual abuse; Adult survivors of child sexual abuse; Incest victims/survivors; Prevention program; Community education; Adolescent survivors of sexual abuse; Male survivors of sexual abuse

CAMBRIDGE

BOSTON AREA RAPE CRISIS CENTER
99 Bishop Richard Allen Dr, Cambridge, MA 02139
Crisis hotline: **(617) 492-RAPE 24 hrs**
Information: (617) 492-8306 9am-5pm (Mon-Fri)
Contact: Maria Altamore, Prog Coord
TYPE OF AGENCY: Rape crisis center
YEARS IN OPERATION: 16
ACCESSIBILITY: Wheelchair accessible; Telecommunications for the hearing impaired (TTY, TDY, etc.) (9am-5pm); Signers for the hearing impaired
CASES SEXUAL ASSAULT/ABUSE (%): 100
CLIENTS/SERVICES: Sexual assault survivors; Marital rape/sexual abuse survivors; Adult survivors of child sexual abuse; Incest victims/survivors; Prevention program; Community education; Adolescent survivors of sexual abuse; Male survivors of sexual abuse

CAMBRIDGE HOSPITAL VICTIMS OF VIOLENCE PROGRAM
1493 Cambridge St, Cambridge, MA 02139
Information: (617) 498-1150 9am-5pm
Contact: Mary Harvey, Dir
TYPE OF AGENCY: Hospital/medical center; Victim/witness assistance program
AREAS SERVED: Middlesex and surrounding area
YEARS IN OPERATION: 5
LANGUAGES: Spanish
ACCESSIBILITY: Wheelchair accessible
CLIENTS/SERVICES: Sexual assault survivors; Marital rape/sexual abuse survivors; Adult survivors of child sexual abuse; Incest victims/survivors; Community education; Adolescent survivors of sexual abuse; Male survivors of sexual abuse
REQUIREMENTS: Must be 14 or older

INCEST SURVIVORS NETWORK
46 Pleasant St, Cambridge, MA 02139
Crisis hotline: **(617) 492-RAPE 24 hrs**
Information: (617) 354-8807 10am-9:30pm
TYPE OF AGENCY: Women's center
SPONSORING ORGANIZATION: Cambridge Women's Center
AREAS SERVED: Middlesex, Suffolk, Norfolk
YEARS IN OPERATION: 7
LANGUAGES: Spanish
ACCESSIBILITY: Wheelchair accessible; Signers for the hearing impaired
DESCRIPTION: An organization of adult female incest and child sexual abuse survivors who have rallied together to provide services for survivors. Offers facilitated support groups, speakers bureau, legislative advocacy, legal resources, and extensive resources for therapists, groups, and networking
CLIENTS/SERVICES: Adult survivors of child sexual abuse; Incest victims/survivors; Community education
SPECIAL PROGRAMS/SERVICES: Totally survivor organized and run

MIDDLESEX COUNTY DISTRICT ATTORNEY'S OFFICE—VICTIM WITNESS SERVICE BUREAU
40 Thorndike St, Cambridge, MA 02141
Information: (617) 494-4604 8:30am-5pm
Contact: Patricia McNamara, Victim Witness Svc Bur Chief
TYPE OF AGENCY: Victim/witness assistance program
AREAS SERVED: Middlesex
YEARS IN OPERATION: 5
LANGUAGES: Spanish, Portuguese, French
ACCESSIBILITY: Wheelchair accessible; Signers for the hearing impaired (case by case basis)
DESCRIPTION: Crisis intervention, information and referral, ongoing support services for crime victims throughout criminal investigation and criminal court process; Priority cases include victims of sexual assault and child sexual abuse
CLIENTS/SERVICES: Sexual assault survivors; Marital rape/sexual abuse survivors; Child victims of sexual abuse; Incest victims/survivors; Community education; Adolescent survivors of sexual abuse; Male survivors of sexual abuse; Publications/media
REQUIREMENTS: For sexual assault and child sexual assault, referrals are accepted even if crime has not yet been reported.
SPECIAL PROGRAMS/SERVICES: Publications: *Multidisciplinary Perspectives on Child Sexual Abuse Intervention*; *Going to Court: A Guide for Young People* (16pp, written for children)

PROSTITUTES UNION OF MASSACHUSETTS (PUMA)
46 Pleasant St, Cambridge, MA 02139
Crisis hotline: **(617) 524-7507 24 hrs**
Information: (617) 524-7507 24 hrs
Contact: Chris Womendez, Pres
TYPE OF AGENCY: Counseling/mental health services
SPONSORING ORGANIZATION: % Women's Center
AREAS SERVED: Interstate
YEARS IN OPERATION: 15
LANGUAGES: Spanish
ACCESSIBILITY: Wheelchair accessible; Telecommunications for the hearing impaired (TTY, TDY, etc.); Signers for the hearing impaired
CASES SEXUAL ASSAULT/ABUSE (%): 75
DESCRIPTION: Provides housing, legal resources, peer support, bail, consciousness raising
CLIENTS/SERVICES: Sexual assault survivors; Adult survivors of child sexual abuse; Incest victims/survivors; Community education; Prostitutes
REQUIREMENTS: Must be over 16; Must be or have been forced to be a prostitute

TAPESTRY, INC
20 Sacramento St, Cambridge, MA 02138
Information: (617) 661-0248
TYPE OF AGENCY: Women's counseling services; Feminist therapy; Substance abuse; Training/research
YEARS IN OPERATION: 13
DESCRIPTION: Psychotherapy services include short- and long-term individual therapy, couples therapy, group therapy, spirituality/meditation, family therapy and workshops. Areas of special expertise include personal growth, violence against women, substance abuse, lesbian life, and adult children of alcoholic/dysfunctional families
CLIENTS/SERVICES: Sexual assault survivors; Marital rape/sexual abuse survivors; Adult survivors of child sexual abuse; Incest victims/survivors; Community education; Lesbians; Bisexuals
REQUIREMENTS: Sliding scale fee

TRANSITION HOUSE
PO Box 530, Harvard Square Station, Cambridge, MA 02238
Crisis hotline: **(617) 661-7203 24 hrs daily**
Information: (617) 354-2676 9am-5pm (Mon-Fri)
Contact: Sharon Vardatira, Admin
TYPE OF AGENCY: Domestic violence program
AREAS SERVED: Suffolk, Middlesex
YEARS IN OPERATION: 13
LANGUAGES: Spanish, Portuguese, French, German, Hebrew, Russian, Italian, Mandarin, Chinese, Sign
ACCESSIBILITY: Telecommunications for the hearing impaired (TTY, TDY, etc.)
CASES SEXUAL ASSAULT/ABUSE (%): 70
CLIENTS/SERVICES: Marital rape/sexual abuse survivors; Child victims of sexual abuse; Incest victims/survivors; Prevention program; Com-

TRANSITION HOUSE *(continued)*
munity education; Adolescent survivors of sexual abuse; Publications/media
SPECIAL PROGRAMS/SERVICES: *Dating Violence Intervention Project,* geared to high school students, uses youth theater, school-based presentations, student assemblies and discussions to present common dating conflicts and nonviolent resolutions/options. Also provides hotline and support groups for those in abusive relationships. Publication: *Peace Begins at Home* children's calendar, a collection of children's art reflecting their feelings about peace and violence in the home ($10); *We Will Not Be Beaten,* 25-minute videocassette ($32) on women breaking free from domestic violence; training manuals on shelter services for women and children ($10 each)

WINGS THERAPY COLLECTIVE
60 ½ Sacramento St, Cambridge, MA 02138
Information: (617) 876-8438 8am-11pm
Contact: Ann Chronis, Psychotherapist
TYPE OF AGENCY: Private practice
AREAS SERVED: Boston area
YEARS IN OPERATION: 13
LANGUAGES: Greek, Turkish, Sign
ACCESSIBILITY: Telecommunications for the hearing impaired (TTY, TDY, etc.); Signers for the hearing impaired
CASES SEXUAL ASSAULT/ABUSE (%): 50
CLIENTS/SERVICES: Sexual assault survivors; Marital rape/sexual abuse survivors; Child victims of sexual abuse; Adult survivors of child sexual abuse; Incest victims/survivors; Adolescent survivors of sexual abuse

CENTERVILLE

MASSACHUSETTS SOCIETY FOR THE PREVENTION OF CRUELTY TO CHILDREN
1550 Falmouth Rd, Centerville, MA 02632
Crisis hotline: **(800) 322-2204 24 hrs daily**
Information: (508) 775-0275 8:30am-5pm
TYPE OF AGENCY: Child sexual abuse services; Child abuse services
YEARS IN OPERATION: 110
LANGUAGES: Spanish, French
ACCESSIBILITY: Wheelchair accessible
DESCRIPTION: Protects children from the danger of abuse, neglect and exploitation in any of its forms; Provides social services, advocacy and education for children and families. Treatment for child sexual abuse/incest offenders modeled on Parents United
CLIENTS/SERVICES: Child victims of sexual abuse; Adult survivors of child sexual abuse; Incest victims/survivors; Prevention program; Community education; Offender treatment program; Adolescent survivors of sexual abuse; Male survivors of sexual abuse

CHELSEA

CHELSEA COMMUNITY COUNSELING CENTER
301 Broadway, Chelsea, MA 02150
Crisis hotline: **(617) 889-HELP 24 hrs**
Information: (617) 889-3300 9am-4:30pm (Mon-Fri)
Contact: Jan Perley, LICSW, Clinic Dir
TYPE OF AGENCY: Counseling/mental health services
SPONSORING ORGANIZATION: North Suffolk Mental Health Association
AREAS SERVED: Chelsea
YEARS IN OPERATION: 15
LANGUAGES: Spanish
ACCESSIBILITY: Wheelchair accessible
CLIENTS/SERVICES: Sexual assault survivors; Marital rape/sexual abuse survivors; Child victims of sexual abuse; Adult survivors of child sexual abuse; Incest victims/survivors; Adolescent survivors of sexual abuse; Male survivors of sexual abuse

CONCORD

MENTAL HEALTH ASSOCIATION OF CENTRAL MIDDLESEX
Community Agencies Bldg, Concord, MA 01742
Crisis hotline: **(508) 263-8777**
Information: (508) 369-7715 9am-5pm
Contact: Louise Davy, Exec Dir
TYPE OF AGENCY: Counseling/mental health services; Child sexual abuse prevention program; Information and referral
AREAS SERVED: Central Middlesex
YEARS IN OPERATION: 32
ACCESSIBILITY: Wheelchair accessible
DESCRIPTION: Provides information, referral, advocacy, education and prevention; Sponsor of Child Assault Prevention Project (CAPP) for elementary schools; Also chairs Child Assault Task Force
CLIENTS/SERVICES: Prevention program; Community education

DEDHAM

NORFOLK COUNTY DISTRICT ATTORNEY—SEXUAL ASSAULT UNIT
618 High St, Dedham, MA 02026
Crisis hotline: **(617) 326-1111 24 hrs**
Information: (617) 329-5440 8:30am-5pm
Contact: Patricia Nigrelli, Dir/Investigator
TYPE OF AGENCY: Victim/witness assistance program
AREAS SERVED: Norfolk
YEARS IN OPERATION: 13
LANGUAGES: Spanish
ACCESSIBILITY: Wheelchair accessible; Telecommunications for the hearing impaired (TTY, TDY, etc.)
CASES SEXUAL ASSAULT/ABUSE (%): 100
CLIENTS/SERVICES: Sexual assault survivors; Marital rape/sexual abuse survivors; Child victims of sexual abuse; Adult survivors of child sexual abuse; Incest victims/survivors; Community education; Adolescent survivors of sexual abuse; Male survivors of sexual abuse

DORCHESTER

COMMUNITY PROGRAM AGAINST SEXUAL ASSAULT (CPASA)
317 Blue Hill Ave, Dorchester, MA 02121
Crisis hotline: **(617) 536-6500 9pm-Midnight**
Information: (617) 427-4470 9am-5pm
Contact: Barbara Bullette, Prog Dir
TYPE OF AGENCY: Rape crisis center
SPONSORING ORGANIZATION: Roxbury Multi-Service Center
AREAS SERVED: Greater Boston neighborhoods
YEARS IN OPERATION: 11
LANGUAGES: Spanish
CASES SEXUAL ASSAULT/ABUSE (%): 100
CLIENTS/SERVICES: Sexual assault survivors; Marital rape/sexual abuse survivors; Adult survivors of child sexual abuse; Incest victims/survivors; Prevention program; Community education; Adolescent survivors of sexual abuse; Male survivors of sexual abuse
REQUIREMENTS: 17 years and older for counseling services
SPECIAL PROGRAMS/SERVICES: Established resource library open to public, which includes materials on women's lives, with focus on people of color

EASTHAMPTON

VALLEY WOMEN'S MARTIAL ARTS, INC
PO Box 1064, 1 Cottage St, Easthampton, MA 01027
Information: (413) 527-0101
Contact: Janet Aalfs, Beth Holt, Head Instructors
TYPE OF AGENCY: Rape prevention program
AREAS SERVED: Hampshire, Hampden, Franklin, Berkshire
YEARS IN OPERATION: 11
LANGUAGES: Spanish
ACCESSIBILITY: Wheelchair accessible
CASES SEXUAL ASSAULT/ABUSE (%): 90
DESCRIPTION: Martial arts school for women and children, teaching karate, arnis (Filipino stick fighting) and self-defense
CLIENTS/SERVICES: Sexual assault survivors; Marital rape/sexual abuse survivors; Child victims of sexual abuse; Adult survivors of child sexual abuse; Incest victims/survivors; Prevention program; Community education; Adolescent survivors of sexual abuse; Healing
REQUIREMENTS: Minimum age is 7 years; Boys and girls 7-12; Girls and women 13 and older
SPECIAL PROGRAMS/SERVICES: Many of the women and children are survivors of sexual assault/abuse; Martial arts including stretching, strengthening, self-defense, visualization, and meditation are parts of their healing process

FALL RIVER

PHOENIX COUNSELING
PO Box 4011, 1001 Eastern Ave, Fall River, MA 02723
Information: (508) 676-6336 9am-9pm (Mon-Fri), 24-hr answering machine
Contact: Barbara Kusinitz, ACSW, Sabrina Gentlewarrior, ACSW, Lic Soc Wkrs
TYPE OF AGENCY: Private practice
AREAS SERVED: Bristol
YEARS IN OPERATION: 1
DESCRIPTION: Wholistic therapy focusing on ameliorating the causes and traumas of all forms of power abuse with special focus on sexual violence. Also provides therapy for lesbian batterers
CLIENTS/SERVICES: Sexual assault survivors; Marital rape/sexual abuse survivors; Child victims of sexual abuse; Adult survivors of child sexual abuse; Incest victims/survivors; Prevention program; Community education; Adolescent survivors of sexual abuse; Male survivors of sexual abuse; Lesbians
REQUIREMENTS: Minimum age 12

WOMEN'S CENTER
386 Stanley St, Fall River, MA 02720
Crisis hotline: **(508) 675-0087 24 hrs**
Information: (508) 675-0087 8:30am-4:30pm
Contact: Susan Cotsoridis, Rape Crisis Coord
TYPE OF AGENCY: Rape crisis center; Domestic violence program
SPONSORING ORGANIZATION: Stanley Street Treatment and Resources
AREAS SERVED: Greater Fall River area
YEARS IN OPERATION: 10
LANGUAGES: Portuguese
ACCESSIBILITY: Wheelchair accessible
CASES SEXUAL ASSAULT/ABUSE (%): 75
DESCRIPTION: Services for survivors of sexual assault and domestic violence; Individual therapy for batterers
CLIENTS/SERVICES: Sexual assault survivors; Marital rape/sexual abuse survivors; Adult survivors of child sexual abuse; Incest victims/survivors; Community education; Adolescent survivors of sexual abuse; Male survivors of sexual abuse

FITCHBURG

BATTERED WOMEN'S RESOURCES, INC
150 Main St, Fitchburg, MA 01420
Crisis hotline: **(508) 342-9355 24 hrs**
Information: (508) 342-2919 8:30am-4:30pm
Contact: Anna Farrell, Exec Dir
TYPE OF AGENCY: Domestic violence program
AREAS SERVED: North Worcester
YEARS IN OPERATION: 10
LANGUAGES: Spanish

BATTERED WOMEN'S RESOURCES, INC
(continued)
ACCESSIBILITY: Telecommunications for the hearing impaired (TTY, TDY, etc.)
CLIENTS/SERVICES: Marital rape/sexual abuse survivors; Community education

FRAMINGHAM

MASSACHUSETTS SOCIETY FOR THE PREVENTION OF CRUELTY TO CHILDREN
46 Park St, 4th Fl, Framingham, MA 01701
Crisis hotline: **(800) 442-3035 24 hrs daily**
Information: (508) 872-8826, 872-8827 8:30am-5pm
TYPE OF AGENCY: Child sexual abuse services; Child abuse services
YEARS IN OPERATION: 110
LANGUAGES: Spanish, French
ACCESSIBILITY: Wheelchair accessible
DESCRIPTION: Protects children from the danger of abuse, neglect and exploitation in any of its forms; Provides social services, advocacy and education for children and families. Treatment for child sexual abuse/incest offenders modeled on Parents United
CLIENTS/SERVICES: Child victims of sexual abuse; Adult survivors of child sexual abuse; Incest victims/survivors; Prevention program; Community education; Offender treatment program; Adolescent survivors of sexual abuse; Male survivors of sexual abuse

METROWEST YOUTH GUIDANCE CENTER
88 Lincoln St, Framingham, MA 02144
Crisis hotline: **(508) 872-3333 24 hrs**
Information: (508) 620-0010 8:30am-9pm (Mon-Thu); 8:30am-5pm (Fri)
Contact: Karen Welling, Parent Child Support Prog Coord
TYPE OF AGENCY: Counseling/mental health services; Child sexual abuse services; Child abuse services
AREAS SERVED: Middlesex
YEARS IN OPERATION: 33
LANGUAGES: Spanish
ACCESSIBILITY: Wheelchair accessible; Telecommunications for the hearing impaired (TTY, TDY, etc.); Signers for the hearing impaired
CASES SEXUAL ASSAULT/ABUSE (%): 25
DESCRIPTION: Provides therapy for children, adolescents and their families, and developmentally delayed adults; Evaluation and treatment for families where physical and/or sexual abuse and/or neglect are issues
CLIENTS/SERVICES: Sexual assault survivors; Marital rape/sexual abuse survivors; Child victims of sexual abuse; Adult survivors of child sexual abuse; Incest victims/survivors; Community education; Offender treatment program; Adolescent survivors of sexual abuse; Male survivors of sexual abuse
REQUIREMENTS: Sex offenders accepted by self referral or by court mandate
SPECIAL PROGRAMS/SERVICES: Group for girl and boy sexual abuse victims aged 4 to 6; Latino girls group in Spanish for ages 11 to 13; Non-Latino group for girls aged 8 to 11; Two senior therapists will be studying use of hypnosis in treating post traumatic stress disorders

GARDNER

NORTH CENTRAL HUMAN SERVICES
31 Lake St, Gardner, MA 01440
Crisis hotline: **(508) 632-9400 24 hrs (emergencies only)**
Information: (508) 632-9400 8am-8pm
Contact: Dya Khalsa, Judy Novick, Sexual Abuse Prog Co-Coords
TYPE OF AGENCY: Counseling/mental health services
AREAS SERVED: Northern Worcester
YEARS IN OPERATION: 6
ACCESSIBILITY: Wheelchair accessible
CASES SEXUAL ASSAULT/ABUSE (%): Adult 15-20; Children 30-40
DESCRIPTION: Individual, family, and group therapy for survivors; Therapy for rapists, child sexual abuse/incest offenders, juvenile sex offenders, and batterers
CLIENTS/SERVICES: Sexual assault survivors; Marital rape/sexual abuse survivors; Child victims of sexual abuse; Adult survivors of child sexual abuse; Incest victims/survivors; Community education; Offender treatment program; Adolescent survivors of sexual abuse; Male survivors of sexual abuse
REQUIREMENTS: Must have an ability to pay for service through insurance or sliding scale fees; HMO payment must be guaranteed before service is initiated

NORTH WORCESTER COUNTY SEXUAL ABUSE PROGRAM
196 Main St, Gardner, MA 01440
Crisis hotline: **(508) 632-9400 24 hrs**
Information: (508) 632-9104, 632-9400 8am-6pm
Contact: Judy Novick, Felicia Hagberg, Prog Coords
TYPE OF AGENCY: Counseling/mental health services; Child sexual abuse services
SPONSORING ORGANIZATION: MA Dept of Social Services; North Central Human Services
AREAS SERVED: Worcester
YEARS IN OPERATION: 5
ACCESSIBILITY: Wheelchair accessible
CLIENTS/SERVICES: Sexual assault survivors; Child victims of sexual abuse; Adult survivors of child sexual abuse; Incest victims/survivors; Community education; Offender treatment program; Adolescent survivors of sexual abuse; Male survivors of sexual abuse

WOMEN'S RESOURCES, INC
20 Parker St, Gardner, MA 01440
Crisis hotline: **(508) 630-1031 24 hrs**
Information: (508) 632-3722
Contact: Tracy Chase, Prog Coord
TYPE OF AGENCY: Domestic violence program
AREAS SERVED: Worcester
YEARS IN OPERATION: 5
LANGUAGES: Spanish
CASES SEXUAL ASSAULT/ABUSE (%): 10
CLIENTS/SERVICES: Marital rape/sexual abuse survivors; Child victims of sexual abuse; Adult survivors of child sexual abuse; Incest victims/survivors; Community education

GREENFIELD

MASSACHUSETTS SOCIETY FOR THE PREVENTION OF CRUELTY TO CHILDREN
479 Main St, Greenfield, MA 01301
Crisis hotline: **(800) 392-6046 24 hrs daily**
Information: (413) 773-3608 9am-5pm
Contact: Judith F Johnson, Dist Exec
TYPE OF AGENCY: Counseling/mental health services; Child sexual abuse services; Child sexual abuse prevention program; Child abuse services; Child abuse prevention program
AREAS SERVED: Franklin, and towns of Athol, Phillipston, Royalston, Petersham
YEARS IN OPERATION: 74
ACCESSIBILITY: Wheelchair accessible
CASES SEXUAL ASSAULT/ABUSE (%): 80
DESCRIPTION: Services for sexual abuse victims, adult survivors and perpetrators, include individual treatment, group work or family systems intervention. Also works with physically/emotionally abused children and their families
CLIENTS/SERVICES: Child victims of sexual abuse; Adult survivors of child sexual abuse; Incest victims/survivors; Prevention program; Community education; Offender treatment program; Adolescent survivors of sexual abuse; Male survivors of sexual abuse
SPECIAL PROGRAMS/SERVICES: Films (*Secrets* and *Two Kinds of Touch*) are used in the schools (preschool through 6th grade) to explore with children their options if they are being abused and/or to alert them to the dangers of sexual abuse

NELCWIT (NEW ENGLAND LEARNING CENTER FOR WOMEN IN TRANSITION)
219 Silver St, Greenfield, MA 01301
Crisis hotline: **(413) 772-0806 24 hrs daily**
Information: (413) 772-0871 9am-4pm (Mon-Fri)
Contact: Mary Kociela, Prog Co-Dir
TYPE OF AGENCY: Rape crisis center; Domestic violence program
AREAS SERVED: Franklin
YEARS IN OPERATION: 13
ACCESSIBILITY: Wheelchair accessible; Signers for the hearing impaired
CASES SEXUAL ASSAULT/ABUSE (%): 98
DESCRIPTION: Provides shelter, counseling, and advocacy services; Community education on rape prevention and self-defense. Sponsors public activities (vigils, etc) to increase awareness of violence and encourage people to take steps to stop the violence in the community
CLIENTS/SERVICES: Sexual assault survivors; Marital rape/sexual abuse survivors; Adult survivors of child sexual abuse; Incest victims/survivors; Prevention program; Community education; Adolescent survivors of sexual abuse

HOLBROOK

CENTER FOR WELLNESS
97 Belcher St, Holbrook, MA 02343
Information: (617) 767-2336 4-7 (Mon); 2-8 (Tue); 9-2 (Wed); 5-8 (Thu)
Contact: Karen Black, Dir
TYPE OF AGENCY: Counseling/mental health services
AREAS SERVED: Norfolk
YEARS IN OPERATION: 8
CASES SEXUAL ASSAULT/ABUSE (%): 60
CLIENTS/SERVICES: Sexual assault survivors; Marital rape/sexual abuse survivors; Child victims of sexual abuse; Adult survivors of child sexual abuse; Incest victims/survivors; Adolescent survivors of sexual abuse; Male survivors of sexual abuse

HOLYOKE

MASSACHUSETTS SOCIETY FOR THE PREVENTION OF CRUELTY TO CHILDREN
1727 Northampton St, Holyoke, MA 01040
Crisis hotline: **(800) 392-6046 24 hrs daily**
Information: (413) 532-9446 8:30am-5pm
TYPE OF AGENCY: Child sexual abuse services; Child abuse services
YEARS IN OPERATION: 110
LANGUAGES: Spanish, French
ACCESSIBILITY: Wheelchair accessible
DESCRIPTION: Protects children from the danger of abuse, neglect and exploitation in any of its forms; Provides social services, advocacy and education for children and families. Treatment for child sexual abuse/incest offenders modeled on Parents United
CLIENTS/SERVICES: Child victims of sexual abuse; Adult survivors of child sexual abuse; Incest victims/survivors; Prevention program; Community education; Offender treatment program; Adolescent survivors of sexual abuse; Male survivors of sexual abuse

HYANNIS

INDEPENDENCE HOUSE
105 Pleasant St, Hyannis, MA 02601
Crisis hotline: **(508) 771-6507 24 hrs (emergency collect calls accepted)**
Information: (508) 771-6507

INDEPENDENCE HOUSE (continued)

TYPE OF AGENCY: Rape crisis center; Domestic violence safehome network
CLIENTS/SERVICES: Sexual assault survivors; Marital rape/sexual abuse survivors; Child victims of sexual abuse; Adult survivors of child sexual abuse; Incest victims/survivors; Community education; Adolescent survivors of sexual abuse

JAMAICA PLAIN

FINEX HOUSE, INC
PO Box 1154, Jamaica Plain, MA 02130
Crisis hotline: **(617) 288-1054 24 hrs**
Information: (617) 436-2002 24 hrs
Contact: Lea Lindbert, Advocate
TYPE OF AGENCY: Domestic violence program
AREAS SERVED: Statewide
YEARS IN OPERATION: 7
LANGUAGES: Spanish, Sign
ACCESSIBILITY: Wheelchair accessible; Telecommunications for the hearing impaired (TTY, TDY, etc.); Signers for the hearing impaired
CASES SEXUAL ASSAULT/ABUSE (%): 50
CLIENTS/SERVICES: Marital rape/sexual abuse survivors; Child victims of sexual abuse; Adult survivors of child sexual abuse; Incest victims/survivors; Blind; Deaf; Prostitutes; Disabled; Publications/media
SPECIAL PROGRAMS/SERVICES: Accessible for women and children who are in wheelchairs, who are blind or deaf or have other disabilities; Has a high security witness protection program and actively supports battered prostitutes. Publication: *Escape: A Handbook for Battered Women Who Have Disabilities*

ELIZABETH STONE HOUSE
PO Box 15, Jamaica Plain, MA 02130
Crisis hotline: **(617) 522-3417 24 hrs**
Information: (617) 522-3417 9am-5pm
TYPE OF AGENCY: Domestic violence program; Counseling/mental health services; Residential treatment facility
YEARS IN OPERATION: 14
LANGUAGES: Spanish
CASES SEXUAL ASSAULT/ABUSE (%): 85
DESCRIPTION: Provides residential services and additional transitional housing for women in emotional distress, including battered women and their children. This is the only residential mental health program in the state that allows women to bring their children with them. Sliding scale fee makes the program accessible to any woman. Approach to mental health issues acknowledges that social pressures such as racism, classism, ageism, sexism, homophobia, and violence against women have a strong effect on the woman's mental health and addresses them as possible causes of the mental health problems. Support groups deal with these issues.
CLIENTS/SERVICES: Sexual assault survivors; Marital rape/sexual abuse survivors; Adult survivors of child sexual abuse; Incest victims/survivors; Community education; Publications/media
REQUIREMENTS: Mental health program supports all distressed women with the exception of drug or alcohol addicts, women with eating disorders, and actively suicidal women
SPECIAL PROGRAMS/SERVICES: Media program: *The Road I Took to You: Stories of Women and Craziness*, video documentary of residents of Elizabeth Stone House addressing the impact of violence, racism and poverty on women's mental health (rental: $75; purchase $200). Publications: *Women and Craziness*, oral histories of ten women who have been residents of Elizabeth Stone House ($5.95); *Elizabeth Stone House How To Handbook* for developing a community-based residential mental health alternative for women, operating a self-help program, working with people in emotional crisis, and developing transitional housing. Spanish-language brochure

LAWRENCE

MASSACHUSETTS SOCIETY FOR THE PREVENTION OF CRUELTY TO CHILDREN
11 Lawrence St, Lawrence, MA 01840
Crisis hotline: **(800) 541-3004 24 hrs daily**
Information: (508) 682-9222 8:30am-5pm
TYPE OF AGENCY: Child sexual abuse services; Child abuse services
YEARS IN OPERATION: 110
LANGUAGES: Spanish, French
ACCESSIBILITY: Wheelchair accessible
DESCRIPTION: Protects children from the danger of abuse, neglect and exploitation in any of its forms; Provides social services, advocacy and education for chilren and families. Treatment for child sexual abuse/incest offenders modeled on Parents United
CLIENTS/SERVICES: Child victims of sexual abuse; Adult survivors of child sexual abuse; Incest victims/survivors; Prevention program; Community education; Offender treatment program; Adolescent survivors of sexual abuse; Male survivors of sexual abuse

WOMEN'S RESOURCE CENTER, INC
454 N Canal St, Lawrence, MA 01841
Crisis hotline: **(800) 542-5212 (rape crisis); (508) 685-2480 (domestic violence) 24 hrs**
Information: (508) 685-2480 9am-5pm
Contact: Anita, Dir; Carmen, Rape Coord
TYPE OF AGENCY: Rape crisis center; Domestic violence program
AREAS SERVED: Lawrence, Methuen, Haverhill, Andover, Boxford cities
YEARS IN OPERATION: 10
LANGUAGES: Spanish, Cambodian
ACCESSIBILITY: Wheelchair accessible
CASES SEXUAL ASSAULT/ABUSE (%): 100
DESCRIPTION: Battered women's program that has added a rape crisis/education program for Latina women
CLIENTS/SERVICES: Sexual assault survivors; Marital rape/sexual abuse survivors; Child victims of sexual abuse; Adult survivors of child sexual abuse; Incest victims/survivors; Prevention program; Community education; Adolescent survivors of sexual abuse; Male survivors of sexual abuse; Ethnic minorities
SPECIAL PROGRAMS/SERVICES: Bilingual brochure (Spanish and English)

LOWELL

ALTERNATIVE HOUSE
PO Box 2096, Highland Station, Lowell, MA 01851
Crisis hotline: **(508) 454-1436 24 hrs**
Information: (508) 458-0274 9am-5pm (Mon-Fri)
Contact: Lisa Christie, Exec Dir
TYPE OF AGENCY: Domestic violence program
AREAS SERVED: Merrimack Valley
YEARS IN OPERATION: 10
LANGUAGES: Spanish
CLIENTS/SERVICES: Marital rape/sexual abuse survivors; Adult survivors of child sexual abuse; Incest victims/survivors; Community education

FAMILY INTERVENTION TEAM
45 Merrimack St, No 200, Lowell, MA 01852
Information: (508) 453-2598 9am-8pm
Contact: Dorothy Wheeler, PhD, Dir
TYPE OF AGENCY: Counseling/mental health services; Child sexual abuse services
SPONSORING ORGANIZATION: Center For Family Development
YEARS IN OPERATION: 4
ACCESSIBILITY: Wheelchair accessible
CASES SEXUAL ASSAULT/ABUSE (%): 100
DESCRIPTION: Provides comprehensive services for victims, survivors, families, couples and offenders; Consultation and training in area
CLIENTS/SERVICES: Child victims of sexual abuse; Adult survivors of child sexual abuse; Incest victims/survivors; Community education; Offender treatment program; Adolescent survivors of sexual abuse; Male survivors of sexual abuse
REQUIREMENTS: Ability to pay or be eligible for payment under Department of Social Services contract

RAPE CRISIS SERVICES OF GREATER LOWELL, INC
% Lowell General Hopsital, 295 Varnum Ave, Lowell, MA 01854
Crisis hotline: **(800) 542-5212 24 hrs**
Information: (508) 452-7721 9am-5pm
Contact: Lisa Ansara, Dir
TYPE OF AGENCY: Rape crisis center; Child sexual abuse prevention program
AREAS SERVED: Middlesex
YEARS IN OPERATION: 13
LANGUAGES: Spanish; will be hiring a Southeast Asian bilingual outreach worker
ACCESSIBILITY: Wheelchair accessible; Signers for the hearing impaired
CASES SEXUAL ASSAULT/ABUSE (%): 90
DESCRIPTION: Provides crisis intervention for victims of sexual assault and prevention through the Child Assault Prevention Program
CLIENTS/SERVICES: Sexual assault survivors; Marital rape/sexual abuse survivors; Child victims of sexual abuse; Adult survivors of child sexual abuse; Incest victims/survivors; Prevention program; Community education
SPECIAL PROGRAMS/SERVICES: Spanish-language brochure

LYNN

ATLANTIC CARE MEDICAL CENTER—RAPE CRISIS SERVICES
212 Boston St, Lynn, MA 01904
Crisis hotline: **(617) 595-7273 (8am-6pm); 598-5100, ext 3555 (after 6pm)**
Information: (617) 595-7273 8am-6pm
TYPE OF AGENCY: Rape crisis center; Hospital/medical center; Counseling/mental health services
CLIENTS/SERVICES: Sexual assault survivors; Child victims of sexual abuse; Adult survivors of child sexual abuse; Incest victims/survivors; Adolescent survivors of sexual abuse; Male survivors of sexual abuse

VICTIM/WITNESS ASSISTANCE PROGRAM
580 Essex St, Lynn, MA 01901
Information: (508) 745-6610 8:30am-4:30pm
Contact: Michaelene O'Neill McCann, Esq, Exec Dir
TYPE OF AGENCY: Victim/witness assistance program; Child sexual abuse services
AREAS SERVED: Essex
YEARS IN OPERATION: 9½
LANGUAGES: Spanish, Khmer
ACCESSIBILITY: Wheelchair accessible
DESCRIPTION: Provides comprehensive victim services, with a special sexual assault unit and a multiagency investigative team for child sexual abuse
CLIENTS/SERVICES: Sexual assault survivors; Marital rape/sexual abuse survivors; Child victims of sexual abuse; Incest victims/survivors; Community education; Adolescent survivors of sexual abuse; Male survivors of sexual abuse
SPECIAL PROGRAMS/SERVICES: Essex County Child Abuse Project involves multidisciplinary teams to investigate child sexual abuse, including an on-going training program and development of data collection/management system

MALDEN

MALDEN POLICE DEPARTMENT—VICTIM ASSISTANCE PROGRAM
200 Pleasant St, Malden, MA 02148
Crisis hotline: **(617) 322-1300 24 hrs**
Information: (617) 397-7171 24 hrs
TYPE OF AGENCY: Victim/witness assistance program
AREAS SERVED: Middlesex
ACCESSIBILITY: Telecommunications for the hearing impaired (TTY, TDY, etc.)
CLIENTS/SERVICES: Sexual assault survivors

SEXUAL ABUSE INVESTIGATION NETWORK (SAIN)
40 Eastern Ave, Malden, MA 02148
Crisis hotline: **(800) 792-5200 24 hrs**
Information: (617) 321-0130 9am-5pm
Contact: Jeff Roberts, SAIN Coord
TYPE OF AGENCY: Victim/witness assistance program; Child sexual abuse services
SPONSORING ORGANIZATION: Massachusetts Department of Social Services and Middlesex County District Attorney's Office
AREAS SERVED: Middlesex
YEARS IN OPERATION: 3
LANGUAGES: Spanish
ACCESSIBILITY: Wheelchair accessible; Signers for the hearing impaired
CASES SEXUAL ASSAULT/ABUSE (%): 100
DESCRIPTION: Coordinates multidisciplinary interview of child victims of sexual abuse; Lessens the trauma to victim and family; Forms an immediate network of police, district attorney, and human service agencies to investigate allegations of sexual abuse
CLIENTS/SERVICES: Child victims of sexual abuse; Community education
REQUIREMENTS: Parental consent for team interview required. Child victim must be of sufficient age/maturity level to make disclosure about abuse, testify in court if necessary

MARLBOROUGH

HEALTH INFORMATION REFERRAL SERVICE, INC
PO Box 449, 169 Pleasant St, Marlborough, MA 01752
Crisis hotline: **(508) 485-RAPE 24 hrs daily**
Information: (508) 481-8290 9am-5pm (Mon-Fri)
Contact: Laura Morrall, Rape Hotline Coord; Bonnie Horka, Child Sexual Assault Prevention Coord
TYPE OF AGENCY: Rape crisis center; Counseling/mental health services; Child sexual abuse services; Child sexual abuse prevention program
YEARS IN OPERATION: 15
LANGUAGES: Spanish, Portuguese
CASES SEXUAL ASSAULT/ABUSE (%): 15
CLIENTS/SERVICES: Sexual assault survivors; Marital rape/sexual abuse survivors; Child victims of sexual abuse; Adult survivors of child sexual abuse; Incest victims/survivors; Prevention program; Community education; Adolescent survivors of sexual abuse; Male survivors of sexual abuse

MILFORD

BLACKSTONE VALLEY RAPE CRISIS TEAM, INC
PO Box 215, Milford, MA 01757
Crisis hotline: **(508) 478-8775 24 hrs 7 days**
Information: (508) 478-8775 9am-5pm (Mon-Fri)
Contact: Mary E Jackson, Dir
TYPE OF AGENCY: Rape crisis center; Child sexual abuse prevention program
AREAS SERVED: Blackstone valley's 14 towns
YEARS IN OPERATION: 10
ACCESSIBILITY: Wheelchair accessible
CASES SEXUAL ASSAULT/ABUSE (%): 100
DESCRIPTION: Comprehensive services for sexual assault victims/survivors; Prevention programs; Feminist martial arts/self-defense program
CLIENTS/SERVICES: Sexual assault survivors; Marital rape/sexual abuse survivors; Child victims of sexual abuse; Adult survivors of child sexual abuse; Incest victims/survivors; Prevention program; Community education; Adolescent survivors of sexual abuse; Male survivors of sexual abuse

NANTUCKET

A SAFE PLACE, INC (ASP)/NANTUCKET CHILD ASSAULT PREVENTION (CAPP)
PO Box 3231, Nantucket, MA 02584
Crisis hotline: **(508) 228-2111 24 hrs**
Information: (508) 228-0561 8:30am-Noon
Contact: Rhonda Thurston, Dir
TYPE OF AGENCY: Rape crisis center; Domestic violence program; Child sexual abuse prevention program
AREAS SERVED: Nantucket Island
YEARS IN OPERATION: 2
ACCESSIBILITY: Wheelchair accessible
CASES SEXUAL ASSAULT/ABUSE (%): 5
DESCRIPTION: A center for victims of sexual assault and domestic violence. ASP provides group counseling, advocacy (medical, legal welfare). Sponsors Nantucket CAPP and is a member of MA CAPP which is a worldwide organization for the prevention of child sexual assault
CLIENTS/SERVICES: Sexual assault survivors; Marital rape/sexual abuse survivors; Adult survivors of child sexual abuse; Incest victims/survivors; Prevention program; Community education

NATICK

WOMEN'S PROTECTIVE SERVICES
251 W Central St, Natick, MA 01760
Crisis hotline: **(617) 651-3300 24 hrs**
Information: (617) 653-4464 9am-5pm
Contact: Francoise M Castellanos, Rape Crisis Counselor
TYPE OF AGENCY: Rape crisis center; Domestic violence program
SPONSORING ORGANIZATION: Boston YWCA
AREAS SERVED: Metro west area
YEARS IN OPERATION: 4
LANGUAGES: Spanish, French
ACCESSIBILITY: Wheelchair accessible
CLIENTS/SERVICES: Sexual assault survivors; Marital rape/sexual abuse survivors; Adult survivors of child sexual abuse; Prevention program; Community education; Adolescent survivors of sexual abuse; Male survivors of sexual abuse; Publications/media
REQUIREMENTS: Must be over 13 years of age
SPECIAL PROGRAMS/SERVICES: Locally produced media programs for education/training

NEW BEDFORD

VICTIM/WITNESS ASSISTANCE PROGRAM
PO Box B-940, New Bedford, MA 02741
Information: (508) 997-0711 9am-5pm
Contact: Donald Gomes, Dir
TYPE OF AGENCY: Victim/witness assistance program
SPONSORING ORGANIZATION: Bristol County District Attorney's Office
AREAS SERVED: Bristol
YEARS IN OPERATION: 3
LANGUAGES: Portuguese, Spanish
ACCESSIBILITY: Wheelchair accessible
CLIENTS/SERVICES: Sexual assault survivors; Marital rape/sexual abuse survivors; Child victims of sexual abuse; Adult survivors of child sexual abuse; Incest victims/survivors

NEWTON CENTER

THE NEXT STEP COUNSELING AND TRAINING CENTER
10 Langley Rd, Ste 200, Newton Center, MA 02159
Information: (617) 332-6601, 332-7868 answering machine after hrs
Contact: Mike Lew, MEd, Co-Dir; Thom Harrigan, Psychotherapist
TYPE OF AGENCY: Private practice; Training/research
AREAS SERVED: Eastern New England, Greater Boston area
YEARS IN OPERATION: 6
LANGUAGES: Italian, German
ACCESSIBILITY: Wheelchair accessible
CASES SEXUAL ASSAULT/ABUSE (%): 70-95
DESCRIPTION: Experienced in working with adult survivors of child sexual abuse, incest and other dysfunctional families. Particular services for male survivors include recovery groups and workshops for gay and heterosexual males. Also services for partners of male and female survivors
CLIENTS/SERVICES: Sexual assault survivors; Marital rape/sexual abuse survivors; Adult survivors of child sexual abuse; Incest victims/survivors; Community education; Adolescent survivors of sexual abuse; Male survivors of sexual abuse; Gay men
REQUIREMENTS: Does not work with offenders or children

NORTH DARTMOUTH

SMU WOMEN'S CENTER
Old Westport Rd, North Dartmouth, MA 02747
Crisis hotline: **(508) 999-8168 12pm-8pm (Mon-Thu)**
Information: (508) 999-8168 12pm-8pm (Mon-Thu)
Contact: Sue Mitchell, Dir
TYPE OF AGENCY: College/university-based services
AREAS SERVED: Southeastern Massachusetts
YEARS IN OPERATION: 9
CLIENTS/SERVICES: Sexual assault survivors; Marital rape/sexual abuse survivors; Adult survivors of child sexual abuse; Incest victims/survivors; Prevention program; Community education

NORTHAMPTON

CIRCA PSYCHOTHERAPY ASSOCIATES FOR WOMEN
160 Main St, Northampton, MA 01060
Information: (413) 586-6471 24 hr answering machine
Contact: Paula Olson, Co-Dir
TYPE OF AGENCY: Counseling/mental health services; Private practice
YEARS IN OPERATION: 10
LANGUAGES: Spanish
CASES SEXUAL ASSAULT/ABUSE (%): 33
CLIENTS/SERVICES: Sexual assault survivors; Marital rape/sexual abuse survivors; Adult survivors of child sexual abuse; Incest victims/survivors
REQUIREMENTS: Serves only women aged 15 and older, couples and families

NECESSITIES/NECESIDADES
16 Center St, Northampton, MA 01060
Crisis hotline: **(413) 586-5066 24 hrs**
Information: (413) 586-1125 9am-5pm
TYPE OF AGENCY: Domestic violence program
AREAS SERVED: Hampshire
LANGUAGES: Spanish
ACCESSIBILITY: Wheelchair accessible (office, but not shelter); Telecommunications for the hearing impaired (TTY, TDY, etc.)
CLIENTS/SERVICES: Marital rape/sexual abuse survivors; Community education

NECESITIES/NECESIDADES *(continued)*
SPECIAL PROGRAMS/SERVICES: Bilingual (Spanish/English) brochure

ORANGE

MASSACHUSETTS SOCIETY FOR THE PREVENTION OF CRUELTY TO CHILDREN
135 E Main St, Orange, MA 01364
Crisis hotline: **(800) 392-6046 24 hrs daily**
Information: (508) 544-7174 8:30am-5pm
TYPE OF AGENCY: Child sexual abuse services; Child abuse services
YEARS IN OPERATION: 110
LANGUAGES: Spanish, French
ACCESSIBILITY: Wheelchair accessible
DESCRIPTION: Protects children from the danger of abuse, neglect and exploitation in any of its forms; Provides social services, advocacy and education for children and families. Treatment for child sexual abuse/incest offenders modeled on Parents United
CLIENTS/SERVICES: Child victims of sexual abuse; Adult survivors of child sexual abuse; Incest victims/survivors; Prevention program; Community education; Offender treatment program; Adolescent survivors of sexual abuse; Male survivors of sexual abuse

PITTSFIELD

MASSACHUSETTS SOCIETY FOR THE PREVENTION OF CRUELTY TO CHILDREN—BERKSHIRE DISTRICT
PO Box 1372, Pittsfield, MA 01201
Crisis hotline: **(413) 442-9434 Evenings; weekends**
Information: (413) 442-6971 8:30am-4:30pm (Mon-Fri)
Contact: Thomas A Duane, District Exec
TYPE OF AGENCY: Child sexual abuse services; Child sexual abuse prevention program; Child abuse services; Child abuse prevention program
AREAS SERVED: Berkshire
YEARS IN OPERATION: 75
CASES SEXUAL ASSAULT/ABUSE (%): 15
DESCRIPTION: Provides preventive and protective services for children and adolescents who have been or may be at risk of physical, sexual or emotional neglect or abuse; Support groups for adult survivors of child sexual abuse
CLIENTS/SERVICES: Child victims of sexual abuse; Adult survivors of child sexual abuse; Incest victims/survivors; Prevention program; Adolescent survivors of sexual abuse

RAPE CRISIS CENTER OF BERKSHIRE COUNTY, INC
18 Charles St, Pittsfield, MA 01201
Crisis hotline: **(413) 443-0089 24 hrs**
Information: (413) 442-6708 9am-5pm
Contact: Roberta Russell, PhD, Exec Dir
TYPE OF AGENCY: Rape crisis center; Child sexual abuse prevention program
AREAS SERVED: Berkshire
YEARS IN OPERATION: 12
LANGUAGES: Spanish, German
ACCESSIBILITY: Wheelchair accessible
CASES SEXUAL ASSAULT/ABUSE (%): 100
DESCRIPTION: Provides comprehensive services for sexual assault/abuse, including crisis counseling and support groups. Also provides group therapy for rapists and child sexual abuse offenders who are in prison
CLIENTS/SERVICES: Sexual assault survivors; Marital rape/sexual abuse survivors; Child victims of sexual abuse; Adult survivors of child sexual abuse; Incest victims/survivors; Prevention program; Community education; Offender treatment program; Adolescent survivors of sexual abuse; Male survivors of sexual abuse
SPECIAL PROGRAMS/SERVICES: Child assault prevention program is based on the national Child Assault Prevention Project. Publication:

It Happens to Boys Too..., a 36-page book for boys 6-12 years of age ($6.50 each)

WOMEN'S SERVICES CENTER
146 1st St, Pittsfield, MA 01201
Crisis hotline: **(413) 443-0089 24 hrs**
Information: (413) 499-2425 9am-5pm (Mon-Fri)
Contact: Catherine Hill, AWARE Coord
TYPE OF AGENCY: Domestic violence program
AREAS SERVED: Berkshire
YEARS IN OPERATION: 14
LANGUAGES: Spanish
ACCESSIBILITY: Wheelchair accessible; Telecommunications for the hearing impaired (TTY, TDY, etc.)
DESCRIPTION: Serves battered women, homeless women, and women in crisis; A referral and support service for women who experience sexual assault or whose children experience sexual assault
CLIENTS/SERVICES: Marital rape/sexual abuse survivors; Community education

PLYMOUTH

SOUTH SHORE WOMEN'S CENTER
14 Main St, Plymouth, MA 02360
Crisis hotline: **(508) 746-2664 24 hrs daily**
Information: (508) 746-2664 9am-5pm (Mon-Fri)
Contact: Linda Rudnick, Exec Dir
TYPE OF AGENCY: Domestic violence program; Child sexual abuse prevention program
AREAS SERVED: Plymouth
YEARS IN OPERATION: 10
CASES SEXUAL ASSAULT/ABUSE (%): 10-15
DESCRIPTION: Provides services and resources for victims of domestic violence, many of whom are victims of sexual assault or incest survivors. One trained counselor handles rape and sexual assault not related to family violence. Group therapy for batterers
CLIENTS/SERVICES: Sexual assault survivors; Marital rape/sexual abuse survivors; Adult survivors of child sexual abuse; Incest victims/survivors; Prevention program; Community education; Adolescent survivors of sexual abuse

QUINCY

DOVE, INC (DOMESTIC VIOLENCE ENDED)
PO Box 287, Quincy, MA 02269
Crisis hotline: **(617) 471-1234**
Information: (617) 471-5087 24 hrs
TYPE OF AGENCY: Domestic violence program
AREAS SERVED: Statewide
YEARS IN OPERATION: 10
CASES SEXUAL ASSAULT/ABUSE (%): 50
CLIENTS/SERVICES: Marital rape/sexual abuse survivors; Community education

SOUTH SHORE THERAPY CENTER
1354 Hancock St, Ste 214, Quincy, MA 02169
Information: (617) 773-0985 9am-9pm
Contact: Tree A Borden, MSW, LICSW, Co-Dir
TYPE OF AGENCY: Private practice
YEARS IN OPERATION: 7
ACCESSIBILITY: Wheelchair accessible
CASES SEXUAL ASSAULT/ABUSE (%): 99
CLIENTS/SERVICES: Sexual assault survivors; Marital rape/sexual abuse survivors; Adult survivors of child sexual abuse; Incest victims/survivors; Community education; Adolescent survivors of sexual abuse; Male survivors of sexual abuse; Healing
REQUIREMENTS: 17 and older; Victim/survivor work only
SPECIAL PROGRAMS/SERVICES: Psychodynamic approach, coupled with psychodramatic work, creative visualization and some bioenergetic work, promotes healing for survivors with recovering memory and dealing with the effects of their victimization. Also addresses addictions and eating disorders

REVERE

COMPREHENSIVE EMERGENCY SERVICES
265 Beach St, Revere, MA 02151
Crisis hotline: **(617) 884-4357 5pm-9am (Mon-Fri); 24 hrs weekends and holidays**
Information: (617) 289-9331 9am-5pm (Mon-Fri)
Contact: Shelley Baer, Prog Dir
TYPE OF AGENCY: Counseling/mental health services; Telephone crisis hotline
SPONSORING ORGANIZATION: North Suffolk Mental Health Association, Inc
AREAS SERVED: Chelsea, Winthrop, Revere
YEARS IN OPERATION: 10
LANGUAGES: Spanish; Cambodian interpreter available
CASES SEXUAL ASSAULT/ABUSE (%): 5
DESCRIPTION: A crisis intervention service; Contracts with the department of social services to provide emergency sexual assault/abuse investigations when DSS is closed; Crisis counseling over the phone; Referrals
CLIENTS/SERVICES: Sexual assault survivors; Child victims of sexual abuse
REQUIREMENTS: The child-at-risk hotline must authorize services after a sexual assault/abuse report is filed; Does emergency investigations as directed by the hotline

ROSLINDALE

FAMILY PROJECT
780 American Legion Hwy, Roslindale, MA 02131
Crisis hotline: **(617) 325-6700 24 hrs**
Information: (617) 325-6700, ext 210 9am-5pm (Mon-Fri)
Contact: Russela Olin, Asst Dir
TYPE OF AGENCY: Counseling/mental health services; Child sexual abuse services; Child abuse services
SPONSORING ORGANIZATION: West-Ros-Park Mental Health Center
AREAS SERVED: Suffolk
YEARS IN OPERATION: 9
ACCESSIBILITY: Wheelchair accessible
CASES SEXUAL ASSAULT/ABUSE (%): 25
DESCRIPTION: Contracted to service department of social service catchment area in Boston. Assesses families where child abuse or neglect (including child sexual abuse) has occurred. Recommends treatment and/or referral
CLIENTS/SERVICES: Child victims of sexual abuse; Adult survivors of child sexual abuse; Incest victims/survivors; Offender treatment program
REQUIREMENTS: Closed referrals from Department of Social Services

SALEM

ESSEX COUNTY DISTRICT ATTORNEY'S OFFICE—VICTIM/WITNESS ASSISTANCE PROGRAM
70 Washington St, Salem, MA 01970
Information: (508) 745-6610 8:30am-4:30pm
Contact: Michaelene O'Neill McCann, Esq, Exec Dir
TYPE OF AGENCY: Victim/witness assistance program; Child sexual abuse services
AREAS SERVED: Essex
YEARS IN OPERATION: 9½
LANGUAGES: Spanish, Khmer
ACCESSIBILITY: Wheelchair accessible
DESCRIPTION: Provides comprehensive victim services, with a special sexual assault unit and a multiagency investigative team for child sexual abuse
CLIENTS/SERVICES: Sexual assault survivors; Marital rape/sexual abuse survivors; Child victims of sexual abuse; Incest victims/survivors; Community education; Adolescent survivors of sexual abuse; Male survivors of sexual abuse

ESSEX COUNTY DISTRICT ATTORNEY'S OFFICE—VICTIM/WITNESS ASSISTANCE PROGRAM (continued)

SPECIAL PROGRAMS/SERVICES: Essex County Child Abuse Project involves multidisciplinary teams to investigate child sexual abuse, including an on-going training program and development of data collection/management system

HELP FOR ABUSED WOMEN AND THEIR CHILDREN (HAWC)
9 Crombie St, Salem, MA 01970
Crisis hotline: **(508) 744-6841 24 hrs**
Information: (508) 744-8552 9am-5pm (Mon-Fri)
Contact: Ann Faulkner, Admin Asst
TYPE OF AGENCY: Domestic violence program
YEARS IN OPERATION: 10
LANGUAGES: Spanish, French, Sign
ACCESSIBILITY: Signers for the hearing impaired
CLIENTS/SERVICES: Marital rape/sexual abuse survivors; Prevention program; Community education
SPECIAL PROGRAMS/SERVICES: Bilingual (Spanish/English) brochure

FLORENCE LUSCOMB WOMEN'S CENTER
352 Lafayette St, Salem, MA 01970
Information: (508) 741-6000, ext 2357 8am-2pm (Mon-Fri), and by appointment
Contact: Lynda Laford, Coord
TYPE OF AGENCY: College/university-based services; Acquaintance/date rape prevention program
SPONSORING ORGANIZATION: Salem State College
AREAS SERVED: North Shore, Boston
YEARS IN OPERATION: 15
DESCRIPTION: Provides referrals for victims; Offers date rape workshops; Sexual abuse library; Crisis counseling; Occasional support groups for sexual assault survivors and adult survivors of child sexual abuse
CLIENTS/SERVICES: Sexual assault survivors; Marital rape/sexual abuse survivors; Adult survivors of child sexual abuse; Incest victims/survivors; Prevention program; Adolescent survivors of sexual abuse; Male survivors of sexual abuse

MASSACHUSETTS SOCIETY FOR THE PREVENTION OF CRUELTY TO CHILDREN (MSPCC)
3 Hawthorne Blvd, Salem, MA 01945
Crisis hotline: **(508) 744-2910 evenings and weekends**
Information: (508) 744-2910 9am-5pm (Mon-Fri); Saturday mornings
Contact: John Cronin, MS, Patricia Griffin, ACSW, LICSW, Co-Dirs
TYPE OF AGENCY: Child sexual abuse services; Child sexual abuse prevention program; Child abuse services
AREAS SERVED: Essex, Middlesex
YEARS IN OPERATION: MSPCC 11, Sexual offender program 4
CASES SEXUAL ASSAULT/ABUSE (%): 25
CLIENTS/SERVICES: Child victims of sexual abuse; Adult survivors of child sexual abuse; Incest victims/survivors; Prevention program; Community education; Offender treatment program; Adolescent survivors of sexual abuse; Male survivors of sexual abuse
REQUIREMENTS: Clients must be evaluated for dangerousness, amenability to treatment. All clients must be pre-trial, on probation, or otherwise connected with the criminal justice system. Client must sign treatment contract, agreeing to 2 year minimum stay in program
SPECIAL PROGRAMS/SERVICES: Slide presentations and videotapes for prevention programs using puppets

SOMERVILLE

SOMERVILLE HOSPITAL—CHILD AND PARENTS PROGRAM
230 Highland, Somerville, MA 02143
Information: (617) 666-4400, ext 184 9am-5pm; referred by emergency room after hrs
Contact: Maggie Mosley, Soc Svcs Dir
TYPE OF AGENCY: Hospital/medical center; Child sexual abuse services; Child sexual abuse prevention program; Child abuse services; Child abuse prevention program
YEARS IN OPERATION: 10
LANGUAGES: Spanish, Portuguese, Haitian, Creole
ACCESSIBILITY: Wheelchair accessible
CASES SEXUAL ASSAULT/ABUSE (%): 50
DESCRIPTION: Provides direct and collateral services for families with children at risk for abuse or neglect
CLIENTS/SERVICES: Sexual assault survivors; Marital rape/sexual abuse survivors; Child victims of sexual abuse; Adult survivors of child sexual abuse; Incest victims/survivors; Prevention program; Community education; Adolescent survivors of sexual abuse; Male survivors of sexual abuse
REQUIREMENTS: Families with children 18 and younger; Must be patients of hospital to receive therapy

SPRINGFIELD

AMBULATORY PEDIATRICS
140 High St, Springfield, MA 01199
Crisis hotline: **(413) 784-2515 24 hrs**
Information: (413) 784-2515 24 hrs
Contact: Edward N Bailey, MD, Sandra Flatow, PNP, Co-Dirs
TYPE OF AGENCY: Hospital/medical center; Child sexual abuse services; Child sexual abuse prevention program
SPONSORING ORGANIZATION: Baystate Medical Center
AREAS SERVED: Western MA
YEARS IN OPERATION: 10
LANGUAGES: Spanish
ACCESSIBILITY: Wheelchair accessible; Telecommunications for the hearing impaired (TTY, TDY, etc.); Signers for the hearing impaired (by request)
CASES SEXUAL ASSAULT/ABUSE (%): 100
CLIENTS/SERVICES: Child victims of sexual abuse; Adult survivors of child sexual abuse; Incest victims/survivors

HAMPDEN COUNTY DISTRICT ATTORNEY—VICTIM/WITNESS SUPPORT PROGRAM
50 State St, Springfield, MA 01103
Information: (413) 781-8100, ext 2026 8:30am-4:30pm (Mon-Fri)
Contact: Eleanor Cress, Dir
TYPE OF AGENCY: Victim/witness assistance program; Child sexual abuse services; Child abuse services
AREAS SERVED: Hampden
YEARS IN OPERATION: 10
LANGUAGES: Spanish
CASES SEXUAL ASSAULT/ABUSE (%): 30-40
CLIENTS/SERVICES: Sexual assault survivors; Marital rape/sexual abuse survivors; Child victims of sexual abuse; Prevention program; Community education; Adolescent survivors of sexual abuse; Male survivors of sexual abuse
REQUIREMENTS: Any victim or witness of a crime in Hampden County; Most services provided after an arrest
SPECIAL PROGRAMS/SERVICES: Multidisciplinary team (pediatrician/social worker/criminal justice and others) interviews children who have been physically or sexually abused. Interviews take place at specially designed clinic at Baystate Medical Center. Victim/Witness staff child specialists and prosecutors are part of team.

MASSACHUSETTS SOCIETY FOR THE PREVENTION OF CRUELTY TO CHILDREN
78 Maple St, Springfield, MA 01105
Crisis hotline: **(800) 392-6046 24 hrs daily**
Information: (413) 734-4978 8:30am-5pm
TYPE OF AGENCY: Child sexual abuse services; Child abuse services
YEARS IN OPERATION: 110
LANGUAGES: Spanish, French
ACCESSIBILITY: Wheelchair accessible
DESCRIPTION: Protects children from the danger of abuse, neglect and exploitation in any of its forms; Provides social services, advocacy and education for children and families. Treatment for child sexual abuse/incest offenders modeled on Parents United
CLIENTS/SERVICES: Child victims of sexual abuse; Adult survivors of child sexual abuse; Incest victims/survivors; Prevention program; Community education; Offender treatment program; Adolescent survivors of sexual abuse; Male survivors of sexual abuse

TAUNTON

MASSACHUSETTS SOCIETY FOR THE PREVENTION OF CRUELTY TO CHILDREN
41 Winthrop St, Taunton, MA 02780
Crisis hotline: **(800) 322-2204 24 hrs**
Information: (508) 822-2770 8:30am-5pm
TYPE OF AGENCY: Child sexual abuse services; Child abuse services
YEARS IN OPERATION: 110
LANGUAGES: Spanish, French
ACCESSIBILITY: Wheelchair accessible
DESCRIPTION: Protects children from the danger of abuse, neglect and exploitation in any of its forms; Provides social services, advocacy and education for children and families. Treatment for child sexual abuse/incest offenders modeled on Parents United
CLIENTS/SERVICES: Child victims of sexual abuse; Adult survivors of child sexual abuse; Incest victims/survivors; Prevention program; Community education; Offender treatment program; Adolescent survivors of sexual abuse; Male survivors of sexual abuse

TAUNTON AREA MENTAL HEALTH CLINIC
175 Dean St, Taunton, MA 02780
Crisis hotline: **(508) 822-2485 After hrs and weekends**
Information: (508) 822-2485 8am-9pm
Contact: Sandy Fyfe, Sexual Abuse Treatment Prog Coord
TYPE OF AGENCY: Counseling/mental health services; Child sexual abuse services
AREAS SERVED: Bristol
YEARS IN OPERATION: 36
LANGUAGES: Portuguese, Spanish
CASES SEXUAL ASSAULT/ABUSE (%): 25
DESCRIPTION: Outpatient mental health clinic specializing in child sexual abuse treatment; Also serves adult victims/survivors of sexual assault
CLIENTS/SERVICES: Sexual assault survivors; Marital rape/sexual abuse survivors; Child victims of sexual abuse; Adult survivors of child sexual abuse; Incest victims/survivors; Prevention program; Community education; Offender treatment program; Adolescent survivors of sexual abuse; Male survivors of sexual abuse
REQUIREMENTS: Survivors eligible for services at reduced or no fee; Sexual offenders must admit to offense and accept full legal responsibility for all sexual offenses

VINEYARD HAVEN

WOMEN'S SUPPORT SERVICES
PO Box 369, Vineyard Haven, MA 02568
Crisis hotline: **(508) 693-0032 24 hrs**
Information: (508) 693-7900 9am-5pm
Contact: Susan Stewart, Prog Mgr
TYPE OF AGENCY: Rape crisis center; Domestic violence program
SPONSORING ORGANIZATION: Martha's Vineyard Community Services
AREAS SERVED: Dukes
YEARS IN OPERATION: 10
ACCESSIBILITY: Wheelchair accessible; Telecommunications for the hearing impaired (TTY, TDY, etc.); Signers for the hearing impaired
CASES SEXUAL ASSAULT/ABUSE (%): 5
CLIENTS/SERVICES: Sexual assault survivors; Marital rape/sexual abuse survivors; Adult survivors of child sexual abuse; Incest victims/survivors; Prevention program; Community education; Male survivors of sexual abuse

WALTHAM

BRANDEIS RAPE AND SEXUAL ASSAULT HOTLINE
Brandeis University Student Senate, Waltham, MA 02254-9110
Crisis hotline: **(617) 736-4774 8pm-3am 7 days**
Information: (617) 736-4773 8pm-3am 7 days, possible daytime hrs
TYPE OF AGENCY: Rape crisis center; College/university-based services; Rape prevention program; Acquaintance/date rape prevention program
SPONSORING ORGANIZATION: Brandeis University
AREAS SERVED: Brandeis University and surrounding area
YEARS IN OPERATION: 5
CASES SEXUAL ASSAULT/ABUSE (%): 100
DESCRIPTION: Short-term counseling and information service with extensive training in stranger, acquaintance, and attempted rape, sexual harassment, lesbian/gay/heterosexual battery, incest and childhood sexual assault
CLIENTS/SERVICES: Sexual assault survivors; Marital rape/sexual abuse survivors; Adult survivors of child sexual abuse; Incest victims/survivors; Prevention program; Community education; Male survivors of sexual abuse; Lesbians; Sexual harassment; Gay men

WARE

VALLEY HUMAN SERVICES, INC
96 South St, Ware, MA 01082
Crisis hotline: **(413) 283-3473 8pm-8am; Weekends**
Information: (413) 967-6241 8am-8pm
Contact: Evalyn Glickman, Exec Dir
TYPE OF AGENCY: Counseling/mental health services; Child sexual abuse services
AREAS SERVED: Hampshire, Hampden, Worcester
YEARS IN OPERATION: 18
ACCESSIBILITY: Wheelchair accessible; Telecommunications for the hearing impaired (TTY, TDY, etc.)
CASES SEXUAL ASSAULT/ABUSE (%): 10
DESCRIPTION: Outpatient mental health center offering individual, family, and group psychotherapy, as well as play therapy for young children; Survivor's groups as well as offenders groups; Special group for mentally retarded offenders
CLIENTS/SERVICES: Sexual assault survivors; Marital rape/sexual abuse survivors; Child victims of sexual abuse; Adult survivors of child sexual abuse; Incest victims/survivors; Offender treatment program; Adolescent survivors of sexual abuse; Male survivors of sexual abuse; Developmentally disabled; Disabled
REQUIREMENTS: Sliding scale fee; Third party payments

WAREHAM

WAREHAM AREA COUNSELING SERVICE, INC
PO Box 245, Wareham, MA 02571
Information: (508) 295-3600 9am-9pm (Mon-Thu); 9am-5pm (Fri)
Contact: B J Scheff, Dir
TYPE OF AGENCY: Counseling/mental health services
AREAS SERVED: Plymouth, Bristol
YEARS IN OPERATION: 18
ACCESSIBILITY: Wheelchair accessible
CASES SEXUAL ASSAULT/ABUSE (%): 20
CLIENTS/SERVICES: Sexual assault survivors; Child victims of sexual abuse; Adult survivors of child sexual abuse; Incest victims/survivors; Prevention program; Adolescent survivors of sexual abuse; Male survivors of sexual abuse

WATERTOWN

BOSTON WOMEN'S HEALTH BOOK COLLECTIVE
47 Nichols Ave, Watertown, MA 02172
Information: (617) 924-0271 Varies
TYPE OF AGENCY: Information center
ACCESSIBILITY: Wheelchair accessible
DESCRIPTION: Non-lending library which has books, newletters, and files of articles on sexual abuse and violence against women; Open to the public several days and one evening per week
CLIENTS/SERVICES: Publications/media

WEBSTER

FORENSIC MENTAL HEALTH ASSOCIATES
RR1, Box 404, Lakeside Beach, Webster, MA 01570
Information: (508) 943-2381
Contact: A Nicholas Groth, Dir
TYPE OF AGENCY: Residential treatment facility; Training/research; Offender treatment
YEARS IN OPERATION: 10
CASES SEXUAL ASSAULT/ABUSE (%): 100
DESCRIPTION: Provides individual and group treatment for rapists and child sexual abuse/incest offenders
CLIENTS/SERVICES: Community education; Offender treatment program; Publications/media
SPECIAL PROGRAMS/SERVICES: Provides a variety of basic and advanced training seminars nationwide on sexual assault victims and offenders encompassing such topics as the investigation, identification, validation, evaluation, and treatment of child sexual abuse; understanding sexual assault in regard to the dynamics of the offense, the motivations of the offender, and the impact on the victim; the assessment and treatment of juvenile and adult sex offenders; and working with adults molested as children, the male victim, the retarded client, the non-abusive spouse in incest families, and allegations of sexual abuse in divorce and custody disputes. Distributor for books in the field of child sexual abuse. Audiotapes available: *The Psychology of Sexual Offenders Against Children* and *Guidelines for Disposition with Regard to Treatment of Sexual Offenders Against Children*, both lectures by A Nicholas Groth ($15 each). Videotapes available: *Working with the Child Sexual Abuse Offender*, interview with A Nicholas Groth, and *Matthew*, an interview of a rapist by A Nicholas Groth in regard to the physical and sexual abuse Matthew experienced as a child and its role in the etiology of his sexual assaultiveness

HUMAN SERVICE CENTER
Thompson Rd, Webster, MA 01570
Crisis hotline: **(508) 943-2600 24 hrs daily**
Information: (508) 943-2600 8:30am-5pm (Mon-Fri)
Contact: Anne Pope, Dir
TYPE OF AGENCY: Hospital/medical center; Counseling/mental health services
SPONSORING ORGANIZATION: Hubbard Regional Hospital
AREAS SERVED: Mid Massachusetts
YEARS IN OPERATION: 15
LANGUAGES: Spanish, Indian
ACCESSIBILITY: Wheelchair accessible; Telecommunications for the hearing impaired (TTY, TDY, etc.); Signers for the hearing impaired
CASES SEXUAL ASSAULT/ABUSE (%): 5
CLIENTS/SERVICES: Sexual assault survivors; Child victims of sexual abuse; Adult survivors of child sexual abuse; Incest victims/survivors; Community education; Adolescent survivors of sexual abuse; Male survivors of sexual abuse

WOBURN

VICTIM WITNESS SERVICES BUREAU
30 Pleasant St, Woburn, MA 01801
Information: (617) 935-7162 8:30am-4:30pm
Contact: Colleen O'Neil, Victim Witness Advocate
TYPE OF AGENCY: Victim/witness assistance program
AREAS SERVED: Middlesex
YEARS IN OPERATION: 10
LANGUAGES: Spanish
ACCESSIBILITY: Wheelchair accessible
CASES SEXUAL ASSAULT/ABUSE (%): 30
CLIENTS/SERVICES: Sexual assault survivors; Marital rape/sexual abuse survivors; Child victims of sexual abuse; Adult survivors of child sexual abuse; Incest victims/survivors; Community education; Adolescent survivors of sexual abuse
REQUIREMENTS: Mainly deals with victims and witnesses of an offense that is being criminally prosecuted

WORCESTER

ASSUMPTION COLLEGE STUDENT DEVELOPMENT CENTER
500 Salisbury St, Worcester, MA 01615-0005
Information: (508) 752-5615, ext 409 8:30am-9pm (Mon-Thu); 8:30am-5pm (Fri)
Contact: N R Castronovo, PhD, Dir
TYPE OF AGENCY: College/university-based services
AREAS SERVED: Assumption College community
LANGUAGES: Russian, Polish
ACCESSIBILITY: Wheelchair accessible
CASES SEXUAL ASSAULT/ABUSE (%): 2
CLIENTS/SERVICES: Sexual assault survivors; Marital rape/sexual abuse survivors; Adult survivors of child sexual abuse; Incest victims/survivors; Prevention program; Male survivors of sexual abuse
REQUIREMENTS: Cost of service is included in tuition for any full-time student.

THE CHILD ASSAULT PREVENTION PROJECT OF GREATER WORCESTER
900 Main St, Worcester, MA 01610
Information: (508) 798-2277 9am-5pm
Contact: Donna Russell, Exec Dir
TYPE OF AGENCY: Child sexual abuse prevention program; Child abuse prevention program
AREAS SERVED: Worcester, Middlesex
YEARS IN OPERATION: 6
LANGUAGES: Spanish, Italian, Sign
CASES SEXUAL ASSAULT/ABUSE (%): 90
DESCRIPTION: Child Assault Prevention (CAP) Project is a primary prevention program dealing with the physical, sexual, and psychological abuse of children for preschoolers, elementary school students, teens, and students with special needs
CLIENTS/SERVICES: Prevention program; Community education

FAMILY SERVICES OF CENTRAL MASSACHUSETTS
31 Harvard St, Worcester, MA 01609
Information: (508) 756-4646 9am-5pm (Tue, Thu, Fri); 9am-9pm (Mon, Wed)
Contact: Jeanne Rosenblatt, Clinical Dir
TYPE OF AGENCY: Counseling/mental health services
AREAS SERVED: Worcester
YEARS IN OPERATION: 100
LANGUAGES: Spanish
ACCESSIBILITY: Wheelchair accessible
CASES SEXUAL ASSAULT/ABUSE (%): 20
DESCRIPTION: Counseling agency for all types of problems, including a therapy group for adult survivors of child sexual abuse
CLIENTS/SERVICES: Adult survivors of child sexual abuse; Incest victims/survivors; Male survivors of sexual abuse
REQUIREMENTS: Must reside or work in the area, be 18 or older and not in need of hospitalization; Sliding scale fee

MASSACHUSETTS SOCIETY FOR THE PREVENTION OF CRUELTY TO CHILDREN
286 Lincoln St, Worcester, MA 01605
Crisis hotline: **(800) 442-3035 24 hrs**
Information: (508) 753-2967 9am-5pm
Contact: Jack Hagenbuch, ARA
TYPE OF AGENCY: Child sexual abuse services; Child sexual abuse prevention program; Child abuse services; Child abuse prevention program
AREAS SERVED: Worcester, Middlesex
YEARS IN OPERATION: 78
LANGUAGES: Spanish
ACCESSIBILITY: Wheelchair accessible; Telecommunications for the hearing impaired (TTY, TDY, etc.)
CASES SEXUAL ASSAULT/ABUSE (%): 15
DESCRIPTION: Provides protective services and counseling for abused children and their families (physical, sexual, emotional abuse); Sponsors Parents United chapter; Provides treatment for child sex abuse offenders; Support groups for female and male adult survivors
CLIENTS/SERVICES: Child victims of sexual abuse; Adult survivors of child sexual abuse; Incest victims/survivors; Prevention program; Community education; Offender treatment program; Adolescent survivors of sexual abuse; Male survivors of sexual abuse
REQUIREMENTS: Must be 18 or younger

MIDDLE DISTRICT ATTORNEY'S OFFICE—VICTIM/WITNESS ASSISTANCE PROGRAM
332 Main St, 7th Fl, Worcester, MA 01608
Information: (508) 792-0214 8:15am-4:45pm
Contact: Anthony Pellegrini, Prog Dir
TYPE OF AGENCY: Victim/witness assistance program; Interagency network
AREAS SERVED: Worcester
YEARS IN OPERATION: 11
LANGUAGES: Spanish
ACCESSIBILITY: Wheelchair accessible
CASES SEXUAL ASSAULT/ABUSE (%): 75
DESCRIPTION: Comprehensive advocacy for victims, witnesses, and family members throughout their involvement with the court system; Focus is on providing information/support services for sexual assault/child sexual abuse victims
CLIENTS/SERVICES: Sexual assault survivors; Marital rape/sexual abuse survivors; Child victims of sexual abuse; Incest victims/survivors; Community education; Adolescent survivors of sexual abuse; Male survivors of sexual abuse; Developmentally disabled
SPECIAL PROGRAMS/SERVICES: Member of the Worcester Area Child Sexual Abuse Task Force, a multiagency group. Its purpose is to raise public awareness, develop and improve services, and promote communication among the various participants

RAPE CRISIS PROGRAM OF WORCESTER, INC
1016 Main St, Worcester, MA 01519
Crisis hotline: **(508) 799-5700 24 hrs daily**
Information: (508) 791-9546 9am-5pm (Mon-Fri)
Contact: Marianne Winters
TYPE OF AGENCY: Rape crisis center
AREAS SERVED: Central Worcester
YEARS IN OPERATION: 16
LANGUAGES: Spanish
ACCESSIBILITY: Wheelchair accessible
CASES SEXUAL ASSAULT/ABUSE (%): 100
CLIENTS/SERVICES: Sexual assault survivors; Marital rape/sexual abuse survivors; Child victims of sexual abuse; Adult survivors of child sexual abuse; Incest victims/survivors; Prevention program; Community education; Adolescent survivors of sexual abuse; Male survivors of sexual abuse
REQUIREMENTS: Counseling for 14 years and older; Medical and legal advocacy for all ages

MICHIGAN

ADRIAN

CALL SOMEONE CONCERNED, INC—SEXUAL ASSAULT PROGRAM
227 N Winter St, Ste 215, Adrian, MI 49221
Crisis hotline: **(517) 263-6737 24 hrs**
Information: (517) 263-6739 8am-11pm
Contact: Lynne Warner, Crisis Ctr Coord
TYPE OF AGENCY: Rape crisis center
AREAS SERVED: Lenawee
YEARS IN OPERATION: 6
LANGUAGES: Spanish
ACCESSIBILITY: Wheelchair accessible
CLIENTS/SERVICES: Sexual assault survivors; Marital rape/sexual abuse survivors; Adult survivors of child sexual abuse; Incest victims/survivors; Prevention program; Community education; Adolescent survivors of sexual abuse; Male survivors of sexual abuse

FAMILY AWARENESS CENTER
317 Erie St, Adrian, MI 49221
Information: (517) 265-5250 8:30am-5pm
Contact: Mary Ann McRobert, Exec Dir
TYPE OF AGENCY: Child sexual abuse services
AREAS SERVED: Lenawee, Hillsdale
YEARS IN OPERATION: 4
ACCESSIBILITY: Wheelchair accessible
CASES SEXUAL ASSAULT/ABUSE (%): 95
DESCRIPTION: Assessment, treatment of child sexual abuse; Services provided for victims, siblings, non-offending parents and offenders
CLIENTS/SERVICES: Child victims of sexual abuse; Adult survivors of child sexual abuse; Incest victims/survivors; Community education; Offender treatment program; Adolescent survivors of sexual abuse; Male survivors of sexual abuse
REQUIREMENTS: Adults Molested as Children and Parents United Groups, no restrictions; Others, current or prior involvement with protective services

ALMA

WOMEN'S AID SERVICE, INC
503 N State, Alma, MI 48801
Information: (517) 463-6014 9am-5pm (Mon-Fri)
TYPE OF AGENCY: Rape crisis center; Domestic violence program; Adolescent program
AREAS SERVED: Isabella, Gratiot, Clare
YEARS IN OPERATION: Women's Aid 10, Sexual assault program 2
DESCRIPTION: Comprehensive services for survivors of sexual assault and domestic violence; Group for batterers (Men Overcoming Violent Experiences) and a group for youth (12-17 years old) who have experienced previous or present violent/abusive relationships
CLIENTS/SERVICES: Sexual assault survivors; Marital rape/sexual abuse survivors; Adult survivors of child sexual abuse; Incest victims/survivors; Community education; Adolescent survivors of sexual abuse; Male survivors of sexual abuse
REQUIREMENTS: Adolescents can receive services with parental permission

ALPENA

SHELTER, INC
PO Box 797, Alpena, MI 49707
Crisis hotline: **(517) 356-9650 24 hrs**
Information: (517) 356-6265 8am-5pm (Mon-Fri)
Contact: Bob Rasche, Exec Dir
TYPE OF AGENCY: Domestic violence program
AREAS SERVED: Alcona, Alpena, Montmorency, Presque Isle, Iosco
YEARS IN OPERATION: 10
DESCRIPTION: Provides temporary safe housing for victims of domestic violence/abuse
CLIENTS/SERVICES: Marital rape/sexual abuse survivors

ANN ARBOR

ASSAULT CRISIS CENTER
2340 E Stadium Blvd, Ann Arbor, MI 48197
Crisis hotline: **(313) 994-1616 24 hrs**
Information: (313) 971-5904 9am-5pm
Contact: Patricia Krohn, Admin
TYPE OF AGENCY: Rape crisis center; Child sexual abuse services
SPONSORING ORGANIZATION: Washtenaw County Community Mental Health Center of Human Services Department
AREAS SERVED: Washtenaw
YEARS IN OPERATION: 13
LANGUAGES: Seek interpreters when necessary
ACCESSIBILITY: Wheelchair accessible
CASES SEXUAL ASSAULT/ABUSE (%): 100
DESCRIPTION: Provides crisis counseling for survivors of sexual assault/abuse; Therapy for child sexual abuse offenders; Feminist self-defense program; Support groups for both female and male survivors are available
CLIENTS/SERVICES: Sexual assault survivors; Marital rape/sexual abuse survivors; Child victims of sexual abuse; Adult survivors of child sexual abuse; Incest victims/survivors; Prevention program; Community education; Offender treatment program; Adolescent survivors of sexual abuse; Male survivors of sexual abuse

CITIZENS' ADVISORY COMMITTEE ON RAPE PREVENTION
PO Box 8647, Ann Arbor, MI 48107
Information: (313) 994-8775 9am-5pm
Contact: Elizabeth Radcliffe, Coord
TYPE OF AGENCY: Rape prevention program
SPONSORING ORGANIZATION: City of Ann Arbor
AREAS SERVED: Washtenaw, City of Ann Arbor
YEARS IN OPERATION: 7
ACCESSIBILITY: Wheelchair accessible; Telecommunications for the hearing impaired (TTY, TDY, etc.)
DESCRIPTION: Focuses on rape (including acquaintance rape) prevention work through educational programs and public policy change; Has worked on general safety ordinances, such as increased lighting, evening transportation, and security in rental housing
CLIENTS/SERVICES: Prevention program; Community education; Publications/media
SPECIAL PROGRAMS/SERVICES: *Breaking Silence* videotape series, defines sexual assault as a crime of power and anger while focusing on survivors' stories and individual and community prevention strategies. Series includes: *Rape by Friends, Dates, and Lovers*, exploring cultural attitudes which support and encourage sexual assault; *Rape in Marriage* exploring legal implications; *Rape of People with Physical Disabilities*; *Fighting the Rape Culture*, featuring community and individual activities to prevent rape and includes information to better understand the cause of rape

DOMESTIC VIOLENCE PROJECT/SAFE HOUSE
PO Box 7052, Ann Arbor, MI 48107
Crisis hotline: **(313) 995-5444 24 hrs**
Information: (313) 973-0242 8am-5pm (Mon-Fri)
Contact: Susan McGee, Dir
TYPE OF AGENCY: Domestic violence program
AREAS SERVED: Washtenaw
YEARS IN OPERATION: 12
CASES SEXUAL ASSAULT/ABUSE (%): 60
DESCRIPTION: Serves survivors of domestic violence, many of whom are also survivors of marital rape
CLIENTS/SERVICES: Marital rape/sexual abuse survivors; Community education

UNIVERSITY OF MICHIGAN—LESBIAN-GAY MALE PROGRAMS OFFICE
3118 Michigan Union, 530 S State St, Ann Arbor, MI 48109
Information: (313) 763-4186 9am-5pm (Mon-Fri)
Contact: Jim Toy, Gay Male Prog Coord; Billie L Edwards, Lesbian Prog Coord
TYPE OF AGENCY: College/university-based services
SPONSORING ORGANIZATION: University of Michigan Counseling Services
AREAS SERVED: Washtenaw, Livingston, Wayne
YEARS IN OPERATION: 17
ACCESSIBILITY: Wheelchair accessible
CASES SEXUAL ASSAULT/ABUSE (%): 50
DESCRIPTION: Provides brief and some long-term therapy; Referral
CLIENTS/SERVICES: Sexual assault survivors; Adult survivors of child sexual abuse; Incest victims/survivors; Male survivors of sexual abuse; Lesbians; Gay men; Bisexuals

UNIVERSITY OF MICHIGAN—LESBIAN-GAY MALE PROGRAMS OFFICE
(continued)

REQUIREMENTS: Lesbians, gay male and bisexual men and women needing counseling and support

UNIVERSITY OF MICHIGAN—SEXUAL ASSAULT PREVENTION AND AWARENESS CENTER
3100 Michigan Union, Ann Arbor, MI 48109
Crisis hotline: **(313) 936-3333 24 hrs**
Information: (313) 763-5865 9am-5pm
Contact: Julie Steiner, Dir
TYPE OF AGENCY: Rape crisis center; College/university-based services; Rape prevention program
AREAS SERVED: University of Michigan
YEARS IN OPERATION: 3
LANGUAGES: Persian
ACCESSIBILITY: Wheelchair accessible; Signers for the hearing impaired
CASES SEXUAL ASSAULT/ABUSE (%): 100
CLIENTS/SERVICES: Sexual assault survivors; Marital rape/sexual abuse survivors; Adult survivors of child sexual abuse; Incest victims/survivors; Prevention program; Community education; Male survivors of sexual abuse
REQUIREMENTS: Must be a University of Michigan student, faculty or staff member

WOMEN'S CRISIS CENTER
PO Box 7413, Ann Arbor, MI 48107
Crisis hotline: **(313) 994-9100 10am-10pm daily**
Information: (313) 761-9475 10am-6pm
Contact: Catherine Fischer, Coord
TYPE OF AGENCY: Women's center
AREAS SERVED: Primarily Washtenaw
YEARS IN OPERATION: 16
DESCRIPTION: Rape crisis services; Feminist martial arts/self defense program
CLIENTS/SERVICES: Sexual assault survivors; Marital rape/sexual abuse survivors; Adult survivors of child sexual abuse; Incest victims/survivors; Community education; Male survivors of sexual abuse

BATTLE CREEK

SAFE PLACE
PO Box 199, Battle Creek, MI 49016
Crisis hotline: **(616) 965-7233 24 hrs daily**
Information: (616) 965-6093 8am-5pm (Mon-Fri)
Contact: William Peck, Exec Dir
TYPE OF AGENCY: Rape crisis center; Domestic violence program
AREAS SERVED: Calhoun, Barry, Eaton
YEARS IN OPERATION: 5
CASES SEXUAL ASSAULT/ABUSE (%): 65
CLIENTS/SERVICES: Sexual assault survivors; Marital rape/sexual abuse survivors; Child victims of sexual abuse; Adult survivors of child sexual abuse; Incest victims/survivors; Prevention program; Community education; Adolescent survivors of sexual abuse; Male survivors of sexual abuse

BAY CITY

BAY COUNTY WOMEN'S CENTER
PO Box 646, Bay City, MI 48706
Crisis hotline: **(517) 686-4551 24 hrs 7 days**
Information: (517) 686-4551 24 hrs 7 days
Contact: Linda Mendez, Sexual Assault Coun
TYPE OF AGENCY: Domestic violence program
AREAS SERVED: Bay, Arenac
YEARS IN OPERATION: 14
ACCESSIBILITY: Wheelchair accessible
DESCRIPTION: Provides shelter for battered women, many of whom are sexual assault survivors; Referrals for children and rape survivors
CLIENTS/SERVICES: Sexual assault survivors; Marital rape/sexual abuse survivors; Child victims of sexual abuse; Adult survivors of child sexual abuse; Incest victims/survivors; Prevention program; Community education; Adolescent survivors of sexual abuse; Male survivors of sexual abuse

LUTHERAN CHILD AND FAMILY SERVICE OF MICHIGAN
PO Box 48, 6019 W Side Saginaw Rd, Bay City, MI 48707
Information: (517) 686-7650 8am-6pm
Contact: Luke Stephan, Family Counselor/Supv
TYPE OF AGENCY: Counseling/mental health services; Child sexual abuse services; Child sexual abuse prevention program; Residential treatment facility
AREAS SERVED: Bay, Saginaw, Midland, Tuscola, Arenac, Huron, Sanilac, Genessee
YEARS IN OPERATION: 8
ACCESSIBILITY: Wheelchair accessible
CASES SEXUAL ASSAULT/ABUSE (%): 50
CLIENTS/SERVICES: Child victims of sexual abuse; Adult survivors of child sexual abuse; Incest victims/survivors; Prevention program; Community education; Offender treatment program; Adolescent survivors of sexual abuse; Male survivors of sexual abuse
REQUIREMENTS: Suspected child sexual abuse cases must be reported to Child Protective Services

BENTON HARBOR

ASSAULT RECOVERY ASSOCIATES
PO Box 1188, Benton Harbor, MI 49022
Information: (616) 983-4242 8am-5pm
Contact: Robin Zollar Smientanka, Co-Founder
TYPE OF AGENCY: Private practice
AREAS SERVED: Statewide
YEARS IN OPERATION: 8
ACCESSIBILITY: Wheelchair accessible
CASES SEXUAL ASSAULT/ABUSE (%): 100
DESCRIPTION: Case/program consultation in area of sexual abuse/assault to human service, law enforcement, medical, educational, legal agencies
CLIENTS/SERVICES: Sexual assault survivors; Marital rape/sexual abuse survivors; Child victims of sexual abuse; Adult survivors of child sexual abuse; Incest victims/survivors; Prevention program; Community education; Offender treatment program; Adolescent survivors of sexual abuse; Male survivors of sexual abuse

BERRIEN COUNTY MENTAL HEALTH
PO Box 547, 1485 M-139, Benton Harbor, MI 49085
Crisis hotline: **(800) 336-0341 24 hrs**
Information: (616) 925-0585
Contact: Ronald Robinson, Unit Supv
TYPE OF AGENCY: Victim/witness assistance program
AREAS SERVED: Berrien
YEARS IN OPERATION: 15
ACCESSIBILITY: Wheelchair accessible
CASES SEXUAL ASSAULT/ABUSE (%): 100
CLIENTS/SERVICES: Sexual assault survivors; Marital rape/sexual abuse survivors; Child victims of sexual abuse; Adult survivors of child sexual abuse; Incest victims/survivors; Community education; Adolescent survivors of sexual abuse

BIG RAPIDS

WOMEN'S INFORMATION SERVICE (WISE)
PO Box 1074, Big Rapids, MI 49307
Crisis hotline: **(616) 796-6600 24 hrs 7 days**
Information: (616) 796-6692 8am-5pm (Mon-Fri)
Contact: Carol Miller, Sexual Assault Prog Coord; Kris Lukens Rose, Dir
TYPE OF AGENCY: Rape crisis center; Domestic violence program
AREAS SERVED: Mecosta, Osceola, Newaygo
YEARS IN OPERATION: 3
ACCESSIBILITY: Wheelchair accessible

CASES SEXUAL ASSAULT/ABUSE (%): 15
CLIENTS/SERVICES: Sexual assault survivors; Marital rape/sexual abuse survivors; Adult survivors of child sexual abuse; Incest victims/survivors; Prevention program; Community education; Adolescent survivors of sexual abuse; Male survivors of sexual abuse
REQUIREMENTS: Must be 14 or older

BRIGHTON

CENTER FOR COUNSELING SERVICES
8137 W Grand River, Ste 6, Brighton, MI 48116
Information: (313) 229-6547 12am-8pm (Mon-Fri)
Contact: Gail Allen, Dir
TYPE OF AGENCY: Private practice
AREAS SERVED: Livingston
YEARS IN OPERATION: 3½
ACCESSIBILITY: Wheelchair accessible
CLIENTS/SERVICES: Sexual assault survivors; Marital rape/sexual abuse survivors; Adult survivors of child sexual abuse; Incest victims/survivors; Adolescent survivors of sexual abuse
REQUIREMENTS: Aged 16 and older

BRONSON

COUNSELING ASSOCIATES
PO Box 207, Bronson, MI 49028
Crisis hotline: **(616) 388-3330 24 hrs**
Information: (517) 369-9212 8am-5pm (Mon-Fri)
Contact: Roberta Adams, Dir/Therapist
TYPE OF AGENCY: Private practice
AREAS SERVED: Branch, St Joseph
YEARS IN OPERATION: 4
ACCESSIBILITY: Wheelchair accessible
CASES SEXUAL ASSAULT/ABUSE (%): 50
DESCRIPTION: Counseling for survivors; Batterers group
CLIENTS/SERVICES: Sexual assault survivors; Marital rape/sexual abuse survivors; Adult survivors of child sexual abuse; Incest victims/survivors; Adolescent survivors of sexual abuse; Male survivors of sexual abuse

CANTON

MAM (MOTHERS AGAINST MOLESTERS)
1156 Stacy, Bldg 57, Canton, MI 48188
Information: (313) 397-9652 24 hrs
TYPE OF AGENCY: Child sexual abuse prevention program
AREAS SERVED: Wayne
YEARS IN OPERATION: 1
DESCRIPTION: Support groups for parents whose children were molested
CLIENTS/SERVICES: Adult survivors of child sexual abuse; Incest victims/survivors; Prevention program; Adolescent survivors of sexual abuse

CARO

THUMB AREA ASSAULT CRISIS CENTER
429 Montague Ave, Caro, MI 48723
Crisis hotline: **(800) 292-3666 24 hrs 7 days**
Information: (517) 673-4121 8:30am-5pm (Mon-Fri)
Contact: Karen Kopka, Prog Coord
TYPE OF AGENCY: Domestic violence program
SPONSORING ORGANIZATION: Human Development Commission
AREAS SERVED: Huron, Lapeer, Sanilac, Tuscola
YEARS IN OPERATION: 9
LANGUAGES: Spanish
ACCESSIBILITY: Wheelchair accessible
CASES SEXUAL ASSAULT/ABUSE (%): 70
CLIENTS/SERVICES: Sexual assault survivors; Marital rape/sexual abuse survivors; Child victims of sexual abuse; Adult survivors of child sexual abuse; Incest victims/survivors; Community education; Adolescent survivors of sexual abuse; Male survivors of sexual abuse

COLDWATER

BRANCH COUNTY COALITION AGAINST DOMESTIC VIOLENCE
PO Box 72, Coldwater, MI 49036
Crisis hotline: **(517) 278-7432 24 hrs**
Information: (517) 278-7432 24 hrs
Contact: Mary Hyslop, Dir
TYPE OF AGENCY: Rape crisis center; Domestic violence program
AREAS SERVED: Branch
YEARS IN OPERATION: 4
LANGUAGES: Spanish
ACCESSIBILITY: Wheelchair accessible
CASES SEXUAL ASSAULT/ABUSE (%): 100
CLIENTS/SERVICES: Sexual assault survivors; Marital rape/sexual abuse survivors; Adult survivors of child sexual abuse; Incest victims/survivors; Prevention program; Community education; Adolescent survivors of sexual abuse

DEARBORN

DEARBORN CRISIS CENTER
5281 Calhoun, Dearborn, MI 48126
Crisis hotline: **(313) 584-7800 11am-11pm (Mon-Fri); 3pm-11pm (Sat, Sun)**
Information: (313) 584-7800
Contact: Rosalie Degregorio, Exec Dir
TYPE OF AGENCY: Crisis intervention program
AREAS SERVED: Wayne
YEARS IN OPERATION: 18
DESCRIPTION: Provides crisis and walk-in counseling and referrals, individual and group counseling, and 24-hour assistance for rape and domestic violence victims
CLIENTS/SERVICES: Sexual assault survivors; Marital rape/sexual abuse survivors; Adult survivors of child sexual abuse; Incest victims/survivors; Prevention program; Community education; Adolescent survivors of sexual abuse; Male survivors of sexual abuse

FOCUS ON WOMEN PROGRAM
5101 Evergreen Rd, Dearborn, MI 48128
Information: (313) 845-9629 9am-4:30pm
Contact: Grace Stewart, PhD, Dir
TYPE OF AGENCY: College/university-based services; Women's center; Rape prevention program
SPONSORING ORGANIZATION: Henry Ford Community College
AREAS SERVED: Wayne
YEARS IN OPERATION: 11
LANGUAGES: French, Arabic
CASES SEXUAL ASSAULT/ABUSE (%): 1
DESCRIPTION: Comprehensive program providing re-entry help, academic programs, access to counseling staff, cultural events, special seminars (divorce, relationships, career changes)
CLIENTS/SERVICES: Community education; Adolescent survivors of sexual abuse; Male survivors of sexual abuse
SPECIAL PROGRAMS/SERVICES: Day-long program focusing on prevention and survival of sexual abuse

DETROIT

DETROIT POLICE DEPARTMENT—RAPE COUNSELING CENTER
4201 St Antoine, Detroit, MI 48201
Crisis hotline: **(313) 832-2530, 224-4487 24 hrs daily**
Information: (313) 832-2530 8am-4:30pm (Mon-Fri)
Contact: Althea M Grant, ACSW, Dir
TYPE OF AGENCY: Rape crisis center; Hospital/medical center; Victim/witness assistance program
SPONSORING ORGANIZATION: Detroit Police Dept
AREAS SERVED: Wayne, Oakland, Macomb
YEARS IN OPERATION: 13
ACCESSIBILITY: Wheelchair accessible; Signers for the hearing impaired
CASES SEXUAL ASSAULT/ABUSE (%): 100
DESCRIPTION: Immediate crisis intervention services for victims and families at the hospital and police station (Sex Crimes Unit); Short-term counseling for walk-in and phone-in clients on 24-hour basis; Court advocacy program; Agency referrals for long-term counseling and other services not available at the Rape Counseling Center
CLIENTS/SERVICES: Sexual assault survivors; Marital rape/sexual abuse survivors; Adult survivors of child sexual abuse; Incest victims/survivors; Prevention program; Community education; Adolescent survivors of sexual abuse; Male survivors of sexual abuse
REQUIREMENTS: Ages 13 and over
SPECIAL PROGRAMS/SERVICES: Spanish language brochure available

FAMILY SERVICE OF DETROIT AND WAYNE COUNTY
220 Bagley, Ste 920, Detroit, MI 48226
Crisis hotline: **(313) 863-0700 24 hrs**
Information: (313) 961-1584 8:30am-5:30pm
Contact: James Naragon, Prog Svcs VPres
TYPE OF AGENCY: Counseling/mental health services; Child sexual abuse services; Child abuse prevention program
AREAS SERVED: Wayne
YEARS IN OPERATION: 50
ACCESSIBILITY: Wheelchair accessible
DESCRIPTION: Family, individual, group, and marital counseling; anatomically correct dolls often used in treatment. Treatment for rapists, batterers, child sexual abuse/incest offenders
CLIENTS/SERVICES: Sexual assault survivors; Marital rape/sexual abuse survivors; Child victims of sexual abuse; Adult survivors of child sexual abuse; Incest victims/survivors; Community education; Offender treatment program; Adolescent survivors of sexual abuse; Male survivors of sexual abuse
SPECIAL PROGRAMS/SERVICES: Parent Infant Beginnings Program provides first-time families with support and training to help prevent child abuse and neglect

HEARTLINE, INC
8201 Sylvester, Detroit, MI 48214
Information: (313) 923-4200 9am-6pm
Contact: M E White, Admin Asst
TYPE OF AGENCY: Domestic violence program
SPONSORING ORGANIZATION: Lutheran Social Services of Michigan
AREAS SERVED: Wayne, Oakland, Macomb
YEARS IN OPERATION: 24
CASES SEXUAL ASSAULT/ABUSE (%): 3
CLIENTS/SERVICES: Sexual assault survivors; Marital rape/sexual abuse survivors; Adult survivors of child sexual abuse; Incest victims/survivors

INTERIM HOUSE
PO Box 456, Detroit, MI 48231
Crisis hotline: **(313) 962-5077 24 hrs**
Information: (313) 962-5077
TYPE OF AGENCY: Domestic violence program
AREAS SERVED: Wayne
YEARS IN OPERATION: 10
LANGUAGES: Spanish
CLIENTS/SERVICES: Marital rape/sexual abuse survivors; Child victims of sexual abuse

NORTHEAST GUIDANCE CENTER
13340 E Warren, Detroit, MI 48215
Crisis hotline: **(313) 224-7000 24 hrs**
Information: (313) 824-8000 8:30am-5pm
Contact: Pat Sims, ACSW, Child Outpatient Supv
TYPE OF AGENCY: Counseling/mental health services
AREAS SERVED: Wayne (east side of Detroit)
YEARS IN OPERATION: 25
DESCRIPTION: Provides mental health services for sexual assault/child sexual abuse victims; Crisis and individual psychotherapy
CLIENTS/SERVICES: Sexual assault survivors; Child victims of sexual abuse; Incest victims/survivors; Adolescent survivors of sexual abuse; Male survivors of sexual abuse

VOICES (VICTIMS OF INCEST/SEXUAL ABUSE CARING EDUCATING SURVIVING)
1035 St Antoine, Detroit, MI 48226
Information: (313) 965-3242 9am-4:30pm (Mon-Fri)
Contact: Cheryl Bedrosian, MSW, CSW, Dir
TYPE OF AGENCY: Child sexual abuse services; Child sexual abuse prevention program
SPONSORING ORGANIZATION: Team for Justice
AREAS SERVED: Wayne, Oakland, Macomb
CASES SEXUAL ASSAULT/ABUSE (%): 100
DESCRIPTION: Offers group counseling for each member of the family where incest/sexual abuse has occurred. In addition, has a group for adults molested as children (modeled after Parents United)
CLIENTS/SERVICES: Child victims of sexual abuse; Adult survivors of child sexual abuse; Incest victims/survivors; Prevention program; Community education; Offender treatment program; Adolescent survivors of sexual abuse; Male survivors of sexual abuse
REQUIREMENTS: Sliding scale fee

WAYNE COUNTY PROSECUTOR'S OFFICE—VICTIM SERVICES
1441 St Antoine, Rm 1120, Frank Murphy Hall of Justice, Detroit, MI 48226
Information: (313) 224-5800 8am-4:30pm (Mon-Fri)
Contact: Kathleen L Quigley, Victim Svcs Dir
TYPE OF AGENCY: Victim/witness assistance program
AREAS SERVED: Wayne
YEARS IN OPERATION: 12
ACCESSIBILITY: Wheelchair accessible
CASES SEXUAL ASSAULT/ABUSE (%): 50
CLIENTS/SERVICES: Sexual assault survivors; Marital rape/sexual abuse survivors; Child victims of sexual abuse; Incest victims/survivors; Community education; Adolescent survivors of sexual abuse; Male survivors of sexual abuse
REQUIREMENTS: Crime must have occurred in Wayne County; Charges must be filed

WAYNE STATE UNIVERSITY—WOMEN'S RESOURCE CENTER AND RE-ENTRY TO EDUCATION PROGRAM
334 Mackenzie Hall, Wayne State University, Detroit, MI 48202
Crisis hotline: **(313) 577-4103, 577-0340 8:30am-5pm (Mon-Fri)**
Information: (313) 577-2006 8:30am-5pm (Mon-Fri)
Contact: Kay Hartley, Academic Svcs Coord
TYPE OF AGENCY: College/university-based services; Rape prevention program
AREAS SERVED: Wayne, Oakland, Macomb, Washtenaw
YEARS IN OPERATION: 12
LANGUAGES: Mandarin Chinese, French, Arabic
ACCESSIBILITY: Wheelchair accessible; Telecommunications for the hearing impaired (TTY, TDY, etc.); Signers for the hearing impaired
CASES SEXUAL ASSAULT/ABUSE (%): 5
DESCRIPTION: Crisis counseling for students and staff who have been sexually assaulted; Incest prevention workshops for parents and for adults who were victims, and workshop on rape prevention. Teaches classes in feminist martial arts/self-defense
CLIENTS/SERVICES: Sexual assault survivors; Prevention program; Community education; Male survivors of sexual abuse
REQUIREMENTS: Open to men and women in community, as well as students and staff

WOMEN'S JUSTICE CENTER
651 E Jefferson, Detroit, MI 48226
Crisis hotline: **(313) 961-7073 24 hrs**, (313) 921-3900 10am-2pm
Information: (313) 961-4057 10am-4pm
Contact: Carol Sullivan, Shelter Dir
TYPE OF AGENCY: Domestic violence program; Legal services agency
AREAS SERVED: Wayne, Oakland, Macomb, Monroe
YEARS IN OPERATION: 13
ACCESSIBILITY: Wheelchair accessible
CASES SEXUAL ASSAULT/ABUSE (%): 30
CLIENTS/SERVICES: Marital rape/sexual abuse survivors

EAST DETROIT

HELP MEI, INC
PO Box 480, East Detroit, MI 48021
Crisis hotline: **(313) 521-4097 24 hrs**
Information: (313) 521-4097 8am-8pm
Contact: Elaine Schweitzer, State Dir
TYPE OF AGENCY: Self-help group
AREAS SERVED: Statewide
YEARS IN OPERATION: 1
ACCESSIBILITY: Wheelchair accessible
CASES SEXUAL ASSAULT/ABUSE (%): 100
DESCRIPTION: Self-help support group for adults sexually abused as children. Expanding program to serve teens and child victims
CLIENTS/SERVICES: Child victims of sexual abuse; Adult survivors of child sexual abuse; Incest victims/survivors; Prevention program; Community education; Adolescent survivors of sexual abuse; Male survivors of sexual abuse
REQUIREMENTS: Must be adult, teen, or child survivor; No perpetrators are served whether or not they are survivors themselves

EAST LANSING

SEXUAL ASSAULT CRISIS AND SAFETY EDUCATION PROGRAM
207 Student Services Bldg, East Lansing, MI 48824
Crisis hotline: **(517) 372-6666 24 hrs**
Information: (517) 355-8270 9am-5pm (Mon-Fri)
Contact: Diane Windischman, Coord
TYPE OF AGENCY: Rape crisis center; College/university-based services; Rape prevention program
SPONSORING ORGANIZATION: Michigan State University
AREAS SERVED: Ingham, Eaton, Clinton
YEARS IN OPERATION: 9
LANGUAGES: French
ACCESSIBILITY: Wheelchair accessible
CASES SEXUAL ASSAULT/ABUSE (%): 80
DESCRIPTION: Provides crisis intervention, hospital and criminal justice system accompaniment, long-term counseling, and support groups for sexual assault survivors and adult survivors of child sexual abuse; Preventive education program includes self-defense workshops and prevention programs for university students
CLIENTS/SERVICES: Sexual assault survivors; Marital rape/sexual abuse survivors; Adult survivors of child sexual abuse; Incest victims/survivors; Prevention program; Community education; Adolescent survivors of sexual abuse; Male survivors of sexual abuse
REQUIREMENTS: Mostly full time MSU students, staff and faculty
SPECIAL PROGRAMS/SERVICES: Offers comprehensive training for residence assistants (500 people) in dealing with sexual assault in the residence halls on campus

ESCANABA

DELTA COUNTY PROSECUTOR'S OFFICE
310 Ludington St, Escanaba, MI 49829
Information: (906) 786-8574
Contact: Cindy Stenberg Russell, Crime Victim Coord
TYPE OF AGENCY: Victim/witness assistance program
AREAS SERVED: Delta
YEARS IN OPERATION: 4
ACCESSIBILITY: Wheelchair accessible
CASES SEXUAL ASSAULT/ABUSE (%): 20
CLIENTS/SERVICES: Sexual assault survivors; Marital rape/sexual abuse survivors; Child victims of sexual abuse; Adult survivors of child sexual abuse; Incest victims/survivors
REQUIREMENTS: Criminal charges against the perpetrator must be filed

FARMINGTON HILLS

JENSEN COUNSELING CENTERS, PC
26105 Orchard Lake Rd, Ste 301, Farmington Hills, MI 48018
Information: (313) 478-4411 24 hrs
Contact: Lee Padula, PhD, Clinician
TYPE OF AGENCY: Counseling/mental health services; Child sexual abuse services; Private practice
AREAS SERVED: Oakland, Wayne, Washtenaw
YEARS IN OPERATION: 9
ACCESSIBILITY: Wheelchair accessible
CASES SEXUAL ASSAULT/ABUSE (%): 20-50
DESCRIPTION: Counseling for survivors and rapists, child sexual abuse/incest offenders, and batterers
CLIENTS/SERVICES: Sexual assault survivors; Marital rape/sexual abuse survivors; Child victims of sexual abuse; Adult survivors of child sexual abuse; Incest victims/survivors; Offender treatment program; Adolescent survivors of sexual abuse; Male survivors of sexual abuse
REQUIREMENTS: Fee for services. The center is JCAH accredited, Blue Cross/Blue Shield approved, Health Alliance Plan (HAP) approved and most health care insurance accepted

FLINT

YWCA OF GREATER FLINT—DOMESTIC VIOLENCE/SEXUAL ASSAULT SERVICES
310 E 3rd St, Flint, MI 48502
Crisis hotline: **(313) 238-SAFE 24 hrs 7 days**
Information: (313) 238-7621 24 hrs 7 days
Contact: Theresa K Cooke, Sexual Assault Therapist
TYPE OF AGENCY: Rape crisis center; Domestic violence program; Child sexual abuse services; Child sexual abuse prevention program
AREAS SERVED: Genesee and surrounding counties
ACCESSIBILITY: Wheelchair accessible; Telecommunications for the hearing impaired (TTY, TDY, etc.); Signers for the hearing impaired
DESCRIPTION: In addition to sexual assault crisis services, feminist martial arts/self-defense program and counseling for sexually abused children, provides support group for parents of sexually abused children, and *You Belong to You* prevention program
CLIENTS/SERVICES: Sexual assault survivors; Marital rape/sexual abuse survivors; Child victims of sexual abuse; Adult survivors of child sexual abuse; Incest victims/survivors; Prevention program; Community education; Offender treatment program; Adolescent survivors of sexual abuse; Male survivors of sexual abuse

GRAND HAVEN

OTTAWA COUNTY PROSECUTING ATTORNEY—VICTIM ASSISTANCE
414 Washington St, Grand Haven, MI 49417
Crisis hotline: **(616) 846-8368 8am-5pm (Mon-Fri)**
Information: (616) 846-8215 8am-5pm (Mon-Fri)
Contact: Deanna M Kirby, Victim Advocate
TYPE OF AGENCY: Victim/witness assistance program
AREAS SERVED: Ottawa
YEARS IN OPERATION: 3
ACCESSIBILITY: Wheelchair accessible
CLIENTS/SERVICES: Sexual assault survivors; Marital rape/sexual abuse survivors; Child victims of sexual abuse; Adult survivors of child sexual abuse; Incest victims/survivors
REQUIREMENTS: Case must be in process of prosecution for crime victim's rights to apply; Referrals on cases not prosecuted

GRAND RAPIDS

CORNERSTONE SEXUAL ASSAULT SERVICES
240 Cherry St SE, 9th Fl, Grand Rapids, MI 49503
Crisis hotline: **(616) 774-3535 24 hrs**
Information: (616) 774-3909
Contact: Amy Giem, Coord
TYPE OF AGENCY: Rape crisis center
CLIENTS/SERVICES: Sexual assault survivors; Adult survivors of child sexual abuse; Community education; Prevention program; Adolescent survivors of sexual abuse; Male survivors of sexual abuse
REQUIREMENTS: Ages 13 and older

KENT COUNTY PROSECUTOR'S OFFICE—VICTIM WITNESS PROGRAM
333 Monroe Ave NW, 416 Hall of Justice, Grand Rapids, MI 49503
Information: (616) 774-6822 8am-5pm (Mon-Fri)
Contact: Mark Gleason, Dir
TYPE OF AGENCY: Victim/witness assistance program
AREAS SERVED: Primarily Kent
YEARS IN OPERATION: 9
LANGUAGES: Spanish
ACCESSIBILITY: Wheelchair accessible; Telecommunications for the hearing impaired (TTY, TDY, etc.); Signers for the hearing impaired (by arrangement)
CASES SEXUAL ASSAULT/ABUSE (%): 5-10
DESCRIPTION: Provides victim advocacy for anyone who must interact with the criminal justice system
CLIENTS/SERVICES: Sexual assault survivors; Marital rape/sexual abuse survivors; Child victims of sexual abuse; Incest victims/survivors; Prevention program; Community education; Adolescent survivors of sexual abuse; Male survivors of sexual abuse

UNITED STATES ATTORNEY'S OFFICE
399 Federal Bldg, Grand Rapids, MI 49503
Crisis hotline: **(616) 456-2404 8:30am-5pm**
Information: (616) 456-2404 8:30am-5pm
Contact: Andrea Morse, Victim/Witness Svcs Coord
TYPE OF AGENCY: Victim/witness assistance program
SPONSORING ORGANIZATION: United States Department of Justice
AREAS SERVED: Western half of Michigan, Upper Peninsula
YEARS IN OPERATION: 3½
LANGUAGES: Spanish
ACCESSIBILITY: Wheelchair accessible
DESCRIPTION: Handles federal cases including child pornography/obscenity and cases of abuse on Indian lands; Assists state victims where services are unavailable

UNITED STATES ATTORNEY'S OFFICE
(continued)

CLIENTS/SERVICES: Sexual assault survivors; Marital rape/sexual abuse survivors; Child victims of sexual abuse; Community education

YWCA SEXUAL ABUSE TREATMENT CENTER
25 Sheldon Blvd SE, Grand Rapids, MI 49503
Crisis hotline: **(616) 774-3535 24 hrs**
Information: (616) 459-4652 8am-7pm (Mon-Thu); 8:30am-5pm (Fri)
Contact: Tom Cottrell, Prog Supv
TYPE OF AGENCY: Domestic violence program; Counseling/mental health services; Child sexual abuse services; Child sexual abuse prevention program
AREAS SERVED: Kent, Barry
YEARS IN OPERATION: 6½
ACCESSIBILITY: Wheelchair accessible
CASES SEXUAL ASSAULT/ABUSE (%): 100
DESCRIPTION: Individual, marital, family, and group counseling for families where incest has been substantiated; Therapy groups for adults molested as children and survivors of rape, both female and male; Assessment, referral, counseling for nonfamilial molestation victims and their families; Individual and group treatment for incest offenders, batterers, and adolescent offenders
CLIENTS/SERVICES: Sexual assault survivors; Marital rape/sexual abuse survivors; Child victims of sexual abuse; Adult survivors of child sexual abuse; Incest victims/survivors; Prevention program; Community education; Offender treatment program; Adolescent survivors of sexual abuse; Male survivors of sexual abuse
REQUIREMENTS: Incest treatment referred through local Children's Protective Services/private pay. Adult survivors: experienced some individual treatment prior to group referral. Rape survivors: same as for adult survivors plus must be 3 months post-rape

HARRISON

WOMEN'S AID SERVICE, INC
185 W Main, Harrison, MI 48625
Information: (517) 539-1046 9am-5pm (Mon-Fri)
TYPE OF AGENCY: Rape crisis center; Domestic violence program; Adolescent program
AREAS SERVED: Isabella, Gratiot, Clare
YEARS IN OPERATION: Women's aid 10, sexual assault program 2
DESCRIPTION: Comprehensive services for survivors of sexual assault and domestic violence; Group for batterers (Men Overcoming Violent Experiences) and a group for youth (12-17 years old) who have experienced previous or present violent/abusive relationships
CLIENTS/SERVICES: Sexual assault survivors; Marital rape/sexual abuse survivors; Adult survivors of child sexual abuse; Incest victims/survivors; Community education; Adolescent survivors of sexual abuse; Male survivors of sexual abuse
REQUIREMENTS: Adolescents can receive services with parental permission

HART

OCEANA COMMUNITY MENTAL HEALTH
601 E Main St, Hart, MI 49420
Crisis hotline: **(616) 873-2108 24 hrs**
Information: (616) 873-2108 9am-5pm
Contact: James Leishman, ACSW, Clinical Svcs Dir
TYPE OF AGENCY: Counseling/mental health services; Child sexual abuse services
AREAS SERVED: Oceana
YEARS IN OPERATION: 15
ACCESSIBILITY: Wheelchair accessible; Signers for the hearing impaired
CASES SEXUAL ASSAULT/ABUSE (%): 10
DESCRIPTION: Provides counseling for community residents, including survivors and incest/child sexual abuse offenders and batterers
CLIENTS/SERVICES: Sexual assault survivors; Marital rape/sexual abuse survivors; Child victims of sexual abuse; Adult survivors of child sexual abuse; Incest victims/survivors; Community education; Offender treatment program; Adolescent survivors of sexual abuse; Male survivors of sexual abuse
REQUIREMENTS: Fee based on ability to pay

HILLSDALE

DOMESTIC HARMONY
PO Box 231, Hillsdale, MI 49242
Crisis hotline: **(517) 439-1454 24 hrs**
Information: (517) 439-1454 8am-5pm (Mon-Fri)
Contact: Kristin Lucas, Exec Dir
TYPE OF AGENCY: Domestic violence program
AREAS SERVED: Hillsdale
YEARS IN OPERATION: 1
ACCESSIBILITY: Wheelchair accessible
CASES SEXUAL ASSAULT/ABUSE (%): 1
DESCRIPTION: Started as a domestic (spousal) violence program. Recently added a small adult sexual assault program
CLIENTS/SERVICES: Sexual assault survivors; Adult survivors of child sexual abuse; Incest victims/survivors; Prevention program

HOLLAND

CENTER FOR WOMEN IN TRANSITION
304 Garden Ave, Holland, MI 49424
Crisis hotline: **(616) 396-4357 24 hrs**
Information: (616) 846-0060, 392-2829, 673-2299 9am-5pm
Contact: Madlyn Perkins, Exec Dir
TYPE OF AGENCY: Rape crisis center; Domestic violence program; Counseling/mental health services; Acquaintance/date rape prevention program; Adolescent program
AREAS SERVED: Allegan, Ottawa
YEARS IN OPERATION: 10
LANGUAGES: Spanish
CASES SEXUAL ASSAULT/ABUSE (%): 50-60
CLIENTS/SERVICES: Sexual assault survivors; Marital rape/sexual abuse survivors; Adult survivors of child sexual abuse; Incest victims/survivors; Community education
SPECIAL PROGRAMS/SERVICES: Prevention programs for adolescents include "Say No" and "Postponing Sexual Involvement". Spanish-language brochure

HOUGHTON

DIAL HELP, INC
PO Box 214, Houghton, MI 49931
Crisis hotline: **(800) 562-7622, (906) 482-4357 24 hrs**
Information: (906) 482-9077 8am-5pm, messages taken 24-hrs
Contact: Robin Johnson, Volunteer/Rape Victim Support Svcs Coord
TYPE OF AGENCY: Rape crisis center
AREAS SERVED: Houghton, Baraga, Keweenaw, Ontonagon
YEARS IN OPERATION: 19
DESCRIPTION: Agency offers support and referral services for victims of sexual assault
CLIENTS/SERVICES: Sexual assault survivors; Marital rape/sexual abuse survivors; Prevention program; Community education; Adolescent survivors of sexual abuse; Male survivors of sexual abuse

HOWELL

SEXUAL ASSAULT RECOVERY ASSISTANCE (SARA)
PO Box 72, Howell, MI 48844
Crisis hotline: **(313) 227-7100 24 hrs**
Information: (517) 548-4228 24 hrs
Contact: Christine Ambrose, Prog Coord
TYPE OF AGENCY: Rape crisis center; Domestic violence program; Child sexual abuse services; Child sexual abuse prevention program
SPONSORING ORGANIZATION: LACASA Livingston Area Council Against Spouse Abuse
AREAS SERVED: Livingston
YEARS IN OPERATION: 2
CASES SEXUAL ASSAULT/ABUSE (%): 100
DESCRIPTION: Counseling for survivors of sexual assault and domestic violence; Individual and group therapy for batterers
CLIENTS/SERVICES: Sexual assault survivors; Marital rape/sexual abuse survivors; Child victims of sexual abuse; Adult survivors of child sexual abuse; Incest victims/survivors; Prevention program; Community education; Adolescent survivors of sexual abuse; Male survivors of sexual abuse
REQUIREMENTS: Minors 14 and under need parental consent after first visit.

WOMEN'S RESOURCE CENTER
PO Box 173, Howell, MI 48843
Information: (517) 548-2090 9am-5pm
Contact: L Howdyshell, Dir
TYPE OF AGENCY: Women's center
AREAS SERVED: Livingston
YEARS IN OPERATION: 8
CASES SEXUAL ASSAULT/ABUSE (%): 10
DESCRIPTION: Provides service for women in transition or crisis: group support, personal counseling, referral
CLIENTS/SERVICES: Adult survivors of child sexual abuse; Incest victims/survivors; Prevention program

IONIA

DOMESTIC VIOLENCE CENTER
108 E Washington, Ionia, MI 48881
Crisis hotline: **(616) 527-3351 4:30pm-8:30am**
Information: (616) 527-1360 8:30am-4:30pm
Contact: Gini Edwards, Counselor/Advocate
TYPE OF AGENCY: Domestic violence program
SPONSORING ORGANIZATION: Eight-Cap, Inc
AREAS SERVED: Ionia, Montcalm
YEARS IN OPERATION: 8
ACCESSIBILITY: Wheelchair accessible (shelter)
CASES SEXUAL ASSAULT/ABUSE (%): 85
DESCRIPTION: Services for domestic violence survivors and group therapy for batterers
CLIENTS/SERVICES: Marital rape/sexual abuse survivors; Community education
REQUIREMENTS: No contact with assailant
SPECIAL PROGRAMS/SERVICES: Interagency council meetings every 2 months, MTD meetings once a month, volunteer training and in-service to community and church groups/private groups

IONIA COUNTY COMMUNITY MENTAL HEALTH
436 W Lincoln, Ionia, MI 48881
Information: (616) 527-1790 24 hrs
Contact: Theresa Anderson-Varney, MA, Outpatient Therapist
TYPE OF AGENCY: Counseling/mental health services; Child sexual abuse services; Child sexual abuse prevention program
AREAS SERVED: Ionia
ACCESSIBILITY: Wheelchair accessible
CASES SEXUAL ASSAULT/ABUSE (%): 25
CLIENTS/SERVICES: Sexual assault survivors; Marital rape/sexual abuse survivors; Child victims of sexual abuse; Adult survivors of child sexual abuse; Incest victims/survivors; Prevention program; Community education; Offend-

IONIA COUNTY COMMUNITY MENTAL HEALTH (continued)

er treatment program; Adolescent survivors of sexual abuse; Male survivors of sexual abuse

IRON MOUNTAIN

CARING HOUSE
1240 S Carpenter, Ste 104, Iron Mountain, MI 49801
Crisis hotline: **(906) 774-5524, 774-1112 24 hr crisis line**
Information: (906) 774-1337 8:30am-4:30pm (Mon-Fri)
Contact: Diane DeSisto, Dir
TYPE OF AGENCY: Rape crisis center; Domestic violence program; Child sexual abuse services
AREAS SERVED: Dickinson, Iron, MI; Florence, Marinette, WI
YEARS IN OPERATION: 6
ACCESSIBILITY: Wheelchair accessible
CASES SEXUAL ASSAULT/ABUSE (%): 30
CLIENTS/SERVICES: Sexual assault survivors; Marital rape/sexual abuse survivors; Child victims of sexual abuse; Adult survivors of child sexual abuse; Incest victims/survivors; Community education; Adolescent survivors of sexual abuse

IRONWOOD

DOMESTIC VIOLENCE ESCAPE (DOVE), INC
PO Box 366, Ironwood, MI 49938
Crisis hotline: **(906) 932-0310 24 hrs**
Information: (906) 932-4990 24 hrs
Contact: Lucia M Patritto, Exec Dir
TYPE OF AGENCY: Domestic violence program
AREAS SERVED: Primarily Gogebic, MI; Iron, WI
YEARS IN OPERATION: 7
LANGUAGES: Finnish, Sign
ACCESSIBILITY: Wheelchair accessible; Signers for the hearing impaired
CASES SEXUAL ASSAULT/ABUSE (%): 30
DESCRIPTION: A domestic violence shelter serving victims of physical, verbal, sexual, and psychological assault; Provides therapy group for adult survivors of childhood sexual assault
CLIENTS/SERVICES: Sexual assault survivors; Marital rape/sexual abuse survivors; Adult survivors of child sexual abuse; Incest victims/survivors; Prevention program; Community education; Male survivors of sexual abuse

LUTHERAN SOCIAL SERVICES OF WISCONSIN AND UPPER MICHIGAN
127 E Ayer St, Ironwood, MI 49938
Information: (906) 932-3902
TYPE OF AGENCY: Counseling/mental health services
DESCRIPTION: Provides individual, group, couple, and family counseling. Many clients have been physically and/or sexually abused
CLIENTS/SERVICES: Sexual assault survivors; Marital rape/sexual abuse survivors; Adult survivors of child sexual abuse; Incest victims/survivors; Adolescent survivors of sexual abuse; Male survivors of sexual abuse

JACKSON

SEXUAL ASSAULT COUNSELING
PO Box 1526, Jackson, MI 47904
Crisis hotline: **(517) 783-2671 24 hrs**
Information: (517) 783-2861 24 hrs
TYPE OF AGENCY: Rape crisis center; Domestic violence program
SPONSORING ORGANIZATION: AWARE, Inc
AREAS SERVED: Jackson
YEARS IN OPERATION: 10
ACCESSIBILITY: Wheelchair accessible; Signers for the hearing impaired
CLIENTS/SERVICES: Sexual assault survivors; Marital rape/sexual abuse survivors; Child victims of sexual abuse; Adult survivors of child sexual abuse; Incest victims/survivors; Prevention program; Community education; Adolescent survivors of sexual abuse; Male survivors of sexual abuse

KALAMAZOO

KALAMAZOO COUNTY PROSECUTING ATTORNEY—VICTIM ASSISTANCE
227 W Michigan Ave, Ste 312, Kalamazoo, MI 49007
Information: (616) 383-8677 8am-5pm
Contact: Fran Bender, Victim Assistance Dir; Gayle Somers, Victim Advocate Spec
TYPE OF AGENCY: Victim/witness assistance program
AREAS SERVED: Kalamazoo
YEARS IN OPERATION: 6
CLIENTS/SERVICES: Sexual assault survivors; Marital rape/sexual abuse survivors; Child victims of sexual abuse

WOMEN'S CENTER
A-331 Ellsworth Hall, Western Michigan University, Kalamazoo, MI 49007
Information: (616) 387-2990 8am-5pm (Mon-Fri)
Contact: Darlene Mosher, Act Dir
TYPE OF AGENCY: College/university-based services
SPONSORING ORGANIZATION: Western Michigan University
AREAS SERVED: Campus community
YEARS IN OPERATION: 12
ACCESSIBILITY: Wheelchair accessible
DESCRIPTION: Information and education for women on campus; Provides programs on sexual assault prevention/education and is developing programs for victim assistance and intervention
CLIENTS/SERVICES: Prevention program
REQUIREMENTS: Member of Western Michigan University faculty, staff, students

YWCA SEXUAL ASSAULT PROGRAM
353 E Michigan Ave, Kalamazoo, MI 49007
Crisis hotline: **(616) 345-3036 24 hrs**
Information: (616) 345-9412
Contact: Grace M Orlando, Dir
TYPE OF AGENCY: Rape crisis center; Child sexual abuse services; Child sexual abuse prevention program; Acquaintance/date rape prevention program
AREAS SERVED: Kalamazoo and outlying districts
YEARS IN OPERATION: 14
ACCESSIBILITY: Wheelchair accessible
CASES SEXUAL ASSAULT/ABUSE (%): 100
CLIENTS/SERVICES: Sexual assault survivors; Marital rape/sexual abuse survivors; Child victims of sexual abuse; Adult survivors of child sexual abuse; Incest victims/survivors; Prevention program; Community education; Adolescent survivors of sexual abuse; Male survivors of sexual abuse
SPECIAL PROGRAMS/SERVICES: Child sexual assault prevention program entitled *You are Special* for children ages 4-13 and 14-17, parents, and teachers ; Child sexual assault prevention program for teenage mothers entitled *Heart to Heart* in cooperation with Ounce of Prevention in Illinois

LANSING

COUNCIL AGAINST DOMESTIC ASSAULT (CADA)
PO Box 14149, Lansing, MI 48901
Crisis hotline: **(517) 372-5572 24 hrs**
Information: (517) 372-5572 24 hrs
Contact: Holly Rosen, Prog Dir
TYPE OF AGENCY: Domestic violence program
AREAS SERVED: Statewide
YEARS IN OPERATION: 12
LANGUAGES: Interpreters available
ACCESSIBILITY: Wheelchair accessible; Signers for the hearing impaired (by arrangement)
CASES SEXUAL ASSAULT/ABUSE (%): 50
CLIENTS/SERVICES: Sexual assault survivors; Marital rape/sexual abuse survivors; Child victims of sexual abuse; Adult survivors of child sexual abuse; Incest victims/survivors; Prevention program; Community education; Adolescent survivors of sexual abuse

INGHAM COUNSELING CENTER
5303 S Cedar St, Lansing, MI 48911
Crisis hotline: **(517) 372-8460 24 hrs**
Information: (517) 393-4030 8am-5:30pm (Mon-Fri)
Contact: Jeffrey L Brown, MSW, Child and Adolescent Outpatient Supv
TYPE OF AGENCY: Counseling/mental health services; Child sexual abuse services
SPONSORING ORGANIZATION: Clinton-Eaton-Ingham Community Mental Health Board
AREAS SERVED: Clinton, Eaton, Ingham
YEARS IN OPERATION: 18
ACCESSIBILITY: Wheelchair accessible; Telecommunications for the hearing impaired (TTY, TDY, etc.); Signers for the hearing impaired
CASES SEXUAL ASSAULT/ABUSE (%): 50
DESCRIPTION: Individual, family, and group psychotherapy for victims of child sexual abuse and their families; Treatment for juvenile and adult perpetrators through individual and group psychotherapy, as well as batterers
CLIENTS/SERVICES: Sexual assault survivors; Marital rape/sexual abuse survivors; Child victims of sexual abuse; Adult survivors of child sexual abuse; Incest victims/survivors; Prevention program; Community education; Offender treatment program; Adolescent survivors of sexual abuse; Male survivors of sexual abuse
REQUIREMENTS: For the child and adolescent outpatient clinic, age range must be between 3 and 18

INGHAM COUNTY SEXUAL ASSAULT TASK FORCE
303 W Kalamazoo, Ste 204, Lansing, MI 48933
Information: (517) 371-2223 11am-3:30pm (Mon-Thu)
Contact: Anne Smiley, Ingham Co Women's Commission Chairperson
TYPE OF AGENCY: Interagency network
SPONSORING ORGANIZATION: Ingham County Women's Commission
AREAS SERVED: Ingham
YEARS IN OPERATION: 10
DESCRIPTION: Informal networking of agencies/individuals committed to increasing communication and services regarding sexual assault via monthly meetings
CLIENTS/SERVICES: Community education

MOVEMENT ARTS, INC
230 Bingham St, Lansing, MI 48912
Information: (517) 485-3868 8am-8pm
Contact: Joan Nelson, Dir
TYPE OF AGENCY: Rape prevention program
AREAS SERVED: Ingham
YEARS IN OPERATION: 4
ACCESSIBILITY: Wheelchair accessible
CASES SEXUAL ASSAULT/ABUSE (%): 15-25
DESCRIPTION: Offers personal safety skills training for women, children, and professionals dealing with explosive individuals
CLIENTS/SERVICES: Sexual assault survivors; Child victims of sexual abuse; Adult survivors of child sexual abuse; Incest victims/survivors; Prevention program; Community education
REQUIREMENTS: Must be 12 or older
SPECIAL PROGRAMS/SERVICES: Offers a twelve-week program for survivors—combines 1 1/4 hours of self-defense training and 1 1/4 hours of support group activity. Co-led by self-defense instructor and therapist

LAPEER

LAPEER COUNTY COMMUNITY MENTAL HEALTH CENTER
1575 Suncrest, Lapeer, MI 48446
Crisis hotline: **(313) 667-0500 24 hrs daily**
Information: (313) 667-0500 24 hrs
Contact: Richard Berman, PhD, Exec Dir
TYPE OF AGENCY: Counseling/mental health services
AREAS SERVED: Lapeer
YEARS IN OPERATION: 15
LANGUAGES: Spanish, Vietnamese (by request)
ACCESSIBILITY: Wheelchair accessible; Telecommunications for the hearing impaired (TTY, TDY, etc.); Signers for the hearing impaired
CASES SEXUAL ASSAULT/ABUSE (%): 1-2
DESCRIPTION: Comprehensive community mental health services, including individual, family, marital, and group counseling
CLIENTS/SERVICES: Sexual assault survivors; Marital rape/sexual abuse survivors; Child victims of sexual abuse; Adult survivors of child sexual abuse; Incest victims/survivors; Prevention program; Community education

LAPEER COUNTY CRIME VICTIM ASSISTANCE
255 Clay St, County Complex Bldg, Lapeer, MI 48446
Information: (313) 667-0326 8:30am-5pm
Contact: Cathy Strong, Victim Rights Coord
TYPE OF AGENCY: Victim/witness assistance program
AREAS SERVED: Lapeer
YEARS IN OPERATION: 3
ACCESSIBILITY: Wheelchair accessible
CASES SEXUAL ASSAULT/ABUSE (%): 15
CLIENTS/SERVICES: Sexual assault survivors; Marital rape/sexual abuse survivors; Child victims of sexual abuse; Adult survivors of child sexual abuse; Incest victims/survivors

LIVONIA

SHUMARD COUNSELING PC
32200 Schoolcraft, Livonia, MI 48150
Crisis hotline: **(313) 425-0396 24 hrs**
Information: (313) 425-0396 24 hrs
Contact: Barbara H Shumard, Dir
TYPE OF AGENCY: Child sexual abuse services; Private practice; Training/research
AREAS SERVED: Wayne, Oakland, Washtenaw, McComb, Livingston
YEARS IN OPERATION: 8
ACCESSIBILITY: Wheelchair accessible
CASES SEXUAL ASSAULT/ABUSE (%): 80
DESCRIPTION: Specializes in working with clients who are traumatized sexually and/or physically and verbally. Provides support groups for female and male survivors. Individual therapy for child sexual abuse/incest offenders
CLIENTS/SERVICES: Sexual assault survivors; Marital rape/sexual abuse survivors; Child victims of sexual abuse; Adult survivors of child sexual abuse; Incest victims/survivors; Offender treatment program; Adolescent survivors of sexual abuse; Male survivors of sexual abuse; Healing
SPECIAL PROGRAMS/SERVICES: David Grove metaphor therapy is used as a way to promote healing without re-traumatizing the clients. It aids in retrieving memories and fostering resolutions and it promotes the individual's spiritual growth and healing

MADISON HEIGHTS

GATEWAY COUNSELING CENTER
26327 John R, Madison Heights, MI 48071
Crisis hotline: **(313) 545-5926 9am-9pm (Mon-Thu); 9am-5pm (Fri); 9am-1pm (Sat)**
Information: (313) 545-5926 9am-9pm (Mon-Thu); 9am-5pm (Fri); 9am-1pm (Sat)
Contact: Sheila Richmond, Act Dir
TYPE OF AGENCY: Counseling/mental health services
AREAS SERVED: Oakland, Wayne, Macomb
YEARS IN OPERATION: 17
ACCESSIBILITY: Wheelchair accessible
CASES SEXUAL ASSAULT/ABUSE (%): 5
CLIENTS/SERVICES: Sexual assault survivors; Child victims of sexual abuse; Adult survivors of child sexual abuse; Incest victims/survivors; Adolescent survivors of sexual abuse; Male survivors of sexual abuse

MARQUETTE

WOMEN'S CENTER
1310 S Front St, Marquette, MI 49855
Crisis hotline: **(906) 226-6611 24 hrs**
Information: (906) 225-1346 8am-5pm (Mon-Fri)
Contact: Ellen L Witt, Sexual Assault Prevention/Response Prog Dir
TYPE OF AGENCY: Rape crisis center; Domestic violence program; Child sexual abuse prevention program; Women's center
AREAS SERVED: Marquette
DESCRIPTION: Provides and coordinates prevention, public information and victim/survivor support and crisis intervention services. Support groups: adult victims/survivors of incest, parents of sexually abused children, rape survivors. Crisis support teams: rape victim support team, adult victim/survivor of incest crisis support group. Prevention: *SAFE* and *How to Say No*
CLIENTS/SERVICES: Sexual assault survivors; Marital rape/sexual abuse survivors; Adult survivors of child sexual abuse; Incest victims/survivors; Prevention program; Community education; Adolescent survivors of sexual abuse

MIDLAND

COUNCIL ON DOMESTIC VIOLENCE AND SEXUAL ASSAULT
PO Box 2289, Midland, MI 48641
Crisis hotline: **(517) 835-6771 24 hrs**
Information: (517) 835-6771 24 hrs
Contact: Carolyn Robb, Sexual Assault Counselor
TYPE OF AGENCY: Rape crisis center; Domestic violence program
AREAS SERVED: Midland, Gladwin
YEARS IN OPERATION: 13
CASES SEXUAL ASSAULT/ABUSE (%): 60
DESCRIPTION: Services for sexual assault and domestic violence survivors; Sponsors batterers educational group (Alternatives to Violence)
CLIENTS/SERVICES: Sexual assault survivors; Marital rape/sexual abuse survivors; Adult survivors of child sexual abuse; Incest victims/survivors; Community education; Adolescent survivors of sexual abuse; Male survivors of sexual abuse

MONROE

FAMILY COUNSELING AND SHELTER SERVICES
6 S Monroe St, Monroe, MI 48161
Crisis hotline: **(313) 242-SAFE 24 hrs**
Information: (313) 241-0180, 241-2380 9am-5pm (Mon, Wed, Fri); 9am-9pm (Tue, Thu)
Contact: Carole Jenne, CSW, PhD, Exec Dir
TYPE OF AGENCY: Domestic violence program; Counseling/mental health services; Child sexual abuse services
AREAS SERVED: Monroe and surrounding area
YEARS IN OPERATION: 22
LANGUAGES: Spanish
CASES SEXUAL ASSAULT/ABUSE (%): 80
DESCRIPTION: Family counseling services; Child abuse/neglect services; Domestic violence services; Treatment for batterers
CLIENTS/SERVICES: Sexual assault survivors; Marital rape/sexual abuse survivors; Child victims of sexual abuse; Adult survivors of child sexual abuse; Incest victims/survivors; Community education; Offender treatment program; Adolescent survivors of sexual abuse; Male survivors of sexual abuse

MOUNT CLEMENS

MACOMB COUNTY CRISIS CENTER
County Bldg, 5th Fl, Mount Clemens, MI 48043
Crisis hotline: **(313) 573-2200 24 hrs 7 days**
Information: (313) 573-2083 8:30am-5pm (Mon-Fri)
Contact: Natalie Hall, Rape Educ Spec
TYPE OF AGENCY: Counseling/mental health services; Telephone crisis hotline
AREAS SERVED: Primarily Macomb
YEARS IN OPERATION: 18
ACCESSIBILITY: Telecommunications for the hearing impaired (TTY, TDY, etc.)
CASES SEXUAL ASSAULT/ABUSE (%): 5
DESCRIPTION: 24-hour telephone crisis counseling agency with public education programs on suicide and rape; Referrals are given for support groups and ongoing counseling
CLIENTS/SERVICES: Sexual assault survivors; Marital rape/sexual abuse survivors; Child victims of sexual abuse; Adult survivors of child sexual abuse; Incest victims/survivors; Prevention program; Community education; Male survivors of sexual abuse

MACOMB FAMILY SERVICES
57 Church St, Mount Clemens, MI 48043
Information: (313) 468-2656 9am-5pm
Contact: Dr Patricia L McDonald, Spec Proj Dir
TYPE OF AGENCY: Counseling/mental health services; Child sexual abuse services
AREAS SERVED: Macomb
YEARS IN OPERATION: 3½
ACCESSIBILITY: Wheelchair accessible
CASES SEXUAL ASSAULT/ABUSE (%): 100
DESCRIPTION: Child sexual abuse trauma team, funded through the Department of Social Services, deals with sexual abuse cases handled by Protective Services. Multidisciplinary team provides medical and psychological evaluation and group treatment for child victims, perpetrators, and non-abusive parents
CLIENTS/SERVICES: Child victims of sexual abuse; Adult survivors of child sexual abuse; Incest victims/survivors; Community education; Offender treatment program; Adolescent survivors of sexual abuse; Male survivors of sexual abuse

NORTH SUBURBAN COUNSELING ASSOCIATES
220 Cass, Mount Clemens, MI 48043
Information: (313) 468-1461 9am-9pm (Mon-Sat)
Contact: June Siebert, Clinic Dir
TYPE OF AGENCY: Private practice
AREAS SERVED: Macomb, Oakland, St Clair, Wayne
YEARS IN OPERATION: 12
ACCESSIBILITY: Wheelchair accessible
CASES SEXUAL ASSAULT/ABUSE (%): 10-20
DESCRIPTION: Private outpatient psychiatric clinic; Services for sexual assault victims and adult survivors of sexual abuse
CLIENTS/SERVICES: Sexual assault survivors; Marital rape/sexual abuse survivors; Child victims of sexual abuse; Adult survivors of child sexual abuse; Incest victims/survivors; Offender treatment program; Adolescent survivors of sexual abuse; Male survivors of sexual abuse
REQUIREMENTS: Ability to pay for services or have insurance

TURNING POINT, INC
PO Box 1123, Mount Clemens, MI 48043
Crisis hotline: **(313) 463-6990 24 hrs**
Information: (313) 463-4430 9am-5pm (Mon-Fri)
Contact: Roxene L Pattyn, Proj Coord
TYPE OF AGENCY: Rape crisis center; Domestic violence program

TURNING POINT, INC *(continued)*
AREAS SERVED: Macomb
YEARS IN OPERATION: 2
ACCESSIBILITY: Wheelchair accessible
CASES SEXUAL ASSAULT/ABUSE (%): 100
CLIENTS/SERVICES: Sexual assault survivors; Marital rape/sexual abuse survivors; Adult survivors of child sexual abuse; Community education; Adolescent survivors of sexual abuse; Male survivors of sexual abuse
REQUIREMENTS: Ages 14 and older

MOUNT PLEASANT

LISTENING EAR CRISIS CENTER—CHILD SEXUAL ABUSE TREATMENT PROGRAM
107 E Illinois Ave, Mount Pleasant, MI 48858
Crisis hotline: **(517) 772-2918 24 hrs**
Information: (517) 772-2919 8am-6pm
Contact: Mike Bell, Children's Svcs Dir
TYPE OF AGENCY: Counseling/mental health services; Child sexual abuse services
AREAS SERVED: Isabella, Montcalm
YEARS IN OPERATION: 18
ACCESSIBILITY: Wheelchair accessible
CLIENTS/SERVICES: Child victims of sexual abuse; Adult survivors of child sexual abuse; Incest victims/survivors; Offender treatment program
REQUIREMENTS: Must be referred via Child Protective Services. Treats offenders if children in treatment

WOMEN'S AID SERVICE, INC
PO Box 743, Mount Pleasant, MI 48804-0743
Crisis hotline: **(517) 772-9168 24 hrs**
Information: (517) 773-0078 9am-5pm (Mon-Fri)
Contact: Amy Barko, Sexual Assault Counselor/Advocate
TYPE OF AGENCY: Rape crisis center; Domestic violence program; Adolescent program
AREAS SERVED: Isabella, Gratiot, Clare
YEARS IN OPERATION: Women's Aid 10, Sexual assault program 2
DESCRIPTION: Comprehensive services for survivors of sexual assault and domestic violence; Group for batterers (Men Overcoming Violent Experiences) and a group for youth (12-17 years old) who have experienced previous or present violent/abusive relationships
CLIENTS/SERVICES: Sexual assault survivors; Marital rape/sexual abuse survivors; Adult survivors of child sexual abuse; Incest victims/survivors; Community education; Adolescent survivors of sexual abuse; Male survivors of sexual abuse
REQUIREMENTS: Adolescents can receive services with parental permission

MUSKEGON

EVERY WOMAN'S PLACE CRISIS CENTER
1706 Peck St, Muskegon, MI 49441
Crisis hotline: **(616) 722-3333 24 hrs**
Information: (616) 726-4493 9am-5pm
Contact: Diane Nye, Crisis Ctr Coord
TYPE OF AGENCY: Rape crisis center; Domestic violence program; Child sexual abuse prevention program
AREAS SERVED: Muskegon
YEARS IN OPERATION: 13
LANGUAGES: Interpreters available
ACCESSIBILITY: Wheelchair accessible
CASES SEXUAL ASSAULT/ABUSE (%): 17
CLIENTS/SERVICES: Sexual assault survivors; Marital rape/sexual abuse survivors; Child victims of sexual abuse; Adult survivors of child sexual abuse; Incest victims/survivors; Prevention program; Community education; Adolescent survivors of sexual abuse
REQUIREMENTS: Must be 18 years old to enter shelter

WEBSTER HOUSE
125 Delaware, Muskegon, MI 49442
Crisis hotline: **(616) 722-2694 24 hrs**
Information: (616) 722-2694 24 hrs
Contact: Richard Basch, Coord
TYPE OF AGENCY: Shelter
SPONSORING ORGANIZATION: Every Woman's Place
AREAS SERVED: Muskegon, Oceana
YEARS IN OPERATION: 12
CASES SEXUAL ASSAULT/ABUSE (%): 70
DESCRIPTION: Provides temporary shelter, individual and family counseling, and independent living for runaways and homeless youth; Works with other community agencies for additional services
CLIENTS/SERVICES: Sexual assault survivors; Incest victims/survivors; Adolescent survivors of sexual abuse
REQUIREMENTS: Runaways ages 12-17; Homeless youth ages 16-19

OAK PARK

THE FEMINIST THERAPY CENTER
21500 Greenfield, Ste 201, Oak Park, MI 48237
Information: (313) 968-1590 24 hr answering service
Contact: Paula Merideth, MA CSW, Dir
TYPE OF AGENCY: Counseling/mental health services; Private practice
AREAS SERVED: Oakland, Wayne
YEARS IN OPERATION: 6
DESCRIPTION: Full-service psychotherapy clinic with a feminist perspective and special focus on women's issues, providing individual, couples, group, and family therapy attending to the needs of women, men, children, and families
CLIENTS/SERVICES: Sexual assault survivors; Marital rape/sexual abuse survivors; Adult survivors of child sexual abuse; Incest victims/survivors; Community education; Adolescent survivors of sexual abuse; Healing
SPECIAL PROGRAMS/SERVICES: Healing experiences for adult women survivors includes working through unresolved grief and re-creating self and family through visualization, ritual and metaphor, art therapy, Gestalt processes. Family sculpting and writing techniques are also used within the supportive environment of a small group of women

PETOSKEY

WOMEN'S RESOURCE CENTER OF NORTHERN MICHIGAN, INC
1515 Howard St, Rm 52, Petoskey, MI 49770
Crisis hotline: **(616) 347-0082 24 hrs**
Information: (616) 347-0067 8:30am-5pm
Contact: Janet M Mancinelli, Exec Dir
TYPE OF AGENCY: Domestic violence program; Child sexual abuse services
AREAS SERVED: Emmet, Otsego, Antrim, Cheboygan, Charlevoix
YEARS IN OPERATION: 10½
CLIENTS/SERVICES: Sexual assault survivors; Marital rape/sexual abuse survivors; Child victims of sexual abuse; Community education; Adolescent survivors of sexual abuse

PONTIAC

CHILD ABUSE AND NEGLECT COUNCIL, COUNTY OF OAKLAND, INC
50 Wayne St, No 204, Pontiac, MI 48058
Information: (313) 332-7173 8:30am-5pm
Contact: Meg Mitzel, Exec Dir
TYPE OF AGENCY: Child sexual abuse prevention program; Child abuse prevention program
AREAS SERVED: Oakland
YEARS IN OPERATION: 11
ACCESSIBILITY: Wheelchair accessible
CLIENTS/SERVICES: Prevention program; Community education
SPECIAL PROGRAMS/SERVICES: In the planning stages of a project entitled CARE (Child Abuse Resource Effort) House based on the National Children's Advocacy Center in Huntsville, AL—coordinating the system's response to child physical and sexual abuse cases. Spanish-language brochures available

HAVEN
PO Box 787, Pontiac, MI 48056
Crisis hotline: **(313) 334-1274 24 hrs**
Information: (313) 334-1284 9am-5pm
Contact: Debi Cain, Exec Dir
TYPE OF AGENCY: Rape crisis center; Domestic violence program; Child sexual abuse services; Child sexual abuse prevention program
AREAS SERVED: Oakland
LANGUAGES: Spanish
ACCESSIBILITY: Wheelchair accessible; Signers for the hearing impaired
DESCRIPTION: Provides short- and long-term services and victim advocacy for survivors of domestic violence, sexual assault, and child sexual abuse; Special counseling programs for adolescent survivors and women in prison; Individual and group therapy for incest offenders and batterers; Parents United Chapter
CLIENTS/SERVICES: Sexual assault survivors; Marital rape/sexual abuse survivors; Child victims of sexual abuse; Adult survivors of child sexual abuse; Incest victims/survivors; Prevention program; Community education; Offender treatment program; Adolescent survivors of sexual abuse; Male survivors of sexual abuse; Prisoners; Disabled
SPECIAL PROGRAMS/SERVICES: Prevention program for differently abled children

OAKLAND FAMILY SERVICES—CHILDREN SERVICES
50 Wayne St, Pontiac, MI 48053
Information: (313) 332-8352 9am-5pm (Mon-Fri); other times by appointment
Contact: Individual and family: Louise R Kerlin, ACSW, Supv/Therapist; Offenders, male victims: John F Neumann, ACS W, Therapist; Group: Cathy Witt, ACSW, Supv/Therapist
TYPE OF AGENCY: Counseling/mental health services; Child sexual abuse services; Child sexual abuse prevention program
AREAS SERVED: Oakland
YEARS IN OPERATION: 67
ACCESSIBILITY: Wheelchair accessible
CASES SEXUAL ASSAULT/ABUSE (%): 70-80
CLIENTS/SERVICES: Sexual assault survivors; Marital rape/sexual abuse survivors; Child victims of sexual abuse; Adult survivors of child sexual abuse; Incest victims/survivors; Prevention program; Community education; Offender treatment program; Adolescent survivors of sexual abuse; Male survivors of sexual abuse
SPECIAL PROGRAMS/SERVICES: Services for clients with multiple personality disorders

WOMEN'S SURVIVAL CENTER
167 W Pike, Pontiac, MI 48053
Crisis hotline: **(313) 335-1520 9am-5pm (Mon-Fri)**
Information: (313) 335-2685 9am-5pm (Mon-Fri)
Contact: Joanne Pepera, I and R Spec
TYPE OF AGENCY: Counseling/mental health services
YEARS IN OPERATION: 10
CASES SEXUAL ASSAULT/ABUSE (%): 20
DESCRIPTION: Women's information-referral services; Individual and group counseling and support; Legal clinic; Employment readiness program
CLIENTS/SERVICES: Sexual assault survivors; Adult survivors of child sexual abuse; Prevention program; Community education

PORT HURON

DOMESTIC ASSAULT/RAPE ELIMINATION SERVICES (DARES)
1625 Pine Grove Ave, Port Huron, MI 49060
Crisis hotline: **(313) 985-5538 24 hrs**
Information: (313) 985-4950 8:30am-5pm
Contact: Carolyn Superczynski, Exec Dir
TYPE OF AGENCY: Rape crisis center; Domestic violence program
AREAS SERVED: St Clair, Sanilac
YEARS IN OPERATION: 10
CLIENTS/SERVICES: Sexual assault survivors; Marital rape/sexual abuse survivors; Community education

SAGINAW

CRISIS INTERVENTION SERVICES (CIS)
500 Hancock, Saginaw, MI 48602
Crisis hotline: **(517) 792-9732 24 hrs**
Information: (517) 799-3822 8am-5pm
Contact: Kenneth T Morris, PhD, CIS Supv
TYPE OF AGENCY: Counseling/mental health services
SPONSORING ORGANIZATION: Saginaw Community Mental Health
AREAS SERVED: Saginaw
YEARS IN OPERATION: 17
LANGUAGES: Interpreters by arrangement
ACCESSIBILITY: Wheelchair accessible; Telecommunications for the hearing impaired (TTY, TDY, etc.); Signers for the hearing impaired (by arrangement)
CASES SEXUAL ASSAULT/ABUSE (%): 1-2
CLIENTS/SERVICES: Sexual assault survivors; Child victims of sexual abuse; Community education

SAGINAW COUNTY SEXUAL ASSAULT CENTER
1226 N Michigan, Saginaw, MI 48602
Crisis hotline: **(517) 755-6565 24 hrs**
Information: (517) 755-6565 9am-5pm (Mon-Fri)
Contact: Pamela M Mays, Prog Dir
TYPE OF AGENCY: Rape crisis center; Child sexual abuse services; Child sexual abuse prevention program
SPONSORING ORGANIZATION: Child and Family Services of Saginaw County
AREAS SERVED: Primarily Saginaw, surrounding counties
YEARS IN OPERATION: 12
LANGUAGES: Spanish
CASES SEXUAL ASSAULT/ABUSE (%): 100
DESCRIPTION: Comprehensive rape crisis and child sexual abuse services and individual therapy for juvenile sex offenders
CLIENTS/SERVICES: Sexual assault survivors; Marital rape/sexual abuse survivors; Child victims of sexual abuse; Adult survivors of child sexual abuse; Incest victims/survivors; Prevention program; Community education; Offender treatment program; Adolescent survivors of sexual abuse; Male survivors of sexual abuse; Preschoolers
SPECIAL PROGRAMS/SERVICES: Provides a preschool prevention program for children ages 3-6 entitled *Happy Bear*, which teaches correct body parts, inappropriate touching and importance of telling someone in a non-threatening manner. In addition to support groups for adult and adolescent survivors, offers a support group for mothers whose children have been sexually abused

UNDERGROUND RAILROAD
PO Box 565, Saginaw, MI 48606
Crisis hotline: **(517) 755-0411 24 hrs**
Information: (517) 755-0411 24 hrs
Contact: Joseph Sedlock, Exec Dir
TYPE OF AGENCY: Domestic violence program; Child sexual abuse prevention program
SPONSORING ORGANIZATION: Sexual Assault Center
AREAS SERVED: Primarily Saginaw, also Genessee and Bay
YEARS IN OPERATION: 10
LANGUAGES: Spanish
CASES SEXUAL ASSAULT/ABUSE (%): 6
DESCRIPTION: $21f
CLIENTS/SERVICES: Sexual assault survivors; Marital rape/sexual abuse survivors; Child victims of sexual abuse; Incest victims/survivors; Prevention program; Adolescent survivors of sexual abuse
SPECIAL PROGRAMS/SERVICES: Child sexual abuse prevention program in shelter and taught in county school system; Group for children dealing with feelings related to sexual abuse and domestic violence; Outreach worker counsels children and identifies sexual abuse victims

SAINT JOHNS

RELIEF AFTER VIOLENT ENCOUNTER
PO Box 472, Saint Johns, MI 48879
Crisis hotline: **(517) 224-RAVE 24 hrs**
Information: (517) 224-4662 9am-5pm
Contact: Janet Holden, Prog Dir
TYPE OF AGENCY: Rape crisis center; Domestic violence program; Interagency network
AREAS SERVED: Clinton, Shiawasse
YEARS IN OPERATION: 4
CASES SEXUAL ASSAULT/ABUSE (%): 50
CLIENTS/SERVICES: Sexual assault survivors; Marital rape/sexual abuse survivors; Child victims of sexual abuse; Adult survivors of child sexual abuse; Prevention program; Community education; Adolescent survivors of sexual abuse; Publications/media
REQUIREMENTS: Must be female and 18 years of age or emancipated minor. Must have been exposed to or threatened with physical and/or emotional abuse by someone with whom there was once a consenting sexual relationship
SPECIAL PROGRAMS/SERVICES: Offers a videotape mini-documentary on relief after violent encounters

SAINT JOSEPH

ASSAULT RECOVERY ASSOCIATES
303 Ridgeway, Saint Joseph, MI 49085
Information: (616) 983-5285
Contact: Gloria Gillespie, Robin Smietanka, Associates
TYPE OF AGENCY: Private practice
AREAS SERVED: Primarily Berrien, Cass, Van Buren, St Joseph
YEARS IN OPERATION: 8
CASES SEXUAL ASSAULT/ABUSE (%): 100
DESCRIPTION: Counseling for survivors and offenders—rapists, batterers, child sexual abuse/incest offenders
CLIENTS/SERVICES: Sexual assault survivors; Marital rape/sexual abuse survivors; Child victims of sexual abuse; Adult survivors of child sexual abuse; Incest victims/survivors; Prevention program; Community education; Offender treatment program; Adolescent survivors of sexual abuse; Male survivors of sexual abuse; Publications/media
SPECIAL PROGRAMS/SERVICES: Slide and video on the pedophile; Tape on prevention; Slide show on information and services

SAULT SAINTE MARIE

CHIPPEWA COUNTY PROSECUTING ATTORNEY—CRIME VICTIM'S ASSISTANCE PROGRAM
Chippewa County Courthouse, Sault Sainte Marie, MI 49783
Crisis hotline: **(906) 635-6364 8am-4pm**
Information: (906) 635-6364 8am-4pm
Contact: Debbie Sirk, Victim Advocate
TYPE OF AGENCY: Victim/witness assistance program
AREAS SERVED: Chippewa
YEARS IN OPERATION: 2
CASES SEXUAL ASSAULT/ABUSE (%): 15
CLIENTS/SERVICES: Sexual assault survivors; Marital rape/sexual abuse survivors; Child victims of sexual abuse; Adult survivors of child sexual abuse; Incest victims/survivors; Community education

EASTERN UPPER PENINSULA DOMESTIC VIOLENCE PROGRAM
PO Box 636, Sault Sainte Marie, MI 49783
Crisis hotline: **(906) 635-0566 24 hrs**
Information: (906) 635-0566
Contact: Doreen Howson, Dir
TYPE OF AGENCY: Rape crisis center; Domestic violence program
AREAS SERVED: Chippewa, Mackinac, Luce
YEARS IN OPERATION: 8
CASES SEXUAL ASSAULT/ABUSE (%): 10
CLIENTS/SERVICES: Sexual assault survivors; Marital rape/sexual abuse survivors; Prevention program; Community education

TAYLOR

CATHOLIC SOCIAL SERVICES OF WAYNE COUNTY
24331 Van Born Rd, Taylor, MI 48180
Information: (313) 292-5690 8:30am-8:30pm (Mon-Fri)
Contact: Nancy L Stein, Soc Wkr
TYPE OF AGENCY: Counseling/mental health services
AREAS SERVED: Wayne
YEARS IN OPERATION: 40
ACCESSIBILITY: Wheelchair accessible
DESCRIPTION: Comprehensive family service agency includes therapy for all types of problems (family, marital, individual and group); Provides in-depth individual and group treatment for sexual abuse survivors
CLIENTS/SERVICES: Sexual assault survivors; Marital rape/sexual abuse survivors; Child victims of sexual abuse; Adult survivors of child sexual abuse; Incest victims/survivors; Adolescent survivors of sexual abuse; Male survivors of sexual abuse
SPECIAL PROGRAMS/SERVICES: Mixed male and female adult incest group

THREE RIVERS

DOMESTIC ASSAULT SHELTER
PO Box 402, Three Rivers, MI 49093
Crisis hotline: **(800) 828-2023 24 hrs**
Information: (616) 279-5122 24 hrs
Contact: Kathy Randall, Sexual Assault Svcs Dir
TYPE OF AGENCY: Rape crisis center; Domestic violence program
AREAS SERVED: St Joseph, Cass, Van Buren
YEARS IN OPERATION: 2
DESCRIPTION: A domestic assault shelter with a 24 hour line for rape victims
CLIENTS/SERVICES: Sexual assault survivors; Marital rape/sexual abuse survivors; Prevention program; Community education

TRAVERSE CITY

INSTITUTE FOR SEX THERAPY, EDUCATION, AND RESEARCH
420 E Front St, Traverse City, MI 49684
Information: (616) 947-2444 9am-5:30pm
Contact: Barbara Jones Smith, PhD, Sexual Abuse/Perpetration Prog Clinical Dir
TYPE OF AGENCY: Counseling/mental health services; Consultation; Training/research
AREAS SERVED: Northern Michigan
YEARS IN OPERATION: 3½
ACCESSIBILITY: Wheelchair accessible; Signers for the hearing impaired
CASES SEXUAL ASSAULT/ABUSE (%): 80

INSTITUTE FOR SEX THERAPY, EDUCATION, AND RESEARCH (continued)

DESCRIPTION: Assessment and treatment of sexual abuse (child through adult), as well as treatment for adolescent and adult offenders; Provides transdisciplinary approach for incest families, as well as sexual dysfunction therapy; Workshops, seminars, and internships for professionals; Case/program consultation; Extensive library of books, audio tapes, and videotapes on human sexuality
CLIENTS/SERVICES: Sexual assault survivors; Marital rape/sexual abuse survivors; Child victims of sexual abuse; Adult survivors of child sexual abuse; Incest victims/survivors; Prevention program; Community education; Offender treatment program; Adolescent survivors of sexual abuse; Male survivors of sexual abuse; Publications/media

MULTIDISCIPLINARY SEXUAL ABUSE TREATMENT PROGRAM
3785 W Townhall Rd, Traverse City, MI 49684
Information: (616) 946-2104 8:30am-5pm (Mon, Wed, Thu, Fri); 8:30am-8:30pm (Tue)
Contact: Chuck Mueller, Family Svc Supv
TYPE OF AGENCY: Child sexual abuse services
SPONSORING ORGANIZATION: Child and Family Services
AREAS SERVED: Grand Traverse, Leelanau, Kalkaska
YEARS IN OPERATION: 3
ACCESSIBILITY: Wheelchair accessible
CASES SEXUAL ASSAULT/ABUSE (%): 100
DESCRIPTION: Assessment and treatment services for child victims of sexual abuse; Individual, group, family, and marital treatment; Parent groups; Adolescent and adult offenders; Victim advocate program; Coordinates community agencies; Community education
CLIENTS/SERVICES: Child victims of sexual abuse; Adult survivors of child sexual abuse; Incest victims/survivors; Community education; Offender treatment program; Adolescent survivors of sexual abuse; Male survivors of sexual abuse; Publications/media
REQUIREMENTS: Clients of probate court, foster care, prevention and protective services within the Department of Social Services
SPECIAL PROGRAMS/SERVICES: Self-help group for adult male and female victims; Multi-county interagency team for child sexual abuse; Recreational therapy program for sexual abuse victims and their families

THIRD LEVEL CRISIS INTERVENTION CENTER, INC
PO Box 1035, Traverse City, MI 49685
Crisis hotline: **(616) 922-4800 24 hrs**
Information: (616) 922-4802 9am-5pm (Mon-Fri)
Contact: Gail Heath, Exec Dir
TYPE OF AGENCY: Counseling/mental health services; Crisis counseling; Telephone hotline; Adolescent program
AREAS SERVED: Grand Traverse, Leelanau, Antrim, Kalkaska, Benzie, Otsego, Emmet, Charleroix, Cheboygan, Crawford, Roscommon, Wexford, Missaukee
YEARS IN OPERATION: 16
ACCESSIBILITY: Wheelchair accessible; Telecommunications for the hearing impaired (TTY, TDY, etc.)
DESCRIPTION: Provides free and confidential crisis counseling, problem assistance, information, and referral; Runaway and youth services; On-site school crisis counseling often is the first point of contact for those who have been assaulted
CLIENTS/SERVICES: Sexual assault survivors; Child victims of sexual abuse; Incest victims/survivors; Adolescent survivors of sexual abuse; Male survivors of sexual abuse

WEST BRANCH

AU SABLE VALLEY COMMUNITY MENTAL HEALTH
511 Griffin, West Branch, MI 48661
Crisis hotline: **(800) 322-0213 24 hrs**
Information: (517) 345-5571 7am-6pm
Contact: John Olesnavage, Prog Dir
TYPE OF AGENCY: Counseling/mental health services
AREAS SERVED: Iosco, Ogeman, Oscoda
YEARS IN OPERATION: 12
ACCESSIBILITY: Wheelchair accessible
CASES SEXUAL ASSAULT/ABUSE (%): 25
DESCRIPTION: Counseling for survivors and individual therapy for perpetrators—rapists, child sexual abuse/incest offenders and batterers
CLIENTS/SERVICES: Sexual assault survivors; Marital rape/sexual abuse survivors; Child victims of sexual abuse; Adult survivors of child sexual abuse; Incest victims/survivors; Prevention program; Community education; Offender treatment program; Adolescent survivors of sexual abuse; Male survivors of sexual abuse
REQUIREMENTS: Children under 14 must have permission from parent or guardian

WESTLAND

FIRST STEP—THE WESTERN WAYNE COUNTY PROJECT ON DOMESTIC ASSAULT
8381 Farmington Rd, Westland, MI 48185
Crisis hotline: **(313) 459-5900 24 hrs**
Information: (313) 525-2230 9am-5pm
Contact: Judy Ellis, Exec Dir
TYPE OF AGENCY: Domestic violence program
AREAS SERVED: Western Wayne (excluding Detroit) and Downriver communities
ACCESSIBILITY: Wheelchair accessible
CLIENTS/SERVICES: Sexual assault survivors; Marital rape/sexual abuse survivors; Adult survivors of child sexual abuse

MINNESOTA

ALBERT LEA

VICTIM'S CRISIS CENTER
PO Box 649, 221 E Clark, Albert Lea, MN 56007
Crisis hotline: **(507) 373-2223 and pagers 5pm-8am (Mon-Fri); 24 hrs (Sat-Sun)**
Information: (507) 373-2223 8am-5pm (Mon-Fri)
Contact: Nona Lindberg, Dir
TYPE OF AGENCY: Rape crisis center; Victim/witness assistance program
AREAS SERVED: Freeborn
YEARS IN OPERATION: 10
LANGUAGES: Spanish
ACCESSIBILITY: Wheelchair accessible
CASES SEXUAL ASSAULT/ABUSE (%): 20
DESCRIPTION: For victims of all crimes, including sexual assault provides advocacy, crisis counseling, support groups, court support, referrals; Group therapy for batterers available
CLIENTS/SERVICES: Sexual assault survivors; Marital rape/sexual abuse survivors; Adult survivors of child sexual abuse; Incest victims/survivors; Community education; Adolescent survivors of sexual abuse
SPECIAL PROGRAMS/SERVICES: Spanish-language brochure available

ALEXANDRIA

LISTENING EAR CRISIS CENTER
111 17th Ave E, Alexandria, MN 56308
Crisis hotline: **(612) 763-6638 24 hrs**
Information: (612) 763-6638 8am-5pm
Contact: Harriet Hopkins, Dir
TYPE OF AGENCY: Rape crisis center; Domestic violence program; Telephone crisis hotline
SPONSORING ORGANIZATION: Douglas County Hospital
AREAS SERVED: Douglas, Grant, Ottertail, Pope, Stevens, Traverse
CLIENTS/SERVICES: Sexual assault survivors; Marital rape/sexual abuse survivors; Child victims of sexual abuse; Adult survivors of child sexual abuse; Incest victims/survivors; Prevention program; Community education; Adolescent survivors of sexual abuse; Male survivors of sexual abuse

AUSTIN

VICTIM'S CRISIS CENTER
1020 1st Dr NW, Austin, MN 55912
Crisis hotline: **(507) 437-6680 24 hrs daily**
Information: (507) 437-6680 8am-4:30pm (Mon-Fri)
Contact: Vickie Potter, Dir
TYPE OF AGENCY: Rape crisis center; Victim/witness assistance program; Child sexual abuse prevention program
AREAS SERVED: Mower
YEARS IN OPERATION: 10
LANGUAGES: Interpreters available
ACCESSIBILITY: Signers for the hearing impaired (by arrangement)
CASES SEXUAL ASSAULT/ABUSE (%): 70
DESCRIPTION: Trained advocates provide support groups and individual counseling for those severely traumatized
CLIENTS/SERVICES: Sexual assault survivors; Marital rape/sexual abuse survivors; Child victims of sexual abuse; Adult survivors of child sexual abuse; Incest victims/survivors; Prevention program; Community education; Adolescent survivors of sexual abuse; Male survivors of sexual abuse

BEMIDJI

IRIS PERSONAL RENEWAL CENTER
722½ Beltrami Ave, Bemidji, MN 56601
Information: (218) 751-5052 9am-5pm (Mon-Fri)
Contact: Susan Smith, Dir/Facilitator
TYPE OF AGENCY: Counseling/mental health services
AREAS SERVED: Beltrami, Cass, Hubbard, Clear Water
YEARS IN OPERATION: 3
CASES SEXUAL ASSAULT/ABUSE (%): 75
CLIENTS/SERVICES: Sexual assault survivors; Marital rape/sexual abuse survivors; Adult survivors of child sexual abuse; Incest victims/survivors; Community education; Adult children of dysfunctional families; Male survivors of sexual abuse; Healing
REQUIREMENTS: Must be 16 or older; Self pay or qualified for Beltrami County funding
SPECIAL PROGRAMS/SERVICES: The model of facilitation used is called *Living Process Facilitation* and is based on the work of Anne Wilson Schaef, PhD. One of its basic premises is that one must be fully aware of and accept one's present to enable him/her to move on and heal. Every person is in a constant process of awareness and heals at his/her own pace. This model also looks at systems and how we internalize their rules and must identify them as a way of changing.

NORTHWOODS COALITION FOR BATTERED WOMEN
PO Box 563, Bemidji, MN 56601
Crisis hotline: **(218) 751-0211 24 hrs**
TYPE OF AGENCY: Domestic violence program
AREAS SERVED: Lake of the Woods, Beltiami, Clearwater, Hubbard, Mahnomen, Cass
YEARS IN OPERATION: 10
ACCESSIBILITY: Telecommunications for the hearing impaired (TTY, TDY, etc.)
CLIENTS/SERVICES: Marital rape/sexual abuse survivors; Child victims of sexual abuse; Adult survivors of child sexual abuse; Incest victims/survivors; Community education; Adolescent survivors of sexual abuse

SEXUAL ASSAULT PROGRAM OF BELTRAMI, CASS, AND HUBBARD COUNTIES
PO Box 1472, Bemidji, MN 56601
Crisis hotline: **(218) 751-0211 24 hrs**
Information: (218) 751-9696 8am-5pm
Contact: Danna Farabee, Prog Dir
TYPE OF AGENCY: Rape crisis center; Child sexual abuse prevention program
AREAS SERVED: Beltrami, Cass, Hubbard, and Red Lake and Leech Lake reservations
YEARS IN OPERATION: 8
ACCESSIBILITY: Wheelchair accessible (Red Lake and Hubbard offices)
CASES SEXUAL ASSAULT/ABUSE (%): 100
CLIENTS/SERVICES: Sexual assault survivors; Marital rape/sexual abuse survivors; Child victims of sexual abuse; Adult survivors of child sexual abuse; Incest victims/survivors; Prevention program; Community education; Adolescent survivors of sexual abuse; Male survivors of sexual abuse; Healing; Publications/media
SPECIAL PROGRAMS/SERVICES: Adapted Illusion Theatre's *Touch* posters for young children, ages 3-10 (cost $50 for set of 11). Encourages healing through writing and journal keeping for sexual assault survivors and adult survivors of child sexual abuse

BLOOMINGTON

THE WOMEN'S RESOURCE CENTER
9700 France Ave S, Normandale Community College, Bloomington, MN 55431
Crisis hotline: **(612) 896-4844 9am-5pm (Mon, Wed, Fri); 9am-8:30pm (Tue, Thu)**
Information: (612) 830-9387 9am-5pm (Mon, Wed, Fri); 9am-8:30pm (Tue, Thu)
Contact: Vivian Rouson-Gossett, Interim Dir
TYPE OF AGENCY: College/university-based services; Rape prevention program
SPONSORING ORGANIZATION: Normandale Community College
AREAS SERVED: Primarily Bloomington metro and south suburbs areas
YEARS IN OPERATION: 7
ACCESSIBILITY: Wheelchair accessible
CASES SEXUAL ASSAULT/ABUSE (%): 5
DESCRIPTION: Offers supportive services and educational programs, referrals, support groups, short-term counseling, information, educational programs related to sexual assault/abuse, as well as feminist martial arts/self-defense
CLIENTS/SERVICES: Sexual assault survivors; Adult survivors of child sexual abuse; Community education; Adolescent survivors of sexual abuse

BRAINERD

NORTHERN PINES MENTAL HEALTH CENTER
County Service Bldg, Brainerd, MN 56401
Information: (218) 829-3235 8am-5pm (Mon-Fri)
Contact: Jim Morrison, Clinical Supv
TYPE OF AGENCY: Rape crisis center; Counseling/mental health services; Child sexual abuse services
AREAS SERVED: Crow Wing, Cass, Todd, Morrison, Wadena
YEARS IN OPERATION: 25
LANGUAGES: Spanish
ACCESSIBILITY: Wheelchair accessible; Telecommunications for the hearing impaired (TTY, TDY, etc.); Signers for the hearing impaired
CASES SEXUAL ASSAULT/ABUSE (%): 70
DESCRIPTION: Sponsors sexual assault advocacy services; Provides treatment services for victims and survivors; Treatment program for incest offenders
CLIENTS/SERVICES: Sexual assault survivors; Marital rape/sexual abuse survivors; Child victims of sexual abuse; Adult survivors of child sexual abuse; Incest victims/survivors; Offender treatment program; Adolescent survivors of sexual abuse; Male survivors of sexual abuse

SEXUAL ASSAULT SERVICES
PO Box 602, Brainerd, MN 56401
Crisis hotline: **(218) 828-1216 24 hrs daily**
Information: (218) 828-1216 24 hrs daily
Contact: Jo Richmond, Sexual Assault Svcs Coord
TYPE OF AGENCY: Rape crisis center; Domestic violence program
SPONSORING ORGANIZATION: Women's Center of Mid-Minnesota
AREAS SERVED: Crow Wing, surrounding area
YEARS IN OPERATION: 10
LANGUAGES: Sign
ACCESSIBILITY: Wheelchair accessible (by arrangement); Telecommunications for the hearing impaired (TTY, TDY, etc.); Signers for the hearing impaired
CASES SEXUAL ASSAULT/ABUSE (%): 100
CLIENTS/SERVICES: Sexual assault survivors; Marital rape/sexual abuse survivors; Child victims of sexual abuse; Adult survivors of child sexual abuse; Incest victims/survivors; Prevention program; Community education; Adolescent survivors of sexual abuse; Male survivors of sexual abuse; Ritualistic abuse victims/survivors
SPECIAL PROGRAMS/SERVICES: Worked with a number of adult and some adolescent victim/survivors of Satanic cult-ritualized abuse. Provides professional training and consultation in this area

BURNSVILLE

SEXUAL ASSAULT SERVICES OF DAKOTA COUNTY
14451 County Rd 11, Burnsville, MN 55337
Crisis hotline: **(612) 431-2424 24 hrs**
Information: (612) 431-2112
Contact: Barbara J Kiffe, Coord
TYPE OF AGENCY: Rape crisis center
SPONSORING ORGANIZATION: Community Action Council
AREAS SERVED: Dakota
YEARS IN OPERATION: 8
ACCESSIBILITY: Wheelchair accessible
CASES SEXUAL ASSAULT/ABUSE (%): 100
CLIENTS/SERVICES: Sexual assault survivors; Marital rape/sexual abuse survivors; Child victims of sexual abuse; Adult survivors of child sexual abuse; Incest victims/survivors; Prevention program; Community education; Adolescent survivors of sexual abuse; Male survivors of sexual abuse; Elderly; Publications/media
SPECIAL PROGRAMS/SERVICES: Locally produced slide show on the elderly.

CENTER CITY

CHISAGO COUNTY ATTORNEY'S OFFICE—VICTIM ASSISTANCE PROGRAM
Chisago County Government Center, Center City, MN 55012
Information: (612) 462-7999, ext 258 8am-4:30pm
Contact: Sara Schlauderaff, Victim Assistance Coord
TYPE OF AGENCY: Victim/witness assistance program
AREAS SERVED: Chisago
YEARS IN OPERATION: 3
ACCESSIBILITY: Wheelchair accessible
CASES SEXUAL ASSAULT/ABUSE (%): 25-30
CLIENTS/SERVICES: Sexual assault survivors; Marital rape/sexual abuse survivors; Child victims of sexual abuse; Adult survivors of child sexual abuse; Incest victims/survivors; Prevention program; Community education; Adolescent survivors of sexual abuse
REQUIREMENTS: Crime committed in Chisago County

CHASKA

SEXUAL VIOLENCE CENTER IN CARVER COUNTY
111000 Bavaria Rd, Chaska, MN 55318
Crisis hotline: **(612) 448-5425 24 hrs daily**
Information: (612) 448-5425 9am-5pm (Mon-Fri)
Contact: Sue Aumer, Prog Coord
TYPE OF AGENCY: Rape crisis center
SPONSORING ORGANIZATION: Sexual Violence Center of Hennepin County
AREAS SERVED: Carver
YEARS IN OPERATION: 6
CASES SEXUAL ASSAULT/ABUSE (%): 100
CLIENTS/SERVICES: Sexual assault survivors; Marital rape/sexual abuse survivors; Child victims of sexual abuse; Adult survivors of child sexual abuse; Incest victims/survivors; Community education; Adolescent survivors of sexual abuse; Male survivors of sexual abuse

CIRCLE PINES

ALEXANDRA HOUSE, INC
PO Box 194, Circle Pines, MN 55014
Crisis hotline: **(612) 780-2330 24 hrs**
Information: (612) 780-2332 9am-5pm
Contact: Pat Prinzevalle, Dir
TYPE OF AGENCY: Domestic violence program
AREAS SERVED: Primarily Anoka
YEARS IN OPERATION: 8
ACCESSIBILITY: Wheelchair accessible; Telecommunications for the hearing impaired (TTY, TDY, etc.); Signers for the hearing impaired
CASES SEXUAL ASSAULT/ABUSE (%): 80-90
CLIENTS/SERVICES: Marital rape/sexual abuse survivors

CROOKSTON

PROJECT SAFE, INC
102 N Broadway, Crookston, MN 56716
Crisis hotline: **(218) 281-2864 24 hrs**
Information: (218) 281-2864 8:30am-5pm
Contact: Nancy Burt, Prog Dir
TYPE OF AGENCY: Rape crisis center; Child sexual abuse services; Child sexual abuse prevention program
AREAS SERVED: Polk, Pennington, Red Lake, Kittson, Marshall
YEARS IN OPERATION: 10
LANGUAGES: Spanish translator available
CASES SEXUAL ASSAULT/ABUSE (%): 100
CLIENTS/SERVICES: Sexual assault survivors; Marital rape/sexual abuse survivors; Child victims of sexual abuse; Adult survivors of child sexual abuse; Incest victims/survivors; Prevention program; Community education; Adolescent survivors of sexual abuse; Male survivors of sexual abuse

DULUTH

PROGRAM FOR AID TO VICTIMS OF SEXUAL ASSAULT, INC
202 Ordean Bldg, Duluth, MN 55806
Crisis hotline: **(218) 723-9929 24 hrs daily**
Information: (218) 726-4751 8:30am-4:30pm (Mon-Fri)
Contact: Susan Askelin, Exec Dir
TYPE OF AGENCY: Rape crisis center; Child sexual abuse prevention program
AREAS SERVED: Lake, Carlton, Southern St Louis
YEARS IN OPERATION: 14
ACCESSIBILITY: Wheelchair accessible; Telecommunications for the hearing impaired (TTY, TDY, etc.); Signers for the hearing impaired (by arrangement)
CASES SEXUAL ASSAULT/ABUSE (%): 100
CLIENTS/SERVICES: Sexual assault survivors; Marital rape/sexual abuse survivors; Child victims of sexual abuse; Adult survivors of child sexual abuse; Incest victims/survivors; Prevention program; Community education; Adolescent survivors of sexual abuse; Male survivors of sexual abuse

ST LOUIS COUNTY VICTIM/WITNESS ASSISTANCE PROGRAM
100 N 5th Ave West, Rm 401, Duluth, MN 55802-1298
Crisis hotline: **(800) 232-1300 24 hrs**
Information: (218) 726-2323 8am-4:30pm
Contact: Paul A Gustad, Dir
TYPE OF AGENCY: Victim/witness assistance program
SPONSORING ORGANIZATION: St Louis County Attorney's Office
AREAS SERVED: St Louis
YEARS IN OPERATION: 12
ACCESSIBILITY: Wheelchair accessible
CASES SEXUAL ASSAULT/ABUSE (%): 20
CLIENTS/SERVICES: Sexual assault survivors; Marital rape/sexual abuse survivors; Child victims of sexual abuse; Adult survivors of child sexual abuse; Incest victims/survivors

WOMEN'S COALITION
PO Box 3205, Duluth, MN 55803
Crisis hotline: **(218) 728-6481 24 hrs**
Information: (218) 728-6481
Contact: Madeliene Tjadn, Legal Advocate
TYPE OF AGENCY: Domestic violence program
AREAS SERVED: St Louis and surrounding counties
YEARS IN OPERATION: 10
ACCESSIBILITY: Telecommunications for the hearing impaired (TTY, TDY, etc.); Signers for the hearing impaired
DESCRIPTION: Provides temporary shelter, emergency assistance, and advocacy for survivors of domestic violence; Counseling for batterers; Feminist martial arts/self-defense training
CLIENTS/SERVICES: Marital rape/sexual abuse survivors; Adult survivors of child sexual abuse; Incest victims/survivors; Prevention program; Community education; Adolescent survivors of sexual abuse

WOMEN'S RESOURCE AND ACTION CENTER
10 University Dr, Duluth, MN 55812
Information: (218) 726-6232 8am-5pm
Contact: Holly Nordquist, Dir
TYPE OF AGENCY: College/university-based services
SPONSORING ORGANIZATION: University of Minnesota-Duluth
YEARS IN OPERATION: 4
ACCESSIBILITY: Wheelchair accessible; Signers for the hearing impaired
CLIENTS/SERVICES: Sexual assault survivors; Prevention program; Sexual harassment

WOMEN'S RESOURCE AND ACTION CENTER *(continued)*

REQUIREMENTS: Client must be a student, staff, or faculty member of the university.

FAIRMONT

SOUTHERN MINNESOTA CRISIS SUPPORT CENTER
Box 214, Fairmont, MN 56031
Crisis hotline: **(507) 235-3456 24 hrs**
Information: (507) 238-2814 10am-3pm (Mon-Fri)
Contact: Sharry Tveit, Chairperson
TYPE OF AGENCY: Counseling/mental health services; Telephone crisis hotline
AREAS SERVED: Martin, Faribault, Watonwan, Jackson, Cottonwood
YEARS IN OPERATION: 10
ACCESSIBILITY: Wheelchair accessible
CASES SEXUAL ASSAULT/ABUSE (%): 12
DESCRIPTION: 24-hour hotline whose primary function is information and referral. Sexual assault and child abuse are two of the main areas. Advocacy and accompaniment to hospital are available in Martin county (city of Fairmont)
CLIENTS/SERVICES: Sexual assault survivors; Child victims of sexual abuse; Community education

FARIBAULT

FARIBAULT VICTIM SUPPORT PROGRAM
PO Box 354, Faribault, MN 55021
Crisis hotline: **(507) 334-2555 24 hrs**
Information: (507) 334-6172
Contact: Betty Aase, Coord
TYPE OF AGENCY: Domestic violence program; Victim/witness assistance program
SPONSORING ORGANIZATION: United Way
AREAS SERVED: Rice
YEARS IN OPERATION: 8
ACCESSIBILITY: Wheelchair accessible; Telecommunications for the hearing impaired (TTY, TDY, etc.); Signers for the hearing impaired
CASES SEXUAL ASSAULT/ABUSE (%): 11
CLIENTS/SERVICES: Sexual assault survivors; Marital rape/sexual abuse survivors; Child victims of sexual abuse; Adult survivors of child sexual abuse; Incest victims/survivors; Prevention program; Community education; Adolescent survivors of sexual abuse; Male survivors of sexual abuse

RICE COUNTY SEXUAL ASSAULT PROGRAM
Faribo Town Square, Faribault, MN 55021
Crisis hotline: **Faribo (507) 334-2555, Northfield (507) 645-5555 24 hrs daily**
Information: (507) 332-2227 9am-1pm
Contact: Sharon Ferris, Coord
TYPE OF AGENCY: Rape crisis center
SPONSORING ORGANIZATION: GRW-CAC, Inc
AREAS SERVED: Rice
YEARS IN OPERATION: 1
ACCESSIBILITY: Wheelchair accessible
CASES SEXUAL ASSAULT/ABUSE (%): 100
CLIENTS/SERVICES: Sexual assault survivors; Marital rape/sexual abuse survivors; Child victims of sexual abuse; Adult survivors of child sexual abuse; Incest victims/survivors; Prevention program; Community education; Adolescent survivors of sexual abuse; Male survivors of sexual abuse
SPECIAL PROGRAMS/SERVICES: Self-esteem programs in support group settings

FERGUS FALLS

WOMEN'S CRISIS CENTER
PO Box 815, Fergus Falls, MN 56537
Crisis hotline: **(218) 739-3359 24 hrs daily**
Information: (218) 739-3486 9am-5pm
Contact: Dianne Long, Coord
TYPE OF AGENCY: Domestic violence program
AREAS SERVED: Grant, Becker, Otter Tail, Clay, Douglas, Wilkin, Pope, Stevens, Traverse
YEARS IN OPERATION: 9½
ACCESSIBILITY: Telecommunications for the hearing impaired (TTY, TDY, etc.)
CASES SEXUAL ASSAULT/ABUSE (%): 50
CLIENTS/SERVICES: Marital rape/sexual abuse survivors; Child victims of sexual abuse; Prevention program; Community education

GRAND RAPIDS

NORTHLAND MENTAL HEALTH CENTER— SEXUAL ASSAULT PROGRAM
215 SE 2nd Ave, Grand Rapids, MN 55744
Crisis hotline: **(218) 326-5008 24 hrs**
Information: (218) 326-1274 8am-5pm
Contact: Mary Ellis Burke, Coord
TYPE OF AGENCY: Rape crisis center; Counseling/mental health services; Child sexual abuse services; Child sexual abuse prevention program
AREAS SERVED: Itasca
YEARS IN OPERATION: 1
ACCESSIBILITY: Wheelchair accessible
CLIENTS/SERVICES: Sexual assault survivors; Marital rape/sexual abuse survivors; Child victims of sexual abuse; Adult survivors of child sexual abuse; Incest victims/survivors; Prevention program; Community education; Offender treatment program; Adolescent survivors of sexual abuse; Male survivors of sexual abuse

HOPKINS

HOPKINS PROJECT, INC
PO Box 272, Hopkins, MN 55343
Crisis hotline: **(612) 933-7422 24 hrs**
Information: (612) 933-7433 24 hrs
Contact: Sandra Hyne, Dir
TYPE OF AGENCY: Domestic violence program
AREAS SERVED: Hennepin
YEARS IN OPERATION: 10
ACCESSIBILITY: Telecommunications for the hearing impaired (TTY, TDY, etc.); Signers for the hearing impaired by request
CASES SEXUAL ASSAULT/ABUSE (%): 10
CLIENTS/SERVICES: Marital rape/sexual abuse survivors

LAKE ELMO

FAMILY VIOLENCE NETWORK
PO Box 854, Lake Elmo, MN 55042
Crisis hotline: **(612) 770-0777 24 hrs**
Information: (612) 770-8544 9am-5pm
Contact: Therese Habisch-Ahlin, Child Advocate
TYPE OF AGENCY: Domestic violence program; Adolescent program
AREAS SERVED: Washington, Eastern Ramsey
YEARS IN OPERATION: 5
LANGUAGES: Spanish
ACCESSIBILITY: Wheelchair accessible; Telecommunications for the hearing impaired (TTY, TDY, etc.)
DESCRIPTION: Provides crisis line, temporary housing, information and referral for battered women and their children; Group therapy for batterers, rapists, child sexual abuse/incest offenders
CLIENTS/SERVICES: Sexual assault survivors; Marital rape/sexual abuse survivors; Child victims of sexual abuse; Adult survivors of child sexual abuse; Incest victims/survivors; Prevention program; Community education; Offender treatment program; Adolescent survivors of sexual abuse

SPECIAL PROGRAMS/SERVICES: ACEPT (Alternative Coping Experiences for Parents and Teens) a program directed at adolescent offenders, who have committed some violent act, and their parents

LITTLE FALLS

MORRISON COUNTY SEXUAL ASSAULT PROGRAM
Rte 5, Box 257, Little Falls, MN 56345
Crisis hotline: **(612) 632-4878**
Information: (612) 632-6647
Contact: Tamara J Feige, Prog Coord
TYPE OF AGENCY: Rape crisis center
AREAS SERVED: Morrison, Todd
YEARS IN OPERATION: 2½
ACCESSIBILITY: Wheelchair accessible; Telecommunications for the hearing impaired (TTY, TDY, etc.)
CASES SEXUAL ASSAULT/ABUSE (%): 100
DESCRIPTION: Provides crisis intervention, support groups, escort services, for survivors of sexual assault/domestic violence; Prevention programs, including feminist martial arts/self-defense
CLIENTS/SERVICES: Sexual assault survivors; Marital rape/sexual abuse survivors; Child victims of sexual abuse; Adult survivors of child sexual abuse; Incest victims/survivors; Prevention program; Community education; Adolescent survivors of sexual abuse; Male survivors of sexual abuse

LUVERNE

SOUTHWESTERN MENTAL HEALTH CENTER
2 Round Wind Rd, Luverne, MN 56156
Crisis hotline: **(800) 642-1525 24 hrs**
Information: (507) 283-9511 8am-5pm (Mon-Fri)
Contact: Vicky Henderson, Mental Health Practitioner
TYPE OF AGENCY: Counseling/mental health services
AREAS SERVED: Cottonwood, Pipestone, Nobles, Rock
YEARS IN OPERATION: 28
ACCESSIBILITY: Wheelchair accessible
CASES SEXUAL ASSAULT/ABUSE (%): 10-15
CLIENTS/SERVICES: Sexual assault survivors; Marital rape/sexual abuse survivors; Child victims of sexual abuse; Adult survivors of child sexual abuse; Incest victims/survivors; Prevention program; Community education; Adolescent survivors of sexual abuse; Male survivors of sexual abuse

MANKATO

SEXUAL ASSAULT SERVICES
410 S 5th St, Mankato, MN 56001
Crisis hotline: **(507) 625-9034 24 hrs**
Information: (507) 625-3031 8am-5pm (Mon-Fri)
TYPE OF AGENCY: Rape crisis center; Child sexual abuse prevention program
SPONSORING ORGANIZATION: Blue Earth County Human Services
AREAS SERVED: Blue Earth
YEARS IN OPERATION: 10
LANGUAGES: Spanish, Southeast Asian translators available
ACCESSIBILITY: Wheelchair accessible; Telecommunications for the hearing impaired (TTY, TDY, etc.); Signers for the hearing impaired
CASES SEXUAL ASSAULT/ABUSE (%): 98
DESCRIPTION: Provides crisis intervention, advocacy, counseling, information and referral services for survivors of sexual assault and their significant others. Prevention programs, including feminist martial arts/self-defense
CLIENTS/SERVICES: Sexual assault survivors; Marital rape/sexual abuse survivors; Child victims of sexual abuse; Adult survivors of child sexual abuse; Incest victims/survivors; Preven-

SEXUAL ASSAULT SERVICES (continued)

tion program; Community education; Adolescent survivors of sexual abuse; Male survivors of sexual abuse
SPECIAL PROGRAMS/SERVICES: Jointly sponsors and supervises a satellite sexual assault services office on the local college campus. Art and play therapy for adult survivors of sexual assault and child sexual abuse

WOMEN'S CENTER
Box 107, Mankato State University, Mankato, MN 56002
Information: (507) 389-6146 7:30am-4:30pm
Contact: Neala Schleuning, Women's Ctr Dir; B J Tesch, Grad Asst
TYPE OF AGENCY: College/university-based services; Child abuse prevention program; Acquaintance/date rape prevention program
SPONSORING ORGANIZATION: Mankato State University
YEARS IN OPERATION: 10
ACCESSIBILITY: Wheelchair accessible
CLIENTS/SERVICES: Sexual assault survivors; Marital rape/sexual abuse survivors; Adult survivors of child sexual abuse; Incest victims/survivors; Community education
SPECIAL PROGRAMS/SERVICES: In-dorm workshops conducted to inform students about sexual assault, type of behavior to lower risk of assault, and awareness of what sexual assault is

MARSHALL

SOUTHWEST MINNESOTA SEXUAL ASSAULT PROGRAM
PO Box 51, Marshall, MN 56258
Crisis hotline: **(507) 532-5764 24 hrs**
Information: (507) 532-5764 9am-5pm
Contact: Gwenn Johnson, Prog Dir
TYPE OF AGENCY: Rape crisis center
AREAS SERVED: Lyon, Redwood
YEARS IN OPERATION: 8
ACCESSIBILITY: Wheelchair accessible
CASES SEXUAL ASSAULT/ABUSE (%): 100
CLIENTS/SERVICES: Sexual assault survivors; Marital rape/sexual abuse survivors; Child victims of sexual abuse; Adult survivors of child sexual abuse; Incest victims/survivors; Prevention program; Community education; Adolescent survivors of sexual abuse; Male survivors of sexual abuse

MINNEAPOLIS

ARTS FOR LIVING
2810 W 42nd St, Minneapolis, MN 55410
Information: (612) 929-2927, 890-5888 9am-5pm
Contact: Elleva Joy McDonald, Music/Movement Psychotherapist
TYPE OF AGENCY: Private practice
YEARS IN OPERATION: 9
ACCESSIBILITY: Wheelchair accessible
CASES SEXUAL ASSAULT/ABUSE (%): 50
DESCRIPTION: Helps people process their feelings, especially the terror, shame, helplessness, anger, and unworthiness associated with sexual abuse. Helps them develop a sense of their freedom, power, and spiritual integrity to replace these feelings
CLIENTS/SERVICES: Sexual assault survivors; Marital rape/sexual abuse survivors; Adult survivors of child sexual abuse; Incest victims/survivors; Adolescent survivors of sexual abuse; Male survivors of sexual abuse; Healing
SPECIAL PROGRAMS/SERVICES: Guided imagery and music psychotherapy in conjunction with hands-on body work

BIHA WOMEN IN ACTION
122 W Franklin Ave, Ste 306, Minneapolis, MN 55411
Information: (612) 870-1193 9am-5pm
Contact: Alice O Lynch, Exec Dir
TYPE OF AGENCY: Domestic violence program; Information and referral
AREAS SERVED: Statewide
YEARS IN OPERATION: 5
ACCESSIBILITY: Wheelchair accessible; Signers for the hearing impaired
CASES SEXUAL ASSAULT/ABUSE (%): 25
DESCRIPTION: Program serving women of color throughout Minnesota by providing education, information, services and workshops on family violence
CLIENTS/SERVICES: Prevention program; Community education; Ethnic minorities; Publications/media
SPECIAL PROGRAMS/SERVICES: Developed three videos for black, Indian, and Hispanic communities on family violence

CHRYSALIS FAMILY AND CHILD TREATMENT PROGRAM/CHRYSALIS MENTAL HEALTH CLINIC
2550 Pillsbury Ave S, Minneapolis, MN 55404
Information: (612) 871-2672 9am-5pm (Mon-Fri)
Contact: Holly Smart, LP-ATR, Sr Therapist
TYPE OF AGENCY: Counseling/mental health services; Child sexual abuse services; Child sexual abuse prevention program
SPONSORING ORGANIZATION: Chrysalis—A Center for Women
AREAS SERVED: Hennepin, Ramsey
YEARS IN OPERATION: 5
CASES SEXUAL ASSAULT/ABUSE (%): 65
DESCRIPTION: Psychotherapy, therapy groups, and support groups in the schools for children, adolescents, parents, and families emphasizing early intervention for child abuse/neglect, a parent's chemical dependency or other family problems. Individual, family and couple therapy focusing on women's concerns; Peer counseling for women; Groups for adult survivors of incest/sexual abuse, adult children of alcoholics, and lesbians; Groups focused on eating disorders, sexuality, co-dependency, and spirituality
CLIENTS/SERVICES: Sexual assault survivors; Marital rape/sexual abuse survivors; Child victims of sexual abuse; Adult survivors of child sexual abuse; Incest victims/survivors; Prevention program; Community education; Adolescent survivors of sexual abuse; Male survivors of sexual abuse; Lesbians; Healing; Publications/media
REQUIREMENTS: Family and child treatment: client must be a child 18 or younger, or a parent. Mental Health Clinic: client must be a woman, or related in some way (spouse, significant other) to a woman client at Chrysalis
SPECIAL PROGRAMS/SERVICES: Creative arts therapies for sexual assault survivors and adult survivors of child sexual abuse (registered art therapist on staff). Slide-lecture on art therapy with sexually abused children

COMMUNITY—UNIVERSITY HEALTH CARE CENTER
2016 16th Ave S, Minneapolis, MN 55404
Information: (612) 627-4774 8:30am-5pm (Mon-Fri)
Contact: Sue Knollenberg, Community Prog Assoc
TYPE OF AGENCY: Hospital/medical center; Counseling/mental health services
AREAS SERVED: Statewide
YEARS IN OPERATION: 3
LANGUAGES: Hmong, Cambodian, Laotian, Vietnamese
DESCRIPTION: Sexual assault program is directed at Southeast Asian refugees. Provides community education, training, counseling, support, and advocacy for sexual assault victims
CLIENTS/SERVICES: Sexual assault survivors; Marital rape/sexual abuse survivors; Child victims of sexual abuse; Adult survivors of child sexual abuse; Incest victims/survivors; Prevention program; Community education; Ethnic minorities
SPECIAL PROGRAMS/SERVICES: Bilingual brochures in four Southeast Asian languages/English (Hmong, Cambodian, Vietnamese, Laotian)

CRIME VICTIM CENTER
822 S 3rd St, Minneapolis, MN 55415
Crisis hotline: **(612) 340-5400 24 hrs**
Information: (612) 340-5400 9am-5pm
Contact: Kathleen Alme, Prog Dir
TYPE OF AGENCY: Victim/witness assistance program
SPONSORING ORGANIZATION: Minnesota Citizens Council on Crime and Justice
AREAS SERVED: Hennepin, Ramsey, Anoka, Scott, Carver, Washington, Dakota
YEARS IN OPERATION: 11
ACCESSIBILITY: Wheelchair accessible
CASES SEXUAL ASSAULT/ABUSE (%): 10
DESCRIPTION: Provides general services for crime victims; Short-term crisis counseling and referrals for sexual assault victims; Feminist martial arts/self-defense program
CLIENTS/SERVICES: Sexual assault survivors; Child victims of sexual abuse; Prevention program; Community education

DIVISION OF INDIAN WORK—SEXUAL ASSAULT PROJECT
3045 Park Ave S, Minneapolis, MN 55407
Crisis hotline: **(612) 827-1795 8am-4:30pm (Mon-Fri)**
Information: (612) 827-1795 8am-4:30pm (Mon-Fri)
Contact: Bonnie Clairmont, Sexual Assault Proj Mgr
TYPE OF AGENCY: Rape crisis center; Counseling/mental health services; Child sexual abuse services; Child sexual abuse prevention program
SPONSORING ORGANIZATION: Greater Minneapolis Council of Churches
AREAS SERVED: Hennepin, Ramsey
YEARS IN OPERATION: 4
ACCESSIBILITY: Wheelchair accessible
CASES SEXUAL ASSAULT/ABUSE (%): 100
CLIENTS/SERVICES: Sexual assault survivors; Marital rape/sexual abuse survivors; Child victims of sexual abuse; Adult survivors of child sexual abuse; Incest victims/survivors; Prevention program; Community education; Adolescent survivors of sexual abuse; Ethnic minorities; Publications/media
SPECIAL PROGRAMS/SERVICES: The "Red Alert Sexual Assault Committee" has three primary objectives: recruit and train more Indian people to do sexual assault work; community education; improve services for rape victims by use of a beeper system for trained people who will be on call during evenings and weekends; In the process of developing an informational, culturally relevant pamphlet on sexual assault within the Indian community and how Indian people are affected by sexual assault; Research project in progress on the issue of incest within Indian families

DOMESTIC ABUSE PROJECT
204 W Franklin, Minneapolis, MN 55404
Information: (612) 874-7063 8:30am-5pm
Contact: Carol Arthur, Exec Dir
TYPE OF AGENCY: Domestic violence program
AREAS SERVED: Hennepin, Dakota
YEARS IN OPERATION: 10
ACCESSIBILITY: Wheelchair accessible
DESCRIPTION: Domestic violence services, including treatment for men who batter
CLIENTS/SERVICES: Marital rape/sexual abuse survivors; Adult survivors of child sexual abuse; Community education

DRIGGS AND ASSOCIATES
2437 Park Ave, Minneapolis, MN 55404
Information: (612) 872-1139 8am-5pm
Contact: John H Driggs, Family and Sexuality Therapist
TYPE OF AGENCY: Private practice
AREAS SERVED: Statewide
YEARS IN OPERATION: 9
CASES SEXUAL ASSAULT/ABUSE (%): 33
DESCRIPTION: Individual, group, and family therapy for victims of sexual abuse; Sexuality therapy
CLIENTS/SERVICES: Sexual assault survivors; Marital rape/sexual abuse survivors; Child victims of sexual abuse; Adult survivors of child sexual abuse; Incest victims/survivors; Adolescent survivors of sexual abuse; Male survivors of sexual abuse

FAMILY AND CHILDREN'S SERVICE
414 S 8th St, Minneapolis, MN 55404
Information: (612) 340-7444 8:15am-4:30pm
Contact: Brier Miller, Family Violence Dept Supv
TYPE OF AGENCY: Counseling/mental health services; Child sexual abuse services
AREAS SERVED: Hennepin, Dakota, Anoka
YEARS IN OPERATION: 109
LANGUAGES: Vietnamese
ACCESSIBILITY: Wheelchair accessible
CASES SEXUAL ASSAULT/ABUSE (%): 25
DESCRIPTION: Provides child sexual assault program for children and their families in cases of nonfamilial child sexual assault
CLIENTS/SERVICES: Sexual assault survivors; Marital rape/sexual abuse survivors; Child victims of sexual abuse; Adult survivors of child sexual abuse; Incest victims/survivors; Prevention program; Community education; Adolescent survivors of sexual abuse; Male survivors of sexual abuse; Lesbians; Prostitutes; Gay men
SPECIAL PROGRAMS/SERVICES: Provides PRIDE program treating teens, women, and men involved in prostitution

ILLUSION THEATER'S PREVENTION PROGRAMS
528 Hennepin Ave, Ste 704, Minneapolis, MN 55403
Information: (612) 339-4944 8:30aam-5pm
Contact: Cordelia Anderson, MA, Prevention Prog Dir
TYPE OF AGENCY: Child sexual abuse prevention program; Theater group; Adolescent program
AREAS SERVED: Statewide and nationwide
YEARS IN OPERATION: 12
ACCESSIBILITY: Wheelchair accessible
DESCRIPTION: Programs to prevent sexual abuse, interpersonal violence and AIDS include educational plays, written materials, videos, and consultation on primary prevention. Touring programs include *Touch* (children), *No Easy Answers* (teens), and *For Adults Only* (adults) on child sexual abuse prevention; *AIDS*, which addresses people's fears and looks at what AIDS teaches about living and humanity; and *Family*, which addresses prevention of interpersonal violence through strengthening the family and includes issues such as: communication, emotional abuse, messages and behaviors learned in our families, men and women's roles, stresses from divorce, chemical dependency, and the feeling of anger vs violent behavior. *Family* includes songs, scenes, slides, and cites alternatives to violence and ideas to strengthen families.
CLIENTS/SERVICES: Prevention program; Community education; Developmentally disabled; Publications/media
REQUIREMENTS: Consultations are free or have a charge, depending upon the length; educational performances and workshops/training sessions have a fee, as do written materials and videotapes. Referrals and information on prevention issues and other programs are provided free of charge
SPECIAL PROGRAMS/SERVICES: Illusion Theater's Licensing Program allows organizations, agencies or theaters to perform the prevention plays *Touch* or *No Easy Answers* in their community. The manual *Showing Promise: Mass Media as a Community Tool for Preventing Sexual Abuse* ($8) describes *Project Abuse* a two-week intensive public service program on child sexual abuse treatment, prosecution, and prevention. WCCO-TV, a CBS affiliate, and Illusion Theater collaborated on the Emmy-award winning program. Several major market stations in collaboration with local agencies have produced their own mass media programming, patterned after *Project Abuse*. Films and videos: *Touch* and *No Easy Answers*. Publications: *No Easy Answers*, sexual abuse curriculum for junior and senior high school students ($29.95); *How to Take the First Steps*, on developing parental and community support ($8.50); *Touch and Sexual Abuse: How to Talk to Your Children*, for parents (50 for $11); *Teaching People with Mental Retardation About Sexual Abuse Prevention* ($4.95); *Building Blocks to Strengthen Families: Developing Skills to Prevent Violence* ($3). (Publications available from Network Publications, 1700 Mission St, Suite 203, Santa Cruz, CA 95061, (408) 429-9822)

INDIAN HEALTH BOARD OF MINNEAPOLIS, INC
1315 E 24th St, Minneapolis, MN 55404
Crisis hotline: **(612) 721-7425 Medical Unit 24 hrs**
Information: (612) 721-3200 Mental Health Unit
Contact: Mike Wilke, L Psychologist, MH Treatment Dir; Margaret Monroe, BSW, Family Violence Coord
TYPE OF AGENCY: Domestic violence program; Counseling/mental health services; Child sexual abuse services
AREAS SERVED: Hennepin
YEARS IN OPERATION: 15
ACCESSIBILITY: Wheelchair accessible
CASES SEXUAL ASSAULT/ABUSE (%): 40
DESCRIPTION: Serves the urban American Indian population. Individual and group therapy for child and adult survivors of physical, psychological, and sexual abuse and treatment for rapists, batterers, and child sexual abuse/incest offenders
CLIENTS/SERVICES: Sexual assault survivors; Marital rape/sexual abuse survivors; Child victims of sexual abuse; Adult survivors of child sexual abuse; Incest victims/survivors; Prevention program; Community education; Offender treatment program; Adolescent survivors of sexual abuse; Male survivors of sexual abuse; Ethnic minorities
REQUIREMENTS: Primarily American Indian

OAK GROVE PSYCHOTHERAPY ASSOCIATES
1111 W 22nd St, Ste 101, Minneapolis, MN 55416
Information: (612) 520-9166 by arrangement
Contact: Beverly Caruso, ACSW, Psychotherapist
TYPE OF AGENCY: Private practice; Acquaintance/date rape prevention program; Interagency network
AREAS SERVED: Hennepin
YEARS IN OPERATION: 2
CASES SEXUAL ASSAULT/ABUSE (%): 75
DESCRIPTION: Provides long- and short-term therapy groups for survivors and their partners, as well as individual therapy for survivors
CLIENTS/SERVICES: Sexual assault survivors; Marital rape/sexual abuse survivors; Adult survivors of child sexual abuse; Incest victims/survivors; Adolescent survivors of sexual abuse
REQUIREMENTS: Adolescents and adults
SPECIAL PROGRAMS/SERVICES: 10-week short-term educational therapy group for incest survivors. 10-week short term educational therapy group for partners of incest survivors. Publication: *Healing: A Handbook for Adult Victims of Child Sexual Abuse* by Beverly Caruso ($12.95)

RAPE AND SEXUAL ASSAULT CENTER
2431 Hennepin S, Minneapolis, MN 55405
Crisis hotline: **(612) 825-4357 24 hrs**
Information: (612) 825-2409 9am-5pm (Mon-Fri)
Contact: Jan Schwartz, Dir
TYPE OF AGENCY: Rape crisis center; Child sexual abuse services; Child sexual abuse prevention program
SPONSORING ORGANIZATION: Neighborhood Involvement Program
AREAS SERVED: Hennepin
YEARS IN OPERATION: 16
ACCESSIBILITY: Wheelchair accessible
CASES SEXUAL ASSAULT/ABUSE (%): 100
DESCRIPTION: Provides comprehensive crisis services, escort services, support groups, counseling, legal advocacy for survivors of sexual assault, 20%-25% of whom are male. Sponsors prevention programs, including feminist martial arts/self-defense. Child sexual abuse treatment program for sexually abused children and non-offending family members. The perpetrator is involved only in the final phase after completing his own primary treatment in another setting. Combination of education and therapy for adult victims of child sexual abuse
CLIENTS/SERVICES: Sexual assault survivors; Marital rape/sexual abuse survivors; Child victims of sexual abuse; Adult survivors of child sexual abuse; Incest victims/survivors; Prevention program; Community education; Adolescent survivors of sexual abuse; Male survivors of sexual abuse
SPECIAL PROGRAMS/SERVICES: Publications: Training manuals on sexual assault/abuse for volunteers/professionals ($12), clergy ($15), parents/teachers about child sexual abuse ($6), and rape crisis center volunteers ($40). Pamphlets on sexual assault for adults ($2) and young adults ($1.50). Curricula for clients: parenting class (versions for normal-functioning and low-functioning adults); self-esteem/safety class (sexual abuse prevention, ages 4-8), sexuality class (victims of sexual abuse), rage and shame class (versions for adult and child survivors of sexual abuse). Game: *Body SAFE Bingo* (ages 6-12). Training videotapes on perpetrators, victimology, crisis intervention, and child sexual abuse I and II. Training audiotapes on family systems, treatment issues pertaining to sexual abuse, and power struggles.

SEXUAL ASSAULT RESOURCE SERVICE
525 Portland Ave, Level 7, Minneapolis, MN 55415
Information: (612) 347-5832 8am-5pm (Mon-Fri); on call 24 hrs
Contact: Linda Ledray, Dir
TYPE OF AGENCY: Rape crisis center; Hospital/medical center; Child sexual abuse services; Training/research
SPONSORING ORGANIZATION: Hennepin County Medical Center
AREAS SERVED: Hennepin, Ramsey, Washington, Dakota
YEARS IN OPERATION: 12
ACCESSIBILITY: Wheelchair accessible; Signers for the hearing impaired
CASES SEXUAL ASSAULT/ABUSE (%): 100
CLIENTS/SERVICES: Sexual assault survivors; Marital rape/sexual abuse survivors; Child victims of sexual abuse; Adult survivors of child sexual abuse; Incest victims/survivors; Community education; Adolescent survivors of sexual abuse; Male survivors of sexual abuse

SEXUAL ASSAULT RESOURCE SERVICE (continued)

REQUIREMENTS: Must be examined at emergency room of a participating hospital; Do not need to report
SPECIAL PROGRAMS/SERVICES: Trained sexual assault nurse clinicians who do the complete evidentiary exam in the emergency room as well as provide crisis counseling and referral; Sexual assault nurse clinician training program (42 CEUS)

SEXUAL VIOLENCE CENTER
1222 W 31st St, Minneapolis, MN 55408
Crisis hotline: **(612) 824-5555 24 hrs**
Information: (612) 824-2864 24 hrs
Contact: Nancy Biele, Exec Dir
TYPE OF AGENCY: Rape crisis center
AREAS SERVED: Hennepin, Carver
ACCESSIBILITY: Wheelchair accessible (Special provision made outside center); Telecommunications for the hearing impaired (TTY, TDY, etc.)
CASES SEXUAL ASSAULT/ABUSE (%): 100
DESCRIPTION: Comprehensive rape crisis services; Sexual harassment support group; Brochure and handbook for victims of sexual exploitation by counselors and therapists
CLIENTS/SERVICES: Sexual assault survivors; Marital rape/sexual abuse survivors; Child victims of sexual abuse; Adult survivors of child sexual abuse; Incest victims/survivors; Prevention program; Community education; Adolescent survivors of sexual abuse; Male survivors of sexual abuse; Sexual harassment; Publications/media
SPECIAL PROGRAMS/SERVICES: The center has been established to facilitate the process of empowerment. Because of the belief about the negative consequences of the imbalance of power in our society, it chooses to operate the organization with a participatory management system which allows for a balance of power for the trinity of its membership bodies (board of dirctors, staff, and volunteers). In this system, no one group of people can make a decision that materially affects another group without consulting and including in that decision making process those who will be affected by that decision. The power as an agency to have an impact on the lives of those victimized by sexual assault and on our society lies in the ability to utilize the strength and creativity of all the members with fairness and respect.

UNIVERSITY OF MINNESOTA, FAMILY PRACTICE DEPARTMENT—PROGRAM IN HUMAN SEXUALITY
2630 University Ave SE, Minneapolis, MN 55414
Information: (612) 627-4360 8am-5pm; Emergencies 24 hrs
Contact: Dr John Kelly, Psychiatrist, Interim Dir
TYPE OF AGENCY: College/university-based services; Hospital/medical center; Counseling/mental health services; Child sexual abuse services; Training/research
SPONSORING ORGANIZATION: University of Minnesota—Department of Family Practice and Community Health
YEARS IN OPERATION: 20
LANGUAGES: Dutch, German
ACCESSIBILITY: Wheelchair accessible
CASES SEXUAL ASSAULT/ABUSE (%): 70
DESCRIPTION: Assessment and treatment of a wide range of sexually-related problems. Individual, couple, family, and group therapy is offered for men, women, adolescents, and children. All services are provided by qualified professionals with specialized training in sex therapy
CLIENTS/SERVICES: Sexual assault survivors; Marital rape/sexual abuse survivors; Child victims of sexual abuse; Adult survivors of child sexual abuse; Incest victims/survivors; Prevention program; Offender treatment program; Adolescent survivors of sexual abuse; Male survivors of sexual abuse
SPECIAL PROGRAMS/SERVICES: Sexual Attitude Reassessment seminars (SAR), 2-day sessions with lectures, media and small-group discussions focusing on sexual issues encountered throughout a person's life. For medical/health care and human services professionals, teachers, lawyers, clergy, students, patients at the Program in Human Sexuality and other interested individuals. Research in sex education and enrichment, sexual dysfunction, sexual identity, sexual abuse, sex offenses, paraphilias, compulsive sexual behavior, and sexual problems related to other physical and mental disorders.

UNIVERSITY OF MINNESOTA—SEXUAL VIOLENCE PROGRAM
101 Eddy Hall, Minneapolis, MN 55455
Crisis hotline: **(612) 626-1300 24 hrs**
Information: (612) 625-6512 8am-4:30pm (Mon-Fri)
Contact: Irene Greene, Dir
TYPE OF AGENCY: Rape crisis center; College/university-based services
SPONSORING ORGANIZATION: University of Minnesota
AREAS SERVED: Hennepin, Ramsey
YEARS IN OPERATION: 2
LANGUAGES: Spanish interpreter available
ACCESSIBILITY: Wheelchair accessible; Telecommunications for the hearing impaired (TTY, TDY, etc.); Signers for the hearing impaired
CASES SEXUAL ASSAULT/ABUSE (%): 99
DESCRIPTION: Provides crisis counseling, advocacy, information, referral, group and individual counseling for adult victims/survivors of sexual assault/exploitation and concerned persons; Education on sexual assault awareness, heterosexism, ageism, racism via workshops and presentations; Political actions such as rallies, victim/survivor speak-out, rape free zone, letter writing
CLIENTS/SERVICES: Sexual assault survivors; Marital rape/sexual abuse survivors; Adult survivors of child sexual abuse; Incest victims/survivors; Prevention program; Community education; Male survivors of sexual abuse; Lesbians; Sexual harassment; Healing
REQUIREMENTS: Services are geared toward the University of Minnesota community
SPECIAL PROGRAMS/SERVICES: Creative visualization, play and art therapy for sexual assault survivors and adult survivors of child sexual abuse. Treatment for women abused by therapists and lesbian battering victims/survivors

UPTOWN MENTAL HEALTH CENTER
2215 Pillsbury Ave, Minneapolis, MN 55404
Information: (612) 871-1111 8:30am-6:30pm
Contact: Mindy Mitnick, Psychologist
TYPE OF AGENCY: Counseling/mental health services
AREAS SERVED: Statewide; Western WI; Northern IA; and the Dakotas
YEARS IN OPERATION: 9
LANGUAGES: Polish
CASES SEXUAL ASSAULT/ABUSE (%): 50-75
DESCRIPTION: Multidisciplinary mental health center providing education and treatment for clients and supervision and consultation for professionals and organizations. Group therapy for female and male survivors. Individual, group and family therapy for rapists, batterers, child sexual abuse/incest offenders, and juvenile sex offenders
CLIENTS/SERVICES: Sexual assault survivors; Marital rape/sexual abuse survivors; Child victims of sexual abuse; Adult survivors of child sexual abuse; Incest victims/survivors; Community education; Offender treatment program; Adolescent survivors of sexual abuse; Male survivors of sexual abuse

WALK-IN COUNSELING CENTER
2421 Chicago Ave S, Minneapolis, MN 55404
Information: (612) 870-0565 9am-5pm (Mon-Fri); 7pm-9pm
Contact: Jeanette Milgram, Consultation/Training Dir
TYPE OF AGENCY: Counseling/mental health services; Information and referral
AREAS SERVED: Hennepin and surrounding areas
YEARS IN OPERATION: 19
ACCESSIBILITY: Wheelchair accessible
CASES SEXUAL ASSAULT/ABUSE (%): 5
DESCRIPTION: Provides easily accessible, short-term counseling and referral without fees
CLIENTS/SERVICES: Sexual assault survivors; Adult survivors of child sexual abuse; Adolescent survivors of sexual abuse; Male survivors of sexual abuse; Sexual harassment
SPECIAL PROGRAMS/SERVICES: Has been, for 14 years, working with the problem of sexual exploitation by psychotherapists and counselors, including clergy, and offers advocacy and some counseling for victims, as well as some assessment of perpetrators, and organizational consultation around this problem. Publication: *Psychotherapist's Sexual Involvement with Clients: Intervention and Prevention* (1988)

WASHBURN CHILD GUIDANCE CENTER
2430 Nicollet Ave S, Minneapolis, MN 55404
Information: (612) 871-1454 8am-8pm (Mon-Wed); 8am-6pm (Thu); 8am-5pm (Fri)
Contact: Dana Fox, PhD, Prog Dir
TYPE OF AGENCY: Counseling/mental health services
AREAS SERVED: Primarily Hennepin
YEARS IN OPERATION: 36
ACCESSIBILITY: Wheelchair accessible
CASES SEXUAL ASSAULT/ABUSE (%): 10-20
DESCRIPTION: Multi-service counseling agency providing family and individual counseling for children and evaluation/assessment of abuse
CLIENTS/SERVICES: Child victims of sexual abuse; Community education; Adolescent survivors of sexual abuse
REQUIREMENTS: Children ages 0-14

WO/MEN'S RENEWAL
2804 Fremont Ave S, Minneapolis, MN 55408
Information: (612) 470-0269, 872-0099 9am-5pm
Contact: Cathy Montgomery, Psychologist
TYPE OF AGENCY: Private practice; Retreat center; Adult survivors services
AREAS SERVED: Statewide
YEARS IN OPERATION: 5
ACCESSIBILITY: Wheelchair accessible
CASES SEXUAL ASSAULT/ABUSE (%): 25-30
DESCRIPTION: Provides a safe environment for individuals to explore their personal emotional issues at a deeper level. Process facilitators are skilled at working with participants who need a safe place to access repressed feelings and memories. Many participants are working with past and present abuse issues
CLIENTS/SERVICES: Sexual assault survivors; Marital rape/sexual abuse survivors; Adult survivors of child sexual abuse; Incest victims/survivors; Male survivors of sexual abuse; Healing
SPECIAL PROGRAMS/SERVICES: Weekend and longer intensive group experiences for women only and for men and women. Wo/Men's Renewal intensives provide an experience in process living. The limiting influence of addictive systems on lives and relationships is explored through the ancient art of storytelling by sharing memories, feelings, and visions of world. The emphasis is upon becoming whole persons as the intellectual, emotional, physical, and spiritual aspects of selves are recognized and nourished during the time together. All intensives are held in country settings with access to the quiet and beauty of nature as well as to a variety of outdoor recreational activities

MINNETONKA

FAMILY THERAPY AND RECOVERY CENTER
1809 Plymouth Rd S, Ste 220, Minnetonka, MN 55343
Information: (612) 545-4494 24 hrs 7 days (answering service)
Contact: Bette Hansen, Prog Dir
TYPE OF AGENCY: Counseling/mental health services; Private practice
AREAS SERVED: Hennepin, Wright, Scott, Ramsey
YEARS IN OPERATION: 4
ACCESSIBILITY: Wheelchair accessible
CASES SEXUAL ASSAULT/ABUSE (%): 25
CLIENTS/SERVICES: Sexual assault survivors; Marital rape/sexual abuse survivors; Child victims of sexual abuse; Adult survivors of child sexual abuse; Incest victims/survivors
REQUIREMENTS: No age requirement; Clients are encouraged to file charges

MORRIS

MORRIS CAMPUS WOMEN'S RESOURCE CENTER
PO Box 696, University of Minnesota, Morris, MN 56267
Information: (612) 589-2211 8:30am-4:30pm
Contact: Janelle Whittingham, MCWC Dir
TYPE OF AGENCY: College/university-based services
SPONSORING ORGANIZATION: University of Minnesota-Morris
AREAS SERVED: Stevens
YEARS IN OPERATION: 20
CASES SEXUAL ASSAULT/ABUSE (%): 20
DESCRIPTION: Provides one-on-one counseling, as well as support groups for victims of sexual assault and incest
CLIENTS/SERVICES: Sexual assault survivors; Child victims of sexual abuse; Adult survivors of child sexual abuse; Incest victims/survivors; Community education; Adolescent survivors of sexual abuse

NORTHFIELD

NORTHFIELD VICTIM SUPPORT PROGRAM
PO Box 171, Northfield, MN 55057
Crisis hotline: **(507) 645-5555 24 hrs daily**
Information: (507) 645-9407
Contact: Deanna Olson, Coord
TYPE OF AGENCY: Counseling/mental health services; Telephone crisis hotline; Information and referral
AREAS SERVED: Rice, Goodhue, Dakota
YEARS IN OPERATION: 10
LANGUAGES: Sign
ACCESSIBILITY: Wheelchair accessible; Signers for the hearing impaired
CASES SEXUAL ASSAULT/ABUSE (%): 10
CLIENTS/SERVICES: Sexual assault survivors; Marital rape/sexual abuse survivors; Child victims of sexual abuse; Adult survivors of child sexual abuse; Incest victims/survivors

OAKDALE

SEXUAL ASSAULT SERVICES
7066 Stillwater Blvd, Oakdale, MN 55119
Crisis hotline: **(612) 777-1117 24 hrs daily**
Information: (612) 777-5222 7:30am-9pm (Mon-Thu); 7:30am-5pm (Fri); 8am-2pm (Sat)
Contact: Karen Hogendorf, Coord
TYPE OF AGENCY: Rape crisis center; Child sexual abuse services; Child sexual abuse prevention program
SPONSORING ORGANIZATION: Human Services, Inc Washington County
AREAS SERVED: Washington
YEARS IN OPERATION: 9
ACCESSIBILITY: Wheelchair accessible
CASES SEXUAL ASSAULT/ABUSE (%): 100
DESCRIPTION: Provides 24-hour telephone crisis services, short-term counseling, support groups, and advocacy with service providers for survivors of sexual assault and their families; Treatment for rapists, child sexual abuse/incest offenders, and batterers
CLIENTS/SERVICES: Sexual assault survivors; Marital rape/sexual abuse survivors; Child victims of sexual abuse; Adult survivors of child sexual abuse; Incest victims/survivors; Prevention program; Community education; Offender treatment program; Adolescent survivors of sexual abuse; Male survivors of sexual abuse

OWATONNA

EXCHANGE CLUB CENTER FOR THE PREVENTION OF CHILD ABUSE OF SOUTHERN MINNESOTA, INC
285 18th St SE, Owatonna, MN 55060
Information: (507) 455-1190, (800) 642-0089 8am-5pm; answering machine after hrs
Contact: Patricia Kniefel, Dir
TYPE OF AGENCY: Child sexual abuse services; Child sexual abuse prevention program; Child abuse services; Child abuse prevention program
AREAS SERVED: Steele, Waseca, Dodge
YEARS IN OPERATION: 5
CLIENTS/SERVICES: Child victims of sexual abuse; Adult survivors of child sexual abuse; Prevention program; Community education
REQUIREMENTS: Families in which abuse has already occurred or families deemed "at risk" of abuse. The family must have at least one child 12 years old or younger to qualify
SPECIAL PROGRAMS/SERVICES: Weekly radio show (5-7 min) offering positive parenting tips to listening audience. 2nd grade sexual abuse prevention education program. Volunteer family aides assist families by providing positive role model, emotional support, and training in parenting skills

SOUTH CENTRAL HUMAN RELATIONS CENTER
215 S Oak, Owatonna, MN 55060
Crisis hotline: **(507) 451-1951 24 hrs**
Information: (507) 451-2630 8am-8pm
Contact: Mark Skrien, Clinical Dir
TYPE OF AGENCY: Counseling/mental health services; Child sexual abuse services
AREAS SERVED: Steele, Waseca, Dodge
YEARS IN OPERATION: 25
ACCESSIBILITY: Wheelchair accessible; Signers for the hearing impaired
CASES SEXUAL ASSAULT/ABUSE (%): 10
DESCRIPTION: Offers a family sexual abuse treatment program serving adult and adolescent perpetrators, victims, spouses and siblings (individual, group, couple and family therapy and support groups)
CLIENTS/SERVICES: Child victims of sexual abuse; Adult survivors of child sexual abuse; Incest victims/survivors; Offender treatment program; Adolescent survivors of sexual abuse
REQUIREMENTS: Perpetrators must be charged; Families must participate

TASK FORCE FOR BATTERED WOMEN AND SEXUAL ASSAULT VICTIMS
PO Box 524, Owatonna, MN 55060
Crisis hotline: **(507) 451-9100 24 hrs**
Information: (507) 451-1897 8am-5pm (Mon-Fri)
Contact: Jackie Ostlund, Exec Dir
TYPE OF AGENCY: Rape crisis center; Domestic violence program
SPONSORING ORGANIZATION: CONTACT
AREAS SERVED: Steele
YEARS IN OPERATION: 8
CASES SEXUAL ASSAULT/ABUSE (%): 40
CLIENTS/SERVICES: Sexual assault survivors; Marital rape/sexual abuse survivors; Adult survivors of child sexual abuse; Incest victims/survivors; Community education
REQUIREMENTS: Must be over the age of 18

PARK RAPIDS

BATTERED WOMEN'S SERVICES OF HUBBARD COUNTY
PO Box 564, Park Rapids, MN 56470
Crisis hotline: **(218) 732-5035 24 hrs daily**
Information: (218) 732-7413 24 hrs daily
Contact: Audrey Husom, Coord
TYPE OF AGENCY: Domestic violence program
AREAS SERVED: Hubbard, Cass, Becker, Waseca
YEARS IN OPERATION: 11
ACCESSIBILITY: Wheelchair accessible; Telecommunications for the hearing impaired (TTY, TDY, etc.)
CASES SEXUAL ASSAULT/ABUSE (%): 50
CLIENTS/SERVICES: Marital rape/sexual abuse survivors; Adult survivors of child sexual abuse; Community education; Adolescent survivors of sexual abuse

PARK RAPIDS—WALKER CLINIC COUNSELING DEPARTMENT
201 E 1st St, Park Rapids, MN 56470
Information: (218) 732-7266 8:30am-5pm
Contact: Gail Anderson, Licensed Psychologist
TYPE OF AGENCY: Hospital/medical center; Private practice
AREAS SERVED: Hubbard, Wadena, Becker, Beltrami
ACCESSIBILITY: Wheelchair accessible
CASES SEXUAL ASSAULT/ABUSE (%): 80
DESCRIPTION: Individual therapy for survivors and for juvenile/adolescent offenders
CLIENTS/SERVICES: Sexual assault survivors; Marital rape/sexual abuse survivors; Child victims of sexual abuse; Adult survivors of child sexual abuse; Incest victims/survivors; Offender treatment program; Adolescent survivors of sexual abuse; Male survivors of sexual abuse; Ritualistic abuse victims/survivors; Healing
SPECIAL PROGRAMS/SERVICES: Works with persons who experience "ego states," "alters," or other forms of dissociation resulting from sexual victimization. The orientation is feminist so that respect for the survivor is the highest value. Experienced in working with victims of Satanic cult sexual victimization. Healing through hypnosis; rituals; play therapy for any age (art, sand, puppets, etc)

ROCHESTER

RAPELINE/SEXUAL ASSAULT PROGRAM
515 2nd St SW, Rochester, MN 55902
Crisis hotline: **(507) 289-0636 24 hrs daily**
Information: (507) 285-8242 8am-5pm (Mon-Fri)
Contact: Debra Anderson, Victim Svcs Coord
TYPE OF AGENCY: Rape crisis center
SPONSORING ORGANIZATION: Community Corrections
AREAS SERVED: Dodge, Olmsted, Fillmore
YEARS IN OPERATION: 12
ACCESSIBILITY: Wheelchair accessible
CASES SEXUAL ASSAULT/ABUSE (%): 95
DESCRIPTION: Provides crisis intervention, escort services, advocacy, and support groups for survivors of sexual abuse and sexual assault; Feminist martial arts/self-defense
CLIENTS/SERVICES: Sexual assault survivors; Marital rape/sexual abuse survivors; Child victims of sexual abuse; Adult survivors of child sexual abuse; Incest victims/survivors; Prevention program; Community education; Adolescent survivors of sexual abuse; Male survivors of sexual abuse; Sexual harassment; Publications/media
SPECIAL PROGRAMS/SERVICES: Program brochures in Vietnamese, Laotian and Hmong languages. Various brochures on child sexual abuse and prevention, parents' guide for talking to children about sexual assault, sexual assault against men, sexual exploitation by

RAPELINE/SEXUAL ASSAULT PROGRAM *(continued)*
therapists, and victim rights. Training manual: *A Teacher's Response to Sexual Abuse*

WOMEN'S SHELTER, INC
PO Box 117, Rochester, MN 55903
Crisis hotline: **(507) 285-1010 24 hrs**
Information: (507) 285-1010 24 hrs
TYPE OF AGENCY: Domestic violence program; Adolescent program
AREAS SERVED: Olmsted, Dodge, Fillmore, Steele, Wabasha, Rice, Mower, Freeborn, Winona, Goodhue, Houston
YEARS IN OPERATION: 10
LANGUAGES: Interpreters available
ACCESSIBILITY: Wheelchair accessible; Telecommunications for the hearing impaired (TTY, TDY, etc.); Signers for the hearing impaired
CASES SEXUAL ASSAULT/ABUSE (%): 40
DESCRIPTION: Provision of safe housing, advocacy, support for battered women and their children; Support groups; Transition housing in separate facility. Many sexual assault survivors also need safe housing
CLIENTS/SERVICES: Sexual assault survivors; Marital rape/sexual abuse survivors; Adult survivors of child sexual abuse; Community education; Publications/media
SPECIAL PROGRAMS/SERVICES: *Breaking Through*, a slide tape on dating violence

ROSEVILLE

UNIVERSITY OF MINNESOTA DEPARTMENT OF SOCIOLOGY
1116 Summer St, Roseville, MN 55113
Information: (612) 631-9409, 489-2430 hrs vary, messages taken
Contact: Lance C Egley
TYPE OF AGENCY: University; Training/research
DESCRIPTION: Research on wife abuse and treatment of wife abuse offenders, including marital rape and marital rape offender treatment. Additional research interests include male survivors of sexual assault/abuse and incest offenders
CLIENTS/SERVICES: Marital rape/sexual abuse survivors; Offender treatment program; Adolescent survivors of sexual abuse; Male survivors of sexual abuse
REQUIREMENTS: Counseling services not offered through department of sociology, only research and consultation
SPECIAL PROGRAMS/SERVICES: Consultation: process of batterer's treatment, stages of change for batterers, interface with legal system, structure of treatment programs

SAINT CLOUD

CENTRAL MINNESOTA SEXUAL ASSAULT CENTER
601½ Mall Germain, Saint Cloud, MN 56301
Crisis hotline: **(612) 251-4357 24 hrs**
Information: (612) 251-4357 9am-5pm
Contact: Denise M Fuller, Exec Dir
TYPE OF AGENCY: Rape crisis center
AREAS SERVED: Benton, Sherburne, Stearns, Mille Lacs, Wright
YEARS IN OPERATION: 11
LANGUAGES: Spanish
ACCESSIBILITY: Signers for the hearing impaired
CASES SEXUAL ASSAULT/ABUSE (%): 100
DESCRIPTION: Provides 24-hour crisis intervention, escort services, and support for sexual abuse survivors. Support groups for female adolescents, male adolescents and women
CLIENTS/SERVICES: Sexual assault survivors; Marital rape/sexual abuse survivors; Child victims of sexual abuse; Adult survivors of child sexual abuse; Incest victims/survivors; Prevention program; Community education; Adolescent survivors of sexual abuse; Male survivors of sexual abuse; Sexual harassment
SPECIAL PROGRAMS/SERVICES: Brochure on sexual exploitation by counselors and therapists

WOMAN HOUSE
Box 195, Saint Cloud, MN 56302
Crisis hotline: **(612) 252-1603 24 hrs**
Information: (612) 253-6900 24 hrs
Contact: Maxine Barnett-Cermele, Dir
TYPE OF AGENCY: Domestic violence program
AREAS SERVED: Benton, Sherburne, Wright, Chisago, Stearns, Isanti, Pine, Mille Lacs, Kennebec
YEARS IN OPERATION: 10
ACCESSIBILITY: Telecommunications for the hearing impaired (TTY, TDY, etc.)
CASES SEXUAL ASSAULT/ABUSE (%): 10-15
DESCRIPTION: Provides shelter for battered women and their children, many of whom have experienced sexual abuse/assault. Group therapy for batterers
CLIENTS/SERVICES: Marital rape/sexual abuse survivors; Adult survivors of child sexual abuse; Prevention program; Community education

SAINT PAUL

CASA DE ESPERANZA
PO Box 74177, Saint Paul, MN 55175
Crisis hotline: **(612) 772-1611 24 hrs daily**
Information: (612) 772-1723 8:30am-5pm
Contact: Pamela Zeller, Exec Dir
TYPE OF AGENCY: Domestic violence program
AREAS SERVED: Ramsey, Hennepin
YEARS IN OPERATION: 6
LANGUAGES: Spanish, Southeast Asian translator services available
ACCESSIBILITY: Telecommunications for the hearing impaired (TTY, TDY, etc.)
CASES SEXUAL ASSAULT/ABUSE (%): 42
CLIENTS/SERVICES: Sexual assault survivors; Marital rape/sexual abuse survivors; Child victims of sexual abuse; Adult survivors of child sexual abuse; Incest victims/survivors; Community education; Adolescent survivors of sexual abuse; Healing

FACE TO FACE HEALTH AND COUNSELING
642 E 7th St, Saint Paul, MN 55106
Information: (612) 772-2539 9am-5pm
Contact: Steve Dopson, MH Prog Dir
TYPE OF AGENCY: Counseling/mental health services; Youth program; Adolescent survivors services
YEARS IN OPERATION: 17
ACCESSIBILITY: Wheelchair accessible
CLIENTS/SERVICES: Sexual assault survivors; Incest victims/survivors; Community education; Adolescent survivors of sexual abuse
REQUIREMENTS: Ages 11-23

FAMILY SERVICES OF GREATER ST PAUL
333 On Sibley St, Ste 500, Saint Paul, MN 55101
Information: (612) 222-0311 8:30am-9pm
Contact: Tim McGuire, Family Counseling Prog Dir
TYPE OF AGENCY: Domestic violence program; Counseling/mental health services; Child sexual abuse services
AREAS SERVED: Ramsey, Dakota, Washington
YEARS IN OPERATION: 92
LANGUAGES: Spanish
ACCESSIBILITY: Wheelchair accessible; Signers for the hearing impaired
CASES SEXUAL ASSAULT/ABUSE (%): 10
DESCRIPTION: Multi-service organization providing counseling services for low-income families; includes a family violence program with individual and family therapy in cases of sexual abuse. The family violence program includes a women's group for women who have been abused, a men's group for batterers, a children's group, and a chapter of Parents Anonymous
CLIENTS/SERVICES: Sexual assault survivors; Marital rape/sexual abuse survivors; Child victims of sexual abuse; Adult survivors of child sexual abuse; Incest victims/survivors

META RESOURCES
Baker Ct 440, 821 Raymond Ave, Saint Paul, MN 55114
Information: (612) 642-9317 24 hrs
Contact: Noel R Larson, PhD, Lic Consult Psychologist
TYPE OF AGENCY: Private practice
YEARS IN OPERATION: 8
ACCESSIBILITY: Wheelchair accessible; Telecommunications for the hearing impaired (TTY, TDY, etc.) (by arrangement); Signers for the hearing impaired (by arrangement)
CASES SEXUAL ASSAULT/ABUSE (%): 30-40
DESCRIPTION: Family and individual therapy for survivors and child sexual abuse/incest offenders
CLIENTS/SERVICES: Sexual assault survivors; Marital rape/sexual abuse survivors; Child victims of sexual abuse; Adult survivors of child sexual abuse; Incest victims/survivors; Offender treatment program; Adolescent survivors of sexual abuse; Male survivors of sexual abuse; Healing
SPECIAL PROGRAMS/SERVICES: Uses a strategic team behind a one-way window for work with difficult families. Works with the whole ecosystem in this way, having the team work with the "system of helpers" sometimes including the foster parents, child protection workers, therapists, lawyers, etc. Also provides wilderness therapy for adult survivors

MIDWAY HOSPITAL CENTER FOR DOMESTIC ABUSE
425 Aldine St, Saint Paul, MN 55104
Crisis hotline: **(612) 641-5584 8am-4:30pm**
Information: (612) 641-5584 8am-4:30pm
Contact: Tom Cytron-Hysom, Dir
TYPE OF AGENCY: Domestic violence program; Child sexual abuse services; Child sexual abuse prevention program
SPONSORING ORGANIZATION: Health East
AREAS SERVED: Ramsey, Washington, Hennepin, Dakota, Anoka
YEARS IN OPERATION: 5
LANGUAGES: Spanish
ACCESSIBILITY: Signers for the hearing impaired (by arrangement)
CASES SEXUAL ASSAULT/ABUSE (%): 20-40
DESCRIPTION: Therapy and advocacy for child sexual abuse victims (especially ages 3-12); Therapy group for adult women incest survivors; Battered women's groups also deal with sexual abuse
CLIENTS/SERVICES: Marital rape/sexual abuse survivors; Child victims of sexual abuse; Adult survivors of child sexual abuse; Incest victims/survivors; Prevention program; Community education; Adolescent survivors of sexual abuse; Male survivors of sexual abuse; Ethnic minorities
SPECIAL PROGRAMS/SERVICES: "Strong and Free": dating violence prevention program for low income, primarily Hispanic and black adolescents in a school setting; "Climb and Grow": a 2-day, outdoor program for 8-12 year olds to help prevent family violence, suicide, drug abuse—a mini-outward bound for children

RAMSEY COUNTY ATTORNEY'S OFFICE—VICTIM/WITNESS ASSISTANCE UNIT
350 St Peter St, Saint Paul, MN 55102
Information: (612) 292-7566 8am-4:30pm
Contact: Mary Biermaier, Dir
TYPE OF AGENCY: Victim/witness assistance program
AREAS SERVED: Ramsey
ACCESSIBILITY: Wheelchair accessible; Signers for the hearing impaired

RAMSEY COUNTY ATTORNEY'S OFFICE—VICTIM/WITNESS ASSISTANCE UNIT (continued)
CLIENTS/SERVICES: Sexual assault survivors; Marital rape/sexual abuse survivors; Child victims of sexual abuse; Incest victims/survivors
REQUIREMENTS: Must be a felony level case charged by the County Attorney's Office

RAMSEY COUNTY COURT—DOMESTIC ABUSE OFFICE
15 W Kellogg, Rm 821, Saint Paul, MN 55102
Information: (612) 292-6680 8am-4:30pm
Contact: Nancy Libman, Supv
TYPE OF AGENCY: Domestic violence program; Legal services agency
AREAS SERVED: Ramsey
YEARS IN OPERATION: 6
LANGUAGES: Interpreters available
ACCESSIBILITY: Telecommunications for the hearing impaired (TTY, TDY, etc.); Signers for the hearing impaired
CASES SEXUAL ASSAULT/ABUSE (%): 10
DESCRIPTION: Interviews clients seeking orders for protection due to domestic violence against adults or children (including sexual assault). Orders for protection are court orders removing the abuser from the home
CLIENTS/SERVICES: Marital rape/sexual abuse survivors; Child victims of sexual abuse; Adult survivors of child sexual abuse; Incest victims/survivors; Community education; Adolescent survivors of sexual abuse; Male survivors of sexual abuse

SEXUAL OFFENSE SERVICES OF RAMSEY COUNTY (SOS)
1619 Dayton Ave, Saint Paul, MN 55104
Crisis hotline: **(612) 298-5898 24 hrs**
Information: (612) 298-5898
TYPE OF AGENCY: Rape crisis center
AREAS SERVED: Ramsey
YEARS IN OPERATION: 12
LANGUAGES: Coordination with Spanish and Southeast Asian program
ACCESSIBILITY: Wheelchair accessible; Signers for the hearing impaired (by arrangement)
CASES SEXUAL ASSAULT/ABUSE (%): 100
DESCRIPTION: Provides direct services for survivors through crisis intervention, escort services, counseling, support groups, and advocacy. Also feminist martial arts/self-defense program
CLIENTS/SERVICES: Sexual assault survivors; Marital rape/sexual abuse survivors; Child victims of sexual abuse; Adult survivors of child sexual abuse; Incest victims/survivors; Prevention program; Community education; Adolescent survivors of sexual abuse; Male survivors of sexual abuse

WILDER COMMUNITY ASSISTANCE PROGRAM
666 Marshall Ave, Saint Paul, MN 55104
Information: (612) 221-0048 8am-5pm
Contact: Mike McGrane, Domestic Abuse Prog Dir
TYPE OF AGENCY: Domestic violence program; Counseling/mental health services
AREAS SERVED: Ramsey, Dakota, Washington, Anoka
YEARS IN OPERATION: 7
ACCESSIBILITY: Wheelchair accessible
DESCRIPTION: Provides individual and group counseling for women who are abused, men who abuse, adolescent victims and perpetrators, and children's groups; Counseling around sexual assault/child sexual abuse as they arise and referrals to appropriate agencies
CLIENTS/SERVICES: Marital rape/sexual abuse survivors; Child victims of sexual abuse

WOMEN OF NATIONS
PO Box 4637, Saint Paul, MN 55104
Crisis hotline: **(612) 292-9487 24 hrs**
Information: (612) 292-9358 8:30am-5pm
TYPE OF AGENCY: Domestic violence program
AREAS SERVED: Ramsey, Hennepin, Anoka, Dakota
YEARS IN OPERATION: 6
ACCESSIBILITY: Wheelchair accessible
DESCRIPTION: Provides supportive services for battered American Indian women and their children. Many battered women receiving services have been sexually assaulted and some of their children molested. Advocates are trained in sexual assault issues for women and children
CLIENTS/SERVICES: Sexual assault survivors; Marital rape/sexual abuse survivors; Child victims of sexual abuse; Adult survivors of child sexual abuse; Incest victims/survivors; Community education; Ethnic minorities
SPECIAL PROGRAMS/SERVICES: "Turning Point" provides legal advocacy for battered American Indian women; Volunteer advocates networking creates advocacy for battered Indian women in both St Paul and Minneapolis 24 hours a day

WOMEN'S ADVOCATES
584-588 Grand Ave, Saint Paul, MN 55102
Crisis hotline: **(612) 227-8284 24 hrs**
Information: (612) 227-9966 9am-5pm
Contact: Lisbeth Wolf, Dir
TYPE OF AGENCY: Domestic violence program
YEARS IN OPERATION: 14
ACCESSIBILITY: Wheelchair accessible; Telecommunications for the hearing impaired (TTY, TDY, etc.)
CASES SEXUAL ASSAULT/ABUSE (%): 45
CLIENTS/SERVICES: Sexual assault survivors; Marital rape/sexual abuse survivors; Child victims of sexual abuse; Adult survivors of child sexual abuse; Incest victims/survivors; Community education

SAINT PETER

INTENSIVE TREATMENT PROGRAM FOR SEXUAL AGGRESSIVES
100 Freeman Dr, Saint Peter, MN 56082
Crisis hotline: **(507) 931-7149 24 hrs**
Information: (507) 931-7150 24 hrs
Contact: Richard K Seely, ITPSA Dir
TYPE OF AGENCY: Hospital/medical center; Residential treatment facility; Offender treatment
SPONSORING ORGANIZATION: Minnesota Security Hospital
AREAS SERVED: Statewide
YEARS IN OPERATION: 14
LANGUAGES: Interpreters available
ACCESSIBILITY: Wheelchair accessible; Telecommunications for the hearing impaired (TTY, TDY, etc.); Signers for the hearing impaired
CASES SEXUAL ASSAULT/ABUSE (%): 100
DESCRIPTION: Treatment for rapists and child sexual abuse/incest offenders who are adjudicated and in need of inpatient care
CLIENTS/SERVICES: Offender treatment program; Deaf/hearing impaired; Disabled
SPECIAL PROGRAMS/SERVICES: Training in human sexuality utilizing the Sexual Attitude Reassessment format. Evaluation services for deaf sexual offenders. Evaluation and treatment opportunities for handicapped offenders. Treatment includes small group therapy; bibliotherapy and writing assignements; human relations class, including topics of human sexuality, sex role sterotyping and communication skills and specialized sexual attitude reassessment seminar for sexually aggressive perpetrators and staff working with sexual assaults

SHAKOPEE

SEXUAL ASSAULT PROGRAM FOR SCOTT COUNTY
325 W 5th Ave, Shakopee, MN 55379
Crisis hotline: **(612) 445-CARE 24 hrs**
Information: (612) 445-2322, ext 296 10am-5pm (Tue, Wed, Thu); secretary answering 8am-4:30pm (Mon-Fri)
Contact: Susan Clark Harris, Prog Coord
TYPE OF AGENCY: Rape crisis center
SPONSORING ORGANIZATION: St Francis Regional Medical Center
AREAS SERVED: Scott, LeSueur upon request
YEARS IN OPERATION: 2
LANGUAGES: Spanish
ACCESSIBILITY: Wheelchair accessible
CASES SEXUAL ASSAULT/ABUSE (%): 100
DESCRIPTION: Crisis intervention; Advocacy; Support in seeking medical, police, and legal services; Community referrals
CLIENTS/SERVICES: Sexual assault survivors; Marital rape/sexual abuse survivors; Child victims of sexual abuse; Adult survivors of child sexual abuse; Incest victims/survivors; Prevention program; Community education; Adolescent survivors of sexual abuse; Male survivors of sexual abuse

SOUTH SAINT PAUL

SOUTH SUBURBAN FAMILY SERVICE
633 S Concord St, South Saint Paul, MN 55075
Information: (612) 451-1434 8:30am-5pm; evenings by appointment
Contact: Harvey Bartz, Exec Dir
TYPE OF AGENCY: Domestic violence program; Counseling/mental health services
AREAS SERVED: Dakota, Washington
YEARS IN OPERATION: 70
LANGUAGES: Spanish
ACCESSIBILITY: Wheelchair accessible
CASES SEXUAL ASSAULT/ABUSE (%): 10
DESCRIPTION: Individual, family, and group counseling; Separate support groups for women in abusive relationships and for batterers; Couples group for those who have individually completed an abuse program
CLIENTS/SERVICES: Sexual assault survivors; Marital rape/sexual abuse survivors; Prevention program; Community education; Offender treatment program; Male survivors of sexual abuse
REQUIREMENTS: Sliding scale fees

VIRGINIA

SEXUAL ASSAULT PROGRAM OF NORTH SAINT LOUIS COUNTY
335 ½ Chestnut St, Virginia, MN 55792
Crisis hotline: **(800) 232-1300 4:30pm-Midnight, weekends**
Information: (218) 749-4725 8:30am-4:30pm
Contact: Kim Riordan, Dir
TYPE OF AGENCY: Rape crisis center; Child sexual abuse services; Child sexual abuse prevention program
AREAS SERVED: North St Louis
YEARS IN OPERATION: 10
CASES SEXUAL ASSAULT/ABUSE (%): 100
CLIENTS/SERVICES: Sexual assault survivors; Marital rape/sexual abuse survivors; Child victims of sexual abuse; Adult survivors of child sexual abuse; Incest victims/survivors; Prevention program; Community education; Adolescent survivors of sexual abuse; Male survivors of sexual abuse
SPECIAL PROGRAMS/SERVICES: Support play groups are for families in which sexual abuse has occurred, including sexually abused children (male and female), siblings in incestuous families, and children of adult survivors of sexual abuse. Children explore concepts such as: what makes a family, empathy, trust, loss, conflict, self-esteem, communication and

SEXUAL ASSAULT PROGRAM OF NORTH SAINT LOUIS COUNTY *(continued)*

awareness of feelings. Discussion topics are centered around activities and play. Parents meet separately to explore parenting issues

WILLMAR

SEXUAL ASSAULT SERVICES PROGRAM/ SHELTER HOUSE
PO Box 787, Willmar, MN 56201
Crisis hotline: **(612) 235-4613, (800) 992-1716 24 hrs**
Information: (612) 235-4613, (800) 992-1716 24 hrs
Contact: Joan Hancock, Asst Coord; Autumn Cole, Unit Dir
TYPE OF AGENCY: Counseling/mental health services; Child sexual abuse services; Child sexual abuse prevention program; Adolescent program
SPONSORING ORGANIZATION: West Central Community Services Center, Inc
AREAS SERVED: Kandiyohi, Meeker, Renville, Swift, Lac Qui Parle, Chippewa, and adjacent areas
YEARS IN OPERATION: 10
LANGUAGES: Spanish
ACCESSIBILITY: Wheelchair accessible; Telecommunications for the hearing impaired (TTY, TDY, etc.); Signers for the hearing impaired
CASES SEXUAL ASSAULT/ABUSE (%): 100
DESCRIPTION: Provides support groups and counseling for victims of sexual assault and child sexual abuse including young male victims, developmentally disabled, and adult survivors. 2 outpatient treatment programs are Family Sexual Abuse Treatment Program and Adolescent Program for Positive Sexual Adjustment. Outreach to Hispanic and Native American communities. Also provides domestic violence shelter. Treatment for rapists, child sexual abuse/incest offenders, and batterers
CLIENTS/SERVICES: Sexual assault survivors; Marital rape/sexual abuse survivors; Child victims of sexual abuse; Adult survivors of child sexual abuse; Incest victims/survivors; Prevention program; Community education; Offender treatment program; Male survivors of sexual abuse; Developmentally disabled; Ethnic minorities
REQUIREMENTS: Sliding scale fee available for participants within the 6-county treatment area
SPECIAL PROGRAMS/SERVICES: Use of hypnosis for adult survivors

WINONA

WOMEN'S RESOURCE CENTER
51 E 4th St, 9 Exchange Bldg, Winona, MN 55987
Crisis hotline: **(507) 452-4440 24 hrs**
Information: (507) 452-4440 9am-5pm
Contact: Constance Hoveland-Belden, Dir
TYPE OF AGENCY: Rape crisis center; Domestic violence program; Child sexual abuse prevention program; Women's center
AREAS SERVED: Winona
YEARS IN OPERATION: 10
LANGUAGES: Interpretrs available
ACCESSIBILITY: Wheelchair accessible
CASES SEXUAL ASSAULT/ABUSE (%): 35
DESCRIPTION: Programs include Sexual Assault Crisis Aid and the Battered Women's Task Force; Crisis intervention and counseling for survivors of sexual assault and domstic violnce; Batterers group available
CLIENTS/SERVICES: Sexual assault survivors; Marital rape/sexual abuse survivors; Child victims of sexual abuse; Adult survivors of child sexual abuse; Incest victims/survivors; Prevention program; Community education; Adolescent survivors of sexual abuse; Male survivors of sexual abuse

WORTHINGTON

NEW WOMEN AGAINST VIOLENCE (WAV)
PO Box 834, Worthington, MN 56187
Crisis hotline: **(800) 642-1525, (507) 376-7671 24 hrs daily**
Information: (507) 376-4311 9am-12pm, 1pm-4pm
Contact: Kathleen Douglas, Coord/Advocate; Carol Wylie, Admis/Advocate
TYPE OF AGENCY: Rape crisis center; Domestic violence program; Child sexual abuse prevention program
AREAS SERVED: Nobles, Rock, Cottonwood, Jackson, Pipestone
YEARS IN OPERATION: 4
LANGUAGES: Spanish and Laotian translators available
ACCESSIBILITY: Wheelchair accessible
CASES SEXUAL ASSAULT/ABUSE (%): 26
CLIENTS/SERVICES: Sexual assault survivors; Marital rape/sexual abuse survivors; Child victims of sexual abuse; Adult survivors of child sexual abuse; Incest victims/survivors; Prevention program; Community education

MISSISSIPPI

BILOXI

GULF COAST WOMEN'S CENTER
PO Box 333, Biloxi, MS 39564
Crisis hotline: **(601) 435-1968 24 hrs**
Information: (601) 436-3809 8am-5pm
Contact: Jane Philo, Exec Dir
TYPE OF AGENCY: Rape crisis center; Domestic violence program
AREAS SERVED: Stone, Pearl River, Hancock, Harrison, Jackson, George
YEARS IN OPERATION: 12
CLIENTS/SERVICES: Sexual assault survivors; Marital rape/sexual abuse survivors; Adult survivors of child sexual abuse; Incest victims/survivors; Prevention program; Community education; Adolescent survivors of sexual abuse; Male survivors of sexual abuse

COLUMBUS

SAFE HAVEN, INC
PO Box 5354, Columbus, MS 39704
Crisis hotline: **(601) 328-0200 24 hrs 7 days**
Information: (601) 328-6118 8am-5pm
Contact: Carolyne D Park, Dir
TYPE OF AGENCY: Domestic violence program
AREAS SERVED: Lowndes, Clay, Oktibbeha, Monroe, Webster, Calhoun, Choctaw, Attala, Montgomery, 3 Alabama counties
YEARS IN OPERATION: 5
CLIENTS/SERVICES: Sexual assault survivors; Marital rape/sexual abuse survivors; Child victims of sexual abuse; Adult survivors of child sexual abuse; Incest victims/survivors; Adolescent survivors of sexual abuse; Male survivors of sexual abuse
REQUIREMENTS: Not equipped to serve mentally retarded, handicapped, or emotionally disturbed individuals

GREENVILLE

RAPE CRISIS COUNSELING OF GREENVILLE
PO Box 426, 4th Circuit Court District, Greenville, MS 38702-0426
Information: (615) 378-2105 8:30am-5pm
Contact: Roxanne Lee, Rape Crisis Prog Coord
TYPE OF AGENCY: Rape crisis center
SPONSORING ORGANIZATION: District Attorney/Victim Witness Program
AREAS SERVED: Washington
CASES SEXUAL ASSAULT/ABUSE (%): 100
CLIENTS/SERVICES: Sexual assault survivors; Child victims of sexual abuse; Adult survivors of child sexual abuse; Prevention program; Community education; Male survivors of sexual abuse

HATTIESBURG

SEXUAL ASSAULT CRISIS CENTER, INC
Southern Station, Box 10016, Hattiesburg, MS 39406
Crisis hotline: **(601) 264-7777 24 hrs**
Information: (601) 264-7078 8am-5pm (Mon-Fri)
Contact: LaNell Lucius, Admin Co-Dir; Angela Watkins, Counseling Co-Dir
TYPE OF AGENCY: Rape crisis center; Child sexual abuse services
AREAS SERVED: Forrest, Lamar, Jones, Perry, Wayne, Greene, Jasper, Jeff Davis, Marion, Covington, Smith
YEARS IN OPERATION: 5
ACCESSIBILITY: Wheelchair accessible; Signers for the hearing impaired
CASES SEXUAL ASSAULT/ABUSE (%): 100
CLIENTS/SERVICES: Sexual assault survivors; Marital rape/sexual abuse survivors; Child victims of sexual abuse; Adult survivors of child sexual abuse; Incest victims/survivors; Prevention program; Community education

JACKSON

CHILD AND FAMILY ASSOCIATES
5740 County Cork Rd, Jackson, MS 39206
Information: (601) 956-7647 8:30am-5pm
Contact: Brenda Chance, Lic Clinical Soc Wkr
TYPE OF AGENCY: Child sexual abuse services; Private practice
YEARS IN OPERATION: 4½
ACCESSIBILITY: Wheelchair accessible
CASES SEXUAL ASSAULT/ABUSE (%): 70
DESCRIPTION: Individual, group, and family psychotherapy for survivors and offenders (rapists, child sexual abuse/incest offenders, and batterers)
CLIENTS/SERVICES: Child victims of sexual abuse; Adult survivors of child sexual abuse; Incest victims/survivors; Prevention program; Community education; Offender treatment program; Adolescent survivors of sexual abuse; Male survivors of sexual abuse
REQUIREMENTS: Primarily court-ordered therapy for sexual offenders

DOMESTIC VIOLENCE SERVICES CENTER
PO Box 2248, Jackson, MS 39225-2248
Information: (601) 352-3300 9am-5pm
Contact: Priscilla Pearson, Clinical Coord
TYPE OF AGENCY: Domestic violence program; Rape prevention program
SPONSORING ORGANIZATION: Catholic Charities, Inc
AREAS SERVED: Statewide
YEARS IN OPERATION: 3
ACCESSIBILITY: Wheelchair accessible
CASES SEXUAL ASSAULT/ABUSE (%): 50
DESCRIPTION: As an adjunct to helping battered families, a therapist is available to help sexually abused children and adolescents. Most victims are court-ordered and referrals come mainly from the welfare department. Also provides treatment for rapists, child sexual abuse/incest offenders and batterers
CLIENTS/SERVICES: Sexual assault survivors; Marital rape/sexual abuse survivors; Child victims of sexual abuse; Adult survivors of child sexual abuse; Incest victims/survivors; Community education; Offender treatment program; Adolescent survivors of sexual abuse; Male survivors of sexual abuse

EXCHANGE CLUB—PARENT/CHILD CENTER
2906 N State St, Ste 105, Jackson, MS 39216
Information: (601) 366-0025
Contact: Becky Williams, Dir
TYPE OF AGENCY: Child sexual abuse services; Child sexual abuse prevention program; Child abuse services; Child abuse prevention program
DESCRIPTION: Prevention and treatment program for child abuse, including child sexual abuse. Provides therapy for victims/survivors, including adolescent male victims. Serves as state chapter of the National Committee for Prevention of Child Abuse
CLIENTS/SERVICES: Child victims of sexual abuse; Adult survivors of child sexual abuse; Incest victims/survivors; Prevention program; Community education; Adolescent survivors of sexual abuse; Male survivors of sexual abuse

JACKSON RAPE CRISIS CENTER
PO Box 2248, Jackson, MS 39225-2248
Crisis hotline: **(601) 982-RAPE 24 hrs**
Information: (601) 355-5520 8:30am-5pm (Mon-Fri)
Contact: Maxine S Lyles, Dir
TYPE OF AGENCY: Rape crisis center; Domestic violence program; Rape prevention program
SPONSORING ORGANIZATION: Catholic Charities, Inc
AREAS SERVED: Hinds, Madison, Rankin
YEARS IN OPERATION: 4½
LANGUAGES: Spanish
ACCESSIBILITY: Wheelchair accessible
CASES SEXUAL ASSAULT/ABUSE (%): 100
CLIENTS/SERVICES: Sexual assault survivors; Marital rape/sexual abuse survivors; Adult survivors of child sexual abuse; Incest victims/survivors; Prevention program; Community education; Adolescent survivors of sexual abuse; Male survivors of sexual abuse
REQUIREMENTS: Adolescents and adult survivors
SPECIAL PROGRAMS/SERVICES: "For Men Only," designed to heighten the sensitivity of men to rape and sexual assault

TUPELO

SAFE, INC SEXUAL ASSAULT PROGRAM
PO Box 985, Tupelo, MS 38802
Crisis hotline: **(800) 527-7233, (601) 841-2273 24 hrs**
Information: (601) 841-9139 24 hrs
Contact: Debbie Messner, Exec Dir
TYPE OF AGENCY: Rape crisis center; Child sexual abuse services; Child sexual abuse prevention program
AREAS SERVED: Alcorn, Itawamba, Lee, Pontotoc, Prentiss, Tishomingo, Monroe
YEARS IN OPERATION: 9
ACCESSIBILITY: Wheelchair accessible
CASES SEXUAL ASSAULT/ABUSE (%): 100
CLIENTS/SERVICES: Sexual assault survivors; Child victims of sexual abuse; Adult survivors of child sexual abuse; Incest victims/survivors; Prevention program; Community education

VICKSBURG

EXCHANGE CLUB OF VICKSBURG—CHILD ABUSE PREVENTION CENTER, INC (CAP)
PO Box 1887, Vicksburg, MS 39180
Crisis hotline: **(601) 634-0557 24 hrs**
Information: (601) 634-0557 24 hrs
Contact: Sharon Hansen, Dir
TYPE OF AGENCY: Child sexual abuse prevention program; Child abuse services; Child abuse prevention program; Interagency network
AREAS SERVED: Warren
YEARS IN OPERATION: 4
ACCESSIBILITY: Wheelchair accessible
CASES SEXUAL ASSAULT/ABUSE (%): 5
DESCRIPTION: Uses volunteer parent aides for abusive families or those at high risk of abuse. Many "high-risk" or abusive parents were physically/sexually abused as children. Parent education, crisis intervention, countywide multidisciplinary child abuse/neglect review team
CLIENTS/SERVICES: Child victims of sexual abuse; Adult survivors of child sexual abuse; Prevention program; Community education

RAPE CRISIS AND SEXUAL ASSAULT SERVICES
PO Box 8056, Vicksburg, MS 39181
Information: (601) 636-4613
TYPE OF AGENCY: Rape crisis center; Counseling/mental health services
SPONSORING ORGANIZATION: Mental Health Association of Warren County
AREAS SERVED: Warren
CASES SEXUAL ASSAULT/ABUSE (%): 100
CLIENTS/SERVICES: Sexual assault survivors; Marital rape/sexual abuse survivors; Child victims of sexual abuse; Adult survivors of child sexual abuse; Incest victims/survivors; Community education

WARREN YAZOO MENTAL HEALTH SERVICE
PO Box 1418, 1315 Adams St, Vicksburg, MS 39180
Crisis hotline: **(601) 638-0031 24 hrs**
Information: (601) 638-0031 8am-5pm
Contact: Don Brown, Dir
TYPE OF AGENCY: Counseling/mental health services
AREAS SERVED: Warren, Yazoo
ACCESSIBILITY: Wheelchair accessible
CLIENTS/SERVICES: Sexual assault survivors; Marital rape/sexual abuse survivors; Child victims of sexual abuse; Adult survivors of child sexual abuse; Incest victims/survivors; Prevention program; Community education; Offender treatment program
REQUIREMENTS: Sliding scale fee

MISSOURI

CHILLICOTHE

THE SURVIVORS
1500 W 3rd St, Chillicothe, MO 64601
Contact: Kathy Jennings, Staff Sponsor
TYPE OF AGENCY: Domestic violence program; Correctional facility; Self-help group
DESCRIPTION: Self-help group for battered women incarcerated at the Chillicothe Correctional Center. In process of developing a support group dealing specifically with sexual abuse.
CLIENTS/SERVICES: Marital rape/sexual abuse survivors; Prisoners

CLAYTON

VICTIM SERVICE COUNCIL
7900 Carondelet Ave, 4th Floor, Clayton, MO 63105
Information: (314) 889-3075 8:30am-4:30pm (Mon-Fri)
Contact: Rhea Oelbaunl, Exec Dir; Marcia Levin, Casewkr
TYPE OF AGENCY: Victim/witness assistance program
SPONSORING ORGANIZATION: St Louis Section, National Council of Jewish Women
AREAS SERVED: St Louis County
YEARS IN OPERATION: 10
ACCESSIBILITY: Wheelchair accessible
CASES SEXUAL ASSAULT/ABUSE (%): 10
CLIENTS/SERVICES: Sexual assault survivors; Marital rape/sexual abuse survivors; Child victims of sexual abuse; Incest victims/survivors; Community education

COLUMBIA

WOMEN'S CENTER
University of Missouri, 229 Brady Commons, Columbia, MO 65211
Information: (314) 882-6621 8:30am-5pm (Mon-Fri)
TYPE OF AGENCY: College/university-based services
YEARS IN OPERATION: 11
ACCESSIBILITY: Wheelchair accessible
CLIENTS/SERVICES: Sexual assault survivors; Marital rape/sexual abuse survivors; Adult survivors of child sexual abuse; Incest victims/survivors; Prevention program

FULTON

SERVE, INC—WATCH HOUSE
2 St Louis Ave, Fulton, MO 65251
Crisis hotline: **(314) 642-3383 24 hrs**
Information: (314) 642-6388 8am-5pm
Contact: Vicki L Buss, Prog Dir
TYPE OF AGENCY: Domestic violence program; Residential treatment facility; Counseling/mental health services
AREAS SERVED: Callaway
YEARS IN OPERATION: 16
DESCRIPTION: Temporary shelter for domestic violence survivors; Residential treatment for chemically dependent women
CLIENTS/SERVICES: Sexual assault survivors; Community education; Adolescent survivors of sexual abuse; Male survivors of sexual abuse

INDEPENDENCE

HEART OF AMERICA FAMILY SERVICES
12401 E 43rd St, Ste 107, Independence, MO 64050
Crisis hotline: **(816) 753-5280 9am-5pm (Mon-Fri)**
Information: (816) 373-7577 9am-5pm (Mon-Fri)
Contact: John Vogt, ACSW, LSCSW, Area Mgr/Clinical Soc Wkr
TYPE OF AGENCY: Counseling/mental health services
AREAS SERVED: Jackson
YEARS IN OPERATION: 40
ACCESSIBILITY: Wheelchair accessible
CASES SEXUAL ASSAULT/ABUSE (%): 5
DESCRIPTION: Provides counseling services for families and individuals who are experiencing life cycle problems, such as marital conflict, alcohol and drug abuse, divorce, emotional problems, violence, and child abuse
CLIENTS/SERVICES: Sexual assault survivors; Marital rape/sexual abuse survivors; Child victims of sexual abuse; Adult survivors of child sexual abuse; Incest victims/survivors; Community education; Adolescent survivors of sexual abuse; Male survivors of sexual abuse

JEFFERSON CITY

JEFFERSON CITY RAPE AND ABUSE CRISIS SERVICE
PO Box 416, Jefferson City, MO 65102
Crisis hotline: **(314) 634-4911 24 hrs daily**
Information: (314) 634-8346 24 hrs daily
Contact: Cheri A Joyce, Exec Dir
TYPE OF AGENCY: Rape crisis center; Domestic violence program
AREAS SERVED: Cole, Callaway, Osage, Moniteau, Miller, Camden, South Boone
YEARS IN OPERATION: 8
ACCESSIBILITY: Wheelchair accessible
CASES SEXUAL ASSAULT/ABUSE (%): 10
CLIENTS/SERVICES: Sexual assault survivors; Marital rape/sexual abuse survivors; Child victims of sexual abuse; Adult survivors of child sexual abuse; Incest victims/survivors; Community education; Adolescent survivors of sexual abuse; Male survivors of sexual abuse

JOPLIN

BARBARA CARTER, MS, PSYCHOLOGIST
740 Illinois, Joplin, MO 64801
Information: (417) 781-4552 (Answering machine)
Contact: Barbara Carter, Psychologist
TYPE OF AGENCY: Private practice
AREAS SERVED: Southwest MO, southeast KS, northeast OK
YEARS IN OPERATION: 10
CASES SEXUAL ASSAULT/ABUSE (%): 85
DESCRIPTION: Individual, family and group therapy for survivors and court mandated counseling for rapists, child sexual abuse offenders, and incest offenders
CLIENTS/SERVICES: Child victims of sexual abuse; Incest victims/survivors; Community education; Offender treatment program; Adolescent survivors of sexual abuse; Male survivors of sexual abuse
REQUIREMENTS: Clients must be at least 21 years old or have parental consent; Charges need not be filed; Offenders must admit crime

JASPER COUNTY PROSECUTOR'S OFFICE—VICTIM SERVICES
6th and Pearl, Joplin, MO 64801
Information: (417) 625-4314 8:30am-5pm
Contact: Dick Godsey, Victim Svc Officer
TYPE OF AGENCY: Victim/witness assistance program
AREAS SERVED: Jasper
YEARS IN OPERATION: 3
CASES SEXUAL ASSAULT/ABUSE (%): 10
CLIENTS/SERVICES: Sexual assault survivors; Child victims of sexual abuse

LAFAYETTE HOUSE
PO Box 1185, Joplin, MO 64802
Crisis hotline: **(417) 782-1772 24 hrs daily**
Information: (417) 782-1772 8am-5pm (Mon-Fri)
Contact: Barbara Carter, Client Svcs Dir
TYPE OF AGENCY: Rape crisis center; Domestic violence program; Residential treatment facility; Counseling/mental health services
AREAS SERVED: Mainly Southwest Missouri but will accept any Missouri resident
YEARS IN OPERATION: 10
CASES SEXUAL ASSAULT/ABUSE (%): 60
DESCRIPTION: Services for domestic violence and sexual assault survivors and for chemically dependent women
CLIENTS/SERVICES: Sexual assault survivors; Marital rape/sexual abuse survivors; Child victims of sexual abuse; Adult survivors of child sexual abuse; Incest victims/survivors; Prevention program; Community education; Adolescent survivors of sexual abuse; Male survivors of sexual abuse

KANSAS CITY

ROSE BROOKS CENTER
PO Box 27067, Kansas City, MO 64110
Crisis hotline: **(816) 861-6100 24 hrs**
Information: (816) 861-3460 8am-5:30pm
Contact: Katherine Parker, Women's Svcs Coord
TYPE OF AGENCY: Domestic violence program
AREAS SERVED: Jackson, Clay, Platte, Johnson, Wyandotte, Ray, Cass
YEARS IN OPERATION: 10
ACCESSIBILITY: Wheelchair accessible
CASES SEXUAL ASSAULT/ABUSE (%): 75
CLIENTS/SERVICES: Sexual assault survivors; Marital rape/sexual abuse survivors; Child victims of sexual abuse; Adult survivors of child sexual abuse; Incest victims/survivors; Prevention program; Community education; Adolescent survivors of sexual abuse

THE CHILDREN'S PLACE
2 E 59th St, Kansas City, MO 64112
Information: (816) 363-1898 8am-5pm (Mon, Tue, Fri); 8am-8pm (Wed, Thu); 8am-1pm (Sat)
Contact: Lynn Peck, Treatment Dir
TYPE OF AGENCY: Counseling/mental health services; Child sexual abuse services
SPONSORING ORGANIZATION: Child Abuse Services Center, Inc
AREAS SERVED: Jackson, Clay, Platte
YEARS IN OPERATION: 10
ACCESSIBILITY: Wheelchair accessible
CASES SEXUAL ASSAULT/ABUSE (%): 60
DESCRIPTION: Serves preschool population in day treatment, extended outpatient services and screenings. Expertise in dealing with young sexually abused children
CLIENTS/SERVICES: Child victims of sexual abuse; Adult survivors of child sexual abuse; Community education; Preschoolers
REQUIREMENTS: Children between the ages of 6 weeks to 6 years

HEART OF AMERICA FAMILY SERVICES
3217 Broadway, Kansas City, MO 64111
Information: (816) 753-5280
Contact: Don L Schempp, Counseling and Treatment Dir
TYPE OF AGENCY: Counseling/mental health services
AREAS SERVED: Platte, Clay, Jackson, MO; Johnson, Wyandotte, KS
YEARS IN OPERATION: 125
LANGUAGES: Spanish
ACCESSIBILITY: Wheelchair accessible
CASES SEXUAL ASSAULT/ABUSE (%): 22
DESCRIPTION: Professional counseling for families and individuals who are experiencing life cycle problems: individual and group therapy for sexually abused children and their families, adolescent and adult survivors of sexual assault/abuse, individual therapy for child sexual abuse/incest offenders and batterers
CLIENTS/SERVICES: Sexual assault survivors; Marital rape/sexual abuse survivors; Child victims of sexual abuse; Adult survivors of child sexual abuse; Incest victims/survivors; Community education; Offender treatment program; Adolescent survivors of sexual abuse; Male survivors of sexual abuse
REQUIREMENTS: Sliding scale fee
SPECIAL PROGRAMS/SERVICES: Provides a homebased treatment program for abusive and neglectful families, involving masters-level therapist and volunteers

JACKSON COUNTY PROSECUTOR'S OFFICE—SEX CRIMES UNIT—VICTIM/WITNESS ASSISTANCE
415 E 12th St, 7-M, Kansas City, MO 64106
Information: (816) 881-3555, 881-3521 8:30am-5pm
Contact: Stacy A Whitworth, Victim/Witness Asst
TYPE OF AGENCY: Victim/witness assistance program
AREAS SERVED: Jackson
YEARS IN OPERATION: 5
LANGUAGES: Interpreters available
ACCESSIBILITY: Wheelchair accessible; Signers for the hearing impaired
CASES SEXUAL ASSAULT/ABUSE (%): 100
CLIENTS/SERVICES: Sexual assault survivors; Child victims of sexual abuse; Male survivors of sexual abuse
REQUIREMENTS: Client must make a police report and charges must be filed.

METROPOLITAN ORGANIZATION TO COUNTER SEXUAL ASSAULT (MOCSA)
3515 Broadway, Ste 301, Kansas City, MO 64111
Crisis hotline: **(816) 531-0233 24 hrs**
Information: (816) 931-4527 8:30am-5pm (Mon-Fri)
Contact: Palle Rilinger, Exec Dir
TYPE OF AGENCY: Rape crisis center; Child sexual abuse services; Child sexual abuse prevention program
AREAS SERVED: Clay, Platte, Jackson, MO; Johnson, Wyandotte, KS
YEARS IN OPERATION: 14
ACCESSIBILITY: Wheelchair accessible
CASES SEXUAL ASSAULT/ABUSE (%): 100
DESCRIPTION: To lessen the ill effects of sexual assault and abuse by treating victims, educating the public in prevention, and improving medical, legal, and psychological treatment of victims through professional training and advocacy; Support groups for female and male survivors available
CLIENTS/SERVICES: Sexual assault survivors; Marital rape/sexual abuse survivors; Child victims of sexual abuse; Adult survivors of child sexual abuse; Incest victims/survivors; Prevention program; Community education; Offender treatment program; Adolescent survivors of sexual abuse; Male survivors of sexual abuse; Publications/media
SPECIAL PROGRAMS/SERVICES: Media program titled *Shattered;* Sponsorship of "An Awareness Day for Adults: The Sexual Abuse/Incest Experience As Seen Through the Eyes of Survivors," a community education speakout

PARENTS UNITED—KANSAS CITY CHAPTER
108 E 117th St, Kansas City, MO 64114
Crisis hotline: **(816) 942-9532 24 hrs**
Information: (816) 942-9532 24 hrs
Contact: William J Norton, PhD, Prof Sponsor
TYPE OF AGENCY: Child sexual abuse services; Child sexual abuse prevention program
SPONSORING ORGANIZATION: Parents United San Jose, California
AREAS SERVED: Jackson
YEARS IN OPERATION: 4
LANGUAGES: Spanish
CASES SEXUAL ASSAULT/ABUSE (%): 100
DESCRIPTION: Support groups for female and male survivors of sexual abuse/assault and their families; Individual and group therapy for rapists, child sexual abuse offenders, incest offenders, and batterers
CLIENTS/SERVICES: Sexual assault survivors; Marital rape/sexual abuse survivors; Child victims of sexual abuse; Adult survivors of child sexual abuse; Incest victims/survivors; Prevention program; Community education; Offender treatment program; Adolescent survivors of sexual abuse; Male survivors of sexual abuse
REQUIREMENTS: Victim and/or family (spouse, siblings, grandparents, perpetrator) must have gone through some sort of legal process and have been referred or advised to seek therapy.

VOICES OF KANSAS CITY
PO Box 30035, Kansas City, MO 64133
TYPE OF AGENCY: Support group; Adult survivors services
AREAS SERVED: Greater Kansas City area
YEARS IN OPERATION: 5
CASES SEXUAL ASSAULT/ABUSE (%): 100
CLIENTS/SERVICES: Adult survivors of child sexual abuse; Incest victims/survivors; Community education
REQUIREMENTS: Adult women incest survivors; Must be 21 or older; Suggests that group members also be in therapy

SAINT CHARLES

BRIDGEWAY COUNSELING SERVICES, INC
114 N Main, Ste 4, Saint Charles, MO 63301
Information: (314) 946-5045, 723-3666 answering service 9am-5pm
Contact: C Lee Richards, Couns
TYPE OF AGENCY: Counseling/mental health services; Substance abuse treatment/counseling
AREAS SERVED: St Charles, St Louis, Warren, Lincoln
YEARS IN OPERATION: 1
CASES SEXUAL ASSAULT/ABUSE (%): 5
DESCRIPTION: Sexual abuse therapy as an adjunct to a drug/alcohol counseling program; Services for sexually abused children and non-offending family members; Parent group, individual and family therapy
CLIENTS/SERVICES: Child victims of sexual abuse; Adult survivors of child sexual abuse; Incest victims/survivors; Adolescent survivors of sexual abuse; Male survivors of sexual abuse
REQUIREMENTS: Sliding scale fee

CATHOLIC FAMILY SERVICE—SAINT CHARLES DISTRICT OFFICE
1360 S 5th St, Rm 396, Saint Charles, MO 63301
Information: (314) 946-6014 9am-5pm; some evenings
Contact: Jo Ann Deiermann, Dist Dir
TYPE OF AGENCY: Counseling/mental health services; Child sexual abuse services
AREAS SERVED: St Charles, Northwest St Louis
YEARS IN OPERATION: 30
ACCESSIBILITY: Wheelchair accessible
CASES SEXUAL ASSAULT/ABUSE (%): 5
CLIENTS/SERVICES: Sexual assault survivors; Marital rape/sexual abuse survivors; Child victims of sexual abuse; Adult survivors of child sexual abuse; Incest victims/survivors; Adolescent survivors of sexual abuse; Male survivors of sexual abuse

THE WOMEN'S CENTER OF BRIDGEWAY COUNSELING SERVICES
125 N 5th St, Saint Charles, MO 63301
Crisis hotline: **(314) 946-3257 24 hrs**
Information: (314) 946-6854 24 hrs
Contact: Pam Moussette, Prog Coord
TYPE OF AGENCY: Domestic violence program; Counseling/mental health services
SPONSORING ORGANIZATION: Bridgeway Counseling Services
AREAS SERVED: St Charles, St Louis, Lincoln, Warren, Franklin
YEARS IN OPERATION: 9
CASES SEXUAL ASSAULT/ABUSE (%): 70
CLIENTS/SERVICES: Sexual assault survivors; Marital rape/sexual abuse survivors; Child victims of sexual abuse; Adult survivors of child sexual abuse; Incest victims/survivors; Prevention program; Community education; Adolescent survivors of sexual abuse

YOUTH IN NEED
320 N 5th St, Saint Charles, MO 63301
Crisis hotline: **(314) 946-3771 24 hrs**
Information: (314) 946-0101 9am-5pm
Contact: James Braun, Exec Dir
TYPE OF AGENCY: Shelter; Adolescent program
AREAS SERVED: St Charles, Franklin, Lincoln, Warren, Pike, and St Louis
YEARS IN OPERATION: 15
DESCRIPTION: Provides crisis intervention and individual, group and family therapy for families. Provides temporary emergency shelter

YOUTH IN NEED (continued)

for adolescents and support groups for sexual abuse survivors
CLIENTS/SERVICES: Sexual assault survivors; Child victims of sexual abuse; Incest victims/survivors; Runaways; Adolescent survivors of sexual abuse; Male survivors of sexual abuse
REQUIREMENTS: Adolescents, ages 10-17 years, and their families; consent of parents or legal guardians

SAINT JOSEPH

FAMILY GUIDANCE CENTER/COMMUNITY MENTAL HEALTH CENTER
910 Edmond, Ste 100, Saint Joseph, MO 64501
Crisis hotline: **(816) 364-2100, (800) 892-5750 24 hrs 7 days**
Information: (816) 364-1502 8am-7pm (Mon-Fri); 8am-5pm (Sat)
Contact: Jean G Brown, MSW, ACSW, Admin
TYPE OF AGENCY: Counseling/mental health services
AREAS SERVED: Andrew, Atchison, Buchanan, Clinton, DeKalb, Gentry, Holt, Nodaway, Worth
YEARS IN OPERATION: 27
ACCESSIBILITY: Wheelchair accessible; Signers for the hearing impaired (by arrangement)
CASES SEXUAL ASSAULT/ABUSE (%): 50
CLIENTS/SERVICES: Sexual assault survivors; Marital rape/sexual abuse survivors; Child victims of sexual abuse; Adult survivors of child sexual abuse; Incest victims/survivors; Prevention program; Community education; Offender treatment program; Adolescent survivors of sexual abuse; Male survivors of sexual abuse; Publications/media
SPECIAL PROGRAMS/SERVICES: Parent-child sex education program series, in which parents and children attend sessions together and discuss sexuality issues. Publication: *Parent-Child Sex Education: A Training Module* ($18.95, 106 pages)

SEXUAL ABUSE PREVENTION PROGRAM
Buchanan County Courthouse, Saint Joseph, MO 64501
Information: (816) 271-1424 8:30am-4:30pm
Contact: Donette Smock, Prog Dir
TYPE OF AGENCY: Child sexual abuse prevention program; Law enforcement agency
SPONSORING ORGANIZATION: Buchanan County Juvenile Office
AREAS SERVED: Buchanan, Andrew, Clinton
YEARS IN OPERATION: 3
DESCRIPTION: Prevention program for children ages 2-8
CLIENTS/SERVICES: Prevention program; Community education

YWCA RAPE CRISIS CENTER
304 N 8th St, Saint Joseph, MO 64501
Crisis hotline: **(816) 232-1225 24 hrs**
Information: (816) 232-4481 8:30am-5pm (Mon-Fri)
Contact: Leona Rivers Jewell, Dir
TYPE OF AGENCY: Rape crisis center; Acquaintance/date rape prevention program
YEARS IN OPERATION: 3
CASES SEXUAL ASSAULT/ABUSE (%): 100
CLIENTS/SERVICES: Sexual assault survivors; Marital rape/sexual abuse survivors; Child victims of sexual abuse; Adult survivors of child sexual abuse; Prevention program; Community education; Adolescent survivors of sexual abuse; Male survivors of sexual abuse
SPECIAL PROGRAMS/SERVICES: Date rape prevention program

SAINT LOUIS

AID FOR VICTIMS OF CRIME
4050 Lindell Blvd, American Red Cross Bldg, 5th Fl, Saint Louis, MO 63108
Crisis hotline: **(314) 652-3623 24 hrs**
Information: (314) 652-9630
Contact: Donna Dowell, Hotline Coord
TYPE OF AGENCY: Victim/witness assistance program
AREAS SERVED: St Louis, St Charles, Jefferson, St Louis City
YEARS IN OPERATION: 16
CLIENTS/SERVICES: Community education

COMPREHENSIVE CLINICAL AND CONSULTING SERVICES
777 S New Ballas Rd, Ste 230 W, Saint Louis, MO 63141
Information: (314) 991-0065 8:30am-10pm (Mon-Thu); 8:30am-6pm (Fri); 9am-1pm (Sat)
Contact: Dr Beth Lipsmeyer, PhD, Psychologist/Pres
TYPE OF AGENCY: Private practice
YEARS IN OPERATION: 2½
ACCESSIBILITY: Wheelchair accessible
CLIENTS/SERVICES: Sexual assault survivors; Marital rape/sexual abuse survivors; Child victims of sexual abuse; Adult survivors of child sexual abuse; Incest victims/survivors; Adolescent survivors of sexual abuse; Male survivors of sexual abuse
REQUIREMENTS: Minors need guardian's consent.

FAMILY AND PERSONAL SUPPORT CENTERS
2650 Olive, Saint Louis, MO 63103
Information: (314) 533-8200 8:30am-4:30pm
Contact: Yvonne Taylor, Inform and 1st appointment Mgr
TYPE OF AGENCY: Counseling/mental health services; Child sexual abuse services
AREAS SERVED: St Louis County and City, Missouri and Illinois counties served by United Way
YEARS IN OPERATION: 128
CASES SEXUAL ASSAULT/ABUSE (%): 50
DESCRIPTION: Provides individual and family counseling, advocacy, and prevention programs; Services for survivors of sexual assault/abuse
CLIENTS/SERVICES: Sexual assault survivors; Marital rape/sexual abuse survivors; Child victims of sexual abuse; Adult survivors of child sexual abuse; Incest victims/survivors; Prevention program; Offender treatment program; Adolescent survivors of sexual abuse; Male survivors of sexual abuse
REQUIREMENTS: For children under 16, parent must be involved. Child abuse must be reported to protective agency, as mandated by law
SPECIAL PROGRAMS/SERVICES: Offers Women Sexually Abused as Children groups which are psychoeducational in nature

FAMILY RESOURCE CENTER
3930 Lindell, Saint Louis, MO 63108
Information: (314) 534-9350 8:30am-5pm (Mon-Fri)
Contact: Jackie Link, MSW, Family Treatment Supv
TYPE OF AGENCY: Child sexual abuse services; Child sexual abuse prevention program
AREAS SERVED: St Louis, St Charles, Jefferson, St Louis City
YEARS IN OPERATION: 13
CASES SEXUAL ASSAULT/ABUSE (%): 40
DESCRIPTION: Home-based and office family therapy; Therapeutic preschool; Treatment program for sexually abused children and their families; Individual and family therapy for incest offenders and batterers
CLIENTS/SERVICES: Sexual assault survivors; Marital rape/sexual abuse survivors; Child victims of sexual abuse; Adult survivors of child sexual abuse; Incest victims/survivors; Prevention program; Community education; Offender treatment program; Adolescent survivors of sexual abuse; Male survivors of sexual abuse; Preschoolers
REQUIREMENTS: Sliding scale fees; Priority is given to children and parents.
SPECIAL PROGRAMS/SERVICES: Therapeutic preschool for children ages 2-5, an intensive day treatment program for children experiencing emotional problems, developmental delays or learning problems. A valuable treatment alternative for the sexually abused and traumatized preschool age child.

HAWTHORN CHILDREN'S PSYCHIATRIC HOSPITAL
5247 Fyler, Saint Louis, MO 63139
Information: (314) 644-8571
Contact: Marla Liberman, Psychologist
TYPE OF AGENCY: Hospital/medical center; Child sexual abuse services; Private practice
SPONSORING ORGANIZATION: Missouri Department of Mental Health
ACCESSIBILITY: Wheelchair accessible
CASES SEXUAL ASSAULT/ABUSE (%): 65
CLIENTS/SERVICES: Child victims of sexual abuse; Adolescent survivors of sexual abuse; Male survivors of sexual abuse

LUTHERAN FAMILY AND CHILDREN SERVICES OF MISSOURI
4625 Lindell Blvd, Ste 501, Saint Louis, MO 63108
Information: (314) 361-2121 8:30am-8:30pm (Mon-Thu); 8:30am-4:30pm (Fri)
Contact: Mara G Berry, Family Life Education Coord
TYPE OF AGENCY: Counseling/mental health services
AREAS SERVED: St Louis, Jefferson
YEARS IN OPERATION: 25
ACCESSIBILITY: Wheelchair accessible
CLIENTS/SERVICES: Child victims of sexual abuse; Adult survivors of child sexual abuse; Community education; Adolescent survivors of sexual abuse; Male survivors of sexual abuse

MAGDALA FOUNDATION
4158 Lindell St, Saint Louis, MO 63108
Information: (314) 652-6004 8am-4:45pm
Contact: Cheryl C Savage, ACSW, Prog Svcs Dir
TYPE OF AGENCY: Counseling/mental health services; Child sexual abuse services; Residential treatment facility; Child abuse services
AREAS SERVED: St Louis City, St Louis County, Jefferson, St Charles
YEARS IN OPERATION: 23
CASES SEXUAL ASSAULT/ABUSE (%): 81
DESCRIPTION: Provides home-based services for sexually abused children and non-offending parents; Works with families in crisis because of other problems, including child physical abuse. Family systems approach, as well as individual and group intervention
CLIENTS/SERVICES: Sexual assault survivors; Marital rape/sexual abuse survivors; Child victims of sexual abuse; Adult survivors of child sexual abuse; Incest victims/survivors; Adolescent survivors of sexual abuse; Male survivors of sexual abuse
REQUIREMENTS: Clients must be referred through the Division of Family Services or pay privately

RAPE PREVENTION SEMINARS, INC
PO Box 31339, Saint Louis, MO 63131
Information: (314) 965-7708 8am-5pm
Contact: Nancy Hightshoe, Principal
TYPE OF AGENCY: Private practice; Rape prevention program; Training/research
AREAS SERVED: St Louis, Jefferson, Franklin, St Charles

RAPE PREVENTION SEMINARS, INC
(continued)

YEARS IN OPERATION: 7
DESCRIPTION: Dedicated to educating and training individuals in the prevention of violent crimes including rape, robbery, and assault; Provides counseling for survivors and their families; Provides training in rape investigation for police officers, military personnel, hospital personnel, rape crisis workers/victim advocates, prosecuting attorneys, etc
CLIENTS/SERVICES: Sexual assault survivors; Marital rape/sexual abuse survivors; Child victims of sexual abuse; Adult survivors of child sexual abuse; Incest victims/survivors; Prevention program; Community education; Adolescent survivors of sexual abuse

RAVEN (RAPE AND VIOLENCE END NOW)
PO Box 24159, Saint Louis, MO 63130
Crisis hotline: **(314) 725-6137 24 hrs**
Information: (314) 725-6137 8am-3pm (Mon-Fri)
Contact: Mark L Robinson, Counseling Coord
TYPE OF AGENCY: Men's program; Male survivors services; Offender treatment
AREAS SERVED: St Louis, Franklin, Jefferson, St Charles, MO; Madison, St Claire, IL
YEARS IN OPERATION: 10
ACCESSIBILITY: Wheelchair accessible
CASES SEXUAL ASSAULT/ABUSE (%): 10
DESCRIPTION: Works with men and adolescent boys to end abuse and help resolve conflicts in intimate relationships. Provides counseling and support groups for male victims/survivors; Classes for men whose partners are survivors of sexual assault/abuse; Treatment for rapists, child sexual abuse/incest offenders, and batterers
CLIENTS/SERVICES: Sexual assault survivors; Child victims of sexual abuse; Adult survivors of child sexual abuse; Incest victims/survivors; Prevention program; Community education; Offender treatment program; Adolescent survivors of sexual abuse; Male survivors of sexual abuse
REQUIREMENTS: Males 13 or older; offenders must admit to abuse and sign a release of information to significant others if a perpetrator. No requirements for survivors
SPECIAL PROGRAMS/SERVICES: Publishes *The Ending Men's Violence National Referral Directory*

ST LOUIS CIRCUIT ATTORNEY'S VICTIM SERVICES
1320 Market St, Rm 221, Saint Louis, MO 63103
Information: (314) 622-4373 9am-5pm (Mon-Thu); 9am-4pm (Fri)
Contact: Julie Swanston, Dir
TYPE OF AGENCY: Victim/witness assistance program
AREAS SERVED: St Louis City
YEARS IN OPERATION: 10
ACCESSIBILITY: Wheelchair accessible; Telecommunications for the hearing impaired (TTY, TDY, etc.); Signers for the hearing impaired
CASES SEXUAL ASSAULT/ABUSE (%): 30
DESCRIPTION: Gives specialized attention to the child victim and the non-abusing parent by working with Division of Family Services and the juvenile court as the case progresses through the criminal justice system; Provides short-term crisis counseling, witness preparation, and referrals
CLIENTS/SERVICES: Sexual assault survivors; Marital rape/sexual abuse survivors; Child victims of sexual abuse; Incest victims/survivors; Community education; Offender treatment program; Adolescent survivors of sexual abuse; Male survivors of sexual abuse
REQUIREMENTS: Works with victims of crime, whether or not their cases are being prosecuted

ST MARTHA'S HALL
PO Box 4950, Saint Louis, MO 63108
Crisis hotline: **(314) 533-1313 8:30am-11pm**
Information: (314) 533-1313 8:30am-11pm
Contact: Michelle Schiller-Ramirez, Exec Dir
TYPE OF AGENCY: Domestic violence program
SPONSORING ORGANIZATION: United Way/Catholic Charities
AREAS SERVED: St Louis Metro Area
YEARS IN OPERATION: 5
LANGUAGES: Spanish
ACCESSIBILITY: Wheelchair accessible
CASES SEXUAL ASSAULT/ABUSE (%): 70
CLIENTS/SERVICES: Sexual assault survivors; Marital rape/sexual abuse survivors; Child victims of sexual abuse; Adult survivors of child sexual abuse; Incest victims/survivors

THE SALVATION ARMY FAMILY HAVEN
3744 Lindell Blvd, Saint Louis, MO 63108
Crisis hotline: **(314) 534-1250, shelter 771-2278 24 hrs**
Information: (314) 534-1250 8:30am-4:30pm (Mon-Fri)
Contact: Lt Violet Doliber, Admin
TYPE OF AGENCY: Domestic violence program; Shelter
AREAS SERVED: St Louis metropolitan area
ACCESSIBILITY: Wheelchair accessible
CASES SEXUAL ASSAULT/ABUSE (%): 15
CLIENTS/SERVICES: Sexual assault survivors; Marital rape/sexual abuse survivors; Child victims of sexual abuse; Adult survivors of child sexual abuse; Incest victims/survivors; Adolescent survivors of sexual abuse; Male survivors of sexual abuse

SEXUAL ABUSE MANAGEMENT PROGRAM
400 S Kingshighway, Saint Louis, MO 63110
Information: (314) 454-6101 8am-7pm (Mon-Fri)
Contact: Lee Ann Taylor, ACSW, Child Abuse/Neglect Management Coord
TYPE OF AGENCY: Hospital/medical center
SPONSORING ORGANIZATION: St Louis Children's Hospital
AREAS SERVED: St Louis metropolitan area
YEARS IN OPERATION: 10
ACCESSIBILITY: Wheelchair accessible; Signers for the hearing impaired (by arrangement)
CASES SEXUAL ASSAULT/ABUSE (%): 100
DESCRIPTION: Crisis counseling, medical/psychosocial evaluations and medical treatment. Interviewing using anatomical dolls and other art forms; videotaping when appropriate. SAM (Sexual Abuse Management) team is composed of physicians, nurses, and social workers
CLIENTS/SERVICES: Child victims of sexual abuse; Community education

SPECIAL ASSESSMENT AND MANAGEMENT CLINIC
1465 S Grand, Saint Louis, MO 63104
Information: (314) 577-5670
TYPE OF AGENCY: Hospital/medical center; Child sexual abuse services; Child sexual abuse prevention program
SPONSORING ORGANIZATION: Cardinal Glennon Children's Hospital
YEARS IN OPERATION: 5½
ACCESSIBILITY: Wheelchair accessible
CASES SEXUAL ASSAULT/ABUSE (%): 100
DESCRIPTION: Provides sexual assault examinations, follow-up medical care, forensic evaluations with colposcope, and videotaped interviews. Referrals for follow-up counseling
CLIENTS/SERVICES: Child victims of sexual abuse; Prevention program; Community education; Adolescent survivors of sexual abuse
REQUIREMENTS: Must be younger than 18
SPECIAL PROGRAMS/SERVICES: Operation Safekid is a child sexual abuse prevention program available for elementary school students, parents, and teachers, day care centers and child care workers, health professionals, and church and community organizations

UNIVERSITY OF MISSOURI, ST LOUIS—COMMUNITY PSYCHOLOGICAL SERVICE
8001 Natural Bridge Rd, Saint Louis, MO 63121-4499
Information: (314) 553-5824 9am-8pm (Mon-Thu), 9am-5pm (Fri)
Contact: Jacob Orlofsky, PhD, Dir; Monica Schnicke, Clinical Asst
TYPE OF AGENCY: College/university-based services; Training/research
AREAS SERVED: St Louis
YEARS IN OPERATION: 11
ACCESSIBILITY: Wheelchair accessible
CASES SEXUAL ASSAULT/ABUSE (%): 5-10
DESCRIPTION: Community psychology clinic associated with the doctoral training program in clinical psychology at the University of Missouri, St Louis. Services include psychotherapy, psychological evaluation, and crisis intervention
CLIENTS/SERVICES: Sexual assault survivors; Adult survivors of child sexual abuse; Male survivors of sexual abuse

UNIVERSITY OF MISSOURI, ST LOUIS—WOMEN'S CENTER
8001 Natural Bridge Rd, Saint Louis, MO 63121
Information: (314) 553-5380 8am-7pm (Mon-Fri)
Contact: Cathy Burack, Dir
TYPE OF AGENCY: College/university-based services
AREAS SERVED: St Louis
YEARS IN OPERATION: 14
ACCESSIBILITY: Wheelchair accessible; Telecommunications for the hearing impaired (TTY, TDY, etc.); Signers for the hearing impaired
CASES SEXUAL ASSAULT/ABUSE (%): 10
CLIENTS/SERVICES: Sexual assault survivors; Marital rape/sexual abuse survivors; Adult survivors of child sexual abuse; Incest victims/survivors; Prevention program; Community education

WOMEN'S COUNSELING COLLECTIVE
7818 Forsyth, Ste 209, Saint Louis, MO 63105
Information: (314) 344-5471 By appointment including evenings
Contact: Debra Kuhn, Ellen Tetlow, Kim Anderson, Collective Members
TYPE OF AGENCY: Counseling/mental health services; Child sexual abuse services; Private practice
AREAS SERVED: St Louis and surrounding counties
YEARS IN OPERATION: 2
CASES SEXUAL ASSAULT/ABUSE (%): 80
DESCRIPTION: Private practice formed in order to provide quality services outside of traditional agency format, with expertise in issues of abuse and women's issues including eating disorders, family violence, lesbian relationships, body image, sexuality, chemical dependency, treatment for female sex offenders
CLIENTS/SERVICES: Sexual assault survivors; Marital rape/sexual abuse survivors; Child victims of sexual abuse; Adult survivors of child sexual abuse; Incest victims/survivors; Community education; Offender treatment program; Adolescent survivors of sexual abuse; Male survivors of sexual abuse; Lesbians
REQUIREMENTS: Fees are charged; Sliding scale available

WOMEN'S SELF HELP CENTER, INC
2838 Olive St, Saint Louis, MO 63103
Crisis hotline: **(314) 531-2003 24 hrs 7 days**
Information: (314) 531-9100 8:30am-5pm (Mon-Fri)
Contact: Gwen Bueckendorf, Education Coord
TYPE OF AGENCY: Rape crisis center; Domestic violence program; Acquaintance/date rape prevention program; Adolescent program
AREAS SERVED: St Louis City, St Louis County and outlying MO and IL counties
YEARS IN OPERATION: 12
LANGUAGES: Spanish

WOMEN'S SELF HELP CENTER, INC
(continued)

ACCESSIBILITY: Wheelchair accessible
CASES SEXUAL ASSAULT/ABUSE (%): 50
CLIENTS/SERVICES: Sexual assault survivors; Marital rape/sexual abuse survivors; Adult survivors of child sexual abuse; Incest victims/survivors; Prevention program; Community education; Adolescent survivors of sexual abuse; Prisoners; Healing; Publications/media
REQUIREMENTS: Client must be female, 17 years or older
SPECIAL PROGRAMS/SERVICES: The center is currently in a joint effort with Progressive Youth Center to implement a prevention program in high schools. Program focuses on violence-free relationships, including physical, emotional and sexual. Has also joined with Craft Alliance to do art therapy with incest survivors. Programs in women's correctional facilities and court advocates work with women entangled in justice system as a result of the abuse in their lives. 30 minute video on agency services and the women served; Volunteer training 3 times a year which consists of 33 hours of training on incest, rape, and battering. Volunteer hotline, speakers, court advocacy

SEDALIA

CITIZENS AGAINST SPOUSE ABUSE, INC (CASA)
PO Box 1371, Sedalia, MO 65301
Crisis hotline: **(816) 827-5555 24 hrs daily**
Information: (816) 827-5559 8am-5pm
Contact: Mary Kay Williams, Exec Dir
TYPE OF AGENCY: Domestic violence program
AREAS SERVED: Pettis, surrounding areas
YEARS IN OPERATION: 5
CASES SEXUAL ASSAULT/ABUSE (%): 70
DESCRIPTION: Serves battered women and their children who may also be sexually abused as well, and on a limited basis, serves as rape advocates
CLIENTS/SERVICES: Sexual assault survivors; Marital rape/sexual abuse survivors; Adult survivors of child sexual abuse; Incest victims/survivors; Prevention program; Community education; Adolescent survivors of sexual abuse

SPRINGFIELD

THE FAMILY CENTER
PO Box 5972, Springfield, MO 65802
Crisis hotline: **(417) 865-1728 24 hrs**
Information: (417) 865-0373 8am-5pm (Mon-Fri)
Contact: Lisa Henning, Crisis Management Spec
TYPE OF AGENCY: Domestic violence program
AREAS SERVED: Cedar, Dade, Polk, Dallas, Laciede, Texas, Shannon, Wright, Webster, Greene, Lawrence, Barry, Stone, Christian, Douglas, Taney, Ozark, Howell, Oregon
YEARS IN OPERATION: 9
CLIENTS/SERVICES: Sexual assault survivors; Marital rape/sexual abuse survivors; Child victims of sexual abuse; Adult survivors of child sexual abuse; Community education

GREENE COUNTY PROSECUTING ATTORNEY—VICTIM/WITNESS SERVICES
Greene County Courthouse, Rm 309, Springfield, MO 65802
Crisis hotline: **(417) 868-4082 8:30am-5pm (Mon-Fri)**
Information: (417) 868-4082 8:30am-5pm (Mon-Fri)
Contact: Paula Tindell, Coord/Advocate
TYPE OF AGENCY: Victim/witness assistance program
AREAS SERVED: Greene
YEARS IN OPERATION: 2
ACCESSIBILITY: Wheelchair accessible; Signers for the hearing impaired
CASES SEXUAL ASSAULT/ABUSE (%): 45
CLIENTS/SERVICES: Sexual assault survivors; Marital rape/sexual abuse survivors; Child victims of sexual abuse; Incest victims/survivors; Community education
REQUIREMENTS: Must file charges

RAPE CRISIS AND SEXUAL ABUSE CENTER
1423 N Jefferson, Springfield, MO 65802
Crisis hotline: **(417) 866-6665 24 hrs**
Information: (417) 836-3765 8am-5pm
Contact: Judy Compere, Exec Dir
TYPE OF AGENCY: Rape crisis center; Child sexual abuse prevention program; Acquaintance/date rape prevention program
AREAS SERVED: Greene
YEARS IN OPERATION: 12
ACCESSIBILITY: Wheelchair accessible; Signers for the hearing impaired
CASES SEXUAL ASSAULT/ABUSE (%): 100
CLIENTS/SERVICES: Sexual assault survivors; Marital rape/sexual abuse survivors; Child victims of sexual abuse; Adult survivors of child sexual abuse; Incest victims/survivors; Prevention program; Community education; Adolescent survivors of sexual abuse; Male survivors of sexual abuse
SPECIAL PROGRAMS/SERVICES: Intensive school based prevention programs in all kindergarten, third and fifth grade elementary classes, all junior high schools and a 3 day program in all high schools. Reach over 10,000 children yearly.

UNIVERSITY CITY

YWCA WOMEN'S RESOURCE CENTER
6665 Delmar Blvd, University City, MO 63130
Information: (314) 726-6665 8:30am-5pm
Contact: Charlene Buckley, Counselor
TYPE OF AGENCY: Counseling/mental health services
AREAS SERVED: St Louis City and County
YEARS IN OPERATION: 2
ACCESSIBILITY: Wheelchair accessible
CASES SEXUAL ASSAULT/ABUSE (%): 40-50
DESCRIPTION: Offers short-term individual counseling for sexual assault survivors; Beginner's 8-week adult survivors groups; On-going 'Phase 2' advanced survivors group; Educational programming; Feminist martial arts/self-defense
CLIENTS/SERVICES: Sexual assault survivors; Marital rape/sexual abuse survivors; Adult survivors of child sexual abuse; Incest victims/survivors; Community education; Adolescent survivors of sexual abuse; Male survivors of sexual abuse

WARRENSBURG

SURVIVAL ADULT ABUSE, INC
PO Box 344, Warrensburg, MO 64093
Crisis hotline: **(816) 429-2847 24 hrs**
Information: (816) 429-1088 9am-3pm
Contact: Barb K Gammeter, Dir
TYPE OF AGENCY: Domestic violence program
AREAS SERVED: Johnson, Henry, Lafayette
YEARS IN OPERATION: 7
LANGUAGES: Spanish, Japanese, Sign, Interpreters available
ACCESSIBILITY: Wheelchair accessible; Signers for the hearing impaired
CASES SEXUAL ASSAULT/ABUSE (%): 75
DESCRIPTION: Provide services for battered women; Provide counseling and hotline crisis advocacy for sexual assault victims; Support groups for male survivors of sexual assault/abuse
CLIENTS/SERVICES: Sexual assault survivors; Marital rape/sexual abuse survivors; Child victims of sexual abuse; Adult survivors of child sexual abuse; Incest victims/survivors; Adolescent survivors of sexual abuse; Male survivors of sexual abuse

MONTANA

BILLINGS

BILLINGS RAPE TASK FORCE
1245 N 29th St, Rm 218, Billings, MT 59101
Crisis hotline: **(406) 259-6506 24 hrs**
Information: (406) 245-6721
Contact: Jean Bradford, Dir
TYPE OF AGENCY: Rape crisis center
AREAS SERVED: Yellowstone and surrounding counties
YEARS IN OPERATION: 13
ACCESSIBILITY: Signers for the hearing impaired
CASES SEXUAL ASSAULT/ABUSE (%): 100
CLIENTS/SERVICES: Sexual assault survivors; Marital rape/sexual abuse survivors; Child victims of sexual abuse; Adult survivors of child sexual abuse; Incest victims/survivors; Community education; Adolescent survivors of sexual abuse; Male survivors of sexual abuse

WOMEN'S STUDIES AND SERVICE CENTER
1500 N 30th St, Billings, MT 59101-0298
Information: (406) 657-2879 8am-5pm (Mon-Fri)
Contact: Sue Hart, Coord
TYPE OF AGENCY: College/university-based services; Rape prevention program
SPONSORING ORGANIZATION: Eastern Montana College
AREAS SERVED: Primarily Yellowstone, eastern Montana
YEARS IN OPERATION: 12
ACCESSIBILITY: Wheelchair accessible; Signers for the hearing impaired (by arrangement)
CASES SEXUAL ASSAULT/ABUSE (%): 5
DESCRIPTION: Provides crisis counseling for sexual assault survivors and education for university students on acquaintance/date rape and personal safety
CLIENTS/SERVICES: Sexual assault survivors; Adult survivors of child sexual abuse; Prevention program; Community education
SPECIAL PROGRAMS/SERVICES: Has sent teams out from office to evaluate workplaces, dormitories, etc in terms of personal safety, and provided employers/residents an "awareness" program

BOZEMAN

ASSESSMENT AND TREATMENT SERVICES
321 E Main, No 405, Bozeman, MT 59715
Crisis hotline: **(406) 586-5125 24 hrs**
Information: (406) 586-5125 9am-7pm (Mon, Wed, Thu, Fri)
Contact: Fred Lemons, Lic Prof Counselor
TYPE OF AGENCY: Private practice; Offender treatment
AREAS SERVED: Gallatin, Park, Silverbow
YEARS IN OPERATION: 3
CASES SEXUAL ASSAULT/ABUSE (%): 80
DESCRIPTION: Provides evaluation and treatment of both adult and adolescent offenders and their families
CLIENTS/SERVICES: Adult survivors of child sexual abuse; Community education; Offender treatment program; Male survivors of sexual abuse
REQUIREMENTS: 13 or older; Legal requirement for treatment preferred; Assessed appropriate for community treatment

WOMEN'S RESOURCE CENTER
15 Hamilton Hall, Montana State University, Bozeman, MT 59717
Information: (406) 994-3836 9am-5pm (Mon-Fri)
Contact: Michelle L Dennis, Dir
TYPE OF AGENCY: College/university-based services
SPONSORING ORGANIZATION: Montana State University
AREAS SERVED: Gallatin
YEARS IN OPERATION: 6
ACCESSIBILITY: Wheelchair accessible
CASES SEXUAL ASSAULT/ABUSE (%): 15
CLIENTS/SERVICES: Sexual assault survivors; Adult survivors of child sexual abuse; Incest victims/survivors; Prevention program; Community education; Adolescent survivors of sexual abuse; Male survivors of sexual abuse

BROWNING

BLACKFEET INDIAN CHILD WELFARE PROGRAM
Box 518, Browning, MT 59417
Information: (406) 338-7806 8am-5pm
TYPE OF AGENCY: Child sexual abuse services; Child abuse services
AREAS SERVED: Glacier, Pondera
YEARS IN OPERATION: 2
CASES SEXUAL ASSAULT/ABUSE (%): 1
CLIENTS/SERVICES: Child victims of sexual abuse; Prevention program; Community education; Ethnic minorities

BUTTE

MENTAL HEALTH SERVICES, INC
2500 Continental Dr, Butte, MT 59701
Crisis hotline: **(406) 723-5489 24 hrs**
Information: (406) 723-5489 8am-7:30pm (Mon-Thu); 8am-5pm (Fri)
Contact: Joan Hays, Office Dir
TYPE OF AGENCY: Counseling/mental health services
AREAS SERVED: Butte-Silverbow, Madison, Jefferson, Deer Lodge, Beaverhead
YEARS IN OPERATION: 12
ACCESSIBILITY: Wheelchair accessible
CASES SEXUAL ASSAULT/ABUSE (%): 30-40
CLIENTS/SERVICES: Sexual assault survivors; Marital rape/sexual abuse survivors; Child victims of sexual abuse; Adult survivors of child sexual abuse; Incest victims/survivors; Community education; Adolescent survivors of sexual abuse; Male survivors of sexual abuse

SAFE SPACE
Box 634, Butte, MT 59703
Crisis hotline: **(406) 782-8511 24 hrs**
Information: (406) 782-2111 9am-5pm
Contact: Marilyn Maney, Exec Dir
TYPE OF AGENCY: Rape crisis center; Domestic violence program
AREAS SERVED: Silver Bow, Beaverhead, Deer Lodge, Powell, Jefferson, Madison
YEARS IN OPERATION: 8
CASES SEXUAL ASSAULT/ABUSE (%): 65
CLIENTS/SERVICES: Sexual assault survivors; Marital rape/sexual abuse survivors; Child victims of sexual abuse; Adult survivors of child sexual abuse; Incest victims/survivors; Community education; Male survivors of sexual abuse
REQUIREMENTS: Client must file charges on the second occurrence of domestic violence upon entering the shelter

COLSTRIP

BATTERED WOMEN'S TASK FORCE, INC
PO Box 1946, Colstrip, MT 59323
Crisis hotline: **(406) 748-2211 24 hrs**
Information: (406) 748-4357 10am-2pm (Mon-Fri)
Contact: Mary Pease, Coord
TYPE OF AGENCY: Domestic violence program
AREAS SERVED: Rosebud, Treasure, Powder River
YEARS IN OPERATION: 8
ACCESSIBILITY: Wheelchair accessible
CASES SEXUAL ASSAULT/ABUSE (%): 2
CLIENTS/SERVICES: Sexual assault survivors; Marital rape/sexual abuse survivors; Adult survivors of child sexual abuse; Incest victims/survivors; Community education; Adolescent survivors of sexual abuse; Male survivors of sexual abuse

FORSYTH

ROSEBUD COUNTY ATTORNEY'S OFFICE—VICTIM/WITNESS ASSISTANCE
Box 69, Rosebud County Courthouse, Forsyth, MT 59327
Information: (406) 356-2236 8am-5pm
Contact: Marvin Quinlan, Jr, County Attorney
TYPE OF AGENCY: Victim/witness assistance program
AREAS SERVED: Rosebud
ACCESSIBILITY: Wheelchair accessible
CASES SEXUAL ASSAULT/ABUSE (%): 10-20

ROSEBUD COUNTY ATTORNEY'S OFFICE—VICTIM/WITNESS ASSISTANCE (continued)

CLIENTS/SERVICES: Sexual assault survivors; Marital rape/sexual abuse survivors; Child victims of sexual abuse; Prevention program; Community education; Offender treatment program
REQUIREMENTS: Charges must be filed or other court action must be taken

GLENDIVE

DAWSON COUNTY SPOUSE ABUSE PROGRAM
PO Box 505, Glendive, MT 59330
Crisis hotline: **(406) 365-6074 24 hrs**
Information: (406) 365-6477 8am-5pm
Contact: Shirley Trangmoe, Coord
TYPE OF AGENCY: Domestic violence program
AREAS SERVED: Dawson, Prairie, Wibaux
YEARS IN OPERATION: 7
ACCESSIBILITY: Wheelchair accessible
CLIENTS/SERVICES: Marital rape/sexual abuse survivors; Community education

EASTERN MONTANA MENTAL HEALTH CENTER
PO Box 1321, Glendive, MT 59330-1321
Crisis hotline: **(406) 365-6074 24 hrs daily**
Information: (406) 365-6075 8am-5pm
Contact: Pete Bruno, MEd, Sex Offender Treatment Prog Dir
TYPE OF AGENCY: Counseling/mental health services; Child sexual abuse services
AREAS SERVED: All of eastern Montana (east of Billings)
DESCRIPTION: Counseling services for survivors; Support groups for female and male survivors of sexual assault/abuse; Individual and group therapy for child sexual abuse offenders, incest offenders, and juvenile sex offenders. Plethysmograph evaluations for offenders
CLIENTS/SERVICES: Sexual assault survivors; Marital rape/sexual abuse survivors; Child victims of sexual abuse; Adult survivors of child sexual abuse; Incest victims/survivors; Prevention program; Offender treatment program; Adolescent survivors of sexual abuse; Male survivors of sexual abuse
REQUIREMENTS: For free services, victim must file

GREAT FALLS

COMMUNITY HELP LINE
113 6th St N, Great Falls, MT 59401
Crisis hotline: **(406) 453-6511, 453-4357 24 hrs**
Information: (406) 761-6010 8:30am-5pm
Contact: Shayna R Dickey, Exec Dir
TYPE OF AGENCY: Counseling/mental health services; Telephone crisis hotline
AREAS SERVED: Primarily Cascade
YEARS IN OPERATION: 3
CLIENTS/SERVICES: Sexual assault survivors; Male survivors of sexual abuse

GIANT SPRINGS COUNSELING ASSOCIATES
510 1st Ave N, Ste 106, Great Falls, MT 59401
Information: (406) 927-5355 8am-5pm (Mon-Fri)
Contact: Janet M Hossack, PhD, Licensed Counselor; George W Hossack EdD, Licensed Psychologist
TYPE OF AGENCY: Child sexual abuse services; Private practice
AREAS SERVED: Cascade
YEARS IN OPERATION: 2
CASES SEXUAL ASSAULT/ABUSE (%): 60
DESCRIPTION: Parents United; Daughters and Sons United; Adults Molested as Children United; Support groups for non-offending parents; Individual and group therapy for juvenile sex offenders; Evaluations of adult sex offenders; Support groups for female and male survivors of sexual abuse/assault
CLIENTS/SERVICES: Sexual assault survivors; Child victims of sexual abuse; Adult survivors of child sexual abuse; Incest victims/survivors; Offender treatment program; Adolescent survivors of sexual abuse; Male survivors of sexual abuse
REQUIREMENTS: Client must have ability to pay via insurance or private source

RAPE VICTIM'S ADVOCACY PROGRAM
PO Box 124, Great Falls, MT 59403
Crisis hotline: **(406) 453-6511 24 hrs**
Information: (406) 761-6010 9am-5pm (Mon-Fri)
Contact: Ardie Battleson, Admin Asst
TYPE OF AGENCY: Rape crisis center
SPONSORING ORGANIZATION: Community Help Line
AREAS SERVED: Cascade
YEARS IN OPERATION: 17
LANGUAGES: Language bank volunteers available
CLIENTS/SERVICES: Sexual assault survivors; Child victims of sexual abuse; Community education; Male survivors of sexual abuse

HAVRE

PARENTS UNITED OF HILL COUNTY
PO Box 7348, Havre, MT 59501
Crisis hotline: **(406) 265-2211 24 hrs**
Information: (406) 265-7831 8am-8pm
Contact: Dr Lawrence Jarvis, Lic Clinical Psychologist
TYPE OF AGENCY: Child sexual abuse services
SPONSORING ORGANIZATION: Havre Clinic, PC
AREAS SERVED: Hill, Blaine, Choteau, Liberty
YEARS IN OPERATION: 5
LANGUAGES: Spanish
ACCESSIBILITY: Wheelchair accessible
CASES SEXUAL ASSAULT/ABUSE (%): 50-75
DESCRIPTION: Sanctioned Parents United, Inc program providing individual, group, marital, and family therapy. Provides an integrated assessment and treatment program primarily for adults molested as children, child victims and child and adult offenders. Does manage some treatment with individuals who are not in the strict sense family, but may be babysitters, close friends, and associates who have not been diagnosed as predatory pedophiles
CLIENTS/SERVICES: Sexual assault survivors; Marital rape/sexual abuse survivors; Child victims of sexual abuse; Adult survivors of child sexual abuse; Incest victims/survivors; Prevention program; Community education; Offender treatment program; Adolescent survivors of sexual abuse; Male survivors of sexual abuse
REQUIREMENTS: Offenders must be adjudicated and a confidentiality waiver is required

HELENA

ASSESSMENT AND TREATMENT SERVICES AND MONTANA PSYCHOTHERAPY
54 N Last Chance Gulch, Helena, MT 59601
Crisis hotline: **(406) 586-5125 24 hrs**
Information: (406) 586-5125 9am-7pm (Mon, Wed, Thu, Fri)
Contact: Fred Lemons, Lic Prof Counselor
TYPE OF AGENCY: Private practice; Offender treatment
AREAS SERVED: Gallatin, Park, Silverbow
YEARS IN OPERATION: 3
CASES SEXUAL ASSAULT/ABUSE (%): 80
DESCRIPTION: Provides evaluation and treatment of both adult and adolescent offenders and their families
CLIENTS/SERVICES: Adult survivors of child sexual abuse; Community education; Offender treatment program; Male survivors of sexual abuse
REQUIREMENTS: 13 or older; Legal requirement for treatment preferred; Assessed appropriate for community treatment

FRIENDSHIP CENTER OF HELENA, INC
1503 Gallatin, Helena, MT 59601
Crisis hotline: **(406) 442-6800 24 hrs**
Information: (406) 442-6800 9am-5pm (Mon-Fri)
Contact: Jill Kennedy, Exec Dir
TYPE OF AGENCY: Domestic violence program; Shelter
AREAS SERVED: Lewis and Clark, Broadwater, Jefferson
YEARS IN OPERATION: 17
CASES SEXUAL ASSAULT/ABUSE (%): 25-30
DESCRIPTION: Provides shelter, counseling, and other supportive services for homeless families and victims of domestic violence and sexual assault.
CLIENTS/SERVICES: Sexual assault survivors; Marital rape/sexual abuse survivors; Child victims of sexual abuse; Adult survivors of child sexual abuse; Incest victims/survivors; Community education

LEWIS AND CLARK COUNTY ATTORNEY—VICTIM/WITNESS ASSISTANCE
228 Broadway, Helena, MT 59601
Information: (406) 443-1010, ext 221 8am-12pm, 1pm-5pm (Mon-Fri)
Contact: Mike McGrath, County Atty
TYPE OF AGENCY: Victim/witness assistance program
AREAS SERVED: Lewis and Clark
YEARS IN OPERATION: 3
LANGUAGES: Language bank
ACCESSIBILITY: Wheelchair accessible; Signers for the hearing impaired
CASES SEXUAL ASSAULT/ABUSE (%): 25-30
CLIENTS/SERVICES: Sexual assault survivors; Marital rape/sexual abuse survivors; Child victims of sexual abuse; Adult survivors of child sexual abuse; Incest victims/survivors; Prevention program; Community education; Adolescent survivors of sexual abuse; Male survivors of sexual abuse
REQUIREMENTS: Clients must report to a law enforcement agency.

SEXUAL ASSAULT TREATMENT PROGRAM
512 Logan St, Helena, MT 59601
Crisis hotline: **(406) 442-0640 24 hrs**
Information: (406) 442-0649
Contact: Ron Silvers MEd LPC, Dir
TYPE OF AGENCY: Counseling/mental health services; Child sexual abuse services
SPONSORING ORGANIZATION: Mental Health Services, Inc
AREAS SERVED: Flathead, Lewis and Clark, Jefferson, Beaverhead, Butte-Silver-Bav, Park, Cascade, Toole, Teton, Hili, Gallston, Broadwater
YEARS IN OPERATION: 2½
CASES SEXUAL ASSAULT/ABUSE (%): 100
DESCRIPTION: Counseling for sexually abused children and their families; Individual and group therapy for child abuse offenders, incest offenders, and adolescent sex offenders; Couples group therapy for offenders and their spouses
CLIENTS/SERVICES: Sexual assault survivors; Marital rape/sexual abuse survivors; Child victims of sexual abuse; Adult survivors of child sexual abuse; Incest victims/survivors; Offender treatment program; Adolescent survivors of sexual abuse
REQUIREMENTS: Serves any child survivor. Adult offenders must pay full fee; Adolescent offenders treated on a sliding scale. All offenders must be involved in the legal system/prosecuted and plead guilty

KALISPELL

CHILD ABUSE PREVENTION COUNCIL
PO Box 246, Kalispell, MT 59903
Information: (406) 752-6565 8am-5pm
TYPE OF AGENCY: Child sexual abuse prevention program; Child abuse prevention program
AREAS SERVED: Flathead
YEARS IN OPERATION: 6
CLIENTS/SERVICES: Prevention program; Community education

VIOLENCE FREE CRISIS LINE
PO Box 1385, Kalispell, MT 59903-1385
Crisis hotline: **(406) 752-7273 24 hrs**
Information: (406) 752-4735 8:30am-12pm (Mon-Fri)
Contact: Janet Cahill, Dir
TYPE OF AGENCY: Rape crisis center; Domestic violence program
AREAS SERVED: Flathead
YEARS IN OPERATION: 12
ACCESSIBILITY: Signers for the hearing impaired
CASES SEXUAL ASSAULT/ABUSE (%): 5
CLIENTS/SERVICES: Sexual assault survivors; Marital rape/sexual abuse survivors; Child victims of sexual abuse; Adult survivors of child sexual abuse; Incest victims/survivors; Prevention program; Community education; Adolescent survivors of sexual abuse

MISSOULA

CHILD AND FAMILY RESOURCE COUNCIL
PO Box 3805, Missoula, MT 59806
Crisis hotline: **(406) 728-KIDS 9am-5pm, (Mon-Fri), after hrs and weekends through answering service**
Information: (406) 728-KIDS 9am-5pm (Mon-Fri)
Contact: Georgina Park, Exec Dir
TYPE OF AGENCY: Counseling/mental health services; Child sexual abuse services; Child sexual abuse prevention program; Child abuse services; Child abuse prevention program
SPONSORING ORGANIZATION: Missoula County Victims Assistance Program
AREAS SERVED: Missoula
YEARS IN OPERATION: 8
DESCRIPTION: Support groups for sexually abused children and adult survivors; Parents Anonymous chapters; Parenting programs and classes
CLIENTS/SERVICES: Marital rape/sexual abuse survivors; Child victims of sexual abuse; Adult survivors of child sexual abuse; Incest victims/survivors; Prevention program; Community education

FRIENDS TO YOUTH
212 W Spruce, Missoula, MT 59802
Information: (406) 728-2662 8am-5pm
Contact: Cindy Bartling, Exec Dir
TYPE OF AGENCY: Counseling/mental health services; Child sexual abuse services; Adolescent program
SPONSORING ORGANIZATION: Missoula County Victim/Witness Assistance Program
AREAS SERVED: Missoula, Rivalli, Lake, Mineral
YEARS IN OPERATION: 13
CASES SEXUAL ASSAULT/ABUSE (%): 30
DESCRIPTION: Provides individual, family, and group counseling for young people ages 10-18
CLIENTS/SERVICES: Child victims of sexual abuse; Incest victims/survivors; Adolescent survivors of sexual abuse
REQUIREMENTS: Clients must be between the ages of 10-18

MISSOULA COUNTY VICTIM'S ASSISTANCE PROGRAM
Missoula County Commissioner's Office, Courthouse Annex, Missoula, MT 59802
Information: (406) 721-5700, ext 224 8am-5pm
Contact: Cynthia B Klette, Prog Coord
TYPE OF AGENCY: Victim/witness assistance program
AREAS SERVED: Missoula
YEARS IN OPERATION: 4
ACCESSIBILITY: Wheelchair accessible
DESCRIPTION: Contracts with community-based nonprofit organizations to provide services related to the sexual assault/child sexual abuse field
CLIENTS/SERVICES: Sexual assault survivors; Marital rape/sexual abuse survivors; Child victims of sexual abuse; Adult survivors of child sexual abuse; Incest victims/survivors; Prevention program; Community education

MISSOULA COUNTY VICTIM'S RESPONSE UNIT
Sheriff's Department, Missoula County Courthouse, Missoula, MT 59802
Information: (406) 721-4700, ext 230, 721-5700, ext 323 8:30am-Noon; 1pm-5pm
Contact: Diane L Morin, Coord
TYPE OF AGENCY: Victim/witness assistance program
SPONSORING ORGANIZATION: Missoula County Victim Assistance Program
AREAS SERVED: Missoula
YEARS IN OPERATION: 3
ACCESSIBILITY: Wheelchair accessible
CASES SEXUAL ASSAULT/ABUSE (%): 10-15
CLIENTS/SERVICES: Sexual assault survivors; Marital rape/sexual abuse survivors; Child victims of sexual abuse; Incest victims/survivors
REQUIREMENTS: Client must file charges in order to qualify for crime victims compensation

WOMEN'S PLACE
521 N Orange St, Missoula, MT 59802
Crisis hotline: **(406) 543-7606 24 hrs**
Information: (406) 543-3320 10am-4pm (Mon-Fri)
Contact: Star Garry, Sexual Assault Prog Coord
TYPE OF AGENCY: Rape crisis center; Child sexual abuse services; Child sexual abuse prevention program
AREAS SERVED: Missoula
YEARS IN OPERATION: 15
LANGUAGES: Spanish
CASES SEXUAL ASSAULT/ABUSE (%): 40
CLIENTS/SERVICES: Sexual assault survivors; Marital rape/sexual abuse survivors; Child victims of sexual abuse; Adult survivors of child sexual abuse; Incest victims/survivors; Prevention program; Community education; Adolescent survivors of sexual abuse; Male survivors of sexual abuse
SPECIAL PROGRAMS/SERVICES: Administers a chapter of Parents United and provides services for families experiencing child sexual abuse through the Parents United counseling program

WOMEN'S RESOURCE CENTER
N Corbin 241, Missoula, MT 59812
Information: (406) 243-4153
Contact: Paula M Pelletier, Volunteers Coord
TYPE OF AGENCY: College/university-based services; Rape prevention program; Acquaintance/date rape prevention program
SPONSORING ORGANIZATION: University of Montana
YEARS IN OPERATION: 20
LANGUAGES: Spanish
ACCESSIBILITY: Signers for the hearing impaired
DESCRIPTION: Provides referral services for women and men on the campus; Sponsors sexual assault awareness programs; Current project is the Date-Rape Teleconference which will be viewed by many teachers and counselors around the state of Montana
CLIENTS/SERVICES: Prevention program; Community education

YWCA BATTERED WOMEN'S SHELTER
1130 W Broadway, Missoula, MT 59802
Crisis hotline: **(406) 542-1944 24 hrs daily**
Information: (406) 542-0028 8am-10pm
Contact: Stacy Sanders, Dir
TYPE OF AGENCY: Domestic violence program; Child sexual abuse prevention program
SPONSORING ORGANIZATION: YWCA; Missoula County Victim/Witness Assistance Program
AREAS SERVED: Missoula, Lake, Sanders, Mineral, Ravalli
YEARS IN OPERATION: 10
CASES SEXUAL ASSAULT/ABUSE (%): 10
CLIENTS/SERVICES: Marital rape/sexual abuse survivors; Prevention program; Community education

POLSON

FAMILY CRISIS AND RESOURCE CENTER
203 Main St, Polson, MT 59860
Crisis hotline: **(406) 676-2518 24 hrs**
Information: (406) 883-3350 9am-4:30pm (Mon-Fri)
Contact: Sandra Penrod, Advocacy Coord
TYPE OF AGENCY: Rape crisis center; Domestic violence program; Child sexual abuse prevention program; Crisis intervention program
AREAS SERVED: Lake
YEARS IN OPERATION: 6
CASES SEXUAL ASSAULT/ABUSE (%): 45
DESCRIPTION: Aid anyone in a crisis situation; Group therapy for batterers
CLIENTS/SERVICES: Sexual assault survivors; Marital rape/sexual abuse survivors; Child victims of sexual abuse; Adult survivors of child sexual abuse; Incest victims/survivors; Prevention program; Community education; Adolescent survivors of sexual abuse; Male survivors of sexual abuse

NEBRASKA

BENKELMAN

DOMESTIC VIOLENCE AND SEXUAL ASSAULT SERVICES
Box 68, Benkelman, NE 69021
Crisis hotline: **(308) 423-2676 24 hrs**
Information: (308) 423-5484 24 hrs
Contact: Wanda G Mindt, Dir
TYPE OF AGENCY: Rape crisis center; Domestic violence program; Child sexual abuse services; Child sexual abuse prevention program
AREAS SERVED: Dundy, Chase
YEARS IN OPERATION: 8
CASES SEXUAL ASSAULT/ABUSE (%): 1
CLIENTS/SERVICES: Sexual assault survivors; Child victims of sexual abuse; Incest victims/survivors; Prevention program; Community education; Adolescent survivors of sexual abuse

BROKEN BOW

CENTRAL NEBRASKA TASK FORCE ON DOMESTIC ABUSE AND SEXUAL ASSAULT SERVICES
PO Box 183, Broken Bow, NE 68822
Crisis hotline: **(308) 872-5988 24 hrs**
Information: (308) 872-5988
Contact: Carol Smith, Dir
TYPE OF AGENCY: Rape crisis center; Domestic violence program; Child sexual abuse prevention program; Private practice
AREAS SERVED: Custer, Loup, Blaine
YEARS IN OPERATION: 9
DESCRIPTION: Provides basic emergency services for domestic abuse and sexual assault victims. Also offers therapy program for batterers; Feminist martial arts/self-defense program
CLIENTS/SERVICES: Sexual assault survivors; Marital rape/sexual abuse survivors; Child victims of sexual abuse; Adult survivors of child sexual abuse; Incest victims/survivors; Prevention program; Community education; Adolescent survivors of sexual abuse; Male survivors of sexual abuse

COLUMBUS

COLUMBUS AREA DOMESTIC VIOLENCE/ SEXUAL ASSAULT PROGRAM
PO Box 573, 1472 28th Ave, Columbus, NE 68601
Crisis hotline: **(402) 564-6677 24 hrs**
Information: (402) 564-1616 8:30am-5pm
Contact: Jamie Snyder, ACSW, Dir
TYPE OF AGENCY: Domestic violence program; Counseling/mental health services; Child sexual abuse services; Child sexual abuse prevention program
SPONSORING ORGANIZATION: Lutheran Family Service
AREAS SERVED: Platte, Nance, Boone, Colfax
YEARS IN OPERATION: 10
CASES SEXUAL ASSAULT/ABUSE (%): 10
DESCRIPTION: Services for survivors of sexual assault and domestic violence; Individual therapy for rapists, child sexual abuse offenders, incest offenders and batterers
CLIENTS/SERVICES: Sexual assault survivors; Marital rape/sexual abuse survivors; Child victims of sexual abuse; Adult survivors of child sexual abuse; Incest victims/survivors; Prevention program; Community education; Offender treatment program; Adolescent survivors of sexual abuse; Male survivors of sexual abuse

CRETE

COORDINATED INTERVENTION SYSTEM FOR DOMESTIC ABUSES (CISDA)
PO Box 73, Crete, NE 68333
Crisis hotline: **(800) 234-4482 24 hrs**
Information: (402) 826-2332 8am-5pm
Contact: Gloria Durman, Exec Dir
TYPE OF AGENCY: Rape crisis center; Domestic violence program; Child sexual abuse services; Child sexual abuse prevention program
AREAS SERVED: Gage, Jefferson, Butler, Polk, Saunders, Saline, York, Seward, Fillmore, Thayer
YEARS IN OPERATION: 10
CASES SEXUAL ASSAULT/ABUSE (%): 35
DESCRIPTION: Comprehensive services for sexual assault and domestic violence survivors; Feminist martial arts/self-defense program
CLIENTS/SERVICES: Sexual assault survivors; Marital rape/sexual abuse survivors; Child victims of sexual abuse; Adult survivors of child sexual abuse; Incest victims/survivors; Prevention program; Community education; Adolescent survivors of sexual abuse; Male survivors of sexual abuse

ELYRIA

LOUP VALLEY TASK FORCE ON DOMESTIC VIOLENCE AND SEXUAL ASSAULT
Box 104, Elyria, NE 68837
Crisis hotline: **(308) 728-7040, 346-HELP 24 hrs**
TYPE OF AGENCY: Rape crisis center; Domestic violence program; Child sexual abuse prevention program
AREAS SERVED: Valley, Sherman, Greeley, Wheeler, Garfield
YEARS IN OPERATION: 9
CASES SEXUAL ASSAULT/ABUSE (%): 20
CLIENTS/SERVICES: Sexual assault survivors; Marital rape/sexual abuse survivors; Adult survivors of child sexual abuse; Incest victims/survivors; Prevention program; Community education; Male survivors of sexual abuse

FREMONT

DOMESTIC ABUSE/SEXUAL ASSAULT CRISIS CENTER
PO Box 622, 33 W 4th St, Ste 1, Fremont, NE 68025
Crisis hotline: **(402) 727-7777 24 hrs**
Information: (402) 721-4340 8am-4pm (Mon-Fri)
Contact: Kathryn Schneider, Exec Dir
TYPE OF AGENCY: Rape crisis center; Domestic violence program
AREAS SERVED: Dodge, Burt, Washington
YEARS IN OPERATION: 6
CASES SEXUAL ASSAULT/ABUSE (%): 40
DESCRIPTION: Services for sexual assault and domestic violence survivors; Anger control group for batterers
CLIENTS/SERVICES: Sexual assault survivors; Marital rape/sexual abuse survivors; Incest victims/survivors; Prevention program; Community education; Adolescent survivors of sexual abuse; Male survivors of sexual abuse
SPECIAL PROGRAMS/SERVICES: Family Effectiveness Training Program that includes all family members. It is a 10-lesson program (2-hour sessions) and has a nursery provided for infants, and classes for 3 ½-8 years, 8-12 years, 13-18 years, and adults. Emphasis is placed on communication, building self-esteem, good disciplinary methods, age appropriate behavior, anger control, stress management.

GORDON

TRI-COUNTY TASK FORCE FOR THE PREVENTION OF DOMESTIC VIOLENCE
109 E 2nd, Gordon, NE 69343
Crisis hotline: **(308) 282-0125 24 hrs**
Information: (308) 282-0126 24 hrs
Contact: Rosella Orosco, Proj Dir
TYPE OF AGENCY: Rape crisis center; Domestic violence program; Child sexual abuse services; Child sexual abuse prevention program
AREAS SERVED: Cherry, Dawes, Sheridan
YEARS IN OPERATION: 1
LANGUAGES: Spanish, Lakota
ACCESSIBILITY: Wheelchair accessible
CASES SEXUAL ASSAULT/ABUSE (%): 50
CLIENTS/SERVICES: Sexual assault survivors; Marital rape/sexual abuse survivors; Child victims of sexual abuse; Adult survivors of child sexual abuse; Incest victims/survivors; Prevention program; Community education; Adolescent survivors of sexual abuse

GRAND ISLAND

CRISIS CENTER, INC
PO Box 1008, Grand Island, NE 68802
Crisis hotline: **(308) 381-0555 (collect calls accepted) 24 hrs**

CRISIS CENTER, INC (continued)
Information: (308) 382-8250 8am-5pm (Mon-Fri)
Contact: Lauri Shultis, Dir
TYPE OF AGENCY: Rape crisis center; Domestic violence program
AREAS SERVED: Hall, Howard, Hamilton, Merrick
YEARS IN OPERATION: 11
LANGUAGES: Laotian and Spanish interpreters available
CASES SEXUAL ASSAULT/ABUSE (%): 25
DESCRIPTION: Services for sexual assault and domestic violence survivors; Therapy program for batterers
CLIENTS/SERVICES: Sexual assault survivors; Marital rape/sexual abuse survivors; Adult survivors of child sexual abuse; Incest victims/survivors; Prevention program; Community education; Male survivors of sexual abuse

HASTINGS

SPOUSE ABUSE/SEXUAL ASSAULT CRISIS CENTER
422 N Hastings, B-2, Hastings, NE 68901
Crisis hotline: **(402) 463-4677 24 hrs**
Information: (402) 463-5810 8:30am-3:30pm
Contact: Rita Hamburger, Exec Dir
TYPE OF AGENCY: Rape crisis center; Domestic violence program; Acquaintance/date rape prevention program
AREAS SERVED: Adams, Clay, Nuckolls, Webster
YEARS IN OPERATION: 5
LANGUAGES: Spanish
CLIENTS/SERVICES: Sexual assault survivors; Marital rape/sexual abuse survivors; Child victims of sexual abuse; Adult survivors of child sexual abuse; Incest victims/survivors; Prevention program; Community education; Adolescent survivors of sexual abuse; Publications/media
SPECIAL PROGRAMS/SERVICES: Media program on date rape

JUNIATA

CHILD ABUSE PREVENTION NETWORK
Rte 2, Box 36, Juniata, NE 68955
Contact: Belva Junker, Pres
TYPE OF AGENCY: Child sexual abuse prevention program; Child abuse prevention program; Interagency network
AREAS SERVED: Adams, Clay, Webster, Nuckolls
YEARS IN OPERATION: 14
ACCESSIBILITY: Wheelchair accessible
DESCRIPTION: Sponsors Bubbylonian Encounter in the schools
CLIENTS/SERVICES: Prevention program; Community education

KEARNEY

THE SAFE CENTER
PO Box 575, 3720 Ave A, Kearney, NE 68848-0575
Crisis hotline: **(308) 237-2599 24 hrs**
Information: (308) 237-2599 9am-3pm
Contact: Judith Dunning, Prog Dir
TYPE OF AGENCY: Domestic violence program
AREAS SERVED: Buffalo, Kearney, Phelps, Harlan, Franklin
YEARS IN OPERATION: 10
CASES SEXUAL ASSAULT/ABUSE (%): 15
CLIENTS/SERVICES: Sexual assault survivors; Marital rape/sexual abuse survivors; Adult survivors of child sexual abuse; Incest victims/survivors; Community education; Male survivors of sexual abuse

LINCOLN

LINCOLN POLICE DEPARTMENT—VICTIM/WITNESS UNIT
233 S 10th St, Lincoln, NE 68508
Information: (402) 471-7181 8am-4:30pm (Mon-Fri)
Contact: JoAnna Koba-Svoboda, Admin
TYPE OF AGENCY: Victim/witness assistance program
AREAS SERVED: Lancaster
YEARS IN OPERATION: 6
ACCESSIBILITY: Wheelchair accessible
CASES SEXUAL ASSAULT/ABUSE (%): 25
CLIENTS/SERVICES: Sexual assault survivors; Marital rape/sexual abuse survivors; Child victims of sexual abuse; Adult survivors of child sexual abuse; Incest victims/survivors; Prevention program; Community education; Adolescent survivors of sexual abuse; Male survivors of sexual abuse; Publications/media
SPECIAL PROGRAMS/SERVICES: Locally-produced media on court procedures and a program on the Victim/Witness Unit services and the experience of victimization

RAPE/SPOUSE ABUSE CRISIS CENTER
1133 H St, Lincoln, NE 68508
Crisis hotline: **(402) 471-7273 24 hrs**
Information: (402) 471-7929 8am-9pm (Mon-Thu); 8am-5pm (Fri); 9am-12pm (Sat)
Contact: Nan Hynes, Prog Dir
TYPE OF AGENCY: Rape crisis center; Domestic violence program; Child sexual abuse services; Child sexual abuse prevention program
SPONSORING ORGANIZATION: Family Services Association
AREAS SERVED: Lancaster
YEARS IN OPERATION: 13
ACCESSIBILITY: Wheelchair accessible; Signers for the hearing impaired
CASES SEXUAL ASSAULT/ABUSE (%): 50
DESCRIPTION: Services for survivors of sexual assault and domestic violence; Individual and group therapy for batterers
CLIENTS/SERVICES: Sexual assault survivors; Marital rape/sexual abuse survivors; Child victims of sexual abuse; Adult survivors of child sexual abuse; Incest victims/survivors; Prevention program; Community education; Adolescent survivors of sexual abuse; Male survivors of sexual abuse

YWCA
1432 N St, Lincoln, NE 68508
Information: (402) 476-2802 9am-9pm
Contact: Jan Deeds, Counseling and Education Dir
TYPE OF AGENCY: Counseling/mental health services
AREAS SERVED: Lancaster
ACCESSIBILITY: Wheelchair accessible
CLIENTS/SERVICES: Sexual assault survivors; Marital rape/sexual abuse survivors; Adult survivors of child sexual abuse; Incest victims/survivors; Prevention program; Adolescent survivors of sexual abuse
REQUIREMENTS: Must be 12 years and older

MCCOOK

DOMESTIC ABUSE/SEXUAL ASSAULT SERVICES
PO Box 714, McCook, NE 69001
Crisis hotline: **(308) 345-5534 24 hrs**
Information: (308) 345-5534 9am-11:30am, 1pm-3:30pm (Mon-Fri)
Contact: Kathy Haas, Dir
TYPE OF AGENCY: Rape crisis center; Domestic violence program
AREAS SERVED: Red Willow, Furnas, Frontier, Hitchcock, Hayes, Chase
YEARS IN OPERATION: 9
ACCESSIBILITY: Wheelchair accessible
CASES SEXUAL ASSAULT/ABUSE (%): 20
CLIENTS/SERVICES: Sexual assault survivors; Marital rape/sexual abuse survivors; Child victims of sexual abuse; Adult survivors of child sexual abuse; Incest victims/survivors; Prevention program; Community education; Adolescent survivors of sexual abuse
REQUIREMENTS: Clients must be 18 years or older or have written parental permission for services.

NORFOLK

NORFOLK TASK FORCE ON DOMESTIC VIOLENCE AND SEXUAL ASSAULT
Box 1711, Norfolk, NE 68701
Crisis hotline: **(402) 379-3798 24 hrs**
Information: (402) 379-3798 9:30am-5:30pm
Contact: Jody Gallop, Dir
TYPE OF AGENCY: Rape crisis center; Domestic violence program
AREAS SERVED: Madison, Stanton, Antelope, Burt, Cuming, Holt, Knox, Cedar
YEARS IN OPERATION: 11
CLIENTS/SERVICES: Sexual assault survivors; Marital rape/sexual abuse survivors; Child victims of sexual abuse; Adult survivors of child sexual abuse; Incest victims/survivors; Community education

NORTH PLATTE

LINCOLN COUNTY ATTORNEY'S OFFICE—VICTIM/WITNESS ASSISTANCE UNIT
Lincoln County Courthouse, North Platte, NE 69101
Crisis hotline: **(308) 534-3438 8am-5pm, answering machine after hrs**
Information: (308) 534-4350 8am-5pm
Contact: Sheila Fleming, Dir
TYPE OF AGENCY: Victim/witness assistance program
AREAS SERVED: Lincoln
YEARS IN OPERATION: 5
ACCESSIBILITY: Wheelchair accessible
CLIENTS/SERVICES: Sexual assault survivors; Marital rape/sexual abuse survivors; Child victims of sexual abuse; Adult survivors of child sexual abuse; Incest victims/survivors; Adolescent survivors of sexual abuse; Male survivors of sexual abuse

RAPE/DOMESTIC ABUSE PROGRAM OF NORTH PLATTE, INC
PO Box 393, North Platte, NE 69103
Crisis hotline: **(308) 534-3495 24 hrs daily**
Information: (308) 532-9240 8am-5pm (Mon-Fri)
Contact: Kathleen Beashore, Dir
TYPE OF AGENCY: Rape crisis center; Domestic violence program
AREAS SERVED: Lincoln, Logan, Hooker, McPherson, Thomas
YEARS IN OPERATION: 4
CASES SEXUAL ASSAULT/ABUSE (%): 10
CLIENTS/SERVICES: Sexual assault survivors; Marital rape/sexual abuse survivors; Child victims of sexual abuse; Adult survivors of child sexual abuse; Incest victims/survivors; Prevention program; Community education; Adolescent survivors of sexual abuse; Male survivors of sexual abuse

OGALLALA

SCIP (SANDHILLS CRISIS INTERVENTION PROGRAM)
PO Box 22, Ogallala, NE 69153
Crisis hotline: **(308) 284-6055 24 hrs**
Information: (308) 284-8311
Contact: Lynn Macomber, Dir
TYPE OF AGENCY: Rape crisis center; Domestic violence program; Private practice
AREAS SERVED: Keith, Arthur, Garden, Grant, Devel, Perkins
YEARS IN OPERATION: 1½

SCIP (SANDHILLS CRISIS INTERVENTION PROGRAM) *(continued)*

CASES SEXUAL ASSAULT/ABUSE (%): 33
DESCRIPTION: To increase knowledge and awareness of the nature and scope of domestic violence and physical, sexual and emotional assault; to establish related ongoing victim emergency assistance and advocacy program; and make the public aware of related resources and services available to them. Teaches feminist martial arts/self-defense
CLIENTS/SERVICES: Sexual assault survivors; Adult survivors of child sexual abuse; Incest victims/survivors; Prevention program; Community education; Adolescent survivors of sexual abuse; Male survivors of sexual abuse
REQUIREMENTS: 18 or older unless with an adult

OMAHA

PARENTS UNITED/DAUGHTERS AND SONS UNITED
1313 Farnam St, Omaha, NE 68102
Information: (402) 595-3521 Douglas County, (402) 339-4294 Sarpy County Mon, Tue
Contact: Teri Wais, MSW, CSW, Dir
TYPE OF AGENCY: Child sexual abuse services
AREAS SERVED: Douglas, Sarpy
YEARS IN OPERATION: 14
CASES SEXUAL ASSAULT/ABUSE (%): 100
DESCRIPTION: Provides a self-help, support group experience for perpetrators, nonoffending spouses, victims, children, and adults molested as children
CLIENTS/SERVICES: Child victims of sexual abuse; Adult survivors of child sexual abuse; Incest victims/survivors; Community education; Adolescent survivors of sexual abuse; Male survivors of sexual abuse
REQUIREMENTS: Children ages 9 or older; Perpetrators must be admitting by 3rd month of involvement

YWCA WOMEN AGAINST VIOLENCE
222 S 29th St, Omaha, NE 68131
Crisis hotline: **(402) 345-7273 24 hrs**
Information: (402) 345-6555 8am-5pm
Contact: Mary Larsen, Dir
TYPE OF AGENCY: Rape crisis center; Domestic violence program; Child sexual abuse services; Child sexual abuse prevention program; Acquaintance/date rape prevention program
AREAS SERVED: Douglas, Sarpy, NE; Pottawatomie, IA
YEARS IN OPERATION: 14
LANGUAGES: Spanish
ACCESSIBILITY: Wheelchair accessible
DESCRIPTION: Provides counseling, crisis services, support groups for sexual assault survivors; Prevention programs geared toward child sexual abuse and acquaintance rape
CLIENTS/SERVICES: Sexual assault survivors; Marital rape/sexual abuse survivors; Child victims of sexual abuse; Adult survivors of child sexual abuse; Prevention program; Community education; Offender treatment program; Adolescent survivors of sexual abuse; Male survivors of sexual abuse

PAPILLION

SARPY COUNTY ATTORNEY'S OFFICE— VICTIM/WITNESS UNIT
Hall of Justice, 1210 Golden Gate Dr, Papillion, NE 68046
Information: (402) 593-2201 8:30am-4:45pm (Mon-Fri)
Contact: Jeffrey Vandenberg, Dir
TYPE OF AGENCY: Victim/witness assistance program; Child sexual abuse services; Adolescent program
AREAS SERVED: Sarpy
YEARS IN OPERATION: 4
LANGUAGES: Spanish

CASES SEXUAL ASSAULT/ABUSE (%): 10
CLIENTS/SERVICES: Sexual assault survivors; Marital rape/sexual abuse survivors; Child victims of sexual abuse; Adult survivors of child sexual abuse; Incest victims/survivors; Community education; Male survivors of sexual abuse
REQUIREMENTS: Majority of cases are being prosecuted through courts.
SPECIAL PROGRAMS/SERVICES: In conjunction with local therapists and law enforcement agencies, this organization has developed a program for victims of sexual assault perpetrated by non-family members, called C.A.R.E. (Children and Adolescents Recovering Emotionally). It is a short-term crisis-intervention, initial counseling program designed for victims and their parents. Further on-going counseling is provided by local agencies and therapists.

SCOTTSBLUFF

DOVES (DOMESTIC VIOLENCE EMERGENCY SERVICES)
PO Box 434, Scottsbluff, NE 69363-0434
Crisis hotline: **(308) 436-HELP 24 hrs**
Information: (308) 632-3683 8am-5pm (Mon-Fri)
Contact: Cheryl Dankers, Dir
TYPE OF AGENCY: Domestic violence program
AREAS SERVED: Banner, Morrill, Kimball, Sioux, Box Butte, Cheyenne, Scottsbluff
YEARS IN OPERATION: 10
LANGUAGES: Lakota and Spanish (by arrangement)
CASES SEXUAL ASSAULT/ABUSE (%): 25
CLIENTS/SERVICES: Sexual assault survivors; Marital rape/sexual abuse survivors; Adult survivors of child sexual abuse; Incest victims/survivors; Community education

WAYNE

HAVEN HOUSE FAMILY SERVICES CENTER
PO Box 44, Wayne, NE 68787
Crisis hotline: **(402) 375-4633 24 hrs**
Information: (402) 375-4633 9am-4pm
Contact: Sara Campbell, Dir
TYPE OF AGENCY: Rape crisis center; Domestic violence program
AREAS SERVED: Wayne, Thurston, Dakota, Dixon, Cedar
YEARS IN OPERATION: 10
ACCESSIBILITY: Wheelchair accessible
CLIENTS/SERVICES: Sexual assault survivors; Marital rape/sexual abuse survivors; Community education
REQUIREMENTS: Minors assisted with parental knowledge, except for referrals to other agencies

NEVADA

ELY

SUPPORT, INC
PO Box 583, Ely, NV 89301
Crisis hotline: **(702) 289-2270 24 hrs**
Information: (702) 289-2270 8am-5pm
Contact: Kathy Scott, Dir
TYPE OF AGENCY: Rape crisis center; Domestic violence program; Child sexual abuse services; Child sexual abuse prevention program
AREAS SERVED: White Pine, Eureka
YEARS IN OPERATION: 7
LANGUAGES: Spanish
CASES SEXUAL ASSAULT/ABUSE (%): 10
DESCRIPTION: Comprehensive services for survivors of domestic violence and sexual assault; Group therapy for batterers
CLIENTS/SERVICES: Sexual assault survivors; Marital rape/sexual abuse survivors; Child victims of sexual abuse; Adult survivors of child sexual abuse; Incest victims/survivors; Prevention program; Community education; Adolescent survivors of sexual abuse; Male survivors of sexual abuse
SPECIAL PROGRAMS/SERVICES: Conducts volunteer training through a class, in conjunction with the local community college (NNCC) for psychology credits

FALLON

DOMESTIC VIOLENCE INTERVENTION
PO Box 2231, Fallon, NV 89406
Crisis hotline: **(800) 992-5757 24 hrs**
Information: (702) 423-1313
Contact: Karen Bentley, Dir
TYPE OF AGENCY: Domestic violence program
AREAS SERVED: Churchill, Pershing, and 2 Indian Reservations
YEARS IN OPERATION: 6
LANGUAGES: Spanish
CLIENTS/SERVICES: Marital rape/sexual abuse survivors; Prevention program; Community education

LAS VEGAS

CHILD SEXUAL ABUSE TREATMENT PROGRAM (C-SAT)
3441 W Sahara, Ste C-3, Las Vegas, NV 89102
Information: (702) 368-1533 9am-5pm (Mon-Fri)
Contact: Sarah Beers, Prog Coord
TYPE OF AGENCY: Child sexual abuse services; Child abuse services
AREAS SERVED: Clark
YEARS IN OPERATION: 4
ACCESSIBILITY: Wheelchair accessible
CASES SEXUAL ASSAULT/ABUSE (%): 100
DESCRIPTION: Group therapy for sexually abused children and their families; Group therapy for incest offenders
CLIENTS/SERVICES: Child victims of sexual abuse; Adult survivors of child sexual abuse; Incest victims/survivors; Community education; Offender treatment program; Adolescent survivors of sexual abuse; Male survivors of sexual abuse; Publications/media
REQUIREMENTS: Child victims must be 8 years or older; Offender must admit to molestation
SPECIAL PROGRAMS/SERVICES: WE CAN (Working to Eliminate Child Abuse and Neglect) offers support groups in schools for all types of abuse and is developing a safety video for the school district

CLARK COUNTY JUVENILE COURT SERVICES—VICTIM ASSISTANCE CENTER
3401 E Bonanza Rd, Las Vegas, NV 89101
Information: (702) 455-5430 8am-5pm
TYPE OF AGENCY: Victim/witness assistance program
AREAS SERVED: Clark
LANGUAGES: Interpreters available
ACCESSIBILITY: Wheelchair accessible
CLIENTS/SERVICES: Child victims of sexual abuse

COMMUNITY ACTION AGAINST RAPE
3441 W Sahara Dr, Las Vegas, NV 89102
Crisis hotline: **(702) 366-1640 24 hrs daily**
Information: (702) 385-2153 8:30am-5pm (Mon-Fri)
Contact: Renata Cirri, Exec Dir
TYPE OF AGENCY: Rape crisis center; Child sexual abuse services; Child sexual abuse prevention program
AREAS SERVED: Clark
YEARS IN OPERATION: 14
LANGUAGES: Spanish
ACCESSIBILITY: Wheelchair accessible; Telecommunications for the hearing impaired (TTY, TDY, etc.); Signers for the hearing impaired
CASES SEXUAL ASSAULT/ABUSE (%): 100
CLIENTS/SERVICES: Sexual assault survivors; Marital rape/sexual abuse survivors; Child victims of sexual abuse; Adult survivors of child sexual abuse; Incest victims/survivors; Prevention program; Community education; Adolescent survivors of sexual abuse; Male survivors of sexual abuse

RETIRED SENIOR VOLUNTEER PROGRAM
1501 Las Vegas Blvd N, Las Vegas, NV 89101
Information: (702) 385-1328 8am-4pm (Mon-Fri)
Contact: Charles E Colletta, Dir
TYPE OF AGENCY: Rape prevention program
SPONSORING ORGANIZATION: Catholic Community Services of Nevada
AREAS SERVED: Clark
YEARS IN OPERATION: 17
ACCESSIBILITY: Wheelchair accessible
DESCRIPTION: Member of Citizen Committee on Victim Rights; Education and prevention training for seniors; Self defense for seniors.
CLIENTS/SERVICES: Prevention program; Community education; Elderly

LOVELOCK

DOMESTIC VIOLENCE INTERVENTION OF PERSHING COUNTY
PO Box 1203, Lovelock, NV 89419
Crisis hotline: **(702) 273-7373, Sheriff 273-2641**
Information: (702) 273-7373 9am-2:30pm (Tue, Wed)
Contact: Chris Bily, Dir
TYPE OF AGENCY: Domestic violence program
SPONSORING ORGANIZATION: Domestic Violence Intervention of Fallon, NV
AREAS SERVED: Pershing
YEARS IN OPERATION: 6 months
LANGUAGES: Spanish translator available
CLIENTS/SERVICES: Sexual assault survivors; Marital rape/sexual abuse survivors; Adult survivors of child sexual abuse; Incest victims/survivors; Prevention program; Community education

RENO

CHILD ASSAULT PREVENTION PROJECT (CAP)
PO Box 8117, Reno, NV 89507
Information: (702) 331-3888 8am-5pm
Contact: Crystal Swank, Exec Dir
TYPE OF AGENCY: Child sexual abuse prevention program
AREAS SERVED: Washoe
YEARS IN OPERATION: 4
DESCRIPTION: Provides workshops for children (preschool through high school) and adults on child assault prevention (physical and sexual abuse) to teach public awareness and skills needed to recognize and deal with dangerous situations
CLIENTS/SERVICES: Prevention program; Community education

COMMUNITY, RUNAWAY AND YOUTH SERVICES (CRYS)
1135 Terminal Way, Ste No 104, Reno, NV 89502
Crisis hotline: **(702) 323-6296 24 hrs**
Information: (702) 323-6296 9am-5pm (Mon-Fri)
Contact: Carol Holliday, Exec Dir
TYPE OF AGENCY: Adolescent program
AREAS SERVED: Washoe
YEARS IN OPERATION: 9
CASES SEXUAL ASSAULT/ABUSE (%): 12
DESCRIPTION: Provides 24-hour crisis intervention counseling for youth and families. After the initial contact, if sexual abuse/molestation has occurred, CRYS refers the individual and/or family to the proper agency. CRYS has two certified sexual abuse counselors on staff

COMMUNITY, RUNAWAY AND YOUTH SERVICES (CRYS) *(continued)*
CLIENTS/SERVICES: Sexual assault survivors; Child victims of sexual abuse; Adolescent survivors of sexual abuse; Male survivors of sexual abuse

FAMILY COUNSELING SERVICE OF NORTHERN NEVADA
777 Sinclair St, Ste 100, Reno, NV 89501
Information: (702) 329-0623 8am-8pm
Contact: Marlene Chrissinger, Admin/Clinic Dir
TYPE OF AGENCY: Counseling/mental health services; Child sexual abuse services
AREAS SERVED: Washoe
YEARS IN OPERATION: 29
ACCESSIBILITY: Wheelchair accessible
CASES SEXUAL ASSAULT/ABUSE (%): 10
DESCRIPTION: Community mental health center under contract with county Child Protection Services agency. Provides specialized program in child sexual abuse, counseling for sexual assault victims, and treatment for child sexual abuse/incest offenders and batterers.
CLIENTS/SERVICES: Sexual assault survivors; Marital rape/sexual abuse survivors; Child victims of sexual abuse; Adult survivors of child sexual abuse; Incest victims/survivors; Offender treatment program
REQUIREMENTS: Child abuse must be reported. Sliding scale fee

NORTHERN NEVADA CHILD/ADOLESCENT SERVICES (NNCAS)
2655 Enterprise Rd, Reno, NV 89512
Crisis hotline: **(702) 688-1600 24 hrs**
Information: (702) 688-1600 8am-5pm (Mon-Fri)
Contact: Darrell Downs, PhD, Outpatient Svcs Dir
TYPE OF AGENCY: Counseling/mental health services; Child sexual abuse services; Residential treatment facility; Adolescent program
SPONSORING ORGANIZATION: Nevada Division of Mental Hygiene, Mental Retardation
AREAS SERVED: Washoe, northern Nevada
YEARS IN OPERATION: 10
LANGUAGES: Spanish
ACCESSIBILITY: Wheelchair accessible
CASES SEXUAL ASSAULT/ABUSE (%): 10-15
DESCRIPTION: Provides mental health services for children, adolescents, and families. Outpatient treatment; Early childhood treatment program; Adolescent and child residential and day treatment; Adolescent community treatment home; Sex offender community treatment home; Abuse victims not involved in investigation
CLIENTS/SERVICES: Child victims of sexual abuse; Incest victims/survivors; Offender treatment program; Adolescent survivors of sexual abuse; Male survivors of sexual abuse
REQUIREMENTS: Nevada resident 18 or younger; Sex offender must be adjudicated

PARENTS UNITED OF WASHOE COUNTY, INC
PO Box 11130, Reno, NV 89520-0027
Information: (702) 328-2342 8am-5pm (Mon-Fri)
Contact: Shirlee Dias, Interim Exec Dir
TYPE OF AGENCY: Child sexual abuse services
AREAS SERVED: Northern NV and outlying northern CA counties
YEARS IN OPERATION: 7
ACCESSIBILITY: Wheelchair accessible
CASES SEXUAL ASSAULT/ABUSE (%): 100
CLIENTS/SERVICES: Sexual assault survivors; Child victims of sexual abuse; Adult survivors of child sexual abuse; Incest victims/survivors; Prevention program; Community education; Offender treatment program; Adolescent survivors of sexual abuse; Male survivors of sexual abuse
REQUIREMENTS: Pedophiles not treated; Program is restricted to cases involving intrafamilial child sexual abuse

PERSONAL DEVELOPMENT CONSULTANTS
1022 Forest St, Reno, NV 89509
Information: (702) 329-4582 7:30am-6:30pm
Contact: Meri Shadley, Chuck Holt, Partners
TYPE OF AGENCY: Private practice
AREAS SERVED: Washoe
YEARS IN OPERATION: 10
CASES SEXUAL ASSAULT/ABUSE (%): 15
CLIENTS/SERVICES: Sexual assault survivors; Marital rape/sexual abuse survivors; Adult survivors of child sexual abuse; Incest victims/survivors; Adolescent survivors of sexual abuse; Male survivors of sexual abuse

RAPE CRISIS CENTER
PO Box 8016, Reno, NV 89507
Crisis hotline: **(702) 323-6111 24 hrs**
Information: (702) 323-4533 24 hrs
Contact: Dianna Sanchez, Coord
TYPE OF AGENCY: Rape crisis center
SPONSORING ORGANIZATION: Crisis Call Center
AREAS SERVED: Washoe, Carson
YEARS IN OPERATION: 10
ACCESSIBILITY: Telecommunications for the hearing impaired (TTY, TDY, etc.)
CASES SEXUAL ASSAULT/ABUSE (%): 20
CLIENTS/SERVICES: Sexual assault survivors; Marital rape/sexual abuse survivors; Prevention program; Community education

SPARKS

COMMITTEE TO AID ABUSED WOMEN
101 15th St, Sparks, NV 89431
Crisis hotline: **(702) 323-6111 5pm-7am (Mon-Fri); 24 hrs (Sat-Sun)**
Information: (702) 358-4150 7am-5pm (Mon-Fri)
Contact: Joni Kaiser, Exec Dir
TYPE OF AGENCY: Domestic violence program
AREAS SERVED: Washoe, northern NV
YEARS IN OPERATION: 11
LANGUAGES: Spanish
ACCESSIBILITY: Wheelchair accessible
CLIENTS/SERVICES: Sexual assault survivors; Marital rape/sexual abuse survivors; Child victims of sexual abuse; Adult survivors of child sexual abuse; Incest victims/survivors; Prevention program; Community education; Publications/media
SPECIAL PROGRAMS/SERVICES: Publications: *Art Exercises with Women*, *Childrens Program Volunteer Manual*, *Parenting Manual*

YERINGTON

LYON COUNTY ALIVE (ALTERNATIVES TO LIVING IN VIOLENT ENVIRONMENTS)
PO Box 130, Yerington, NV 89447
Crisis hotline: **(702) 463-4009, 577-2781 24 hrs**
Information: (702) 463-4466 10am-4pm (Tue-Fri)
Contact: Diana Mominee, Coord
TYPE OF AGENCY: Rape crisis center; Domestic violence program
AREAS SERVED: Lyon
YEARS IN OPERATION: 1
ACCESSIBILITY: Wheelchair accessible
CLIENTS/SERVICES: Sexual assault survivors; Marital rape/sexual abuse survivors; Adult survivors of child sexual abuse; Prevention program; Community education

NEW HAMPSHIRE

BERLIN

RESPONSE TO SEXUAL AND DOMESTIC VIOLENCE
54 Willow St, Berlin, NH 03570
Crisis hotline: **(800) 336-6289 24 hrs**
Information: (603) 752-2040 8:30am-4:30pm
Contact: Donna L Cummings, Prog Coord
TYPE OF AGENCY: Rape crisis center; Domestic violence program
SPONSORING ORGANIZATION: Coos County Family Health Services, Inc
AREAS SERVED: Coos
YEARS IN OPERATION: 8
LANGUAGES: French
ACCESSIBILITY: Wheelchair accessible
CASES SEXUAL ASSAULT/ABUSE (%): 5
CLIENTS/SERVICES: Sexual assault survivors; Marital rape/sexual abuse survivors; Community education

CLAREMONT

WOMEN'S SUPPORTIVE SERVICES
11 School St, Claremont, NH 03743
Crisis hotline: **(603) 543-0155 24 hrs**
Information: (603) 542-8338 9am-4:30pm (Mon-Fri)
Contact: Deborah J Mozden, Dir
TYPE OF AGENCY: Rape crisis center; Domestic violence program; Child sexual abuse services
AREAS SERVED: Sullivan
YEARS IN OPERATION: 10
ACCESSIBILITY: Signers for the hearing impaired
CASES SEXUAL ASSAULT/ABUSE (%): 15
DESCRIPTION: Services for sexual assault and domestic violence survivors; Feminist martial arts/self-defense program
CLIENTS/SERVICES: Sexual assault survivors; Marital rape/sexual abuse survivors; Child victims of sexual abuse; Adult survivors of child sexual abuse; Incest victims/survivors; Community education; Adolescent survivors of sexual abuse; Male survivors of sexual abuse

CONCORD

RAPE AND DOMESTIC VIOLENCE CRISIS CENTER
PO Box 1344, Concord, NH 03302-1344
Crisis hotline: **(800) 852-3388, (603) 225-9000 24 hrs**
Information: (603) 225-7376 9am-4pm
Contact: Nancy A Francoeur, Exec Dir
TYPE OF AGENCY: Rape crisis center; Domestic violence program; Child sexual abuse prevention program
AREAS SERVED: Merrimack County
YEARS IN OPERATION: 11
LANGUAGES: Spanish, French, Thai, Cambodian, Iranian, Japanese, others by arrangement
ACCESSIBILITY: Telecommunications for the hearing impaired (TTY, TDY, etc.); Signers for the hearing impaired
CASES SEXUAL ASSAULT/ABUSE (%): 15
CLIENTS/SERVICES: Sexual assault survivors; Marital rape/sexual abuse survivors; Adult survivors of child sexual abuse; Incest victims/survivors; Prevention program; Community education; Male survivors of sexual abuse

DERRY

SEXUAL ASSAULT RECOVERY THRU AWARENESS AND HOPE—SARAH, INC
PO Box 1485, Derry, NH 03038
Information: (603) 432-8782 9am-5pm
Contact: Lyn Pine, Co-Founder/Chairperson of Board
TYPE OF AGENCY: Self-help groups; Adult survivors services
AREAS SERVED: Rockingham, Hillsborough
YEARS IN OPERATION: 3
ACCESSIBILITY: Wheelchair accessible
CASES SEXUAL ASSAULT/ABUSE (%): 100
DESCRIPTION: Support groups for survivors of incest/sexual abuse, including one group at Concord State Prison. SARAH recognizes that the trauma of sexual abuse needs to be validated before recovery can begin. Through recovery meetings, speaking engagements and workshops, SARAH seeks to break the cycle of abuse
CLIENTS/SERVICES: Adult survivors of child sexual abuse; Incest victims/survivors; Community education; Adolescent survivors of sexual abuse; Male survivors of sexual abuse; Prisoners
REQUIREMENTS: 17 years and older, male and female, preferably in therapy and with intake interview
SPECIAL PROGRAMS/SERVICES: Meetings are facilitator led. The facilitators are survivors who have made sufficient progress in their own recovery (SARAH member for at least 6 months) to be there each week so others may work on their recovery. This helps in strengthening the sense of self-empowerment and calls upon this person to recognize skills she/he thought she/he did not have

DOVER

SEXUAL ABUSE TREATMENT PROGRAM (SATP)
130 Central Ave, Dover, NH 03820
Crisis hotline: **(603) 742-0630 24 hrs**
Information: (603) 742-0630 8:30am-5pm
Contact: Paul K Katz, ACSW, SATP Mgr
TYPE OF AGENCY: Counseling/mental health services; Child sexual abuse services; Child sexual abuse prevention program
SPONSORING ORGANIZATION: Strafford Guidance Center, Inc
AREAS SERVED: Strafford
YEARS IN OPERATION: SATP 3, Agency 34
ACCESSIBILITY: Wheelchair accessible; Signers for the hearing impaired
CASES SEXUAL ASSAULT/ABUSE (%): 25-30
DESCRIPTION: SATP operates within a community mental health center, serving adult/child victims, non-offending parents, siblings, families, adolescent/adult sex offenders, and batterers
CLIENTS/SERVICES: Sexual assault survivors; Child victims of sexual abuse; Adult survivors of child sexual abuse; Incest victims/survivors; Prevention program; Community education; Offender treatment program; Adolescent survivors of sexual abuse; Male survivors of sexual abuse
REQUIREMENTS: No requirements for victims and families. Offenders must be followed by legal system for entry

STRAFFORD COUNTY HUMAN SERVICES
PO Box 799, Dover, NH 03820
Crisis hotline: **(603) 742-8078 8:30am-4:30pm**
Information: (603) 742-1469 8:30am-4:30pm
Contact: Betty Stowell, Juvenile Intervention Worker/Court Appointed Case Mgr
TYPE OF AGENCY: Counseling/mental health services
AREAS SERVED: Strafford
YEARS IN OPERATION: 12
ACCESSIBILITY: Wheelchair accessible
DESCRIPTION: Provides referral services as well as juvenile intervention services; County mediation program and parent support groups
CLIENTS/SERVICES: Child victims of sexual abuse

LEBANON

COUNSELING CENTER OF LEBANON
Box 10, 23 Old Etna Rd, Lebanon, NH 03766
Information: (603) 448-1101 8am-5pm (Mon-Fri)
Contact: Bill Ballantyne, Treatment Team Coord
TYPE OF AGENCY: Counseling/mental health services; Child sexual abuse services
SPONSORING ORGANIZATION: West Central Services, Inc
AREAS SERVED: Sullivan, lower Grafton, upper valley VT communities
YEARS IN OPERATION: 18
ACCESSIBILITY: Wheelchair accessible
DESCRIPTION: Counseling services, including individual and group therapy for sexual assault survivors, sexually abused children, adolescents and adult survivors. Comprehensive treatment program for child sexual abuse/incest offenders
CLIENTS/SERVICES: Sexual assault survivors; Marital rape/sexual abuse survivors; Child victims of sexual abuse; Adult survivors of child

COUNSELING CENTER OF LEBANON
(continued)

sexual abuse; Incest victims/survivors; Community education; Offender treatment program; Adolescent survivors of sexual abuse; Male survivors of sexual abuse
REQUIREMENTS: Offenders must be charged and adjudicated as a sexual offender

DOMESTIC VIOLENCE AND SEXUAL ASSAULT PROGRAM OF THE UPPER VALLEY
58 Hanover St, Lebanon, NH 03766
Crisis hotline: **(603) 448-5525 24 hrs**
Information: (603) 448-5922 9am-4:30pm (Mon-Thu)
Contact: Lyn Staack, Prog Dir
TYPE OF AGENCY: Rape crisis center; Domestic violence program
SPONSORING ORGANIZATION: Women's Information Services (WISE)
AREAS SERVED: Windsor, Orange, VT; Southern Grafton, NH
YEARS IN OPERATION: 15
LANGUAGES: Spanish, French, Italian, Chinese
ACCESSIBILITY: Signers for the hearing impaired
CASES SEXUAL ASSAULT/ABUSE (%): 12
CLIENTS/SERVICES: Sexual assault survivors; Marital rape/sexual abuse survivors; Child victims of sexual abuse; Adult survivors of child sexual abuse; Incest victims/survivors; Prevention program; Community education

HEADREST
14 Church St, Box 221, Lebanon, NH 03766
Crisis hotline: **(603) 448-4400 24 hrs**
Information: (603) 448-4872 9am-5pm
Contact: Bob Sandoe, Dir
TYPE OF AGENCY: Counseling/mental health services; Telephone crisis counseling
AREAS SERVED: The upper valley of NH and VT
YEARS IN OPERATION: 17
CASES SEXUAL ASSAULT/ABUSE (%): 5-10
CLIENTS/SERVICES: Sexual assault survivors; Child victims of sexual abuse; Adult survivors of child sexual abuse; Incest victims/survivors; Male survivors of sexual abuse

MANCHESTER

HILLSBOROUGH COUNTY ATTORNEY'S OFFICE—VICTIM/WITNESS SERVICES
300 Chestnut St, Manchester, NH 03101
Information: (603) 627-5605 9am-5pm
Contact: Catherine McNaughton, Dir
TYPE OF AGENCY: Victim/witness assistance program
AREAS SERVED: Hillsborough
YEARS IN OPERATION: 10
ACCESSIBILITY: Wheelchair accessible
CASES SEXUAL ASSAULT/ABUSE (%): 90
CLIENTS/SERVICES: Sexual assault survivors; Marital rape/sexual abuse survivors; Child victims of sexual abuse; Adult survivors of child sexual abuse; Incest victims/survivors; Community education; Male survivors of sexual abuse
REQUIREMENTS: Assist victims who have, or are considering, filing charges

WOMEN'S CRISIS SERVICE
72 Concord St, Manchester, NH 03101
Crisis hotline: **(603) 668-2299 24 hrs daily**
Information: (603) 625-5785 9am-5pm (Mon-Fri)
Contact: Jeannette Sheldon, Dir
TYPE OF AGENCY: Rape crisis center; Domestic violence program
SPONSORING ORGANIZATION: YWCA
AREAS SERVED: Hillsborough
YEARS IN OPERATION: 12
LANGUAGES: Spanish and other translators available
ACCESSIBILITY: Wheelchair accessible
CASES SEXUAL ASSAULT/ABUSE (%): 17
DESCRIPTION: Provides direct services for victims of rape and battering; Prevention services for children and adolescents; Feminist martial arts/self-defense program
CLIENTS/SERVICES: Sexual assault survivors; Marital rape/sexual abuse survivors; Adult survivors of child sexual abuse; Incest victims/survivors; Prevention program; Community education; Adolescent survivors of sexual abuse; Prisoners
SPECIAL PROGRAMS/SERVICES: Education and support groups in prison for female survivors of rape, child abuse, and battery, and for women who have committed a violent crime as a result of living in violence. Services include educational program on understanding violence and power, and control relationships; One-on-one peer counseling while in prison; Outreach to inmates at halfway house

NASHUA

RAPE AND ASSAULT SUPPORT SERVICES
PO Box 217, Nashua, NH 03061
Crisis hotline: **(603) 883-3044 24 hrs**
Information: (603) 883-5521, ext 2208 8:30am-4:30pm
Contact: Deborah Fauth, Prog Dir
TYPE OF AGENCY: Rape crisis center; Domestic violence program; Child sexual abuse services; Child sexual abuse prevention program
AREAS SERVED: Hillsborough, Rockingham
YEARS IN OPERATION: 12
LANGUAGES: Spanish
CASES SEXUAL ASSAULT/ABUSE (%): 33
CLIENTS/SERVICES: Sexual assault survivors; Marital rape/sexual abuse survivors; Child victims of sexual abuse; Adult survivors of child sexual abuse; Incest victims/survivors; Prevention program; Community education; Adolescent survivors of sexual abuse; Male survivors of sexual abuse

PLYMOUTH

CENTER FOR WOMEN'S SERVICES
Bagley House, Plymouth, NH 03264
Information: (603) 536-5000, ext 2387 8am-4:30pm
Contact: Beverly N Hart, Dir/Couns
TYPE OF AGENCY: College/university-based services; Acquaintance/date rape prevention program
SPONSORING ORGANIZATION: Plymouth State College
AREAS SERVED: Plymouth state college only
YEARS IN OPERATION: 7
ACCESSIBILITY: Wheelchair accessible
DESCRIPTION: Provides crisis counseling and support groups for sexual assault survivors; Programs on sexual harassment and violence in relationships, among many topics; Prevention programs on date/acquaintance rape
CLIENTS/SERVICES: Sexual assault survivors; Prevention program; Community education; Sexual harassment
REQUIREMENTS: Must be a student at Plymouth State College

PLYMOUTH AREA CRISIS SERVICES
PO Box 53, Plymouth, NH 03264
Crisis hotline: **(603) 536-1659 24 hrs**
Information: (603) 563-3423 8am-4pm (Mon-Fri)
Contact: Andi Lee, Prog Dir
TYPE OF AGENCY: Rape crisis center; Domestic violence program
AREAS SERVED: Southeastern Grafton
YEARS IN OPERATION: 7
LANGUAGES: Spanish, French, Danish
CLIENTS/SERVICES: Sexual assault survivors; Marital rape/sexual abuse survivors; Adult survivors of child sexual abuse; Incest victims/survivors; Community education; Male survivors of sexual abuse

PORTSMOUTH

SEACOAST MENTAL HEALTH CENTER
1145 Sagamore Rd, Portsmouth, NH 03801
Crisis hotline: **(603) 431-6703 24 hrs**
Information: (603) 431-6703
Contact: Kay Wagner, Children/Youth Svcs Dir
TYPE OF AGENCY: Counseling/mental health services
AREAS SERVED: Rockingham
YEARS IN OPERATION: 25
LANGUAGES: French
ACCESSIBILITY: Wheelchair accessible
CASES SEXUAL ASSAULT/ABUSE (%): 60
DESCRIPTION: Counseling and group therapy for victims/survivors and rapists, child sexual abuse and incest offenders
CLIENTS/SERVICES: Sexual assault survivors; Marital rape/sexual abuse survivors; Child victims of sexual abuse; Adult survivors of child sexual abuse; Incest victims/survivors; Offender treatment program; Adolescent survivors of sexual abuse; Male survivors of sexual abuse

WOMEN'S RESOURCE CENTER
1 Junkins Ave, Portsmouth, NH 03801
Crisis hotline: **(800) 852-3311 9am-5pm**
Information: (603) 436-4107 24 hrs, Advocates on call
Contact: Linda Juvanty, Svcs Dir
TYPE OF AGENCY: Rape crisis center; Child sexual abuse services; Child sexual abuse prevention program
AREAS SERVED: Rockingham, Strafford
YEARS IN OPERATION: 10
LANGUAGES: Spanish
ACCESSIBILITY: Wheelchair accessible
CASES SEXUAL ASSAULT/ABUSE (%): 100
CLIENTS/SERVICES: Sexual assault survivors; Marital rape/sexual abuse survivors; Child victims of sexual abuse; Adult survivors of child sexual abuse; Incest victims/survivors; Prevention program; Community education

NEW JERSEY

BELVEDERE

DOMESTIC ABUSE AND RAPE CRISIS CENTER, INC
PO Box 423, Belvedere, NJ 07823
Crisis hotline: **(201) 475-8408 24 hrs**
Information: (201) 475-4420
Contact: Bonnie Lawrence
TYPE OF AGENCY: Rape crisis center; Domestic violence program
AREAS SERVED: Warren
LANGUAGES: Spanish speaking interpreter available
CLIENTS/SERVICES: Sexual assault survivors; Marital rape/sexual abuse survivors; Adult survivors of child sexual abuse; Incest victims/survivors; Community education

BRANT BEACH

THE SEXUAL ABUSE AND ASSAULT PROGRAM
4700 Long Beach Blvd, Brant Beach, NJ 08005
Crisis hotline: **(609) 494-1090, (201) 370-4090 24 hrs**
Information: (609) 494-1554 9am-9pm (Mon-Fri); 9am-1pm (Sat)
Contact: Teresa Gray Lewis, Prog Coord
TYPE OF AGENCY: Rape crisis center; Counseling/mental health services; Child sexual abuse services
SPONSORING ORGANIZATION: St Francis Counseling Service
AREAS SERVED: Ocean
YEARS IN OPERATION: 3½
LANGUAGES: Spanish
ACCESSIBILITY: Wheelchair accessible
CASES SEXUAL ASSAULT/ABUSE (%): 100
DESCRIPTION: Crisis intervention and ongoing therapy for victims/survivors; Individual therapy for child sexual abuse/incest offenders and batterers
CLIENTS/SERVICES: Sexual assault survivors; Marital rape/sexual abuse survivors; Child victims of sexual abuse; Adult survivors of child sexual abuse; Incest victims/survivors; Prevention program; Community education; Offender treatment program; Adolescent survivors of sexual abuse; Male survivors of sexual abuse; Healing
SPECIAL PROGRAMS/SERVICES: Marathon weekends for mothers of incest victims groups; Adolescent incest survivors groups involve a weekend (at a borrowed house near the ocean) of therapy, recreation, education, and socializing

BRIDGETON

CUMBERLAND COUNTY PROSECUTOR'S OFFICE—SEXUAL ASSAULT UNIT
43 Fayette St, CN01, Bridgeton, NJ 08302
Crisis hotline: **(609) 451-8010 After 4:30pm**
Information: (609) 451-8000, ext 474 8:30am-4:30pm
Contact: Beth P Evans, Victim-Witness Coord
TYPE OF AGENCY: Victim/witness assistance program
AREAS SERVED: Cumberland
ACCESSIBILITY: Wheelchair accessible
CASES SEXUAL ASSAULT/ABUSE (%): 50
DESCRIPTION: Provides court information and support; Witness preparation; Court accompaniment; Referrals
CLIENTS/SERVICES: Sexual assault survivors; Marital rape/sexual abuse survivors; Child victims of sexual abuse; Adult survivors of child sexual abuse; Incest victims/survivors; Community education; Adolescent survivors of sexual abuse
REQUIREMENTS: Must file criminal charges

BRIDGEWATER

SOMERSET COALITION FOR PREVENTION AND TREATMENT OF SEXUAL ABUSE
500 N Bridge St, Bridgewater, NJ 08807
Information: (201) 725-2800
Contact: Katrina Monroe, EdM, Coord
TYPE OF AGENCY: Rape crisis center; Child sexual abuse services; Child sexual abuse prevention program; Interagency network
SPONSORING ORGANIZATION: Richard Hall Community Mental Health Center
AREAS SERVED: Somerset
DESCRIPTION: Coalition of agencies and individuals united in an effort to implement and support programs to combat child and adult sexual abuse and its effects. Provides direct services for victims/survivors, as well as, information and referral, sponsorship of the Child Assault Prevention (CAP) Project, agency coordination, and biennial conferences.
CLIENTS/SERVICES: Sexual assault survivors; Marital rape/sexual abuse survivors; Child victims of sexual abuse; Adult survivors of child sexual abuse; Incest victims/survivors; Prevention program; Community education

BURLINGTON

PROVIDENCE HOUSE/WILLINGBORO SHELTER
PO Box 424, Burlington, NJ 08016
Crisis hotline: **(609) 871-7551 24 hrs**
Information: (609) 871-7551, 871-7552 9am-5pm
Contact: Jean Metz, Prog Supv; Rochelle Smith, Prog Coord
TYPE OF AGENCY: Domestic violence program
SPONSORING ORGANIZATION: Catholic Charities—Diocese of Trenton
AREAS SERVED: Burlington
YEARS IN OPERATION: 11
LANGUAGES: Spanish, German
ACCESSIBILITY: Wheelchair accessible; Telecommunications for the hearing impaired (TTY, TDY, etc.)
CLIENTS/SERVICES: Marital rape/sexual abuse survivors; Child victims of sexual abuse; Adult survivors of child sexual abuse; Incest victims/survivors; Community education; Offender treatment program

CAMDEN

CAMDEN COUNTY PROSECUTOR'S OFFICE
518 Market St, Parkade Bldg, 4th Fl, Camden, NJ 08101
Crisis hotline: **(800) 242-0804**
Information: (609) 757-8400 8:30am-4:30pm
Contact: Linda Burkett, Victim-Witness Coord
TYPE OF AGENCY: Victim/witness assistance program
AREAS SERVED: Camden County
YEARS IN OPERATION: 1½
LANGUAGES: Spanish interpreter available
CASES SEXUAL ASSAULT/ABUSE (%): 20
CLIENTS/SERVICES: Sexual assault survivors; Child victims of sexual abuse; Community education
REQUIREMENTS: Must file charges

FAMILY COUNSELING SERVICE
217 S 6th St, Camden, NJ 08103
Information: (609) 964-1990 9am-9pm (Mon-Thu); 9am-5pm (Fri)
Contact: Nate Terrell, Indiv and Family Therapy Prog Coord
TYPE OF AGENCY: Counseling/mental health services; Child sexual abuse services
AREAS SERVED: Camden, Gloucester
YEARS IN OPERATION: 60
LANGUAGES: Spanish
CASES SEXUAL ASSAULT/ABUSE (%): 10
DESCRIPTION: Individual, group, and family therapy for survivors; Community day care for children with special needs; Treatment for rapists, batterers, child sexual abuse/incest offenders, and adolescent sex offenders
CLIENTS/SERVICES: Sexual assault survivors; Marital rape/sexual abuse survivors; Child victims of sexual abuse; Adult survivors of child sexual abuse; Incest victims/survivors; Community education; Offender treatment program; Adolescent survivors of sexual abuse; Male survivors of sexual abuse; Preschoolers

CAPE MAY COURT HOUSE

COALITION AGAINST RAPE AND ABUSE (CARA)
Box 43, Cape May Court House, NJ 08210
Crisis hotline: **(609) 522-6489 24 hrs**
Information: (609) 522-6489
Contact: Jade Deignan
TYPE OF AGENCY: Rape crisis center
AREAS SERVED: Cape May
CLIENTS/SERVICES: Sexual assault survivors; Child victims of sexual abuse; Adult survivors of child sexual abuse; Incest victims/survivors; Community education

COLLINGSWOOD

WAR (WOMEN AGAINST RAPE)
PO Box 346, Collingswood, NJ 08108
Crisis hotline: **(609) 858-7800 24 hrs**
Information: (609) 858-7800 24 hrs
Contact: Joan McKenna, Dir
TYPE OF AGENCY: Rape crisis center; Child sexual abuse prevention program
AREAS SERVED: Burlington, Gloucester, Camden
YEARS IN OPERATION: 15
LANGUAGES: Spanish, Chinese
ACCESSIBILITY: Wheelchair accessible; Signers for the hearing impaired
CASES SEXUAL ASSAULT/ABUSE (%): 97
DESCRIPTION: Comprehensive rape crisis services, including support groups for female and male survivors of sexual abuse/assault and emergency shelter for victims of sexual assault. Prevention programs for persons of all ages, including senior citizens
CLIENTS/SERVICES: Sexual assault survivors; Marital rape/sexual abuse survivors; Child victims of sexual abuse; Adult survivors of child sexual abuse; Incest victims/survivors; Prevention program; Community education; Adolescent survivors of sexual abuse; Male survivors of sexual abuse; Elderly

EAST ORANGE

EAST ORANGE GENERAL HOSPITAL—CRISIS INTERVENTION UNIT
300 Central Ave, East Orange, NJ 07019
Crisis hotline: **(201) 672-9685, 672-9686 24 hrs**
Information: (201) 672-9685, 672-9686 24 hrs
Contact: Susan Herman, RN, Crisis Intervention Unit Dept Mgr
TYPE OF AGENCY: Hospital/medical center
AREAS SERVED: Essex
YEARS IN OPERATION: 9
LANGUAGES: Translators available
ACCESSIBILITY: Wheelchair accessible
DESCRIPTION: Provides brief crisis counseling for individuals (adults and children) who are victims of sexual assault/abuse. Patients are referred to other agencies for follow-up treatment. Patients are also medically treated in the emergency room and interviewed by the local police
CLIENTS/SERVICES: Sexual assault survivors; Marital rape/sexual abuse survivors; Child victims of sexual abuse; Male survivors of sexual abuse
REQUIREMENTS: Children are treated with parental/guardian consent

ELMER

SALEM COUNTY RAPE CRISIS CENTER
PO Box 655, Elmer, NJ 08318
Crisis hotline: **(609) 935-6655 24 hrs**
Information: (609) 935-6655 24 hrs
Contact: Marsha Charlton, Dir
TYPE OF AGENCY: Rape crisis center; Child sexual abuse prevention program
AREAS SERVED: Salem
YEARS IN OPERATION: 10
LANGUAGES: Sign
ACCESSIBILITY: Signers for the hearing impaired
CASES SEXUAL ASSAULT/ABUSE (%): 100
CLIENTS/SERVICES: Sexual assault survivors; Marital rape/sexual abuse survivors; Child victims of sexual abuse; Adult survivors of child sexual abuse; Incest victims/survivors; Prevention program; Community education; Adolescent survivors of sexual abuse; Male survivors of sexual abuse

FLEMINGTON

HUNTERDON MEDICAL CENTER—COMMUNITY MENTAL HEALTH CENTER
Rte 31, Flemington, NJ 08822
Information: (201) 788-6401 hrs vary
Contact: D Bjorn Olson, PhD, Staff Psychologist
TYPE OF AGENCY: Hospital/medical center; Counseling/mental health services
AREAS SERVED: Primarily Hunterdon; Surrounding counties by request
YEARS IN OPERATION: 2½
ACCESSIBILITY: Wheelchair accessible
CASES SEXUAL ASSAULT/ABUSE (%): 100
DESCRIPTION: Provides services for sexually abused children, sexual assault survivors, and adolescent sex offenders
CLIENTS/SERVICES: Sexual assault survivors; Child victims of sexual abuse; Incest victims/survivors; Offender treatment program; Adolescent survivors of sexual abuse

WOMEN'S CRISIS SERVICES, INC
3 Main St, Flemington, NJ 08804
Crisis hotline: **(201) 788-4044 24 hrs**
Information: (201) 788-4044 8am-6pm
Contact: Shirley Smith, Dir
TYPE OF AGENCY: Rape crisis center; Domestic violence program
AREAS SERVED: Hunterdon
YEARS IN OPERATION: 9
LANGUAGES: Spanish
ACCESSIBILITY: Telecommunications for the hearing impaired (TTY, TDY, etc.)
CASES SEXUAL ASSAULT/ABUSE (%): 10
DESCRIPTION: Services for sexual assault and domestic violence survivors; Individual and group therapy for batterers
CLIENTS/SERVICES: Sexual assault survivors; Marital rape/sexual abuse survivors; Adult survivors of child sexual abuse; Incest victims/survivors; Prevention program; Community education; Adolescent survivors of sexual abuse

FREEHOLD

INSTITUTE FOR APPLIED PSYCHOLOGY
75 W Main St, Freehold, NJ 07728
Crisis hotline: **(201) 431-2663 24 hrs**
Information: (201) 431-2663 24 hrs answering service
Contact: Dr Martin Krupnick, Exec Dir
TYPE OF AGENCY: Private practice
AREAS SERVED: Monmouth, Ocean, Middlesex, Mercer, available to others
YEARS IN OPERATION: 7
CASES SEXUAL ASSAULT/ABUSE (%): 50
CLIENTS/SERVICES: Sexual assault survivors; Marital rape/sexual abuse survivors; Child victims of sexual abuse; Adult survivors of child sexual abuse; Incest victims/survivors; Offender treatment program; Adolescent survivors of sexual abuse; Male survivors of sexual abuse

PROBATION OFFENDERS PROGRAM
75 W Main St, Freehold, NJ 07728
Information: (201) 431-2663 9am-5pm
Contact: John Smack, Probation Officer/Prog Dir, Martin Krupnick, PsyD, Prog Consultant
TYPE OF AGENCY: Probation department; Offender treatment
SPONSORING ORGANIZATION: Monmouth County Probation Department
AREAS SERVED: Monmouth
YEARS IN OPERATION: 4
CASES SEXUAL ASSAULT/ABUSE (%): 100
DESCRIPTION: Screens all juvenile sex offenders to determine their eligibility for community-based treatment; Provides individual, group, and family therapy for juvenile sex offenders
CLIENTS/SERVICES: Offender treatment program

GLASSBORO

GLOUCESTER COUNTY RAPE ASSAULT PREVENTION PROGRAM
16 E High St, Glassboro, NJ 08028
Information: (609) 881-5921
Contact: Colleen Buckley
TYPE OF AGENCY: Rape crisis center
AREAS SERVED: Gloucester
CLIENTS/SERVICES: Sexual assault survivors; Child victims of sexual abuse; Adult survivors of child sexual abuse; Incest victims/survivors; Community education

WOMEN'S REFERRAL CENTER
7 State St, Glassboro, NJ 08028
Crisis hotline: **(800) 322-8092 24 hrs**
Information: (609) 881-7045 9am-5pm
Contact: Paul Stratton, Counseling Svcs Mgr
TYPE OF AGENCY: Information and referral
SPONSORING ORGANIZATION: Together, Inc
AREAS SERVED: Statewide
YEARS IN OPERATION: 18
ACCESSIBILITY: Telecommunications for the hearing impaired (TTY, TDY, etc.)
CASES SEXUAL ASSAULT/ABUSE (%): 10
CLIENTS/SERVICES: Sexual assault survivors; Marital rape/sexual abuse survivors; Child victims of sexual abuse; Adult survivors of child sexual abuse; Incest victims/survivors

HACKENSACK

ALTERNATIVES TO DOMESTIC VIOLENCE
21 Main St, Court Plaza S, Hackensack, NJ 07601
Crisis hotline: **(201) 487-8484 24 hrs**
Information: (201) 487-8484 9am-9pm (Mon-Thu); 9am-5pm (Fri)
TYPE OF AGENCY: Domestic violence program; Counseling/mental health services; Adolescent program
SPONSORING ORGANIZATION: Bergen County Department of Human Services
AREAS SERVED: Bergen
YEARS IN OPERATION: 12
ACCESSIBILITY: Wheelchair accessible
CASES SEXUAL ASSAULT/ABUSE (%): 4
DESCRIPTION: Comprehensive services for domestic violence survivors; Adolescent specialist on staff to intervene with teen dating abuse
CLIENTS/SERVICES: Sexual assault survivors; Marital rape/sexual abuse survivors; Adult survivors of child sexual abuse; Incest victims/survivors; Prevention program; Community education

BERGEN COUNTY COALITION AGAINST SEXUAL ASSAULT
285 Passaic St, Hackensack, NJ 07601
Crisis hotline: **(201) 487-2227 24 hrs**
Information: (201) 488-7110 9am-4pm (Mon-Fri)
TYPE OF AGENCY: Child sexual abuse prevention program; Interagency network
SPONSORING ORGANIZATION: YWCA of Hackensack
AREAS SERVED: Bergen
YEARS IN OPERATION: 3
LANGUAGES: Spanish
ACCESSIBILITY: Wheelchair accessible
CASES SEXUAL ASSAULT/ABUSE (%): 60
CLIENTS/SERVICES: Sexual assault survivors; Marital rape/sexual abuse survivors; Child victims of sexual abuse; Adult survivors of child sexual abuse; Incest victims/survivors; Community education; Adolescent survivors of sexual abuse; Male survivors of sexual abuse

BERGEN COUNTY PROSECUTOR'S OFFICE—VICTIM/WITNESS ADVOCACY
Bergen County Courthouse, Hackensack, NJ 07601
Crisis hotline: **(201) 646-2057 9am-4:30pm (Mon-Fri)**
Information: (201) 646-2057 9am-4:30pm (Mon-Fri)
Contact: Mary Pillarella, County Coord
TYPE OF AGENCY: Victim/witness assistance program; Child sexual abuse services; Child sexual abuse prevention program
AREAS SERVED: Bergen
YEARS IN OPERATION: 10
LANGUAGES: Spanish
ACCESSIBILITY: Wheelchair accessible
CASES SEXUAL ASSAULT/ABUSE (%): 85
DESCRIPTION: In addition to victim assistance services and court orientation and accompaniment, sponsors Survivors of Rape, a support group for adult female survivors of rape
CLIENTS/SERVICES: Sexual assault survivors; Marital rape/sexual abuse survivors; Child victims of sexual abuse; Adult survivors of child sexual abuse; Incest victims/survivors; Prevention program; Community education; Adolescent survivors of sexual abuse; Male survivors of sexual abuse

BERGEN COUNTY RAPE CRISIS CENTER
285 Passaic St, Hackensack, NJ 07601
Crisis hotline: **(201) 487-2227 24 hrs**
Information: (201) 488-7110 9am-4pm
Contact: Jill Greenbaum, Dir
TYPE OF AGENCY: Rape crisis center
SPONSORING ORGANIZATION: YWCA
AREAS SERVED: Primarily Bergen
YEARS IN OPERATION: 13
LANGUAGES: Spanish
ACCESSIBILITY: Wheelchair accessible
CASES SEXUAL ASSAULT/ABUSE (%): 99
CLIENTS/SERVICES: Sexual assault survivors; Marital rape/sexual abuse survivors; Child victims of sexual abuse; Adult survivors of child sexual abuse; Prevention program; Community education; Adolescent survivors of sexual abuse; Male survivors of sexual abuse
SPECIAL PROGRAMS/SERVICES: Volunteer training program highlights special needs of different populations: female/male, lesbian/gay, child, adolescent, elderly, physically disabled, significant others (lovers, husbands, parents)

FAMILY SERVICES OF BERGEN COUNTY, INC
10 Banta Pl, Hackensack, NJ 07601
Information: (201) 342-9200 9am-9pm (Mon, Wed, Thu); 9am-5pm (Tue, Fri)
Contact: Tricia DeBartolome, Professional Svcs Dir
TYPE OF AGENCY: Counseling/mental health services
AREAS SERVED: Bergen, Passaic, Union, Hudson
YEARS IN OPERATION: 89
LANGUAGES: Spanish
ACCESSIBILITY: Wheelchair accessible
CASES SEXUAL ASSAULT/ABUSE (%): 15-20
DESCRIPTION: Individual and family counseling; Groups and case management services for families; Special programs for elderly, AIDS, adult and adolescent survivors of incest and their families, and sexually abused children
CLIENTS/SERVICES: Sexual assault survivors; Marital rape/sexual abuse survivors; Child victims of sexual abuse; Adult survivors of child sexual abuse; Incest victims/survivors; Prevention program; Community education; Adolescent survivors of sexual abuse; Male survivors of sexual abuse

HIGHLAND PARK

FAMILY SERVICE ASSOCIATION OF MIDDLESEX COUNTY
901 Raritan Ave, Highland Park, NJ 08904
Contact: Belle Meisler, Supv
TYPE OF AGENCY: Counseling/mental health services; Child sexual abuse services
AREAS SERVED: Middlesex, South
YEARS IN OPERATION: 7
CASES SEXUAL ASSAULT/ABUSE (%): 100
DESCRIPTION: South county program provides counseling and support services for victims of sexual assault/child sexual abuse. Program is funded by Division of Youth and Family Services
CLIENTS/SERVICES: Sexual assault survivors; Child victims of sexual abuse; Adult survivors of child sexual abuse; Adolescent survivors of sexual abuse
REQUIREMENTS: Clients must be referred through New Jersey Division of Youth and Family Services

HIGHTSTOWN

FAMILY SERVICE PRINCETON AREA
169 S Main St, Hightstown, NJ 08520
Information: (609) 448-0056 9am-9pm (Mon-Thu); 9am-5pm (Fri)
TYPE OF AGENCY: Counseling/mental health services
AREAS SERVED: Mercer, Middlesex
YEARS IN OPERATION: 90
CLIENTS/SERVICES: Marital rape/sexual abuse survivors; Child victims of sexual abuse; Adult survivors of child sexual abuse; Incest victims/survivors

HOBOKEN

ST MARY'S MENTAL HEALTH CENTER
314 Clinton St, Hoboken, NJ 07030
Crisis hotline: **(201) 795-5505 24 hrs**
Information: (201) 792-8200 9am-5pm (Mon-Fri)
Contact: Helene Pinsky, Clinical Soc Wkr
TYPE OF AGENCY: Hospital/medical center; Counseling/mental health services; Child sexual abuse services; Child sexual abuse prevention program
AREAS SERVED: Hudson
YEARS IN OPERATION: 2½
CASES SEXUAL ASSAULT/ABUSE (%): 100
DESCRIPTION: Incest and sexual abuse unit is a community-based outpatient treatment program that serves survivors and juvenile offenders of intra- or extrafamilial sexual abuse. Groups for non-offending mothers whose children have been abused and for pre-adolescent female victims/survivors
CLIENTS/SERVICES: Child victims of sexual abuse; Incest victims/survivors; Prevention program; Community education; Offender treatment program; Adolescent survivors of sexual abuse
REQUIREMENTS: Clients must be referred from either the court or DYFS (child protective agency). In the case of an offender, referral is accepted only after sentencing.

JERSEY CITY

HUDSON COUNTY PROSECUTOR'S OFFICE—SEXUAL ASSAULT VICTIM ASSISTANCE (SAVA) UNIT
595 Newark Ave, Jersey City, NJ 07306
Crisis hotline: **(201) 451-7282 24 hrs**
Information: (201) 451-7282, 795-6508 24 hrs
Contact: Donald Racek, Lt in charge of SAVA
TYPE OF AGENCY: Victim/witness assistance program
AREAS SERVED: Hudson
YEARS IN OPERATION: 10
LANGUAGES: Spanish
ACCESSIBILITY: Wheelchair accessible (by request); Telecommunications for the hearing impaired (TTY, TDY, etc.) (by request); Signers for the hearing impaired (by request)
CASES SEXUAL ASSAULT/ABUSE (%): 25
CLIENTS/SERVICES: Sexual assault survivors; Marital rape/sexual abuse survivors; Child victims of sexual abuse; Adult survivors of child sexual abuse; Incest victims/survivors; Prevention program; Community education

SERVICES TO VICTIMS OF SEXUAL ASSAULT
176 Palisade Ave, Jersey City, NJ 07306
Crisis hotline: **(201) 795-8375 24 hrs**
Information: (201) 795-8375
Contact: Linda Young, MS, Coord
TYPE OF AGENCY: Rape crisis center; Hospital/medical center
SPONSORING ORGANIZATION: Christ Hospital Community Mental Health Center
AREAS SERVED: Hudson
YEARS IN OPERATION: 3
LANGUAGES: Spanish
ACCESSIBILITY: Wheelchair accessible
CASES SEXUAL ASSAULT/ABUSE (%): 100
DESCRIPTION: Comprehensive rape crisis services, support groups for female and male survivors and counseling for people who have been sexually abused by doctors, therapists, etc
CLIENTS/SERVICES: Sexual assault survivors; Marital rape/sexual abuse survivors; Child victims of sexual abuse; Adult survivors of child sexual abuse; Incest victims/survivors; Prevention program; Community education; Adolescent survivors of sexual abuse; Male survivors of sexual abuse
REQUIREMENTS: No offenders or violent acting-out types; Because of limited staff there may be a waiting list or a local referral may be made
SPECIAL PROGRAMS/SERVICES: The coordinator produces and hosts local cable TV programs and writes newspaper articles on sexual abuse issues or matters related to the exploitation of women. In the process of increasing services for men, and trying to remove the stigma they feel about being victims. Bilingual brochure (Spanish/English)

KEYPORT

WOMEN'S RESOURCE AND SURVIVAL CENTER
10-16 Broad St, Keyport, NJ 07735
Crisis hotline: **(201) 264-4111 24 hrs**
Information: (201) 264-4111 24 hrs
Contact: Darlene Averick, Sexual Assault Prog Coord
TYPE OF AGENCY: Rape crisis center; Domestic violence program
AREAS SERVED: Monmouth, Ocean
YEARS IN OPERATION: 10
LANGUAGES: Spanish
ACCESSIBILITY: Telecommunications for the hearing impaired (TTY, TDY, etc.)
DESCRIPTION: Sponsors three adult incest survivors groups; Provides comprehensive rape crisis and domestic violence services. Feminist martial arts/self-defense program also available
CLIENTS/SERVICES: Sexual assault survivors; Marital rape/sexual abuse survivors; Child victims of sexual abuse; Adult survivors of child sexual abuse; Incest victims/survivors; Prevention program; Community education; Adolescent survivors of sexual abuse; Male survivors of sexual abuse

LAKEWOOD

SHORE MENTAL HEALTH CENTER
700 Airport Rd, Lakewood, NJ 08701
Information: (201) 367-4700 8am-9pm
Contact: Lu Ann M Albanese, MSW, ACSW, Staff Soc Wkr
TYPE OF AGENCY: Counseling/mental health services
AREAS SERVED: Ocean
ACCESSIBILITY: Wheelchair accessible
CASES SEXUAL ASSAULT/ABUSE (%): 3
CLIENTS/SERVICES: Adult survivors of child sexual abuse
REQUIREMENTS: Clients must be 18 or older

LAMBERTVILLE

COUNSELING CENTER OF LAMBERTVILLE
83 Douglas St, Lambertville, NJ 08530
Information: (609) 397-2760 8am-9pm
Contact: Ken Singer, Clinical Dir
TYPE OF AGENCY: Private practice
YEARS IN OPERATION: 6
LANGUAGES: Spanish
CASES SEXUAL ASSAULT/ABUSE (%): 75
CLIENTS/SERVICES: Adult survivors of child sexual abuse; Incest victims/survivors; Offender treatment program; Male survivors of sexual abuse
SPECIAL PROGRAMS/SERVICES: Runs ongoing support/therapy group for male adult incest survivors through Parents United Chapter; Involved with adult male survivors treatment provider network and on the National Task Force on Juvenile Sexual Offenders

LIVINGSTON

SEXUAL ASSAULT SUPPORT SERVICE
Old Short Hills Rd, Livingston, NJ 07039
Information: (201) 533-5180
Contact: Nancy Denburg
TYPE OF AGENCY: Rape crisis center; Hospital/medical center
SPONSORING ORGANIZATION: St Barnabas Medical Center—Emergency Room
AREAS SERVED: Essex
CLIENTS/SERVICES: Sexual assault survivors; Child victims of sexual abuse; Community education

LUMBERTON

CROSSROADS PROGRAMS, INC
Box 321, Lumberton, NJ 08048
Crisis hotline: **(609) 261-5400 24 hrs**
Information: (609) 267-6666 9am-5pm (Mon-Fri)
Contact: Lynn Sternberg, Community Development Spec
TYPE OF AGENCY: Counseling/mental health services
AREAS SERVED: Burlington and surrounding area
CLIENTS/SERVICES: Sexual assault survivors; Child victims of sexual abuse; Adult survivors of child sexual abuse; Incest victims/survivors; Offender treatment program; Adolescent survivors of sexual abuse
REQUIREMENTS: Members of perpetrators group are referred through the courts

MAYS LANDING

ATLANTIC COUNTY OFFICE OF VICTIM WITNESS ADVOCACY
PO Box 2002, 19th Ave at Rte 40, Mays Landing, NJ 08330
Crisis hotline: **(609) 645-5808 9am-5pm (Mon-Fri)**
Information: (609) 625-7000, ext 5287 9am-5pm (Mon-Fri)
Contact: Jacqueline J Buoy, Victim Witness Coord
TYPE OF AGENCY: Victim/witness assistance program
SPONSORING ORGANIZATION: Atlantic County Prosecutor
AREAS SERVED: Atlantic
YEARS IN OPERATION: 2
ACCESSIBILITY: Wheelchair accessible
CASES SEXUAL ASSAULT/ABUSE (%): 35
CLIENTS/SERVICES: Sexual assault survivors; Marital rape/sexual abuse survivors; Child victims of sexual abuse; Adult survivors of child sexual abuse; Incest victims/survivors; Community education; Adolescent survivors of sexual abuse; Male survivors of sexual abuse

METUCHEN

MIDDLESEX COUNTY RAPE CRISIS INTERVENTION CENTER
PO Box 151, Metuchen, NJ 08840
Crisis hotline: **(201) 321-6800 24 hrs**
Information: (201) 321-6800, ext 466 8:30am-4:15pm
Contact: Mary Skidmore Taylor, Coord; Ruth Anne Koenick, Coord
TYPE OF AGENCY: Rape crisis center; Child sexual abuse services
SPONSORING ORGANIZATION: Roosevelt Hospital
AREAS SERVED: Middlesex
YEARS IN OPERATION: 13
LANGUAGES: Spanish
ACCESSIBILITY: Wheelchair accessible
CASES SEXUAL ASSAULT/ABUSE (%): 100
CLIENTS/SERVICES: Sexual assault survivors; Marital rape/sexual abuse survivors; Child victims of sexual abuse; Adult survivors of child sexual abuse; Incest victims/survivors; Prevention program; Community education; Adolescent survivors of sexual abuse; Male survivors of sexual abuse

MILLVILLE

CUMBERLAND COUNTY GUIDANCE CENTER—SEXUAL ASSAULT PROGRAM
PO Box 808, RD 1, Carmel Rd, Millville, NJ 08332
Crisis hotline: **(609) 455-5555 24 hrs**
Information: (609) 825-6810 9am-5pm (Mon, Wed, Fri); 9am-10pm (Tue, Thu)
Contact: Jeff Harvey, Sexual Assault Prog Coord
TYPE OF AGENCY: Rape crisis center; Counseling/mental health services; Child sexual abuse services; Child sexual abuse prevention program
AREAS SERVED: Cumberland
YEARS IN OPERATION: 4½
LANGUAGES: Spanish
ACCESSIBILITY: Wheelchair accessible
DESCRIPTION: Crisis intervention and long-term counseling for survivors of sexual assault/sexual abuse and their families; Individual and group therapy for rapists, child sexual abuse offenders, incest offenders, batterers, and adolescent sex offenders
CLIENTS/SERVICES: Sexual assault survivors; Marital rape/sexual abuse survivors; Child victims of sexual abuse; Adult survivors of child sexual abuse; Incest victims/survivors; Prevention program; Community education; Offender treatment program; Adolescent survivors of sexual abuse; Male survivors of sexual abuse
SPECIAL PROGRAMS/SERVICES: Bilingual (English/Spanish) brochure

MONTCLAIR

NORTH ESSEX HELPLINE
60 S Fullerton Ave, Montclair, NJ 07042
Crisis hotline: **(201) 744-1954 24 hrs**
Contact: Sandy Norgren
TYPE OF AGENCY: Rape crisis center
AREAS SERVED: Essex
CLIENTS/SERVICES: Sexual assault survivors; Child victims of sexual abuse; Adult survivors of child sexual abuse; Incest victims/survivors

MOORESTOWN

CONTACT OF BURLINGTON COUNTY
Box 333, Moorestown, NJ 08057
Crisis hotline: **(609) 234-8888, 267-8500, 871-4700, children's Contact-a-Friend line 261-2200 24 hrs**
Information: (609) 234-2223 8:30am-4:30pm
Contact: Joan K Willett, Inform and Referral
TYPE OF AGENCY: Counseling/mental health services; Telephone "warmline"; Information and referral
AREAS SERVED: Burlington
YEARS IN OPERATION: 15
CASES SEXUAL ASSAULT/ABUSE (%): 2
DESCRIPTION: Telephone helpline for all types of help and information-referral, including special "warm line" for children.
CLIENTS/SERVICES: Sexual assault survivors; Child victims of sexual abuse; Adult survivors of child sexual abuse; Incest victims/survivors

MORRIS PLAINS

FAMILY THERAPY CENTER OF MORRIS COUNTY, PC
172 Speedwell Ave, Morris Plains, NJ 07950
Information: (201) 263-1078
TYPE OF AGENCY: Child sexual abuse services; Private practice
AREAS SERVED: Morris
YEARS IN OPERATION: 1
CASES SEXUAL ASSAULT/ABUSE (%): 85
CLIENTS/SERVICES: Sexual assault survivors; Marital rape/sexual abuse survivors; Child victims of sexual abuse; Adult survivors of child sexual abuse; Incest victims/survivors; Adolescent survivors of sexual abuse; Male survivors of sexual abuse

MORRISTOWN

MORRIS COUNTY PROSECUTOR'S OFFICE—VICTIM/WITNESS ASSISTANCE UNIT
Hall of Records, Morristown, NJ 07960
Information: (201) 285-6200 8:30am-4:30pm
Contact: Patricia Poore, ACSW, CSW, MSW
TYPE OF AGENCY: Victim/witness assistance program
AREAS SERVED: Morris
YEARS IN OPERATION: 2
ACCESSIBILITY: Wheelchair accessible
CLIENTS/SERVICES: Sexual assault survivors; Marital rape/sexual abuse survivors; Child victims of sexual abuse; Male survivors of sexual abuse
REQUIREMENTS: Case must be "founded" and pursued by the prosecutor's office

THE PARENTING CENTER
100 Madison Ave, Morristown, NJ 07960
Information: (201) 540-5648 8am-10pm (Mon-Thu); 8am-5pm (Fri)
Contact: Dr Jeffrey Segal, Coord
TYPE OF AGENCY: Hospital/medical center; Child sexual abuse services
SPONSORING ORGANIZATION: Morristown Memorial Hospital
AREAS SERVED: Statewide
YEARS IN OPERATION: 10
ACCESSIBILITY: Wheelchair accessible
CASES SEXUAL ASSAULT/ABUSE (%): 70
DESCRIPTION: Outpatient clinic within a hospital providing individual, group, marital and family therapy for victims of sexual assault/abuse. Individual therapy for child sexual abuse/incest offenders, and batterers
CLIENTS/SERVICES: Sexual assault survivors; Marital rape/sexual abuse survivors; Child victims of sexual abuse; Adult survivors of child sexual abuse; Incest victims/survivors; Prevention program; Community education; Adolescent survivors of sexual abuse; Male survivors of sexual abuse

MOUNT HOLLY

FAMILY SERVICE OF BURLINGTON COUNTY
PO Box 588, Mount Holly, NJ 08060
Crisis hotline: **(609) 261-4970 9am-7pm daily, 24-hr answering service**
Information: (609) 267-5928 9am-5pm daily, 24-hr answering service
Contact: Lynn Millard, Prog Supv
TYPE OF AGENCY: Counseling/mental health services; Child sexual abuse services; Child abuse services
AREAS SERVED: Burlington
YEARS IN OPERATION: 25
LANGUAGES: Spanish
ACCESSIBILITY: Wheelchair accessible; Signers for the hearing impaired
CASES SEXUAL ASSAULT/ABUSE (%): 35
DESCRIPTION: The Strengthening Families Through Social Services Program is specifically funded by the State of New Jersey for the treatment of families in which child physical and sexual abuse is a factor. Counseling Program provides short- and long-term therapy for victims/survivors and treatment for rapists, child sexual abuse/incest offenders, and batterers
CLIENTS/SERVICES: Sexual assault survivors; Marital rape/sexual abuse survivors; Child victims of sexual abuse; Adult survivors of child sexual abuse; Incest victims/survivors; Prevention program; Community education; Offender treatment program; Adolescent survivors of sexual abuse; Male survivors of sexual abuse
REQUIREMENTS: Strengthening Families Through Social Services program clients must be referred by NJ Division of Youth and Family Services. No restrictions on provision of service in Counseling Program

NEPTUNE CITY

MONMOUTH COUNTY BOARD SOCIAL SERVICES—FAMILY SERVICES DIVISION
1900 Corlies Ave, Neptune City, NJ 07753
Information: (201) 988-4300 8:30am-4:30pm
Contact: Mary Jo Albartus, Soc Wkr Supv; Kati Boehler, Soc Wkr Spec
TYPE OF AGENCY: Counseling/mental health services
AREAS SERVED: Monmouth
YEARS IN OPERATION: 4
LANGUAGES: Spanish
ACCESSIBILITY: Wheelchair accessible
DESCRIPTION: Crisis intervention and counseling for adult and child survivors of incest/sexual abuse; Chapter of Parents Anonymous; Group therapy for child sexual abuse, incest, and adolescent sex offenders
CLIENTS/SERVICES: Sexual assault survivors; Marital rape/sexual abuse survivors; Child victims of sexual abuse; Adult survivors of child sexual abuse; Incest victims/survivors; Community education; Offender treatment program; Adolescent survivors of sexual abuse; Male survivors of sexual abuse

NEW BRUNSWICK

PROSECUTOR'S OFFICE OF VICTIM WITNESS ADVOCACY
PO Box 71, New Brunswick, NJ 08903
Crisis hotline: **(201) 321-6800 24 hrs**
Information: (201) 745-3394 8:30am-4:15pm; 24-hr beeper
Contact: Jayne A Guarino, Victim Witness Coord
TYPE OF AGENCY: Victim/witness assistance program
AREAS SERVED: Middlesex
YEARS IN OPERATION: 5
LANGUAGES: Interpreters available
ACCESSIBILITY: Wheelchair accessible; Signers for the hearing impaired
CASES SEXUAL ASSAULT/ABUSE (%): 10-15
CLIENTS/SERVICES: Sexual assault survivors; Marital rape/sexual abuse survivors; Child victims of sexual abuse; Adult survivors of child sexual abuse; Incest victims/survivors; Community education
REQUIREMENTS: Must file charges

WOMEN AWARE, INC
5 Elm Row, Rm 306, New Brunswick, NJ 08903
Crisis hotline: **(201) 249-4504 24 hrs**
Information: (201) 937-9525 9am-4:30pm (Mon-Fri)
TYPE OF AGENCY: Domestic violence program
AREAS SERVED: Middlesex and vicinity
YEARS IN OPERATION: 10
LANGUAGES: Spanish
ACCESSIBILITY: Telecommunications for the hearing impaired (TTY, TDY, etc.)
DESCRIPTION: Provides shelter, hotline, support groups for battered/abused women; Group for mothers of incest victims
CLIENTS/SERVICES: Marital rape/sexual abuse survivors; Community education

WOMENS' SUPPORT AND RESOURCE CENTER
56 College Ave, New Brunswick, NJ 08901
Crisis hotline: **(201) 828-7273 hrs vary**
Information: (201) 828-7273 hrs vary
Contact: Celeste Campos, VP
TYPE OF AGENCY: College/university-based services; Counseling/mental health services
AREAS SERVED: Statewide
YEARS IN OPERATION: 14
CASES SEXUAL ASSAULT/ABUSE (%): 25
CLIENTS/SERVICES: Sexual assault survivors; Information and referral

NEWARK

THE APOSTLES' HOUSE PARENT AIDE PROGRAM
18 Grant St, Newark, NJ 07104
Contact: Elsa Ramirez, Parent Aide Prog Dir
TYPE OF AGENCY: Counseling/mental health services; Child sexual abuse prevention program; Child abuse prevention program; Shelter
AREAS SERVED: Essex
YEARS IN OPERATION: 6
LANGUAGES: Spanish
DESCRIPTION: Uses community paraprofessionals who work with families at risk of child abuse and neglect, including child sexual abuse
CLIENTS/SERVICES: Child victims of sexual abuse; Adult survivors of child sexual abuse; Incest victims/survivors; Prevention program; Community education; Adolescent survivors of sexual abuse
REQUIREMENTS: Families are referred by Division of Youth and Family Services or by previous client families

ESSEX COUNTY FAMILY VIOLENCE PROGRAM
755 S Orange Ave, Newark, NJ 07106
Crisis hotline: **(201) 484-4446 24 hrs 7 days**
Information: (201) 484-1704 8:30am-5pm (Mon-Fri)
Contact: Sr Rita, Coord
TYPE OF AGENCY: Domestic violence program
SPONSORING ORGANIZATION: Babyland Nursery, Inc
YEARS IN OPERATION: 10
LANGUAGES: Spanish
ACCESSIBILITY: Telecommunications for the hearing impaired (TTY, TDY, etc.)
CLIENTS/SERVICES: Marital rape/sexual abuse survivors; Community education

SEXUAL ASSAULT AND RAPE ANALYSIS (SARA) UNIT
1 Lincoln Ave, Rm 203, Newark, NJ 07104
Crisis hotline: **(201) 733-7273 Daily (Mon-Fri)**
Information: (201) 733-7273 Daily (Mon-Fri)
Contact: Lt Thomas E Grill
TYPE OF AGENCY: Victim/witness assistance program
SPONSORING ORGANIZATION: Newark, New Jersey Police Department
AREAS SERVED: Essex
YEARS IN OPERATION: 13
LANGUAGES: Spanish, Polish
ACCESSIBILITY: Wheelchair accessible
CASES SEXUAL ASSAULT/ABUSE (%): 100
CLIENTS/SERVICES: Community education
REQUIREMENTS: Sexual assault victims must make a formal complaint to a court of law.

UNITED HOSPITALS MEDICAL CENTER AND CHILDREN'S HOSPITAL OF NEW JERSEY
15 S 9th St, Newark, NJ 07107
Information: (201) 268-8499 9am-5pm
Contact: Peggy Foster, Sexual Assault Unit Co Dir
TYPE OF AGENCY: Rape crisis center; Hospital/medical center; Child sexual abuse services
AREAS SERVED: Essex, statewide consultation
YEARS IN OPERATION: 13
LANGUAGES: Spanish, Translators available
ACCESSIBILITY: Wheelchair accessible; Telecommunications for the hearing impaired (TTY, TDY, etc.)
CASES SEXUAL ASSAULT/ABUSE (%): 100
DESCRIPTION: Provides medical exams and any needed medical treatment, as well as crisis counseling; Special clinic for children CORTS (children of rape trauma syndrom); Short-term treatment groups for children
CLIENTS/SERVICES: Sexual assault survivors; Marital rape/sexual abuse survivors; Child victims of sexual abuse; Adult survivors of child sexual abuse; Incest victims/survivors; Prevention program; Community education; Adolescent survivors of sexual abuse; Male survivors of sexual abuse

NEWTON

DOMESTIC ABUSE PROGRAM OF SAMARITAN INN (DASI)
PO Box 321, Newton, NJ 07860
Crisis hotline: **(201) 875-1211 24 hrs**
Information: (201) 875-1211 9am-5pm (Mon-Fri)
Contact: Cheryl Fox, Dir
TYPE OF AGENCY: Domestic violence program
AREAS SERVED: Sussex
YEARS IN OPERATION: 4
ACCESSIBILITY: Telecommunications for the hearing impaired (TTY, TDY, etc.); Signers for the hearing impaired
CASES SEXUAL ASSAULT/ABUSE (%): 50
DESCRIPTION: Comprehensive services for battered women and their children, Group therapy and educational groups for batterers
CLIENTS/SERVICES: Marital rape/sexual abuse survivors; Community education

PROJECT AGAINST SEXUAL ASSAULT ABUSE
175 High St, Newton, NJ 07860
Crisis hotline: **(201) 875-1211 24 hrs**
Information: (201) 579-8340
Contact: Jacquelynn Konzelman
TYPE OF AGENCY: Rape crisis center
SPONSORING ORGANIZATION: Newton Memorial Hospital
AREAS SERVED: Sussex
CLIENTS/SERVICES: Sexual assault survivors; Child victims of sexual abuse; Adult survivors of child sexual abuse; Incest victims/survivors; Community education

NORTHFIELD

ATLANTIC COUNTY WOMEN'S CENTER
PO Box 311, Northfield, NJ 08225
Crisis hotline: **(609) 646-6767 24 hrs**
Information: (609) 646-4376 9am-5pm
Contact: Deirdre A Razzi, Rape Care Supv

ATLANTIC COUNTY WOMEN'S CENTER
(continued)

TYPE OF AGENCY: Rape crisis center; Domestic violence program; Child sexual abuse services; Child sexual abuse prevention program
AREAS SERVED: Atlantic
YEARS IN OPERATION: 5
LANGUAGES: Spanish
ACCESSIBILITY: Wheelchair accessible; Telecommunications for the hearing impaired (TTY, TDY, etc.); Signers for the hearing impaired (by arrangement)
CASES SEXUAL ASSAULT/ABUSE (%): 40
DESCRIPTION: Services for survivors of sexual assault and domestic violence; Feminist martial arts/self-defense program; Group therapy and hotline for batterers
CLIENTS/SERVICES: Sexual assault survivors; Marital rape/sexual abuse survivors; Child victims of sexual abuse; Adult survivors of child sexual abuse; Incest victims/survivors; Prevention program; Community education; Adolescent survivors of sexual abuse; Male survivors of sexual abuse
SPECIAL PROGRAMS/SERVICES: State certification program for volunteers consists of 40 hour training sessions.

ORANGE

FAMILY SERVICE AND CHILD GUIDANCE CENTER OF THE ORANGES, MAPLEWOOD AND MILLBURN
395 S Center St, Orange, NJ 07050
Information: (201) 675-3817 9am-9pm (Mon-Fri)
Contact: Jonathan Hauser, PhD, Staff Psychologist
TYPE OF AGENCY: Counseling/mental health services; Child sexual abuse services
AREAS SERVED: Essex
YEARS IN OPERATION: 100
LANGUAGES: Spanish
CASES SEXUAL ASSAULT/ABUSE (%): 25-33
DESCRIPTION: Provides psychotherapy for children, including child victims of sexual abuse, families, and couples
CLIENTS/SERVICES: Marital rape/sexual abuse survivors; Child victims of sexual abuse; Adolescent survivors of sexual abuse

PRINCETON

FAMILY SERVICE PRINCETON AREA
120 John St, Princeton, NJ 08542
Information: (609) 924-2098 9am-9pm (Mon-Thu); 9am-5pm (Fri)
Contact: M Ballard, Admin Asst
TYPE OF AGENCY: Counseling/mental health services
AREAS SERVED: Mercer, Middlesex
YEARS IN OPERATION: 90
DESCRIPTION: Individual, couple, and family therapy on issues of relationships, alcoholism, communication
CLIENTS/SERVICES: Sexual assault survivors; Marital rape/sexual abuse survivors; Child victims of sexual abuse; Adult survivors of child sexual abuse; Incest victims/survivors; Male survivors of sexual abuse
REQUIREMENTS: Sliding scale fee

SHARE (SEXUAL HARASSMENT/ASSAULT ADVISING, RESOURCES, AND EDUCATION) PROGRAM
McCosh Health Center, Princeton University, Princeton, NJ 08544-1004
Information: (609) 452-3310 9am-5pm
Contact: Myra Hindus, Dir
TYPE OF AGENCY: College/university-based services
SPONSORING ORGANIZATION: Princeton University
AREAS SERVED: University community
YEARS IN OPERATION: 2
ACCESSIBILITY: Wheelchair accessible
DESCRIPTION: Provides counseling and advice for victims of sexual harassment and sexual assault; Educational and training programs, including workshops and panels directed at students, staff, and faculty
CLIENTS/SERVICES: Sexual assault survivors; Marital rape/sexual abuse survivors; Adult survivors of child sexual abuse; Prevention program; Community education; Male survivors of sexual abuse; Sexual harassment
REQUIREMENTS: Must be student, staff, or faculty member of the university
SPECIAL PROGRAMS/SERVICES: Designing workshops on sexual assault and male/female relationships which are aimed at male and mixed audiences, and are conducted by specially trained pairs of male/female peer educators

SALEM

SALEM COUNTY PROSECUTOR'S OFFICE—VICTIM-WITNESS ADVOCACY
94 Market St, Salem, NJ 08079
Crisis hotline: **(609) 935-HELP 24 hrs**
Information: (609) 935-7510, ext 526 8:30am-4:30pm
Contact: Suzanne Sturmfels, Coord
TYPE OF AGENCY: Victim/witness assistance program
AREAS SERVED: Salem
YEARS IN OPERATION: 1
ACCESSIBILITY: Wheelchair accessible
CASES SEXUAL ASSAULT/ABUSE (%): 50
CLIENTS/SERVICES: Sexual assault survivors; Child victims of sexual abuse; Adult survivors of child sexual abuse; Prevention program; Community education; Adolescent survivors of sexual abuse
REQUIREMENTS: Clients must file charges

SOMERVILLE

SOMERSET RAPE CRISIS SERVICE
95 Franklin St, Somerville, NJ 08876
Crisis hotline: **(201) 526-7444 24 hrs 7 days**
Information: (201) 526-8005 9am-7pm (Mon-Fri)
Contact: Linda Hipp, Dir
TYPE OF AGENCY: Rape crisis center
SPONSORING ORGANIZATION: Somerset Family Planning Service
AREAS SERVED: Somerset
YEARS IN OPERATION: ½
ACCESSIBILITY: Wheelchair accessible
CASES SEXUAL ASSAULT/ABUSE (%): 100
CLIENTS/SERVICES: Sexual assault survivors; Adult survivors of child sexual abuse; Incest victims/survivors; Prevention program; Community education; Male survivors of sexual abuse

SOUTH ORANGE

THE YOUTH CENTER OF FAMILY SERVICE AND CHILD GUIDANCE CENTER OF THE ORANGES, MAPLEWOOD AND MILLBURN
122 Irvington Ave, South Orange, NJ 07079
Information: (201) 763-8940 9am-9pm (Mon-Thu), 9am-5pm (Fri)
Contact: Daniel H Gallagher, PhD, Dir
TYPE OF AGENCY: Counseling/mental health services; Child sexual abuse services
AREAS SERVED: South Orange and Maplewood towns in Essex County
YEARS IN OPERATION: 10
LANGUAGES: German, Sign
ACCESSIBILITY: Wheelchair accessible; Signers for the hearing impaired
CASES SEXUAL ASSAULT/ABUSE (%): 10
DESCRIPTION: Provides outpatient mental health counseling and related services for children, families and couples, including situations of sexual abuse
CLIENTS/SERVICES: Marital rape/sexual abuse survivors; Child victims of sexual abuse; Adolescent survivors of sexual abuse
REQUIREMENTS: Children to age 18, couples

STRATFORD

DIAGNOSTIC CENTER FOR VICTIMIZED CHILDREN
301 S Central Plaza, Stratford, NJ 08084
Crisis hotline: **(609) 346-7036 9am-6pm**
Information: (609) 346-7036 9am-6pm
Contact: Dr M Finkel, Acting Chair, Dept of Pediatrics
TYPE OF AGENCY: Hospital/medical center; Child sexual abuse services
SPONSORING ORGANIZATION: University of Medicine and Dentistry of New Jersey-School of Osteopathic Medicine, Department of Pediatrics
AREAS SERVED: Statewide services
YEARS IN OPERATION: 6
ACCESSIBILITY: Wheelchair accessible
CASES SEXUAL ASSAULT/ABUSE (%): 95
DESCRIPTION: Medical consultant for sexually abused children; Multidisciplinary team—child psychologist, MSW, child psychiatrist
CLIENTS/SERVICES: Child victims of sexual abuse; Community education; Adolescent survivors of sexual abuse

TOMS RIVER

OCEAN COUNTY COMMISSION ON THE STATUS OF WOMEN
40 Hadley Ave, Toms River, NJ 08753
Information: (201) 929-2136
Contact: Ann Finnegan
TYPE OF AGENCY: Women's commission; Information and referral
AREAS SERVED: Ocean
CLIENTS/SERVICES: Sexual assault survivors; Community education

OCEAN COUNTY OFFICE OF VICTIM WITNESS ADVOCACY
CN 2191, Rm 123, Toms River, NJ 08754
Information: (201) 929-2195 9am-5pm
Contact: Susan Herbert, Victim Witness Coord
TYPE OF AGENCY: Victim/witness assistance program
SPONSORING ORGANIZATION: Ocean County Prosecutor's Office
AREAS SERVED: Ocean
YEARS IN OPERATION: 1
LANGUAGES: Spanish
ACCESSIBILITY: Wheelchair accessible
CASES SEXUAL ASSAULT/ABUSE (%): 10
CLIENTS/SERVICES: Sexual assault survivors; Marital rape/sexual abuse survivors; Child victims of sexual abuse; Adult survivors of child sexual abuse; Incest victims/survivors; Adolescent survivors of sexual abuse; Male survivors of sexual abuse

TRENTON

MERCER COUNTY PROSECUTOR'S OFFICE—OFFICE OF VICTIM/WITNESS ADVOCACY
PO Box 8068, Mercer County Courthouse, Trenton, NJ 08650
Information: (609) 989-6428 8:30am-4:30pm
Contact: Mary Effie Raney, Victim/Witness Coord
TYPE OF AGENCY: Victim/witness assistance program; Child sexual abuse services
AREAS SERVED: Mercer County (13 townships)
YEARS IN OPERATION: 10
ACCESSIBILITY: Wheelchair accessible
CLIENTS/SERVICES: Sexual assault survivors; Marital rape/sexual abuse survivors; Child victims of sexual abuse; Adult survivors of child sexual abuse; Incest victims/survivors; Com-

MERCER COUNTY PROSECUTOR'S OFFICE—OFFICE OF VICTIM/WITNESS ADVOCACY *(continued)*
munity education; Male survivors of sexual abuse
SPECIAL PROGRAMS/SERVICES: County has established a child sexual assault/abuse interview room, where the child victim can be interviewed by the law enforcement officials in a positive environment.

MERCER COUNTY RAPE CRISIS PROGRAM
140 E Hanover St, Trenton, NJ 08608
Crisis hotline: **(609) 989-9332 24 hrs**
Information: (609) 989-9592 9am-5pm (Mon-Fri)
Contact: Phyllis Knighten, Dir
TYPE OF AGENCY: Rape crisis center
SPONSORING ORGANIZATION: YWCA of Trenton, New Jersey, Inc
AREAS SERVED: Mercer and surrounding area
YEARS IN OPERATION: 7
LANGUAGES: Sign
ACCESSIBILITY: Wheelchair accessible; Telecommunications for the hearing impaired (TTY, TDY, etc.); Signers for the hearing impaired
CASES SEXUAL ASSAULT/ABUSE (%): 100
CLIENTS/SERVICES: Sexual assault survivors; Marital rape/sexual abuse survivors; Adult survivors of child sexual abuse; Incest victims/survivors; Prevention program; Community education

PARENTS UNITED OF MERCER COUNTY, INC
39 N Clinton Ave, Trenton, NJ 08607
Information: (609) 394-5157 9am-5pm (Mon-Fri)
Contact: Ed Rosado, Co-Coord; Audrey Snyder, Co-Coord
TYPE OF AGENCY: Child sexual abuse services
SPONSORING ORGANIZATION: Family Growth Program
AREAS SERVED: Entire state
YEARS IN OPERATION: 8
CASES SEXUAL ASSAULT/ABUSE (%): 100
DESCRIPTION: Group treatment for individuals and families affected by intrafamilial child sexual abuse; Group therapy for child sexual abuse offenders, incest offenders, and adolescent offenders
CLIENTS/SERVICES: Child victims of sexual abuse; Adult survivors of child sexual abuse; Incest victims/survivors; Offender treatment program; Adolescent survivors of sexual abuse; Male survivors of sexual abuse
REQUIREMENTS: Adolescent and adult offenders must admit to sex abuse charges and be currently involved in individual therapy. It is recommended that all survivors be in individual therapy as well.

WESTFIELD

UNION COUNTY RAPE CRISIS CENTER
300 North Ave E, Westfield, NJ 07090
Crisis hotline: **(201) 233-7273 24 hrs**
Information: (201) 233-7273
Contact: Jennifer Pruden
TYPE OF AGENCY: Rape crisis center
AREAS SERVED: Union
CLIENTS/SERVICES: Sexual assault survivors; Child victims of sexual abuse; Adult survivors of child sexual abuse; Incest victims/survivors; Community education; Adolescent survivors of sexual abuse

NEW MEXICO

ALAMOGORDO

CENTER OF PROTECTIVE ENVIRONMENT
PO Box 1180, Alamogordo, NM 88310
Crisis hotline: **(505) 437-2673 24 hrs**
Information: (505) 434-3622 9am-5pm
Contact: Josie Jaramillo, Dir
TYPE OF AGENCY: Domestic violence program
AREAS SERVED: Otero
YEARS IN OPERATION: 9
LANGUAGES: Spanish
ACCESSIBILITY: Wheelchair accessible
CASES SEXUAL ASSAULT/ABUSE (%): 25
DESCRIPTION: Domestic violence services, including individual and group therapy for batterers
CLIENTS/SERVICES: Marital rape/sexual abuse survivors; Child victims of sexual abuse; Adult survivors of child sexual abuse; Incest victims/survivors; Prevention program; Community education; Adolescent survivors of sexual abuse; Male survivors of sexual abuse

COUNSELING CENTER
1408 8th St, Alamogordo, NM 88310
Crisis hotline: **(505) 437-8680 24 hrs**
Information: (505) 437-7404 8am-5pm (Mon-Fri); evenings by appointment
Contact: Nina Aguilar, Therapist
TYPE OF AGENCY: Counseling/mental health services
SPONSORING ORGANIZATION: Otero County Mental Health Association
AREAS SERVED: Otero, Lincoln
YEARS IN OPERATION: 15
LANGUAGES: Spanish, Farsi, Norwegian
ACCESSIBILITY: Wheelchair accessible
CASES SEXUAL ASSAULT/ABUSE (%): 45
CLIENTS/SERVICES: Sexual assault survivors; Marital rape/sexual abuse survivors; Child victims of sexual abuse; Adult survivors of child sexual abuse; Incest victims/survivors; Offender treatment program; Adolescent survivors of sexual abuse; Male survivors of sexual abuse

ALBUQUERQUE

ALBUQUERQUE COUNSELING COOPERATIVE, INC
1010 Tijeras NW, Albuquerque, NM 87102
Information: (505) 247-2966 9am-5pm, answering machine after hrs
Contact: Peggy Norton, Admin Coord
TYPE OF AGENCY: Counseling/mental health services; Private practice
AREAS SERVED: Bernalillo, Valencia, Sandoval
YEARS IN OPERATION: 15
LANGUAGES: French, Spanish
ACCESSIBILITY: Wheelchair accessible
CASES SEXUAL ASSAULT/ABUSE (%): 60
DESCRIPTION: Purpose is to empower people to take control of their lives, including understanding the role past abuse has taken in their lives. Two counselors are skilled with play therapy and work well with children in abusive situations
CLIENTS/SERVICES: Sexual assault survivors; Marital rape/sexual abuse survivors; Child victims of sexual abuse; Adult survivors of child sexual abuse; Incest victims/survivors; Adolescent survivors of sexual abuse; Male survivors of sexual abuse

ALBUQUERQUE RAPE CRISIS CENTER
1025 Hermosa SE, Albuquerque, NM 87108
Crisis hotline: **(505) 266-7711 24 hrs**
Information: (505) 266-7711 8am-5pm
Contact: Ann Eisler, MSW, Clinical Dir
TYPE OF AGENCY: Rape crisis center; Child sexual abuse services; Child sexual abuse prevention program
SPONSORING ORGANIZATION: University of New Mexico
AREAS SERVED: Bernalillo
YEARS IN OPERATION: 15
LANGUAGES: Spanish
ACCESSIBILITY: Wheelchair accessible; Signers for the hearing impaired
CASES SEXUAL ASSAULT/ABUSE (%): 100
DESCRIPTION: 24-hour victim's crisis services including hotline, hospital crisis intervention and support; Ongoing professional counseling on appointment basis; Support groups for female and male survivors; Feminist martial arts program
CLIENTS/SERVICES: Sexual assault survivors; Marital rape/sexual abuse survivors; Child victims of sexual abuse; Adult survivors of child sexual abuse; Incest victims/survivors; Prevention program; Community education; Adolescent survivors of sexual abuse; Male survivors of sexual abuse; Healing
SPECIAL PROGRAMS/SERVICES: Art and wilderness therapy programs available for sexual assault survivors

COMMON BOND, INC
PO Box 26836, Albuquerque, NM 87125
Crisis hotline: **Lesbian: (505) 255-7288; Gay: (505) 266-8041 7pm-10pm**
Information: Lesbian: (505) 255-7288; Gay: (505) 266-8041 7-10pm (Sun-Sat-most nights)
Contact: Mary M Gray, Common Bond Brd of Dirs, Helpline Chair
TYPE OF AGENCY: Counseling/mental health services; Telephone crisis hotline; Information and referral
AREAS SERVED: Primarily Bernalillo
YEARS IN OPERATION: 3
ACCESSIBILITY: Wheelchair accessible
CASES SEXUAL ASSAULT/ABUSE (%): 1-5
CLIENTS/SERVICES: Sexual assault survivors; Community education; Lesbians; Gay men

FAMILY AND CHILDREN'S SERVICES, INC—PSYCHOTHERAPY AND COUNSELING DIVISION
1503 University Blvd NE, Albuquerque, NM 87102
Crisis hotline: **(505) 243-2551 8am-5:30pm (Mon, Thu, Fri); 8am-8:30pm (Tue); 8am-6:30pm (Wed)**
Information: (505) 243-2551 8am-5:30pm (Mon, Thu, Fri); 8am-8:30pm (Tue); 8am-6:30pm (Wed)
Contact: W R Franz, ACSW, Supv; Jennifer Dritt, MSW, Clinical Soc Wkr
TYPE OF AGENCY: Counseling/mental health services
AREAS SERVED: Primarily Bernalillo
YEARS IN OPERATION: 37
LANGUAGES: Spanish
ACCESSIBILITY: Wheelchair accessible
CASES SEXUAL ASSAULT/ABUSE (%): 10
DESCRIPTION: Comprehensive outpatient mental health program, including treatment for sexually abused children and their families, adults who were victims as children, and perpetrators. Individual, couple, and family therapy for rapists, batterers, and child sexual abuse/incest offenders
CLIENTS/SERVICES: Sexual assault survivors; Marital rape/sexual abuse survivors; Child victims of sexual abuse; Adult survivors of child sexual abuse; Incest victims/survivors; Community education; Adolescent survivors of sexual abuse; Male survivors of sexual abuse
SPECIAL PROGRAMS/SERVICES: Parentcraft offers educational and support programs for parents to enhance their parenting skills and increase their understanding of child development. Includes extensive series of workshops, courses, and support groups. WarmLine (243-2616), a non-crisis, non-medical telephone consultation line open from 9am-12 noon (Mon-Fri) for parents with problems related to being a parent or concerns about their young child. Bi-monthly newsletter and library of resource material

FAMILY RECOVERY
11000 Candelaria NE, Albuquerque, NM 87111
Information: (505) 293-5146 8am-5pm (Mon-Fri)
Contact: Cheryl Parkin, Prog Dir
TYPE OF AGENCY: Private practice
AREAS SERVED: Bernalillo
YEARS IN OPERATION: 6½
ACCESSIBILITY: Wheelchair accessible
CASES SEXUAL ASSAULT/ABUSE (%): 80
DESCRIPTION: Long-term and crisis therapy with adults and children from dysfunctional families; many clients have been sexually abused
CLIENTS/SERVICES: Sexual assault survivors; Marital rape/sexual abuse survivors; Child victims of sexual abuse; Adult survivors of child sexual abuse; Incest victims/survivors; Adolescent survivors of sexual abuse; Healing

FAMILY RECOVERY (continued)
REQUIREMENTS: Ability to pay fee
SPECIAL PROGRAMS/SERVICES: Healing for adult survivors of sexual assault and childhood sexual abuse using psychodrama, intensive experiential work, Gestalt, and body work

INCEST SURVIVORS ANONYMOUS (ISA)
8300 Constitution NE, Albuquerque, NM 87110
Contact: Lauri Dillingham
TYPE OF AGENCY: Self-help group
YEARS IN OPERATION: 3
CASES SEXUAL ASSAULT/ABUSE (%): 100
DESCRIPTION: 12-step support group for incest survivors, 2 mixed groups and one for men only
CLIENTS/SERVICES: Marital rape/sexual abuse survivors; Adult survivors of child sexual abuse; Incest victims/survivors; Male survivors of sexual abuse

PARENTS UNITED
PO Box 6573, Albuquerque, NM 87197
Crisis hotline: **(505) 344-7727 24 hrs 7 days**
Information: (505) 345-8938 9am-5pm
Contact: Marilyn Finkelstein, Prog Dir
TYPE OF AGENCY: Child sexual abuse services; Adolescent program
SPONSORING ORGANIZATION: All Faiths Receiving Home
AREAS SERVED: Bernalillo
YEARS IN OPERATION: 2
CASES SEXUAL ASSAULT/ABUSE (%): 100
DESCRIPTION: Group treatment for sexually abused children and their families, including offenders; Daughters and Sons United; Adults Molested as Children; Wilderness trips for adolescent survivors.
CLIENTS/SERVICES: Child victims of sexual abuse; Adult survivors of child sexual abuse; Incest victims/survivors; Community education; Offender treatment program; Adolescent survivors of sexual abuse; Male survivors of sexual abuse; Healing

PASO NUEVO COUNSELING SERVICE
510 2nd St NW, No 220, Albuquerque, NM 87102
Crisis hotline: **(505) 247-8853 24 hrs**
Information: (505) 247-8853 24 hrs
Contact: Judith Fleischman, Dir/Therapist
TYPE OF AGENCY: Private practice
YEARS IN OPERATION: 6
ACCESSIBILITY: Wheelchair accessible
CASES SEXUAL ASSAULT/ABUSE (%): 100
CLIENTS/SERVICES: Sexual assault survivors; Marital rape/sexual abuse survivors; Adult survivors of child sexual abuse; Incest victims/survivors; Offender treatment program; Male survivors of sexual abuse

PROGRAMS FOR CHILDREN
2600 Marble Ave NE, Albuquerque, NM 87106
Information: (505) 843-2190 8am-5pm, other hrs by appointment
Contact: Natalie Porter, PhD, Prog for Children Dir; Allis Curran, MSW, Sexual Abuse Proj Dir; Gloria Sandoval, Intake Wkr
TYPE OF AGENCY: College/university-based services; Child sexual abuse services
SPONSORING ORGANIZATION: University of New Mexico Mental Health Programs
AREAS SERVED: Bernalillo and surrounding counties
YEARS IN OPERATION: 20
LANGUAGES: Spanish
ACCESSIBILITY: Wheelchair accessible; Signers for the hearing impaired (by arrangement)
CASES SEXUAL ASSAULT/ABUSE (%): 50
DESCRIPTION: Provides individual, group, and family therapy, and evaluation for children and adolescents, sexually abused children and juvenile sex offenders. Also provides group therapy for adult survivors of child sexual abuse
CLIENTS/SERVICES: Child victims of sexual abuse; Adult survivors of child sexual abuse; Incest victims/survivors; Prevention program; Community education; Offender treatment program; Adolescent survivors of sexual abuse; Male survivors of sexual abuse
REQUIREMENTS: Children and adolescents up to age 18

SEXUAL ASSAULT TREATMENT SERVICES, INC
2201 San Pedro NE, Bldg 2, Ste 222, Albuquerque, NM 87110
Information: (505) 883-4373 7am-7pm
Contact: Caryl Trotter, Pres/Counselor; Stefani Atwood, Counselor/Private Practice
TYPE OF AGENCY: Private practice
AREAS SERVED: Bernalillo, Sandoval
YEARS IN OPERATION: 5½
ACCESSIBILITY: Wheelchair accessible
CASES SEXUAL ASSAULT/ABUSE (%): 80
DESCRIPTION: Provides psychotherapy for adult survivors of sexual abuse, particularly incest; Family therapy for incest offenders
CLIENTS/SERVICES: Sexual assault survivors; Marital rape/sexual abuse survivors; Adult survivors of child sexual abuse; Incest victims/survivors; Community education; Adolescent survivors of sexual abuse; Male survivors of sexual abuse

UNIVERSITY OF NEW MEXICO—SEX OFFENDER RESEARCH AND TREATMENT PROGRAM
Dept of Psychology, University of New Mexico, Albuquerque, NM 87131
Information: (505) 277-5164 8am-5pm
Contact: Michael Dougher, Assoc Prof of Psychology
TYPE OF AGENCY: College/university-based services; Offender treatment
AREAS SERVED: Statewide
YEARS IN OPERATION: 8
ACCESSIBILITY: Wheelchair accessible
CASES SEXUAL ASSAULT/ABUSE (%): 100
DESCRIPTION: Assessment and treatment of men who sexually abuse children, using behavioral and cognitive therapy and individual and group therapy
CLIENTS/SERVICES: Offender treatment program
REQUIREMENTS: Child molester, nonviolent, nonpsychotic. Ability to pay

ARTESIA

ARTESIA COUNSELING AND RESOURCE CENTER
PO Box 620, 801 Bush Ave, Artesia, NM 88210
Crisis hotline: **(505) 746-6222 24 hrs**
Information: (505) 746-9848 8am-6pm
Contact: Cynde Gibson, Sex Crimes Coord
TYPE OF AGENCY: Counseling/mental health services; Child sexual abuse services
CLIENTS/SERVICES: Sexual assault survivors; Marital rape/sexual abuse survivors; Child victims of sexual abuse; Adult survivors of child sexual abuse; Incest victims/survivors; Offender treatment program; Adolescent survivors of sexual abuse

CARLSBAD

CARLSBAD BATTERED FAMILIES SHELTER
PO Box 2396, Carlsbad, NM 88220
Crisis hotline: **(505) 885-4615 24 hrs**
Information: (505) 887-2549 various
Contact: Terri Hines, Prog Dir
TYPE OF AGENCY: Domestic violence program
AREAS SERVED: Primarily Eddy
YEARS IN OPERATION: 6
LANGUAGES: Spanish
ACCESSIBILITY: Wheelchair accessible
CASES SEXUAL ASSAULT/ABUSE (%): 25-30
CLIENTS/SERVICES: Sexual assault survivors; Marital rape/sexual abuse survivors; Child victims of sexual abuse; Adult survivors of child sexual abuse; Incest victims/survivors; Prevention program; Community education; Adolescent survivors of sexual abuse

CARLSBAD MENTAL HEALTH ASSOCIATION
701 N Canal, Carlsbad, NM 88220
Crisis hotline: **(505) 885-8888 24 hrs**
Information: (505) 885-4836 8am-6pm
Contact: Marian G Morris, EdD, Chief Exec Off
TYPE OF AGENCY: Rape crisis center; Counseling/mental health services; Child sexual abuse services
AREAS SERVED: Eddy
YEARS IN OPERATION: 3
LANGUAGES: Spanish
ACCESSIBILITY: Wheelchair accessible
CLIENTS/SERVICES: Sexual assault survivors; Marital rape/sexual abuse survivors; Child victims of sexual abuse; Adult survivors of child sexual abuse; Incest victims/survivors; Community education

CLOVIS

MENTAL HEALTH RESOURCES, INC
3620 N Prince, Ste C, Clovis, NM 88101
Crisis hotline: **(800) 432-2159 24 hrs**
Information: (505) 769-2345 9am-6pm
TYPE OF AGENCY: Rape crisis center; Counseling/mental health services
CLIENTS/SERVICES: Sexual assault survivors; Marital rape/sexual abuse survivors; Child victims of sexual abuse; Adult survivors of child sexual abuse; Incest victims/survivors; Adolescent survivors of sexual abuse; Male survivors of sexual abuse

DEMING

DEMING CRISIS CENTER
109 E Pine St, Deming, NM 88030
Crisis hotline: **(505) 546-2655 (Sheriff's Dept) 24 hrs**
Information: (505) 546-2272 9am-3pm
TYPE OF AGENCY: Crisis intervention program
CLIENTS/SERVICES: Sexual assault survivors

FARMINGTON

FAMILY CRISIS CENTER, INC (FCCI)
115 Corcorran Dr, Farmington, NM 87401
Crisis hotline: **(505) 325-1906 24 hrs**
Information: (505) 325-3549, 325-1906 8am-5pm
Contact: Marge Atkinson, Exec Dir
TYPE OF AGENCY: Domestic violence program
AREAS SERVED: San Juan
YEARS IN OPERATION: 10
LANGUAGES: Navajo
ACCESSIBILITY: Wheelchair accessible
CASES SEXUAL ASSAULT/ABUSE (%): 75
CLIENTS/SERVICES: Sexual assault survivors; Marital rape/sexual abuse survivors; Adult survivors of child sexual abuse

PRESBYTERIAN MEDICAL SERVICES—COMMUNITY COUNSELING CENTER
724 W Animas, Farmington, NM 87401
Crisis hotline: **(505) 325-1906 24 hrs**
Information: (505) 325-0238 8am-6pm
Contact: Robin Ross, MA, Therapist
TYPE OF AGENCY: Hospital/medical center; Counseling/mental health services; Child sexual abuse services
AREAS SERVED: San Juan
YEARS IN OPERATION: 5
LANGUAGES: Navajo
ACCESSIBILITY: Wheelchair accessible
CASES SEXUAL ASSAULT/ABUSE (%): 25

PRESBYTERIAN MEDICAL SERVICES—COMMUNITY COUNSELING CENTER
(continued)

DESCRIPTION: Provides individual and group therapy for survivors and child sexual abuse/incest offenders
CLIENTS/SERVICES: Sexual assault survivors; Marital rape/sexual abuse survivors; Child victims of sexual abuse; Adult survivors of child sexual abuse; Incest victims/survivors; Offender treatment program; Adolescent survivors of sexual abuse; Male survivors of sexual abuse
REQUIREMENTS: Sex offender treatment program requests clients to be court mandated to treatment

RAGSDALE AND ASSOCIATES COUNSELING SERVICES
2110 N Sullivan, Farmington, NM 87401
Information: (505) 327-7472 8am-5pm
Contact: J W Ragsdale, Therapist/Dir
TYPE OF AGENCY: Private practice
AREAS SERVED: San Juan
YEARS IN OPERATION: 3
ACCESSIBILITY: Wheelchair accessible
CASES SEXUAL ASSAULT/ABUSE (%): 50
DESCRIPTION: Primary therapeutic interventions for both victims and offenders within the context of a comprehensive outpatient counseling service. Offender treatment for rapists, child sexual assault/incest offenders, and batterers
CLIENTS/SERVICES: Sexual assault survivors; Marital rape/sexual abuse survivors; Child victims of sexual abuse; Adult survivors of child sexual abuse; Incest victims/survivors; Community education; Offender treatment program; Adolescent survivors of sexual abuse; Male survivors of sexual abuse
REQUIREMENTS: Fee for service

RAPE CRISIS TEAM
801 W Maple, Farmington, NM 87401
Crisis hotline: **(505) 325-5011, 325-1906 24 hrs 7 days**
Information: (505) 325-5011 8am-4:30pm
Contact: Nancy Wilhite, MA, Dir
TYPE OF AGENCY: Hospital/medical center
SPONSORING ORGANIZATION: San Juan Regional Medical Center
AREAS SERVED: San Juan
YEARS IN OPERATION: ½
LANGUAGES: Spanish, Navajo interpreter available
ACCESSIBILITY: Wheelchair accessible
DESCRIPTION: Rape crisis team members (male and female) meet victims in emergency room and stay with them during police investigation. Victims then are referred to PMS Mental Health for counseling and victims advocate at district attorney's office
CLIENTS/SERVICES: Sexual assault survivors; Marital rape/sexual abuse survivors; Child victims of sexual abuse; Male survivors of sexual abuse

HOBBS

OPTION, INC
PO Box 2213, Hobbs, NM 88240
Crisis hotline: **(505) 397-1576 24 hrs**
Information: (505) 397-1576
TYPE OF AGENCY: Domestic violence program
AREAS SERVED: Lea
YEARS IN OPERATION: 10
LANGUAGES: Spanish
CLIENTS/SERVICES: Marital rape/sexual abuse survivors; Child victims of sexual abuse; Adult survivors of child sexual abuse; Incest victims/survivors
REQUIREMENTS: Victims of domestic abuse; Children must be accompanied by a parent to stay in shelter; Protective service for adults

RAPE CRISIS CENTER
920 W Broadway, Hobbs, NM 88240
Crisis hotline: **(505) 393-6633 24 hrs**
Information: (505) 393-3168 24 hrs
Contact: Carla R Clark, MA, Sexual Assault Coord
TYPE OF AGENCY: Rape crisis center; Domestic violence program; Child sexual abuse services; Child sexual abuse prevention program
SPONSORING ORGANIZATION: The Guidance Center of Lea County, Inc
AREAS SERVED: Lea and surrounding area
YEARS IN OPERATION: 17
LANGUAGES: Spanish
ACCESSIBILITY: Wheelchair accessible; Signers for the hearing impaired
CASES SEXUAL ASSAULT/ABUSE (%): 80
CLIENTS/SERVICES: Sexual assault survivors; Marital rape/sexual abuse survivors; Child victims of sexual abuse; Adult survivors of child sexual abuse; Incest victims/survivors; Prevention program; Community education; Offender treatment program; Adolescent survivors of sexual abuse; Male survivors of sexual abuse
SPECIAL PROGRAMS/SERVICES: Use of ceramics and drawing in art therapy with children

LAGUNA

LAGUNA FAMILY SHELTER PROGRAM
PO Box 194, Laguna, NM 87026
Crisis hotline: **(505) 552-6666, 552-6667 police dept 24 hrs**
Information: (505) 552-9701 8am-4:30pm
Contact: Robin Brassie, Family Coun
TYPE OF AGENCY: Domestic violence program
AREAS SERVED: Cibola
YEARS IN OPERATION: 5
CASES SEXUAL ASSAULT/ABUSE (%): 7
DESCRIPTION: Tribally-operated program providing information and referral services, individual counseling, shelter, and advocacy for survivors of domestic violence/sexual assault; Treatment program for rapists, child sexual abuse/incest offenders and batterers
CLIENTS/SERVICES: Sexual assault survivors; Marital rape/sexual abuse survivors; Child victims of sexual abuse; Adult survivors of child sexual abuse; Incest victims/survivors; Prevention program; Community education; Offender treatment program; Adolescent survivors of sexual abuse; Ethnic minorities

LAS CRUCES

LA CASA, INC
PO Box 2463, Las Cruces, NM 88004
Crisis hotline: **(505) 526-6661 24 hrs**
Information: (505) 526-2819 9am-3pm
Contact: Suzan Martinez de Gonzales, Dir
TYPE OF AGENCY: Domestic violence program
AREAS SERVED: Dona Anna
YEARS IN OPERATION: 7
LANGUAGES: Spanish
ACCESSIBILITY: Wheelchair accessible
CASES SEXUAL ASSAULT/ABUSE (%): 30
CLIENTS/SERVICES: Marital rape/sexual abuse survivors; Child victims of sexual abuse; Adult survivors of child sexual abuse

NEW MEXICO STATE UNIVERSITY—COUNSELING AND STUDENT DEVELOPMENT
Box 3575, Las Cruces, NM 88003
Crisis hotline: **(505) 646-3311 campus police 24 hrs**
Information: (505) 646-2731 8am-5pm
Contact: Dr Patricia R Wolf, Counseling and Student Development Dir
TYPE OF AGENCY: College/university-based services
AREAS SERVED: Campus wide
ACCESSIBILITY: Wheelchair accessible
CASES SEXUAL ASSAULT/ABUSE (%): 25
CLIENTS/SERVICES: Sexual assault survivors; Marital rape/sexual abuse survivors; Adult survivors of child sexual abuse; Incest victims/survivors; Prevention program; Community education; Adolescent survivors of sexual abuse; Male survivors of sexual abuse
REQUIREMENTS: Clients must be associated with the university: students, faculty or staff

LAS VEGAS

SANGRE DE CRISTO COMMUNITY MENTAL HEALTH SERVICES
116 Bridge St, Las Vegas, NM 87701
Crisis hotline: **(505) 425-3558 24 hrs**
Information: (505) 454-1451 8am-5pm
Contact: Sande Hawley, Sexual Abuse Counselor
TYPE OF AGENCY: Counseling/mental health services; Child sexual abuse services; Child sexual abuse prevention program; Residential treatment facility
AREAS SERVED: San Miguel
YEARS IN OPERATION: 9
LANGUAGES: Spanish
ACCESSIBILITY: Wheelchair accessible; Telecommunications for the hearing impaired (TTY, TDY, etc.)
DESCRIPTION: Provides support services for chronic mentally ill persons; Sexual abuse counseling for victims and offenders; Individual, family, marital counseling
CLIENTS/SERVICES: Sexual assault survivors; Marital rape/sexual abuse survivors; Child victims of sexual abuse; Adult survivors of child sexual abuse; Incest victims/survivors; Prevention program; Community education; Offender treatment program; Adolescent survivors of sexual abuse; Male survivors of sexual abuse

LOS ALAMOS

CHARTER COUNSELING CENTER
600 6th St, Ste 102, Los Alamos, NM 87504
Information: (505) 662-5545 7am-7pm
Contact: Ellen Schechner, MA, ATR, Art Psychotherapist
TYPE OF AGENCY: Hospital/medical center; Counseling/mental health services
YEARS IN OPERATION: 2
ACCESSIBILITY: Wheelchair accessible
CASES SEXUAL ASSAULT/ABUSE (%): 50
CLIENTS/SERVICES: Child victims of sexual abuse; Adult survivors of child sexual abuse; Incest victims/survivors; Adolescent survivors of sexual abuse; Male survivors of sexual abuse

LOS ALAMOS WOMEN'S CENTER
PO Box 1337, Los Alamos, NM 87544
Crisis hotline: **(505) 662-5299 24 hrs (answering machine)**
Information: (505) 662-5299 9am-3pm (Mon); 1pm-3pm (Tue); 9am-11am, 1pm-3pm (Wed); 11am-1pm (Thu); 9am-11am, 1pm-3pm (Fri)
Contact: Marie Gosling, Svcs Coord
TYPE OF AGENCY: Domestic violence program; Women's center
AREAS SERVED: Los Alamos, Santa Fe, Espanola
YEARS IN OPERATION: 13
CASES SEXUAL ASSAULT/ABUSE (%): 2
DESCRIPTION: Services for survivors of sexual assault and domestic violence; Feminist martial arts/self-defense
CLIENTS/SERVICES: Sexual assault survivors; Marital rape/sexual abuse survivors; Adult survivors of child sexual abuse; Incest victims/survivors; Community education
SPECIAL PROGRAMS/SERVICES: Help Our Sisters Fund (donations). Small amount of money provides a woman in any kind of financial crisis or to a woman experiencing difficult times. Social concerns committee (a group of five professional women) gives women long or short-term support and help in many areas.

LOS LUNAS

SEXUAL OFFENDERS PROGRAM
PO Drawer 1328, Los Lunas, NM 87031
Information: (505) 865-1622, ext 351 8am-4:30pm
Contact: Mark Gould, Psychologist II
TYPE OF AGENCY: Correctional facility; Offender treatment
SPONSORING ORGANIZATION: Central New Mexico Correctional Facility
AREAS SERVED: Statewide
YEARS IN OPERATION: 8
ACCESSIBILITY: Wheelchair accessible
CASES SEXUAL ASSAULT/ABUSE (%): 30
DESCRIPTION: Individual, group, marital, and family therapy for incest offenders, child sexual abuse offenders, and rapists. Psychoeducational modules for group therapy
CLIENTS/SERVICES: Offender treatment program
REQUIREMENTS: Adult men incarcerated for sexual offenses in the state of NM

MESCALERO

MENTAL HEALTH SERVICES—MESCALERO INDIAN HEALTH SERVICE HOSPITAL
PO Box 155, Mescalero, NM 88340
Crisis hotline: **(505) 671-4441 24 hrs**
Information: (505) 671-4814 8am-4:30pm (Mon-Fri)
Contact: Jeff Schroeder, PhD, MH Svcs Dir
TYPE OF AGENCY: Hospital/medical center; Counseling/mental health services
SPONSORING ORGANIZATION: Indian Health Service
AREAS SERVED: Mescalero Apache Reservation
YEARS IN OPERATION: 20
LANGUAGES: Apache
ACCESSIBILITY: Wheelchair accessible
CASES SEXUAL ASSAULT/ABUSE (%): 10-15
DESCRIPTION: Full spectrum of mental health services, crisis intervention; counseling; referral; advocacy in sexual assault cases; individual, marital, family counseling for survivors
CLIENTS/SERVICES: Sexual assault survivors; Marital rape/sexual abuse survivors; Child victims of sexual abuse; Adult survivors of child sexual abuse; Incest victims/survivors; Ethnic minorities
REQUIREMENTS: Enrolled member of any federally recognized Native American tribe; spouses, children, or wards of enrolled member; member of local professional/support community (federal employees)

PORTALES

ROOSEVELT COUNTY RAPE CRISIS ADVOCACY
300 E 1st St, Portales, NM 88130
Crisis hotline: **(800) 432-2159 24 hrs**
Information: (505) 359-1221 9am-6pm
Contact: Mary Sweeney, Counselor
TYPE OF AGENCY: Rape crisis center; Counseling/mental health services
SPONSORING ORGANIZATION: Mental Health Resources, Inc
AREAS SERVED: Roosevelt
CLIENTS/SERVICES: Sexual assault survivors; Marital rape/sexual abuse survivors; Child victims of sexual abuse; Adult survivors of child sexual abuse; Incest victims/survivors; Adolescent survivors of sexual abuse; Male survivors of sexual abuse

ROSWELL

COUNSELING ASSOCIATES, INC
Box 749, Roswell, NM 88202
Crisis hotline: **(505) 623-1480 24 hrs**
Information: (505) 623-1480 9am-5:30pm
TYPE OF AGENCY: Rape crisis center; Counseling/mental health services
CLIENTS/SERVICES: Sexual assault survivors; Marital rape/sexual abuse survivors; Child victims of sexual abuse; Adult survivors of child sexual abuse; Incest victims/survivors; Offender treatment program; Adolescent survivors of sexual abuse; Male survivors of sexual abuse

ROSWELL REFUGE FOR BATTERED ADULTS
PO Box 184, Roswell, NM 88202-9987
Crisis hotline: **(505) 624-0666 24 hrs**
Information: (505) 624-0666 8am-5pm
Contact: Kathryn Chaney, Exec Dir
TYPE OF AGENCY: Domestic violence program
AREAS SERVED: Chaves, northern Eddy
YEARS IN OPERATION: 7
LANGUAGES: Spanish
ACCESSIBILITY: Wheelchair accessible
CASES SEXUAL ASSAULT/ABUSE (%): 35
CLIENTS/SERVICES: Marital rape/sexual abuse survivors; Child victims of sexual abuse; Community education; Adolescent survivors of sexual abuse

SANTA FE

PARENT ASSISTANCE CENTER
1421 Luisa St, Ste R, Santa Fe, NM 87501
Crisis hotline: **(505) 982-8686 24 hrs**
Information: (505) 982-8686 8:30am-4:30pm
Contact: Phyllis Leavitt, Parents United Coord
TYPE OF AGENCY: Child sexual abuse services; Child sexual abuse prevention program
SPONSORING ORGANIZATION: Parents United
AREAS SERVED: Santa Fe and surrounding counties
YEARS IN OPERATION: 3 (Parents United)
LANGUAGES: Spanish
ACCESSIBILITY: Wheelchair accessible
CASES SEXUAL ASSAULT/ABUSE (%): 100
DESCRIPTION: Individual and group therapy for sexually abused children and their families; Parents United chapter; Treatment for adolescent offenders
CLIENTS/SERVICES: Sexual assault survivors; Marital rape/sexual abuse survivors; Child victims of sexual abuse; Adult survivors of child sexual abuse; Incest victims/survivors; Offender treatment program; Adolescent survivors of sexual abuse; Male survivors of sexual abuse
REQUIREMENTS: Clients must be ages 3 years and older; Offenders must admit to crime; Extra-familial offenders not accepted; Chemically dependent clients must be in treatment for their substance abuse

SANTA FE MOUNTAIN CENTER
Rte 4, Box 34C, Santa Fe, NM 87501
Information: (505) 983-6158 8:30am-5pm
Contact: Rose Sanchez, Proj Dir
TYPE OF AGENCY: Counseling/mental health services
AREAS SERVED: Statewide
YEARS IN OPERATION: 10
ACCESSIBILITY: Signers for the hearing impaired
CASES SEXUAL ASSAULT/ABUSE (%): 1
DESCRIPTION: Wilderness therapy for adult survivors
CLIENTS/SERVICES: Sexual assault survivors; Marital rape/sexual abuse survivors; Child victims of sexual abuse; Adult survivors of child sexual abuse; Incest victims/survivors; Healing
REQUIREMENTS: Client must currently be in therapy and must return to therapy after the course; Fee information upon request for service

SANTA FE RAPE CRISIS CENTER, INC
PO Box 16346, Santa Fe, NM 87506
Crisis hotline: **(505) 473-7818 24 hrs daily**
Information: (505) 473-7818 8am-5pm
Contact: Christine Ertl, Exec Dir
TYPE OF AGENCY: Rape crisis center; Child sexual abuse services; Child sexual abuse prevention program
AREAS SERVED: Santa Fe, Rio Arriba, Los Alamos
YEARS IN OPERATION: 14
LANGUAGES: Spanish
ACCESSIBILITY: Wheelchair accessible; Signers for the hearing impaired
CASES SEXUAL ASSAULT/ABUSE (%): 100
CLIENTS/SERVICES: Sexual assault survivors; Marital rape/sexual abuse survivors; Child victims of sexual abuse; Adult survivors of child sexual abuse; Incest victims/survivors; Prevention program; Community education; Adolescent survivors of sexual abuse; Male survivors of sexual abuse; Healing
SPECIAL PROGRAMS/SERVICES: Art therapy; Wilderness experience; Self-defense classes for adult survivors of sexual assault

SILVER CITY

BORDER AREA MENTAL HEALTH SERVICES, INC
PO Box 677, Silver City, NM 88062
Crisis hotline: **(505) 538-3488 24 hrs**
Information: (505) 388-4412 9am-6pm
Contact: Judi Matthews, MSW, Prog Supv
TYPE OF AGENCY: Counseling/mental health services
AREAS SERVED: Grant, Luna, Catron, Hidalgo
YEARS IN OPERATION: 13
LANGUAGES: Spanish
ACCESSIBILITY: Wheelchair accessible
CASES SEXUAL ASSAULT/ABUSE (%): 25
DESCRIPTION: Community mental health agency with a broad range of services, including crisis intervention, and coordination with local hospital. Individual treatment for sex offenders and batterers
CLIENTS/SERVICES: Sexual assault survivors; Marital rape/sexual abuse survivors; Child victims of sexual abuse; Adult survivors of child sexual abuse; Incest victims/survivors; Prevention program; Community education; Offender treatment program; Adolescent survivors of sexual abuse; Male survivors of sexual abuse

TAOS

COMMUNITY AGAINST RAPE, INC
Box 3170, Taos, NM 87571
Crisis hotline: **(505) 758-2910 24 hrs**
Information: (505) 758-8871 8am-5pm
Contact: Jean Clawson, Coord
TYPE OF AGENCY: Rape crisis center; Child sexual abuse prevention program
AREAS SERVED: Taos
YEARS IN OPERATION: 11
LANGUAGES: Spanish
CASES SEXUAL ASSAULT/ABUSE (%): 100
CLIENTS/SERVICES: Sexual assault survivors; Marital rape/sexual abuse survivors; Child victims of sexual abuse; Adult survivors of child sexual abuse; Incest victims/survivors; Prevention program; Community education; Adolescent survivors of sexual abuse; Male survivors of sexual abuse; Prisoners
SPECIAL PROGRAMS/SERVICES: Use of *Kid Ability* prevention program for elementary grades. Art therapy in some group sessions; Wilderness therapy through Santa Fe Mt Center; Sweats for adult survivors of sexual assault and child sexual abuse

TUCUMCARI

MENTAL HEALTH RESOURCES, INC
300 S 2nd, Tucumcari, NM 88401
Crisis hotline: **(800) 432-2159 24 hrs**
Information: (505) 461-3013 9am-6pm
TYPE OF AGENCY: Rape crisis center; Counseling/mental health services
CLIENTS/SERVICES: Sexual assault survivors; Marital rape/sexual abuse survivors; Child victims of sexual abuse; Adult survivors of child sexual abuse; Incest victims/survivors; Adoles-

MENTAL HEALTH RESOURCES, INC
(continued)

cent survivors of sexual abuse; Male survivors of sexual abuse

WHITE SANDS MISSILE RANGE

FAMILY ADVOCACY
215 Loki, White Sands Missile Range, NM 88002
Information: (505) 678-3933 8am-5pm
Contact: Dawn Sumner, Family Advocacy Outreach Worker
TYPE OF AGENCY: Counseling/mental health services; Military services
SPONSORING ORGANIZATION: Army Community Service
AREAS SERVED: White Sands Missile Range community
CASES SEXUAL ASSAULT/ABUSE (%): 2-3
CLIENTS/SERVICES: Sexual assault survivors; Marital rape/sexual abuse survivors; Child victims of sexual abuse; Adult survivors of child sexual abuse; Incest victims/survivors; Community education; Adolescent survivors of sexual abuse; Male survivors of sexual abuse
REQUIREMENTS: Post residents only

NEW YORK

ALBANY

ALBANY COUNTY RAPE CRISIS CENTER
112 State St, Rm 1100, Albany, NY 12208
Crisis hotline: **(518) 445-7547 24 hrs**
Information: (518) 447-7100 9am-5pm (Mon-Fri)
Contact: Judith V Condo, Dir
TYPE OF AGENCY: Rape crisis center
AREAS SERVED: Albany
YEARS IN OPERATION: 13
ACCESSIBILITY: Wheelchair accessible
CASES SEXUAL ASSAULT/ABUSE (%): 100
CLIENTS/SERVICES: Sexual assault survivors; Marital rape/sexual abuse survivors; Child victims of sexual abuse; Adult survivors of child sexual abuse; Incest victims/survivors; Prevention program; Community education; Adolescent survivors of sexual abuse; Male survivors of sexual abuse; Publications/media
SPECIAL PROGRAMS/SERVICES: Has a yearly conference on sexual abuse issues (videotapes available). Also offers videotape on child sexual abuse

EQUINOX COUNSELING CENTER
214 Lark St, Albany, NY 12210
Crisis hotline: **(518) 436-6000 24 hrs**
Information: (518) 434-6135 9am-5pm (Mon-Fri)
Contact: Susan Cox, PhD, Assoc Exec Dir
TYPE OF AGENCY: Counseling/mental health services
SPONSORING ORGANIZATION: Equinox, Inc
AREAS SERVED: Capital district of New York State
YEARS IN OPERATION: 20
ACCESSIBILITY: Telecommunications for the hearing impaired (TTY, TDY, etc.) (hotline number)
CASES SEXUAL ASSAULT/ABUSE (%): 25
DESCRIPTION: Individual, couple, family, and group counseling specializing in issues related to substance abuse. Provides counseling groups for adult female incest survivors
CLIENTS/SERVICES: Adult survivors of child sexual abuse; Incest victims/survivors; Adolescent survivors of sexual abuse; Male survivors of sexual abuse
REQUIREMENTS: Sliding scale fees

FORENSIC MENTAL HEALTH ASSOCIATES
437 Western Ave, Albany, NY 12203
Information: (518) 489-7971 8am-10pm
Contact: Richard Hamill, PhD, Dir
TYPE OF AGENCY: Private practice
YEARS IN OPERATION: 7
CASES SEXUAL ASSAULT/ABUSE (%): 85
DESCRIPTION: Provides evaluations and treatment services for child and adult survivors of sexual abuse/assault, adult and juvenile sex offenders (rapists and child sexual abuse/incest offenders) and batterers, and families in which incest has occurred. Professional and organizational consultant services available
CLIENTS/SERVICES: Sexual assault survivors; Marital rape/sexual abuse survivors; Child victims of sexual abuse; Adult survivors of child sexual abuse; Incest victims/survivors; Community education; Offender treatment program; Adolescent survivors of sexual abuse; Male survivors of sexual abuse; Developmentally disabled
SPECIAL PROGRAMS/SERVICES: Currently has seven ongoing therapy groups for adult sex offenders, including two groups for men who have abused male children and a group for intellectually impaired offenders

ST ANNE INSTITUTE—SEX ABUSE PREVENTION SERVICES
160 N Main Ave, Albany, NY 12206
Crisis hotline: **(518) 489-7411 24 hrs**
Information: (518) 489-7411 24 hrs
Contact: M Etcheverry, Preventive Svcs Dir
TYPE OF AGENCY: Child sexual abuse services
AREAS SERVED: Albany, Rensselaer, Schnectady, Saratoga, Washington, Warren
YEARS IN OPERATION: 6
ACCESSIBILITY: Telecommunications for the hearing impaired (TTY, TDY, etc.)
CASES SEXUAL ASSAULT/ABUSE (%): 100
CLIENTS/SERVICES: Child victims of sexual abuse; Adult survivors of child sexual abuse; Incest victims/survivors; Community education; Offender treatment program; Adolescent survivors of sexual abuse
REQUIREMENTS: For incest prevention services, victim of incest must be under age 18 for family to qualify and be referred by Dept of Social Services in contract counties; For juvenile sex offender project, offender must be under age 21 who abused a child. Referrals are open in contract counties. No fees in either program. Clients are either voluntary or court-ordered.

ALBION

RAPE CRISIS SERVICE OF PLANNED PARENTHOOD
151 Platt St, Albion, NY 14411
Crisis hotline: **(800) 527-1757 24 hrs**
Information: (716) 589-5682 9am-5pm (Mon-Fri)
Contact: Michelle Phillips, Coord
TYPE OF AGENCY: Rape crisis center; Child sexual abuse services; Child sexual abuse prevention program
AREAS SERVED: Orleans
YEARS IN OPERATION: 3
CASES SEXUAL ASSAULT/ABUSE (%): 100
CLIENTS/SERVICES: Sexual assault survivors; Marital rape/sexual abuse survivors; Child victims of sexual abuse; Adult survivors of child sexual abuse; Incest victims/survivors; Prevention program; Community education

AMSTERDAM

FULTON COUNTY AND MONTGOMERY COUNTY RAPE CRISIS SERVICE
24 Division St, Amsterdam City Center, Amsterdam, NY 12010
Crisis hotline: **(800) 446-2345 24 hrs**
Information: (518) 843-4367 9am-4pm (Mon-Fri)
Contact: Deborah Gilbert, Team Leader
TYPE OF AGENCY: Rape crisis center; Counseling/mental health services
AREAS SERVED: Fulton, Montgomery
YEARS IN OPERATION: 15
ACCESSIBILITY: Wheelchair accessible
CASES SEXUAL ASSAULT/ABUSE (%): 100
CLIENTS/SERVICES: Sexual assault survivors; Marital rape/sexual abuse survivors; Adult survivors of child sexual abuse; Incest victims/survivors; Prevention program; Community education; Adolescent survivors of sexual abuse; Male survivors of sexual abuse
REQUIREMENTS: Clients under age 13 are referred elsewhere for counseling

AUBURN

SEXUAL ASSAULT VICTIM'S ADVOCATE RESOURCE
PO Box 71, Auburn, NY 13021
Crisis hotline: **(315) 252-2112 24 hrs**
Information: (315) 253-0657 9am-4:30pm (Mon-Fri)
Contact: Doreen Henry, Dir
TYPE OF AGENCY: Rape crisis center; Child sexual abuse services; Child sexual abuse prevention program
AREAS SERVED: Cayuga
YEARS IN OPERATION: 9
LANGUAGES: Spanish, Sign
ACCESSIBILITY: Wheelchair accessible; Signers for the hearing impaired
CASES SEXUAL ASSAULT/ABUSE (%): 100
CLIENTS/SERVICES: Sexual assault survivors; Marital rape/sexual abuse survivors; Child victims of sexual abuse; Adult survivors of child sexual abuse; Incest victims/survivors; Prevention program; Community education; Adolescent survivors of sexual abuse; Male survivors of sexual abuse

BATAVIA

RAPE CRISIS SERVICE OF PLANNED PARENTHOOD—GENESEE COUNTY
Masse Mall, Ste 24, Batavia, NY 14020
Crisis hotline: **(800) 527-1757 24 hrs**
Information: (716) 344-0541 9am-5pm
Contact: Karin Brown-Joseph, Coord

RAPE CRISIS SERVICE OF PLANNED PARENTHOOD—GENESEE COUNTY
(continued)
TYPE OF AGENCY: Rape crisis center; Child sexual abuse prevention program
SPONSORING ORGANIZATION: Planned Parenthood
AREAS SERVED: Genesee
YEARS IN OPERATION: 5
ACCESSIBILITY: Wheelchair accessible
CASES SEXUAL ASSAULT/ABUSE (%): 95
CLIENTS/SERVICES: Sexual assault survivors; Marital rape/sexual abuse survivors; Child victims of sexual abuse; Adult survivors of child sexual abuse; Incest victims/survivors; Prevention program; Community education; Adolescent survivors of sexual abuse; Male survivors of sexual abuse; Elderly
SPECIAL PROGRAMS/SERVICES: Brochure geared toward rape awareness for older women

BAYSHORE

YMCA FAMILY SERVICES
PO Box 242P, 4 Fourth Ave, Bayshore, NY 11706
Information: (516) 665-1173 9am-8pm (Mon-Fri)
Contact: Jacquelyn Schwicke, Proj Dir
TYPE OF AGENCY: Counseling/mental health services; Child sexual abuse services
SPONSORING ORGANIZATION: YMCA of Long Island, Inc
AREAS SERVED: Town of Islip only
YEARS IN OPERATION: 8
ACCESSIBILITY: Wheelchair accessible
CASES SEXUAL ASSAULT/ABUSE (%): 50-65
DESCRIPTION: Youth and family crisis center; Social worker therapists provide individual, family, and group counseling for victims, mothers, offenders; CPS case management; Court intervention; Expert witnesses
CLIENTS/SERVICES: Sexual assault survivors; Marital rape/sexual abuse survivors; Child victims of sexual abuse; Adult survivors of child sexual abuse; Incest victims/survivors; Prevention program; Community education; Offender treatment program; Adolescent survivors of sexual abuse; Male survivors of sexual abuse

BEDFORD HILLS

BEDFORD HILLS CORRECTIONAL FACILITY—FAMILY VIOLENCE PROGRAM
247 Harris Rd, Bedford Hills, NY 10507
Information: (914) 241-3100, ext 462 9am-5pm
Contact: M Sharon Smolick, Coord
TYPE OF AGENCY: Correctional facility
SPONSORING ORGANIZATION: New York State Department of Correctional Services/Division for Women
AREAS SERVED: New York State incarcerated women
YEARS IN OPERATION: 1
LANGUAGES: Spanish
CASES SEXUAL ASSAULT/ABUSE (%): 10-20
DESCRIPTION: The project is an outgrowth of the testimony provided by incarcerated women at a public hearing in 1985. Many women, in describing the relationship between family violence and incarceration, disclose incest and rape as life experiences/traumas
CLIENTS/SERVICES: Sexual assault survivors; Marital rape/sexual abuse survivors; Adult survivors of child sexual abuse; Incest victims/survivors; Community education; Offender treatment program

BELLMORE

RUNAWAY HOT LINE
2740 Martin Ave, Bellmore, NY 11710
Crisis hotline: **(516) 489-6066, 679-1111 24 hrs**
Information: (516) 826-0244 24 hrs
Contact: Anne Russo, Proj Dir
TYPE OF AGENCY: Counseling/mental health services; Telephone crisis hotline; Adolescent program
SPONSORING ORGANIZATION: Middle Earth Crisis Center
AREAS SERVED: Nassau
YEARS IN OPERATION: 18
CLIENTS/SERVICES: Sexual assault survivors; Marital rape/sexual abuse survivors; Child victims of sexual abuse; Adult survivors of child sexual abuse; Incest victims/survivors; Prevention program; Community education; Prisoners

BINGHAMTON

ALTERNATIVES COUNSELING CENTER, INC
37 Mill St, Binghamton, NY 13903
Information: (607) 722-1836 8am-5pm (Mon, Thu, Fri); 8am-10pm (Tue, Wed)
Contact: Charles E Kramer, Dir
TYPE OF AGENCY: Counseling/mental health services
AREAS SERVED: Broome, Tioga, Chenango
YEARS IN OPERATION: 10
CASES SEXUAL ASSAULT/ABUSE (%): 20
DESCRIPTION: Individual therapy for survivors and rapists, incest/child sexual abuse offenders, and batterers
CLIENTS/SERVICES: Sexual assault survivors; Marital rape/sexual abuse survivors; Child victims of sexual abuse; Adult survivors of child sexual abuse; Incest victims/survivors; Offender treatment program; Adolescent survivors of sexual abuse; Male survivors of sexual abuse

RAPE AND ABUSE CRISIS CENTER, INC
PO Box 836, Binghamton, NY 13902
Crisis hotline: **(607) 722-4256 24 hrs**
Information: (607) 723-3200 8:30am-5pm (Mon-Fri)
Contact: Kathy Magee, Exec Dir
TYPE OF AGENCY: Rape crisis center; Domestic violence program; Child sexual abuse prevention program; Acquaintance/date rape prevention program; Adolescent program
AREAS SERVED: Broome
YEARS IN OPERATION: 10
ACCESSIBILITY: Wheelchair accessible
CASES SEXUAL ASSAULT/ABUSE (%): 70
CLIENTS/SERVICES: Sexual assault survivors; Marital rape/sexual abuse survivors; Child victims of sexual abuse; Adult survivors of child sexual abuse; Incest victims/survivors; Prevention program; Community education; Adolescent survivors of sexual abuse; Male survivors of sexual abuse
SPECIAL PROGRAMS/SERVICES: Child Assault Prevention Program (CAP) teaches sexual abuse prevention to elementary school children. CAP uses a series of role plays to help children recognize and avoid dangerous situations. Youth Assault Prevention Program (YAP) teaches prevention to junior and senior high students through film and group discussion.

YWCA EMERGENCY HOUSING PROGRAM (INTERFAITH ROOMS)
80 Hawley St, Binghamton, NY 13901
Crisis hotline: **(607) 772-0340 24 hrs**
Information: (607) 772-0340 24 hrs
Contact: Debra G Beardsell, Emergency Housing Coord
TYPE OF AGENCY: Shelter
AREAS SERVED: Broome and surrounding area
YEARS IN OPERATION: 9
ACCESSIBILITY: Wheelchair accessible
CASES SEXUAL ASSAULT/ABUSE (%): 3
DESCRIPTION: Provides emergency housing for women for up to 30 days if sexual abuse is the main issue. Usually refers to the SOS shelter, as well as for counseling and treatment. If SOS shelter is unavailable, housing is provided
CLIENTS/SERVICES: Sexual assault survivors; Marital rape/sexual abuse survivors; Child victims of sexual abuse; Adult survivors of child sexual abuse; Incest victims/survivors; Adolescent survivors of sexual abuse
REQUIREMENTS: Homeless and 16 years or older

BRONX

BRONX DISTRICT ATTORNEY'S OFFICE—CRIME VICTIM ASSISTANCE UNIT
215 E 161st St, 4th Fl, Bronx, NY 10451
Information: (212) 590-2115 8:30am-5:30pm (Mon-Fri)
Contact: Karen D Andrews, Supv
TYPE OF AGENCY: Victim/witness assistance program
AREAS SERVED: The Bronx
YEARS IN OPERATION: 12
LANGUAGES: Spanish, interpreters available for other languages
ACCESSIBILITY: Wheelchair accessible
CASES SEXUAL ASSAULT/ABUSE (%): 20-25
CLIENTS/SERVICES: Sexual assault survivors; Marital rape/sexual abuse survivors; Child victims of sexual abuse; Adult survivors of child sexual abuse; Incest victims/survivors; Community education; Adolescent survivors of sexual abuse; Male survivors of sexual abuse
SPECIAL PROGRAMS/SERVICES: Spanish-language brochure available

BRONX MUNICIPAL HOSPITAL CENTER—JACOBI HOSPITAL PEDIATRIC EMERGENCY ROOM
Pelham Pkwy S and Eastchester Rd, Bronx, NY 10461
Information: (212) 430-8421 9am-5pm (Mon-Fri)
Contact: Karen Tillquist, Soc Wkr
TYPE OF AGENCY: Hospital/medical center; Child sexual abuse services
AREAS SERVED: Bronx
ACCESSIBILITY: Wheelchair accessible
CASES SEXUAL ASSAULT/ABUSE (%): 80
CLIENTS/SERVICES: Sexual assault survivors; Marital rape/sexual abuse survivors; Child victims of sexual abuse; Adult survivors of child sexual abuse; Incest victims/survivors; Community education; Adolescent survivors of sexual abuse; Male survivors of sexual abuse
REQUIREMENTS: Pediatric emergency room ages 1 month-19 years

CHILD VICTIM UNIT
900 Sheridan Ave, Rm 62-38, Bronx, NY 10451
Information: (212) 590-2371 9am-5pm (Mon-Fri)
Contact: Randy Weintraub, Coord
TYPE OF AGENCY: Victim/witness assistance program; Child sexual abuse services
SPONSORING ORGANIZATION: Victim Services Agency
AREAS SERVED: Bronx
YEARS IN OPERATION: 4
LANGUAGES: Spanish
CASES SEXUAL ASSAULT/ABUSE (%): 20
DESCRIPTION: Assists child victims of crime by other children through family court process; Provides short-term and court-related counseling for sexual abuse victims, as well as concrete services and legal advocacy
CLIENTS/SERVICES: Child victims of sexual abuse; Adolescent survivors of sexual abuse
REQUIREMENTS: Clients must be 3-20 years of age or family of victims
SPECIAL PROGRAMS/SERVICES: Spanish-language brochure available

CITIZENS ADVICE BUREAU
2050 Grand Concourse, Bronx, NY 10457
Crisis hotline: **(212) 731-0720 9am-5pm**
Information: (212) 731-0720 9am-3:30pm
Contact: Norma Alamo, Sexual Abuse/Domestic Violence Counselor
TYPE OF AGENCY: Counseling/mental health services; Information and referral

CITIZENS ADVICE BUREAU (continued)
AREAS SERVED: New York
YEARS IN OPERATION: 17
LANGUAGES: Spanish, African
ACCESSIBILITY: Signers for the hearing impaired
CASES SEXUAL ASSAULT/ABUSE (%): 5
DESCRIPTION: Provides information and referral; Elder abuse counselor; Senior crime victims program; Advocacy for homeless families; AIDS education; Domestic violence/sexual abuse counselor who provides supportive counseling, advocacy and referral for shelter placement, emergency entitlements, therapy, and day care
CLIENTS/SERVICES: Sexual assault survivors; Marital rape/sexual abuse survivors; Adult survivors of child sexual abuse; Incest victims/survivors; Community education; Elderly

JEWISH BOARD OF FAMILY AND CHILDREN'S SERVICES
990 Pelham Pkwy S, Bronx, NY 10461
Information: (212) 931-2600 9am-8pm (Mon, Thu); 9am-5pm (Tue, Wed, Fri)
Contact: Annaclare Van Daley, Supv
TYPE OF AGENCY: Counseling/mental health services
AREAS SERVED: Bronx
YEARS IN OPERATION: 50
LANGUAGES: Spanish, Hebrew
CASES SEXUAL ASSAULT/ABUSE (%): 10
DESCRIPTION: Psychotherapy and social services for children and their families who are having emotional, social, interpersonal difficulties
CLIENTS/SERVICES: Sexual assault survivors; Marital rape/sexual abuse survivors; Child victims of sexual abuse; Adult survivors of child sexual abuse; Incest victims/survivors; Community education; Adolescent survivors of sexual abuse; Male survivors of sexual abuse
REQUIREMENTS: Nonsectarian, sliding scale fee

KINGSBRIDGE HEIGHTS COMMUNITY CENTER
3101 Kingsbridge Terr, Bronx, NY 10463
Information: (212) 884-0700
TYPE OF AGENCY: Counseling/mental health services; Child sexual abuse services; Adolescent survivors services
DESCRIPTION: Sexual assault services for adolescents
CLIENTS/SERVICES: Sexual assault survivors; Adolescent survivors of sexual abuse; Male survivors of sexual abuse

NORTH CENTRAL BRONX HOSPITAL
3424 Kossuth Ave, Bronx, NY 10475
Crisis hotline: **(212) 519-3030 24 hrs**
Information: (212) 519-4785 9am-5pm
Contact: Esther Abalos, CSW, Supv I
TYPE OF AGENCY: Hospital/medical center; Child sexual abuse services
AREAS SERVED: Westchester, Bronx, New York, Queens, Brooklyn
YEARS IN OPERATION: 10
LANGUAGES: Spanish, Albanian
ACCESSIBILITY: Wheelchair accessible
CLIENTS/SERVICES: Sexual assault survivors; Marital rape/sexual abuse survivors; Child victims of sexual abuse; Adult survivors of child sexual abuse; Incest victims/survivors

BROOKLYN

BROOKLYN WOMEN'S ANTI-RAPE EXCHANGE
30 3rd Ave, Brooklyn, NY 11217
Information: (718) 330-0310
Contact: Marie Philip
TYPE OF AGENCY: Rape crisis center
SPONSORING ORGANIZATION: Brooklyn YWCA Women's Center
CLIENTS/SERVICES: Sexual assault survivors; Community education

CANARSIE AWARE, INC
1205 Rockaway Ave, Brooklyn, NY 11236
Information: (718) 257-3195 9am-5pm
Contact: Suzanne Biddiscombe, Prog Psychologist
TYPE OF AGENCY: Counseling/mental health services; Substance abuse treatment/counseling; Adolescent program
SPONSORING ORGANIZATION: Canarsie Youth Center
YEARS IN OPERATION: 20
LANGUAGES: Spanish
DESCRIPTION: Treats teenagers, young adults, and their families, many of whom have histories of sexual abuse, experiencing substance abuse difficulties
CLIENTS/SERVICES: Child victims of sexual abuse; Adult survivors of child sexual abuse; Prevention program; Community education; Adolescent survivors of sexual abuse
REQUIREMENTS: Ages 13 through 25 with a history of substance abuse, family crisis and delinquent behavior; Parents are required to attend groups and counseling sessions

NEW YORK CITY SELF-HELP CLEARINGHOUSE, INC
PO Box 022812, Brooklyn, NY 11202
Crisis hotline: **(718) 596-6000 8:30am-4:30pm**
Information: (718) 596-6000 8:30am-4:30pm
TYPE OF AGENCY: Information and referral services
AREAS SERVED: Kings, Manhattan
YEARS IN OPERATION: 10
LANGUAGES: Spanish
CASES SEXUAL ASSAULT/ABUSE (%): 10
DESCRIPTION: Referrals to existing self-help groups that address various issues
CLIENTS/SERVICES: Sexual assault survivors; Marital rape/sexual abuse survivors; Child victims of sexual abuse; Adult survivors of child sexual abuse; Incest victims/survivors; Offender treatment program

OUTREACH AND ADVOCACY PROJECT FOR BATTERED WOMEN
PO Box 200279, Brooklyn, NY 11220
Information: (212) 439-4612 10am-6pm (Mon-Fri)
Contact: Darlene Johnson, Aftercare Coord
TYPE OF AGENCY: Domestic violence program
SPONSORING ORGANIZATION: The Center for the Elimination of Violence in the Family, Inc
CASES SEXUAL ASSAULT/ABUSE (%): 90
DESCRIPTION: Provides outreach for formerly battered women and advocacy to improve legal, educational, and political rights of battered women. The history of battered women usually includes marital rape and/or incest, rape, child abuse
CLIENTS/SERVICES: Marital rape/sexual abuse survivors; Adult survivors of child sexual abuse; Community education; Healing
SPECIAL PROGRAMS/SERVICES: 17-week empowerment training program includes meditation skills for stress management, centering, growth and manifestation, healing. Topic Discussion introduces choices, assertiveness training, and an increase in self-esteem. Skills training introduces clients to job and financial skills and other everyday skills. Outside agencies are encouraged to participate so that there is a network of people working with women after the crisis intervention period.

PEOPLE AGAINST SEXUAL ABUSE, INC (PASA)
26 Court St, Ste 315, Brooklyn, NY 11242-1102
Information: (718) 834-9467 9am-5pm
Contact: Kathy Dee Zasloff, Exec Dir
TYPE OF AGENCY: Child sexual abuse prevention program; Rape prevention program; Acquaintance/date rape prevention program; Interagency network
AREAS SERVED: New York City area (5 boroughs)
YEARS IN OPERATION: 5
DESCRIPTION: Provides primary prevention education and training in the contexts of sex abuse, exploitation and victimization; Provides information and referral for survivor services, and advocacy for anyone (including offenders) who has been involved in a sexually violent experience; Library
CLIENTS/SERVICES: Prevention program; Community education
REQUIREMENTS: Workshops are free in the Borough of Brooklyn with a sliding scale for other requesting agencies
SPECIAL PROGRAMS/SERVICES: Workshops include such topics as, "Teaching Personal Safety," "Adolescent Dating Dilemmas," "Law Related Education," "Body Mind Coordination Techniques and Skills," "Mythology of Sexual Violence: Are Men Sexually Assaulted and Are Women Sexual Offenders?" and "Communivision: Media as a Learning Tool." Personal safety training focuses on communication skills (both verbal and nonverbal), space awareness and body mind coordination training, stress relaxation strategies, wholistic and wellness strategies, and use of sound, music, and guided imagery techniques as the foundation of their work and play shops. Teams of men and women known as Prevention Advocates teach personal safety. Bridges to Common Ground links people from varied disciplines and fields such as drug and substance abuse, suicide prevention, mental health, psychology, juvenile justice, crime prevention, law and law enforcement, health education, education, and alternative health care. Provides a forum which identifies interagency, interdisciplinary and interpersonal common grounds.

RAPE CRISIS INTERVENTION PROGRAM AND SOCIAL WORK DEPARTMENT
354 Henry St, Brooklyn, NY 11201
Crisis hotline: **(718) 780-1459 24 hrs**
Information: (718) 780-1459, 780-1962 Emergency Dept 24 hrs
Contact: Harriet Lessel, Coord
TYPE OF AGENCY: Rape crisis center; Hospital/medical center
SPONSORING ORGANIZATION: Long Island College Hospital
AREAS SERVED: Kings and surrounding area
YEARS IN OPERATION: 4
LANGUAGES: Spanish
ACCESSIBILITY: Wheelchair accessible; Signers for the hearing impaired
CASES SEXUAL ASSAULT/ABUSE (%): 100, child sexual abuse 5
DESCRIPTION: Rape Crisis Intervention Program provides 24-hour medical care and emotional support for rape survivors brought to the emergency room. Follow-up individual and group counseling and advocacy. Social Work Dept provides protocol in emergency room and serves child sexual abuse survivors. Social work available weekdays and weekends for assessment and referral
CLIENTS/SERVICES: Sexual assault survivors; Marital rape/sexual abuse survivors; Child victims of sexual abuse; Community education; Adolescent survivors of sexual abuse; Male survivors of sexual abuse

VICTIM SERVICES AGENCY—CHILD VICTIM UNIT
283 Adams St, Brooklyn, NY 11201
Crisis hotline: **(212) 577-7777 24 hrs 7 days**
Information: (718) 834-7432 9am-5pm (Mon-Fri)
Contact: Leslie Heller, Soc Wkr
TYPE OF AGENCY: Victim/witness assistance program; Child sexual abuse services
AREAS SERVED: Brooklyn
YEARS IN OPERATION: 5
LANGUAGES: Creole
ACCESSIBILITY: Wheelchair accessible
CASES SEXUAL ASSAULT/ABUSE (%): 60-70

VICTIM SERVICES AGENCY—CHILD VICTIM UNIT *(continued)*
DESCRIPTION: Designed to minimize the impact of crime on victims and their families; Provides counseling, court orientation, emergency assistance, referrals, advocacy regarding housing and school transfers for child victims who have been sexually assaulted by other children and adolescents
CLIENTS/SERVICES: Sexual assault survivors; Child victims of sexual abuse; Adult survivors of child sexual abuse; Community education; Adolescent survivors of sexual abuse
REQUIREMENTS: Must be a Brooklyn resident; Children between the ages of 0-16

VICTIM SERVICES AGENCY—FAMILY ASSISTANCE PROJECT
210 Joralemon St, Rm 608, Brooklyn, NY 11201
Information: (718) 834-6689 9am-5pm (Mon-Fri); evening hrs by appointment
Contact: Barbara Becker Bruno, Proj Dir
TYPE OF AGENCY: Victim/witness assistance program
SPONSORING ORGANIZATION: Kings County District Attorney's Office (Co-sponsor)
AREAS SERVED: Kings
YEARS IN OPERATION: 3
LANGUAGES: Spanish
ACCESSIBILITY: Wheelchair accessible
CASES SEXUAL ASSAULT/ABUSE (%): 100
DESCRIPTION: Long-term treatment program for child victims of incest and their family members, including the offenders
CLIENTS/SERVICES: Child victims of sexual abuse; Adult survivors of child sexual abuse; Incest victims/survivors; Community education; Offender treatment program; Adolescent survivors of sexual abuse; Male survivors of sexual abuse
REQUIREMENTS: Offenders must be mandated for treatment by criminal, supreme or family court and must meet certain psychological criteria; Other family members may be voluntary or court-mandated clients

BROOKLYN HEIGHTS

CRIME VICTIMS' COUNSELING SERVICES, INC
PO Box 023003, Brooklyn Heights, NY 11202-0060
Information: (718) 875-5862 9am-5pm (Mon-Fri); answering machine after hrs
Contact: Shelley Neiderbach, PhD, Exec Dir
TYPE OF AGENCY: Victim/witness assistance program; Training/research
AREAS SERVED: Nassau, Suffolk, Westchester, Hudson, Berlen
YEARS IN OPERATION: 8
CASES SEXUAL ASSAULT/ABUSE (%): 20-25
DESCRIPTION: Provides reduction of post-traumatic stress disorder for crime victims through group counseling
CLIENTS/SERVICES: Sexual assault survivors; Adult survivors of child sexual abuse; Incest victims/survivors; Community education; Adolescent survivors of sexual abuse; Male survivors of sexual abuse
REQUIREMENTS: Males and females over 12 years of age
SPECIAL PROGRAMS/SERVICES: Training in post-traumatic stress disorder, designed individually for various organizations. Publication: *Invisible Wounds: Crime Victims Speak* by Shelley Neiderbach (Haworth Press, 1986)

BUFFALO

ADVOCATE PROGRAM FOR VICTIMS OF SEXUAL ASSAULT
3258 Main St, Buffalo, NY 14214
Crisis hotline: **(716) 834-3131 24 hrs**
Information: (716) 834-3131
Contact: Sharon Simon
TYPE OF AGENCY: Rape crisis center
SPONSORING ORGANIZATION: Suicide Prevention and Crisis Service
CLIENTS/SERVICES: Sexual assault survivors; Child victims of sexual abuse; Adult survivors of child sexual abuse; Incest victims/survivors; Prevention program; Community education; Adolescent survivors of sexual abuse; Male survivors of sexual abuse

CHILD AND ADOLESCENT PSYCHIATRIC CLINIC, INC
3350 Main St, Buffalo, NY 14214
Information: (716) 835-4011 9am-9pm (Mon-Thu); 9am-1pm (Fri)
Contact: Jen E Henry, CSW, ACSW, Sexual Trauma Treatment Prog Dir
TYPE OF AGENCY: Counseling/mental health services; Child sexual abuse services
AREAS SERVED: Erie
YEARS IN OPERATION: 52
LANGUAGES: Translators available
ACCESSIBILITY: Wheelchair accessible; Signers for the hearing impaired
CASES SEXUAL ASSAULT/ABUSE (%): 20-25
DESCRIPTION: The Sexual Trauma Treatment Program provides specialized treatment for children and families who have been affected by sexual abuse; Treatment for rapists, child sexual abuse/incest offenders, and batterers
CLIENTS/SERVICES: Child victims of sexual abuse; Adult survivors of child sexual abuse; Incest victims/survivors; Community education; Offender treatment program; Adolescent survivors of sexual abuse; Male survivors of sexual abuse
REQUIREMENTS: Children and adolescents to age 19 and their families; Adult survivors of child sexual abuse only when adult is parent of a sexually abused child

CHILD AND FAMILY SERVICES OF BUFFALO AND ERIE COUNTY
330 Delaware Ave, Buffalo, NY 14202
Information: (716) 842-2750 9am-5pm, evenings by appointment
Contact: Joan Clarke, ACSW
TYPE OF AGENCY: Domestic violence program; Counseling/mental health services; Child sexual abuse prevention program; Residential treatment facility
AREAS SERVED: Erie
YEARS IN OPERATION: 100
LANGUAGES: Spanish
DESCRIPTION: Family counseling; Family mental health; Foster care and adoption; Residential care for males ages 6-12; Domestic violence shelter; Community based domestic violence program
CLIENTS/SERVICES: Sexual assault survivors; Marital rape/sexual abuse survivors; Child victims of sexual abuse; Adult survivors of child sexual abuse; Incest victims/survivors; Prevention program; Community education

CITIZENS COMMITTEE ON RAPE, SEXUAL ASSAULT, AND SEXUAL ABUSE, INC
95 Franklin St, Rm 230, Buffalo, NY 14202
Information: (716) 846-7879 9am-5pm (Mon-Fri)
Contact: Ann Marie Tucker, Coord
TYPE OF AGENCY: Child sexual abuse prevention program; Rape prevention program; Acquaintance/date rape prevention program
SPONSORING ORGANIZATION: Erie County Citizens Committee on Rape and Sexual Assault
AREAS SERVED: Erie
YEARS IN OPERATION: 4

ACCESSIBILITY: Wheelchair accessible
CASES SEXUAL ASSAULT/ABUSE (%): 100
DESCRIPTION: Addresses all aspects of sexual violence through community education and professional training to encourage reporting, a sensitive response to victims, and prevention; To encourage and facilitate coordination of services addressing sexual violence
CLIENTS/SERVICES: Prevention program; Community education
SPECIAL PROGRAMS/SERVICES: A school-based prevention curriculum for grades K-6 entitled *Teach Personal Safety* is available for purchase. A grade 7-12 curriculum is in development; a ten-hour teacher training is available. A videotape on the broad topic of sexual violence including incest, acquaintance rape, marital rape, male victims and female and adolescent perpetrators, entitled *Suffering in Silence: Sexual Assault Survivors* is available for purchase

CRIME VICTIM ASSISTANCE
1081 Broadway, Buffalo, NY 14212
Information: (716) 897-4100 8:30am-4:30pm
Contact: Lorraine Mangin, Coord
TYPE OF AGENCY: Victim/witness assistance program; Counseling/mental health services
SPONSORING ORGANIZATION: Neighborhood Information Center
AREAS SERVED: Erie
YEARS IN OPERATION: 17
LANGUAGES: Polish
ACCESSIBILITY: Wheelchair accessible
CASES SEXUAL ASSAULT/ABUSE (%): 1
CLIENTS/SERVICES: Sexual assault survivors
SPECIAL PROGRAMS/SERVICES: Polish-language brochure

VICTIM ASSISTANCE AND ADVOCACY ORGANIZATION
155 Lawn Ave, Buffalo, NY 14207
Information: (716) 876-8108 8:30am-5pm (Mon-Fri)
Contact: Martha Dippel, Prog Coord
TYPE OF AGENCY: Victim/witness assistance program
AREAS SERVED: Erie (North, Northwest, Upper and Lower Westside, village of Kenmore, Town of Tonawanda); Niagara (City of North Tonawanda)
YEARS IN OPERATION: 8
ACCESSIBILITY: Wheelchair accessible
CASES SEXUAL ASSAULT/ABUSE (%): 25
CLIENTS/SERVICES: Sexual assault survivors; Marital rape/sexual abuse survivors; Child victims of sexual abuse; Adult survivors of child sexual abuse; Incest victims/survivors; Community education

CAIRO

GREENE COUNTY MENTAL HEALTH CENTER
Rte 3, Box 905, Cairo, NY 12413
Information: (518) 943-3300 9am-9pm (Mon); 9am-5pm (Tue-Fri)
Contact: David C Fleming, Assoc Psychologist
TYPE OF AGENCY: Counseling/mental health services
AREAS SERVED: Greene
YEARS IN OPERATION: 25-30
ACCESSIBILITY: Wheelchair accessible
CASES SEXUAL ASSAULT/ABUSE (%): 5-10
CLIENTS/SERVICES: Sexual assault survivors; Marital rape/sexual abuse survivors; Child victims of sexual abuse; Adult survivors of child sexual abuse; Incest victims/survivors; Adolescent survivors of sexual abuse; Male survivors of sexual abuse

CAMBRIDGE

RAPE CRISIS FOR WASHINGTON COUNTY
1 Myrtle Ave, Mary McClellan Hospital, Cambridge, NY 12816
Crisis hotline: **(518) 747-6412 24 hrs**
Information: (518) 677-3019
Contact: Jan Wolski, Dir
TYPE OF AGENCY: Rape crisis center
AREAS SERVED: Washington
YEARS IN OPERATION: 1
ACCESSIBILITY: Wheelchair accessible
CASES SEXUAL ASSAULT/ABUSE (%): 100
CLIENTS/SERVICES: Sexual assault survivors; Marital rape/sexual abuse survivors; Child victims of sexual abuse; Adult survivors of child sexual abuse; Incest victims/survivors; Community education; Adolescent survivors of sexual abuse; Male survivors of sexual abuse

CANANDAIGUA

RAPE CRISIS SERVICE—ONTARIO COUNTY
181 S Main St, Kindeblock, Ste 9, Canandaigua, NY 14424
Crisis hotline: **(800) 527-1757 24 hrs**
Information: (716) 394-5820 9am-5pm (Mon-Fri)
Contact: Joy M Skatharoudis, Coord
TYPE OF AGENCY: Rape crisis center
SPONSORING ORGANIZATION: Planned Parenthood of Rochester and the Genesee Valley, Inc
AREAS SERVED: Ontario
YEARS IN OPERATION: 2
LANGUAGES: Spanish
ACCESSIBILITY: Wheelchair accessible; Telecommunications for the hearing impaired (TTY, TDY, etc.) (Monroe County); Signers for the hearing impaired (Monroe County)
CASES SEXUAL ASSAULT/ABUSE (%): 100
CLIENTS/SERVICES: Sexual assault survivors; Marital rape/sexual abuse survivors; Child victims of sexual abuse; Adult survivors of child sexual abuse; Incest victims/survivors; Prevention program; Community education; Adolescent survivors of sexual abuse; Male survivors of sexual abuse

CANTON

CAVA RAPE CRISIS CENTER (CITIZENS AGAINST VIOLENT ACTS, INC)
PO Box 174, Canton, NY 13617
Crisis hotline: **(315) 265-2422 (Reachout) after office hrs**
Information: (315) 386-3777 9am-5pm (Mon-Fri)
Contact: Jennifer Bixby, Dir
TYPE OF AGENCY: Rape crisis center; Child sexual abuse services; Child sexual abuse prevention program; Acquaintance/date rape prevention program
AREAS SERVED: St Lawrence
YEARS IN OPERATION: 5
CASES SEXUAL ASSAULT/ABUSE (%): 100
DESCRIPTION: Provides counseling and legal advocacy for victims of sexual assault, as well as an incest offender program and a teen rape prevention program
CLIENTS/SERVICES: Sexual assault survivors; Marital rape/sexual abuse survivors; Child victims of sexual abuse; Adult survivors of child sexual abuse; Incest victims/survivors; Prevention program; Community education; Offender treatment program; Adolescent survivors of sexual abuse; Male survivors of sexual abuse

ST LAWRENCE VALLEY RENEWAL HOUSE FOR VICTIMS OF FAMILY VIOLENCE
Box 468, Canton, NY 13617
Crisis hotline: **(315) 265-2422 After hrs and weekends**
Information: (315) 379-9845 7:30am-5:30pm (Mon-Fri); crisis calls accepted during office hrs
Contact: Carol Drew, Dir
TYPE OF AGENCY: Domestic violence program
AREAS SERVED: St Lawrence
YEARS IN OPERATION: 6
CASES SEXUAL ASSAULT/ABUSE (%): 10
DESCRIPTION: Provides safe housing, support groups, and advocacy for survivors of domestic violence/sexual assault; Self-help group for batterers
CLIENTS/SERVICES: Marital rape/sexual abuse survivors; Community education

CARMEL

SEXUAL ASSAULT CRISIS COUNSELING
Stonewalk Ninham Rd, Carmel, NY 10512
Crisis hotline: **(914) 225-4300 (sheriff) 24 hrs**
Information: (914) 225-2650 24 hrs
Contact: R Maureen Salvestrini, Dir
TYPE OF AGENCY: Victim/witness assistance program
AREAS SERVED: Putnam
YEARS IN OPERATION: 13
ACCESSIBILITY: Wheelchair accessible
CASES SEXUAL ASSAULT/ABUSE (%): 100
DESCRIPTION: Crisis intervention and counseling for victims/survivors, including support groups for female and male survivors; Treatment for rapists and child sexual abuse/incest offenders
CLIENTS/SERVICES: Sexual assault survivors; Child victims of sexual abuse; Adult survivors of child sexual abuse; Incest victims/survivors; Prevention program; Community education; Offender treatment program; Adolescent survivors of sexual abuse; Male survivors of sexual abuse; Gay men
REQUIREMENTS: Client must report

COBLESKILL

SCHOHARIE COUNTY RAPE CRISIS SERVICE
23 Main St, Cobleskill, NY 12043
Crisis hotline: **(518) 234-4949 24 hrs**
Information: (518) 234-4844 9am-4pm (Mon-Fri)
Contact: Deborah Gilbert, Team Leader
TYPE OF AGENCY: Rape crisis center; Counseling/mental health services
SPONSORING ORGANIZATION: Planned Parenthood
AREAS SERVED: Schoharie
YEARS IN OPERATION: 15
ACCESSIBILITY: Wheelchair accessible
CASES SEXUAL ASSAULT/ABUSE (%): 100
CLIENTS/SERVICES: Sexual assault survivors; Marital rape/sexual abuse survivors; Adult survivors of child sexual abuse; Incest victims/survivors; Prevention program; Community education; Adolescent survivors of sexual abuse; Male survivors of sexual abuse
REQUIREMENTS: Clients under age 13 are referred elsewhere for counseling

COLD SPRINGS

MEN'S WORKSHOPS
26 Chestnut St, Cold Springs, NY 10516
Information: (914) 225-9491
Contact: Steve Dill, Co-Dir
TYPE OF AGENCY: Domestic violence program; Men's program
AREAS SERVED: Putnam
YEARS IN OPERATION: 4
DESCRIPTION: Offers services to all men, with particular emphasis on domestic violence batterer's program; Counsels sexual assault victims and secondary victims (men)
CLIENTS/SERVICES: Sexual assault survivors; Marital rape/sexual abuse survivors; Adult survivors of child sexual abuse; Incest victims/survivors; Prevention program; Male survivors of sexual abuse

CORNING

CHOICE PROGRAM OF FAMILY SERVICES SOCIETY
11 E Pulteney St, Corning, NY 14830
Information: (607) 962-3148 9am-5pm
Contact: Norman White, Coord
TYPE OF AGENCY: Counseling/mental health services; Child sexual abuse services; Adolescent program
YEARS IN OPERATION: 6
ACCESSIBILITY: Wheelchair accessible
CASES SEXUAL ASSAULT/ABUSE (%): 100
DESCRIPTION: Family treatment approach for child sexual abuse; Individual, group, and family therapy for child sexual abuse/incest and adolescent sex offenders
CLIENTS/SERVICES: Child victims of sexual abuse; Adult survivors of child sexual abuse; Incest victims/survivors; Community education; Offender treatment program; Adolescent survivors of sexual abuse; Male survivors of sexual abuse
SPECIAL PROGRAMS/SERVICES: Developing adolescent offender and victim treatment programs. Plans to move toward working with youth service program to develop a preventive program for youth at risk. By working with adolescent youths who have been victims, hopes to interrupt the transition from victim to offender. Working to develop adult incest survivors week-end therapy groups

CORTLAND

AID TO WOMEN VICTIMS OF VIOLENCE
14 Clayton Ave, Cortland, NY 13045
Crisis hotline: **(607) 756-4779 24 hrs**
Information: (607) 753-3639 8:30am-4:30pm
Contact: Kathleen J Tariq, AWVV Prog Dir
TYPE OF AGENCY: Rape crisis center; Domestic violence program; Victim/witness assistance program; Child sexual abuse prevention program
SPONSORING ORGANIZATION: YWCA of Cortland
AREAS SERVED: Cortland
YEARS IN OPERATION: 10
LANGUAGES: Spanish, German
ACCESSIBILITY: Wheelchair accessible
CASES SEXUAL ASSAULT/ABUSE (%): 10
CLIENTS/SERVICES: Sexual assault survivors; Marital rape/sexual abuse survivors; Child victims of sexual abuse; Adult survivors of child sexual abuse; Incest victims/survivors; Prevention program; Community education; Adolescent survivors of sexual abuse; Male survivors of sexual abuse
SPECIAL PROGRAMS/SERVICES: Coalition for Children, another program of the YWCA, offers big brother/sister program for children from ages 3-8 who are from violent or troubled homes

DELHI

DELAWARE OPPORTUNITIES, INC—SAFE AGAINST VIOLENCE
47 Main St, Delhi, NY 13753
Crisis hotline: **(607) 746-6278 24 hrs**
Information: (607) 746-2992 9am-5pm
Contact: Lauren Mandel, Rape Crisis Outreach Educator; Barbara Madero, SAV Coord
TYPE OF AGENCY: Rape crisis center; Domestic violence program; Victim/witness assistance program
AREAS SERVED: Delaware
YEARS IN OPERATION: 5
LANGUAGES: Spanish and Hebrew interpreters
ACCESSIBILITY: Wheelchair accessible; Signers for the hearing impaired
CASES SEXUAL ASSAULT/ABUSE (%): 75
CLIENTS/SERVICES: Sexual assault survivors; Marital rape/sexual abuse survivors; Child victims of sexual abuse; Adult survivors of child

DELAWARE OPPORTUNITIES, INC—SAFE AGAINST VIOLENCE (continued)

sexual abuse; Incest victims/survivors; Prevention program; Community education; Adolescent survivors of sexual abuse; Male survivors of sexual abuse

ELIZABETHTOWN

END DV PROGRAM
PO Box 115, Elizabethtown, NY 12932
Crisis hotline: **(518) 873-9240 24 hrs**
Information: (518) 873-9240, 873-9241 9am-5pm (Mon-Fri)
Contact: Cathy Henrichs, Exec Dir
TYPE OF AGENCY: Domestic violence program
SPONSORING ORGANIZATION: Citizens' Domestic Violence and Criminal Justice Planning Corporation of Essex County
AREAS SERVED: Primarily Essex
YEARS IN OPERATION: 4
CASES SEXUAL ASSAULT/ABUSE (%): 10
CLIENTS/SERVICES: Marital rape/sexual abuse survivors; Child victims of sexual abuse; Community education; Adolescent survivors of sexual abuse; Male survivors of sexual abuse

ELMIRA

NEIGHBORHOOD JUSTICE PROJECT OF THE SOUTHERN TIER, INC
451 E Market St, Elmira, NY 14901
Crisis hotline: **(607) 962-6774 24 hrs**
Information: (607) 734-3338 24 hrs
Contact: Tammy Bennett-Davis, Victims Svcs Spec-Corning office; Susan G King, Coord
TYPE OF AGENCY: Rape crisis center; Counseling/mental health services; Child sexual abuse prevention program; Victim assistance program
AREAS SERVED: Chemung, Schuyler, Steuben
YEARS IN OPERATION: 7
LANGUAGES: Spanish, Sign
ACCESSIBILITY: Wheelchair accessible; Telecommunications for the hearing impaired (TTY, TDY, etc.); Signers for the hearing impaired
CASES SEXUAL ASSAULT/ABUSE (%): 25
DESCRIPTION: Provides comprehensive services for all crime victims; Advocacy; Escort services; Short-term crisis counseling; School-based programs; Referral services; Transportation; Assistance with crime victim compensation
CLIENTS/SERVICES: Sexual assault survivors; Marital rape/sexual abuse survivors; Child victims of sexual abuse; Adult survivors of child sexual abuse; Incest victims/survivors; Prevention program; Community education; Adolescent survivors of sexual abuse; Male survivors of sexual abuse

ENDICOTT

WOMEN AGAINST VIOLENCE (WAV)
PO Box 434, Endicott, NY 13760
Crisis hotline: **(607) 785-0089, 785-6143 24 hrs daily**
Information: (607) 785-0089, 785-6143 24 hrs daily
Contact: Bridget or Florence, Representatives
TYPE OF AGENCY: Domestic violence program
AREAS SERVED: Broome
YEARS IN OPERATION: 2
CASES SEXUAL ASSAULT/ABUSE (%): 100
DESCRIPTION: Nonresidential domestic violence organization providing advocacy (in the courts, at the police departments, hospitals, DSS, and in schools); Moving services for abused/battered women and their families; peer support, and crisis intervention via phone
CLIENTS/SERVICES: Marital rape/sexual abuse survivors; Adult survivors of child sexual abuse; Incest victims/survivors; Community education; Male survivors of sexual abuse

FLUSHING

POMONOK NEIGHBORHOOD CENTER
67-09 Kissena Blvd, Flushing, NY 11367
Information: (718) 591-6060 9am-9pm
Contact: Ellen Waldman, Counseling Spec
TYPE OF AGENCY: Victim/witness assistance program; Counseling/mental health services
AREAS SERVED: Queens
YEARS IN OPERATION: 32
LANGUAGES: Spanish, Yiddish
ACCESSIBILITY: Wheelchair accessible
DESCRIPTION: Provides various services for the neighborhood, including a crime victim assistance program. This program offers court-related assistance, lock replacement, escorts to police, hospital, and court. Also counseling for individuals and families, and a crime prevention program
CLIENTS/SERVICES: Sexual assault survivors; Marital rape/sexual abuse survivors; Adult survivors of child sexual abuse; Prevention program; Community education; Adolescent survivors of sexual abuse; Male survivors of sexual abuse

QUEENS COLLEGE WOMEN'S CENTER
SU Box 26, Flushing, NY 11367
Information: (718) 263-5668 9am-5:30pm (Mon-Fri)
Contact: Katy German, Pres
TYPE OF AGENCY: College/university-based services
SPONSORING ORGANIZATION: Queens College
ACCESSIBILITY: Wheelchair accessible
DESCRIPTION: Support group which meets once a week, facilitated by a professional counselor, for both survivors of abuse and women who are presently in abusive situations
CLIENTS/SERVICES: Sexual assault survivors; Marital rape/sexual abuse survivors; Adult survivors of child sexual abuse; Incest victims/survivors; Adolescent survivors of sexual abuse

FOREST HILLS

WOMEN'S COUNSELING AND THERAPY CENTER
112-11 68th Dr, Forest Hills, NY 11375
Information: (718) 268-3077 8am-9pm
Contact: Sandra G Fishman, Dir
TYPE OF AGENCY: Counseling/mental health services; Private practice
AREAS SERVED: Queens
YEARS IN OPERATION: 8
CLIENTS/SERVICES: Sexual assault survivors; Adult survivors of child sexual abuse; Incest victims/survivors
REQUIREMENTS: 18 and older; Minimal fee

FRANKLIN SQUARE

WEST NASSAU MENTAL HEALTH CENTER
365 Franklin Ave, Franklin Square, NY 11010
Information: (516) 437-8060 9am-5pm (Mon, Fri); 9am-9pm (Tue, Wed, Thu); 9am-2:30pm (Sat)
Contact: David Ackerman, ACSW, Clinical Svcs Coord; Pat Weiboldt, CSW, Intake Coord
TYPE OF AGENCY: Counseling/mental health services
AREAS SERVED: Nassau
YEARS IN OPERATION: 30
CASES SEXUAL ASSAULT/ABUSE (%): 10
DESCRIPTION: One of 5 agencies in the county designated to provide sexual abuse treatment for survivors and child sexual abuse, incest offenders and batterers
CLIENTS/SERVICES: Sexual assault survivors; Marital rape/sexual abuse survivors; Child victims of sexual abuse; Adult survivors of child sexual abuse; Incest victims/survivors; Community education; Offender treatment program; Adolescent survivors of sexual abuse; Male survivors of sexual abuse

FREDONIA

AMICAE, INC: HOTLINE FOR RAPE AND BATTERING
PO Box 23, Fredonia, NY 14063
Crisis hotline: **(716) 672-8484 24 hrs**
Information: (716) 664-1895, 672-8423 9am-5pm (Mon-Fri)
Contact: Dawn R Chase, Exec Dir
TYPE OF AGENCY: Rape crisis center; Domestic violence program; Acquaintance/date rape prevention program
AREAS SERVED: Chautauqua
YEARS IN OPERATION: 9½
LANGUAGES: Spanish, Swedish, Belgian
ACCESSIBILITY: Wheelchair accessible (Jamestown only)
CASES SEXUAL ASSAULT/ABUSE (%): 25
CLIENTS/SERVICES: Sexual assault survivors; Marital rape/sexual abuse survivors; Child victims of sexual abuse; Adult survivors of child sexual abuse; Incest victims/survivors; Prevention program; Community education; Adolescent survivors of sexual abuse; Ethnic minorities

FREEPORT

THE CHILDREN'S ALCOHOL RESOURCE AND EDUCATION CENTER
87 Church St, Freeport, NY 11520
Information: (516) 378-2992 9am-5pm (Mon, Wed, Fri); 9am-9pm (Tue, Thu)
Contact: Mary Lou Jones, ACSW, Dir
TYPE OF AGENCY: Counseling/mental health services
SPONSORING ORGANIZATION: South Shore Child Guidance Center
AREAS SERVED: Nassau
YEARS IN OPERATION: 4
CASES SEXUAL ASSAULT/ABUSE (%): 25-50
DESCRIPTION: Treats children of alcoholics and substance abusers and their families; Individual therapy for incest offenders
CLIENTS/SERVICES: Child victims of sexual abuse; Community education; Offender treatment program; Adolescent survivors of sexual abuse
REQUIREMENTS: Related only to clients who have been affected by drugs/alcohol abuse

SOUTH SHORE CHILD GUIDANCE CENTER
17 W Merrick Rd, Freeport, NY 11520
Information: (516) 868-3030 9am-5pm (Wed, Fri); 9am-9pm (Mon, Tue, Thu)
Contact: Murray Felson, CSW, Exec Dir
TYPE OF AGENCY: Counseling/mental health services; Child sexual abuse services
AREAS SERVED: Nassau
YEARS IN OPERATION: 29
LANGUAGES: Spanish
CASES SEXUAL ASSAULT/ABUSE (%): 5
DESCRIPTION: Outpatient psychiatric services for children and teenagers, with supportive services for parents; Special program for sexually abused children; Crisis intervention program
CLIENTS/SERVICES: Child victims of sexual abuse; Incest victims/survivors; Adolescent survivors of sexual abuse
REQUIREMENTS: 1½ to 18 years of age and parents

GARDEN CITY

CRIME VICTIMS AND RAPE COUNSELING
Box 701, Garden City, NY 11530
Crisis hotline: **Rape hotline (516) 222-2293 24 hrs**
Information: (516) 228-7410 8:30am-4:30pm (Mon-Fri)
Contact: Lois A Carey, Dir
TYPE OF AGENCY: Rape crisis center; Consultation; Training/research

CRIME VICTIMS AND RAPE COUNSELING (continued)

SPONSORING ORGANIZATION: Adelphi University, School of Social Work, Social Service Center
AREAS SERVED: Nassau
ACCESSIBILITY: Wheelchair accessible
DESCRIPTION: Provides counseling, and support groups for survivors; Training, educational materials, conferences, lectures, technical assistance, and individualized in-service training for professionals
CLIENTS/SERVICES: Sexual assault survivors; Marital rape/sexual abuse survivors; Child victims of sexual abuse; Adult survivors of child sexual abuse; Incest victims/survivors; Community education; Adolescent survivors of sexual abuse; Publications/media
SPECIAL PROGRAMS/SERVICES: Crime victims resource center has a comprehensive library of articles, books, and films, develops training manuals, bibliographies and literature reviews, and has a hotline for professionals and volunteers working with victims/survivors. Also sponsors training institutes for professionals and volunteers, including a 20-hour interdisciplinary program on "Working With Victims of Rape, Incest, and Sexual Assault" (3 times a year)

PHENIX I
Box 7167, Garden City, NY 11530
Information: (516) 379-4731 by appointment (Calls are answered between 10:30am-11:30am; later calls will be returned within 24 hrs)
Contact: E Sue Blume, CSW, Dir
TYPE OF AGENCY: Counseling/mental health services; Private practice; Women's counseling services; Training/research
AREAS SERVED: Nassau, Suffolk, Queens, Brooklyn, Manhattan
CASES SEXUAL ASSAULT/ABUSE (%): 80
DESCRIPTION: Provides therapy for women, adult children of alcoholics, lesbians, and their families, bereavement and adult incest survivors and their "significant others."
CLIENTS/SERVICES: Adult survivors of child sexual abuse; Incest victims/survivors; Community education; Adolescent survivors of sexual abuse; Lesbians; Healing; Publications/media
REQUIREMENTS: Over 16 years old; Women only (Will see male partners, siblings, etc of clients)
SPECIAL PROGRAMS/SERVICES: Publications: *The Incest Survivor's Aftereffects Check List* (free upon request with SASE); Offers training and community presentations on aftereffects of incest and other women's issues and lesbian/gay issues.

GENESEO

RAPE CRISIS SERVICE OF LIVINGSTON COUNTY
4241 Lakeville Rd, Geneseo, NY 14454
Crisis hotline: **(800) 527-1757 24 hrs, 7 days**
Information: (716) 243-0576
Contact: Laurie Snyder, Coord
TYPE OF AGENCY: Rape crisis center
SPONSORING ORGANIZATION: Planned Parenthood
AREAS SERVED: Livingston
YEARS IN OPERATION: 1½
CASES SEXUAL ASSAULT/ABUSE (%): 100
CLIENTS/SERVICES: Sexual assault survivors; Marital rape/sexual abuse survivors; Child victims of sexual abuse; Adult survivors of child sexual abuse; Incest victims/survivors; Prevention program; Community education; Adolescent survivors of sexual abuse; Male survivors of sexual abuse

GLENS FALLS

ADIRONDACK PREVENTION SERVICES, INC
48 Lawrence St, Glens Falls, NY 12801
Crisis hotline: **(518) 793-6696, 793-5888 24 hrs**
Information: (518) 792-1268 24 hrs
Contact: Kathleen Lefebvre, Exec Dir
TYPE OF AGENCY: Rape crisis center; Domestic violence program; Child sexual abuse prevention program
AREAS SERVED: Warren, Washington
YEARS IN OPERATION: 18
ACCESSIBILITY: Wheelchair accessible
CASES SEXUAL ASSAULT/ABUSE (%): 6
CLIENTS/SERVICES: Sexual assault survivors; Marital rape/sexual abuse survivors; Child victims of sexual abuse; Prevention program; Community education; Adolescent survivors of sexual abuse; Male survivors of sexual abuse

GLOVERSVILLE

THE FAMILY COUNSELING CENTER OF FULTON COUNTY
113 Bleecker St, Gloversville, NY 12078
Crisis hotline: **(518) 725-5300 (domestic violence) 24 hrs**
Information: (518) 725-4310 9am-8:30pm (Mon-Thu); 9am-5pm (Fri)
Contact: Sharon Brace, Exec Dir
TYPE OF AGENCY: Domestic violence program; Counseling/mental health services; Child sexual abuse services; Child sexual abuse prevention program
AREAS SERVED: Fulton, Montgomery, Hamilton
YEARS IN OPERATION: 12
ACCESSIBILITY: Wheelchair accessible
CASES SEXUAL ASSAULT/ABUSE (%): 40
DESCRIPTION: Individual, marriage, and family counseling, youth counseling, and crisis services for domestic violence survivors; Therapy for sexually abused children, adolescents and adults and their families. Individual and group therapy for batterers
CLIENTS/SERVICES: Sexual assault survivors; Marital rape/sexual abuse survivors; Child victims of sexual abuse; Adult survivors of child sexual abuse; Incest victims/survivors; Prevention program; Community education; Adolescent survivors of sexual abuse

GOSHEN

ORANGE COUNTY CRIME VICTIM ASSISTANCE PROGRAM
Orange County Government Center, Goshen, NY 10924
Crisis hotline: **(914) 294-5156 5pm-9am, answering machine**
Information: (914) 343-7981 9am-5pm (Mon-Fri)
Contact: William J Slaughter, III, Probation Supv
TYPE OF AGENCY: Victim/witness assistance program
SPONSORING ORGANIZATION: Orange County Probation Department
AREAS SERVED: Orange
YEARS IN OPERATION: 7
ACCESSIBILITY: Wheelchair accessible
CASES SEXUAL ASSAULT/ABUSE (%): 15
CLIENTS/SERVICES: Sexual assault survivors; Marital rape/sexual abuse survivors; Child victims of sexual abuse; Incest victims/survivors; Male survivors of sexual abuse
REQUIREMENTS: For compensation client must report to police and cooperate in prosecution

RAPE SURVIVOR ADVOCACY PROGRAM
223 Main St, Goshen, NY 10940
Crisis hotline: **(800) 832-1200 24 hrs**
Information: (914) 294-7411 8am-5pm
Contact: Lauren Keely, Prog Coord; Debbie de Jong, Sexual Assault Prevention Programs Coord
TYPE OF AGENCY: Rape crisis center; Counseling/mental health services; Child sexual abuse prevention program
SPONSORING ORGANIZATION: The Mental Health Association
AREAS SERVED: Orange, Sullivan, Ulster
YEARS IN OPERATION: 9
LANGUAGES: Spanish
CASES SEXUAL ASSAULT/ABUSE (%): 100
DESCRIPTION: Provides rape crisis intervention services and hospital emergency room accompaniment; Support groups for adolescent and adult rape survivors; Self-defense and self-esteem techniques and prevention education for women and children
CLIENTS/SERVICES: Sexual assault survivors; Marital rape/sexual abuse survivors; Child victims of sexual abuse; Adult survivors of child sexual abuse; Incest victims/survivors; Prevention program; Community education; Adolescent survivors of sexual abuse; Male survivors of sexual abuse

HARTSDALE

CHILD SEXUAL ABUSE TREATMENT CENTER
141 N Central Ave, Hartsdale, NY 10530
Crisis hotline: **(914) 949-0043 24 hrs**
Information: (914) 949-6761 9am-9pm (Mon-Thu)
Contact: Patricia Lemp, CSW, Dir
TYPE OF AGENCY: Child sexual abuse services
SPONSORING ORGANIZATION: Westchester Jewish Community Services
AREAS SERVED: Westchester
YEARS IN OPERATION: 5
ACCESSIBILITY: Wheelchair accessible
CASES SEXUAL ASSAULT/ABUSE (%): 100
DESCRIPTION: Family, individual, and group treatment for victims of incest, nonoffending parent, and offending parent
CLIENTS/SERVICES: Child victims of sexual abuse; Adult survivors of child sexual abuse; Incest victims/survivors; Prevention program; Community education; Offender treatment program; Adolescent survivors of sexual abuse; Male survivors of sexual abuse

HAUPPAUGE

SUFFOLK COUNTY DISTRICT ATTORNEY'S OFFICE—FAMILY CRIME BUREAU
Bldg 151, Veteran's Memorial Hwy, Hauppauge, NY 11788
Information: (516) 360-5230 9am-5pm (Mon-Fri)
Contact: Mary Werner, Bur Chief
TYPE OF AGENCY: Victim/witness assistance program
AREAS SERVED: Suffolk
YEARS IN OPERATION: 10
LANGUAGES: Spanish
ACCESSIBILITY: Wheelchair accessible; Telecommunications for the hearing impaired (TTY, TDY, etc.); Signers for the hearing impaired
CASES SEXUAL ASSAULT/ABUSE (%): 90
CLIENTS/SERVICES: Sexual assault survivors; Marital rape/sexual abuse survivors; Child victims of sexual abuse; Adult survivors of child sexual abuse; Incest victims/survivors; Adolescent survivors of sexual abuse; Male survivors of sexual abuse
REQUIREMENTS: All cases go through the screening bureau

VICTIMS INFORMATION BUREAU OF SUFFOLK
515 Rte 111, Hauppauge, NY 11788
Crisis hotline: **(516) 360-3606 24 hrs 7 days**
Information: (516) 360-3730 9am-9pm (Mon-Fri)
Contact: Lynn C Cugini, CSW, Asst Dir
TYPE OF AGENCY: Rape crisis center; Domestic violence program
AREAS SERVED: Suffolk
YEARS IN OPERATION: 13

VICTIMS INFORMATION BUREAU OF SUFFOLK *(continued)*

LANGUAGES: Spanish
ACCESSIBILITY: Wheelchair accessible
CASES SEXUAL ASSAULT/ABUSE (%): 20
DESCRIPTION: Provides crisis services and counseling for survivors of sexual assault and domestic violence; Batterers program
CLIENTS/SERVICES: Sexual assault survivors; Marital rape/sexual abuse survivors; Child victims of sexual abuse; Adult survivors of child sexual abuse; Incest victims/survivors; Community education; Adolescent survivors of sexual abuse; Male survivors of sexual abuse

HEMPSTEAD

JEWISH COMMUNITY SERVICES OF LONG ISLAND
50 Clinton St, Hempstead, NY 11550
Crisis hotline: **(516) 485-5710 9am-9pm (Mon-Fri)**
Information: (516) 485-5710 9am-9pm (Mon-Fri)
Contact: Edna Lenchner, Sr Caseworker
TYPE OF AGENCY: Counseling/mental health services; Child sexual abuse services
AREAS SERVED: Nassau, Suffolk, Queens
YEARS IN OPERATION: 40
ACCESSIBILITY: Wheelchair accessible
CASES SEXUAL ASSAULT/ABUSE (%): 25
DESCRIPTION: Provides family counseling services, including individual, group, couple, and family therapy; Special project for survivors of childhood sexual abuse; Counseling for rape victims, current victims of sexual abuse (children and adults), and families of victims
CLIENTS/SERVICES: Sexual assault survivors; Marital rape/sexual abuse survivors; Child victims of sexual abuse; Adult survivors of child sexual abuse; Incest victims/survivors; Prevention program; Adolescent survivors of sexual abuse; Male survivors of sexual abuse

NASSAU COALITION ON CHILD ABUSE AND NEGLECT
353 Fulton Ave, Hempstead, NY 11550
Information: (516) 481-7784 9am-5pm
Contact: Jean Forman, Exec Dir
TYPE OF AGENCY: Child sexual abuse prevention program; Interagency network
AREAS SERVED: Nassau
YEARS IN OPERATION: 10
DESCRIPTION: Network of over 70 agencies and organizations dedicated to the prevention of child abuse through awareness, advocacy, development of effective intervention, and professional training
CLIENTS/SERVICES: Child victims of sexual abuse; Incest victims/survivors; Prevention program; Community education
SPECIAL PROGRAMS/SERVICES: Child Abuse Coordination and Treatment Team coordinates efforts of Child Protective Services, law enforcement and treatment agencies working with sexually abused children. Effort includes case coordination, training, and program planning. Sexual Abuse Study and Treatment Team for therapists working with sexually abused children and their families. Meets regularly to discuss treatment experiences and to improve clinical skills. Sex Offender Study and Treatment Team for therapists treating the intrafamilial sex offender. Meets regularly to discuss treatment experiences and to improve clinical skills

PSYCHOLOGICALLY AND PHYSICALLY ABUSED PERSONS CENTER
Hofstra University, Hempstead, NY 11550
Information: (516) 560-5624 9am-5pm (Mon-Fri)
Contact: Dr Irene Gillman, Dir
TYPE OF AGENCY: College/university-based services
SPONSORING ORGANIZATION: Hofstra University
AREAS SERVED: Statewide

YEARS IN OPERATION: 10
ACCESSIBILITY: Wheelchair accessible
CASES SEXUAL ASSAULT/ABUSE (%): 20
CLIENTS/SERVICES: Sexual assault survivors; Marital rape/sexual abuse survivors; Child victims of sexual abuse; Adult survivors of child sexual abuse; Incest victims/survivors

RUNAWAY YOUTH COORDINATING COUNCIL, INC (RYCC)
45 Main St, 2nd Fl, Hempstead, NY 11550
Crisis hotline: **(516) 489-6066 24 hrs 7 days through backup service**
Information: (516) 489-6066 9am-5pm (Mon-Fri)
Contact: Joel Flax, Exec Dir
TYPE OF AGENCY: Child sexual abuse services; Child sexual abuse prevention program; Shelter; Adolescent program
AREAS SERVED: Nassau
YEARS IN OPERATION: 13
LANGUAGES: Spanish, Hebrew, Sign
ACCESSIBILITY: Wheelchair accessible; Signers for the hearing impaired
CLIENTS/SERVICES: Child victims of sexual abuse; Incest victims/survivors; Prevention program; Community education; Adolescent survivors of sexual abuse
REQUIREMENTS: Must be under 21 years of age or their parent or guardian

HUDSON

COLUMBIA-GREENE RAPE CRISIS CENTER
PO Box 1073, Hudson, NY 12534
Crisis hotline: **(518) 758-6696 24 hrs**
Information: (518) 828-5556 8:30am-4:30pm
Contact: Jean Schild, Dir
TYPE OF AGENCY: Rape crisis center
AREAS SERVED: Columbia, Greene
YEARS IN OPERATION: 7
ACCESSIBILITY: Signers for the hearing impaired
CASES SEXUAL ASSAULT/ABUSE (%): 100
CLIENTS/SERVICES: Sexual assault survivors; Marital rape/sexual abuse survivors; Child victims of sexual abuse; Adult survivors of child sexual abuse; Incest victims/survivors; Prevention program; Community education; Adolescent survivors of sexual abuse; Male survivors of sexual abuse; Preschoolers
SPECIAL PROGRAMS/SERVICES: Volunteer training; Video program: *Critter Jitters,* a child sexual abuse prevention education video and teachers manual for children 3-8 years of age ($175). Emphasizes that "Touching Should Feel Safe and Happy" and demonstrates what to do if it doesn't. Mime, music, song, poetry, and movement are included as students and their teacher play the *Critter Jitters* game about saying "no" to unwanted and uncomfortable touch

INDIAN LAKE

RAPE PREVENTION/CRISIS INTERVENTION OF HAMILTON COUNTY
85 White Birch Ln, Indian Lake, NY 12842
Crisis hotline: **(518) 793-5888 24 hrs**
Information: (518) 648-5911 9am-4pm
Contact: Claire Schultz, Coord
TYPE OF AGENCY: Rape crisis center; Child sexual abuse prevention program
SPONSORING ORGANIZATION: Warren-Hamilton Community Action Agency
AREAS SERVED: Hamilton
YEARS IN OPERATION: 1
ACCESSIBILITY: Wheelchair accessible
CASES SEXUAL ASSAULT/ABUSE (%): 95
CLIENTS/SERVICES: Sexual assault survivors; Marital rape/sexual abuse survivors; Child victims of sexual abuse; Adult survivors of child sexual abuse; Incest victims/survivors; Prevention program; Community education; Adolescent survivors of sexual abuse; Male survivors of sexual abuse

ISLIP TERRACE

LONG ISLAND WOMEN'S COALITION, INC (LIWC)
PO Box 183, Islip Terrace, NY 11787
Crisis hotline: **(516) 666-8833 24 hrs**
Information: (516) 666-7181
Contact: Jo Anne Sanders, Exec Dir
TYPE OF AGENCY: Domestic violence program
AREAS SERVED: Suffolk
YEARS IN OPERATION: 12
LANGUAGES: Spanish
ACCESSIBILITY: Wheelchair accessible
CLIENTS/SERVICES: Marital rape/sexual abuse survivors; Child victims of sexual abuse; Incest victims/survivors; Community education

ITHACA

CHILD SEXUAL ABUSE PROJECT
PO Box 164, Ithaca, NY 14851
Crisis hotline: **(607) 277-5000 24 hrs**
Information: (607) 277-3203 9am-5pm
Contact: Louise Miller, Prog Coord
TYPE OF AGENCY: Domestic violence program; Child sexual abuse services; Child sexual abuse prevention program
SPONSORING ORGANIZATION: Tompkins County Task Force for Battered Women
AREAS SERVED: Tompkins
YEARS IN OPERATION: 7
CASES SEXUAL ASSAULT/ABUSE (%): 100
DESCRIPTION: Provides advocacy, crisis intervention, and support services for young victims of sexual abuse/assault and for family members. Support group for girls ages 12-18 who are survivors of sexual abuse
CLIENTS/SERVICES: Sexual assault survivors; Child victims of sexual abuse; Incest victims/survivors; Prevention program; Community education; Adolescent survivors of sexual abuse; Male survivors of sexual abuse
REQUIREMENTS: Must be under 18 years of age
SPECIAL PROGRAMS/SERVICES: Slide-tape program on agency services

ITHACA RAPE CRISIS, INC
PO Box 713, Ithaca, NY 14850
Crisis hotline: **(607) 272-1616 24 hrs**
Information: (607) 273-5589 9:30am-5:30pm (Mon-Fri)
Contact: Kathleen Seibel, Exec Dir; Bonnie Shelley, CSW, Cous Svcs Coord
TYPE OF AGENCY: Rape crisis center
AREAS SERVED: Tompkins
YEARS IN OPERATION: 15
ACCESSIBILITY: Wheelchair accessible
CASES SEXUAL ASSAULT/ABUSE (%): 100
DESCRIPTION: Provides short-term counseling, advocacy, crisis intervention, and support groups for survivors of sexual assault, their families, and friends. Feminist martial arts/self-defense
CLIENTS/SERVICES: Sexual assault survivors; Marital rape/sexual abuse survivors; Adult survivors of child sexual abuse; Incest victims/survivors; Prevention program; Community education; Adolescent survivors of sexual abuse; Male survivors of sexual abuse
REQUIREMENTS: Ages 15 and older
SPECIAL PROGRAMS/SERVICES: Sensitivity training for police department

SUICIDE PREVENTION AND CRISIS SERVICE
Box 312, Ithaca, NY 14851
Crisis hotline: **(607) 272-1616 24 hrs**
Information: (607) 272-1505 9am-5pm
Contact: M Dyer, Exec Dir
TYPE OF AGENCY: Counseling/mental health services; Telephone crisis hotline; Adolescent program
AREAS SERVED: Tompkins, Yates
YEARS IN OPERATION: 20
LANGUAGES: Translators as needed

SUICIDE PREVENTION AND CRISIS SERVICE *(continued)*
DESCRIPTION: 24-hour crisis intervention; Telephone counseling; Emergency outreach; Face-to-face counseling; Adolescent outreach
CLIENTS/SERVICES: Sexual assault survivors; Child victims of sexual abuse; Community education

JAMAICA

QUEENS HOSPITAL CENTER RAPE CRISIS PROGRAM
82-68 164th St, Jamaica, NY 11432
Crisis hotline: **(718) 990-3188 9am-5pm**
Information: (718) 990-3188 9am-5pm
Contact: Gayle Raskin, Sexual Assault Coord
TYPE OF AGENCY: Rape crisis center; Hospital/medical center
AREAS SERVED: Queens
YEARS IN OPERATION: 4
ACCESSIBILITY: Wheelchair accessible
CASES SEXUAL ASSAULT/ABUSE (%): 100
DESCRIPTION: Provides a variety of services for sexual assault survivors; Rape companion program, 24 hours in emergency room
CLIENTS/SERVICES: Sexual assault survivors; Marital rape/sexual abuse survivors; Adult survivors of child sexual abuse; Incest victims/survivors; Community education

VICTIM SERVICES AGENCY
89-31 161st St, Jamaica, NY 11432
Crisis hotline: **(212) 577-7777 24 hrs**
Information: (718) 291-2555
TYPE OF AGENCY: Victim assistance program
CLIENTS/SERVICES: Sexual assault survivors; Marital rape/sexual abuse survivors; Child victims of sexual abuse; Community education; Adolescent survivors of sexual abuse; Male survivors of sexual abuse

WOMEN HELPING WOMEN
PO Box 3002, Jamaica, NY 11431
Crisis hotline: **(718) 539-9111 8am-11pm**
Information: (718) 539-9111 8am-11pm
Contact: Elizabeth Minturn, Dir
TYPE OF AGENCY: Domestic violence program
AREAS SERVED: New York City
YEARS IN OPERATION: 8
CASES SEXUAL ASSAULT/ABUSE (%): 100
CLIENTS/SERVICES: Marital rape/sexual abuse survivors

JAMESTOWN

FAMILY VIOLENCE/SEXUAL ASSAULT NETWORK
401 N Main St, Jamestown, NY 14701
Crisis hotline: **(716) 484-0052 24 hrs**
Information: (716) 485-1137 9am-5pm
Contact: Karen Luciano, Dir
TYPE OF AGENCY: Rape crisis center; Domestic violence program
SPONSORING ORGANIZATION: YWCA
AREAS SERVED: Chautauqua
YEARS IN OPERATION: 5
CASES SEXUAL ASSAULT/ABUSE (%): 45
CLIENTS/SERVICES: Sexual assault survivors; Marital rape/sexual abuse survivors; Child victims of sexual abuse; Adult survivors of child sexual abuse; Incest victims/survivors; Community education; Adolescent survivors of sexual abuse

KINGSTON

CRIME VICTIMS ASSISTANCE PROGRAM
1 Pearl St, Kingston, NY 12401
Crisis hotline: **(914) 437-0020 evenings, weekends, holidays**
Information: (914) 331-9300, ext 444, 443 9am-5pm (Mon-Fri)
Contact: Gail Jaffe, Educ Coord
TYPE OF AGENCY: Victim/witness assistance program
SPONSORING ORGANIZATION: Ulster County Probation Department
AREAS SERVED: Ulster
YEARS IN OPERATION: 10
CLIENTS/SERVICES: Sexual assault survivors; Marital rape/sexual abuse survivors; Child victims of sexual abuse; Adult survivors of child sexual abuse; Incest victims/survivors; Prevention program; Community education; Adolescent survivors of sexual abuse; Male survivors of sexual abuse

SUPPORT GROUP FOR SURVIVORS OF SEXUAL ABUSE
209 Clinton Ave, Kingston, NY 12401
Information: (914) 338-6844 11am-1pm (Wed)
Contact: Maggie Severe, Facilitator
TYPE OF AGENCY: Counseling/mental health services
SPONSORING ORGANIZATION: YWCA
AREAS SERVED: Ulster
YEARS IN OPERATION: 2
CASES SEXUAL ASSAULT/ABUSE (%): 100
CLIENTS/SERVICES: Adult survivors of child sexual abuse; Incest victims/survivors

MAHOPAC

PUTNAM-NORTH WESTCHESTER WOMEN'S RESOURCE CENTER
2 Mahopac Plaza, Mahopac, NY 10541
Crisis hotline: **(914) 628-2166 24 hrs**
Information: (914) 628-9284
Contact: JoAnne De Paola, Exec Dir
TYPE OF AGENCY: Rape crisis center; Domestic violence program
CLIENTS/SERVICES: Sexual assault survivors; Adult survivors of child sexual abuse; Prevention program; Community education; Male survivors of sexual abuse

MALONE

NORTH STAR MENTAL HEALTH SERVICES
130 Park St, Malone, NY 12953
Information: North end of county (518) 483-3261; South end of county 891-5535 8am-5pm (Mon-Fri)
Contact: Roger L March, CSW, Malone Assoc Dir; Phyllis Magnus, CSW, Saranac Lake Assoc Dir
TYPE OF AGENCY: Counseling/mental health services
AREAS SERVED: Franklin
ACCESSIBILITY: Wheelchair accessible
DESCRIPTION: Counseling services for survivors and offenders—rapists, child sexual abuse/incest offenders, and batterers
CLIENTS/SERVICES: Sexual assault survivors; Marital rape/sexual abuse survivors; Child victims of sexual abuse; Adult survivors of child sexual abuse; Incest victims/survivors; Offender treatment program; Adolescent survivors of sexual abuse; Male survivors of sexual abuse

MANHASSET

NORTH SHORE CHILD AND FAMILY GUIDANCE CENTER
1495 Northern Blvd, Manhasset, NY 11030
Information: (516) 627-6671 9am-5pm (Mon, Wed, Fri); 9am-9pm (Tue, Thu)
Contact: Barbara Applebaum, Prog Coord
TYPE OF AGENCY: Counseling/mental health services; Child sexual abuse services; Child sexual abuse prevention program
AREAS SERVED: Queens, Nassau, Suffolk
YEARS IN OPERATION: 30
LANGUAGES: Spanish
ACCESSIBILITY: Wheelchair accessible
CLIENTS/SERVICES: Sexual assault survivors; Marital rape/sexual abuse survivors; Child victims of sexual abuse; Adult survivors of child sexual abuse; Incest victims/survivors; Prevention program; Community education; Offender treatment program

MOUNT KISCO

NORTHERN WESTCHESTER GUIDANCE CLINIC—CHILD AND ADOLESCENT SEXUAL ABUSE PROJECT
344 Main St, Mount Kisco, NY 10549
Information: (914) 666-4646 9am-7pm (Mon-Thu); 9am-5pm (Fri)
Contact: Christine Masters, PhD, Proj Dir
TYPE OF AGENCY: Counseling/mental health services; Child sexual abuse services
AREAS SERVED: Westchester
YEARS IN OPERATION: 5
ACCESSIBILITY: Wheelchair accessible
CASES SEXUAL ASSAULT/ABUSE (%): 12
CLIENTS/SERVICES: Sexual assault survivors; Child victims of sexual abuse; Incest victims/survivors; Community education; Adolescent survivors of sexual abuse
REQUIREMENTS: Child sexual abuse victims 21 and younger

MOUNT VERNON

MOUNT VERNON COMMUNITY SERVICE CENTER
100 E 1st St, 5th Fl, Mount Vernon, NY 10550
Information: (914) 664-7171 9am-5pm
Contact: Valerie Johnstone, Ctr Admin
TYPE OF AGENCY: Counseling/mental health services
SPONSORING ORGANIZATION: Westchester County Department of Community Mental Health
AREAS SERVED: Westchester
YEARS IN OPERATION: 10
LANGUAGES: Spanish
ACCESSIBILITY: Signers for the hearing impaired
CASES SEXUAL ASSAULT/ABUSE (%): 5
DESCRIPTION: Individual and group counseling for survivors/victims; Individual therapy for child sexual abuse offenders and batterers
CLIENTS/SERVICES: Sexual assault survivors; Child victims of sexual abuse; Adult survivors of child sexual abuse; Incest victims/survivors; Community education; Offender treatment program; Adolescent survivors of sexual abuse; Male survivors of sexual abuse

RAPE CRISIS HELPLINE
229 S 7th Ave, Mount Vernon, NY 10550
Crisis hotline: **(914) 684-9877 24 hrs daily**
Information: (914) 667-1610 9am-5pm (Mon, Tue, Wed)
TYPE OF AGENCY: Counseling/mental health services; Victim assistance program
SPONSORING ORGANIZATION: Westchester Community Opportunity Program, Victims Assistance Services
AREAS SERVED: Westchester
YEARS IN OPERATION: 7
LANGUAGES: Spanish
ACCESSIBILITY: Wheelchair accessible
CASES SEXUAL ASSAULT/ABUSE (%): 20
DESCRIPTION: Provides comprehensive services for all crime victims and their families; Rape crisis services are a distinct program component
CLIENTS/SERVICES: Sexual assault survivors; Marital rape/sexual abuse survivors; Child victims of sexual abuse; Adult survivors of child sexual abuse; Incest victims/survivors; Prevention program; Community education; Adolescent survivors of sexual abuse; Male survivors of sexual abuse

NEW BREMEN

HELP HOTLINE
PO Box 111, New Bremen, NY 13367
Crisis hotline: **(315) 376-4357 24 hrs**
Information: (315) 376-8202 8am-4pm
Contact: Carol Batchelor, Coord
TYPE OF AGENCY: Rape crisis center; Child sexual abuse prevention program
SPONSORING ORGANIZATION: Lewis County Opportunities, Inc
AREAS SERVED: Lewis
YEARS IN OPERATION: 3
LANGUAGES: Spanish
ACCESSIBILITY: Wheelchair accessible; Telecommunications for the hearing impaired (TTY, TDY, etc.)
CASES SEXUAL ASSAULT/ABUSE (%): 100
CLIENTS/SERVICES: Sexual assault survivors; Marital rape/sexual abuse survivors; Child victims of sexual abuse; Adult survivors of child sexual abuse; Incest victims/survivors; Prevention program; Community education; Adolescent survivors of sexual abuse; Male survivors of sexual abuse

NEW CITY

VOLUNTEER COUNSELING SERVICE OF ROCKLAND COUNTY, INC
151 S Main St, New City, NY 10956
Information: (914) 634-5729 9am-9pm (Mon-Thu) 9am-5pm (Fri)
Contact: Phyllis B Frank, Asst Dir
TYPE OF AGENCY: Counseling/mental health services
AREAS SERVED: Rockland
YEARS IN OPERATION: 18
CASES SEXUAL ASSAULT/ABUSE (%): 15
CLIENTS/SERVICES: Sexual assault survivors; Child victims of sexual abuse; Adult survivors of child sexual abuse; Incest victims/survivors; Adolescent survivors of sexual abuse

NEW HYDE PARK

PLAYING IT SAFE
999 Herricks Rd, Herricks Community Center, New Hyde Park, NY 11040
Information: (516) 741-0620 9am-5pm (Mon-Fri)
Contact: Paula Geonie, Pres
TYPE OF AGENCY: Child sexual abuse prevention program; Crime prevention
SPONSORING ORGANIZATION: LIAISON, Inc
AREAS SERVED: New York City, Nassau, Suffolk, Westchester
YEARS IN OPERATION: 6
ACCESSIBILITY: Wheelchair accessible
DESCRIPTION: Liaison, Inc, a volunteer crime prevention program has twelve different programs serving people of all ages. "Playing It Safe" is a nonthreatening approach to child safety concerning abuse, abduction and general safety rules for children ages 3-7
CLIENTS/SERVICES: Prevention program; Community education; Preschoolers; Publications/media
SPECIAL PROGRAMS/SERVICES: Publications: *Playing It Safe* is available in curriculum form for areas outside the New York area ($25). *Playing It Safe* book for children ($1.00 each), brochure ($.50 each), and stickers ($.25 each)

NEW ROCHELLE

FAMILY VIOLENCE PROGRAM
16 Guion Pl, New Rochelle, NY 10801
Crisis hotline: **(914) 632-5000, ext 3420 12pm-8:30pm (Mon, Wed); 9am-5pm (Tue, Thu, Fri)**
Information: (914) 632-5000, ext 3420 9am-5pm (Mon-Fri)
Contact: Annette Packard and Vera Stein, ACSWs
TYPE OF AGENCY: Domestic violence program
SPONSORING ORGANIZATION: Kirschenbaum Mental Health Center
AREAS SERVED: Westchester
YEARS IN OPERATION: 10
LANGUAGES: Spanish
CASES SEXUAL ASSAULT/ABUSE (%): 10
DESCRIPTION: Domestic violence program principally dealing with spouse abuse and adult incest survivors; Individual therapy for incest offenders and batterers
CLIENTS/SERVICES: Marital rape/sexual abuse survivors; Adult survivors of child sexual abuse; Incest victims/survivors; Community education; Offender treatment program; Male survivors of sexual abuse
REQUIREMENTS: Must be 18 or older; Sliding scale fee charged for service

RAPE CRISIS HELPLINE
95 Lincoln Ave, New Rochelle, NY 10801
Crisis hotline: **(914) 684-9877 24 hrs daily**
Information: (914) 636-3050 9am-5pm (Thu, Fri)
TYPE OF AGENCY: Rape crisis center; Victim/witness assistance program
SPONSORING ORGANIZATION: Westchester Community Opportunity Program, Victims Assistance Services
AREAS SERVED: Westchester
YEARS IN OPERATION: 7
LANGUAGES: Spanish
ACCESSIBILITY: Wheelchair accessible
CASES SEXUAL ASSAULT/ABUSE (%): 20
DESCRIPTION: Provides comprehensive services for all crime victims and their families; Rape crisis services are a distinct program component
CLIENTS/SERVICES: Sexual assault survivors; Marital rape/sexual abuse survivors; Child victims of sexual abuse; Adult survivors of child sexual abuse; Incest victims/survivors; Prevention program; Community education; Adolescent survivors of sexual abuse; Male survivors of sexual abuse

NEW YORK

AMERICAN INDIAN COMMUNITY HOUSE
842 Broadway, 8th Fl, New York, NY 10003
Information: (212) 598-0100 9am-5pm
Contact: Clifford Limpy, Ch Soc Wkr
TYPE OF AGENCY: Counseling/mental health services; Information and referral
AREAS SERVED: New York City
YEARS IN OPERATION: 20
LANGUAGES: Indian languages
DESCRIPTION: Nonprofit organization serving Native Americans; Provides referrals for sexual assault survivors
CLIENTS/SERVICES: Sexual assault survivors; Ethnic minorities

ASAAC—CENTER FOR ADULTS SEXUALLY ABUSED AS CHILDREN
81 Irving Pl, Ste 1C, New York, NY 10003
Information: (212) 486-7102
Contact: Rory M McDonald, CSW, Ina H Anisfeld, Co-Dirs
TYPE OF AGENCY: Counseling/mental health services
AREAS SERVED: New York City and surrounding area
YEARS IN OPERATION: 4
CASES SEXUAL ASSAULT/ABUSE (%): 100
CLIENTS/SERVICES: Adult survivors of child sexual abuse; Incest victims/survivors; Male survivors of sexual abuse
REQUIREMENTS: Must be 18 or older

ASIAN FAMILY SERVICES
48 Henry St, Basement, New York, NY 10002
Crisis hotline: **(212) 962-1182 9am-5pm (Mon-Fri)**
Information: (212) 233-9830 9am-5pm (Mon-Wed, Fri); 9am-7pm (Thu)
Contact: Amelia Chu, Prog Dir
TYPE OF AGENCY: Domestic violence program; Counseling/mental health services; Child abuse prevention program
SPONSORING ORGANIZATION: Chinese-American Planning Council, Inc
AREAS SERVED: New York City
YEARS IN OPERATION: 4
LANGUAGES: Chinese, Korean
CASES SEXUAL ASSAULT/ABUSE (%): 30
DESCRIPTION: Counseling; Crisis intervention and follow-up; Advocacy; Information and referral; Parenting aides
CLIENTS/SERVICES: Sexual assault survivors; Marital rape/sexual abuse survivors; Child victims of sexual abuse; Adult survivors of child sexual abuse; Incest victims/survivors; Prevention program; Community education; Adolescent survivors of sexual abuse; Ethnic minorities
REQUIREMENTS: At least one child under 18 who is at risk of foster care placement
SPECIAL PROGRAMS/SERVICES: Developing bilingual training materials and curriculum on child abuse (physical, sexual, and emotional); Adolescent discussion group is also being planned

ASIAN-AMERICAN MENTAL HEALTH SERVICES—JAPANESE UNIT
236 W 72nd St, New York, NY 10023
Crisis hotline: **(212) 787-7741 9am-5pm**
Information: (212) 787-7741 9am-5pm
Contact: Fumi Raith, Soc Wkr Supv
TYPE OF AGENCY: Counseling/mental health services; Child sexual abuse services
SPONSORING ORGANIZATION: Hamilton-Madison House
AREAS SERVED: New York City
YEARS IN OPERATION: 5
LANGUAGES: Japanese
ACCESSIBILITY: Wheelchair accessible
CASES SEXUAL ASSAULT/ABUSE (%): 1
DESCRIPTION: Provides mental health services for Japanese-speaking population, including treatment for rapists, batterers, and child sexual abuse/incest offenders
CLIENTS/SERVICES: Sexual assault survivors; Marital rape/sexual abuse survivors; Child victims of sexual abuse; Adult survivors of child sexual abuse; Incest victims/survivors; Prevention program; Community education; Offender treatment program; Adolescent survivors of sexual abuse; Male survivors of sexual abuse; Ethnic minorities
REQUIREMENTS: Sliding scale fee
SPECIAL PROGRAMS/SERVICES: Bilingual (Japanese/English) brochure

INTENSIVE SERVICES TO FAMILIES DEPARTMENT
6 E 94th St, New York, NY 10128
Crisis hotline: **(212) 369-0300 24 hrs 7 days**
Information: (212) 369-0300 9am-5pm (Tue, Thu, Fri); 9am-8:30pm (Mon, Wed)
Contact: Margaret Fluhr, Intensive Svcs to Families Prog Dir
TYPE OF AGENCY: Child sexual abuse services; Child sexual abuse prevention program; Child abuse services; Child abuse prevention program
SPONSORING ORGANIZATION: Spence-Chapin Services to Families and Children
AREAS SERVED: 5 boroughs of New York City
YEARS IN OPERATION: 16
LANGUAGES: Spanish, French
ACCESSIBILITY: Wheelchair accessible
DESCRIPTION: Provides extensive clinical, case management and advocacy services for severely dysfunctional families with a high incidence of physical, emotional, and sexual abuse, and neglect. Goal is to keep families together (prevent children from entering foster care), improve the emotional and social functioning of all family members, and prevent a recurrence of the abuse

INTENSIVE SERVICES TO FAMILIES DEPARTMENT (continued)

CLIENTS/SERVICES: Marital rape/sexual abuse survivors; Child victims of sexual abuse; Adult survivors of child sexual abuse; Incest victims/survivors; Community education; Adolescent survivors of sexual abuse; Male survivors of sexual abuse
REQUIREMENTS: There must be a child under 18 in the home (or a pregnant woman); Must reside within New York City; Parents/guardians must be involved in treatment in addition to the children

THE KARATE SCHOOL FOR WOMEN/KARATE FOR KIDS
149 Bleecker St, New York, NY 10012
Information: (212) 982-4739 9am-9pm
Contact: Roberta Schire, Dir
TYPE OF AGENCY: Rape prevention program
AREAS SERVED: Manhattan, Brooklyn, Bronx
YEARS IN OPERATION: 12
LANGUAGES: Spanish, French
CASES SEXUAL ASSAULT/ABUSE (%): 30
DESCRIPTION: Karate instruction for women and children. Beginners (ages 4-10) learn basic punches, blocks, and kicks. Assertiveness games are a regular part of the class, and concepts of self-defense are sensitively introduced. At the intermediate and advanced levels, children practice more difficult basics as well as kata and sparring
CLIENTS/SERVICES: Sexual assault survivors; Marital rape/sexual abuse survivors; Child victims of sexual abuse; Adult survivors of child sexual abuse; Incest victims/survivors; Prevention program; Community education; Preschoolers
REQUIREMENTS: Children's classes are for ages 4-11

LESBIAN SWITCHBOARD
208 W 13th St, New York, NY 10011
Crisis hotline: **(212) 741-2610 6pm-10pm (Mon-Fri)**
TYPE OF AGENCY: Counseling/mental health services; Telephone crisis hotline; Information and referral
AREAS SERVED: New York, New Jersey, Connecticut
YEARS IN OPERATION: 15
LANGUAGES: Hebrew, Spanish
CASES SEXUAL ASSAULT/ABUSE (%): 10-15
DESCRIPTION: Volunteer-staffed phone line which provides peer counseling, information and referrals (legal, medical, etc) especially for the lesbian community
CLIENTS/SERVICES: Sexual assault survivors; Marital rape/sexual abuse survivors; Adult survivors of child sexual abuse; Incest victims/survivors; Lesbians

MID-LIFE WOMEN'S CRISIS SUPPORT GROUP
25 W 64th St, New York, NY 10023
Crisis hotline: **(212) 491-5882 24 hrs (answering machine)**
Information: (212) 491-5882 24 hrs (answering machine)
Contact: Adrian Tiemann, PhD, MSW, Dir
TYPE OF AGENCY: Private practice
YEARS IN OPERATION: 3
ACCESSIBILITY: Wheelchair accessible
CASES SEXUAL ASSAULT/ABUSE (%): 10
CLIENTS/SERVICES: Sexual assault survivors; Child victims of sexual abuse; Adult survivors of child sexual abuse; Incest victims/survivors; Offender treatment program; Adolescent survivors of sexual abuse; Male survivors of sexual abuse
REQUIREMENTS: Ages 35-60, female, for support groups, other ages and sexes for counseling/psychotherapy. Will see self-referred abusers

SPECIAL PROGRAMS/SERVICES: Affiliated with Foundation of Thanatology, does crisis counseling with people facing life threatening illness/events, such as major surgery. Uses a holistic healing approach based on Milton Erickson's work/therapy to help people maximize their use of inner resources

MOUNT SINAI MEDICAL CENTER—RAPE CRISIS INTERVENTION PROGRAM
1 Gustave L Levy Place, Box 1170, New York, NY 10029
Crisis hotline: **(212) 241-5461 24 hrs daily**
Information: (212) 241-5461 9am-5pm (Mon-Fri)
Contact: Iona Siegel, Dir; Joan Dauhajve, Asst Dir
TYPE OF AGENCY: Rape crisis center; Hospital/medical center
AREAS SERVED: Manhattan
YEARS IN OPERATION: 5
LANGUAGES: Spanish
ACCESSIBILITY: Wheelchair accessible
CASES SEXUAL ASSAULT/ABUSE (%): 99
DESCRIPTION: Offers advocacy for victims seen in the emergency room; Individual and support group counseling for men and women; Provides training in feminist martial arts/self-defense
CLIENTS/SERVICES: Sexual assault survivors; Marital rape/sexual abuse survivors; Adult survivors of child sexual abuse; Incest victims/survivors; Prevention program; Community education; Adolescent survivors of sexual abuse; Male survivors of sexual abuse
REQUIREMENTS: Must be 17 or older
SPECIAL PROGRAMS/SERVICES: Bilingual brochure (Spanish/English)

NEW YORK ASIAN WOMEN'S CENTER, INC
39 Bowery, Box 375, New York, NY 10002
Crisis hotline: **(212) 941-1192 6pm-9pm (Tue, Wed); Other hrs message will be returned within 24 hrs**
Information: (212) 941-1192 Mon-Fri (calls will be returned before 5pm)
Contact: Barbara Chang, Ctr Coord
TYPE OF AGENCY: Domestic violence program; Child sexual abuse prevention program
AREAS SERVED: New York City (all 5 boroughs)
YEARS IN OPERATION: 7
LANGUAGES: Chinese, Japanese, Korean
ACCESSIBILITY: Wheelchair accessible
CASES SEXUAL ASSAULT/ABUSE (%): 8
DESCRIPTION: Provides direct services for battered Asian women and their dependents; Short-term crisis counseling for sexually assaulted/abused Asian women and children
CLIENTS/SERVICES: Sexual assault survivors; Marital rape/sexual abuse survivors; Child victims of sexual abuse; Adult survivors of child sexual abuse; Prevention program; Community education; Adolescent survivors of sexual abuse; Ethnic minorities

NEW YORK CITY GAY AND LESBIAN ANTI-VIOLENCE PROJECT
208 W 13th St, New York, NY 10011
Crisis hotline: **(212) 807-0197 24 hrs**
Information: (212) 807-6761 10am-6pm (Mon-Fri)
Contact: Nina Kaminsky, Clinical Dir
TYPE OF AGENCY: Victim/witness assistance program
AREAS SERVED: New York City greater metropolitan area
YEARS IN OPERATION: 8
LANGUAGES: Spanish
CASES SEXUAL ASSAULT/ABUSE (%): 10
DESCRIPTION: Provides counseling, advocacy, information for survivors of anti-gay and anti-lesbian violence, sexual assault, domestic violence, and other types of victimization. Special programs for lesbian and male survivors of sexual assault

CLIENTS/SERVICES: Sexual assault survivors; Marital rape/sexual abuse survivors; Adult survivors of child sexual abuse; Incest victims/survivors; Community education; Male survivors of sexual abuse; Lesbians; Gay men
REQUIREMENTS: Must be 18 or older
SPECIAL PROGRAMS/SERVICES: Brochure about sexual assault of lesbians in an English/Spanish edition and male sexual assault brochure in Spanish and English

NEW YORK CITY TASK FORCE AGAINST SEXUAL ASSAULT
250 Church St, Rm 625-A, New York, NY 10013
Crisis hotline: **(212) 553-5083 9am-6pm**
Information: (212) 433-7298 9am-6pm
Contact: Chezia Carraway, Coord
TYPE OF AGENCY: Interagency network
SPONSORING ORGANIZATION: City of New York Human Resources Administration
AREAS SERVED: New York City
YEARS IN OPERATION: 8
LANGUAGES: Spanish
CASES SEXUAL ASSAULT/ABUSE (%): 90
DESCRIPTION: A coalition of professionals and groups dedicated to the elimination of sexual violence. Focuses on public education, coordination of services, development of policy guidelines, and dissemination of printed materials on rape, incest, child sexual abuse, and sexual harassment
CLIENTS/SERVICES: Prevention program; Community education

NEW YORK COUNTY DISTRICT ATTORNEY'S OFFICE—WITNESS AID SERVICES UNIT
1 Hogan Pl, New York, NY 10013
Crisis hotline: **(212) 553-9040, 553-9041 8am-midnight**
Information: (212) 553-9040, 553-9041 8am-midnight
Contact: Thomas Alessandro, Dir
TYPE OF AGENCY: Victim/witness assistance program
AREAS SERVED: New York
YEARS IN OPERATION: 12
LANGUAGES: Spanish
ACCESSIBILITY: Wheelchair accessible
CLIENTS/SERVICES: Sexual assault survivors; Marital rape/sexual abuse survivors; Child victims of sexual abuse; Adult survivors of child sexual abuse; Incest victims/survivors; Community education; Adolescent survivors of sexual abuse; Male survivors of sexual abuse
REQUIREMENTS: Victim must cooperate with the prosecution of the case

NEW YORK FOUNDLING HOSPITAL—CHILD ABUSE PREVENTION SERVICES
18 W 18th St, 8th Fl, New York, NY 10011
Crisis hotline: **(800) 635-1522 9am-5pm (Mon-Fri), (800) 342-3720 (weekends, holidays, evenings)**
Information: (212) 727-6900 9am-5pm (Mon-Fri)
TYPE OF AGENCY: Hospital/medical center; Child sexual abuse services; Child abuse services
CLIENTS/SERVICES: Child victims of sexual abuse; Offender treatment program; Adolescent survivors of sexual abuse; Male survivors of sexual abuse

NEW YORK WOMEN AGAINST RAPE
666 Broadway, Rm 610, New York, NY 10012
Crisis hotline: **(212) 777-4000 Victim Services 24 hrs; Incest helpline 8am-8pm (Mon-Sat)**
Information: (212) 477-0819 9am-5pm
Contact: Lucy N Friedman, Exec Dir
TYPE OF AGENCY: Rape crisis center; Child sexual abuse prevention program; Acquaintance/date rape prevention program; Theater group
AREAS SERVED: All 5 boroughs of New York City
YEARS IN OPERATION: 16
LANGUAGES: Spanish
ACCESSIBILITY: Wheelchair accessible

NEW YORK WOMEN AGAINST RAPE
(continued)

DESCRIPTION: Programs in family and criminal courts in 10 communities, in schools and police precincts, as well as special programs serving domestic violence, child sexual abuse, rape, elder abuse victims, families of homicide victims; Group therapy available for child sexual abuse offenders and batterers
CLIENTS/SERVICES: Sexual assault survivors; Marital rape/sexual abuse survivors; Child victims of sexual abuse; Adult survivors of child sexual abuse; Incest victims/survivors; Prevention program; Community education; Adolescent survivors of sexual abuse; Male survivors of sexual abuse; Publications/media
SPECIAL PROGRAMS/SERVICES: Acting Out, a teen theater project which uses drama to deal with issues of sexual assault, has recently produced a music video about child and teenage sexual abuse. SAPPS, Sexual Assault Prevention Project in the Schools and Streets, is another program for teenagers, offering counseling and community education to the Lower East Side in English and Spanish. Bilingual brochures (Spanish and English)

NEW YORK WOMEN AGAINST RAPE
666 Broadway, Rm 610, New York, NY 10012
Crisis hotline: **(212) 777-4000 victim services 24 hrs**
Information: (212) 477-0819 9am-5pm
Contact: Margie Metsch
TYPE OF AGENCY: Rape crisis center; Child sexual abuse prevention program; Acquaintance/date rape prevention program
AREAS SERVED: All 5 boroughs of New York City
YEARS IN OPERATION: 16
LANGUAGES: Spanish
ACCESSIBILITY: Wheelchair accessible
DESCRIPTION: Programs in family and criminal courts in 10 communities, in schools and police precincts, as well as special programs serving domestic violence, child sexual abuse, rape, and elder abuse victims, families of homicide victims; Group therapy available for child sexual abuse offenders and batterers
CLIENTS/SERVICES: Sexual assault survivors; Marital rape/sexual abuse survivors; Child victims of sexual abuse; Adult survivors of child sexual abuse; Incest victims/survivors; Prevention program; Community education; Adolescent survivors of sexual abuse; Male survivors of sexual abuse; Publications/media
SPECIAL PROGRAMS/SERVICES: *Acting Out*, a teen theater project which uses drama to deal with issues of sexual assault, has recently produced a music video about child and teenage sexual abuse. SAPPS, Sexual Assault Prevention Program in the Schools and Streets, is another program for teenagers, offering counseling and community education to the lower East Side in English and Spanish. Bilingual brochures available

PREVENTIVE SERVICES PROGRAM
150 E 45th St, New York, NY 10017
Crisis hotline: **(212) 949-4800 24 hrs**
Information: (212) 949-4904 9am-5pm (Mon-Fri)
Contact: Gerri Berger, On-site Supv
TYPE OF AGENCY: Counseling/mental health services; Child sexual abuse prevention program; Child abuse prevention program
SPONSORING ORGANIZATION: Children's Aid Society
AREAS SERVED: Manhattan
YEARS IN OPERATION: 15
LANGUAGES: Spanish
ACCESSIBILITY: Wheelchair accessible
CASES SEXUAL ASSAULT/ABUSE (%): 10
DESCRIPTION: Provides a range of mandated preventive services, including homemaker service, casework counseling, parent aide services, referrals for medical care and psychotherapy for families at-risk of child abuse, including sexual abuse
CLIENTS/SERVICES: Sexual assault survivors; Marital rape/sexual abuse survivors; Child victims of sexual abuse; Adult survivors of child sexual abuse; Incest victims/survivors; Prevention program; Community education; Adolescent survivors of sexual abuse
REQUIREMENTS: There must be children at home, under the age of 18, who are at risk of foster care

RAPE CRISIS INTERVENTION PROGRAM
622 W 168th St, New York, NY 10032
Information: (212) 305-9060
Contact: Filomena Critelli, Coord
TYPE OF AGENCY: Rape crisis center; Hospital/medical center
SPONSORING ORGANIZATION: Presbyterian Hospital
AREAS SERVED: Primarily Upper Manhattan
YEARS IN OPERATION: 10
LANGUAGES: Spanish
CASES SEXUAL ASSAULT/ABUSE (%): 100
CLIENTS/SERVICES: Sexual assault survivors; Marital rape/sexual abuse survivors; Community education; Adolescent survivors of sexual abuse; Male survivors of sexual abuse
REQUIREMENTS: 12 years and older
SPECIAL PROGRAMS/SERVICES: Bilingual brochure (Spanish and English)

RAPE INTERVENTION PROGRAM/CRIME VICTIM ASSESSMENT PROJECT (RIP/CVAP)
411 W 114th St, No 5A, New York, NY 10025
Crisis hotline: **(212) 523-4728 6pm-8am**
Information: (212) 523-4728 9am-5pm
Contact: Susan Xenarios, Proj Dir
TYPE OF AGENCY: Rape crisis center; Domestic violence program; Hospital/medical center; Victim/witness assistance program; Child sexual abuse services; Child sexual abuse prevention program; Acquaintance/date rape prevention program
SPONSORING ORGANIZATION: St Luke's/Roosevelt Hospital Center
AREAS SERVED: New York City, Tri-state area
YEARS IN OPERATION: 11
LANGUAGES: Spanish
ACCESSIBILITY: Wheelchair accessible
CASES SEXUAL ASSAULT/ABUSE (%): 75
DESCRIPTION: Provides crisis intervention and short-term counseling in the hospital emergency room for all survivors of sexual assault and other violent crimes; Support groups for female rape survivors, battered women; Currently developing a group for male sexual assault survivors
CLIENTS/SERVICES: Sexual assault survivors; Marital rape/sexual abuse survivors; Child victims of sexual abuse; Adult survivors of child sexual abuse; Incest victims/survivors; Prevention program; Community education; Adolescent survivors of sexual abuse; Male survivors of sexual abuse
SPECIAL PROGRAMS/SERVICES: RIP/CVAP has a resource center that is available to the general public. Collection includes books, journals, and videos addressing the issues of sexual assault, domestic violence, child sexual abuse and incest, AIDS, victimology and literature pertaining to the gay/lesbian community, and women of color. Also runs a prevention program for New York City junior high and high school youth

RHEEDLEN PLACE
457 W 51st St, New York, NY 10019
Crisis hotline: **(212) 866-0700 24 hrs**
Information: (212) 315-1707 8:30am-8pm
Contact: Michael Arsham, Prog Dir
TYPE OF AGENCY: Counseling/mental health services; Child sexual abuse services; Child abuse services; Shelter
SPONSORING ORGANIZATION: Rheedlen Foundation
AREAS SERVED: Manhattan Community Planning Districts 4 and 5
YEARS IN OPERATION: 4
LANGUAGES: Spanish
DESCRIPTION: Preventive service program works to avert foster care placement of children at risk. Provides counseling for survivors and rapists, batterers, and child sexual abuse/incest offenders; In-home counseling for at-risk families; Short-term emergency shelter for abused children
CLIENTS/SERVICES: Sexual assault survivors; Marital rape/sexual abuse survivors; Child victims of sexual abuse; Adult survivors of child sexual abuse; Incest victims/survivors; Prevention program; Community education; Offender treatment program; Adolescent survivors of sexual abuse; Male survivors of sexual abuse

SEXUAL BEHAVIOR CLINIC
Box 17, 722 W 168th St, New York, NY 10032
Information: (212) 960-5851 9am-5pm
Contact: Judith V Becker, PhD, Clinic Dir
TYPE OF AGENCY: Hospital/medical center
SPONSORING ORGANIZATION: New York State Psychiatric Institute
AREAS SERVED: Statewide
YEARS IN OPERATION: 10
ACCESSIBILITY: Wheelchair accessible
CASES SEXUAL ASSAULT/ABUSE (%): 100
DESCRIPTION: Provides evaluation and treatment for adolescent perpetrators of sexual crimes
CLIENTS/SERVICES: Offender treatment program
REQUIREMENTS: Must be nonpsychotic male between the ages of 13 and 18

STEPS TO END FAMILY VIOLENCE
104 E 107th St, New York, NY 10029
Information: (212) 876-0367 9am-7pm (Mon-Thu); 9am-5pm (Fri)
Contact: Sr Mary Nerney, Dir
TYPE OF AGENCY: Domestic violence program; Counseling/mental health services
SPONSORING ORGANIZATION: Edwin Gould Services for Children
AREAS SERVED: New York City
YEARS IN OPERATION: 1
LANGUAGES: Spanish
CASES SEXUAL ASSAULT/ABUSE (%): 75
DESCRIPTION: Court intervention, advocacy, and comprehensive services for women who have been abused, and then are arrested for defending themselves and/or their children
CLIENTS/SERVICES: Sexual assault survivors; Marital rape/sexual abuse survivors; Child victims of sexual abuse; Adult survivors of child sexual abuse; Incest victims/survivors; Community education

VICTIM SERVICES AGENCY
2 Lafayette St, 3rd Fl, New York, NY 10007
Crisis hotline: **Incest Helpline (212) 227-3000; Other crime victims (212) 577-7777 8am-8pm (Mon-Sat)**
Information: (212) 577-7700 9am-5pm
Contact: Jane Barker, Clinical Svcs Dir
TYPE OF AGENCY: Victim/witness assistance program; Child sexual abuse services; Child sexual abuse prevention program
AREAS SERVED: New York City metropolitan area
YEARS IN OPERATION: 10
LANGUAGES: Spanish
ACCESSIBILITY: Wheelchair accessible
CASES SEXUAL ASSAULT/ABUSE (%): 100
DESCRIPTION: Offers emergency assistance and short- and long-term counseling for victims of crime including sexual assault/child sexual abuse; Family assistance project is a long-term treatment program for victims of incest and their families; Provides services for runaways, domestic violence; Family counseling; Group therapy for incest offenders and batterers
CLIENTS/SERVICES: Sexual assault survivors; Marital rape/sexual abuse survivors; Child victims of sexual abuse; Adult survivors of child

VICTIM SERVICES AGENCY (continued)

sexual abuse; Incest victims/survivors; Prevention program; Community education; Offender treatment program; Adolescent survivors of sexual abuse; Male survivors of sexual abuse
REQUIREMENTS: For Helpline and Hotline, there are no requirements. Some of VSA's specialized counseling programs do have residency or age restrictions. Hotlines can provide appropriate referrals
SPECIAL PROGRAMS/SERVICES: The Incest Helpline, a telephone hotline service for incest victims and survivors is the first of its kind; Bilingual (Spanish/English) brochures available

VICTIM TREATMENT CENTER
329 E 62nd St, New York, NY 10021
Information: (212) 838-4333 9am-8pm (Mon-Fri)
Contact: Jill Stultz, CSW, Victim Treatment Ctr Dir
TYPE OF AGENCY: Victim/witness assistance program; Counseling/mental health services; Training/research
SPONSORING ORGANIZATION: Karen Horney Clinic
YEARS IN OPERATION: 14
LANGUAGES: French
CASES SEXUAL ASSAULT/ABUSE (%): 25
DESCRIPTION: Short-term counseling for victims of stranger-related crime; Individual and group treatment for adult survivors of child sexual abuse
CLIENTS/SERVICES: Sexual assault survivors; Adult survivors of child sexual abuse; Incest victims/survivors; Community education; Adolescent survivors of sexual abuse; Male survivors of sexual abuse
REQUIREMENTS: Adults. Cases involving younger survivors may be considered on an individual basis if the perpetrator is absent and monitoring is not required
SPECIAL PROGRAMS/SERVICES: Sponsors conferences, seminars, etc, on issues related to victimization, including sexual assault and survivors of child sexual abuse

VICTIMS FOR VICTIMS NEW YORK CHAPTER
PO Box 2089, Canal St Station, New York, NY 10013
Information: (212) 431-1200
Contact: Kathie Callaghan, Support Grp Dir
TYPE OF AGENCY: Victim/witness assistance program; Self-help group
AREAS SERVED: New York City
YEARS IN OPERATION: 4
CASES SEXUAL ASSAULT/ABUSE (%): 65
DESCRIPTION: Self-help organization run by volunteers which offers the following services for victims of violent crime: emotional support via telephone; peer support group; information and referral
CLIENTS/SERVICES: Sexual assault survivors

VICTIMS OF VIOLENT ASSAULT ASSISTANCE PROGRAM
1st Ave and 27th St, Rm GC49, New York, NY 10016
Information: (212) 561-3755 9am-6pm
Contact: Alex Deas, Prog Dir
TYPE OF AGENCY: Hospital/medical center
SPONSORING ORGANIZATION: Bellevue Hospital Center
AREAS SERVED: New York
YEARS IN OPERATION: 8
LANGUAGES: Spanish
ACCESSIBILITY: Wheelchair accessible
CASES SEXUAL ASSAULT/ABUSE (%): 60
DESCRIPTION: Emergency medical treatment and special evidence collection by nurse practitioners for female and male rape victims over 18; Follow-up counseling (individuals, couples, and families); Support groups; Follow-up medical evaluation; Information and referral
CLIENTS/SERVICES: Sexual assault survivors; Marital rape/sexual abuse survivors; Adult survivors of child sexual abuse; Incest victims/survivors; Prevention program; Community education; Adolescent survivors of sexual abuse; Male survivors of sexual abuse
REQUIREMENTS: Must be 18 or older
SPECIAL PROGRAMS/SERVICES: The use of the nurse practitioner for the medical examination and evidence collection for adult sexual assault survivors in the emergency room is unique in New York State and ensures that the sexual assault survivor receives immediate, thorough and quality care in the emergency room, hastening the resolution of rape trauma syndrome and enhancing the victims' ability to successfully prosecute their assailant

VICTIMS SERVICES AGENCY
155 W 72nd St, Rm 607, New York, NY 10024
Crisis hotline: **(212) 227-3000 24 hrs 7 days**
Information: (212) 874-0724 9am-5pm (Mon-Fri)
TYPE OF AGENCY: Victim/witness assistance program
LANGUAGES: Spanish
CLIENTS/SERVICES: Sexual assault survivors; Adult survivors of child sexual abuse; Incest victims/survivors; Prevention program; Community education; Adolescent survivors of sexual abuse

WOMEN'S ACTION ALLIANCE, INC
370 Lexington Ave, Ste 603, New York, NY 10017
Information: (212) 532-8330 9am-5pm (Mon-Fri)
Contact: Ellen C Leuchs, Information and Referral Svcs
TYPE OF AGENCY: Information and referral; Women's organization
AREAS SERVED: Primarily New York City, has national listings
YEARS IN OPERATION: 16
DESCRIPTION: Provides information and referral on women's concerns, primarily in the New York City area and some national resources; National projects include a women's center network; Women's Alcohol and Drug Education Project, and sex-fair education
CLIENTS/SERVICES: Community education

WOMEN'S COUNSELING PROJECT, INC
3001 Broadway, Reid Hall, Barnard College, New York, NY 10027
Information: (212) 854-3063 10am-5pm (Mon-Thu)
Contact: Anita Laviola, Coord
TYPE OF AGENCY: Information and referral; Women's center
AREAS SERVED: Greater metropolitan area
YEARS IN OPERATION: 18
LANGUAGES: Spanish
CASES SEXUAL ASSAULT/ABUSE (%): 6
DESCRIPTION: Refers women callers to the proper professional, whether legal, health, mental health, or abuse; Peer counseling
CLIENTS/SERVICES: Sexual assault survivors; Marital rape/sexual abuse survivors; Child victims of sexual abuse; Adult survivors of child sexual abuse; Incest victims/survivors

WOMEN'S INSTITUTE FOR PSYCHOTHERAPY
105 W 13th St, New York, NY 10011
Crisis hotline: **(516) 267-8896 Weekends**
Information: (212) 741-1278
Contact: Jean Mundy, Psychologist
TYPE OF AGENCY: Private practice
AREAS SERVED: New York City, Suffolk
YEARS IN OPERATION: 10
CASES SEXUAL ASSAULT/ABUSE (%): 5
CLIENTS/SERVICES: Sexual assault survivors; Marital rape/sexual abuse survivors; Child victims of sexual abuse; Adult survivors of child sexual abuse; Incest victims/survivors; Adolescent survivors of sexual abuse

WOMEN'S THERAPY CENTER INSTITUTE
80 E 11th St, Rm 101, New York, NY 10003
Information: (212) 420-1974
Contact: Margery Rosenthal, Admin
TYPE OF AGENCY: Training/research
AREAS SERVED: New York City metropolitan area
YEARS IN OPERATION: 7
CLIENTS/SERVICES: Sexual assault survivors; Adult survivors of child sexual abuse; Incest victims/survivors

NEWARK

RAPE CRISIS SERVICE
165 E Union St, Newark, NY 14513
Crisis hotline: **(800) 527-1757 24 hrs**
Information: (315) 331-1171 9am-4pm (Mon-Fri)
Contact: Laurie J Mundy, Coord
TYPE OF AGENCY: Rape crisis center
SPONSORING ORGANIZATION: Planned Parenthood
AREAS SERVED: Wayne
YEARS IN OPERATION: 8
ACCESSIBILITY: Wheelchair accessible
CASES SEXUAL ASSAULT/ABUSE (%): 30
CLIENTS/SERVICES: Sexual assault survivors; Marital rape/sexual abuse survivors; Child victims of sexual abuse; Adult survivors of child sexual abuse; Incest victims/survivors; Community education; Adolescent survivors of sexual abuse; Male survivors of sexual abuse

NEWBURGH

ORANGE COUNTY SAFE HOMES PROJECT, INC
PO Box 649, Newburgh, NY 12550
Crisis hotline: **(914) 562-5340 24 hrs**
Information: (914) 562-5365
Contact: Eileen Maddock, Exec Dir
TYPE OF AGENCY: Domestic violence program
AREAS SERVED: Orange
YEARS IN OPERATION: 3
LANGUAGES: Spanish
CASES SEXUAL ASSAULT/ABUSE (%): 5
DESCRIPTION: Primarily domestic violence services, but clients include marital rape survivors
CLIENTS/SERVICES: Marital rape/sexual abuse survivors; Community education

NIAGARA FALLS

RAPE CRISIS SERVICES OF NIAGARA COUNTY
775 3rd St, Niagara Falls, NY 14302
Crisis hotline: **(716) 285-3518 24 hrs**
Information: (716) 285-9636
Contact: Stefani Perakis
TYPE OF AGENCY: Rape crisis center
CLIENTS/SERVICES: Sexual assault survivors; Marital rape/sexual abuse survivors; Child victims of sexual abuse; Adult survivors of child sexual abuse; Incest victims/survivors; Prevention program; Community education; Adolescent survivors of sexual abuse; Male survivors of sexual abuse

NORWICH

CRIME VICTIMS/WITNESS ASSISTANCE PROGRAM
19 Prospect St, Norwich, NY 13815
Crisis hotline: **(607) 334-3532 24 hrs**
Information: (607) 334-3532 9am-5pm (Mon-Fri)
Contact: Kathleen Libby, Crime Victims Advocate
TYPE OF AGENCY: Victim/witness assistance program; Counseling/mental health services; Child sexual abuse services; Child sexual abuse prevention program
SPONSORING ORGANIZATION: Catholic Charities of Chenango County

CRIME VICTIMS/WITNESS ASSISTANCE PROGRAM *(continued)*
AREAS SERVED: Chenango
CASES SEXUAL ASSAULT/ABUSE (%): 60
DESCRIPTION: Services for survivors, as well as feminist martial arts/self-defense program
CLIENTS/SERVICES: Sexual assault survivors; Marital rape/sexual abuse survivors; Child victims of sexual abuse; Adult survivors of child sexual abuse; Incest victims/survivors; Prevention program; Community education; Adolescent survivors of sexual abuse; Male survivors of sexual abuse

OCEANSIDE

FAMILY CRISIS PROGRAM
Oceanside, NY 11572
Crisis hotline: **(516) 764-8664 8am-10pm (Mon-Thu); 8am-5pm (Fri, Sat)**
Information: (516) 763-3942 8am-10pm (Mon-Thu); 8am-5pm (Fri, Sat)
Contact: Judy Kitzes, CSW (R), Family Crisis Prog Supv
TYPE OF AGENCY: Rape crisis center; Domestic violence program; Hospital/medical center; Victim/witness assistance program; Child sexual abuse services
SPONSORING ORGANIZATION: Mental Health Clinic, South Nassau Community Hospital
AREAS SERVED: Nassau
YEARS IN OPERATION: 10
LANGUAGES: Spanish, French
CASES SEXUAL ASSAULT/ABUSE (%): 100
DESCRIPTION: Family Crisis Program counsels sexually abused children and their parents and siblings including the offender (incest offenders only). Support groups available. Crime Victims Counseling Center provides crisis counseling for victims of rape and street crime. Domestic violence program for survivors and treatment for batterers
CLIENTS/SERVICES: Sexual assault survivors; Marital rape/sexual abuse survivors; Child victims of sexual abuse; Adult survivors of child sexual abuse; Incest victims/survivors; Offender treatment program; Adolescent survivors of sexual abuse; Male survivors of sexual abuse
REQUIREMENTS: Sliding scale fee for Family Crisis Program
SPECIAL PROGRAMS/SERVICES: Groups for incest mothers, offender fathers, and the victim and siblings of all ages. Special parent training programs for mothers who need this help. Flat weekly out-of-pocket charge to encourage families to take part in a variety of programs including dyadic, group and family sessions each week

OLEAN

AVOW—AID TO VICTIMS OR WITNESSES
210 E Elm St, Olean, NY 14760
Crisis hotline: **(716) 945-3970 24 hrs**
Information: (716) 373-4027 9am-5pm (Mon-Fri)
Contact: Ned Watson, Prog Coord
TYPE OF AGENCY: Victim/witness assistance program
SPONSORING ORGANIZATION: Cattaraugus Community Action, Inc
AREAS SERVED: Allegany, Cattaraugus
YEARS IN OPERATION: 2
CASES SEXUAL ASSAULT/ABUSE (%): 85
CLIENTS/SERVICES: Sexual assault survivors; Marital rape/sexual abuse survivors; Child victims of sexual abuse; Adult survivors of child sexual abuse; Incest victims/survivors; Community education; Adolescent survivors of sexual abuse; Male survivors of sexual abuse

RAPE CRISIS PROGRAM
210 E Elm St, Olean, NY 14760
Crisis hotline: **(716) 945-3970 24 hrs**
Information: (716) 373-4027 9am-5pm (Mon-Fri)
Contact: Michele A Coletti, Rape Crisis Prog Coord; Sue Wymer, Coord
TYPE OF AGENCY: Rape crisis center; Domestic violence program; Counseling/mental health services
SPONSORING ORGANIZATION: Cattaraugus Community Action
AREAS SERVED: Cattaraugus, Allegany
YEARS IN OPERATION: 1
ACCESSIBILITY: Wheelchair accessible
CASES SEXUAL ASSAULT/ABUSE (%): 100
DESCRIPTION: Crisis intervention; Victim assistance; Short-term counseling; Support groups; Emergency shelter
CLIENTS/SERVICES: Sexual assault survivors; Marital rape/sexual abuse survivors; Child victims of sexual abuse; Adult survivors of child sexual abuse; Incest victims/survivors; Prevention program; Community education

ONEIDA

VICTIMS OF VIOLENCE
134 Vanderbilt Ave, Oneida, NY 13421
Crisis hotline: **(315) 366-5000 24 hrs**
Information: (315) 363-0048 9am-4:30pm
Contact: Cheryl Matzke, Prog Coord
TYPE OF AGENCY: Rape crisis center; Domestic violence program
SPONSORING ORGANIZATION: Programs and Domiciles, Inc
AREAS SERVED: Madison
YEARS IN OPERATION: 1
ACCESSIBILITY: Wheelchair accessible
CLIENTS/SERVICES: Sexual assault survivors; Marital rape/sexual abuse survivors; Prevention program; Community education; Male survivors of sexual abuse

ONEONTA

RAPE CRISIS SERVICES
32 Main St, Oneonta, NY 13820
Crisis hotline: **(607) 432-8088 24 hrs**
Information: (607) 432-8937 8am-4pm
Contact: Francine Lopomo, Dir
TYPE OF AGENCY: Rape crisis center; Child sexual abuse services; Child sexual abuse prevention program
SPONSORING ORGANIZATION: Opportunities for Otsego
AREAS SERVED: Otsego
YEARS IN OPERATION: 11
ACCESSIBILITY: Wheelchair accessible
CASES SEXUAL ASSAULT/ABUSE (%): 100
CLIENTS/SERVICES: Sexual assault survivors; Marital rape/sexual abuse survivors; Child victims of sexual abuse; Adult survivors of child sexual abuse; Incest victims/survivors; Prevention program; Community education; Adolescent survivors of sexual abuse; Male survivors of sexual abuse

OSWEGO

OSWEGO HOSPITAL MENTAL HEALTH DIVISION
74 Bunner St, Oswego, NY 13126
Crisis hotline: **(315) 343-8162 24 hrs daily**
Information: (315) 343-8162 8am-4:30pm
TYPE OF AGENCY: Hospital/medical center; Counseling/mental health services; Child sexual abuse services
AREAS SERVED: Oswego
YEARS IN OPERATION: 24
LANGUAGES: Spanish
ACCESSIBILITY: Wheelchair accessible
DESCRIPTION: Hospital-based mental health center providing inpatient and outpatient therapy for victims/survivors and rapists, child sexual abuse/incest offenders, batterers
CLIENTS/SERVICES: Sexual assault survivors; Marital rape/sexual abuse survivors; Child victims of sexual abuse; Adult survivors of child sexual abuse; Incest victims/survivors; Offender treatment program; Male survivors of sexual abuse
REQUIREMENTS: Individuals below age 13 are not admitted for inpatient services

SAF (SERVICES TO AID FAMILIES)
101 W Utica St, Oswego, NY 13126
Crisis hotline: **(315) 342-1600 24 hrs**
Information: (315) 342-1544 9am-5pm
Contact: Antoinette Fallon, Victim Svcs Coord; Robin Braunstein, SAF Div Dir
TYPE OF AGENCY: Rape crisis center; Domestic violence program; Child sexual abuse prevention program
SPONSORING ORGANIZATION: Oswego County Opportunities
AREAS SERVED: Oswego
YEARS IN OPERATION: Domestic violence 10, Rape crisis 4
LANGUAGES: Spanish and Chinese by request
ACCESSIBILITY: Wheelchair accessible
CASES SEXUAL ASSAULT/ABUSE (%): 30-40
DESCRIPTION: Services for survivors of sexual assault and domestic violence; Prevention programs for different groups, including developmentally disabled adults and children
CLIENTS/SERVICES: Sexual assault survivors; Marital rape/sexual abuse survivors; Child victims of sexual abuse; Adult survivors of child sexual abuse; Incest victims/survivors; Prevention program; Community education; Adolescent survivors of sexual abuse; Male survivors of sexual abuse

OWEGO

VICTIM/WITNESS ASSISTANCE CENTER
55 North Ave, Owego, NY 13827
Crisis hotline: **(607) 687-6866 24 hrs**
Information: (607) 687-6866 9am-5pm (Mon-Fri)
Contact: Rose Garrity, Exec Dir
TYPE OF AGENCY: Victim/witness assistance program; Child sexual abuse prevention program
AREAS SERVED: Tioga
YEARS IN OPERATION: 3
LANGUAGES: Italian
ACCESSIBILITY: Telecommunications for the hearing impaired (TTY, TDY, etc.); Signers for the hearing impaired
CASES SEXUAL ASSAULT/ABUSE (%): 50
CLIENTS/SERVICES: Sexual assault survivors; Marital rape/sexual abuse survivors; Child victims of sexual abuse; Adult survivors of child sexual abuse; Incest victims/survivors; Prevention program; Community education; Adolescent survivors of sexual abuse; Male survivors of sexual abuse

PEEKSKILL

NORTHERN WESTCHESTER SHELTER PEEKSKILL OFFICE
925 South St, Peekskill, NY 10566
Crisis hotline: **(914) 747-0707 24 hrs**
Information: (914) 736-2330 9am-5pm (Mon-Fri), and two evenings
Contact: Holly Look, Outreach Coord
TYPE OF AGENCY: Domestic violence program
SPONSORING ORGANIZATION: Crime Victims
AREAS SERVED: Westchester
CLIENTS/SERVICES: Marital rape/sexual abuse survivors; Adult survivors of child sexual abuse; Community education

PLATTSBURGH

CRIME VICTIM/SEXUAL ASSAULT PROGRAM
36 Brinkerhoff St, Plattsburgh, NY 12901
Crisis hotline: **(800) DIAL SOS 24 hrs daily**
Information: (518) 561-2330 8am-5pm
Contact: Nancy Travis, Prog Coord

CRIME VICTIM/SEXUAL ASSAULT PROGRAM (continued)
TYPE OF AGENCY: Rape crisis center; Victim/witness assistance program; Child sexual abuse services; Child sexual abuse prevention program
SPONSORING ORGANIZATION: CEF Crisis Helpline
AREAS SERVED: Clinton, Essex, Franklin
YEARS IN OPERATION: 18
ACCESSIBILITY: Wheelchair accessible
CASES SEXUAL ASSAULT/ABUSE (%): 90
DESCRIPTION: Outreach for victims of any type of violent crime, particularly sexual assault victims; Provides individual and group counseling and medical and legal advocacy; Support groups for adolescents, children and adult male and female survivors
CLIENTS/SERVICES: Sexual assault survivors; Marital rape/sexual abuse survivors; Child victims of sexual abuse; Adult survivors of child sexual abuse; Incest victims/survivors; Prevention program; Community education; Adolescent survivors of sexual abuse; Male survivors of sexual abuse; Preschoolers
SPECIAL PROGRAMS/SERVICES: Education program uses a puppet show which is presented to preverbal and minimal verbal children. The emphasis is on safe and unsafe touch.

STOP CENTER ON DOMESTIC VIOLENCE
159 Margaret St, Plattsburgh, NY 12901
Crisis hotline: **(518) 563-6904 24 hrs**
Information: (518) 563-6904 9am-5pm (Mon-Fri)
Contact: Susan Kelley, Prog Dir
TYPE OF AGENCY: Domestic violence program
SPONSORING ORGANIZATION: Clinton County Mental Health Association
AREAS SERVED: Clinton
YEARS IN OPERATION: 8
ACCESSIBILITY: Wheelchair accessible
CASES SEXUAL ASSAULT/ABUSE (%): 30-50
CLIENTS/SERVICES: Marital rape/sexual abuse survivors; Community education

POUGHKEEPSIE

DUTCHESS COUNTY CRIME VICTIMS ASSISTANCE PROGRAM
North Rd, Poughkeepsie, NY 12601
Crisis hotline: **Emergency (914) 431-8220 After hrs and weekends**
Information: (914) 431-8808 9am-5pm
Contact: Jean Craven, Dir
TYPE OF AGENCY: Victim/witness assistance program
SPONSORING ORGANIZATION: Saint Francis Hospital
AREAS SERVED: Dutchess
YEARS IN OPERATION: 12
ACCESSIBILITY: Wheelchair accessible
CASES SEXUAL ASSAULT/ABUSE (%): 50-70
DESCRIPTION: Short- and long-term therapy; Medical services; Witness preparation
CLIENTS/SERVICES: Sexual assault survivors; Marital rape/sexual abuse survivors; Child victims of sexual abuse; Adult survivors of child sexual abuse; Incest victims/survivors; Prevention program; Community education; Adolescent survivors of sexual abuse

DUTCHESS COUNTY DEPARTMENT OF MENTAL HYGIENE (DC/DMH)
230 North Rd, Poughkeepsie, NY 12601
Crisis hotline: **(914) 485-9700 24 hrs**
Information: (914) 485-9700 9am-9pm (Mon, Tue, Thu); 9am-5pm (Wed, Fri)
Contact: Kenneth M Glatt, PhD, Commissioner
TYPE OF AGENCY: Counseling/mental health services; Child sexual abuse services
AREAS SERVED: Dutchess
YEARS IN OPERATION: 20
LANGUAGES: Spanish
ACCESSIBILITY: Wheelchair accessible; Telecommunications for the hearing impaired (TTY, TDY, etc.); Signers for the hearing impaired
CASES SEXUAL ASSAULT/ABUSE (%): 10
DESCRIPTION: Counseling for perpetrators or victims of sexual assault/child abuse; Treatment for rapists, child sexual abuse/incest offenders, and batterers
CLIENTS/SERVICES: Sexual assault survivors; Marital rape/sexual abuse survivors; Child victims of sexual abuse; Adult survivors of child sexual abuse; Incest victims/survivors; Community education; Offender treatment program; Adolescent survivors of sexual abuse; Male survivors of sexual abuse
SPECIAL PROGRAMS/SERVICES: Coordinates with other relevant county agencies Family Incest Program (FIP). DSS/CPS, probation, the district attorney's office, and DC/DMH meet monthly to coordinate the care and treatment of these families

RIVERDALE

SHARING
5500 Fieldston Rd, Riverdale, NY 10471
Information: (212) 543-2244 8am-11pm, and answering machine
Contact: Monique Lang, Founder/Psychotherapist
TYPE OF AGENCY: Private practice
AREAS SERVED: Westchester; New York City
YEARS IN OPERATION: 10
LANGUAGES: French, Spanish
CLIENTS/SERVICES: Sexual assault survivors; Marital rape/sexual abuse survivors; Adult survivors of child sexual abuse; Incest victims/survivors; Healing
REQUIREMENTS: Client must be able to come to the office; Fee charged—eligible for CVB reimbursement if client is eligible
SPECIAL PROGRAMS/SERVICES: Often includes male and female survivors in ongoing groups. The ½-day workshops use meditation, visualization, healing, and ritual, as well as traditional psychotherapy and group work. Healing involves integrating psychotherapy, laying on of hands, visualization, body work, psychodrama, and art therapy depending on clients needs

ROCHESTER

ALTERNATIVES FOR BATTERED WOMEN
PO Box 39601, Rochester, NY 14604
Crisis hotline: **(716) 232-7353 24 hrs 7 days**
Information: (716) 232-7353 9am-5pm (Mon-Fri)
TYPE OF AGENCY: Domestic violence program
AREAS SERVED: Monroe
YEARS IN OPERATION: 9
LANGUAGES: Spanish, German
ACCESSIBILITY: Wheelchair accessible; Telecommunications for the hearing impaired (TTY, TDY, etc.); Signers for the hearing impaired (by appointment)
CASES SEXUAL ASSAULT/ABUSE (%): 20
CLIENTS/SERVICES: Marital rape/sexual abuse survivors; Adult survivors of child sexual abuse; Community education

MONROE COUNTY DISTRICT ATTORNEY—DOMESTIC VIOLENCE BUREAU
Hall of Justice Civic Center Plaza, Ste 201, Rochester, NY 14534
Information: (716) 428-5423 9am-5pm
Contact: Terry M Servis, Spec Asst DA
TYPE OF AGENCY: Domestic violence program; Victim/witness assistance program
AREAS SERVED: Monroe
YEARS IN OPERATION: 9
ACCESSIBILITY: Wheelchair accessible
CASES SEXUAL ASSAULT/ABUSE (%): 70
CLIENTS/SERVICES: Sexual assault survivors; Child victims of sexual abuse

REGIONAL RAPE CRISIS SERVICE
114 University Ave, Rochester, NY 14605
Crisis hotline: **(800) 527-1757 24 hrs**
Information: (716) 546-2777 24 hrs
Contact: Laurie Long, Regional Dir
TYPE OF AGENCY: Rape crisis center; Child sexual abuse prevention program
SPONSORING ORGANIZATION: Planned Parenthood of Rochester and the Genesee Valley, Inc
AREAS SERVED: Monroe, Wayne, Ontario, Livingston, Genesee, Orleans
YEARS IN OPERATION: 15
ACCESSIBILITY: Wheelchair accessible; Telecommunications for the hearing impaired (TTY, TDY, etc.); Signers for the hearing impaired
CASES SEXUAL ASSAULT/ABUSE (%): 99
DESCRIPTION: Legal and medical advocacy; Court accompaniment; Individual, group, short-term post-crisis counseling; Crisis intervention
CLIENTS/SERVICES: Sexual assault survivors; Marital rape/sexual abuse survivors; Child victims of sexual abuse; Adult survivors of child sexual abuse; Incest victims/survivors; Community education; Adolescent survivors of sexual abuse; Male survivors of sexual abuse
SPECIAL PROGRAMS/SERVICES: Spanish-language brochure. Media program: Police training/RCS video is under development

ROCHESTER POLICE DEPARTMENT—VICTIM ASSISTANCE UNIT
150 S Plymouth Ave, Rochester, NY 14614
Information: (716) 428-6630 8am-5pm (Mon-Fri)
Contact: Karel Kurst-Swanger, Victim Svc Coord
TYPE OF AGENCY: Victim/witness assistance program
AREAS SERVED: City of Rochester
YEARS IN OPERATION: 12
LANGUAGES: Interpreters available
ACCESSIBILITY: Wheelchair accessible; Signers for the hearing impaired
CLIENTS/SERVICES: Sexual assault survivors; Marital rape/sexual abuse survivors; Community education
REQUIREMENTS: Clients must file charges

SARANAC LAKE

TRI LAKES COMMUNITY CENTER, INC
PO Box 589, Saranac Lake, NY 12983
Crisis hotline: **(518) 891-3173 24 hrs**
Information: (518) 891-3173 24 hrs
Contact: Patricia A Gailus, Exec Dir
TYPE OF AGENCY: Rape crisis center; Domestic violence program; Child sexual abuse services; Child sexual abuse prevention program
AREAS SERVED: Franklin, Lower Essex
YEARS IN OPERATION: 10
LANGUAGES: Spanish
CASES SEXUAL ASSAULT/ABUSE (%): 20-30
CLIENTS/SERVICES: Sexual assault survivors; Marital rape/sexual abuse survivors; Child victims of sexual abuse; Adult survivors of child sexual abuse; Incest victims/survivors; Prevention program; Community education; Adolescent survivors of sexual abuse; Male survivors of sexual abuse

SCHENECTADY

INFOLINE OF THE HUMAN SERVICES PLANNING COUNCIL
432 State St, Rm 220, Schenectady, NY 12308
Information: (315) 372-3395, Information and referral 374-2244 8:30am-5pm
Contact: Deborah N Gilbert, INFOLINE Dir
TYPE OF AGENCY: Information and referral
AREAS SERVED: Schenectady
YEARS IN OPERATION: 10
CASES SEXUAL ASSAULT/ABUSE (%): 1
DESCRIPTION: Comprehensive telephone information and referral service

INFOLINE OF THE HUMAN SERVICES PLANNING COUNCIL *(continued)*
CLIENTS/SERVICES: Sexual assault survivors; Marital rape/sexual abuse survivors; Child victims of sexual abuse; Adult survivors of child sexual abuse; Incest victims/survivors

NORTHEAST PARENT AND CHILD SOCIETY—SEXUAL ABUSE TREATMENT PROGRAM
122A Park Ave, Schenectady, NY 12304
Information: (518) 393-2194 9am-5pm, evenings by appointment
Contact: Angela Baris, CSW, Prog Supv
TYPE OF AGENCY: Counseling/mental health services; Child sexual abuse services
AREAS SERVED: Schenectady
YEARS IN OPERATION: 1½
ACCESSIBILITY: Wheelchair accessible
CASES SEXUAL ASSAULT/ABUSE (%): 100
DESCRIPTION: Provides psychotherapeutic treatment for child victims, non-offending parents and child sexual abuse/incest offenders
CLIENTS/SERVICES: Child victims of sexual abuse; Incest victims/survivors; Community education; Offender treatment program; Adolescent survivors of sexual abuse
REQUIREMENTS: Children ages 3-17; Referrals must come through Schenectady County Department of Social Services

RAPE CRISIS SERVICE—PLANNED PARENTHOOD OF SCHENECTADY AND AFFILIATED COUNTIES
414 Union St, Schenectady, NY 12305
Crisis hotline: **(518) 346-2266 24 hrs**
Information: (518) 374-5236, 374-5353 9am-4pm (Mon-Fri)
Contact: Deborah Gilbert, Team Leader
TYPE OF AGENCY: Rape crisis center; Counseling/mental health services
AREAS SERVED: Schenectady
YEARS IN OPERATION: 15
ACCESSIBILITY: Wheelchair accessible
CASES SEXUAL ASSAULT/ABUSE (%): 100
CLIENTS/SERVICES: Sexual assault survivors; Marital rape/sexual abuse survivors; Adult survivors of child sexual abuse; Incest victims/survivors; Prevention program; Community education; Adolescent survivors of sexual abuse; Male survivors of sexual abuse
REQUIREMENTS: Clients under age 13 are referred elsewhere for counseling

SCHOHARIE

SCHOHARIE COUNTY MENTAL HEALTH CENTER
PO Box 160, County Office Bldg, 3rd Fl, Schoharie, NY 12157
Crisis hotline: **(518) 295-8114 5pm-8:30am, weekends and holidays**
Information: (518) 295-8336 8:30am-5pm (Mon-Fri)
Contact: Timothy C Donovan, CSW/ACSW, Psychiatric Soc Wkr Supv
TYPE OF AGENCY: Counseling/mental health services
AREAS SERVED: Schoharie
YEARS IN OPERATION: 20
ACCESSIBILITY: Wheelchair accessible
DESCRIPTION: Individual and group therapies for victims/survivors; Individual therapy for rapists, batterers, and child sexual abuse/incest offenders
CLIENTS/SERVICES: Sexual assault survivors; Marital rape/sexual abuse survivors; Child victims of sexual abuse; Adult survivors of child sexual abuse; Incest victims/survivors; Offender treatment program; Adolescent survivors of sexual abuse; Male survivors of sexual abuse
REQUIREMENTS: Accepts insurance, Medicaid, has sliding scale fee. CPS and police statements for minor victims must be in place for new disclosures prior to beginning abuse-specific treatment except for crisis services. Post-disclosure physical exam recommended prior to beginning treatment

SMITHTOWN

VICTIMS INFORMATION BUREAU OF SUFFOLK
22 Lawrence Ave, Smithtown, NY 11787
Crisis hotline: **(516) 360-3606 24 hrs**
Information: (516) 360-3730 9am-5pm (Mon-Fri)
Contact: Susan B Brown, Community Svcs Coord; Pamela Johnston, Exec Dir
TYPE OF AGENCY: Rape crisis center; Domestic violence program; Child sexual abuse services; Acquaintance/date rape prevention program
AREAS SERVED: Suffolk
YEARS IN OPERATION: 12
LANGUAGES: Spanish
CASES SEXUAL ASSAULT/ABUSE (%): 25-40
DESCRIPTION: Services for victims of domestic violence, rape, incest, and sexual assault; Emergency room companions assist victims of rape and sexual assault at hospital; Group therapy for batterers available
CLIENTS/SERVICES: Sexual assault survivors; Marital rape/sexual abuse survivors; Child victims of sexual abuse; Adult survivors of child sexual abuse; Incest victims/survivors; Prevention program; Community education; Adolescent survivors of sexual abuse; Male survivors of sexual abuse
SPECIAL PROGRAMS/SERVICES: Brochure on "Date Rape"; Group for parents of adolescent survivors

SPRING VALLEY

ROCKLAND FAMILY SHELTER—RAPE CRISIS PROGRAM
39 S Main St, Spring Valley, NY 10977
Crisis hotline: **(914) 425-0112 24 hrs 7 days**
Information: (914) 425-0112 9am-5pm (Mon-Fri)
Contact: Jean Albertson, Rape Crisis Coord
TYPE OF AGENCY: Rape crisis center; Domestic violence program
AREAS SERVED: Rockland
YEARS IN OPERATION: 4
CASES SEXUAL ASSAULT/ABUSE (%): 100
CLIENTS/SERVICES: Sexual assault survivors; Marital rape/sexual abuse survivors; Child victims of sexual abuse; Adult survivors of child sexual abuse; Incest victims/survivors; Prevention program; Community education; Adolescent survivors of sexual abuse

STATEN ISLAND

SOCIETY FOR SEAMEN'S CHILDREN—TEEN ADVOCACY PROGRAM PREVENTION UNIT
26 Bay St, Staten Island, NY 10301
Crisis hotline: **(718) 273-2727 9am-8pm (Mon-Fri)**
Information: (718) 447-7666 9am-8pm (Mon-Fri)
Contact: Diane Sjolin, Teen Advocacy Dir; Pat Frank, Prevention Unit Supv
TYPE OF AGENCY: Adolescent program
AREAS SERVED: Staten Island
YEARS IN OPERATION: 6
CASES SEXUAL ASSAULT/ABUSE (%): 5-10
DESCRIPTION: Works primarily with adolescents and families, including runaway and homeless youth and those at-risk of abuse
CLIENTS/SERVICES: Prevention program; Community education; Adolescent survivors of sexual abuse
REQUIREMENTS: Adolescents and families

VICTIM SERVICES AGENCY
67 Targee St, Staten Island Criminal Court, Staten Island, NY 10304
Crisis hotline: **(212) 577-7777 24 hrs 7 days**
Information: (718) 727-7555 9am-5pm (Mon-Fri)
Contact: Maureen Italiano, Soc Wkr
TYPE OF AGENCY: Victim/witness assistance program
AREAS SERVED: Richmond
YEARS IN OPERATION: 8
CASES SEXUAL ASSAULT/ABUSE (%): 20
CLIENTS/SERVICES: Sexual assault survivors; Marital rape/sexual abuse survivors; Child victims of sexual abuse; Adult survivors of child sexual abuse; Incest victims/survivors; Adolescent survivors of sexual abuse; Male survivors of sexual abuse

STONY BROOK

RESPONSE OF SUFFOLK COUNTY, INC
PO Box 300, Stony Brook, NY 11790
Crisis hotline: **(516) 751-7500 24 hrs**
Contact: Arlene Stevens, Exec Dir
TYPE OF AGENCY: Counseling/mental health services; Telephone crisis hotline
AREAS SERVED: Suffolk
YEARS IN OPERATION: 17
DESCRIPTION: 24-hour crisis intervention; Suicide prevention hotline with resource and referral components
CLIENTS/SERVICES: Sexual assault survivors; Child victims of sexual abuse

SYRACUSE

ONONDAGA COUNTY SHERIFF'S DEPARTMENT—ABUSED PERSON'S UNIT
407 S State St, Syracuse, NY 13202
Crisis hotline: **(315) 425-3092 24 hrs**
Information: (315) 425-3092
Contact: Sgt Chris Young
TYPE OF AGENCY: Victim/witness assistance program; Child sexual abuse services
AREAS SERVED: Onondaga
YEARS IN OPERATION: 10
LANGUAGES: Interpreters available
ACCESSIBILITY: Telecommunications for the hearing impaired (TTY, TDY, etc.); Signers for the hearing impaired
CASES SEXUAL ASSAULT/ABUSE (%): 90
DESCRIPTION: Investigates all child abuse, physical, sexual, and neglect; Investigates all adult sex crimes
CLIENTS/SERVICES: Sexual assault survivors; Marital rape/sexual abuse survivors; Child victims of sexual abuse; Adult survivors of child sexual abuse; Incest victims/survivors; Community education; Adolescent survivors of sexual abuse
SPECIAL PROGRAMS/SERVICES: Developed a 0-3 day child sexual abuse intervention program which is a joint effort of law enforcement, child protective services, and rape crisis

RAPE CRISIS CENTER OF SYRACUSE, INC
423 W Onondaga St, Syracuse, NY 13202
Crisis hotline: **(315) 422-7273**
Information: (315) 422-7273
Contact: Katherine O'Connell
TYPE OF AGENCY: Rape crisis center; Child sexual abuse prevention program
CLIENTS/SERVICES: Sexual assault survivors

VICTIM WITNESS ASSISTANCE CENTER
Public Safety Bldg, Rm 112, Syracuse, NY 13202
Crisis hotline: **(315) 474-7011 24 hrs**
Information: (315) 473-2891 9am-4pm (Mon-Fri)
Contact: Maria Galvin, Jeanne Moon, Co-Coords
TYPE OF AGENCY: Victim/witness assistance program
SPONSORING ORGANIZATION: The Volunteer Center
AREAS SERVED: Onondaga, Madison, Oswego
YEARS IN OPERATION: 24
ACCESSIBILITY: Wheelchair accessible; Telecommunications for the hearing impaired (TTY, TDY, etc.); Signers for the hearing impaired (by arrangement)

VICTIM WITNESS ASSISTANCE CENTER *(continued)*

CASES SEXUAL ASSAULT/ABUSE (%): 1
CLIENTS/SERVICES: Sexual assault survivors; Child victims of sexual abuse; Community education

VOLUNTEER CENTER "HELPLINE"
115 E Jefferson St, Syracuse, NY 13202
Crisis hotline: **(315) 474-7011 24 hrs 7 days**
Information: (315) 474-7011 9am-5pm
Contact: Mary Anne Ruff, Helpline Dir
TYPE OF AGENCY: Victim/witness assistance program; Counseling/mental health services; Information and referral service
SPONSORING ORGANIZATION: The Volunteer Center, Inc
AREAS SERVED: Onondaga
YEARS IN OPERATION: 22
LANGUAGES: Interpreters by arrangement
ACCESSIBILITY: Wheelchair accessible; Telecommunications for the hearing impaired (TTY, TDY, etc.)
CASES SEXUAL ASSAULT/ABUSE (%): 2
CLIENTS/SERVICES: Sexual assault survivors; Marital rape/sexual abuse survivors; Child victims of sexual abuse; Adult survivors of child sexual abuse; Incest victims/survivors
REQUIREMENTS: Must be resident of Onondaga County or border areas of adjacent counties
SPECIAL PROGRAMS/SERVICES: Victim-Witness Assistance Program operated cooperatively with the local Rape Crisis Center, Onondaga County's District Attorney's Office and Helpline

WOMEN'S INFORMATION CENTER
601 Allen St, Syracuse, NY 13210
Information: (315) 478-4636 9am-5pm (Mon-Fri)
Contact: Kathy Belge, Co-Dir
TYPE OF AGENCY: Information and referral; Women's center
AREAS SERVED: Onondaga
YEARS IN OPERATION: 17
ACCESSIBILITY: Wheelchair accessible
DESCRIPTION: Referral service for agencies serving sexual assault survivors. Offers space for support groups to meet, and occasionally runs self-defense classes for women
CLIENTS/SERVICES: Sexual assault survivors; Adult survivors of child sexual abuse; Incest victims/survivors

TROY

RAPE CRISIS PROGRAM FOR RENSSELAER COUNTY
2215 Burdett Ave, Samaritan Hospital, Troy, NY 12180
Crisis hotline: **(518) 271-3257 24 hrs**
Information: (518) 271-3445 8am-5pm
Contact: Ellen C Schell, Dir
TYPE OF AGENCY: Rape crisis center
AREAS SERVED: Rensselaer
YEARS IN OPERATION: 8
ACCESSIBILITY: Wheelchair accessible
CASES SEXUAL ASSAULT/ABUSE (%): 100
DESCRIPTION: Comprehensive rape crisis services; Provides feminist martial arts/self-defense program
CLIENTS/SERVICES: Sexual assault survivors; Marital rape/sexual abuse survivors; Child victims of sexual abuse; Adult survivors of child sexual abuse; Incest victims/survivors; Prevention program; Community education; Adolescent survivors of sexual abuse; Male survivors of sexual abuse

SETON CATHOLIC FAMILY AND COMMUNITY SERVICES
240 2nd St, Troy, NY 12180
Information: (518) 274-9245 8:30am-5pm
TYPE OF AGENCY: Counseling/mental health services; Child sexual abuse services; Parenting programs
AREAS SERVED: Rensselear
YEARS IN OPERATION: 90
DESCRIPTION: Provides respite day care to prevent abuse; Parenting programs
CLIENTS/SERVICES: Child victims of sexual abuse; Prevention program; Community education; Male survivors of sexual abuse; Preschoolers
REQUIREMENTS: Daycare must be referred by child protective services; Ages 1½-5 years; Parent education for anyone

UNITY HOUSE FAMILIES IN CRISIS
2900 5th Ave, Troy, NY 12180
Crisis hotline: **(518) 272-2370 24 hrs**
Information: (518) 272-2370 24 hrs
Contact: Susan Bowers, Dir
TYPE OF AGENCY: Domestic violence program; Child sexual abuse prevention program; Acquaintance/date rape prevention program
AREAS SERVED: Primarily Albany, Rensselaer
YEARS IN OPERATION: 10
LANGUAGES: Spanish, interpreters available for Chinese, Japanese, and Portuguese languages
ACCESSIBILITY: Wheelchair accessible (Shelter only)
CASES SEXUAL ASSAULT/ABUSE (%): 50
CLIENTS/SERVICES: Sexual assault survivors; Marital rape/sexual abuse survivors; Child victims of sexual abuse; Adult survivors of child sexual abuse; Incest victims/survivors; Prevention program; Community education; Adolescent survivors of sexual abuse; Male survivors of sexual abuse; Healing
SPECIAL PROGRAMS/SERVICES: Dance and art therapy for child and adult survivors. School-based prevention education in elementary, jr high and high schools, providing written educative materials, exercises on violence, anger, conflict resolution, Good Touch, Bad Touch, rape, coping skills. Serves as consultant and educator to school faculty

UTICA

YWCA RAPE CRISIS SERVICE
1000 Cornelia St, Utica, NY 13502
Crisis hotline: **(315) 733-0665 24 hrs**
Information: (315) 732-2159, 793-0057 9am-5pm (Mon-Fri)
Contact: Tina Utley Edwards, YWCA Crisis Svcs Dir
TYPE OF AGENCY: Rape crisis center; Child sexual abuse services; Child sexual abuse prevention program; Shelter; Acquaintance/date rape prevention program
AREAS SERVED: Oneida, Herkimer
YEARS IN OPERATION: 10
ACCESSIBILITY: Telecommunications for the hearing impaired (TTY, TDY, etc.); Signers for the hearing impaired
CASES SEXUAL ASSAULT/ABUSE (%): 100
DESCRIPTION: Provides crisis intervention and legal advocacy for victims of sexual assault; Emergency housing for sexually abused children in YWCA Hall House; Prevention program for high school students on acquaintance rape and dating violence; Feminist martial arts/self-defense program
CLIENTS/SERVICES: Sexual assault survivors; Marital rape/sexual abuse survivors; Child victims of sexual abuse; Adult survivors of child sexual abuse; Incest victims/survivors; Prevention program; Community education; Adolescent survivors of sexual abuse; Male survivors of sexual abuse

VALHALLA

RUNAWAY AND HOMELESS YOUTH PROGRAM
PO Box 276, Valhalla, NY 10595
Crisis hotline: **(914) 997-1583 24 hrs**
Information: (914) 347-4242 24 hrs
Contact: Sid Portnoy, CSW, Prog Dir
TYPE OF AGENCY: Child sexual abuse services; Shelter; Adolescent program
SPONSORING ORGANIZATION: Volunteers of America
AREAS SERVED: Westchester
ACCESSIBILITY: Wheelchair accessible
CASES SEXUAL ASSAULT/ABUSE (%): 10-15
DESCRIPTION: 24-hour service for runaways, including care house if necessary
CLIENTS/SERVICES: Child victims of sexual abuse; Incest victims/survivors

WATERTOWN

JEFFERSON COUNTY WOMEN'S CENTER
131 Franklin St, Watertown, NY 13601
Crisis hotline: **(315) 782-1855 24 hrs**
Information: (315) 782-1823 8am-5pm
Contact: Doreen Fairchild, Rape Crisis Coord
TYPE OF AGENCY: Rape crisis center; Domestic violence program; Child sexual abuse prevention program
AREAS SERVED: Jefferson, Lewis, St Lawrence
YEARS IN OPERATION: 10
LANGUAGES: Spanish, German
ACCESSIBILITY: Wheelchair accessible; Signers for the hearing impaired
CASES SEXUAL ASSAULT/ABUSE (%): 30
DESCRIPTION: Provides medical and legal advocacy and referrals for victims of domestic violence and sexual assault, as well as counseling services, support groups, and a feminist martial arts/self-defense program
CLIENTS/SERVICES: Sexual assault survivors; Marital rape/sexual abuse survivors; Child victims of sexual abuse; Adult survivors of child sexual abuse; Incest victims/survivors; Prevention program; Community education; Adolescent survivors of sexual abuse; Male survivors of sexual abuse

WATKINS GLEN

NEIGHBORHOOD JUSTICE PROJECT
PO Box 366, Watkins Glen, NY 14814
Crisis hotline: **(607) 734-3338 Evenings and days closed**
Information: (607) 535-4757 9am-5pm (Mon-Fri)
Contact: Ruth Helfinstine, Victim Svcs Coord
TYPE OF AGENCY: Victim/witness assistance program; Counseling/mental health services
AREAS SERVED: Schuyler
YEARS IN OPERATION: 6
ACCESSIBILITY: Wheelchair accessible
CASES SEXUAL ASSAULT/ABUSE (%): 40
CLIENTS/SERVICES: Sexual assault survivors; Marital rape/sexual abuse survivors; Child victims of sexual abuse; Adult survivors of child sexual abuse; Incest victims/survivors; Prevention program; Community education; Adolescent survivors of sexual abuse; Male survivors of sexual abuse

WHITE PLAINS

THE CENTER FOR PREVENTIVE PSYCHIATRY, INC
19 Greenridge Ave, White Plains, NY 10605
Information: (914) 949-7680 24 hrs
Contact: Sylvia Bloom, Community Relations Dir
TYPE OF AGENCY: Counseling/mental health services; Child sexual abuse services
AREAS SERVED: Westchester
YEARS IN OPERATION: 23
LANGUAGES: German, Spanish, Italian, Hebrew, French

THE CENTER FOR PREVENTIVE PSYCHIATRY, INC *(continued)*
ACCESSIBILITY: Wheelchair accessible
CASES SEXUAL ASSAULT/ABUSE (%): 10
DESCRIPTION: Provides early childhood therapy and situational crisis intervention for children and adults faced with a traumatic external event in the recent past. In addition to the direct treatment service, consultation to other agencies, community groups, and schools in the area of sexual abuse are provided
CLIENTS/SERVICES: Sexual assault survivors; Marital rape/sexual abuse survivors; Child victims of sexual abuse; Adult survivors of child sexual abuse; Incest victims/survivors; Prevention program; Community education

DOMESTIC VIOLENCE AND CHILD ABUSE BUREAU
110 Grove St, White Plains, NY 10601
Crisis hotline: **(914) 285-3000 8:30am-5pm**
Information: (914) 285-3000 8:30am-5pm
Contact: Jeanine Ferris Pirro, Asst DA
TYPE OF AGENCY: Domestic violence program; Victim/witness assistance program; Child sexual abuse services
SPONSORING ORGANIZATION: Westchester County District Attorney
AREAS SERVED: Westchester
YEARS IN OPERATION: 10
LANGUAGES: Spanish
CASES SEXUAL ASSAULT/ABUSE (%): 100
DESCRIPTION: Victims of domestic violence, child assault, and sexual abuse are interviewed with a view toward prosecution and ancillary services including networking with therapists, doctors, shelter, social service and mental health professionals.
CLIENTS/SERVICES: Sexual assault survivors; Marital rape/sexual abuse survivors; Child victims of sexual abuse; Community education

RAPE CRISIS HELPLINE
3 Carhart Ave, White Plains, NY 10605
Crisis hotline: **(914) 684-9877 24 hrs daily**
Information: (914) 684-6871 9am-5pm (Mon-Fri)
Contact: Barbara Carbone, Rape Crisis Helpline Coord; Toni Downes, ACSW, Dir
TYPE OF AGENCY: Rape crisis center; Victim/witness assistance program; Counseling/mental health services
SPONSORING ORGANIZATION: Westchester Community Opportunity Program, Victims Assistance Services
AREAS SERVED: Westchester
YEARS IN OPERATION: 7
LANGUAGES: Spanish
ACCESSIBILITY: Wheelchair accessible
CASES SEXUAL ASSAULT/ABUSE (%): 20
DESCRIPTION: Provides comprehensive services for all crime victims and their families; Rape crisis services are a distinct program component
CLIENTS/SERVICES: Sexual assault survivors; Marital rape/sexual abuse survivors; Child victims of sexual abuse; Adult survivors of child sexual abuse; Incest victims/survivors; Prevention program; Community education; Adolescent survivors of sexual abuse; Male survivors of sexual abuse

WESTCHESTER COALITION OF FAMILY VIOLENCE AGENCIES
112 E Post Rd, White Plains, NY 10601
Information: (914) 285-5972
TYPE OF AGENCY: Domestic violence program; Interagency network
SPONSORING ORGANIZATION: Westchester County Office for Women
DESCRIPTION: Provides a coordinated and cooperative approach to the eradication of family violence in all its forms
CLIENTS/SERVICES: Marital rape/sexual abuse survivors; Child victims of sexual abuse; Incest victims/survivors; Adult survivors of child sexual abuse; Community education
SPECIAL PROGRAMS/SERVICES: Annual Family Violence Conference in October (Domestic Violence Awareness Month)

WISH (WOMEN-IN-SELF-HELP)
468 Rosedale Ave, White Plains, NY 10605
Crisis hotline: **(914) 946-5757 9am-4pm**
Information: (914) 946-5757 9am-4pm
Contact: Mildred Kaplan, Dir
TYPE OF AGENCY: Counseling/mental health services; Telephone "Warmline"
AREAS SERVED: Westche
YEARS IN OPERATION: 12
LANGUAGES: Japanese
CASES SEXUAL ASSAULT/ABUSE (%): 1
CLIENTS/SERVICES: Sexual assault survivors; Marital rape/sexual abuse survivors; Child victims of sexual abuse; Adult survivors of child sexual abuse; Incest victims/survivors

WOODMERE

PENINSULA COUNSELING CENTER
124 Franklin Pl, Woodmere, NY 11598
Information: (516) 569-6600 9am-9pm (Mon-Fri)
Contact: Irene Schulman, Family Support Prog Dir
TYPE OF AGENCY: Counseling/mental health services; Child sexual abuse services; Child abuse services
AREAS SERVED: Nassau
YEARS IN OPERATION: 18
LANGUAGES: Spanish, Yiddish
ACCESSIBILITY: Wheelchair accessible
DESCRIPTION: The Family Support Program deals solely with physical and sexual abuse in families; Counseling also available for rape survivors and adult survivors of child sexual abuse
CLIENTS/SERVICES: Sexual assault survivors; Marital rape/sexual abuse survivors; Child victims of sexual abuse; Adult survivors of child sexual abuse; Incest victims/survivors; Prevention program; Community education; Offender treatment program; Adolescent survivors of sexual abuse; Male survivors of sexual abuse

YONKERS

RAPE CRISIS HELPLINE
201 Palisades Ave, Yonkers, NY 10701
Crisis hotline: **(914) 684-9877 24 hrs daily**
Information: (914) 965-0217 9am-5pm (Mon-Fri)
TYPE OF AGENCY: Rape crisis center; Victim/witness assistance program; Counseling/mental health services
SPONSORING ORGANIZATION: Westchester Community Opportunity Program, Victims Assistance Services
AREAS SERVED: Westchester
YEARS IN OPERATION: 7
LANGUAGES: Spanish
ACCESSIBILITY: Wheelchair accessible
CASES SEXUAL ASSAULT/ABUSE (%): 20
DESCRIPTION: Provides comprehensive services for all crime victims and their families; Rape crisis services are a distinct program component
CLIENTS/SERVICES: Sexual assault survivors; Marital rape/sexual abuse survivors; Child victims of sexual abuse; Adult survivors of child sexual abuse; Incest victims/survivors; Prevention program; Community education; Adolescent survivors of sexual abuse; Male survivors of sexual abuse

NORTH CAROLINA

ASHEBORO

RANDOLPH COUNTY FAMILY CRISIS CENTER
PO Box 2161, Asheboro, NC 27204
Crisis hotline: **(919) 629-4159 24 hrs daily**
Information: (919) 629-4159 8am-5pm
Contact: Iris Voss, Victims of Sexual Assault Prog Dir
TYPE OF AGENCY: Rape crisis center; Domestic violence program; Child sexual abuse services; Child sexual abuse prevention program
AREAS SERVED: Randolph
CASES SEXUAL ASSAULT/ABUSE (%): 34
DESCRIPTION: Services for survivors of domestic violence and sexual assault; Group therapy for batterers
CLIENTS/SERVICES: Sexual assault survivors; Marital rape/sexual abuse survivors; Child victims of sexual abuse; Adult survivors of child sexual abuse; Incest victims/survivors; Prevention program; Community education; Adolescent survivors of sexual abuse; Male survivors of sexual abuse

ASHEVILLE

ASHEVILLE POLICE DEPARTMENT—VICTIM ASSISTANCE PROGRAM
PO Box 7148, Asheville, NC 28807
Crisis hotline: **(704) 252-1110 24 hrs**
Information: (704) 259-5912 8:30am-5pm
Contact: Jan Phillips, Victim Advocate
TYPE OF AGENCY: Victim/witness assistance program
AREAS SERVED: Buncombe
YEARS IN OPERATION: 1
ACCESSIBILITY: Wheelchair accessible; Telecommunications for the hearing impaired (TTY, TDY, etc.); Signers for the hearing impaired
CASES SEXUAL ASSAULT/ABUSE (%): 25-30
CLIENTS/SERVICES: Sexual assault survivors; Marital rape/sexual abuse survivors; Child victims of sexual abuse; Incest victims/survivors; Community education

BUNCOMBE COUNTY RAPE CRISIS CENTER, INC
PO Box 7453, Asheville, NC 28807
Crisis hotline: **(704) 255-7576 24 hrs**
Information: (704) 252-0562 9am-5pm (Mon-Fri)
Contact: Leigh Dudasik, Exec Dir
TYPE OF AGENCY: Rape crisis center; Child sexual abuse prevention program
SPONSORING ORGANIZATION: Rape Crisis Center, Inc
AREAS SERVED: Buncombe
YEARS IN OPERATION: 14
LANGUAGES: Interpreters available
ACCESSIBILITY: Wheelchair accessible; Telecommunications for the hearing impaired (TTY, TDY, etc.); Signers for the hearing impaired
CASES SEXUAL ASSAULT/ABUSE (%): 100
CLIENTS/SERVICES: Sexual assault survivors; Marital rape/sexual abuse survivors; Child victims of sexual abuse; Adult survivors of child sexual abuse; Incest victims/survivors; Prevention program; Community education; Adolescent survivors of sexual abuse; Male survivors of sexual abuse; Healing
REQUIREMENTS: Children under the age of 16 are referred to local professionals specializing in the treatment of child sexual abuse
SPECIAL PROGRAMS/SERVICES: Buncombe and Henderson Counties child sexual abuse task forces. Arts therapy through music, writing, dancing, pottery, drawing, storytelling. Child care and meals throughout court processes; Self-advocacy for those who want to speak out. Scrapbooks of support system with photos, poetry, and letters. "Funny Tummy Feelings" prevention program; Cycle of Abuse Community Education Program.

FAMILY MENDING
50 S French Broad, Asheville, NC 28801
Information: (704) 253-9314 8:30am-8pm
Contact: Gene Myers, Coord
TYPE OF AGENCY: Counseling/mental health services; Child sexual abuse services
SPONSORING ORGANIZATION: Family Services Center
AREAS SERVED: Buncombe
YEARS IN OPERATION: 8
ACCESSIBILITY: Wheelchair accessible
CLIENTS/SERVICES: Sexual assault survivors; Marital rape/sexual abuse survivors; Child victims of sexual abuse; Adult survivors of child sexual abuse; Incest victims/survivors; Offender treatment program; Adolescent survivors of sexual abuse; Male survivors of sexual abuse
REQUIREMENTS: Children must have permission of guardian for treatment
SPECIAL PROGRAMS/SERVICES: Use of psychodrama with sexually abused children

BOLIVIA

DISTRICT ATTORNEY'S OFFICE—RAPE/SEXUAL ABUSE VICTIM SERVICES
Brunswick County Courthouse, Bolivia, NC 28422
Crisis hotline: **(919) 253-4494 24 hrs**
Information: (919) 253-4447 8:30am-5pm
Contact: Elena Peterson, Dir
TYPE OF AGENCY: Rape crisis center; Victim/witness assistance program
AREAS SERVED: Brunswick, Columbus, Bladen
YEARS IN OPERATION: 2
ACCESSIBILITY: Wheelchair accessible
CASES SEXUAL ASSAULT/ABUSE (%): 100
DESCRIPTION: Provides 24-hour crisis intervention services with victim advocacy. Program is the first rape crisis center in NC that is based in a district attorney's office
CLIENTS/SERVICES: Sexual assault survivors; Marital rape/sexual abuse survivors; Child victims of sexual abuse; Adult survivors of child sexual abuse; Incest victims/survivors; Prevention program; Community education; Adolescent survivors of sexual abuse; Male survivors of sexual abuse

BOONE

OASIS, INC (OPPOSING ABUSE WITH SERVICE, INFORMATION, AND SHELTER)
PO Box 1591, Boone, NC 28607
Crisis hotline: **(704) 262-5035 24 hrs**
Information: (704) 264-1532 9am-5pm (Mon-Fri)
Contact: Dawn Wilson, Exec Dir
TYPE OF AGENCY: Rape crisis center; Domestic violence program; Child sexual abuse prevention program
AREAS SERVED: Watauga, Ashe, Avery, Alleghany
YEARS IN OPERATION: 10
LANGUAGES: Interpreters available
ACCESSIBILITY: Wheelchair accessible
CASES SEXUAL ASSAULT/ABUSE (%): 18
CLIENTS/SERVICES: Sexual assault survivors; Marital rape/sexual abuse survivors; Child victims of sexual abuse; Adult survivors of child sexual abuse; Incest victims/survivors; Prevention program; Community education; Adolescent survivors of sexual abuse; Male survivors of sexual abuse

BURLINGTON

RAPE CRISIS ALLIANCE OF ALAMANCE COUNTY, INC
PO Box 673, Burlington, NC 27216
Crisis hotline: **(919) 227-6220 24 hrs**
Information: (919) 228-0813 9am-5pm
Contact: Brenda Gum, Dir
TYPE OF AGENCY: Rape crisis center
AREAS SERVED: Alamance
YEARS IN OPERATION: 10
CASES SEXUAL ASSAULT/ABUSE (%): 100
CLIENTS/SERVICES: Sexual assault survivors; Marital rape/sexual abuse survivors; Adult survivors of child sexual abuse; Prevention program; Community education

CARRBORO

TRIANGLE WOMEN'S MARTIAL ARTS CENTER
PO Box 381, Carrboro, NC 27510
Information: (919) 682-7262 9am-9pm
Contact: Kathy Hopwood, Dir-Chief Instructor
TYPE OF AGENCY: Rape prevention program

TRIANGLE WOMEN'S MARTIAL ARTS CENTER *(continued)*

AREAS SERVED: Durham, Orange, Chatham, Wake
YEARS IN OPERATION: 9
DESCRIPTION: Provides short- and long-term in-depth training in self-defense and safety skills for women and children; Sponsors special classes for survivors of sexual assault which focuses on empowering and healing through the study of self-defense training
CLIENTS/SERVICES: Sexual assault survivors; Marital rape/sexual abuse survivors; Child victims of sexual abuse; Adult survivors of child sexual abuse; Incest victims/survivors; Prevention program; Community education; Adolescent survivors of sexual abuse; Healing
SPECIAL PROGRAMS/SERVICES: Workshops and classes: "Empowering the Warrior Within", healing for women survivors; "Confrontation-Assertiveness Training", verbal self-defense skills; "Body Wisdom", focuses on physical training and feedback to develop physical strength not based on muscle body strength but using inner (KI) energy awareness

CHAPEL HILL

NORTH CAROLINA MEMORIAL HOSPITAL EMERGENCY DEPARTMENT
Manning Dr, Chapel Hill, NC 27514
Crisis hotline: **(919) 967-7273 24 hrs**
Information: (919) 966-4721 24 hrs
TYPE OF AGENCY: Hospital/medical center; Child sexual abuse services
AREAS SERVED: Orange
ACCESSIBILITY: Wheelchair accessible; Telecommunications for the hearing impaired (TTY, TDY, etc.)
DESCRIPTION: Rape crisis center advocates are available 24 hours daily
CLIENTS/SERVICES: Sexual assault survivors; Marital rape/sexual abuse survivors; Child victims of sexual abuse; Adult survivors of child sexual abuse; Incest victims/survivors

ORANGE COUNTY RAPE CRISIS CENTER
PO Box 871, Chapel Hill, NC 27514
Crisis hotline: **(919) 967-7273 24 hrs**
Information: (919) 968-4647 9am-5pm (Mon-Fri); answering machine 24 hrs
Contact: Mary Ann Chap, Dir
TYPE OF AGENCY: Rape crisis center; Rape prevention program; Acquaintance/date rape prevention program
AREAS SERVED: Orange
YEARS IN OPERATION: 14
LANGUAGES: Spanish
CASES SEXUAL ASSAULT/ABUSE (%): 100
DESCRIPTION: Provides crisis services, legal and medical advocacy, support groups for victims of sexual assault; Child advocates are volunteers who provide support, accompaniment, and advocacy for child and teen victims, adult survivors of child sexual abuse, non-abusing family and friends, and serve as a resource for teachers, health care providers, etc
CLIENTS/SERVICES: Sexual assault survivors; Marital rape/sexual abuse survivors; Child victims of sexual abuse; Adult survivors of child sexual abuse; Incest victims/survivors; Prevention program; Community education; Adolescent survivors of sexual abuse; Male survivors of sexual abuse
SPECIAL PROGRAMS/SERVICES: Prevention programs for children and adolescents: "You Are a Special Person" (preschool and early elementary); "Talking About Touching" (upper elementary); "My Body, My Rights" (junior high); "When Sex Is Forced" (high school on date/acquaintance rape). Adult programs focus on date/acquaintance rape, supporting a victim of sexual assault, overview of sexual assault, legal definition of sexual assault and the line between sex and rape, and child sexual abuse and its prevention

CHARLOTTE

CLINICAL AND FORENSIC CONSULTANTS
9015 J M Keynes Dr, Ste 14, Charlotte, NC 28213
Crisis hotline: **(704) 547-8790 24 hrs**
Information: (704) 547-1483 7am-9pm (Mon-Fri); 9am-5pm (Sat)
Contact: Faye E Sultan, PhD, Dir
TYPE OF AGENCY: Private practice
AREAS SERVED: Mecklenburg, Union, Cabarrus
YEARS IN OPERATION: 6
ACCESSIBILITY: Wheelchair accessible
CASES SEXUAL ASSAULT/ABUSE (%): 70
DESCRIPTION: Both individual and group psychotherapy available for survivors and rapists, child sexual abuse/incest offenders, and batterers
CLIENTS/SERVICES: Sexual assault survivors; Marital rape/sexual abuse survivors; Child victims of sexual abuse; Adult survivors of child sexual abuse; Incest victims/survivors; Community education; Offender treatment program; Adolescent survivors of sexual abuse; Male survivors of sexual abuse
REQUIREMENTS: Low fee slots and payment plans available. Treatment cost reimbursed by most major insurance carriers

INFORMATION AND REFERRAL SERVICE
301 S Brevard St, Charlotte, NC 28202
Crisis hotline: **(704) 788-1156 Cabarrus County; (704) 373-0982 Mecklenburg County; (704) 289-8102 Union County all 24 hrs**
Information: (704) 788-1156 Cabarrus County; (704) 373-0982 Mecklenburg County; (704) 289-8102 Union County
Contact: Karen T Miller, Asst Dir
TYPE OF AGENCY: Information and referral
SPONSORING ORGANIZATION: United Way of Central Carolinas, Inc
AREAS SERVED: Cabarrus, Mecklenburg, Union
YEARS IN OPERATION: 12
ACCESSIBILITY: Wheelchair accessible; Telecommunications for the hearing impaired (TTY, TDY, etc.)
CLIENTS/SERVICES: Sexual assault survivors

UNITED FAMILY SERVICES VICTIM ASSISTANCE
301 S Brevard St, Charlotte, NC 28202
Information: (704) 332-9034
Contact: James Johnson
TYPE OF AGENCY: Counseling/mental health services; Victim assistance program
AREAS SERVED: Mecklenburg
CLIENTS/SERVICES: Crime victims

VICTIM ASSISTANCE/RAPE CRISIS
825 E 4th St, Charlotte, NC 28202
Crisis hotline: **(704) 375-9900 24 hrs daily**
Information: (704) 336-2190 8:30am-5pm
Contact: Annette Morrison, Dir
TYPE OF AGENCY: Rape crisis center; Victim/witness assistance program; Counseling/mental health services
SPONSORING ORGANIZATION: United Family Services
AREAS SERVED: Mecklenburg
YEARS IN OPERATION: 10
ACCESSIBILITY: Wheelchair accessible
CASES SEXUAL ASSAULT/ABUSE (%): 33
CLIENTS/SERVICES: Sexual assault survivors; Marital rape/sexual abuse survivors; Child victims of sexual abuse; Adult survivors of child sexual abuse; Incest victims/survivors; Community education; Adolescent survivors of sexual abuse; Male survivors of sexual abuse
REQUIREMENTS: Charges do not have to be filed

WOMAN REACH, INC
605 The Gallery, Midtown Sq, Charlotte, NC 28204
Crisis hotline: **(704) 334-3614 10am-5pm (Mon-Fri); 10am-2pm (Sat)**
Information: (704) 334-3614 9am-9pm (Mon-Thu); 10am-4pm (Fri, Sat)
Contact: Fran Saxon, Exec Dir
TYPE OF AGENCY: Women's center
AREAS SERVED: Mecklenburg, Union, Cabarras
YEARS IN OPERATION: 11
ACCESSIBILITY: Wheelchair accessible
CASES SEXUAL ASSAULT/ABUSE (%): 6
DESCRIPTION: Peer counseling; Support; Recovery education
CLIENTS/SERVICES: Sexual assault survivors; Marital rape/sexual abuse survivors; Adult survivors of child sexual abuse; Incest victims/survivors; Community education; Adolescent survivors of sexual abuse

CLYDE

HAYWOOD PEDIATRICS
102 Hospital Dr, No 9, Clyde, NC 28721
Crisis hotline: **(704) 452-2211 24 hrs**
Information: (704) 452-2211 24 hrs
Contact: Harry F Manes, Family Therapist
TYPE OF AGENCY: Hospital/medical center; Private practice
AREAS SERVED: Haywood
CASES SEXUAL ASSAULT/ABUSE (%): 5
DESCRIPTION: Medical practice for children and adolescents. Therapist associate of practice is trained in working with sexually abused children and adolescents
CLIENTS/SERVICES: Child victims of sexual abuse; Adult survivors of child sexual abuse; Incest victims/survivors; Adolescent survivors of sexual abuse

DURHAM

PARK PSYCHOLOGICAL SERVICES/PARK PSYCHOSOCIAL RESOURCE CENTER
1906 Hwy 54, Ste 200-D, Durham, NC 27713
Crisis hotline: **(800) 412-9825 24 hrs**
Information: (919) 544-2565 8am-5pm (Mon, Wed, Fri); 8am-9pm (Tue, Thu)
Contact: William Scarborough, PhD, Licensed Practicing Psychologist
TYPE OF AGENCY: Private practice; Training/research
AREAS SERVED: Durham, Wake, Orange, Chatham
YEARS IN OPERATION: 4
ACCESSIBILITY: Wheelchair accessible; Telecommunications for the hearing impaired (TTY, TDY, etc.)
CASES SEXUAL ASSAULT/ABUSE (%): 40
DESCRIPTION: Counseling for survivors and families involved in child sexual abuse; Support groups for female and male survivors of sexual assault/abuse; Individual and group therapy for rapists, child sexual abuse offenders, incest offenders, and batterers. Staff includes psychologists, social workers, and psychiatric/medical consultant
CLIENTS/SERVICES: Sexual assault survivors; Marital rape/sexual abuse survivors; Child victims of sexual abuse; Adult survivors of child sexual abuse; Incest victims/survivors; Community education; Offender treatment program; Adolescent survivors of sexual abuse; Male survivors of sexual abuse
SPECIAL PROGRAMS/SERVICES: Annual workshop for all groups in treating this population

RAPE CRISIS OF DURHAM
413 E Chapel Hill St, No 207, Durham, NC 27701
Crisis hotline: **(919) 683-8628 24 hrs daily**
Information: (919) 682-2264 9am-5pm (Mon-Fri)
Contact: Cris South, RN, Exec Dir

RAPE CRISIS OF DURHAM (continued)
TYPE OF AGENCY: Rape crisis center; Child sexual abuse prevention program; Residential treatment facility
AREAS SERVED: Durham
YEARS IN OPERATION: 5
LANGUAGES: Spanish, French
ACCESSIBILITY: Signers for the hearing impaired (by arrangement)
CASES SEXUAL ASSAULT/ABUSE (%): 20
CLIENTS/SERVICES: Sexual assault survivors; Marital rape/sexual abuse survivors; Child victims of sexual abuse; Adult survivors of child sexual abuse; Incest victims/survivors; Prevention program; Community education; Adolescent survivors of sexual abuse; Male survivors of sexual abuse
SPECIAL PROGRAMS/SERVICES: Safe touch programs for children aged 5 to 12; Personal safety and awareness programs for adolescents; Date/acquaintance programs for adolescents

THE YWCA RAPE CRISIS CENTER
809 Proctor St, Durham, NC 27707
Crisis hotline: **(919) 683-1595 24 hrs**
Information: (919) 688-4396 24 hrs
Contact: Sian McLean, Dir
TYPE OF AGENCY: Rape crisis center; Child sexual abuse services; Child sexual abuse prevention program
SPONSORING ORGANIZATION: The Durham YWCA
AREAS SERVED: Durham
YEARS IN OPERATION: 4
LANGUAGES: French
ACCESSIBILITY: Wheelchair accessible
CASES SEXUAL ASSAULT/ABUSE (%): 100
DESCRIPTION: Provides crisis and counseling services, support groups, accompaniment and advocacy for all victims of sexual assault; Teaches feminist martial arts/self-defense
CLIENTS/SERVICES: Sexual assault survivors; Marital rape/sexual abuse survivors; Child victims of sexual abuse; Adult survivors of child sexual abuse; Incest victims/survivors; Prevention program; Community education; Adolescent survivors of sexual abuse; Male survivors of sexual abuse
SPECIAL PROGRAMS/SERVICES: In process of establishing a "Courtwatch" program in the local courts, based on the MADD (Mothers Against Drunk Driving) model

ELIZABETH CITY

CRIMES AGAINST WOMEN TASK FORCE, INC—T/A ALBEMARLE HOPELINE
PO Box 2064, Elizabeth City, NC 27906-2064
Crisis hotline: **(919) 338-3011 24 hrs**
Information: (919) 338-5338, 338-1646 9am-5pm
Contact: Patricia J Kepler, Exec Dir
TYPE OF AGENCY: Rape crisis center; Child sexual abuse services; Child sexual abuse prevention program; Adolescent program
AREAS SERVED: Pasquotank, Currituck, Camden, Perquimans, Gates, Chowan
YEARS IN OPERATION: 6½
CASES SEXUAL ASSAULT/ABUSE (%): 76
DESCRIPTION: Provides needed support and services for adult and child victims of sexual assault, including short- and long-term counseling
CLIENTS/SERVICES: Sexual assault survivors; Marital rape/sexual abuse survivors; Child victims of sexual abuse; Adult survivors of child sexual abuse; Incest victims/survivors; Prevention program; Community education; Adolescent survivors of sexual abuse; Male survivors of sexual abuse
SPECIAL PROGRAMS/SERVICES: The results from a 1987-88 staff research study on teen dating violence in area high schools is being used as a base in creating a program on awareness and prevention for adolescents. "Good Touch-Bad Touch" brochure written for children

ELIZABETHTOWN

BLADEN COUNTY MENTAL HEALTH CENTER
PO Box 1176, Elizabethtown, NC 28337
Crisis hotline: **(800) 672-8255 24 hrs daily**
Information: (919) 862-3165 8:30am-5pm (Mon-Fri)
Contact: Jeff Campbell, Clinical Supv
TYPE OF AGENCY: Counseling/mental health services
SPONSORING ORGANIZATION: Southeastern Regional Mental Health Center
AREAS SERVED: Bladen
YEARS IN OPERATION: 15
ACCESSIBILITY: Wheelchair accessible
CASES SEXUAL ASSAULT/ABUSE (%): 2
DESCRIPTION: Provides outpatient mental health services for assault/abuse victims, domestic violence victims, and offenders
CLIENTS/SERVICES: Sexual assault survivors; Marital rape/sexual abuse survivors; Child victims of sexual abuse; Adult survivors of child sexual abuse; Incest victims/survivors; Offender treatment program; Adolescent survivors of sexual abuse; Male survivors of sexual abuse
REQUIREMENTS: Must be a resident of Bladen County

FAYETTEVILLE

GUARDIAN AD LITEM
PO Box 363, Cumberland County Courthouse, Fayetteville, NC 28302
Information: (919) 486-1348 8am-5pm
Contact: Brownie Smathers, Prog Coord
TYPE OF AGENCY: Victim/witness assistance program; Child sexual abuse services; Child abuse services; Child advocacy
SPONSORING ORGANIZATION: Administration Office of the Courts
AREAS SERVED: Cumberland, Hoke
YEARS IN OPERATION: 3½
ACCESSIBILITY: Wheelchair accessible
CASES SEXUAL ASSAULT/ABUSE (%): 38
DESCRIPTION: Provides advocate and attorney for children in juvenile court proceedings alleging abuse/neglect
CLIENTS/SERVICES: Child victims of sexual abuse; Incest victims/survivors; Prevention program; Community education
REQUIREMENTS: Petition filed by Department of Social Services with the Juvenile Court alleging abuse or neglect.

RAPE CRISIS VOLUNTEERS OF CUMBERLAND COUNTY
108 Highland Ave, Fayetteville, NC 28302
Crisis hotline: **(919) 484-6101**
Information: (919) 485-7273
Contact: Pat Jensen
TYPE OF AGENCY: Rape crisis center
AREAS SERVED: Cumberland
CLIENTS/SERVICES: Sexual assault survivors

FOREST CITY

PATH, INC (PREVENTION OF ABUSE IN THE HOME)
PO Box 1075, Forest City, NC 28043
Crisis hotline: **(704) 245-8595 24 hrs**
Information: (704) 245-8595 24 hrs
Contact: Kim Hooper, Exec Dir
TYPE OF AGENCY: Rape crisis center; Domestic violence program; Child sexual abuse services; Child abuse services
AREAS SERVED: Rutherford; Surrounding counties on a space-available basis
YEARS IN OPERATION: 7
ACCESSIBILITY: Wheelchair accessible
CASES SEXUAL ASSAULT/ABUSE (%): 15
DESCRIPTION: Provides services for victims of domestic violence, rape/sexual assault, child abuse and neglect, and child sexual abuse, including 24-hour crisis intervention, emergency shelter, counseling, support groups, court and agency advocacy
CLIENTS/SERVICES: Sexual assault survivors; Marital rape/sexual abuse survivors; Child victims of sexual abuse; Adult survivors of child sexual abuse; Incest victims/survivors; Prevention program; Community education; Adolescent survivors of sexual abuse; Male survivors of sexual abuse

GASTONIA

BATTERED SPOUSE PROGRAM OF GASTON COUNTY
PO Box 10, Gastonia, NC 28053
Crisis hotline: **(704) 867-4357 After 5pm (Mon-Fri); 24 hrs (Sat, Sun, and Holidays)**
Information: (704) 866-3679 8am-5pm (Mon-Fri)
Contact: Barbara A Robinson, Allied Svcs Admin
TYPE OF AGENCY: Domestic violence program
SPONSORING ORGANIZATION: Gaston County Department of Social Services
AREAS SERVED: Gaston, Lincoln; other counties as space permits
YEARS IN OPERATION: 6
CASES SEXUAL ASSAULT/ABUSE (%): 20
DESCRIPTION: Provides shelter and other services for battered women and their children; Temporary housing for male survivors
CLIENTS/SERVICES: Sexual assault survivors; Marital rape/sexual abuse survivors; Prevention program; Community education; Male survivors of sexual abuse

GREENSBORO

DISTRICT ATTORNEY'S OFFICE—VICTIM/WITNESS ASSISTANCE
PO Box 2378, Greensboro, NC 27402
Information: (919) 334-5584 8am-5pm
Contact: Catherine Shaw, Victim Witness Asst
TYPE OF AGENCY: Victim/witness assistance program
SPONSORING ORGANIZATION: Box 2378
AREAS SERVED: Guilford
YEARS IN OPERATION: 1½
ACCESSIBILITY: Wheelchair accessible; Signers for the hearing impaired
CASES SEXUAL ASSAULT/ABUSE (%): 10
CLIENTS/SERVICES: Sexual assault survivors; Marital rape/sexual abuse survivors; Child victims of sexual abuse
REQUIREMENTS: Cases in which the offender has been charged almost exclusively but will help anyone who calls with information and with victims compensation applications

TURNING POINT
1301 N Elm St, Greensboro, NC 27401
Information: (919) 373-1345
Contact: Jane Cauthen, Dir
TYPE OF AGENCY: Rape crisis center; Domestic violence program
SPONSORING ORGANIZATION: Family and Childrens Service
DESCRIPTION: Provides shelter for battered women; Rape crisis line and rape companion to assist and support victim after assault; Steppingstones Play School, drop in child care for children of mothers in crisis; Focus, court mandated counseling program for male batterers, family and individual counseling; Good Beginnings, parent education program
CLIENTS/SERVICES: Sexual assault survivors; Marital rape/sexual abuse survivors; Child victims of sexual abuse; Incest victims/survivors; Prevention program

GREENVILLE

REAL CRISIS INTERVENTION, INC
312 E 10th St, Greenville, NC 27858
Crisis hotline: **(919) 758-HELP 24 hrs**
Information: (919) 758-HELP 24 hrs
Contact: Mary L Smith, Exec Dir
TYPE OF AGENCY: Rape crisis center
AREAS SERVED: Pitt
YEARS IN OPERATION: 17
ACCESSIBILITY: Wheelchair accessible
CASES SEXUAL ASSAULT/ABUSE (%): 2
CLIENTS/SERVICES: Sexual assault survivors; Child victims of sexual abuse; Adult survivors of child sexual abuse; Incest victims/survivors; Prevention program; Community education; Adolescent survivors of sexual abuse; Male survivors of sexual abuse

HAVELOCK

THE COUNSELING CENTER
10 E Plaza, Havelock, NC 28532
Crisis hotline: **(919) 247-3023, 638-5995**
Information: (919) 447-3900 10am-7pm (Mon-Fri)
Contact: Betty Skulstad, ACSW, Dir
TYPE OF AGENCY: Counseling/mental health services; Child sexual abuse services; Private practice
AREAS SERVED: Craven, Carteret, Jones, Pamlico
YEARS IN OPERATION: 1
ACCESSIBILITY: Wheelchair accessible
CASES SEXUAL ASSAULT/ABUSE (%): 40
DESCRIPTION: Individual and group therapy for survivors, including support groups for male survivors; Parents United chapter onsite
CLIENTS/SERVICES: Sexual assault survivors; Marital rape/sexual abuse survivors; Child victims of sexual abuse; Adult survivors of child sexual abuse; Incest victims/survivors; Prevention program; Community education; Offender treatment program; Adolescent survivors of sexual abuse; Male survivors of sexual abuse
REQUIREMENTS: Sliding scale fees; Accepts major health insurance plans

HENDERSON

FAMILY VIOLENCE INTERVENTION PROGRAM OF REGION K
PO Box 1988, Henderson, NC 27536
Crisis hotline: **(919) 492-9693**
Information: (919) 492-0659
Contact: Carolyn Gray
TYPE OF AGENCY: Domestic violence program
AREAS SERVED: Vance, Franklin, Person, Granville, Warren
CLIENTS/SERVICES: Sexual assault survivors; Marital rape/sexual abuse survivors

HENDERSONVILLE

HENDERSON COUNTY RAPE CRISIS CENTER
PO Box 2461, Hendersonville, NC 28793
Crisis hotline: **(704) 692-3931 24 hrs**
Information: (704) 692-3931 9am-5pm
Contact: Janice Maney, Coord
TYPE OF AGENCY: Rape crisis center; Child sexual abuse prevention program
SPONSORING ORGANIZATION: Rape Crisis Center, Inc
AREAS SERVED: Henderson
YEARS IN OPERATION: 2½
LANGUAGES: Spanish, interpreters available
ACCESSIBILITY: Telecommunications for the hearing impaired (TTY, TDY, etc.) (by request); Signers for the hearing impaired (by request)
CASES SEXUAL ASSAULT/ABUSE (%): 100
CLIENTS/SERVICES: Sexual assault survivors; Marital rape/sexual abuse survivors; Child victims of sexual abuse; Adult survivors of child sexual abuse; Incest victims/survivors; Prevention program; Community education; Adolescent survivors of sexual abuse; Male survivors of sexual abuse; Healing
REQUIREMENTS: Children under the age of 16 are referred to local professionals specializing in the treatment of child sexual abuse
SPECIAL PROGRAMS/SERVICES: Exhibit of survivors' work titled "The Invisible Wound—Healing From Sexual Assault" funded by North Carolina Arts Council. Buncombe and Henderson Counties child sexual abuse task forces. Arts therapy through music, writing, dancing, pottery, drawing, storytelling. Child care and meals throughout court processes; Self advocacy for those who want to speak out. Scrapbooks of support system with photos, poetry, and letters. "Funny Tummy Feelings" prevention program; Cycle of Abuse Community Education Program

HICKORY

AID TO VICTIMS OF SEXUAL ASSAULT
PO Box 665, Hickory, NC 28603
Crisis hotline: **911, (704) 322-6243 24 hrs daily**
Information: (704) 322-6011 8am-5pm
Contact: Debbie Benfield, Exec Dir
TYPE OF AGENCY: Rape crisis center; Child sexual abuse prevention program; Acquaintance/date rape prevention program
AREAS SERVED: Catawba
YEARS IN OPERATION: 6
CASES SEXUAL ASSAULT/ABUSE (%): 95
CLIENTS/SERVICES: Sexual assault survivors; Marital rape/sexual abuse survivors; Child victims of sexual abuse; Adult survivors of child sexual abuse; Incest victims/survivors; Prevention program; Community education; Adolescent survivors of sexual abuse
SPECIAL PROGRAMS/SERVICES: Art therapy program for survivors of sexual assault

JACKSONVILLE

CRIST CLINIC FOR WOMEN
200 Memorial Dr, Jacksonville, NC 28540
Information: (919) 353-2715 9am-4pm
Contact: Dr T Crist, Dir
TYPE OF AGENCY: Hospital/medical center
YEARS IN OPERATION: 16
LANGUAGES: Greek, Spanish
ACCESSIBILITY: Wheelchair accessible
CASES SEXUAL ASSAULT/ABUSE (%): 1
CLIENTS/SERVICES: Sexual assault survivors; Marital rape/sexual abuse survivors; Child victims of sexual abuse; Prevention program; Community education; Adolescent survivors of sexual abuse

GUARDIAN AD LITEM PROGRAM
625 Court St, Onslow County Courthouse, Jacksonville, NC 28540
Information: (919) 346-5335 8am-5pm
Contact: Jean Hawley, Prog Coord
TYPE OF AGENCY: Child sexual abuse services; Child advocacy
SPONSORING ORGANIZATION: Administrative Office of the Courts, North Carolina
AREAS SERVED: Onslow, Jones, Duplin, Sampson
YEARS IN OPERATION: 3
LANGUAGES: Spanish
CASES SEXUAL ASSAULT/ABUSE (%): 24
DESCRIPTION: A Guardian ad Litem is appointed to represent the "best interest of the child," advocates for services for the child or family, monitors the progress of the child throughout the legal proceedings, and reports significant changes/needs to the court. The program provides an attorney to represent and protect the child's legal rights during litigation
CLIENTS/SERVICES: Child victims of sexual abuse; Community education
REQUIREMENTS: Petition filed by Department of Social Services in District Juvenile Court; age: birth to 18 years

ONSLOW COUNTY WOMEN'S CENTER
PO Box 1622, Jacksonville, NC 28541
Crisis hotline: **(919) 347-4000 24 hrs**
Information: (919) 347-4000 9am-4pm
Contact: Darlene Study, Sexual Assault Couns
TYPE OF AGENCY: Rape crisis center; Domestic violence program; Child sexual abuse prevention program
AREAS SERVED: Onslow, Carteret, Pender, Duplin, Jones
YEARS IN OPERATION: 5
ACCESSIBILITY: Wheelchair accessible
CASES SEXUAL ASSAULT/ABUSE (%): 20
DESCRIPTION: Services for survivors of sexual assault and domestic violence; Feminist martial arts/self defense program
CLIENTS/SERVICES: Sexual assault survivors; Marital rape/sexual abuse survivors; Child victims of sexual abuse; Adult survivors of child sexual abuse; Incest victims/survivors; Prevention program; Community education; Adolescent survivors of sexual abuse; Male survivors of sexual abuse; Publications/media
SPECIAL PROGRAMS/SERVICES: Media program: Sexual Assault Myths

LENOIR

SHELTER HOME OF CALDWELL COUNTY
PO Box 426, Lenoir, NC 28645
Crisis hotline: **(704) 758-0888 24 hrs daily**
Information: (704) 758-0888 8am-5pm (Mon-Fri)
Contact: Georgie Stone, Exec Dir
TYPE OF AGENCY: Rape crisis center; Domestic violence program
AREAS SERVED: Caldwell
YEARS IN OPERATION: 10
LANGUAGES: French, German
ACCESSIBILITY: Wheelchair accessible; Signers for the hearing impaired
CASES SEXUAL ASSAULT/ABUSE (%): 10
DESCRIPTION: Works with the community to prevent family violence and sexual assault through direct services for victims and community education; Psychoeducational therapy for batterers
CLIENTS/SERVICES: Sexual assault survivors; Marital rape/sexual abuse survivors; Child victims of sexual abuse; Adult survivors of child sexual abuse; Incest victims/survivors; Prevention program; Community education; Adolescent survivors of sexual abuse; Male survivors of sexual abuse

LEXINGTON

DAVIDSON COUNTY DOMESTIC VIOLENCE SERVICES, INC
PO Box 1231, Lexington, NC 27293
Crisis hotline: **(919) 476-1131, (704) 249-8974 24 hrs**
Information: (704) 243-1934, 243-1628 6:30am-10:30pm
Contact: Sandra S Steadman, Exec Dir
TYPE OF AGENCY: Domestic violence program
AREAS SERVED: Davidson
YEARS IN OPERATION: 8
ACCESSIBILITY: Wheelchair accessible
DESCRIPTION: Provides comprehensive services for victims of domestic violence and their children, including shelter, counseling, and a children's program; Therapy for batterers
CLIENTS/SERVICES: Marital rape/sexual abuse survivors; Community education

LILLINGTON

RAPE CRISIS INTERVENTION OF HARNETT COUNTY
PO Box 1473, Lillington, NC 27546
Crisis hotline: **(919) 893-2118 24 hrs**
Information: (919) 893-5088
Contact: Vickie Whitley, Dir
TYPE OF AGENCY: Rape crisis center
AREAS SERVED: Harnett

RAPE CRISIS INTERVENTION OF HARNETT COUNTY *(continued)*
YEARS IN OPERATION: 1
CASES SEXUAL ASSAULT/ABUSE (%): 57
DESCRIPTION: Services for sexual assault survivors; Feminist martial arts/self-defense and other prevention programs
CLIENTS/SERVICES: Sexual assault survivors; Marital rape/sexual abuse survivors; Child victims of sexual abuse; Adult survivors of child sexual abuse; Incest victims/survivors; Prevention program; Community education

MANTEO

OUTER BANKS HOTLINE
PO Box 1417, Manteo, NC 27954
Crisis hotline: **(919) 473-3366, 995-4555 (Hatteras Island)**
Information: (919) 473-5121
Contact: Lynn S Bryant
TYPE OF AGENCY: Rape crisis center
AREAS SERVED: Dare
CLIENTS/SERVICES: Sexual assault survivors

MARSHALL

MARSHALL COUNTY RAPE CRISIS CENTER, INC
PO Box 395, Marshall, NC 28793
Crisis hotline: **(704) 649-3912 24 hrs**
Information: (704) 649-3912 9am-5pm
Contact: Leigh Dudasik, Exec Dir
TYPE OF AGENCY: Rape crisis center; Child sexual abuse prevention program
SPONSORING ORGANIZATION: Rape Crisis Center, Inc
AREAS SERVED: Madison
YEARS IN OPERATION: 2½
LANGUAGES: Interpreters available
ACCESSIBILITY: Telecommunications for the hearing impaired (TTY, TDY, etc.) (by request); Signers for the hearing impaired (by request)
CASES SEXUAL ASSAULT/ABUSE (%): 100
CLIENTS/SERVICES: Sexual assault survivors; Marital rape/sexual abuse survivors; Adult survivors of child sexual abuse; Incest victims/survivors; Prevention program; Community education; Adolescent survivors of sexual abuse; Male survivors of sexual abuse; Healing
REQUIREMENTS: Children under the age of 16 are referred to local professionals specializing in the treatment of child sexual abuse
SPECIAL PROGRAMS/SERVICES: Buncombe and Henderson Counties child sexual abuse task force. Arts therapy through music, writing, dancing, pottery, drawing, storytelling. Child care and meals throughout the court processes. Self-advocacy for those who want to speak out. Scrapbooks of support system with photos, poetry, and letters. "Funny Tummy Feelings" prevention program; Cycle of Abuse Community Education Program.

MONROE

UNION COUNTY RAPE CRISIS COMPANIONS
PO Box 1110, Monroe, NC 28110
Crisis hotline: **(704) 283-7770 24 hrs**
Information: (704) 283-7770 9am-5pm
Contact: Luzette Maynard, Coord
TYPE OF AGENCY: Rape crisis center; Child sexual abuse services; Child sexual abuse prevention program
SPONSORING ORGANIZATION: Union County Crime Prevention
AREAS SERVED: Union
YEARS IN OPERATION: 8
ACCESSIBILITY: Wheelchair accessible
CASES SEXUAL ASSAULT/ABUSE (%): 100
CLIENTS/SERVICES: Sexual assault survivors; Marital rape/sexual abuse survivors; Child victims of sexual abuse; Adult survivors of child sexual abuse; Incest victims/survivors; Prevention program; Community education; Adolescent survivors of sexual abuse

MOREHEAD CITY

CARTERET COUNTY RAPE CRISIS PROGRAM
Webb Civic Center, 9th and Evans St, Morehead City, NC 28557
Crisis hotline: **(919) 247-3023 24 hrs daily**
Information: (919) 726-6730 8:30am-5pm
Contact: Jane Butler, Dir
TYPE OF AGENCY: Rape crisis center; Child sexual abuse services; Child sexual abuse prevention program
SPONSORING ORGANIZATION: Helpline of Carteret County
AREAS SERVED: Carteret
YEARS IN OPERATION: 3
LANGUAGES: Translators available through the hospital
ACCESSIBILITY: Wheelchair accessible; Signers for the hearing impaired
CASES SEXUAL ASSAULT/ABUSE (%): 100
CLIENTS/SERVICES: Sexual assault survivors; Marital rape/sexual abuse survivors; Child victims of sexual abuse; Adult survivors of child sexual abuse; Incest victims/survivors; Prevention program; Community education; Adolescent survivors of sexual abuse; Male survivors of sexual abuse

MORGANTON

OPTIONS, INC
PO Box 2512, Morganton, NC 28655
Crisis hotline: **(704) 438-9444 24 hrs**
Information: (704) 438-9444 8am-5pm (Mon-Fri)
Contact: Lynn Ballance, Sexual Assault Couns
TYPE OF AGENCY: Victim/witness assistance program; Child sexual abuse services; Child sexual abuse prevention program
AREAS SERVED: Burke
YEARS IN OPERATION: 3
ACCESSIBILITY: Telecommunications for the hearing impaired (TTY, TDY, etc.); Signers for the hearing impaired
CASES SEXUAL ASSAULT/ABUSE (%): 35
DESCRIPTION: Provides peer counseling and crisis intervention for all victims of violent crime, including adult and child victims of sexual assault; Conducts a clinical therapy group for child victims and their mothers
CLIENTS/SERVICES: Sexual assault survivors; Marital rape/sexual abuse survivors; Child victims of sexual abuse; Adult survivors of child sexual abuse; Incest victims/survivors; Prevention program; Community education; Adolescent survivors of sexual abuse; Male survivors of sexual abuse

MURPHY

REACH, INC
PO Box 977, Murphy, NC 28906
Crisis hotline: **(704) 837-8064 24 hrs**
Information: (704) 837-8064 9am-5pm
Contact: Robin Mauney, Dir
TYPE OF AGENCY: Rape crisis center; Domestic violence program; Child sexual abuse prevention program
AREAS SERVED: Cherokee, Clay, Graham
YEARS IN OPERATION: 7
ACCESSIBILITY: Wheelchair accessible
CASES SEXUAL ASSAULT/ABUSE (%): 20
CLIENTS/SERVICES: Sexual assault survivors; Marital rape/sexual abuse survivors; Child victims of sexual abuse; Adult survivors of child sexual abuse; Incest victims/survivors; Prevention program; Community education; Adolescent survivors of sexual abuse; Male survivors of sexual abuse

NEW BERN

NEUSE-TRENT RAPE ASSISTANCE PROGRAM
PO Box 1285, New Bern, NC 28560
Crisis hotline: **(919) 638-5995 24 hrs**
Information: (919) 636-3381 8:30am-5pm
Contact: Patricia Gay Welch, Prog Dir
TYPE OF AGENCY: Rape crisis center
SPONSORING ORGANIZATION: Craven County Council on Women
AREAS SERVED: Craven, Jones, Pamilca
YEARS IN OPERATION: 6
ACCESSIBILITY: Wheelchair accessible
CASES SEXUAL ASSAULT/ABUSE (%): 100
DESCRIPTION: Provides 24-hour crisis line, hospital companions, court advocates for victims of sexual assault; Provides temporary shelter for rape victims and courtesy kits at all local emergency rooms
CLIENTS/SERVICES: Sexual assault survivors; Marital rape/sexual abuse survivors; Child victims of sexual abuse; Adult survivors of child sexual abuse; Incest victims/survivors; Prevention program; Community education; Adolescent survivors of sexual abuse
SPECIAL PROGRAMS/SERVICES: *Mock Rape Trial* film

PINEHURST

SANDHILLS CENTER FOR MENTAL HEALTH, MENTAL RETARDATION, SUBSTANCE ABUSE
PO Drawer 639, Pinehurst, NC 28374
Crisis hotline: **(919) 295-6853 24 hrs 7 days**
Information: (919) 295-6853 8:30am-5pm
Contact: Deborah Rich, MS, Child Svcs Coord
TYPE OF AGENCY: Counseling/mental health services; Child sexual abuse services
AREAS SERVED: Anson, Montgomery, Richmond, Moore, Hoke
ACCESSIBILITY: Wheelchair accessible; Signers for the hearing impaired
CASES SEXUAL ASSAULT/ABUSE (%): 70
DESCRIPTION: Child and family services program provides individual, group, family psychotherapy for any mental health and related problems
CLIENTS/SERVICES: Sexual assault survivors; Marital rape/sexual abuse survivors; Child victims of sexual abuse; Adult survivors of child sexual abuse; Incest victims/survivors; Community education; Offender treatment program; Adolescent survivors of sexual abuse; Male survivors of sexual abuse

PITTSBORO

FAMILY VIOLENCE AND RAPE CRISIS VOLUNTEERS IN CHATHAM COUNTY
PO Box 1105, Pittsboro, NC 27312
Crisis hotline: **(919) 929-0479, 742-5612 24 hrs**
Information: (919) 542-5445 9am-5pm (Mon-Fri)
Contact: Jo Sanders, Dir
TYPE OF AGENCY: Rape crisis center; Domestic violence program; Child sexual abuse prevention program
AREAS SERVED: Chatham
YEARS IN OPERATION: 6
LANGUAGES: Spanish interpreters by arrangement
ACCESSIBILITY: Wheelchair accessible
CASES SEXUAL ASSAULT/ABUSE (%): 15-20
DESCRIPTION: Crisis intervention for victims of domestic violence and sexual assault; Group therapy is available for batterers
CLIENTS/SERVICES: Sexual assault survivors; Marital rape/sexual abuse survivors; Child victims of sexual abuse; Prevention program; Community education

RALEIGH

THE CHILD SEXUAL ABUSE TEAM
3000 New Bern Ave, Raleigh, NC 27610
Crisis hotline: **(800) 4 A CHILD 8am-5pm**
Information: (919) 755-8493 8am-5pm
Contact: Kim Crews, Sexual Abuse Coun; V Denise Everett, MD
TYPE OF AGENCY: Hospital/medical center; Child sexual abuse services
SPONSORING ORGANIZATION: Wake Medical Center
AREAS SERVED: Wake, Johnston, Franklin, Granville, Lee, Vance, Warren
YEARS IN OPERATION: 7
LANGUAGES: Spanish
ACCESSIBILITY: Wheelchair accessible
CASES SEXUAL ASSAULT/ABUSE (%): 100
DESCRIPTION: Evaluation and counseling for victims of sexual assault/abuse and their families; Education and consultation to community agencies; Research and research projects relating to child sexual abuse
CLIENTS/SERVICES: Child victims of sexual abuse; Incest victims/survivors; Community education
REQUIREMENTS: Major emphasis on children 12 years or younger, consideration given to children over 12 on a case-by-case basis

INTERACT
PO Box 11096, Raleigh, NC 27604
Crisis hotline: **(919) 755-6661 24 hrs**
Information: (919) 755-6453 9am-5pm (Mon-Fri)
Contact: Kathy J Sutenall, Rape Crisis Prog Dir
TYPE OF AGENCY: Rape crisis center; Domestic violence program
SPONSORING ORGANIZATION: United Way
AREAS SERVED: Wake
YEARS IN OPERATION: 10
ACCESSIBILITY: Wheelchair accessible; Signers for the hearing impaired
CASES SEXUAL ASSAULT/ABUSE (%): 40
CLIENTS/SERVICES: Sexual assault survivors; Marital rape/sexual abuse survivors; Child victims of sexual abuse; Adult survivors of child sexual abuse; Incest victims/survivors; Prevention program; Community education; Adolescent survivors of sexual abuse; Male survivors of sexual abuse

ROANOKE RAPIDS

HALIFAX COUNTY MENTAL HEALTH CENTER
PO Drawer 1199, 210 Smith Church Rd, Roanoke Rapids, NC 27870
Crisis hotline: **(919) 537-2909 (night), 537-6174 (day)**
Information: (919) 537-6174
Contact: Lois Batton, Dir
TYPE OF AGENCY: Counseling/mental health services
AREAS SERVED: Halifax
CLIENTS/SERVICES: Sexual assault survivors; Adolescent survivors of sexual abuse

SALISBURY

THE RAPE, CHILD AND FAMILY ABUSE CRISIS COUNCIL OF SALISBURY-ROWAN, INC
127 W Council St, Salisbury, NC 28144
Crisis hotline: **(704) 636-9222 24 hrs**
Information: (704) 636-4718 8:30am-5pm
Contact: Elizabeth Cress, Exec Dir
TYPE OF AGENCY: Rape crisis center; Domestic violence program
SPONSORING ORGANIZATION: United Way
AREAS SERVED: Rowan
YEARS IN OPERATION: 10
DESCRIPTION: Provides crisis services and support groups for rape and domestic violence victims
CLIENTS/SERVICES: Sexual assault survivors; Marital rape/sexual abuse survivors; Child victims of sexual abuse; Adult survivors of child sexual abuse; Incest victims/survivors; Prevention program; Community education

SANFORD

FAMILY VIOLENCE AND RAPE CRISIS ASSOCIATION OF LEE COUNTY
PO Box 3191, Sanford, NC 27331
Crisis hotline: **(919) 774-4520**
Information: (919) 774-8923
Contact: Sherry Owensby, Dir
TYPE OF AGENCY: Rape crisis center; Domestic violence program
AREAS SERVED: Lee, Harnett
CLIENTS/SERVICES: Sexual assault survivors

LEE-HARNETT MENTAL HEALTH CENTER
130 Carbonton Rd, Sanford, NC 27330
Crisis hotline: **(919) 774-4520 24 hrs**
Information: (919) 774-6521
Contact: Jim Rockwell, Children's Svcs SWIII
TYPE OF AGENCY: Counseling/mental health services
AREAS SERVED: Lee, Harnett
YEARS IN OPERATION: 20
LANGUAGES: Spanish
ACCESSIBILITY: Wheelchair accessible
CLIENTS/SERVICES: Sexual assault survivors; Marital rape/sexual abuse survivors; Child victims of sexual abuse; Adult survivors of child sexual abuse; Incest victims/survivors; Offender treatment program; Adolescent survivors of sexual abuse; Male survivors of sexual abuse

SHELBY

CHILD ABUSE PREVENTION SERVICES, INC
PO Box 3000, Shelby, NC 28151-3000
Information: (704) 487-1278, 487-1404 9am-4pm
Contact: Gale A Kirk, Act Dir
TYPE OF AGENCY: Child sexual abuse services; Child sexual abuse prevention program; Child abuse services; Child abuse prevention program
AREAS SERVED: Cabarrus
YEARS IN OPERATION: 8
ACCESSIBILITY: Wheelchair accessible
DESCRIPTION: Super Kids Program teaches the children to recognize sexual abuse. A majority of children in Super Kids Program are or have been sexually abused or are in a situation that could lead to sexual abuse.
CLIENTS/SERVICES: Child victims of sexual abuse; Adult survivors of child sexual abuse; Incest victims/survivors; Prevention program; Community education
REQUIREMENTS: Many clients are court-ordered or referred by Department of Social Services and Mental Health Agency
SPECIAL PROGRAMS/SERVICES: Family Tree Event: provides parents and their children an opportunity to spend quality time together in a supportive environment and to practice newly acquired skills. Evenings at the community college watching plays or listening to music programs, making ice cream, reading to each other or learning to play games with the children

CLEVELAND COUNTY ABUSE PREVENTION COUNCIL, INC
PO Box 2895, Shelby, NC 28151
Crisis hotline: **(704) 481-0043 24 hrs**
Information: (704) 487-7129 24 hrs
Contact: Ellen Blair Brackett, Volunteer Coord/Admin Asst
TYPE OF AGENCY: Rape crisis center; Domestic violence program
AREAS SERVED: Cleveland and surrounding counties
YEARS IN OPERATION: Agency 3 years; Program 2½ years
CASES SEXUAL ASSAULT/ABUSE (%): 10
CLIENTS/SERVICES: Sexual assault survivors; Marital rape/sexual abuse survivors; Child victims of sexual abuse; Adult survivors of child sexual abuse; Incest victims/survivors; Community education; Adolescent survivors of sexual abuse; Male survivors of sexual abuse

SMITHFIELD

HARBOR, INC
PO Box 1903, Smithfield, NC 27577
Crisis hotline: **(919) 934-6161 24 hrs**
Information: (919) 934-0233 8am-5pm
Contact: Adelaide Brooks, Dir
TYPE OF AGENCY: Rape crisis center; Domestic violence program
AREAS SERVED: Johnston
YEARS IN OPERATION: 5
LANGUAGES: Spanish
DESCRIPTION: Provides crisis counseling, temporary shelter, victim advocacy and accompaniment, and referrals for survivors of rape and family violence
CLIENTS/SERVICES: Sexual assault survivors; Marital rape/sexual abuse survivors; Child victims of sexual abuse; Community education

SOUTHERN PINES

FRIEND TO FRIEND
455 SE Broad St, Southern Pines, NC 28387
Information: (919) 692-1022
Contact: Janet Norfleet, Crisis Coord
TYPE OF AGENCY: Rape crisis center
AREAS SERVED: Moore
CLIENTS/SERVICES: Sexual assault survivors

STATESVILLE

JUBILEE HOUSE COMMUNITY
906 5th St, Statesville, NC 28677
Crisis hotline: **(704) 872-7638 24 hrs**
Information: (704) 872-4045 9am-10pm
Contact: Margaret Carpenter, Pat Floerke
TYPE OF AGENCY: Rape crisis center; Domestic violence program
AREAS SERVED: Iredell, Davie, Yadkin, Rowan, Catawba, Alexander
YEARS IN OPERATION: 9
LANGUAGES: French, Spanish, Mandarin Chinese, German
ACCESSIBILITY: Wheelchair accessible; Signers for the hearing impaired
CASES SEXUAL ASSAULT/ABUSE (%): 85
CLIENTS/SERVICES: Sexual assault survivors; Marital rape/sexual abuse survivors; Child victims of sexual abuse; Adult survivors of child sexual abuse; Incest victims/survivors; Community education; Adolescent survivors of sexual abuse; Male survivors of sexual abuse
SPECIAL PROGRAMS/SERVICES: Interagency task force creating multidisciplinary approaches to the needs of victims of domestic violence. Clergywoman on staff works with other clergypeople to help them understand the patriarchal roots of sexual violence, and rethink/recreate a Biblical response. She is available to work with programs in learning how to reach and work with clergy.

SYLVA

REACH OF JACKSON COUNTY
PO Box 1828, Sylva, NC 28779
Crisis hotline: **(704) 586-2459 24 hrs**
Information: (704) 586-8969 9am-5pm (Mon-Fri)
Contact: Elizabeth Worley, Dir
TYPE OF AGENCY: Rape crisis center; Domestic violence program
AREAS SERVED: Macon, Jackson
YEARS IN OPERATION: 5
CASES SEXUAL ASSAULT/ABUSE (%): 2

REACH OF JACKSON COUNTY
(continued)

CLIENTS/SERVICES: Sexual assault survivors; Marital rape/sexual abuse survivors; Adult survivors of child sexual abuse; Incest victims/survivors; Prevention program; Community education; Male survivors of sexual abuse
REQUIREMENTS: Must be over 18 years of age

TROY

THE CRISIS COUNCIL, INC
PO Box O, Troy, NC 27371
Crisis hotline: **(919) 572-3747 24 hrs**
Information: (919) 572-3749 8am-5pm
Contact: Mareida Grossman, MSW, Exec Dir
TYPE OF AGENCY: Rape crisis center; Domestic violence program
AREAS SERVED: Montgomery, Stanly, Anson, Moore
YEARS IN OPERATION: 3½
CASES SEXUAL ASSAULT/ABUSE (%): 16
CLIENTS/SERVICES: Sexual assault survivors; Marital rape/sexual abuse survivors; Adult survivors of child sexual abuse; Incest victims/survivors; Prevention program; Community education; Offender treatment program; Adolescent survivors of sexual abuse; Male survivors of sexual abuse

WASHINGTON

OPTIONS: TO DOMESTIC VIOLENCE AND SEXUAL ASSAULT
PO Box 1387, 211 N Market St, Washington, NC 27889
Crisis hotline: **(800) 682-0767 24 hrs**
Information: (919) 946-3219 8:30am-5pm
Contact: Sally Vanderzell, Exec Dir
TYPE OF AGENCY: Rape crisis center; Domestic violence program
AREAS SERVED: Beaufort, Hyde, Martin, Tyrell, Washington
YEARS IN OPERATION: 5
CASES SEXUAL ASSAULT/ABUSE (%): 10
DESCRIPTION: Serves victims of domestic violence, sexual assault, and child abuse. Provides a 24-hour crisis line, information, referral, court and medical accompaniment, and shelter; Feminist martial arts/self-defense program
CLIENTS/SERVICES: Sexual assault survivors; Marital rape/sexual abuse survivors; Child victims of sexual abuse; Prevention program; Community education; Adolescent survivors of sexual abuse

WAYNESVILLE

REACH OF HAYWOOD COUNTY
PO Box 206, Waynesville, NC 28786
Crisis hotline: **(704) 456-7898 24 hrs**
Information: (704) 456-7898 9am-5pm
Contact: Kris Gillet, Dir
TYPE OF AGENCY: Rape crisis center; Domestic violence program; Child sexual abuse prevention program
AREAS SERVED: Haywood
YEARS IN OPERATION: 3
ACCESSIBILITY: Wheelchair accessible
CASES SEXUAL ASSAULT/ABUSE (%): 25
CLIENTS/SERVICES: Sexual assault survivors; Marital rape/sexual abuse survivors; Child victims of sexual abuse; Adult survivors of child sexual abuse; Incest victims/survivors; Prevention program; Community education; Adolescent survivors of sexual abuse; Male survivors of sexual abuse

WILKESBORO

SHELTERED AID TO FAMILIES IN EMERGENCY (SAFE), INC
Box 445, Wilkesboro, NC 28697
Crisis hotline: **(919) 838-7233 24 hrs daily**
Information: (919) 667-7656 9am-5pm
Contact: Lil Barrett, Dir; Mary Taylor, Victim Assistance Coord
TYPE OF AGENCY: Rape crisis center; Domestic violence program; Child sexual abuse services; Child sexual abuse prevention program
AREAS SERVED: Wilkes
YEARS IN OPERATION: 8
ACCESSIBILITY: Wheelchair accessible; Telecommunications for the hearing impaired (TTY, TDY, etc.); Signers for the hearing impaired
DESCRIPTION: Comprehensive services for survivors of sexual assault and domestic violence, including support groups for female and male survivors and feminist martial arts/self-defense
CLIENTS/SERVICES: Sexual assault survivors; Marital rape/sexual abuse survivors; Child victims of sexual abuse; Adult survivors of child sexual abuse; Incest victims/survivors; Prevention program; Community education; Adolescent survivors of sexual abuse; Male survivors of sexual abuse

WILMINGTON

RAPE CRISIS CENTER
415 Grace St, Wilmington, NC 28401
Crisis hotline: **(919) 763-3695, (800) 672-2903 in NC 24 hrs**
Information: (919) 762-4255 9am-5pm
Contact: Carolyn Brown, Rape Crisis Spec; Margaret Weller, Dir
TYPE OF AGENCY: Rape crisis center; Child sexual abuse prevention program
SPONSORING ORGANIZATION: Cape Fear Substance Abuse Center
AREAS SERVED: New Hanover, Pender
YEARS IN OPERATION: 8
CASES SEXUAL ASSAULT/ABUSE (%): 100
DESCRIPTION: Comprehensive rape crisis services; Prevention programs on child sexual abuse; Feminist martial arts/self-defense
CLIENTS/SERVICES: Sexual assault survivors; Marital rape/sexual abuse survivors; Child victims of sexual abuse; Adult survivors of child sexual abuse; Incest victims/survivors; Prevention program; Community education; Adolescent survivors of sexual abuse; Male survivors of sexual abuse

WINSTON-SALEM

RAPE RESPONSE
610 Coliseum Dr, Winston-Salem, NC 27106
Crisis hotline: **(919) 722-4457 24 hrs**
Information: (919) 722-4457 8:30am-5pm (Mon-Fri)
Contact: Carolyn Williams, Educ Prevention and Community Dev Svcs Coord
TYPE OF AGENCY: Rape crisis center; Domestic violence program; Counseling/mental health services
SPONSORING ORGANIZATION: Family Services, Inc
AREAS SERVED: Forsyth, Stokes, Davie, Yadkin
YEARS IN OPERATION: 6
ACCESSIBILITY: Wheelchair accessible
CASES SEXUAL ASSAULT/ABUSE (%): 100
CLIENTS/SERVICES: Sexual assault survivors; Marital rape/sexual abuse survivors; Child victims of sexual abuse; Adult survivors of child sexual abuse; Incest victims/survivors; Prevention program; Community education; Adolescent survivors of sexual abuse; Male survivors of sexual abuse

NORTH DAKOTA

BEULAH

MERCER COUNTY WOMEN'S ACTION AND RESOURCE CENTER
PO Box 940, Beulah, ND 58523
Crisis hotline: **(701) 873-2274, 748-2274 24 hrs**
Information: (701) 873-2274, 748-2274 10am-4pm (Mon-Fri)
Contact: Shari Stroup, Exec Dir
TYPE OF AGENCY: Rape crisis center; Domestic violence program
AREAS SERVED: Mercer, Oliver, Dunn
YEARS IN OPERATION: 9
ACCESSIBILITY: Wheelchair accessible
CASES SEXUAL ASSAULT/ABUSE (%): 35
CLIENTS/SERVICES: Sexual assault survivors; Marital rape/sexual abuse survivors; Adult survivors of child sexual abuse; Incest victims/survivors; Prevention program; Community education; Adolescent survivors of sexual abuse; Male survivors of sexual abuse
REQUIREMENTS: Must be 15 or older

BISMARCK

ABUSED ADULT RESOURCE CENTER
PO Box 167, Bismarck, ND 58502
Crisis hotline: **(800) 472-2911 24 hrs**
Information: (701) 222-8370 9am-5pm
Contact: Diane Zainhofsky, Prog Dir
TYPE OF AGENCY: Domestic violence program
AREAS SERVED: Burleigh, Morton, Emmons, Grant, Kidder, Oliver, Sheridan, Sioux, Logan, Wells
YEARS IN OPERATION: 11
CASES SEXUAL ASSAULT/ABUSE (%): 10
CLIENTS/SERVICES: Marital rape/sexual abuse survivors; Prevention program; Community education

OUR KIDS NEED TO KNOW
2016 N Grandview Ln, Bismarck, ND 58501
Information: (701) 258-6697 8am-5pm
Contact: Ann L Schmitz, Coord
TYPE OF AGENCY: Child sexual abuse prevention program
AREAS SERVED: Burleigh, Morton
YEARS IN OPERATION: 4½
CLIENTS/SERVICES: Prevention program; Community education
SPECIAL PROGRAMS/SERVICES: Prevention for 2nd graders; consisting of two 30-minute segments (film, roleplay, discussion, and coloring page)

RAPE CRISIS CENTER
221 N 5th St, 2nd Fl, Bismarck, ND 58501
Crisis hotline: **(701) 222-8782 24 hrs**
Information: (701) 222-8775 11:30am-3:30pm
Contact: Melanie Bean, Coord
TYPE OF AGENCY: Rape crisis center
AREAS SERVED: Burleigh, Morton
YEARS IN OPERATION: 9
CASES SEXUAL ASSAULT/ABUSE (%): 100
CLIENTS/SERVICES: Sexual assault survivors; Marital rape/sexual abuse survivors; Child victims of sexual abuse; Adult survivors of child sexual abuse; Incest victims/survivors; Prevention program; Community education

WEST CENTRAL HUMAN SERVICE CENTER
600 S 2nd St, Bismarck, ND 58504
Crisis hotline: **(701) 255-3090 24 hrs**
Information: (701) 255-3090
Contact: Mary Lee Steele, ACSW, LCSW, Soc Wkr III
TYPE OF AGENCY: Counseling/mental health services; Child sexual abuse services
AREAS SERVED: Burleigh, Morton, Sioux, Kidder, Oliver, McClean, Mercer, Sheridan, Emmons, Grant
YEARS IN OPERATION: 14
ACCESSIBILITY: Wheelchair accessible
CASES SEXUAL ASSAULT/ABUSE (%): 25
DESCRIPTION: Counseling for sexually abused children; Adults molested as children group; Individual, group, and dyad therapy for child sexual abuse offenders, incest offenders, batterers and adolescent offenders
CLIENTS/SERVICES: Child victims of sexual abuse; Adult survivors of child sexual abuse; Incest victims/survivors; Offender treatment program; Adolescent survivors of sexual abuse; Male survivors of sexual abuse
REQUIREMENTS: Minors must have consent of a parent, although one appointment is allowed without the consent.

DEVILS LAKE

SAFE ALTERNATIVES FOR ABUSED FAMILIES
PO Box 657, Devils Lake, ND 58301
Crisis hotline: **(701) 662-5050 24 hrs**
Information: (701) 662-7378 24 hrs
Contact: Pat Roed, Exec Dir
TYPE OF AGENCY: Rape crisis center; Domestic violence program; Child sexual abuse prevention program
AREAS SERVED: Ramsey, Benson, Eddy and surrounding area
YEARS IN OPERATION: 9
LANGUAGES: German, Sign
ACCESSIBILITY: Signers for the hearing impaired
CASES SEXUAL ASSAULT/ABUSE (%): 100
CLIENTS/SERVICES: Sexual assault survivors; Marital rape/sexual abuse survivors; Adult survivors of child sexual abuse; Incest victims/survivors; Prevention program; Community education
REQUIREMENTS: Must be 18 years of age or older, unless child is with a battered or abused parent

DICKINSON

DOMESTIC VIOLENCE AND RAPE CRISIS CENTER
PO Box 1081, Dickinson, ND 58601
Crisis hotline: **(701) 225-4506 24 hrs**
Information: (701) 225-4506 24 hrs
Contact: Lisa Bjergaard, Volunteer: Public Educ Coord
TYPE OF AGENCY: Rape crisis center; Domestic violence program
AREAS SERVED: Stark, Hettinger, Adams, Bowman, Slope, Golden Valley, Billings, ½ of Dunn
YEARS IN OPERATION: 10
CASES SEXUAL ASSAULT/ABUSE (%): 14
CLIENTS/SERVICES: Sexual assault survivors; Marital rape/sexual abuse survivors; Child victims of sexual abuse; Adult survivors of child sexual abuse; Incest victims/survivors; Prevention program; Community education; Adolescent survivors of sexual abuse; Male survivors of sexual abuse

ELLENDALE

KEDISH HOUSE
PO Box 322, Ellendale, ND 58436
Crisis hotline: **(701) 349-3611 24 hrs**
Information: (701) 349-4729 9:30am-5pm
Contact: Sharron Brady, Proj Dir
TYPE OF AGENCY: Domestic violence safehome network
AREAS SERVED: Dickey, Logan, La Moure, Sargent, McIntosh
CLIENTS/SERVICES: Marital rape/sexual abuse survivors

FARGO

CASS COUNTY VICTIM/WITNESS ASSISTANCE PROGRAM
PO Box 2806, Cass County Courthouse, Fargo, ND 58108
Information: (701) 241-5850 8am-5pm (Mon-Fri)
Contact: Peg Winters, Dir; Shona Dockter, Casewkr
TYPE OF AGENCY: Victim/witness assistance program
SPONSORING ORGANIZATION: Cass County State's Attorney
AREAS SERVED: Cass
YEARS IN OPERATION: 2
LANGUAGES: German
ACCESSIBILITY: Wheelchair accessible
CASES SEXUAL ASSAULT/ABUSE (%): 15
CLIENTS/SERVICES: Sexual assault survivors; Marital rape/sexual abuse survivors; Child victims of sexual abuse; Adult survivors of child sexual abuse; Incest victims/survivors; Com-

CASS COUNTY VICTIM/WITNESS ASSISTANCE PROGRAM *(continued)*

munity education; Adolescent survivors of sexual abuse
SPECIAL PROGRAMS/SERVICES: Volunteers work on public awareness projects during National Victim's Rights Week. Two volunteers do court monitoring to keep the public aware, to be sure that laws are being enforced, to support law enforcement, and to keep this program informed regarding any unusual circumstance surrounding a case.

INCEST AWARENESS PROJECT
Box 8122, Fargo, ND 58109
Crisis hotline: **(701) 235-SEEK 24 hrs**
Information: (701) 281-1728 8am-5pm
Contact: Gwen Rust, Developer and Pres
TYPE OF AGENCY: Volunteer-non profit corp
AREAS SERVED: All of ND, Central Eastern MN
YEARS IN OPERATION: 2
CASES SEXUAL ASSAULT/ABUSE (%): 100
DESCRIPTION: Communication network; Provides therapy, mutual strength and support for adult incest survivors
CLIENTS/SERVICES: Adult survivors of child sexual abuse; Incest victims/survivors; Community education; Male survivors of sexual abuse; Healing; Publications/media
SPECIAL PROGRAMS/SERVICES: Encourages incest victims to break the silence of incest through the newsletter and by speaking to public and private groups. Victims are empowering themselves through self-help groups which are led by trained facilitators. A 16-hour training program for self-help group leaders is sponsored 3 times a year by the project. The organization is run by a volunteer board of directors, 2/3 of which is composed of victims, 1/3 non-victim. Holding 1st annual retreat for victims called "Celebrating Our New Beginning," which includes creative arts, drama, ritual, and other healing methods. Membership in the project brings the member *Breaking the Silence* newsletter 6 times a year.

RAPE AND ABUSE CRISIS CENTER
PO Box 2984, Fargo, ND 58108
Crisis hotline: **(701) 293-7273 24 hrs**
Information: (701) 293-7273 24 hrs
Contact: Ann Heilman, Exec Dir
TYPE OF AGENCY: Rape crisis center; Domestic violence program; Child sexual abuse services; Child sexual abuse prevention program; Child abuse prevention program
AREAS SERVED: Cass, Clay, Wilken, Ottertail, Traill
YEARS IN OPERATION: 10
LANGUAGES: Spanish
ACCESSIBILITY: Wheelchair accessible
CASES SEXUAL ASSAULT/ABUSE (%): 40
DESCRIPTION: Comprehensive services for sexual assault survivors, including support groups for female and male survivors of sexual assault/abuse; Group therapy for batterers
CLIENTS/SERVICES: Sexual assault survivors; Marital rape/sexual abuse survivors; Child victims of sexual abuse; Adult survivors of child sexual abuse; Incest victims/survivors; Prevention program; Community education; Adolescent survivors of sexual abuse; Male survivors of sexual abuse; Developmentally disabled; Preschoolers; Publications/media
SPECIAL PROGRAMS/SERVICES: Sexual abuse prevention materials are available. "Red Flag Green Flag Program" focuses on the prevention of sexual and physical abuse of children and includes a 30-page coloring book (in English and Spanish) and a facilitator's program guide. *T Is for Touching* is a filmstrip/videotape program for children ages 3-6. *The Woodrow Project* is for the developmentally disabled and includes a facilitator's manual and videotape which provide details of the program. *New Beginnings* is a 60-page facilitator's manual for implementing a support group for female adolescent sexual assault survivors. *Annie* is a story booklet, written in the language of a child, about a little girl who is afraid to tell anyone when she is touched by someone in a way she doesn't like. In addition to the materials, a one-day training program is available for schools, social services, crisis centers, police departments, parents, and others interested in preventing child sexual abuse.

THE VILLAGE FAMILY SERVICE CENTER
PO Box 7398, Fargo, ND 58109-7398
Information: (701) 235-6433 8am-5pm
Contact: Mary Ann Donaldson, Clinic Svcs Co-Dir
TYPE OF AGENCY: Counseling/mental health services; Training/research
ACCESSIBILITY: Wheelchair accessible
CASES SEXUAL ASSAULT/ABUSE (%): 33-50
DESCRIPTION: The Incest Treatment Program is one special issues program within this family services organization, offering individual and group therapy for adult survivors of childhood incest.
CLIENTS/SERVICES: Adult survivors of child sexual abuse; Incest victims/survivors
REQUIREMENTS: Sliding scale fee
SPECIAL PROGRAMS/SERVICES: Agency has been actively involved in research regarding adult incest survivors since 1982; also has developed client aid materials, as well as a questionnaire to measure clinical change

VOICES OF FARGO-MOORHEAD
Box 8122, Fargo, ND 58109-8122
Crisis hotline: **(701) 235-SEEK 24 hrs**
Contact: Beth Senn, Board of Dir Pres
TYPE OF AGENCY: Adult survivors services; Self-help groups
AREAS SERVED: Cass, ND; Clay, MN
YEARS IN OPERATION: 4
CASES SEXUAL ASSAULT/ABUSE (%): 100
DESCRIPTION: Self-help groups for adult survivors of childhood sexual abuse/incest, facilitated by trained survivors who are also working on their issues. Also provides speakers to aid in public education
CLIENTS/SERVICES: Adult survivors of child sexual abuse; Incest victims/survivors; Community education
REQUIREMENTS: Adults 18 and older

GRAFTON

DOMESTIC VIOLENCE PROGRAM OF WALSH COUNTY
422 Hill Ave, Grafton, ND 58237
Crisis hotline: **(701) 352-3059 24 hrs 7 days**
Information: (701) 352-0647 9am-5pm
Contact: Bobbi Carson, Dir
TYPE OF AGENCY: Domestic violence program
AREAS SERVED: Walsh
YEARS IN OPERATION: 6
LANGUAGES: Spanish
CASES SEXUAL ASSAULT/ABUSE (%): 5
CLIENTS/SERVICES: Sexual assault survivors; Marital rape/sexual abuse survivors; Child victims of sexual abuse; Incest victims/survivors; Prevention program; Community education

GRAND FORKS

ABUSE AND RAPE CRISIS CENTER
111 S 4th St, Grand Forks, ND 58201
Crisis hotline: **(701) 746-8900 24 hrs**
Information: (701) 746-0405 8:30am-5pm
Contact: Beth Benson, Exec Dir
TYPE OF AGENCY: Rape crisis center; Domestic violence program
YEARS IN OPERATION: 9
ACCESSIBILITY: Wheelchair accessible
CASES SEXUAL ASSAULT/ABUSE (%): 20
DESCRIPTION: Crisis intervention and support groups for survivors of sexual assault and domestic violence; Batterers group available
CLIENTS/SERVICES: Sexual assault survivors; Marital rape/sexual abuse survivors; Community education; Offender treatment program; Adolescent survivors of sexual abuse; Male survivors of sexual abuse
REQUIREMENTS: Child victims who are assaulted by custodial adults must go through Grand Forks County Social Services. Serves minor children, primarily adolescents, who are raped by someone other than a custodial adult.

WOMEN'S CENTER
Box 105, 305 Hamline St, Grand Forks, ND 58201
Information: (701) 777-4300 9am-4:30pm (Mon-Fri)
Contact: Nancy Nienhuis, Coord
TYPE OF AGENCY: College/university-based services; Acquaintance/date rape prevention program
SPONSORING ORGANIZATION: University of North Dakota
AREAS SERVED: Grand Forks
YEARS IN OPERATION: 16
ACCESSIBILITY: Wheelchair accessible
CASES SEXUAL ASSAULT/ABUSE (%): 1
DESCRIPTION: Provides advocacy, education, support for the university and surrounding community; Provides education on sexual assault and sets up individual and group counseling; Two VOICES (Victims of Incest Can Emerge Survivors) groups; Acquaintance rape prevention programs and workshops
CLIENTS/SERVICES: Incest victims/survivors; Community education; Adolescent survivors of sexual abuse

HARWOOD

FREE-TO-GROW COUNSELING CENTER
RR 1, Box 190, Harwood, ND 58042
Information: (701) 281-1728 8am-5pm
Contact: Gwen Rust, Owner/Counselor
TYPE OF AGENCY: Private practice
YEARS IN OPERATION: 2
CASES SEXUAL ASSAULT/ABUSE (%): 75
CLIENTS/SERVICES: Sexual assault survivors; Marital rape/sexual abuse survivors; Child victims of sexual abuse; Adult survivors of child sexual abuse; Incest victims/survivors; Community education; Adolescent survivors of sexual abuse; Male survivors of sexual abuse; Lesbians; Healing
REQUIREMENTS: Ability to pay fee
SPECIAL PROGRAMS/SERVICES: Specialty is incest and its recovery process, with emphasis on healing the inner wounded child using guided imagery. Special emphasis groups: incest and sexuality; incest and spirituality; secondary victims therapy group; mothers and daughters therapy group; incest therapy for lesbians

JAMESTOWN

SAFE SHELTER
PO Box 1934, Jamestown, ND 58402
Crisis hotline: **(701) 251-2300 24 hrs**
Information: (701) 251-2300 9am-5pm (Mon-Fri)
Contact: Lynne Tally, Dir
TYPE OF AGENCY: Rape crisis center; Domestic violence program
AREAS SERVED: Stutsman and surrounding area
YEARS IN OPERATION: 7
CASES SEXUAL ASSAULT/ABUSE (%): 25
CLIENTS/SERVICES: Sexual assault survivors; Marital rape/sexual abuse survivors; Adult survivors of child sexual abuse; Incest victims/survivors; Prevention program; Community education; Adolescent survivors of sexual abuse; Male survivors of sexual abuse

LISBON

WOMEN'S ADVOCACY NETWORK
Box 919, Lisbon, ND 58054
Crisis hotline: **(701) 683-5097 24 hrs**
Information: (701) 683-5097 24 hrs
Contact: Kris Carlson, Volunteer Dir
TYPE OF AGENCY: Rape crisis center; Domestic violence program
AREAS SERVED: Ransom
CASES SEXUAL ASSAULT/ABUSE (%): 20
CLIENTS/SERVICES: Sexual assault survivors; Marital rape/sexual abuse survivors; Prevention program; Community education

MEKINOCK

TURTLE TRAIL COUNSELING CENTER
PO Box 43, Mekinock, ND 58258
Crisis hotline: **(701) 594-4886 6am-Midnight**
Information: (701) 594-4886 8am-5pm
Contact: Sandra J Parsons, Owner
TYPE OF AGENCY: Counseling/mental health services
AREAS SERVED: Grand Forks, NE North Dakota; NW Minnesota
YEARS IN OPERATION: 1
LANGUAGES: Spanish
CASES SEXUAL ASSAULT/ABUSE (%): 25-30
DESCRIPTION: Counseling services for women and concerning women's issues. Comprehensive services for adult and adolescent sexual assault survivors and adult survivors of child sexual abuse. Also provides support groups for male survivors and treatment for batterers. Board member of Directors of the Incest Awareness Project for North Dakota
CLIENTS/SERVICES: Sexual assault survivors; Marital rape/sexual abuse survivors; Adult survivors of child sexual abuse; Incest victims/survivors; Community education; Adolescent survivors of sexual abuse; Male survivors of sexual abuse
SPECIAL PROGRAMS/SERVICES: Sunflower, 40-acre farm and rural educational/cultural center for women, is available as a healing space for survivors. Workshops, retreats and celebrations are held at Sunflower

MINOT

GATEWAYS
315 S Main St, No 307-A, Minot, ND 58701
Information: (701) 838-4606 9am-6pm
Contact: Jane Hull, Therapist
TYPE OF AGENCY: Private practice
AREAS SERVED: Ward
YEARS IN OPERATION: 2
ACCESSIBILITY: Wheelchair accessible
CASES SEXUAL ASSAULT/ABUSE (%): 50
CLIENTS/SERVICES: Sexual assault survivors; Marital rape/sexual abuse survivors; Adult survivors of child sexual abuse; Incest victims/survivors; Adolescent survivors of sexual abuse; Male survivors of sexual abuse; Healing
REQUIREMENTS: Client must be 14 years or older.
SPECIAL PROGRAMS/SERVICES: Treatment for post-traumatic stress symptoms; Guided imagery and group experiences for healing of memories; Anger work, memory retrieval; Gestalt; Self-esteem and boundary work; Awareness and education about addiction issues; Addiction counseling.

WOMEN'S ACTION PROGRAM—DOMESTIC VIOLENCE CRISIS CENTER
Box 881, Minot, ND 58702
Crisis hotline: **(701) 857-2000 24 hrs**
Information: (701) 852-2258 9am-5pm
Contact: Linda K Grotelueschen, Exec Dir
TYPE OF AGENCY: Rape crisis center; Domestic violence program
AREAS SERVED: Ward, McHenry, Renville, Pierce, Bottineau
YEARS IN OPERATION: 10
CASES SEXUAL ASSAULT/ABUSE (%): 10
CLIENTS/SERVICES: Sexual assault survivors; Marital rape/sexual abuse survivors; Adult survivors of child sexual abuse; Prevention program; Community education

ROLLA

PARENTS UNITED, TURTLE MOUNTAIN COUNTIES CHAPTER
Box 519, Rolla, ND 58367
Crisis hotline: **(701) 477-5623 4:30pm-8am**
Information: (701) 477-3141 8am-4:30pm
Contact: Marlys Hiatt, Licensed Soc Wkr III
TYPE OF AGENCY: Child sexual abuse services
SPONSORING ORGANIZATION: Rolette County Social Services
AREAS SERVED: Rolette
YEARS IN OPERATION: 6
ACCESSIBILITY: Wheelchair accessible
CLIENTS/SERVICES: Child victims of sexual abuse; Adult survivors of child sexual abuse; Incest victims/survivors; Prevention program; Community education; Offender treatment program

VALLEY CITY

ABUSED PERSONS OUTREACH CENTER
Box 508, Valley City, ND 58072
Crisis hotline: **(701) 845-0072 24 hrs**
Information: (701) 845-0078 10am-4pm (Mon-Fri)
Contact: Zita Braun, Prog Dir
TYPE OF AGENCY: Rape crisis center; Domestic violence program
AREAS SERVED: Barnes County area
YEARS IN OPERATION: 1½
LANGUAGES: Spanish, German, French, Czech, Vietnamese, Interpreters available; Sign
ACCESSIBILITY: Signers for the hearing impaired
CASES SEXUAL ASSAULT/ABUSE (%): 10
CLIENTS/SERVICES: Sexual assault survivors; Marital rape/sexual abuse survivors; Adult survivors of child sexual abuse; Community education; Adolescent survivors of sexual abuse; Male survivors of sexual abuse
REQUIREMENTS: Minor children are referred to Social Services and to the State Attorney's Office

WILLISTON

FAMILY CRISIS SHELTER
PO Box 1893, Williston, ND 58801
Crisis hotline: **(701) 572-9111 24 hrs**
Information: (701) 572-0757 8am-5pm (Mon-Fri)
Contact: Laurine Baxter, Dir
TYPE OF AGENCY: Rape crisis center; Domestic violence program
AREAS SERVED: Williams, McKenzie, Divide
YEARS IN OPERATION: 9
CASES SEXUAL ASSAULT/ABUSE (%): 99
CLIENTS/SERVICES: Sexual assault survivors; Marital rape/sexual abuse survivors; Adult survivors of child sexual abuse; Incest victims/survivors; Prevention program; Community education; Adolescent survivors of sexual abuse; Male survivors of sexual abuse

WILLIAMS COUNTY VICTIM/WITNESS ASSISTANCE PROGRAM
PO Box 2047, Williston, ND 58802-2047
Information: (701) 572-6373, ext 30 9am-5pm
Contact: Vikki Lorenz, Victim's Advocate
TYPE OF AGENCY: Victim/witness assistance program
SPONSORING ORGANIZATION: Williams County State's Attorney's Office
AREAS SERVED: Williams
YEARS IN OPERATION: 2
ACCESSIBILITY: Wheelchair accessible
CASES SEXUAL ASSAULT/ABUSE (%): 15
CLIENTS/SERVICES: Sexual assault survivors; Marital rape/sexual abuse survivors; Child victims of sexual abuse; Adult survivors of child sexual abuse; Incest victims/survivors; Community education; Adolescent survivors of sexual abuse; Male survivors of sexual abuse

OHIO

AKRON

SUMMIT COUNTY PSYCHOLOGICAL ASSOCIATES
277 S Broadway, Akron, OH 44308
Information: (216) 535-8181 24 hrs
Contact: Dr James A Orlando, Clinical Psychologist/Dir
TYPE OF AGENCY: Child sexual abuse services; Child sexual abuse prevention program; Private practice
AREAS SERVED: Summit, Portage, Geauga, Medina
YEARS IN OPERATION: 4
ACCESSIBILITY: Wheelchair accessible
CASES SEXUAL ASSAULT/ABUSE (%): 50
DESCRIPTION: Specialization includes, but is not limited to, sexual assault/abuse survivors and offenders (rapists, child sexual abuse/incest offenders, batterers)
CLIENTS/SERVICES: Sexual assault survivors; Marital rape/sexual abuse survivors; Child victims of sexual abuse; Adult survivors of child sexual abuse; Incest victims/survivors; Offender treatment program; Adolescent survivors of sexual abuse; Male survivors of sexual abuse

YWCA RAPE CRISIS CENTER
146 S High St, Akron, OH 44308
Crisis hotline: **(216) 434-7273, (800) 433-7273 24 hrs**
Information: (216) 253-6131 9am-5pm (Mon-Fri)
Contact: Terri Heckman, Dir
TYPE OF AGENCY: Rape crisis center; Acquaintance/date rape prevention program
SPONSORING ORGANIZATION: YWCA
AREAS SERVED: Summit, Medina, Portage
YEARS IN OPERATION: 18
ACCESSIBILITY: Wheelchair accessible; Telecommunications for the hearing impaired (TTY, TDY, etc.); Signers for the hearing impaired
CASES SEXUAL ASSAULT/ABUSE (%): 100
DESCRIPTION: Provides 24-hour crisis intervention, advocacy, prevention education for victims of sexual assault and incest; Date rape prevention program in local high schools; Self-defense classes
CLIENTS/SERVICES: Sexual assault survivors; Marital rape/sexual abuse survivors; Adult survivors of child sexual abuse; Incest victims/survivors; Prevention program; Community education; Adolescent survivors of sexual abuse; Male survivors of sexual abuse
REQUIREMENTS: Clients younger than 16 must have parental permission to receive counseling
SPECIAL PROGRAMS/SERVICES: This is the only 1-800 toll-free hotline serving all of the US; Offers 24-hour crisis intervention and nationwide referrals

ASHTABULA

CONTACT ASHTABULA COUNTY, INC
Box 674, Ashtabula, OH 44004
Crisis hotline: **(216) 998-2607 24 hrs daily**
Information: (216) 998-2609 9am-4pm
TYPE OF AGENCY: Counseling/mental health services; Telephone crisis hotline; Information and referral
AREAS SERVED: Ashtabula
YEARS IN OPERATION: 16
DESCRIPTION: Telephone helpline for crisis counseling, information and referral, suicide prevention, and general support
CLIENTS/SERVICES: Sexual assault survivors; Adult survivors of child sexual abuse; Incest victims/survivors

RAPE CRISIS SERVICES OF HOMESAFE
PO Box 702, Ashtabula, OH 44004
Crisis hotline: **(216) 992-2727 24 hrs daily**
Information: (216) 992-2727 8am-4:30pm (Mon-Fri)
Contact: Cindy Herner, Case Mgr
TYPE OF AGENCY: Rape crisis center; Domestic violence program
SPONSORING ORGANIZATION: Homesafe
AREAS SERVED: Ashtabula
YEARS IN OPERATION: 3½
LANGUAGES: Spanish
CASES SEXUAL ASSAULT/ABUSE (%): 100
CLIENTS/SERVICES: Sexual assault survivors; Marital rape/sexual abuse survivors; Adult survivors of child sexual abuse; Incest victims/survivors; Prevention program; Community education; Adolescent survivors of sexual abuse
REQUIREMENTS: Survivors must request services

ATHENS

ATHENS COUNTY PROSECUTOR'S VICTIM ASSISTANCE PROGRAM
Courthouse, Athens, OH 45701
Information: (614) 592-3208 8am-4pm (Mon-Fri)
Contact: Mura R Goldfarb, Dir
TYPE OF AGENCY: Victim/witness assistance program; Child sexual abuse services
AREAS SERVED: Athens
YEARS IN OPERATION: 1½
ACCESSIBILITY: Wheelchair accessible; Signers for the hearing impaired (with prior notice)
CLIENTS/SERVICES: Sexual assault survivors; Marital rape/sexual abuse survivors; Child victims of sexual abuse; Adult survivors of child sexual abuse; Incest victims/survivors; Community education; Adolescent survivors of sexual abuse; Male survivors of sexual abuse
SPECIAL PROGRAMS/SERVICES: Presently applying for funding for a multidisciplinary approach to dealing with child sexual abuse; Hopes to provide training for prosecutors, judges, police, foster parents, and guardians ad litem and to set up a therapeutic foster care network, as well as to attempt to humanize the court process for children

CARELINE SURVIVOR ADVOCACY
28 W Stimson Ave, Athens, OH 45701
Crisis hotline: **(614) 593-3344 24 hrs**
Information: (614) 592-3091 8am-5pm (Mon, Wed, Fri); 8am-8pm (Tues, Thurs)
Contact: Mark Sutton, Hotline Svcs Dir; Lesli Johnson, Outpatient Svcs Dir, Sexual Abuse Treatment Team Coord; Cheryl Cesta, Survivor Advocates, Rape Prevention Education
TYPE OF AGENCY: Rape crisis center; Counseling/mental health services; Child sexual abuse prevention program; Counseling/mental health services; Telephone crisis hotline; Information and referral
SPONSORING ORGANIZATION: Tri-County Mental Health and Counseling Services, Inc
AREAS SERVED: Athens, Hocking, Vinton
YEARS IN OPERATION: 18
ACCESSIBILITY: Wheelchair accessible
CASES SEXUAL ASSAULT/ABUSE (%): Survivor Advocates 100, Clinic population 50
DESCRIPTION: Programs include: Sexual Assault and Survivor Advocacy Program and the Child Assault Prevention Project; Rape crisis program; Treatment for survivors of child sexual abuse and their families; Treatment for child sexual abuse and incest offenders
CLIENTS/SERVICES: Sexual assault survivors; Marital rape/sexual abuse survivors; Child victims of sexual abuse; Adult survivors of child sexual abuse; Incest victims/survivors; Prevention program; Community education; Adolescent survivors of sexual abuse; Male survivors of sexual abuse; Publications/media
SPECIAL PROGRAMS/SERVICES: Media program: *How Will I Tell*, which follows a rape survivor through hospital and police proceedings and describes the Sexual Assault Survivor Advocacy Program.

CHILD SEXUAL ABUSE TREATMENT PROGRAM (CSATP)
PO Box 1046, Athens, OH 45701
Information: (614) 592-3061 8:30am-4:30pm
Contact: Janey S Coon, Intake Supv
TYPE OF AGENCY: Victim/witness assistance program; Counseling/mental health services; Child sexual abuse services; Interagency network
SPONSORING ORGANIZATION: Athens County Children Services and Tri-County Mental Health and Counseling
AREAS SERVED: Athens
YEARS IN OPERATION: 5
ACCESSIBILITY: Wheelchair accessible
CASES SEXUAL ASSAULT/ABUSE (%): 100
DESCRIPTION: Athens County Children Services conducts investigations of child sexual assault cases. As a result of an increasing number of

CHILD SEXUAL ABUSE TREATMENT PROGRAM (CSATP) *(continued)*

cases, CSATP was formed to help deal with victims and families. Team approach (ACCS, Tri-County Mental Health and Counseling and court system) to counseling for sexually abused children and their families and for adolescent and adult sex offenders
CLIENTS/SERVICES: Child victims of sexual abuse; Adult survivors of child sexual abuse; Incest victims/survivors; Prevention program; Community education; Offender treatment program; Adolescent survivors of sexual abuse; Male survivors of sexual abuse

MY SISTER'S PLACE
PO Box 1158, Athens, OH 45701
Crisis hotline: **(614) 593-3402, (800) 443-3402 24 hrs daily**
Information: (614) 594-8337
TYPE OF AGENCY: Domestic violence program
AREAS SERVED: Athens, Hocking, Vinton
YEARS IN OPERATION: 10
CLIENTS/SERVICES: Marital rape/sexual abuse survivors; Child victims of sexual abuse; Adult survivors of child sexual abuse; Incest victims/survivors; Adolescent survivors of sexual abuse

BATAVIA

CLERMONT COUNSELING CENTER
2291 Bauer Rd, Batavia, OH 45103
Crisis hotline: **(513) 724-7900 24 hrs**
Information: (513) 732-7370 8:30am-6pm
Contact: Linda L Loy, Child Abuse Prevention Prog Dir
TYPE OF AGENCY: Counseling/mental health services; Child sexual abuse services; Child sexual abuse prevention program; Interagency network
AREAS SERVED: Clermont
YEARS IN OPERATION: 6
ACCESSIBILITY: Wheelchair accessible; Telecommunications for the hearing impaired (TTY, TDY, etc.)
CASES SEXUAL ASSAULT/ABUSE (%): 40
DESCRIPTION: Provides comprehensive county-wide treatment services for families, children and offenders; Public awareness of treatment/prevention services and programs
CLIENTS/SERVICES: Sexual assault survivors; Marital rape/sexual abuse survivors; Child victims of sexual abuse; Adult survivors of child sexual abuse; Incest victims/survivors; Prevention program; Community education; Offender treatment program; Adolescent survivors of sexual abuse; Male survivors of sexual abuse
REQUIREMENTS: Parent program requires that if court-referred, parents sign legal agreement to complete 16-week program with release of information to court and Children's Protective Services
SPECIAL PROGRAMS/SERVICES: Incest Treatment Team: interagency treatment team meets monthly to discuss clinical issues/treatment for children and families. Sex Abuse Task Force: Interagency team from all county agencies who meet quarterly to plan training, community liaisons

CLERMONT COUNTY PROSECUTOR'S OFFICE—VICTIM/WITNESS ASSISTANCE PROGRAM
285 Main St, Batavia, OH 45103
Crisis hotline: **(513) 724-7900 24 hrs**
Information: (513) 732-7112 8:30am-5pm
Contact: James A Shriver, Asst Prosecutor/Prog Dir
TYPE OF AGENCY: Victim/witness assistance program
AREAS SERVED: Clermont
YEARS IN OPERATION: 1
ACCESSIBILITY: Wheelchair accessible

CASES SEXUAL ASSAULT/ABUSE (%): 30
CLIENTS/SERVICES: Sexual assault survivors; Child victims of sexual abuse; Incest victims/survivors; Adolescent survivors of sexual abuse; Male survivors of sexual abuse
REQUIREMENTS: Crime must have occurred in Clermont County; Client must report crime to law enforcement; Case does not have to be prosecuted for victim to receive services

CLERMONT COUNTY YOUTH SERVICES COORDINATING COUNCIL
2085-A Front Wheel Dr, Batavia, OH 45103
Information: (513) 724-1150 9am-5pm (Tue, Wed, Thu)
Contact: Karen E Long, Dir
TYPE OF AGENCY: Counseling/mental health services; Child sexual abuse prevention program; Adolescent program; Interagency network
AREAS SERVED: Clermont
YEARS IN OPERATION: 7
ACCESSIBILITY: Wheelchair accessible
DESCRIPTION: Networks with youth-serving agencies to provide services for sexually abused children and also provides training on sexual abuse and coordinates prevention programs for the schools
CLIENTS/SERVICES: Prevention program; Community education
REQUIREMENTS: Ages birth to 18 years

CANTON

CHILD AND FAMILY ADVOCACY CENTER
217 2nd St, 402 Bliss Tower, Canton, OH 44702
Crisis hotline: **(216) 452-6000 24 hrs**
Information: (216) 456-8555
Contact: Sue Ellyn Haas, MA, Coord
TYPE OF AGENCY: Child sexual abuse services
SPONSORING ORGANIZATION: Crisis Intervention Center/Child and Adolescent Service Center
AREAS SERVED: Stark
YEARS IN OPERATION: 1½
ACCESSIBILITY: Wheelchair accessible
CASES SEXUAL ASSAULT/ABUSE (%): 100
DESCRIPTION: Provides individual and group therapy for child and adolescent survivors of sexual abuse, including family therapy
CLIENTS/SERVICES: Child victims of sexual abuse; Incest victims/survivors; Community education; Adolescent survivors of sexual abuse
REQUIREMENTS: Must be 18 or younger

RAPE CRISIS
618 2nd St NW, Canton, OH 44703
Crisis hotline: **(216) 452-1111 24 hrs**
Information: (216) 453-0146 8:30am-4:30pm (Mon-Fri)
Contact: Kathleen Trissel, Rape Crisis Dir
TYPE OF AGENCY: Rape crisis center; Counseling/mental health services
SPONSORING ORGANIZATION: American Red Cross
AREAS SERVED: Stark
YEARS IN OPERATION: 13
ACCESSIBILITY: Wheelchair accessible
CLIENTS/SERVICES: Sexual assault survivors; Marital rape/sexual abuse survivors; Child victims of sexual abuse; Adult survivors of child sexual abuse; Incest victims/survivors; Prevention program; Community education; Adolescent survivors of sexual abuse; Male survivors of sexual abuse

CHARDON

RAVENWOOD CENTER
12557 Ravenwood Dr, Chardon, OH 44024
Crisis hotline: **(216) 564-9555 24 hrs**
Information: (216) 285-3568 9am-9pm (Mon-Thu); 9am-5pm (Fri)
Contact: Vicki Clark, Sexual Abuse Treatment Prog Coord
TYPE OF AGENCY: Counseling/mental health services; Child sexual abuse services

SPONSORING ORGANIZATION: Geauga County Department of Human Services
AREAS SERVED: Geauga
YEARS IN OPERATION: 2
ACCESSIBILITY: Wheelchair accessible; Telecommunications for the hearing impaired (TTY, TDY, etc.)
CLIENTS/SERVICES: Sexual assault survivors; Child victims of sexual abuse; Adult survivors of child sexual abuse; Incest victims/survivors; Prevention program; Community education; Offender treatment program; Adolescent survivors of sexual abuse; Male survivors of sexual abuse
REQUIREMENTS: The offender must be held legally responsible
SPECIAL PROGRAMS/SERVICES: Full-time investigator deals with reports of intrafamily child sexual abuse and works with an investigative social worker

VICTIM/WITNESS ASSISTANCE PROGRAM
231 Main St, Courthouse Annex, Chardon, OH 44024
Crisis hotline: **(216) 564-9555 24 hrs**
Information: (216) 285-2222 8am-4:30pm
Contact: Rosemary Galayda, Prog Dir
TYPE OF AGENCY: Victim/witness assistance program
AREAS SERVED: Geauga
YEARS IN OPERATION: 3
ACCESSIBILITY: Wheelchair accessible
CASES SEXUAL ASSAULT/ABUSE (%): 43
CLIENTS/SERVICES: Sexual assault survivors; Marital rape/sexual abuse survivors; Child victims of sexual abuse; Adult survivors of child sexual abuse; Incest victims/survivors; Adolescent survivors of sexual abuse

CHILLICOTHE

SCIOTO PAINT VALLEY MENTAL HEALTH CENTER
4449 State Rte 159, Chillicothe, OH 45601
Crisis hotline: **(614) 773-4357 24 hrs daily**
Information: (614) 775-1260 8am-5pm
TYPE OF AGENCY: Counseling/mental health services
AREAS SERVED: Ross, Pickaway, Pike, Highland, Fayette
YEARS IN OPERATION: 20
LANGUAGES: Vietnamese, French, Spanish interpreters available
ACCESSIBILITY: Wheelchair accessible; Telecommunications for the hearing impaired (TTY, TDY, etc.); Signers for the hearing impaired
DESCRIPTION: Provides individual and group counseling for victims and their families; Individual and group therapy for batterers
CLIENTS/SERVICES: Sexual assault survivors; Marital rape/sexual abuse survivors; Child victims of sexual abuse; Adult survivors of child sexual abuse; Incest victims/survivors; Adolescent survivors of sexual abuse; Male survivors of sexual abuse

CINCINNATI

A GROWING PLACE
9656 Sycamore Trace Ct, Cincinnati, OH 45242
Information: (513) 984-3907 9am-9pm
Contact: Harold Nordeman, Gail Nordeman, Owners/Dirs
TYPE OF AGENCY: Child sexual abuse services; Private practice; Parenting programs
AREAS SERVED: Hamilton, Clermont
YEARS IN OPERATION: 15
CASES SEXUAL ASSAULT/ABUSE (%): 45
DESCRIPTION: An educational counseling and consulting center based on the philosophy that people are important and need healthy individual growth, responsibility and high self-esteem. Offers client-oriented programs; Consultation with industry and institutions desiring communication programs and seminars;

A GROWING PLACE (continued)
Training of professionals and/or paraprofessionals; Problem-solving sessions for individuals, families and groups
CLIENTS/SERVICES: Sexual assault survivors; Marital rape/sexual abuse survivors; Child victims of sexual abuse; Adult survivors of child sexual abuse; Incest victims/survivors; Prevention program; Community education; Adolescent survivors of sexual abuse; Male survivors of sexual abuse
SPECIAL PROGRAMS/SERVICES: Class on "Self-Esteem: A Family Affair" for building self-esteem while learning parenting skills. Content includes communication skills, child development, problem solving, affirmations, and personality theory based on transactional analysis. Also conducts "Intensive Parenting Experience" (1-, 2-, or 3-day weekends) to facilitate the growth of people who want to improve or replace an unwanted parenting experience or create a primary parenting experience which was not available due to the absence of one parent. Individuals go through a series of developmental stages from conception to adulthood; these stages are recycled throughout life, providing an opportunity for individuals to claim an increase in their own personal power

UNIVERSITY OF CINCINNATI—OFFICE OF WOMEN'S PROGRAMS AND SERVICES
350 Tangeman University Center, ML 179, Cincinnati, OH 45221
Information: (513) 475-4401 8am-5pm
Contact: Nancy Spence, Dir
TYPE OF AGENCY: College/university-based services; Rape prevention program; Acquaintance/date rape prevention program
SPONSORING ORGANIZATION: University of Cincinnati
DESCRIPTION: Crisis counseling and support groups for female and male survivors, as well as acquaintance/date rape prevention programs and a resource library
CLIENTS/SERVICES: Sexual assault survivors; Prevention program; Community education; Adolescent survivors of sexual abuse; Male survivors of sexual abuse; Publications/media
REQUIREMENTS: Serves students, faculty, and staff members of the university
SPECIAL PROGRAMS/SERVICES: SOAR (Students Organize Against Rape) is a university student group of men and women which, after an 8-10 week training, gives 2-hour prevention programs on date rape for student organizations and groups; Sound/slide shows, each about 20 minutes long: *No, Please, No: Acquaintance and Date Rape* examines how attitudes and behaviors in male-female interactions contribute to date rape; *I'm Black and Blue: Rape from Image to Reality*—through exploration of advertising, album and book-cover design, popular music, magazines, films, comics, videos, and pornography, a connection is made between the rape as a crime of aggression and ubiquitous images of anti-female violence; *Increasing Your Chances: Tips and Techniques for Rape Prevention*, practical, easy-to-remember advice and simple techniques for preventing rape

VICTIM SERVICES
1000 Main St, Courthouse Rm 220, Cincinnati, OH 45202
Information: (513) 632-8794 8am-4pm
Contact: Nancy Rankin, Dir
TYPE OF AGENCY: Victim/witness assistance program
SPONSORING ORGANIZATION: Hamilton County Probation (Cincinnati)
AREAS SERVED: Hamilton
YEARS IN OPERATION: 5
ACCESSIBILITY: Wheelchair accessible
CASES SEXUAL ASSAULT/ABUSE (%): 33
CLIENTS/SERVICES: Sexual assault survivors; Marital rape/sexual abuse survivors; Child victims of sexual abuse; Incest victims/survivors

VICTIM'S RIGHTS ADVOCACY
PO Box 30128, Cincinnati, OH 45230
Information: (513) 232-2162
Contact: Katie Williams Murphy, Jacqueline G Ferneding, Dirs
TYPE OF AGENCY: Victim/witness assistance program
AREAS SERVED: Hamilton, Statewide legislative advocacy
YEARS IN OPERATION: ½
CASES SEXUAL ASSAULT/ABUSE (%): 100
DESCRIPTION: VRA advocates for changes in Ohio laws affecting victims of sexual assault specifically and victims of crime generally, including a constitutional amendment to enumerate the rights of victims. Also provides advocacy in the criminal justice system for individual victims of sexual assault
CLIENTS/SERVICES: Sexual assault survivors; Marital rape/sexual abuse survivors; Adult survivors of child sexual abuse; Community education

WOMEN HELPING WOMEN, INC
216 E 9th St, Cincinnati, OH 45202
Crisis hotline: **(513) 381-5610 24 hrs**
Information: (513) 381-6003 7am-6pm
Contact: Helen Magers, Exec Dir
TYPE OF AGENCY: Rape crisis center; Domestic violence program; Child sexual abuse services; Child sexual abuse prevention program
AREAS SERVED: Hamilton
YEARS IN OPERATION: 15
ACCESSIBILITY: Wheelchair accessible
CASES SEXUAL ASSAULT/ABUSE (%): 65
CLIENTS/SERVICES: Sexual assault survivors; Marital rape/sexual abuse survivors; Child victims of sexual abuse; Adult survivors of child sexual abuse; Incest victims/survivors; Prevention program; Community education; Adolescent survivors of sexual abuse; Male survivors of sexual abuse

CLEVELAND

CLEVELAND RAPE CRISIS CENTER
3101 Euclid Ave, Ste 711, Cleveland, OH 44115
Crisis hotline: **(216) 391-3912 24 hrs**
Information: (216) 391-3914 8:30am-5pm (Mon-Fri)
Contact: Cindy Lee, Exec Dir
TYPE OF AGENCY: Rape crisis center; Child sexual abuse prevention program
AREAS SERVED: Cuyahoga
YEARS IN OPERATION: 15
ACCESSIBILITY: Wheelchair accessible
CASES SEXUAL ASSAULT/ABUSE (%): 90-95
CLIENTS/SERVICES: Sexual assault survivors; Marital rape/sexual abuse survivors; Adult survivors of child sexual abuse; Incest victims/survivors; Prevention program; Community education; Adolescent survivors of sexual abuse; Male survivors of sexual abuse
REQUIREMENTS: Children must be 12 or older.

TEMPLUM HOUSE
PO Box 5466, Cleveland, OH 44101
Crisis hotline: **(216) 631-2275 24 hrs**
Information: (216) 631-0211 24 hrs
Contact: Sonia Ferencik, Children's Prog Coord; Cathleen Alexander, Assoc Dir
TYPE OF AGENCY: Domestic violence program; Child sexual abuse prevention program; Shelter; Adolescent program
SPONSORING ORGANIZATION: Cleveland Women, Inc
YEARS IN OPERATION: 10
LANGUAGES: Language bank available
ACCESSIBILITY: Signers for the hearing impaired
CASES SEXUAL ASSAULT/ABUSE (%): 65-70
DESCRIPTION: Provides crisis shelter for battered and homeless women and children and support groups for women and children who are survivors of sexual assault and physical violence
CLIENTS/SERVICES: Sexual assault survivors; Marital rape/sexual abuse survivors; Child victims of sexual abuse; Adult survivors of child sexual abuse; Incest victims/survivors; Prevention program; Community education; Adolescent survivors of sexual abuse; Male survivors of sexual abuse
SPECIAL PROGRAMS/SERVICES: "What's Love Got To Do With It?" a performance for teens, by a teen acting troupe, explores violence in family, dating, and peer relationships

WESTSIDE ADOLESCENT SERVICE NETWORK
3000 Bridge Ave, Cleveland, OH 44108
Information: (216) 771-7297 9am-3pm
Contact: Secundra Beasley, Youth Outreach Wkr
TYPE OF AGENCY: Child sexual abuse prevention program; Adolescent program
AREAS SERVED: Cuyahoga
YEARS IN OPERATION: 5
CASES SEXUAL ASSAULT/ABUSE (%): 35
DESCRIPTION: Teens Speak Out! Talks to teens (12-18) about child abuse, incest, sexual assault, and neglect. The goal is two-fold: Stop teens from further abuse occurring in their own lives and ability to help friends in abusive situations
CLIENTS/SERVICES: Prevention program; Community education
REQUIREMENTS: Ages 12-18

WITNESS/VICTIM CENTER OF CUYAHOGA COUNTY
1215 W 3rd St, Cleveland, OH 44113
Information: (216) 443-7345 8:30am-4:30pm
Contact: Carla Kole, Child Sexual Assault Counselor
TYPE OF AGENCY: Victim/witness assistance program
AREAS SERVED: Cuyahoga
YEARS IN OPERATION: 13
LANGUAGES: Language bank available
ACCESSIBILITY: Wheelchair accessible; Signers for the hearing impaired
DESCRIPTION: Provides criminal justice advocacy and comprehensive victim services, including elder abuse therapist on staff, treatment program for batterers, individual/group counseling for battered women
CLIENTS/SERVICES: Sexual assault survivors; Marital rape/sexual abuse survivors; Child victims of sexual abuse; Adult survivors of child sexual abuse; Incest victims/survivors; Community education; Adolescent survivors of sexual abuse; Male survivors of sexual abuse; Elderly
SPECIAL PROGRAMS/SERVICES: Peer volunteer program links a person of the same age who was previously a crime victim and has been through the criminal justice system with the victim

WOMEN TOGETHER
PO Box 03541, Cleveland, OH 44103
Crisis hotline: **(216) 391-4357 24 hrs**
Information: (216) 431-6267 9am-5pm (Mon-Fri)
Contact: Patricia Gillette, Exec Dir
TYPE OF AGENCY: Domestic violence program
AREAS SERVED: Cuyahoga
YEARS IN OPERATION: 12
LANGUAGES: Spanish
ACCESSIBILITY: Wheelchair accessible
CLIENTS/SERVICES: Marital rape/sexual abuse survivors

COLUMBUS

AFFIRMATIONS: A CENTER FOR PSYCHOTHERAPY AND GROWTH
918 S Front St, Columbus, OH 43206
Information: (614) 445-8277 24 hrs
Contact: Howard Fradkin, PhD, Psychologist; Kate Kitchen, LSW, MSW, Clinical Soc Wkr
TYPE OF AGENCY: Counseling/mental health services; Private practice; Men's program
AREAS SERVED: Primarily Franklin
YEARS IN OPERATION: 4
CASES SEXUAL ASSAULT/ABUSE (%): 50
DESCRIPTION: Therapy groups and specialization in working with gay and bisexual men
CLIENTS/SERVICES: Sexual assault survivors; Marital rape/sexual abuse survivors; Child victims of sexual abuse; Adult survivors of child sexual abuse; Incest victims/survivors; Offender treatment program; Adolescent survivors of sexual abuse; Male survivors of sexual abuse; Gay men; Bisexuals
REQUIREMENTS: Ability to pay; Accept insurance and Medicaid; Clients are primarily adults

ALPATHA HEALING CENTER
815 N High St, Ste 8, Columbus, OH 43215
Crisis hotline: **(614) 294-7979 phone machine 10am-7pm**
Information: (614) 294-7979 10am-7pm, or by appointment
Contact: Lana Wall, MSW
TYPE OF AGENCY: Counseling/mental health services; Training/research
AREAS SERVED: Franklin and surrounding areas
YEARS IN OPERATION: 1
ACCESSIBILITY: Wheelchair accessible; Telecommunications for the hearing impaired (TTY, TDY, etc.); Signers for the hearing impaired
DESCRIPTION: Couple, group, and individual therapy; Issues of focus include substance abuse recovery, victimization recovery—adult survivors of childhood physical, sexual, and emotional abuse, rape, domestic violence, and other dysfunctional family dynamics; Special emphasis on gay and lesbian communities; Professional training, workshops, and seminars available
CLIENTS/SERVICES: Sexual assault survivors; Marital rape/sexual abuse survivors; Adult survivors of child sexual abuse; Incest victims/survivors; Prevention program; Community education; Offender treatment program; Male survivors of sexual abuse; Lesbians; Gay men; Healing
SPECIAL PROGRAMS/SERVICES: Massage used as a form of healing for sexual assault survivors

CHILD ABUSE PROGRAM
700 Children's Dr, Columbus, OH 43205
Crisis hotline: **(800) 282-KIDS 24 hrs**
Information: (614) 461-2504 8am-5pm (Mon-Fri)
Contact: Chas Johnson, MD, Dir
TYPE OF AGENCY: Hospital/medical center; Child sexual abuse services; Child abuse services; Training/research
SPONSORING ORGANIZATION: Children's Hospital
AREAS SERVED: Franklin and surrounding area
YEARS IN OPERATION: 10
LANGUAGES: Translators available
ACCESSIBILITY: Wheelchair accessible; Signers for the hearing impaired
CASES SEXUAL ASSAULT/ABUSE (%): 70
DESCRIPTION: Multidisciplinary child abuse team of 14 professionals provides medical, nursing, and psychosocial assessments; comprehensive medical treatment and follow-up; and psychological evaluation
CLIENTS/SERVICES: Child victims of sexual abuse; Incest victims/survivors; Prevention program; Community education; Adolescent survivors of sexual abuse; Publications/media
REQUIREMENTS: Children ages birth to 18 years

SPECIAL PROGRAMS/SERVICES: One-stop interviews; Interdisciplinary university-based education; Medical student research training; Child development fellow training; Mini-residencies; Home study kit for nurse, MD, CME credit. Media programs: slide sets, slide-tape presentations, videos, booklets, and abuse reporting forms on the areas of child abuse and child sexual abuse. A set of five tests have been developed to survey knowledge and attitudes of adults pertaining to children (child development, discipline, ideal child, temperaments) to be used prior to educational programs ($5 for set of 5; $1.50 each)

CHOICES FOR VICTIMS OF DOMESTIC VIOLENCE
PO Box 06157, Columbus, OH 43206
Crisis hotline: **(614) 224-4663 24 hrs**
Information: (614) 224-4663 24 hrs
Contact: Gail Heller, Exec Dir
TYPE OF AGENCY: Domestic violence program
AREAS SERVED: Franklin, Delaware, Madison, Pickaway, Union
YEARS IN OPERATION: 10
LANGUAGES: Translators available
ACCESSIBILITY: Wheelchair accessible; Telecommunications for the hearing impaired (TTY, TDY, etc.); Signers for the hearing impaired
CLIENTS/SERVICES: Marital rape/sexual abuse survivors; Incest victims/survivors; Community education

CLINTONVILLE COUNSELING SERVICES
3840 N High St, Columbus, OH 43214
Information: (614) 261-1126 By appointment
Contact: Jerry Jones, Counselor; Roseann Umana, Psychologist
TYPE OF AGENCY: Private practice
YEARS IN OPERATION: 5
ACCESSIBILITY: Signers for the hearing impaired
CASES SEXUAL ASSAULT/ABUSE (%): 90
CLIENTS/SERVICES: Sexual assault survivors; Marital rape/sexual abuse survivors; Child victims of sexual abuse; Adult survivors of child sexual abuse; Incest victims/survivors; Adolescent survivors of sexual abuse; Male survivors of sexual abuse
REQUIREMENTS: Fee for service program but accepts Medicaid, etc

COUNSELING AND CONSULTATION SERVICE
1739 N High St, No 446-C, Columbus, OH 43210-1392
Information: (614) 292-5766 8am-5pm (Mon-Fri)
Contact: Louise Douce, Dir
TYPE OF AGENCY: College/university-based services
SPONSORING ORGANIZATION: Ohio State University
AREAS SERVED: Ohio State University students
YEARS IN OPERATION: 40
LANGUAGES: Spanish
ACCESSIBILITY: Wheelchair accessible
CASES SEXUAL ASSAULT/ABUSE (%): 2
DESCRIPTION: Counseling and psychological services for OSU students. Provides individual and group counseling for incest survivors; Rape survivors counseling is both crisis intervention and follow-up. Individual therapy available for sex offenders and batterers
CLIENTS/SERVICES: Sexual assault survivors; Marital rape/sexual abuse survivors; Adult survivors of child sexual abuse; Incest victims/survivors; Offender treatment program; Adolescent survivors of sexual abuse; Male survivors of sexual abuse
REQUIREMENTS: Registered OSU student

FAMILY SUPPORT PROGRAM
700 Children's Dr, Columbus, OH 43205
Information: (614) 461-2100 8am-5pm; answering machine until 9pm
Contact: Deborah D Sendek, Dir

TYPE OF AGENCY: Hospital/medical center; Child sexual abuse services
SPONSORING ORGANIZATION: Columbus Children's Hospital
AREAS SERVED: Central Ohio
YEARS IN OPERATION: 7
ACCESSIBILITY: Wheelchair accessible; Telecommunications for the hearing impaired (TTY, TDY, etc.); Signers for the hearing impaired
CASES SEXUAL ASSAULT/ABUSE (%): 100
DESCRIPTION: Offers evaluation and treatment services for child and adolescent victims of sexual abuse, including psychological and social assessment and individual, family and group therapies. Also provides treatment for child sexual abuse/incest offenders and adolescent sex offenders
CLIENTS/SERVICES: Child victims of sexual abuse; Incest victims/survivors; Community education; Offender treatment program; Adolescent survivors of sexual abuse; Male survivors of sexual abuse
REQUIREMENTS: Ages 3 through 10
SPECIAL PROGRAMS/SERVICES: Interagency child abuse team meeting involves staff from social services, psychology, and medical personnel from Children's Hospital; Staff from local child protective services and police personnel also included in cases of child sexual and physical abuse. This interagency team looks at interventions and evaluates progress

FRANKLIN COUNTY PROSECUTOR'S OFFICE—VICTIM WITNESS ASSISTANCE PROGRAM
369 S High St, Columbus, OH 43215
Information: (614) 462-3555 8am-5pm
Contact: Barbara Felty, Dir
TYPE OF AGENCY: Victim/witness assistance program
AREAS SERVED: Franklin
YEARS IN OPERATION: 12
ACCESSIBILITY: Wheelchair accessible; Telecommunications for the hearing impaired (TTY, TDY, etc.); Signers for the hearing impaired
CASES SEXUAL ASSAULT/ABUSE (%): 95
CLIENTS/SERVICES: Sexual assault survivors; Marital rape/sexual abuse survivors; Child victims of sexual abuse; Incest victims/survivors; Community education; Adolescent survivors of sexual abuse; Male survivors of sexual abuse
REQUIREMENTS: Victim must report abuse/assault and go before the grand jury for an indictment

INCEST RESEARCH AND TREATMENT INSTITUTE
1601 W 5th Ave, Ste 202, Columbus, OH 43212
Information: (614) 869-4192 8am-5pm (Mon-Fri)
Contact: Martha Zanetis, Founder, Board Pres
TYPE OF AGENCY: Private practice; Training/research
AREAS SERVED: Franklin, Madison
YEARS IN OPERATION: 2
CASES SEXUAL ASSAULT/ABUSE (%): 100
DESCRIPTION: Offers training for professionals and contracts with local resources for traditional counseling, art therapy, mind-body work, massage, self-defense. Focus is on adult survivors of incest, particularly underserved populations (men and economically disadvantaged). Also provides individual therapy for child sexual abuse offenders.
CLIENTS/SERVICES: Adult survivors of child sexual abuse; Incest victims/survivors; Prevention program; Community education; Offender treatment program; Adolescent survivors of sexual abuse; Male survivors of sexual abuse; Healing
REQUIREMENTS: Adolescent-adult survivors of incest

KARATE TEMPLE
1377 Studer Ave, Columbus, OH 43206
Information: (614) 443-1025
Contact: Melanie Fine, Head Instructor
TYPE OF AGENCY: Rape prevention program
AREAS SERVED: Franklin
YEARS IN OPERATION: 4
ACCESSIBILITY: Wheelchair accessible
DESCRIPTION: Provides karate classes for children, women, and men; Teaches self-defense classes for women, emphasizing assertiveness training, rape prevention awareness, as well as actual physical self-defense techniques
CLIENTS/SERVICES: Sexual assault survivors; Marital rape/sexual abuse survivors; Adult survivors of child sexual abuse
REQUIREMENTS: Minimum age is 7 for children's classes; Fees are charged but may be waived

MOUNT CARMEL SHARE
854 W Town St, Columbus, OH 43222
Information: (614) 224-6700 8:30am-7:30pm
Contact: Virginia Okeeffe, Dir
TYPE OF AGENCY: Hospital/medical center; Counseling/mental health services
AREAS SERVED: Franklin
YEARS IN OPERATION: 7
LANGUAGES: Spanish
CASES SEXUAL ASSAULT/ABUSE (%): 80
DESCRIPTION: Chemical dependency outpatient agency, with special programs for women many of whom have experienced incest and violence; Support groups for male and female survivors
CLIENTS/SERVICES: Adult survivors of child sexual abuse; Incest victims/survivors; Community education; Male survivors of sexual abuse
REQUIREMENTS: Must be 18 or older; Fee for service

HANNAH NEIL CENTER/WILLSON FAMILY AND CHILD GUIDANCE CLINIC
301 Obetz Rd, Columbus, OH 43207
Information: (614) 497-0122 8am-8pm (Mon-Fri)
Contact: Judith Siehl, Therapist
TYPE OF AGENCY: Counseling/mental health services; Child sexual abuse services; Residential treatment facility
AREAS SERVED: Franklin, Licking, Guernsey, Pickaway
YEARS IN OPERATION: 15
ACCESSIBILITY: Wheelchair accessible; Telecommunications for the hearing impaired (TTY, TDY, etc.); Signers for the hearing impaired
CASES SEXUAL ASSAULT/ABUSE (%): 20
DESCRIPTION: Outpatient treatment program for children and adolescents that operates from a family systems theory base. The clinic has developed expertise in working with victims of sexual abuse and adolescent sexual offenders, including family sessions and work with adult offenders if a member of the family
CLIENTS/SERVICES: Child victims of sexual abuse; Adult survivors of child sexual abuse; Incest victims/survivors; Prevention program; Community education; Offender treatment program; Adolescent survivors of sexual abuse
REQUIREMENTS: Mental health services for families when a child or adolescent is the identified patient

OHIO WOMEN MARTIAL ARTISTS
1462 Summit St, Columbus, OH 43201
Information: (614) 268-6873
Contact: Julie Harmon, PhD, Instructor
TYPE OF AGENCY: Rape prevention program
AREAS SERVED: Franklin and surrounding area
YEARS IN OPERATION: 4
ACCESSIBILITY: Wheelchair accessible
CASES SEXUAL ASSAULT/ABUSE (%): 50-75
DESCRIPTION: Teaches self-defense and martial arts to children and women; Counseling services for women, children, families related to abuse/neglect/survivorship

CLIENTS/SERVICES: Sexual assault survivors; Marital rape/sexual abuse survivors; Child victims of sexual abuse; Adult survivors of child sexual abuse; Incest victims/survivors; Prevention program; Community education

M A ORCUTT, PHD, AND ASSOCIATES
4889 Sinclair Rd, Ste 115, Columbus, OH 43229
Crisis hotline: **(614) 848-8448 24 hrs (answering machine with emergency number on the message)**
Information: (614) 848-8448 9am-4pm
Contact: Mary Anne Orcutt, PhD, Psychologist
TYPE OF AGENCY: Private practice
AREAS SERVED: Statewide
YEARS IN OPERATION: 6
LANGUAGES: French
ACCESSIBILITY: Wheelchair accessible
CASES SEXUAL ASSAULT/ABUSE (%): 20-25
DESCRIPTION: Staff is 4 females and 1 male, all trained to deal with persons who have been physically, sexually, or psychologically abused
CLIENTS/SERVICES: Sexual assault survivors; Marital rape/sexual abuse survivors; Child victims of sexual abuse; Adult survivors of child sexual abuse; Incest victims/survivors; Offender treatment program

RAPE EDUCATION AND PREVENTION PROGRAM
408 Ohio Union, 1739 N High St, Columbus, OH 43210-1392
Information: (614) 292-0479, 292-8473 9am-5pm
Contact: Sue Green, Prog Coord
TYPE OF AGENCY: College/university-based services; Consultation
SPONSORING ORGANIZATION: The Ohio State University Office of Student Life
AREAS SERVED: Franklin
YEARS IN OPERATION: 5
ACCESSIBILITY: Wheelchair accessible
CASES SEXUAL ASSAULT/ABUSE (%): 100
DESCRIPTION: Comprehensive rape prevention program educating women and men on all issues concerning rape, including the societal conditions which allow it to exist; Five-week self-defense courses for women; Workshops about rape and racism; Educational workshops for men; Support groups for sexual assault survivors; Crisis intervention; Basic educational workshops about sexual assault
CLIENTS/SERVICES: Sexual assault survivors; Marital rape/sexual abuse survivors; Adult survivors of child sexual abuse; Incest victims/survivors; Prevention program; Community education; Male survivors of sexual abuse; Sexual harassment; Ethnic minorities; Publications/media
SPECIAL PROGRAMS/SERVICES: Offers two-hour workshops that are culturally-specific and look at rape and racism within an Africentric worldview. Also offers two-hour educational programs for men so they may examine the behaviors and attitudes they exhibit which contribute to the problem of rape. Individuals and agencies can write to REPP for copies of curriculum guides for the men's program and a copy of a script for the Black women's rape prevention workshop. Consultation services available to other universities.

ST ANTHONY RAPE TREATMENT CENTER
1492 E Broad St, Columbus, OH 43205
Information: (614) 251-3000 8:30am-5pm
Contact: Marsha Browning, Dir
TYPE OF AGENCY: Rape crisis center; Hospital/medical center
SPONSORING ORGANIZATION: St Anthony Medical Center
AREAS SERVED: Franklin and surrounding counties
YEARS IN OPERATION: 9
ACCESSIBILITY: Wheelchair accessible; Signers for the hearing impaired
CASES SEXUAL ASSAULT/ABUSE (%): 100

DESCRIPTION: Provides comprehensive services, including medical treatment, legal information, crisis intervention, and referrals to other area service providers
CLIENTS/SERVICES: Sexual assault survivors; Marital rape/sexual abuse survivors; Community education; Adolescent survivors of sexual abuse; Male survivors of sexual abuse
REQUIREMENTS: Must be 14 or older
SPECIAL PROGRAMS/SERVICES: Worked very closely with the local police department and prosecutor's office to establish protocol used; Victims are treated as a priority in the emergency room and brought immediately to the treatment area; Victims receive no bill for services in the emergency room

WOMEN AGAINST RAPE
PO Box 02084, Columbus, OH 43202
Crisis hotline: **(614) 221-4447 24 hrs**
Information: (614) 291-9751 9am-5pm (Mon-Fri)
Contact: Tami Snyder, Rape Crisis Center Coord
TYPE OF AGENCY: Rape crisis center
AREAS SERVED: Franklin
YEARS IN OPERATION: 17
ACCESSIBILITY: Wheelchair accessible; Telecommunications for the hearing impaired (TTY, TDY, etc.)
CASES SEXUAL ASSAULT/ABUSE (%): 100
DESCRIPTION: Comprehensive rape crisis and rape prevention services, including feminist martial arts/self-defense program
CLIENTS/SERVICES: Sexual assault survivors; Marital rape/sexual abuse survivors; Child victims of sexual abuse; Adult survivors of child sexual abuse; Incest victims/survivors; Prevention program; Community education
SPECIAL PROGRAMS/SERVICES: In-home rape prevention workshops; Door-to-door community outreach project

COSHOCTON

COSHOCTON COUNTY CRISIS HOTLINE
709 Main St, Coshocton, OH 43812
Crisis hotline: **(614) 622-3457 24 hrs**
Information: (614) 622-0033 8am-5pm
Contact: Kathie Brahaney, Exec Dir
TYPE OF AGENCY: Counseling/mental health services; Telephone crisis hotline; Information and referral services
SPONSORING ORGANIZATION: Coshocton County Drug and Alcohol Council
AREAS SERVED: Coshocton
YEARS IN OPERATION: 16
ACCESSIBILITY: Wheelchair accessible; Telecommunications for the hearing impaired (TTY, TDY, etc.); Signers for the hearing impaired
CLIENTS/SERVICES: Sexual assault survivors; Child victims of sexual abuse; Incest victims/survivors

DAYTON

DAYTON FREE CLINIC AND COUNSELING CENTER
1133 Salem Ave, Dayton, OH 45406
Information: (513) 278-9481 11am-8pm (Mon-Thu)
Contact: Dr J Lamar Johnson, Counseling Coord
TYPE OF AGENCY: Hospital/medical center
AREAS SERVED: Montgomery, Greene
YEARS IN OPERATION: 18
CASES SEXUAL ASSAULT/ABUSE (%): 5
CLIENTS/SERVICES: Sexual assault survivors; Child victims of sexual abuse; Adult survivors of child sexual abuse; Incest victims/survivors; Offender treatment program; Adolescent survivors of sexual abuse; Male survivors of sexual abuse

GRACE HOUSE SEXUAL ABUSE RESOURCE CENTER
301 Forest Ave, Dayton, OH 45405
Crisis hotline: **(513) 449-1555 24 hrs**
Information: (513) 449-1555 9am-5pm
Contact: Zenith Lawrence, Dir
TYPE OF AGENCY: Counseling/mental health services; Child sexual abuse services
AREAS SERVED: Montgomery, Clark, Greene, Preble, Miami, Clinton, Hamilton
YEARS IN OPERATION: 3½
ACCESSIBILITY: Wheelchair accessible; Signers for the hearing impaired
CASES SEXUAL ASSAULT/ABUSE (%): 100
DESCRIPTION: Counseling for sexually abused children and their families, including offenders; Sponsors Parents United and Daughters and Sons United chapters
CLIENTS/SERVICES: Child victims of sexual abuse; Adult survivors of child sexual abuse; Incest victims/survivors; Community education; Offender treatment program; Adolescent survivors of sexual abuse; Male survivors of sexual abuse; Healing
REQUIREMENTS: Will not treat clients who are actively using drugs and/or alcohol. Will not treat offenders who have been diagnosed as fixated pedophiles
SPECIAL PROGRAMS/SERVICES: Art and music therapy for child and adult survivors

MONTGOMERY COUNTY SHERIFF'S OFFICE—VICTIM/WITNESS ASSISTANCE
330 W 2nd St, Dayton, OH 45422
Crisis hotline: **(513) 225-4357 24 hrs**
Information: (513) 225-4665 8:30am-4:30pm
Contact: Claudia L Martin, Victim Advocate
TYPE OF AGENCY: Victim/witness assistance program
AREAS SERVED: Montgomery
LANGUAGES: Interpreters available
ACCESSIBILITY: Wheelchair accessible; Telecommunications for the hearing impaired (TTY, TDY, etc.); Signers for the hearing impaired
CASES SEXUAL ASSAULT/ABUSE (%): 10
CLIENTS/SERVICES: Sexual assault survivors; Marital rape/sexual abuse survivors; Child victims of sexual abuse; Incest victims/survivors; Prevention program; Community education; Adolescent survivors of sexual abuse; Male survivors of sexual abuse
REQUIREMENTS: Must file a police report

SEXUAL ABUSE RESOURCE CENTER
224 N Wilkinson St, Dayton, OH 45419
Information: (513) 226-0780 8:30am-5pm
Contact: Kathleen Zupan, Sexual Abuse Resource Coord
TYPE OF AGENCY: Child sexual abuse prevention program; Information center; Training/research
SPONSORING ORGANIZATION: Planned Parenthood Association of Miami Valley
AREAS SERVED: Montgomery
YEARS IN OPERATION: 1½
ACCESSIBILITY: Wheelchair accessible
CLIENTS/SERVICES: Prevention program; Community education; Developmentally disabled; Publications/media
SPECIAL PROGRAMS/SERVICES: Resource library of print and nonprint materials for parents, children, and professionals; Anatomically correct dolls available for loan; Resource materials on prevention education for mentally retarded and developmentally disabled individuals

STOP CHILD ABUSE AND NEGLECT (SCAN)
184 Salem Ave, Dayton, OH 45406
Crisis hotline: **(513) 278-5846, 372-1040 24 hrs**
Information: (513) 222-9481 8:30am-5pm
Contact: Sheila Drennen, SCAN Clinical Coord
TYPE OF AGENCY: Child sexual abuse services; Child sexual abuse prevention program; Child abuse services; Child abuse prevention program

SPONSORING ORGANIZATION: Family Service Association
AREAS SERVED: Montgomery, Greene, Preble
YEARS IN OPERATION: 12
ACCESSIBILITY: Wheelchair accessible; Telecommunications for the hearing impaired (TTY, TDY, etc.); Signers for the hearing impaired
CASES SEXUAL ASSAULT/ABUSE (%): 75
DESCRIPTION: Comprehensive child physical/sexual abuse and neglect prevention and treatment services. Treatment services focus on child sexual abuse victims, adult survivors, families and adolescent and adult offenders (rapists, child sexual abuse/incest offenders)
CLIENTS/SERVICES: Sexual assault survivors; Marital rape/sexual abuse survivors; Child victims of sexual abuse; Adult survivors of child sexual abuse; Incest victims/survivors; Prevention program; Community education; Offender treatment program; Adolescent survivors of sexual abuse; Male survivors of sexual abuse
REQUIREMENTS: Some groups have age restrictions

YWCA BATTERED WOMAN PROJECT
141 W 3rd St, Dayton, OH 45402
Crisis hotline: **(513) 222-0874 24 hrs**
Information: (513) 222-0874 24 hrs
Contact: Kathy Bohachek, Dir
TYPE OF AGENCY: Domestic violence program
SPONSORING ORGANIZATION: Young Women's Christian Association
AREAS SERVED: Montgomery
YEARS IN OPERATION: 12
CASES SEXUAL ASSAULT/ABUSE (%): 30
CLIENTS/SERVICES: Community education; Adolescent survivors of sexual abuse

DEFIANCE

NORTHWESTERN OHIO RAPE CRISIS INTERVENTION
424 Wayne Ave, Defiance, OH 43512
Crisis hotline: **(419) 782-1100 24 hrs**
Information: (419) 782-4906 8am-5pm
Contact: Kathryn Oberow, Jennifer Shoub, Coords
TYPE OF AGENCY: Rape crisis center
AREAS SERVED: Defiance, Fulton, Henry, Paulding, Williams
YEARS IN OPERATION: 2
LANGUAGES: Spanish and Sign by arrangement
ACCESSIBILITY: Wheelchair accessible; Telecommunications for the hearing impaired (TTY, TDY, etc.); Signers for the hearing impaired (by arrangement)
CASES SEXUAL ASSAULT/ABUSE (%): 100
CLIENTS/SERVICES: Sexual assault survivors; Marital rape/sexual abuse survivors; Child victims of sexual abuse; Adult survivors of child sexual abuse; Incest victims/survivors; Prevention program; Community education; Adolescent survivors of sexual abuse; Male survivors of sexual abuse

DELAWARE

GRADY MEMORIAL HOSPITAL—RAPE PREVENTION PROJECT
561 W Central Ave, Delaware, OH 43015
Information: (614) 369-8711, ext 2569 8am-4pm
Contact: Jeanne Frentsos, RN, Rape Prevention Proj Coord
TYPE OF AGENCY: Hospital/medical center; Child sexual abuse prevention program; Rape prevention program
AREAS SERVED: Delaware
YEARS IN OPERATION: ½
ACCESSIBILITY: Wheelchair accessible; Signers for the hearing impaired
DESCRIPTION: Provides medical services for adult and child survivors; Prevention programs, including feminist martial arts/self-defense

CLIENTS/SERVICES: Sexual assault survivors; Child victims of sexual abuse; Prevention program; Community education

EATON

PREBLE COUNTY COUNSELING CENTER
101 N Barron St, Eaton, OH 45320
Crisis hotline: **(513) 456-1166 24 hrs daily**
Information: (513) 456-1166 9am-5pm (Mon-Fri)
Contact: Barbara Evans, Battered Women/VOCA Dir
TYPE OF AGENCY: Domestic violence program; Victim/witness assistance program; Counseling/mental health services
AREAS SERVED: Preble
YEARS IN OPERATION: 3
ACCESSIBILITY: Wheelchair accessible
CASES SEXUAL ASSAULT/ABUSE (%): 40
DESCRIPTION: Individual and group counseling for battered women and victims of crime
CLIENTS/SERVICES: Sexual assault survivors; Marital rape/sexual abuse survivors; Child victims of sexual abuse; Adult survivors of child sexual abuse; Incest victims/survivors; Offender treatment program; Adolescent survivors of sexual abuse; Male survivors of sexual abuse

FINDLAY

HANCOCK COUNTY COUNCIL ON DOMESTIC VIOLENCE
PO Box 496, Findlay, OH 45840
Crisis hotline: **(419) 422-4766 24 hrs daily**
Information: (419) 422-4766 24 hrs daily
Contact: Judy Lowe, Exec Dir
TYPE OF AGENCY: Domestic violence program; Child sexual abuse services; Child sexual abuse prevention program
AREAS SERVED: Hancock and surrounding areas
YEARS IN OPERATION: 7
CASES SEXUAL ASSAULT/ABUSE (%): 80
DESCRIPTION: Provides emergency/crisis shelter for women and their children in immediate danger of physical, sexual, or emotional abuse; Individual therapy for batterers
CLIENTS/SERVICES: Sexual assault survivors; Marital rape/sexual abuse survivors; Child victims of sexual abuse; Adult survivors of child sexual abuse; Incest victims/survivors; Prevention program; Community education; Adolescent survivors of sexual abuse

FOSTORIA

FIRST STEP DOMESTIC VIOLENCE SHELTER
PO Box 1103, Fostoria, OH 44830
Crisis hotline: **(419) 435-7300 24 hrs**
Information: (419) 435-7300 24 hrs
Contact: Terri Mercer, Exec Dir
TYPE OF AGENCY: Domestic violence program
AREAS SERVED: Sandusky, Seneca, Wood, Wyandot
YEARS IN OPERATION: 7
ACCESSIBILITY: Wheelchair accessible; Signers for the hearing impaired
CASES SEXUAL ASSAULT/ABUSE (%): 60
DESCRIPTION: Provides support groups for domestic violence survivors; Rape crisis training; Treatment for batterers
CLIENTS/SERVICES: Sexual assault survivors; Marital rape/sexual abuse survivors; Child victims of sexual abuse; Adult survivors of child sexual abuse; Incest victims/survivors; Community education; Offender treatment program; Adolescent survivors of sexual abuse; Male survivors of sexual abuse

FREMONT

SANDUSKY COUNTY DEPARTMENT OF HUMAN SERVICES—CHILDREN'S SERVICES UNIT
PO Box 890, 500 W State St, Fremont, OH 43420
Crisis hotline: **(419) 334-3891 24 hrs**
Information: (419) 334-3891
TYPE OF AGENCY: Counseling/mental health services; Child sexual abuse services; Child sexual abuse prevention program
AREAS SERVED: Sandusky
LANGUAGES: Spanish
ACCESSIBILITY: Wheelchair accessible
DESCRIPTION: Investigation and supportive services for abused, neglected, and dependent children and their families; Case management; Prevention programs through community education and awareness
CLIENTS/SERVICES: Child victims of sexual abuse; Incest victims/survivors; Prevention program; Community education
REQUIREMENTS: Must be resident of Sandusky County; Children or families having children 18 or younger, or 21 if handicapped

HAMILTON

YWCA SHELTER FOR BATTERED PERSONS AND THEIR CHILDREN
244 Dayton St, Hamilton, OH 45011
Crisis hotline: **(800) 543-1399, (513) 863-7099 24 hrs daily**
Information: (513) 863-4762 7am-5pm
Contact: Leta Kranbuhl, Rape Svcs Coord
TYPE OF AGENCY: Rape crisis center
AREAS SERVED: Butler
YEARS IN OPERATION: 1
DESCRIPTION: Domestic violence shelter which recently received a grant to provide comprehensive, coordinated services for survivors of rape and sexual assault
CLIENTS/SERVICES: Sexual assault survivors; Marital rape/sexual abuse survivors; Adult survivors of child sexual abuse; Incest victims/survivors; Prevention program; Community education

HILLSBORO

HIGHLAND COUNTY DOMESTIC VIOLENCE TASK FORCE
108 Erin Court, Hillsboro, OH 45133
Crisis hotline: **(513) 393-9946, 393-9904 24 hrs**
Information: (513) 393-9946 8am-5pm (Mon, Wed, Fri); 8am-8pm (Tue, Thu)
Contact: Janet Carroll, Women's Advocate of Highland County
TYPE OF AGENCY: Domestic violence program
AREAS SERVED: Highland
DESCRIPTION: Provides domestic violence safehomes and referrals
CLIENTS/SERVICES: Marital rape/sexual abuse survivors; Community education

JACKSON

COMMUNITY ASSAULT PREVENTION SERVICES
PO Box 207, Jackson, OH 45640
Crisis hotline: **(614) 286-6611 24 hrs**
Information: (614) 286-6611
Contact: Carol Edwards
TYPE OF AGENCY: Rape crisis center
AREAS SERVED: Jackson
CLIENTS/SERVICES: Prevention program

JEFFERSON

VICTIM OF CRIME ASSISTANCE PROGRAM
25 W Jefferson St, Jefferson, OH 44047
Crisis hotline: **(216) 576-0055 24 hrs**
Information: (216) 576-0055 24 hrs
Contact: Glen Osburn, Coord
TYPE OF AGENCY: Victim/witness assistance program
AREAS SERVED: Ashtabula
YEARS IN OPERATION: 2
ACCESSIBILITY: Wheelchair accessible
CASES SEXUAL ASSAULT/ABUSE (%): 4
CLIENTS/SERVICES: Sexual assault survivors; Marital rape/sexual abuse survivors; Child victims of sexual abuse; Community education
REQUIREMENTS: Crime must be reported to police within 72 hours

KENT

SAFER FUTURES
302 N DePeyster St, Kent, OH 44240
Crisis hotline: **(216) 678-HELP 24 hrs**
Information: (216) 678-3911 9am-5pm (Mon-Fri)
Contact: Susan Denning, Dir
TYPE OF AGENCY: Domestic violence program
SPONSORING ORGANIZATION: Family and Community Services of Catholic Charities
AREAS SERVED: Portage
YEARS IN OPERATION: 1
ACCESSIBILITY: Signers for the hearing impaired
CASES SEXUAL ASSAULT/ABUSE (%): 25
CLIENTS/SERVICES: Marital rape/sexual abuse survivors

TOWNHALL II
PO Box 781, 225 E College Ave, Kent, OH 44240-0781
Crisis hotline: **(216) 678-HELP 24 hrs**
Information: (216) 678-3006
Contact: Helena Roubanes
TYPE OF AGENCY: Rape crisis center; Telephone crisis hotline
AREAS SERVED: Portage
CLIENTS/SERVICES: Sexual assault survivors; Adult survivors of child sexual abuse; Incest victims/survivors; Community education

LANCASTER

FAIRFIELD FAMILY COUNSELING
1592 Granville Pike, Lancaster, OH 43130
Crisis hotline: **(614) 687-8255 24 hrs**
Information: (614) 687-0606 8am-9pm (Mon, Thur); 8am-5pm (Tues, Wed, Fri)
Contact: Carolyn Huddle, Assault Treatment Spec
TYPE OF AGENCY: Counseling/mental health services
AREAS SERVED: Primarily Fairfield
YEARS IN OPERATION: 3
ACCESSIBILITY: Wheelchair accessible
CLIENTS/SERVICES: Sexual assault survivors; Marital rape/sexual abuse survivors; Adult survivors of child sexual abuse; Incest victims/survivors; Prevention program; Community education; Male survivors of sexual abuse
REQUIREMENTS: Must be 18 or older
SPECIAL PROGRAMS/SERVICES: Provides group therapy for adult incest victims and codependent groups for all victims to process learned helplessness and other self-defeating patterns of behavior resulting from victimization experiences

LEBANON

WARREN COUNTY FAMILY ABUSE SHELTER, INC
570 N State, Route 741, Lebanon, OH 45036
Crisis hotline: **(800) 932-3366 After hrs and weekends**
Information: (513) 932-6301 8am-6pm
Contact: Janet Hoffman, Exec Dir
TYPE OF AGENCY: Domestic violence program
AREAS SERVED: Warren
YEARS IN OPERATION: 5
CASES SEXUAL ASSAULT/ABUSE (%): 5
DESCRIPTION: Provides shelter for domestic violence survivors and crisis services for sexual assault survivors
CLIENTS/SERVICES: Sexual assault survivors; Marital rape/sexual abuse survivors; Adult survivors of child sexual abuse; Community education; Adolescent survivors of sexual abuse; Male survivors of sexual abuse

WARREN COUNTY PROSECUTOR'S OFFICE
313 E Warren St, Law Bldg, Lebanon, OH 45036
Crisis hotline: **(513) 932-4040 24 hrs**
Information: (513) 933-1335 8:30am-4:30pm (Mon-Fri)
Contact: Chris Haynes, Victim Advocate
TYPE OF AGENCY: Victim/witness assistance program
AREAS SERVED: Warren
YEARS IN OPERATION: 7
CASES SEXUAL ASSAULT/ABUSE (%): 5-10
CLIENTS/SERVICES: Sexual assault survivors; Marital rape/sexual abuse survivors; Child victims of sexual abuse; Adult survivors of child sexual abuse; Incest victims/survivors; Community education; Adolescent survivors of sexual abuse

LIMA

CRIME VICTIM SERVICES, INC
PO Box 962, Lima, OH 45802-0962
Information: (419) 222-8656 8am-5pm (Mon-Fri)
Contact: David Voth, Exec Dir
TYPE OF AGENCY: Victim/witness assistance program
AREAS SERVED: Allen
YEARS IN OPERATION: 7
LANGUAGES: Spanish
ACCESSIBILITY: Wheelchair accessible; Signers for the hearing impaired
CASES SEXUAL ASSAULT/ABUSE (%): 10
CLIENTS/SERVICES: Sexual assault survivors; Marital rape/sexual abuse survivors; Child victims of sexual abuse; Community education
SPECIAL PROGRAMS/SERVICES: Victim and convicted offender mediation/meeting for victims to get answers and express feelings for healing and closure and through which offenders see personal effects of their crimes

CROSS ROADS CRISIS CENTER
Box 643, Lima, OH 45802
Crisis hotline: **(419) 228-4357 24 hrs**
Information: (419) 228-6692 24 hrs
Contact: James M Ottarson, Exec Dir
TYPE OF AGENCY: Rape crisis center; Domestic violence program
AREAS SERVED: Allen, Hardin
YEARS IN OPERATION: 9
CASES SEXUAL ASSAULT/ABUSE (%): 25
CLIENTS/SERVICES: Sexual assault survivors; Marital rape/sexual abuse survivors; Child victims of sexual abuse; Adult survivors of child sexual abuse; Community education; Adolescent survivors of sexual abuse

LOGAN

CARELINE SURVIVOR ADVOCACY
47 N Market St, Logan, OH 43138
Crisis hotline: **(614) 385-8484 24 hrs**
Information: (614) 385-6594
TYPE OF AGENCY: Rape crisis center; Counseling/mental health services; Child sexual abuse prevention program; Telephone crisis hotline; Information and referral
SPONSORING ORGANIZATION: Tri-County Mental Health and Counseling Service, Inc
AREAS SERVED: Hocking

CARELINE SURVIVOR ADVOCACY
(continued)
YEARS IN OPERATION: 18
DESCRIPTION: Programs include: Sexual assault and survivor advocacy program and the Child Assault Prevention Project; Rape crisis program; Treatment for survivors of child sexual abuse and their families; Treatment for child sexual abuse and incest offenders
CLIENTS/SERVICES: Sexual assault survivors; Marital rape/sexual abuse survivors; Child victims of sexual abuse; Adult survivors of child sexual abuse; Incest victims/survivors; Prevention program; Community education; Offender treatment program; Adolescent survivors of sexual abuse; Male survivors of sexual abuse; Publications/media
SPECIAL PROGRAMS/SERVICES: Media program: *How Will I Tell,* which follows a rape survivor through hospital and police proceedings and describes the sexual assault survivor advocacy program.

LONDON

MADISON COUNTY PROSECUTOR'S OFFICE—VICTIM/WITNESS DIVISION
23 W High St, London, OH 43140
Information: (614) 852-2259 8:30am-4pm (Mon-Fri)
Contact: Judy A Pierce, Dir
TYPE OF AGENCY: Victim/witness assistance program
AREAS SERVED: Madison
YEARS IN OPERATION: 1 month
ACCESSIBILITY: Wheelchair accessible
CLIENTS/SERVICES: Sexual assault survivors; Marital rape/sexual abuse survivors; Child victims of sexual abuse; Community education

MANSFIELD

THE DOMESTIC VIOLENCE SHELTER, INC
PO Box 1524, Mansfield, OH 44901
Crisis hotline: **(419) 526-4450 24 hrs daily**
Information: (419) 526-4450 8:30am-4:30pm
Contact: Rosemary Smith, Prog Supv
TYPE OF AGENCY: Domestic violence program
AREAS SERVED: Richland, Ashland, Huron
YEARS IN OPERATION: 10
CLIENTS/SERVICES: Sexual assault survivors; Marital rape/sexual abuse survivors; Adult survivors of child sexual abuse

HELPLINE—ASAP
741 Scholl Rd, Mansfield, OH 44907
Crisis hotline: **(419) 522-4357 24 hrs**
Information: (419) 522-4357
Contact: Kim Hildreth
TYPE OF AGENCY: Rape crisis center; Telephone crisis hotline; Information and referral
SPONSORING ORGANIZATION: The Center for Individual and Family Services
AREAS SERVED: Richland
CLIENTS/SERVICES: Sexual assault survivors; Marital rape/sexual abuse survivors; Child victims of sexual abuse; Adult survivors of child sexual abuse; Incest victims/survivors; Adolescent survivors of sexual abuse; Male survivors of sexual abuse

MARION

TURNING POINT
PO Box 822, Marion, OH 43302
Crisis hotline: **(800) 232-6505 in Ohio; (614) 382-8988 24 hrs daily**
Information: (614) 382-9192 8am-4:30pm
Contact: Alice-Kay Hilderbrand, Exec Dir; Lori Thomas, Prog Dir
TYPE OF AGENCY: Domestic violence program
SPONSORING ORGANIZATION: Concerned Citizens Against Violence Against Women, Inc
AREAS SERVED: Crawford, Delaware, Marion, Morrow, Union, Wyandot
YEARS IN OPERATION: 9
ACCESSIBILITY: Signers for the hearing impaired
CASES SEXUAL ASSAULT/ABUSE (%): 26
DESCRIPTION: Comprehensive domestic violence shelter, with individual therapy for batterers
CLIENTS/SERVICES: Sexual assault survivors; Marital rape/sexual abuse survivors; Child victims of sexual abuse; Adult survivors of child sexual abuse; Incest victims/survivors; Prevention program; Community education; Children of victims; Adolescent survivors of sexual abuse; Male survivors of sexual abuse

VICTIM ASSISTANCE PROGRAM
333 W Center St, Marion, OH 43302
Crisis hotline: **(614) 387-7200 24 hrs**
Information: (614) 387-4401 8:30am-5pm
Contact: Judy Mount, Victim Advocate
TYPE OF AGENCY: Victim/witness assistance program; Counseling/mental health services
SPONSORING ORGANIZATION: Marion Area Counseling Center, Inc
AREAS SERVED: Marion
YEARS IN OPERATION: 2
ACCESSIBILITY: Wheelchair accessible
CLIENTS/SERVICES: Sexual assault survivors; Marital rape/sexual abuse survivors; Child victims of sexual abuse; Adult survivors of child sexual abuse; Incest victims/survivors; Prevention program; Community education

MARYSVILLE

VICTIMS OF CRIME ASSISTANCE PROGRAM
715 S Plum, Marysville, OH 43040
Crisis hotline: **(513) 644-6363 24 hrs**
Information: (513) 644-9192 24 hrs
Contact: Bruce Adams, Prog Coord
TYPE OF AGENCY: Victim/witness assistance program; Counseling/mental health services
SPONSORING ORGANIZATION: Charles B. Mills Center
AREAS SERVED: Union
YEARS IN OPERATION: 2
LANGUAGES: As needed
ACCESSIBILITY: Wheelchair accessible; Signers for the hearing impaired
CASES SEXUAL ASSAULT/ABUSE (%): 5
DESCRIPTION: Provides crisis intervention, short- and long-term therapy for victims of sexual assault/child sexual abuse and adult survivors; Individual and group therapy for sex offenders and batterers
CLIENTS/SERVICES: Sexual assault survivors; Marital rape/sexual abuse survivors; Child victims of sexual abuse; Adult survivors of child sexual abuse; Incest victims/survivors; Community education; Offender treatment program; Adolescent survivors of sexual abuse; Male survivors of sexual abuse

MCARTHUR

CARELINE SURVIVOR ADVOCACY
313½ W Main St, McArthur, OH 45651
Crisis hotline: **(614) 596-5211 24 hrs**
Information: (614) 596-4809
TYPE OF AGENCY: Rape crisis center; Counseling/mental health services; Child sexual abuse prevention program; Telephone crisis hotline; Information and referral
SPONSORING ORGANIZATION: Tri-County Mental Health and Counseling Service, Inc
AREAS SERVED: Vinton
YEARS IN OPERATION: 18
DESCRIPTION: Programs include: Sexual assault and survivor advocacy program and the Child Assault Prevention Project; Rape crisis program; Treatment for survivors of child sexual abuse and their families; Treatment for child sexual abuse and incest offenders
CLIENTS/SERVICES: Sexual assault survivors; Marital rape/sexual abuse survivors; Child victims of sexual abuse; Adult survivors of child sexual abuse; Incest victims/survivors; Prevention program; Community education; Offender treatment program; Adolescent survivors of sexual abuse; Male survivors of sexual abuse; Publications/media
SPECIAL PROGRAMS/SERVICES: Media program: *How Will I Tell,* which follows a rape survivor through hospital and police proceedings and describes the sexual assault survivor advocacy program.

MOUNT GILEAD

MORROW COUNTY SEXUAL ABUSE PREVENTION AND EDUCATION TEAM
27 W High St, Mount Gilead, OH 43338
Information: (419) 947-9111
Contact: Carol Curl, Dept Human Svcs Dir
TYPE OF AGENCY: Child sexual abuse services
DESCRIPTION: Coordinated services and multi-disciplinary approach to treatment of child sexual abuse. Provides support groups for offenders, non-offending parents, and adolescent victims
CLIENTS/SERVICES: Child victims of sexual abuse; Community education; Offender treatment program; Male survivors of sexual abuse

MOUNT VERNON

NEW DIRECTIONS
Box 453, Mount Vernon, OH 43050
Crisis hotline: **(614) 397-4357 24 hrs**
Information: (614) 397-4357 8am-5pm
Contact: Mary Hendrickson, Dir
TYPE OF AGENCY: Rape crisis center; Domestic violence program
AREAS SERVED: Knox
YEARS IN OPERATION: 6
DESCRIPTION: Services for victims/survivors of sexual assault and domestic violence; Batterers group
CLIENTS/SERVICES: Sexual assault survivors; Marital rape/sexual abuse survivors; Prevention program; Community education; Adolescent survivors of sexual abuse

NAPOLEON

CENTER FOR ABUSE PREVENTION AND TREATMENT, INC
104 E Washington St, Napoleon, OH 43545
Information: (419) 592-0540
Contact: Lois Hanna, Dir
TYPE OF AGENCY: Counseling/mental health services; Child sexual abuse services; Child sexual abuse prevention program
AREAS SERVED: Henry, Williams, Defiance, Fulton
YEARS IN OPERATION: 1
ACCESSIBILITY: Wheelchair accessible
CASES SEXUAL ASSAULT/ABUSE (%): 100
CLIENTS/SERVICES: Sexual assault survivors; Marital rape/sexual abuse survivors; Child victims of sexual abuse; Adult survivors of child sexual abuse; Incest victims/survivors; Prevention program; Community education; Offender treatment program; Adolescent survivors of sexual abuse; Male survivors of sexual abuse

NEW PHILADELPHIA

HARBOR HOUSE, INC
PO Box 6102, Monroe Mall, New Philadelphia, OH 44663
Crisis hotline: **(216) 364-1374 24 hrs**
Information: (216) 343-2778 9am-5pm
Contact: Suzanne R Abel, Exec Dir
TYPE OF AGENCY: Domestic violence program
AREAS SERVED: Tuscarawas, Carroll
YEARS IN OPERATION: 4

HARBOR HOUSE, INC *(continued)*
ACCESSIBILITY: Signers for the hearing impaired
CLIENTS/SERVICES: Marital rape/sexual abuse survivors; Child victims of sexual abuse; Adult survivors of child sexual abuse; Incest victims/survivors; Community education

NEWARK

NEW BEGINNINGS
126 W Church St, Newark, OH 43055
Crisis hotline: **(614) 345-4498 24 hrs**
Information: (614) 349-8719 24 hrs
Contact: Carolyn Cutter, Prog Dir
TYPE OF AGENCY: Domestic violence program
SPONSORING ORGANIZATION: Family Counseling Services
AREAS SERVED: Licking
YEARS IN OPERATION: 5
ACCESSIBILITY: Wheelchair accessible; Signers for the hearing impaired
CASES SEXUAL ASSAULT/ABUSE (%): 75
CLIENTS/SERVICES: Marital rape/sexual abuse survivors; Community education

PSYCHOLOGICAL ASSOCIATES, INC
60 Messimer Dr, Newark, OH 43055
Crisis hotline: **(614) 366-0386 24 hrs**
Information: (614) 522-5252 8am-8:30pm
Contact: William P McFarren, EdD, Wendy T Schoff, PhD, Psychologists
TYPE OF AGENCY: Child sexual abuse services; Private practice
AREAS SERVED: Licking, Knox, Cochocton, Muskingdum, Perry
YEARS IN OPERATION: 9
ACCESSIBILITY: Wheelchair accessible; Signers for the hearing impaired
CASES SEXUAL ASSAULT/ABUSE (%): 10-20
CLIENTS/SERVICES: Sexual assault survivors; Marital rape/sexual abuse survivors; Child victims of sexual abuse; Adult survivors of child sexual abuse; Incest victims/survivors; Community education; Adolescent survivors of sexual abuse; Male survivors of sexual abuse
REQUIREMENTS: Fee for services

RAPE CRISIS CENTER
843 N 21st St, Newark, OH 43055
Crisis hotline: **(614) 345-HELP 24 hrs**
Information: (614) 366-3377
Contact: Nancy Heller, Counselor; Louisa Hext, Education Dir
TYPE OF AGENCY: Rape crisis center; Counseling/mental health services
SPONSORING ORGANIZATION: Planned Parenthood of East Central Ohio (PPECO)
AREAS SERVED: Licking
CLIENTS/SERVICES: Sexual assault survivors; Prevention program; Adolescent survivors of sexual abuse; Male survivors of sexual abuse

NILES

"HELP ME"
PO Box 621, Niles, OH 44446
Crisis hotline: **(216) 747-2696, 393-1565 24 hrs**
Information: (216) 395-4656 9am-9pm
Contact: Carol Wilt, Natl Dir; Karen Madden, Founder
TYPE OF AGENCY: Counseling/mental health services; Private practice; Self-help group
AREAS SERVED: Trumbull, Mahoning, Astabulla, Columbiana, OH; Detroit, MI
YEARS IN OPERATION: 3
CASES SEXUAL ASSAULT/ABUSE (%): 100
DESCRIPTION: Educates adolescent and adult survivors, helping professions, and the general public about the effects of child sexual abuse. Provides support groups for female and male survivors and their families and friends
CLIENTS/SERVICES: Adult survivors of child sexual abuse; Incest victims/survivors; Prevention program; Community education; Adolescent survivors of sexual abuse; Male survivors of sexual abuse

NORTON

HELMUTH PSYCHOLOGICAL ASSOCIATES, INC
3725 S Cleveland Massillon Rd, Greenridge Plaza, Norton, OH 44203
Contact: Victoria Kepler, MA, LPC
TYPE OF AGENCY: Child sexual abuse services; Private practice
DESCRIPTION: Counseling for victims/survivors and child sexual abuse/incest offenders, with a holistic and Christian philosophy. Spiritual healing weekends available twice a year.
CLIENTS/SERVICES: Child victims of sexual abuse; Adult survivors of child sexual abuse; Incest victims/survivors; Prevention program; Community education; Offender treatment program; Adolescent survivors of sexual abuse; Male survivors of sexual abuse; Healing

OXFORD

OXFORD CRISIS AND REFERRAL CENTER
111 E Walnut, Oxford, OH 45056
Crisis hotline: **(513) 523-4146 24 hrs**
Information: (513) 523-4149 9am-5pm
Contact: Laura Rothfuss, Asst Dir
TYPE OF AGENCY: Counseling/mental health services
AREAS SERVED: Butler
YEARS IN OPERATION: 7
ACCESSIBILITY: Wheelchair accessible
CASES SEXUAL ASSAULT/ABUSE (%): 5
CLIENTS/SERVICES: Sexual assault survivors; Marital rape/sexual abuse survivors; Child victims of sexual abuse; Adult survivors of child sexual abuse; Incest victims/survivors; Community education; Adolescent survivors of sexual abuse; Male survivors of sexual abuse

PAINESVILLE

FORBES HOUSE
PO Box 702, Painesville, OH 44077
Crisis hotline: **(216) 354-6838 24 hrs**
Information: (216) 354-6838 9am-5pm (Mon-Fri)
Contact: Kathie Tryon, Exec Dir
TYPE OF AGENCY: Domestic violence program
AREAS SERVED: Lake
YEARS IN OPERATION: 8
ACCESSIBILITY: Signers for the hearing impaired (on referral)
CASES SEXUAL ASSAULT/ABUSE (%): 60
CLIENTS/SERVICES: Marital rape/sexual abuse survivors; Child victims of sexual abuse

SEXUAL ASSAULT CENTER OF LAKE COUNTY
1 New Market Mall, B-201, Painesville, OH 44077
Crisis hotline: **(513) 354-6838, 953-0600 24 hrs**
Information: (513) 354-6838, 953-0600 8am-5pm
Contact: Peggy Taylor, Dir
TYPE OF AGENCY: Rape crisis center; Child sexual abuse prevention program
AREAS SERVED: Lake
YEARS IN OPERATION: 9
ACCESSIBILITY: Wheelchair accessible; Telecommunications for the hearing impaired (TTY, TDY, etc.)
CASES SEXUAL ASSAULT/ABUSE (%): 100
CLIENTS/SERVICES: Sexual assault survivors; Marital rape/sexual abuse survivors; Child victims of sexual abuse; Adult survivors of child sexual abuse; Incest victims/survivors; Prevention program; Community education; Adolescent survivors of sexual abuse; Male survivors of sexual abuse
SPECIAL PROGRAMS/SERVICES: Works closely with county police and prosecutors; Provides special room for children with a one-way mirror and videotaping equipment available for police use

PORTSMOUTH

SOUTHERN OHIO TASK FORCE ON DOMESTIC VIOLENCE
PO Box 754, Portsmouth, OH 45662
Crisis hotline: **(614) 354-1010 24 hrs**
Information: (614) 456-8217 24 hrs
Contact: Marilyn Nevison, Exec Dir
TYPE OF AGENCY: Domestic violence program
AREAS SERVED: Adams, Sciato, Lawrence
YEARS IN OPERATION: 9
CLIENTS/SERVICES: Marital rape/sexual abuse survivors; Prevention program; Community education; Adolescent survivors of sexual abuse

E W THROCKMORTON AND ASSOCIATES
428 Chillicothe St, Ste 222, Portsmouth, OH 45662
Crisis hotline: **(614) 354-8806 24 hrs**
Information: (614) 354-8806 9am-5pm
Contact: E Warren Throckmorton, Dir
TYPE OF AGENCY: Private practice
AREAS SERVED: Pike, Scioto, Lawrence
YEARS IN OPERATION: 2
ACCESSIBILITY: Wheelchair accessible
CASES SEXUAL ASSAULT/ABUSE (%): 25-30
CLIENTS/SERVICES: Marital rape/sexual abuse survivors; Child victims of sexual abuse; Adult survivors of child sexual abuse; Incest victims/survivors; Offender treatment program
REQUIREMENTS: Ability to pay for services or have third party payer

SAINT CLAIRSVILLE

WOMEN'S TRI-COUNTY HELP CENTER, INC
PO Box 494, 155 W Main St, Saint Clairsville, OH 43950
Crisis hotline: **(304) 234-8161 24 hrs daily**
Information: (614) 695-5441 8:30am-9pm (Mon, Wed); 8:30am-5pm (Tue, Thu, Fri)
Contact: Linda Wallace, Exec Dir
TYPE OF AGENCY: Rape crisis center; Domestic violence program; Child sexual abuse services; Child sexual abuse prevention program; Acquaintance/date rape prevention program
AREAS SERVED: Belmont, Harrison, Monroe
YEARS IN OPERATION: 8
ACCESSIBILITY: Wheelchair accessible; Telecommunications for the hearing impaired (TTY, TDY, etc.); Signers for the hearing impaired
CASES SEXUAL ASSAULT/ABUSE (%): 40
DESCRIPTION: Provides individual and group therapy for female and male survivors of family violence and sexual assault; 24-hour phone and face-to-face crisis intervention; Hospital and legal advocacy; Adult survivors counseling group; Therapy for batterers. Member of sexual assault task force involved with child sexual assault protocol
CLIENTS/SERVICES: Sexual assault survivors; Marital rape/sexual abuse survivors; Child victims of sexual abuse; Adult survivors of child sexual abuse; Incest victims/survivors; Prevention program; Community education; Adolescent survivors of sexual abuse; Male survivors of sexual abuse; Publications/media
SPECIAL PROGRAMS/SERVICES: Student production of date rape video

SIDNEY

NEW CHOICES, INC
PO Box 452, Sidney, OH 45365
Crisis hotline: **(800) 351-7347 24 hrs**
Information: (513) 498-7261 9am-4pm
Contact: Barbara Voress, Admin Dir
TYPE OF AGENCY: Domestic violence program
AREAS SERVED: Shelby
YEARS IN OPERATION: 7
CASES SEXUAL ASSAULT/ABUSE (%): 99

NEW CHOICES, INC *(continued)*
CLIENTS/SERVICES: Marital rape/sexual abuse survivors; Prevention program; Community education

SPRINGFIELD

PROJECT WOMAN
1101 E High St, Ste A, Springfield, OH 45505
Crisis hotline: **(513) 325-3707 24 hrs**
Information: (513) 328-5306 9am-5pm (Mon-Fri)
Contact: Donna B Hart, Exec Dir
TYPE OF AGENCY: Rape crisis center; Domestic violence program
YEARS IN OPERATION: 14
LANGUAGES: Translators available
ACCESSIBILITY: Wheelchair accessible; Telecommunications for the hearing impaired (TTY, TDY, etc.); Signers for the hearing impaired
CASES SEXUAL ASSAULT/ABUSE (%): 3
CLIENTS/SERVICES: Sexual assault survivors; Marital rape/sexual abuse survivors; Child victims of sexual abuse; Adult survivors of child sexual abuse; Incest victims/survivors; Prevention program; Community education; Adolescent survivors of sexual abuse; Male survivors of sexual abuse; Prisoners
REQUIREMENTS: Minors need parental consent; No shelter facilities for adolescent boys
SPECIAL PROGRAMS/SERVICES: Female offender program provides creative outlets, counseling, follow-up for incarcerated females

STEUBENVILLE

ALIVE, INC
PO Box 866, Steubenville, OH 43952
Crisis hotline: **(614) 283-3444 24 hrs**
Information: (614) 283-3444 24 hrs
Contact: Michael Gromczewski, Exec Dir
TYPE OF AGENCY: Domestic violence program
SPONSORING ORGANIZATION: United Way
AREAS SERVED: Jefferson
YEARS IN OPERATION: 8
ACCESSIBILITY: Wheelchair accessible
CASES SEXUAL ASSAULT/ABUSE (%): 30
DESCRIPTION: Domestic violence services; Individual therapy for batterers
CLIENTS/SERVICES: Sexual assault survivors; Marital rape/sexual abuse survivors; Adult survivors of child sexual abuse; Community education

TOLEDO

YW RAPE CRISIS CENTER
1018 Jefferson Ave, Toledo, OH 43624
Crisis hotline: **(419) 241-7273 24 hrs**
Information: (419) 241-7006 9am-5pm (Mon-Fri)
Contact: Pam Van Camp, Dir
TYPE OF AGENCY: Rape crisis center; Child sexual abuse services; Child sexual abuse prevention program
SPONSORING ORGANIZATION: YWCA of Greater Toledo
AREAS SERVED: Lucas, Wood, Fulton, Ottawa, Sandusky
YEARS IN OPERATION: 15
LANGUAGES: Spanish
ACCESSIBILITY: Wheelchair accessible; Telecommunications for the hearing impaired (TTY, TDY, etc.); Signers for the hearing impaired
CASES SEXUAL ASSAULT/ABUSE (%): 100
DESCRIPTION: Provides comprehensive rape crisis services and therapy for sexually abused children; Treatment for rapists and batterers; Participation in juvenile sex offender treatment team; Feminist martial arts/self-defense
CLIENTS/SERVICES: Sexual assault survivors; Marital rape/sexual abuse survivors; Child victims of sexual abuse; Adult survivors of child sexual abuse; Incest victims/survivors; Prevention program; Community education; Offender treatment program; Adolescent survivors of sexual abuse; Male survivors of sexual abuse; Publications/media
SPECIAL PROGRAMS/SERVICES: Media program: *Rape Aftermath: How I Can Help*

TROY

MIAMI COUNTY PROSECUTOR'S OFFICE—VICTIM WITNESS PROGRAM
201 W Main St, Safety Bldg, Troy, OH 45373
Crisis hotline: **Sheriff's Dept (513) 335-8378 24 hrs via pager**
Information: (513) 335-8341, ext 2381 8am-4pm (Mon-Fri)
Contact: Shirley Utz, Victim Witness Coord
TYPE OF AGENCY: Victim/witness assistance program
AREAS SERVED: Miami
YEARS IN OPERATION: 3
ACCESSIBILITY: Wheelchair accessible; Signers for the hearing impaired
CASES SEXUAL ASSAULT/ABUSE (%): 85
CLIENTS/SERVICES: Sexual assault survivors; Marital rape/sexual abuse survivors; Child victims of sexual abuse; Prevention program; Community education; Adolescent survivors of sexual abuse; Male survivors of sexual abuse

WARREN

FAMILY SERVICE ASSOCIATION
1704 North Rd SE, Warren, OH 44484
Information: (216) 856-2907, 530-0395 8:30am-8pm (Mon, Thu) 8:30am-5pm (Tue, Wed, Fri)
Contact: George Kovach, Clinical Svcs Dir
TYPE OF AGENCY: Counseling/mental health services
AREAS SERVED: Trumbull
YEARS IN OPERATION: 50
ACCESSIBILITY: Wheelchair accessible
CASES SEXUAL ASSAULT/ABUSE (%): 20-25
DESCRIPTION: Counseling for survivors and offenders—child sexual abuse/incest offenders and batterers
CLIENTS/SERVICES: Sexual assault survivors; Marital rape/sexual abuse survivors; Child victims of sexual abuse; Adult survivors of child sexual abuse; Incest victims/survivors; Community education; Offender treatment program; Adolescent survivors of sexual abuse; Male survivors of sexual abuse

RAPE CRISIS TEAM OF TRUMBULL COUNTY, INC
PO Box 1743, Warren, OH 44482
Crisis hotline: **(216) 393-1565 24 hrs**
Information: (216) 393-1565 24 hrs
Contact: Mary Lapolla, Team/Board Member
TYPE OF AGENCY: Rape crisis center; Child sexual abuse prevention program; Rape prevention program
AREAS SERVED: Trumbull
YEARS IN OPERATION: 14
LANGUAGES: Greek, Italian
ACCESSIBILITY: Wheelchair accessible; Signers for the hearing impaired
CASES SEXUAL ASSAULT/ABUSE (%): 100
DESCRIPTION: Provides crisis intervention counseling and advocacy in hospital and law enforcement settings for rape and sexual abuse victims; Prevention programs including feminist martial/self-defense
CLIENTS/SERVICES: Sexual assault survivors; Marital rape/sexual abuse survivors; Child victims of sexual abuse; Adult survivors of child sexual abuse; Prevention program; Community education; Adolescent survivors of sexual abuse; Male survivors of sexual abuse
SPECIAL PROGRAMS/SERVICES: Holds NRA-approved handgun safety courses to familiarize women with guns. It teaches each woman to disassemble, clean, and accurately shoot the weapon. New volunteers take the rape prevention and self-defense class to facilitate awareness and safety when they go out on a rape call

TRUMBULL COUNTY PROSECUTOR'S OFFICE—VICTIM/WITNESS DIVISION
160 High St, Warren, OH 44481
Crisis hotline: **(216) 841-0444 24 hrs**
Information: (216) 841-0444 8:30am-4:30pm
Contact: Jacqueline Coury, Dir
TYPE OF AGENCY: Victim/witness assistance program
AREAS SERVED: Trumbull
YEARS IN OPERATION: 3
ACCESSIBILITY: Wheelchair accessible; Signers for the hearing impaired
CASES SEXUAL ASSAULT/ABUSE (%): 30-40
CLIENTS/SERVICES: Sexual assault survivors; Marital rape/sexual abuse survivors; Child victims of sexual abuse; Adult survivors of child sexual abuse; Incest victims/survivors; Prevention program; Community education
REQUIREMENTS: Charges need not be filed

WOOSTER

CHILD SEXUAL ABUSE INSTITUTE OF OHIO
PO Box 453, Wooster, OH 44691
Information: (216) 263-0579 9am-5pm (Mon-Fri)
Contact: Victoria Kepler Didato, Dir
TYPE OF AGENCY: Child sexual abuse services; Consultation; Training/research
AREAS SERVED: Statewide
YEARS IN OPERATION: 7
ACCESSIBILITY: Wheelchair accessible
CASES SEXUAL ASSAULT/ABUSE (%): 100
DESCRIPTION: Provides consultation and training for professionals in the area of child sexual abuse. Seminar topics include: interview techniques with victim/offender; cultural conditioning which contributes to abuse; behavioral cues victims of trauma exhibit in childhood; triggers and rituals associated with the trauma and how to "defuse" them; understanding sexual dysfunctions and their origins in abuse; understanding family dynamics; interpreting artwork of sexually abused children; six levels of victim guilt and how to work through them; offender profiles—male vs female, fixated vs regressed.
CLIENTS/SERVICES: Community education; Adolescent survivors of sexual abuse; Male survivors of sexual abuse

EVERY WOMAN'S HOUSE, INC
225 N Grant St, Wooster, OH 44691
Crisis hotline: **(216) 263-1020 24 hrs**
Information: (216) 263-6021 8:30am-5pm (Mon-Fri)
Contact: Tammy Beckett, Exec Dir
TYPE OF AGENCY: Domestic violence program
AREAS SERVED: Wayne, Holmes
YEARS IN OPERATION: 9
ACCESSIBILITY: Wheelchair accessible; Telecommunications for the hearing impaired (TTY, TDY, etc.); Signers for the hearing impaired
CASES SEXUAL ASSAULT/ABUSE (%): 50
DESCRIPTION: Provides services for families experiencing domestic violence: 24-hour emergency shelter, children's program, and individual and group counseling. Another Way is a self-help group experience, professionally facilitated to teach men alternatives to violence and abusive behavior
CLIENTS/SERVICES: Sexual assault survivors; Marital rape/sexual abuse survivors; Child victims of sexual abuse; Adult survivors of child sexual abuse; Prevention program; Community education; Offender treatment program; Adolescent survivors of sexual abuse; Male survivors of sexual abuse

WORTHINGTON

WILBRIDGE CONSULTATION CENTER
73 E Wilson Bridge Rd, Ste B4, Worthington, OH 43085
Information: (614) 885-2411 24 hr answering service
Contact: Kristen Elliott, Natl Cert Couns
TYPE OF AGENCY: Private practice
AREAS SERVED: Greater Columbus area
YEARS IN OPERATION: 2½
CASES SEXUAL ASSAULT/ABUSE (%): 25-35
CLIENTS/SERVICES: Sexual assault survivors; Marital rape/sexual abuse survivors; Child victims of sexual abuse; Adult survivors of child sexual abuse; Incest victims/survivors

XENIA

GREENE COUNTY PROSECUTOR'S OFFICE—VICTIM/WITNESS DIVISION
45 N Detroit St, Xenia, OH 45385
Crisis hotline: **(513) 376-5034 24 hrs**
Information: (513) 376-5087 8am-5pm (Mon-Fri)
Contact: Jeannette M Adkins, Dir
TYPE OF AGENCY: Victim/witness assistance program; Child sexual abuse prevention program; Rape prevention program; Acquaintance/date rape prevention program
AREAS SERVED: Greene
YEARS IN OPERATION: 7
ACCESSIBILITY: Wheelchair accessible; Signers for the hearing impaired
CASES SEXUAL ASSAULT/ABUSE (%): 50
CLIENTS/SERVICES: Sexual assault survivors; Marital rape/sexual abuse survivors; Child victims of sexual abuse; Adult survivors of child sexual abuse; Incest victims/survivors; Prevention program; Community education; Adolescent survivors of sexual abuse; Male survivors of sexual abuse
SPECIAL PROGRAMS/SERVICES: Extensive child sexual abuse prevention programs for second, fourth, and sixth graders, as well as acquaintance rape prevention for junior high school students; Rape prevention materials for college-level students

YOUNGSTOWN

BATTERED PERSONS' CRISIS CENTER
PO Box 1255, Youngstown, OH 44501
Crisis hotline: **(800) 438-1167 (statewide), (216) 744-5101 24 hrs**
Information: (216) 744-5374 24 hrs
Contact: Ruth Ciotti, Rape Crisis Coord
TYPE OF AGENCY: Rape crisis center; Domestic violence program
AREAS SERVED: Columbiana, Mahoning
YEARS IN OPERATION: 10
ACCESSIBILITY: Wheelchair accessible
CASES SEXUAL ASSAULT/ABUSE (%): 20
CLIENTS/SERVICES: Sexual assault survivors; Marital rape/sexual abuse survivors; Adult survivors of child sexual abuse; Prevention program; Community education; Adolescent survivors of sexual abuse; Male survivors of sexual abuse

HELP HOTLINE, INC
PO Box 46, Youngstown, OH 44501
Crisis hotline: **(216) 747-2696, 426-9355, 424-7767 24 hrs**
Information: (216) 747-5111 8am-6pm
Contact: Dolores M Elias, LPCC, Exec Dir
TYPE OF AGENCY: Victim/witness assistance program; Counseling/mental health services; Information and referral; Telephone crisis hotline
AREAS SERVED: Mahoning, Columbiana
YEARS IN OPERATION: 17
LANGUAGES: Spanish interpreter
ACCESSIBILITY: Telecommunications for the hearing impaired (TTY, TDY, etc.)
DESCRIPTION: 24-hour crisis intervention/suicide prevention; 24-hour victims of crime hotline; Direct link (by beeper) to caseworkers and counselors for face-to-face services after hours, weekends and holidays. Also provides victims assistance services and support
CLIENTS/SERVICES: Sexual assault survivors; Marital rape/sexual abuse survivors; Child victims of sexual abuse; Adult survivors of child sexual abuse; Incest victims/survivors; Community education

MAHONING COUNTY CHILDREN SERVICES
2801 Market St, Youngstown, OH 44507
Crisis hotline: **(216) 783-0411 24 hrs**
Information: (216) 783-0411 8:30am-4:30pm
TYPE OF AGENCY: Counseling/mental health services; Child sexual abuse prevention program; Child abuse prevention program
AREAS SERVED: Mahoning
ACCESSIBILITY: Wheelchair accessible
DESCRIPTION: Mandated by law to investigate, assess, and provide casework services for abused or neglected children in Mahoning County. Prevention program for preschool through high school
CLIENTS/SERVICES: Prevention program; Community education

MAHONING COUNTY PROSECUTOR— VICTIM/WITNESS PROGRAM
120 Market St, Youngstown, OH 44460
Crisis hotline: **(216) 747-2696 24 hrs**
Information: (216) 740-2333 8:30am-4:30pm
Contact: Edie Smith, Crisis Couns
TYPE OF AGENCY: Victim/witness assistance program; Child sexual abuse services; Child sexual abuse prevention program
AREAS SERVED: Mahoning
YEARS IN OPERATION: 3
ACCESSIBILITY: Wheelchair accessible
CASES SEXUAL ASSAULT/ABUSE (%): 25
CLIENTS/SERVICES: Sexual assault survivors; Marital rape/sexual abuse survivors; Child victims of sexual abuse; Adult survivors of child sexual abuse; Incest victims/survivors; Prevention program; Community education; Adolescent survivors of sexual abuse; Male survivors of sexual abuse; Elderly
REQUIREMENTS: Must file police report within 72 hours of the crime
SPECIAL PROGRAMS/SERVICES: Presents a program using a *Lucky Duck Puppet* to help children say "No" to "Bad Touches," geared toward children ages 3 to 7; Trains senior citizen volunteers; Developing a program that specificallly deals with physical abuse, working closely with the schools

RAPE INFORMATION AND COUNSELING
535 Marmion, Youngstown, OH 44502
Crisis hotline: **(216) 782-3936 24 hrs**
Information: (216) 782-3936 8am-4:30pm
Contact: Linda Botirius, Prog Dir
TYPE OF AGENCY: Rape crisis center
SPONSORING ORGANIZATION: Family Service Agency
AREAS SERVED: Mahoning
YEARS IN OPERATION: 20
CASES SEXUAL ASSAULT/ABUSE (%): 100
CLIENTS/SERVICES: Sexual assault survivors; Marital rape/sexual abuse survivors; Child victims of sexual abuse; Adult survivors of child sexual abuse; Incest victims/survivors; Prevention program; Community education; Adolescent survivors of sexual abuse; Male survivors of sexual abuse

ZANESVILLE

SIX COUNTY, INC—MUSKINGUM COUNSELING CENTER
2845 Bell St, Zanesville, OH 43701
Crisis hotline: **(800) 344-5818, (614) 453-5818 24 hrs**
Information: (614) 454-9766 8am-5pm (Mon-Fri)
Contact: James McDonald, Mgr
TYPE OF AGENCY: Counseling/mental health services; Child sexual abuse services
AREAS SERVED: Muskingum, Coshocton, Guernsey, Perry, Noble, Morgan
YEARS IN OPERATION: 20
LANGUAGES: Chinese
ACCESSIBILITY: Wheelchair accessible
CASES SEXUAL ASSAULT/ABUSE (%): 10
DESCRIPTION: Outpatient, adult inpatient C and E; Partial hospitalization; Emergency services; Outpatient sexual assault treatment; Support groups for male and female survivors; Therapy for child sexual abuse/incest offenders and batterers
CLIENTS/SERVICES: Sexual assault survivors; Marital rape/sexual abuse survivors; Child victims of sexual abuse; Adult survivors of child sexual abuse; Incest victims/survivors; Prevention program; Community education; Offender treatment program; Adolescent survivors of sexual abuse; Male survivors of sexual abuse
SPECIAL PROGRAMS/SERVICES: Video training for ER staff and on legal system

OKLAHOMA

ADA

AREA SERVICES FOR BATTERED WOMEN, INC
PO Box 2274, Ada, OK 74820
Crisis hotline: **(405) 436-3504 24 hrs**
Information: (405) 436-3504 8am-5pm
Contact: Marilee Roberts, Exec Dir
TYPE OF AGENCY: Domestic violence program
AREAS SERVED: Pontotoc, Marshall, Atoka, Coal, Hughes, Carter, Garvin, Love, Bryan, Johnston, Seminole, Murray
YEARS IN OPERATION: 8
CASES SEXUAL ASSAULT/ABUSE (%): 15
CLIENTS/SERVICES: Sexual assault survivors; Marital rape/sexual abuse survivors; Child victims of sexual abuse; Adult survivors of child sexual abuse; Prevention program; Community education; Adolescent survivors of sexual abuse; Male survivors of sexual abuse

DISTRICT ATTORNEY'S OFFICE—VICTIM WITNESS CENTER
PO Box 146, Ada, OK 74820
Information: (405) 332-0378 9am-5pm; After 5 (405) 332-3834
Contact: Ann Armstrong, Coord
TYPE OF AGENCY: Victim/witness assistance program
AREAS SERVED: Pontotoc, Seminole, Hughes
YEARS IN OPERATION: 3
CASES SEXUAL ASSAULT/ABUSE (%): 10
CLIENTS/SERVICES: Sexual assault survivors; Marital rape/sexual abuse survivors; Child victims of sexual abuse
REQUIREMENTS: With claims to Crime Victims Comp Board, there are several requirements.

ANTLERS

SOUTHEASTERN OKLAHOMA SERVICES FOR ABUSED WOMEN
PO Box 185, Antlers, OK 74523
Crisis hotline: **(405) 298-5575 24 hrs**
Information: (405) 298-5575 24 hrs
Contact: Pat Payne, Exec Dir
TYPE OF AGENCY: Domestic violence program
AREAS SERVED: Choctaw, McCurtain, Pushmataha
YEARS IN OPERATION: 7
CASES SEXUAL ASSAULT/ABUSE (%): 6
CLIENTS/SERVICES: Sexual assault survivors; Marital rape/sexual abuse survivors; Child victims of sexual abuse; Adult survivors of child sexual abuse; Incest victims/survivors; Prevention program; Community education; Adolescent survivors of sexual abuse

BARTLESVILLE

SEXUAL ASSAULT SAFETY CENTER
PO Box 2016, Bartlesville, OK 74005
Crisis hotline: **(918) 336-1188 24 hrs**
Information: (918) 336-1188 8am-5pm (Mon-Fri)
Contact: Bobbe Hornback, Pres-SASC Board of Dir
TYPE OF AGENCY: Rape crisis center; Domestic violence program
AREAS SERVED: Washington
YEARS IN OPERATION: 2½
LANGUAGES: French, Spanish
CASES SEXUAL ASSAULT/ABUSE (%): 100
DESCRIPTION: Comprehensive rape crisis services and prevention programs; Services for domestic violence survivors; Individual and group therapy for batterers including feminist martial arts/self-defense
CLIENTS/SERVICES: Sexual assault survivors; Marital rape/sexual abuse survivors; Child victims of sexual abuse; Adult survivors of child sexual abuse; Incest victims/survivors; Prevention program; Community education; Adolescent survivors of sexual abuse; Male survivors of sexual abuse
REQUIREMENTS: Must be of legal age

WASHINGTON COUNTY DISTRICT ATTORNEY—VICTIM/WITNESS PROGRAM
420 S Johnstone, Bartlesville, OK 74003
Information: (918) 336-4320 8am-5pm (Mon-Fri)
Contact: Beth Dow, Victim-Witness Coord
TYPE OF AGENCY: Victim/witness assistance program
AREAS SERVED: Washington, Nowata
YEARS IN OPERATION: 6
ACCESSIBILITY: Wheelchair accessible
CASES SEXUAL ASSAULT/ABUSE (%): 10-15
CLIENTS/SERVICES: Sexual assault survivors; Marital rape/sexual abuse survivors; Child victims of sexual abuse; Community education

WOMEN AND CHILDREN IN CRISIS, INC
PO Box 2016, Bartlesville, OK 74005
Crisis hotline: **(918) 336-1188 24 hrs**
Information: (918) 336-1188 9am-5pm
Contact: Faye Marlowe-Holden, Exec Dir
TYPE OF AGENCY: Domestic violence program
AREAS SERVED: Washington, Nowata, Osage
YEARS IN OPERATION: 6
LANGUAGES: Spanish, French
CASES SEXUAL ASSAULT/ABUSE (%): 60
CLIENTS/SERVICES: Marital rape/sexual abuse survivors

CHICKASHA

WOMEN'S SERVICE AND FAMILY RESOURCE CENTER
PO Box 1539, Chickasha, OK 73023
Crisis hotline: **(405) 222-1818, Toll free ask operator for Enterprise 53000 24 hrs**
Information: Chickasha (405) 222-1819, El Reno (405) 262-4455 9am-5pm (Mon-Fri)
Contact: Jenny Roberts, Exec Dir
TYPE OF AGENCY: Rape crisis center; Domestic violence program; Child sexual abuse prevention program
AREAS SERVED: Grady, Canadian
YEARS IN OPERATION: 8
LANGUAGES: Spanish
ACCESSIBILITY: Wheelchair accessible; Signers for the hearing impaired
CASES SEXUAL ASSAULT/ABUSE (%): 20
DESCRIPTION: Services for survivors of sexual assault and domestic violence; Non-offending parent support in cases of incest; Feminist martial arts/self defense program
CLIENTS/SERVICES: Sexual assault survivors; Marital rape/sexual abuse survivors; Child victims of sexual abuse; Adult survivors of child sexual abuse; Incest victims/survivors; Prevention program; Community education; Adolescent survivors of sexual abuse; Male survivors of sexual abuse

CHOCTAW

TRI-CITY YOUTH AND FAMILY CENTER, INC
PO Box 695, Choctaw, OK 73020
Information: (405) 390-8131 8:30am-6pm (Mon-Thu); 8:30am-3pm (Fri)
Contact: Joy L Leuthard, Exec Dir
TYPE OF AGENCY: Counseling/mental health services; Child sexual abuse services
AREAS SERVED: Eastern Oklahoma
YEARS IN OPERATION: 14½
ACCESSIBILITY: Wheelchair accessible; Signers for the hearing impaired
CASES SEXUAL ASSAULT/ABUSE (%): 50
DESCRIPTION: Counseling for survivors; Individual and family therapy for child sexual abuse offenders, incest offenders and batterers
CLIENTS/SERVICES: Sexual assault survivors; Marital rape/sexual abuse survivors; Child victims of sexual abuse; Adult survivors of child sexual abuse; Incest victims/survivors; Community education; Offender treatment program; Adolescent survivors of sexual abuse; Male survivors of sexual abuse

CLINTON

ACTION ASSOCIATES, INC
PO Box 1534, Clinton, OK 73601
Crisis hotline: **(405) 323-2604 24 hrs**
Information: (405) 323-0838 8am-5pm
Contact: Mary Rayner, RN, Exec Dir
TYPE OF AGENCY: Rape crisis center; Domestic violence program
AREAS SERVED: Western Oklahoma
YEARS IN OPERATION: 9
LANGUAGES: Spanish, Sign, French, German, Asiatic, Hindu
ACCESSIBILITY: Wheelchair accessible; Signers for the hearing impaired
CASES SEXUAL ASSAULT/ABUSE (%): 100
DESCRIPTION: Services for survivors of sexual assault and domestic violence; Individual and group therapy for batterers
CLIENTS/SERVICES: Sexual assault survivors; Marital rape/sexual abuse survivors; Child victims of sexual abuse; Adult survivors of child sexual abuse; Incest victims/survivors; Prevention program; Community education; Offender treatment program; Adolescent survivors of sexual abuse

EDMOND

MORGAN, MORGAN AND ASSOCIATES
909 Glen Eagles Dr, Edmond, OK 73013
Crisis hotline: **(405) 755-2002 24 hrs**
Information: (405) 755-2002 8am-5pm
Contact: Catherine Morgan, PhD, Psychologist
TYPE OF AGENCY: Private practice
AREAS SERVED: Metro Oklahoma city area
YEARS IN OPERATION: 6
ACCESSIBILITY: Signers for the hearing impaired
CASES SEXUAL ASSAULT/ABUSE (%): 70
CLIENTS/SERVICES: Sexual assault survivors; Marital rape/sexual abuse survivors; Child victims of sexual abuse; Adult survivors of child sexual abuse; Incest victims/survivors; Community education; Adolescent survivors of sexual abuse; Male survivors of sexual abuse
REQUIREMENTS: Insurance assignment is accepted but client portion must be paid at the time service is provided

ENID

DISTRICT ATTORNEY'S OFFICE—VICTIM WITNESS CENTER
Garfield County Courthouse, Enid, OK 73701
Information: (405) 233-5228 8am-5pm
Contact: Billie Dempewolf, Coord
TYPE OF AGENCY: Victim/witness assistance program
AREAS SERVED: Garfield, Grant, Canadian, Blaine, Kingfisher
YEARS IN OPERATION: 6½
LANGUAGES: Spanish
ACCESSIBILITY: Wheelchair accessible
CASES SEXUAL ASSAULT/ABUSE (%): 10
CLIENTS/SERVICES: Sexual assault survivors; Marital rape/sexual abuse survivors; Child victims of sexual abuse; Community education
REQUIREMENTS: Client must file charges.

NORTHWEST OKLAHOMA PASTORAL CARE ASSOCIATION, INC
PO Box 3165, 302 N Independence, Enid, OK 73702
Crisis hotline: **(405) 234-1111 24 hrs**
Information: (405) 237-8400 9am-9:30pm (Mon, Tue, Thu); 9am-5pm (Wed, Fri, Sat)
Contact: Nan Rowe, Exec Dir
TYPE OF AGENCY: Counseling/mental health services; Pastoral counseling
AREAS SERVED: Northwest Oklahoma
YEARS IN OPERATION: 25
LANGUAGES: Spanish
ACCESSIBILITY: Wheelchair accessible; Telecommunications for the hearing impaired (TTY, TDY, etc.)
CASES SEXUAL ASSAULT/ABUSE (%): 70-80
DESCRIPTION: Provides Christian family counseling in the area of sexual assault/abuse, including support groups for female and male survivors of sexual assault/abuse; Individual, group, and family therapy for rapists, child sexual abuse offenders, incest offenders and batterers
CLIENTS/SERVICES: Sexual assault survivors; Marital rape/sexual abuse survivors; Child victims of sexual abuse; Adult survivors of child sexual abuse; Incest victims/survivors; Prevention program; Community education; Adolescent survivors of sexual abuse; Male survivors of sexual abuse
SPECIAL PROGRAMS/SERVICES: In-depth psychotherapy for victims of abuse—adult, adolescent, child, male and female—called "Primal Integration Therapy."

YWCA CRISIS CENTER
525 S Quincy, Enid, OK 73701
Crisis hotline: **(405) 234-7644 24 hrs**
Information: (405) 234-7581 8am-5pm
Contact: Suzi Powell, Crisis Ctr Dir
TYPE OF AGENCY: Rape crisis center; Domestic violence program
AREAS SERVED: Primarily Garfield, Grant, Major, Kingfisher, Blaine
YEARS IN OPERATION: 10
LANGUAGES: Spanish, Vietnamese
ACCESSIBILITY: Wheelchair accessible; Signers for the hearing impaired
CASES SEXUAL ASSAULT/ABUSE (%): 65
CLIENTS/SERVICES: Sexual assault survivors; Marital rape/sexual abuse survivors; Adult survivors of child sexual abuse; Incest victims/survivors; Prevention program; Community education

FORT SILL

ARMY COMMUNITY SERVICE
PO Box 33097, Fort Sill, OK 73503
Information: (405) 351-5018, 351-6801 7:30am-4pm
Contact: Yvonne Kearns, Family Advocacy Prog Mgr
TYPE OF AGENCY: Counseling/mental health services; Military services
AREAS SERVED: Comanche and outlying area
YEARS IN OPERATION: 20
LANGUAGES: Spanish
ACCESSIBILITY: Wheelchair accessible
DESCRIPTION: Provides emergency social services, information and referral, and prevention/education classes on many topics, including sexual assault/child sexual abuse
CLIENTS/SERVICES: Sexual assault survivors; Child victims of sexual abuse; Prevention program; Community education
REQUIREMENTS: Client must be on active duty or retired military or their dependents. Education classes and sexual abuse prevention available for civilians on request

IDABEL

DISTRICT ATTORNEY'S OFFICE—VICTIM/WITNESS PROGRAM
McCurtain County Courthouse, Idabel, OK 74745
Information: (405) 286-7611 8am-5pm
Contact: Reed Blankenship, Victim/Witness Coord-Investigator
TYPE OF AGENCY: Victim/witness assistance program
SPONSORING ORGANIZATION: District #17
AREAS SERVED: McCurtain, Choctaw, Pushmataha
CASES SEXUAL ASSAULT/ABUSE (%): 2
CLIENTS/SERVICES: Sexual assault survivors; Child victims of sexual abuse
REQUIREMENTS: Charges need not be filed; however, investigations are related to the prosecution field. If the facts can be proven, charges are filed and case is prosecuted

LAWTON

FORMERLY ABUSED CHILDREN EMERGING IN SOCIETY (FACES)
3501 SW "F" Ave, Lawton, OK 73505
Information: (405) 248-0471 9am-5pm
Contact: Julie May, Dir
TYPE OF AGENCY: Counseling/mental health services
SPONSORING ORGANIZATION: Center for Creative Living
AREAS SERVED: Comanche, Stephens, Caddo, Cotton, McClain
YEARS IN OPERATION: 3
ACCESSIBILITY: Wheelchair accessible; Signers for the hearing impaired
CASES SEXUAL ASSAULT/ABUSE (%): 100
CLIENTS/SERVICES: Adult survivors of child sexual abuse; Incest victims/survivors; Male survivors of sexual abuse
REQUIREMENTS: Client must be over 18 years of age

NEW DIRECTIONS, INC
PO Box 1684, Lawton, OK 73502
Crisis hotline: **(405) 357-2500**
Information: (405) 357-6141
Contact: Susan Clark
TYPE OF AGENCY: Rape crisis center; Domestic violence program
CLIENTS/SERVICES: Sexual assault survivors

NEWKIRK

DISTRICT ATTORNEY'S VICTIM/WITNESS PROGRAM
Courthouse, Newkirk, OK 74647
Information: (405) 362-2571 8:30am-4:30pm
Contact: Jodie Frazier, Victim/Witness Coord
TYPE OF AGENCY: Victim/witness assistance program
AREAS SERVED: Kay, Noble
YEARS IN OPERATION: 7
ACCESSIBILITY: Wheelchair accessible
CLIENTS/SERVICES: Sexual assault survivors; Child victims of sexual abuse

NORMAN

BETHESDA ALTERNATIVE, INC
204 Woodcrest Dr, Norman, OK 73071
Information: (405) 364-0333 9am-5pm (Mon-Fri)
Contact: Candace McCaffrey, PhD, Exec Dir
TYPE OF AGENCY: Child sexual abuse services; Private practice
AREAS SERVED: Cleveland, Oklahoma, McClain
YEARS IN OPERATION: 7
ACCESSIBILITY: Wheelchair accessible; Signers for the hearing impaired
CASES SEXUAL ASSAULT/ABUSE (%): 100
DESCRIPTION: Comprehensive child sexual abuse treatment program, providing therapeutic services for children (ages 4-18) who have been sexually abused, for offenders, and for other related family members (primarily mothers), and for adult survivors of incest
CLIENTS/SERVICES: Child victims of sexual abuse; Adult survivors of child sexual abuse; Incest victims/survivors; Community education; Offender treatment program; Adolescent survivors of sexual abuse; Preschoolers
REQUIREMENTS: Children's program: ages 3-18, not psychotic or mentally retarded. Offender program: prefer men with legal charge and supervision; must make two-year commitment to program, not psychotic or mentally retarded; must take some degree of responsibility for behavior

BETHESDA ALTERNATIVE, INC
(continued)

SPECIAL PROGRAMS/SERVICES: Offers a specialized 12-week program with both a therapeutic and educational/prevention forcus for preschool children who have been sexually abused. There is a concurrent parent education group. Utilizes play and art therapy, as well as the use of video for therapeutic intervention in problem areas such as body image and poor self-concept.

WOMEN'S RESOURCE CENTER
PO Box 5089, Norman, OK 73070
Crisis hotline: **(405) 360-0590 24 hrs**
Information: (405) 364-9424 8:30am-5pm (Mon-Fri)
Contact: Judy Harper, Exec Dir
TYPE OF AGENCY: Rape crisis center; Domestic violence program; Child sexual abuse prevention program
AREAS SERVED: Cleveland, McClain
YEARS IN OPERATION: 13
LANGUAGES: Spanish
CASES SEXUAL ASSAULT/ABUSE (%): 50
CLIENTS/SERVICES: Sexual assault survivors; Marital rape/sexual abuse survivors; Adult survivors of child sexual abuse; Incest victims/survivors; Prevention program; Community education; Adolescent survivors of sexual abuse

OKLAHOMA CITY

DISTRICT ATTORNEY'S OFFICE—VICTIM ASSISTANCE CENTER
320 Robert S Kerr, Ste 627, Oklahoma City, OK 73132
Information: (405) 278-1633 8am-5pm
Contact: Lyn Bolding, Victim Advocate
TYPE OF AGENCY: Victim/witness assistance program
AREAS SERVED: Oklahoma
YEARS IN OPERATION: 7
CLIENTS/SERVICES: Sexual assault survivors; Marital rape/sexual abuse survivors; Child victims of sexual abuse; Adult survivors of child sexual abuse; Incest victims/survivors; Prevention program; Community education

PARENTS ASSISTANCE CENTER—SEXUAL ABUSE TREATMENT PROGRAM
323 NW 10th, Oklahoma City, OK 73103
Crisis hotline: **(405) 232-8226 24 hrs**
Information: (405) 232-8226 8am-5pm
Contact: Dr Richard Kishur, Prog Dir
TYPE OF AGENCY: Counseling/mental health services; Child sexual abuse services; Child abuse services
AREAS SERVED: Oklahoma
YEARS IN OPERATION: 12
CASES SEXUAL ASSAULT/ABUSE (%): 25-30
DESCRIPTION: Counseling for sexually abused children and their families; Support groups for female and male survivors of sexual assault/abuse; Group therapy for rapists, child sexual abuse offenders, incest offenders, and batterers
CLIENTS/SERVICES: Child victims of sexual abuse; Adult survivors of child sexual abuse; Incest victims/survivors; Prevention program; Community education; Offender treatment program; Adolescent survivors of sexual abuse; Male survivors of sexual abuse
REQUIREMENTS: Children 6 years and older, all family members

PASSAGEWAYS CENTER
3000 United Founders Blvd, No 11, Oklahoma City, OK 73112
Information: (405) 842-6980 9am-5pm (Mon-Fri)
Contact: Ruth Ann Mertens, PhD, Dir
TYPE OF AGENCY: Private practice
AREAS SERVED: Statewide
YEARS IN OPERATION: 5
ACCESSIBILITY: Wheelchair accessible
CASES SEXUAL ASSAULT/ABUSE (%): 60
DESCRIPTION: Offers evaluation and both child/adolescent and family therapy for sexually abused children 2-18 years of age. Also court-related evaluations of child and family relative to abuse allegations in custody cases
CLIENTS/SERVICES: Child victims of sexual abuse; Adult survivors of child sexual abuse; Incest victims/survivors; Community education; Adolescent survivors of sexual abuse; Male survivors of sexual abuse
REQUIREMENTS: Children 2-18 years and adults

UNIVERSITY OF OKLAHOMA HEALTH SCIENCES CENTER—CHILD STUDY CENTER
1100 NE 13th St, Oklahoma City, OK 73117
Information: (405) 271-6816 8am-5pm
Contact: Diane J Willis, PhD, Child Study Ctr Asst Dir/Dir of Psychological Svcs
TYPE OF AGENCY: Hospital/medical center; Child sexual abuse services
AREAS SERVED: Statewide
ACCESSIBILITY: Wheelchair accessible
CASES SEXUAL ASSAULT/ABUSE (%): 15-17
DESCRIPTION: Assesses and treats children with exceptional disorders such as developmental problems, emotional-behavioral problems, learning disorders, etc
CLIENTS/SERVICES: Child victims of sexual abuse; Incest victims/survivors; Prevention program; Adolescent survivors of sexual abuse
REQUIREMENTS: Ages 0-16

YWCA RAPE CRISIS CENTER
415 NW 5th St, Oklahoma City, OK 73102
Crisis hotline: **(405) 524-7273 24 hrs**
Information: (405) 232-6199 8am-5pm
Contact: Crystal Hines, Rape Crisis Coord
TYPE OF AGENCY: Rape crisis center; Domestic violence program
SPONSORING ORGANIZATION: YWCA Crisis Intervention Services
AREAS SERVED: Oklahoma
YEARS IN OPERATION: 8
LANGUAGES: Spanish translator available
ACCESSIBILITY: Telecommunications for the hearing impaired (TTY, TDY, etc.)
CLIENTS/SERVICES: Sexual assault survivors; Marital rape/sexual abuse survivors; Child victims of sexual abuse; Prevention program; Community education; Adolescent survivors of sexual abuse

PONCA CITY

DOMESTIC VIOLENCE PROGRAM OF NORTH CENTRAL OKLAHOMA, INC
PO Box 85, Ponca City, OK 74602
Crisis hotline: **(405) 762-2873 24 hrs**
Information: (405) 762-3603 8am-11pm
Contact: Christy Dulick, Prog Coord
TYPE OF AGENCY: Domestic violence program
AREAS SERVED: Payne, Osage, Noble, Kay, Pawnee
YEARS IN OPERATION: 10
CASES SEXUAL ASSAULT/ABUSE (%): 70
CLIENTS/SERVICES: Sexual assault survivors; Marital rape/sexual abuse survivors; Adult survivors of child sexual abuse; Community education

STILLWATER

STILLWATER DOMESTIC VIOLENCE SERVICES, INC
PO Box 1059, Stillwater, OK 74076
Crisis hotline: **(405) 624-3020 24 hrs**
Information: (405) 624-2517 9am-5pm (Mon-Fri)
Contact: Jane Vantine, Exec Dir
TYPE OF AGENCY: Rape crisis center; Domestic violence program
AREAS SERVED: Payne, Osage, Kay, Pawnee, Noble
YEARS IN OPERATION: 10
ACCESSIBILITY: Signers for the hearing impaired
CASES SEXUAL ASSAULT/ABUSE (%): 20
CLIENTS/SERVICES: Sexual assault survivors; Marital rape/sexual abuse survivors; Child victims of sexual abuse; Adult survivors of child sexual abuse; Incest victims/survivors; Prevention program; Community education; Adolescent survivors of sexual abuse; Male survivors of sexual abuse

TAHLEQUAH

HELP IN CRISIS
PO Box 1975, Tahlequah, OK 74465
Crisis hotline: **(918) 456-4357 24 hrs**
Information: (918) 456-0673
Contact: Pamela Moore, Exec Dir
TYPE OF AGENCY: Rape crisis center; Domestic violence program
AREAS SERVED: Cherokee, Adair, Sequoyah, Wagoner
YEARS IN OPERATION: 6
ACCESSIBILITY: Wheelchair accessible; Telecommunications for the hearing impaired (TTY, TDY, etc.)
CASES SEXUAL ASSAULT/ABUSE (%): 25
CLIENTS/SERVICES: Sexual assault survivors; Marital rape/sexual abuse survivors; Child victims of sexual abuse; Adult survivors of child sexual abuse; Incest victims/survivors; Community education

TULSA

CALL RAPE, INC
2121 S Columbia, Ste 420, Tulsa, OK 74114
Crisis hotline: **(918) 744-7273 24 hrs daily**
Information: (918) 744-7361 8am-5pm (Mon-Fri)
Contact: Gloria Dialectic, PhD, Exec Dir
TYPE OF AGENCY: Rape crisis center
AREAS SERVED: Tulsa, Creek, Rogers, Okmulgee, Mayes
YEARS IN OPERATION: 13
CASES SEXUAL ASSAULT/ABUSE (%): 100
CLIENTS/SERVICES: Sexual assault survivors; Marital rape/sexual abuse survivors; Child victims of sexual abuse; Prevention program; Community education; Adolescent survivors of sexual abuse; Male survivors of sexual abuse

CHILD ABUSE NETWORK CENTER
1502 S Denver, Tulsa, OK 74119
Information: (918) 599-7881 9am-4pm
Contact: Dianne Dessauer, Proj Dir
TYPE OF AGENCY: Victim/witness assistance program; Child sexual abuse services; Child abuse services; Interagency network
SPONSORING ORGANIZATION: Child Abuse Network, Inc
AREAS SERVED: Tulsa
YEARS IN OPERATION: 1
DESCRIPTION: Interdisciplinary planning to strengthen the response to child abuse; Includes DA's Crimes Against Children Task Force which coordinates investigation process (interviews, medical exam, victim witness, child development)
CLIENTS/SERVICES: Community education

FAMILY SEXUAL ABUSE TREATMENT PROGRAM (FSATP)
650 S Peoria, Tulsa, OK 74120
Information: (918) 587-9471 8:30am-8pm (Mon, Wed); 8:30am-5:30pm (Tue, Thu, Fri)
Contact: J Adams-Westcott, PhD, Prog Supv
TYPE OF AGENCY: Child sexual abuse services; Child sexual abuse prevention program
SPONSORING ORGANIZATION: Family and Children's Service, Inc
AREAS SERVED: Tulsa and contiguous counties
YEARS IN OPERATION: 8
ACCESSIBILITY: Wheelchair accessible
CASES SEXUAL ASSAULT/ABUSE (%): 100

FAMILY SEXUAL ABUSE TREATMENT PROGRAM (FSATP) *(continued)*

DESCRIPTION: Counseling for sexually abused children and their families; Personal safety training for preschool children; Individual, group, and family therapy for child sexual abuse offenders, incest offenders, and adolescent offenders and their families
CLIENTS/SERVICES: Child victims of sexual abuse; Adult survivors of child sexual abuse; Incest victims/survivors; Prevention program; Community education; Offender treatment program; Adolescent survivors of sexual abuse; Male survivors of sexual abuse; Preschoolers

TULSA COUNTY DISTRICT ATTORNEY— VICTIM/WITNESS CENTER
707 Tulsa County Courthouse, Tulsa, OK 74103
Information: (918) 584-4230 8am-5pm (Mon-Fri)
Contact: Mary Jo Speaker, Victim-Witness Coord
TYPE OF AGENCY: Victim/witness assistance program
AREAS SERVED: Tulsa
YEARS IN OPERATION: 6
ACCESSIBILITY: Wheelchair accessible
CASES SEXUAL ASSAULT/ABUSE (%): 10-15
CLIENTS/SERVICES: Sexual assault survivors; Marital rape/sexual abuse survivors; Child victims of sexual abuse

WOODWARD

DISTRICT ATTORNEY'S OFFICE—VICTIM/WITNESS PROGRAM
1600 Main, Woodward, OK 73801
Crisis hotline: **(800) 522-7233 24 hrs**
Information: (405) 256-8616 9am-5pm
Contact: Pam Rodgers, Victim/Witness Coord
TYPE OF AGENCY: Victim/witness assistance program
AREAS SERVED: Woodward, Woods, Major, Dewey, Alfalfa
YEARS IN OPERATION: 3
ACCESSIBILITY: Wheelchair accessible
CLIENTS/SERVICES: Sexual assault survivors; Marital rape/sexual abuse survivors; Child victims of sexual abuse; Incest victims/survivors; Prevention program; Community education
REQUIREMENTS: Incident must be reported to law enforcement; Client must be willing to file charges

NORTHWEST DOMESTIC CRISIS SERVICES, INC
1515 Main, Woodward, OK 73801
Crisis hotline: **(405) 256-8712 24 hrs**
Information: (405) 256-1215 8am-5pm (Mon-Fri)
Contact: Deanne Griffin, Exec Dir
TYPE OF AGENCY: Domestic violence program
AREAS SERVED: Alfalfa, Beaver, Cimarron, Dewey, Ellis, Harper, Major, Texas, Woods, Woodward
YEARS IN OPERATION: 8
LANGUAGES: Spanish translator
CASES SEXUAL ASSAULT/ABUSE (%): 40
CLIENTS/SERVICES: Sexual assault survivors; Marital rape/sexual abuse survivors; Community education

OREGON

BAKER

MAY DAY, INC
2101 Main St, Baker, OR 97814
Crisis hotline: **(503) 523-5903 24 hrs**
Information: (503) 523-4134 9:30am-1:30pm
Contact: Becky Hansen, Prog Coord
TYPE OF AGENCY: Rape crisis center; Domestic violence program
AREAS SERVED: Baker
YEARS IN OPERATION: 3
ACCESSIBILITY: Wheelchair accessible; Signers for the hearing impaired
CASES SEXUAL ASSAULT/ABUSE (%): 50
CLIENTS/SERVICES: Sexual assault survivors; Marital rape/sexual abuse survivors; Adult survivors of child sexual abuse; Prevention program; Community education; Adolescent survivors of sexual abuse; Male survivors of sexual abuse

BEAVERTON

CENTER FOR BEHAVIORAL INTERVENTION
4560 SW 110th, No 200, Beaverton, OR 97005
Information: (503) 644-2772 9am-5pm
Contact: Cory Jewell, Asst Dir
TYPE OF AGENCY: Private practice; Offender treatment; Training/research
AREAS SERVED: Clark, Washington, Clackamas, Multnomah, Yamhill, Clatsop, Tillamook
YEARS IN OPERATION: 6
CASES SEXUAL ASSAULT/ABUSE (%): 100
DESCRIPTION: Evaluation and treatment of juvenile and adult sex offenders and their families. Therapy includes aversion conditioning, men's group therapy, couples group therapy, family therapy, and nonvictim sibling treatment
CLIENTS/SERVICES: Marital rape/sexual abuse survivors; Child victims of sexual abuse; Adult survivors of child sexual abuse; Incest victims/survivors; Prevention program; Community education; Offender treatment program; Adolescent survivors of sexual abuse; Male survivors of sexual abuse
REQUIREMENTS: Offender must be court mandated to successfully complete this program

ST MARY'S BOYS HOME
16535 SW Tualatin Valley Hwy, Beaverton, OR 97006
Information: (503) 649-5651 24 hrs
Contact: Pat Connell, Treatment Dir; Loyal F Marsh, PhD, Assoc Dir
TYPE OF AGENCY: Child sexual abuse services; Residential treatment facility; Adolescent program; Offender treatment
AREAS SERVED: Statewide
YEARS IN OPERATION: 100
CASES SEXUAL ASSAULT/ABUSE (%): 25
DESCRIPTION: Treats adolescent sexual offenders and deals with related abuse problems. Also works with parents
CLIENTS/SERVICES: Child victims of sexual abuse; Offender treatment program; Adolescent survivors of sexual abuse; Male survivors of sexual abuse
REQUIREMENTS: Must be adjudicated, unless 12 or younger; Cannot be grossly retarded or overly psychotic (Ages 10-18)

BEND

CENTRAL OREGON BATTERING AND RAPE ALLIANCE (COBRA)
PO Box 1086, Bend, OR 97709
Crisis hotline: **(800) 356-2369, (503) 389-7021 24 hrs**
Information: (503) 382-9227 8am-5pm
Contact: Donna Gordon, Exec Coord
TYPE OF AGENCY: Rape crisis center; Domestic violence program
AREAS SERVED: Deschutes, Jefferson, Crook
YEARS IN OPERATION: 11
LANGUAGES: Spanish, Russian, French
ACCESSIBILITY: Wheelchair accessible
CASES SEXUAL ASSAULT/ABUSE (%): 80
CLIENTS/SERVICES: Sexual assault survivors; Marital rape/sexual abuse survivors; Child victims of sexual abuse; Adult survivors of child sexual abuse; Incest victims/survivors; Prevention program; Community education; Adolescent survivors of sexual abuse

BOARDMAN

MORROW COUNTY MENTAL HEALTH SERVICE
PO Box 261, Boardman, OR 97818
Information: (503) 481-2911, 676-9161 9am-5pm
TYPE OF AGENCY: Counseling/mental health services; Private practice
AREAS SERVED: Morrow, Wheeler, Gilliam
DESCRIPTION: Community mental health agency with separate sex offender/victim programs. Clinical member of Association for Behavioral Treatment of Sex Abuse
CLIENTS/SERVICES: Sexual assault survivors; Marital rape/sexual abuse survivors; Child victims of sexual abuse; Adult survivors of child sexual abuse; Incest victims/survivors; Offender treatment program; Adolescent survivors of sexual abuse; Male survivors of sexual abuse
REQUIREMENTS: Crime must be reported to law enforcement

CORVALLIS

CENTER AGAINST RAPE AND DOMESTIC VIOLENCE
PO Box 914, Corvallis, OR 97339
Crisis hotline: **(503) 754-0110 24 hrs**
Information: (503) 758-0219 9am-5pm (Mon-Fri)
Contact: George Grosch, Resource Developer
TYPE OF AGENCY: Rape crisis center; Domestic violence program
AREAS SERVED: Linn, Benton
YEARS IN OPERATION: 10
DESCRIPTION: Services for sexual assault and domestic violence survivors, including feminist martial arts/self-defense
CLIENTS/SERVICES: Sexual assault survivors; Marital rape/sexual abuse survivors; Child victims of sexual abuse; Adult survivors of child sexual abuse; Incest victims/survivors; Prevention program; Community education; Adolescent survivors of sexual abuse

THE DALLES

WASCO COUNTY DISTRICT ATTORNEY'S OFFICE—VICTIM/WITNESS ASSISTANCE
Wasco County Courthouse, Rm 411, The Dalles, OR 97058
Information: (503) 296-4611
Contact: Eddie Illingworth, Prog Coord
TYPE OF AGENCY: Victim/witness assistance program
AREAS SERVED: Wasco
YEARS IN OPERATION: 2½
CASES SEXUAL ASSAULT/ABUSE (%): 5
CLIENTS/SERVICES: Sexual assault survivors; Marital rape/sexual abuse survivors; Child victims of sexual abuse; Incest victims/survivors
REQUIREMENTS: Must be a victim of a crime reported in the state of Oregon

ENTERPRISE

WALLOWA COUNTY DISTRICT ATTORNEY'S OFFICE—VICTIM/WITNESS ASSISTANCE PROGRAM
PO Box 158, Enterprise, OR 97828
Information: (503) 426-3197 on call
Contact: Judy Wandschneider, Victim/Witness Prog Coord
TYPE OF AGENCY: Victim/witness assistance program; Interagency network
AREAS SERVED: Wallowa
YEARS IN OPERATION: 4
DESCRIPTION: District attorney and coordinator of the program are both members of county interagency child abuse team; Cases involving sexual abuse are given high priority by this team; DA's office coordinator prepares child for court and stays with the child throughout the legal experience and follow-up

WALLOWA COUNTY DISTRICT ATTORNEY'S OFFICE—VICTIM/WITNESS ASSISTANCE PROGRAM *(continued)*
CLIENTS/SERVICES: Child victims of sexual abuse; Developmentally disabled

EUGENE

CHOICES—CREATING HEALTHY OPTIONS IN CONFRONTING EXPLOITIVE SEXUALITY
1258 High, Eugene, OR 97401
Information: (503) 343-7643 24 hrs
Contact: Steven E Mussack, PhD, Prog Dir
TYPE OF AGENCY: Counseling/mental health services; Child sexual abuse services; Private practice
AREAS SERVED: Lane, Lynn, Benton, Marion, Lincoln, Deschutes, Douglas
YEARS IN OPERATION: 4
CASES SEXUAL ASSAULT/ABUSE (%): 80
DESCRIPTION: Provides community-based intervention for offenders, victims, and families in which sexual abuse has occurred. Programs for MED clients and incest treatment project geared to intrafamilial sexual abuse
CLIENTS/SERVICES: Marital rape/sexual abuse survivors; Child victims of sexual abuse; Adult survivors of child sexual abuse; Incest victims/survivors; Community education; Offender treatment program; Adolescent survivors of sexual abuse; Male survivors of sexual abuse; Developmentally disabled

EUGENE FAMILY INSTITUTE
1258 High St, Eugene, OR 97401
Information: (503) 342-4863 24 hrs
Contact: Steven Mussack, PhD, Training Consultant
TYPE OF AGENCY: Counseling/mental health services; Child sexual abuse services; Private practice; Training/research
AREAS SERVED: Lane, Lynn, Benton, Marion, Lincoln, Deschutes, Douglas
YEARS IN OPERATION: 1
CASES SEXUAL ASSAULT/ABUSE (%): 30
DESCRIPTION: Therapy for victims/survivors (including MED clients) and for rapists and child sexual abuse/incest offenders. Provides clinical training and supervision for interns, residents, and practicing professionals in the multiple facets of sexual abuse intervention
CLIENTS/SERVICES: Marital rape/sexual abuse survivors; Child victims of sexual abuse; Adult survivors of child sexual abuse; Incest victims/survivors; Community education; Offender treatment program; Adolescent survivors of sexual abuse; Male survivors of sexual abuse; Developmentally disabled
REQUIREMENTS: Will not accept clients with life-threatening conditions, active non-medicated psychosis or substance abuse as a primary diagnosis

FAMILY SHELTER
969 Hwy 99 N, Eugene, OR 97402
Crisis hotline: **(503) 689-7156 24 hrs**
Information: (503) 689-7156 24 hrs
Contact: Char Hall, Domestic Violence Prog Mgr
TYPE OF AGENCY: Domestic violence program; Shelter
SPONSORING ORGANIZATION: Eugene Emergency Housing
YEARS IN OPERATION: 12
LANGUAGES: Spanish translation available
ACCESSIBILITY: Wheelchair accessible
DESCRIPTION: Provides emergency shelter for homeless families and domestic violence victims
CLIENTS/SERVICES: Sexual assault survivors; Marital rape/sexual abuse survivors; Community education
REQUIREMENTS: Victims of domestic violence need to be referred by Womenspace, a local women's shelter (503) 485-6513 and must be homeless with at least one child under 18

LANE COUNTY VICTIM/WITNESS SERVICES
400 Lane County Courthouse, Eugene, OR 97401
Information: (503) 687-4523 8am-5:30pm (Mon-Fri)
Contact: Lori R Nelson, Dir
TYPE OF AGENCY: Victim/witness assistance program
AREAS SERVED: Lane
YEARS IN OPERATION: 3½
ACCESSIBILITY: Wheelchair accessible
CASES SEXUAL ASSAULT/ABUSE (%): 15-20
CLIENTS/SERVICES: Sexual assault survivors; Marital rape/sexual abuse survivors; Child victims of sexual abuse; Incest victims/survivors; Community education

RAPE CRISIS NETWORK
358 W 10th Ave, Eugene, OR 97401
Crisis hotline: **(503) 485-6700 24 hrs**
Information: (503) 485-6701 9am-5pm
Contact: LaVerne Gagehabib, Dir
TYPE OF AGENCY: Rape crisis center; Child sexual abuse prevention program
AREAS SERVED: Lane
YEARS IN OPERATION: 11
LANGUAGES: Sign
ACCESSIBILITY: Telecommunications for the hearing impaired (TTY, TDY, etc.); Signers for the hearing impaired
CASES SEXUAL ASSAULT/ABUSE (%): 100
DESCRIPTION: Provides preventive/reactive support for sexual assault survivors and their friends, including support for survivors of incidents ranging from obscene phone calls to violent rape to past incest; Support groups for survivors of rape, sexual assault and incest; Self-defense information; Men Against Rape support groups for rapists
CLIENTS/SERVICES: Sexual assault survivors; Marital rape/sexual abuse survivors; Adult survivors of child sexual abuse; Incest victims/survivors; Prevention program; Community education; Adolescent survivors of sexual abuse; Male survivors of sexual abuse; Developmentally disabled; Disabled
REQUIREMENTS: Referrals only for those 13 and younger
SPECIAL PROGRAMS/SERVICES: Program for children called "Safe Touch" for K-5th grades; Outreach program for rural, low-income, and alternatively abled communities, including community education programs in ASL (Sign) for the hearing impaired, and designed for mentally retarded persons

WOMENSPACE
PO Box 5485, Eugene, OR 97405
Crisis hotline: **(503) 485-6513 24 hrs daily**
Information: (503) 485-8232 24 hrs daily
Contact: Freddie Tryk, Dir
TYPE OF AGENCY: Domestic violence program
AREAS SERVED: Lane
YEARS IN OPERATION: 12
LANGUAGES: Spanish; Translators available
ACCESSIBILITY: Wheelchair accessible; Signers for the hearing impaired (by request)
CASES SEXUAL ASSAULT/ABUSE (%): 40
DESCRIPTION: Provides shelter and services focused on domestic violence, but many clients are marital rape/incest survivors. Also works with Rape Crisis Network to house sexual assault victims in danger and need of shelter where appropriate. Provides men's anger management group for abusers
CLIENTS/SERVICES: Marital rape/sexual abuse survivors; Child victims of sexual abuse; Adult survivors of child sexual abuse; Incest victims/survivors; Prevention program; Community education; Adolescent survivors of sexual abuse; Lesbians
SPECIAL PROGRAMS/SERVICES: Sponsors Lesbian Battering Support Group. Provides transitional housing (1-4 months) for 5 women and their children after leaving shelter

GOLD BEACH

OASIS SHELTER HOME
PO Box 746, Gold Beach, OR 97444
Crisis hotline: **(503) 247-6331 24 hrs**
Information: (503) 247-7011 10am-3pm
Contact: Sue Golay, Dir
TYPE OF AGENCY: Domestic violence program
AREAS SERVED: Curry
LANGUAGES: Spanish, German, Cherokee
ACCESSIBILITY: Wheelchair accessible
CASES SEXUAL ASSAULT/ABUSE (%): 10
CLIENTS/SERVICES: Sexual assault survivors; Marital rape/sexual abuse survivors; Prevention program; Community education

PROSECUTOR'S VICTIM/WITNESS ASSISTANCE PROGRAM
PO Box 746, Gold Beach, OR 97444
Crisis hotline: **(503) 247-6331 24 hrs**
Information: (503) 247-7011 10am-3pm
Contact: Sue Golay, Coord
TYPE OF AGENCY: Domestic violence program; Victim/witness assistance program
AREAS SERVED: Curry
YEARS IN OPERATION: 10
LANGUAGES: Spanish, German, Cherokee
ACCESSIBILITY: Wheelchair accessible
CASES SEXUAL ASSAULT/ABUSE (%): 10
CLIENTS/SERVICES: Sexual assault survivors; Marital rape/sexual abuse survivors; Prevention program; Community education

GRANTS PASS

FAMILY FRIENDS
360 SE "H" St, Ste A, Grants Pass, OR 97526
Information: (503) 476-4248 8am-5pm (Mon-Fri)
Contact: Jeff Henderson, Exec Dir
TYPE OF AGENCY: Child sexual abuse services; Child sexual abuse prevention program; Child abuse services; Child abuse prevention program
AREAS SERVED: Josephine, Jackson, Douglas
YEARS IN OPERATION: 4
CASES SEXUAL ASSAULT/ABUSE (%): 75
DESCRIPTION: Provides outpatient treatment for victims of child sexual, physical, and emotional abuse; Serves as the regional resource center for the Oregon Chapter of the National Committee for the Prevention of Child Abuse
CLIENTS/SERVICES: Sexual assault survivors; Child victims of sexual abuse; Adult survivors of child sexual abuse; Incest victims/survivors; Prevention program; Community education; Adolescent survivors of sexual abuse; Male survivors of sexual abuse
REQUIREMENTS: Abuse victims between ages of 2 and adulthood
SPECIAL PROGRAMS/SERVICES: Sponsorship of "Spiderman" that visited the Rogue Valley in 1988 and talked with children about child abuse

FAMILY OFFENDER PROGRAM
PO Box 189, Grants Pass, OR 97526
Information: (503) 474-3120 8am-5pm
Contact: Phil Backes, Prog Coord
TYPE OF AGENCY: Counseling/mental health services; Child sexual abuse services; Child sexual abuse prevention program
AREAS SERVED: Josephine
YEARS IN OPERATION: 8
CASES SEXUAL ASSAULT/ABUSE (%): 100
CLIENTS/SERVICES: Sexual assault survivors; Marital rape/sexual abuse survivors; Child victims of sexual abuse; Adult survivors of child sexual abuse; Incest victims/survivors; Prevention program; Community education; Offend-

FAMILY OFFENDER PROGRAM
(continued)

er treatment program; Adolescent survivors of sexual abuse; Male survivors of sexual abuse
REQUIREMENTS: The offender must be charged, have no previous sexually related arrests, and take full responsibility for offense, and must not have used force during offense
SPECIAL PROGRAMS/SERVICES: Interagency teams consisting of family's therapist, group therapist, probation officer, child's therapist, program coordinator, and occasionally foster parents meet quarterly to maintain consistency in treatment process. These meetings also assist in family reunification process, when applicable

WOMEN'S CRISIS SUPPORT TEAM
748 NW 5th St, Grants Pass, OR 97526
Crisis hotline: **(503) 479-HELP 24 hrs**
Information: (503) 479-9349 8am-5pm (Mon-Fri)
Contact: Esther Jackson, Dir
TYPE OF AGENCY: Rape crisis center; Domestic violence program; Child sexual abuse prevention program
SPONSORING ORGANIZATION: Women's Coalition of Josephine County
AREAS SERVED: Josephine, Northern Jackson, Southern Douglas
YEARS IN OPERATION: 11
LANGUAGES: Interpreters available for Filipino and other Asian and Hispanic languages
ACCESSIBILITY: Signers for the hearing impaired
CASES SEXUAL ASSAULT/ABUSE (%): 60
CLIENTS/SERVICES: Sexual assault survivors; Marital rape/sexual abuse survivors; Prevention program; Community education; Adolescent survivors of sexual abuse

HILLSBORO

RAPE CRISIS CENTER
PO Box 73, Hillsboro, OR 97123
Crisis hotline: **(503) 640-5311 24 hrs**
Contact: Marilyn Oldfield, Dir
TYPE OF AGENCY: Rape crisis center; Victim/witness assistance program; Public school system; Child sexual abuse services; Child sexual abuse prevention program
AREAS SERVED: Washington
YEARS IN OPERATION: 11
LANGUAGES: Spanish
CASES SEXUAL ASSAULT/ABUSE (%): 100
CLIENTS/SERVICES: Sexual assault survivors; Marital rape/sexual abuse survivors; Adult survivors of child sexual abuse; Incest victims/survivors; Prevention program; Community education; Offender treatment program; Adolescent survivors of sexual abuse; Male survivors of sexual abuse

HOOD RIVER

CRIME VICTIM ASSISTANCE PROGRAM
County Courthouse, District Attorney's Office, Hood River, OR 97031
Information: (503) 386-3103 8am-5pm (Mon-Fri)
Contact: Jackie Henson, Dir
TYPE OF AGENCY: Victim/witness assistance program
AREAS SERVED: Hood River
YEARS IN OPERATION: 4
LANGUAGES: Spanish
ACCESSIBILITY: Wheelchair accessible
CLIENTS/SERVICES: Sexual assault survivors; Child victims of sexual abuse
REQUIREMENTS: Must report the crime and cooperate in efforts to prosecute the assailant

KLAMATH FALLS

VICTIMS' ASSISTANCE PROGRAM
316 Main St, District Attorney's Office, Klamath Falls, OR 97601
Information: (503) 883-5147 8:30am-5pm (Mon-Fri)
Contact: Charlene Divine, Victim's Asst Coord
TYPE OF AGENCY: Victim/witness assistance program
AREAS SERVED: Klamath
YEARS IN OPERATION: 6
ACCESSIBILITY: Wheelchair accessible
CASES SEXUAL ASSAULT/ABUSE (%): 16
CLIENTS/SERVICES: Sexual assault survivors; Marital rape/sexual abuse survivors; Child victims of sexual abuse; Incest victims/survivors; Prevention program; Community education
REQUIREMENTS: Clients must file charges

LA GRANDE

TASK FORCE ON DOMESTIC VIOLENCE AND SEXUAL ASSAULT
PO Box 173, La Grande, OR 97850
Crisis hotline: **(503) 963-9261 24 hrs**
Information: (503) 963-7226 9am-1pm
Contact: Annie Fleser, Prog Coord
TYPE OF AGENCY: Rape crisis center; Domestic violence program
AREAS SERVED: Union, Wallowa
YEARS IN OPERATION: 9
LANGUAGES: Spanish interpreters available
CASES SEXUAL ASSAULT/ABUSE (%): 10
CLIENTS/SERVICES: Sexual assault survivors; Marital rape/sexual abuse survivors; Adult survivors of child sexual abuse; Incest victims/survivors; Prevention program; Community education; Male survivors of sexual abuse
REQUIREMENTS: Must be 18 or older for services; Referrals for juveniles

LAKEVIEW

CRISIS INTERVENTION CENTER
11 N "G" St, Lakeview, OR 97630
Crisis hotline: **(800) 338-1590 24 hrs daily**
Information: (503) 947-2449 10am-2pm (Mon-Fri)
Contact: Sharon Piercy, Dir
TYPE OF AGENCY: Domestic violence program
AREAS SERVED: Lake
YEARS IN OPERATION: 5
ACCESSIBILITY: Wheelchair accessible
CASES SEXUAL ASSAULT/ABUSE (%): 5
DESCRIPTION: Services for rural women who are survivors of domestic violence and sexual assault include counseling and a support group for women
CLIENTS/SERVICES: Sexual assault survivors; Marital rape/sexual abuse survivors; Adult survivors of child sexual abuse; Incest victims/survivors; Community education; Adolescent survivors of sexual abuse

LINCOLN CITY

LINCOLN SHELTER AND SERVICES, INC
PO Box 426, Lincoln City, OR 97367
Crisis hotline: **(503) 994-5959, Newport (503) 265-7726 24 hrs**
Information: (503) 994-3365, Newport (503) 265-2040 9am-1pm
Contact: GayLynn Pack, Dir
TYPE OF AGENCY: Rape crisis center; Domestic violence program
AREAS SERVED: Lincoln
YEARS IN OPERATION: 9
ACCESSIBILITY: Wheelchair accessible
CASES SEXUAL ASSAULT/ABUSE (%): 40
CLIENTS/SERVICES: Sexual assault survivors; Marital rape/sexual abuse survivors; Child victims of sexual abuse; Adult survivors of child sexual abuse; Incest victims/survivors; Prevention program; Community education; Adolescent survivors of sexual abuse; Male survivors of sexual abuse
REQUIREMENTS: Anyone who is affected by domestic or sexual violence is eligible for services. Minors must be accompanied by a parent or guardian to be sheltered

MADRAS

JEFFERSON COUNTY DISTRICT ATTORNEY'S OFFICE—VICTIM ASSISTANCE PROGRAM
657 C St, Courthouse, Madras, OR 97741
Information: (503) 475-2286
Contact: Pam Middlestetter, Victim Prog Dir
TYPE OF AGENCY: Victim/witness assistance program
AREAS SERVED: Jefferson
YEARS IN OPERATION: 3
LANGUAGES: Spanish
ACCESSIBILITY: Wheelchair accessible
CASES SEXUAL ASSAULT/ABUSE (%): 30
CLIENTS/SERVICES: Sexual assault survivors; Marital rape/sexual abuse survivors; Child victims of sexual abuse; Adult survivors of child sexual abuse; Incest victims/survivors; Adolescent survivors of sexual abuse; Male survivors of sexual abuse
REQUIREMENTS: Must report offense; No need to file charges

MARYHURST

CLACKAMAS ADOLESCENT INTERVENTION SERVICES, INC
PO Box 113, Maryhurst Campus, Maryhurst, OR 97036
Crisis hotline: **(503) 657-0683 evenings and weekends**
Information: (503) 635-0554 8:30am-5pm
Contact: Richard King, Dir
TYPE OF AGENCY: Child sexual abuse services; Adolescent program; Offender treatment
AREAS SERVED: Clackamas, Washington, Multnomah
YEARS IN OPERATION: 6
LANGUAGES: Spanish
ACCESSIBILITY: Wheelchair accessible
CASES SEXUAL ASSAULT/ABUSE (%): 100
DESCRIPTION: Provides services for adolescent victims and perpetrators of sexual abuse. Services include: group, individual, and parent counseling, psychological testing and assessment, screening, educational/social skills training, parent education and professional training
CLIENTS/SERVICES: Sexual assault survivors; Child victims of sexual abuse; Adult survivors of child sexual abuse; Incest victims/survivors; Prevention program; Community education; Offender treatment program; Adolescent survivors of sexual abuse; Male survivors of sexual abuse
REQUIREMENTS: Adolescent sexual offender program: 12-18 years with arrest record. Child sexual offender program: 4-12 years. Child and adolescent sexual abuse victims program: 4-18 years

McMINNVILLE

LUTHERAN FAMILY SERVICE OF YAMHILL COUNTY
819 N Hwy 99 W, Ste B, McMinnville, OR 97128
Information: (503) 472-4020 9am-5pm; 24-hr answering service
Contact: Kathleen Horgan, Dir
TYPE OF AGENCY: Counseling/mental health services
AREAS SERVED: Yamhill
YEARS IN OPERATION: 6
ACCESSIBILITY: Wheelchair accessible
CASES SEXUAL ASSAULT/ABUSE (%): 40

LUTHERAN FAMILY SERVICE OF YAMHILL COUNTY *(continued)*

DESCRIPTION: Provides family counseling, including the following special programs: Adults molested as children (individual and group counseling), anger control program for batterers, and teen group

CLIENTS/SERVICES: Sexual assault survivors; Marital rape/sexual abuse survivors; Child victims of sexual abuse; Adult survivors of child sexual abuse; Incest victims/survivors; Community education; Adolescent survivors of sexual abuse; Male survivors of sexual abuse

YAMHILL COUNTY DISTRICT ATTORNEY'S OFFICE—CRIME VICTIM ASSISTANCE PROGRAM (CVAP)
535 E 5th St, McMinnville, OR 97128
Crisis hotline: **(503) 472-9371, ext 210 24 hrs daily**
Information: (503) 472-9371, ext 210 8:30am-5pm
Contact: Kathleen Robbins, CVAP Dir
TYPE OF AGENCY: Victim/witness assistance program; Child sexual abuse prevention program
AREAS SERVED: Yamhill
YEARS IN OPERATION: 1
LANGUAGES: Spanish translator available
ACCESSIBILITY: Wheelchair accessible
CASES SEXUAL ASSAULT/ABUSE (%): 7-10
DESCRIPTION: Provides emotional support and guidance throughout the court process; Police and hospital escort; Works with families of victims; Presents child abuse awareness/risk reduction presentation to school children, grades K through college level
CLIENTS/SERVICES: Sexual assault survivors; Child victims of sexual abuse; Incest victims/survivors; Prevention program; Community education
REQUIREMENTS: Encourages victims to report, but not necessary for emotional support/guidance

MEDFORD

DUNN HOUSE—RAPE CRISIS: SEXUAL AND DOMESTIC VIOLENCE INTERVENTION
PO Box 819, Medford, OR 97501
Crisis hotline: **(503) 779-HELP 24 hrs daily**
Information: (503) 779-1111, 779-2112 9am-2pm
Contact: Angie Lindquist, Prog Asst
TYPE OF AGENCY: Rape crisis center; Domestic violence program; Child sexual abuse prevention program
SPONSORING ORGANIZATION: Crisis Intervention Services
AREAS SERVED: Jackson
YEARS IN OPERATION: 5
CLIENTS/SERVICES: Sexual assault survivors; Marital rape/sexual abuse survivors; Child victims of sexual abuse; Adult survivors of child sexual abuse; Incest victims/survivors; Prevention program; Community education; Adolescent survivors of sexual abuse; Male survivors of sexual abuse

JACKSON COUNTY DISTRICT ATTORNEY—CRIME VICTIM/WITNESS ASSISTANCE PROGRAM
10 S Oakdale, County Courthouse, Medford, OR 97501
Information: (503) 776-7520 8am-5pm
Contact: Emma L Adams, Dir
TYPE OF AGENCY: Victim/witness assistance program
AREAS SERVED: Jackson
YEARS IN OPERATION: 5
LANGUAGES: Spanish by arrangement
ACCESSIBILITY: Wheelchair accessible
CASES SEXUAL ASSAULT/ABUSE (%): 5
DESCRIPTION: Provides crime victims and witnesses involved in the criminal justice system with ongoing emotional support, information and referral, and short-term counseling, whether or not the perpetrator of the crime has been arrested
CLIENTS/SERVICES: Sexual assault survivors; Marital rape/sexual abuse survivors; Child victims of sexual abuse; Incest victims/survivors; Community education; Adolescent survivors of sexual abuse; Male survivors of sexual abuse
REQUIREMENTS: Client must file charges for most services; short-term counseling and referrals provided for any victim of a crime whether charges have been filed or not

SHALOM CHRISTIAN COUNSELING CENTER
18 Vancouver, Medford, OR 97504
Crisis hotline: **(503) 772-9987 evenings**
Information: (503) 772-9987
Contact: William Vaughters, Dir
TYPE OF AGENCY: Counseling/mental health services
AREAS SERVED: Jackson, Josephine
YEARS IN OPERATION: 12
ACCESSIBILITY: Wheelchair accessible
CASES SEXUAL ASSAULT/ABUSE (%): 20
DESCRIPTION: Provides psychological, emotional, and if applicable, spiritual healing in mental health related problems (depression, anxiety, family conflict, sexual, and physical abuse, etc)
CLIENTS/SERVICES: Sexual assault survivors; Marital rape/sexual abuse survivors; Child victims of sexual abuse; Adult survivors of child sexual abuse; Incest victims/survivors; Community education; Adolescent survivors of sexual abuse; Male survivors of sexual abuse

YOUTHWORKS, INC
1032 W Main, Medford, OR 97501
Crisis hotline: **(503) 779-HELP 24 hrs**
Information: (503) 779-2393 8am-5pm
Contact: Harriet Saturen, Adolescent and Family Counselor; Roland Gangstee, Prog Mgr
TYPE OF AGENCY: Counseling/mental health services; Child sexual abuse services; Adolescent program
AREAS SERVED: Jackson
YEARS IN OPERATION: 10
ACCESSIBILITY: Wheelchair accessible; Signers for the hearing impaired
CASES SEXUAL ASSAULT/ABUSE (%): 50
DESCRIPTION: Individual and group counseling for sexually abused children and adolescents; Group counseling for non-offending parents. Individual and group therapy for adolescent sex offenders
CLIENTS/SERVICES: Sexual assault survivors; Child victims of sexual abuse; Incest victims/survivors; Community education; Offender treatment program; Adolescent survivors of sexual abuse
REQUIREMENTS: For victim/survivor services: ages 6-18 and parents; for offender services: adolescent sex offenders who have been adjudicated and mandated to treatment

MILL CITY

CANYON CRISIS CENTER
PO Box 500, 310 NW Santiam Blvd, Mill City, OR 97360
Crisis hotline: **(503) 897-2327 24 hrs**
Information: (503) 897-2327 9am-5pm (Mon-Thu)
Contact: Lorie J Kelley, Volunteer Coord
TYPE OF AGENCY: Rape crisis center; Domestic violence program; Child sexual abuse prevention program
AREAS SERVED: Marion, Linn
YEARS IN OPERATION: 3
CASES SEXUAL ASSAULT/ABUSE (%): 12
CLIENTS/SERVICES: Sexual assault survivors; Marital rape/sexual abuse survivors; Child victims of sexual abuse; Adult survivors of child sexual abuse; Incest victims/survivors; Prevention program; Community education; Adolescent survivors of sexual abuse; Male survivors of sexual abuse

MILWAUKIE

CLACKAMAS WOMAN'S SERVICES
PO Box 22547, Milwaukie, OR 97222
Crisis hotline: **(503) 654-2288 24 hrs**
Information: (503) 654-2807 8am-5pm
Contact: Laurie Cox, Agency Dir
TYPE OF AGENCY: Domestic violence program
YEARS IN OPERATION: 2
CLIENTS/SERVICES: Marital rape/sexual abuse survivors; Child victims of sexual abuse; Adult survivors of child sexual abuse; Incest victims/survivors; Community education; Adolescent survivors of sexual abuse
SPECIAL PROGRAMS/SERVICES: Spanish-language brochure

NORTH BEND

COOS COUNTY WOMEN'S CRISIS SERVICE
PO Box 791, North Bend, OR 97459
Crisis hotline: **(503) 756-7000 24 hrs daily**
Information: (503) 756-7864 7am-10pm
Contact: Doreen S Binder, Admin
TYPE OF AGENCY: Rape crisis center; Domestic violence program; Child sexual abuse services
AREAS SERVED: Coos, Curry, western Douglas
YEARS IN OPERATION: 9½
ACCESSIBILITY: Wheelchair accessible
CASES SEXUAL ASSAULT/ABUSE (%): 70
CLIENTS/SERVICES: Sexual assault survivors; Marital rape/sexual abuse survivors; Child victims of sexual abuse; Adult survivors of child sexual abuse; Incest victims/survivors; Prevention program; Community education; Adolescent survivors of sexual abuse

ONTARIO

ALEXANDRIA ASSOCIATES
911 SW 3rd St, Ontario, OR 97914
Information: (503) 889-8938 9am-6pm
Contact: Jan Hindman
TYPE OF AGENCY: Child sexual abuse services; Child sexual abuse prevention program; Private practice; Consultation
AREAS SERVED: Malheur, Grant, Harney, Baker, Union
YEARS IN OPERATION: 3
LANGUAGES: Spanish
CASES SEXUAL ASSAULT/ABUSE (%): 99
CLIENTS/SERVICES: Sexual assault survivors; Marital rape/sexual abuse survivors; Child victims of sexual abuse; Adult survivors of child sexual abuse; Incest victims/survivors; Prevention program; Community education; Offender treatment program; Adolescent survivors of sexual abuse; Male survivors of sexual abuse

RTAT, INC (RESTITUTION TREATMENT AND TRAINING)
PO Box 800, Ontario, OR 97914
Information: (503) 889-9194 10am-5pm
Contact: Lucy Hutchens, Prog Coord
TYPE OF AGENCY: Counseling/mental health services; Child sexual abuse services; Consultation; Training/research
AREAS SERVED: Malheur
YEARS IN OPERATION: 3
LANGUAGES: Spanish
ACCESSIBILITY: Wheelchair accessible
CASES SEXUAL ASSAULT/ABUSE (%): 100
DESCRIPTION: Provides a coordinating body for all local providers of treatment for child sexual abuse; Support groups for male and female survivors; Group therapy for adult and juvenile sex offenders; Training in sexual arousal control; Polygraph monitoring; After-care support groups
CLIENTS/SERVICES: Child victims of sexual abuse; Adult survivors of child sexual abuse; Incest victims/survivors; Prevention program; Com-

RTAT, INC (RESTITUTION TREATMENT AND TRAINING) (continued)
munity education; Offender treatment program; Adolescent survivors of sexual abuse; Male survivors of sexual abuse; Publications/media
REQUIREMENTS: Offenders must plead guilty and be mandated into program
SPECIAL PROGRAMS/SERVICES: Training and consultation services for professionals working in the field of child sexual abuse. Training is available on the following topics: organization of a child sexual abuse interagency team and treatment program, group treatment goals and techniques, restitution treatment philosophy, prevention and self-protection for children. Three-day on-site demonstration includes observation of primary treatment group, observation of aftercare treatment groups, attendance at interagency abuse team, attendance at case staffing meeting, four hours of individual consultation, and program materials. Slide-tape *After You Tell,* process from report to treatment

OREGON CITY

CLACKAMAS COUNTY DISTRICT ATTORNEY—VICTIM ASSISTANCE DIVISION
708 Main St, Delta Bldg, Oregon City, OR 97045
Crisis hotline: **(503) 655-8616 24 hrs**
Information: (503) 655-8616 8am-5pm
Contact: Sharon O'Shea, Dir
TYPE OF AGENCY: Victim/witness assistance program; Child sexual abuse services; Child sexual abuse prevention program
AREAS SERVED: Clackamas
YEARS IN OPERATION: 11
LANGUAGES: Interpreters available as needed
ACCESSIBILITY: Wheelchair accessible
CASES SEXUAL ASSAULT/ABUSE (%): 50
CLIENTS/SERVICES: Sexual assault survivors; Marital rape/sexual abuse survivors; Child victims of sexual abuse; Adult survivors of child sexual abuse; Incest victims/survivors; Prevention program; Community education; Adolescent survivors of sexual abuse; Male survivors of sexual abuse

PENDLETON

DOMESTIC VIOLENCE SERVICES
PO Box 152, Pendleton, OR 97801
Crisis hotline: **(503) 278-0241 24 hrs**
Information: (503) 276-3322 8am-5pm (Mon-Fri)
Contact: Lyndall Hurse, Dir; Eileen A Edwards, Sexual Assasult Advocate
TYPE OF AGENCY: Rape crisis center; Domestic violence program
AREAS SERVED: Umatilla, Morrow
YEARS IN OPERATION: 11
LANGUAGES: Spanish interpreter available
ACCESSIBILITY: Signers for the hearing impaired
CASES SEXUAL ASSAULT/ABUSE (%): 40
DESCRIPTION: Provides emergency services for domestic violence and sexual assault survivors; VOCA grant is a joint project with District Attorney's Office Victim/Witness program; Adults Molested as Children (AMAC) group; Therapy for batterers; Martial arts/self-defense program available for survivors
CLIENTS/SERVICES: Sexual assault survivors; Marital rape/sexual abuse survivors; Child victims of sexual abuse; Adult survivors of child sexual abuse; Incest victims/survivors; Community education; Adolescent survivors of sexual abuse; Male survivors of sexual abuse; Healing
SPECIAL PROGRAMS/SERVICES: Provides relaxation and creative visualization art therapy within the AMAC group

PORTLAND

BRADLEY-ANGLE HOUSE, INC
PO Box 14694, Portland, OR 97214
Crisis hotline: **(503) 281-2442 24 hrs**
Information: (503) 281-3540 9am-9pm
Contact: Jo Seidl, Shelter Coord
TYPE OF AGENCY: Domestic violence program
YEARS IN OPERATION: 13
CASES SEXUAL ASSAULT/ABUSE (%): 100
CLIENTS/SERVICES: Sexual assault survivors; Marital rape/sexual abuse survivors; Adult survivors of child sexual abuse; Incest victims/survivors; Community education

CARES (CHILD ABUSE RESPONSE AND EVALUATION SERVICES)
2801 N Gantenbeen Ave, Portland, OR 97229
Information: (503) 280-4943 8:30am-5pm
Contact: Karen Pancheau, Prog Sec
TYPE OF AGENCY: Hospital/medical center; Child sexual abuse services
SPONSORING ORGANIZATION: Emanuel Hospital and Health Center
AREAS SERVED: Washington, Clackamas, Multnomah
YEARS IN OPERATION: 2
LANGUAGES: Interpreters available
ACCESSIBILITY: Wheelchair accessible; Signers for the hearing impaired
CASES SEXUAL ASSAULT/ABUSE (%): 90
DESCRIPTION: Provides a one-time medical examination and interview with alleged child victim of abuse and neglect. The interview is videotaped to avoid further multiple interviews
CLIENTS/SERVICES: Child victims of sexual abuse; Community education
REQUIREMENTS: 0-13 years of age. Must meet intake criteria of prioritization of CARES services

COMMUNITY ADVOCATES
10531 SW Capitol Hwy, Portland, OR 97219
Information: (503) 245-4033 9am-4pm (Mon-Fri)
Contact: Belle Bennett, Exec Dir
TYPE OF AGENCY: Child sexual abuse prevention program; Rape prevention program
AREAS SERVED: Multnomah, Washington, Clackamas
YEARS IN OPERATION: 7
ACCESSIBILITY: Signers for the hearing impaired
CASES SEXUAL ASSAULT/ABUSE (%): 30
DESCRIPTION: 2 programs: Kids Can for children ages 3-12, their parents and teachers; and assertiveness and self-defense classes (feminist-based) for women and girls ages 12 and older. Many of the women and children who participate in the classes are survivors of sexual assault/abuse. Also offers crisis counseling and referral
CLIENTS/SERVICES: Prevention program; Community education
SPECIAL PROGRAMS/SERVICES: Kids Can program is based on the CAP (Child Assault Prevention) model. Serves preschoolers through 5th graders. Has incorporated emotional abuse, physical abuse, and neglect into this sexual assault prevention curriculum. Publications: ($2 each): *Touch That Hurts, Talking With Children About Sexual Abuse* (for parents); *Color Me Safe and Strong and Free* (children's coloring book on prevention); *Fighting Chance—Assertiveness, Rape Avoidance and Self- Defense for Women*

EASTMORELAND CONSULTING
8332 SE 13th, Portland, OR 97202
Crisis hotline: **(503) 273-7230 24 hrs**
Information: (503) 238-4622 24 hrs
Contact: J Ross Neder, PhD
TYPE OF AGENCY: Private practice; Offender treatment
AREAS SERVED: Multnomah, Clackamus, Washington
YEARS IN OPERATION: 4
ACCESSIBILITY: Wheelchair accessible
CASES SEXUAL ASSAULT/ABUSE (%): 50
DESCRIPTION: Treatment of sex offenders, rapists, child sexual abuse/incest offenders, and batterers; Treatment of victims of abuse in general and victims of cult abuse in particular. Specializes in associative disorders and religosity issues
CLIENTS/SERVICES: Adult survivors of child sexual abuse; Incest victims/survivors; Offender treatment program; Male survivors of sexual abuse; Ritualistic abuse victims/survivors

ECHOES COUNSELING SERVICES
PO Box 86231, Portland, OR 97206
Information: (503) 293-2800 10am-8pm (Mon-Fri); Saturday appointments by arrangement
Contact: Wendy Ann Wood, MA, Clinical Dir
TYPE OF AGENCY: Counseling/mental health services; Private practice
AREAS SERVED: Washington, Multnomah, Clackamas, Clark, Columbia
YEARS IN OPERATION: 5
ACCESSIBILITY: Wheelchair accessible; Signers for the hearing impaired
CASES SEXUAL ASSAULT/ABUSE (%): 95
DESCRIPTION: Provides supportive, directive, eclectic therapy for survivors of sexual abuse. Counselors are professionally trained in the inner healing, spiritual, emotional, sexual and personal recovery of those traumatized by sexual abuse and/or assault, including ritual abuse; Creative arts therapy
CLIENTS/SERVICES: Sexual assault survivors; Marital rape/sexual abuse survivors; Child victims of sexual abuse; Adult survivors of child sexual abuse; Incest victims/survivors; Prevention program; Community education; Adolescent survivors of sexual abuse; Male survivors of sexual abuse; Ritualistic abuse victims/survivors; Healing
REQUIREMENTS: Sliding scale fee
SPECIAL PROGRAMS/SERVICES: Art therapy, play therapy, journal writing, spiritual recovery for adult survivors of sexual assault and childhood sexual abuse. Development of personal life notebook for clients with amnesic childhoods. Support group for new mothers who were molested as children and partners groups for men whose partners have been sexually abused

LUTHERAN FAMILY SERVICE
605 SE 39th Ave, Portland, OR 97214
Information: (503) 231-7480 8am-5pm (Mon-Fri)
Contact: Annette Selmer, AMAC Prog Dir
TYPE OF AGENCY: Counseling/mental health services
AREAS SERVED: Multnomah, Clackamas, Washington
YEARS IN OPERATION: 35
ACCESSIBILITY: Wheelchair accessible; Telecommunications for the hearing impaired (TTY, TDY, etc.)
CASES SEXUAL ASSAULT/ABUSE (%): 35
DESCRIPTION: AMAC (Adults Molested as Children) program works with male and female survivors and their partners; ACOA (Adult Children of Alcoholics) group for survivors; Group using hypnotherapy; Works with sexually abused children; Uses art therapy for children and adults; Teaches feminist martial arts/self-defense
CLIENTS/SERVICES: Sexual assault survivors; Marital rape/sexual abuse survivors; Child victims of sexual abuse; Adult survivors of child sexual abuse; Incest victims/survivors; Community education; Adolescent survivors of sexual abuse; Male survivors of sexual abuse

KEVIN B MCGOVERN, PHD AND ASSOCIATES
1225 NW Murray Rd, Ste 214, Portland, OR 97229
Crisis hotline: **(503) 644-6600 24 hrs**
Information: (503) 644-6600 9am-5pm (Mon-Fri)

KEVIN B MCGOVERN, PHD AND ASSOCIATES (continued)
Contact: Kevin B McGovern, PhD, Clinical Psychologist
TYPE OF AGENCY: Child sexual abuse services; Child sexual abuse prevention program; Private practice; Interagency network; Training/research
YEARS IN OPERATION: 14
CASES SEXUAL ASSAULT/ABUSE (%): 40
DESCRIPTION: Individual and group treatment for rapists and child sexual abuse/incest offenders; Educational materials and seminars on child sexual abuse
CLIENTS/SERVICES: Prevention program; Community education; Offender treatment program; Adolescent survivors of sexual abuse; Male survivors of sexual abuse; Developmentally disabled
SPECIAL PROGRAMS/SERVICES: Publications: *Preventing Sexual Abuse* (quarterly newsletter, $25); *Alice Doesn't Babysit Anymore* (storybook, $8.95); *Be Safe...Be Aware* (board game, $35). Seminar tapes: *Child Sexual Abuse: Do Children Lie or Adults Misperceive?* (16 tapes at $120, or $10 each); *Inside the Criminal Mind...and Sexual Deviancy* (13 tapes at $100, or $10 each); *The Societal Problems of Sexual Deviancy: What Remedies Are Available?* (14 tapes at $110, or $10 each); *The System as Perpetrator: Is the System Offending or Defending Victims of Sexual Abuse?* (15 tapes at $120, or $10 each)

MEN'S RESOURCE CENTER
2036 SE Morrison, Portland, OR 97214
Information: (503) 235-3433 By appointment
Contact: Bob Weinreich, Psychologist
TYPE OF AGENCY: Domestic violence program; Men's program
AREAS SERVED: Portland metro area
YEARS IN OPERATION: 12
ACCESSIBILITY: Wheelchair accessible
CASES SEXUAL ASSAULT/ABUSE (%): 10-15
DESCRIPTION: Comprehensive counseling services for men, their partners and families; Comprehensive domestic violence program; Specific services for adult men molested as children
CLIENTS/SERVICES: Sexual assault survivors; Marital rape/sexual abuse survivors; Child victims of sexual abuse; Adult survivors of child sexual abuse; Incest victims/survivors; Male survivors of sexual abuse
REQUIREMENTS: Sliding scale fees

MULTNOMAH COUNTY DISTRICT ATTORNEY—VICTIM'S ASSISTANCE PROGRAM
1021 SW 4th, No 804, Portland, OR 97204
Information: (503) 248-3222 8am-5pm (Mon-Fri)
Contact: Douglass Evan Beloof, Dir
TYPE OF AGENCY: Victim/witness assistance program
AREAS SERVED: Multnomah
YEARS IN OPERATION: 14
LANGUAGES: Translators available
ACCESSIBILITY: Wheelchair accessible; Signers for the hearing impaired
CLIENTS/SERVICES: Sexual assault survivors; Marital rape/sexual abuse survivors; Child victims of sexual abuse; Incest victims/survivors; Community education; Adolescent survivors of sexual abuse; Male survivors of sexual abuse

MULTNOMAH COUNTY JUVENILE JUSTICE DIVISION
1401 NE 68th Ave, Portland, OR 97213
Information: (503) 248-3460 8am-5pm daily
Contact: Sandy Wygant, Phil Lingelbach, Juvenile Court Counselors
TYPE OF AGENCY: Adolescent program; Offender treatment
AREAS SERVED: Multnomah
YEARS IN OPERATION: 8
ACCESSIBILITY: Wheelchair accessible
DESCRIPTION: Specialized program for adolescent sex offenders which includes group process, intensive case service, and education on sexuality and sexual assault
CLIENTS/SERVICES: Offender treatment program
REQUIREMENTS: Youth adjudicated for and found to have committed a sexual offense but presenting risk level allowing for remaining in the community

PORTLAND COUNSELING AND PSYCHOTHERAPY ASSOCIATES
1525 NE Weidler, Portland, OR 97232
Information: (503) 287-7006
Contact: Dr Mark Kohen
TYPE OF AGENCY: Private practice
YEARS IN OPERATION: 10
CASES SEXUAL ASSAULT/ABUSE (%): 15-20
CLIENTS/SERVICES: Sexual assault survivors; Marital rape/sexual abuse survivors; Adult survivors of child sexual abuse; Incest victims/survivors; Community education; Adolescent survivors of sexual abuse; Male survivors of sexual abuse
REQUIREMENTS: Age 4 and over

PORTLAND POLICE BUREAU—SEXUAL ASSAULT PREVENTION ADULT PROGRAM
1111 SW 2nd, No 1552, Portland, OR 97204
Information: (503) 796-3139 8:30am-5pm (Mon-Fri)
Contact: Mary Otto, Dir
TYPE OF AGENCY: Child abuse prevention program; Acquaintance/date rape prevention program
AREAS SERVED: City of Portland
YEARS IN OPERATION: 10
ACCESSIBILITY: Wheelchair accessible
CASES SEXUAL ASSAULT/ABUSE (%): 100
DESCRIPTION: Provides education on prevention of sexual assault and acquaintance/date rape; Self-defense training for teenage and adult women (class is called "Women Strength")
CLIENTS/SERVICES: Prevention program; Community education

PORTLAND WOMEN'S CRISIS LINE
PO Box 42610, Portland, OR 97242-0610
Crisis hotline: **(503) 235-5333 24 hrs**
Information: (503) 232-9751 9am-5pm (Mon-Fri)
Contact: Tess Wiseheart, Exec Dir
TYPE OF AGENCY: Rape crisis center; Domestic violence program
AREAS SERVED: Clackamas, Multnomah, Washington
YEARS IN OPERATION: 16
LANGUAGES: Spanish
ACCESSIBILITY: Telecommunications for the hearing impaired (TTY, TDY, etc.); Signers for the hearing impaired
CASES SEXUAL ASSAULT/ABUSE (%): 10
DESCRIPTION: Provides crisis counseling and intervention for victims of sexual assault, rape, domestic violence, and child abuse. Services include referrals for shelter, counseling, medical and legal services, transportation from danger to safety; Ongoing rape support groups; Public education on domestic and sexual violence
CLIENTS/SERVICES: Sexual assault survivors; Marital rape/sexual abuse survivors; Child victims of sexual abuse; Adult survivors of child sexual abuse; Incest victims/survivors; Community education; Adolescent survivors of sexual abuse; Male survivors of sexual abuse

RAPE SURVIVORS, INC
PO Box 42248, Portland, OR 97242-0248
Information: (503) 241-6033 24 hrs
Contact: Glenda Langager, Dir
TYPE OF AGENCY: Counseling/mental health services; Self-help group
AREAS SERVED: Multnomah, Clackamas, Washington, Coos
YEARS IN OPERATION: 2
ACCESSIBILITY: Wheelchair accessible
CASES SEXUAL ASSAULT/ABUSE (%): 100
DESCRIPTION: Eight weekly sessions for sexual assault survivors dealing with education about all aspects of sexual assault and the assaulter; includes assertiveness training, coping and recovery skills; Provides victimization program for incarcerated juvenile sex offenders
CLIENTS/SERVICES: Sexual assault survivors; Marital rape/sexual abuse survivors; Prevention program; Community education; Offender treatment program; Adolescent survivors of sexual abuse; Prisoners

SEXUAL ABUSE CLINIC
8332 SE 13th, Portland, OR 97202
Information: (503) 238-1632 9am-4pm (Mon-Fri)
Contact: Laren Bays
TYPE OF AGENCY: Private practice; Offender treatment
AREAS SERVED: Washington, Multnomah, Clackamas
YEARS IN OPERATION: 3
ACCESSIBILITY: Wheelchair accessible
CASES SEXUAL ASSAULT/ABUSE (%): 90
CLIENTS/SERVICES: Offender treatment program

SVOI, INC (SILENT VICTIMS OF INNOCENCE)
PO Box 86231, Portland, OR 97206
Crisis hotline: **(503) 293-2800 24 hrs**
Contact: Wendy Wood, Exec Dir
TYPE OF AGENCY: Counseling/mental health services; Child sexual abuse services
AREAS SERVED: Pacific Northwest
YEARS IN OPERATION: 7
CASES SEXUAL ASSAULT/ABUSE (%): 100
DESCRIPTION: Assists adults who were molested as children and families in crisis due to the trauma of sexual abuse; Provides information and referral, legal assistance, support groups, legislative advocacy, literature and materials, and a speakers bureau
CLIENTS/SERVICES: Sexual assault survivors; Child victims of sexual abuse; Adult survivors of child sexual abuse; Incest victims/survivors; Prevention program; Community education; Adolescent survivors of sexual abuse; Male survivors of sexual abuse

WEST WOMEN'S AND CHILDREN'S SHELTER
2010 NW Kearney Ave, Portland, OR 97209
Crisis hotline: **(503) 224-7718 24 hrs**
Information: (503) 224-7718 24 hrs
Contact: Allanya Guenther, Dir
TYPE OF AGENCY: Shelter
SPONSORING ORGANIZATION: Burnside Community Council
AREAS SERVED: Multnomah, Clackamas, Washington
YEARS IN OPERATION: 8
ACCESSIBILITY: Wheelchair accessible
CASES SEXUAL ASSAULT/ABUSE (%): 80-85
DESCRIPTION: Transitional services for homeless women and children; Case management; Information and referral; Legal assistance; Education on domestic violence; Child play therapy; Parenting skills education; Employment assistance; Medical/dental clinic referrals
CLIENTS/SERVICES: Marital rape/sexual abuse survivors; Child victims of sexual abuse; Adult survivors of child sexual abuse; Incest victims/survivors
REQUIREMENTS: Must not be chronically mentally ill, active prostitute, current drug/alcohol abuser; Must be willing to work toward change of homelessness

YWCA WOMEN'S RESOURCE CENTER
1111 SW 10th Ave, Portland, OR 97205
Crisis hotline: **(503) 223-6281 24 hrs**
Information: (503) 223-6281, ext 232 9am-5pm
Contact: Dorothy Steele, Emergency Svcs Dir

YWCA WOMEN'S RESOURCE CENTER
(continued)

TYPE OF AGENCY: Domestic violence program; Counseling/mental health services; Child sexual abuse services
AREAS SERVED: Multnomah, Tri-County
YEARS IN OPERATION: 10
ACCESSIBILITY: Wheelchair accessible
CASES SEXUAL ASSAULT/ABUSE (%): 35
CLIENTS/SERVICES: Sexual assault survivors; Marital rape/sexual abuse survivors; Child victims of sexual abuse; Adult survivors of child sexual abuse; Incest victims/survivors; Community education; Adolescent survivors of sexual abuse

PRINEVILLE

CROOK COUNTY VICTIMS' ASSISTANCE PROGRAM
Crook County Courthouse, Prineville, OR 97754
Information: (503) 447-4158 8:30am-12pm, 1pm-5pm
Contact: Marney Nance Close, Victims' Asst
TYPE OF AGENCY: Victim/witness assistance program
SPONSORING ORGANIZATION: District Attorney's Office
AREAS SERVED: Crook
YEARS IN OPERATION: 3
ACCESSIBILITY: Wheelchair accessible
CLIENTS/SERVICES: Sexual assault survivors; Marital rape/sexual abuse survivors; Child victims of sexual abuse; Adult survivors of child sexual abuse; Incest victims/survivors
REQUIREMENTS: Incident must be reported to a law enforcement agency

ROSEBURG

ADOLESCENT SPECIAL OFFENDERS PROGRAM
1036 SE Douglas, Rm 206, Roseburg, OR 97470
Crisis hotline: **(503) 673-6641 (United Parents) 24 hrs**
Information: (503) 440-3328 7am-5pm
Contact: Nancy Griffith, Spec Offenders Prog Coord
TYPE OF AGENCY: Child sexual abuse services; Adolescent program; Offender treatment
AREAS SERVED: Douglas
YEARS IN OPERATION: 11
ACCESSIBILITY: Wheelchair accessible
CASES SEXUAL ASSAULT/ABUSE (%): 100
DESCRIPTION: Deals with families involved with sexual abuse. The offender pleads guilty to a sexual offense in court and is placed in the program for 5 years. The family receives individual, family, mother-daughter, father-daughter, multifamily counseling. Services involve an interagency approach, including district attorney's office, probation and parole, mental health services, and children's services
CLIENTS/SERVICES: Child victims of sexual abuse; Adult survivors of child sexual abuse; Incest victims/survivors; Community education; Offender treatment program; Adolescent survivors of sexual abuse; Male survivors of sexual abuse
REQUIREMENTS: Client must admit guilt in court; family must be willing to become involved in a program of psychotherapy

BATTERED PERSONS' ADVOCACY
PO Box 1942, Roseburg, OR 97470
Crisis hotline: **(503) 673-6641 24 hrs daily**
Information: (503) 673-7867
Contact: Linda Dunn, Case Manager
TYPE OF AGENCY: Domestic violence program
AREAS SERVED: Douglas
YEARS IN OPERATION: 10
ACCESSIBILITY: Signers for the hearing impaired
CLIENTS/SERVICES: Marital rape/sexual abuse survivors; Adult survivors of child sexual abuse; Prevention program; Community education

DOUGLAS COUNTY DISTRICT ATTORNEY'S OFFICE—VICTIM/WITNESS ASSISTANCE PROGRAM
PO Box 1006, Justice Bldg, Roseburg, OR 07470
Information: (503) 440-4388 8am-5pm
Contact: Lila DuQuette, Victims' Asst Dir
TYPE OF AGENCY: Victim/witness assistance program
AREAS SERVED: Douglas
YEARS IN OPERATION: 12
LANGUAGES: Interpreters on call
ACCESSIBILITY: Signers for the hearing impaired
DESCRIPTION: Provides services for all crime victims. Rape advocacy program provides 24-hour service for sexual assault victims. CSD handles all incest cases
CLIENTS/SERVICES: Sexual assault survivors; Marital rape/sexual abuse survivors; Child victims of sexual abuse; Adult survivors of child sexual abuse; Community education; Adolescent survivors of sexual abuse; Male survivors of sexual abuse

SAINT HELENS

COLUMBIA COUNTY WOMEN'S RESOURCE CENTER
PO Box 22, Saint Helens, OR 97051
Crisis hotline: **(503) 397-6161 24 hrs**
Information: (503) 397-6161 9am-5pm (Mon-Fri)
Contact: Pat Anderson, Volunteer Svcs Coord
TYPE OF AGENCY: Rape crisis center; Domestic violence program; Child sexual abuse prevention program; Women's center
AREAS SERVED: Columbia
YEARS IN OPERATION: 10
LANGUAGES: Spanish interpreters on call; Language bank
CASES SEXUAL ASSAULT/ABUSE (%): 2
DESCRIPTION: Legal and medical advocacy; Community education; Peer counseling; Support groups; Referral; CAP (Child Assault Prevention) Program
CLIENTS/SERVICES: Sexual assault survivors; Marital rape/sexual abuse survivors; Adult survivors of child sexual abuse; Incest victims/survivors; Prevention program; Community education; Adolescent survivors of sexual abuse; Male survivors of sexual abuse

SALEM

CORRECTIONAL TREATMENT PROGRAMS—SEX OFFENDER UNIT
Oregon State Hospital, Salem, OR 97310
Information: (503) 378-2077 8am-5pm
Contact: Robert Freeman-Longo, Unit Dir
TYPE OF AGENCY: Correctional facility; Offender treatment
AREAS SERVED: Statewide
YEARS IN OPERATION: 10
CASES SEXUAL ASSAULT/ABUSE (%): 100
DESCRIPTION: Provides assessment and treatment of sexual offenders. Components include: group therapy, aversive arousal counter conditioning, education, and social skills training
CLIENTS/SERVICES: Offender treatment program; Prisoners
REQUIREMENTS: Client must have been convicted of a sex offense and be a current inmate in a correctional facility

MARION COUNTY DISTRICT ATTORNEY—VICTIM/WITNESS ASSISTANCE PROGRAM
100 High St NE, County Courthouse, Rm 99, Salem, OR 97301
Information: (503) 588-5253 8am-5pm (Mon-Fri)
Contact: Karylinn D Huntting-Echols, Dir
TYPE OF AGENCY: Victim/witness assistance program
AREAS SERVED: Marion
YEARS IN OPERATION: 8
LANGUAGES: Spanish
ACCESSIBILITY: Wheelchair accessible; Signers for the hearing impaired
CLIENTS/SERVICES: Sexual assault survivors; Marital rape/sexual abuse survivors; Child victims of sexual abuse; Incest victims/survivors; Prevention program; Community education

MID VALLEY COUNSELING CENTER
876 Welcome Way SE, Salem, OR 97302
Crisis hotline: **(503) 364-6093 24 hrs**
Information: (503) 364-6093 24 hrs
Contact: Randall L Green, PhD, Clinical Psychologist
TYPE OF AGENCY: Counseling/mental health services
AREAS SERVED: Marion, Linn, Benton, Polk
YEARS IN OPERATION: 10
CASES SEXUAL ASSAULT/ABUSE (%): 7
DESCRIPTION: Provides child, adult, marital and family therapy modalities. 70% of the clientele have some Christian affiliation. Offers ex-offender evaluation and group services for rapists, child sexual abuse/incest offenders, and batterers
CLIENTS/SERVICES: Sexual assault survivors; Marital rape/sexual abuse survivors; Child victims of sexual abuse; Adult survivors of child sexual abuse; Incest victims/survivors; Offender treatment program; Adolescent survivors of sexual abuse; Male survivors of sexual abuse

SPRINGFIELD

SPRINGFIELD CHILD ABUSE RESOURCES
1030 G St, Springfield, OR 97477
Information: (503) 746-3376 8:30am-5pm (Mon-Fri)
Contact: Anne Mascall, Admin Asst
TYPE OF AGENCY: Child sexual abuse services; Child sexual abuse prevention program; Residential treatment facility; Private practice; Child abuse services; Child abuse prevention program; Training/research
AREAS SERVED: Lane
YEARS IN OPERATION: 5
ACCESSIBILITY: Wheelchair accessible
CASES SEXUAL ASSAULT/ABUSE (%): 100
DESCRIPTION: Provides education/training programs about child abuse to the community; Direct services include low cost family counseling, counseling of the victimized child, children's treatment group, women victimized as children support group, and a residential program for abused children. Also provides group therapy for child sexual abuse offenders
CLIENTS/SERVICES: Child victims of sexual abuse; Adult survivors of child sexual abuse; Incest victims/survivors; Prevention program; Community education; Offender treatment program
SPECIAL PROGRAMS/SERVICES: SCAR annual events include the annual Western Regional Symposium on Child Abuse and Sexual Assault, and the Week-Of-Our-Children each year on the seven days preceding Christmas. Symposium videotapes available to attendees. The Jasper Mountain Program includes comprehensive residential treatment to moderately or severely disturbed children, most of whom have been physically/sexually abused. Treatment modalities include: environmental, psychotherapeutic, behavioral and self-esteem components. Innovative aspects include biofeedback and meditation training, video feedback program, equestrian training and gardening as well as crafts and a strong recreation program

TILLAMOOK

WOMEN'S CRISIS CENTER
PO Box 187, Tillamook, OR 97141
Crisis hotline: **(503) 842-9486 24 hrs**
Information: (503) 842-9486 9am-5pm
Contact: Rachel Perry, Coord
TYPE OF AGENCY: Domestic violence program
AREAS SERVED: Tillamook
YEARS IN OPERATION: 5½
LANGUAGES: Spanish, Sign
ACCESSIBILITY: Wheelchair accessible; Telecommunications for the hearing impaired (TTY, TDY, etc.); Signers for the hearing impaired
CASES SEXUAL ASSAULT/ABUSE (%): 50-75
DESCRIPTION: Offers shelter in local safe-homes, peer counseling, support groups for victims of domestic violence, most of whom are also victims of rape/sexual abuse. Advocacy for parent/child victims of sexual abuse
CLIENTS/SERVICES: Sexual assault survivors; Marital rape/sexual abuse survivors; Child victims of sexual abuse; Adult survivors of child sexual abuse; Incest victims/survivors; Prevention program; Community education; Adolescent survivors of sexual abuse

VALE

MALHEUR COUNTY DISTRICT ATTORNEY—VICTIM/WITNESS ASSISTANCE PROGRAM
251 B St W, Box 6, Vale, OR 97918
Information: (503) 473-5155 8am-5pm
Contact: Mary Pinkston, Dir
TYPE OF AGENCY: Victim/witness assistance program
AREAS SERVED: Malheur
ACCESSIBILITY: Wheelchair accessible
CASES SEXUAL ASSAULT/ABUSE (%): 33
CLIENTS/SERVICES: Sexual assault survivors; Marital rape/sexual abuse survivors; Child victims of sexual abuse; Community education
REQUIREMENTS: Offers services and information for those who do not press charges and for those who do

PENNSYLVANIA

ALTOONA

SEXUAL ASSAULT VOLUNTEER EFFORT (SAVE)
2022 Broad Ave, Altoona, PA 16601
Crisis hotline: **(814) 944-3585 24 hrs**
Information: (814) 944-3583 8:30am-5pm (Mon-Fri)
Contact: Anna Fleck, SAVE Coord
TYPE OF AGENCY: Rape crisis center; Domestic violence program; Counseling/mental health services
SPONSORING ORGANIZATION: Family and Children's Service
AREAS SERVED: Blair
YEARS IN OPERATION: 10
ACCESSIBILITY: Wheelchair accessible
CASES SEXUAL ASSAULT/ABUSE (%): 100
DESCRIPTION: Crisis and supportive counseling for victims of sexual assault; Assistance with compensation claims; Batterers support group (Men Helping Men)
CLIENTS/SERVICES: Sexual assault survivors; Marital rape/sexual abuse survivors; Child victims of sexual abuse; Adult survivors of child sexual abuse; Incest victims/survivors; Community education; Adolescent survivors of sexual abuse; Male survivors of sexual abuse

ARDLSEY

ARDSLEY KARATE CLUB
Spear and Central Aves, Ardlsey, PA 19038
Information: (215) 576-1630 10am-5pm (Mon-Fri)
Contact: Eresa Galetti, Head Instructor
TYPE OF AGENCY: Rape prevention program
SPONSORING ORGANIZATION: Ardsley Community Center
AREAS SERVED: Montgomery, Bucks, Philadelphia
YEARS IN OPERATION: 6
LANGUAGES: Spanish
DESCRIPTION: Teaches Tae Kwon Do (Korean Karate) and self-defense ("Fight Back", a course in self empowerment), both with a feminist philosophy. Provides courses at Temple University, University of Penn, Women's Centers, etc. The self-defense courses are very realistically physical, and participants are also encouraged to talk about the violence and abuse that brought them to the classes. Outreach to gay and lesbian community, as well as older men and women
CLIENTS/SERVICES: Sexual assault survivors; Adult survivors of child sexual abuse; Incest victims/survivors; Prevention program

BEAVER

WOMEN'S CENTER OF BEAVER COUNTY
PO Box 397, Beaver, PA 15009
Crisis hotline: **(412) 775-0131 24 hrs**
Information: (412) 775-0131 9am-5pm
Contact: Jill Marsilio-Colonna, Prog Dir
TYPE OF AGENCY: Rape crisis center; Domestic violence program; Child sexual abuse services; Child sexual abuse prevention program
AREAS SERVED: Beaver
YEARS IN OPERATION: 10
CASES SEXUAL ASSAULT/ABUSE (%): 40
CLIENTS/SERVICES: Sexual assault survivors; Marital rape/sexual abuse survivors; Child victims of sexual abuse; Adult survivors of child sexual abuse; Incest victims/survivors; Prevention program; Community education; Adolescent survivors of sexual abuse; Male survivors of sexual abuse

BELLEFONTE

CENTRE COUNTY VICTIM/WITNESS ADVOCATE
County Courthouse, No 404, Bellefonte, PA 16823
Crisis hotline: **(814) 355-6736 24 hrs**
Information: (814) 355-6735 8:30am-5pm
Contact: Dawn G McKee, Victim Advocate
TYPE OF AGENCY: Victim/witness assistance program
AREAS SERVED: Centre
YEARS IN OPERATION: 2½
ACCESSIBILITY: Wheelchair accessible
CLIENTS/SERVICES: Sexual assault survivors; Marital rape/sexual abuse survivors; Child victims of sexual abuse
REQUIREMENTS: Crime must have occurred in Centre County; Client must prosecute

BLOOMSBURG

WOMEN'S CENTER
111 N Market St, Bloomsburg, PA 17815
Crisis hotline: **(717) 784-6631 24 hrs**
Information: (717) 784-6631 24 hrs
Contact: Melissa Dyas, Exec Dir
TYPE OF AGENCY: Rape crisis center; Domestic violence program
AREAS SERVED: Columbia, Montour, Northumberland, lower Luzerne
YEARS IN OPERATION: 14
CASES SEXUAL ASSAULT/ABUSE (%): 30
CLIENTS/SERVICES: Sexual assault survivors; Marital rape/sexual abuse survivors; Child victims of sexual abuse; Adult survivors of child sexual abuse; Incest victims/survivors; Prevention program; Community education; Adolescent survivors of sexual abuse; Male survivors of sexual abuse

BROOKVILLE

THE RAPE CRISIS CENTER, INC
301 Main St, Brookville, PA 15825
Crisis hotline: **(814) 849-7274 24 hrs**
Information: (814) 849-5303 8:30am-4:30pm (Mon-Fri)
Contact: Julie Copen, Exec Dir
TYPE OF AGENCY: Rape crisis center; Child sexual abuse services; Child sexual abuse prevention program
AREAS SERVED: Clarion, Jefferson
YEARS IN OPERATION: 8
ACCESSIBILITY: Signers for the hearing impaired
CASES SEXUAL ASSAULT/ABUSE (%): 100
CLIENTS/SERVICES: Sexual assault survivors; Marital rape/sexual abuse survivors; Child victims of sexual abuse; Adult survivors of child sexual abuse; Incest victims/survivors; Prevention program; Community education

BUTLER

CENTER ON RAPE AND ASSAULT (CORA)
PO Box 2236, Butler, PA 16003-2236
Crisis hotline: **(412) 272-7273, 287-7769 9am-4pm (Mon-Fri); 24-hr hotline**
Information: (412) 282-7275, 282-1277 9am-4pm (Mon-Fri)
Contact: Sharon M Schmittlein, PR/Educ Coord
TYPE OF AGENCY: Rape crisis center; Child sexual abuse prevention program; Acquaintance/date rape prevention program
AREAS SERVED: Butler
YEARS IN OPERATION: 10
CASES SEXUAL ASSAULT/ABUSE (%): 89
CLIENTS/SERVICES: Sexual assault survivors; Marital rape/sexual abuse survivors; Child victims of sexual abuse; Adult survivors of child sexual abuse; Incest victims/survivors; Prevention program; Community education; Adolescent survivors of sexual abuse; Male survivors of sexual abuse
SPECIAL PROGRAMS/SERVICES: Prevention programs include: Child Assault Prevention (CAP) program, for grade school children; "Dealing With Assault Through Education" (DATE) for junior and senior high students; Self-defense classes for women

CHAMBERSBURG

WOMEN IN NEED, INC (WIN)/VICTIM HELP SERVICES
PO Box 25, Chambersburg, PA 17201
Crisis hotline: **(717) 264-4444, (800) 621-6660 24 hrs**
Information: (717) 264-3056 9am-5pm
Contact: Barb Selman, Counseling Coord

WOMEN IN NEED, INC (WIN)/VICTIM HELP SERVICES *(continued)*

TYPE OF AGENCY: Rape crisis center; Domestic violence program; Victim/witness assistance program; Child sexual abuse services; Child sexual abuse prevention program
AREAS SERVED: Franklin, Fulton, Adams
YEARS IN OPERATION: 12
ACCESSIBILITY: Wheelchair accessible; Signers for the hearing impaired
CASES SEXUAL ASSAULT/ABUSE (%): 33
DESCRIPTION: Provides counseling, court advocacy, support groups and shelter for sexual assault survivors, domestic violence survivors, and other victims of crime
CLIENTS/SERVICES: Sexual assault survivors; Marital rape/sexual abuse survivors; Child victims of sexual abuse; Adult survivors of child sexual abuse; Incest victims/survivors; Prevention program; Community education; Adolescent survivors of sexual abuse; Male survivors of sexual abuse

CLARION

CHILDREN AND YOUTH SERVICES
214 S 7th Ave, Ste 209, Clarion, PA 16214
Crisis hotline: **(814) 226-7020 24 hrs**
Information: (814) 226-9280 24 hrs
Contact: Bud Neely, Admin
TYPE OF AGENCY: Counseling/mental health services; Child sexual abuse services
AREAS SERVED: Clarion
YEARS IN OPERATION: 21
ACCESSIBILITY: Wheelchair accessible
CASES SEXUAL ASSAULT/ABUSE (%): 10
CLIENTS/SERVICES: Child victims of sexual abuse
REQUIREMENTS: Ages birth to 18

CLARION COUNTY COUNSELING CENTER
214 S 7th Ave, Clarion, PA 16214
Crisis hotline: **(814) 226-7223 24 hrs**
Information: (814) 226-6252 8:30am-4:30pm (Mon, Wed, Thu, Fri); 8:30am-7:30pm (Tue)
Contact: Martina Lawrito, Psych Svcs Assoc II
TYPE OF AGENCY: Counseling/mental health services
AREAS SERVED: Clarion
YEARS IN OPERATION: 7
ACCESSIBILITY: Wheelchair accessible
CASES SEXUAL ASSAULT/ABUSE (%): 8-10
CLIENTS/SERVICES: Sexual assault survivors; Marital rape/sexual abuse survivors; Child victims of sexual abuse; Adult survivors of child sexual abuse; Incest victims/survivors; Offender treatment program; Adolescent survivors of sexual abuse; Male survivors of sexual abuse

STOP ABUSE FOR EVERYONE, INC
PO Box 108, Clarion, PA 16214
Crisis hotline: **(814) 226-SAFE, 226-7020 SAFE 9am-4:30pm (Mon-Fri); 7020 evenings and weekends**
Information: (814) 226-8481 9am-4:30pm
Contact: Debra Arner, Legal Advocate
TYPE OF AGENCY: Domestic violence program
AREAS SERVED: Clarion
YEARS IN OPERATION: 4
ACCESSIBILITY: Wheelchair accessible
CASES SEXUAL ASSAULT/ABUSE (%): 25
CLIENTS/SERVICES: Sexual assault survivors; Marital rape/sexual abuse survivors; Adult survivors of child sexual abuse; Prevention program; Community education

DOYLESTOWN

NETWORK OF VICTIM ASSISTANCE (NOVA)
30 W Oakland Ave, Doylestown, PA 18901
Crisis hotline: **(215) 752-3596 24 hrs**
Information: (215) 348-5664 9am-4:30pm
Contact: Toyita B Raffel, Exec Dir
TYPE OF AGENCY: Victim/witness assistance program; Counseling/mental health services
AREAS SERVED: Bucks
YEARS IN OPERATION: 15
LANGUAGES: Spanish
CASES SEXUAL ASSAULT/ABUSE (%): 85
CLIENTS/SERVICES: Sexual assault survivors; Child victims of sexual abuse; Adult survivors of child sexual abuse; Incest victims/survivors; Prevention program; Community education; Adolescent survivors of sexual abuse; Male survivors of sexual abuse
REQUIREMENTS: Must live in Bucks County

A WOMAN'S PLACE
PO Box 299, Doylestown, PA 18901
Crisis hotline: **(215) 348-9780, 752-8035 24 hrs**
Information: (215) 348-9780, 752-8035
Contact: Gale Hewitt, Act Dir
TYPE OF AGENCY: Domestic violence program
AREAS SERVED: Bucks
YEARS IN OPERATION: 12
ACCESSIBILITY: Telecommunications for the hearing impaired (TTY, TDY, etc.)
CLIENTS/SERVICES: Marital rape/sexual abuse survivors; Child victims of sexual abuse

DUBOIS

CLEARFIELD-JEFFERSON COMMUNITY MENTAL HEALTH CENTER
100 Caldwell Dr, DuBois, PA 15801
Crisis hotline: **(814) 371-1105 24 hrs**
Contact: William R Young, MH Ctr Crisis Supv
TYPE OF AGENCY: Counseling/mental health services; Child sexual abuse services
AREAS SERVED: Clearfield, Jefferson
YEARS IN OPERATION: 17
ACCESSIBILITY: Wheelchair accessible
CASES SEXUAL ASSAULT/ABUSE (%): 1-2
CLIENTS/SERVICES: Sexual assault survivors; Marital rape/sexual abuse survivors; Child victims of sexual abuse; Adult survivors of child sexual abuse; Incest victims/survivors; Offender treatment program; Adolescent survivors of sexual abuse; Male survivors of sexual abuse

ERIE

ERIE COUNTY RAPE CRISIS CENTER, INC
313 Wallace St, Erie, PA 16507
Crisis hotline: **(814) 870-7087 24 hrs**
Information: (814) 870-7087 9am-5pm
Contact: Susanne M Porowski, Exec Dir
TYPE OF AGENCY: Rape crisis center; Child sexual abuse services; Child sexual abuse prevention program
AREAS SERVED: Erie
YEARS IN OPERATION: 15
LANGUAGES: Interpreters for hearing impaired and Spanish available
ACCESSIBILITY: Wheelchair accessible
CASES SEXUAL ASSAULT/ABUSE (%): 80
CLIENTS/SERVICES: Sexual assault survivors; Marital rape/sexual abuse survivors; Child victims of sexual abuse; Adult survivors of child sexual abuse; Incest victims/survivors; Prevention program; Community education; Adolescent survivors of sexual abuse; Male survivors of sexual abuse

ERIE HOTLINE
110 W 10th St, Erie, PA 16501
Crisis hotline: **(814) 453-5656 24 hrs**
Information: (814) 456-2937 8:30am-5pm
Contact: Judy Glembocki, Asst Dir
TYPE OF AGENCY: Counseling/mental health services; Telephone crisis hotline; Information and referral
SPONSORING ORGANIZATION: United Way of Erie County
AREAS SERVED: Erie
YEARS IN OPERATION: 17
ACCESSIBILITY: Telecommunications for the hearing impaired (TTY, TDY, etc.)
CASES SEXUAL ASSAULT/ABUSE (%): 3
CLIENTS/SERVICES: Sexual assault survivors; Marital rape/sexual abuse survivors; Child victims of sexual abuse; Adult survivors of child sexual abuse; Incest victims/survivors

FOLSOM

SENIOR VICTIM SERVICES, INC OF DELAWARE COUNTY
9th and Morton Ave, Folsom, PA 19033
Information: (215) 586-0537 8:30am-5pm; after hrs answering service
Contact: Jonathan Stolley, Dir
TYPE OF AGENCY: Victim/witness assistance program
AREAS SERVED: Delaware
YEARS IN OPERATION: 11
ACCESSIBILITY: Wheelchair accessible
CASES SEXUAL ASSAULT/ABUSE (%): 3
DESCRIPTION: Provides comprehensive victim assistance for persons 55 or older; Works with other county agencies to provide assistance for elderly sexual assault victims; Court escort/accompaniment
CLIENTS/SERVICES: Sexual assault survivors; Prevention program; Community education; Elderly
REQUIREMENTS: Must be 55 or older

GETTYSBURG

SURVIVORS, INC
PO Box 3572, Gettysburg, PA 17325
Crisis hotline: **(717) 334-9777 24 hrs**
Information: (717) 334-0589 8:30am-5pm
Contact: Claudia McCarthy, Exec Dir
TYPE OF AGENCY: Rape crisis center; Domestic violence program
AREAS SERVED: Adams
YEARS IN OPERATION: 5½
LANGUAGES: Interpreters available through language bank
ACCESSIBILITY: Wheelchair accessible
CLIENTS/SERVICES: Sexual assault survivors; Marital rape/sexual abuse survivors; Child victims of sexual abuse; Adult survivors of child sexual abuse; Incest victims/survivors; Prevention program; Community education; Adolescent survivors of sexual abuse

GREENSBURG

WOMEN'S SERVICES OF WESTMORELAND COUNTY, INC
PO Box 246, Greensburg, PA 15601-0246
Crisis hotline: **(412) 836-1122 24 hrs daily**
Information: (412) 837-9540 8:30am-4:30pm (Mon-Fri)
Contact: Norma F Samide, Exec Dir
TYPE OF AGENCY: Rape crisis center; Domestic violence program; Child sexual abuse services; Child sexual abuse prevention program
AREAS SERVED: Westmoreland
YEARS IN OPERATION: 12
CASES SEXUAL ASSAULT/ABUSE (%): 24
CLIENTS/SERVICES: Sexual assault survivors; Marital rape/sexual abuse survivors; Child victims of sexual abuse; Adult survivors of child sexual abuse; Incest victims/survivors; Prevention program; Community education; Adolescent survivors of sexual abuse; Male survivors of sexual abuse

HARRISBURG

YWCA RAPE CRISIS SERVICES
215 Market St, Harrisburg, PA 17101
Crisis hotline: **(717) 238-7273 24 hrs**
Information: (717) 238-7273 9am-7pm
Contact: D Jo Sterner, Rape Crisis Svcs Dir
TYPE OF AGENCY: Rape crisis center; Child sexual abuse services; Child sexual abuse prevention program

YWCA RAPE CRISIS SERVICES
(continued)

SPONSORING ORGANIZATION: YWCA of the Greater Harrisburg Area
AREAS SERVED: Cumberland, Dauphin, Perry
YEARS IN OPERATION: 10
LANGUAGES: Spanish
ACCESSIBILITY: Wheelchair accessible; Telecommunications for the hearing impaired (TTY, TDY, etc.)
CASES SEXUAL ASSAULT/ABUSE (%): 52
CLIENTS/SERVICES: Sexual assault survivors; Marital rape/sexual abuse survivors; Child victims of sexual abuse; Adult survivors of child sexual abuse; Incest victims/survivors; Prevention program; Community education; Adolescent survivors of sexual abuse; Male survivors of sexual abuse; Healing
SPECIAL PROGRAMS/SERVICES: Support group at drug and alcohol inpatient treatment program; 3-day retreat for adult incest survivors at the YWCA's day camp facility; Speaks to offenders during offender treatment group

HUMMELSTOWN

WOMEN IN CRISIS
RD No 1, Box 314-A, Hummelstown, PA 17036
Crisis hotline: **(800) 992-1101, (717) 534-1101 24 hrs**
Information: (717) 534-1103 8am-4pm
Contact: Peggy Lorah, Counseling Coord
TYPE OF AGENCY: Domestic violence program
AREAS SERVED: Dauphin, Cumberland, Lebanon, Perry
CASES SEXUAL ASSAULT/ABUSE (%): 30
CLIENTS/SERVICES: Marital rape/sexual abuse survivors; Community education; Adolescent survivors of sexual abuse

INDIANA

ALICE PAUL HOUSE
PO Box 417, Indiana, PA 15701
Crisis hotline: **(412) 349-4444 24 hrs**
Information: (412) 349-4444 8am-5pm
Contact: Lenore Patton, Exec Dir
TYPE OF AGENCY: Rape crisis center; Domestic violence program
AREAS SERVED: Indiana
YEARS IN OPERATION: 6
LANGUAGES: Spanish, German, French translators available
ACCESSIBILITY: Wheelchair accessible; Signers for the hearing impaired
CASES SEXUAL ASSAULT/ABUSE (%): 35
CLIENTS/SERVICES: Sexual assault survivors; Marital rape/sexual abuse survivors; Child victims of sexual abuse; Adult survivors of child sexual abuse; Incest victims/survivors; Prevention program; Community education; Adolescent survivors of sexual abuse; Male survivors of sexual abuse

JOHNSTOWN

VICTIM SERVICES, INC
334 Southmont Blvd, Johnstown, PA 15905
Crisis hotline: **(814) 535-2551, 443-1555, (800) 452-0218 24 hrs**
Information: (814) 535-2551
Contact: Rosalie Danchanko, Exec Dir
TYPE OF AGENCY: Rape crisis center; Victim/witness assistance program; Child sexual abuse prevention program
AREAS SERVED: Cambria, Somerset, Bedford
YEARS IN OPERATION: 5
LANGUAGES: Italian
ACCESSIBILITY: Wheelchair accessible; Telecommunications for the hearing impaired (TTY, TDY, etc.); Signers for the hearing impaired
CASES SEXUAL ASSAULT/ABUSE (%): 85

DESCRIPTION: Comprehensive services for victims; Support groups for adolescent and adult survivors; Witness preparation; Prevention programs for children and adolescents
CLIENTS/SERVICES: Sexual assault survivors; Marital rape/sexual abuse survivors; Child victims of sexual abuse; Adult survivors of child sexual abuse; Incest victims/survivors; Prevention program; Community education; Adolescent survivors of sexual abuse; Male survivors of sexual abuse; Elderly; Publications/media
SPECIAL PROGRAMS/SERVICES: Home security/safety program for the elderly; 1-hour documentary on agency called "The Victim's World"

KITTANNING

HAVIN (HELPING ABUSE VICTIMS IN NEED), INC
PO Box 983, Kittanning, PA 16201
Crisis hotline: **(412) 548-8888 24 hrs daily**
Information: (412) 543-1180 8am-5pm (Mon-Fri)
Contact: Betsy Smith, Exec Dir
TYPE OF AGENCY: Rape crisis center; Domestic violence program; Child sexual abuse services; Child sexual abuse prevention program
AREAS SERVED: Armstrong
YEARS IN OPERATION: 9
LANGUAGES: French, Spanish
ACCESSIBILITY: Wheelchair accessible; Signers for the hearing impaired
CASES SEXUAL ASSAULT/ABUSE (%): 42
CLIENTS/SERVICES: Sexual assault survivors; Marital rape/sexual abuse survivors; Child victims of sexual abuse; Adult survivors of child sexual abuse; Incest victims/survivors; Prevention program; Community education

LANCASTER

LANCASTER SHELTER FOR ABUSED WOMEN
PO Box 359, Lancaster, PA 17603
Crisis hotline: **(717) 299-1249 24 hrs**
Information: (717) 299-9776 8am-12 midnight
Contact: Donna Glover, Dir
TYPE OF AGENCY: Domestic violence program
SPONSORING ORGANIZATION: Community Action Program
AREAS SERVED: Lancaster County and city
YEARS IN OPERATION: 12
LANGUAGES: Spanish translator available
ACCESSIBILITY: Wheelchair accessible
CLIENTS/SERVICES: Marital rape/sexual abuse survivors; Community education

RAPE AID AND PREVENTION
501 W James St, Lancaster, PA 17603
Crisis hotline: **(717) 392-7273 24 hrs**
Information: (717) 392-7273 9am-4:30pm
Contact: Deb Bard, Direct Svcs Supv
TYPE OF AGENCY: Rape crisis center
AREAS SERVED: Lancaster
YEARS IN OPERATION: 14
CASES SEXUAL ASSAULT/ABUSE (%): 100
CLIENTS/SERVICES: Sexual assault survivors; Marital rape/sexual abuse survivors; Child victims of sexual abuse; Adult survivors of child sexual abuse; Incest victims/survivors; Prevention program; Community education; Adolescent survivors of sexual abuse; Male survivors of sexual abuse

VICTIM/WITNESS SERVICES PROGRAM
PO Box 3480, 50 N Duke St, Lancaster, PA 17603-1881
Information: (717) 299-8048 8:30am-5pm
Contact: Debra Akers Wissler, Prog Dir
TYPE OF AGENCY: Victim/witness assistance program
SPONSORING ORGANIZATION: Lancaster County Office of the District Attorney
AREAS SERVED: Lancaster
YEARS IN OPERATION: 2½

ACCESSIBILITY: Wheelchair accessible
CLIENTS/SERVICES: Sexual assault survivors; Marital rape/sexual abuse survivors; Child victims of sexual abuse; Community education; Adolescent survivors of sexual abuse; Male survivors of sexual abuse

LANSDALE

FAMILY SERVICE
713 W Main St, Lansdale, PA 19446
Information: (215) 368-0985 Mon, Wed, Thu 9am-9pm, Tue, Fri 9am-5pm, answering machine after hrs
Contact: Larry Fiebert, MSW, ACSW, Branch Supv
TYPE OF AGENCY: Counseling/mental health services; Child sexual abuse services; Child sexual abuse prevention program; Child abuse services; Child abuse prevention program; Child advocacy; Acquaintance/date rape prevention program; Interagency network
YEARS IN OPERATION: Over 25
LANGUAGES: Spanish
ACCESSIBILITY: Wheelchair accessible
CASES SEXUAL ASSAULT/ABUSE (%): 15
CLIENTS/SERVICES: Sexual assault survivors; Marital rape/sexual abuse survivors; Child victims of sexual abuse; Adult survivors of child sexual abuse; Incest victims/survivors; Prevention program; Community education; Adolescent survivors of sexual abuse; Male survivors of sexual abuse; Preschoolers; Sexual harassment; Disabled; Elderly

LEBANON

LEBANON COUNTY DISTRICT ATTORNEY'S OFFICE—VICTIM/WITNESS PROGRAM
400 S 8th St, Municipal Bldg, Rm 402, Lebanon, PA 17042
Crisis hotline: **(717) 273-8846 answering machine**
Information: (717) 273-8846 8:30am-4:30pm
Contact: June L Lloyd, Victim/Witness Coord
TYPE OF AGENCY: Victim/witness assistance program
AREAS SERVED: Lebanon
YEARS IN OPERATION: 2½
LANGUAGES: Interpreters available
ACCESSIBILITY: Wheelchair accessible; Telecommunications for the hearing impaired (TTY, TDY, etc.)
CLIENTS/SERVICES: Sexual assault survivors; Marital rape/sexual abuse survivors; Child victims of sexual abuse; Incest victims/survivors; Community education; Male survivors of sexual abuse
REQUIREMENTS: Clients must file charges

RAPE CRISIS SERVICES OF LEBANON COUNTY
PO Box 836, Lebanon, PA 17036
Crisis hotline: **(717) 272-5308 24 hrs**
Information: (717) 270-2253 9am-5pm
Contact: Jenny Murphy-Shifflet, Exec Dir
TYPE OF AGENCY: Rape crisis center
AREAS SERVED: Lebanon
YEARS IN OPERATION: 5
CASES SEXUAL ASSAULT/ABUSE (%): 100
CLIENTS/SERVICES: Sexual assault survivors; Marital rape/sexual abuse survivors; Child victims of sexual abuse; Adult survivors of child sexual abuse; Incest victims/survivors; Prevention program; Community education; Adolescent survivors of sexual abuse; Male survivors of sexual abuse

LEWISBURG

SUSQUEHANNA VALLEY WOMEN IN TRANSITION
PO Box 170, Lewisburg, PA 17837
Crisis hotline: **(717) 523-6482 24 hrs**
Information: (717) 523-1134 8am-5pm
Contact: Jaime Grant, Dir Svc Coord
TYPE OF AGENCY: Rape crisis center; Domestic violence program
AREAS SERVED: Union, Snyder, Upper Northumberland
YEARS IN OPERATION: 13
LANGUAGES: Spanish
CASES SEXUAL ASSAULT/ABUSE (%): 25
CLIENTS/SERVICES: Sexual assault survivors; Marital rape/sexual abuse survivors; Child victims of sexual abuse; Adult survivors of child sexual abuse; Incest victims/survivors; Prevention program; Community education; Adolescent survivors of sexual abuse; Male survivors of sexual abuse

LEWISTOWN

MIFFLIN COUNTY ABUSE NETWORK
PO Box 268, Lewistown, PA 17044
Crisis hotline: **(717) 242-2444 24 hrs**
Information: (717) 242-0351 8:30am-4:30pm
Contact: Marlyn Pupo, Prog Coord
TYPE OF AGENCY: Rape crisis center; Domestic violence program
AREAS SERVED: Mifflin, Juniata
YEARS IN OPERATION: 5
CASES SEXUAL ASSAULT/ABUSE (%): 25
CLIENTS/SERVICES: Sexual assault survivors; Marital rape/sexual abuse survivors; Child victims of sexual abuse; Adult survivors of child sexual abuse; Incest victims/survivors; Prevention program; Community education; Adolescent survivors of sexual abuse; Male survivors of sexual abuse

LITITZ

LUTHERAN SOCIAL SERVICES—EAST REGION
600 E Main St, Lititz, PA 17543
Information: (717) 626-1171, 272-5641 8:30am-4:30pm
Contact: Ted Hummel, Pastoral Counselor
TYPE OF AGENCY: Counseling/mental health services
AREAS SERVED: Lebanon, Lancaster
YEARS IN OPERATION: 25
CASES SEXUAL ASSAULT/ABUSE (%): 15
CLIENTS/SERVICES: Sexual assault survivors; Marital rape/sexual abuse survivors; Child victims of sexual abuse; Adult survivors of child sexual abuse; Adolescent survivors of sexual abuse

SEXUAL ASSAULT CENTER OF LANCASTER COUNTY
209 E Lincoln Ave, Lititz, PA 17543
Crisis hotline: **(717) 291-2393 24 hrs**
Information: (717) 626-0746 9am-5pm
Contact: Terry Wentling, Direct Svcs Supv
TYPE OF AGENCY: Rape crisis center; Child sexual abuse services
AREAS SERVED: Lancaster
YEARS IN OPERATION: 1
LANGUAGES: Interpreters available as needed
CASES SEXUAL ASSAULT/ABUSE (%): 100
DESCRIPTION: Crisis counseling from the moment of reporting the rape (at hospital, police department) through the court system; Advocacy for victim; Transportation; Referrals for therapy; Support groups; Consultation on courtroom procedures; Support groups for male survivors
CLIENTS/SERVICES: Sexual assault survivors; Marital rape/sexual abuse survivors; Child victims of sexual abuse; Adult survivors of child sexual abuse; Incest victims/survivors; Prevention program; Community education; Adolescent survivors of sexual abuse; Male survivors of sexual abuse

LOCK HAVEN

VICTIM/WITNESS PROGRAM
PO Box 725, Clinton County Courthouse Annex, Lock Haven, PA 17745
Crisis hotline: **(717) 748-2936 Communication center 24 hrs**
Information: (717) 893-4054
Contact: Karen Rockey, Victim/Witness Coord
TYPE OF AGENCY: Victim/witness assistance program
SPONSORING ORGANIZATION: Pennsylvania Commission on Crime and Delinquency
AREAS SERVED: Clinton
YEARS IN OPERATION: 1½
CASES SEXUAL ASSAULT/ABUSE (%): 10
CLIENTS/SERVICES: Sexual assault survivors; Child victims of sexual abuse; Community education

MANSFIELD

TIOGA COUNTY WOMEN'S COALITION
PO Box 503, Mansfield, PA 16933
Crisis hotline: **(800) 332-6718 24 hrs**
Information: (717) 662-7228 9am-4pm
Contact: Carol Johnson, Sexual Assault Prog Coord
TYPE OF AGENCY: Rape crisis center; Domestic violence program
AREAS SERVED: Tioga
YEARS IN OPERATION: 2
ACCESSIBILITY: Wheelchair accessible; Signers for the hearing impaired
CLIENTS/SERVICES: Sexual assault survivors; Marital rape/sexual abuse survivors; Child victims of sexual abuse; Adult survivors of child sexual abuse; Incest victims/survivors; Prevention program; Community education; Adolescent survivors of sexual abuse; Male survivors of sexual abuse

MEADVILLE

WOMEN'S SERVICES, INC
PO Box 637, Meadville, PA 16335
Crisis hotline: **(814) 333-9766 24 hrs**
Information: (814) 724-4637, 333-1058 8am-5pm (Mon-Fri)
Contact: Deanna Ferraino, Sexual Assault Coord
TYPE OF AGENCY: Rape crisis center; Domestic violence program
AREAS SERVED: Crawford
YEARS IN OPERATION: 10
LANGUAGES: Interpreters available
ACCESSIBILITY: Wheelchair accessible; Telecommunications for the hearing impaired (TTY, TDY, etc.)
CASES SEXUAL ASSAULT/ABUSE (%): 50
DESCRIPTION: Identifies the needs of women in Crawford County and develops and facilitates services meeting those needs. Contained within this structure is Victim Support Services, which provides specialized services for sexual assault/abuse victims and their families
CLIENTS/SERVICES: Sexual assault survivors; Marital rape/sexual abuse survivors; Child victims of sexual abuse; Adult survivors of child sexual abuse; Incest victims/survivors; Prevention program; Community education; Adolescent survivors of sexual abuse; Male survivors of sexual abuse
SPECIAL PROGRAMS/SERVICES: Maintains a Domestic Violence/Sexual Assault Advisory Committee whose purposes are: to coordinate activities between Women's Services, Inc and other agencies to avoid duplication of services; to assess the effectiveness of Women Services, Inc in meeting the needs of clients; to generate ideas to aid in short- and long-range planning; to serve as a consulting body. The committee consists of board members, client representatives, program coordinators, volunteers and other interested community members

MONTROSE

MONTROSE COMMUNITY COUNSELING CENTER
PO Box 312, 60 Church St, Montrose, PA 18801
Information: (717) 278-9492 24 hrs answering machine
Contact: Paul W Towers, Co-Dir
TYPE OF AGENCY: Counseling/mental health services
AREAS SERVED: Susquehanna, Wyoming
YEARS IN OPERATION: 2
CASES SEXUAL ASSAULT/ABUSE (%): 85
DESCRIPTION: Provides individual, marital and family therapy for all ages, including survivors of sex abuse, rape, verbal and emotional abuse. Treatment for sex offenders (rapists, child sexual abuse/incest offenders) and batterers
CLIENTS/SERVICES: Sexual assault survivors; Marital rape/sexual abuse survivors; Child victims of sexual abuse; Adult survivors of child sexual abuse; Incest victims/survivors; Community education; Offender treatment program; Adolescent survivors of sexual abuse; Male survivors of sexual abuse
REQUIREMENTS: For offenders: must be through the district attorney's office, court-ordered or referred from probation office

NEW CASTLE

WOMEN'S SHELTER/RAPE CRISIS CENTER
PO Box 1422, New Castle, PA 16103
Crisis hotline: **(412) 652-9036 24 hrs**
Information: (412) 652-9206 24 hrs
Contact: Bonnie Robinson, Exec Dir
TYPE OF AGENCY: Rape crisis center; Domestic violence program
AREAS SERVED: Lawrence
YEARS IN OPERATION: 8
CASES SEXUAL ASSAULT/ABUSE (%): 30
CLIENTS/SERVICES: Sexual assault survivors; Marital rape/sexual abuse survivors; Child victims of sexual abuse; Adult survivors of child sexual abuse; Incest victims/survivors; Prevention program; Community education; Adolescent survivors of sexual abuse; Male survivors of sexual abuse

NORRISTOWN

FAMILY SERVICE OF MONTGOMERY COUNTY
801 W Main St, Norristown, PA 19401
Information: (215) 272-1520 9am-5pm (Tue, Fri); 9am-9pm (Mon, Wed, Thu)
Contact: Donna F Derr, PhD, Family/Community Educ Dir
TYPE OF AGENCY: Counseling/mental health services; Child sexual abuse services; Child sexual abuse prevention program
AREAS SERVED: Montgomery and surrounding areas
YEARS IN OPERATION: 50
ACCESSIBILITY: Wheelchair accessible
CASES SEXUAL ASSAULT/ABUSE (%): 50
DESCRIPTION: Counseling, support groups, and workshops for a variety of issues, including dating violence, child sexual abuse prevention (ages 4-9), addiction, and parenting programs; Support groups for adult male and female survivors of child sexual abuse; Support groups for partners of adults who were sexually abused as children
CLIENTS/SERVICES: Sexual assault survivors; Marital rape/sexual abuse survivors; Child victims of sexual abuse; Adult survivors of child sexual abuse; Incest victims/survivors; Prevention program; Community education; Adoles-

FAMILY SERVICE OF MONTGOMERY COUNTY *(continued)*
cent survivors of sexual abuse; Male survivors of sexual abuse

LAUREL HOUSE
PO Box 764, Norristown, PA 19401
Crisis hotline: **(215) 643-3150 24 hrs**
Contact: Sarah Bolton, Children's Prog Coord; Nancy Hopkins, Prog Dir
TYPE OF AGENCY: Domestic violence program
SPONSORING ORGANIZATION: Pennsylvania Coalition Against Domestic Violence
AREAS SERVED: Montgomery and others
YEARS IN OPERATION: 8
ACCESSIBILITY: Wheelchair accessible; Telecommunications for the hearing impaired (TTY, TDY, etc.)
DESCRIPTION: Provides shelter for battered women and their dependent children. Many women were sexually assaulted by current abuser, as well as victims of child sexual abuse; Also provides therapy for batterers
CLIENTS/SERVICES: Sexual assault survivors; Marital rape/sexual abuse survivors; Child victims of sexual abuse; Adult survivors of child sexual abuse; Incest victims/survivors; Community education

VICTIM SERVICES CENTER OF MONTGOMERY COUNTY, INC
527 Swede St, Norristown, PA 19401
Crisis hotline: **(215) 277-5200, ASSIST-1 24 hrs**
Information: (215) 277-0932 8:30am-4:30pm (Mon-Fri)
Contact: L C Gilhool, Exec Dir
TYPE OF AGENCY: Rape crisis center; Victim/witness assistance program; Child abuse prevention program; Acquaintance/date rape prevention program
AREAS SERVED: Montgomery
YEARS IN OPERATION: 14
CASES SEXUAL ASSAULT/ABUSE (%): 72
DESCRIPTION: Provides supportive services for all victims of sexual assault and their families; Educational services on sexual assault and the means to avoid victimization for all age levels
CLIENTS/SERVICES: Sexual assault survivors; Marital rape/sexual abuse survivors; Child victims of sexual abuse; Adult survivors of child sexual abuse; Incest victims/survivors; Prevention program; Community education; Adolescent survivors of sexual abuse; Male survivors of sexual abuse
SPECIAL PROGRAMS/SERVICES: Comprehensive personal safety program for school children on several levels: "Good Touch, Bad Touch" for preschool and elementary school children; a program for junior high or middle school students on child sexual abuse; program on acquaintance rape for high school students

PHILADELPHIA

ADULT PROBATION DEPARTMENT—VICTIM SERVICES UNIT
121 N Broad St, Ste 309, Philadelphia, PA 19107
Information: (215) 686-7745 9am-5pm
Contact: Frank N Menna, Proj Mgr
TYPE OF AGENCY: Victim/witness assistance program
AREAS SERVED: Philadelphia
YEARS IN OPERATION: 3
CASES SEXUAL ASSAULT/ABUSE (%): 30
CLIENTS/SERVICES: Sexual assault survivors; Marital rape/sexual abuse survivors; Child victims of sexual abuse; Adult survivors of child sexual abuse; Incest victims/survivors; Adolescent survivors of sexual abuse

GAY AND LESBIAN PEER COUNSELING
3601 Locust Walk, Rm 4, Philadelphia, PA 19104
Crisis hotline: **(215) 898-8888, 386-6110 4pm-10pm (Mon-Thu); 4pm-7pm (Fri)**
Information: (215) 898-8888, 386-6110 4pm-10pm (Mon-Thu); 4pm-7pm (Fri)
TYPE OF AGENCY: Counseling/mental health services
YEARS IN OPERATION: 12
CASES SEXUAL ASSAULT/ABUSE (%): 5
DESCRIPTION: Short-term peer counseling; Crisis counseling
CLIENTS/SERVICES: Sexual assault survivors; Marital rape/sexual abuse survivors; Adult survivors of child sexual abuse; Incest victims/survivors; Adolescent survivors of sexual abuse; Male survivors of sexual abuse; Developmentally disabled; Lesbians; Gay men

PENN WOMEN'S CENTER
3417 Spruce St, 119 Houston Hall, Philadelphia, PA 19104
Information: (215) 898-8611, 898-8612 9am-5pm (Mon-Fri); answering machine for other hrs
Contact: Gloria M Gay, MSW, Asst Dir
TYPE OF AGENCY: College/university-based services
SPONSORING ORGANIZATION: University of Pennsylvania
AREAS SERVED: Philadelphia
YEARS IN OPERATION: 15
LANGUAGES: Spanish, German
ACCESSIBILITY: Wheelchair accessible
CLIENTS/SERVICES: Sexual assault survivors; Marital rape/sexual abuse survivors; Adult survivors of child sexual abuse; Incest victims/survivors; Prevention program; Community education
SPECIAL PROGRAMS/SERVICES: Sponsorship of national conference Ending Campus Violence (Fall 1988)

JOSEPH J PETERS INSTITUTE
260 S Broad St, Ste 220, Philadelphia, PA 19102-3814
Information: (215) 893-0600 9am-9pm (Mon, Thu); 9am-8pm (Tue); 9am-7pm (Wed); 9am-5pm (Fri)
TYPE OF AGENCY: Counseling/mental health services; Child sexual abuse services; Training/research; Offender treatment
AREAS SERVED: Philadelphia, Bucks, Montgomery, Chester
YEARS IN OPERATION: 33
LANGUAGES: Interpreters by arrangement
ACCESSIBILITY: Wheelchair accessible
CASES SEXUAL ASSAULT/ABUSE (%): 100
DESCRIPTION: Provides therapy for victims/survivors; Treatment for rapists, child sexual abuse/incest offenders, pedophiles, exhibitionists, physicians who have been unethically or illegally sexually involved with others, sex offenders incarcerated at the State Correctional Institution at Graterford
CLIENTS/SERVICES: Sexual assault survivors; Marital rape/sexual abuse survivors; Child victims of sexual abuse; Adult survivors of child sexual abuse; Incest victims/survivors; Offender treatment program; Prisoners; Sexual harassment; Publications/media
SPECIAL PROGRAMS/SERVICES: Training is available in evaluation and treatment of child and adolescent sexual abuse, rapists, pedophiles/child molesters, incest offenders, sex offenders in a prison setting, and multiple personality disorder. Publications (monographs and reprint articles) on these topics. Videotapes (4, 45 minutes each) on *Intrafamilial Child Sexual Abuse Assessment Interview*

PHILADELPHIA DISTRICT ATTORNEY'S OFFICE—CHILD ABUSE PROSECUTION UNIT
1421 Arch St, Philadelphia, PA 19102
Information: (215) 686-8721 8:30am-5pm
Contact: Mary Achilles, Victim Svcs Dir
TYPE OF AGENCY: Victim/witness assistance program; Child sexual abuse services; Child abuse services
AREAS SERVED: Philadelphia
ACCESSIBILITY: Wheelchair accessible; Signers for the hearing impaired
CLIENTS/SERVICES: Child victims of sexual abuse

PHILADELPHIA SEXUAL ABUSE PROJECT
6038 Wissahickon Ave, Philadelphia, PA 19144
Information: (215) 844-7566 answering machine
Contact: Pamela Freeman, Therapist
TYPE OF AGENCY: Private practice
AREAS SERVED: Philadelphia, Montgomery, Delaware, Bucks, Chester, New Jersey
YEARS IN OPERATION: 5
CASES SEXUAL ASSAULT/ABUSE (%): 100
CLIENTS/SERVICES: Sexual assault survivors; Marital rape/sexual abuse survivors; Adult survivors of child sexual abuse; Incest victims/survivors; Healing
REQUIREMENTS: 18 years of age and over
SPECIAL PROGRAMS/SERVICES: Specializes in healing and recovery groups for adult women survivors of childhood sexual abuse. Groups are time-limited (12-16 weeks), requiring women to do some reading, to keep a journal, and to set a goal for their time in group. Uses a Gestalt method with the emphasis on the individual woman's experience.

SPRING GARDEN PSYCHOLOGICAL ASSOCIATES
2236 Mt Vernon St, Philadelphia, PA 19130
Information: (215) 642-1494, 978-6810 9am-7pm
Contact: Sandra Block Steiker, Asst Dir
TYPE OF AGENCY: Private practice
AREAS SERVED: Philadelphia, Delaware, Montgomery, Bucks, Lancaster
YEARS IN OPERATION: 5
CASES SEXUAL ASSAULT/ABUSE (%): 50
DESCRIPTION: Specializes in evaluation and treatment of children, adolescent and adult survivors, parents, and child sexual abuse/incest offenders and batterers; Individual, couple and family treatment provided
CLIENTS/SERVICES: Sexual assault survivors; Marital rape/sexual abuse survivors; Child victims of sexual abuse; Adult survivors of child sexual abuse; Incest victims/survivors; Offender treatment program; Adolescent survivors of sexual abuse; Male survivors of sexual abuse
REQUIREMENTS: Client is responsible for payment

WOMEN AGAINST ABUSE
PO Box 15738, Philadelphia, PA 19101
Crisis hotline: **(215) 386-7777 24 hrs**
Information: (215) 386-1280 9am-5pm
Contact: Diane Hall, Shelter Dir
TYPE OF AGENCY: Domestic violence program
AREAS SERVED: Statewide, National Hotline Connection
YEARS IN OPERATION: 10
LANGUAGES: Spanish
ACCESSIBILITY: Wheelchair accessible
CASES SEXUAL ASSAULT/ABUSE (%): 75
CLIENTS/SERVICES: Sexual assault survivors; Marital rape/sexual abuse survivors; Child victims of sexual abuse; Adult survivors of child sexual abuse; Community education; Adolescent survivors of sexual abuse; Healing
SPECIAL PROGRAMS/SERVICES: Counseling includes art therapy, movement therapy, massage and fun ways to express anger

WOMEN IN DIALOGUE
PO Box 11795, Philadelphia, PA 19101
Information: (215) 844-1066 Vary; 24 hr answering machine
Contact: Mary Hawryshkiw, Activities Coord
TYPE OF AGENCY: Victim/witness assistance program
AREAS SERVED: Mainly Philadelphia area
YEARS IN OPERATION: 8
LANGUAGES: Ukrainian
DESCRIPTION: Provides information on financial compensation for victims/survivors of rape and other violent crimes; Publishes *Every*

WOMEN IN DIALOGUE (continued)

Woman's Handbook on Compensation for Rape and Other Violent Crimes in Pennsylvania with information on applying to the PA Victim Compensation Board and on filing a civil suit against an offender or a third party (employer, landlord, etc); Gives workshops in the community; Speaks at conferences on the issue of compensation for rape victims; Refers women for counseling and other direct services
CLIENTS/SERVICES: Community education; Publications/media

WOMEN IN TRANSITION
125 S 9th St, Ste 502, Philadelphia, PA 19107
Crisis hotline: **(215) 922-7500 24 hrs**
Information: (215) 922-7177 9am-8pm (Mon-Fri)
Contact: Annie Peskofsky, Assoc Dir
TYPE OF AGENCY: Domestic violence program; Women's center
AREAS SERVED: Philadelphia, Montgomery, Bucks, Delaware, Chester
YEARS IN OPERATION: 16
ACCESSIBILITY: Wheelchair accessible
CASES SEXUAL ASSAULT/ABUSE (%): 15-20
CLIENTS/SERVICES: Adult survivors of child sexual abuse; Incest victims/survivors; Prevention program; Community education; Adolescent survivors of sexual abuse
SPECIAL PROGRAMS/SERVICES: Teen dating violence prevention program

WOMEN ORGANIZED AGAINST RAPE (WOAR)
125 S 9th St, Ste 601, Philadelphia, PA 19107
Crisis hotline: **(215) 922-3434 24 hrs**
Information: (215) 922-7400 9am-5pm
Contact: Karen Kulp, Exec Dir; Meloney Sallie, Comm Ed and Training Dir
TYPE OF AGENCY: Rape crisis center; Child sexual abuse services; Child sexual abuse prevention program
AREAS SERVED: Philadelphia
YEARS IN OPERATION: 16
LANGUAGES: Spanish
ACCESSIBILITY: Wheelchair accessible; Signers for the hearing impaired (consultants)
CASES SEXUAL ASSAULT/ABUSE (%): 100
CLIENTS/SERVICES: Sexual assault survivors; Marital rape/sexual abuse survivors; Child victims of sexual abuse; Adult survivors of child sexual abuse; Incest victims/survivors; Prevention program; Community education; Adolescent survivors of sexual abuse; Male survivors of sexual abuse; Ethnic minorities; Publications/media
SPECIAL PROGRAMS/SERVICES: Publications: *Rape Is...* ($.15); *Teens Your Right to Know* ($.15); *We Can Help* ($1.00, available in Spanish); Comic book ($.15); *Touching Can Be Fun* ($.15, available in Spanish); *Family/Juvenile Court* ($1.00); *Rape and the Older Woman* ($1.00); *When the Defendant Is a Juvenile* ($1.00, available in Spanish); *Taking Control: A Personal Safety Handbook* ($1.00, available in Spanish); *Articles on Rape* ($1.00); *Child Abuse Is a Secret* ($.15, available in Spanish); *Do It Yourself Self-Defense* ($.25); *Safety on Public Transportation* ($.10); *Women's Self-Defense Course* ($3.00). Special caucus for women of color. Brochures on child sexual abuse, rape, and prevention and awareness for teens

WOMEN'S LAW PROJECT
125 S 9th St Ste 401, Philadelphia, PA 19107
Crisis hotline: **(215) 928-9801 9am-5pm (Mon-Fri)**
Contact: Dabney Miller, Education Coord
TYPE OF AGENCY: Legal services agency; Information and referral
YEARS IN OPERATION: 15
CLIENTS/SERVICES: Sexual assault survivors; Adult survivors of child sexual abuse; Incest victims/survivors

WOMEN'S THERAPY CENTER
1930 Chestnut St, Ste 1703, Philadelphia, PA 19103
Information: (215) 567-1111 24 hr answering service
Contact: Joan Biordi, Admin Coord
TYPE OF AGENCY: Counseling/mental health services
AREAS SERVED: Philadelphia, Montgomery, Delaware
YEARS IN OPERATION: 16
ACCESSIBILITY: Wheelchair accessible
CASES SEXUAL ASSAULT/ABUSE (%): 35
CLIENTS/SERVICES: Sexual assault survivors; Marital rape/sexual abuse survivors; Adult survivors of child sexual abuse; Incest victims/survivors
REQUIREMENTS: Female 16 or older; Ability to pay according to sliding fee scale

PITTSBURGH

ALLEGHENY COUNTY CENTER FOR VICTIMS OF VIOLENT CRIME
1520 Penn Ave, Penn-Liberty Plaza, Pittsburgh, PA 15222
Crisis hotline: **(412) 392-8582 24 hrs**
Information: (412) 392-8582 8:30am-4:30pm
Contact: Mary Alice Gorman, Exec Dir
TYPE OF AGENCY: Victim/witness assistance program
AREAS SERVED: Allegheny
YEARS IN OPERATION: 14
LANGUAGES: Italian
ACCESSIBILITY: Wheelchair accessible
CASES SEXUAL ASSAULT/ABUSE (%): 54
CLIENTS/SERVICES: Sexual assault survivors; Marital rape/sexual abuse survivors; Child victims of sexual abuse; Adult survivors of child sexual abuse; Incest victims/survivors; Prevention program; Community education; Adolescent survivors of sexual abuse; Male survivors of sexual abuse; Elderly; Publications/media
SPECIAL PROGRAMS/SERVICES: Elderly crime prevention brochure; Entire volunteer training program on video-cassettes

ALLE-KISKI AREA HOPE CENTER
2120 Freeport Rd, Pittsburgh, PA 15068
Crisis hotline: **(412) 339-HOPE 24 hrs**
Information: (412) 339-2500 9am-5pm
Contact: Stephanie Ragni, Exec Dir
TYPE OF AGENCY: Domestic violence program
AREAS SERVED: Allegheny, Westmoreland
YEARS IN OPERATION: 9
LANGUAGES: Spanish
ACCESSIBILITY: Wheelchair accessible
CASES SEXUAL ASSAULT/ABUSE (%): 50
CLIENTS/SERVICES: Marital rape/sexual abuse survivors; Adult survivors of child sexual abuse; Incest victims/survivors

FAMILY RESOURCES
429 Forbes Ave, Ste 412, Pittsburgh, PA 15219
Crisis hotline: **(412) 562-9440 24 hrs**
Information: (412) 562-9440 24 hrs
Contact: Cynthia A Snyder, Parents United Coord
TYPE OF AGENCY: Child sexual abuse services
AREAS SERVED: Allegheny
YEARS IN OPERATION: 16
ACCESSIBILITY: Wheelchair accessible
CASES SEXUAL ASSAULT/ABUSE (%): 100
DESCRIPTION: Parents United and Parents Anonymous support groups work with incest families, including male and female survivors, non-offending parents, and perpetrators; Individual and group therapy for child sexual abuse/incest offenders
CLIENTS/SERVICES: Child victims of sexual abuse; Adult survivors of child sexual abuse; Incest victims/survivors; Offender treatment program; Adolescent survivors of sexual abuse; Male survivors of sexual abuse

PITTSBURGH ACTION AGAINST RAPE (PAAR)
3712 Forbes Ave, Pittsburgh, PA 15213
Crisis hotline: **(412) 765-2731 24 hrs**
Information: (412) 682-0219 9am-5pm (Mon-Fri)
Contact: Molly Knox, Exec Dir
TYPE OF AGENCY: Rape crisis center
AREAS SERVED: Allegheny
YEARS IN OPERATION: 16
CASES SEXUAL ASSAULT/ABUSE (%): 100
DESCRIPTION: Provides free services for child and adult survivors of sexual assault and their significant others, including medical and legal advocacy, counseling, and groups for male and female survivors; Community training and education programs
CLIENTS/SERVICES: Sexual assault survivors; Marital rape/sexual abuse survivors; Child victims of sexual abuse; Adult survivors of child sexual abuse; Incest victims/survivors; Prevention program; Community education; Adolescent survivors of sexual abuse; Male survivors of sexual abuse; Publications/media
SPECIAL PROGRAMS/SERVICES: In the process of creating an agency video

WOMEN'S CENTER AND SHELTER OF GREATER PITTSBURGH
PO Box 9024, Pittsburgh, PA 15224
Crisis hotline: **(412) 687-8005 24 hrs**
Information: (412) 687-8017 9am-5pm
Contact: Janet S Metz, Training Dir
TYPE OF AGENCY: Domestic violence program; Adolescent program
AREAS SERVED: Allegheny
YEARS IN OPERATION: 14
LANGUAGES: Spanish, German, French, Yiddish, Portuguese, Russian
ACCESSIBILITY: Wheelchair accessible; Signers for the hearing impaired
DESCRIPTION: Provides crisis intervention to women and children victims of domestic violence (including sexual abuse); Prevention programs on dating violence to high school and university students
CLIENTS/SERVICES: Marital rape/sexual abuse survivors; Child victims of sexual abuse; Adult survivors of child sexual abuse; Incest victims/survivors; Prevention program; Community education; Adolescent survivors of sexual abuse; Ethnic minorities; Publications/media
REQUIREMENTS: Must be a victim of domestic violence
SPECIAL PROGRAMS/SERVICES: Dating violence prevention programs for high school students; Outreach project to Afro-American women victims of domestic violence in public housing projects; Slide-tape program depicting emergency room situations. Specialized consulting and training on the dynamics and scope of domestic violence for those working in the medical setting with a focus on emergency room care of abused women. Materials include *Domestic Violence: A Focus on the Emergency Room Care of Abused Women* (manual); *In Need of Special Attention* (28-minute film on emergency room interventions); 12-minute slide program on identification and care of abused women

YWCA OF GREATER PITTSBURGH
305 Wood St, Pittsburgh, PA 15222
Information: (412) 391-5100, ext 253; 771-TEEN 9am-5pm; TEEN 7pm-11pm
Contact: Judy Gettle, PhD, Counseling and Women's Svcs Dir
TYPE OF AGENCY: Legal services agency; Counseling/mental health services
AREAS SERVED: Allegheny and surrounding area
YEARS IN OPERATION: 7
ACCESSIBILITY: Wheelchair accessible
CASES SEXUAL ASSAULT/ABUSE (%): 30
CLIENTS/SERVICES: Adult survivors of child sexual abuse; Incest victims/survivors; Community education; Adolescent survivors of sexual abuse

POTTSTOWN

THE POTTSTOWN YWCA PARENT'S SUPPORT GROUP PROGRAM
315 King St, Pottstown, PA 19464
Information: (215) 323-1888
Contact: Kathleen Wilson, Prog Dir
TYPE OF AGENCY: Counseling/mental health services; Child abuse services; Child abuse prevention program
AREAS SERVED: Chester, Montgomery
YEARS IN OPERATION: 2
ACCESSIBILITY: Wheelchair accessible
CASES SEXUAL ASSAULT/ABUSE (%): 20
DESCRIPTION: Sponsors a Parents Anonymous chapter
CLIENTS/SERVICES: Adult survivors of child sexual abuse; Incest victims/survivors; Prevention program; Community education

POTTSVILLE

THE RAPE CRISIS CENTER OF SCHUYLKILL COUNTY
325 S Centre St, Pottsville, PA 17901
Crisis hotline: **(717) 622-6220 24 hrs**
Information: (717) 628-2965 10am-3pm
Contact: Mary Beth Semerod, Dir
TYPE OF AGENCY: Rape crisis center
AREAS SERVED: Schuylkill
YEARS IN OPERATION: 5
ACCESSIBILITY: Signers for the hearing impaired
CASES SEXUAL ASSAULT/ABUSE (%): 100
CLIENTS/SERVICES: Sexual assault survivors; Marital rape/sexual abuse survivors; Child victims of sexual abuse; Adult survivors of child sexual abuse; Incest victims/survivors; Prevention program; Community education; Adolescent survivors of sexual abuse; Male survivors of sexual abuse

READING

BERKS WOMEN IN CRISIS
PO Box 803, Reading, PA 19603
Information: (215) 373-2053 24 hrs
Contact: Nanette Balmer, Exec Dir
TYPE OF AGENCY: Domestic violence program
AREAS SERVED: Berks
YEARS IN OPERATION: 8
LANGUAGES: Spanish
ACCESSIBILITY: Wheelchair accessible
CASES SEXUAL ASSAULT/ABUSE (%): 16% current, 80% past sexual abuse
CLIENTS/SERVICES: Community education; Offender treatment program

CRIME VICTIM CENTER
230 N 5th St, Ste 101, Reading, PA 19601
Crisis hotline: **(215) 372-RAPE, 37C-RIME 24 hrs**
Information: (215) 372-4065 8am-5pm
Contact: Jan Mareditne Baily, Exec Dir; Linda Fink, Victim Svcs Supv
TYPE OF AGENCY: Rape crisis center; Victim/witness assistance program
AREAS SERVED: Berks
YEARS IN OPERATION: 15
LANGUAGES: Spanish
ACCESSIBILITY: Wheelchair accessible
CASES SEXUAL ASSAULT/ABUSE (%): 60
CLIENTS/SERVICES: Sexual assault survivors; Marital rape/sexual abuse survivors; Child victims of sexual abuse; Adult survivors of child sexual abuse; Incest victims/survivors; Prevention program; Community education; Adolescent survivors of sexual abuse; Male survivors of sexual abuse; Publications/media
SPECIAL PROGRAMS/SERVICES: Media program: *Journey Towards Justice,* adult courtroom orientation (videotape)

RIDGEWAY

CAPSEA, INC/CITIZENS AGAINST PHYSICAL SEXUAL AND EMOTIONAL ABUSE, INC
Box 464, Ridgeway, PA 15853
Crisis hotline: **(814) 772-1227 24 hrs daily**
Information: (814) 772-3838 8:30am-5pm
Contact: Karen Roberts, Exec Dir
TYPE OF AGENCY: Rape crisis center; Domestic violence program; Child sexual abuse prevention program
AREAS SERVED: Elk, Cameron
YEARS IN OPERATION: 10
ACCESSIBILITY: Wheelchair accessible; Signers for the hearing impaired
CASES SEXUAL ASSAULT/ABUSE (%): 15
CLIENTS/SERVICES: Sexual assault survivors; Marital rape/sexual abuse survivors; Child victims of sexual abuse; Adult survivors of child sexual abuse; Incest victims/survivors; Prevention program; Community education; Adolescent survivors of sexual abuse; Male survivors of sexual abuse

SCRANTON

WOMEN'S RESOURCE CENTER
PO Box 975, Scranton, PA 18501-0975
Crisis hotline: **(717) 346-4671 24 hrs**
Information: (717) 346-4671 9am-5pm (Mon-Fri)
Contact: Maribeth Woody, Exec Dir
TYPE OF AGENCY: Rape crisis center; Domestic violence program; Child abuse services; Child sexual abuse prevention program
AREAS SERVED: Lackawanna, Susquehanna
YEARS IN OPERATION: 11
ACCESSIBILITY: Telecommunications for the hearing impaired (TTY, TDY, etc.)
CASES SEXUAL ASSAULT/ABUSE (%): 30
CLIENTS/SERVICES: Sexual assault survivors; Marital rape/sexual abuse survivors; Child victims of sexual abuse; Adult survivors of child sexual abuse; Incest victims/survivors; Prevention program; Community education; Adolescent survivors of sexual abuse; Male survivors of sexual abuse
REQUIREMENTS: Services are free and confidential to any person stating that they have been a victim of sexual assault or domestic violence

SHARON

ALTERNATIVES FOR WOMEN/ADVOCACY, RESOURCES AND EDUCATION (AW/ARE)
54 S Sharpsville Ave, Sharon, PA 16146
Crisis hotline: **(412) 981-1457 24 hrs**
Information: (412) 981-3753 9am-5pm
Contact: Laura Moore, Exec Dir
TYPE OF AGENCY: Rape crisis center; Domestic violence program; Child sexual abuse services
AREAS SERVED: Mercer
YEARS IN OPERATION: 12
CLIENTS/SERVICES: Sexual assault survivors; Marital rape/sexual abuse survivors; Child victims of sexual abuse; Adult survivors of child sexual abuse; Incest victims/survivors; Community education; Adolescent survivors of sexual abuse; Male survivors of sexual abuse; Sexual harassment

STATE COLLEGE

CENTRE COUNTY WOMEN'S RESOURCE CENTER
140 W Nittany Ave, State College, PA 16801
Crisis hotline: **(814) 234-5050 24 hrs 7 days**
Information: (814) 234-5222 9am-7pm (Mon-Fri)
Contact: Karin Wiedemann, Sexual Assault Svcs Coord/Child Advocate
TYPE OF AGENCY: Rape crisis center; Domestic violence program; Child sexual abuse prevention program
AREAS SERVED: Centre
YEARS IN OPERATION: 13
ACCESSIBILITY: Wheelchair accessible
DESCRIPTION: Provides services for survivors of domestic violence and sexual assault (both women and children)
CLIENTS/SERVICES: Sexual assault survivors; Marital rape/sexual abuse survivors; Child victims of sexual abuse; Adult survivors of child sexual abuse; Incest victims/survivors; Prevention program; Community education; Adolescent survivors of sexual abuse; Male survivors of sexual abuse; Publications/media
SPECIAL PROGRAMS/SERVICES: Provides Child Assault Prevention (CAP) program, for elementary school children, church groups, scouts, etc. Holds a Sexual Assault Speakout every spring and participates in a mock rape trial and Take Back the Night March at Penn State University. Publishes a sexual assault anthology, *Surviving Sexual Assault: Writings by Survivors* (1987), which is available for purchase at $3.00. Publishes *The Connection,* a bimonthly newsletter

STROUDSBURG

WOMEN'S RESOURCES OF MONROE COUNTY, INC
30 N 7th St, Stroudsburg, PA 18360
Crisis hotline: **(717) 421-4000 24 hrs daily**
Information: (717) 421-4200 9am-5pm (Mon-Fri)
Contact: Mollie Whalen, Exec Dir
TYPE OF AGENCY: Rape crisis center; Domestic violence program; Child sexual abuse services; Child sexual abuse prevention program
AREAS SERVED: Monroe, Pike
YEARS IN OPERATION: 10
LANGUAGES: Interpreters available
CASES SEXUAL ASSAULT/ABUSE (%): 35
CLIENTS/SERVICES: Sexual assault survivors; Marital rape/sexual abuse survivors; Child victims of sexual abuse; Adult survivors of child sexual abuse; Incest victims/survivors; Prevention program; Community education; Adolescent survivors of sexual abuse; Male survivors of sexual abuse

TITUSVILLE

TITUSVILLE YWCA WOMEN'S CENTER
201 N Franklin St, Titusville, PA 16354
Crisis hotline: **(800) 828-7474, (814) 827-9777 24 hrs**
Information: (814) 827-2746 9am-4pm
Contact: Betty Kradel, Dir
TYPE OF AGENCY: Rape crisis center; Domestic violence program; Child sexual abuse services; Child sexual abuse prevention program
AREAS SERVED: Crawford, Venango
YEARS IN OPERATION: 10
CASES SEXUAL ASSAULT/ABUSE (%): 20
CLIENTS/SERVICES: Sexual assault survivors; Marital rape/sexual abuse survivors; Child victims of sexual abuse; Adult survivors of child sexual abuse; Incest victims/survivors; Prevention program; Community education; Adolescent survivors of sexual abuse

TOWANDA

ABUSE AND RAPE CRISIS CENTER
PO Box 186, Towanda, PA 18848
Crisis hotline: **(717) 265-9101 24 hrs**
Information: (717) 265-5333 9am-5pm
Contact: Karen Robinson, Dir Svcs Supv
TYPE OF AGENCY: Rape crisis center; Domestic violence program; Child sexual abuse prevention program
AREAS SERVED: Bradford
YEARS IN OPERATION: 5
CLIENTS/SERVICES: Sexual assault survivors; Marital rape/sexual abuse survivors; Child victims of sexual abuse; Adult survivors of child sexual abuse; Incest victims/survivors; Preven-

ABUSE AND RAPE CRISIS CENTER *(continued)*
tion program; Community education; Adolescent survivors of sexual abuse

TUNKHANNOCK

VICTIMS RESOURCE CENTER
106 ½ Warren St, Tunkhannock, PA 18657
Crisis hotline: **(717) 836-5544 24 hrs**
Information: (717) 836-5844 8:30am-4:30pm
Contact: Janet Pencek, Prog Coord
TYPE OF AGENCY: Victim/witness assistance program; Child sexual abuse prevention program
AREAS SERVED: Luzerne, Wyoming
YEARS IN OPERATION: 2
LANGUAGES: French, Creole, Spanish
ACCESSIBILITY: Telecommunications for the hearing impaired (TTY, TDY, etc.)
CASES SEXUAL ASSAULT/ABUSE (%): 50
CLIENTS/SERVICES: Sexual assault survivors; Marital rape/sexual abuse survivors; Child victims of sexual abuse; Adult survivors of child sexual abuse; Incest victims/survivors; Prevention program; Community education; Adolescent survivors of sexual abuse; Male survivors of sexual abuse

UNIONTOWN

COMMUNITY RESOURCES OF FAYETTE COUNTY, INC
78 Morgantown St, Uniontown, PA 15401
Crisis hotline: **(412) 437-3737 24 hrs**
Information: (412) 438-1470 9am-5pm
Contact: Janet A Maxwell, Exec Dir
TYPE OF AGENCY: Rape crisis center; Child sexual abuse services; Child sexual abuse prevention program; Child abuse prevention program
SPONSORING ORGANIZATION: Women's Resource Center
AREAS SERVED: Fayette
YEARS IN OPERATION: 13
CASES SEXUAL ASSAULT/ABUSE (%): 80
DESCRIPTION: Provides survivors of sexual violence and child abuse with 24-hour hotline, referrals, support/counseling, and advocacy. Also Parents Anonymous program
CLIENTS/SERVICES: Sexual assault survivors; Marital rape/sexual abuse survivors; Child victims of sexual abuse; Adult survivors of child sexual abuse; Incest victims/survivors; Prevention program; Community education; Adolescent survivors of sexual abuse; Male survivors of sexual abuse

WASHINGTON

CARE RAPE CRISIS CENTER
80 E Chestnut St, Washington, PA 15301
Crisis hotline: **(412) 222-7150 24 hrs 7 days**
Information: (412) 228-2200 9am-5pm (Mon-Fri)
Contact: Alice Lohr, Sexual Assault Svcs Dir
TYPE OF AGENCY: Rape crisis center; Child sexual abuse services; Child sexual abuse prevention program
SPONSORING ORGANIZATION: The CARE Center
AREAS SERVED: Washington, Greene
YEARS IN OPERATION: 6
ACCESSIBILITY: Wheelchair accessible
CASES SEXUAL ASSAULT/ABUSE (%): 100
DESCRIPTION: Provides support services, counseling, and accompaniment for victims of sexual assault and their families
CLIENTS/SERVICES: Sexual assault survivors; Marital rape/sexual abuse survivors; Child victims of sexual abuse; Adult survivors of child sexual abuse; Incest victims/survivors; Prevention program; Community education; Adolescent survivors of sexual abuse; Male survivors of sexual abuse

WAYNE

WOMEN'S RESOURCE CENTER
PO Box 309, 113 W Wayne Ave, Wayne, PA 19087
Information: (215) 687-6391 9:30am-4pm (Mon, Thu); 9:30am-4pm, 7pm-9pm (Wed)
TYPE OF AGENCY: Information and referral; Women's center
AREAS SERVED: Montgomery, Delaware, Chester, Philadelphia, Buck, Berks
YEARS IN OPERATION: 14½
CASES SEXUAL ASSAULT/ABUSE (%): 2
CLIENTS/SERVICES: Sexual assault survivors; Marital rape/sexual abuse survivors; Adult survivors of child sexual abuse; Incest victims/survivors; Community education; Adolescent survivors of sexual abuse

WEST CHESTER

CRIME VICTIMS CENTER OF CHESTER COUNTY
236 W Market St, West Chester, PA 19382
Crisis hotline: **(215) 692-7273, 692-7420 24 hrs**
Information: (215) 692-1926
Contact: Pat DeMajistre, Community Outreach Dir
TYPE OF AGENCY: Rape crisis center; Victim/witness assistance program
AREAS SERVED: Chester
YEARS IN OPERATION: 15
LANGUAGES: Spanish
CASES SEXUAL ASSAULT/ABUSE (%): 70
CLIENTS/SERVICES: Sexual assault survivors; Marital rape/sexual abuse survivors; Child victims of sexual abuse; Adult survivors of child sexual abuse; Incest victims/survivors; Prevention program; Community education; Adolescent survivors of sexual abuse; Male survivors of sexual abuse

WEST HAZLETON

VICTIMS RESOURCE CENTER
107 Madison Ave, West Hazleton, PA 18201
Crisis hotline: **(717) 454-7200 24 hrs**
Information: (717) 823-0766 9am-5pm
Contact: Mary Claire Mullen, Victim Svcs Dir
TYPE OF AGENCY: Victim/witness assistance program; Child sexual abuse services; Child sexual abuse prevention program
AREAS SERVED: Luzerne, Wyoming
YEARS IN OPERATION: 15
ACCESSIBILITY: Wheelchair accessible (will provide services in home); Telecommunications for the hearing impaired (TTY, TDY, etc.) (through helpline (717) 829-1341); Signers for the hearing impaired (by arrangement)
CASES SEXUAL ASSAULT/ABUSE (%): 75
DESCRIPTION: Comprehensive services for crime victims, advocacy, and educational programming; Long-term counseling; Support groups for male and female survivors; Group therapy for children; Experienced in working with children and adults with disabilities
CLIENTS/SERVICES: Sexual assault survivors; Marital rape/sexual abuse survivors; Child victims of sexual abuse; Adult survivors of child sexual abuse; Incest victims/survivors; Prevention program; Community education; Adolescent survivors of sexual abuse; Male survivors of sexual abuse; Disabled; Publications/media
SPECIAL PROGRAMS/SERVICES: Videotapes and workbooks for children on prevention

WILKES-BARRE

VICTIMS RESOURCE CENTER
79 W Union St, Wilkes-Barre, PA 18701-1409
Crisis hotline: **(717) 823-0765, 836-5544, 454-7200, (800) 331-3261 24 hrs**
Information: (717) 823-0766 9am-5pm
Contact: Mary Claire Mullen, Victim Svcs Dir
TYPE OF AGENCY: Rape crisis center; Victim/witness assistance program; Child sexual abuse services; Child sexual abuse prevention program
AREAS SERVED: Luzerne, Wyoming
YEARS IN OPERATION: 15
ACCESSIBILITY: Wheelchair accessible (will provide services in home); Telecommunications for the hearing impaired (TTY, TDY, etc.) (through helpline (717) 829-1341); Signers for the hearing impaired (by arrangement)
CASES SEXUAL ASSAULT/ABUSE (%): 75
DESCRIPTION: Comprehensive services for crime victims, advocacy, and educational programming; Long-term counseling; Support groups for male and female survivors; Group therapy for children; Experienced in working with children and adults with disabilities
CLIENTS/SERVICES: Sexual assault survivors; Marital rape/sexual abuse survivors; Child victims of sexual abuse; Adult survivors of child sexual abuse; Incest victims/survivors; Prevention program; Community education; Adolescent survivors of sexual abuse; Male survivors of sexual abuse; Disabled; Publications/media
SPECIAL PROGRAMS/SERVICES: Videotapes and workbooks for children on prevention

WILLIAMSPORT

WISE OPTIONS FOR WOMEN
815 W 4th St, Williamsport, PA 17701
Crisis hotline: **(717) 323-8167 24 hrs**
Information: (717) 323-8167 24 hrs
Contact: Arlene Shaheen, Dir
TYPE OF AGENCY: Rape crisis center; Domestic violence program
SPONSORING ORGANIZATION: YWCA
AREAS SERVED: Lycoming
YEARS IN OPERATION: 11
LANGUAGES: Polish
ACCESSIBILITY: Telecommunications for the hearing impaired (TTY, TDY, etc.)
CLIENTS/SERVICES: Sexual assault survivors; Marital rape/sexual abuse survivors; Child victims of sexual abuse; Adult survivors of child sexual abuse; Incest victims/survivors; Prevention program; Community education; Adolescent survivors of sexual abuse; Male survivors of sexual abuse

YORK

ACESS-YORK, INC
PO Box 743, York, PA 17405
Crisis hotline: **(717) 846-5400, (800) 262-8444 24 hrs**
Information: (717) 846-5400 8am-4pm
Contact: Deb Markel, Counselor
TYPE OF AGENCY: Domestic violence program
AREAS SERVED: York
YEARS IN OPERATION: 10
LANGUAGES: Spanish
ACCESSIBILITY: Signers for the hearing impaired (by arrangement)
CLIENTS/SERVICES: Marital rape/sexual abuse survivors; Community education

RAPE AND VICTIM ASSISTANCE CENTER
PO Box 892, York, PA 17405
Crisis hotline: **(717) 854-3131, (800) 422-3204 24 hrs**
Information: (717) 848-3535 8:30am-4:30pm
Contact: Karen Hook, Exec Dir
TYPE OF AGENCY: Rape crisis center; Child sexual abuse services; Child sexual abuse prevention program
AREAS SERVED: York
YEARS IN OPERATION: 15
CASES SEXUAL ASSAULT/ABUSE (%): 90
CLIENTS/SERVICES: Sexual assault survivors; Marital rape/sexual abuse survivors; Child victims of sexual abuse; Adult survivors of child sexual abuse; Incest victims/survivors; Prevention program; Community education; Adolescent survivors of sexual abuse; Male survivors of sexual abuse

RHODE ISLAND

CRANSTON

RHODE ISLAND RAPE CRISIS CENTER
1660 Broad St, Cranston, RI 02905
Crisis hotline: **(401) 941-2400 (collect calls accepted) 24 hrs**
Information: (401) 941-2400
Contact: Peg Langhammer, Dir; Wenny Kusuma, Community Relations Coord
TYPE OF AGENCY: Rape crisis center; Child sexual abuse prevention program; Child assault prevention (CAP) project; Acquaintance/date rape prevention program
AREAS SERVED: Statewide
DESCRIPTION: Comprehensive rape crisis services for the state of Rhode Island; Prevention programs include the Child Assault Awareness (CAP) Project and the Adolescent Assault Awareness Program
CLIENTS/SERVICES: Sexual assault survivors; Marital rape/sexual abuse survivors; Child victims of sexual abuse; Adult survivors of child sexual abuse; Incest victims/survivors; Prevention program; Community education; Adolescent survivors of sexual abuse; Male survivors of sexual abuse

WOMEN'S CENTER
600 Mt Pleasant Ave, Cranston, RI 02908
Information: (401) 456-8474 9am-4pm (Mon-Fri)
Contact: M Healey-Cohen, Dir
TYPE OF AGENCY: College/university-based services
SPONSORING ORGANIZATION: Rhode Island College
YEARS IN OPERATION: 10
DESCRIPTION: Counseling by appointment or on a walk-in basis is offered. Also, the library maintains up-to-date publications for the use of all students
CLIENTS/SERVICES: Sexual assault survivors; Marital rape/sexual abuse survivors; Adult survivors of child sexual abuse; Incest victims/survivors; Prevention program; Community education

PROVIDENCE

EAST SIDE CENTER, INC
173 Waterman St, Providence, RI 02906
Information: (401) 351-1501 9am-6pm
Contact: Diane M Petrella, Admin Dir
TYPE OF AGENCY: Private practice
AREAS SERVED: Rhode Island, Southeastern Massachusetts
YEARS IN OPERATION: 3½
CASES SEXUAL ASSAULT/ABUSE (%): 70
DESCRIPTION: Counseling for sexually abused children and their families; Individual, group, and family therapy for child sexual abuse offenders and incest offenders
CLIENTS/SERVICES: Sexual assault survivors; Marital rape/sexual abuse survivors; Child victims of sexual abuse; Adult survivors of child sexual abuse; Incest victims/survivors; Offender treatment program; Adolescent survivors of sexual abuse; Male survivors of sexual abuse
REQUIREMENTS: Cases of child sexual abuse must be reported to state child protective agency

WOMEN'S CENTER OF RHODE ISLAND, INC
45 E Transit St, Providence, RI 02906
Crisis hotline: **(401) 861-2760 24 hrs daily**
Information: (401) 861-2760 9am-9pm
Contact: Anne Grant, Exec Dir
TYPE OF AGENCY: Domestic violence program; Shelter
YEARS IN OPERATION: 12
LANGUAGES: Spanish
CLIENTS/SERVICES: Marital rape/sexual abuse survivors; Community education

WAKEFIELD

WOMEN'S RESOURCE CENTER OF SOUTH COUNTY
PO Box 791, Wakefield, RI 02880
Crisis hotline: **(401) 539-2569 24 hrs**
Information: (401) 783-9351 9am-5pm (Mon-Fri)
Contact: Marilyn S Goodman, Asst Dir
TYPE OF AGENCY: Domestic violence program; Child sexual abuse services; Child sexual abuse prevention program
AREAS SERVED: Washington
YEARS IN OPERATION: 10
LANGUAGES: Spanish, Swedish, French
ACCESSIBILITY: Wheelchair accessible
CASES SEXUAL ASSAULT/ABUSE (%): 35
DESCRIPTION: Provides counseling for adults sexually abused as children and sexually abused children; Expressive therapy; Group therapy for batterers
CLIENTS/SERVICES: Sexual assault survivors; Marital rape/sexual abuse survivors; Child victims of sexual abuse; Adult survivors of child sexual abuse; Incest victims/survivors; Prevention program; Community education; Adolescent survivors of sexual abuse; Male survivors of sexual abuse

SOUTH CAROLINA

AIKEN

AIKEN COALITION TO ASSIST ABUSED PERSONS
PO Box 1293, Aiken, SC 29802
Crisis hotline: **(803) 648-9900 5pm-9am (Mon-Fri); 24 hrs (Sat-Sun)**
Information: (803) 649-0480 9am-5pm (Mon-Fri)
Contact: Mary Jo Thomas, Exec Dir
TYPE OF AGENCY: Rape crisis center; Domestic violence program; Child sexual abuse prevention program; Acquaintance/date rape prevention program
AREAS SERVED: Aiken, Edgefield
YEARS IN OPERATION: 8
ACCESSIBILITY: Wheelchair accessible
CASES SEXUAL ASSAULT/ABUSE (%): 10
CLIENTS/SERVICES: Sexual assault survivors; Marital rape/sexual abuse survivors; Adult survivors of child sexual abuse; Incest victims/survivors; Prevention program; Community education; Adolescent survivors of sexual abuse; Male survivors of sexual abuse; Publications/media
REQUIREMENTS: Sexual assault victims must be 18 or older, or be referred by the SC Department of Social Services
SPECIAL PROGRAMS/SERVICES: Offers video program on date rape

AIKEN COUNTY SHERIFF'S DEPARTMENT—VICTIM ASSISTANCE PROGRAM
PO Box 462, Aiken, SC 29802-0462
Crisis hotline: **(803) 642-1761 24 hrs**
Information: (803) 642-1790 8:30am-5pm
Contact: Anne W Wolf, Victim Assistance Coord
TYPE OF AGENCY: Victim/witness assistance program
AREAS SERVED: Aiken
YEARS IN OPERATION: 6 months
LANGUAGES: German
CASES SEXUAL ASSAULT/ABUSE (%): 6
CLIENTS/SERVICES: Sexual assault survivors; Child victims of sexual abuse; Community education; Male survivors of sexual abuse
REQUIREMENTS: Must report the crime

THE CHILDREN'S PLACE
604 Park Ave, Aiken, SC 29801
Information: (803) 649-9714 8:30am-4:30pm
Contact: Ann P Suich, Exec Dir
TYPE OF AGENCY: Child sexual abuse services; Child abuse services
SPONSORING ORGANIZATION: Services Council of Aiken County
AREAS SERVED: Aiken
YEARS IN OPERATION: 4
CASES SEXUAL ASSAULT/ABUSE (%): 20
DESCRIPTION: Therapeutic day treatment center for physically, sexually, emotionally abused and/or neglected children. Treatment is comprehensive, individualized, and highly structured. The program is staffed by a multi-disciplinary team which includes a developmental specialist, mental health counselor, speech therapist, and a registered nurse
CLIENTS/SERVICES: Child victims of sexual abuse; Incest victims/survivors; Preschoolers
REQUIREMENTS: Ages 3 to 5

SECOND JUDICIAL CIRCUIT SOLICITOR'S OFFICE
PO Box 2327, Aiken, SC 29802
Crisis hotline: **(803) 259-1727 Central dispatch 24-hrs for rape crisis center**
Information: (803) 259-7992 Barnwell; 642-1557 Aiken 8:30am-5pm
Contact: Wren S Hart, Victim Assistance Prog Coord
TYPE OF AGENCY: Victim/witness assistance program
AREAS SERVED: Aiken, Barnwell, Bamberg
YEARS IN OPERATION: 4
ACCESSIBILITY: Wheelchair accessible (Aiken)
CASES SEXUAL ASSAULT/ABUSE (%): 25
CLIENTS/SERVICES: Sexual assault survivors; Marital rape/sexual abuse survivors; Child victims of sexual abuse; Community education; Adolescent survivors of sexual abuse; Male survivors of sexual abuse
REQUIREMENTS: Client must cooperate with police and prosecution

ANDERSON

ANDERSON PASTORAL COUNSELING AND CONSULTATION SERVICE
612 Bonham Ct, Anderson, SC 29621
Information: (803) 261-3939 8am-5pm, and 1 evening a week
Contact: Nancy C Welch, Marriage and Family Therapist
TYPE OF AGENCY: Private practice
AREAS SERVED: Anderson, Oconee, Pickens, Hartwell
YEARS IN OPERATION: 10
CASES SEXUAL ASSAULT/ABUSE (%): 5-10
CLIENTS/SERVICES: Sexual assault survivors; Marital rape/sexual abuse survivors; Child victims of sexual abuse; Adult survivors of child sexual abuse; Incest victims/survivors; Adolescent survivors of sexual abuse; Male survivors of sexual abuse

CRISIS MINISTRIES
PO Box 1925, Anderson, SC 29622
Crisis hotline: **(803) 226-0297 Anderson, 459-9650 Abbeville, 882-9912 Oconee, 868-9964 Pickens 24 hrs 7 days**
Information: (803) 226-0297
Contact: Archie L Morgan, Exec Dir
TYPE OF AGENCY: Rape crisis center; Counseling/mental health services; Child sexual abuse services; Child sexual abuse prevention program; Adolescent program
AREAS SERVED: Anderson, Oconee, Pickens, Abbeville
YEARS IN OPERATION: 19
CASES SEXUAL ASSAULT/ABUSE (%): 10
DESCRIPTION: Crisis intervention and counseling for victims/survivors; Treatment for rapists, child sexual abuse/incest offenders, and batterers. Other programs geared toward adolescents in crisis and those in prison
CLIENTS/SERVICES: Sexual assault survivors; Marital rape/sexual abuse survivors; Child victims of sexual abuse; Adult survivors of child sexual abuse; Incest victims/survivors; Prevention program; Community education; Offender treatment program; Adolescent survivors of sexual abuse; Male survivors of sexual abuse

VICTIM/WITNESS ASSISTANCE
PO Box 4046, Anderson, SC 29621
Information: (803) 260-4046
Contact: Anne Ewing, V/W Asst; Denise McCurry, Child V/W Asst
TYPE OF AGENCY: Victim/witness assistance program
SPONSORING ORGANIZATION: 10th Judicial Solicitor, George M Ducworth
AREAS SERVED: Anderson, Oconee
YEARS IN OPERATION: 6
CLIENTS/SERVICES: Sexual assault survivors; Child victims of sexual abuse
REQUIREMENTS: Criminal charges must be filed by police officers or individuals

BARNWELL

BARNWELL COUNTY HELP LINE
PO Box 262, Barnwell, SC 29812
Crisis hotline: **(803) 259-3333, 259-1727 (beeper service) 24 hrs**
Information: (803) 259-5396 8:30am-5pm
Contact: Terri Jowers Willis, Coord
TYPE OF AGENCY: Rape crisis center; Domestic violence program; Telephone crisis hotline
AREAS SERVED: Bamberg, Allendale, Barnell
CLIENTS/SERVICES: Sexual assault survivors; Marital rape/sexual abuse survivors; Child victims of sexual abuse; Adult survivors of child sexual abuse; Incest victims/survivors; Adolescent survivors of sexual abuse; Male survivors of sexual abuse

BEAUFORT

CHARTER COUNSELING CENTER OF BEAUFORT
140 S Ribaut Rd, Ste 106, Beaufort, SC 29902
Crisis hotline: **(912) 354-3911 24 hrs daily**
Information: (803) 524-9091 8:30am-5pm
Contact: Royce V Malphrus, MA, Dir
TYPE OF AGENCY: Private practice
SPONSORING ORGANIZATION: Charter Hospital of Savannah
AREAS SERVED: Beaufort, Jasper, Hampton, Allendale, Colleton
YEARS IN OPERATION: 2
ACCESSIBILITY: Wheelchair accessible
CASES SEXUAL ASSAULT/ABUSE (%): 25
DESCRIPTION: Provides individual, marital, group, and family therapy in the community; Assists with psychiatric and substance abuse hospitalizations.
CLIENTS/SERVICES: Sexual assault survivors; Child victims of sexual abuse; Adult survivors of child sexual abuse; Incest victims/survivors; Community education; Adolescent survivors of sexual abuse; Male survivors of sexual abuse

CHILD ABUSE PREVENTION ASSOCIATION
PO Box 531, Beaufort, SC 29901
Information: (803) 524-4350 9am-5pm
Contact: Susan Cato, Exec Dir
TYPE OF AGENCY: Child sexual abuse services; Child sexual abuse prevention program; Child abuse services; Child abuse prevention program; Child advocacy; Shelter; Adolescent program
AREAS SERVED: Beaufort
YEARS IN OPERATION: 9
CASES SEXUAL ASSAULT/ABUSE (%): 50
DESCRIPTION: Provides emergency short-term shelter for abused and neglected children; Sponsors Guardian Ad Litem program to advocate for children in family court; Provides support groups for adult survivors of child sexual abuse
CLIENTS/SERVICES: Child victims of sexual abuse; Adult survivors of child sexual abuse; Incest victims/survivors; Prevention program; Community education
REQUIREMENTS: Shelter care for children from birth to age 18

CITIZENS AGAINST RAPE
PO Box 1919, Beaufort, SC 29901-1919
Crisis hotline: **(800) 637-RAPE 24 hrs**
Information: (803) 525-6699 24 hrs
Contact: Gaye Oglesby, Exec Dir
TYPE OF AGENCY: Rape crisis center
SPONSORING ORGANIZATION: Rape Crisis Center of the Lowcountry
AREAS SERVED: Beaufort, Jasper, Hampton, Colleton, Allendale
YEARS IN OPERATION: 5
CASES SEXUAL ASSAULT/ABUSE (%): 100
CLIENTS/SERVICES: Sexual assault survivors; Marital rape/sexual abuse survivors; Child victims of sexual abuse; Adult survivors of child sexual abuse; Prevention program; Community education

COASTAL EMPIRE MENTAL HEALTH CENTER
125 S Ribaut Rd, Beaufort, SC 29902
Crisis hotline: **(800) 922-7844 24 hrs**
Information: (803) 524-3378 8:30am-5pm
Contact: Dennis M Young, Asst Dir
TYPE OF AGENCY: Counseling/mental health services
AREAS SERVED: Beaufort, Jasper, Colleton, Hampton, Allendale
YEARS IN OPERATION: 15
LANGUAGES: Spanish
ACCESSIBILITY: Wheelchair accessible
CASES SEXUAL ASSAULT/ABUSE (%): 5-10
CLIENTS/SERVICES: Sexual assault survivors; Marital rape/sexual abuse survivors; Child victims of sexual abuse; Adult survivors of child sexual abuse; Incest victims/survivors; Community education

CAMDEN

COUNSELING SERVICES OF CAMDEN
1202 Broad St, Camden, SC 29020
Information: (803) 432-5337 9am-5pm
Contact: Kay Barlow
TYPE OF AGENCY: Private practice
YEARS IN OPERATION: 2
DESCRIPTION: Individual counseling for survivors and child sexual abuse offenders
CLIENTS/SERVICES: Sexual assault survivors; Child victims of sexual abuse; Adult survivors of child sexual abuse; Incest victims/survivors; Offender treatment program; Adolescent survivors of sexual abuse

KERSHAW COUNTY COALITION AGAINST SEXUAL ASSAULT, INC
PO Box 282, Camden, SC 29020
Crisis hotline: **(803) 425-4357 24 hrs**
Information: (803) 425-4357 9:30am-5pm
Contact: Carolyn Morris, Dir
TYPE OF AGENCY: Rape crisis center; Child sexual abuse services; Child sexual abuse prevention program
AREAS SERVED: Kershaw, Lee
YEARS IN OPERATION: 3
CASES SEXUAL ASSAULT/ABUSE (%): 100
DESCRIPTION: 24-hour counseling, hospital and law enforcement accompaniment for rape survivors. Counseling, play therapy, and videotaping for court testimony for children who have been sexually abused
CLIENTS/SERVICES: Sexual assault survivors; Marital rape/sexual abuse survivors; Child victims of sexual abuse; Adult survivors of child sexual abuse; Prevention program; Community education; Adolescent survivors of sexual abuse; Male survivors of sexual abuse

CHARLESTON

CHARLESTON AREA MENTAL HEALTH CENTER
30 Lockwood Dr, Charleston, SC 29401
Crisis hotline: **(803) 727-2000 24 hrs**
Information: (803) 727-2000
Contact: Sharon Cox, MH Counselor
TYPE OF AGENCY: Counseling/mental health services
AREAS SERVED: Charleston
YEARS IN OPERATION: 30
ACCESSIBILITY: Wheelchair accessible
CASES SEXUAL ASSAULT/ABUSE (%): 25
CLIENTS/SERVICES: Sexual assault survivors; Marital rape/sexual abuse survivors; Child victims of sexual abuse; Adult survivors of child sexual abuse; Incest victims/survivors; Community education; Offender treatment program; Adolescent survivors of sexual abuse; Male survivors of sexual abuse
REQUIREMENTS: Child and adolescent services: under 18 years of age who has been abused. Adults: sliding scale fee

CRIME VICTIMS RESEARCH AND TREATMENT CENTER (CVC)
171 Ashley Ave, Charleston, SC 29425-0742
Information: (803) 792-2945 9am-5pm
Contact: Julie A Lipovsky, PhD, Instructor
TYPE OF AGENCY: Victim/witness assistance program; Training/research
SPONSORING ORGANIZATION: Medical University of South Carolina Department of Psychiatry
AREAS SERVED: Charleston, Dorchester, Berkeley
YEARS IN OPERATION: 11
ACCESSIBILITY: Wheelchair accessible
CASES SEXUAL ASSAULT/ABUSE (%): 90
DESCRIPTION: Provides evaluation and treatment of psychological effects of criminal victimization, including individual, group, and family therapy; Child sexual abuse/incest offenders and batterers therapy; Training of mental health professionals; Public policy/child advocacy work
CLIENTS/SERVICES: Sexual assault survivors; Marital rape/sexual abuse survivors; Child victims of sexual abuse; Adult survivors of child sexual abuse; Incest victims/survivors; Community education; Offender treatment program; Adolescent survivors of sexual abuse; Male survivors of sexual abuse
SPECIAL PROGRAMS/SERVICES: Research program includes projects dealing with family functioning in incest families, child as victim/witness in criminal justice system, and characteristics of incest offenders

MEDICAL UNIVERSITY OF SOUTH CAROLINA—CHILDREN'S HOSPITAL
Medical University of South Carolina Children's Hospital, Charleston, SC 29425
Crisis hotline: **(803) 792-3826 24 hrs**
Information: (803) 792-2618 8:30am-5pm (Mon-Fri); Emergencies (803) 792-2123 page operator
Contact: Sara E Schuh, MD, Assoc Prof Pediatrics
TYPE OF AGENCY: Hospital/medical center; Child sexual abuse services; Training/research
AREAS SERVED: Statewide
YEARS IN OPERATION: 9
LANGUAGES: Interpreters available
ACCESSIBILITY: Wheelchair accessible; Signers for the hearing impaired (by arrangement)
CASES SEXUAL ASSAULT/ABUSE (%): 60
DESCRIPTION: Provides sexual assault treatment and supportive counseling for all ages through the Sexual Assault Center. Additional evaluation and treatment are available through the Children's Hospital and CURC
CLIENTS/SERVICES: Child victims of sexual abuse; Community education
REQUIREMENTS: For Children's Hospital, to age 18; For Sexual Assault Center, must file charges or report to child protection agency

PARENTS UNITED, DORCHESTER COUNTY
171 Ashley Ave, Charleston, SC 29425
Crisis hotline: **(803) 871-9445 24 hrs**
Information: (803) 873-8483 8am-10pm
Contact: Sarah Stanley, MSN, RN, CS, Prof Coord
TYPE OF AGENCY: Child sexual abuse services
SPONSORING ORGANIZATION: Psychiatric Nursing Department Institute of Psychiatry, MUSC
AREAS SERVED: Dorchester, Berkley, Charleston
YEARS IN OPERATION: 6
ACCESSIBILITY: Wheelchair accessible
CASES SEXUAL ASSAULT/ABUSE (%): 100
CLIENTS/SERVICES: Sexual assault survivors; Child victims of sexual abuse; Adult survivors of child sexual abuse; Incest victims/survivors; Community education; Offender treatment program; Adolescent survivors of sexual abuse; Male survivors of sexual abuse

PEOPLE AGAINST RAPE
701 E Bay St, BTC Box 1101, Charleston, SC 29403
Crisis hotline: **(803) 722-7273 24 hrs**
Information: (803) 722-7273 9am-5pm
Contact: Charlotte Heimbaugh, Victim Svc Coord
TYPE OF AGENCY: Rape crisis center; Child sexual abuse prevention program; Consultation; Acquaintance/date rape prevention program
AREAS SERVED: Charleston, Dorchester, Berkeley
YEARS IN OPERATION: 14
LANGUAGES: Spanish interpreters available
ACCESSIBILITY: Wheelchair accessible; Signers for the hearing impaired
CASES SEXUAL ASSAULT/ABUSE (%): 100

PEOPLE AGAINST RAPE *(continued)*
DESCRIPTION: Crisis counseling; Rape victims escort to hospital; Police and court escort and support; Prison program for rapists
CLIENTS/SERVICES: Sexual assault survivors; Marital rape/sexual abuse survivors; Child victims of sexual abuse; Adult survivors of child sexual abuse; Incest victims/survivors; Prevention program; Community education; Offender treatment program; Adolescent survivors of sexual abuse; Male survivors of sexual abuse
SPECIAL PROGRAMS/SERVICES: "Metaphysical" approach in support group for rape survivors; Police training; Acquaintance assault curriculum for adolescents; Consultation for setting up new rape crisis centers

CHARLESTON HEIGHTS

HOTLINE, INC
PO Box 71583, Charleston Heights, SC 29415-1583
Crisis hotline: **(803) 744-4357 (HELP), (800) 922-2283 SC only 24 hrs daily**
Information: (803) 747-3007 9am-5pm (Mon-Fri)
Contact: Charlotte Anderson, Exec Dir
TYPE OF AGENCY: Counseling/mental health services; Telephone crisis hotline; Information and referral
AREAS SERVED: Charleston, Dorchester, Berkeley
YEARS IN OPERATION: 18
CASES SEXUAL ASSAULT/ABUSE (%): 1
CLIENTS/SERVICES: Sexual assault survivors; Child victims of sexual abuse; Male survivors of sexual abuse

CLEMSON

HELPING HANDS OF CLEMSON, INC
PO Box 561, Clemson, SC 29633
Information: (803) 654-6154 8am-6pm
Contact: Jean E Tulli, Dir
TYPE OF AGENCY: Child sexual abuse services; Shelter; Adolescent program
AREAS SERVED: Pickens, Anderson, Oconee, Greenville
YEARS IN OPERATION: 5
DESCRIPTION: Operates an emergency shelter for abused children (licensed for 40)
CLIENTS/SERVICES: Child victims of sexual abuse; Incest victims/survivors; Community education
REQUIREMENTS: Girls ages birth to 18; Boys ages birth to 13

COLUMBIA

CAVE—CITIZENS AGAINST VIOLENT CRIME
PO Drawer 5895, Columbia, SC 29250
Crisis hotline: **(803) 252-CAVE 24 hrs 7 days**
Information: (803) 252-2283 24 hrs 7 days answer machine
Contact: Ray Rossi, State Pres
TYPE OF AGENCY: Victim/witness assistance program
AREAS SERVED: Statewide
YEARS IN OPERATION: 4
CASES SEXUAL ASSAULT/ABUSE (%): 20
DESCRIPTION: Assists victims of violent crime; Assistance before, after, and during the trial process and continued through the parole process
CLIENTS/SERVICES: Sexual assault survivors

CHILD ABUSE AND NEGLECT INTERDISCIPLINARY TRAINING PROJECT
College of Social Work, Columbia, SC 29208
Information: (803) 777-8109 9am-5pm (Mon-Fri)
Contact: Arlene Bowers Andrews, Proj Dir; Ana Lopez-DeFede, Training Dir
TYPE OF AGENCY: College/university-based services; Child sexual abuse services; Child sexual abuse prevention program; Child abuse services; Training/research
SPONSORING ORGANIZATION: University of South Carolina
AREAS SERVED: Statewide
YEARS IN OPERATION: 1
LANGUAGES: Spanish
ACCESSIBILITY: Wheelchair accessible
CASES SEXUAL ASSAULT/ABUSE (%): 50
DESCRIPTION: Advanced professional training for master's and doctoral students in criminal justice, education, health, law, medicine, nursing, psychology, social work to prepare graduate students for interdisciplinary work with survivors and perpetrators of child sexual assault and child abuse. Training in program/policy development pertaining to victimization and survivor services, as well as clinical training
CLIENTS/SERVICES: Child victims of sexual abuse; Adult survivors of child sexual abuse; Incest victims/survivors; Prevention program; Community education
SPECIAL PROGRAMS/SERVICES: How to be Your Own Best Hero teaches children to resist sexual abuse

COUNSELING AND READJUSTMENT SERVICES
1804 Hampton St, Columbia, SC 29201
Crisis hotline: **(803) 765-0700 24 hrs**
Information: (803) 765-0700 24 hrs
Contact: Lawrence H Bergmann, PhD, Co-Dir
TYPE OF AGENCY: Counseling/mental health services
AREAS SERVED: Richland, Lexington, Kershaw, Barnwell, Aiken, Bamburg, York
YEARS IN OPERATION: 7
ACCESSIBILITY: Wheelchair accessible; Signers for the hearing impaired (by request)
CASES SEXUAL ASSAULT/ABUSE (%): 30
DESCRIPTION: Agency is a post-trauma treatment center providing services for survivors of violence, as well as those experiencing work and duty-related stress
CLIENTS/SERVICES: Sexual assault survivors; Marital rape/sexual abuse survivors; Child victims of sexual abuse; Adult survivors of child sexual abuse; Incest victims/survivors; Community education; Adolescent survivors of sexual abuse; Male survivors of sexual abuse
REQUIREMENTS: Sliding scale fee

PROVIDENCE HOME WOMEN'S SHELTER
3425 N Main St, Columbia, SC 29203
Information: (803) 779-4706 8:30am-5pm
Contact: Kathy Riley, Dir
TYPE OF AGENCY: Shelter
AREAS SERVED: Statewide
YEARS IN OPERATION: 26
DESCRIPTION: Provides home shelters for all women including victims of sexual assault, in need of emergency services
CLIENTS/SERVICES: Sexual assault survivors; Marital rape/sexual abuse survivors
REQUIREMENTS: Adult women 18 or older in need of housing, with no other support systems in place

RAPE CRISIS NETWORK
PO Box 50121, Columbia, SC 29205
Crisis hotline: **(803) 252-8393 24 hrs**
Information: (803) 252-8393 9am-5pm
Contact: Lyn Phillips, MSW, Exec Dir
TYPE OF AGENCY: Rape crisis center
AREAS SERVED: Richland, Lexington, Newberry, Fairfield
YEARS IN OPERATION: 5
LANGUAGES: Translators available
ACCESSIBILITY: Signers for the hearing impaired
CASES SEXUAL ASSAULT/ABUSE (%): 100
CLIENTS/SERVICES: Sexual assault survivors; Marital rape/sexual abuse survivors; Child victims of sexual abuse; Adult survivors of child sexual abuse; Incest victims/survivors; Prevention program; Community education; Offender treatment program; Adolescent survivors of sexual abuse; Male survivors of sexual abuse
SPECIAL PROGRAMS/SERVICES: Assists with corrections therapy program for sex offenders through two-session education/sensitization program for rapists in a maximum-security prison

RICHLAND MEMORIAL HOSPITAL
5 Richland Medical Park, Columbia, SC 29203
Crisis hotline: **(803) 765-7000 24 hrs**
Information: (803) 765-7000 24 hrs
Contact: Karen Hansen, Soc Wkr Asst Dir
TYPE OF AGENCY: Hospital/medical center
AREAS SERVED: Richland
YEARS IN OPERATION: 5
ACCESSIBILITY: Wheelchair accessible; Signers for the hearing impaired
DESCRIPTION: Provides medical treatment and collection of medical evidence in cases of sexual assault/abuse against adults and children; Referrals for support and follow-up
CLIENTS/SERVICES: Sexual assault survivors; Child victims of sexual abuse
REQUIREMENTS: Client must file charges with police to receive protocol (collection of physical evidence and medical exam)

SISTERCARE, INC
PO Box 1029, Columbia, SC 29202
Crisis hotline: **(803) 765-9428 24 hrs daily**
Information: (803) 799-5477 8:30am-5pm
Contact: Nancy Barton, Exec Dir
TYPE OF AGENCY: Domestic violence program
AREAS SERVED: Richland, Lexington, Newberry, Kershaw, Fairfield
YEARS IN OPERATION: 7
ACCESSIBILITY: Wheelchair accessible
CASES SEXUAL ASSAULT/ABUSE (%): 33
DESCRIPTION: Services for domestic violence survivors; Shelter for referrals from local rape crisis network; Group therapy and couple groups therapy for batterers
CLIENTS/SERVICES: Sexual assault survivors; Marital rape/sexual abuse survivors; Adult survivors of child sexual abuse; Incest victims/survivors; Prevention program; Community education; Adolescent survivors of sexual abuse

SOUTH CAROLINA GUARDIAN AD LITEM PROGRAM
SC GAL Program, TRIO Programs, University of South Carolina, Columbia, SC 29208
Information: (803) 777-5127 8:30am-5pm
Contact: Jonathan Cowles, Assoc Dir
TYPE OF AGENCY: Child sexual abuse services; Child abuse services; Child advocacy
SPONSORING ORGANIZATION: TRIO Programs, University of South Carolina, College of Humanities and Social Sciences
AREAS SERVED: Statewide
YEARS IN OPERATION: 5
CASES SEXUAL ASSAULT/ABUSE (%): 30
DESCRIPTION: Programs provide training/supervision for volunteer (Guardians ad Litem) GALs to represent the best interest of abused and neglected children involved in family court (civil) proceedings
CLIENTS/SERVICES: Child victims of sexual abuse; Community education

CONWAY

SEXUAL ASSAULT PREVENTION/ INTERVENTION PROGRAM
PO Drawer 1076, Conway, SC 29526
Crisis hotline: **(803) 248-7213, 448-RAPE 24 hrs**
Information: (803) 248-7213 24 hrs (after hrs emergency line)
Contact: Christine Thomas, Svcs to Women Coord
TYPE OF AGENCY: Counseling/mental health services

SEXUAL ASSAULT PREVENTION/INTERVENTION PROGRAM (continued)

SPONSORING ORGANIZATION: Waccamaw Center for Mental Health
AREAS SERVED: Harry, Georgetown, Williamsburg
YEARS IN OPERATION: 6
ACCESSIBILITY: Wheelchair accessible
CLIENTS/SERVICES: Sexual assault survivors; Adult survivors of child sexual abuse

EASLEY

RAPE CRISIS COUNCIL OF PICKENS COUNTY, INC
PO Box 998, Easley, SC 29641
Crisis hotline: **(803) 878-7268 24 hrs**
Information: (803) 878-7268 8:30am-5pm
Contact: Debbie S Barnes, Exec Dir
TYPE OF AGENCY: Rape crisis center; Child sexual abuse prevention program
AREAS SERVED: Pickens
YEARS IN OPERATION: 3
CASES SEXUAL ASSAULT/ABUSE (%): 100
DESCRIPTION: Provides advocacy, referrals, support groups for survivors of sexual assault; Feminist martial arts/self-defense program
CLIENTS/SERVICES: Sexual assault survivors; Marital rape/sexual abuse survivors; Child victims of sexual abuse; Adult survivors of child sexual abuse; Incest victims/survivors; Prevention program; Community education; Adolescent survivors of sexual abuse; Male survivors of sexual abuse

EDGEFIELD

EDGEFIELD COUNTY RAPE CRISIS CENTER
PO Box 211, Edgefield, SC 29824
Crisis hotline: **(803) 275-3033 24 hrs**
Information: (803) 275-3033 24 hrs
Contact: Jenifer C Edwards, Prog Coord
TYPE OF AGENCY: Rape crisis center
AREAS SERVED: Edgefield
YEARS IN OPERATION: 1
ACCESSIBILITY: Wheelchair accessible
CASES SEXUAL ASSAULT/ABUSE (%): 100
CLIENTS/SERVICES: Sexual assault survivors; Marital rape/sexual abuse survivors; Adult survivors of child sexual abuse; Incest victims/survivors; Prevention program; Community education; Male survivors of sexual abuse
REQUIREMENTS: For minors (under age of 18) offers crisis counseling and referral to Dept of Social Services

FLORENCE

PEE DEE COALITION AGAINST DOMESTIC AND SEXUAL ASSAULT
PO Box 2152, Florence, SC 29503
Crisis hotline: **(803) 669-4600 24 hrs**
Information: (803) 669-4694 9am-5pm
Contact: Ellen C Hamilton, Exec Dir
TYPE OF AGENCY: Rape crisis center; Domestic violence program; Child sexual abuse services; Child sexual abuse prevention program
AREAS SERVED: Florence, Darlington, Marion, Marlboro, Chesterfield, Dillon
YEARS IN OPERATION: 1½
CASES SEXUAL ASSAULT/ABUSE (%): 40
CLIENTS/SERVICES: Sexual assault survivors; Marital rape/sexual abuse survivors; Child victims of sexual abuse; Adult survivors of child sexual abuse; Incest victims/survivors; Prevention program; Community education; Adolescent survivors of sexual abuse; Male survivors of sexual abuse

GREENVILLE

CHILD/ADOLESCENT SERVICES
715 Grove Rd, Greenville, SC 29609
Crisis hotline: **(803) 233-4357 24 hrs daily**
Information: (803) 235-0186 8:30am-5pm (Mon-Fri)
Contact: Carl Lancaster, Proj Admin
TYPE OF AGENCY: Counseling/mental health services
SPONSORING ORGANIZATION: Greenville Mental Health Center
AREAS SERVED: Greenville
YEARS IN OPERATION: Center 35, Sexual abuse program 7
ACCESSIBILITY: Wheelchair accessible; Telecommunications for the hearing impaired (TTY, TDY, etc.); Signers for the hearing impaired
CASES SEXUAL ASSAULT/ABUSE (%): 12-15
DESCRIPTION: Provides mental health treatment for mildly, moderately, and severely emotionally disturbed children and adolescents. Specialized program provides treatment for incest victims, mothers of these victims, and the offenders
CLIENTS/SERVICES: Child victims of sexual abuse; Incest victims/survivors; Offender treatment program; Adolescent survivors of sexual abuse; Male survivors of sexual abuse
REQUIREMENTS: Between the ages of 2 and 18 years

EMPLOYEE COUNSELING AND ASSISTANCE
638 E Washington St, Greenville, SC 29601
Crisis hotline: **(803) 232-8633 Rape crisis; 233-4357 Helpline 24 hrs**
Information: (803) 242-1807, 235-5184
Contact: Ginger Culbertson, Clinical Soc Wkr/Professional Counselor
TYPE OF AGENCY: Private practice
AREAS SERVED: Greenville, Greenwood, Laurens
YEARS IN OPERATION: 6
LANGUAGES: German
CASES SEXUAL ASSAULT/ABUSE (%): 5
DESCRIPTION: Provides short- and long-term counseling, including clients who have experienced domestic violence, spouse rape and rape by strangers
CLIENTS/SERVICES: Sexual assault survivors; Marital rape/sexual abuse survivors; Adult survivors of child sexual abuse; Incest victims/survivors; Adolescent survivors of sexual abuse; Healing
REQUIREMENTS: 18 years or older; Sliding scale fee
SPECIAL PROGRAMS/SERVICES: NLP therapy and use of drawing and painting to express feelings and ventilate

JUSTICE FOR SEXUALLY ABUSED CHILDREN
30 Palmetto Estates, Greenville, SC 29611
Crisis hotline: **(803) 233-4357 24 hrs**
Information: (803) 294-1569 24 hors
Contact: Cathy Redmond, SC State Office Pres
TYPE OF AGENCY: Child sexual abuse services; Child sexual abuse prevention program
YEARS IN OPERATION: 2
CASES SEXUAL ASSAULT/ABUSE (%): 100
CLIENTS/SERVICES: Child victims of sexual abuse; Adult survivors of child sexual abuse; Incest victims/survivors; Community education; Adolescent survivors of sexual abuse; Male survivors of sexual abuse

LINDER, WADDELL AND ASSOCIATES
14 Lavinia Ave, Greenville, SC 29601
Information: (803) 233-5279 9am-5pm
Contact: Chrys J Harris, PhD, Clinical Associate
TYPE OF AGENCY: Private practice
AREAS SERVED: Greenville, Spartanburg, Anderson, Pickens
YEARS IN OPERATION: 10
ACCESSIBILITY: Wheelchair accessible
CASES SEXUAL ASSAULT/ABUSE (%): 10
DESCRIPTION: All therapists are trained marriage and family therapists with membership in AAMFT. Specialty includes neuro-linguistic programming, treatment for post-traumatic stress disorder (and reaction), anxiety and panic disorders, and general psychotherapy. Contract to treat individuals and families in the local victim/witness program
CLIENTS/SERVICES: Sexual assault survivors; Marital rape/sexual abuse survivors; Child victims of sexual abuse; Adult survivors of child sexual abuse; Incest victims/survivors; Prevention program; Community education; Adolescent survivors of sexual abuse; Male survivors of sexual abuse

RAPE CRISIS COUNCIL OF GREENVILLE
104 Chapman, Greenville, SC 29605
Crisis hotline: **(803) 232-8633 24 hrs**
Information: (803) 232-8633 8:30am-5pm
Contact: Allene Thompson, Exec Dir
TYPE OF AGENCY: Rape crisis center
CLIENTS/SERVICES: Sexual assault survivors; Child victims of sexual abuse; Adult survivors of child sexual abuse; Incest victims/survivors; Prevention program; Community education; Adolescent survivors of sexual abuse

SHELTER FOR FAMILIES OF DOMESTIC VIOLENCE
301 University Ridge, Ste 5500, Greenville, SC 29601-3674
Crisis hotline: **(803) 233-4357 24 hrs**
Information: (803) 232-2434 8:30am-5pm
Contact: Vicki Ernest, Prog Dir
TYPE OF AGENCY: Domestic violence program
SPONSORING ORGANIZATION: Family Counseling Center-Greenville
AREAS SERVED: Greenville, Spartanburg, Anderson, Oconee, Pickens
YEARS IN OPERATION: 10
CASES SEXUAL ASSAULT/ABUSE (%): 75
DESCRIPTION: Provides emergency shelter service for abused women and their children; Treatment for batterers
CLIENTS/SERVICES: Marital rape/sexual abuse survivors; Child victims of sexual abuse; Adult survivors of child sexual abuse; Incest victims/survivors; Community education; Adolescent survivors of sexual abuse

VICTIM WITNESS ASSISTANCE PROGRAM
Greenville County Courthouse Annex, Ste 101, Greenville, SC 29601
Information: (803) 298-8647 8:30am-5pm
Contact: Jayne Crisp, Prog Dir
TYPE OF AGENCY: Victim/witness assistance program
SPONSORING ORGANIZATION: 13th Judicial Circuit Solicitor's Office
AREAS SERVED: Greenville, Pickens
YEARS IN OPERATION: 10
CLIENTS/SERVICES: Sexual assault survivors; Marital rape/sexual abuse survivors; Child victims of sexual abuse; Adult survivors of child sexual abuse; Incest victims/survivors; Prevention program; Community education; Adolescent survivors of sexual abuse; Male survivors of sexual abuse

GREENWOOD

RAPE CRISIS COUNCIL OF GREENWOOD
PO Box 70, Greenwood, SC 29646
Crisis hotline: **(803) 223-4357, (800) 223-4357 toll free in-state 24 hrs**
Contact: Cornelia Walker
TYPE OF AGENCY: Rape crisis center
AREAS SERVED: Primarily Greenwood
YEARS IN OPERATION: 10
CASES SEXUAL ASSAULT/ABUSE (%): 100
CLIENTS/SERVICES: Sexual assault survivors; Community education

RAPE CRISIS COUNCIL OF GREENWOOD *(continued)*
REQUIREMENTS: Adults only; Department of Social Services handles child sexual abuse cases

HAMPTON

SOLICITOR'S OFFICE—VICTIM/WITNESS PROGRAM
PO Box 457, Hampton, SC 29924
Information: (803) 943-3580 8am-5pm, other hrs by appointment
Contact: LaClaire W Laffitte, Dir
TYPE OF AGENCY: Victim/witness assistance program
AREAS SERVED: Hampton, Allendale, Colleton, Jasper, Beaufort
YEARS IN OPERATION: 3
CLIENTS/SERVICES: Sexual assault survivors; Marital rape/sexual abuse survivors; Child victims of sexual abuse; Adult survivors of child sexual abuse; Incest victims/survivors
REQUIREMENTS: Victims of crimes which come into the court system

HARTSVILLE

OFFICE OF SOLICITOR—VICTIM WITNESS ASSISTANCE
PO Box 2555, Hartsville, SC 29550
Information: (803) 332-0193 9am-5pm
Contact: Ann G Atkins, Victim/Witness Advocate
TYPE OF AGENCY: Victim/witness assistance program
AREAS SERVED: Marlboro, Darlington, Chesterfield, Dillon
CLIENTS/SERVICES: Sexual assault survivors; Marital rape/sexual abuse survivors; Child victims of sexual abuse; Incest victims/survivors
REQUIREMENTS: Charges must be filed

LANCASTER

CATAWBA MENTAL HEALTH CENTER—LANCASTER OFFICE
208 W Meeting St, Lancaster, SC 29745
Crisis hotline: **(803) 285-7888 24 hrs 7 days**
Information: (803) 285-7456 8:30am-5pm (Mon-Fri)
Contact: Casey Smith, ACSW, Child Adolescent Svcs MH Counselor III
TYPE OF AGENCY: Counseling/mental health services
AREAS SERVED: Lancaster
YEARS IN OPERATION: 15
ACCESSIBILITY: Wheelchair accessible
CASES SEXUAL ASSAULT/ABUSE (%): 39
CLIENTS/SERVICES: Child victims of sexual abuse; Adult survivors of child sexual abuse; Incest victims/survivors; Adolescent survivors of sexual abuse; Male survivors of sexual abuse

LANCASTER COUNTY RAPE CRISIS CENTER
111 N York St, Lancaster, SC 29720
Crisis hotline: **(803) 286-1214, 286-5232 24 hrs daily**
Information: (803) 286-5232
Contact: Ann V Beckham, Exec Dir
TYPE OF AGENCY: Rape crisis center
AREAS SERVED: Lancaster
YEARS IN OPERATION: 2
CASES SEXUAL ASSAULT/ABUSE (%): 87
DESCRIPTION: Provides educational, health, and psychological programs for victims of incest, sexual assault/abuse, and attempted sexual assault. Includes crisis intervention, face-to-face counseling, legal and medical advocacy, support groups for female and male survivors
CLIENTS/SERVICES: Sexual assault survivors; Marital rape/sexual abuse survivors; Child victims of sexual abuse; Adult survivors of child sexual abuse; Incest victims/survivors; Prevention program; Community education; Adolescent survivors of sexual abuse; Male survivors of sexual abuse

SOUTH CAROLINA GUARDIAN AD LITEM PROGRAM
PO Box 1507, Lancaster, SC 29720
Information: (803) 286-6064
Contact: Jeannie Hegler, Coord
TYPE OF AGENCY: Child sexual abuse services; Child advocacy
AREAS SERVED: Lancaster
YEARS IN OPERATION: 2
CASES SEXUAL ASSAULT/ABUSE (%): 80
DESCRIPTION: Trained volunteers make a full investigation of all reports and appear in court to represent the best interests of the child
CLIENTS/SERVICES: Child victims of sexual abuse; Incest victims/survivors; Community education

LEXINGTON

LEXINGTON COUNTY SHERIFF'S DEPT
PO Box 639, 521 Gibson Rd, Lexington, SC 29072
Information: (803) 359-8230 24 hrs
Contact: Melissa Lee, Victim Assistance Officer
TYPE OF AGENCY: Victim/witness assistance program
AREAS SERVED: Lexington
YEARS IN OPERATION: 4
ACCESSIBILITY: Wheelchair accessible
DESCRIPTION: Law enforcement related and the first to be in contact with victims; Assists in obtaining aid and counseling; Explains the procedures of the law enforcement system
CLIENTS/SERVICES: Sexual assault survivors; Marital rape/sexual abuse survivors; Child victims of sexual abuse; Prevention program; Community education
REQUIREMENTS: Must report offense

ORANGEBURG

OFFICE OF SOLICITOR—VICTIM WITNESS ASSISTANCE
PO Box 1525, Orangeburg, SC 29116-1525
Information: (803) 533-1000 8:30am-5pm
Contact: Brenda S Brant, Victim/Witness Advocate
TYPE OF AGENCY: Victim/witness assistance program
SPONSORING ORGANIZATION: First Judicial Circuit
AREAS SERVED: Orangeburg, Dorchester, Calhoun
YEARS IN OPERATION: 3
ACCESSIBILITY: Wheelchair accessible
CLIENTS/SERVICES: Sexual assault survivors; Marital rape/sexual abuse survivors; Child victims of sexual abuse; Incest victims/survivors; Community education; Publications/media
SPECIAL PROGRAMS/SERVICES: Locally produced media programs on the *Victim/Witness Assistance Program in South Carolina* and *Crime Victim Compensation*

TRI COUNTY CITIZENS AGAINST SEXUAL ASSAULT (CASA)
PO Box 1568, Orangeburg, SC 29116-1568
Crisis hotline: **(803) 534-2272 24 hrs**
Information: (803) 534-2448 9am-6pm
Contact: Gilda Cobb Hunter, Exec Dir
TYPE OF AGENCY: Rape crisis center
AREAS SERVED: Orangeburg, Bamberg, Calhoun
YEARS IN OPERATION: 9
ACCESSIBILITY: Wheelchair accessible
CASES SEXUAL ASSAULT/ABUSE (%): 100
CLIENTS/SERVICES: Sexual assault survivors; Marital rape/sexual abuse survivors; Child victims of sexual abuse; Adult survivors of child sexual abuse; Prevention program; Community education; Adolescent survivors of sexual abuse; Male survivors of sexual abuse

RIDGELAND

COASTAL EMPIRE MENTAL HEALTH
PO Box 1216, Ridgeland, SC 29936
Crisis hotline: **(800) 922-7844 5pm-8:30am**
Information: (803) 726-8030 8:30am-5pm
Contact: Dana G Mullins, Office Supv/MHC II
TYPE OF AGENCY: Counseling/mental health services
AREAS SERVED: Jasper
YEARS IN OPERATION: 15
ACCESSIBILITY: Wheelchair accessible
CASES SEXUAL ASSAULT/ABUSE (%): 1-5
CLIENTS/SERVICES: Sexual assault survivors; Marital rape/sexual abuse survivors; Child victims of sexual abuse; Adult survivors of child sexual abuse; Incest victims/survivors; Adolescent survivors of sexual abuse; Male survivors of sexual abuse

ROCK HILL

SOUTH CAROLINA VOLUNTEER GUARDIAN AD LITEM PROGRAM
PO Box 8032 CRS, Rock Hill, SC 29731
Information: (803) 327-9997 9am-5pm (Mon-Fri)
Contact: Lynn Snowber-Marini, Circuit Coord
TYPE OF AGENCY: Child sexual abuse services; Child abuse services; Child advocacy
SPONSORING ORGANIZATION: USC Trio Programs
AREAS SERVED: York, Union
YEARS IN OPERATION: ½
ACCESSIBILITY: Wheelchair accessible
CASES SEXUAL ASSAULT/ABUSE (%): 58
DESCRIPTION: Provides trained volunteers to serve as guardians ad litem for abused and neglected children. The GAL advocates the best interests of the child by conducting an independent investigation, preparing a written report, and appearing in court
CLIENTS/SERVICES: Child victims of sexual abuse; Community education
REQUIREMENTS: Report of child abuse/neglect to Department of Social Services

YORK COUNTY RAPE CRISIS COUNCIL, INC
166 Dotson St, Rock Hill, SC 29730
Crisis hotline: **(803) 327-2012 24 hrs**
Information: (803) 327-2012 9am-5pm
Contact: Irene S Price, Pres
TYPE OF AGENCY: Rape crisis center; Domestic violence program; Child sexual abuse prevention program; Acquaintance/date rape prevention program
AREAS SERVED: York, Chester
YEARS IN OPERATION: 12
LANGUAGES: Hebrew
ACCESSIBILITY: Wheelchair accessible
CASES SEXUAL ASSAULT/ABUSE (%): 100
DESCRIPTION: Services for sexual assault survivors; Prevention programs for adolescents and university students; Feminist martial arts/self-defense
CLIENTS/SERVICES: Sexual assault survivors; Marital rape/sexual abuse survivors; Child victims of sexual abuse; Adult survivors of child sexual abuse; Incest victims/survivors; Prevention program; Community education; Adolescent survivors of sexual abuse; Male survivors of sexual abuse

SPARTANBURG

COUNCIL ON SEXUAL ASSAULT OF SPARTANBURG
175 Alabama St, Spartanburg, SC 29302
Crisis hotline: **(803) 591-4344 24 hrs**
Information: (803) 585-9569 9am-5pm
Contact: Elaine Hudson, Exec Dir
TYPE OF AGENCY: Rape crisis center; Child sexual abuse services
AREAS SERVED: Spartanburg
YEARS IN OPERATION: 3
CASES SEXUAL ASSAULT/ABUSE (%): 100

COUNCIL ON SEXUAL ASSAULT OF SPARTANBURG *(continued)*

CLIENTS/SERVICES: Sexual assault survivors; Marital rape/sexual abuse survivors; Child victims of sexual abuse; Adult survivors of child sexual abuse; Incest victims/survivors; Prevention program; Community education; Adolescent survivors of sexual abuse; Male survivors of sexual abuse

FAMILY CARE COUNCIL
PO Box 2413, Spartanburg, SC 29304
Information: (803) 591-2273 8am-8pm
Contact: Nancy Hodges, Coord
TYPE OF AGENCY: Child sexual abuse prevention program; Child abuse prevention program
AREAS SERVED: Spartanburg
YEARS IN OPERATION: 4½
ACCESSIBILITY: Wheelchair accessible
DESCRIPTION: Child abuse prevention, including Parents Anonymous chapter
CLIENTS/SERVICES: Adult survivors of child sexual abuse; Prevention program; Community education; Adolescent survivors of sexual abuse

SPARTANBURG COUNTY GUARDIAN AD LITEM PROGRAM
PO Box 5286, Spartanburg, SC 29302
Information: (803) 574-8550 9am-5pm
Contact: Sylvia Lynn Gillotte, Circuit Coord
TYPE OF AGENCY: Child sexual abuse services; Child abuse services; Child advocacy
AREAS SERVED: Spartanburg, Cherokee
YEARS IN OPERATION: 3
LANGUAGES: French, German, Afrikaans
CASES SEXUAL ASSAULT/ABUSE (%): 35
DESCRIPTION: Volunteers serve as court-appointed special advocates (guardians ad litem) for abused and neglected children in Department of Social Services Family Court cases
CLIENTS/SERVICES: Child victims of sexual abuse; Incest victims/survivors; Community education
REQUIREMENTS: Cases referred by Dept of Social Services and the solicitor's office

VICTIM/WITNESS ASSISTANCE PROGRAM
Spartanburg County Courthouse, Spartanburg, SC 29301
Information: (803) 596-2575 8:30am-5pm
Contact: Laura H Rogers, Victim/Witness Program Coord
TYPE OF AGENCY: Victim/witness assistance program
SPONSORING ORGANIZATION: 7th Circuit Solicitor's Office
AREAS SERVED: Spartanburg, Cherokee
YEARS IN OPERATION: 4
ACCESSIBILITY: Wheelchair accessible
CASES SEXUAL ASSAULT/ABUSE (%): 10
CLIENTS/SERVICES: Sexual assault survivors; Marital rape/sexual abuse survivors; Child victims of sexual abuse; Prevention program; Adolescent survivors of sexual abuse; Male survivors of sexual abuse

SUMMERVILLE

CENTER FOR COUNSELING AND DEVELOPMENT
PO Box 1942, Summerville, SC 29484-1942
Information: (803) 871-3041 Secretary hrs 8:30am-5:30pm; Therapist hrs 10am-9pm; Answering service after hrs
Contact: Priscilla H Taylor, PhD, Dir
TYPE OF AGENCY: Private practice
AREAS SERVED: Berkeley, Charleston, Dorchester
YEARS IN OPERATION: 5
ACCESSIBILITY: Wheelchair accessible
DESCRIPTION: Counseling for victims/survivors, including support groups for female and male survivors; Treatment for rapists and child sexual abuse/incest offenders
CLIENTS/SERVICES: Child victims of sexual abuse; Adult survivors of child sexual abuse; Incest victims/survivors; Offender treatment program; Adolescent survivors of sexual abuse; Male survivors of sexual abuse

PARENTS UNITED
300 B-4 N Cedar St, Summerville, SC 29483
Information: (803) 873-8483
Contact: Margaret Germann, MSN, RN, CS, Professional Coord
TYPE OF AGENCY: Child sexual abuse services
SPONSORING ORGANIZATION: Psychological Nursing Departments, MUSC
AREAS SERVED: Dorchester, Berkley, Charleston
YEARS IN OPERATION: 6
ACCESSIBILITY: Wheelchair accessible
CASES SEXUAL ASSAULT/ABUSE (%): 100
DESCRIPTION: Group therapy for the family of the sexually abused child, including child sexual abuse/incest offenders and adult survivors of child sexual abuse. Groups include Parents United, Daughters and Sons United and Adults Molested as Children United
CLIENTS/SERVICES: Child victims of sexual abuse; Adult survivors of child sexual abuse; Incest victims/survivors; Community education; Offender treatment program; Adolescent survivors of sexual abuse; Male survivors of sexual abuse
REQUIREMENTS: Children 7 or older; Crime must be reported

SUMTER

SANTEE-WATEREE MENTAL HEALTH CENTER
PO Box 1946, 215 N Magnolia St, Sumter, SC 29151
Crisis hotline: **(803) 775-9364 24 hrs**
Information: (803) 775-9364 8:30am-5pm
Contact: Ken McLeod, ACSW, Spec Svcs Coord
TYPE OF AGENCY: Counseling/mental health services
AREAS SERVED: Sumter, Clarendon, Kershaw, Lee
YEARS IN OPERATION: 25
ACCESSIBILITY: Wheelchair accessible
CASES SEXUAL ASSAULT/ABUSE (%): 10
DESCRIPTION: Crisis intervention, assessment, diagnosis, and treatment services are provided for child and adult victims of sexual assault. Also provides treatment for rapists, child sexual abuse/incest offenders, and batterers
CLIENTS/SERVICES: Sexual assault survivors; Marital rape/sexual abuse survivors; Child victims of sexual abuse; Adult survivors of child sexual abuse; Incest victims/survivors; Community education; Offender treatment program; Adolescent survivors of sexual abuse; Male survivors of sexual abuse

YWCA OF THE SUMTER AREA, INC
246 Church St, Sumter, SC 29150
Crisis hotline: **(803) 773-HELP 24 hrs daily**
Information: (803) 773-7158 9am-5pm
Contact: Theodis Parsons Palmer, Exec Dir
TYPE OF AGENCY: Rape crisis center; Domestic violence program; Child sexual abuse services; Child sexual abuse prevention program; Acquaintance/date rape prevention program
AREAS SERVED: Sumter, Lee, Clarendon
YEARS IN OPERATION: 21
ACCESSIBILITY: Wheelchair accessible
DESCRIPTION: Provides shelter, group and individual counseling and advocacy for survivors of sexual assault/family violence; Prevention programs include *Kid Safe,* for preschool and elementary children, and *Teen Safe*
CLIENTS/SERVICES: Sexual assault survivors; Marital rape/sexual abuse survivors; Child victims of sexual abuse; Adult survivors of child sexual abuse; Incest victims/survivors; Prevention program; Community education; Adolescent survivors of sexual abuse; Male survivors of sexual abuse

WESTMINSTER

RECOVERY MOUNTAIN, INC
PO Box 341, Westminster, SC 29693
Crisis hotline: **(803) 647-6470 24 hrs**
Contact: Frank W Hix, Admin
TYPE OF AGENCY: Domestic violence program
SPONSORING ORGANIZATION: U-Way of Oconee County
AREAS SERVED: Oconee
YEARS IN OPERATION: 7
CASES SEXUAL ASSAULT/ABUSE (%): 10
DESCRIPTION: Provides help for all types of abuse
CLIENTS/SERVICES: Marital rape/sexual abuse survivors; Child victims of sexual abuse; Prevention program; Community education

YORK

YORK COUNTY SOLICITOR'S OFFICE— VICTIM/WITNESS ASSISTANCE PROGRAM
PO Box 726, York, SC 29745
Information: (803) 684-8524 8:30am-5pm
Contact: Janice Gillespie, Dir
TYPE OF AGENCY: Victim/witness assistance program
AREAS SERVED: York, Union
YEARS IN OPERATION: 4
CASES SEXUAL ASSAULT/ABUSE (%): 20
CLIENTS/SERVICES: Sexual assault survivors; Marital rape/sexual abuse survivors; Child victims of sexual abuse; Incest victims/survivors; Community education

SOUTH DAKOTA

ABERDEEN

RESOURCE CENTER FOR WOMEN
317 S Kline, Aberdeen, SD 57401
Crisis hotline: **(605) 226-1212 24 hrs**
Information: (605) 226-1212 8am-5pm
Contact: Barbara Bergen, Counselor
TYPE OF AGENCY: Rape crisis center; Domestic violence program; Child sexual abuse services; Child sexual abuse prevention program
SPONSORING ORGANIZATION: United Way
AREAS SERVED: Brown, Day, Marshall, Edmonds, Potter, Walworth, McPherson, Campbell
YEARS IN OPERATION: 11
ACCESSIBILITY: Wheelchair accessible
DESCRIPTION: Services for survivors of sexual assault and domestic violence; Feminist martial arts/self-defense
CLIENTS/SERVICES: Sexual assault survivors; Marital rape/sexual abuse survivors; Child victims of sexual abuse; Adult survivors of child sexual abuse; Incest victims/survivors; Prevention program; Community education; Adolescent survivors of sexual abuse

DEADWOOD

STATE'S ATTORNEY'S OFFICE
78-80 Sherman St, Deadwood, SD 57732
Information: (605) 578-1707 8am-5pm (Mon-Fri)
Contact: Jeffry Bloomberg, State's Attorney; Janice Crangle, Victim Asst
TYPE OF AGENCY: Victim/witness assistance program
AREAS SERVED: Lawrence
ACCESSIBILITY: Wheelchair accessible
CLIENTS/SERVICES: Sexual assault survivors; Marital rape/sexual abuse survivors; Child victims of sexual abuse; Adult survivors of child sexual abuse; Incest victims/survivors; Community education
REQUIREMENTS: Criminal charges pending

EAGLE BUTTE

SACRED HEART CENTER/WOMEN'S SHELTER
Box 110, Eagle Butte, SD 57625
Crisis hotline: **(605) 964-SAFE 24 hrs**
Information: (605) 964-6062 9am-5pm (Mon-Fri)
Contact: Br Jim Muller, SCJ, Dir
TYPE OF AGENCY: Domestic violence program; Counseling/mental health services; Shelter; Adolescent program
SPONSORING ORGANIZATION: Sacred Heart Priests and Brothers
AREAS SERVED: Dewey, Zeibach, Corson
YEARS IN OPERATION: 3
LANGUAGES: Lakota
ACCESSIBILITY: Wheelchair accessible
CASES SEXUAL ASSAULT/ABUSE (%): 10
DESCRIPTION: Provides crisis services and shelter for survivors of sexual assault and domestic violence; Adolescent crisis shelter
CLIENTS/SERVICES: Sexual assault survivors; Child victims of sexual abuse; Community education; Adolescent survivors of sexual abuse

HOT SPRINGS

HOT SPRINGS CRISIS INTERVENTION TEAM
PO Box 882, Hot Springs, SD 57747
Crisis hotline: **(605) 745-6070 24 hrs**
Information: (605) 745-4678 24 hrs
Contact: Barb Kloppel, Chair
TYPE OF AGENCY: Rape crisis center; Domestic violence program
AREAS SERVED: Fall River
YEARS IN OPERATION: 12
CASES SEXUAL ASSAULT/ABUSE (%): 98
DESCRIPTION: Services for survivors of sexual assault and domestic violence; Treatment program for batterers
CLIENTS/SERVICES: Sexual assault survivors; Marital rape/sexual abuse survivors; Community education; Adolescent survivors of sexual abuse; Male survivors of sexual abuse

HURON

HURON YWCA
17 5th SW, Huron, SD 57350
Crisis hotline: **(605) 352-9433 24 hrs**
Information: (605) 352-2793 9am-4pm
Contact: Carla Micheel, Exec Dir
TYPE OF AGENCY: Domestic violence program
AREAS SERVED: Beadle
YEARS IN OPERATION: 4
ACCESSIBILITY: Wheelchair accessible
CLIENTS/SERVICES: Marital rape/sexual abuse survivors; Community education

PIERRE

MISSOURI SHORES WOMEN'S RESOURCE CENTER
104 E Capitol Ave, Hughes County Courthouse, Pierre, SD 57501
Crisis hotline: **(605) 224-6224 24 hrs daily**
Information: (605) 224-0259 9am-Noon (Mon-Fri)
Contact: Dedra Shaw, Crisis Coun
TYPE OF AGENCY: Domestic violence program
AREAS SERVED: Hughes, Stanley, Lyman, Hyde, Buffalo, Jones, Sully
YEARS IN OPERATION: 10
CASES SEXUAL ASSAULT/ABUSE (%): 60
CLIENTS/SERVICES: Sexual assault survivors; Marital rape/sexual abuse survivors; Adult survivors of child sexual abuse; Incest victims/survivors; Community education

RAPID CITY

VICTIMS ASSISTANCE PROGRAM
300 Kansas City St, Rapid City, SD 57701
Information: (605) 394-2191 7am-5pm
Contact: Vicky Wicks, Victim's Asst
TYPE OF AGENCY: Victim/witness assistance program
SPONSORING ORGANIZATION: Pennington County
AREAS SERVED: Pennington
YEARS IN OPERATION: ½
ACCESSIBILITY: Wheelchair accessible
CASES SEXUAL ASSAULT/ABUSE (%): 5
CLIENTS/SERVICES: Sexual assault survivors; Marital rape/sexual abuse survivors; Child victims of sexual abuse; Incest victims/survivors; Community education
REQUIREMENTS: Any victim of any crime may receive assistance. However, ability to assist is greatly improved if the victim reports the crime and then follows through with prosecution.

WOMEN AGAINST VIOLENCE, INC
PO Box 3042, Rapid City, SD 57709
Crisis hotline: **(605) 341-4808 24 hrs**
Information: (605) 341-3292, Shelter 348-5227 8am-5pm; Shelter 7:30am-10:30pm
Contact: Suzann Ecker, Exec Dir
TYPE OF AGENCY: Rape crisis center; Domestic violence program
AREAS SERVED: Western South Dakota
YEARS IN OPERATION: 10
LANGUAGES: Lakota
ACCESSIBILITY: Wheelchair accessible; Signers for the hearing impaired
CASES SEXUAL ASSAULT/ABUSE (%): 15
CLIENTS/SERVICES: Sexual assault survivors; Marital rape/sexual abuse survivors; Adult survivors of child sexual abuse; Incest victims/survivors; Prevention program; Community education

SIOUX FALLS

CHILDREN'S INN
615 S Grange, Sioux Falls, SD 57104
Crisis hotline: **(605) 338-4880 24 hrs**
Information: (605) 338-4880
Contact: Marlene K Weires, Dir
TYPE OF AGENCY: Domestic violence program
AREAS SERVED: Minnehaha, Lincoln, Union, McCook, Turner
YEARS IN OPERATION: 11
LANGUAGES: Translators available

CHILDREN'S INN (continued)
ACCESSIBILITY: Telecommunications for the hearing impaired (TTY, TDY, etc.); Signers for the hearing impaired
CASES SEXUAL ASSAULT/ABUSE (%): 75
CLIENTS/SERVICES: Sexual assault survivors; Marital rape/sexual abuse survivors; Child victims of sexual abuse; Prevention program; Community education

CITIZENS AGAINST RAPE AND DOMESTIC VIOLENCE
PO Box 876, Sioux Falls, SD 57101-0876
Crisis hotline: **(605) 339-4357 24 hrs daily**
Information: (605) 339-4357 8am-5pm (Mon-Fri)
Contact: Renae Battista-Turbak, Rape Crisis Prog Dir
TYPE OF AGENCY: Rape crisis center; Domestic violence program
AREAS SERVED: Minnehaha and immediate surrounding counties
YEARS IN OPERATION: 11
ACCESSIBILITY: Wheelchair accessible; Telecommunications for the hearing impaired (TTY, TDY, etc.); Signers for the hearing impaired
CASES SEXUAL ASSAULT/ABUSE (%): 100
DESCRIPTION: Crisis intervention and counseling for survivors of sexual assault, including support groups for female and male survivors. Men Against Violence—trained male volunteers who do public education programs on domestic violence and sexual assault. Family violence project—26-week treatment program for batterers
CLIENTS/SERVICES: Sexual assault survivors; Marital rape/sexual abuse survivors; Adult survivors of child sexual abuse; Prevention program; Community education; Adolescent survivors of sexual abuse; Male survivors of sexual abuse
REQUIREMENTS: Anyone under the age of 13 is referred to the Department of Social Service.

MCKENNAN HOSPITAL—SEXUAL TRAUMA PROGRAM
800 E 21st St, Sioux Falls, SD 57101
Crisis hotline: **(605) 334-6645 24 hrs daily**
Information: (605) 339-8075 24 hrs by pager
Contact: Barb Haddican, MSW, ACSW, Psychiatric Soc Wkr
TYPE OF AGENCY: Hospital/medical center
YEARS IN OPERATION: 1
ACCESSIBILITY: Wheelchair accessible; Telecommunications for the hearing impaired (TTY, TDY, etc.); Signers for the hearing impaired (by arrangement)
CASES SEXUAL ASSAULT/ABUSE (%): 33-50
CLIENTS/SERVICES: Sexual assault survivors; Marital rape/sexual abuse survivors; Child victims of sexual abuse; Adult survivors of child sexual abuse; Incest victims/survivors

SPEARFISH

WOMEN IN CRISIS COALITION, INC
PO Box 486, Spearfish, SD 57783
Crisis hotline: **(605) 652-7825 24 hrs**
Information: (605) 652-7825
Contact: Zindie Meyers, Office Mgr
TYPE OF AGENCY: Rape crisis center; Domestic violence program; Acquaintance/date rape prevention program
AREAS SERVED: Lawrence, Butte, Meade
YEARS IN OPERATION: 9
CASES SEXUAL ASSAULT/ABUSE (%): 95
CLIENTS/SERVICES: Sexual assault survivors; Marital rape/sexual abuse survivors; Community education
SPECIAL PROGRAMS/SERVICES: In-service workshops in public schools on dating violence and rape

VERMILLION

PSYCHOLOGICAL SERVICES CENTER
414 E Clark St, Vermillion, SD 57069
Crisis hotline: **(605) 677-5354 7pm-2am**
Information: (605) 677-5354 8am-5pm
Contact: Patricia Petretic-Jackson, PhD, Assoc Prof Psychology
TYPE OF AGENCY: College/university-based services; Counseling/mental health services; Acquaintance/date rape prevention program; Training/research
SPONSORING ORGANIZATION: University of South Dakota
AREAS SERVED: Southeastern SD; Northwestern IA
YEARS IN OPERATION: 17
ACCESSIBILITY: Wheelchair accessible
CASES SEXUAL ASSAULT/ABUSE (%): 50
DESCRIPTION: Crisis intervention and short- and long-term treatment for victims/survivors. Also provides individual therapy for child sexual abuse offenders and batterers. Has dual purpose of supervised training of graduate students in APA approved clinical psychology training program and service provision
CLIENTS/SERVICES: Sexual assault survivors; Marital rape/sexual abuse survivors; Child victims of sexual abuse; Adult survivors of child sexual abuse; Incest victims/survivors; Prevention program; Community education; Offender treatment program; Adolescent survivors of sexual abuse; Male survivors of sexual abuse
SPECIAL PROGRAMS/SERVICES: Prevention programs: acquaintance rape training of residence hall staff for educational program for prevention in college-age group

YANKTON

WOMEN'S CENTER/SHELTER
PO Box 675, 510 Broadway, Yankton, SD 57078
Crisis hotline: **(605) 665-1448 24 hrs**
Information: (605) 665-4811 24 hrs
Contact: Beacy Nelson, Dir
TYPE OF AGENCY: Domestic violence program
SPONSORING ORGANIZATION: Contact Center
AREAS SERVED: Yankton, Bon Homme, Hutchinson
YEARS IN OPERATION: 7
CASES SEXUAL ASSAULT/ABUSE (%): 95
CLIENTS/SERVICES: Marital rape/sexual abuse survivors; Adult survivors of child sexual abuse; Prevention program; Community education

TENNESSEE

ALCOA

HAVEN HOUSE
PO Box 134, Alcoa, TN 37701
Crisis hotline: **(615) 982-1087 24 hrs 7 days**
Information: (615) 982-1087 9am-5pm
Contact: Peggy Cantrell, Dir
TYPE OF AGENCY: Domestic violence program
AREAS SERVED: Blount, Loudon, Monroe
YEARS IN OPERATION: 5
ACCESSIBILITY: Wheelchair accessible; Signers for the hearing impaired (by arrangement)
CASES SEXUAL ASSAULT/ABUSE (%): 25
CLIENTS/SERVICES: Sexual assault survivors; Marital rape/sexual abuse survivors; Child victims of sexual abuse; Adult survivors of child sexual abuse; Incest victims/survivors

CHATTANOOGA

FAMILY AND CHILDREN'S SERVICES OF CHATTANOOGA, TENNESSEE
323 High St, Chattanooga, TN 37402
Crisis hotline: **(615) 755-2700 24 hrs**
Information: (615) 755-2800 8am-6pm (Mon-Thu); 8am-12pm (Fri)
Contact: Peg Johnson, MA, Family Violence Prog Coord; Kathryn Drake, LCSW, Clinical Counseling Coord
TYPE OF AGENCY: Domestic violence program; Counseling/mental health services; Child sexual abuse services; Residential treatment facility
AREAS SERVED: Hamilton, surrounding area including N GA
YEARS IN OPERATION: 89
LANGUAGES: Interpreters available
ACCESSIBILITY: Wheelchair accessible; Telecommunications for the hearing impaired (TTY, TDY, etc.); Signers for the hearing impaired
CASES SEXUAL ASSAULT/ABUSE (%): 25
DESCRIPTION: Contracts with Tennessee Department of Human Service to provide therapy for children, adolescents, perpetrators, non-offending parents in cases of sexual abuse; Also provides counseling for adult survivors and batterers
CLIENTS/SERVICES: Sexual assault survivors; Marital rape/sexual abuse survivors; Child victims of sexual abuse; Adult survivors of child sexual abuse; Incest victims/survivors; Prevention program; Community education; Offender treatment program; Adolescent survivors of sexual abuse; Male survivors of sexual abuse

CROSSVILLE

BATTERED WOMEN, INC
PO Box 3063, Crossville, TN 38557
Crisis hotline: **(800) 641-3434 24 hrs**
Information: (615) 456-0747 8am-5pm (Mon-Fri)
Contact: Marianne Blevins, Exec Dir
TYPE OF AGENCY: Domestic violence program
AREAS SERVED: Cumberland, Fentress, Bledsoe, Morgan, Rhea, Van Buren
YEARS IN OPERATION: 4
CASES SEXUAL ASSAULT/ABUSE (%): 20
DESCRIPTION: Provides shelter, referrals, and crisis counseling for survivors of domestic violence/sexual assault
CLIENTS/SERVICES: Sexual assault survivors; Marital rape/sexual abuse survivors; Child victims of sexual abuse; Adult survivors of child sexual abuse; Community education; Adolescent survivors of sexual abuse

DYERSBURG

NORTHWEST SAFELINE
PO Box 1831, 108 N King, Dyersburg, TN 38025-1831
Crisis hotline: **(901) 285-7233 24 hrs**
Information: (901) 285-6470 8:30am-4:30pm
Contact: Brenda Cherry, Dir
TYPE OF AGENCY: Rape crisis center; Domestic violence program
AREAS SERVED: Dyer, Lake, Obion, Weakley, Lauderdale
YEARS IN OPERATION: 4
ACCESSIBILITY: Wheelchair accessible; Signers for the hearing impaired (by arrangement)
CASES SEXUAL ASSAULT/ABUSE (%): 100
CLIENTS/SERVICES: Sexual assault survivors; Marital rape/sexual abuse survivors; Community education

JACKSON

BATTERED SPOUSE PROJECT
PO Box 2066, Jackson, TN 38302-2066
Information: (901) 645-7961 8:30am-5pm (Mon-Fri)
Contact: Tommie Moore, Paralegal
TYPE OF AGENCY: Domestic violence program; Legal services agency
SPONSORING ORGANIZATION: West Tennessee Legal Services
AREAS SERVED: McNairy
YEARS IN OPERATION: 1
ACCESSIBILITY: Wheelchair accessible
CLIENTS/SERVICES: Marital rape/sexual abuse survivors; Child victims of sexual abuse; Community education
REQUIREMENTS: Client must be income eligible

EXCHANGE CLUB—CARL PERKINS CENTER FOR THE PREVENTION OF CHILD ABUSE
PO Box 447, Jackson, TN 38302
Crisis hotline: **(901) 424-7900, (800) 522-0277 24 hrs**
Information: (901) 424-7900 8am-5pm
Contact: Pam Nash, Exec Dir
TYPE OF AGENCY: Child sexual abuse prevention program
AREAS SERVED: Madison, satellite offices in Chester, Henderson, Hardeman, Gibson
YEARS IN OPERATION: 6
ACCESSIBILITY: Wheelchair accessible
CASES SEXUAL ASSAULT/ABUSE (%): 5
CLIENTS/SERVICES: Sexual assault survivors; Marital rape/sexual abuse survivors; Adult survivors of child sexual abuse; Incest victims/survivors; Prevention program; Community education; Offender treatment program; Male survivors of sexual abuse

WO/MEN'S RESOURCE AND RAPE ASSISTANCE PROGRAM
416 E Lafayette, Jackson, TN 38301
Crisis hotline: **(901) 423-0700 24 hrs daily**
Information: (901) 423-0700 8am-5pm
Contact: Patsy Numan, Exec Dir
TYPE OF AGENCY: Rape crisis center; Domestic violence program; Child sexual abuse services; Child sexual abuse prevention program
AREAS SERVED: West Tennessee
YEARS IN OPERATION: 17
ACCESSIBILITY: Wheelchair accessible
CASES SEXUAL ASSAULT/ABUSE (%): 40
DESCRIPTION: Provides counseling, advocacy, and accompaniment services, and emergency shelter for survivors of sexual assault and domestic violence; Feminist martial arts/self-defense program; Public education
CLIENTS/SERVICES: Sexual assault survivors; Marital rape/sexual abuse survivors; Child victims of sexual abuse; Adult survivors of child sexual abuse; Incest victims/survivors; Prevention program; Community education; Adolescent survivors of sexual abuse; Male survivors of sexual abuse

JOHNSON CITY

CASA (COURT APPOINTED SPECIAL ADVOCATE)
PO Box 21820A, Johnson City, TN 37614-0002
Information: (615) 929-6651 8am-4:30pm
Contact: Charles Charlton, Reg Dir
TYPE OF AGENCY: Child sexual abuse services; Child abuse services; Child advocacy
SPONSORING ORGANIZATION: East Tennessee State University, Department of Sociology
AREAS SERVED: Washington, Sullivan
YEARS IN OPERATION: 3
ACCESSIBILITY: Wheelchair accessible
DESCRIPTION: Trained volunteers serve as advocates for children whose home placement is being decided by the juvenile court—usually as a result of abuse or neglect. Independently investigate a case by talking with the child, family members, neighbors, school officials, and others, and by reviewing all records and documents pertaining to the child. Submits

CASA (COURT APPOINTED SPECIAL ADVOCATE) (continued)
recommendations to the court as to what placement serves the interests of the child
CLIENTS/SERVICES: Child victims of sexual abuse
REQUIREMENTS: Court must appoint the advocate

WINGS (WOMEN IN NEED GROWING STRONG)
PO Box 1715, Johnson City, TN 37601-1715
Crisis hotline: **(615) 926-8901 24 hrs**
Information: (615) 926-8901 8am-5pm
Contact: Rebecca McCobin, Shelter Dir
TYPE OF AGENCY: Domestic violence program
SPONSORING ORGANIZATION: Salvation Army
AREAS SERVED: Greene, Unicoi, Carter, Washington, Sullivan
YEARS IN OPERATION: 5
CASES SEXUAL ASSAULT/ABUSE (%): 25
CLIENTS/SERVICES: Marital rape/sexual abuse survivors; Adult survivors of child sexual abuse; Incest victims/survivors

KNOXVILLE

PROJECT AGAINST SEXUAL ABUSE OF APPALACHIAN CHILDREN
2602 E 5th Ave, Knoxville, TN 37909
Information: (615) 524-2653 8:30am-5pm (Mon-Fri)
Contact: Kathryn Dean, Dir
TYPE OF AGENCY: Counseling/mental health services; Child sexual abuse services; Child sexual abuse prevention program; Consultation; Training/research
SPONSORING ORGANIZATION: Child and Family Services
AREAS SERVED: Sixteen-county area in East Tennessee
YEARS IN OPERATION: 10
ACCESSIBILITY: Wheelchair accessible
CASES SEXUAL ASSAULT/ABUSE (%): 100
DESCRIPTION: Treatment of sexually abused children and their families and adult survivors (groups for female and male survivors), including individual, group, marital, and family therapy. Counseling for adolescent sex offenders and child sexual abuse/incest offenders
CLIENTS/SERVICES: Child victims of sexual abuse; Adult survivors of child sexual abuse; Incest victims/survivors; Prevention program; Community education; Offender treatment program; Adolescent survivors of sexual abuse; Male survivors of sexual abuse
SPECIAL PROGRAMS/SERVICES: The teaching and training component of the PASAAC program is called the Knoxville Institute for Sexual Abuse Treatment Training. KISATT provides specialized training yearly to hundreds of professionals representing a range of disciplines in the coordination, investigation, and treatment of child sexual abuse. Most recently, KISATT developed a model sex abuse training package for thirty-five runaway shelters throughout the Southeastern United States. PASAAC also conducted federally-funded research on the experience of males as victims of child sexual abuse and evaluation of the relative effectiveness of prevention programs.

SEXUAL ASSAULT CRISIS CENTER
6409 Deane Hill Dr, Knoxville, TN 37919
Crisis hotline: **(615) 522-7273 24 hrs**
Information: (615) 558-9040 8:30am-5pm (Mon-Fri)
Contact: Eileen Kogen, Exec Dir
TYPE OF AGENCY: Rape crisis center
AREAS SERVED: Eastern Tennessee
YEARS IN OPERATION: 16
CASES SEXUAL ASSAULT/ABUSE (%): 100
DESCRIPTION: Comprehensive rape crisis services; Feminist martial arts/self-defense and prevention programs for children and adolescents
CLIENTS/SERVICES: Sexual assault survivors; Marital rape/sexual abuse survivors; Adult survivors of child sexual abuse; Incest victims/survivors; Prevention program; Community education; Adolescent survivors of sexual abuse; Male survivors of sexual abuse
SPECIAL PROGRAMS/SERVICES: Self-defense videotape in production. WOMANSSOURCE is a year-long series of creative healing workshops, held monthly in outdoor retreat settings, for women who are survivors of incest and child sexual abuse. Each daylong workshop focuses on creative activities that reflect themes of the specific season. Creative activities throughout the year include mask- and shield making, mandala paintings, journal writing, musical instrument and songmaking, movement exploration and dance, collage, mobiles, and stick sculpture

LAWRENCEBURG

THE SHELTER, INC
PO Box 894, Lawrenceburg, TN 38464
Crisis hotline: **(615) 762-1115 24 hrs**
Contact: Virginia Kilburn, Dir
TYPE OF AGENCY: Domestic violence program
AREAS SERVED: Lawrence, Wayne, Giles, Lewis
YEARS IN OPERATION: 3
CASES SEXUAL ASSAULT/ABUSE (%): 60
CLIENTS/SERVICES: Sexual assault survivors; Marital rape/sexual abuse survivors; Adult survivors of child sexual abuse; Incest victims/survivors; Community education

MEMPHIS

EXCHANGE CLUB—CHILD ABUSE PREVENTION CENTER
4230 Elvis Presley Blvd, No 209, Memphis, TN 38116
Crisis hotline: **(901) 332-1111 24 hrs**
Information: (901) 332-1111 8am-4:30pm
Contact: Liz Banks, Exec Dir
TYPE OF AGENCY: Child sexual abuse services; Child sexual abuse prevention program; Child abuse prevention program
AREAS SERVED: Shelby
YEARS IN OPERATION: 4
ACCESSIBILITY: Wheelchair accessible
CASES SEXUAL ASSAULT/ABUSE (%): 75
CLIENTS/SERVICES: Child victims of sexual abuse; Adult survivors of child sexual abuse; Incest victims/survivors; Prevention program; Community education; Adolescent survivors of sexual abuse; Male survivors of sexual abuse

MEMPHIS POLICE DEPARTMENT—CHILD ABUSE SQUAD
201 Poplar, Rm 11-27, Memphis, TN 38104
Crisis hotline: **(901) 529-7120 24 hrs**
Information: (901) 576-5220
Contact: Walter Crews, Capt
TYPE OF AGENCY: Victim/witness assistance program; Child sexual abuse services; Child abuse services
AREAS SERVED: Shelby
YEARS IN OPERATION: 2
ACCESSIBILITY: Wheelchair accessible; Signers for the hearing impaired
CASES SEXUAL ASSAULT/ABUSE (%): 95
CLIENTS/SERVICES: Child victims of sexual abuse; Incest victims/survivors; Prevention program; Community education; Offender treatment program; Adolescent survivors of sexual abuse; Male survivors of sexual abuse
REQUIREMENTS: Child sexual abuse: 13 and younger; 13-17 years of age if perpetrator is in custodial situation (babysitter, teacher, etc); Physical abuse if victim is hospitalized

MEMPHIS RAPE CRISIS CENTER/CHILD VICTIM ADVOCATE PROGRAM
2600 Poplar, Ste 208, Memphis, TN 38112
Crisis hotline: **(901) 528-2161 24 hrs**
Information: (901) 323-5437 24 hrs
Contact: Brenda Cassinello, Child Advocate
TYPE OF AGENCY: Rape crisis center; Child sexual abuse services
AREAS SERVED: Shelby
YEARS IN OPERATION: 12
LANGUAGES: Translators available by arrangement
ACCESSIBILITY: Wheelchair accessible; Signers for the hearing impaired
CASES SEXUAL ASSAULT/ABUSE (%): 100
DESCRIPTION: Provides comprehensive services for sexual assault/abuse victims, including crisis intervention, evidence collection, and escort services. Forensic serologist handles evidence and serves as expert witness
CLIENTS/SERVICES: Sexual assault survivors; Marital rape/sexual abuse survivors; Child victims of sexual abuse; Adult survivors of child sexual abuse; Incest victims/survivors; Community education; Adolescent survivors of sexual abuse; Male survivors of sexual abuse

MURFREESBORO

DOMESTIC VIOLENCE PROGRAM
PO Box 2652, Murfreesboro, TN 37133
Crisis hotline: **(615) 896-2012 24 hrs**
Information: (615) 896-8976 8:30am-4:30pm
Contact: Jackie Fhety, Victim Advocate
TYPE OF AGENCY: Domestic violence program
AREAS SERVED: Rutherford
YEARS IN OPERATION: 3
LANGUAGES: Interpreters available
ACCESSIBILITY: Wheelchair accessible
CLIENTS/SERVICES: Marital rape/sexual abuse survivors; Community education

RUTHERFORD COUNTY GUIDANCE CENTER/SEXUAL ABUSE TREATMENT PROGRAM
PO Box 1559, Murfreesboro, TN 37133-1559
Information: (615) 893-0770 8am-5pm (Mon-Fri)
Contact: Elise Waring-Vincent, MSSW, Sexual Abuse Prog Coord
TYPE OF AGENCY: Counseling/mental health services; Child sexual abuse services
AREAS SERVED: Rutherford, Cannon
YEARS IN OPERATION: 5
ACCESSIBILITY: Wheelchair accessible
CASES SEXUAL ASSAULT/ABUSE (%): 10
DESCRIPTION: Comprehensive community mental health center with a child sexual abuse treatment program that provides mental health treatment for the victims, perpetrators, and families within a coordinated, interagency framework
CLIENTS/SERVICES: Child victims of sexual abuse; Adult survivors of child sexual abuse; Incest victims/survivors; Offender treatment program; Adolescent survivors of sexual abuse; Male survivors of sexual abuse

NASHVILLE

COMPREHENSIVE CHILD ABUSE PROGRAM
176 Thompson Ln, Ste 100, Nashville, TN 37211
Information: (615) 333-3100 (Comprehensive Child Abuse Program); 834-3240 (Luton Mental Health Center) 8am-8pm (Mon, Tue, Wed); 8am-6pm (Thur); 8am-Noon (Fri)
Contact: Marie C Savinelli, LCSW, CCAP Coord
TYPE OF AGENCY: Counseling/mental health services; Child sexual abuse services
SPONSORING ORGANIZATION: Luton Mental Health Center
AREAS SERVED: Davidson
YEARS IN OPERATION: 3
ACCESSIBILITY: Wheelchair accessible
CASES SEXUAL ASSAULT/ABUSE (%): 100% in CCAP

COMPREHENSIVE CHILD ABUSE PROGRAM (continued)

DESCRIPTION: Comprehensive Child Abuse Program provides an array of evaluation, treatment, training, and consultation services in the area of child sexual abuse using a multidisciplinary team approach and serves victims, perpetrators, and family members. Adult Outpatient Division provides therapy for rape victims/survivors. Also provides therapy for adolescent sex offenders and batterers
CLIENTS/SERVICES: Sexual assault survivors; Marital rape/sexual abuse survivors; Child victims of sexual abuse; Adult survivors of child sexual abuse; Incest victims/survivors; Community education; Offender treatment program; Adolescent survivors of sexual abuse; Male survivors of sexual abuse
REQUIREMENTS: Adult perpetrators of children must admit to offense(s). Sliding scale fee structure is only available to residents of the catchment area

METROPOLITAN POLICE DEPARTMENT—VICTIM INTERVENTION PROGRAM
200 James Robertson Pkwy, Nashville, TN 37201
Information: (615) 742-7773 8:30am-4:30pm
Contact: Amy Griffith, Act Dir
TYPE OF AGENCY: Victim/witness assistance program
YEARS IN OPERATION: 13
ACCESSIBILITY: Signers for the hearing impaired (by arrangement)
CASES SEXUAL ASSAULT/ABUSE (%): 80-90
CLIENTS/SERVICES: Sexual assault survivors; Marital rape/sexual abuse survivors; Child victims of sexual abuse; Prevention program; Community education; Adolescent survivors of sexual abuse; Male survivors of sexual abuse

NASHVILLE COALITION ON CHILD ABUSE
2012 21st Ave S, Nashville, TN 37212
Information: (615) 385-2221 8:30am-5pm
Contact: Mary N Baker, Coord
TYPE OF AGENCY: Child sexual abuse services; Child abuse services; Interagency network
AREAS SERVED: Davidson
YEARS IN OPERATION: 1
DESCRIPTION: Collaborative, community-wide network of service agencies dedicated to strengthening interagency relationships, coordination, and communication in order to improve the services for children and families
CLIENTS/SERVICES: Community education

OASIS CENTER, INC
PO Box 121648, Nashville, TN 37212
Crisis hotline: **(615) 327-4455 24 hrs daily**
Information: (615) 329-8036 24 hrs daily
Contact: Judy Freudenthal, Counseling Dir
TYPE OF AGENCY: Counseling/mental health services; Child sexual abuse services; Child sexual abuse prevention program; Shelter; Adolescent program
AREAS SERVED: Davidson and surrounding counties
YEARS IN OPERATION: 19
ACCESSIBILITY: Wheelchair accessible; Signers for the hearing impaired (as needed)
CASES SEXUAL ASSAULT/ABUSE (%): 40-80
DESCRIPTION: Provides comprehensive services for youth and their families, with an emphasis on empowerment. Many services support youth who may be victims of sexual abuse, especially the groups for sexually abused females.
CLIENTS/SERVICES: Sexual assault survivors; Incest victims/survivors; Prevention program; Community education; Adolescent survivors of sexual abuse
REQUIREMENTS: Ages 13-17 and their families

RAPE AND SEXUAL ABUSE CENTER OF DAVIDSON COUNTY
PO Box 120831, Nashville, TN 37212
Crisis hotline: **(615) 327-1110 24 hrs**
Information: (615) 259-9055 8:30am-4:30pm
Contact: Norma Calway-Fagen, Exec Dir
TYPE OF AGENCY: Rape crisis center
AREAS SERVED: Middle TN
YEARS IN OPERATION: 11
ACCESSIBILITY: Wheelchair accessible; Signers for the hearing impaired
CASES SEXUAL ASSAULT/ABUSE (%): 100
DESCRIPTION: Provides basic services for victims of sexual assault/abuse: Support/counseling, support groups, hospital/police/DA accompaniment and witness preparation. Offender treatment programs for adolescent perpetrators and for incest offenders. Feminist martial arts/self-defense program available
CLIENTS/SERVICES: Sexual assault survivors; Marital rape/sexual abuse survivors; Child victims of sexual abuse; Adult survivors of child sexual abuse; Incest victims/survivors; Prevention program; Community education; Offender treatment program; Adolescent survivors of sexual abuse; Male survivors of sexual abuse

THE SALVATION ARMY
PO Box 24236, Nashville, TN 37215
Crisis hotline: **(615) 255-3435 24 hrs**
Information: (615) 242-0411 24 hrs
Contact: Robyn Minton, Soc Svcs Coord
TYPE OF AGENCY: Shelter
YEARS IN OPERATION: 99
ACCESSIBILITY: Wheelchair accessible
CASES SEXUAL ASSAULT/ABUSE (%): 80
CLIENTS/SERVICES: Sexual assault survivors; Marital rape/sexual abuse survivors; Child victims of sexual abuse; Adult survivors of child sexual abuse; Incest victims/survivors; Adolescent survivors of sexual abuse; Male survivors of sexual abuse

WOMEN'S COUNSELING SERVICES
115 28th Ave N, Nashville, TN 37203
Information: (615) 329-1656 24-hr answering machine
Contact: Judy Eron, LCSW
TYPE OF AGENCY: Private practice
AREAS SERVED: Davidson, Williamson, Cheatham, Dickson
YEARS IN OPERATION: 13
ACCESSIBILITY: Wheelchair accessible
CASES SEXUAL ASSAULT/ABUSE (%): 33
DESCRIPTION: Individual, family, and group services for all survivors
CLIENTS/SERVICES: Sexual assault survivors; Marital rape/sexual abuse survivors; Child victims of sexual abuse; Adult survivors of child sexual abuse; Incest victims/survivors; Adolescent survivors of sexual abuse; Male survivors of sexual abuse

NEWPORT

SAFE SPACE
PO Box 831, Newport, TN 37821
Crisis hotline: **(615) 623-3125 24 hrs**
Information: (615) 623-3125 24 hrs
Contact: Dianne Levy, Exec Dir
TYPE OF AGENCY: Domestic violence program
AREAS SERVED: Cooke, Jefferson, Sevier
YEARS IN OPERATION: 13
LANGUAGES: Spanish, German translators
ACCESSIBILITY: Signers for the hearing impaired (translator)
CASES SEXUAL ASSAULT/ABUSE (%): 50
CLIENTS/SERVICES: Marital rape/sexual abuse survivors; Adult survivors of child sexual abuse

SELMER

ADVOCATES FOR PEACEFUL HOMES
Box 1032, Selmer, TN 38375
Information: (901) 645-3505, 645-5784
Contact: Charlie Murphy, Chairman
TYPE OF AGENCY: Domestic violence program
SPONSORING ORGANIZATION: First Presbyterian Church
CLIENTS/SERVICES: Marital rape/sexual abuse survivors; Community education

TEXAS

ABILENE

THE ABILENE RAPE CRISIS CENTER
PO Box 122, Abilene, TX 79604
Crisis hotline: **(915) 677-7895 24 hrs daily**
Information: (915) 677-7895 8:30am-5pm
Contact: Judy Edwards, Dir
TYPE OF AGENCY: Rape crisis center; Child sexual abuse services; Child sexual abuse prevention program
SPONSORING ORGANIZATION: Division of the Mental Health Mental Retardation Center
AREAS SERVED: Taylor, Jones, Callahan
YEARS IN OPERATION: 11
CASES SEXUAL ASSAULT/ABUSE (%): 100
DESCRIPTION: Provides comprehensive support services for victims of sexual assault, including liaison with police, medical services, district attorney. Specialized services for children. Splits caseload with Child Protective Services
CLIENTS/SERVICES: Sexual assault survivors; Marital rape/sexual abuse survivors; Child victims of sexual abuse; Adult survivors of child sexual abuse; Incest victims/survivors; Prevention program; Community education; Adolescent survivors of sexual abuse; Male survivors of sexual abuse
SPECIAL PROGRAMS/SERVICES: WHO programs (We Help Ourselves) for preschool-12th grades emphasizing safety measures that should be taken to avoid becoming a victim of crime

NOAH PROJECT, INC
1802 Grape St, Abilene, TX 79602
Information: (915) 676-7107 24 hrs
Contact: D Foster, Prog Dir
TYPE OF AGENCY: Domestic violence program
YEARS IN OPERATION: 9
LANGUAGES: Spanish
ACCESSIBILITY: Wheelchair accessible
DESCRIPTION: Provides shelter, counseling, and referrals for survivors of family violence (sexual, physical, psychological abuse)
CLIENTS/SERVICES: Sexual assault survivors; Marital rape/sexual abuse survivors; Child victims of sexual abuse; Adult survivors of child sexual abuse; Incest victims/survivors; Community education; Adolescent survivors of sexual abuse

ALPINE

ALPINE WOMEN'S CENTER
PO Box 1470, Alpine, TX 79831
Crisis hotline: **(915) 837-2242 24 hrs**
Information: (915) 837-7254 8am-5pm (Mon-Fri)
Contact: Gaylan Corbin, Dir
TYPE OF AGENCY: Rape crisis center; Domestic violence program
AREAS SERVED: Brewster, Pecos, Presidio, Terrell, Jeff Davis
YEARS IN OPERATION: 7

LANGUAGES: Spanish
CLIENTS/SERVICES: Sexual assault survivors; Marital rape/sexual abuse survivors; Child victims of sexual abuse; Adult survivors of child sexual abuse; Prevention program; Community education; Male survivors of sexual abuse

AMARILLO

RAPE CRISIS/DOMESTIC VIOLENCE CENTER
804 S Bryan, No 214, Amarillo, TX 79106
Crisis hotline: **(806) 373-8022, 373-2787 24 hrs**
Information: (806) 373-8533 8:30am-5pm
Contact: Lori Sikes, Rape Crisis Dir
TYPE OF AGENCY: Rape crisis center; Domestic violence program
CLIENTS/SERVICES: Sexual assault survivors; Marital rape/sexual abuse survivors; Child victims of sexual abuse; Adult survivors of child sexual abuse; Incest victims/survivors; Adolescent survivors of sexual abuse; Male survivors of sexual abuse

ANGLETON

HELPLINE, INFORMATION AND REFERRAL
PO Box 909, Angleton, TX 77515
Information: (409) 849-4404 8am-4:30pm (Mon-Fri)
Contact: Esther Bernard, Comm Svcs Dir
TYPE OF AGENCY: Information and referral
SPONSORING ORGANIZATION: United Way of Brazoria County
AREAS SERVED: Brazoria
YEARS IN OPERATION: 8
LANGUAGES: Spanish
ACCESSIBILITY: Wheelchair accessible
DESCRIPTION: An information and referral service for sexually abused persons among others; Educational materials
CLIENTS/SERVICES: Sexual assault survivors

WOMEN'S CENTER OF BRAZORIA COUNTY
PO Box 476, Angleton, TX 77515
Crisis hotline: **(409) 849-5166, (800) 243-5788 24 hrs**
Information: (409) 849-9553 9am-4pm
Contact: Jan Hein, Sexual Assault Coord
TYPE OF AGENCY: Rape crisis center; Domestic violence program
AREAS SERVED: Brazoria
YEARS IN OPERATION: 5
LANGUAGES: Spanish
ACCESSIBILITY: Signers for the hearing impaired
CASES SEXUAL ASSAULT/ABUSE (%): 35
CLIENTS/SERVICES: Sexual assault survivors; Marital rape/sexual abuse survivors; Adult survivors of child sexual abuse; Prevention program; Community education; Adolescent survivors of sexual abuse; Male survivors of sexual abuse

REQUIREMENTS: For sexual assault group, client must be 18 or older
SPECIAL PROGRAMS/SERVICES: Bilingual (Spanish/English) brochure

ARLINGTON

ARLINGTON HANDICAPPED ASSOCIATION
600 New York, Arlington, TX 76010
Information: (817) 460-6691 9am-4pm
Contact: Pamela Moorman, Exec Dir
TYPE OF AGENCY: Counseling/mental health services; Child sexual abuse prevention program
AREAS SERVED: Tarrant, Dallas
YEARS IN OPERATION: 11
ACCESSIBILITY: Wheelchair accessible; Signers for the hearing impaired
CASES SEXUAL ASSAULT/ABUSE (%): 5
DESCRIPTION: Develops, defines, and implements needs of the handicapped of Arlington and surrounding areas
CLIENTS/SERVICES: Prevention program; Community education; Disabled

ARLINGTON POLICE DEPARTMENT— COMMUNITY SERVICES SECTION
PO Box 1065, Arlington, TX 76010
Information: (817) 459-5725 8am-4pm (Mon-Fri)
Contact: Sgt A Jay Six, Supv
TYPE OF AGENCY: Child sexual abuse prevention program; Rape prevention program; Acquaintance/date rape prevention program
AREAS SERVED: City of Arlington
YEARS IN OPERATION: 16
DESCRIPTION: Primary public education provider for the police department; "Stranger-danger" presentations to children; Gives rape prevention and personal safety programs to secondary school students and adults; "Date Rape" classes for secondary students; Programs for handicapped scheduled, provided the group supplies their own interpreter
CLIENTS/SERVICES: Prevention program; Community education; Disabled

TEXAS DEPARTMENT OF HUMAN SERVICES
PO Box 5128, 631 106th St, Arlington, TX 76011
Crisis hotline: **(800) 252-5400 24 hrs**
Information: (817) 649-5154 8am-5pm
Contact: Ethel B Crear, Protective Svcs to Families and Children Regional Dir
TYPE OF AGENCY: Counseling/mental health services; Child sexual abuse services; Child abuse services; Interagency network
AREAS SERVED: Dallas, Tarrant, Ellis, Kaufman, Collin, Hunt, Rockwall, Navarro, Johnson, Somervell, Denton, Grayson, Fannin, Cooke, Wise, Erath, Hood, Palo Pinto, Parker
YEARS IN OPERATION: 49
LANGUAGES: Spanish

TEXAS DEPARTMENT OF HUMAN SERVICES (continued)

ACCESSIBILITY: Wheelchair accessible; Telecommunications for the hearing impaired (TTY, TDY, etc.); Signers for the hearing impaired
CASES SEXUAL ASSAULT/ABUSE (%): 20
DESCRIPTION: Mandated by law to investigate referrals of child abuse/neglect; Provides on-going services for the entire family of sexual abuse victims; Support groups; Therapy; Casework services
CLIENTS/SERVICES: Child victims of sexual abuse; Offender treatment program; Adolescent survivors of sexual abuse
REQUIREMENTS: Referral must have been made to the agency reporting that a child has been abused/neglected for an investigation to begin
SPECIAL PROGRAMS/SERVICES: Sexual abuse group treatment program; COR (Concerned Offenders Respond), a group of adults who have successfully completed the group treatment program and help families beginning treatment deal with some of their feelings; Tarrant County Sexual Abuse Advisory Council made up of community agencies and law enforcement departments

AUSTIN

AUSTIN CHILD GUIDANCE CENTER
810 W 45th, Austin, TX 78701
Information: (512) 451-ACGC 8:30am-8:30pm
Contact: Donald J Zappone, Exec Dir
TYPE OF AGENCY: Counseling/mental health services; Child sexual abuse services
AREAS SERVED: Travis and surrounding counties
YEARS IN OPERATION: 37
LANGUAGES: Spanish
ACCESSIBILITY: Wheelchair accessible; Telecommunications for the hearing impaired (TTY, TDY, etc.); Signers for the hearing impaired
CASES SEXUAL ASSAULT/ABUSE (%): 25-33
DESCRIPTION: Promotes mental health of children and families through a multidisciplinary team; Individual, family, and group therapy; Psychiatric and psychological examinations
CLIENTS/SERVICES: Child victims of sexual abuse; Community education
REQUIREMENTS: Must be 18 or younger

AUSTIN POLICE DEPARTMENT—VICTIM SERVICES DIVISION
715 E 8th St, Austin, TX 78701
Crisis hotline: **911 request "Crisis team" 24 hrs**
Information: (512) 480-5037 8am-7pm (Mon-Fri); 10am-6pm (Sat, Sun)
Contact: Ann Hutchison McDavid, Div Mgr
TYPE OF AGENCY: Domestic violence program; Victim/witness assistance program
SPONSORING ORGANIZATION: City of Austin
AREAS SERVED: Travis, surrounding counties by request
YEARS IN OPERATION: 9
LANGUAGES: Spanish
ACCESSIBILITY: Wheelchair accessible; Telecommunications for the hearing impaired (TTY, TDY, etc.) (through 911); Signers for the hearing impaired (by arrangement)
CASES SEXUAL ASSAULT/ABUSE (%): 16
DESCRIPTION: Provides crisis intervention, short-term counseling, referral, education, advocacy, support for crime victims; Counseling for battered women; Specialized child abuse counselors obtain videotape statements from child victims; Crisis team available nights at scene of crime or victim's home; Crisis counseling and referrals available for juvenile/adolescent sex offenders, adult sex offenders, incest offenders, and batterers
CLIENTS/SERVICES: Sexual assault survivors; Marital rape/sexual abuse survivors; Child victims of sexual abuse; Adult survivors of child sexual abuse; Incest victims/survivors; Prevention program; Community education; Adolescent survivors of sexual abuse; Male survivors of sexual abuse; Prostitutes
SPECIAL PROGRAMS/SERVICES: HOPE program—Counseling and coordination of community services for prostitutes; Creation of "Critical Incident" team with school district; Bilingual (Spanish/English) brochure available

AUSTIN PSYCHOTHERAPY ASSOCIATES
1001 W 31st, Ste 200, Austin, TX 78705
Information: (512) 459-5431
Contact: Marylein Davies, CSW-ACP
TYPE OF AGENCY: Private practice
AREAS SERVED: Travis and surrounding areas
YEARS IN OPERATION: 8
ACCESSIBILITY: Wheelchair accessible; Telecommunications for the hearing impaired (TTY, TDY, etc.); Signers for the hearing impaired
CASES SEXUAL ASSAULT/ABUSE (%): 40-60
DESCRIPTION: Serves adults and children survivors of sexual abuse and other family violence
CLIENTS/SERVICES: Sexual assault survivors; Marital rape/sexual abuse survivors; Child victims of sexual abuse; Adult survivors of child sexual abuse; Incest victims/survivors; Community education; Adolescent survivors of sexual abuse; Healing
REQUIREMENTS: Ages 4 and older
SPECIAL PROGRAMS/SERVICES: Use of Gestalt techniques, art therapy, games, written assignments, and role play (preparation for confrontation)

AUSTIN RAPE CRISIS CENTER
4326 James Casey, Austin, TX 78745
Crisis hotline: **(512) 440-7273 24 hrs**
Information: (512) 445-5776, 440-7297 8am-5:30pm
Contact: Sue Wendelin, Direct Svcs Coord
TYPE OF AGENCY: Rape crisis center; Acquaintance/date rape prevention program
AREAS SERVED: Travis
YEARS IN OPERATION: 14
LANGUAGES: Spanish
ACCESSIBILITY: Signers for the hearing impaired
CASES SEXUAL ASSAULT/ABUSE (%): 76
DESCRIPTION: Provides survivors of sexual assault with 24-hour hotline, counseling, advocacy, and support groups for incest survivors, male loved ones of survivors, Spanish-speaking women, and teenagers
CLIENTS/SERVICES: Sexual assault survivors; Marital rape/sexual abuse survivors; Child victims of sexual abuse; Incest victims/survivors; Prevention program; Community education; Adolescent survivors of sexual abuse; Male survivors of sexual abuse; Sexual harassment; Publications/media
SPECIAL PROGRAMS/SERVICES: Works with Texas NOW on offering a support group for victims of sexual harassment. Received a grant to do a videotape on violence-free relationships for middle-school (6-9th grades) students (rape prevention/avoidance)

CHILD AND FAMILY SERVICE, INC
2001 Chicon, Austin, TX 78722
Information: (512) 478-1648 8:30am-8:30pm (Mon-Thur); 8:30am-5pm (Fri)
Contact: Patti R Ricker, CSW/ACP
TYPE OF AGENCY: Counseling/mental health services
AREAS SERVED: Travis
LANGUAGES: Spanish
ACCESSIBILITY: Wheelchair accessible
CLIENTS/SERVICES: Sexual assault survivors; Marital rape/sexual abuse survivors; Child victims of sexual abuse; Adult survivors of child sexual abuse; Incest victims/survivors; Community education; Adolescent survivors of sexual abuse; Male survivors of sexual abuse
SPECIAL PROGRAMS/SERVICES: 8-week groups "Beginning to Heal" for incest survivors; Long term group psychotherapy for incest survivors

DAYGLO FAMILY TREATMENT PROGRAM
PO Box 13345, Austin, TX 78711
Information: (512) 479-6158 9am-5pm
Contact: Ann Stanley, Unit Mgr
TYPE OF AGENCY: Counseling/mental health services; Child sexual abuse services; Child sexual abuse prevention program; Child abuse services
AREAS SERVED: Travis, Williams, Bastrop, Hays, Caldwell, Burnet
YEARS IN OPERATION: 17
LANGUAGES: Spanish
CASES SEXUAL ASSAULT/ABUSE (%): 80
DESCRIPTION: Treatment groups for preschoolers, outdoor group therapy for children ages 7 to 12, sexual abuse group for female teens, group for mothers of sexually abused children, group for child sexual abuse/incest offenders
CLIENTS/SERVICES: Child victims of sexual abuse; Adult survivors of child sexual abuse; Incest victims/survivors; Prevention program; Community education; Offender treatment program; Adolescent survivors of sexual abuse; Male survivors of sexual abuse; Preschoolers
REQUIREMENTS: Sliding scale fee
SPECIAL PROGRAMS/SERVICES: Dayglo Zilker Park Program offers intensive outdoor treatment with noncompetitive activities in both large and small groups. Children work on issues related to their abuse and peer relations. Dayglo Preschool Program offers group therapy for preschool-aged victims of sexual abuse

FAMILY DEVELOPMENT CENTER (FDC)
PO Box 1748, Austin, TX 78767
Information: (512) 473-9220 8am-5pm
Contact: Cherlyn Townsend, Victim Witness Dir
TYPE OF AGENCY: Victim/witness assistance program; Child sexual abuse services
SPONSORING ORGANIZATION: Travis County District Attorney
AREAS SERVED: Travis, Bastrop, Williamson
YEARS IN OPERATION: 1
LANGUAGES: Spanish
ACCESSIBILITY: Signers for the hearing impaired
CASES SEXUAL ASSAULT/ABUSE (%): 100
DESCRIPTION: Provides assessment, referral, group therapy for families of incest, including incest offenders; Support groups for male survivors
CLIENTS/SERVICES: Child victims of sexual abuse; Adult survivors of child sexual abuse; Incest victims/survivors; Community education; Offender treatment program; Adolescent survivors of sexual abuse; Male survivors of sexual abuse
REQUIREMENTS: Incest must be present

PEBBLE PROJECT
1100 W 31st, Austin, TX 78705
Information: (512) 454-4722 8am-5pm
TYPE OF AGENCY: Child sexual abuse prevention program; Child Assault Prevention (CAP) Project
DESCRIPTION: Sponsors Child Assault Prevention (CAP) Project; Facilitates groups in the schools for sexually and physically abused children
CLIENTS/SERVICES: Child victims of sexual abuse; Prevention program; Community education

TRAVIS COUNTY DISTRICT ATTORNEY'S OFFICE—VICTIM/WITNESS PROGRAM
PO Box 1748, Austin, TX 78767
Information: (512) 473-9449
Contact: Beth Ann Larsen, Victim Witness Advocate
TYPE OF AGENCY: Victim/witness assistance program
AREAS SERVED: Travis
CLIENTS/SERVICES: Sexual assault survivors

Austin

WOMEN'S COUNSELING AND RESOURCE CENTER
2330 Guadalupe, Austin, TX 78705
Information: (512) 472-3053, 472-2064 9am-7pm (Mon-Thu); 9am-4pm (Fri)
Contact: Micki O'Brien, Dir
TYPE OF AGENCY: Counseling/mental health services
SPONSORING ORGANIZATION: University YWCA
AREAS SERVED: Travis
YEARS IN OPERATION: 15
LANGUAGES: Spanish
CASES SEXUAL ASSAULT/ABUSE (%): 10-25
DESCRIPTION: Low cost, short-term counseling for women and couples; Specializes in suicide and crisis intervention; Staff is trained in working with sexual assault survivors and in treating adult survivors of incest and/or abuse. Also offers groups for survivors of childhood abuse and dysfunctional families and assault trauma
CLIENTS/SERVICES: Sexual assault survivors; Marital rape/sexual abuse survivors; Adult survivors of child sexual abuse; Incest victims/survivors
REQUIREMENTS: 18 or older

YOUTH AND FAMILY RESOURCE CENTER
3708-B S 2nd St, Austin, TX 78704
Crisis hotline: **(512) 441-8336 24 hrs**
Information: (512) 447-5639 9am-6pm
Contact: Bill Wren, YFRC Coord
TYPE OF AGENCY: Counseling/mental health services; Child sexual abuse services; Shelter; Adolescent program
SPONSORING ORGANIZATION: Middle Earth Unlimited, Inc
AREAS SERVED: Travis and surrounding areas
YEARS IN OPERATION: 5
LANGUAGES: Spanish
ACCESSIBILITY: Wheelchair accessible
CASES SEXUAL ASSAULT/ABUSE (%): 70
DESCRIPTION: Provides crisis intervention services for youth and their families; Emergency shelter for youth; Crisis counseling; Psychotherapy; Life skills training
CLIENTS/SERVICES: Child victims of sexual abuse; Incest victims/survivors; Prevention program; Community education; Adolescent survivors of sexual abuse
REQUIREMENTS: For shelter or counseling services must be aged 10-17; For independent living must be ages 16-21

BASTROP

FAMILY CRISIS CENTER
PO Box 736, Bastrop, TX 78602
Crisis hotline: **(512) 321-7755 24 hrs**
Information: (512) 321-7760 8am-5pm
Contact: Debbie Bresette, Exec Dir
TYPE OF AGENCY: Rape crisis center; Domestic violence program; Child sexual abuse prevention program; Adolescent program
AREAS SERVED: Bastrop, Fayette, Lee
YEARS IN OPERATION: 5
LANGUAGES: Spanish, German
ACCESSIBILITY: Signers for the hearing impaired
CASES SEXUAL ASSAULT/ABUSE (%): 90
DESCRIPTION: Services for survivors of sexual assault and domestic violence; Support groups for male and female survivors of sexual assault/abuse; Teen hotline; Child Assault Prevention Program
CLIENTS/SERVICES: Sexual assault survivors; Marital rape/sexual abuse survivors; Child victims of sexual abuse; Adult survivors of child sexual abuse; Incest victims/survivors; Prevention program; Community education; Adolescent survivors of sexual abuse; Male survivors of sexual abuse

BAY CITY

MATAGORDA COUNTY WOMEN'S CRISIS CENTER
PO Box 1820, Bay City, TX 77414
Crisis hotline: **(409) 245-9299, (800) 451-9235 24 hrs**
Information: (409) 245-9109 8am-5pm
Contact: Jennifer Weldon, Dir
TYPE OF AGENCY: Rape crisis center; Domestic violence program
CLIENTS/SERVICES: Sexual assault survivors; Marital rape/sexual abuse survivors; Child victims of sexual abuse; Adult survivors of child sexual abuse; Incest victims/survivors; Prevention program; Community education; Adolescent survivors of sexual abuse; Male survivors of sexual abuse

BAYTOWN

BAYTOWN AREA WOMEN'S CENTER
PO Box 3735, Baytown, TX 77522
Crisis hotline: **(713) 422-2292 24 hrs**
Information: (713) 427-2421, 422-9173 8am-5pm (Mon-Fri)
Contact: Rebecca Jasso, Exec Dir; Karen Branson, CSW, Outreach Coord
TYPE OF AGENCY: Rape crisis center; Domestic violence program; Child sexual abuse services
AREAS SERVED: Harris, Liberty, Chambers
YEARS IN OPERATION: 6
LANGUAGES: Spanish, French
ACCESSIBILITY: Wheelchair accessible
CASES SEXUAL ASSAULT/ABUSE (%): 50
CLIENTS/SERVICES: Sexual assault survivors; Marital rape/sexual abuse survivors; Child victims of sexual abuse; Adult survivors of child sexual abuse; Incest victims/survivors; Prevention program; Community education; Adolescent survivors of sexual abuse; Male survivors of sexual abuse

BEAUMONT

RAPE AND SUICIDE CRISIS OF SOUTHEAST TEXAS, INC
PO Box 5011, Beaumont, TX 77706
Crisis hotline: **(409) 835-3355 (collect calls accepted)**
Information: (409) 832-6530
Contact: Marty Belt
TYPE OF AGENCY: Rape crisis center
CLIENTS/SERVICES: Sexual assault survivors

BIG SPRING

RAPE CRISIS/VICTIM SERVICES
PO Box 1693, Big Spring, TX 79721-1693
Crisis hotline: **(915) 263-3312 24 hrs**
Information: (915) 263-3312, 267-3626 24 hrs
Contact: Cecelia McKenzie, Exec Dir
TYPE OF AGENCY: Rape crisis center; Victim/witness assistance program
AREAS SERVED: Howard, Martin, Borden, Glasscock, Mitchell
YEARS IN OPERATION: 4
LANGUAGES: Spanish, Sign
ACCESSIBILITY: Wheelchair accessible; Telecommunications for the hearing impaired (TTY, TDY, etc.); Signers for the hearing impaired
CASES SEXUAL ASSAULT/ABUSE (%): 20-25
DESCRIPTION: Provides crisis intervention and other services for sexual assault/abuse victims and victims of other crimes
CLIENTS/SERVICES: Sexual assault survivors; Marital rape/sexual abuse survivors; Child victims of sexual abuse; Adult survivors of child sexual abuse; Incest victims/survivors; Prevention program; Community education; Adolescent survivors of sexual abuse; Male survivors of sexual abuse

BROWNSVILLE

CAMERON COUNTY DISTRICT ATTORNEY'S OFFICE—VICTIM ASSISTANCE PROGRAM
974 E Harrison St, Brownsville, TX 78520
Information: (512) 544-0849 8am-5pm
Contact: Carmen Robles, Victim Assistance Coord
TYPE OF AGENCY: Victim/witness assistance program
AREAS SERVED: Cameron
YEARS IN OPERATION: 3
LANGUAGES: Spanish
CASES SEXUAL ASSAULT/ABUSE (%): 12
CLIENTS/SERVICES: Sexual assault survivors; Marital rape/sexual abuse survivors; Child victims of sexual abuse; Adult survivors of child sexual abuse; Incest victims/survivors

BRYAN

BRAZOS COUNTY RAPE CRISIS CENTER, INC
PO Box 3082, Bryan, TX 77805
Crisis hotline: **(409) 779-7273 24 hrs daily**
Information: (409) 779-0041 8am-5pm (Mon-Fri)
Contact: Linda Castoria, Exec Dir
TYPE OF AGENCY: Rape crisis center; Child sexual abuse services; Child sexual abuse prevention program; Private practice; Acquaintance/date rape prevention program
AREAS SERVED: Brazos, Robertson, Burleson
YEARS IN OPERATION: 4½
LANGUAGES: Spanish
ACCESSIBILITY: Wheelchair accessible; Signers for the hearing impaired
CASES SEXUAL ASSAULT/ABUSE (%): 100
DESCRIPTION: Provides support/counseling for survivors of sexual assault, one-to-one and group; Escort service to hospitals, police, and court. Feminist martial arts/self-defense program available. Support group for adult female survivors and separate group for family members and friends of survivors
CLIENTS/SERVICES: Sexual assault survivors; Marital rape/sexual abuse survivors; Child victims of sexual abuse; Adult survivors of child sexual abuse; Incest victims/survivors; Prevention program; Community education; Adolescent survivors of sexual abuse; Male survivors of sexual abuse
SPECIAL PROGRAMS/SERVICES: Date rape presentation (film and skit) for adolescents

PHOEBE'S HOME
PO Box 3490, Bryan, TX 77805
Crisis hotline: **(409) 775-5355 24 hrs daily**
Information: (409) 823-2471 8:30am-5pm (Mon-Fri)
Contact: Liz Jackson, Admin
TYPE OF AGENCY: Domestic violence program
SPONSORING ORGANIZATION: Twin City Mission
AREAS SERVED: Brazis, Burleson, Grimes, Robertson¹
YEARS IN OPERATION: 9
LANGUAGES: Spanish
ACCESSIBILITY: Wheelchair accessible
DESCRIPTION: Serves battered women and their children. Many battered women's children have been sexually abused, and many of the women were sexually molested as children. Treatment for batterers
CLIENTS/SERVICES: Sexual assault survivors; Marital rape/sexual abuse survivors; Child victims of sexual abuse; Adult survivors of child sexual abuse; Incest victims/survivors; Community education

CLEBURNE

JOHNSON COUNTY FAMILY CRISIS CENTER
PO Box 43, Cleburne, TX 76033
Crisis hotline: **(817) 641-2332 24 hrs**
Information: (817) 641-2332 8am-5pm
Contact: Fran Pansini, Dir
TYPE OF AGENCY: Rape crisis center; Domestic violence program
AREAS SERVED: Johnson, Somervell, Hood, Hill
YEARS IN OPERATION: 5
LANGUAGES: Spanish
CASES SEXUAL ASSAULT/ABUSE (%): 50
DESCRIPTION: 24-hour rape crisis/family crisis hotlines; Individual and group peer/professional counseling; Female and male sexual assault and incest victims support groups; Anger control; Grief recovery; Assertiveness training; Shelter for victims of violence; Treatment for batterers
CLIENTS/SERVICES: Sexual assault survivors; Marital rape/sexual abuse survivors; Child victims of sexual abuse; Adult survivors of child sexual abuse; Incest victims/survivors; Prevention program; Community education; Adolescent survivors of sexual abuse; Male survivors of sexual abuse

CORPUS CHRISTI

CRISIS SERVICES
4906-B Everhart, Corpus Christi, TX 78411
Crisis hotline: **(512) 993-7410 24 hrs**
Information: (512) 993-7416 8am-5pm (Mon-Fri)
Contact: Becky Barker, Sexual Assault Prog Coord
TYPE OF AGENCY: Victim/witness assistance program; Counseling/mental health services; Child sexual abuse services; Child sexual abuse prevention program
AREAS SERVED: Nueces, Bee, San Patricio, Jim Wells, Kleberg, Aransas
YEARS IN OPERATION: 4
ACCESSIBILITY: Wheelchair accessible; Telecommunications for the hearing impaired (TTY, TDY, etc.); Signers for the hearing impaired (by arrangement)
CASES SEXUAL ASSAULT/ABUSE (%): 100
DESCRIPTION: Individual and group counseling for victims; Escort to hospital, police department, district attorney's office, and court; Witness preparation for court testimony
CLIENTS/SERVICES: Sexual assault survivors; Marital rape/sexual abuse survivors; Child victims of sexual abuse; Adult survivors of child sexual abuse; Incest victims/survivors; Prevention program; Community education; Adolescent survivors of sexual abuse; Male survivors of sexual abuse

NUECES COUNTY DISTRICT ATTORNEY—VICTIM/WITNESS ASSISTANCE
901 Leopard St, Corpus Christi, TX 78404
Information: (512) 888-0410 8am-5pm
Contact: Rosa Maria Cervantes
TYPE OF AGENCY: Victim/witness assistance program
AREAS SERVED: Nueces
YEARS IN OPERATION: 4
LANGUAGES: Spanish
ACCESSIBILITY: Wheelchair accessible
CASES SEXUAL ASSAULT/ABUSE (%): 10
CLIENTS/SERVICES: Sexual assault survivors; Marital rape/sexual abuse survivors; Child victims of sexual abuse; Community education

DALLAS

DALLAS COUNTY RAPE CRISIS AND CHILD SEXUAL ABUSE CENTER
PO Box 35728, Dallas, TX 75235
Crisis hotline: **(214) 653-8740 24 hrs**
Information: (214) 653-8740 8am-5pm (Mon-Fri)
Contact: Gail B Inman, MA, Asst Staff Coord
TYPE OF AGENCY: Rape crisis center; Child sexual abuse services; Child sexual abuse prevention program; Interagency network
AREAS SERVED: Dallas
YEARS IN OPERATION: 14
LANGUAGES: Spanish; blind and deaf interpreters by request
ACCESSIBILITY: Wheelchair accessible; Signers for the hearing impaired
CASES SEXUAL ASSAULT/ABUSE (%): 100
DESCRIPTION: Criminal justice system integration and support; Assist victims, family and friends to return to pre-assault functioning and recovery; Serves as a liaison and training tool for the criminal justice system, the community, and other professionals; Provides feminist martial arts/self-defense program
CLIENTS/SERVICES: Sexual assault survivors; Marital rape/sexual abuse survivors; Child victims of sexual abuse; Adult survivors of child sexual abuse; Incest victims/survivors; Prevention program; Community education; Adolescent survivors of sexual abuse; Male survivors of sexual abuse; Publications/media
SPECIAL PROGRAMS/SERVICES: Member of Sexual Assault Interagency Council of Dallas Metroplex with DHS, all area police departments, District Attorney's office, offender treatment services, victim advocate groups, hospitals. Peer-counseling training tape interviews with victims.

FAMILY PSYCHOLOGY INSTITUTE OF DALLAS
3798 Forest Ln, Ste 2, Dallas, TX 75244
Information: (214) 350-6537 24 hrs
Contact: Robert P Littlefield, PhD, Psychologist; Sue James, MS, Clinical Assoc
TYPE OF AGENCY: Private practice
AREAS SERVED: Dallas, Denton, Collin, Tarrant
YEARS IN OPERATION: 12
ACCESSIBILITY: Wheelchair accessible
CASES SEXUAL ASSAULT/ABUSE (%): 15
DESCRIPTION: Family systems approach to treating child sexual abuse; Individual and group therapy for child sexual abuse offenders, incest offenders, and batterers
CLIENTS/SERVICES: Sexual assault survivors; Marital rape/sexual abuse survivors; Child victims of sexual abuse; Adult survivors of child sexual abuse; Incest victims/survivors; Community education; Offender treatment program; Adolescent survivors of sexual abuse; Male survivors of sexual abuse

INCEST RECOVERY ASSOCIATION
6200 N Central Expressway, Ste 209, Dallas, TX 75206
Information: (214) 373-6607 9am-5pm (Mon-Fri)
Contact: Alice A Zaccarello, Exec Dir
TYPE OF AGENCY: Counseling/mental health services
AREAS SERVED: Dallas and surrounding counties
YEARS IN OPERATION: 5
ACCESSIBILITY: Wheelchair accessible
CASES SEXUAL ASSAULT/ABUSE (%): 100
DESCRIPTION: Provides services for adult survivors of childhood incest; Group therapy for adult and adolescent female and male survivors
CLIENTS/SERVICES: Adult survivors of child sexual abuse; Incest victims/survivors; Community education; Adolescent survivors of sexual abuse; Male survivors of sexual abuse
REQUIREMENTS: For adolescent program must be between 10 and 17; Adult program must be 18 or older

MENTAL HEALTH ASSOCIATION OF DALLAS COUNTY
2500 Maple Ave, Dallas, TX 75201-1998
Information: (214) 871-2420 8:30am-8pm
Contact: C Dale McEowen, Asst Dir
TYPE OF AGENCY: Counseling/mental health services; Child sexual abuse prevention program; Child abuse services
AREAS SERVED: 42
LANGUAGES: Spanish
CASES SEXUAL ASSAULT/ABUSE (%): 10
CLIENTS/SERVICES: Prevention program; Community education
SPECIAL PROGRAMS/SERVICES: The WHO (We Help Ourselves) program is in over 95 cities nationwide. It is presented in educational settings from preschool to college. It helps youth have a plan for personal safety, know how to respond to difficult or uncomfortable situations, and teaches them to ask for help from trusted adults. It addresses physical, sexual, and emotional abuse, street danger, home safety, peer pressure, and other possible forms of victimization while building self-esteem. Usually the program is delivered through trained counselors within the school system. There is a preschool program, along with K-3rd, 4-6th, 7-9th, 10-12th grades, and college program.

PARKLAND MEMORIAL HOSPITAL
5201 Harry Hines Blvd, Dallas, TX 76039
Crisis hotline: **(214) 590-8000 24 hrs**
Contact: Dr Irving Stone, Dir of Evidence Collection
TYPE OF AGENCY: Hospital/medical center
SPONSORING ORGANIZATION: Dallas County Hospital
AREAS SERVED: Dallas
LANGUAGES: Spanish translator available by request
ACCESSIBILITY: Wheelchair accessible; Signers for the hearing impaired
DESCRIPTION: Provides rape examination and evidence collection (under contract with Dallas County); Works with Rape Crisis Center in individual and family counseling for sexual assault victims
CLIENTS/SERVICES: Sexual assault survivors; Marital rape/sexual abuse survivors; Child victims of sexual abuse
REQUIREMENTS: Client must file charges

SOUTHERN METHODIST UNIVERSITY—HUMAN RESOURCE WOMEN'S CENTER
Box 172, Southern Methodist University, Dallas, TX 75275
Information: (214) 987-4997 8:30am-5pm (Mon-Fri)
Contact: Lindley Doran, Dir
TYPE OF AGENCY: College/university-based services
SPONSORING ORGANIZATION: Southern Methodist University
YEARS IN OPERATION: 14
CASES SEXUAL ASSAULT/ABUSE (%): 75
DESCRIPTION: Counseling; Support; Information; Referrals; Feminist martial arts/self-defense available
CLIENTS/SERVICES: Sexual assault survivors; Marital rape/sexual abuse survivors; Adult survivors of child sexual abuse; Incest victims/survivors; Prevention program; Adolescent survivors of sexual abuse; Male survivors of sexual abuse; Sexual harassment
REQUIREMENTS: Must be an SMU student, faculty or staff member

VICTIMS OUTREACH
PO Box 515727, Dallas, TX 75251-5727
Crisis hotline: **(214) 233-5184 24 hrs**
Information: (214) 233-5184 9am-5pm (Mon-Fri)
Contact: Patricia A (Patsy) Day, Exec Dir
TYPE OF AGENCY: Victim/witness assistance program
AREAS SERVED: Dallas, Collin, Denton, Ellis, Hunt, Kaufman, Eastern Tarrant
YEARS IN OPERATION: 2
LANGUAGES: Spanish by arrangement
ACCESSIBILITY: Wheelchair accessible; Signers for the hearing impaired
CASES SEXUAL ASSAULT/ABUSE (%): 13

VICTIMS OUTREACH (continued)

DESCRIPTION: Comprehensive services available for victims, families, friends, and survivors of violent crime, ages 12 and older as an adjunct to crisis intervention and counseling offered by Rape Crisis and Child Sexual Abuse Center; Support groups for male and female survivors
CLIENTS/SERVICES: Sexual assault survivors; Marital rape/sexual abuse survivors; Adult survivors of child sexual abuse; Incest victims/survivors; Community education; Adolescent survivors of sexual abuse; Male survivors of sexual abuse
REQUIREMENTS: Must be 12 or older
SPECIAL PROGRAMS/SERVICES: Beginning an areawide child exploitation network of law enforcement, prosecutors, mental health, and victim assistance providers

YWCA WOMEN'S RESOURCE CENTER
4621 Ross Ave, Dallas, TX 75204
Information: (214) 821-9595 9am-5pm
Contact: Susan Lauterbach, Prog Dir
TYPE OF AGENCY: Counseling/mental health services
AREAS SERVED: Dallas
YEARS IN OPERATION: 10
LANGUAGES: Spanish
ACCESSIBILITY: Wheelchair accessible
CASES SEXUAL ASSAULT/ABUSE (%): 18
DESCRIPTION: Individual and group support counseling; Alcohol/drug abuse counseling; Legal counseling; Employment counseling
CLIENTS/SERVICES: Sexual assault survivors; Marital rape/sexual abuse survivors; Adult survivors of child sexual abuse; Incest victims/survivors; Community education; Adolescent survivors of sexual abuse; Male survivors of sexual abuse
REQUIREMENTS: Sliding fee scale

DENTON

DENTON COUNTY FRIENDS OF THE FAMILY, INC
PO Box 623, Denton, TX 76202
Crisis hotline: **(817) 382-7273 24 hrs**
Information: (817) 387-5131 24 hrs
Contact: Linda Schubert, Exec Dir
TYPE OF AGENCY: Rape crisis center; Domestic violence program; Child sexual abuse services
AREAS SERVED: Denton, Wise, Cooke, Collin
YEARS IN OPERATION: 8
LANGUAGES: Spanish, Chinese
ACCESSIBILITY: Wheelchair accessible
CASES SEXUAL ASSAULT/ABUSE (%): 50
DESCRIPTION: Shelter and support services for victims of family violence, sexual assault, and/or child sexual abuse; Denton and Lewisville outreach service centers for counseling; Sexual harassment services; Support groups for male survivors; Individual and group therapy for batterers
CLIENTS/SERVICES: Sexual assault survivors; Marital rape/sexual abuse survivors; Child victims of sexual abuse; Adult survivors of child sexual abuse; Incest victims/survivors; Prevention program; Community education; Adolescent survivors of sexual abuse; Male survivors of sexual abuse; Sexual harassment

EL PASO

DISTRICT ATTORNEY'S OFFICE—VICTIM WITNESS ASSISTANCE PROGRAM
303 City-County Bldg, El Paso, TX 79901
Crisis hotline: **(915) 546-2091 8am-5pm**
Information: (915) 546-2091 8am-5pm
Contact: Jesse Carrasco, Victim/Witness Coord
TYPE OF AGENCY: Victim/witness assistance program
AREAS SERVED: El Paso
YEARS IN OPERATION: 5
LANGUAGES: Spanish
ACCESSIBILITY: Wheelchair accessible
CASES SEXUAL ASSAULT/ABUSE (%): 10
CLIENTS/SERVICES: Sexual assault survivors; Child victims of sexual abuse; Community education

EL PASO RAPE CRISIS SERVICES
PO Box 9997, El Paso, TX 79990
Crisis hotline: **(915) 779-1800 24 hrs**
Information: (915) 779-7130 8am-5pm
Contact: Aracelis Turner, Rape Crisis Supv
TYPE OF AGENCY: Rape crisis center
SPONSORING ORGANIZATION: Life Management Center
AREAS SERVED: El Paso
YEARS IN OPERATION: 14
LANGUAGES: Spanish
ACCESSIBILITY: Telecommunications for the hearing impaired (TTY, TDY, etc.)
CASES SEXUAL ASSAULT/ABUSE (%): 100
DESCRIPTION: Provides crisis intervention for victims of sexual assault and their families at the hospital and throughout the legal processes. Offers support groups for female and male survivors.
CLIENTS/SERVICES: Sexual assault survivors; Marital rape/sexual abuse survivors; Child victims of sexual abuse; Adult survivors of child sexual abuse; Incest victims/survivors; Prevention program; Community education; Adolescent survivors of sexual abuse; Male survivors of sexual abuse

SEXUAL ABUSE TREATMENT CENTER
1733 Curie, Ste 204, El Paso, TX 79902
Information: (915) 542-1582 Hours by appointment, evening and weekend hrs available; Available 24 hrs for emergencies
Contact: Norma W Reed, Clinical Soc Wkr
TYPE OF AGENCY: Private practice
AREAS SERVED: El Paso, TX; Dona Ana, NM
YEARS IN OPERATION: 4
LANGUAGES: Spanish
ACCESSIBILITY: Wheelchair accessible; Signers for the hearing impaired
CASES SEXUAL ASSAULT/ABUSE (%): 75
DESCRIPTION: Counseling for survivors and offenders—rapists and child sexual abuse/incest offenders
CLIENTS/SERVICES: Sexual assault survivors; Marital rape/sexual abuse survivors; Child victims of sexual abuse; Adult survivors of child sexual abuse; Incest victims/survivors; Offender treatment program; Adolescent survivors of sexual abuse; Male survivors of sexual abuse

FORT WORTH

DISTRICT ATTORNEY—VICTIM ASSISTANCE
200 W Belknap, Fort Worth, TX 76196-0201
Information: (817) 877-2740 7:45am-4:45pm (Mon-Fri)
Contact: Shari Shanafelt, Cir
TYPE OF AGENCY: Victim/witness assistance program
AREAS SERVED: Tarrant
YEARS IN OPERATION: 4
LANGUAGES: Spanish
CLIENTS/SERVICES: Sexual assault survivors; Marital rape/sexual abuse survivors; Child victims of sexual abuse; Community education
REQUIREMENTS: Client must file charges; Services are extended to felony crime victims where an offender is charged and a case is accepted for filing by the District Attorney's Office

FORT WORTH POLICE DEPARTMENT—CRIME PREVENTION UNIT
925 Taylor St, Fort Worth, TX 76102
Information: (817) 870-6600 8am-5pm (Mon-Fri)
Contact: Tim Ellis, Sgt
TYPE OF AGENCY: Victim/witness assistance program; Crime prevention unit; Child abuse prevention program; Rape prevention program; Acquaintance/date rape prevention program
AREAS SERVED: Tarrant
YEARS IN OPERATION: 20
LANGUAGES: Spanish
DESCRIPTION: Educational arm for the police department; Serves as a liaison between citizens and the police department; Education and training on rape, date rape, and risk reducers; Provides self-protection program and brochure for women; Child abuse prevention program for children; Acquaintance rape prevention program for high school and university students
CLIENTS/SERVICES: Prevention program; Community education

MICSAIT PROGRAM (MULTIDISCIPLINARY INSTITUTE FOR CHILD SEXUAL ABUSE INTERVENTION AND TREATMENT)
4801 Marine Creek Pkwy, Fort Worth, TX 76179
Information: (817) 232-7758 8am-9pm (CST)
Contact: Jane D Bingham, Asst Dean/Prog Coord
TYPE OF AGENCY: Community college; Training/research
SPONSORING ORGANIZATION: Tarrant County Junior College
AREAS SERVED: Statewide
YEARS IN OPERATION: 5
ACCESSIBILITY: Wheelchair accessible; Signers for the hearing impaired
DESCRIPTION: Statewide training facility for professionals involved in the investigation, intervention, or treatment of child sexual abuse, including law enforcement, child protective services, victim witness programs, probation, mental health, and medical fields. Basic curriculum is a weeklong seminar, including such topics as overview of child sexual abuse, family dynamics in incest cases, dynamics and typology of the offender, investigation and interviewing approach in cases of child sexual abuse, the role of criminal courts, case preparation for court proceedings, treatment referrals and modalities. Advanced workshops (2 days in length) are presented throughout the year. An annual statewide conference brings in national experts
CLIENTS/SERVICES: Community education; Adolescent survivors of sexual abuse

PARENTING GUIDANCE CENTER
2928 W 5th St, Fort Worth, TX 76107
Information: (817) 332-6348 8:30am-9pm (Mon-Thu); 8:30am-5pm (Fri)
Contact: Barney Hisanaga, Clinical Dir
TYPE OF AGENCY: Counseling/mental health services; Child sexual abuse services; Child abuse services; Child abuse prevention program
AREAS SERVED: Tarrant
YEARS IN OPERATION: 13
LANGUAGES: Spanish
ACCESSIBILITY: Wheelchair accessible
CASES SEXUAL ASSAULT/ABUSE (%): 25
DESCRIPTION: Prevention of child abuse and neglect; Promotion of positive parenting skills; Individual, group, and family counseling; Play therapy for children; Community education, Warm Line (817) 332-6399 from noon to 3pm (Mon-Fri) on parenting issues
CLIENTS/SERVICES: Child victims of sexual abuse; Adult survivors of child sexual abuse; Incest victims/survivors

PARENTS UNITED
1025 S Jennings, Ste 103, Fort Worth, TX 76104
Crisis hotline: **(817) 877-3440 24 hrs**
Information: (817) 877-3440 24 hrs
Contact: Rita Foust, MA ACP-PR/CADAC
TYPE OF AGENCY: Child sexual abuse services
SPONSORING ORGANIZATION: The Treatment Place
AREAS SERVED: Tarrant and outlying
YEARS IN OPERATION: 5

PARENTS UNITED (continued)

ACCESSIBILITY: Wheelchair accessible
CASES SEXUAL ASSAULT/ABUSE (%): 100
CLIENTS/SERVICES: Child victims of sexual abuse; Adult survivors of child sexual abuse; Incest victims/survivors; Offender treatment program; Adolescent survivors of sexual abuse; Male survivors of sexual abuse
REQUIREMENTS: Must be 16 and older
SPECIAL PROGRAMS/SERVICES: This is a support group for those involved in sexual abuse

PROFESSIONAL ALLIANCE COUNSELING AND CONSULTATION CENTER
3101 E 1st, Fort Worth, TX 76111
Information: (817) 838-7478 24 hrs
Contact: Deborah L Moore, Psychotherapist
TYPE OF AGENCY: Private practice; Offender treatment
AREAS SERVED: Tarrant, Parker, Johnson, Denton
YEARS IN OPERATION: 6
LANGUAGES: Spanish
ACCESSIBILITY: Wheelchair accessible
CASES SEXUAL ASSAULT/ABUSE (%): 99
DESCRIPTION: Individual and group therapy for victims of sexual abuse/sexual assault, including groups for female and male survivors. Treatment of sex offenders through control and modification of behavior and cognitive process; Biofeedback using the penile plethysmograph. Treatment for male and female offenders, juvenile sex offenders, mentally retarded offenders, rapists, child sexual abuse/incest offenders and batterers
CLIENTS/SERVICES: Sexual assault survivors; Marital rape/sexual abuse survivors; Child victims of sexual abuse; Adult survivors of child sexual abuse; Incest victims/survivors; Community education; Offender treatment program; Adolescent survivors of sexual abuse; Male survivors of sexual abuse; Developmentally disabled

RAPE CRISIS PROGRAM
1723 Hemphill, Fort Worth, TX 76110
Crisis hotline: **(817) 92-RAPES 24 hrs**
Information: (817) 927-4039 9am-5pm
Contact: Linda Braswell, Dir
TYPE OF AGENCY: Rape crisis center; Child sexual abuse services; Child sexual abuse prevention program
SPONSORING ORGANIZATION: Women's Center
AREAS SERVED: Parker, Tarrant
YEARS IN OPERATION: 9
ACCESSIBILITY: Wheelchair accessible
CASES SEXUAL ASSAULT/ABUSE (%): 100
CLIENTS/SERVICES: Sexual assault survivors; Marital rape/sexual abuse survivors; Child victims of sexual abuse; Adult survivors of child sexual abuse; Incest victims/survivors; Prevention program; Community education; Adolescent survivors of sexual abuse; Male survivors of sexual abuse
SPECIAL PROGRAMS/SERVICES: "Play It Safe!" is a model prevention program with a script for K-6 grades. Incest groups are didactic in nature and run approximately 16 weeks each.

TARRANT COUNTY MENTAL HEALTH/MENTAL RETARDATION
2400 NW 24th St, Fort Worth, TX 76106
Crisis hotline: **(817) 927-5544 24 hrs**
Information: (817) 625-4301 8am-8pm (Mon, Wed, Thu); 8am-5pm (Tue, Fri)
Contact: Ezio Leite, MEd, LPC, Prog Mgr
TYPE OF AGENCY: Counseling/mental health services
AREAS SERVED: Tarrant
YEARS IN OPERATION: 19
ACCESSIBILITY: Wheelchair accessible; Telecommunications for the hearing impaired (TTY, TDY, etc.); Signers for the hearing impaired
DESCRIPTION: Structured program for the treatment of perpetrators of child sexual abuse and individual counseling for victims of sexual abuse; Provides individual and group therapy for rapists and batterers
CLIENTS/SERVICES: Offender treatment program
REQUIREMENTS: Offenders are on probation/parole for sex offenses against children, are court-ordered and 18 or older; may also be admitted on voluntary basis

THE TREATMENT PLACE
1025 S Jennings, Ste 103, Fort Worth, TX 76104
Information: (817) 877-3440 8am-8pm, 24 hrs for emergencies
Contact: Rita Foust, MA, CSW, ACP, PR/CAD-AC
TYPE OF AGENCY: Child sexual abuse services; Private practice; Offender treatment
AREAS SERVED: Tarrant and outlying
YEARS IN OPERATION: 5
ACCESSIBILITY: Wheelchair accessible
CASES SEXUAL ASSAULT/ABUSE (%): 80
CLIENTS/SERVICES: Sexual assault survivors; Marital rape/sexual abuse survivors; Child victims of sexual abuse; Adult survivors of child sexual abuse; Incest victims/survivors; Community education; Offender treatment program; Adolescent survivors of sexual abuse; Male survivors of sexual abuse
SPECIAL PROGRAMS/SERVICES: Program for chemically dependent sexual offenders. This is the only program combining both problems/issues

GAINESVILLE

COOKE COUNTY FRIENDS OF THE FAMILY
PO Box 1221, Gainesville, TX 76240
Crisis hotline: **(817) 665-2873 24 hrs**
Information: (817) 665-2877 9am-5pm
Contact: Becky Bryant, Ed
TYPE OF AGENCY: Rape crisis center
AREAS SERVED: Cooke
YEARS IN OPERATION: 5
LANGUAGES: Spanish
ACCESSIBILITY: Wheelchair accessible
CASES SEXUAL ASSAULT/ABUSE (%): 20
CLIENTS/SERVICES: Sexual assault survivors; Marital rape/sexual abuse survivors; Child victims of sexual abuse; Adult survivors of child sexual abuse; Incest victims/survivors; Community education; Adolescent survivors of sexual abuse; Male survivors of sexual abuse

GALVESTON

WOMEN'S RESOURCE AND CRISIS CENTER OF GALVESTON COUNTY, INC
PO Box 1545, Galveston, TX 77553
Crisis hotline: **(409) 765-SAFE, 925-HELP, (713) 332-HELP 24 hrs**
Information: (409) 763-1441 8am-5pm (Mon-Fri)
Contact: Barbara Quiroz, Exec Dir
TYPE OF AGENCY: Rape crisis center; Domestic violence program
AREAS SERVED: Galveston
YEARS IN OPERATION: 10
LANGUAGES: Spanish
ACCESSIBILITY: Wheelchair accessible; Signers for the hearing impaired
CLIENTS/SERVICES: Sexual assault survivors; Marital rape/sexual abuse survivors; Child victims of sexual abuse; Adult survivors of child sexual abuse; Incest victims/survivors; Prevention program; Community education; Adolescent survivors of sexual abuse; Male survivors of sexual abuse

GARLAND

THE GALAXY CENTER
451 W Ave D, Garland, TX 75040
Information: (214) 272-4429 10am-9pm (Mon-Thu); 10am-6pm (Fri); 9am-3pm (Sat)
Contact: Elaine Ply, Exec Dir
TYPE OF AGENCY: Counseling/mental health services; Child sexual abuse services
AREAS SERVED: Dallas
YEARS IN OPERATION: 13
LANGUAGES: Spanish
ACCESSIBILITY: Wheelchair accessible
CASES SEXUAL ASSAULT/ABUSE (%): 33
DESCRIPTION: Services for victims and adult survivors of incest; Treatment program for mothers of incest victims, child sexual abuse offenders, incest offenders
CLIENTS/SERVICES: Child victims of sexual abuse; Adult survivors of child sexual abuse; Incest victims/survivors; Offender treatment program; Adolescent survivors of sexual abuse
REQUIREMENTS: If under age, the client must have permission from custodial parent unless it is an emergency situation; Clients must file charges or notify the appropriate authorities

GRAND PRAIRIE

CHILDREN FIRST CENTER
PO Box 531733, Grand Prairie, TX 75053-1733
Crisis hotline: **(214) 264-0604 24 hrs**
Information: (214) 264-0604 10am-6pm
Contact: Carolyn Odom, Interim Dir
TYPE OF AGENCY: Child sexual abuse services; Private practice
AREAS SERVED: Dallas, Tarrant
YEARS IN OPERATION: 11
LANGUAGES: Spanish
CLIENTS/SERVICES: Child victims of sexual abuse; Adult survivors of child sexual abuse; Prevention program

HARKER HEIGHTS

ASSOCIATED COUNSELING SERVICES
455 E Central Texas Expwy, Harker Heights, TX 76543
Information: (817) 699-3103 8am-7pm (Mon-Fri)
Contact: Janis Curran, Therapist
TYPE OF AGENCY: Private practice
AREAS SERVED: Coryell, Bell
YEARS IN OPERATION: 5
LANGUAGES: Korean interpreter available
ACCESSIBILITY: Wheelchair accessible
CASES SEXUAL ASSAULT/ABUSE (%): 60
DESCRIPTION: Counseling for survivors and for child sexual abuse offenders, incest offenders, and batterers
CLIENTS/SERVICES: Sexual assault survivors; Marital rape/sexual abuse survivors; Child victims of sexual abuse; Adult survivors of child sexual abuse; Incest victims/survivors; Community education; Offender treatment program; Adolescent survivors of sexual abuse; Male survivors of sexual abuse

HARLINGEN

FAMILY CRISIS CENTER, INC
2220 Haine Dr, No 32, Harlingen, TX 78550
Crisis hotline: **(512) 423-9304, 544-7273 24 hrs**
Information: (512) 423-9304, 544-7273 8am-6pm (Mon-Fri)
Contact: Melissa Reyna, Rape Crisis Coord
TYPE OF AGENCY: Rape crisis center; Domestic violence program
AREAS SERVED: Cameron, Willacy
YEARS IN OPERATION: 8
LANGUAGES: Spanish
ACCESSIBILITY: Wheelchair accessible
CASES SEXUAL ASSAULT/ABUSE (%): 50
CLIENTS/SERVICES: Sexual assault survivors; Marital rape/sexual abuse survivors; Child victims of sexual abuse; Adult survivors of child

FAMILY CRISIS CENTER, INC (continued)
sexual abuse; Incest victims/survivors; Prevention program; Community education

HOUSTON

AID TO VICTIMS OF DOMESTIC ABUSE
5009 Caroline, Houston, TX 77004
Information: (713) 520-8620 9am-4pm (Mon-Fri)
Contact: Rhonda Serson, Dir
TYPE OF AGENCY: Domestic violence program
AREAS SERVED: Harris
YEARS IN OPERATION: 8
LANGUAGES: Spanish
ACCESSIBILITY: Wheelchair accessible
CASES SEXUAL ASSAULT/ABUSE (%): 25
CLIENTS/SERVICES: Marital rape/sexual abuse survivors

CHILD ADVOCATES, INC
6425 Chimney Rock, Houston, TX 77081
Information: (713) 661-1596 8:30am-5:30pm
Contact: Martha E Braniff, Exec Dir
TYPE OF AGENCY: Legal services agency; Child advocacy
AREAS SERVED: Harris
YEARS IN OPERATION: 4
LANGUAGES: Spanish
CASES SEXUAL ASSAULT/ABUSE (%): 25
DESCRIPTION: Provides trained court appointed special advocate volunteers for abused/neglected children in the court system, including sexually abused children
CLIENTS/SERVICES: Child victims of sexual abuse; Incest victims/survivors; Community education

CITY OF HOUSTON DEPARTMENT OF HEALTH AND HUMAN SERVICES—SEXUAL ASSAULT PROGRAM
8000 N Stadium Dr, Houston, TX 77054
Information: (713) 794-9360 8am-5pm
Contact: Vivian R Miles, MSW, CSW, ACP, Sexual Assault Prog Coord
TYPE OF AGENCY: Hospital/medical center
AREAS SERVED: Harris
YEARS IN OPERATION: 12
ACCESSIBILITY: Wheelchair accessible
CASES SEXUAL ASSAULT/ABUSE (%): 100
DESCRIPTION: Short- and long-term individual counseling for victims/survivors
CLIENTS/SERVICES: Sexual assault survivors; Marital rape/sexual abuse survivors; Child victims of sexual abuse; Adult survivors of child sexual abuse; Incest victims/survivors; Prevention program; Community education; Adolescent survivors of sexual abuse; Male survivors of sexual abuse

CRISIS HOTLINE
PO Box 130866, Houston, TX 77219
Crisis hotline: **Central Houston (713) 228-1505, Bay area (713) 333-5111 24 hrs 7 days**
Information: (713) 527-9864 answering machine
Contact: Hotline volunteer
TYPE OF AGENCY: Counseling/mental health services; Telephone crisis hotline; Information and referral
SPONSORING ORGANIZATION: Crisis Intervention of Houston, Inc
AREAS SERVED: Harris, Montgomery, Fort Bend, Waller
YEARS IN OPERATION: 18
LANGUAGES: Spanish
CASES SEXUAL ASSAULT/ABUSE (%): 4
DESCRIPTION: 24-hour crisis intervention/suicide prevention telephone service, providing crisis counseling and specific information and referral on a comprehensive range of topics, including sexual assault and child and elderly abuse.
CLIENTS/SERVICES: Sexual assault survivors; Marital rape/sexual abuse survivors; Child victims of sexual abuse; Adult survivors of child sexual abuse; Incest victims/survivors; Prevention program; Community education

GUNTER AND ASSOCIATES
6666 Harwin, Houston, TX 77006
Crisis hotline: **(713) 266-5400 24 hrs**
Information: (713) 266-5400 24 hrs
Contact: Jim Gunter, Dir
TYPE OF AGENCY: Child sexual abuse services; Child sexual abuse prevention program; Private practice
AREAS SERVED: Harris, Ft Bend
YEARS IN OPERATION: 12
LANGUAGES: Spanish
ACCESSIBILITY: Wheelchair accessible
CASES SEXUAL ASSAULT/ABUSE (%): 20-25
DESCRIPTION: Provides individual, family, and group therapies for survivors of sexual abuse; Works with perpetrators (rapists, batterers, child sexual abuse/incest offenders) in individual and group settings. Able to provide free therapy for victims of crime.
CLIENTS/SERVICES: Sexual assault survivors; Marital rape/sexual abuse survivors; Child victims of sexual abuse; Adult survivors of child sexual abuse; Incest victims/survivors; Prevention program; Community education; Offender treatment program; Adolescent survivors of sexual abuse; Male survivors of sexual abuse; Healing
REQUIREMENTS: Ages 6 and older; Sliding scale fee
SPECIAL PROGRAMS/SERVICES: Trauma resolution therapies, art therapy, play therapy, ROPES for adult survivors of sexual assault and child sexual abuse

THE HART GROUP
5300 Memorial Dr, Ste 350, Houston, TX 77007
Information: (713) 864-3200 8am-9pm
Contact: Rion Hart, PhD
TYPE OF AGENCY: Private practice
AREAS SERVED: Harris, Galveston
YEARS IN OPERATION: 4
ACCESSIBILITY: Wheelchair accessible
CASES SEXUAL ASSAULT/ABUSE (%): 15-20
CLIENTS/SERVICES: Sexual assault survivors; Marital rape/sexual abuse survivors; Child victims of sexual abuse; Adult survivors of child sexual abuse; Incest victims/survivors; Community education; Adolescent survivors of sexual abuse

POST OAK PSYCHIATRY ASSOCIATES
17115 Red Oak Dr, Ste 109, Houston, TX 77090
Information: (713) 893-4111 8am-5pm
Contact: Pamela Silverman, CSW, ACP, Social Wkr Dir
TYPE OF AGENCY: Private practice
AREAS SERVED: Harris, Montgomery
YEARS IN OPERATION: 20
ACCESSIBILITY: Wheelchair accessible
CLIENTS/SERVICES: Sexual assault survivors; Marital rape/sexual abuse survivors; Child victims of sexual abuse; Adult survivors of child sexual abuse; Incest victims/survivors; Adolescent survivors of sexual abuse; Male survivors of sexual abuse

RAPE CRISIS PROGRAM
4 Chelsea, Houston, TX 77006
Crisis hotline: **(713) 528-RAPE 24 hrs**
Information: (713) 528-6798 9am-5pm (Mon-Fri)
Contact: Cassandra Thomas, Dir
TYPE OF AGENCY: Rape crisis center; Domestic violence program
SPONSORING ORGANIZATION: Houston Area Women's Center
AREAS SERVED: Harris
YEARS IN OPERATION: 8
LANGUAGES: Spanish, French, Russian, German
ACCESSIBILITY: Wheelchair accessible; Signers for the hearing impaired
CASES SEXUAL ASSAULT/ABUSE (%): 100
DESCRIPTION: Provides services for survivors of sexual assault, their family, and friends. Promotes public awareness of sexual assault issues. Feminist martial arts/self-defense program available
CLIENTS/SERVICES: Sexual assault survivors; Marital rape/sexual abuse survivors; Child victims of sexual abuse; Adult survivors of child sexual abuse; Prevention program; Community education; Adolescent survivors of sexual abuse; Male survivors of sexual abuse; Publications/media
SPECIAL PROGRAMS/SERVICES: Locally produced videotapes with medical, law enforcement, and court professionals on their roles in dealing with survivors

SPRING BRANCH/MEMORIAL FAMILY OUTREACH AND HARRIS COUNTY CHILDREN'S PROTECTIVE SERVICES
11612 Memorial Dr, Houston, TX 77024
Information: (713) 974-4825 24 hrs
Contact: Frances Jones, Pres
TYPE OF AGENCY: Child sexual abuse prevention program; Child abuse services; Child abuse prevention program
AREAS SERVED: Harris
YEARS IN OPERATION: 6
DESCRIPTION: Provides volunteers who work with at-risk families; Presents programs for grades K-12 on recognizing inappropriate sexual behavior, "WHO (We Help Ourselves)"; "STEP (Systematic Training for Effective Parenting)," parenting classes; Telephone counseling; Resource referral
CLIENTS/SERVICES: Prevention program; Community education

TASK FORCE ON FAMILY VIOLENCE
University of Houston Law Center, Houston, TX 77204-6380
Information: (713) 749-4816
Contact: Laura Oreu, Faculty Sponsor; Anne Schuette, Pres
TYPE OF AGENCY: Domestic violence program; College/university-based services; Legal services agency
SPONSORING ORGANIZATION: University of Houston Law Center
AREAS SERVED: Ft Bend, Montgomery, Harris
YEARS IN OPERATION: ½
DESCRIPTION: Law student organization with 2 main purposes: To educate themselves on family, civil and criminal law relating to family violence; Community service by presenting legal information to the women's shelters in Houston and surrounding areas
CLIENTS/SERVICES: Marital rape/sexual abuse survivors; Community education

BEN TAUB GENERAL HOSPITAL
1502 Taub Loop, Houston, TX 77030
Crisis hotline: **(713) 791-7300 24 hrs daily**
Information: (713) 791-7388 8am-4:30pm
Contact: Elizabeth Green, RN, Patient Advocate
TYPE OF AGENCY: Hospital/medical center
AREAS SERVED: Harris
YEARS IN OPERATION: 30
LANGUAGES: Spanish; translators for other languages available
ACCESSIBILITY: Wheelchair accessible; Telecommunications for the hearing impaired (TTY, TDY, etc.)
DESCRIPTION: Has sexual assault nurse examiners and training for all registered nurses in the care of sexual assault survivors
CLIENTS/SERVICES: Sexual assault survivors; Marital rape/sexual abuse survivors; Child victims of sexual abuse; Adult survivors of child sexual abuse; Incest victims/survivors

VICTIM ASSISTANCE CENTER, INC
914 Preston, Ste 800, Houston, TX 77002
Information: (713) 221-5625 8am-5pm
Contact: Marinelle Timmons, Exec Dir

VICTIM ASSISTANCE CENTER, INC
(continued)
TYPE OF AGENCY: Victim/witness assistance program
AREAS SERVED: Harris
YEARS IN OPERATION: 1
LANGUAGES: Spanish by request
ACCESSIBILITY: Wheelchair accessible
CASES SEXUAL ASSAULT/ABUSE (%): 10
CLIENTS/SERVICES: Sexual assault survivors; Marital rape/sexual abuse survivors; Child victims of sexual abuse; Adult survivors of child sexual abuse; Incest victims/survivors; Adolescent survivors of sexual abuse
REQUIREMENTS: A police report must be filed within 72 hours of offense and victim must be willing to press charges in order to apply for crime victims compensation

WEINBERGER, HALL, AND ASSOCIATES, PC
4140 SW Fwy, Ste 401, Houston, TX 77027
Crisis hotline: **(713) 623-0800 24 hrs**
Information: (713) 623-0800 8:30am-8pm (Mon-Fri); Crisis appointments as needed
Contact: Karyn D Hall, PhD, Lic Clinical Psychologist
TYPE OF AGENCY: Private practice
AREAS SERVED: Harris
YEARS IN OPERATION: 13
LANGUAGES: Spanish
ACCESSIBILITY: Wheelchair accessible
CASES SEXUAL ASSAULT/ABUSE (%): 10
DESCRIPTION: Specializes in children and adolescents with emotional problems and their families
CLIENTS/SERVICES: Sexual assault survivors; Marital rape/sexual abuse survivors; Child victims of sexual abuse; Adolescent survivors of sexual abuse
REQUIREMENTS: Fee for service but assignment of insurance accepted

WEST HOUSTON PSYCHOLOGICAL ASSOCIATES
1011 Hwy 6 S, Ste 311, Houston, TX 77077
Crisis hotline: **(713) 496-7185 24 hrs**
Information: (713) 496-7185 24 hrs
Contact: Carolyn Ivens, PhD
TYPE OF AGENCY: Child sexual abuse services; Private practice
AREAS SERVED: Harris, Ft Bend
YEARS IN OPERATION: 5
LANGUAGES: Spanish
ACCESSIBILITY: Wheelchair accessible
CASES SEXUAL ASSAULT/ABUSE (%): 85
CLIENTS/SERVICES: Child victims of sexual abuse; Adult survivors of child sexual abuse; Incest victims/survivors; Offender treatment program; Adolescent survivors of sexual abuse; Male survivors of sexual abuse

WHO (WE HELP OURSELVES) PROGRAM
2211 Norfolk, No 810, Houston, TX 77098
Information: (713) 523-8963 8:30am-4:30pm
Contact: Janet Pozmantier, Children's Svcs/WHO Prog Dir
TYPE OF AGENCY: Counseling/mental health services; Child sexual abuse prevention program; Child abuse prevention program
SPONSORING ORGANIZATION: Mental Health Association of Houston and Harris County
AREAS SERVED: Harris
YEARS IN OPERATION: 35
LANGUAGES: Spanish
ACCESSIBILITY: Wheelchair accessible
DESCRIPTION: WHO is an anti-victimization education program for children 3-18 years of age. Five different age-appropriate presentations are available: preschoolers, kindergarten-3rd grade, 4th-6th grade, 7th-9th grade, and 10th-12th grade.
CLIENTS/SERVICES: Prevention program; Community education; Publications/media

SPECIAL PROGRAMS/SERVICES: Media program: video-based curriculum program, *Grown Ups and Downs*, to help adults feel comfortable assisting victimized children. The curriculum includes a short videotape depicting adults confronted with children disclosing three types of abuse (physical, sexual, and emotional) in three different vignettes. The Curriculum Guide and Discussion Text provides factual information to assist in leading group discussion to explore the attitudes, myths, and fears which prevent adults from responding appropriately to an abused child

YOUTH VICTIM/WITNESS PROGRAM
3217 Montrose Blvd, Houston, TX 77035
Crisis hotline: **(713) 520-9110 8:30am-5pm**
Information: (713) 520-9110 8:30am-5pm
Contact: Pamela R Hobbs, Prog Dir
TYPE OF AGENCY: Victim/witness assistance program
SPONSORING ORGANIZATION: Houston Metropolitan Ministries
AREAS SERVED: Harris
YEARS IN OPERATION: 4½
LANGUAGES: Spanish
ACCESSIBILITY: Wheelchair accessible
CASES SEXUAL ASSAULT/ABUSE (%): 85
DESCRIPTION: Provides a link to the entire criminal justice system; Court escort; Helps the family cope with the victimization and enable the child to participate in the legal system with the least amount of trauma; Parent support groups available
CLIENTS/SERVICES: Child victims of sexual abuse; Community education; Adolescent survivors of sexual abuse
REQUIREMENTS: Must be 18 or younger
SPECIAL PROGRAMS/SERVICES: Only victim assistance program for children in Texas that is not part of the system, enhancing the ability to serve as advocates for victimized children

HUNTSVILLE

WALKER COUNTY FAMILY VIOLENCE COUNCIL
PO Box 1893, Huntsville, TX 77342-1893
Crisis hotline: **(409) 291-3369 24 hrs**
Information: (409) 291-3529 8am-5pm (Mon-Fri)
Contact: Ruth Knight, Sexual Assault Advocate
TYPE OF AGENCY: Rape crisis center; Domestic violence program
AREAS SERVED: Walker, New Waverly
YEARS IN OPERATION: ½
LANGUAGES: Spanish
CASES SEXUAL ASSAULT/ABUSE (%): 5
CLIENTS/SERVICES: Sexual assault survivors; Marital rape/sexual abuse survivors; Child victims of sexual abuse; Adult survivors of child sexual abuse; Incest victims/survivors; Community education; Adolescent survivors of sexual abuse; Male survivors of sexual abuse

KERRVILLE

HILL COUNTRY CRISIS COUNCIL
PO Box 1817, Kerrville, TX 78029
Crisis hotline: **(512) 257-2400 24 hrs**
Information: (512) 257-7088 24 hrs
Contact: Larry Arnold, Outreach Coord
TYPE OF AGENCY: Rape crisis center; Domestic violence program
AREAS SERVED: Bandera, Gillespie, Kendall, Kerr
YEARS IN OPERATION: 4
LANGUAGES: Spanish (on call)
ACCESSIBILITY: Wheelchair accessible; Signers for the hearing impaired (on call)
CASES SEXUAL ASSAULT/ABUSE (%): 33
DESCRIPTION: Provides hotline, shelter, counseling, and advocacy for victims of domestic violence and sexual assault. Individual and group therapy for batterers

CLIENTS/SERVICES: Sexual assault survivors; Marital rape/sexual abuse survivors; Child victims of sexual abuse; Adult survivors of child sexual abuse; Incest victims/survivors; Prevention program; Community education; Adolescent survivors of sexual abuse; Male survivors of sexual abuse
REQUIREMENTS: Children must have parent approval

KILGORE

KILGORE COMMUNITY CRISIS CENTER
905 Broadway, Kilgore, TX 75662
Crisis hotline: **(214) 984-2377 24 hrs**
Information: (214) 984-2377 8am-5pm
Contact: Gerdie Headen, Exec Dir
TYPE OF AGENCY: Rape crisis center; Domestic violence program; Victim/witness assistance program
AREAS SERVED: Gregg, Rusk
YEARS IN OPERATION: 4
ACCESSIBILITY: Wheelchair accessible
CASES SEXUAL ASSAULT/ABUSE (%): 35
CLIENTS/SERVICES: Sexual assault survivors; Marital rape/sexual abuse survivors; Child victims of sexual abuse; Adult survivors of child sexual abuse; Incest victims/survivors; Prevention program; Community education

KILLEEN

FAMILIES IN CRISIS, INC—RAPE CRISIS CENTER
PO Box 25, Killeen, TX 76540
Crisis hotline: **(817) 634-8309 24 hrs daily**
Information: (817) 634-1184 8am-5pm
Contact: Natalie Tolley, Sexual Assault Prog Coord
TYPE OF AGENCY: Rape crisis center; Domestic violence program; Child sexual abuse services; Child sexual abuse prevention program
AREAS SERVED: Bell, Coryell, Hamilton
YEARS IN OPERATION: 10
LANGUAGES: Spanish
ACCESSIBILITY: Wheelchair accessible
CASES SEXUAL ASSAULT/ABUSE (%): 100
DESCRIPTION: Comprehensive services for survivors of sexual assault and domestic violence; Support groups for female and male survivors
CLIENTS/SERVICES: Sexual assault survivors; Marital rape/sexual abuse survivors; Child victims of sexual abuse; Adult survivors of child sexual abuse; Incest victims/survivors; Prevention program; Community education; Adolescent survivors of sexual abuse; Male survivors of sexual abuse

KINGSVILLE

KLEBERG COUNTY FAMILY GUIDANCE SERVICES
729 W Nettie, Kingsville, TX 78363
Information: (512) 592-6446 9am-5pm (Mon, Wed, Fri); 9am-8pm (Tue, Thu)
Contact: Nancy W Casey, Admin Asst
TYPE OF AGENCY: Counseling/mental health services
AREAS SERVED: Kleberg, Jim Wells, Nueces
YEARS IN OPERATION: 16
ACCESSIBILITY: Wheelchair accessible
CLIENTS/SERVICES: Sexual assault survivors; Marital rape/sexual abuse survivors; Child victims of sexual abuse; Adult survivors of child sexual abuse; Incest victims/survivors; Adolescent survivors of sexual abuse; Male survivors of sexual abuse

LAREDO

LAREDO STATE CENTER-MENTAL HEALTH MENTAL RETARDATION—SEXUAL ASSAULT CENTER
PO Box 1835, Laredo, TX 78041
Crisis hotline: **(512) 724-1919 24 hrs**
Information: (512) 723-2926 8am-5pm
Contact: Gloria N Landin, Rape Crisis Coun
TYPE OF AGENCY: Rape crisis center; Child sexual abuse services; Child sexual abuse prevention program
AREAS SERVED: Webb, Zapata, Jim Hogg, Starr
YEARS IN OPERATION: 6
LANGUAGES: Spanish
ACCESSIBILITY: Wheelchair accessible
CASES SEXUAL ASSAULT/ABUSE (%): 100
DESCRIPTION: Short- and long-term counseling for victims and significant others; Accompaniment after assault and throughout medical exam and through the legal process if the victim chooses to prosecute; Group therapy programs for rapists, child sexual abuse offenders, and incest offenders
CLIENTS/SERVICES: Sexual assault survivors; Marital rape/sexual abuse survivors; Child victims of sexual abuse; Adult survivors of child sexual abuse; Incest victims/survivors; Prevention program; Community education; Offender treatment program; Adolescent survivors of sexual abuse; Male survivors of sexual abuse

LONGVIEW

EAST TEXAS ASSOCIATION FOR ABUSED FAMILIES
PO Box 347, Longview, TX 75606
Crisis hotline: **(800) 441-5555 24 hrs**
Information: (214) 757-9308 24 hrs
Contact: Doyle D Dietz, Exec Dir
TYPE OF AGENCY: Rape crisis center; Domestic violence program
AREAS SERVED: Gregg, Harrison, Upshur, Camp, Rusk, Panola, Marion
YEARS IN OPERATION: 6
ACCESSIBILITY: Wheelchair accessible
CASES SEXUAL ASSAULT/ABUSE (%): 30
CLIENTS/SERVICES: Sexual assault survivors; Marital rape/sexual abuse survivors; Child victims of sexual abuse; Adult survivors of child sexual abuse; Incest victims/survivors; Community education; Adolescent survivors of sexual abuse; Male survivors of sexual abuse

LUBBOCK

LUBBOCK COUNTY—CRIMINAL DISTRICT ATTORNEY VICTIM/WITNESS ASSISTANCE
PO Box 10536, Lubbock, TX 79408
Information: (806) 741-8043 8:30am-5pm (Mon-Fri)
Contact: Jane Piercy, Victim/Witness Coord
TYPE OF AGENCY: Victim/witness assistance program
AREAS SERVED: Lubbock
YEARS IN OPERATION: 2
ACCESSIBILITY: Wheelchair accessible
CASES SEXUAL ASSAULT/ABUSE (%): 15
CLIENTS/SERVICES: Sexual assault survivors; Marital rape/sexual abuse survivors; Child victims of sexual abuse; Incest victims/survivors
REQUIREMENTS: Usually a client must have filed charges, but counseling and referral for those who don't wish to pursue criminal charges are provided

LUBBOCK RAPE CRISIS CENTER, INC
PO Box 2000, Lubbock, TX 79457
Crisis hotline: **(806) 763-7273 24 hrs daily**
Information: (806) 763-3232 24 hrs daily
Contact: Becky Cannon, Exec Dir
TYPE OF AGENCY: Rape crisis center; Child sexual abuse services; Child sexual abuse prevention program
YEARS IN OPERATION: 14
LANGUAGES: Spanish
ACCESSIBILITY: Wheelchair accessible; Signers for the hearing impaired
CASES SEXUAL ASSAULT/ABUSE (%): 100
CLIENTS/SERVICES: Sexual assault survivors; Marital rape/sexual abuse survivors; Child victims of sexual abuse; Adult survivors of child sexual abuse; Incest victims/survivors; Prevention program; Community education; Adolescent survivors of sexual abuse; Male survivors of sexual abuse; Publications/media
SPECIAL PROGRAMS/SERVICES: Publications: *Rapists Don't Discriminate!* (for survivors of sexual assault); *Sexual Assault Prevention Through Awareness* (for community education)

WOMEN'S PROTECTIVE SERVICES
1706 23rd, Ste 104, Lubbock, TX 79411
Crisis hotline: **(806) 765-8393 24 hrs**
Information: (806) 747-6491 9am-5pm (Mon-Fri)
Contact: Suzanne Foley, Regional Outreach Victim/Volunteer Coord
TYPE OF AGENCY: Domestic violence program
AREAS SERVED: Lubbock, Bailey, Lamb, Cochran, Hockley, Terry, Crosby, Dickens, King, Yoakum, Lynn, Garza
YEARS IN OPERATION: 10
LANGUAGES: Spanish
ACCESSIBILITY: Wheelchair accessible
CASES SEXUAL ASSAULT/ABUSE (%): 50
CLIENTS/SERVICES: Sexual assault survivors; Marital rape/sexual abuse survivors; Child victims of sexual abuse; Community education; Adolescent survivors of sexual abuse

MCALLEN

MUJERES UNIDAS/WOMEN TOGETHER FOUNDATION
420 N 21st, McAllen, TX 78501
Crisis hotline: **(512) 630-4878 24 hrs**
Information: (512) 630-4878 9am-5pm
Contact: Estella DeAnda, Exec Dir
TYPE OF AGENCY: Rape crisis center; Domestic violence program; Child sexual abuse prevention program
AREAS SERVED: Hidalgo, Starr
YEARS IN OPERATION: 12
LANGUAGES: Spanish
ACCESSIBILITY: Wheelchair accessible
CLIENTS/SERVICES: Sexual assault survivors; Marital rape/sexual abuse survivors; Child victims of sexual abuse; Adult survivors of child sexual abuse; Incest victims/survivors; Prevention program; Community education; Adolescent survivors of sexual abuse; Male survivors of sexual abuse
SPECIAL PROGRAMS/SERVICES: Brochures in Spanish and English

MCKINNEY

COLLIN COUNTY RAPE CRISIS CENTER
PO Box 73, McKinney, TX 75069
Crisis hotline: **(800) 234-RAPE, (214) 548-RAPE (local number) 24 hrs**
Information: (214) 548-RAPE 9am-5pm (Mon-Fri)
Contact: Carol Finch, Exec Dir
TYPE OF AGENCY: Rape crisis center
AREAS SERVED: Collin
YEARS IN OPERATION: 6
ACCESSIBILITY: Wheelchair accessible
CASES SEXUAL ASSAULT/ABUSE (%): 100
CLIENTS/SERVICES: Sexual assault survivors; Marital rape/sexual abuse survivors; Child victims of sexual abuse; Adult survivors of child sexual abuse; Incest victims/survivors; Prevention program; Community education; Adolescent survivors of sexual abuse; Male survivors of sexual abuse

MIDLAND

MIDLAND RAPE CRISIS CENTER
PO Box 10081, Midland, TX 79702
Crisis hotline: **(915) 682-7273 24 hrs daily**
Information: (915) 682-7273 24 hrs daily
Contact: Laura Walker, Dir
TYPE OF AGENCY: Rape crisis center; Child sexual abuse services; Child sexual abuse prevention program; Acquaintance/date rape prevention program
AREAS SERVED: Midland
YEARS IN OPERATION: 8
ACCESSIBILITY: Wheelchair accessible
CASES SEXUAL ASSAULT/ABUSE (%): 100
CLIENTS/SERVICES: Sexual assault survivors; Marital rape/sexual abuse survivors; Child victims of sexual abuse; Adult survivors of child sexual abuse; Incest victims/survivors; Prevention program; Community education; Adolescent survivors of sexual abuse; Male survivors of sexual abuse
SPECIAL PROGRAMS/SERVICES: Prevention programs for children include filmstrip/film: *Speak Up, Say NO!* (K-2nd grade); *For Pete's Sake, Tell!* (3-4 grades); *No More Secrets* (5-6 grades). Programs for adults include: talking with children about child sexual abuse, acquaintance/date rape prevention and rape facts and prevention strategies

PERMIAN BASIN CENTER FOR BATTERED WOMEN AND THEIR CHILDREN
PO Box 2942, Midland, TX 79702
Crisis hotline: **(915) 683-1300 24 hrs**
Information: (915) 683-1300 24 hrs
Contact: Marlene Bruce, Soc Svcs Coord
TYPE OF AGENCY: Domestic violence program
AREAS SERVED: Midland, Ector, Loving, Andrews, Reeves, Winkler, Borden, Crane, Upton, Howard, Glasscock, Martin, Gaines, Dawson
YEARS IN OPERATION: 10
LANGUAGES: Spanish interpreter available
ACCESSIBILITY: Wheelchair accessible
CASES SEXUAL ASSAULT/ABUSE (%): 5
DESCRIPTION: Comprehensive domestic violence services and Batterers Anonymous group
CLIENTS/SERVICES: Marital rape/sexual abuse survivors; Prevention program; Community education
REQUIREMENTS: Serves adult victims of family violence

NACOGDOCHES

NACOGDOCHES RAPE CRISIS HOTLINE
PO Box 2385, Nacogdoches, TX 75963
Crisis hotline: **(409) 560-0393 6pm-7am daily**
TYPE OF AGENCY: Rape crisis center
CLIENTS/SERVICES: Sexual assault survivors

WOMEN'S SHELTER OF EAST TEXAS, INC
PO Box 569, Nacogdoches, TX 75961
Crisis hotline: **(800) 828-SAFE 24 hrs**
Information: (409) 569-1018 8am-5pm (Mon-Fri)
Contact: Mary McKinley, Exec Dir
TYPE OF AGENCY: Domestic violence program
AREAS SERVED: Angelina, Houston, Nacogdoches, Trinity, San Jacinto, Polk, Shelby, San Augustine, Sabine
YEARS IN OPERATION: 9
LANGUAGES: Spanish speaking volunteers
CASES SEXUAL ASSAULT/ABUSE (%): 20-25
CLIENTS/SERVICES: Marital rape/sexual abuse survivors; Child victims of sexual abuse

ODESSA

ECTOR COUNTY DISTRICT ATTORNEY'S OFFICE—VICTIM ASSISTANCE
Ector County Courthouse, Rm, No 305, Odessa, TX 79761
Information: (915) 335-3035 8:30am-5pm
Contact: Natalie Warren, Victim's Asst
TYPE OF AGENCY: Victim/witness assistance program
AREAS SERVED: Ector
YEARS IN OPERATION: 5
ACCESSIBILITY: Wheelchair accessible
CASES SEXUAL ASSAULT/ABUSE (%): 25-30
CLIENTS/SERVICES: Sexual assault survivors; Marital rape/sexual abuse survivors; Child victims of sexual abuse; Incest victims/survivors
REQUIREMENTS: Client must have filed charges and the case must be indicted by the grand jury, or client may be referred by another agency

ODESSA RAPE CRISIS CENTER
PO Box 7741, Odessa, TX 79760
Crisis hotline: **(915) 366-7273 24 hrs**
Information: (915) 333-2527 8:30am-5pm (Mon-Fri)
Contact: Julia Ladd, Exec Dir
TYPE OF AGENCY: Rape crisis center
AREAS SERVED: Ector, Andrews, Crane, Ward, Winkler
YEARS IN OPERATION: 6
LANGUAGES: Spanish
ACCESSIBILITY: Wheelchair accessible
CASES SEXUAL ASSAULT/ABUSE (%): 100
CLIENTS/SERVICES: Sexual assault survivors; Marital rape/sexual abuse survivors; Child victims of sexual abuse; Adult survivors of child sexual abuse; Incest victims/survivors; Prevention program; Community education; Adolescent survivors of sexual abuse; Male survivors of sexual abuse

PAIGE

STRESS AND TRAUMA RECOVERY CENTER
Rte 1, 809 Ponderosa Loop, Paige, TX 78659
Crisis hotline: **(512) 321-7291 Evenings and weekends**
Information: (512) 321-9204 8am-5pm (Mon-Fri)
Contact: Barbara Franco, Dir
TYPE OF AGENCY: Private practice
AREAS SERVED: Bastrop, Lee, Fayette, Travis
YEARS IN OPERATION: 1
LANGUAGES: Spanish
CASES SEXUAL ASSAULT/ABUSE (%): 30-40
CLIENTS/SERVICES: Sexual assault survivors; Marital rape/sexual abuse survivors; Adult survivors of child sexual abuse; Incest victims/survivors; Prevention program; Community education; Offender treatment program; Adolescent survivors of sexual abuse; Male survivors of sexual abuse; Healing
SPECIAL PROGRAMS/SERVICES: Specializes in traumatic stress (post-traumatic stress disorder) and provides current, proven techniques for trauma resolution. Focuses on intervention in compulsive/addictive responses to trauma, includes family members when possible. Healing through staff spiritual advisor for support services, meditation training, and Indian sweat lodge ritual

PAMPA

TRALEE CRISIS CENTER FOR WOMEN, INC
PO Box 2880, Pampa, TX 79066-2880
Crisis hotline: **(806) 669-1788 24 hrs daily**
Information: (806) 669-1131 8:30am-5pm
Contact: Judy Warner, Dir
TYPE OF AGENCY: Rape crisis center; Domestic violence program; Victim/witness assistance program; Child sexual abuse services; Child sexual abuse prevention program; Private practice
AREAS SERVED: Carson, Collingsworth, Donley, Gray, Hemphill, Hutchinson, Roberts, Wheeler
YEARS IN OPERATION: 4
LANGUAGES: Spanish
ACCESSIBILITY: Wheelchair accessible; Signers for the hearing impaired
CASES SEXUAL ASSAULT/ABUSE (%): 22-28
DESCRIPTION: Provides comprehensive services for survivors of domestic violence, sexual assault, and other crimes. Also provides feminist martial arts/self defense
CLIENTS/SERVICES: Sexual assault survivors; Marital rape/sexual abuse survivors; Child victims of sexual abuse; Adult survivors of child sexual abuse; Incest victims/survivors; Prevention program; Community education; Adolescent survivors of sexual abuse

PARIS

FAMILY HAVEN CRISIS AND RESOURCE CENTER, INC
PO Box 1453, Paris, TX 75460
Crisis hotline: **(214) 784-6842 24 hrs**
Information: (214) 784-6842 8:30am-5:30pm (Mon-Fri)
Contact: Julie Abbett, Legal Advocate
TYPE OF AGENCY: Domestic violence program
AREAS SERVED: Lamar, Titus, Franklin, Hopkins, Red River, Delta
YEARS IN OPERATION: 4
ACCESSIBILITY: Wheelchair accessible
CASES SEXUAL ASSAULT/ABUSE (%): 50
DESCRIPTION: Provides shelter for battered women and their children; Counseling; Legal advocacy; Assistance with transportation (to court, job interviews, etc); Housing; Hospital, police, and court accompaniment for sexual assault victims; Crime scene counseling and treatment for batterers
CLIENTS/SERVICES: Sexual assault survivors; Marital rape/sexual abuse survivors; Child victims of sexual abuse; Adult survivors of child sexual abuse; Incest victims/survivors; Community education; Offender treatment program; Adolescent survivors of sexual abuse; Male survivors of sexual abuse

PASADENA

THE BRIDGE OVER TROUBLED WATERS, INC
PO Box 3488, Pasadena, TX 77536
Crisis hotline: **(713) 473-2801 24 hrs**
Information: (713) 472-0753 9am-5pm
Contact: Diane Bryant, Outreach Dir
TYPE OF AGENCY: Rape crisis center; Domestic violence program
AREAS SERVED: Southeast Harris
YEARS IN OPERATION: 10
LANGUAGES: Spanish
ACCESSIBILITY: Wheelchair accessible
DESCRIPTION: Intake hotline for Parents United; Victim advocacy; Accompaniment for family violence and sexual assault victims; Non-residential support groups
CLIENTS/SERVICES: Sexual assault survivors; Marital rape/sexual abuse survivors; Adult survivors of child sexual abuse; Incest victims/survivors; Prevention program; Community education

PERRYTON

PANHANDLE CRISIS CENTER
PO Box 502, Perryton, TX 79070
Crisis hotline: **(806) 435-5008 24 hrs (answering service 5pm-9am)**
Information: (806) 435-5008, 435-5013 24 hrs (answering service)
Contact: Helen A Bussey, Dir
TYPE OF AGENCY: Rape crisis center; Domestic violence program
AREAS SERVED: Ochiltree, Hansford, Lipscomb
YEARS IN OPERATION: 4
LANGUAGES: Spanish
ACCESSIBILITY: Wheelchair accessible
CASES SEXUAL ASSAULT/ABUSE (%): 14
CLIENTS/SERVICES: Sexual assault survivors; Marital rape/sexual abuse survivors; Adult survivors of child sexual abuse; Incest victims/survivors; Prevention program; Community education

PLAINVIEW

HALE COUNTY RAPE CRISIS CENTER
PO Box 326, Plainview, TX 79073-0326
Crisis hotline: **(806) 293-7273 24 hrs**
Information: (806) 293-9772 8am-5pm
Contact: Sandy Howard, Exec Dir
TYPE OF AGENCY: Rape crisis center; Domestic violence program
CLIENTS/SERVICES: Sexual assault survivors; Marital rape/sexual abuse survivors; Child victims of sexual abuse; Adult survivors of child sexual abuse; Incest victims/survivors; Prevention program; Community education; Adolescent survivors of sexual abuse; Male survivors of sexual abuse

RICHMOND

CRIMINAL DISTRICT ATTORNEY'S OFFICE—VICTIM WITNESS PROGRAM
Ft Bend County Courthouse, Richmond, TX 77469
Information: (713) 461-4460 8am-5pm
Contact: Sherry Stavinoha, Victim Witness Coord
TYPE OF AGENCY: Victim/witness assistance program
AREAS SERVED: Fort Bend
YEARS IN OPERATION: 1½
ACCESSIBILITY: Wheelchair accessible
CLIENTS/SERVICES: Sexual assault survivors; Marital rape/sexual abuse survivors; Child victims of sexual abuse; Incest victims/survivors; Community education; Adolescent survivors of sexual abuse

FORT BEND COUNTY WOMEN'S REFUGE, INC
PO Box 183, Richmond, TX 77469
Crisis hotline: **(713) 342-HELP 24 hrs 7 days**
Information: (713) 342-0251 8:30am-4:30pm (Mon-Thu); 8:30am-Noon (Fri)
Contact: Maria Emerson, Exec Dir
TYPE OF AGENCY: Rape crisis center; Domestic violence program
AREAS SERVED: Fort Bend
YEARS IN OPERATION: 4
LANGUAGES: Spanish, French
ACCESSIBILITY: Wheelchair accessible
CASES SEXUAL ASSAULT/ABUSE (%): 75
CLIENTS/SERVICES: Sexual assault survivors; Marital rape/sexual abuse survivors; Adult survivors of child sexual abuse; Incest victims/survivors; Prevention program; Community education; Male survivors of sexual abuse

ROUND ROCK

WILLIAMSON COUNTY CRISIS CENTER
211 Commerce Cove, No 103, Round Rock, TX 78680
Crisis hotline: **(512) 255-1212 24 hrs**
Information: (512) 255-1278 8am-12pm, 1pm-5pm (Mon-Fri)
Contact: Susan Wukasch, Prog Dir
TYPE OF AGENCY: Rape crisis center; Domestic violence program
SPONSORING ORGANIZATION: Williamson-Burnet County Opportunities, Inc
AREAS SERVED: Williamson
YEARS IN OPERATION: 5
LANGUAGES: Spanish translation available
ACCESSIBILITY: Wheelchair accessible
CASES SEXUAL ASSAULT/ABUSE (%): 33

WILLIAMSON COUNTY CRISIS CENTER
(continued)

CLIENTS/SERVICES: Sexual assault survivors; Marital rape/sexual abuse survivors; Child victims of sexual abuse; Adult survivors of child sexual abuse; Incest victims/survivors; Prevention program; Community education; Adolescent survivors of sexual abuse; Male survivors of sexual abuse

SAN ANGELO

RAPE CRISIS SERVICES FOR CONCHO VALLEY
244 N Magdalen, San Angelo, TX 76903
Crisis hotline: **(915) 658-8888 24 hrs**
Information: (915) 655-8965
Contact: Rosemary Klingler, Dir
TYPE OF AGENCY: Rape crisis center; Child sexual abuse prevention program; Child Assault Prevention (CAP) Project
SPONSORING ORGANIZATION: Mental Health Mental Retardation Services for Concho Valley
CLIENTS/SERVICES: Sexual assault survivors; Marital rape/sexual abuse survivors; Child victims of sexual abuse; Adult survivors of child sexual abuse; Incest victims/survivors; Prevention program; Community education; Adolescent survivors of sexual abuse; Male survivors of sexual abuse

SAN ANTONIO

ALAMO AREA RAPE CRISIS CENTER
PO Box 27802, San Antonio, TX 78227
Crisis hotline: **(512) 349-7273 24 hrs**
Information: (512) 674-4900 8:30am-5pm
Contact: Sherry Abbott, Exec Dir
TYPE OF AGENCY: Rape crisis center; Child sexual abuse services; Child sexual abuse prevention program
AREAS SERVED: Bexar
YEARS IN OPERATION: 13
LANGUAGES: Spanish
ACCESSIBILITY: Signers for the hearing impaired
CASES SEXUAL ASSAULT/ABUSE (%): 100
DESCRIPTION: Crisis intervention for victims of sexual assault and their families; Support groups for female and male victims; Legal follow-up for victims going through the legal system. Offender treatment program under development
CLIENTS/SERVICES: Sexual assault survivors; Marital rape/sexual abuse survivors; Child victims of sexual abuse; Adult survivors of child sexual abuse; Incest victims/survivors; Prevention program; Community education; Adolescent survivors of sexual abuse; Male survivors of sexual abuse

CHILD ADVOCATES SAN ANTONIO
600 Mission Rd, San Antonio, TX 78210
Crisis hotline: **(512) 531-1072 9am-5pm**
Information: (512) 531-1072 9am-5pm
Contact: Ellinor Forland, Exec Dir
TYPE OF AGENCY: Child sexual abuse services; Child abuse services; Child advocacy
AREAS SERVED: Bexar
YEARS IN OPERATION: 5
LANGUAGES: Spanish
CASES SEXUAL ASSAULT/ABUSE (%): 30
DESCRIPTION: Serves as the voice in court for abused and neglected children who are placed in foster care, through the use of court appointed volunteers advocating for timely, permanent placement of the children into stable and nurturing families
CLIENTS/SERVICES: Child victims of sexual abuse; Incest victims/survivors

CITY OF SAN ANTONIO, DEPARTMENT OF HUMAN RESOURCES AND SERVICES—CHILDREN'S RESOURCES DIVISION
PO Box 839966, San Antonio, TX 78283-3966
Information: (512) 299-7671 7:45am-4:30pm (Mon-Fri)
TYPE OF AGENCY: Child sexual abuse services; Child sexual abuse prevention program
AREAS SERVED: Bexar
YEARS IN OPERATION: 4
LANGUAGES: Spanish
ACCESSIBILITY: Wheelchair accessible
CASES SEXUAL ASSAULT/ABUSE (%): 85
DESCRIPTION: Provides services for child victims and their families in nonfamilial sexual abuse cases. State provides services for all other child victims
CLIENTS/SERVICES: Child victims of sexual abuse; Prevention program; Community education; Adolescent survivors of sexual abuse
REQUIREMENTS: For direct services, victims must be 17 or younger and have offense report on file

FAMILY OUTREACH OF SAN ANTONIO
215 W Poplar, San Antonio, TX 78212
Information: (512) 225-4943 8:30am-5pm
Contact: Chris Boyle, Casework Mgr
TYPE OF AGENCY: Child sexual abuse prevention program
AREAS SERVED: Bexar
YEARS IN OPERATION: 13
LANGUAGES: Spanish
CASES SEXUAL ASSAULT/ABUSE (%): 25
DESCRIPTION: Prevention agency that uses trained volunteers to serve as Parent Aides; Teaches parenting skills classes; Teaches children personal safety rules
CLIENTS/SERVICES: Prevention program; Community education
SPECIAL PROGRAMS/SERVICES: STAR (Safety Through Assertive Response) is an assertiveness training program for children that teaches them how to protect themselves and how to recognize inappropriate touching. Different programs for preschool through 3rd grades, 4th-6th grades, and junior/senior high school students

FAMILY SEX ABUSE TREATMENT PROGRAM
230 Pereida St, San Antonio, TX 78210
Information: (513) 226-3391 8:30am-5pm (Mon-Fri)
Contact: John Dauer, ACSW, ACP, Coord
TYPE OF AGENCY: Counseling/mental health services; Child sexual abuse services
SPONSORING ORGANIZATION: Family Service Association
AREAS SERVED: Bexar
YEARS IN OPERATION: 10
LANGUAGES: Spanish
ACCESSIBILITY: Wheelchair accessible
CASES SEXUAL ASSAULT/ABUSE (%): 100
DESCRIPTION: Long-term outpatient psychotherapy for incest families, including incest offenders; Groups include Parents United, Adults Molested as Children, and Daughters United
CLIENTS/SERVICES: Child victims of sexual abuse; Adult survivors of child sexual abuse; Incest victims/survivors; Offender treatment program; Adolescent survivors of sexual abuse; Male survivors of sexual abuse; Publications/media
REQUIREMENTS: All offenders must admit to the crime; Child victims must be 6 or older
SPECIAL PROGRAMS/SERVICES: Video interviews with incest family members

SAN MARCOS

HAYS COUNTY WOMEN'S CENTER
PO Box 234, San Marcos, TX 78667
Crisis hotline: **(512) 396-4357 24 hrs**
Information: (512) 396-3404 8am-5pm
Contact: Lacey Sloan, Sexual Assault Svcs Coord
TYPE OF AGENCY: Rape crisis center; Domestic violence program
AREAS SERVED: Hays, Caldwell, Comal
YEARS IN OPERATION: 8
LANGUAGES: Spanish
ACCESSIBILITY: Wheelchair accessible
CASES SEXUAL ASSAULT/ABUSE (%): 50
DESCRIPTION: Provides 24-hour crisis response, counseling, social work and other supportive services for victims of family violence, sexual assault and child sexual abuse. Support groups available for adolescent, female, and male survivors; feminist martial arts/self-defense program available. Treatment program under development for incest offenders
CLIENTS/SERVICES: Sexual assault survivors; Marital rape/sexual abuse survivors; Child victims of sexual abuse; Adult survivors of child sexual abuse; Incest victims/survivors; Prevention program; Community education; Adolescent survivors of sexual abuse; Male survivors of sexual abuse; Healing
SPECIAL PROGRAMS/SERVICES: Healing for adult survivors of child sexual abuse through creative arts (poetry, writing, artwork); Wilderness therapy; Use of stones, crystals, smudging. Wilderness therapy and tube floats for adolescent survivors.

SHERMAN

CRISIS CENTER
PO Box 2112, Sherman, TX 75091
Crisis hotline: **(214) 893-5615 24 hrs**
Information: (214) 893-3909 8am-5pm
Contact: Leta Koch, Exec Dir
TYPE OF AGENCY: Rape crisis center; Domestic violence program
AREAS SERVED: Grayson, Fannin
YEARS IN OPERATION: 13
LANGUAGES: Spanish, German, and other translators available
ACCESSIBILITY: Wheelchair accessible; Signers for the hearing impaired (by arrangement)
CASES SEXUAL ASSAULT/ABUSE (%): 15
CLIENTS/SERVICES: Sexual assault survivors; Marital rape/sexual abuse survivors; Child victims of sexual abuse; Adult survivors of child sexual abuse; Incest victims/survivors; Prevention program; Community education; Adolescent survivors of sexual abuse

SOUR LAKE

WOMEN'S AND CHILDREN'S SHELTER OF SOUTHEAST TEXAS
PO Box 6606, Sour Lake, TX 77659
Crisis hotline: **(800) 621-8882 24 hrs daily**
Information: (409) 832-7575 8:30am-4:30pm
Contact: Betty J Tucker, Dir
TYPE OF AGENCY: Domestic violence program
SPONSORING ORGANIZATION: Family Services Association, Inc
AREAS SERVED: Hardin, Jefferson, Orange, Newton, Jasper, Chambers, Liberty
YEARS IN OPERATION: 11
LANGUAGES: Spanish
ACCESSIBILITY: Signers for the hearing impaired
CASES SEXUAL ASSAULT/ABUSE (%): 70
DESCRIPTION: Safe house protection; Advocacy; Counseling; Referrals to social service agencies; Treatment for rapists, child sexual abusers, incest offenders, and batterers
CLIENTS/SERVICES: Sexual assault survivors; Marital rape/sexual abuse survivors; Community education; Offender treatment program

TEXARKANA

DOMESTIC VIOLENCE PREVENTION, INC—BATTERED WOMEN SHELTER AND SEXUAL ASSAULT SERVICES
PO Box 712, Texarkana, TX 75504
Crisis hotline: **(214) 793-HELP 24 hrs (collect calls accepted)**
Information: (214) 794-4000
Contact: Vicki Janoe, Dir; Betty Hines, Sexual Assault Svcs Advocate
TYPE OF AGENCY: Rape crisis center; Domestic violence program
AREAS SERVED: Bowie, Cass, Marion, Morris, TX; Miller, Little River, Sevier, Hempstad, Howard, AR
DESCRIPTION: Comprehensive services for victims/survivors of sexual and domestic violence, including victims of cult/ritualistic abuse; Prevention programs for the differently abled, the elderly, and for single persons
CLIENTS/SERVICES: Sexual assault survivors; Marital rape/sexual abuse survivors; Child victims of sexual abuse; Adult survivors of child sexual abuse; Incest victims/survivors; Prevention program; Community education; Adolescent survivors of sexual abuse; Male survivors of sexual abuse; Ritualistic abuse victims/survivors; Disabled; Elderly

TYLER

EAST TEXAS CRISIS CENTER
1314 S Fleishel St, No 100, Tyler, TX 75791
Crisis hotline: **(800) 333-0358, (214) 595-5591 24 hrs**
Information: (214) 595-3199 8am-5:30pm (Mon-Fri)
Contact: Trent Goodwin, Victim Svc Dir
TYPE OF AGENCY: Rape crisis center; Domestic violence program; Victim/witness assistance program
AREAS SERVED: Smith, Wood, Rains, Van Zandt, Henderson, Anderson
YEARS IN OPERATION: 10
LANGUAGES: Spanish
ACCESSIBILITY: Wheelchair accessible; Telecommunications for the hearing impaired (TTY, TDY, etc.)
CASES SEXUAL ASSAULT/ABUSE (%): 25
DESCRIPTION: Comprehensive program/crisis intervention providing a full range of services for victims of crime; 24-hour hotline offers emotional support and information
CLIENTS/SERVICES: Sexual assault survivors; Marital rape/sexual abuse survivors; Child victims of sexual abuse; Adolescent survivors of sexual abuse; Male survivors of sexual abuse; Preschoolers
SPECIAL PROGRAMS/SERVICES: Antivictimization programs for daycare children including training the daycare workers, with parents invited to attend

VICTORIA

HOPE OF SOUTH TEXAS
PO Box 2237, Victoria, TX 77902-2237
Crisis hotline: **(512) 573-3600 24 hrs**
Information: (512) 573-5868 8am-5pm
Contact: Candy White, Admin
TYPE OF AGENCY: Rape crisis center
AREAS SERVED: Victoria, Calhoun, Dewitt, Goliad, Jackson, Lavaca, Gonzales
YEARS IN OPERATION: 3
LANGUAGES: Spanish
CASES SEXUAL ASSAULT/ABUSE (%): 90
CLIENTS/SERVICES: Sexual assault survivors; Marital rape/sexual abuse survivors; Child victims of sexual abuse; Adult survivors of child sexual abuse; Incest victims/survivors; Community education; Adolescent survivors of sexual abuse; Male survivors of sexual abuse

WACO

CENTER FOR ACTION AGAINST SEXUAL ASSAULT
201 W Waco Dr, Ste 213, Waco, TX 76707
Crisis hotline: **(817) 752-1113 24 hrs**
Information: (817) 752-9330 8:30am-5pm (Mon-Fri)
Contact: Sherri Sunaz, Educ Coord
TYPE OF AGENCY: Rape crisis center; Child sexual abuse services; Child sexual abuse prevention program; Acquaintance/date rape prevention program
AREAS SERVED: McLennan, Falls, Freestone, Limestone, Hill, Bosque
YEARS IN OPERATION: 7
LANGUAGES: Spanish
ACCESSIBILITY: Wheelchair accessible; Signers for the hearing impaired
CASES SEXUAL ASSAULT/ABUSE (%): 100
DESCRIPTION: Comprehensive rape crisis services, including support groups for female and male survivors; Prevention for children, adolescents, and university students and a special prevention program for senior citizens
CLIENTS/SERVICES: Sexual assault survivors; Marital rape/sexual abuse survivors; Child victims of sexual abuse; Adult survivors of child sexual abuse; Incest victims/survivors; Prevention program; Community education; Adolescent survivors of sexual abuse; Male survivors of sexual abuse; Elderly

WICHITA FALLS

FIRST STEP, INC
PO Box 773, Wichita Falls, TX 76307
Crisis hotline: **(817) 767-4933 24 hrs**
Information: (817) 767-3330 8am-5:30pm (Mon-Fri)
Contact: Beverly Edsall, Rape Crisis Coun
TYPE OF AGENCY: Rape crisis center; Domestic violence program
AREAS SERVED: Wichita
YEARS IN OPERATION: 12
LANGUAGES: Spanish
CASES SEXUAL ASSAULT/ABUSE (%): 100
CLIENTS/SERVICES: Sexual assault survivors; Marital rape/sexual abuse survivors; Child victims of sexual abuse; Adult survivors of child sexual abuse; Incest victims/survivors; Prevention program; Community education; Adolescent survivors of sexual abuse; Male survivors of sexual abuse

THE WOODLANDS

MONTGOMERY COUNTY WOMEN'S CENTER—RAPE CRISIS PROGRAM
PO Box 8666, The Woodlands, TX 77387
Crisis hotline: **(409) 539-5757, (713) 292-4338 24 hrs**
Information: (713) 367-8003 9am-5pm (Mon-Fri)
Contact: Sue Colbert, Outreach Coord; Nancy Harrington, Exec Dir
TYPE OF AGENCY: Rape crisis center; Domestic violence program
AREAS SERVED: Montgomery
YEARS IN OPERATION: 6
LANGUAGES: French, Spanish
ACCESSIBILITY: Signers for the hearing impaired
CASES SEXUAL ASSAULT/ABUSE (%): 100
DESCRIPTION: Provides crisis services for survivors of family violence and sexual assault through safe shelter, counseling, support groups, systems advocacy and accompaniment, and public education. Also provides feminist martial arts/self-defense program
CLIENTS/SERVICES: Sexual assault survivors; Marital rape/sexual abuse survivors; Child victims of sexual abuse; Adult survivors of child sexual abuse; Incest victims/survivors; Community education; Adolescent survivors of sexual abuse; Male survivors of sexual abuse

UTAH

LOGAN

BEAR RIVER MENTAL HEALTH SERVICES, INC
PO Box 683, Logan, UT 84321
Crisis hotline: **(801) 752-0750 24 hrs**
Information: (801) 752-0750, 734-9449 (Box Elder County) 24 hrs
Contact: Trent Wentz, PhD, Cache/Rich County Svcs Dir; Chuck Sharp, MS, Box Elder Svcs Dir
TYPE OF AGENCY: Counseling/mental health services
AREAS SERVED: Cache, Rich, Box Elder
ACCESSIBILITY: Wheelchair accessible
CASES SEXUAL ASSAULT/ABUSE (%): 5
CLIENTS/SERVICES: Sexual assault survivors; Marital rape/sexual abuse survivors; Child victims of sexual abuse; Adult survivors of child sexual abuse; Incest victims/survivors; Community education; Adolescent survivors of sexual abuse; Male survivors of sexual abuse

CITIZENS AGAINST PHYSICAL AND SEXUAL ABUSE (CAPSA)
PO Box 3617, Logan, UT 84321
Crisis hotline: **(801) 753-2500 24 hrs**
Information: (801) 752-4493 24 hrs
Contact: Susan Briggs, Dir
TYPE OF AGENCY: Rape crisis center; Domestic violence program
SPONSORING ORGANIZATION: Bear River Area Government
AREAS SERVED: Cache, Rich, Box Elder, UT; Southern ID; Western WY
YEARS IN OPERATION: 9
LANGUAGES: Spanish
ACCESSIBILITY: Wheelchair accessible
CASES SEXUAL ASSAULT/ABUSE (%): 50
DESCRIPTION: Crisis intervention for victims of rape; Legal and medical advocacy; Long-term counseling and support groups for victims; Emergency shelter for up to 72 hours if needed
CLIENTS/SERVICES: Sexual assault survivors; Marital rape/sexual abuse survivors; Adult survivors of child sexual abuse; Incest victims/survivors; Prevention program; Community education; Adolescent survivors of sexual abuse

OGDEN

THE REGIONAL TREATMENT CENTER FOR SEXUAL ABUSE
3595 Washington Blvd, Ste 204, Ogden, UT 84403
Information: (801) 394-7548 9am-5pm
Contact: Tamara Robinette, Dir
TYPE OF AGENCY: Counseling/mental health services; Child sexual abuse services
AREAS SERVED: Weber, Davis, Morgan, Box Elder
YEARS IN OPERATION: 7
CASES SEXUAL ASSAULT/ABUSE (%): 100
DESCRIPTION: Counseling for sexually abused children and their families; Group therapy for incest offenders
CLIENTS/SERVICES: Child victims of sexual abuse; Adult survivors of child sexual abuse; Incest victims/survivors; Community education; Offender treatment program; Adolescent survivors of sexual abuse; Male survivors of sexual abuse
REQUIREMENTS: Clients must file charges. Offenders must be in a private counseling service or residential facility.

VICTIM/WITNESS COUNCIL
Municipal Bldg, 7th Fl, Ogden, UT 84401
Crisis hotline: **911 24 hrs**
Information: (801) 399-8672 7am-4pm
Contact: Shari Vander Heide, Victim/Witness Coord
TYPE OF AGENCY: Victim/witness assistance program
SPONSORING ORGANIZATION: Weber County Attorney's Office
AREAS SERVED: Weber
YEARS IN OPERATION: 7
CASES SEXUAL ASSAULT/ABUSE (%): 20
CLIENTS/SERVICES: Sexual assault survivors; Marital rape/sexual abuse survivors; Child victims of sexual abuse; Adult survivors of child sexual abuse; Incest victims/survivors; Prevention program; Community education; Offender treatment program; Adolescent survivors of sexual abuse; Male survivors of sexual abuse; Publications/media
SPECIAL PROGRAMS/SERVICES: Booklet for elementary students; Secondary school court DOSA program, an orientation to the court system and a court tour

YOUR COMMUNITY CONNECTION
2261 Adams Ave, Ogden, UT 84401
Crisis hotline: **(801) 392-7273 24 hrs**
Information: (801) 394-9456 8am-5pm
Contact: Marilyn Mills, Child Treat Coord; Laura Roe, Women's Crisis Ctr Coord
TYPE OF AGENCY: Rape crisis center; Domestic violence program
SPONSORING ORGANIZATION: United Way
AREAS SERVED: Weber, Davis, Box Elder, Morgan
YEARS IN OPERATION: 48
CLIENTS/SERVICES: Sexual assault survivors; Marital rape/sexual abuse survivors; Child victims of sexual abuse; Adult survivors of child sexual abuse; Incest victims/survivors; Prevention program; Community education; Adolescent survivors of sexual abuse; Male survivors of sexual abuse
REQUIREMENTS: Must be 17 or older

PARK CITY

THE COUNSELING INSTITUTE
PO Box 566, Park City, UT 84060
Crisis hotline: **(801) 649-2426 9am-5pm**
Information: (801) 649-2426 9am-5pm
Contact: James P Wheeler, ACSW, Dir
TYPE OF AGENCY: Counseling/mental health services; Child sexual abuse services; Child sexual abuse prevention program; Child abuse services; Child abuse prevention program
AREAS SERVED: Summit, Wasatch
YEARS IN OPERATION: 6
CASES SEXUAL ASSAULT/ABUSE (%): 20
CLIENTS/SERVICES: Sexual assault survivors; Marital rape/sexual abuse survivors; Child victims of sexual abuse; Adult survivors of child sexual abuse; Incest victims/survivors; Prevention program; Community education; Offender treatment program; Adolescent survivors of sexual abuse; Male survivors of sexual abuse
REQUIREMENTS: Fees based on a sliding scale
SPECIAL PROGRAMS/SERVICES: Primary prevention curriculum on Positive Parenting for 9th grade students. The curriculum includes experiential exercises and is taught in eleven sessions

PROVO

CENTER FOR WOMEN AND CHILDREN IN CRISIS, INC
PO Box 1075, Provo, UT 84603
Crisis hotline: **(801) 377-5500 24 hrs daily**
Information: (801) 374-9351, 374-9352 8am-5pm
Contact: Exec Dir
TYPE OF AGENCY: Rape crisis center; Domestic violence program
AREAS SERVED: Utah, Wasatch, Summit
YEARS IN OPERATION: 4½
CASES SEXUAL ASSAULT/ABUSE (%): 20
CLIENTS/SERVICES: Sexual assault survivors; Marital rape/sexual abuse survivors; Child victims of sexual abuse; Adult survivors of child sexual abuse; Community education

PARENTS UNITED OF UTAH VALLEY
PO Box 1464, Provo, UT 84603
Information: (801) 374-9952 9am-5pm
Contact: Lynn M Roundy, Dir
TYPE OF AGENCY: Child sexual abuse services
AREAS SERVED: Utah, Wasatch, Summit
YEARS IN OPERATION: 5
CASES SEXUAL ASSAULT/ABUSE (%): 100
DESCRIPTION: Assists sexual abuse and incest victims ages 8-adult, offenders and non-offending spouses to work through their concerns in a group therapy format
CLIENTS/SERVICES: Child victims of sexual abuse; Adult survivors of child sexual abuse; Incest victims/survivors; Community education; Offender treatment program; Adolescent survi-

PARENTS UNITED OF UTAH VALLEY
(continued)

vors of sexual abuse; Male survivors of sexual abuse

SALT LAKE CITY

CLINIC FOR COUNSELING AND PSYCHOTHERAPY, INC AND NORTHWEST PASSAGE, INC
24 M St, No 1, Salt Lake City, UT 84103
Crisis hotline: **(801) 364-3138 24 hrs**
Information: (801) 363-9017 9am-7pm
Contact: Robert D Card, PhD, Pres; Craig Hansen, LCSW, Dir
TYPE OF AGENCY: Correctional facility; Residential treatment facility; Private practice; Offender treatment
AREAS SERVED: Statewide
YEARS IN OPERATION: Clinic 22, NWP 3
LANGUAGES: German
ACCESSIBILITY: Wheelchair accessible
CASES SEXUAL ASSAULT/ABUSE (%): 75
DESCRIPTION: Evaluation and treatment of sex abusers (rapists and child sexual abuse/incest offenders) on an outpatient basis. NWP is a residential treatment facility providing court-ordered 24-hour supervision and treatment for sex offenders. Frequently treats adults who are victims/survivors of sexual abuse as children, or victims of a more current rape. Offender treatment includes individual and group therapy, conditioning therapies, and classes for abusers on criminal thinking, sex education, and assertiveness training
CLIENTS/SERVICES: Sexual assault survivors; Marital rape/sexual abuse survivors; Adult survivors of child sexual abuse; Incest victims/survivors; Offender treatment program; Adolescent survivors of sexual abuse; Male survivors of sexual abuse
REQUIREMENTS: Works with adults or late teenagers. Charges must be filed (for both perpetrators and victims) if within the statute of limitations and if perpetrator can be located

FAMILY SUPPORT CENTER
2003 Lake St, Salt Lake City, UT 84105
Crisis hotline: **(801) 487-7500 24 hrs**
Information: (801) 487-7500
Contact: Elaine Ortman, RN, MS Clinical Dir
TYPE OF AGENCY: Counseling/mental health services; Child sexual abuse services; Child sexual abuse prevention program
AREAS SERVED: Statewide
YEARS IN OPERATION: 11
CASES SEXUAL ASSAULT/ABUSE (%): 100
DESCRIPTION: Psychological and corroborative assessments; Individual, marital, family, and group therapy; Crisis intervention; Networks with community agencies; AMAC groups; Parent support group
CLIENTS/SERVICES: Sexual assault survivors; Marital rape/sexual abuse survivors; Child victims of sexual abuse; Adult survivors of child sexual abuse; Incest victims/survivors; Prevention program; Community education; Adolescent survivors of sexual abuse; Male survivors of sexual abuse

SALT LAKE RAPE CRISIS CENTER
2035 S 1300 E, Salt Lake City, UT 84105
Crisis hotline: **(801) 467-7273 24 hrs**
Information: (801) 467-7282 8am-5pm
Contact: Christine Watters, Dir
TYPE OF AGENCY: Rape crisis center
YEARS IN OPERATION: 14
LANGUAGES: Spanish
ACCESSIBILITY: Wheelchair accessible
CASES SEXUAL ASSAULT/ABUSE (%): 98
CLIENTS/SERVICES: Sexual assault survivors; Marital rape/sexual abuse survivors; Child victims of sexual abuse; Adult survivors of child sexual abuse; Incest victims/survivors; Prevention program; Community education; Adolescent survivors of sexual abuse; Male survivors of sexual abuse

VICTIM COUNSELING UNIT
231 E 400 S, Salt Lake City, UT 84111
Crisis hotline: **(801) 483-5444 5pm-8am**
Information: (801) 363-7911 8am-5pm (Mon-Fri)
Contact: Julie Branch, Prog Dir
TYPE OF AGENCY: Victim/witness assistance program
SPONSORING ORGANIZATION: Valley Mental Health
AREAS SERVED: Salt Lake
YEARS IN OPERATION: 12
LANGUAGES: Spanish
ACCESSIBILITY: Wheelchair accessible
CASES SEXUAL ASSAULT/ABUSE (%): 85
CLIENTS/SERVICES: Sexual assault survivors; Marital rape/sexual abuse survivors; Child victims of sexual abuse; Adult survivors of child sexual abuse; Community education; Adolescent survivors of sexual abuse; Male survivors of sexual abuse
REQUIREMENTS: Referrals through police departments and attorneys.

WOMEN'S RESOURCE CENTER
293 Union Bldg, Salt Lake City, UT 84112
Information: (801) 581-8030 8am-5pm (Mon-Fri)
Contact: Beverly Purrington, Dir
TYPE OF AGENCY: College/university-based services; Child abuse prevention program; Acquaintance/date rape prevention program
SPONSORING ORGANIZATION: University of Utah
AREAS SERVED: Primarily Salt Lake and Utah; statewide
YEARS IN OPERATION: 16
LANGUAGES: Spanish
ACCESSIBILITY: Wheelchair accessible
CASES SEXUAL ASSAULT/ABUSE (%): 70
DESCRIPTION: Counseling for women students who have experienced or are experiencing sexual assault/abuse and marital rape. Seminars and support groups, including sexual harassment, self-defense, date rape prevention
CLIENTS/SERVICES: Sexual assault survivors; Marital rape/sexual abuse survivors; Adult survivors of child sexual abuse; Incest victims/survivors; Prevention program; Adolescent survivors of sexual abuse; Sexual harassment
REQUIREMENTS: First priority to faculty, staff, and students at the University; Community residents served on space available basis
SPECIAL PROGRAMS/SERVICES: Collaborated with an intern from the counseling center who had summarized the literature on sexual assault (especially date/acquaintance rape) and collected information on possible programs to implement for and/or by men to reduce sexual assault on campus. Began implementing new programs based on this research

YWCA WOMEN IN JEOPARDY
322 E 300 S, Salt Lake City, UT 84111
Crisis hotline: **(801) 355-2804 24 hrs**
Information: (801) 355-2804 8am-5pm
Contact: Kathryn Warner, Res Asst
TYPE OF AGENCY: Domestic violence program
YEARS IN OPERATION: 11
LANGUAGES: Spanish
ACCESSIBILITY: Wheelchair accessible; Signers for the hearing impaired
CLIENTS/SERVICES: Marital rape/sexual abuse survivors; Prevention program; Community education

VERMONT

BARRE

VERMONT VICTIM ASSISTANCE PROGRAM—WASHINGTON COUNTY
255 N Main St, Barre, VT 05641
Information: (802) 479-1074 8:30am-4:30pm
Contact: Aimee M'E Bunting, Victim Advocate
TYPE OF AGENCY: Victim/witness assistance program
AREAS SERVED: Washington
YEARS IN OPERATION: 2
LANGUAGES: French
ACCESSIBILITY: Wheelchair accessible; Telecommunications for the hearing impaired (TTY, TDY, etc.); Signers for the hearing impaired by arrangement
CASES SEXUAL ASSAULT/ABUSE (%): 40
CLIENTS/SERVICES: Sexual assault survivors; Child victims of sexual abuse
REQUIREMENTS: Charges must be filed with the State's Attorney's Office. Will work with clients before a criminal case is declared

BENNINGTON

BENNINGTON COUNTY VICTIM ADVOCATE
State's Attorney's Office, 1 Veterans Memorial Dr, Bennington, VT 05201
Information: (802) 442-8116 8:30am-3pm
Contact: Cecelia Brown, Victim Advocate
TYPE OF AGENCY: Victim/witness assistance program
SPONSORING ORGANIZATION: Vermont Victim Assistance Program
AREAS SERVED: Bennington
YEARS IN OPERATION: 2
ACCESSIBILITY: Wheelchair accessible
CASES SEXUAL ASSAULT/ABUSE (%): 40
CLIENTS/SERVICES: Sexual assault survivors; Marital rape/sexual abuse survivors; Child victims of sexual abuse; Adult survivors of child sexual abuse; Incest victims/survivors; Community education; Adolescent survivors of sexual abuse; Male survivors of sexual abuse
REQUIREMENTS: Crime must be reported to law enforcement agency.

PAVE (PROJECT AGAINST VIOLENT ENCOUNTERS)
PO Box 227, Bennington, VT 05201
Crisis hotline: **(802) 442-2111 24 hrs**
Information: (802) 442-2370 10:30am-4:30pm (Mon-Fri)
Contact: Barbara Acosta, Prog Coord
TYPE OF AGENCY: Domestic violence program
AREAS SERVED: Primarily Bennington
YEARS IN OPERATION: 8
LANGUAGES: Spanish
CASES SEXUAL ASSAULT/ABUSE (%): 12
CLIENTS/SERVICES: Sexual assault survivors; Adult survivors of child sexual abuse; Community education; Male survivors of sexual abuse; Male survivors of sexual abuse

PSYCHOTHERAPY ASSOCIATES
226 Union St, Bennington, VT 05201
Crisis hotline: **(802) 442-3520 24 hrs**
Information: (802) 442-3520
Contact: Louis Propp, PsyD, Psychologist
TYPE OF AGENCY: Child sexual abuse services; Private practice
AREAS SERVED: Bennington and surrounding areas
YEARS IN OPERATION: 10
ACCESSIBILITY: Wheelchair accessible
CASES SEXUAL ASSAULT/ABUSE (%): 25
DESCRIPTION: Therapy for stress-related disorders with psychological and psychiatric interventions; Individual therapy for child sexual abuse offenders and batterers
CLIENTS/SERVICES: Sexual assault survivors; Marital rape/sexual abuse survivors; Child victims of sexual abuse; Adult survivors of child sexual abuse; Incest victims/survivors; Offender treatment program; Adolescent survivors of sexual abuse; Male survivors of sexual abuse
REQUIREMENTS: Health or medical insurance

BRATTLEBORO

WINDHAM COUNTY STATE'S ATTORNEY— VICTIM ASSISTANCE PROGRAM
PO Box 785, Brattleboro, VT 05301
Information: (802) 257-7122 8am-4:30pm
Contact: Martha Stockwell, Victim Advocate
TYPE OF AGENCY: Victim/witness assistance program
AREAS SERVED: Windham
YEARS IN OPERATION: 2½
ACCESSIBILITY: Wheelchair accessible
CASES SEXUAL ASSAULT/ABUSE (%): 30
CLIENTS/SERVICES: Sexual assault survivors; Marital rape/sexual abuse survivors; Child victims of sexual abuse; Community education; Male survivors of sexual abuse
REQUIREMENTS: Must report crime to law enforcement

WOMEN'S CRISIS CENTER
PO Box 933, Brattleboro, VT 05301
Crisis hotline: **(802) 254-6954 24 hrs**
Information: (802) 257-7364 9am-5pm (Mon-Fri)
Contact: Ann Darling, Exec Dir
TYPE OF AGENCY: Rape crisis center; Domestic violence program; Child sexual abuse services
AREAS SERVED: Windham, Windsor, Bennington, VT; Cheshire, NH
YEARS IN OPERATION: 10
ACCESSIBILITY: Wheelchair accessible; Signers for the hearing impaired (by arrangement)
CASES SEXUAL ASSAULT/ABUSE (%): 6
CLIENTS/SERVICES: Sexual assault survivors; Marital rape/sexual abuse survivors; Child victims of sexual abuse; Adult survivors of child sexual abuse; Incest victims/survivors; Prevention program; Community education

BRISTOL

ADDISON COUNTY WOMEN IN CRISIS
6 Main St, Bristol, VT 05443
Crisis hotline: **(802) 453-2838 24 hrs**
Information: (802) 453-2838 10am-4pm
Contact: Carol Gibson-Warnoch, Dir
TYPE OF AGENCY: Rape crisis center; Domestic violence program
AREAS SERVED: Addison
YEARS IN OPERATION: 9
CASES SEXUAL ASSAULT/ABUSE (%): 25
CLIENTS/SERVICES: Sexual assault survivors; Marital rape/sexual abuse survivors; Child victims of sexual abuse; Adult survivors of child sexual abuse; Incest victims/survivors; Prevention program; Community education; Adolescent survivors of sexual abuse; Male survivors of sexual abuse

BURLINGTON

BEHAVIOR THERAPY AND PSYCHOTHERAPY CENTER
University of Vermont Department of Psychology, Burlington, VT 05405
Crisis hotline: **(802) 656-2661 6pm-8am**
Information: (802) 656-2661 8am-6pm
Contact: Karen Fondacaro, PhD, Clinical Psychologist
TYPE OF AGENCY: College/university-based services; Counseling/mental health services; Training/research
AREAS SERVED: Chittenden and surrounding counties
YEARS IN OPERATION: 13
ACCESSIBILITY: Wheelchair accessible
DESCRIPTION: Provides services for many psychological problems, while providing training for graduate students in the clinical psychology program. Regarding sexual abuse, provides treatment group for sex offenders, group and individual therapy for adolescent offenders, education/support group for parents of children who have been sexually abused, and family, individual, and marital therapy for incest cases
CLIENTS/SERVICES: Sexual assault survivors; Marital rape/sexual abuse survivors; Child victims of sexual abuse; Adult survivors of child sexual abuse; Incest victims/survivors; Community education; Offender treatment program

CHAMPLAIN VALLEY VICTIM SERVICES
415 S Willard St, Burlington, VT 05401
Information: (802) 864-4513 8am-6pm
Contact: Meg Foster, CSW, Dir
TYPE OF AGENCY: Victim/witness assistance program; Child sexual abuse services; Private practice; Child abuse services
SPONSORING ORGANIZATION: Vermont Victim Services Network
AREAS SERVED: Chittenden, Franklin, Grand Isle
YEARS IN OPERATION: 3
ACCESSIBILITY: Wheelchair accessible
CASES SEXUAL ASSAULT/ABUSE (%): 75
CLIENTS/SERVICES: Sexual assault survivors; Child victims of sexual abuse; Adult survivors of child sexual abuse; Incest victims/survivors; Community education; Adolescent survivors of sexual abuse
SPECIAL PROGRAMS/SERVICES: Provides social work services on contract for rural elementary schools to assist personnel in reporting suspected abuse and neglect

CHITTENDEN COUNTY STATE'S ATTORNEY'S OFFICE—VICTIM/WITNESS PROGRAM
PO Box 27, Burlington, VT 05402
Crisis hotline: **(802) 863-2865, or local police 24 hrs by pager**
Information: (802) 863-2865 8am-4:30pm
Contact: Doris Clayton-Viens, Victim-Witness Advocate
TYPE OF AGENCY: Victim/witness assistance program
AREAS SERVED: Chittenden
YEARS IN OPERATION: 2
LANGUAGES: Interpreters by arrangement
ACCESSIBILITY: Wheelchair accessible; Signers for the hearing impaired (by arrangement)
CASES SEXUAL ASSAULT/ABUSE (%): 30
CLIENTS/SERVICES: Sexual assault survivors; Marital rape/sexual abuse survivors; Child victims of sexual abuse; Prevention program; Community education; Adolescent survivors of sexual abuse; Male survivors of sexual abuse
REQUIREMENTS: Client must file a report with police.

WOMEN HELPING BATTERED WOMEN
PO Box 1535, Burlington, VT 05402
Crisis hotline: **(802) 658-1996 24 hrs daily**
Information: (802) 658-3131
Contact: Deb Baird, Public Inform Coord
TYPE OF AGENCY: Domestic violence program
AREAS SERVED: Chittenden
YEARS IN OPERATION: 14
LANGUAGES: French
ACCESSIBILITY: Wheelchair accessible; Telecommunications for the hearing impaired (TTY, TDY, etc.); Signers for the hearing impaired (by arrangement)
DESCRIPTION: Provides crisis services for battered women who have experienced physical, emotional, financial, as well as sexual abuse. Refers sexual assault victims to the Rape Crisis Center in Burlington
CLIENTS/SERVICES: Sexual assault survivors; Marital rape/sexual abuse survivors; Child victims of sexual abuse; Adult survivors of child sexual abuse; Incest victims/survivors; Prevention program; Community education

WOMEN'S ORGANIZATION AND RESOURCE CENTER
WORC Billings Student Center, Burlington, VT 05401
Information: (802) 860-1663 Answering machine
Contact: Beth Mintz, Advisor
TYPE OF AGENCY: College/university-based services; Rape prevention program
SPONSORING ORGANIZATION: University of Vermont
AREAS SERVED: Primarily university community, Burlington area
YEARS IN OPERATION: 16
ACCESSIBILITY: Wheelchair accessible
DESCRIPTION: Provides education to the university community about rape, battering, and pornography; Organized Take Back the Night marches and Rape Awareness Week; Sponsors speakers and shows films; Carries out direct political action
CLIENTS/SERVICES: Community education

WOMEN'S RAPE CRISIS CENTER
PO Box 92, Burlington, VT 05402
Crisis hotline: **(802) 863-1236 24 hrs**
Information: (802) 864-0555 9am-3pm (Mon-Fri)
Contact: Jamie Shaw, Coord/Dir
TYPE OF AGENCY: Rape crisis center; Child sexual abuse services; Residential treatment facility
AREAS SERVED: Mostly Chittenden
YEARS IN OPERATION: 15
LANGUAGES: Sign interpreter available
ACCESSIBILITY: Signers for the hearing impaired (by arrangement)
CASES SEXUAL ASSAULT/ABUSE (%): 100
DESCRIPTION: Provides a 24-hour hotline for victims/survivors of sexual assault (abuse and incest), their families and friends, accompaniment, legal advocacy, information and referrals. Conducts sexual assault awareness/prevention programs with a focus on the colleges and high schools. Co-sponsors feminist martial arts/self-defense program
CLIENTS/SERVICES: Sexual assault survivors; Marital rape/sexual abuse survivors; Child victims of sexual abuse; Adult survivors of child sexual abuse; Incest victims/survivors; Prevention program; Community education; Adolescent survivors of sexual abuse; Male survivors of sexual abuse

CHELSEA

ORANGE COUNTY SAFELINE
Box 254, Chelsea, VT 05038
Crisis hotline: **(800) 248-0432 24 hrs**
Information: (802) 685-4514 8am-4pm (Mon-Fri)
Contact: Rachel Beede, Maryann Zavez, Co-coords
TYPE OF AGENCY: Rape crisis center; Domestic violence program
SPONSORING ORGANIZATION: Central Vermont Community Action Council, Inc
AREAS SERVED: Orange
YEARS IN OPERATION: 1
CLIENTS/SERVICES: Sexual assault survivors; Marital rape/sexual abuse survivors; Prevention program; Community education

HARDWICK

AID TO WOMEN IN ABUSE AND RAPE EMERGENCIES (AWARE)
PO Box 307, Hardwick, VT 05843
Crisis hotline: **(802) 472-6463 24 hrs daily**
Information: (802) 472-6464 9am-12pm (Mon, Wed, Fri, Sat)
Contact: Martha Zweig, Office Coord
TYPE OF AGENCY: Rape crisis center; Domestic violence program
AREAS SERVED: Caledonia, parts of Lamoille and Orleans
YEARS IN OPERATION: 4
CASES SEXUAL ASSAULT/ABUSE (%): 20
CLIENTS/SERVICES: Sexual assault survivors; Marital rape/sexual abuse survivors; Adult survivors of child sexual abuse; Adolescent survivors of sexual abuse

MIDDLEBURY

COUNSELING SERVICE OF ADDISON COUNTY
89 Main St, Middlebury, VT 05753
Crisis hotline: **(802) 388-7641 24 hrs daily**
Information: (802) 388-6751 9am-9pm (Mon-Fri)
TYPE OF AGENCY: Counseling/mental health services
AREAS SERVED: Addison
YEARS IN OPERATION: 30
ACCESSIBILITY: Wheelchair accessible; Telecommunications for the hearing impaired (TTY, TDY, etc.); Signers for the hearing impaired
CASES SEXUAL ASSAULT/ABUSE (%): 25
CLIENTS/SERVICES: Sexual assault survivors; Marital rape/sexual abuse survivors; Child victims of sexual abuse; Adult survivors of child sexual abuse; Incest victims/survivors; Prevention program; Community education; Offender treatment program; Adolescent survivors of sexual abuse; Male survivors of sexual abuse

MONTPELIER

RESOLUTIONS
PO Box 1249, Montpelier, VT 05602
Information: (802) 223-2088 9am-5pm
Contact: Saul Schoenberg, Dir
TYPE OF AGENCY: Private practice; Offender treatment
SPONSORING ORGANIZATION: Institute of Professional Practice
AREAS SERVED: Washington, Lamoille, Caledonia, Orleans
YEARS IN OPERATION: 4
CASES SEXUAL ASSAULT/ABUSE (%): 100
DESCRIPTION: Community-based adult and adolescent sex offender population; Post-adjudication; Group and individual, cognitive behavioral, relapse-prevention model. Forensic psychosexual evaluations
CLIENTS/SERVICES: Offender treatment program
REQUIREMENTS: Adjudicated, not in denial, convicted of sexual offense, waiver of confidentiality, sign treatment contract, behavioral procedures, fee-for-service

SEXUAL ASSAULT CRISIS TEAM OF WASHINGTON COUNTY, INC
PO Box 1313, Montpelier, VT 05602
Crisis hotline: **(802) 223-7755 24 hrs**
Information: (802) 223-7755 varying
Contact: Harriet Beeman, Coord
TYPE OF AGENCY: Rape crisis center
AREAS SERVED: Washington
YEARS IN OPERATION: 4
ACCESSIBILITY: Wheelchair accessible
CASES SEXUAL ASSAULT/ABUSE (%): 100
CLIENTS/SERVICES: Sexual assault survivors; Marital rape/sexual abuse survivors; Adult survivors of child sexual abuse; Incest victims/survivors; Community education; Male survivors of sexual abuse

MORRISVILLE

CLARINA HOWARD NICHOLS CENTER
PO Box 517, Morrisville, VT 05661
Crisis hotline: **(802) 888-5256 24 hrs**
Information: (802) 888-5256 9am-5pm (Mon-Fri)
Contact: Judy Rex, Dir
TYPE OF AGENCY: Rape crisis center; Domestic violence program
AREAS SERVED: Lamoille
YEARS IN OPERATION: Rape crisis program 3
LANGUAGES: French
CASES SEXUAL ASSAULT/ABUSE (%): 100
DESCRIPTION: Provides services for victims/survivors of sexual assault and domestic violence; Feminist martial arts/self-defense program
CLIENTS/SERVICES: Sexual assault survivors; Marital rape/sexual abuse survivors; Child victims of sexual abuse; Adult survivors of child sexual abuse; Incest victims/survivors; Prevention program; Community education; Adolescent survivors of sexual abuse

NEWPORT

ABATE ONE
4 Court Sq, Newport, VT 05855
Crisis hotline: **(802) 334-2855 24 hrs**
Information: (802) 334-2855 9am-3pm
Contact: Ilene C Elliott, Exec Dir
TYPE OF AGENCY: Rape crisis center; Domestic violence program; Child sexual abuse prevention program
AREAS SERVED: Orleans, northern Essex
YEARS IN OPERATION: 8
CASES SEXUAL ASSAULT/ABUSE (%): 50
CLIENTS/SERVICES: Sexual assault survivors; Marital rape/sexual abuse survivors; Child victims of sexual abuse; Adult survivors of child sexual abuse; Incest victims/survivors; Prevention program; Community education; Adolescent survivors of sexual abuse

NORTH CLARENDON

ST FRANCIS CENTER FOR PERSONAL GROWTH
Box 57, Creek Rd, North Clarendon, VT 05759
Crisis hotline: **(802) 775-5652 as needed**
Information: (802) 775-5652 8am-6pm
Contact: Connie E Naitove, Psychotherapist and Multi-Arts Therapist
TYPE OF AGENCY: Counseling/mental health services; Private practice
AREAS SERVED: Counties within 60 miles of Rutland, VT, and within 60 miles of Hanover, NH (these include VT, NH, NY, and MA)
YEARS IN OPERATION: 11
LANGUAGES: French, Spanish
ACCESSIBILITY: Wheelchair accessible
CASES SEXUAL ASSAULT/ABUSE (%): 30-50
DESCRIPTION: Counseling services for victims/survivors and offenders, using the tools of Transactional Analysis and Gestalt therapy.
CLIENTS/SERVICES: Sexual assault survivors; Marital rape/sexual abuse survivors; Child victims of sexual abuse; Adult survivors of child sexual abuse; Incest victims/survivors; Prevention program; Community education; Offender treatment program; Creative arts therapy; Adolescent survivors of sexual abuse; Male survivors of sexual abuse; Prisoners
REQUIREMENTS: Ability to pay, eligibility for available grants of or insurance coverage
SPECIAL PROGRAMS/SERVICES: Offers training courses, workshops and lectures on the use of the arts therapies (art, drama, poetry, dance, and therapeutic recreation) with victims, survivors and offenders. These workshops include a book with basic data, techniques, references, etc

RUTLAND

RUTLAND COUNTY WOMEN'S NETWORK AND SHELTER
PO Box 313, Rutland, VT 05701
Crisis hotline: **(802) 775-3232 24 hrs**
Information: (802) 775-6788 8am-5pm
Contact: Jody Estenfeld, Sexual Assault Coord; Tamara Trombley, Asst Sexual Assault Coord/Mgr
TYPE OF AGENCY: Rape crisis center; Domestic violence program; Child sexual abuse services; Child sexual abuse prevention program
AREAS SERVED: Rutland, Windsor
YEARS IN OPERATION: 7
CASES SEXUAL ASSAULT/ABUSE (%): 30
DESCRIPTION: Services for sexual assault and domestic violence survivors; Individual and group therapy for batterers
CLIENTS/SERVICES: Sexual assault survivors; Marital rape/sexual abuse survivors; Child victims of sexual abuse; Adult survivors of child sexual abuse; Incest victims/survivors; Prevention program; Community education; Adolescent survivors of sexual abuse; Male survivors of sexual abuse

VERMONT EDUCATIONAL SUPPORT ASSOCIATES, INC
162 N Main St, Rutland, VT 05701
Information: (802) 775-6331 8am-5pm
Contact: William L Cunningham, PhD, Clinical Dir
TYPE OF AGENCY: Private practice; Offender treatment
AREAS SERVED: Rutland, Bennington, Windsor, Orange, Windham
YEARS IN OPERATION: 4
ACCESSIBILITY: Wheelchair accessible
CASES SEXUAL ASSAULT/ABUSE (%): 90
CLIENTS/SERVICES: Sexual assault survivors; Marital rape/sexual abuse survivors; Child victims of sexual abuse; Adult survivors of child sexual abuse; Incest victims/survivors; Community education; Offender treatment program; Adolescent survivors of sexual abuse; Male survivors of sexual abuse
REQUIREMENTS: To receive services as a sex offender, the adolescent or adult must be on probation or under contract with a court diversion board
SPECIAL PROGRAMS/SERVICES: In addition to a male adolescent sex offender treatment group, has started a female adolescent sex offender treatment group

VERMONT VICTIM ASSISTANCE PROGRAM
PO Box 6284, Rutland, VT 05701
Information: (802) 775-2531 7:30am-5pm
Contact: Lynne Black, Victim Asst
TYPE OF AGENCY: Victim/witness assistance program
SPONSORING ORGANIZATION: Rutland County State's Attorney's Office
AREAS SERVED: Rutland
YEARS IN OPERATION: 2
ACCESSIBILITY: Wheelchair accessible
CASES SEXUAL ASSAULT/ABUSE (%): 50
CLIENTS/SERVICES: Sexual assault survivors; Child victims of sexual abuse; Community education
REQUIREMENTS: Client must report incident to the police.

SAINT ALBANS

THE FAMILY CENTER—DOMESTIC VIOLENCE AND SEXUAL ASSAULT PREVENTION PROGRAM
86 N Main St, Saint Albans, VT 05478
Crisis hotline: **Sheriff (802) 524-2121, 868-4866 After hrs**
Information: (802) 524-6574, (800) 527-7748, Enosburg outreach (802) 933-4915 8:30am-4:30pm
Contact: Lynda Blanchard, Anne Baxter, Co-Dirs
TYPE OF AGENCY: Rape crisis center; Domestic violence program; Child sexual abuse prevention program
AREAS SERVED: Franklin, Grand Isle
YEARS IN OPERATION: 9
LANGUAGES: French
CASES SEXUAL ASSAULT/ABUSE (%): 15-20
DESCRIPTION: Services for survivors of sexual assault and domestic violence; Group for non-offending parents of sexually abused children
CLIENTS/SERVICES: Sexual assault survivors; Marital rape/sexual abuse survivors; Child victims of sexual abuse; Adult survivors of child sexual abuse; Incest victims/survivors; Prevention program; Community education; Adolescent survivors of sexual abuse; Male survivors of sexual abuse

SAINT JOHNSBURY

UMBRELLA RAPE CRISIS TEAM
1 Prospect St, Saint Johnsbury, VT 05819
Crisis hotline: **(802) 748-8141 24 hrs**
Information: (802) 748-8645 8:30am-4:30pm
Contact: Diane Wemple, Rape Crisis Team Asst
TYPE OF AGENCY: Rape crisis center; Child sexual abuse services; Child sexual abuse prevention program
SPONSORING ORGANIZATION: The Umbrella, Inc
AREAS SERVED: Caledonia, Orleans, Essex, Franklin, Lamoille, VT; Coos, Grafton, NH
YEARS IN OPERATION: 11
LANGUAGES: French
ACCESSIBILITY: Wheelchair accessible
CASES SEXUAL ASSAULT/ABUSE (%): 100
DESCRIPTION: Comprehensive rape crisis services; Support group for parents of sexually abused children
CLIENTS/SERVICES: Sexual assault survivors; Marital rape/sexual abuse survivors; Child victims of sexual abuse; Adult survivors of child sexual abuse; Incest victims/survivors; Prevention program; Community education; Adolescent survivors of sexual abuse; Male survivors of sexual abuse; Publications/media
SPECIAL PROGRAMS/SERVICES: Courtwatch, a community volunteer organization, monitors all legal proceedings against accused offenders and/or assists victim in courtroom protocol. Publications: *Courtwatch Manual, Surviving Sexual Abuse, Surviving the Sexual Abuse of Your Child*. Films/videotapes: *TLC: Talk, Listen, Care* sexual abuse prevention video for parents

SPRINGFIELD

NEW BEGINNINGS
100 River St, Springfield, VT 05156
Crisis hotline: **(802) 885-2050 24 hrs**
Information: (802) 885-2368 9am-5pm (Mon-Fri)
Contact: Teri Lamb, Exec Dir
TYPE OF AGENCY: Rape crisis center; Domestic violence program
AREAS SERVED: Windsor, North Windham
YEARS IN OPERATION: 8
LANGUAGES: French
ACCESSIBILITY: Wheelchair accessible
CASES SEXUAL ASSAULT/ABUSE (%): 10
CLIENTS/SERVICES: Sexual assault survivors; Marital rape/sexual abuse survivors; Child victims of sexual abuse; Adult survivors of child sexual abuse; Incest victims/survivors; Prevention program; Community education; Adolescent survivors of sexual abuse

STOWE

MOUNTAIN AFFILIATES IN PSYCHOLOGY
PO Box 424, Stowe, VT 05672
Crisis hotline: **(802) 253-7337 7am-11pm**
Information: (802) 253-7337 7am-11pm
Contact: Rodger Kessler, Dir
TYPE OF AGENCY: Private practice
YEARS IN OPERATION: 7
ACCESSIBILITY: Wheelchair accessible
CLIENTS/SERVICES: Sexual assault survivors; Marital rape/sexual abuse survivors; Child victims of sexual abuse; Adult survivors of child sexual abuse; Incest victims/survivors; Prevention program; Community education; Offender treatment program; Adolescent survivors of sexual abuse; Male survivors of sexual abuse

WHITE RIVER JUNCTION

THE FAMILY PLACE
34 Gates St, White River Junction, VT 05001
Information: (802) 296-2545 7:30am-5:30pm, evenings by appointment
Contact: Christie Jacobsen, Exec Dir
TYPE OF AGENCY: Counseling/mental health services; Child sexual abuse prevention program; Private practice; Child abuse services; Child abuse prevention program
AREAS SERVED: Windsor and Southern Orange, VT; Grafton, NH
YEARS IN OPERATION: 7
ACCESSIBILITY: Wheelchair accessible

THE FAMILY PLACE *(continued)*

CASES SEXUAL ASSAULT/ABUSE (%): 50% of parents of children are survivors of abuse (sexual, physical, emotional), 5% of children

DESCRIPTION: Prevention-oriented parent-child center, empowering young children and their families. Integrates *Children Are People* and *Child Assault Prevention* curricula. Sponsors parent support groups and chapter of Parents Anonymous

CLIENTS/SERVICES: Sexual assault survivors; Marital rape/sexual abuse survivors; Child victims of sexual abuse; Adult survivors of child sexual abuse; Incest victims/survivors; Prevention program; Community education; Preschoolers; Healing; Publications/media

REQUIREMENTS: Families with young children (prenatal-12); Therapeutic services available on sliding scale fee

SPECIAL PROGRAMS/SERVICES: Creating a video and workbook for teachers of young children and parents called *Promoting Healthy Preschoolers: Body, Mind and Spirit*. The focus is on prevention and includes the following topics: communication, dealing with feelings, building self-esteem, empowerment, and personal safety. Use of metaphor, inner child and therapeutic touch for healing of adult survivors of sexual assault and child sexual abuse

WINDSOR COUNTY VICTIM ASSISTANCE PROGRAM

Box 488, White River Junction, VT 05001
Information: (802) 295-8870 8am-5pm
Contact: Terri Satterlee, Victim Advocate

TYPE OF AGENCY: Victim/witness assistance program
AREAS SERVED: Windsor
YEARS IN OPERATION: 2½
ACCESSIBILITY: Wheelchair accessible
CASES SEXUAL ASSAULT/ABUSE (%): 20
CLIENTS/SERVICES: Sexual assault survivors; Child victims of sexual abuse; Community education; Male survivors of sexual abuse
REQUIREMENTS: Client must file criminal charges

VIRGINIA

ALEXANDRIA

FAIRFAX COUNTY VICTIM ASSISTANCE NETWORK
8119 Holland Rd, Alexandria, VA 22306
Crisis hotline: **(703) 360-7273 24 hrs**
Information: (703) 360-6910 Days and evenings (Mon-Sat)
Contact: Anne Van Ryzin, Coord
TYPE OF AGENCY: Rape crisis center; Domestic violence program; Counseling/mental health services; Child sexual abuse prevention program; Acquaintance/date rape prevention program
SPONSORING ORGANIZATION: Mount Vernon Center for Community Mental Health
AREAS SERVED: Fairfax County, Cities of Fairfax and Falls Church
YEARS IN OPERATION: 13
LANGUAGES: Spanish
ACCESSIBILITY: Wheelchair accessible; Telecommunications for the hearing impaired (TTY, TDY, etc.); Signers for the hearing impaired
CASES SEXUAL ASSAULT/ABUSE (%): 40
DESCRIPTION: Countywide network of prevention, education, and direct victim services related to sexual assault and domestic violence; Support groups for survivors of sexual assault, domestic violence, and parents of children who have been sexually assaulted by someone other than a family member; Seminars on the effects of sexual assault are available for concerned men
CLIENTS/SERVICES: Sexual assault survivors; Marital rape/sexual abuse survivors; Child victims of sexual abuse; Prevention program; Community education; Adolescent survivors of sexual abuse; Male survivors of sexual abuse; Preschoolers
SPECIAL PROGRAMS/SERVICES: Community education: "Who Do You Tell," for children ages 5-11 and/or their parents; "Touch" workshops, film developed by Illusion Theatre for adults and children; "Building Blocks for Safety," program for teachers and parents of preschoolers and daycare providers; "A Touchy Subject," program for parents and adult caretakers, depicting situations in which adults discuss sexual abuse prevention with preschool and school-aged children; "Teen Rape/Acquaintance Rape" program; "A Time to Tell—Teen Sexual Abuse," a film about acquaintance rape and incest; Sexual assault/rape awareness and precaution programs for adults; Sexual assault/rape awareness and intervention program for those providing care for the victim (medical, legal, and social service care providers)

NORTHERN VIRGINIA FAMILY SERVICE
3321 Duke St, Alexandria, VA 22314
Information: (703) 370-3223 9am-9pm (Mon, Tue, Wed); 9am-5pm (Thu, Fri)
Contact: Jim Alexander, Admin Supv
TYPE OF AGENCY: Counseling/mental health services
YEARS IN OPERATION: 64
ACCESSIBILITY: Wheelchair accessible
CASES SEXUAL ASSAULT/ABUSE (%): 10
DESCRIPTION: Family service agency oriented to short-term individual, couple, and family therapy
CLIENTS/SERVICES: Sexual assault survivors; Marital rape/sexual abuse survivors; Child victims of sexual abuse; Adult survivors of child sexual abuse; Incest victims/survivors; Adolescent survivors of sexual abuse

RAPE VICTIM COMPANION PROGRAM
2525 Mt Vernon Ave, Unit 6, Alexandria, VA 22301
Crisis hotline: **(703) 683-7273 24 hrs**
Information: (703) 838-0970 9am-6pm
Contact: Kathy Hagans, Health and Safety Coord
TYPE OF AGENCY: Rape crisis center; Child sexual abuse services
SPONSORING ORGANIZATION: City of Alexandria Office on Women
AREAS SERVED: City of Alexandria
YEARS IN OPERATION: 14
ACCESSIBILITY: Wheelchair accessible; Telecommunications for the hearing impaired (TTY, TDY, etc.); Signers for the hearing impaired
CASES SEXUAL ASSAULT/ABUSE (%): 100
DESCRIPTION: Works as advocate for rape victims from crisis intervention through court advocacy and for children who are victims of nonfamilial sexual assault. Feminist martial arts/self-defense program available. Anger management groups for batterers
CLIENTS/SERVICES: Sexual assault survivors; Marital rape/sexual abuse survivors; Child victims of sexual abuse; Adult survivors of child sexual abuse; Incest victims/survivors; Prevention program; Community education; Publications/media
SPECIAL PROGRAMS/SERVICES: Videotape program *Seeking Justice*, describes one victim's attempt to prosecute a rape case

SCAN (STOP CHILD ABUSE NOW) OF NORTHERN VIRGINIA
216 S Peyton St, Alexandria, VA 22314
Information: (703) 836-1820 9am-4pm
Contact: Vicki Almquist, Pres
TYPE OF AGENCY: Child sexual abuse prevention program; Child abuse prevention program; Child advocacy
AREAS SERVED: Fairfax, Loudoun, Arlington, Prince William, Alexandria
YEARS IN OPERATION: 1½
CLIENTS/SERVICES: Prevention program; Community education
SPECIAL PROGRAMS/SERVICES: Has two court appointed special advocate (CASA) programs, in Alexandria and Fairfax Counties. Trained volunteers represent a child's best interest in cases of abuse or neglect

AMHERST

AMHERST COUNTY VICTIM/WITNESS PROGRAM
PO Box 358, Amherst, VA 24521
Information: (804) 946-9316 9am-5pm (Mon-Fri)
Contact: Gregory N Britto, Asst Commonwealth's Attorney
TYPE OF AGENCY: Victim/witness assistance program
SPONSORING ORGANIZATION: Amherst County Commonwealth's Attorney's Office
AREAS SERVED: Amherst
YEARS IN OPERATION: 3
ACCESSIBILITY: Wheelchair accessible
CASES SEXUAL ASSAULT/ABUSE (%): 5
CLIENTS/SERVICES: Sexual assault survivors; Child victims of sexual abuse

ARLINGTON

THE ARLINGTON COMMUNITY TEMPORARY SHELTER
PO Box 1285, Arlington, VA 22210
Crisis hotline: **(703) 237-0881 24 hrs**
Information: (703) 536-1849 24 hrs
Contact: Rhonda Wilbien, Exec Dir
TYPE OF AGENCY: Domestic violence program
AREAS SERVED: Arlington
YEARS IN OPERATION: 9
LANGUAGES: Spanish
ACCESSIBILITY: Wheelchair accessible
CLIENTS/SERVICES: Marital rape/sexual abuse survivors; Adult survivors of child sexual abuse; Prevention program; Community education

NORTHERN VIRGINIA HOTLINE
PO Box 187, Arlington, VA 22210
Crisis hotline: **(703) 527-4077 24 hrs 7 days**
Contact: Marty Pearl, Dir
TYPE OF AGENCY: Counseling/mental health services; Telephone crisis hotline; Information and referral
AREAS SERVED: Arlington, Fairfax, Loudoun, Prince William, City of Alexandria, VA; DC; Montgomery, Prince Georges, Charles, MD
YEARS IN OPERATION: 19
DESCRIPTION: Provides 24-hour 7-day listening service for all types of calls. For sexual assault/child abuse calls: talks with the caller, gets him/her to safety, offers referrals for follow-through care with local agencies

NORTHERN VIRGINIA HOTLINE
(continued)

CLIENTS/SERVICES: Sexual assault survivors; Marital rape/sexual abuse survivors; Child victims of sexual abuse; Adult survivors of child sexual abuse; Incest victims/survivors

RAPE AND DOMESTIC VIOLENCE SERVICES OF ARLINGTON
1725 N George Mason Dr, Arlington, VA 22205
Crisis hotline: **(703) 358-4848 24 hrs**
Information: (703) 358-5150 9am-5pm
Contact: Marie-France Michand, MH Therapist/Community Educator
TYPE OF AGENCY: Counseling/mental health services; Child sexual abuse prevention program
AREAS SERVED: Arlington
LANGUAGES: Spanish, French, Creole, German
ACCESSIBILITY: Wheelchair accessible; Signers for the hearing impaired
CLIENTS/SERVICES: Sexual assault survivors; Marital rape/sexual abuse survivors; Adult survivors of child sexual abuse; Incest victims/survivors; Community education

BRISTOL

BRISTOL CRISIS CENTER
PO Box 642, Bristol, VA 24201
Crisis hotline: **(703) 466-2312 24 hrs**
Information: (703) 466-2218 8am-5pm
Contact: Donna Shortt, Sexual Assault Prog Coord
TYPE OF AGENCY: Rape crisis center; Domestic violence program
AREAS SERVED: Washington, Bristol, VA; Sullivan, Bristol, TN
YEARS IN OPERATION: 1½
ACCESSIBILITY: Wheelchair accessible
CASES SEXUAL ASSAULT/ABUSE (%): 10
CLIENTS/SERVICES: Sexual assault survivors; Marital rape/sexual abuse survivors; Child victims of sexual abuse; Adult survivors of child sexual abuse; Incest victims/survivors; Prevention program; Community education; Adolescent survivors of sexual abuse; Male survivors of sexual abuse

VICTIM/WITNESS ASSISTANCE PROGRAM
497 Cumberland St, City Hall, Bristol, VA 24201
Information: (703) 466-5988 9am-5pm
Contact: Jo Thurston, Dir
TYPE OF AGENCY: Victim/witness assistance program
AREAS SERVED: Washington, City of Bristol
YEARS IN OPERATION: 3
ACCESSIBILITY: Wheelchair accessible
CASES SEXUAL ASSAULT/ABUSE (%): 10
CLIENTS/SERVICES: Sexual assault survivors; Marital rape/sexual abuse survivors; Child victims of sexual abuse; Adult survivors of child sexual abuse; Incest victims/survivors; Community education; Adolescent survivors of sexual abuse; Male survivors of sexual abuse

CHARLOTTESVILLE

SEXUAL ASSAULT RESOURCE AGENCY (SARA)
PO Box 6705, Charlottesville, VA 22906
Crisis hotline: **(804) 977-7273 24 hrs daily**
Information: (804) 295-7273 9am-6pm
Contact: Annette Grimm, Exec Dr
TYPE OF AGENCY: Rape crisis center; Child sexual abuse services; Child sexual abuse prevention program
AREAS SERVED: Albemarle, Fluvanna, Louisa, Greene, Nelson, Orange
YEARS IN OPERATION: 14
LANGUAGES: Spanish, French
ACCESSIBILITY: Signers for the hearing impaired
CASES SEXUAL ASSAULT/ABUSE (%): 100

CLIENTS/SERVICES: Sexual assault survivors; Marital rape/sexual abuse survivors; Child victims of sexual abuse; Adult survivors of child sexual abuse; Incest victims/survivors; Prevention program; Community education

SHELTER FOR HELP IN EMERGENCY
PO Box 3013, Charlottesville, VA 22903
Crisis hotline: **(804) 293-8509 24 hrs**
Information: (804) 293-6155 24 hrs
Contact: Deborah D Cobb, Exec Dir; Ceara Sullivan, Client Svcs
TYPE OF AGENCY: Domestic violence program
AREAS SERVED: Fluvanna, Greene, Louisa, Nelson, and city of Charlottesville
YEARS IN OPERATION: 10
ACCESSIBILITY: Wheelchair accessible; Signers for the hearing impaired
CASES SEXUAL ASSAULT/ABUSE (%): 25
DESCRIPTION: Emergency shelter for survivors of domestic violence/sexual abuse; Information, referral, advocacy, and support groups for abused women; Self-help groups for batterers
CLIENTS/SERVICES: Sexual assault survivors; Marital rape/sexual abuse survivors; Adult survivors of child sexual abuse; Prevention program; Community education

TASK FORCE ON CHILD SEXUAL VICTIMIZATION
413 E Market St, Charlottesville, VA 22901
Crisis hotline: **(804) 972-1800, 295-RAPE 24 hrs**
Information: (804) 972-1800
Contact: Susan Karlson, Child Sexual Abuse Svcs Advocate
TYPE OF AGENCY: Counseling/mental health services; Child sexual abuse services
SPONSORING ORGANIZATION: Region Ten Community Services Board
AREAS SERVED: Charlottesville, Albemarle, Greene, Louisa, Fluvanna, Nelson
YEARS IN OPERATION: 2
ACCESSIBILITY: Wheelchair accessible; Signers for the hearing impaired (by arrangement)
CASES SEXUAL ASSAULT/ABUSE (%): 100
DESCRIPTION: Counseling for sexually abused children and adolescents, and adult survivors of child sexual abuse. Coordination of and referrals for offender treatment
CLIENTS/SERVICES: Child victims of sexual abuse; Adult survivors of child sexual abuse; Incest victims/survivors; Community education; Adolescent survivors of sexual abuse; Male survivors of sexual abuse

CHESTERFIELD

CHESTERFIELD COUNTY SHERIFF'S OFFICE—VICTIM-WITNESS ASSISTANCE PROGRAM
PO Box 554, Chesterfield, VA 23832
Crisis hotline: **(804) 796-HELP 24 hrs**
Information: (804) 796-7087 8:30am-5pm
Contact: Penny W Staver, Dir
TYPE OF AGENCY: Victim/witness assistance program
AREAS SERVED: Chesterfield
YEARS IN OPERATION: 3
CASES SEXUAL ASSAULT/ABUSE (%): 25
CLIENTS/SERVICES: Sexual assault survivors; Marital rape/sexual abuse survivors; Child victims of sexual abuse; Incest victims/survivors; Community education
REQUIREMENTS: Crime must have occurred in Chesterfield County

CULPEPER

ASSOCIATES FOR GROWTH
763 Madison Rd, Culpeper, VA 22701
Crisis hotline: **(703) 825-9566 24 hrs**
Information: (703) 825-9566 9am-8pm
Contact: Susan L Vignola, LCSW
TYPE OF AGENCY: Child sexual abuse services; Private practice

AREAS SERVED: Culpeper, Madison, Orange, Rappahamock, Fauquier, Spotsylvania
YEARS IN OPERATION: 6
ACCESSIBILITY: Wheelchair accessible
CASES SEXUAL ASSAULT/ABUSE (%): 20
CLIENTS/SERVICES: Sexual assault survivors; Marital rape/sexual abuse survivors; Child victims of sexual abuse; Adult survivors of child sexual abuse; Incest victims/survivors; Community education; Offender treatment program; Adolescent survivors of sexual abuse; Male survivors of sexual abuse

SERVICES TO ABUSED FAMILIES, INC/WOMEN'S ABUSE SHELTER
PO Box 402, Culpeper, VA 22701
Crisis hotline: **(703) 825-8876 24 hrs**
Information: (703) 825-8876 9am-5pm
Contact: Samuel D Vala, Exec Dir
TYPE OF AGENCY: Domestic violence program
AREAS SERVED: Culpeper, Fauquier, Madison, Orange, Rappahannock
YEARS IN OPERATION: 8
CLIENTS/SERVICES: Marital rape/sexual abuse survivors; Prevention program; Community education; Publications/media
SPECIAL PROGRAMS/SERVICES: Offers videotape programs to educate public about sexual abuse

DANVILLE

DOVES, INC—RAPE CRISIS SERVICES
PO Box 2381, Danville, VA 24541
Crisis hotline: **(804) 791-1400 24 hrs 7 days**
Information: (804) 799-3683 9am-5pm (Mon-Fri)
Contact: Barbara Jo Brown, Exec Dir
TYPE OF AGENCY: Rape crisis center
AREAS SERVED: Danville city, Pittsylvania
YEARS IN OPERATION: 5
CASES SEXUAL ASSAULT/ABUSE (%): 100
CLIENTS/SERVICES: Sexual assault survivors; Marital rape/sexual abuse survivors; Adult survivors of child sexual abuse; Incest victims/survivors; Prevention program; Community education; Male survivors of sexual abuse

FAIRFAX

FAIRFAX COUNTY POLICE DEPARTMENT—VICTIM/WITNESS ASSISTANCE PROGRAM
4100 Chain Bridge Rd, Fairfax, VA 22030
Information: (703) 246-2141, Police dept 691-2131 8am-4:30pm; on call through police dept after hrs
Contact: Virginia Johnson, Volunteer Coord
TYPE OF AGENCY: Victim/witness assistance program
AREAS SERVED: Fairfax
YEARS IN OPERATION: 2
LANGUAGES: Interpreters available
ACCESSIBILITY: Wheelchair accessible
CASES SEXUAL ASSAULT/ABUSE (%): 25
CLIENTS/SERVICES: Sexual assault survivors; Marital rape/sexual abuse survivors; Child victims of sexual abuse; Adult survivors of child sexual abuse; Incest victims/survivors; Community education

PARENTS UNITED
10301 Democracy Ln, Fairfax, VA 22030
Information: (703) 246-7518 8am-4:30pm
Contact: Meriam S Rogan, Community Relations Planner
TYPE OF AGENCY: Child sexual abuse services
SPONSORING ORGANIZATION: Fairfax DSS and Woodburn Mental Health Center
AREAS SERVED: Fairfax, Arlington
YEARS IN OPERATION: 5
ACCESSIBILITY: Wheelchair accessible
CASES SEXUAL ASSAULT/ABUSE (%): 100
DESCRIPTION: Professionally facilitated self-help group for sexual abusers, their partners; Adults Molested As Children (AMACS)

PARENTS UNITED *(continued)*

CLIENTS/SERVICES: Sexual assault survivors; Child victims of sexual abuse; Adult survivors of child sexual abuse; Incest victims/survivors; Offender treatment program

REQUIREMENTS: Abusers must acknowledge responsibility for the abuse; All members must be in or have completed an individual treatment program

FREDERICKSBURG

FREDERICKSBURG AREA RAPE CRISIS PROGRAM
PO Box 1276, Fredericksburg, VA 22402
Crisis hotline: **(703) 371-1666 24 hrs**
Information: (703) 371-1666
Contact: Cynthia Huff, Admin Coord
TYPE OF AGENCY: Rape crisis center
AREAS SERVED: Stafford, King George, Spotsylvania, Caroline, City of Fredericksburg
YEARS IN OPERATION: 2
LANGUAGES: French
CASES SEXUAL ASSAULT/ABUSE (%): 100
CLIENTS/SERVICES: Sexual assault survivors; Marital rape/sexual abuse survivors; Adult survivors of child sexual abuse; Incest victims/survivors; Community education; Adolescent survivors of sexual abuse; Male survivors of sexual abuse
SPECIAL PROGRAMS/SERVICES: Media program on date rape

RAPPAHANNOCK COUNCIL ON DOMESTIC VIOLENCE
PO Box 5923, Fredericksburg, VA 22403
Crisis hotline: **(703) 371-1212 24 hrs**
Information: (703) 373-9373 24 hrs (office phone reverts to hotline)
Contact: Natalie Davis, Exec Dir
TYPE OF AGENCY: Domestic violence program
AREAS SERVED: Fredericksburg, Stafford, King George, Caroline, Spotsylvania
YEARS IN OPERATION: 11
LANGUAGES: Interpreters available
ACCESSIBILITY: Wheelchair accessible; Telecommunications for the hearing impaired (TTY, TDY, etc.); Signers for the hearing impaired
CASES SEXUAL ASSAULT/ABUSE (%): 12
DESCRIPTION: Assistance for survivors of domestic violence/abuse; Shelter for abused women and their children; Court advocacy; Individual and group counseling for women and children; Group counseling for men who have been abusive
CLIENTS/SERVICES: Sexual assault survivors; Marital rape/sexual abuse survivors; Prevention program; Community education

FRONT ROYAL

WARREN COUNTY COUNCIL ON DOMESTIC VIOLENCE
PO Box 1831, Front Royal, VA 22630
Crisis hotline: **(703) 635-9062 24 hrs**
Information: (703) 635-9062 9am-5pm (Mon-Fri)
Contact: Judi Becker-Greenfield, Exec Dir
TYPE OF AGENCY: Domestic violence program
AREAS SERVED: Warren, Frederick, Rockingham
YEARS IN OPERATION: 1
CLIENTS/SERVICES: Sexual assault survivors; Marital rape/sexual abuse survivors; Community education

HAMPTON

THE PENINSULA PARENTS UNITED/ DAUGHTERS AND SONS UNITED
PO Box 7315, 1520 Aberdeen Rd, Hampton, VA 23666
Information: (804) 838-1960 9am-5pm (Mon-Fri)
Contact: Mary Helen T Jackson, MSW, Prog Coord
TYPE OF AGENCY: Child sexual abuse services
SPONSORING ORGANIZATION: Peninsula Family Service, Inc
AREAS SERVED: Hampton, Newport News, York
YEARS IN OPERATION: 1½
ACCESSIBILITY: Wheelchair accessible
CASES SEXUAL ASSAULT/ABUSE (%): 100
DESCRIPTION: Self help supportive group counseling for families involved in intrafamilial child sexual abuse; Groups for pre- and adolescent male and female victims; Offenders group; Non-offending spouses group; Orientation group for all new adults
CLIENTS/SERVICES: Child victims of sexual abuse; Adult survivors of child sexual abuse; Incest victims/survivors; Community education; Offender treatment program; Adolescent survivors of sexual abuse; Male survivors of sexual abuse
REQUIREMENTS: Must be 8 or older; All cases must be reported

VIRGINIA PENINSULA COUNCIL ON DOMESTIC VIOLENCE
PO Box 561, Hampton, VA 23669
Crisis hotline: **(804) 723-7774 24 hrs daily**
Information: (804) 722-2261 8:30am-4:30pm
Contact: Sonya McKeithan, Child Abuse Treatment Coord
TYPE OF AGENCY: Domestic violence program; Child sexual abuse services
AREAS SERVED: Hampton, Newport News, Poquoson, Yorktown cities
YEARS IN OPERATION: Child sexual abuse treatment 3; Shelter program 10
LANGUAGES: Spanish
CASES SEXUAL ASSAULT/ABUSE (%): 25-30
DESCRIPTION: Domestic violence services support groups for children identified as being sexually abused by non-caretakers and the non-offending parents
CLIENTS/SERVICES: Child victims of sexual abuse; Adult survivors of child sexual abuse; Prevention program; Community education

HARRISONBURG

CITIZENS AGAINST SEXUAL ASSAULT (CASA) OF HARRISONBURG, ROCKINGHAM COUNTY
162 S Main St, Harrisonburg, VA 22801
Information: (703) 434-2848 9am-5pm (Mon-Fri)
Contact: Joseph G Lynch, Sec
TYPE OF AGENCY: Rape crisis center
AREAS SERVED: Rockingham
YEARS IN OPERATION: 1
CASES SEXUAL ASSAULT/ABUSE (%): 100
CLIENTS/SERVICES: Sexual assault survivors; Marital rape/sexual abuse survivors; Child victims of sexual abuse; Adult survivors of child sexual abuse; Incest victims/survivors; Community education; Adolescent survivors of sexual abuse; Male survivors of sexual abuse

FAMILY COUNSELING SERVICES, INC
162 S Main S, Harrisonburg, VA 22801
Information: (703) 434-2848 9am-5pm, 24-hr answering service
Contact: Joseph G Lynch, LCSW, Dir
TYPE OF AGENCY: Private practice
AREAS SERVED: Rockingham
YEARS IN OPERATION: 4
CASES SEXUAL ASSAULT/ABUSE (%): 35-40
DESCRIPTION: Male and female therapist for adult survivors of sexual assault; Individual counseling for survivors; individual and group therapy for offenders (child sexual abuse/incest offenders and batterers)
CLIENTS/SERVICES: Sexual assault survivors; Marital rape/sexual abuse survivors; Child victims of sexual abuse; Adult survivors of child sexual abuse; Incest victims/survivors; Community education; Offender treatment program; Adolescent survivors of sexual abuse; Male survivors of sexual abuse
REQUIREMENTS: Fee for service

SHENANDOAH VALLEY SEX OFFENDER TREATMENT PROGRAM
162 S Main St, Harrisonburg, VA 22801
Information: (703) 434-2848 9am-5pm
Contact: Joseph Lynch, LCSW
TYPE OF AGENCY: Private practice; Offender treatment
AREAS SERVED: Rockingham
YEARS IN OPERATION: 4
CASES SEXUAL ASSAULT/ABUSE (%): 100
DESCRIPTION: Group therapy for adolescent and adult sex offenders (including child sexual abuse/incest offenders) and their families. Phallometric testing by plethysmograph. Support group for offenders in addition to group therapy and a separate spouse support group
CLIENTS/SERVICES: Offender treatment program
REQUIREMENTS: Some court involvement requiring treatment

HOPEWELL

HOPEWELL VICTIM/WITNESS ASSISTANCE PROGRAM
300 N Main St, Hopewell, VA 23860
Information: (804) 541-2352 8:30am-5pm (Mon-Fri); on call service available
Contact: Carla Stewart, Victim/Witness Assistance Dir
TYPE OF AGENCY: Victim/witness assistance program
SPONSORING ORGANIZATION: Department of Criminal Justice Services
AREAS SERVED: Hopewell
YEARS IN OPERATION: 2½
CASES SEXUAL ASSAULT/ABUSE (%): 10
CLIENTS/SERVICES: Sexual assault survivors; Marital rape/sexual abuse survivors; Child victims of sexual abuse; Adult survivors of child sexual abuse; Incest victims/survivors; Community education

LEESBURG

LOUDOUN COUNTY MENTAL HEALTH CENTER
8 South St SW, Leesburg, VA 22075
Crisis hotline: **(703) 777-0320 24 hrs daily**
Information: (703) 777-0320
Contact: Frances Goldman, Outpatient Supv
TYPE OF AGENCY: Counseling/mental health services; Child sexual abuse services
AREAS SERVED: Loudoun
YEARS IN OPERATION: 20
ACCESSIBILITY: Wheelchair accessible
CASES SEXUAL ASSAULT/ABUSE (%): 10
CLIENTS/SERVICES: Sexual assault survivors; Marital rape/sexual abuse survivors; Child victims of sexual abuse; Adult survivors of child sexual abuse; Incest victims/survivors; Prevention program; Community education; Offender treatment program; Adolescent survivors of sexual abuse; Male survivors of sexual abuse

VICTIM WITNESS OFFICE
20 E Market St, Leesburg, VA 22075
Crisis hotline: **(703) 777-3399 24 hrs**
Information: (703) 777-0417
Contact: Irene Wodell, Dir
TYPE OF AGENCY: Victim/witness assistance program
AREAS SERVED: Loudoun
YEARS IN OPERATION: 11
LANGUAGES: Interpreters available
ACCESSIBILITY: Wheelchair accessible; Signers for the hearing impaired
CLIENTS/SERVICES: Sexual assault survivors; Marital rape/sexual abuse survivors; Child victims of sexual abuse; Adult survivors of child sexual abuse; Incest victims/survivors; Community education; Adolescent survivors of sexual abuse; Male survivors of sexual abuse

LEXINGTON

COMMONWEALTH ATTORNEY'S OFFICE—VICTIM/WITNESS ASSISTANCE PROGRAM
6 E Washington St, Lexington, VA 24450
Information: (703) 463-9649 9am-5pm daily
Contact: Mirchana Everhart, Victim-Witness Coord
TYPE OF AGENCY: Victim/witness assistance program
AREAS SERVED: City of Lexington, Rockbridge County
YEARS IN OPERATION: 10
CASES SEXUAL ASSAULT/ABUSE (%): 15-20
CLIENTS/SERVICES: Sexual assault survivors; Marital rape/sexual abuse survivors; Child victims of sexual abuse; Adolescent survivors of sexual abuse
REQUIREMENTS: Client must file criminal charges

LYNCHBURG

LYNCHBURG COMMONWEALTH ATTORNEY'S OFFICE—VICTIM/WITNESS ASSISTANCE PROGRAM
PO Box 1539, Lynchburg, VA 24503
Information: (804) 847-1593
Contact: Susan Clark, Victim Witness Coord
TYPE OF AGENCY: Victim/witness assistance program
AREAS SERVED: Lynchburg City
YEARS IN OPERATION: 3
ACCESSIBILITY: Wheelchair accessible
CLIENTS/SERVICES: Sexual assault survivors; Marital rape/sexual abuse survivors; Child victims of sexual abuse; Incest victims/survivors; Community education
REQUIREMENTS: Must file charges

THE PREVENTION CENTER FOR CHILD ABUSE AND NEGLECT OF CENTRAL VIRGINIA
PO Box 3039, Rivermont Station, Lynchburg, VA 24503
Information: (804) 384-5000 8:30am-5pm
Contact: Laura H Knaup, Exec Dir
TYPE OF AGENCY: Child sexual abuse services; Child sexual abuse prevention program; Child abuse services; Child abuse prevention program
AREAS SERVED: Amherst, Appomattox, Bedford, Campbell
YEARS IN OPERATION: 1
ACCESSIBILITY: Wheelchair accessible
CASES SEXUAL ASSAULT/ABUSE (%): 50
DESCRIPTION: Community education; Volunteer parent aides for families in crisis and in need of support; Group therapy for incest offenders; Sponsorship of Parents Anonymous, Parents United, Daughters and Sons United, and Adults Molested as Children support groups
CLIENTS/SERVICES: Child victims of sexual abuse; Adult survivors of child sexual abuse; Incest victims/survivors; Community education; Adolescent survivors of sexual abuse; Male survivors of sexual abuse

RAPE COMPANION PROGRAM
Tate Springs Rd, Lynchburg, VA 24501
Crisis hotline: **(804) 528-2046, 528-2033 24 hrs**
Information: (804) 528-2046
Contact: Donna Nash, Advocacy Coord
TYPE OF AGENCY: Rape crisis center
SPONSORING ORGANIZATION: Lynchburg General Hospital
AREAS SERVED: Amherst, Campbell, Bedford, Lynchburg, Appomattox, Altavista
YEARS IN OPERATION: 6
CASES SEXUAL ASSAULT/ABUSE (%): 100
CLIENTS/SERVICES: Sexual assault survivors; Community education

MANASSAS

PARENTS UNITED, INC OF PRINCE WILLIAM COUNTY, VIRGINIA
9311 Lee Ave, Manassas, VA 22110
Crisis hotline: **(703) 368-4141 24 hrs**
Information: (703) 335-6200 8am-5pm (Mon-Fri)
Contact: Mark Kirchberg, Coord
TYPE OF AGENCY: Child sexual abuse services
AREAS SERVED: Prince William, Stafford
YEARS IN OPERATION: 4
ACCESSIBILITY: Wheelchair accessible
CASES SEXUAL ASSAULT/ABUSE (%): 100
DESCRIPTION: Therapeutic, self-help group for families who have experienced incest. Provides chance to discuss various behavior and relationship patterns that contribute to incestuous acts
CLIENTS/SERVICES: Adult survivors of child sexual abuse; Incest victims/survivors; Prevention program; Offender treatment program
REQUIREMENTS: Offender must be a family member with significant age difference between the offender and the victim. Court involvement is a prerequisite

PRINCE WILLIAM COUNTY MENTAL HEALTH CENTER
8807 Sudley Rd, Manassas, VA 22110
Crisis hotline: **(703) 361-3101 24 hrs daily**
Information: (703) 361-3101 Manassas, (703) 221-4163 8:30am-9pm (Mon-Thu); 8:30am-5pm (Fri)
Contact: Arnold Woodruff, MH Dir
TYPE OF AGENCY: Counseling/mental health services
SPONSORING ORGANIZATION: Prince William County Community Services Board
AREAS SERVED: Prince William
YEARS IN OPERATION: 20
LANGUAGES: Spanish, Cambodian
ACCESSIBILITY: Wheelchair accessible
CASES SEXUAL ASSAULT/ABUSE (%): 5
CLIENTS/SERVICES: Sexual assault survivors; Marital rape/sexual abuse survivors; Child victims of sexual abuse; Adult survivors of child sexual abuse; Incest victims/survivors; Offender treatment program; Adolescent survivors of sexual abuse; Male survivors of sexual abuse

SEXUAL ASSAULT VICTIMS ADVOCACY SERVICES (SAVAS)
PO Box 1834, Manassas, VA 22110
Crisis hotline: **(703) 368-4141 24 hrs daily**
Information: (703) 368-9626 9:30am-5pm (Mon-Fri)
Contact: Peggy Harris, Dir
TYPE OF AGENCY: Rape crisis center; Child sexual abuse services; Child sexual abuse prevention program
AREAS SERVED: Prince William
YEARS IN OPERATION: 5
CASES SEXUAL ASSAULT/ABUSE (%): 100
CLIENTS/SERVICES: Sexual assault survivors; Marital rape/sexual abuse survivors; Child victims of sexual abuse; Adult survivors of child sexual abuse; Incest victims/survivors; Prevention program; Community education; Adolescent survivors of sexual abuse; Male survivors of sexual abuse

MARTINSVILLE

CITIZENS AGAINST FAMILY VIOLENCE, INC
PO Box 210, Martinsville, VA 24114
Crisis hotline: **(703) 632-8701 24 hrs**
Information: (703) 632-8701 24 hrs
Contact: Lynn Wehlau, Exec Dir
TYPE OF AGENCY: Domestic violence program
AREAS SERVED: Henry, Patrick, Franklin, Pittsylvania
YEARS IN OPERATION: 8
ACCESSIBILITY: Wheelchair accessible
CLIENTS/SERVICES: Marital rape/sexual abuse survivors; Adult survivors of child sexual abuse; Prevention program; Community education

NEWPORT NEWS

COMMONWEALTH ATTORNEY'S OFFICE—VICTIM/WITNESS ASSISTANCE PROGRAM
247 28th St, 3rd Fl, Newport News, VA 23607
Information: (804) 244-0941 8am-5pm (Mon-Fri)
Contact: Jerry Kiser, VW Coord
TYPE OF AGENCY: Victim/witness assistance program
AREAS SERVED: Newport News
YEARS IN OPERATION: 2
ACCESSIBILITY: Wheelchair accessible
DESCRIPTION: Assists victims in overcoming their victimization; Works with child sexual abuse cases when the defendant is a noncaretaker
CLIENTS/SERVICES: Sexual assault survivors; Marital rape/sexual abuse survivors; Child victims of sexual abuse; Community education
SPECIAL PROGRAMS/SERVICES: Sponsor of conference on Advanced Treatment Issues in Child Sexual Abuse

SEXUAL ASSAULT DIVISION
6901 Huntington Ave, Newport News, VA 23607
Crisis hotline: **(804) 245-0041 24 hrs**
Information: (804) 244-0594 8am-5pm
Contact: Kathleen M Giles, Sexual Assault Svcs Coord
TYPE OF AGENCY: Rape crisis center; Child sexual abuse prevention program
SPONSORING ORGANIZATION: CONTACT Peninsula, Inc
AREAS SERVED: Hampton, Newport News, York, Poquoson
YEARS IN OPERATION: 14
ACCESSIBILITY: Telecommunications for the hearing impaired (TTY, TDY, etc.)
CASES SEXUAL ASSAULT/ABUSE (%): 100
DESCRIPTION: Provides hotline and companion/advocacy services for medical, police and court procedures for all victims of sexual assault and their families. Provides services for child victims of non-caretaker molestation and support groups for male and female adult victims of rape
CLIENTS/SERVICES: Sexual assault survivors; Marital rape/sexual abuse survivors; Child victims of sexual abuse; Adult survivors of child sexual abuse; Incest victims/survivors; Prevention program; Community education; Adolescent survivors of sexual abuse; Male survivors of sexual abuse
REQUIREMENTS: No treatment for child victims of incest

NORFOLK

NAVY FAMILY SERVICES CENTER
8910 Hampton Blvd, Norfolk, VA 23505
Crisis hotline: **(804) 444-NAVY 24 hrs**
Information: (804) 444-2102 8:30am-5pm
TYPE OF AGENCY: Counseling/mental health services; Military services
AREAS SERVED: Cities served are Norfolk, Virginia Beach, Chesapeake, Portsmouth, Newport News, Hampton
YEARS IN OPERATION: 9
ACCESSIBILITY: Wheelchair accessible
CASES SEXUAL ASSAULT/ABUSE (%): 15-20
CLIENTS/SERVICES: Sexual assault survivors; Child victims of sexual abuse; Adult survivors of child sexual abuse; Prevention program; Community education; Offender treatment program; Male survivors of sexual abuse
REQUIREMENTS: Military personnel on active duty, retired, or personnel's dependent

NORFOLK COMMONWEALTH'S ATTORNEY—VICTIM/WITNESS ASSISTANCE PROGRAM
800 E City Hall Ave, Ste 600, Norfolk, VA 23510
Crisis hotline: **(804) 625-3514** 8am-5pm
Information: (804) 625-3514 8am-5pm
Contact: Debra A Mills, Victim/Witness Coord
TYPE OF AGENCY: Victim/witness assistance program
AREAS SERVED: Norfolk
YEARS IN OPERATION: 3
ACCESSIBILITY: Wheelchair accessible
CLIENTS/SERVICES: Sexual assault survivors; Child victims of sexual abuse; Incest victims/survivors; Community education; Publications/media
REQUIREMENTS: Client must file charges
SPECIAL PROGRAMS/SERVICES: Children testifying in court receive program coloring book designed to assist with legal terminology and assist with attorney/client support

PARENTS UNITED OF VIRGINIA, INC/ HUMAN POTENTIALS
c/o 1176 Pickett Rd, Ste B, Norfolk, VA 23502
Information: (804) 461-3358
Contact: Fae Deaton, LCSW, LPC, Dir
TYPE OF AGENCY: Child sexual abuse services
YEARS IN OPERATION: 9
ACCESSIBILITY: Wheelchair accessible
CASES SEXUAL ASSAULT/ABUSE (%): 100
CLIENTS/SERVICES: Child victims of sexual abuse; Adult survivors of child sexual abuse; Incest victims/survivors; Prevention program; Community education; Offender treatment program; Adolescent survivors of sexual abuse; Male survivors of sexual abuse

PSYCHOTHERAPY RESOURCES OF NORFOLK (PRN)
330 W Brambleton Ave, Ste 206, Norfolk, VA 23510
Crisis hotline: **(804) 640-0400** 24 hrs 7 days
Information: (804) 640-0400 8:30am-9pm (Mon-Thu), coverage by pager
Contact: Elizabeth Gay, Betty Kedrock, Co-Dirs
TYPE OF AGENCY: Private practice
AREAS SERVED: Norfolk
YEARS IN OPERATION: 1
ACCESSIBILITY: Wheelchair accessible
CASES SEXUAL ASSAULT/ABUSE (%): 60
DESCRIPTION: PRN is a private practice offering psychotherapy for individuals, couples, and families, in addition to consultation and training to colleagues. Perspective is systemic and feminist. Offers 12-week groups for survivors of sexual assault and incest year-round, and have just begun a group for survivors of sexual assault who have multiple personalities
CLIENTS/SERVICES: Sexual assault survivors; Marital rape/sexual abuse survivors; Child victims of sexual abuse; Adult survivors of child sexual abuse; Incest victims/survivors; Community education; Offender treatment program; Multiple personality; Adolescent survivors of sexual abuse; Male survivors of sexual abuse; Healing
SPECIAL PROGRAMS/SERVICES: Weekend workshop for survivors "Moving Beyond Survival," workshops on "Women and Anger," "Female Sexuality," "Mother Daughter Connection." Case consultations for the local rape crisis center run and coordinate support groups

RESPONSE SEXUAL ASSAULT SUPPORT SERVICES
253 W Freemason St, Norfolk, VA 23510
Crisis hotline: **(804) 622-4300** 24 hrs
Information: (804) 622-4300 9am-5pm (Mon-Fri)
Contact: Nancy Brock, Exec Dir
TYPE OF AGENCY: Rape crisis center; Child sexual abuse prevention program; Rape prevention program
AREAS SERVED: Norfolk, Virginia Beach, Portsmouth, Chesapeake, Suffolk cities
YEARS IN OPERATION: 14
ACCESSIBILITY: Wheelchair accessible; Signers for the hearing impaired (by arrangement)
CASES SEXUAL ASSAULT/ABUSE (%): 100
DESCRIPTION: Provides 24-hour hotline, crisis counseling, accompaniment services and support groups for survivors. Also offers program in feminist martial arts/self-defense
CLIENTS/SERVICES: Sexual assault survivors; Marital rape/sexual abuse survivors; Child victims of sexual abuse; Adult survivors of child sexual abuse; Incest victims/survivors; Prevention program; Community education; Adolescent survivors of sexual abuse; Male survivors of sexual abuse
SPECIAL PROGRAMS/SERVICES: Prevention programs include "Some Secrets Hurt," puppet show on child sexual abuse prevention for children ages 7-12; sexual assault awareness and personal safety programs sponsored by employers and developed to fit the specific needs of employee groups in the workplace

YWCA WOMEN IN CRISIS PROGRAM
253 W Freemason St, Norfolk, VA 23510
Crisis hotline: **(804) 625-5570** 24 hrs daily
Information: (804) 625-4248 9am-5pm (Mon-Fri)
Contact: Dr Alice Twining, Coord
TYPE OF AGENCY: Domestic violence program
SPONSORING ORGANIZATION: YWCA of South Hampton Roads
AREAS SERVED: South Hampton Roads cities of Norfolk, Virginia Beach, Portsmouth, Chesapeake
YEARS IN OPERATION: 5
LANGUAGES: Spanish, other language interpreters by arrangement
ACCESSIBILITY: Wheelchair accessible
CASES SEXUAL ASSAULT/ABUSE (%): 40
CLIENTS/SERVICES: Marital rape/sexual abuse survivors; Child victims of sexual abuse; Adult survivors of child sexual abuse; Incest victims/survivors; Community education
REQUIREMENTS: Cannot accept male children 14 and older, but can offer free motel lodging for 3 days

PORTSMOUTH

CHILD AND FAMILY SERVICES
1805 Airline Blvd, Portsmouth, VA 23707
Information: (804) 397-2121 8:30am-9pm (Mon, Wed); 8:30am-5pm (Tue, Thu, Fri)
Contact: Dorothy Evans, Exec Dir
TYPE OF AGENCY: Counseling/mental health services
YEARS IN OPERATION: 30
ACCESSIBILITY: Wheelchair accessible
CASES SEXUAL ASSAULT/ABUSE (%): 25
CLIENTS/SERVICES: Sexual assault survivors; Marital rape/sexual abuse survivors; Child victims of sexual abuse; Adult survivors of child sexual abuse; Incest victims/survivors; Community education; Offender treatment program

COMMONWEALTH ATTORNEY'S VICTIM/ WITNESS PROGRAM
PO Box 1417, Portsmouth, VA 23705
Information: (804) 393-8581 8:30am-5pm
Contact: Theresa J Saunders, Victim/Witness Dir
TYPE OF AGENCY: Victim/witness assistance program; Child sexual abuse prevention program
AREAS SERVED: City of Portsmouth
YEARS IN OPERATION: 13
ACCESSIBILITY: Wheelchair accessible; Telecommunications for the hearing impaired (TTY, TDY, etc.) (by request); Signers for the hearing impaired (be request)
CASES SEXUAL ASSAULT/ABUSE (%): 20
CLIENTS/SERVICES: Sexual assault survivors; Marital rape/sexual abuse survivors; Child victims of sexual abuse; Adult survivors of child sexual abuse; Incest victims/survivors; Prevention program; Community education; Adolescent survivors of sexual abuse; Male survivors of sexual abuse
REQUIREMENTS: Crime must have been reported to police

HELP AND EMERGENCY RESPONSE
PO Box 1515, Portsmouth, VA 23705
Crisis hotline: **(804) 393-9449** 24 hrs daily
Information: (804) 393-7833 8am-5pm
Contact: Elizabeth Brickhouse, Exec Dir
TYPE OF AGENCY: Domestic violence program; Child sexual abuse prevention program
AREAS SERVED: Portsmouth, Chesapeake, Suffolk, Virginia Beach, Norfolk
YEARS IN OPERATION: 3½
LANGUAGES: Spanish
ACCESSIBILITY: Signers for the hearing impaired (by arrangement)
CASES SEXUAL ASSAULT/ABUSE (%): 80
CLIENTS/SERVICES: Marital rape/sexual abuse survivors; Child victims of sexual abuse; Adult survivors of child sexual abuse; Incest victims/survivors; Prevention program; Community education

PURCELLEVILLE

LOUDOUN ABUSED WOMEN'S SHELTER
PO Box 875, Purcellville, VA 22132
Crisis hotline: **(703) 777-6552** 24 hrs
Information: (703) 777-6552 9am-6pm
Contact: Sandra Scalidi, Dir; Carmen Howell, Shelter Mgr; Pam Stutz, Advocate-Coord
TYPE OF AGENCY: Domestic violence program; Rape prevention program
AREAS SERVED: Loudoun
YEARS IN OPERATION: 4
LANGUAGES: Spanish, Portuguese, French
CASES SEXUAL ASSAULT/ABUSE (%): 50
DESCRIPTION: Comprehensive domestic violence program, including a program for teens on date rape prevention
CLIENTS/SERVICES: Sexual assault survivors; Marital rape/sexual abuse survivors; Child victims of sexual abuse; Adult survivors of child sexual abuse; Incest victims/survivors; Community education; Male survivors of sexual abuse

RADFORD

WOMEN'S RESOURCE CENTER OF THE NEW RIVER VALLEY
PO Box 306, Radford, VA 24141
Crisis hotline: **(703) 639-1123** 24 hrs
Information: (703) 639-9592 24 hrs
Contact: Betty B Jones, Sexual Assault Svcs Coord
TYPE OF AGENCY: Rape crisis center; Domestic violence program; Child sexual abuse prevention program
AREAS SERVED: Giles, Montgomery, Floyd, Pulaski, City of Radford
YEARS IN OPERATION: 11
CASES SEXUAL ASSAULT/ABUSE (%): 40
DESCRIPTION: Provides services for survivors of domestic violence and sexual assault and their families, including crisis counseling and support groups for female and male survivors
CLIENTS/SERVICES: Sexual assault survivors; Marital rape/sexual abuse survivors; Child victims of sexual abuse; Adult survivors of child sexual abuse; Incest victims/survivors; Prevention program; Community education; Adolescent survivors of sexual abuse; Male survivors of sexual abuse; Healing; Publications/media
SPECIAL PROGRAMS/SERVICES: Provides healing through creative arts and wilderness therapy. Also training video for presentation in schools

RICHMOND

RAPE CRISIS OUTREACH PROGRAM/ WOMEN'S ADVOCACY PROGRAM
6 N 5th St, Richmond, VA 23219
Crisis hotline: **(804) 643-0888 24 hrs 7 days**
Information: (804) 643-6761 9am-5pm (Mon-Fri)
Contact: Lawrencine Smith, Rape Svcs Coord; Amy Kite, Rape Program Development Coord
TYPE OF AGENCY: Rape crisis center; Domestic violence program
SPONSORING ORGANIZATION: YWCA
AREAS SERVED: Henrico, Chesterfield, Goochland, Hanover
YEARS IN OPERATION: 10
ACCESSIBILITY: Wheelchair accessible; Telecommunications for the hearing impaired (TTY, TDY, etc.) (hotline); Signers for the hearing impaired (by arrangement)
CASES SEXUAL ASSAULT/ABUSE (%): 100
CLIENTS/SERVICES: Sexual assault survivors; Marital rape/sexual abuse survivors; Adult survivors of child sexual abuse; Incest victims/survivors; Prevention program; Community education; Adolescent survivors of sexual abuse; Male survivors of sexual abuse

RICHMOND CITY COMMONWEALTH ATTORNEY—VICTIM/WITNESS SERVICES
800 E Marshall St, Rm 211, Richmond, VA 23219
Information: (804) 780-8045
Contact: Melissa Lennon, Victim Witness Coord
TYPE OF AGENCY: Victim/witness assistance program
CLIENTS/SERVICES: Sexual assault survivors; Marital rape/sexual abuse survivors; Child victims of sexual abuse; Adult survivors of child sexual abuse; Prevention program; Community education; Male survivors of sexual abuse

ROANOKE

COMMONWEALTH ATTORNEY'S OFFICE—VICTIM/WITNESS PROGRAM
315 Church Ave, Roanoke, VA 24016
Crisis hotline: **(703) 981-2683 Answering machine after 5:30pm**
Information: (703) 981-2683 8am-5:30pm
Contact: Mary Ann Myers, Dir
TYPE OF AGENCY: Victim/witness assistance program
AREAS SERVED: Roanoke City
YEARS IN OPERATION: 4
ACCESSIBILITY: Wheelchair accessible
CASES SEXUAL ASSAULT/ABUSE (%): 20
CLIENTS/SERVICES: Sexual assault survivors; Marital rape/sexual abuse survivors; Child victims of sexual abuse; Adult survivors of child sexual abuse; Incest victims/survivors; Community education
REQUIREMENTS: Most cases have charges pending, however victims are not turned away because charges have not been filed

PARENTS UNITED OF ROANOKE VALLEY
325 W Campbell Ave, 2nd Fl, Roanoke, VA 24016
Information: (703) 344-3579 8:30am-4:30pm
Contact: Bob Yost, Self-Help Group Coord
TYPE OF AGENCY: Child sexual abuse services; Child sexual abuse prevention program; Child abuse services; Child abuse prevention program; Interagency network
SPONSORING ORGANIZATION: Child Abuse and Neglect Coordinating Council of Roanoke Valley
AREAS SERVED: Roanoke, Botetourt, Craig
YEARS IN OPERATION: 7
CASES SEXUAL ASSAULT/ABUSE (%): 100
DESCRIPTION: Child Abuse and Neglect Coordinating Council promotes, advocates, and assists in the development of a coordinated service system directed at the early diagnosis, comprehensive treatment, and prevention of child abuse and neglect, including sexual abuse prevention education and sponsorship of support groups for families that have experienced incest; Support groups available for incest offenders
CLIENTS/SERVICES: Child victims of sexual abuse; Adult survivors of child sexual abuse; Incest victims/survivors; Prevention program; Community education; Offender treatment program; Adolescent survivors of sexual abuse; Male survivors of sexual abuse
SPECIAL PROGRAMS/SERVICES: Monthly mental health professionals forum, an opportunity on a monthly basis for mental health professionals from public and private settings to meet for the purpose of case consultation and education

SEXUAL ASSAULT RESPONSE AND AWARENESS (SARA)
920 S Jefferson St, Ste 400, Roanoke, VA 24016
Crisis hotline: **(703) 981-9352 24 hrs daily**
Information: (703) 981-9318 9am-5pm (Mon-Fri)
Contact: Teresa C Berry, MS, SARA Coord
TYPE OF AGENCY: Rape crisis center
SPONSORING ORGANIZATION: Mental Health Services of the Roanoke Valley
AREAS SERVED: Roanoke and Salem cities, Botetourt and Roanoke counties
YEARS IN OPERATION: 10
ACCESSIBILITY: Wheelchair accessible
CASES SEXUAL ASSAULT/ABUSE (%): 100
CLIENTS/SERVICES: Sexual assault survivors; Marital rape/sexual abuse survivors; Child victims of sexual abuse; Adult survivors of child sexual abuse; Incest victims/survivors; Prevention program; Community education; Adolescent survivors of sexual abuse; Male survivors of sexual abuse

TRUST—ROANOKE VALLEY TROUBLE CENTER
360 Washington Ave SW, Roanoke, VA 24016
Crisis hotline: **(703) 344-1948 24 hrs**
Information: (703) 345-8859 8am-5pm
Contact: Stuart Israel, Exec Dir
TYPE OF AGENCY: Counseling/mental health services
AREAS SERVED: Roanoke City, Roanoke County, Salem City, Botetourt, Craig
YEARS IN OPERATION: 18
ACCESSIBILITY: Telecommunications for the hearing impaired (TTY, TDY, etc.)
CASES SEXUAL ASSAULT/ABUSE (%): 4-5
CLIENTS/SERVICES: Sexual assault survivors; Marital rape/sexual abuse survivors; Child victims of sexual abuse; Adult survivors of child sexual abuse; Incest victims/survivors; Adolescent survivors of sexual abuse; Male survivors of sexual abuse

SALEM

COMMONWEALTH ATTORNEY'S OFFICE—VICTIM/WITNESS ASSISTANCE PROGRAM
305 E Main St, Salem, VA 24153
Information: (703) 387-6174 8am-5pm
Contact: Sandra Thrasher
TYPE OF AGENCY: Victim/witness assistance program
AREAS SERVED: Roanoke, Vinton
ACCESSIBILITY: Wheelchair accessible
CLIENTS/SERVICES: Sexual assault survivors; Child victims of sexual abuse; Incest victims/survivors

STAUNTON

ALTERNATIVES FOR ABUSED ADULTS
PO Box 1414, Staunton, VA 24401
Crisis hotline: **(703) 942-HELP, 886-6800 24 hrs**
Information: (703) 886-4001 8:30am-4pm (Mon-Fri)
Contact: Joyce Thompson, Dir
TYPE OF AGENCY: Domestic violence program
AREAS SERVED: Augusta
YEARS IN OPERATION: 10
CLIENTS/SERVICES: Marital rape/sexual abuse survivors; Child victims of sexual abuse; Adult survivors of child sexual abuse; Incest victims/survivors; Community education

PEOPLE AGAINST RAPE
PO Box 2415, Staunton, VA 24401
Crisis hotline: **(703) 885-7273 24 hrs**
Information: (703) 885-7273
Contact: Robyn Douglas, Prog Coord
TYPE OF AGENCY: Rape crisis center; Child sexual abuse services; Child sexual abuse prevention program
AREAS SERVED: Staunton, Waynesboro, Augusta, and surrounding counties
YEARS IN OPERATION: 11
CASES SEXUAL ASSAULT/ABUSE (%): 100
DESCRIPTION: Crisis intervention; Victim assistance; Prevention education; Escort for rape victims through medical, police, and legal procedures; Wilderness therapy program under development
CLIENTS/SERVICES: Sexual assault survivors; Marital rape/sexual abuse survivors; Child victims of sexual abuse; Adult survivors of child sexual abuse; Incest victims/survivors; Prevention program; Community education; Adolescent survivors of sexual abuse; Male survivors of sexual abuse

TAZEWELL

TAZEWELL COUNTY OFFICE OF THE COMMONWEALTH'S ATTORNEY—VICTIM/WITNESS ASSISTANCE PROGRAM
PO Box 871, Tazewell, VA 24651
Crisis hotline: **(703) 988-5966 (Sheriff's Dept) 24 hrs**
Information: (703) 988-7541, ext 332 8:30am-5pm
Contact: Dianne Altizer, Dir
TYPE OF AGENCY: Victim/witness assistance program
AREAS SERVED: Tazewell
YEARS IN OPERATION: 2½
CASES SEXUAL ASSAULT/ABUSE (%): 5
CLIENTS/SERVICES: Sexual assault survivors; Marital rape/sexual abuse survivors; Child victims of sexual abuse; Incest victims/survivors; Community education; Adolescent survivors of sexual abuse; Male survivors of sexual abuse
REQUIREMENTS: Client is encouraged to file charges and participate in prosecution

VICTIMS OF SEXUAL ASSAULT PROGRAM
PO Box 487, Tazewell, VA 24651
Crisis hotline: **(703) 988-5583, 988-5584 24 hrs (contact sheriff department)**
Information: (703) 988-5583, 988-5584 8am-3:30pm
Contact: Anne Wildman, Coord
TYPE OF AGENCY: Rape crisis center; Child sexual abuse services; Child sexual abuse prevention program
SPONSORING ORGANIZATION: Clinch Valley Community Action
AREAS SERVED: Tazewell, Buchanan, Russell
YEARS IN OPERATION: 1½
ACCESSIBILITY: Wheelchair accessible
CASES SEXUAL ASSAULT/ABUSE (%): 100
DESCRIPTION: Provides assistance for adults or children, male or female, who have been sexually assaulted. Works closely with the social services department in dealng with child sexual abuse. Provides support groups for female and male survivors
CLIENTS/SERVICES: Sexual assault survivors; Marital rape/sexual abuse survivors; Child victims of sexual abuse; Adult survivors of child sexual abuse; Incest victims/survivors; Prevention program; Community education; Adoles-

VICTIMS OF SEXUAL ASSAULT PROGRAM *(continued)*
cent survivors of sexual abuse; Male survivors of sexual abuse

VIRGINIA BEACH

COMMONWEALTH'S ATTORNEY'S OFFICE—VICTIM/WITNESS PROGRAM, VIRGINIA BEACH
Municipal Center, Virginia Beach, VA 23456
Crisis hotline: **(804) 427-4401 9am-5pm; recordings 5:30pm-8:30am**
Information: (804) 427-4401 8am-5pm
Contact: Lee-Hope Thrasher, Victim/Witness Coord
TYPE OF AGENCY: Victim/witness assistance program
AREAS SERVED: Virginia Beach
YEARS IN OPERATION: 7
ACCESSIBILITY: Wheelchair accessible
CLIENTS/SERVICES: Sexual assault survivors; Marital rape/sexual abuse survivors; Child victims of sexual abuse; Adult survivors of child sexual abuse; Incest victims/survivors; Prevention program; Community education; Male survivors of sexual abuse

COUNSELING ASSOCIATES
2940 N Lynnhaven Rd, Ste 100, Virginia Beach, VA 23452
Information: (804) 486-6515 8am-6pm
Contact: Jean C Holcombe, EdD, Lic Prof Couns
TYPE OF AGENCY: Private practice
AREAS SERVED: Hampton Roads, Tidewater
YEARS IN OPERATION: 3
ACCESSIBILITY: Wheelchair accessible
CASES SEXUAL ASSAULT/ABUSE (%): 50
CLIENTS/SERVICES: Sexual assault survivors; Marital rape/sexual abuse survivors; Child victims of sexual abuse; Adult survivors of child sexual abuse; Incest victims/survivors; Adolescent survivors of sexual abuse; Healing
REQUIREMENTS: Mandatory reporting of child abuse
SPECIAL PROGRAMS/SERVICES: Uses imagery and music to assist client in reliving and fully processing the trauma, whether in childhood or a more recent occurrance. Has a transpersonal psychology (wholistic) background

WILLIAMSBURG

COMMONWEALTH ATTORNEY'S OFFICE—VICTIM/WITNESS ASSISTANCE
PO Box 333, Williamsburg, VA 23187
Information: (804) 229-6080 8am-5pm
Contact: Lynn Thomas, Victim/Witness Coord
TYPE OF AGENCY: Victim/witness assistance program
AREAS SERVED: James City
LANGUAGES: Japanese, Spanish
ACCESSIBILITY: Wheelchair accessible; Signers for the hearing impaired
CLIENTS/SERVICES: Sexual assault survivors; Child victims of sexual abuse; Incest victims/survivors
REQUIREMENTS: Victims must file charges

WILLIAMSBURG TASK FORCE ON BATTERED WOMEN/SEXUAL ASSAULT
PO Box 1079, Williamsburg, VA 23187
Crisis hotline: **(804) 229-7585 24 hrs**
Information: (804) 229-3661 9am-5pm
Contact: Ronnie Long, Sexual Assault Svcs Coord
TYPE OF AGENCY: Rape crisis center; Domestic violence program
AREAS SERVED: James City, York, Williamsburg
YEARS IN OPERATION: 2½
CLIENTS/SERVICES: Sexual assault survivors; Marital rape/sexual abuse survivors; Child victims of sexual abuse; Adult survivors of child sexual abuse; Incest victims/survivors; Prevention program; Community education; Adolescent survivors of sexual abuse; Male survivors of sexual abuse

WINCHESTER

THE SHELTER FOR ABUSED WOMEN
PO Box 14, Winchester, VA 22601
Crisis hotline: **(703) 667-6466 24 hrs**
Information: (703) 667-6466 24 hrs
Contact: Donna Carpenter, Exec Dir
TYPE OF AGENCY: Domestic violence program
AREAS SERVED: Clarke, Frederick, Warren, Shenandoah, Page
YEARS IN OPERATION: 7
DESCRIPTION: Provides emergency housing and services for female victims of domestic violence and their children, who may also have been victims of sexual abuse; Treatment for batterers
CLIENTS/SERVICES: Marital rape/sexual abuse survivors; Child victims of sexual abuse; Community education

WYTHEVILLE

FAMILY RESOURCE CENTER/SEXUAL ASSAULT PROGRAM
PO Box 612, Wytheville, VA 24382
Crisis hotline: **(703) 228-7141 24 hrs**
Information: (703) 228-7141 8:30am-5pm (variable)
Contact: Regina Pack Eller, Sexual Assault Svcs Coord
TYPE OF AGENCY: Rape crisis center; Domestic violence program; Child sexual abuse prevention program
AREAS SERVED: Wythe, Smyth, Bland, Grayson, Carroll, City of Galax
YEARS IN OPERATION: 3
LANGUAGES: French, Spanish, and Oriental language interpreters available
ACCESSIBILITY: Wheelchair accessible
CLIENTS/SERVICES: Sexual assault survivors; Marital rape/sexual abuse survivors; Child victims of sexual abuse; Adult survivors of child sexual abuse; Incest victims/survivors; Prevention program; Community education; Adolescent survivors of sexual abuse; Male survivors of sexual abuse

YORKTOWN

YORK COUNTY COMMONWEALTH'S ATTORNEY—VICTIM/WITNESS ASSISTANCE
PO Box C, Yorktown, VA 23690
Information: (804) 898-0043 8:30am-5pm
Contact: Barbara Seibert, Victim/Witness Coord
TYPE OF AGENCY: Victim/witness assistance program
AREAS SERVED: York County, City of Poquoson
YEARS IN OPERATION: 2½
CASES SEXUAL ASSAULT/ABUSE (%): 20
CLIENTS/SERVICES: Sexual assault survivors; Marital rape/sexual abuse survivors; Child victims of sexual abuse; Incest victims/survivors; Community education

WASHINGTON

ABERDEEN

GRAYS HARBOR RAPE CRISIS
PO Box 423, Aberdeen, WA 98520
Crisis hotline: **(206) 532-HELP 24 hrs**
Information: (206) 532-HELP 24 hrs
Contact: Alysa Ruddell, Board Pres; Keith Krueger, Board VPres
TYPE OF AGENCY: Rape crisis center; Child sexual abuse prevention program
AREAS SERVED: Grays Harbor
YEARS IN OPERATION: 8
LANGUAGES: Spanish, Sign
ACCESSIBILITY: Signers for the hearing impaired
CASES SEXUAL ASSAULT/ABUSE (%): 90
DESCRIPTION: Advocacy for victims of sexual assault; Community education; Support groups for female and male survivors
CLIENTS/SERVICES: Sexual assault survivors; Marital rape/sexual abuse survivors; Child victims of sexual abuse; Adult survivors of child sexual abuse; Incest victims/survivors; Prevention program; Community education; Adolescent survivors of sexual abuse; Male survivors of sexual abuse

ASOTIN

PROSECUTOR'S OFFICE—CRIME VICTIM WITNESS ASSISTANCE
PO Box 220, Asotin, WA 99402
Information: (509) 243-4161 9am-5pm
Contact: Ethel L Ellis, Prog Coord
TYPE OF AGENCY: Victim/witness assistance program
AREAS SERVED: Asotin
YEARS IN OPERATION: 5
CLIENTS/SERVICES: Sexual assault survivors; Marital rape/sexual abuse survivors; Child victims of sexual abuse; Incest victims/survivors

BAINBRIDGE ISLAND

ASAP—ADVOCATES FOR SEXUALLY ASSAULTED PEOPLE
PO Box 11678, Bainbridge Island, WA 98110
Crisis hotline: **(206) 842-1920, 697-3844 (collect calls accepted) 24 hrs**
Information: (206) 842-1930 9am-4pm (Mon-Fri)
Contact: Jan Horning, Exec Dir
TYPE OF AGENCY: Rape crisis center
AREAS SERVED: Kitsap
YEARS IN OPERATION: 2
LANGUAGES: Spanish
ACCESSIBILITY: Wheelchair accessible; Signers for the hearing impaired
CASES SEXUAL ASSAULT/ABUSE (%): 100
CLIENTS/SERVICES: Sexual assault survivors; Marital rape/sexual abuse survivors; Child victims of sexual abuse; Adult survivors of child sexual abuse; Incest victims/survivors; Prevention program; Community education; Adolescent survivors of sexual abuse; Male survivors of sexual abuse

BELLEVUE

BELLEVUE COMMUNITY COLLEGE—WOMEN'S RESOURCE CENTER
PO Box 92700, 3000 Landerholm Cir, Rm A102, Bellevue, WA 98009
Information: (206) 641-2279 8am-4:30pm
Contact: Rennie Lallatin, Displaced Homemaker Coord
TYPE OF AGENCY: College/university-based services
AREAS SERVED: King
YEARS IN OPERATION: 15
ACCESSIBILITY: Wheelchair accessible
CASES SEXUAL ASSAULT/ABUSE (%): 20
DESCRIPTION: Primarily a referral service; Peer counselors; Displaced homemaker program; Offers support for women at the college and surrounding communities with workshops, seminars, and support groups
CLIENTS/SERVICES: Sexual assault survivors; Marital rape/sexual abuse survivors; Adult survivors of child sexual abuse; Incest victims/survivors; Community education

CORRECTIONAL SPECIALTIES
201 116th Ave NE, Bellevue, WA 98004
Crisis hotline: **(206) 453-1234 8am-9pm (Mon-Sat)**
Information: (206) 453-1234 8am-9pm (Mon-Sat)
Contact: Tim Kahn, MSW, Juvenile Svcs Dir
TYPE OF AGENCY: Child sexual abuse services; Private practice; Training/research; Offender treatment
AREAS SERVED: King, Snohomish
YEARS IN OPERATION: 8
LANGUAGES: Spanish
CASES SEXUAL ASSAULT/ABUSE (%): 80
DESCRIPTION: Treatment of sexual deviancy and services for victims and families where sexual abuse has been an issue. Group and individual therapy, including behavioral methods, for adolescent and adult offenders (including female sex offenders)—rapists, child sex abuse/incest offenders and batterers
CLIENTS/SERVICES: Child victims of sexual abuse; Adult survivors of child sexual abuse; Incest victims/survivors; Community education; Offender treatment program; Adolescent survivors of sexual abuse; Male survivors of sexual abuse; Publications/media
REQUIREMENTS: Offenders must sign comprehensive treatment agreement
SPECIAL PROGRAMS/SERVICES: Comprehensive training programs for residential treatment staff, mental health counselors, and criminal justice system personnel in understanding and treating sexual offenders. Complete training manuals available upon request.

BELLINGHAM

CHRYSALIS THERAPY CENTER
214 N Commercial, Bellingham, WA 98225
Information: (206) 647-2643 8am-8pm, 24-hr answering service
Contact: Tamar Groffman, ACSW, Therapist
TYPE OF AGENCY: Child sexual abuse services; Private practice
SPONSORING ORGANIZATION: Domestic Violence and Sexual Assault
AREAS SERVED: Whatcom, Skagit, Island
YEARS IN OPERATION: 5½
CASES SEXUAL ASSAULT/ABUSE (%): 50-75
CLIENTS/SERVICES: Sexual assault survivors; Marital rape/sexual abuse survivors; Child victims of sexual abuse; Adult survivors of child sexual abuse; Incest victims/survivors; Adolescent survivors of sexual abuse; Male survivors of sexual abuse
REQUIREMENTS: Able to pay or have insurance or funding source

SOAP BOX PLAYERS
PO Box 159, Bellingham, WA 98227
Information: (206) 734-5121 9am-5pm
Contact: Patricia A Kelly, Educ Theatre Prog Dir
TYPE OF AGENCY: Counseling/mental health services; Child sexual abuse prevention program; Theater group
SPONSORING ORGANIZATION: Coalition for Child Advocacy
AREAS SERVED: Whatcom, Island, San Juan, Pacific Northwest
YEARS IN OPERATION: 8
ACCESSIBILITY: Wheelchair accessible; Signers for the hearing impaired
CASES SEXUAL ASSAULT/ABUSE (%): 50
DESCRIPTION: Uses theatre as a medium to teach sexual abuse prevention skills to children and adults, as well as parenting and coping skills to parents and teens through dramatization. *The Touching Problem* children's program is a 45-minute theater presentation using roleplay to teach protection skills to children; how to say "no" to touch that seems scary or uncomfortable; how to identify touching problems; how to tell someone about the problem; and who their community support system is. In the adult program the players enact skits that demonstrate profiles of a victim, an offender, a confrontation between a mother and her brother, a mother talking about touching problems with her son, and a teacher providing support for a child who has disclosed that she is a victim
CLIENTS/SERVICES: Prevention program; Community education; Preschoolers; Healing; Publications/media

SOAP BOX PLAYERS *(continued)*
SPECIAL PROGRAMS/SERVICES: Media programs: *The Touching Problem* film or video, showing how a child deals with the unwelcome touch of a relative; *Foster Parents: Giving Children a Second Chance*, based on the theatrical foster parent show. Publications: Prevention curricula for preschoolers and for K-6th grades; *The Touching Problem* script and information on creating a theater group ($125 for entire program, $25 for single copy of script); Children's book *Touching* ($5.95). Also sells anatomically correct dolls.

WESTERN WASHINGTON UNIVERSITY—WOMEN'S CENTER
Viking Union 211, Western Washington University, Bellingham, WA 98225
Crisis hotline: **(206) 734-7271, 384-1485 24 hrs daily**
Information: (206) 676-3460, ext 5461
Contact: Laura Vance, Coord
TYPE OF AGENCY: College/university-based services; Child abuse prevention program; Acquaintance/date rape prevention program
AREAS SERVED: Whatcom
YEARS IN OPERATION: 62
ACCESSIBILITY: Wheelchair accessible; Signers for the hearing impaired
CASES SEXUAL ASSAULT/ABUSE (%): 5
DESCRIPTION: Provides peer counseling and referrals; Film series about rape/incest in residence halls
CLIENTS/SERVICES: Sexual assault survivors; Marital rape/sexual abuse survivors; Adult survivors of child sexual abuse; Incest victims/survivors; Community education

WHATCOM COUNTY CRISIS SERVICES—RAPE RELIEF
124 E Holly St, Bellingham, WA 98225
Crisis hotline: **(206) 734-7271 24 hrs**
Information: (206) 671-5714 8:30am-4:30pm
Contact: Jude de Fatta, Prog Mgr
TYPE OF AGENCY: Rape crisis center
AREAS SERVED: Whatcom
YEARS IN OPERATION: 14
ACCESSIBILITY: Wheelchair accessible; Telecommunications for the hearing impaired (TTY, TDY, etc.)
CASES SEXUAL ASSAULT/ABUSE (%): 100
DESCRIPTION: Provides 24-hour crisis intervention services, education and training, referrals and advocacy for members of the community through the use of trained community volunteers; Feminist martial arts/self-defense
CLIENTS/SERVICES: Sexual assault survivors; Marital rape/sexual abuse survivors; Adult survivors of child sexual abuse; Incest victims/survivors; Prevention program; Community education; Adolescent survivors of sexual abuse; Male survivors of sexual abuse

WOMENCARE SHELTER
1026 N Forest, No 201, Bellingham, WA 98225
Crisis hotline: **(206) 734-3438 24 hrs**
Information: (206) 671-8539 9am-1pm (Tue-Fri)
Contact: Kay Porter, Asst Admin
TYPE OF AGENCY: Domestic violence program
AREAS SERVED: Primarily Whatcom
YEARS IN OPERATION: 10
LANGUAGES: Spanish
CASES SEXUAL ASSAULT/ABUSE (%): 50
CLIENTS/SERVICES: Marital rape/sexual abuse survivors; Child victims of sexual abuse; Adult survivors of child sexual abuse; Prevention program; Community education

BREMERTON

KITSAP SEXUAL ASSAULT CENTER/RAPE RESPONSE
PO Box 1327, Bremerton, WA 98310
Crisis hotline: **(206) 479-8500 24 hrs**
Information: (206) 479-1788 9am-5pm (Mon-Fri)
Contact: Martha Wescott, Exec Dir
TYPE OF AGENCY: Rape crisis center; Child sexual abuse services; Child sexual abuse prevention program
AREAS SERVED: Kitsap
YEARS IN OPERATION: 13
LANGUAGES: Interpreters by arrangement
CLIENTS/SERVICES: Sexual assault survivors; Marital rape/sexual abuse survivors; Child victims of sexual abuse; Adult survivors of child sexual abuse; Incest victims/survivors; Prevention program; Community education

CHEHALIS

CARE (COUNTY ABUSE AND RAPE EMERGENCY) SERVICES
PO Box 337, Chehalis, WA 98532
Crisis hotline: **(206) 748-6601, 748-6602, (800) 458-3080 24 hrs daily**
Information: (206) 748-0547 8am-5pm
Contact: Ginny Brockman, Prog Admin
TYPE OF AGENCY: Rape crisis center; Domestic violence program; Child sexual abuse services
SPONSORING ORGANIZATION: Lewis County Hotline and Care Services
AREAS SERVED: Lewis
YEARS IN OPERATION: 8
LANGUAGES: Spanish
ACCESSIBILITY: Wheelchair accessible
CASES SEXUAL ASSAULT/ABUSE (%): 10-15
CLIENTS/SERVICES: Sexual assault survivors; Marital rape/sexual abuse survivors; Child victims of sexual abuse; Adult survivors of child sexual abuse; Incest victims/survivors; Prevention program; Community education; Adolescent survivors of sexual abuse; Male survivors of sexual abuse; Publications/media
SPECIAL PROGRAMS/SERVICES: Videotape/workshop for clergy; Videotape, audiotape, and book library for training staff in providing education to community groups, individual counseling, or for use in support groups

CLARKSTON

DEVELOPMENTAL AND RESIDENTIAL SERVICES
1603 Dustan Loop, Clarkston, WA 99403
Crisis hotline: **(208) 799-8026 24 hr paging**
Information: (509) 758-9842 8am-4pm (Mon-Fri)
Contact: Adele Plouffe, Dir
TYPE OF AGENCY: Counseling/mental health services
AREAS SERVED: Asotin
YEARS IN OPERATION: 15
ACCESSIBILITY: Wheelchair accessible
CLIENTS/SERVICES: Sexual assault survivors; Male survivors of sexual abuse; Developmentally disabled

COLFAX

WHITMAN COUNTY PROSECUTOR'S OFFICE—VICTIM/WITNESS UNIT
PO Box 30, Colfax, WA 99111
Information: (509) 397-3449 7:30am-5pm
Contact: Lori Colpron, Victim/Witness Coord
TYPE OF AGENCY: Victim/witness assistance program
AREAS SERVED: Whitman
YEARS IN OPERATION: 5
ACCESSIBILITY: Wheelchair accessible
CASES SEXUAL ASSAULT/ABUSE (%): 10
CLIENTS/SERVICES: Marital rape/sexual abuse survivors; Child victims of sexual abuse

COLVILLE

ALTERNATIVES TO VIOLENCE
260 N Oak, Colville, WA 99114
Crisis hotline: **(509) 684-6139 24 hrs**
Information: (509) 684-3796 8am-5pm
Contact: Joyce McNeil, Mary Fossum, Dirs
TYPE OF AGENCY: Rape crisis center; Domestic violence program
AREAS SERVED: Stevens
YEARS IN OPERATION: 9
ACCESSIBILITY: Wheelchair accessible
CASES SEXUAL ASSAULT/ABUSE (%): 25
CLIENTS/SERVICES: Sexual assault survivors; Marital rape/sexual abuse survivors; Child victims of sexual abuse; Adult survivors of child sexual abuse; Incest victims/survivors; Prevention program; Community education; Adolescent survivors of sexual abuse; Male survivors of sexual abuse

ELLENSBURG

KITTITAS SEXUAL ASSAULT UNIT
220 W 4th Ave, Ellensburg, WA 98926
Crisis hotline: **(509) 925-4168 24 hrs**
Information: (509) 925-9861 8am-5pm
Contact: Fran Dew, Coord
TYPE OF AGENCY: Rape crisis center; Counseling/mental health services
SPONSORING ORGANIZATION: Central Washington Comprehensive Mental Health
AREAS SERVED: Kittitas
ACCESSIBILITY: Wheelchair accessible
CASES SEXUAL ASSAULT/ABUSE (%): 100
CLIENTS/SERVICES: Sexual assault survivors; Adult survivors of child sexual abuse; Community education

EVERETT

COUNSELING SERVICES CENTER
3207 Oakes Ave, Everett, WA 98201
Crisis hotline: **(206) 259-4822 24 hrs**
Information: (206) 259-4822 9am-5pm; evenings and weekends by arrangement
Contact: Dolores Righi, ACSW, MS, Marital and Family Therapist
TYPE OF AGENCY: Counseling/mental health services; Child sexual abuse services; Private practice
AREAS SERVED: Snohomish, Island, Skagit
YEARS IN OPERATION: 10
ACCESSIBILITY: Wheelchair accessible
CASES SEXUAL ASSAULT/ABUSE (%): 40
DESCRIPTION: Provides individual, marital, family and group therapy for all ages; Play therapy for survivors; Incest survivors group for adult women; Works with the mother-daughter dyad in cases of adolescent victims of incest; Extensive individual therapy with rape victims, including preparing them for court
CLIENTS/SERVICES: Sexual assault survivors; Marital rape/sexual abuse survivors; Child victims of sexual abuse; Adult survivors of child sexual abuse; Incest victims/survivors; Adolescent survivors of sexual abuse; Male survivors of sexual abuse

PROVIDENCE SEXUAL ASSAULT CENTER
PO Box 1067, Everett, WA 98206
Crisis hotline: **(206) 252-4800 24 hrs**
Information: (206) 258-7844
Contact: Patricia L Cowan, Dir
TYPE OF AGENCY: Rape crisis center; Child sexual abuse services; Child sexual abuse prevention program
SPONSORING ORGANIZATION: Providence Hospital of Everett
AREAS SERVED: Snohomish, part of Island
YEARS IN OPERATION: 10
LANGUAGES: Spanish
CASES SEXUAL ASSAULT/ABUSE (%): 99

PROVIDENCE SEXUAL ASSAULT CENTER *(continued)*

CLIENTS/SERVICES: Sexual assault survivors; Marital rape/sexual abuse survivors; Child victims of sexual abuse; Adult survivors of child sexual abuse; Incest victims/survivors; Prevention program; Community education; Adolescent survivors of sexual abuse; Male survivors of sexual abuse
SPECIAL PROGRAMS/SERVICES: Child Victim Assistance Project places one Sexual Assault Center staff person within the Sheriff's Office to conduct preliminary investigative interviews with child victims in either a room especially designed for children, or in the child's home. This "investigative assistant" prepares a detailed report for the detective assigned to the case. The detective then completes the investigation, conducting interviews with the alleged offender and other witnesses. Following the initial interview with the child, a volunteer advocate provides supportive services for the child and/or his or her non-offending family members. These services include: information/referral, crisis intervention and assessment, on-going peer support counseling, access to parent support groups, and court advocacy services. Supervised Visitation Services (fee charged) provides supervision for children at risk who are visiting a mentally ill, neglecting, abusive or offending parent or a noncustodial parent with a history of attempted abduction and/or noncompliance with visitation orders. Provides supervision for prescheduled visits with the philosophy that the child is the primary client, and that his/her physical and emotional well-being supercedes the needs or wishes of the visiting parent(s). Also provides, upon request, reports to the court and/or documentation of the visit including a report of the circumstances under which the visit took place.

STOP ABUSE
2731 10th St, Everett, WA 98201
Crisis hotline: **(206) 252-2873 24 hrs**
Information: (206) 258-3543 9am-5pm (Mon-Fri)
Contact: Vicki Orena, Dir
TYPE OF AGENCY: Domestic violence program
AREAS SERVED: Statewide; Snohomish, King for counseling
YEARS IN OPERATION: 12
ACCESSIBILITY: Wheelchair accessible
CASES SEXUAL ASSAULT/ABUSE (%): 40
DESCRIPTION: Services for domestic violence survivors and individual therapy for batterers
CLIENTS/SERVICES: Marital rape/sexual abuse survivors; Child victims of sexual abuse; Adult survivors of child sexual abuse; Incest victims/survivors; Community education; Male survivors of sexual abuse

FEDERAL WAY

ASSOCIATES IN COUNSELING
33305 1st Ave S, Ste 206, Federal Way, WA 98003
Information: (206) 838-8070 9am-11pm (Mon-Thu)
Contact: Robert L Macy, Dir; Marsha T Macy, Clinical Dir
TYPE OF AGENCY: Private practice
AREAS SERVED: King, Pierce
YEARS IN OPERATION: 10
ACCESSIBILITY: Wheelchair accessible
CASES SEXUAL ASSAULT/ABUSE (%): 90
DESCRIPTION: Provides a comprehensive, community-based program specializing in the treatment of sex offenders and their families. For offender, assessment of physiological arousal using the penile plethysmograph. Support groups for wives/mothers of sex offenders. Counseling of victims/survivors, including support groups for female and male survivors and services for victims of ritual abuse

CLIENTS/SERVICES: Sexual assault survivors; Marital rape/sexual abuse survivors; Child victims of sexual abuse; Adult survivors of child sexual abuse; Incest victims/survivors; Community education; Offender treatment program; Adolescent survivors of sexual abuse; Male survivors of sexual abuse; Ritualistic abuse victims/survivors
REQUIREMENTS: Treats victims of sexual assault including ritual abuse; Accepts offenders into program whether or not they are court-ordered

FORKS

FORKS ABUSE PROGRAM
PO Box 1775, Forks, WA 98331
Crisis hotline: **(206) 374-2273 24 hrs**
Information: (206) 374-2273
Contact: Margaret Baso, Coord
TYPE OF AGENCY: Rape crisis center; Domestic violence program
AREAS SERVED: Clallam, Jefferson
YEARS IN OPERATION: 10
LANGUAGES: Korean and Spanish interpreters available
ACCESSIBILITY: Wheelchair accessible
CASES SEXUAL ASSAULT/ABUSE (%): 20
CLIENTS/SERVICES: Sexual assault survivors; Marital rape/sexual abuse survivors; Adult survivors of child sexual abuse; Incest victims/survivors; Community education; Adolescent survivors of sexual abuse; Male survivors of sexual abuse

FORT LEWIS

ARMY FAMILY ADVOCACY PROGRAM (FAP)
AFZH-PAW-C, Bldg 5219, Fort Lewis, WA 98433-5000
Information: (206) 967-7166 7:30am-4:30pm (Mon-Fri)
Contact: Billie A Stewart, Soc Wrk Svcs Chief, FAP Mgr
TYPE OF AGENCY: Counseling/mental health services; Child sexual abuse prevention program; Military services
SPONSORING ORGANIZATION: Army Community Service
AREAS SERVED: Pierce, Thurston
YEARS IN OPERATION: 23
ACCESSIBILITY: Wheelchair accessible
CASES SEXUAL ASSAULT/ABUSE (%): 10-15
CLIENTS/SERVICES: Marital rape/sexual abuse survivors; Child victims of sexual abuse; Prevention program; Community education; Offender treatment program
REQUIREMENTS: Active duty or retired Army or family member, or Department of Defense civilian employee

FRIDAY HARBOR

SAN JUAN COUNTY PROSECUTING ATTORNEY—VICTIM/WITNESS PROGRAM
PO Box 760, Friday Harbor, WA 98250
Information: (206) 378-4101 8:30am-4:30pm
Contact: Pam Murray, Admin
TYPE OF AGENCY: Victim/witness assistance program
AREAS SERVED: San Juan
YEARS IN OPERATION: 7
CASES SEXUAL ASSAULT/ABUSE (%): 5
CLIENTS/SERVICES: Sexual assault survivors; Child victims of sexual abuse

KELSO

COWLITZ COUNTY SEXUAL ASSAULT
PO Box 877, Kelso, WA 98626
Crisis hotline: **(206) 636-8452 24 hrs**
Information: (206) 425-1176 8am-5pm (Mon-Fri)
Contact: Marlene Watkins, Sexual Assault Coord
TYPE OF AGENCY: Domestic violence program

SPONSORING ORGANIZATION: Emergency Support Shelter
AREAS SERVED: Cowlitz
YEARS IN OPERATION: ½
LANGUAGES: Interpreters by request
ACCESSIBILITY: Wheelchair accessible
CLIENTS/SERVICES: Sexual assault survivors; Marital rape/sexual abuse survivors; Child victims of sexual abuse; Adult survivors of child sexual abuse; Incest victims/survivors; Community education

EMERGENCY SUPPORT SHELTER
PO Box 877, Kelso, WA 98626
Crisis hotline: **(206) 636-8471 24 hrs daily**
Information: (206) 425-1176 8am-5pm (Mon-Fri)
Contact: Jennifer Neilson, Exec Dir
TYPE OF AGENCY: Domestic violence program
AREAS SERVED: Cowlitz, Wahkiakum
CLIENTS/SERVICES: Sexual assault survivors; Marital rape/sexual abuse survivors; Child victims of sexual abuse; Adult survivors of child sexual abuse; Community education; Male survivors of sexual abuse

KENNEWICK

BENTON COUNTY PROSECUTOR'S OFFICE
7320 W Quinault Ave, Kennewick, WA 99336
Information: (509) 735-3591 8am-5pm
Contact: Laurie Louden, Victim/Witness Coord
TYPE OF AGENCY: Victim/witness assistance program
AREAS SERVED: Benton
CASES SEXUAL ASSAULT/ABUSE (%): 25-30
CLIENTS/SERVICES: Sexual assault survivors; Marital rape/sexual abuse survivors; Child victims of sexual abuse; Adult survivors of child sexual abuse; Incest victims/survivors; Community education; Adolescent survivors of sexual abuse; Male survivors of sexual abuse

JUVENILE JUSTICE CENTER
5606 W Canal Pl, Ste 106, Kennewick, WA 99336
Information: (509) 783-2151 7am-7pm (Mon-Fri)
Contact: Don McCullough, Merideth Ingraham, Probation Couns
TYPE OF AGENCY: Probation program; Adolescent program
SPONSORING ORGANIZATION: Benton/Franklin Counties Juvenile Court
AREAS SERVED: Benton, Franklin, Walla Walla
CASES SEXUAL ASSAULT/ABUSE (%): 10
DESCRIPTION: Processes all illegal infractions by youths under the age of 18; Treats needs of adjudicated juvenile sex offenders through weekly groups, individual, and family therapy sessions
CLIENTS/SERVICES: Offender treatment program
REQUIREMENTS: Each juvenile sex offender must be an adjudicated youth residing within the Benton-Franklin County area

KENT

DOMESTIC ABUSE WOMEN'S NETWORK (DAWN)
PO Box 1521, Kent, WA 98035
Crisis hotline: **(206) 854-7867 24 hrs**
Information: (206) 852-5529 9am-5pm
Contact: Diane A Evergreen, Exec Dir
TYPE OF AGENCY: Domestic violence program
AREAS SERVED: South King
YEARS IN OPERATION: 8
LANGUAGES: Translators as needed
ACCESSIBILITY: Telecommunications for the hearing impaired (TTY, TDY, etc.); Signers for the hearing impaired (arranged)
CASES SEXUAL ASSAULT/ABUSE (%): 80-90
CLIENTS/SERVICES: Marital rape/sexual abuse survivors; Community education

LYNNWOOD

THE BELLSHIRE PSYCHOLOGY GROUP
18631 Alderwood Blvd, Ste 306, Lynnwood, WA 98037
Crisis hotline: **(206) 771-3248 24 hr answering service**
Information: (206) 771-3248 9am-5pm (Mon-Thu), evening appointments by special arrangement
Contact: Judith Hartsook, PhD, Shirley Baron, PhD, Psychologists
TYPE OF AGENCY: Private practice
AREAS SERVED: King, Snohomish, Skagit
YEARS IN OPERATION: 9
ACCESSIBILITY: Wheelchair accessible
CASES SEXUAL ASSAULT/ABUSE (%): 15-20
DESCRIPTION: Offers individual and couples therapy for adults, including women with histories of incest or sexual abuse. Occasional treatment of abusive spouse if spouse is treatable
CLIENTS/SERVICES: Sexual assault survivors; Marital rape/sexual abuse survivors; Adult survivors of child sexual abuse; Incest victims/survivors; Male survivors of sexual abuse
REQUIREMENTS: Adults; must be able to pay for services

EDMONDS COMMUNITY COLLEGE—WOMEN'S PROGRAMS
20000 68th Ave W, Lynnwood, WA 98036
Information: (206) 771-1585 9am-4pm (Mon-Thu); 9am-12pm (Fri)
Contact: Ruth McCormick, Womens Prog Coord
TYPE OF AGENCY: College/university-based services
AREAS SERVED: South Snohomish
YEARS IN OPERATION: 1
ACCESSIBILITY: Wheelchair accessible
DESCRIPTION: General services for women in the community; Support group for survivors of childhood sexual trauma; Women in abusive relationships group
CLIENTS/SERVICES: Adult survivors of child sexual abuse

WORLD FOR WOMEN, INC
PO Box 5627, Lynnwood, WA 98046
Crisis hotline: **(206) 258-4357 24 hrs**
Information: (206) 774-9843 9am-5pm
Contact: Teri Eyster, Counseling Coord
TYPE OF AGENCY: Counseling/mental health services; Private practice
SPONSORING ORGANIZATION: United Way
AREAS SERVED: Snohomish
YEARS IN OPERATION: 13
ACCESSIBILITY: Wheelchair accessible
CASES SEXUAL ASSAULT/ABUSE (%): 33
DESCRIPTION: Promotes well-being of women through counseling, classes, career development, shared housing, and emergency housing
CLIENTS/SERVICES: Sexual assault survivors; Marital rape/sexual abuse survivors; Child victims of sexual abuse; Adult survivors of child sexual abuse; Incest victims/survivors; Prevention program; Community education; Adolescent survivors of sexual abuse
REQUIREMENTS: Must be 11 or older

MONROE

WASHINGTON DEPARTMENT OF CORRECTIONS—SEX OFFENDER TREATMENT PROGRAM
Twin Rivers Correctional Center, Monroe, WA 98272
Information: (206) 794-2361 8am-4:30pm
Contact: Barbara Schwartz, PhD, Dir
TYPE OF AGENCY: Correctional facility; Offender treatment
AREAS SERVED: Statewide
YEARS IN OPERATION: 3/4
LANGUAGES: Spanish
ACCESSIBILITY: Wheelchair accessible
CASES SEXUAL ASSAULT/ABUSE (%): 100
DESCRIPTION: Treatment of incarcerated sex offenders, many of whom are also victims. Some services available for their families. Consultation on sentencing and supervision
CLIENTS/SERVICES: Community education; Offender treatment program; Prisoners
REQUIREMENTS: Incarcerated for sex offense, crime committed since 7/1/87, admits guilt, volunteers for treatment

MOUNT VERNON

SKAGIT COUNTY PROSECUTING ATTORNEY'S OFFICE—VICTIM/WITNESS ASSISTANCE UNIT
Courthouse Annex, Mount Vernon, WA 98273
Information: (206) 336-9460 8:30am-4:40pm (Mon-Fri)
Contact: Gretchen Paque, Dir
TYPE OF AGENCY: Victim/witness assistance program; Child sexual abuse prevention program
AREAS SERVED: Skagit
YEARS IN OPERATION: 9
LANGUAGES: Sign
ACCESSIBILITY: Wheelchair accessible; Signers for the hearing impaired
CASES SEXUAL ASSAULT/ABUSE (%): 65
CLIENTS/SERVICES: Sexual assault survivors; Marital rape/sexual abuse survivors; Child victims of sexual abuse; Adult survivors of child sexual abuse; Incest victims/survivors; Prevention program; Community education; Adolescent survivors of sexual abuse; Male survivors of sexual abuse
REQUIREMENTS: Crime must be reported to law enforcement; Victim/survivor must be willing to participate in the prosecution process

SKAGIT RAPE RELIEF AND BATTERED WOMEN'S SERVICES
PO Box 301, Mount Vernon, WA 98273
Crisis hotline: **(206) 336-2162 24 hrs**
Information: (206) 336-9591 8:30am-4:30pm (Mon-Fri)
Contact: Deborah Lynn, Dir
TYPE OF AGENCY: Rape crisis center; Domestic violence program
AREAS SERVED: Skagit
YEARS IN OPERATION: 9
LANGUAGES: Spanish
CASES SEXUAL ASSAULT/ABUSE (%): 25
CLIENTS/SERVICES: Sexual assault survivors; Marital rape/sexual abuse survivors; Adult survivors of child sexual abuse; Incest victims/survivors; Prevention program; Community education; Adolescent survivors of sexual abuse; Male survivors of sexual abuse

NASELLE

PACIFIC COUNTY CRISIS SUPPORT NETWORK
HCR 78, Box 336, Naselle, WA 98638
Crisis hotline: **(800) 562-6025 24 hrs**
Information: (206) 487-7191 9am-3pm
Contact: Jerralo Keenan, Dir
TYPE OF AGENCY: Rape crisis center; Domestic violence program; Child sexual abuse services; Child sexual abuse prevention program
AREAS SERVED: Pacific, West Wahkiakum
YEARS IN OPERATION: 5
LANGUAGES: Finnish, Spanish
ACCESSIBILITY: Telecommunications for the hearing impaired (TTY, TDY, etc.)
CASES SEXUAL ASSAULT/ABUSE (%): 50
CLIENTS/SERVICES: Sexual assault survivors; Marital rape/sexual abuse survivors; Child victims of sexual abuse; Adult survivors of child sexual abuse; Incest victims/survivors; Prevention program; Community education; Adolescent survivors of sexual abuse; Male survivors of sexual abuse

NEWPORT

FAMILY CRISIS NETWORK
Box 959, Newport, WA 99156
Crisis hotline: **(509) 447-5483 24 hrs**
Information: (509) 447-2274
Contact: Wini Oberdorfer, Prog Dir
TYPE OF AGENCY: Rape crisis center; Domestic violence program; Child sexual abuse services; Child sexual abuse prevention program
AREAS SERVED: Pend Oreille, WA; West Bonner, ID
YEARS IN OPERATION: 6
ACCESSIBILITY: Signers for the hearing impaired
CASES SEXUAL ASSAULT/ABUSE (%): 10
DESCRIPTION: Provides crisis intervention services: support, counseling, legal advocacy, and accompaniment through hospital/police/legal proceedings. Offers support groups for both female and male survivors
CLIENTS/SERVICES: Sexual assault survivors; Marital rape/sexual abuse survivors; Child victims of sexual abuse; Adult survivors of child sexual abuse; Incest victims/survivors; Prevention program; Community education; Adolescent survivors of sexual abuse; Male survivors of sexual abuse

PEND OREILLE COUNTY PROSECUTING ATTORNEY—VICTIM/WITNESS ASSISTANCE PROGRAM
PO Box 5000, Newport, WA 99156-5070
Information: (509) 447-4414 8:30am-4:30pm
Contact: Barbara Drake, Prog Coord
TYPE OF AGENCY: Victim/witness assistance program
AREAS SERVED: Pend Oreille
YEARS IN OPERATION: 5
ACCESSIBILITY: Wheelchair accessible
CASES SEXUAL ASSAULT/ABUSE (%): 4
CLIENTS/SERVICES: Sexual assault survivors; Marital rape/sexual abuse survivors; Child victims of sexual abuse; Incest victims/survivors
REQUIREMENTS: To apply for compensation benefits, the crime must be reported within 72 hours of occurrence unless victim is unable to do so

OAK HARBOR

CADA (CITIZENS AGAINST DOMESTIC ABUSE AND SEXUAL ASSAULT)
PO Box 190, Oak Harbor, WA 98277
Crisis hotline: **(206) 675-2232 24 hrs daily**
Information: (206) 675-7781, Langley office (206) 321-4181 9am-4pm (Mon-Thu)
Contact: Vicki Jones, Exec Dir
TYPE OF AGENCY: Rape crisis center; Domestic violence program
AREAS SERVED: Island
YEARS IN OPERATION: 7
LANGUAGES: Filipino interpreter
ACCESSIBILITY: Wheelchair accessible
CASES SEXUAL ASSAULT/ABUSE (%): 20
CLIENTS/SERVICES: Sexual assault survivors; Marital rape/sexual abuse survivors; Adult survivors of child sexual abuse; Incest victims/survivors; Prevention program; Community education; Adolescent survivors of sexual abuse; Male survivors of sexual abuse

OLYMPIA

FEMINISTS IN SELF-DEFENSE TRAINING (FIST)
PO Box 1883, Olympia, WA 98507
Information: (206) 438-0288 8am-5pm (Mon-Fri)
Contact: Debbie Leung, Coord
TYPE OF AGENCY: Rape prevention program
AREAS SERVED: Thurston, Mason, Pierce
YEARS IN OPERATION: 9
ACCESSIBILITY: Wheelchair accessible (with notice); Signers for the hearing impaired (with notice)

FEMINISTS IN SELF-DEFENSE TRAINING (FIST) (continued)

DESCRIPTION: Provides sexual assault prevention information for women and children which emphasizes every person's right to choose whichever options they feel are best suited to their preferences and needs; Information on all types of assault is provided, as well as info/practice on a wide range of prevention options which include safety ideas, assertiveness, and fighting skills
CLIENTS/SERVICES: Sexual assault survivors; Marital rape/sexual abuse survivors; Child victims of sexual abuse; Adult survivors of child sexual abuse; Incest victims/survivors; Prevention program; Community education; Adolescent survivors of sexual abuse
REQUIREMENTS: Classes for junior high age through adult

HEARTSPARKLE PLAYERS
PO Box 1883, Olympia, WA 98507
Information: (206) 943-6772 8am-6pm
TYPE OF AGENCY: Child sexual abuse prevention program; Theater group
AREAS SERVED: Thurston, Mason
YEARS IN OPERATION: 5
DESCRIPTION: Education program that does prevention work through the medium of theater for school-aged children, 5-8 years old. In the process of writing a script for preschoolers
CLIENTS/SERVICES: Prevention program; Community education; Publications/media
REQUIREMENTS: Ages 5-8
SPECIAL PROGRAMS/SERVICES: Media program: Video describing program and discussing prevention work

PUGET SOUND LEGAL ASSISTANCE FOUNDATION
529 W 4th Ave, Olympia, WA 98501
Information: (206) 943-6260 8:30am-5pm
TYPE OF AGENCY: Legal services agency
AREAS SERVED: Mason, Thurston
YEARS IN OPERATION: 15
ACCESSIBILITY: Wheelchair accessible
DESCRIPTION: Provides family law representation for victims of spousal sexual abuse and for parents of sexually abused children
CLIENTS/SERVICES: Marital rape/sexual abuse survivors; Child victims of sexual abuse
REQUIREMENTS: Low-income persons or persons 60 or older who live in Mason or Thurston County

SAFEPLACE: RAPE RELIEF/WOMEN'S SHELTER SERVICES
PO Box 1605, Olympia, WA 98507
Crisis hotline: **(206) 754-6300 24 hrs**
Information: (206) 786-8754 9am-5pm (Mon-Fri)
Contact: Tyra Lindquist, Admin; Charlotte Wheeler, Crisis Intervention Svcs Coord
TYPE OF AGENCY: Rape crisis center; Domestic violence program; Child sexual abuse services
AREAS SERVED: Thurston
YEARS IN OPERATION: 8
LANGUAGES: Spanish, Cambodian
ACCESSIBILITY: Wheelchair accessible; Signers for the hearing impaired (on call)
CASES SEXUAL ASSAULT/ABUSE (%): 20
CLIENTS/SERVICES: Sexual assault survivors; Marital rape/sexual abuse survivors; Child victims of sexual abuse; Adult survivors of child sexual abuse; Incest victims/survivors; Prevention program; Community education; Adolescent survivors of sexual abuse; Male survivors of sexual abuse

OMAK

THE SUPPORT CENTER
PO Box 2058, Omak, WA 98841
Crisis hotline: **(509) 826-3221 24 hrs**
Information: (509) 826-3221 8am-4pm
Contact: Margo Amelong, Asst Prog Dir
TYPE OF AGENCY: Rape crisis center; Domestic violence program
AREAS SERVED: Okanogan
YEARS IN OPERATION: 10
CASES SEXUAL ASSAULT/ABUSE (%): 25
DESCRIPTION: Provides basic services for victims of sexual assault/abuse: 24-hour hotline, support/counseling, referrals, escort services to hospital, police, district attorney's office. Videotaping of child victims for court testimony.
CLIENTS/SERVICES: Sexual assault survivors; Marital rape/sexual abuse survivors; Child victims of sexual abuse; Adult survivors of child sexual abuse; Incest victims/survivors; Prevention program; Community education; Adolescent survivors of sexual abuse; Male survivors of sexual abuse

PASCO

FRANKLIN COUNTY PROSECUTING ATTORNEY—VICTIM/WITNESS ASSISTANCE
PO Box 1160, Pasco, WA 99301
Information: (509) 545-3543 8:30am-Noon, 1pm-5pm (Mon-Fri)
Contact: Debbie Brasil, Coord
TYPE OF AGENCY: Victim/witness assistance program
AREAS SERVED: Franklin
YEARS IN OPERATION: 4
CLIENTS/SERVICES: Sexual assault survivors; Marital rape/sexual abuse survivors; Child victims of sexual abuse; Adult survivors of child sexual abuse; Incest victims/survivors

PORT ANGELES

SAFEHOME/SEXUAL ASSAULT PROGRAM
PO Box 1858, 708 E 8th, Port Angeles, WA 98362
Crisis hotline: **(206) 452-HELP 24 hrs**
Information: (206) 452-3811 9am-5pm (Mon-Fri)
Contact: Mary Ann Minor, Prog Coord
TYPE OF AGENCY: Rape crisis center; Domestic violence program; Child sexual abuse services; Child sexual abuse prevention program
SPONSORING ORGANIZATION: Umbrella Community Services
AREAS SERVED: Clallam
YEARS IN OPERATION: 6
CASES SEXUAL ASSAULT/ABUSE (%): 10
DESCRIPTION: Provides victim advocacy through the medical and court systems along with crisis counseling. Sexual Assault Treatment Program (SATP) for long-term therapy
CLIENTS/SERVICES: Sexual assault survivors; Marital rape/sexual abuse survivors; Child victims of sexual abuse; Adult survivors of child sexual abuse; Incest victims/survivors; Prevention program; Community education; Adolescent survivors of sexual abuse; Male survivors of sexual abuse

PORT TOWNSEND

THE DOMESTIC VIOLENCE/SEXUAL ASSAULT PROGRAM OF EASTERN JEFFERSON COUNTY
PO Box 743, Port Townsend, WA 98368
Crisis hotline: **(206) 385-5291 24 hrs**
Information: (206) 385-5291 9am-5pm
Contact: Patricia A Teal, Prog Dir
TYPE OF AGENCY: Rape crisis center; Domestic violence program; Child sexual abuse services; Child sexual abuse prevention program
AREAS SERVED: Eastern Jefferson
YEARS IN OPERATION: 10
LANGUAGES: Spanish, French, Hindi, Vrdu
ACCESSIBILITY: Wheelchair accessible
CASES SEXUAL ASSAULT/ABUSE (%): 40
DESCRIPTION: Services for survivors of sexual assault and domestic violence, including support groups for female and male survivors of sexual abuse/assault
CLIENTS/SERVICES: Sexual assault survivors; Marital rape/sexual abuse survivors; Child victims of sexual abuse; Adult survivors of child sexual abuse; Incest victims/survivors; Prevention program; Community education; Adolescent survivors of sexual abuse; Male survivors of sexual abuse

RENTON

FAMILY SERVICES
305 S 43rd St, Renton, WA 98055
Information: (206) 226-1253 9am-5pm (Mon-Fri); 5pm-9pm (Mon-Fri) answering machine
Contact: Barbara Sardarov, Branch Office Dir
TYPE OF AGENCY: Counseling/mental health services
AREAS SERVED: King, Pierce
YEARS IN OPERATION: 80
ACCESSIBILITY: Wheelchair accessible
CASES SEXUAL ASSAULT/ABUSE (%): 60
DESCRIPTION: Counseling agency providing individual, family, couple, and group counseling, including services for clients with a presenting problem of sexual assault
CLIENTS/SERVICES: Sexual assault survivors; Marital rape/sexual abuse survivors; Child victims of sexual abuse; Adult survivors of child sexual abuse; Incest victims/survivors; Community education; Adolescent survivors of sexual abuse; Male survivors of sexual abuse
REQUIREMENTS: Fee charged

KING COUNTY RAPE RELIEF
1025 S 3rd, Ste C, Renton, WA 98055
Information: (206) 226-5062 9am-5pm
Contact: Mary Ellen Stone, Dir
TYPE OF AGENCY: Rape crisis center; Child sexual abuse prevention program; Acquaintance/date rape prevention program
AREAS SERVED: King (victim services); Nationwide (education)
LANGUAGES: SE Asian languages
ACCESSIBILITY: Wheelchair accessible
CASES SEXUAL ASSAULT/ABUSE (%): 100
CLIENTS/SERVICES: Sexual assault survivors; Marital rape/sexual abuse survivors; Child victims of sexual abuse; Adult survivors of child sexual abuse; Incest victims/survivors; Prevention program; Community education; Adolescent survivors of sexual abuse; Male survivors of sexual abuse; Ethnic minorities; Publications/media
REQUIREMENTS: Primary service area is King County outside the city of Seattle
SPECIAL PROGRAMS/SERVICES: Publications: *So What's It to Me? Sexual Assault Information for Guys* ($4.50, Activity guide $14); *Top Secret: Sexual Assault Information for Teenagers Only* ($4.50, Discussion guide: $13.75); *Where Do I Start? A Parent's Guide for Talking to Teens About Acquaintance Rape* ($2); *Talking to Children/Talking to Parents About Sexual Assault* ($12.50); *He Told Me Not to Tell* ($2.50, also available in Spanish); *Be Aware, Be Safe*, for Southeast Asian teenagers ($1.25); *Helping Your Child to be Safe*, for Southeast Asian parents ($1.25, English-Khmer-Lao edition, English-Vietnamese-Chinese edition). Media programs: staff have been involved in *Child Sexual Abuse: A Solution* (6 filmstrips for children, teachers, and parents); *Child Sexual Abuse: What Your Children Should Know* (5 films or videos originally aired on PBS in 1983; programs for parents, grades K-3, grades 4-7, grades 7-12, and senior high students featuring staff from King County Rape Relief and the Illusion Theater).

REPUBLIC

FERRY COUNTY COMMUNITY SERVICES
PO Box 907, Republic, WA 99166
Crisis hotline: **(509) 775-3132 24 hrs**
Information: (509) 775-3341 8am-4pm; 24-hr on call
Contact: Linda Visness, Vista-Sexual Assault
TYPE OF AGENCY: Counseling/mental health services; Child sexual abuse services; Child sexual abuse prevention program
AREAS SERVED: Ferry
YEARS IN OPERATION: 10
ACCESSIBILITY: Wheelchair accessible
CLIENTS/SERVICES: Sexual assault survivors; Marital rape/sexual abuse survivors; Child victims of sexual abuse; Adult survivors of child sexual abuse; Incest victims/survivors; Prevention program; Community education; Adolescent survivors of sexual abuse; Male survivors of sexual abuse

RICHLAND

BENTON-FRANKLIN RAPE RELIEF AND SEXUAL ASSAULT PROGRAM
PO Box 9, Richland, WA 99352
Crisis hotline: **(509) 946-2377 24 hrs daily**
Information: (509) 946-2377 8am-5pm
Contact: Mary Sisk, Dir; Lynn Crook, Education Coord
TYPE OF AGENCY: Rape crisis center
AREAS SERVED: Benton, Franklin
YEARS IN OPERATION: 11
LANGUAGES: Spanish, access to language bank
ACCESSIBILITY: Wheelchair accessible; Telecommunications for the hearing impaired (TTY, TDY, etc.)
CASES SEXUAL ASSAULT/ABUSE (%): 100
DESCRIPTION: Offers crisis counseling and victim assistance for survivors of sexual assault and families and friends; Feminist martial arts/self-defense program
CLIENTS/SERVICES: Sexual assault survivors; Marital rape/sexual abuse survivors; Child victims of sexual abuse; Adult survivors of child sexual abuse; Incest victims/survivors; Prevention program; Community education; Adolescent survivors of sexual abuse; Male survivors of sexual abuse

SEATTLE

ABUSED DEAF WOMEN'S ADVOCACY SERVICES
2366 Eastlake Ave E, Ste 305, Seattle, WA 98102
Crisis hotline: **(206) 774-2501 (TTY) 24 hrs**
Information: (206) 726-0093 9am-5pm (Mon-Fri)
Contact: Marilyn J Smith, Exec Dir
TYPE OF AGENCY: Rape crisis center; Domestic violence program; Child sexual abuse services; Child sexual abuse prevention program
AREAS SERVED: King
YEARS IN OPERATION: 3
LANGUAGES: Sign
ACCESSIBILITY: Wheelchair accessible; Telecommunications for the hearing impaired (TTY, TDY, etc.); Signers for the hearing impaired
CASES SEXUAL ASSAULT/ABUSE (%): 35
DESCRIPTION: Provides services that are culturally and linguistically relevant for victims of sexual assault and domestic violence who are deaf or deaf-blind; Provides education for these two communities
CLIENTS/SERVICES: Sexual assault survivors; Marital rape/sexual abuse survivors; Child victims of sexual abuse; Adult survivors of child sexual abuse; Incest victims/survivors; Prevention program; Community education; Deaf/hearing impaired; Deaf-blind; Adolescent survivors of sexual abuse; Male survivors of sexual abuse; Disabled

ALTERNATIVES TO FEAR
2811 E Madison, Ste 208, Seattle, WA 98112
Information: (206) 328-5347
Contact: Py Bateman
TYPE OF AGENCY: Child sexual abuse prevention program; Rape prevention program; Acquaintance/date rape prevention program
DESCRIPTION: Presents sexual assault prevention programs to different groups—children, teens, adult women, elderly, the disabled. Available for consultation, training, and speaking engagements
CLIENTS/SERVICES: Prevention program; Community education; Disabled; Elderly; Publications/media
SPECIAL PROGRAMS/SERVICES: Publications: *Acquaintance Rape: Awareness and Prevention for Teenagers* (16 p, $4); *Where Do I Start? A Parent's Guide to Talking to Teens* (50 p, $4) *Macho: Is That What I Really Want?* (48 p, $4); *Fear Into Anger*, self-defense manual with step-by-step directions and photographs (123 p, $11.95); *Peace of Mind*, a booklet for senior citizens (30 p, $4)

ASIAN COUNSELING AND REFERRAL SERVICE
1032 S Jackson, Ste 200, Seattle, WA 98104
Information: (206) 461-3606 8:30am-5pm
Contact: Ann Christian, Assoc Dir
TYPE OF AGENCY: Victim/witness assistance program; Counseling/mental health services
AREAS SERVED: King
YEARS IN OPERATION: 16
LANGUAGES: Vietnamese, Tagalog, Ilocano, Samoan, Korean, Cantonese, Toishanese, Laotian, Mien, Japanese, Cambodian
ACCESSIBILITY: Wheelchair accessible
CASES SEXUAL ASSAULT/ABUSE (%): 1
DESCRIPTION: VOCA (Victim of Crime Act) program provides counseling for Asian children who have been physically or sexually abused
CLIENTS/SERVICES: Child victims of sexual abuse; Adolescent survivors of sexual abuse; Disabled; Ethnic minorities
REQUIREMENTS: Clients must be under the age of 18

CATHERINE BOOTH HOUSE
PO Box 20128, Seattle, WA 98102
Crisis hotline: **(206) 324-7271, 324-4943 24 hrs**
Information: (206) 324-7271, 324-4943 24 hrs
Contact: Elizabeth Avalos, Resource Coord
TYPE OF AGENCY: Domestic violence program; Child sexual abuse services; Child sexual abuse prevention program
SPONSORING ORGANIZATION: Salvation Army
AREAS SERVED: King
YEARS IN OPERATION: 12
LANGUAGES: Spanish, French
ACCESSIBILITY: Wheelchair accessible; Telecommunications for the hearing impaired (TTY, TDY, etc.)
CASES SEXUAL ASSAULT/ABUSE (%): 50
DESCRIPTION: Confidentially located shelter for battered women and their children, many of whom have been sexually abused; Assesses sexual abuse; Accompanies victims to medical and legal services; Advocacy; Feminist counseling
CLIENTS/SERVICES: Sexual assault survivors; Marital rape/sexual abuse survivors; Child victims of sexual abuse; Adult survivors of child sexual abuse; Incest victims/survivors; Prevention program; Community education; Adolescent survivors of sexual abuse

CONSEJO COUNSELING AND REFERRAL SERVICE
3808 S Angeline, Seattle, WA 98118
Information: (206) 461-4880 8:30am-5pm
Contact: Jorge R Chacon, Exec Dir
TYPE OF AGENCY: Counseling/mental health services; Child sexual abuse services; Child sexual abuse prevention program; Child abuse prevention program
AREAS SERVED: King and adjacent counties
YEARS IN OPERATION: 10
LANGUAGES: Spanish
ACCESSIBILITY: Wheelchair accessible; Telecommunications for the hearing impaired (TTY, TDY, etc.)
CASES SEXUAL ASSAULT/ABUSE (%): 10
DESCRIPTION: Provides culturally sensitive bilingual services for the low-income Chicano/Latino population. Family violence prevention program which includes a child abuse/neglect prevention component
CLIENTS/SERVICES: Sexual assault survivors; Marital rape/sexual abuse survivors; Child victims of sexual abuse; Adult survivors of child sexual abuse; Prevention program; Community education; Adolescent survivors of sexual abuse; Ethnic minorities

FEMINIST KARATE UNION
5429 Russell Ave NW, Seattle, WA 98107
Information: (206) 789-4561 24-hr answering machine
Contact: Linda Kenoyer, Chief Instructor
TYPE OF AGENCY: Rape prevention program
AREAS SERVED: King
YEARS IN OPERATION: 17
ACCESSIBILITY: Wheelchair accessible; Signers for the hearing impaired (program being developed)
DESCRIPTION: Teaches karate and self-defense for women and children. This knowledge empowers women and children and helps them to combat and prevent sexual assault
CLIENTS/SERVICES: Prevention program; Community education
REQUIREMENTS: All women accepted; Children's classes, boys must be 12 or younger

45TH STREET COMMUNITY HEALTH CLINIC
1629 N 45th St, Seattle, WA 98103
Information: (206) 633-3350 8:30am-9:30pm (Mon, Wed); 8:30am-5:30pm (Tue, Fri); 8:30am-2pm (Sat)
TYPE OF AGENCY: Hospital/medical center
AREAS SERVED: King
YEARS IN OPERATION: 17
LANGUAGES: Spanish, German
ACCESSIBILITY: Wheelchair accessible; Signers for the hearing impaired (by arrangement)
CASES SEXUAL ASSAULT/ABUSE (%): 5
DESCRIPTION: Comprehensive medical and dental care provided for low-income residents of north Seattle and north King County; Rape examinations; Referrals for counseling and low-cost legal services
CLIENTS/SERVICES: Sexual assault survivors; Child victims of sexual abuse
REQUIREMENTS: Low-income, Northend resident

HARBORVIEW MEDICAL CENTER—BATTERED WOMEN'S PROGRAM
325 9th Ave, Seattle, WA 98104
Crisis hotline: **(800) 562-6025 24 hrs**
Information: (206) 223-5418 9am-5pm (Mon-Fri)
Contact: P Yager, MSW, D Forsberg, MSW
TYPE OF AGENCY: Domestic violence program; Hospital/medical center
AREAS SERVED: King
YEARS IN OPERATION: 1
ACCESSIBILITY: Wheelchair accessible; Telecommunications for the hearing impaired (TTY, TDY, etc.); Signers for the hearing impaired
DESCRIPTION: Funded to provide specialized domestic violence services for mentally ill or homeless victims
CLIENTS/SERVICES: Marital rape/sexual abuse survivors

KING COUNTY PROSECUTING ATTORNEY'S OFFICE—VICTIM ASSISTANCE UNIT
516 3rd Ave, Rm, No E542, Seattle, WA 98104
Information: (206) 296-9552 8:30am-4:30pm (Mon-Fri)
Contact: Ralyn Baird, Dir

KING COUNTY PROSECUTING ATTORNEY'S OFFICE—VICTIM ASSISTANCE UNIT *(continued)*
TYPE OF AGENCY: Victim/witness assistance program
AREAS SERVED: King
YEARS IN OPERATION: 13
ACCESSIBILITY: Wheelchair accessible
CASES SEXUAL ASSAULT/ABUSE (%): 25
CLIENTS/SERVICES: Sexual assault survivors; Marital rape/sexual abuse survivors; Child victims of sexual abuse; Adult survivors of child sexual abuse; Incest victims/survivors; Community education; Male survivors of sexual abuse
REQUIREMENTS: Criminal charges must be filed with the prosecuting attorney's office

KING COUNTY PROSECUTOR'S OFFICE—SPECIAL ASSAULT UNIT (SAU)
516 3rd Ave, Seattle, WA 98106
Information: (206) 296-9466 8:30am-4:30pm
Contact: E K Brom, Victim Svcs Coord
TYPE OF AGENCY: Victim/witness assistance program
AREAS SERVED: King
YEARS IN OPERATION: 3
ACCESSIBILITY: Wheelchair accessible; Signers for the hearing impaired
CASES SEXUAL ASSAULT/ABUSE (%): 70
DESCRIPTION: Prosecutes all felony level criminal cases against adults in the following crime categories: sexual assault of adults, sexual abuse of children, physical abuse of children, sexual exploitation, and felony domestic violence; Provides advocacy and witness preparation
CLIENTS/SERVICES: Sexual assault survivors; Marital rape/sexual abuse survivors; Child victims of sexual abuse; Incest victims/survivors; Community education; Male survivors of sexual abuse
REQUIREMENTS: Police report and referral to SAU for consideration of filing charges

LESBIAN RESOURCE CENTER
1208 E Pine, Seattle, WA 98122
Crisis hotline: **(206) 322-3953 2pm-7pm (Mon-Fri)**
Information: (206) 322-3953
Contact: Hope Sandler, Co-Dir
TYPE OF AGENCY: Women's center
AREAS SERVED: King
YEARS IN OPERATION: 17
ACCESSIBILITY: Wheelchair accessible; Telecommunications for the hearing impaired (TTY, TDY, etc.)
CLIENTS/SERVICES: Community education; Lesbians

NEW BEGINNINGS SHELTER FOR BATTERED WOMEN AND THEIR CHILDREN
PO Box 75125, Seattle, WA 98125-0125
Crisis hotline: **(206) 522-9472 24 hrs daily**
Information: (206) 522-9474 9am-5pm (Mon-Fri)
Contact: Mary Pontarolo, Exec Dir
TYPE OF AGENCY: Domestic violence program; Child sexual abuse services
AREAS SERVED: Statewide
YEARS IN OPERATION: 12
LANGUAGES: Spanish
ACCESSIBILITY: Telecommunications for the hearing impaired (TTY, TDY, etc.); Signers for the hearing impaired (by arrangement)
CASES SEXUAL ASSAULT/ABUSE (%): 15
CLIENTS/SERVICES: Marital rape/sexual abuse survivors; Child victims of sexual abuse; Adult survivors of child sexual abuse; Incest victims/survivors; Community education; Adolescent survivors of sexual abuse

NORTHWEST TREATMENT ASSOCIATES
315 W Galer, Seattle, WA 98119
Information: (206) 283-8099 9am-10pm (Mon-Thu); 9am-4pm (Fri)
Contact: Roger Wolfe, Co-Dir
TYPE OF AGENCY: Private practice; Offender treatment
AREAS SERVED: Statewide
YEARS IN OPERATION: 12
CASES SEXUAL ASSAULT/ABUSE (%): 98
DESCRIPTION: Provides comprehensive treatment for child sexual abuse/incest offenders and batterers
CLIENTS/SERVICES: Offender treatment program
REQUIREMENTS: 18 or older, nonpsychotic, normal intellectual functioning

SEATTLE COUNSELING SERVICES FOR SEXUAL MINORITIES
1505 Broadway, Seattle, WA 98122
Crisis hotline: **(206) 329-8707 12pm-9pm**
Information: (206) 329-8737 9am-6pm (Mon-Fri)
Contact: Doug Fisher, Emergency Svcs Prog Mgr
TYPE OF AGENCY: Counseling/mental health services; Telephone crisis hotline; Information and referral
AREAS SERVED: Primarily King
YEARS IN OPERATION: 20
ACCESSIBILITY: Signers for the hearing impaired (by arrangement)
CASES SEXUAL ASSAULT/ABUSE (%): 5-7
DESCRIPTION: Provides a full range of therapeutic services for the lesbian/gay community; Various issues presented including the impact of any kind of abuse on the individuals' ability to create a healthy life
CLIENTS/SERVICES: Male survivors of sexual abuse; Lesbians; Gay men

SEATTLE INSTITUTE FOR SEX THERAPY, EDUCATION, AND RESEARCH (SISTER)
100 NE 56th, Seattle, WA 98105
Information: (206) 522-8588 8am-6pm (Mon-Fri)
Contact: Elizabeth Rae Larson, Co-Dir
TYPE OF AGENCY: Counseling/mental health services
AREAS SERVED: King and surrounding areas
YEARS IN OPERATION: 13
ACCESSIBILITY: Wheelchair accessible
CASES SEXUAL ASSAULT/ABUSE (%): 50
DESCRIPTION: Counseling specializing in sexuality issues, including the treatment of sexual recovery from sexual trauma and exploitation. Workshops and evening programs presented on topics pertaining to sexuality
CLIENTS/SERVICES: Sexual assault survivors; Marital rape/sexual abuse survivors; Adult survivors of child sexual abuse; Community education; Sexuality issues; Adolescent survivors of sexual abuse; Male survivors of sexual abuse; Publications/media
REQUIREMENTS: Services appropriate to adolescents and adults
SPECIAL PROGRAMS/SERVICES: Publication: free booklet entitled *Recovering from Rape: Healing Your Sexuality*

SEATTLE POLICE DEPARTMENT—VICTIM ASSISTANCE SECTION
610 3rd Ave, Seattle, WA 98104
Information: (206) 684-7777 8am-4:30pm
Contact: Barbara Kendziorek, Dir
TYPE OF AGENCY: Victim/witness assistance program
AREAS SERVED: City of Seattle
YEARS IN OPERATION: 10
LANGUAGES: Chinese, Cantonese, Mandarin
ACCESSIBILITY: Wheelchair accessible
CASES SEXUAL ASSAULT/ABUSE (%): 30
CLIENTS/SERVICES: Sexual assault survivors; Marital rape/sexual abuse survivors; Child victims of sexual abuse; Community education
REQUIREMENTS: Crime must be reported to police; Must be a felony-level, person-to-person crime

SEATTLE RAPE RELIEF
1825 S Jackson, Ste 102, Seattle, WA 98144
Crisis hotline: **(206) 632-7273 24 hrs**
Information: (206) 325-5531 9am-5pm (Mon-Fri)
Contact: Leslie Shinsato, Office/Crisis Line Mgr
TYPE OF AGENCY: Rape crisis center
AREAS SERVED: City of Seattle
YEARS IN OPERATION: 16
LANGUAGES: Chinese, Mien, Laotian, Hmong
ACCESSIBILITY: Wheelchair accessible; Telecommunications for the hearing impaired (TTY, TDY, etc.)
CASES SEXUAL ASSAULT/ABUSE (%): 95
CLIENTS/SERVICES: Sexual assault survivors; Marital rape/sexual abuse survivors; Child victims of sexual abuse; Adult survivors of child sexual abuse; Incest victims/survivors; Prevention program; Community education; Adolescent survivors of sexual abuse; Developmentally disabled; Male survivors of sexual abuse; Disabled; Ethnic minorities; Publications/media
SPECIAL PROGRAMS/SERVICES: Legal Outreach Coordinator provides legal advocacy for victims who choose to report and go through the legal system. Provides special outreach services for the Black community and an Asian Outreach Program that includes a "Helpline". It is a crisis line that provides crisis intervention counseling and advocacy for Southeast Asian people. Counselors speak the different languages of Southeast Asia, thereby eliminating the need for interpreters. The Asian Outreach Program has produced a media program, *We Have the Right to Protect Ourselves*. The Disabilities Project provides training and consultation on specialized sexual abuse treatment and prevention services designed for children and adults with physical, sensory, visual, or developmental disabilities. Publications include: *Choices: Self Protection Workbooks for Persons with Physical Disabilities, Visual Impairments and Deaf/Hearing Impairments* (3 workbooks, $5 each; also available in large print and audio cassette for the visually impaired); *A Curriculum for Developing an Awareness; of Sexual Abuse and Self Protection Techniques* (includes lesson plans, filmstrips and group activities. Ages 6-11: $125; ages 12 to adult: $495); 2 staff training manuals on working with people with disabilities ($45 each), one for rape crisis staff and volunteers and one for teachers, school counselors, and school nurses for developing a special education prevention program within the school district

SEATTLE YOUTH AND COMMUNITY SERVICES
1020 Virginia St, Seattle, WA 98111
Crisis hotline: **(206) 725-8888 24 hrs**
Information: (206) 622-3187 9am-5pm
Contact: Ray Jagaer, Prog Mgr
TYPE OF AGENCY: Child sexual abuse services; Child sexual abuse prevention program; Residential treatment facility; Shelter; Adolescent program
AREAS SERVED: King
YEARS IN OPERATION: 16
ACCESSIBILITY: Wheelchair accessible
DESCRIPTION: Targets youth who are, or at risk of becoming, prostitutes. Also targets other sexually exploited persons
CLIENTS/SERVICES: Sexual assault survivors; Child victims of sexual abuse; Incest victims/survivors; Prevention program; Community education; Adolescent survivors of sexual abuse; Male survivors of sexual abuse; Prostitutes
REQUIREMENTS: Ages 11-18

SEXUAL ASSAULT CENTER OF HARBORVIEW MEDICAL CENTER
325 9th Ave ZA-07, Seattle, WA 98104
Information: (206) 223-3047 8am-5pm

SEXUAL ASSAULT CENTER OF HARBORVIEW MEDICAL CENTER
(continued)

TYPE OF AGENCY: Rape crisis center; Child sexual abuse services
DESCRIPTION: Provides medical care, crisis counseling, and advocacy with the criminal justice system for female and male victims of sexual assault. Extensive counseling and support for sexually abused children and their families
CLIENTS/SERVICES: Sexual assault survivors; Child victims of sexual abuse; Adult survivors of child sexual abuse; Incest victims/survivors; Community education; Adolescent survivors of sexual abuse; Male survivors of sexual abuse

WOMEN'S INFORMATION CENTER
Cunningham Hall AJ-50, University of Washington, Seattle, WA 98195
Information: (206) 545-1090 9am-5pm (Mon, Tue, Wed, Fri); 9am-9pm (Thu)
Contact: Angela Ginorio, Dir
TYPE OF AGENCY: College/university-based services
SPONSORING ORGANIZATION: University of Washington
AREAS SERVED: King
YEARS IN OPERATION: 10
LANGUAGES: Spanish
ACCESSIBILITY: Wheelchair accessible; Telecommunications for the hearing impaired (TTY, TDY, etc.)
CASES SEXUAL ASSAULT/ABUSE (%): 1
DESCRIPTION: Primarily an information center; Has extensive information and referral data base, of which sexual assault related referrals is a part. Has a community library and operates a re-entry program for women. In addition, has a women's art gallery, sponsors noncredit classes, and produces special events (such as the 1987 Women's Humor Festival).
CLIENTS/SERVICES: Sexual assault survivors; Marital rape/sexual abuse survivors; Child victims of sexual abuse; Adult survivors of child sexual abuse; Incest victims/survivors

SHELTON

RECOVERY: AID TO VICTIMS OF SEXUAL AND DOMESTIC ABUSE
Box 1132, Shelton, WA 98584
Crisis hotline: **(800) 562-6025 24 hrs**
Information: (206) 426-5878 10am-5pm (Mon-Fri)
Contact: Debi VanBuskirk, Sexual Assault Coord
TYPE OF AGENCY: Rape crisis center; Domestic violence program; Child sexual abuse services
AREAS SERVED: Mason
YEARS IN OPERATION: 8½
ACCESSIBILITY: Wheelchair accessible
CASES SEXUAL ASSAULT/ABUSE (%): 75
CLIENTS/SERVICES: Sexual assault survivors; Marital rape/sexual abuse survivors; Child victims of sexual abuse; Adult survivors of child sexual abuse; Incest victims/survivors; Community education; Adolescent survivors of sexual abuse; Male survivors of sexual abuse

THE SEXUAL ABUSE CLINIC, SHELTON OFFICE
PO Box 927, Shelton, WA 98584
Information: (206) 426-6113
Contact: Beth Bruno, MA, Therapist
TYPE OF AGENCY: Private practice; Offender treatment
SPONSORING ORGANIZATION: The Sexual Abuse Clinic, Portland Office
AREAS SERVED: Grays Harbor, Mason, Thurston
YEARS IN OPERATION: 1½
CASES SEXUAL ASSAULT/ABUSE (%): 100
DESCRIPTION: Provides individual and group therapies for rapists and child sexual abuse/incest offenders
CLIENTS/SERVICES: Community education; Offender treatment program
REQUIREMENTS: Adult offenders only

SPOKANE

GROWTH COUNSELING SERVICES
PO Box 141622, 202 Pines Rd, Spokane, WA 99214-1622
Information: (509) 928-5321 24 hrs by pager
Contact: Wayne Hough or Carol Hough, Co-Dirs
TYPE OF AGENCY: Private practice
AREAS SERVED: Spokane, Stevens
YEARS IN OPERATION: 7
ACCESSIBILITY: Wheelchair accessible
CASES SEXUAL ASSAULT/ABUSE (%): 75
CLIENTS/SERVICES: Sexual assault survivors; Marital rape/sexual abuse survivors; Child victims of sexual abuse; Adult survivors of child sexual abuse; Incest victims/survivors; Prevention program; Community education; Offender treatment program; Adolescent survivors of sexual abuse; Male survivors of sexual abuse
REQUIREMENTS: Must meet reporting requirements for minors

PARENTS UNITED
PO Box 141622, Spokane, WA 99214-1622
Crisis hotline: **(509) 928-8010 24 hrs daily via pager**
Information: (509) 928-5321 10am-8pm (Mon-Thu)
Contact: Carol Hough, United Couns Admin
TYPE OF AGENCY: Child sexual abuse services
SPONSORING ORGANIZATION: United Counseling Services
AREAS SERVED: Spokane, Stevens
YEARS IN OPERATION: 2
ACCESSIBILITY: Wheelchair accessible
CASES SEXUAL ASSAULT/ABUSE (%): 95
DESCRIPTION: Sponsors Parents United and Adults Molested as Children and offers group and individual therapy for people dealing with the effects of childhood sexual abuse
CLIENTS/SERVICES: Sexual assault survivors; Marital rape/sexual abuse survivors; Adult survivors of child sexual abuse; Incest victims/survivors; Community education; Offender treatment program; Adolescent survivors of sexual abuse; Male survivors of sexual abuse
REQUIREMENTS: Any offense against a person under age must be reported

RAPE CRISIS NETWORK
S 7 Howard, Ste 200, Spokane, WA 99201
Crisis hotline: **(509) 624-RAPE 24 hrs daily**
Information: (509) 747-8224 8:30am-5pm (Mon-Fri)
Contact: Shirley Cannon, Prog Supv
TYPE OF AGENCY: Rape crisis center; Child sexual abuse services; Child sexual abuse prevention program
SPONSORING ORGANIZATION: Lutheran Social Services of Washington and Idaho
AREAS SERVED: Spokane
YEARS IN OPERATION: 14
ACCESSIBILITY: Wheelchair accessible
CASES SEXUAL ASSAULT/ABUSE (%): 95
DESCRIPTION: Clinical treatment, individual, group, and family therapy for victims/survivors of child sexual abuse, incest, or rape and their non-offending family members; Prevention/education, advocacy, court accompaniment, medical and legal systems support, and support groups for both female and male survivors
CLIENTS/SERVICES: Sexual assault survivors; Marital rape/sexual abuse survivors; Child victims of sexual abuse; Adult survivors of child sexual abuse; Incest victims/survivors; Prevention program; Community education; Adolescent survivors of sexual abuse; Male survivors of sexual abuse
REQUIREMENTS: Child sexual abuse must be determined by Child Protective Services and/or police prior to acceptance

SPECIAL PROGRAMS/SERVICES: Locally produced film: *Age Makes No Difference*

SPOKANE COUNTY PROSECUTING ATTORNEY—VICTIM/WITNESS ASSISTANCE UNIT
W 1100 Mallon Public Safety Bldg, Spokane, WA 99260
Information: (509) 456-3646 8:30am-5pm
Contact: Dorothy Scott, Dir
TYPE OF AGENCY: Victim/witness assistance program
AREAS SERVED: Spokane
YEARS IN OPERATION: 10
ACCESSIBILITY: Wheelchair accessible
CLIENTS/SERVICES: Sexual assault survivors; Marital rape/sexual abuse survivors; Child victims of sexual abuse; Incest victims/survivors; Adolescent survivors of sexual abuse; Male survivors of sexual abuse

STEVENSON

SKAMANIA COUNTY COUNCIL ON DOMESTIC VIOLENCE AND SEXUAL ASSAULT
PO Box 477, Stevenson, WA 98648
Crisis hotline: **(800) 562-6025 24 hrs**
Information: (509) 427-5636 8am-5pm (Mon-Fri)
Contact: Renee Torres, Prog Coord
TYPE OF AGENCY: Rape crisis center; Domestic violence program; Child sexual abuse prevention program
AREAS SERVED: Skamania
YEARS IN OPERATION: 10
LANGUAGES: Spanish, French, Sign interpreters
ACCESSIBILITY: Wheelchair accessible; Signers for the hearing impaired
CASES SEXUAL ASSAULT/ABUSE (%): 5-10
CLIENTS/SERVICES: Sexual assault survivors; Marital rape/sexual abuse survivors; Child victims of sexual abuse; Adult survivors of child sexual abuse; Incest victims/survivors; Prevention program; Community education

SUNNYSIDE

LOWER VALLEY CRISIS AND SUPPORT SERVICES
PO Box 93, Sunnyside, WA 98944
Crisis hotline: **(509) 837-6689 24 hrs**
Information: (509) 837-6689 24 hrs
TYPE OF AGENCY: Rape crisis center; Domestic violence program; Child sexual abuse services; Child sexual abuse prevention program
AREAS SERVED: Yakima and part of Benton
YEARS IN OPERATION: 10
LANGUAGES: Spanish
ACCESSIBILITY: Wheelchair accessible
CASES SEXUAL ASSAULT/ABUSE (%): Ricki Tebaldi, Exec Dir
DESCRIPTION: Basic hotline, support/counseling, and escort services for sexual assault survivors; Support groups for female and male survivors; Therapy program for batterers
CLIENTS/SERVICES: Sexual assault survivors; Marital rape/sexual abuse survivors; Child victims of sexual abuse; Adult survivors of child sexual abuse; Incest victims/survivors; Prevention program; Community education; Adolescent survivors of sexual abuse; Male survivors of sexual abuse

TACOMA

CENTER FOR CHILD ABUSE PREVENTION SERVICES
949 Market St, Ste 411, Tacoma, WA 98402
Crisis hotline: **(206) 572-5541 24 hrs**
Information: (206) 572-5541 9am-4:30pm
Contact: Jim Teverbaugh, Exec Dir
TYPE OF AGENCY: Child sexual abuse prevention program
AREAS SERVED: Pierce

CENTER FOR CHILD ABUSE PREVENTION SERVICES *(continued)*
YEARS IN OPERATION: 15
ACCESSIBILITY: Wheelchair accessible
CASES SEXUAL ASSAULT/ABUSE (%): 50
DESCRIPTION: Prevention through community education and training
CLIENTS/SERVICES: Prevention program; Community education; Adolescent survivors of sexual abuse
SPECIAL PROGRAMS/SERVICES: Two multi-disciplinary case consultation teams; Project "Safeplace": youth in crisis can go to designated safeplace sites and be connected with a trained volunteer for help; "Parenting Plus": a family development program for high risk parents

PIERCE COUNTY RAPE RELIEF
1901 S 19th, Ste A-302, Allenmore Medical Center, Bldg A, Tacoma, WA 98405
Crisis hotline: **(206) 474-7273 24 hrs**
Information: (206) 597-6424 8am-4:30pm (Mon-Fri)
Contact: Maureen MacNamara, Exec Dir; Kay Wylie, Direct Svcs Dir
TYPE OF AGENCY: Rape crisis center
AREAS SERVED: Pierce
YEARS IN OPERATION: 15
LANGUAGES: Spanish
ACCESSIBILITY: Wheelchair accessible; Telecommunications for the hearing impaired (TTY, TDY, etc.); Signers for the hearing impaired (by request)
CASES SEXUAL ASSAULT/ABUSE (%): 100
CLIENTS/SERVICES: Sexual assault survivors; Marital rape/sexual abuse survivors; Adult survivors of child sexual abuse; Incest victims/survivors; Prevention program; Community education; Adolescent survivors of sexual abuse; Male survivors of sexual abuse
SPECIAL PROGRAMS/SERVICES: Uses animal-assisted therapy as treatment modality for support group. (Specially trained dog attends group and provides companionship in order to make disclosure and healing less lonely)

YWCA WOMEN'S SUPPORT SHELTER
405 Broadway, Tacoma, WA 98402
Crisis hotline: **(206) 383-2593 24 hrs**
Information: (206) 272-4181 8am-5pm (Mon-Fri)
Contact: Dee Arscheene, Shelter Mgr
TYPE OF AGENCY: Domestic violence program
AREAS SERVED: Pierce
YEARS IN OPERATION: 13
LANGUAGES: Korean
ACCESSIBILITY: Wheelchair accessible
CLIENTS/SERVICES: Marital rape/sexual abuse survivors; Child victims of sexual abuse; Adult survivors of child sexual abuse; Prevention program; Community education; Adolescent survivors of sexual abuse

VANCOUVER

CLARK COUNTY PROSECUTING ATTORNEY—VICTIM/WITNESS UNIT
1101 Harney St, Vancouver, WA 98660
Information: (206) 699-2008 8am-5pm (Mon-Fri)
Contact: Amy Kendis, Justice Prog Admin
TYPE OF AGENCY: Victim/witness assistance program
AREAS SERVED: Clark
YEARS IN OPERATION: 9
CASES SEXUAL ASSAULT/ABUSE (%): 20
CLIENTS/SERVICES: Sexual assault survivors; Marital rape/sexual abuse survivors; Child victims of sexual abuse; Adult survivors of child sexual abuse; Incest victims/survivors; Adolescent survivors of sexual abuse
SPECIAL PROGRAMS/SERVICES: Jointly recruits and trains volunteer advocates with the YWCA Sexual Assault, Domestic Violence, and Guardian Ad Litem Programs; Received national recognition for the cooperative effort

YWCA CLARK COUNTY SEXUAL ASSAULT PROGRAM
1115 Esther St, Vancouver, WA 98660
Crisis hotline: **(206) 695-0501 24 hrs**
Information: (206) 696-0167 9am-5pm
Contact: Joan Renner, Dir
TYPE OF AGENCY: Rape crisis center; Child sexual abuse services; Child sexual abuse prevention program
AREAS SERVED: Clark
YEARS IN OPERATION: 7½
LANGUAGES: Interpreters for Spanish and SE Asian languages available
ACCESSIBILITY: Signers for the hearing impaired
CASES SEXUAL ASSAULT/ABUSE (%): 100
CLIENTS/SERVICES: Sexual assault survivors; Marital rape/sexual abuse survivors; Child victims of sexual abuse; Adult survivors of child sexual abuse; Incest victims/survivors; Prevention program; Community education; Male survivors of sexual abuse; Publications/media
SPECIAL PROGRAMS/SERVICES: Sexual assault service provider group; Media programs *Call It Rape* and *Teen Acquaintance Rape* video

WALLA WALLA

COMMUNITY ABUSE AND ASSAULT CENTER
PO Box 1773, Walla Walla, WA 99362
Crisis hotline: **(509) 529-3377 24 hrs**
Information: (509) 529-3300
Contact: Bev Hintz, Assoc Dir
TYPE OF AGENCY: Rape crisis center; Domestic violence program; Child sexual abuse services; Child sexual abuse prevention program
AREAS SERVED: Walla Walla
YEARS IN OPERATION: 12
LANGUAGES: Spanish
CASES SEXUAL ASSAULT/ABUSE (%): 45
CLIENTS/SERVICES: Sexual assault survivors; Marital rape/sexual abuse survivors; Child victims of sexual abuse; Adult survivors of child sexual abuse; Incest victims/survivors; Prevention program; Community education; Offender treatment program; Adolescent survivors of sexual abuse; Male survivors of sexual abuse

WATERVILLE

DOUGLAS COUNTY PROSECUTING ATTORNEY
PO Box M, Waterville, WA 98858
Information: (509) 884-9446, 745-8535 8am-5pm
Contact: Judith L McCauley, Pros Atty
TYPE OF AGENCY: Victim/witness assistance program
AREAS SERVED: Douglas
YEARS IN OPERATION: 6
ACCESSIBILITY: Wheelchair accessible
CASES SEXUAL ASSAULT/ABUSE (%): 10
CLIENTS/SERVICES: Sexual assault survivors
REQUIREMENTS: Client must be willing to testify in criminal proceedings

WENATCHEE

CHELAN COUNTY PROSECUTING ATTORNEY—VICTIM WITNESS UNIT
PO Box 2596, Wenatchee, WA 98801
Information: (509) 664-5206 8:30am-5pm
Contact: Sharon Roe, Victim Witness Coord
TYPE OF AGENCY: Victim/witness assistance program
AREAS SERVED: Chelan
YEARS IN OPERATION: 5
LANGUAGES: Interpreters available
ACCESSIBILITY: Wheelchair accessible
CASES SEXUAL ASSAULT/ABUSE (%): 20
CLIENTS/SERVICES: Sexual assault survivors; Marital rape/sexual abuse survivors; Child victims of sexual abuse; Incest victims/survivors; Community education; Adolescent survivors of sexual abuse; Male survivors of sexual abuse

WENATCHEE RAPE CRISIS AND DOMESTIC VIOLENCE CENTER
PO Box 2704, Wenatchee, WA 98807
Crisis hotline: **(509) 663-7446 24 hrs**
Information: (509) 663-1952 9am-5pm (Mon-Fri)
Contact: Sharen Fisher, Exec Dir
TYPE OF AGENCY: Rape crisis center; Domestic violence program; Child sexual abuse services; Child sexual abuse prevention program
AREAS SERVED: Chelan, Douglas
YEARS IN OPERATION: 10
LANGUAGES: Spanish
ACCESSIBILITY: Wheelchair accessible
CASES SEXUAL ASSAULT/ABUSE (%): 40
CLIENTS/SERVICES: Sexual assault survivors; Marital rape/sexual abuse survivors; Child victims of sexual abuse; Adult survivors of child sexual abuse; Incest victims/survivors; Community education

YAKIMA

PROSECUTOR'S OFFICE—VICTIM/WITNESS ASSISTANCE UNIT
Courthouse, Rm 329, Yakima, WA 98901
Information: (509) 575-4141 8:30am-5pm
Contact: Robyn B Cyr, Admin
TYPE OF AGENCY: Victim/witness assistance program; Child sexual abuse services
AREAS SERVED: Yakima
YEARS IN OPERATION: 10
LANGUAGES: Spanish
ACCESSIBILITY: Wheelchair accessible; Signers for the hearing impaired
CASES SEXUAL ASSAULT/ABUSE (%): 30-40
DESCRIPTION: Assists law enforcement and child protective services in the investigation and interviewing of children who have been physically or sexually abused; Provides legal advocacy
CLIENTS/SERVICES: Sexual assault survivors; Marital rape/sexual abuse survivors; Child victims of sexual abuse; Adult survivors of child sexual abuse; Incest victims/survivors; Prevention program; Community education; Adolescent survivors of sexual abuse
REQUIREMENTS: Case must be reported to law enforcement for investigation and/or proceeding to prosecution

SEXUAL ASSAULT UNIT
PO Box 959, Yakima, WA 98907
Crisis hotline: **(509) 575-4200, (800) 572-8122 24 hrs**
Information: (509) 575-4084 8am-5pm
Contact: Fran Dew, Coord
TYPE OF AGENCY: Rape crisis center; Counseling/mental health services
AREAS SERVED: Yakima
YEARS IN OPERATION: 16
ACCESSIBILITY: Wheelchair accessible
CASES SEXUAL ASSAULT/ABUSE (%): 100
CLIENTS/SERVICES: Sexual assault survivors; Adult survivors of child sexual abuse; Community education

WEST VIRGINIA

BECKLEY

WOMEN'S RESOURCE CENTER
PO Box 1476, Beckley, WV 25802-1476
Crisis hotline: **(304) 255-2559 24 hrs 7 days**
Information: (304) 255-2559 24 hrs
Contact: Deborah Short, Exec Dir; Carlotta Smith, Coun
TYPE OF AGENCY: Domestic violence program
AREAS SERVED: Raleigh, Fayette, Mercer, McDowell, Nicholas, Summers, Wyoming
YEARS IN OPERATION: 5
ACCESSIBILITY: Telecommunications for the hearing impaired (TTY, TDY, etc.)
CASES SEXUAL ASSAULT/ABUSE (%): 50
DESCRIPTION: Provides shelter, counseling, and other support services for victims of domestic violence and sexual abuse; Treatment programs for marital rape/sexual abuse offenders
CLIENTS/SERVICES: Sexual assault survivors; Marital rape/sexual abuse survivors; Child victims of sexual abuse; Adult survivors of child sexual abuse; Incest victims/survivors; Prevention program; Community education; Offender treatment program; Adolescent survivors of sexual abuse; Male survivors of sexual abuse

BLACKSVILLE

HAVEN (HELP FOR ABUSED VICTIMS WITH EMERGENCY NEEDS)
PO Box 72, Blacksville, WV 26521
Crisis hotline: **(304) 432-8209 24 hrs daily**
Information: (304) 432-8211 8am-5pm
Contact: Claire Claude-McFall, Board Member-Coord
TYPE OF AGENCY: Hospital/medical center; Counseling/mental health services; Telephone crisis hotline
AREAS SERVED: Monongalia, Wetzel, WV; Green, PA
YEARS IN OPERATION: 1
CASES SEXUAL ASSAULT/ABUSE (%): 5-10
CLIENTS/SERVICES: Sexual assault survivors; Child victims of sexual abuse; Adult survivors of child sexual abuse; Incest victims/survivors; Adolescent survivors of sexual abuse; Male survivors of sexual abuse

CHARLESTON

FAMILY SERVICE OF KANAWHA VALLEY (SEXUAL ASSAULT SERVICES)
922 Quarrier St, Ste 201, Embleton Bldg, Charleston, WV 25301
Crisis hotline: **(304) 340-3676 24 hrs**
Information: (304) 340-3676 9am-5pm (Mon, Wed, Fri); 12pm-8pm (Tue, Thu)
Contact: Susan Barrows, Dir
TYPE OF AGENCY: Rape crisis center; Counseling/mental health services; Child sexual abuse services
YEARS IN OPERATION: 10
ACCESSIBILITY: Wheelchair accessible; Telecommunications for the hearing impaired (TTY, TDY, etc.) (by arrangement); Signers for the hearing impaired (by arrangement)
CASES SEXUAL ASSAULT/ABUSE (%): 100
DESCRIPTION: Employs an adult offender therapist, juvenile sex offender therapist, victim therapist, rape therapist, and part-time group co-therapist for the purpose of providing therapy for both victims and offenders (child sexual abuse/incest offenders) Has rape crisis volunteer program for crisis intervention and accompaniment to hospital emergency room. Facilitates 9-10 groups weekly: teens, girls, boys, Adults Molested as Children, Parents United, couples, offenders (adult and juvenile), mothers (non-offending parents), and "hands-off" offenders group
CLIENTS/SERVICES: Sexual assault survivors; Marital rape/sexual abuse survivors; Child victims of sexual abuse; Adult survivors of child sexual abuse; Incest victims/survivors; Community education; Offender treatment program; Adolescent survivors of sexual abuse; Male survivors of sexual abuse
SPECIAL PROGRAMS/SERVICES: Videotaping is sometimes used while working with family members, and with victims permission, the tapes are shown to parents

RESOLVE FAMILY ABUSE PROGRAM
1114 Quarrier St, Charleston, WV 25301
Crisis hotline: **(304) 340-3549 24 hrs**
Information: (304) 340-3549 8:30am-4:30pm (Mon-Fri)
Contact: Alicia McCormick, Dir
TYPE OF AGENCY: Domestic violence program
SPONSORING ORGANIZATION: YWCA
YEARS IN OPERATION: 8
ACCESSIBILITY: Wheelchair accessible
CASES SEXUAL ASSAULT/ABUSE (%): 80
DESCRIPTION: Serves victims of domestic violence who have also experienced sexual abuse; Treatment programs for batterers
CLIENTS/SERVICES: Marital rape/sexual abuse survivors; Adult survivors of child sexual abuse; Community education; Adolescent survivors of sexual abuse; Male survivors of sexual abuse

WOMEN'S COUNSELING CENTER OF WEST VIRGINIA
PO Box 6254, Charleston, WV 25302
Information: (304) 342-3724 9am-9pm
Contact: Lynn R Hartz, PhD, Pres
TYPE OF AGENCY: Private practice
AREAS SERVED: Kanawha, Putnam
YEARS IN OPERATION: 13
DESCRIPTION: Individual, couple, family, and group counseling; Addictions counseling; Hypnotherapy; Massage therapy
CLIENTS/SERVICES: Sexual assault survivors; Marital rape/sexual abuse survivors; Child victims of sexual abuse; Adult survivors of child sexual abuse; Incest victims/survivors; Community education; Adolescent survivors of sexual abuse; Male survivors of sexual abuse; Healing

CLARKSBURG

CRISS-CROSS, INC
PO Box 1831, Clarksburg, WV 26330
Crisis hotline: **(800) 352-6513 24 hrs**
Information: (304) 623-6681 8:30am-5pm (Mon-Fri)
Contact: Sandra Miller, Hotline Coord
TYPE OF AGENCY: Information and referral
AREAS SERVED: Statewide
YEARS IN OPERATION: 2
DESCRIPTION: Provides 24-hour reporting of child or adult abuse, neglect or exploitation, and domestic violence
CLIENTS/SERVICES: Sexual assault survivors; Child victims of sexual abuse

ELKINS

WOMEN'S AID IN CRISIS (WAIC)
PO Box 2062, Elkins, WV 26241
Crisis hotline: **(304) 636-3232 4pm-8:30am and weekends**
Information: (304) 636-8433 8:30am-4pm (Mon-Fri)
Contact: Susie Rebert, Dir
TYPE OF AGENCY: Rape crisis center; Domestic violence program; Child sexual abuse prevention program
AREAS SERVED: Barbour, Braxton, Upshur, Tucker, Randolph, Webster
YEARS IN OPERATION: 10
LANGUAGES: Spanish, French
CASES SEXUAL ASSAULT/ABUSE (%): 10
DESCRIPTION: Sexual assault and domestic violence shelter and counseling service; Treatment program for batterers
CLIENTS/SERVICES: Sexual assault survivors; Marital rape/sexual abuse survivors; Adult survivors of child sexual abuse; Incest victims/survivors; Prevention program; Community education; Adolescent survivors of sexual abuse; Male survivors of sexual abuse

FAIRMONT

HOPE, INC TASK FORCE ON DOMESTIC VIOLENCE
PO Box 626, Fairmont, WV 26555
Crisis hotline: **(304) 367-1100 24 hrs**
Information: (304) 367-1100 24 hrs
Contact: Harriet Sutton, Exec Dir; Anne Martin, Victim Svcs Coord
TYPE OF AGENCY: Rape crisis center; Domestic violence program; Child sexual abuse services; Child sexual abuse prevention program
AREAS SERVED: Marion, Harrison, Doddridge, Lewis, Gilmer
YEARS IN OPERATION: 8
ACCESSIBILITY: Wheelchair accessible
CLIENTS/SERVICES: Sexual assault survivors; Marital rape/sexual abuse survivors; Child victims of sexual abuse; Adult survivors of child sexual abuse; Incest victims/survivors; Prevention program; Community education; Male survivors of sexual abuse

HUNTINGTON

CABELL COUNTY CHILD PROTECTION TEAM, INC
1304 5th Ave, Huntington, WV 25701
Information: (304) 523-9587 9am-5pm (Mon-Fri)
Contact: Laurie McKeown, Coord
TYPE OF AGENCY: Child sexual abuse prevention program; Child abuse services; Child abuse prevention program; Child advocacy; Interagency network
AREAS SERVED: Primarily Cabell, and neighboring counties
YEARS IN OPERATION: 2½
DESCRIPTION: Chapter of the West Virginia Committee for Prevention of Child Abuse; Presents the Child Assault Prevention (CAP) project in the elementary schools; Facilitates a Parents Anonymous group; Works on assault prevention for disabled teens; Starting West Virginia's first Court Appointed Special Advocate (CASA) project
CLIENTS/SERVICES: Prevention program; Community education; Disabled

CONTACT RAPE CRISIS COUNSELING TEAM (RCCT)
PO Box 2963, Huntington, WV 25729
Crisis hotline: **(304) 523-3448 24 hrs**
Information: (304) 523-3447 9am-5pm
Contact: Julie Damewood, Exec Dir
TYPE OF AGENCY: Rape crisis center; Counseling/mental health services
SPONSORING ORGANIZATION: CONTACT Huntington, Inc
AREAS SERVED: Cabell, Wayne, Lincoln, Putnam
YEARS IN OPERATION: 18
ACCESSIBILITY: Telecommunications for the hearing impaired (TTY, TDY, etc.)
CASES SEXUAL ASSAULT/ABUSE (%): 100 (RCCT)
CLIENTS/SERVICES: Sexual assault survivors; Child victims of sexual abuse; Adult survivors of child sexual abuse; Incest victims/survivors; Community education; Adolescent survivors of sexual abuse; Male survivors of sexual abuse

FAMILY SERVICE, INC
1304 5th Ave, Huntington, WV 25701
Information: (304) 523-9454 9am-6pm (Mon-Fri)
Contact: Barbara Tinsman, Exec Dir
TYPE OF AGENCY: Counseling/mental health services; Child sexual abuse services; Child sexual abuse prevention program
AREAS SERVED: Cabell, Wayne, Lincoln, Putnam, WV; Lawrence, OH
YEARS IN OPERATION: 50
ACCESSIBILITY: Wheelchair accessible
CASES SEXUAL ASSAULT/ABUSE (%): 30
DESCRIPTION: Treatment programs for child sexual abuse and incest offenders
CLIENTS/SERVICES: Sexual assault survivors; Marital rape/sexual abuse survivors; Child victims of sexual abuse; Adult survivors of child sexual abuse; Incest victims/survivors; Prevention program; Community education; Offender treatment program; Adolescent survivors of sexual abuse

PRESTERA CENTER FOR MENTAL HEALTH SERVICES, INC
3375 Rte 60 E, Huntington, WV 25705
Crisis hotline: **(304) 525-7851 24 hrs**
Information: (304) 525-7851
Contact: Dr Michael J Hughes, Clinicial Dir
TYPE OF AGENCY: Counseling/mental health services
AREAS SERVED: Cabell, Lincoln, Mason, Wayne
YEARS IN OPERATION: 21
ACCESSIBILITY: Wheelchair accessible; Telecommunications for the hearing impaired (TTY, TDY, etc.)
CASES SEXUAL ASSAULT/ABUSE (%): 15
CLIENTS/SERVICES: Sexual assault survivors; Marital rape/sexual abuse survivors; Child victims of sexual abuse; Adult survivors of child sexual abuse; Incest victims/survivors; Adolescent survivors of sexual abuse; Male survivors of sexual abuse

KEYSER

FAMILY CRISIS CENTER, INC
PO Box 207, Keyser, WV 26726
Crisis hotline: **(304) 788-6061 24 hrs**
Information: (304) 788-6061 8:30am-4:30pm (Mon-Fri)
Contact: Margaret Chaney, Exec Dir
TYPE OF AGENCY: Rape crisis center; Domestic violence program
AREAS SERVED: Mineral, Hardy, Hampshire, Grant, Pendleton
YEARS IN OPERATION: 5
CASES SEXUAL ASSAULT/ABUSE (%): 2
DESCRIPTION: Provides crisis intervention and counseling for sexual assault victims/survivors, as well as domestic violence survivors
CLIENTS/SERVICES: Sexual assault survivors; Marital rape/sexual abuse survivors; Adult survivors of child sexual abuse; Incest victims/survivors; Community education

LEWISBURG

FAMILY REFUGE CENTER
PO Box 249, Lewisburg, WV 24901
Crisis hotline: **(304) 645-6334 24 hrs 7 days**
Information: (304) 645-6334, 645-6355 9am-5pm (Mon-Fri)
Contact: Trudy Laurenson, Dir; Stephanie Mendelson, Children's Advocate
TYPE OF AGENCY: Domestic violence program
AREAS SERVED: Greenbrier, Pocahontas, Monroe
YEARS IN OPERATION: 8
CASES SEXUAL ASSAULT/ABUSE (%): 18
DESCRIPTION: Provides direct services for domestic violence survivors and abusers; Develops community awareness and responsiveness through various programs
CLIENTS/SERVICES: Sexual assault survivors; Marital rape/sexual abuse survivors; Child victims of sexual abuse; Adult survivors of child sexual abuse; Incest victims/survivors; Prevention program; Community education; Adolescent survivors of sexual abuse; Male survivors of sexual abuse

MARTINSBURG

SHENANDOAH WOMEN'S CENTER
PO Box 1083, Martinsburg, WV 25401
Crisis hotline: **(304) 263-8292 24 hrs**
Information: (304) 263-8522 9am-5pm (Mon-Fri); available some Sat
Contact: Pam Shouse, Susan McIntyre, Co-Dirs
TYPE OF AGENCY: Rape crisis center; Domestic violence program
AREAS SERVED: Jefferson, Berkeley, Morgan
YEARS IN OPERATION: 12
CASES SEXUAL ASSAULT/ABUSE (%): 25
CLIENTS/SERVICES: Sexual assault survivors; Marital rape/sexual abuse survivors; Child victims of sexual abuse; Adult survivors of child sexual abuse; Incest victims/survivors; Prevention program; Community education; Adolescent survivors of sexual abuse; Male survivors of sexual abuse

MORGANTOWN

RAPE AND DOMESTIC VIOLENCE INFORMATION CENTER
PO Box 4228, Morgantown, WV 26505
Crisis hotline: **(304) 292-5100 24 hrs**
Information: (304) 292-5100 9am-5pm (Mon-Fri)
Contact: Judy King Smith, Dir
TYPE OF AGENCY: Rape crisis center; Domestic violence program; Child sexual abuse prevention program
AREAS SERVED: Monongalia, Taylor, Preston, Wetzel
YEARS IN OPERATION: 15
CASES SEXUAL ASSAULT/ABUSE (%): 30-50
CLIENTS/SERVICES: Sexual assault survivors; Marital rape/sexual abuse survivors; Child victims of sexual abuse; Adult survivors of child sexual abuse; Incest victims/survivors; Prevention program; Community education; Adolescent survivors of sexual abuse; Male survivors of sexual abuse

PARKERSBURG

THE FAMILY CRISIS INTERVENTION CENTER
PO Box 695, Parkersburg, WV 26102
Crisis hotline: **(304) 428-2333 24 hrs**
Information: (304) 428-3707 8am-4:30pm (Mon-Fri)
Contact: Sue Casto, Exec Dir
TYPE OF AGENCY: Domestic violence program
AREAS SERVED: Calhoun, Jackson, Pleasants, Roane, Ritchis, Tyler, Wirt, Wood
YEARS IN OPERATION: 6
ACCESSIBILITY: Wheelchair accessible
CASES SEXUAL ASSAULT/ABUSE (%): 40
DESCRIPTION: Comprehensive services for domestic violence survivors; Individual therapy and support group for batterers
CLIENTS/SERVICES: Sexual assault survivors; Marital rape/sexual abuse survivors; Child victims of sexual abuse; Adult survivors of child sexual abuse; Community education; Male survivors of sexual abuse

WELCH

SAFE, INC—STOP ABUSIVE FAMILY ENVIRONMENTS
PO Box 234, Welch, WV 24801
Crisis hotline: **(304) 436-8330 (McDowell County Jail) Nights and weekends**
Information: (304) 436-8117 9am-5pm (Mon-Fri)
Contact: Betty J Lester, Prog Coord
TYPE OF AGENCY: Domestic violence program
AREAS SERVED: McDowell, Wyoming
YEARS IN OPERATION: 4
ACCESSIBILITY: Wheelchair accessible
CASES SEXUAL ASSAULT/ABUSE (%): 10
CLIENTS/SERVICES: Sexual assault survivors; Marital rape/sexual abuse survivors; Child victims of sexual abuse; Community education

WEST HAMLIN

PRESTERA CENTER—LINCOLN COUNTY OFFICE (SATELLITE)
Rte 3, Box 208, West Hamlin, WV 25571
Crisis hotline: **(800) 642-3434 24 hrs**
Information: (304) 824-5790 8:30am-5pm
Contact: Eila Phailbus, Prog Supv
TYPE OF AGENCY: Counseling/mental health services
SPONSORING ORGANIZATION: Prestera Center (Huntington, WV)
AREAS SERVED: Lincoln
YEARS IN OPERATION: 8
CASES SEXUAL ASSAULT/ABUSE (%): 1-2
DESCRIPTION: Comprehensive mental health services
CLIENTS/SERVICES: Sexual assault survivors; Marital rape/sexual abuse survivors; Child victims of sexual abuse; Adult survivors of child sexual abuse; Incest victims/survivors; Offender treatment program; Adolescent survivors of sexual abuse

WHEELING

SEXUAL ASSAULT HELP CENTER (UPPER OHIO VALLEY)
PO Box 6764, Wheeling, WV 26003
Crisis hotline: **(304) 234-8161 24 hrs**
Information: (304) 234-1783 8am-4:30pm (Mon-Fri)
Contact: Barbara Rice, Exec Dir
TYPE OF AGENCY: Rape crisis center; Child sexual abuse services; Child sexual abuse prevention program; Adolescent program
AREAS SERVED: Marshall, Ohio, Hancock, Brooke
YEARS IN OPERATION: 10
ACCESSIBILITY: Telecommunications for the hearing impaired (TTY, TDY, etc.)
CASES SEXUAL ASSAULT/ABUSE (%): 100
CLIENTS/SERVICES: Sexual assault survivors; Marital rape/sexual abuse survivors; Child victims of sexual abuse; Adult survivors of child sexual abuse; Incest victims/survivors; Prevention program; Community education; Adolescent survivors of sexual abuse; Male survivors of sexual abuse; Developmentally disabled
SPECIAL PROGRAMS/SERVICES: Prevention programs in most area schools; Two special projects targeting at-risk youths: the first is for adolescents in group homes, and the second is for mentally retarded children

WILLIAMSON

TUG VALLEY RECOVERY SHELTER
PO Box 863, Williamson, WV 25661
Crisis hotline: **(304) 235-6121 24 hrs**
Information: (304) 235-6121 9am-5pm
Contact: Susan Julian, Women's Advocate
TYPE OF AGENCY: Rape crisis center; Domestic violence program; Child sexual abuse services; Child sexual abuse prevention program
AREAS SERVED: Mingo, Logan
YEARS IN OPERATION: 4
CLIENTS/SERVICES: Sexual assault survivors; Marital rape/sexual abuse survivors; Child victims of sexual abuse; Adult survivors of child sexual abuse; Incest victims/survivors; Prevention program; Community education; Adolescent survivors of sexual abuse

WISCONSIN

ANTIGO

AVAIL
612 Clermont St, Antigo, WI 54409
Crisis hotline: **(715) 623-5767 24 hrs**
Information: (715) 623-5177 8am-5pm
Contact: Patricia McKinney, Sexual Assault Coord
TYPE OF AGENCY: Rape crisis center; Domestic violence program
AREAS SERVED: Langlade
YEARS IN OPERATION: 7
CLIENTS/SERVICES: Sexual assault survivors; Marital rape/sexual abuse survivors; Adult survivors of child sexual abuse; Incest victims/survivors; Prevention program; Community education
REQUIREMENTS: Must be 18 or older

APPLETON

OUTAGAMIE COUNTY DOMESTIC ABUSE PROGRAM—"HARBOR HOUSE"
401 S Elm St, Appleton, WI 54911
Crisis hotline: **(414) 832-1666 24 hrs**
Information: (414) 832-1667 24 hrs
Contact: Marlene Kteily, Dir
TYPE OF AGENCY: Domestic violence program
AREAS SERVED: Outagamie, Calumet
YEARS IN OPERATION: 4
LANGUAGES: Spanish, Arabic, French
DESCRIPTION: Comprehensive domestic violence services and individual and group therapy for batterers
CLIENTS/SERVICES: Marital rape/sexual abuse survivors; Child victims of sexual abuse; Prevention program; Community education; Offender treatment program

SEXUAL ASSAULT CRISIS CENTER
PO Box 344, Appleton, WI 54912
Crisis hotline: **(414) 733-8119 24 hrs**
Information: (414) 733-8119 8:30am-12:30pm
Contact: Bonnie Coonen, Dir
TYPE OF AGENCY: Rape crisis center; Child sexual abuse services; Child sexual abuse prevention program
YEARS IN OPERATION: 10
CLIENTS/SERVICES: Sexual assault survivors; Marital rape/sexual abuse survivors; Child victims of sexual abuse; Adult survivors of child sexual abuse; Incest victims/survivors; Prevention program; Community education; Adolescent survivors of sexual abuse; Male survivors of sexual abuse
SPECIAL PROGRAMS/SERVICES: Annual "Sexual Abuse Awareness Week" that includes Illusion Theater (Minneapolis MN) performing "No Easy Answers," "Touch," and "Family" for area schools and families, as well as a speech for professionals on "Making Courts Safe for Children." Also provides protective behaviors programs in schools.

BALSAM LAKE

COMMUNITY REFERRAL AGENCY, INC/ "WELCOME HOME" SHELTER
PO Box 182, Balsam Lake, WI 54810
Crisis hotline: **(715) 485-3171 24 hrs**
Information: (715) 485-3171 8am-5pm
Contact: Ann van der Paardt, Dir
TYPE OF AGENCY: Rape crisis center; Domestic violence program
AREAS SERVED: Polk, Burnett
YEARS IN OPERATION: 2
CASES SEXUAL ASSAULT/ABUSE (%): .5
CLIENTS/SERVICES: Sexual assault survivors; Marital rape/sexual abuse survivors; Adult survivors of child sexual abuse; Community education; Male survivors of sexual abuse

BEAVER DAM

PEOPLE AGAINST A VIOLENT ENVIRONMENT (PAVE)
Box 561, Beaver Dam, WI 53916
Crisis hotline: **(414) 887-3785, after hours 386-2411 9am-4pm**
Information: (414) 887-3785 9am-4pm (Mon-Fri)
Contact: Rene Will, Dir
TYPE OF AGENCY: Rape crisis center; Domestic violence program
AREAS SERVED: Dodge and all of Watertown
YEARS IN OPERATION: 8
LANGUAGES: Spanish
ACCESSIBILITY: Wheelchair accessible; Signers for the hearing impaired
CLIENTS/SERVICES: Sexual assault survivors; Marital rape/sexual abuse survivors; Prevention program; Community education; Adolescent survivors of sexual abuse

BELOIT

BELOIT MEMORIAL HOSPITAL
1969 W Hart Rd, Beloit, WI 53511
Crisis hotline: **(608) 364-5151**
Information: (608) 364-5130
TYPE OF AGENCY: Hospital/medical center
AREAS SERVED: Rock
CLIENTS/SERVICES: Sexual assault survivors; Marital rape/sexual abuse survivors; Child victims of sexual abuse; Adolescent survivors of sexual abuse; Male survivors of sexual abuse

BLACK RIVER FALLS

JACKSON COUNTY VICTIM/WITNESS ASSISTANCE
Courthouse, 307 Main St, Black River Falls, WI 54615
Information: (715) 284-0242 8am-4:30pm
Contact: Hazel Moen, Coord
TYPE OF AGENCY: Victim/witness assistance program
AREAS SERVED: Jackson
YEARS IN OPERATION: 4
ACCESSIBILITY: Wheelchair accessible
CLIENTS/SERVICES: Sexual assault survivors; Child victims of sexual abuse; Adult survivors of child sexual abuse; Community education; Adolescent survivors of sexual abuse
REQUIREMENTS: Victim must file a complaint with the proper agency

CEDARBURG

COPE—OZAUKEE COUNTY HOTLINE
Box 723, Cedarburg, WI 53012
Crisis hotline: **(414) 377-2673, Enterprise 2673 24 hrs 7 days**
Information: (414) 377-1477 9am-11pm
Contact: Dorothy Dyhen, Exec Dir
TYPE OF AGENCY: Counseling/mental health services; Telephone crisis hotline; Information and referral
SPONSORING ORGANIZATION: COPE Services, Inc
AREAS SERVED: Ozaukee, Milwaukee, Washington, Sheboygan
YEARS IN OPERATION: 10
CASES SEXUAL ASSAULT/ABUSE (%): .5
DESCRIPTION: Information, referral, and crisis intervention line. Referrals to treatment centers, support groups, victim/witness coordinators, and shelters. In a life-threatening situation, sends emergency services to the caller
CLIENTS/SERVICES: Sexual assault survivors; Marital rape/sexual abuse survivors; Child victims of sexual abuse; Adult survivors of child sexual abuse; Incest victims/survivors

CHIPPEWA FALLS

CHIPPEWA COUNTY DISTRICT ATTORNEY—VICTIM/WITNESS PROGRAM
711 N Bridge St, Chippewa Falls, WI 54729
Information: (715) 723-1831 8am-5pm
Contact: Thomas A Starr, District Attorney
TYPE OF AGENCY: Victim/witness assistance program
AREAS SERVED: Chippewa
YEARS IN OPERATION: 1
ACCESSIBILITY: Wheelchair accessible
CASES SEXUAL ASSAULT/ABUSE (%): 30

CHIPPEWA COUNTY DISTRICT ATTORNEY—VICTIM/WITNESS PROGRAM *(continued)*
CLIENTS/SERVICES: Sexual assault survivors; Marital rape/sexual abuse survivors; Child victims of sexual abuse
REQUIREMENTS: Must file charges

FAMILY SUPPORT CENTER
28 E Columbia St, Chippewa Falls, WI 54729
Crisis hotline: **(715) 723-1811 5pm-8am and weekends**
Information: (715) 723-1138 8am-5pm (Mon-Fri)
Contact: Tracy Bredeson, Exec Dir
TYPE OF AGENCY: Domestic violence program; Child sexual abuse services; Child sexual abuse prevention program
AREAS SERVED: Chippewa, Eau Claire
YEARS IN OPERATION: 8
LANGUAGES: Sign
ACCESSIBILITY: Wheelchair accessible; Signers for the hearing impaired
CASES SEXUAL ASSAULT/ABUSE (%): Children 75, adults 15
DESCRIPTION: Domestic abuse services (safehomes, support groups, crisis line); Protective behaviors, sexual abuse prevention education program for schools, grades K-12; Therapy for children, many of whom were sexually abused; Parent counseling and education; Support group for mothers of sexually abused children; Sponsors NOVUS; Individual and group counseling and a support group for batterers
CLIENTS/SERVICES: Sexual assault survivors; Marital rape/sexual abuse survivors; Child victims of sexual abuse; Adult survivors of child sexual abuse; Incest victims/survivors; Prevention program; Community education; Male survivors of sexual abuse

EAU CLAIRE

BOLTON REFUGE HOUSE, INC
PO Box 482, Eau Claire, WI 54702
Crisis hotline: **(715) 834-9578 24 hrs**
Information: (715) 834-0628 24 hrs
Contact: Ann McKinley, Sexual Assault Svcs Coord; Gerald Wilkie, Dir
TYPE OF AGENCY: Domestic violence program
AREAS SERVED: Eau Claire, Chippewa, Dunn, Trempealeau, Clark, Jackson, Pepin
YEARS IN OPERATION: 11
ACCESSIBILITY: Signers for the hearing impaired (as needed)
CASES SEXUAL ASSAULT/ABUSE (%): 35
DESCRIPTION: Domestic abuse shelter; Crisis line, shelter, advocacy, counseling, and support groups for incest and sexual assault survivors; Groups for mothers of child sexual abuse victims; Staff participation in a family incest treatment program; Individual and group therapy for incest offenders and batterers
CLIENTS/SERVICES: Sexual assault survivors; Marital rape/sexual abuse survivors; Child victims of sexual abuse; Adult survivors of child sexual abuse; Incest victims/survivors; Community education; Offender treatment program; Adolescent survivors of sexual abuse; Male survivors of sexual abuse; Healing
SPECIAL PROGRAMS/SERVICES: Provides healing through camping, retreats, and rituals for adult sexual assault survivors; Offers music therapy program for child sexual abuse victims

THE GUIDANCE CLINIC, INC
202 Graham Ave, Eau Claire, WI 54701
Crisis hotline: **(715) 834-6040 24 hrs**
Information: (715) 832-3471 8am-5pm (Mon, Thu, Fri); 8am-9pm (Tue, Wed)
Contact: Michael Weiser, Dir
TYPE OF AGENCY: Counseling/mental health services
AREAS SERVED: Eau Claire
YEARS IN OPERATION: 36
ACCESSIBILITY: Wheelchair accessible
CASES SEXUAL ASSAULT/ABUSE (%): 5
DESCRIPTION: Offers family court-ordered incest treatment; Survivors group for adult females sexually abused as children; Group therapy for adolescent sex offenders
CLIENTS/SERVICES: Sexual assault survivors; Child victims of sexual abuse; Adult survivors of child sexual abuse; Incest victims/survivors; Prevention program; Community education; Offender treatment program; Adolescent survivors of sexual abuse
REQUIREMENTS: Offender must have been legally prosecuted and court-ordered into the program

REGIONAL SEXUAL ASSAULT TREATMENT CENTER
1221 Whipple St, Eau Claire, WI 54702-4105
Crisis hotline: **(715) 839-7273 24 hrs**
Information: (715) 839-3311
TYPE OF AGENCY: Hospital/medical center
SPONSORING ORGANIZATION: Lutheran Hospital
AREAS SERVED: Eau Claire, Dunn, Chippewa
CLIENTS/SERVICES: Sexual assault survivors; Marital rape/sexual abuse survivors; Child victims of sexual abuse; Adolescent survivors of sexual abuse; Male survivors of sexual abuse

ELKHORN

WALWORTH COUNTY DISTRICT ATTORNEY'S OFFICE—VICTIM/WITNESS ASSISTANCE PROGRAM
PO Box 1001, Elkhorn, WI 53121
Information: (414) 741-4310 8am-5pm
Contact: Mary B Reeves, Victim/Witness Coord
TYPE OF AGENCY: Victim/witness assistance program
AREAS SERVED: Walworth
YEARS IN OPERATION: 2
ACCESSIBILITY: Wheelchair accessible
DESCRIPTION: Court information and support
CLIENTS/SERVICES: Sexual assault survivors; Child victims of sexual abuse

ELLSWORTH

PIERCE COUNTY OFFICE OF THE DISTRICT ATTORNEY—VICTIM/WITNESS ASSISTANCE
PO Box 808, Pierce County Courthouse, Ellsworth, WI 54011
Information: (715) 273-3531, ext 320 8:30am-4:30pm
Contact: Ann Gustafson, Prog Coord
TYPE OF AGENCY: Victim/witness assistance program
AREAS SERVED: Pierce
YEARS IN OPERATION: 3
ACCESSIBILITY: Wheelchair accessible; Telecommunications for the hearing impaired (TTY, TDY, etc.); Signers for the hearing impaired (by arrangement)
CASES SEXUAL ASSAULT/ABUSE (%): 10-15
DESCRIPTION: Provides court-related services and makes referrals to appropriate community resources. Program coordinator is a member of county sex abuse treatment team.
CLIENTS/SERVICES: Sexual assault survivors; Marital rape/sexual abuse survivors; Child victims of sexual abuse; Adult survivors of child sexual abuse; Incest victims/survivors; Community education; Adolescent survivors of sexual abuse
REQUIREMENTS: Victim must report crime

FOND DU LAC

FOND DU LAC COUNTY HEALTH CARE CENTER
459 E 1st St, Fond du Lac, WI 54935
Crisis hotline: **(414) 929-3535 24 hrs**
Information: (414) 929-3555 8am-4:30pm
Contact: Ellen A Ballwanz, Psychiatric Soc Wkr
TYPE OF AGENCY: Counseling/mental health services
AREAS SERVED: Fond du Lac
YEARS IN OPERATION: 17
LANGUAGES: Spanish
ACCESSIBILITY: Wheelchair accessible; Telecommunications for the hearing impaired (TTY, TDY, etc.)
CASES SEXUAL ASSAULT/ABUSE (%): 20
DESCRIPTION: Counseling for survivors of sexual assault/abuse and for rapists, and child sexual abuse/incest offenders
CLIENTS/SERVICES: Sexual assault survivors; Marital rape/sexual abuse survivors; Child victims of sexual abuse; Adult survivors of child sexual abuse; Incest victims/survivors; Community education; Offender treatment program; Adolescent survivors of sexual abuse; Male survivors of sexual abuse

FOND DU LAC COUNTY VICTIM/WITNESS ASSISTANCE
160 S Macy St, Fond du Lac, WI 54935
Information: (414) 929-3050 8am-4:30pm (Mon-Fri)
Contact: B J Bradley, Coord
TYPE OF AGENCY: Victim/witness assistance program
SPONSORING ORGANIZATION: Prosecutor's Office
AREAS SERVED: Fond du Lac
YEARS IN OPERATION: 7
LANGUAGES: Interpreters available
ACCESSIBILITY: Wheelchair accessible; Signers for the hearing impaired
CASES SEXUAL ASSAULT/ABUSE (%): 45
CLIENTS/SERVICES: Sexual assault survivors; Marital rape/sexual abuse survivors; Child victims of sexual abuse; Incest victims/survivors; Community education
REQUIREMENTS: Must be a victim of a crime, whether a prosecution is pending or not

FRIENDS AWARE OF VIOLENT RELATIONSHIPS
PO Box 1752, Fond du Lac, WI 54936-1752
Crisis hotline: **(414) 923-1700 24 hrs**
Information: (414) 922-7760 9am-4:30pm
Contact: Lea A Kitz, Exec Dir
TYPE OF AGENCY: Domestic violence program
AREAS SERVED: Fond du Lac
YEARS IN OPERATION: 6
LANGUAGES: Spanish interpreters available
DESCRIPTION: Shelter; Legal advocacy; Transportation; 24-hour crisis phone; Group therapy for batterers
CLIENTS/SERVICES: Sexual assault survivors; Marital rape/sexual abuse survivors; Community education

GREEN BAY

DISTRICT ATTORNEY'S OFFICE—VICTIM/WITNESS ASSISTANCE PROGRAM
PO Box 1600, 300 E Walnut St, Green Bay, WI 54301
Information: (414) 436-4300 8am-4:30pm
Contact: Karen H Dorau, Coord
TYPE OF AGENCY: Victim/witness assistance program
AREAS SERVED: Brown
YEARS IN OPERATION: 4½
LANGUAGES: Interpreters available
ACCESSIBILITY: Wheelchair accessible; Signers for the hearing impaired
CASES SEXUAL ASSAULT/ABUSE (%): 15

DISTRICT ATTORNEY'S OFFICE—VICTIM/WITNESS ASSISTANCE PROGRAM (continued)
CLIENTS/SERVICES: Sexual assault survivors; Child victims of sexual abuse; Incest victims/survivors
REQUIREMENTS: Client must report incident to a law enforcement agency and report must be forwarded to the District Attorney's Office for opinion or prosecution

SEXUAL ASSAULT CENTER—FAMILY SERVICE ASSOCIATION
131 S Madison St, Green Bay, WI 54301
Crisis hotline: **(414) 433-0584**
Information: (414) 437-7071
Contact: Susan Cohen
TYPE OF AGENCY: Rape crisis center
CLIENTS/SERVICES: Sexual assault survivors

HALES CORNERS

FAMILY SOCIAL AND PSYCHOTHERAPY SERVICES
5300 S 108, Ste 9, Hales Corners, WI 53130
Information: (414) 529-0600 9am-9pm (Mon-Fri); 9am-5pm (Sat)
Contact: Mary Ann Grochowski, Clinic Dir
TYPE OF AGENCY: Counseling/mental health services; Child sexual abuse services; Private practice
AREAS SERVED: Waukesha, Milwaukee
YEARS IN OPERATION: 19
ACCESSIBILITY: Wheelchair accessible
CASES SEXUAL ASSAULT/ABUSE (%): 25
DESCRIPTION: Outpatient mental health facility, including treatment for incest families, sexual abuse victims, and rapists, child sexual abuse/incest offenders, and batterers
CLIENTS/SERVICES: Sexual assault survivors; Marital rape/sexual abuse survivors; Child victims of sexual abuse; Adult survivors of child sexual abuse; Incest victims/survivors; Community education; Offender treatment program; Adolescent survivors of sexual abuse; Male survivors of sexual abuse
REQUIREMENTS: Eligibility for crime victim compensation or health insurance which covers outpatient mental health services or ability to pay privately

JANESVILLE

ROCK COUNTY 51.42 BOARD
PO Box 351, Janesville, WI 53545
Crisis hotline: **(608) 755-2625 24 hrs**
Information: (608) 755-2715 Janesville, 362-9033 Beloit 8:30am-5pm
Contact: Juanita Marin, MH Coord
TYPE OF AGENCY: Counseling/mental health services
AREAS SERVED: Rock
YEARS IN OPERATION: 20
LANGUAGES: Spanish by request
ACCESSIBILITY: Wheelchair accessible; Telecommunications for the hearing impaired (TTY, TDY, etc.); Signers for the hearing impaired (by request)
DESCRIPTION: Counseling services available for adults and children who have been sexually assaulted/abused, as well as for rapists, child sexual abuse/incest offenders and batterers
CLIENTS/SERVICES: Sexual assault survivors; Marital rape/sexual abuse survivors; Child victims of sexual abuse; Adult survivors of child sexual abuse; Incest victims/survivors; Community education; Offender treatment program; Adolescent survivors of sexual abuse; Male survivors of sexual abuse

ROCK COUNTY VICTIM/WITNESS ASSISTANCE PROGRAM
51 S Main St, Janesville, WI 53545
Information: (608) 755-2069 8am-5pm (Mon-Fri)
Contact: Janice R Hilson, Coord
TYPE OF AGENCY: Victim/witness assistance program
AREAS SERVED: Rock
YEARS IN OPERATION: 3
ACCESSIBILITY: Wheelchair accessible; Signers for the hearing impaired
CASES SEXUAL ASSAULT/ABUSE (%): 20
CLIENTS/SERVICES: Sexual assault survivors; Child victims of sexual abuse; Community education
REQUIREMENTS: Must report the offense and file a criminal complaint

JEFFERSON

JEFFERSON COUNTY HUMAN SERVICES DEPARTMENT
N3995 Annex Rd, Jefferson, WI 53549
Crisis hotline: **(414) 674-3105 24 hrs**
Information: (414) 674-3105 24 hrs
Contact: Jacqueline M Schuh, Human Svcs Supv
TYPE OF AGENCY: Counseling/mental health services; Child sexual abuse services
AREAS SERVED: Jefferson
YEARS IN OPERATION: 10
ACCESSIBILITY: Wheelchair accessible; Telecommunications for the hearing impaired (TTY, TDY, etc.); Signers for the hearing impaired
CASES SEXUAL ASSAULT/ABUSE (%): 60
DESCRIPTION: Assessment; Evaluation; Treatment; Individual, family, couple, and group counseling
CLIENTS/SERVICES: Sexual assault survivors; Marital rape/sexual abuse survivors; Child victims of sexual abuse; Adult survivors of child sexual abuse; Incest victims/survivors; Community education; Offender treatment program; Adolescent survivors of sexual abuse; Male survivors of sexual abuse

JUNEAU

DODGE COUNTY DISTRICT ATTORNEY—VICTIM/WITNESS PROGRAM
Legal Services Bldg, Juneau, WI 53039
Information: (414) 386-4411 8am-4:30pm
Contact: Kevin Schram, DA
TYPE OF AGENCY: Victim/witness assistance program
AREAS SERVED: Dodge
ACCESSIBILITY: Wheelchair accessible
CASES SEXUAL ASSAULT/ABUSE (%): 5
CLIENTS/SERVICES: Sexual assault survivors; Child victims of sexual abuse
REQUIREMENTS: Reports accepted only from police/sheriff agencies

KENOSHA

KENOSHA COUNTY DISTRICT ATTORNEY'S OFFICE—VICTIM/WITNESS PROGRAM
912 56th St, Rm 312, Kenosha, WI 53140
Information: (414) 656-6480 8am-5pm
Contact: Lynn M Copen, Coord
TYPE OF AGENCY: Victim/witness assistance program
AREAS SERVED: Kenosha
YEARS IN OPERATION: 7
LANGUAGES: Interpreters available
ACCESSIBILITY: Wheelchair accessible
CASES SEXUAL ASSAULT/ABUSE (%): 10
CLIENTS/SERVICES: Marital rape/sexual abuse survivors; Child victims of sexual abuse; Adult survivors of child sexual abuse; Incest victims/survivors; Community education
REQUIREMENTS: Cases referred to District Attorney for review or by request of law enforcement agency

LUTHERAN SOCIAL SERVICES
5820 3rd Ave, Kenosha, WI 53140
Information: (414) 658-3154
Contact: Norma Tellier, Psychologist
TYPE OF AGENCY: Counseling/mental health services; Child sexual abuse services; Private practice
AREAS SERVED: Kenosha
YEARS IN OPERATION: 3
CASES SEXUAL ASSAULT/ABUSE (%): 20
DESCRIPTION: Provides therapy for individuals, groups and families; Group services for children, teenagers and adults
CLIENTS/SERVICES: Sexual assault survivors; Child victims of sexual abuse; Adult survivors of child sexual abuse; Incest victims/survivors; Community education; Adolescent survivors of sexual abuse; Male survivors of sexual abuse

PUCCI AND ASSOCIATES
1202 60th St, Ste 109, Kenosha, WI 53140
Crisis hotline: **(414) 657-7188 24 hrs**
Information: (414) 652-9830 By appointment
Contact: Linda M Pucci, PhD, Lic Psychologist/Clinic Dir
TYPE OF AGENCY: Counseling/mental health services; Private practice
YEARS IN OPERATION: 5
ACCESSIBILITY: Wheelchair accessible
CASES SEXUAL ASSAULT/ABUSE (%): 30
DESCRIPTION: Outpatient mental health facility serving children, youth, and families, including survivors of childhood sexual abuse. Direct services are primarily evaluation and/or therapy/counseling for children, youth, families, parents and adult survivors
CLIENTS/SERVICES: Child victims of sexual abuse; Adult survivors of child sexual abuse; Incest victims/survivors; Community education; Adolescent survivors of sexual abuse; Male survivors of sexual abuse

SEXUAL ASSAULT TREATMENT CENTER
3556 7th Ave, Kenosha, WI 53142
Crisis hotline: **(414) 658-1717 24 hrs daily**
Information: (414) 656-3898 8am-4pm
Contact: Kathy Heinzman, Sexual Assault Supv
TYPE OF AGENCY: Rape crisis center; Hospital/medical center; Child sexual abuse services; Child sexual abuse prevention program
SPONSORING ORGANIZATION: St Catherine's Hospital
AREAS SERVED: Kenosha, Racine, WI; Lake, IL
YEARS IN OPERATION: 10
ACCESSIBILITY: Wheelchair accessible; Telecommunications for the hearing impaired (TTY, TDY, etc.)
CASES SEXUAL ASSAULT/ABUSE (%): Sexual assault 20%, sexual abuse 92%
DESCRIPTION: 24-hour crisis counseling; Advocacy services; Comprehensive medical services; Court support; Law enforcement advocacy
CLIENTS/SERVICES: Sexual assault survivors; Marital rape/sexual abuse survivors; Child victims of sexual abuse; Adult survivors of child sexual abuse; Incest victims/survivors; Prevention program; Community education; Adolescent survivors of sexual abuse; Male survivors of sexual abuse
SPECIAL PROGRAMS/SERVICES: Prevention program entitled "Taking Care of Me" for K-12 grades uses cartoon touch cards, bookmarks, stickers, and color book. Currently working on parent handbook on sexual abuse

WOMEN'S HORIZONS, INC
PO Box 792, Kenosha, WI 53141
Crisis hotline: **(414) 652-1846 24 hrs 7 days**
Information: (414) 652-1846 9am-5pm (Mon-Fri)
Contact: Judy Arnold, Dir
TYPE OF AGENCY: Domestic violence program
AREAS SERVED: Kenosha
YEARS IN OPERATION: 13
LANGUAGES: Spanish

WOMEN'S HORIZONS, INC (continued)
CASES SEXUAL ASSAULT/ABUSE (%): 20
CLIENTS/SERVICES: Sexual assault survivors; Marital rape/sexual abuse survivors; Adult survivors of child sexual abuse; Incest victims/survivors; Community education

YOUTH AND FAMILY SERVICES
3514 60th St, Kenosha, WI 53140
Information: (414) 654-3566
Contact: Norma Tellier, Psychologist
TYPE OF AGENCY: Counseling/mental health services; Child sexual abuse services; Private practice
AREAS SERVED: Kenosha
YEARS IN OPERATION: 3
CASES SEXUAL ASSAULT/ABUSE (%): 20
DESCRIPTION: Provides therapy for individuals, groups and families; Group services for children, teenagers and adults
CLIENTS/SERVICES: Sexual assault survivors; Child victims of sexual abuse; Adult survivors of child sexual abuse; Incest victims/survivors; Community education; Adolescent survivors of sexual abuse; Male survivors of sexual abuse

KESHENA

NE-NAIAH-KAHA-KOK
PO Box 82, Keshena, WI 54135
Information: (715) 799-4398 8am-4:30pm
Contact: Beatrice Olson Brunette, Dir
TYPE OF AGENCY: Domestic violence program; Counseling/mental health services
AREAS SERVED: Menominee
YEARS IN OPERATION: 1
CLIENTS/SERVICES: Sexual assault survivors; Marital rape/sexual abuse survivors; Adult survivors of child sexual abuse; Prevention program; Community education; Male survivors of sexual abuse; Healing; Ethnic minorities
SPECIAL PROGRAMS/SERVICES: The Medicine Wheel Human Development and Personal Awareness Training Program offers training to assist people in forming a positive self-image while creating a spiritual bond of Native American traditional culture. Training areas include Medicine Wheel/Circle of Life; personal growth and development; domestic abuse; sexual, physical and verbal abuse; spiritual advising; parenting and family enrichment; healing from substance abuse

LA CROSSE

FAMILY AND CHILDREN'S CENTER
2507 Weston, La Crosse, WI 54601
Information: (608) 788-6333 8am-7pm
Contact: Mary Wentz, Clinical Supv
TYPE OF AGENCY: Counseling/mental health services; Child sexual abuse services
AREAS SERVED: La Crosse, Monroe, Houston
YEARS IN OPERATION: 100
ACCESSIBILITY: Wheelchair accessible; Signers for the hearing impaired
CASES SEXUAL ASSAULT/ABUSE (%): 80
DESCRIPTION: Offers sexual abuse treatment groups for adult female survivors of incest/sexual abuse and individual counseling for survivors (adults and children)
CLIENTS/SERVICES: Sexual assault survivors; Marital rape/sexual abuse survivors; Child victims of sexual abuse; Adult survivors of child sexual abuse; Incest victims/survivors; Community education; Adolescent survivors of sexual abuse; Male survivors of sexual abuse
REQUIREMENTS: Sliding scale fee

HUMAN DEVELOPMENT ASSOCIATES
115 5th Ave S, Ste 301, La Crosse, WI 54601
Information: (608) 784-8688 8am-6pm (Mon-Fri)
Contact: Patricia B Richgels, Co-Dir/Therapist
TYPE OF AGENCY: Private practice
AREAS SERVED: Statewide
YEARS IN OPERATION: 4
ACCESSIBILITY: Wheelchair accessible
CASES SEXUAL ASSAULT/ABUSE (%): 20
DESCRIPTION: Individual, couple, and family therapy, including group therapy for female and male survivors and individual therapy for child sexual abuse/incest offenders and batterers
CLIENTS/SERVICES: Sexual assault survivors; Marital rape/sexual abuse survivors; Child victims of sexual abuse; Adult survivors of child sexual abuse; Incest victims/survivors; Offender treatment program; Adolescent survivors of sexual abuse; Male survivors of sexual abuse
REQUIREMENTS: Minor clients must have parent's consent after first session

LA CROSSE COUNTY DISTRICT ATTORNEY'S OFFICE—VICTIM/WITNESS ASSISTANCE PROGRAM
La Crosse County Courthouse, La Crosse, WI 54601
Information: (608) 785-9604 8:30am-5pm
Contact: Bonnie Sacia, Victim/Witness Coord
TYPE OF AGENCY: Victim/witness assistance program
AREAS SERVED: La Crosse
YEARS IN OPERATION: 4
ACCESSIBILITY: Wheelchair accessible; Signers for the hearing impaired
CASES SEXUAL ASSAULT/ABUSE (%): 3
CLIENTS/SERVICES: Sexual assault survivors; Marital rape/sexual abuse survivors; Child victims of sexual abuse; Incest victims/survivors; Community education; Male survivors of sexual abuse

NEW HORIZONS WOMEN'S SHELTER
PO Box 2031, La Crosse, WI 54601
Crisis hotline: **(608) 784-6419 24 hrs**
Information: (608) 784-6419
Contact: Barbara Jensen, Dir
TYPE OF AGENCY: Domestic violence program
SPONSORING ORGANIZATION: YWCA
AREAS SERVED: LaCrosse, Trempeleau, Monroe, Jackson, Vernon, Juneau, Crawford, Dane
YEARS IN OPERATION: 10
ACCESSIBILITY: Wheelchair accessible
CASES SEXUAL ASSAULT/ABUSE (%): 100
CLIENTS/SERVICES: Sexual assault survivors; Marital rape/sexual abuse survivors; Adult survivors of child sexual abuse; Incest victims/survivors; Prevention program; Community education; Adolescent survivors of sexual abuse

SEXUAL ABUSE TREATMENT AND SUPPORT PROGRAM
1910 South Ave, La Crosse, WI 54601
Crisis hotline: **(800) 362-8255 WI, (800) 356-9588 MN and IA 24 hrs 7 days**
Information: (608) 785-0530, ext 3845 8am-5pm (Mon-Fri)
Contact: Janis Elder, Coord; Beth Hartmann, Medical Social Svcs Dir
TYPE OF AGENCY: Hospital/medical center; Child sexual abuse services; Child sexual abuse prevention program
SPONSORING ORGANIZATION: Lutheran Hospital—La Crosse
AREAS SERVED: Trempealeau, Monroe, Vernon, Crawford, La Crosse
YEARS IN OPERATION: 3
ACCESSIBILITY: Wheelchair accessible; Telecommunications for the hearing impaired (TTY, TDY, etc.); Signers for the hearing impaired
CASES SEXUAL ASSAULT/ABUSE (%): 100
DESCRIPTION: Group and individual treatment for child victims, non-abusing parents and adult survivors of child sexual abuse; Volunteer support for victims of child sexual abuse and the non-abusing parent during both treatment and legal proceedings; Outreach treatment program provides therapy and volunteer support for child victims and adult survivors in three rural counties
CLIENTS/SERVICES: Sexual assault survivors; Marital rape/sexual abuse survivors; Child victims of sexual abuse; Adult survivors of child sexual abuse; Incest victims/survivors; Prevention program; Community education; Adolescent survivors of sexual abuse; Male survivors of sexual abuse
REQUIREMENTS: Child victims cases must be validated by county social services department
SPECIAL PROGRAMS/SERVICES: Publication *Child Sexual Abuse Awarenss and Prevention Manual*

LADYSMITH

TIME-OUT FAMILY ABUSE SHELTER, INC
PO Box 406, Ladysmith, WI 54848
Crisis hotline: **(715) 532-7089 24 hrs**
Information: (715) 532-6976
TYPE OF AGENCY: Domestic violence program
AREAS SERVED: Rusk, Price, Sawyer, Barron, Washburn
YEARS IN OPERATION: 8
ACCESSIBILITY: Wheelchair accessible
CLIENTS/SERVICES: Marital rape/sexual abuse survivors; Community education

MADISON

DANE COUNTY ADVOCATES FOR BATTERED WOMEN
PO Box 1145, Madison, WI 53711
Crisis hotline: **(608) 251-4445 24 hrs**
Information: (608) 251-1237 9am-4:30pm (Mon-Fri)
Contact: Anne Valentine, Exec Dir
TYPE OF AGENCY: Domestic violence program; Acquaintance/date rape prevention program
AREAS SERVED: Dane
YEARS IN OPERATION: 10
LANGUAGES: Translators for Southeast Asian, Spanish, Portuguese, French, Arabic, Hindu, Urdu, Tamali
ACCESSIBILITY: Wheelchair accessible; Signers for the hearing impaired
DESCRIPTION: Counseling and shelter for battered women and their children; Screening and referral for child abuse and child sexual abuse; Legal assistance; Community education
CLIENTS/SERVICES: Marital rape/sexual abuse survivors; Child victims of sexual abuse; Adult survivors of child sexual abuse; Incest victims/survivors; Prevention program; Community education
SPECIAL PROGRAMS/SERVICES: Prevention program on dating violence for high school and college age women

DANE COUNTY DISTRICT ATTORNEY—VICTIM/WITNESS UNIT
210 Martin Luther King Jr Blvd, Rm 305, Madison, WI 53709
Information: (608) 266-4211 7:45am-4:30pm
Contact: Gillian Lawrence, Dir
TYPE OF AGENCY: Victim/witness assistance program
AREAS SERVED: Dane
YEARS IN OPERATION: 10
ACCESSIBILITY: Wheelchair accessible; Telecommunications for the hearing impaired (TTY, TDY, etc.); Signers for the hearing impaired (by arrangement)
CASES SEXUAL ASSAULT/ABUSE (%): 10
CLIENTS/SERVICES: Sexual assault survivors; Marital rape/sexual abuse survivors; Child victims of sexual abuse; Incest victims/survivors; Community education

DANE COUNTY RAPE CRISIS CENTER
128 E Olin Ave, Madison, WI 53713
Crisis hotline: **(608) 251-7273 24 hrs**
Information: (608) 251-5126 9am-5pm
Contact: Normajean Bunton, Exec Dir

DANE COUNTY RAPE CRISIS CENTER
(continued)

TYPE OF AGENCY: Rape crisis center; Rape prevention program
AREAS SERVED: Dane
YEARS IN OPERATION: 15
LANGUAGES: Spanish, Interpreters as needed
ACCESSIBILITY: Wheelchair accessible; Telecommunications for the hearing impaired (TTY, TDY, etc.); Signers for the hearing impaired (by arrangement)
CASES SEXUAL ASSAULT/ABUSE (%): 100
DESCRIPTION: Assists survivors and potential victims, their friends and family members in recovery; Services to combat sexual harassment
CLIENTS/SERVICES: Sexual assault survivors; Marital rape/sexual abuse survivors; Child victims of sexual abuse; Adult survivors of child sexual abuse; Incest victims/survivors; Prevention program; Community education; Adolescent survivors of sexual abuse; Male survivors of sexual abuse; Sexual harassment

FAMILY SEXUAL ABUSE TREATMENT, INC
1605 Monroe St, Madison, WI 53711
Information: (608) 251-4013 8am-5pm (Mon-Fri)
Contact: Jill Cohen Kolb, Exec Dir
TYPE OF AGENCY: Child sexual abuse services; Training/research; Interagency network
AREAS SERVED: Dane
YEARS IN OPERATION: 5
ACCESSIBILITY: Wheelchair accessible
CASES SEXUAL ASSAULT/ABUSE (%): 100
DESCRIPTION: Coordinates treatment for families involved with incest; Makes referrals to appropriate public and private agencies and develops a treatment team to plan for treatment, and monitor family progress. Also trains other professionals in the areas of treatment and assessment of intrafamilial sexual abuse
CLIENTS/SERVICES: Child victims of sexual abuse; Adult survivors of child sexual abuse; Incest victims/survivors; Community education; Adolescent survivors of sexual abuse; Male survivors of sexual abuse
SPECIAL PROGRAMS/SERVICES: Sponsorship of Midwest Conference on Child Sexual Abuse and Incest

FAMILY THERAPY CENTER OF MADISON, INC
6400 Enterprise Ln, Ste 211, Madison, WI 53719
Information: (608) 276-9191 24 hrs (answering machine after hrs)
Contact: John M Bailey, PhD, Dir
TYPE OF AGENCY: Private practice
AREAS SERVED: Statewide
YEARS IN OPERATION: 6
ACCESSIBILITY: Wheelchair accessible
CASES SEXUAL ASSAULT/ABUSE (%): 10-15
DESCRIPTION: A general psychotherapy and family therapy clinic, specializing in assessing and treating child and adult victims of sexual assault, adult survivors of childhood sexual abuse, incest families, and offenders—rapists, child sexual abuse/incest offenders and batterers
CLIENTS/SERVICES: Sexual assault survivors; Marital rape/sexual abuse survivors; Child victims of sexual abuse; Adult survivors of child sexual abuse; Incest victims/survivors; Community education; Offender treatment program; Adolescent survivors of sexual abuse; Male survivors of sexual abuse

ADA JAMES WOMEN'S COUNSELING SERVICE
710 University Ave, Madison, WI 53703
Crisis hotline: **(608) 262-5731 9am-5pm (Mon-Fri)**
Information: (608) 262-8093 9am-5pm (Mon-Fri)
Contact: Deborah Ptak, Coord
TYPE OF AGENCY: College/university-based services
SPONSORING ORGANIZATION: Ada James Women's Center
AREAS SERVED: Dane
YEARS IN OPERATION: 6
ACCESSIBILITY: Wheelchair accessible
CASES SEXUAL ASSAULT/ABUSE (%): 40
DESCRIPTION: Free and confidential peer counseling, and support groups developed and facilitated by women; Training involves issues related to incest and sexual abuse survivors
CLIENTS/SERVICES: Sexual assault survivors; Marital rape/sexual abuse survivors; Adult survivors of child sexual abuse; Incest victims/survivors; Prevention program; Community education; Male survivors of sexual abuse
REQUIREMENTS: Services open to university and community women and men

LIVES UNLIMITED PSYCHOTHERAPY AND RESOURCE CENTER
401 Wisconsin Ave, Madison, WI 53703
Information: (608) 256-3733 8am-6pm (Mon-Fri)
Contact: Pat Browne, Mare Chapman, Elthea Steidemann, Therapists
TYPE OF AGENCY: Counseling/mental health services Feminist therapy; Private practice
AREAS SERVED: Dane
YEARS IN OPERATION: 8
ACCESSIBILITY: Wheelchair accessible; Signers for the hearing impaired
CASES SEXUAL ASSAULT/ABUSE (%): 60
CLIENTS/SERVICES: Sexual assault survivors; Marital rape/sexual abuse survivors; Child victims of sexual abuse; Adult survivors of child sexual abuse; Incest victims/survivors; Community education; Adolescent survivors of sexual abuse; Male survivors of sexual abuse

PARENTAL STRESS CENTER AND OASIS PROGRAM
1506 Madison St, Madison, WI 53711
Crisis hotline: **(608) 251-2266 24 hrs**
Information: (608) 251-9464 9am-4pm
Contact: Fran Nelson, Agency Dir; Stephanie Smith, Prog Coord
TYPE OF AGENCY: Counseling/mental health services; Child sexual abuse services; Child sexual abuse prevention program; Child abuse services
AREAS SERVED: Dane
YEARS IN OPERATION: 10
ACCESSIBILITY: Telecommunications for the hearing impaired (TTY, TDY, etc.)
CASES SEXUAL ASSAULT/ABUSE (%): 100
DESCRIPTION: OASIS (a chapter of Parents United) is a group treatment program offering help for children and adults from sexually abusive families. Groups for child victims ages 5-18, adult survivors of intrafamilial sexual abuse, adult perpetrators of sexual abuse, and nonabusive parents of sexually abused children
CLIENTS/SERVICES: Child victims of sexual abuse; Adult survivors of child sexual abuse; Incest victims/survivors; Community education; Offender treatment program; Adolescent survivors of sexual abuse; Male survivors of sexual abuse
REQUIREMENTS: Services available for victims/survivors ages 5 and older. Abuse of all minor age clients must be reported. Perpetrators must be court-ordered into treatment and absent from the home; Adult survivors must be in individual therapy at the same time as they participate in group
SPECIAL PROGRAMS/SERVICES: Adult program offers groups whose members include adult survivors, perpetrators, and non-abusing parents. This group setting is a more advanced form of treatment for survivors. Survivors are encouraged to have undergone prior healing work before starting this program

THE RAINBOW PROJECT, INC
409 E Main St, Madison, WI 53703
Information: (608) 255-7356 9am-5pm, plus emergency services
Contact: Sharyl J Kato Nilson, Dir
TYPE OF AGENCY: Domestic violence program; Counseling/mental health services; Child sexual abuse services; Child sexual abuse prevention program; Child abuse services; Child abuse prevention program
AREAS SERVED: Dane
YEARS IN OPERATION: 9
ACCESSIBILITY: Wheelchair accessible (by arrangement); Signers for the hearing impaired (by arrangement)
CASES SEXUAL ASSAULT/ABUSE (%): 36
DESCRIPTION: Comprehensive long-term treatment for children and families affected by family violence (including child physical and sexual abuse), providing assessment/evaluation of individual children, parents, and parent-child relationship; Provides individual, couple, family counseling, and children and parents group; Consultation/training; Parent education; Referral service; Interagency coordination; Follow-up services
CLIENTS/SERVICES: Child victims of sexual abuse; Adult survivors of child sexual abuse; Prevention program; Community education; Preschoolers; Publications/media
REQUIREMENTS: Children (infants-6 years) and their families at high risk or who have experienced abuse or neglect, including sexual abuse and witnessing family violence
SPECIAL PROGRAMS/SERVICES: Consultation and training for teachers and child care workers on identification and effects of sexual abuse on young child victims and their families; Guidelines for referral to other treatment and support services; Training on sexual abuse prevention materials and activities for preschool aged children; Curriculum developed for pre- and primary school ages on problem solving alternatives to violence for teachers to use in classroom setting

THE UNITED
PO Box 310, Madison, WI 53701
Crisis hotline: **(608) 255-4297 9am-4pm, 7pm-10pm (Mon-Fri)**
Information: (608) 255-8582 9am-4pm (Mon-Fri)
Contact: Doug Bauder, Coord
TYPE OF AGENCY: Counseling/mental health services; Telephone crisis hotline; Information and referral
AREAS SERVED: Dane
YEARS IN OPERATION: 10
CASES SEXUAL ASSAULT/ABUSE (%): 5
DESCRIPTION: Works toward the creation of a safe, positive environment for lesbians and gays. Provides crisis and information phone line, advocacy, support groups, and community outreach and education
CLIENTS/SERVICES: Sexual assault survivors; Marital rape/sexual abuse survivors; Child victims of sexual abuse; Adult survivors of child sexual abuse; Incest victims/survivors; Community education; Adolescent survivors of sexual abuse; Male survivors of sexual abuse; Lesbians; Gay men

WOMEN'S PSYCHOTHERAPY CENTRE OF WISCONSIN
16 N Carroll St, No 710, Madison, WI 53703
Information: (608) 255-4747 24-hr answering machine
Contact: Tamar Zick, Clinic Dir
TYPE OF AGENCY: Counseling/mental health services; Private practice
AREAS SERVED: Statewide
YEARS IN OPERATION: 1
ACCESSIBILITY: Wheelchair accessible
CASES SEXUAL ASSAULT/ABUSE (%): 30
CLIENTS/SERVICES: Sexual assault survivors; Marital rape/sexual abuse survivors; Adult survivors of child sexual abuse; Incest victims/survivors; Community education; Offender treatment program; Adolescent survivors of sexual abuse

WOMEN'S TRANSIT AUTHORITY
306 N Brooks St, Madison, WI 53715
Crisis hotline: **(608) 263-1700 (ride service) 7pm-2am**
Information: (608) 256-3710 10am-2pm
Contact: Rebecca Smith, Dir
TYPE OF AGENCY: Rape prevention program
AREAS SERVED: City of Madison
YEARS IN OPERATION: 15
ACCESSIBILITY: Wheelchair accessible; Telecommunications for the hearing impaired (TTY, TDY, etc.)
CASES SEXUAL ASSAULT/ABUSE (%): 45
DESCRIPTION: A rape prevention ride service run by women for women; Provides safe, no-cost rides for women having no other means of transportation, from 7pm-2am
CLIENTS/SERVICES: Sexual assault survivors; Adult survivors of child sexual abuse; Incest victims/survivors; Prevention program; Community education; Adolescent survivors of sexual abuse
REQUIREMENTS: Provides rides for both male and female children aged 12 and younger accompanied by an adult (person 13 or older)

MANITOWOC

DOMESTIC VIOLENCE CENTER
PO Box 1142, Manitowoc, WI 54221-1142
Crisis hotline: **(414) 684-5770 24 hrs**
Information: (414) 684-5770 8:30am-4:30pm
TYPE OF AGENCY: Domestic violence program
AREAS SERVED: Manitowoc, Calumet
YEARS IN OPERATION: 12
LANGUAGES: Hmong interpreters available
ACCESSIBILITY: Wheelchair accessible; Signers for the hearing impaired (by arrangement)
CASES SEXUAL ASSAULT/ABUSE (%): 75
CLIENTS/SERVICES: Sexual assault survivors; Marital rape/sexual abuse survivors; Child victims of sexual abuse; Adult survivors of child sexual abuse; Incest victims/survivors

SEXUAL ASSAULT TREATMENT PROGRAM
2300 Western Ave, Manitowoc, WI 54220
Crisis hotline: **(414) 684-2233 24 hrs**
Information: (414) 684-2450
TYPE OF AGENCY: Hospital/medical center
SPONSORING ORGANIZATION: Holy Family Medical Center
AREAS SERVED: Manitowoc
CLIENTS/SERVICES: Sexual assault survivors; Marital rape/sexual abuse survivors; Child victims of sexual abuse; Adolescent survivors of sexual abuse; Male survivors of sexual abuse

MARINETTE

BAY AREA MEDICAL CENTER
3100 Shore Dr, Marinette, WI 54143
Crisis hotline: **(715) 735-6621 24 hrs**
Information: (715) 735-6621
Contact: Ann Bresnahan, Soc Wkr
TYPE OF AGENCY: Hospital/medical center
AREAS SERVED: Marinette, Menominee
ACCESSIBILITY: Wheelchair accessible
CASES SEXUAL ASSAULT/ABUSE (%): 5-10
DESCRIPTION: Medical hospital and emergency room services; Provides crisis counseling and referral to appropriate agencies
CLIENTS/SERVICES: Sexual assault survivors; Child victims of sexual abuse

SHELTER
400 Wells St, Marinette, WI 54143
Crisis hotline: **(715) 735-6656 24 hrs daily**
Information: (715) 735-6656 24 hrs daily
Contact: Robert Jarentowski, Marinette Co Unified Brd Short-term Svcs Mgr
TYPE OF AGENCY: Domestic violence program
SPONSORING ORGANIZATION: Marinette County Unified Board
AREAS SERVED: Marinette, Menominee, Oconto, Florence, WI; Menominee, MI
YEARS IN OPERATION: 9
CLIENTS/SERVICES: Sexual assault survivors; Marital rape/sexual abuse survivors; Community education

MARSHFIELD

THE PERSONAL DEVELOPMENT CENTER, INC
604 E 4th St, Marshfield, WI 54449
Crisis hotline: **(715) 384-5555 24 hrs**
Information: (715) 384-2971 9am-3pm
Contact: Mary B James, Dir
TYPE OF AGENCY: Rape crisis center; Domestic violence program
AREAS SERVED: Wood and surrounding counties
YEARS IN OPERATION: 10
LANGUAGES: Spanish
ACCESSIBILITY: Wheelchair accessible
CASES SEXUAL ASSAULT/ABUSE (%): 50
CLIENTS/SERVICES: Sexual assault survivors; Marital rape/sexual abuse survivors; Adult survivors of child sexual abuse; Incest victims/survivors; Community education; Adolescent survivors of sexual abuse

MEDFORD

TAYLOR COUNTY CITIZENS AGAINST DOMESTIC ABUSE
PO Box 224, Medford, WI 54451
Crisis hotline: **(715) 748-5140 24 hrs daily**
Information: (715) 748-3131 8:30am-12:30pm
Contact: Carol Roush, Dir/Advocate
TYPE OF AGENCY: Domestic violence program
AREAS SERVED: Taylor
YEARS IN OPERATION: 4
ACCESSIBILITY: Wheelchair accessible
CASES SEXUAL ASSAULT/ABUSE (%): 1
CLIENTS/SERVICES: Sexual assault survivors; Marital rape/sexual abuse survivors; Adult survivors of child sexual abuse; Community education

TAYLOR COUNTY VICTIM WITNESS ASSISTANCE PROGRAM
224 S 2nd St, Medford, WI 54451
Information: (715) 748-3131 8:30am-12:30pm
Contact: Carol Roush, Victim Witness Spec
TYPE OF AGENCY: Victim/witness assistance program
AREAS SERVED: Taylor
YEARS IN OPERATION: 4
ACCESSIBILITY: Wheelchair accessible
CLIENTS/SERVICES: Marital rape/sexual abuse survivors; Adult survivors of child sexual abuse; Incest victims/survivors

MENOMONIE

CRIME VICTIM ASSISTANCE PROGRAM
PO Box 700, Menomonie, WI 54751
Crisis hotline: **(715) 232-1348 5pm-8am, weekends, holidays**
Information: (715) 235-7890 8am-4:30pm
Contact: Shirley Fredrickson, Dir
TYPE OF AGENCY: Domestic violence program; Victim/witness assistance program; Counseling/mental health services; Telephone crisis hotline
SPONSORING ORGANIZATION: West Central Domestic Abuse Project, Inc
AREAS SERVED: Dunn
YEARS IN OPERATION: 2
CASES SEXUAL ASSAULT/ABUSE (%): 30
DESCRIPTION: Provides services for battered women and all crime victims whether or not the crime has been reported to law enforcement. Provides 24-hour crisis line for adult sexual assault victims.
CLIENTS/SERVICES: Sexual assault survivors

MILWAUKEE

BEACON SUPPORT GROUP
PO Box 11544, Milwaukee, WI 53211
Crisis hotline: **(414) 963-1444 9am-10:30pm (Mon-Fri)**
Information: (414) 963-1444 for business message 9am-10:30pm (Mon-Fri)
Contact: Katie Schmidt, Pres
TYPE OF AGENCY: Self-help group
AREAS SERVED: Milwaukee
YEARS IN OPERATION: 6
ACCESSIBILITY: Wheelchair accessible
CASES SEXUAL ASSAULT/ABUSE (%): 100
DESCRIPTION: Self-help support for survivors of sexual assault/abuse provided by other survivors who've completed a group facilitator training course.
CLIENTS/SERVICES: Sexual assault survivors; Marital rape/sexual abuse survivors; Adult survivors of child sexual abuse; Incest victims/survivors; Community education; Adolescent survivors of sexual abuse
REQUIREMENTS: Must be 16 or older

CITY OF MILWAUKEE—COMMON COUNCIL TASK FORCE ON SEXUAL ASSAULT AND DOMESTIC VIOLENCE
200 E Wells St, City Hall, Rm 205, Milwaukee, WI 53202
Crisis hotline: **(414) 278-2997 Recordings 5pm-8am**
Information: (414) 278-2997 8am-5pm
Contact: Terry Perry, Coord
TYPE OF AGENCY: Interagency network
AREAS SERVED: Milwaukee
YEARS IN OPERATION: 10
LANGUAGES: Spanish
ACCESSIBILITY: Wheelchair accessible
DESCRIPTION: Works with caregivers, government, police, the media, and the community to examine issues, assist with policy clarifications and legislation in the areas of sexual assault, domestic violence and child abuse. In addition, monitors provision of services to area residents and police/court enforcement of public policy
CLIENTS/SERVICES: Prevention program; Community education; Sexual harassment
SPECIAL PROGRAMS/SERVICES: Among other projects developed by the Task Force, currently working on a project to be run by the Archdiocese of the area to provide services for those survivors of child sexual abuse (teens and adults) perpetrated by a church authority and for parishes who have experienced child sexual abuse perpetrated by a priest, nun, lay teacher, staff. Task Force has recently revised the policy of Milwaukee public schools in dealing with peer sexual assaults and has been involved in the development of programs for juvenile sex offenders

THE COUNSELING CENTER OF MILWAUKEE, INC
2038 N Bartlett Ave, Milwaukee, WI 53202
Crisis hotline: **(414) 271-9523 24 hrs**
Information: (414) 271-2565 9am-8pm
Contact: Maryann Clesceri, SafePath Proj Coord
TYPE OF AGENCY: Counseling/mental health services; Child sexual abuse prevention program; Shelter; Acquaintance/date rape prevention program; Adolescent program
AREAS SERVED: Milwaukee and surrounding area
YEARS IN OPERATION: 4
ACCESSIBILITY: Wheelchair accessible
CASES SEXUAL ASSAULT/ABUSE (%): 75
DESCRIPTION: The SafePath youth program consists of 24-hour hotline for victims of sexual abuse; Individual and family counseling for victims; Temporary shelter (Pathfinders); Support groups for teenaged mothers who have been sexually abused, and juvenile sex offender groups. Prevention programs include Positive Alternatives for Youth (PAY) and Prevention Is Kids Stuff (PIKS); Peer Helpers pro-

**THE COUNSELING CENTER OF MIL-
WAUKEE, INC** *(continued)*
gram trains high school students and their
teachers, churches, and community groups to
work with their peers.
CLIENTS/SERVICES: Sexual assault survivors;
Marital rape/sexual abuse survivors; Child victims of sexual abuse; Adult survivors of child
sexual abuse; Incest victims/survivors; Prevention program; Community education; Offender treatment program; Adolescent survivors of
sexual abuse; Male survivors of sexual abuse
REQUIREMENTS: The Counseling Program has no
age restrictions. PathFinders only serves 12-17
year olds. The prevention education program
services run in all school levels. SafePath program serves 10-21 year olds

LAKE SHORE CLINIC
1442 N Farwell Ave, Milwaukee, WI 53202
Information: (414) 278-0492 by appointment
Contact: Kathleen Neville, Psychotherapist
TYPE OF AGENCY: Private practice
AREAS SERVED: Greater Milwaukee area
YEARS IN OPERATION: 19
ACCESSIBILITY: Wheelchair accessible
CASES SEXUAL ASSAULT/ABUSE (%): 15
CLIENTS/SERVICES: Sexual assault survivors;
Marital rape/sexual abuse survivors; Child victims of sexual abuse; Adult survivors of child
sexual abuse; Incest victims/survivors

**MILWAUKEE COUNTY CHILDREN'S
COURT—VICTIM/WITNESS SERVICE**
10201 W Watertown Plank Rd, Milwaukee, WI
53226
Information: (414) 257-4527 8:30am-5pm
Contact: Bobbi Moebius, Dir
TYPE OF AGENCY: Victim/witness assistance program
SPONSORING ORGANIZATION: Lutheran Social
Services
AREAS SERVED: Milwaukee
YEARS IN OPERATION: 8
LANGUAGES: Spanish
ACCESSIBILITY: Wheelchair accessible
CASES SEXUAL ASSAULT/ABUSE (%): 10
DESCRIPTION: Provides comprehensive services
for all victims and witnesses of juvenile crime
whose cases are prosecuted by the District
Attorney's Office Juvenile Division; Specialized services are provided for sexual assault
victims
CLIENTS/SERVICES: Sexual assault survivors;
Child victims of sexual abuse; Community
education; Adolescent survivors of sexual
abuse; Publications/media
REQUIREMENTS: Victims of juvenile offenders;
Offenders must be 18 or younger
SPECIAL PROGRAMS/SERVICES: "What's It Like
Going to Court?" brochure written for children

MILWAUKEE WOMEN'S CENTER
611 N Broadway, Ste 230, Milwaukee, WI 53202
Crisis hotline: **(414) 671-6140 24 hrs daily**
Information: (414) 272-6199 9am-5pm (Mon-Fri);
evenings by appointment
TYPE OF AGENCY: Domestic violence program;
Counseling/mental health services
AREAS SERVED: Milwaukee
YEARS IN OPERATION: 7
LANGUAGES: Spanish
ACCESSIBILITY: Wheelchair accessible; Signers for
the hearing impaired
CASES SEXUAL ASSAULT/ABUSE (%): 15
DESCRIPTION: Provides services for families affected by domestic violence, sexual assault,
and alcohol or drug abuse: shelter for victims,
individual and group counseling for child sexual abuse/incest survivors and offenders and
batterers
CLIENTS/SERVICES: Sexual assault survivors;
Marital rape/sexual abuse survivors; Adult survivors of child sexual abuse; Incest victims/
survivors; Community education; Offender
treatment program; Male survivors of sexual
abuse
REQUIREMENTS: Must be over 18 years of age

**NORTHWEST GENERAL HOSPITAL—
DOMESTIC ABUSE PROJECT**
5310 W Capitol Dr, Milwaukee, WI 53216
Crisis hotline: **(414) 447-8634 24 hrs**
Contact: Donna K Johnson, Dir
TYPE OF AGENCY: Domestic violence program;
Hospital/medical center
YEARS IN OPERATION: 8
ACCESSIBILITY: Wheelchair accessible
DESCRIPTION: Provides counseling, medical services, advocacy, and referral designed specifically for needs of battered women. Provides
group therapy for batterers ("Nevermore") and
a separate group for battered women
CLIENTS/SERVICES: Marital rape/sexual abuse survivors

**PARENTS ANONYMOUS OF GREATER
MILWAUKEE**
PO Box 11415, Milwaukee, WI 53211
Crisis hotline: **(414) 963-0566 9am-5pm (Mon-Fri)**
Information: (414) 963-1835 9am-5pm (Mon-Fri)
Contact: Rosalie Cowdin, Sexual Abuse Prog
Coord
TYPE OF AGENCY: Child abuse services
AREAS SERVED: Greater Milwaukee area
YEARS IN OPERATION: 10
ACCESSIBILITY: Wheelchair accessible
CASES SEXUAL ASSAULT/ABUSE (%): 50
DESCRIPTION: Provides self-help support groups
for perpetrators, non-offending parents, teen
victims and female and male adult survivors
of sexual abuse
CLIENTS/SERVICES: Adult survivors of child sexual abuse; Incest victims/survivors; Community education; Offender treatment program;
Adolescent survivors of sexual abuse; Male
survivors of sexual abuse
REQUIREMENTS: Perpetrator must admit at some
basic level; Cases must be reported to
authorities

PATHFINDERS—SAFEPATH PROJECT
1614 E Kane Pl, Milwaukee, WI 53202
Crisis hotline: **(414) 271-9523 24 hrs**
Information: (414) 271-9523 24 hrs
Contact: Robin Ahrens, Prog Dir
TYPE OF AGENCY: Child sexual abuse services;
Shelter; Adolescent program
SPONSORING ORGANIZATION: The Counseling
Center of Milwaukee
AREAS SERVED: Metro Milwaukee area
(Milwaukee, Ozaukee, Waukesha, Washington)
YEARS IN OPERATION: 18
CASES SEXUAL ASSAULT/ABUSE (%): 28
DESCRIPTION: Provides shelter and counseling
services for runaway and homeless teens and
family members, many of whom have been
victims of sexual abuse. Nonresidential counseling for teen and preteen victims of sexual
abuse and their families. Treatment program
for adolescent sex offenders
CLIENTS/SERVICES: Sexual assault survivors;
Child victims of sexual abuse; Community
education; Offender treatment program; Adolescent survivors of sexual abuse; Male survivors of sexual abuse
REQUIREMENTS: 12-17 years for shelter

SEXUAL ASSAULT COUNSELING UNIT
821 W State St, Milwaukee, WI 53233
Information: (414) 278-4617 8:30am-5pm
Contact: Ann Ranfranz, Dir
TYPE OF AGENCY: Victim/witness assistance program
SPONSORING ORGANIZATION: Milwaukee County District Attorney's Office
AREAS SERVED: Milwaukee
YEARS IN OPERATION: 14
LANGUAGES: Spanish
ACCESSIBILITY: Wheelchair accessible; Signers for
the hearing impaired
CASES SEXUAL ASSAULT/ABUSE (%): 100
CLIENTS/SERVICES: Sexual assault survivors;
Marital rape/sexual abuse survivors; Child victims of sexual abuse; Incest victims/survivors;
Community education; Adolescent survivors
of sexual abuse; Male survivors of sexual
abuse

**SEXUAL ASSAULT TREATMENT CENTER
OF GREATER MILWAUKEE**
2000 W Kilbourn Ave, Milwaukee, WI 53233
Crisis hotline: **(414) 937-5555 24 hrs daily**
Information: (414) 937-5471 8am-4:30pm
Contact: Marlene Putz, RN
TYPE OF AGENCY: Hospital/medical center
SPONSORING ORGANIZATION: Sinai Samaritan
Medical Center
AREAS SERVED: Milwaukee and surrounding area
(Washington, Racine, Ozaukeee, Waukesha)
YEARS IN OPERATION: 13
ACCESSIBILITY: Wheelchair accessible; Telecommunications for the hearing impaired (TTY,
TDY, etc.)
CASES SEXUAL ASSAULT/ABUSE (%): 100
DESCRIPTION: Interviews; Medicolegal evidence
collection; STD's and pregnancy tests; Referrals for medical check up; Counseling
CLIENTS/SERVICES: Sexual assault survivors;
Marital rape/sexual abuse survivors; Child victims of sexual abuse; Adult survivors of child
sexual abuse; Incest victims/survivors; Prevention program; Community education; Male
survivors of sexual abuse; Disabled

**THE TRAINING INSTITUTE—PLANNED
PARENTHOOD OF WISCONSIN**
744 N 4th St, Milwaukee, WI 53203
Information: (414) 271-8045 8am-5pm
Contact: Ruth Cohen, PhD, Educ and Training
Dir
TYPE OF AGENCY: Counseling/mental health services; Training/research
DESCRIPTION: Grant received from the Wisconsin Council on Developmental Disabilities to
develop education and training programs on
sexual abuse and sexuality for professionals
who work with the developmentally disabled
population in Wisconsin; Offers demonstration lessons and workshops for parents
CLIENTS/SERVICES: Prevention program; Community education

MONROE

GREEN HAVEN FAMILY ADVOCATES, INC
PO Box 181, Monroe, WI 53566
Crisis hotline: **(608) 325-7711 24 hrs 7 days**
Information: (608) 325-6489 9am-5pm (Mon-Thu)
TYPE OF AGENCY: Domestic violence program
AREAS SERVED: Green
YEARS IN OPERATION: 6
LANGUAGES: Spanish, German, French
ACCESSIBILITY: Signers for the hearing impaired
CASES SEXUAL ASSAULT/ABUSE (%): 30-35
CLIENTS/SERVICES: Sexual assault survivors;
Marital rape/sexual abuse survivors; Adult survivors of child sexual abuse; Incest victims/
survivors; Community education; Adolescent
survivors of sexual abuse

OSHKOSH

SEXUAL ABUSE SERVICES
201 Ceape Ave, Oshkosh, WI 54901
Crisis hotline: **(414) 426-1460, 722-8150 24 hrs**
Information: (414) 426-1460, 722-8150
Contact: Mary Wiatrowski, Dir
TYPE OF AGENCY: Rape crisis center; Child sexual abuse services; Child sexual abuse prevention program; Acquaintance/date rape prevention program
AREAS SERVED: Winnebago

SEXUAL ABUSE SERVICES (continued)

YEARS IN OPERATION: 10
LANGUAGES: Interpreters as needed
ACCESSIBILITY: Wheelchair accessible; Telecommunications for the hearing impaired (TTY, TDY, etc.); Signers for the hearing impaired
CASES SEXUAL ASSAULT/ABUSE (%): 100
DESCRIPTION: Provides crisis intervention, short-term counseling, therapy groups, support groups, advocacy services for adult, teen, and child survivors of sexual assault; Interagency family treatment program for child sexual abuse and incest; Structured therapy groups for female and male survivors; Sexual Perpetrators Anonymous support group for incest/child sexual abuse offenders; Works with rapists in conjunction with corrections
CLIENTS/SERVICES: Sexual assault survivors; Marital rape/sexual abuse survivors; Child victims of sexual abuse; Adult survivors of child sexual abuse; Incest victims/survivors; Prevention program; Community education; Offender treatment program; Adolescent survivors of sexual abuse; Male survivors of sexual abuse; Publications/media
SPECIAL PROGRAMS/SERVICES: Locally produced videotapes on father/daughter relationships and what happens after a report of child sexual abuse; In-school prevention program which reaches children throughout the county in grades 1, 3, 5, and 7, and is expanding to include high school presentations

PLATTEVILLE

FAMILY ADVOCATES, INC
PO Box 705, Platteville, WI 53818
Crisis hotline: **(608) 348-3838 24 hrs**
Information: (608) 348-5995 8:30am-5pm
Contact: Rita Udelhoven, Sexual Assault Svcs Coord
TYPE OF AGENCY: Rape crisis center; Domestic violence program
AREAS SERVED: Grant, Iowa, Lafayette, Crawford
YEARS IN OPERATION: 2
CASES SEXUAL ASSAULT/ABUSE (%): 33
CLIENTS/SERVICES: Sexual assault survivors; Marital rape/sexual abuse survivors; Adult survivors of child sexual abuse; Incest victims/survivors; Prevention program; Community education; Male survivors of sexual abuse
REQUIREMENTS: Must be 18 years of age or older

RACINE

LIGHTHOUSE COUNSELING ASSOCIATES
5605 Washington Ave, Racine, WI 53406
Crisis hotline: **(414) 886-1240 24 hrs**
Information: (414) 886-1240 8am-6pm
Contact: David Nichols, PhD, Dir
TYPE OF AGENCY: Counseling/mental health services; Private practice
AREAS SERVED: Racine, Kenosha
YEARS IN OPERATION: 5
LANGUAGES: Spanish
ACCESSIBILITY: Wheelchair accessible
CASES SEXUAL ASSAULT/ABUSE (%): 10-20
CLIENTS/SERVICES: Sexual assault survivors; Marital rape/sexual abuse survivors; Child victims of sexual abuse; Adult survivors of child sexual abuse; Incest victims/survivors; Offender treatment program; Adolescent survivors of sexual abuse; Male survivors of sexual abuse

RACINE COUNTY DISTRICT ATTORNEY'S OFFICE—VICTIM/WITNESS PROGRAM
730 Wisconsin Ave, Racine, WI 53405
Information: (414) 636-3889 8am-5pm
Contact: Marianne Jensen, Dir
TYPE OF AGENCY: Victim/witness assistance program
AREAS SERVED: Racine
YEARS IN OPERATION: 7
ACCESSIBILITY: Wheelchair accessible
CASES SEXUAL ASSAULT/ABUSE (%): 30
CLIENTS/SERVICES: Sexual assault survivors; Child victims of sexual abuse
REQUIREMENTS: Case must be referred to law enforcement

WOMEN'S RESOURCE CENTER
PO Box 1764, Racine, WI 53401
Information: (414) 633-3233 24 hrs
Contact: Maria Scott, Board Directors Pres
TYPE OF AGENCY: Rape crisis center; Domestic violence program
AREAS SERVED: Racine
YEARS IN OPERATION: 11
CLIENTS/SERVICES: Sexual assault survivors; Marital rape/sexual abuse survivors; Adult survivors of child sexual abuse; Incest victims/survivors; Community education; Adolescent survivors of sexual abuse

REEDSBURG

SAUK COUNTY HUMAN SERVICES
425 6th St, Reedsburg, WI 53959
Crisis hotline: **(608) 356-7035, 524-4391**
Information: (608) 356-7035, 524-4391 8am-4:30pm (Mon, Wed, Thu, Fri); 8am-9pm (Tue)
Contact: Julie Chiplitski, MSSW
TYPE OF AGENCY: Counseling/mental health services
AREAS SERVED: Sauk, Juneau, Richland
YEARS IN OPERATION: 1
ACCESSIBILITY: Wheelchair accessible
CASES SEXUAL ASSAULT/ABUSE (%): 5
CLIENTS/SERVICES: Marital rape/sexual abuse survivors; Child victims of sexual abuse; Adult survivors of child sexual abuse; Incest victims/survivors; Community education; Offender treatment program; Adolescent survivors of sexual abuse; Male survivors of sexual abuse
REQUIREMENTS: Perpetrator must be adjudicated

RHINELANDER

TRI-COUNTY COUNCIL ON DOMESTIC VIOLENCE AND SEXUAL ASSAULT
PO Box 233, Rhinelander, WI 54501
Crisis hotline: **(715) 362-6800 24 hrs daily**
Information: (715) 362-6841
Contact: Karen Jurgens, Sexual Assault Prog Coord
TYPE OF AGENCY: Rape crisis center; Domestic violence program
AREAS SERVED: Forest, Oneida, Vilas
YEARS IN OPERATION: 9
CASES SEXUAL ASSAULT/ABUSE (%): 60-75
DESCRIPTION: Assists victims of past/current sexual abuse through rehabilitation and reporting processes. Offers support groups for both female and male survivors
CLIENTS/SERVICES: Sexual assault survivors; Marital rape/sexual abuse survivors; Child victims of sexual abuse; Adult survivors of child sexual abuse; Incest victims/survivors; Prevention program; Community education; Adolescent survivors of sexual abuse; Male survivors of sexual abuse
REQUIREMENTS: Offenses against juveniles must be reported

RICHLAND CENTER

PASSAGES—A PROGRAM FOR VICTIMS OF DOMESTIC ABUSE AND SEXUAL ASSAULT
PO Box 121, Richland Center, WI 53581
Crisis hotline: **(608) 647-2720 24 hrs**
Information: (608) 647-6317 8:30am-5pm (Mon-Fri)
Contact: Terry Yanke, Direct Svcs Coord
TYPE OF AGENCY: Rape crisis center; Domestic violence program
AREAS SERVED: Richland, Sauk, Juneau
YEARS IN OPERATION: 2
CASES SEXUAL ASSAULT/ABUSE (%): 100
DESCRIPTION: Provides short-term counseling, advocacy, and support groups for victims/survivors of sexual assault and domestic violence; Feminist martial arts/self-defense program
CLIENTS/SERVICES: Sexual assault survivors; Marital rape/sexual abuse survivors; Child victims of sexual abuse; Adult survivors of child sexual abuse; Incest victims/survivors; Prevention program; Community education

RIVER FALLS

TURNINGPOINT FOR VICTIMS OF DOMESTIC ABUSE, INC
PO Box 304, River Falls, WI 54022
Crisis hotline: **(715) 425-6751, (800) 338-2882 WI only 24 hrs**
Information: (715) 425-6751, (800) 338-2882 WI only 9am-5pm
Contact: Jill Zimmerman, Exec Dir
TYPE OF AGENCY: Domestic violence program
AREAS SERVED: Pierce, St Croix, Dunn, Pepin
YEARS IN OPERATION: 9½
LANGUAGES: Spanish and Sign interpreters available
ACCESSIBILITY: Wheelchair accessible; Signers for the hearing impaired
CASES SEXUAL ASSAULT/ABUSE (%): 25
CLIENTS/SERVICES: Sexual assault survivors; Marital rape/sexual abuse survivors; Child victims of sexual abuse; Adult survivors of child sexual abuse; Incest victims/survivors; Prevention program; Community education

SHEBOYGAN

SHEBOYGAN MEMORIAL MEDICAL CENTER—SEXUAL ASSAULT TREATMENT CENTER
2629 N 7th, Sheboygan, WI 53081
Crisis hotline: **(414) 459-5553 24 hrs**
Contact: Teresa Leffel, Soc Wkr
TYPE OF AGENCY: Rape crisis center; Hospital/medical center
AREAS SERVED: Surrounding counties
YEARS IN OPERATION: 17
LANGUAGES: Interpreters as needed
ACCESSIBILITY: Wheelchair accessible; Signers for the hearing impaired
CASES SEXUAL ASSAULT/ABUSE (%): 100
DESCRIPTION: Medical examination, evidence collection, crisis counseling, professional counseling, and legal advocacy
CLIENTS/SERVICES: Sexual assault survivors; Marital rape/sexual abuse survivors; Child victims of sexual abuse; Adult survivors of child sexual abuse; Prevention program; Community education; Adolescent survivors of sexual abuse; Male survivors of sexual abuse
REQUIREMENTS: Parent's authorization for children under the age of 18 unless court-ordered or temporary custody obtained by Department of Social Services

VICTIM/WITNESS ASSISTANCE
615 N 6th St, Sheboygan, WI 53081
Information: (414) 459-3099 24 hrs
Contact: Susan Hein, Supv
TYPE OF AGENCY: Victim/witness assistance program
AREAS SERVED: Sheboygan
YEARS IN OPERATION: 4½
LANGUAGES: Spanish, Hmong by arrangement
ACCESSIBILITY: Signers for the hearing impaired
CASES SEXUAL ASSAULT/ABUSE (%): 25
CLIENTS/SERVICES: Sexual assault survivors; Marital rape/sexual abuse survivors; Child victims of sexual abuse; Adult survivors of child sexual abuse; Incest victims/survivors; Prevention program; Community education

SPARTA

MONROE COUNTY DISTRICT ATTORNEY'S OFFICE—VICTIM/WITNESS ASSISTANCE PROGRAM
PO Box 536, Sparta, WI 54656
Information: (608) 269-8779 8am-Noon, 12:30pm-4:30pm
Contact: Karen Rengert, Victim/Witness Coord
TYPE OF AGENCY: Victim/witness assistance program
AREAS SERVED: Monroe
YEARS IN OPERATION: 2
ACCESSIBILITY: Wheelchair accessible
CASES SEXUAL ASSAULT/ABUSE (%): 7
CLIENTS/SERVICES: Sexual assault survivors; Child victims of sexual abuse; Adult survivors of child sexual abuse; Incest victims/survivors; Community education; Adolescent survivors of sexual abuse; Male survivors of sexual abuse

STEVENS POINT

FAMILY CRISIS CENTER
1503 Water St, Stevens Point, WI 54481
Crisis hotline: **(715) 344-8508 24 hrs**
Information: (715) 344-8508 8:30am-4:30pm
Contact: Toni Frostman, Dir
TYPE OF AGENCY: Domestic violence program
AREAS SERVED: Portage, Waushara, Adams, Waupaca
YEARS IN OPERATION: 10
LANGUAGES: Hmong and Spanish interpreters available
CASES SEXUAL ASSAULT/ABUSE (%): 20
DESCRIPTION: Provides 24-hour crisis intervention and shelter for survivors of domestic violence and liaison with sexual assault victims services advocates. Batterers' group
CLIENTS/SERVICES: Marital rape/sexual abuse survivors; Child victims of sexual abuse; Adult survivors of child sexual abuse; Incest victims/survivors; Adolescent survivors of sexual abuse; Male survivors of sexual abuse

SEXUAL ASSAULT VICTIM SERVICES, INC
PO Box 992, Stevens Point, WI 54481
Crisis hotline: **(715) 344-8508 24 hrs**
Contact: Teresa Summerton, Pres
TYPE OF AGENCY: Rape crisis center
AREAS SERVED: Portage
YEARS IN OPERATION: 6
CASES SEXUAL ASSAULT/ABUSE (%): 100
CLIENTS/SERVICES: Sexual assault survivors; Prevention program; Community education

STURGEON BAY

HELP OF DOOR COUNTY, INC
PO Box 319, Sturgeon Bay, WI 54235
Crisis hotline: **(414) 743-8818 24 hrs**
Information: (414) 743-8818 8am-4:30pm (Mon-Fri)
Contact: Gay Pustaver, Dir
TYPE OF AGENCY: Rape crisis center; Counseling/mental health services; Domestic violence program
AREAS SERVED: Door, Kewaunee
YEARS IN OPERATION: 10
CASES SEXUAL ASSAULT/ABUSE (%): 10% of crisis calls; 43% of domestic violence cases
DESCRIPTION: Coordinates support groups for child victims of sexual assault and non-abusing parents; Adult victims receive immediate and short-term counseling and assistance with criminal reporting and prosecution; Batterers groups available
CLIENTS/SERVICES: Sexual assault survivors; Marital rape/sexual abuse survivors; Child victims of sexual abuse; Adult survivors of child sexual abuse; Incest victims/survivors; Community education; Adolescent survivors of sexual abuse; Male survivors of sexual abuse

SUPERIOR

CENTER AGAINST SEXUAL AND DOMESTIC ABUSE
2231 Catlin Ave, Superior, WI 54880
Crisis hotline: **(715) 392-3136 24 hrs**
Information: (715) 392-3136 8am-5pm
Contact: Brita Rekve, Dir
TYPE OF AGENCY: Rape crisis center; Domestic violence program; Child sexual abuse services; Child sexual abuse prevention program
AREAS SERVED: Douglas, Bayfield, Ashland, Washburn, Burnett
YEARS IN OPERATION: 5
ACCESSIBILITY: Wheelchair accessible
CASES SEXUAL ASSAULT/ABUSE (%): 25
DESCRIPTION: Provides crisis counseling, escort/advocacy with the medical and legal systems; Support groups for sexual assault/abuse victims and their families; Rural outreach program
CLIENTS/SERVICES: Sexual assault survivors; Marital rape/sexual abuse survivors; Child victims of sexual abuse; Adult survivors of child sexual abuse; Incest victims/survivors; Prevention program; Community education; Adolescent survivors of sexual abuse; Male survivors of sexual abuse

DISTRICT ATTORNEY'S OFFICE—VICTIM/WITNESS ASSISTANCE
1313 Belknap St, Superior, WI 54880
Information: (715) 394-0349 8am-4:30pm
Contact: Darlene Olson, Victim/Witness Spec
TYPE OF AGENCY: Victim/witness assistance program; Child sexual abuse services
AREAS SERVED: Douglas
YEARS IN OPERATION: 10
ACCESSIBILITY: Wheelchair accessible
DESCRIPTION: Interviews child victims and prepares them for court testimony; Referrals for counseling; Prevention work with children
CLIENTS/SERVICES: Sexual assault survivors; Child victims of sexual abuse; Incest victims/survivors; Prevention program; Community education; Offender treatment program; Male survivors of sexual abuse
SPECIAL PROGRAMS/SERVICES: Family incest treatment program, a multiagency approach to working with the entire family (including the offender) to see that further sexual abuse does not recur in the family

HUMAN RESOURCE CENTER
39 N 25th St E, Superior, WI 54880
Crisis hotline: **(715) 392-8216 24 hrs daily**
Information: (715) 392-8216 8:30am-4:30pm (Mon, Wed, Fri); 8:30am-8pm (Tue, Thu)
Contact: Bob Kinderman, Exec Dir
TYPE OF AGENCY: Counseling/mental health services
AREAS SERVED: Douglas
YEARS IN OPERATION: 40
ACCESSIBILITY: Wheelchair accessible
DESCRIPTION: Individual, group, and family counseling; Psychiatric coverage; Testing and evaluation
CLIENTS/SERVICES: Sexual assault survivors; Child victims of sexual abuse; Adult survivors of child sexual abuse; Incest victims/survivors; Offender treatment program; Adolescent survivors of sexual abuse; Male survivors of sexual abuse

THIENSVILLE

AWARENESS COUNSELING SERVICES
216 Green Bay Rd, Ste 206, Thiensville, WI 53092
Information: (414) 242-5153
Contact: Lee B Raffel, Therapist/Owner
TYPE OF AGENCY: Child sexual abuse services; Private practice
AREAS SERVED: Milwaukee, Ozaukee, Washington, Waukesha
YEARS IN OPERATION: 11½
DESCRIPTION: Holistic psychotherapy to meet the emotional demands of anyone who has been sexually assaulted, raped, molested or incestuously abused. Clients participate in a learning and growing experience integrating their physical, emotional and spiritual well being
CLIENTS/SERVICES: Sexual assault survivors; Marital rape/sexual abuse survivors; Child victims of sexual abuse; Adult survivors of child sexual abuse; Incest victims/survivors; Adolescent survivors of sexual abuse; Male survivors of sexual abuse

WAUKESHA

WAUKESHA COUNTY DISTRICT ATTORNEY'S OFFICE—VICTIM/WITNESS PROGRAM
515 W Moreland Blvd, Waukesha, WI 53188
Information: (414) 548-7071 8am-4:30pm (Mon-Fri)
Contact: Gerry Wuerslin, Coord
TYPE OF AGENCY: Victim/witness assistance program
AREAS SERVED: Waukesha
YEARS IN OPERATION: 9
LANGUAGES: Interpreters available
ACCESSIBILITY: Wheelchair accessible
CASES SEXUAL ASSAULT/ABUSE (%): 7
CLIENTS/SERVICES: Sexual assault survivors; Child victims of sexual abuse; Community education

WOMEN AND FAMILIES' PSYCHOTHERAPY RESOURCES, INC
707 W Moreland Blvd, Waukesha, WI 53188-2432
Crisis hotline: **(414) 542-0123 24 hrs**
Information: (414) 542-0123 24 hrs
Contact: Ramona Powers, Clinic Dir
TYPE OF AGENCY: Private practice
AREAS SERVED: Waukesha, Washington, Ozaukee
YEARS IN OPERATION: 8
CASES SEXUAL ASSAULT/ABUSE (%): 35-40
DESCRIPTION: Therapy for victims/survivors and offenders—rapists, child sexual abuse/incest offenders and batterers
CLIENTS/SERVICES: Sexual assault survivors; Marital rape/sexual abuse survivors; Child victims of sexual abuse; Adult survivors of child sexual abuse; Incest victims/survivors; Community education; Offender treatment program; Adolescent survivors of sexual abuse; Male survivors of sexual abuse

THE WOMEN'S CENTER, INC
726 N East Ave, Waukesha, WI 53186
Crisis hotline: **(414) 542-3828 24 hrs**
Information: (414) 547-4600 8:30am-5pm (Mon-Fri)
Contact: Jeri Shryock, Victim Svcs Coord
TYPE OF AGENCY: Rape crisis center; Domestic violence program; Child sexual abuse services; Child sexual abuse prevention program
AREAS SERVED: Waukesha
YEARS IN OPERATION: 11
LANGUAGES: Spanish, Sign
ACCESSIBILITY: Telecommunications for the hearing impaired (TTY, TDY, etc.); Signers for the hearing impaired
CASES SEXUAL ASSAULT/ABUSE (%): 50
DESCRIPTION: Provides advocacy, support, crisis counseling, support groups, hospital, police, and district attorney accompaniment. Group therapy and art/play therapy for child survivors
CLIENTS/SERVICES: Sexual assault survivors; Marital rape/sexual abuse survivors; Child victims of sexual abuse; Adult survivors of child sexual abuse; Incest victims/survivors; Prevention program; Community education; Adolescent survivors of sexual abuse; Male survivors of sexual abuse

WAUPACA

VICTIM/WITNESS ASSISTANCE PROGRAM
109 S Main St, Waupaca, WI 54981
Information: (715) 258-8872 8am-4pm
Contact: Sarah Schmidt, Victim/Witness Coord
TYPE OF AGENCY: Victim/witness assistance program
SPONSORING ORGANIZATION: State of Wisconsin and Waupaca County
AREAS SERVED: Waupaca
YEARS IN OPERATION: 4
LANGUAGES: Interpreters available
ACCESSIBILITY: Wheelchair accessible (by arrangement); Telecommunications for the hearing impaired (TTY, TDY, etc.) (by arrangement); Signers for the hearing impaired (by arrangement)
CASES SEXUAL ASSAULT/ABUSE (%): 10
CLIENTS/SERVICES: Sexual assault survivors; Marital rape/sexual abuse survivors; Child victims of sexual abuse; Adult survivors of child sexual abuse; Incest victims/survivors; Community education; Adolescent survivors of sexual abuse; Male survivors of sexual abuse
REQUIREMENTS: Must be involved in a criminal case

WAUSAU

NORTH CENTRAL HEALTH CARE FACILITIES
1100 Lake View Dr, Wausau, WI 54401
Crisis hotline: **(715) 845-4326 24 hrs**
Information: (715) 848-4600 8am-10pm
Contact: Sue Saeger, Clinical Soc Wkr
TYPE OF AGENCY: Counseling/mental health services
AREAS SERVED: Marathon, Lincoln, Langlade
YEARS IN OPERATION: 15
ACCESSIBILITY: Wheelchair accessible; Telecommunications for the hearing impaired (TTY, TDY, etc.); Signers for the hearing impaired
DESCRIPTION: Outpatient and inpatient mental health services; Intrafamilial child sexual abuse treatment program; Treatment for incest offenders and adolescent sex offenders
CLIENTS/SERVICES: Sexual assault survivors; Child victims of sexual abuse; Adult survivors of child sexual abuse; Incest victims/survivors; Offender treatment program; Adolescent survivors of sexual abuse; Male survivors of sexual abuse

THE WOMEN'S COMMUNITY, INC—SEXUAL ASSAULT VICTIM SERVICE
PO Box 6215, 329 4th St, Wausau, WI 54402-6215
Crisis hotline: **(715) 842-7323 24 hrs**
Information: (715) 842-5663 8am-5pm
Contact: Vickie Popanz, Prog Dir
TYPE OF AGENCY: Rape crisis center; Domestic violence program; Child sexual abuse services
AREAS SERVED: Marathon, Wood, Lincoln
YEARS IN OPERATION: 2
CASES SEXUAL ASSAULT/ABUSE (%): 100
CLIENTS/SERVICES: Sexual assault survivors; Marital rape/sexual abuse survivors; Child victims of sexual abuse; Adult survivors of child sexual abuse; Incest victims/survivors; Community education; Adolescent survivors of sexual abuse; Male survivors of sexual abuse

WEST BEND

FRIENDS OF ABUSED FAMILIES
PO Box 117, West Bend, WI 53095
Crisis hotline: **(414) 334-7298 (West Bend), 673-7298 (Hartford), 255-9488 (Germantown) 24 hrs daily**
Information: (414) 334-5598 8am-4pm (Mon-Fri)
Contact: Vickie L Bladow, Dir Svc Coord
TYPE OF AGENCY: Domestic violence program
AREAS SERVED: Washington
YEARS IN OPERATION: 2
ACCESSIBILITY: Wheelchair accessible
CASES SEXUAL ASSAULT/ABUSE (%): 75-80
CLIENTS/SERVICES: Marital rape/sexual abuse survivors; Child victims of sexual abuse; Adult survivors of child sexual abuse; Incest victims/survivors; Prevention program; Community education
SPECIAL PROGRAMS/SERVICES: Prevention coordinator works in the high schools with adolescent females ages 12-18 on many issues. At present a needs assessment is helping her to determine the most prevalent concerns. Will soon be a resource center for all of southeastern Wisconsin

WISCONSIN RAPIDS

WOOD COUNTY DISTRICT ATTORNEY'S OFFICE—VICTIM/WITNESS SERVICES
PO Box 8095, Courthouse, 400 Market St, Wisconsin Rapids, WI 54495-8095
Information: (715) 421-8580 8am-Noon, 1pm-4:45pm
Contact: Marcia Kuehnast, Prog Coord
TYPE OF AGENCY: Victim/witness assistance program
AREAS SERVED: Wood
YEARS IN OPERATION: 2½
ACCESSIBILITY: Wheelchair accessible; Signers for the hearing impaired (by arrangement)
CASES SEXUAL ASSAULT/ABUSE (%): 90
CLIENTS/SERVICES: Sexual assault survivors; Marital rape/sexual abuse survivors; Child victims of sexual abuse; Incest victims/survivors; Prevention program; Community education
REQUIREMENTS: Charges must first be filed by District Attorney's Office

WYOMING

BASIN

CRISIS AND EMERGENCY SERVICES (CARES)
PO Box 931, Basin, WY 82410
Crisis hotline: **(307) 568-3334 24 hrs**
Information: (307) 568-2020 8am-5pm (Mon-Fri)
Contact: D L Irvine, Dir
TYPE OF AGENCY: Rape crisis center; Domestic violence program; Counseling/mental health services; Child sexual abuse services; Child sexual abuse prevention program
SPONSORING ORGANIZATION: Big Horn County Counseling
AREAS SERVED: Big Horn
YEARS IN OPERATION: 4
LANGUAGES: Spanish
ACCESSIBILITY: Wheelchair accessible
CASES SEXUAL ASSAULT/ABUSE (%): 10
CLIENTS/SERVICES: Sexual assault survivors; Marital rape/sexual abuse survivors; Child victims of sexual abuse; Adult survivors of child sexual abuse; Incest victims/survivors; Prevention program; Community education; Offender treatment program; Adolescent survivors of sexual abuse; Male survivors of sexual abuse

CASPER

WOMEN'S SELF HELP CENTER
341 E "E" St, Casper, WY 82604
Crisis hotline: **(307) 235-2814 24 hrs daily**
Information: (307) 235-2814 24 hrs daily
TYPE OF AGENCY: Rape crisis center; Domestic violence program; Child sexual abuse services
AREAS SERVED: Natrona
YEARS IN OPERATION: 10
LANGUAGES: Spanish interpreter available
ACCESSIBILITY: Wheelchair accessible
CASES SEXUAL ASSAULT/ABUSE (%): 20-30
CLIENTS/SERVICES: Sexual assault survivors; Marital rape/sexual abuse survivors; Child victims of sexual abuse; Adult survivors of child sexual abuse; Incest victims/survivors; Prevention program; Community education; Adolescent survivors of sexual abuse; Male survivors of sexual abuse

CHEYENNE

SAFE HOUSE/SEXUAL ASSAULT SERVICES, INC
PO Box 1621, Cheyenne, WY 82003
Crisis hotline: **(307) 637-SAFE 24 hrs**
Information: (307) 634-8655 8am-5pm (Mon-Fri)
Contact: Pat Fairbanks, Exec Dir
TYPE OF AGENCY: Rape crisis center; Domestic violence program; Child sexual abuse prevention program
AREAS SERVED: Laramie
YEARS IN OPERATION: 9
LANGUAGES: Spanish interpreters available
ACCESSIBILITY: Wheelchair accessible; Signers for the hearing impaired
CASES SEXUAL ASSAULT/ABUSE (%): 60
DESCRIPTION: Support and advocacy for survivors of sexual assault and domestic violence; Support groups for female and male survivors; Shelter available for male survivors; Self defense classes
CLIENTS/SERVICES: Sexual assault survivors; Marital rape/sexual abuse survivors; Child victims of sexual abuse; Adult survivors of child sexual abuse; Incest victims/survivors; Prevention program; Community education; Adolescent survivors of sexual abuse; Male survivors of sexual abuse
SPECIAL PROGRAMS/SERVICES: Personal Care Kits containing a sweatsuit, socks, underwear, personal hygiene supplies and the agency brochure are distributed to all hospital emergency rooms. *Protective Behaviors for Children Program* teaches prevention. *The Victim/Witness Program* provides legal advocacy for adults and children. *Rural Outreach Program* accepts collect calls, travels to see clients in their home, and is increasing the number of rural volunteers

CODY

CRISIS INTERVENTION SERVICES
PO Box 1324, Cody, WY 82414
Crisis hotline: **(307) 754-3737 Powell, 587-7801 Cody 24 hrs**
Information: (307) 587-3545 9am-5pm (Mon-Fri)
Contact: Annette Coggins, Exec Dir
TYPE OF AGENCY: Rape crisis center; Domestic violence program
AREAS SERVED: Park
YEARS IN OPERATION: 7
ACCESSIBILITY: Wheelchair accessible
CASES SEXUAL ASSAULT/ABUSE (%): 25
CLIENTS/SERVICES: Sexual assault survivors; Marital rape/sexual abuse survivors; Child victims of sexual abuse; Adult survivors of child sexual abuse; Incest victims/survivors; Prevention program; Community education; Adolescent survivors of sexual abuse; Male survivors of sexual abuse

DOUGLAS

CONVERSE COUNTY COALITION AGAINST FAMILY VIOLENCE
PO Box 692, Douglas, WY 82633
Crisis hotline: **(307) 358-4800 24 hrs**
Information: (307) 358-6148 9am-5pm
Contact: Gaye M Cameron, Dir
TYPE OF AGENCY: Rape crisis center; Domestic violence program
AREAS SERVED: Converse
YEARS IN OPERATION: 5
LANGUAGES: Spanish
ACCESSIBILITY: Wheelchair accessible; Signers for the hearing impaired
CASES SEXUAL ASSAULT/ABUSE (%): 25
DESCRIPTION: Services for survivors of domestic violence and sexual assault; Individual and group therapy for batterers
CLIENTS/SERVICES: Sexual assault survivors; Marital rape/sexual abuse survivors; Child victims of sexual abuse; Adult survivors of child sexual abuse; Incest victims/survivors; Prevention program; Community education; Adolescent survivors of sexual abuse; Male survivors of sexual abuse

EVANSTON

UINTA COUNTY COUNSELING SERVICE
350 Uinta View Dr, Ste 302, Evanston, WY 82930
Crisis hotline: **(307) 789-7916**
Information: (307) 789-7915 8:30am-5pm (Mon-Fri)
Contact: Allan Volman, Dir
TYPE OF AGENCY: Counseling/mental health services
AREAS SERVED: Uinta
YEARS IN OPERATION: 9
ACCESSIBILITY: Wheelchair accessible
CASES SEXUAL ASSAULT/ABUSE (%): 15
CLIENTS/SERVICES: Sexual assault survivors; Marital rape/sexual abuse survivors; Child victims of sexual abuse; Adult survivors of child sexual abuse; Incest victims/survivors; Offender treatment program

UINTA COUNTY SEXUAL ASSAULT—FAMILY VIOLENCE TASK FORCE
350 Uinta View Dr, No 208, Evanston, WY 82930
Crisis hotline: **(307) 789-7315 24 hrs**
Information: (307) 789-3628 8:30am-5pm
Contact: Nancy Dawson, Exec Dir
TYPE OF AGENCY: Rape crisis center; Domestic violence program
AREAS SERVED: Uinta
YEARS IN OPERATION: 7
ACCESSIBILITY: Wheelchair accessible
CLIENTS/SERVICES: Sexual assault survivors; Child victims of sexual abuse; Adult survivors of child sexual abuse; Incest victims/survivors; Prevention program

GILLETTE

CAMPBELL COUNTY PROSECUTING ATTORNEY'S OFFICE—VICTIM/WITNESS COORDINATOR
500 S Gillette Ave, Gillette, WY 82716
Information: (307) 682-4310 8am-5pm
Contact: Margretta S Perry, Victim/Witness Coord
TYPE OF AGENCY: Victim/witness assistance program
AREAS SERVED: Campbell
YEARS IN OPERATION: 1
LANGUAGES: Spanish translator available
ACCESSIBILITY: Wheelchair accessible; Signers for the hearing impaired (by arrangement)
CASES SEXUAL ASSAULT/ABUSE (%): 1
CLIENTS/SERVICES: Sexual assault survivors; Marital rape/sexual abuse survivors; Child victims of sexual abuse; Adult survivors of child sexual abuse; Incest victims/survivors; Community education; Adolescent survivors of sexual abuse; Male survivors of sexual abuse; Publications/media
SPECIAL PROGRAMS/SERVICES: Publication: coloring book for children going to court. The text describes the pictures, beginning with a child "sharing his story" with an adult he trusts, to follow-up counseling after court

GILLETTE ABUSE REFUGE FOUNDATION
Box 3110, Gillette, WY 82717
Crisis hotline: **(307) 686-8070 24 hrs**
Information: (307) 686-8071 8:30am-5pm
Contact: Pattie Kinney, Office Coord
TYPE OF AGENCY: Rape crisis center; Domestic violence program
AREAS SERVED: Campbell
YEARS IN OPERATION: 6
ACCESSIBILITY: Wheelchair accessible
CASES SEXUAL ASSAULT/ABUSE (%): 20
CLIENTS/SERVICES: Sexual assault survivors; Marital rape/sexual abuse survivors; Child victims of sexual abuse; Adult survivors of child sexual abuse; Incest victims/survivors; Prevention program; Community education; Male survivors of sexual abuse

WYOMING REGIONAL COUNSELING CENTER
900 W 6th St, Gillette, WY 82716
Crisis hotline: **(307) 687-5379, 682-4762 24 hrs**
Information: (307) 687-5517, 682-4762 8am-5pm
Contact: William F Heineke, EdD, County Coord
TYPE OF AGENCY: Hospital/medical center; Counseling/mental health services; Child sexual abuse services
SPONSORING ORGANIZATION: Campbell County Memorial Hospital
AREAS SERVED: Campbell, Crook, Johnson
YEARS IN OPERATION: 25
LANGUAGES: Spanish
ACCESSIBILITY: Wheelchair accessible
CASES SEXUAL ASSAULT/ABUSE (%): 30
DESCRIPTION: Treats families in which incest has occurred by providing them with group and individual therapy. Also treats children abused from within and without the family system. Treats adolescent sex offenders and their families, incest offenders and batterers (Men's Impulse Control Group)
CLIENTS/SERVICES: Marital rape/sexual abuse survivors; Child victims of sexual abuse; Adult survivors of child sexual abuse; Incest victims/survivors; Offender treatment program; Adolescent survivors of sexual abuse; Male survivors of sexual abuse
REQUIREMENTS: Sliding scale fee; Adult and juvenile offenders must be court-ordered into treatment

JACKSON

TETON COUNTY TASK FORCE ON FAMILY VIOLENCE AND SEXUAL ASSAULT
PO Box 1328, Jackson, WY 83001
Crisis hotline: **(307) 733-7466 24 hrs**
Information: (307) 733-3711 9am-5pm (Mon-Fri)
Contact: Maureen Rozee, Dir
TYPE OF AGENCY: Rape crisis center; Domestic violence program
AREAS SERVED: Teton
YEARS IN OPERATION: 7
LANGUAGES: Chinese, Vietnamese, Spanish, French, German interpreters available
CASES SEXUAL ASSAULT/ABUSE (%): 10
CLIENTS/SERVICES: Sexual assault survivors; Marital rape/sexual abuse survivors; Adult survivors of child sexual abuse; Incest victims/survivors; Prevention program; Community education; Male survivors of sexual abuse
SPECIAL PROGRAMS/SERVICES: Assertiveness training for men and women

KEMMERER

THE TURNING POINT
Box 64, Kemmerer, WY 83101
Crisis hotline: **(307) 877-9209, Afton outreach (307) 886-9491 24 hrs**
Information: (307) 877-6834, Afton outreach (307) 886-9072 Kemmerer 9am-5pm; Afton 9am-3pm
Contact: Beth Green, Linda McNeel, Co-Dirs
TYPE OF AGENCY: Rape crisis center; Domestic violence program; Child sexual abuse prevention program
AREAS SERVED: Lincoln
YEARS IN OPERATION: 7
LANGUAGES: Spanish
ACCESSIBILITY: Wheelchair accessible
CASES SEXUAL ASSAULT/ABUSE (%): 8
CLIENTS/SERVICES: Sexual assault survivors; Marital rape/sexual abuse survivors; Adult survivors of child sexual abuse; Incest victims/survivors; Prevention program; Community education; Male survivors of sexual abuse
REQUIREMENTS: Minors are referred to social services

LANDER

FREMONT COUNSELING SERVICE
748 Main, Lander, WY 82520
Crisis hotline: **(307) 332-2231 24 hrs daily**
Information: (307) 332-2231 24 hrs daily
Contact: Betty Sorensen, Area Coord
TYPE OF AGENCY: Counseling/mental health services; Child sexual abuse services
AREAS SERVED: Fremont
YEARS IN OPERATION: 18
ACCESSIBILITY: Wheelchair accessible
CASES SEXUAL ASSAULT/ABUSE (%): 10
DESCRIPTION: Individual and group counseling for survivors and offenders (rapists, child sexual abuse/incest offenders and batterers)
CLIENTS/SERVICES: Sexual assault survivors; Child victims of sexual abuse; Adult survivors of child sexual abuse; Incest victims/survivors; Community education; Offender treatment program; Adolescent survivors of sexual abuse; Male survivors of sexual abuse

LARAMIE

CATHEDRAL HOME FOR CHILDREN
Box E, Laramie, WY 82070
Information: (307) 745-8997 8am-5pm
Contact: Sharon Kava, Couns
TYPE OF AGENCY: Child sexual abuse services; Residential treatment facility; Adolescent program
AREAS SERVED: Statewide
YEARS IN OPERATION: 80
CASES SEXUAL ASSAULT/ABUSE (%): 50
DESCRIPTION: Provides long-term residential treatment for emotionally disturbed adolescents ages 12-18. The population has experienced many types of trauma, including sexual abuse. Also provides therapy for child sexual abuse offenders
CLIENTS/SERVICES: Sexual assault survivors; Child victims of sexual abuse; Incest victims/survivors; Offender treatment program; Adolescent survivors of sexual abuse
REQUIREMENTS: Ages 12-18

SAFE PROJECT
Box 665, Laramie, WY 82070
Crisis hotline: **(307) 745-3556 24 hrs**
Information: (307) 742-2273 8:30am-4:30pm
Contact: Kelli Johnson, Dir
TYPE OF AGENCY: Rape crisis center; Domestic violence program; Child sexual abuse services; Child sexual abuse prevention program
AREAS SERVED: Albany
YEARS IN OPERATION: 8
LANGUAGES: Spanish interpreter available
CASES SEXUAL ASSAULT/ABUSE (%): 60
CLIENTS/SERVICES: Sexual assault survivors; Marital rape/sexual abuse survivors; Child victims of sexual abuse; Adult survivors of child sexual abuse; Incest victims/survivors; Prevention program; Community education; Adolescent survivors of sexual abuse; Male survivors of sexual abuse

LOVELL

CARES
441 Montana Ave, Lovell, WY 82431
Crisis hotline: **(307) 548-2333 24 hrs**
Information: (307) 548-6543 8am-5pm (Mon-Fri)
Contact: Mary Alice Tew, Coord
TYPE OF AGENCY: Rape crisis center; Domestic violence program; Child sexual abuse prevention program
AREAS SERVED: Big Horn
YEARS IN OPERATION: 5
ACCESSIBILITY: Wheelchair accessible
CASES SEXUAL ASSAULT/ABUSE (%): 20
CLIENTS/SERVICES: Sexual assault survivors; Marital rape/sexual abuse survivors; Child victims of sexual abuse; Adult survivors of child sexual abuse; Incest victims/survivors; Prevention program; Community education; Adolescent survivors of sexual abuse

LUSK

EASTERN WYOMING MENTAL HEALTH CENTER—SEXUAL ASSAULT/ABUSE SERVICES
207 S Main, Lusk, WY 82225
Crisis hotline: **(307) 358-2846, 334-3666 8am-5pm; on call 24 hrs**
Information: (307) 334-3666 8am-5pm; on call 24 hrs
Contact: V Jewell Taylor, Niobrara Co MH Coord/Therapist
TYPE OF AGENCY: Counseling/mental health services
AREAS SERVED: Niobrara
YEARS IN OPERATION: 15
ACCESSIBILITY: Wheelchair accessible; Signers for the hearing impaired
CASES SEXUAL ASSAULT/ABUSE (%): 75-85
DESCRIPTION: Individual and group counseling for survivors; Individual and group therapy for child sexual abuse offenders and batterers
CLIENTS/SERVICES: Sexual assault survivors; Marital rape/sexual abuse survivors; Child victims of sexual abuse; Adult survivors of child sexual abuse; Incest victims/survivors; Community education; Offender treatment program; Adolescent survivors of sexual abuse; Male survivors of sexual abuse
REQUIREMENTS: Sliding scale fee

HELPMATE
PO Box 89, Lusk, WY 82225
Crisis hotline: **(307) 334-2608 24 hrs**
Information: (307) 334-3416 8:30am-12pm
Contact: Judy Phipps, Dir
TYPE OF AGENCY: Rape crisis center; Domestic violence program; Child sexual abuse prevention program; Residential treatment facility
AREAS SERVED: Niobrara
YEARS IN OPERATION: 4
ACCESSIBILITY: Wheelchair accessible
CLIENTS/SERVICES: Sexual assault survivors; Marital rape/sexual abuse survivors; Child victims of sexual abuse; Adult survivors of child sexual abuse; Incest victims/survivors; Prevention program; Community education; Adolescent survivors of sexual abuse; Male survivors of sexual abuse
SPECIAL PROGRAMS/SERVICES: Adult survivors of child sexual abuse group at women's prison

PINEDALE

SUBLETTE COUNTY SAFV TASK FORCE
PO Box 1236, Pinedale, WY 82941
Crisis hotline: **(800) 445-7233 24 hrs daily**
Information: (307) 367-6305 9am-5pm (Mon-Fri)
TYPE OF AGENCY: Rape crisis center; Domestic violence program; Child sexual abuse services; Child sexual abuse prevention program
AREAS SERVED: Sublette
YEARS IN OPERATION: 5
ACCESSIBILITY: Wheelchair accessible
CASES SEXUAL ASSAULT/ABUSE (%): 15
CLIENTS/SERVICES: Sexual assault survivors; Marital rape/sexual abuse survivors; Child victims of sexual abuse; Incest victims/survivors; Prevention program; Community education

RAWLINS

CARBON COUNTY CITIZENS ORGANIZED TO SEE VIOLENCE ENDED (COVE)
Box 713, Rawlins, WY 82301
Crisis hotline: **(307) 324-7144 24 hrs**
Information: (307) 324-7071 8am-5pm
Contact: Pauline Gonzales, Dir
TYPE OF AGENCY: Rape crisis center; Domestic violence program; Child sexual abuse services; Child sexual abuse prevention program
AREAS SERVED: Carbon
YEARS IN OPERATION: 5
LANGUAGES: Spanish
ACCESSIBILITY: Wheelchair accessible
CASES SEXUAL ASSAULT/ABUSE (%): 40
DESCRIPTION: Services for survivors of sexual assault and domestic violence; Feminist martial arts/self defense program
CLIENTS/SERVICES: Sexual assault survivors; Marital rape/sexual abuse survivors; Child victims of sexual abuse; Adult survivors of child sexual abuse; Incest victims/survivors; Prevention program; Community education; Adolescent survivors of sexual abuse; Male survivors of sexual abuse

RIVERTON

FREMONT COUNTY ALLIANCE AGAINST DOMESTIC VIOLENCE AND SEXUAL ASSAULT
PO Box 1127, Riverton, WY 82501
Crisis hotline: **(307) 856-4734 24 hrs**
Information: (307) 856-0942 24 hrs
Contact: Tami Stouffer, Jacque Taylor, Ann Rossi, Jan Cline, Dirs
TYPE OF AGENCY: Rape crisis center; Domestic violence program; Child sexual abuse prevention program
AREAS SERVED: Fremont
YEARS IN OPERATION: 7
CLIENTS/SERVICES: Sexual assault survivors; Marital rape/sexual abuse survivors; Adult survivors of child sexual abuse; Incest victims/survivors; Prevention program; Community education; Male survivors of sexual abuse

WYOMING STATE HONOR FARM
PO Box 32, Riverton, WY 82501
Information: (307) 856-9578
Contact: James M Gamble, Supt
TYPE OF AGENCY: Offender treatment
DESCRIPTION: Treatment of identified offenders in a minimum security, residential setting
CLIENTS/SERVICES: Adult survivors of child sexual abuse; Offender treatment program; Male survivors of sexual abuse

ROCK SPRINGS

SWEETWATER COUNTY TASK FORCE ON SEXUAL ASSAULT
450 S Main St, Rock Springs, WY 82901
Crisis hotline: **(307) 382-4381, 875-3381 24 hrs**
Information: (307) 382-4381, 875-3381 9am-5pm (Mon-Fri)
Contact: Mary Ann Clark, Advocate Coord
TYPE OF AGENCY: Rape crisis center; Child sexual abuse services; Child sexual abuse prevention program
AREAS SERVED: Sweetwater
YEARS IN OPERATION: 13
LANGUAGES: Spanish; Interpreters for other languages
CASES SEXUAL ASSAULT/ABUSE (%): 100
DESCRIPTION: Comprehensive rape crisis services with support groups for female and male survivors of sexual abuse/assault
CLIENTS/SERVICES: Sexual assault survivors; Marital rape/sexual abuse survivors; Child victims of sexual abuse; Adult survivors of child sexual abuse; Incest victims/survivors; Prevention program; Community education; Adolescent survivors of sexual abuse; Male survivors of sexual abuse

SHERIDAN

BLANCHARD AND ASSOCIATES
PO Box 378, 1 E Alger St, Sheridan, WY 82801
Information: (307) 674-6309 8am-5pm
Contact: Geral Blanchard, MA, Dir
TYPE OF AGENCY: Private practice; Offender treatment
AREAS SERVED: Northeastern WY
YEARS IN OPERATION: 7
ACCESSIBILITY: Wheelchair accessible
CASES SEXUAL ASSAULT/ABUSE (%): 75
DESCRIPTION: Provides individual and group counseling for victims of physical/sexual assault, the offenders and their families. Support groups for female and male survivors. Offender treatment for rapists, child sexual abuse/incest offenders, and batterers
CLIENTS/SERVICES: Sexual assault survivors; Marital rape/sexual abuse survivors; Child victims of sexual abuse; Adult survivors of child sexual abuse; Incest victims/survivors; Prevention program; Community education; Offender treatment program; Adolescent survivors of sexual abuse; Male survivors of sexual abuse; Publications/media
REQUIREMENTS: Client must file charges
SPECIAL PROGRAMS/SERVICES: Publication: *Sex Offender Treatment: A Psychoeducational Model*, a manual for treating sex offenders. Especially useful in prisons and deals with sexual addiction issues

NORTHERN WYOMING MENTAL HEALTH CENTER
1221 W 5th St, Sheridan, WY 82801
Crisis hotline: **(307) 674-4405, 674-4496 after hours 24 hrs**
Information: (307) 674-4405 8am-5pm
Contact: Mick Pattinson, PhD, Deputy Dir
TYPE OF AGENCY: Counseling/mental health services; Child sexual abuse services

AREAS SERVED: Sheridan, Johnson, Weston, Crook
YEARS IN OPERATION: 22
LANGUAGES: Spanish
ACCESSIBILITY: Wheelchair accessible
CASES SEXUAL ASSAULT/ABUSE (%): 20
DESCRIPTION: Counseling for survivors, including female and male survivors; Treatment for child sexual abuse/incest offenders and juvenile sex offenders
CLIENTS/SERVICES: Sexual assault survivors; Marital rape/sexual abuse survivors; Child victims of sexual abuse; Adult survivors of child sexual abuse; Incest victims/survivors; Offender treatment program; Adolescent survivors of sexual abuse; Male survivors of sexual abuse

PIEDMONT PSYCHOLOGICAL PRACTICE
319 W Dow, Sheridan, WY 82801
Crisis hotline: **(307) 672-2468 24 hrs**
Information: (307) 672-2468 24 hrs
Contact: Dr Ray Leugers, Lic Psychologist
TYPE OF AGENCY: Private practice
AREAS SERVED: Sheridan, Johnson, Campbell
YEARS IN OPERATION: 4
ACCESSIBILITY: Wheelchair accessible
CASES SEXUAL ASSAULT/ABUSE (%): 35
CLIENTS/SERVICES: Sexual assault survivors; Marital rape/sexual abuse survivors; Child victims of sexual abuse; Adult survivors of child sexual abuse; Incest victims/survivors; Adolescent survivors of sexual abuse

WOMEN'S CENTER
PO Box 581, Sheridan, WY 82801
Crisis hotline: **(307) 672-3222**
Information: (307) 672-7471
Contact: Charlotte Jenkins
TYPE OF AGENCY: Rape crisis center
CLIENTS/SERVICES: Women's center

SUNDANCE

CROOK COUNTY FAMILY VIOLENCE AND SEXUAL ASSAULT SERVICES
PO Box 128, Sundance, WY 82729
Crisis hotline: **(307) 283-2620 24 hrs 7 days**
Information: (307) 283-2415 9am-4pm
Contact: June Scribner, Prog Dir
TYPE OF AGENCY: Rape crisis center; Domestic violence program; Child sexual abuse prevention program
AREAS SERVED: Crook
YEARS IN OPERATION: 5
CLIENTS/SERVICES: Sexual assault survivors; Marital rape/sexual abuse survivors; Child victims of sexual abuse; Adult survivors of child sexual abuse; Incest victims/survivors; Prevention program; Community education
REQUIREMENTS: Persons under 19 years of age are referred to social services.

THERMOPOLIS

HOT SPRINGS COUNTY COUNSELING SERVICES
121 S 4th St, Thermopolis, WY 82443
Crisis hotline: **(307) 864-3121 24 hrs**
Information: (307) 864-5292 8am-5pm (Mon-Fri)
Contact: Steve Mincer, Dir
TYPE OF AGENCY: Counseling/mental health services
AREAS SERVED: Hot Springs
YEARS IN OPERATION: 12
ACCESSIBILITY: Wheelchair accessible
CASES SEXUAL ASSAULT/ABUSE (%): 5
CLIENTS/SERVICES: Sexual assault survivors; Marital rape/sexual abuse survivors; Child victims of sexual abuse; Adult survivors of child sexual abuse; Incest victims/survivors; Adolescent survivors of sexual abuse; Male survivors of sexual abuse

HOT SPRINGS CRISIS LINE
PO Box 824, 427 Big Horn, Thermopolis, WY 82443
Crisis hotline: **(307) 864-2131 24 hrs**
Information: (307) 864-2131 9am-5pm
Contact: Lorraine Detterrera, Prog Dir
TYPE OF AGENCY: Rape crisis center; Child sexual abuse prevention program
AREAS SERVED: Hot Springs and surrounding counties
YEARS IN OPERATION: 5
LANGUAGES: Spanish
CASES SEXUAL ASSAULT/ABUSE (%): 50
CLIENTS/SERVICES: Sexual assault survivors; Marital rape/sexual abuse survivors; Child victims of sexual abuse; Adult survivors of child sexual abuse; Incest victims/survivors; Prevention program; Community education; Adolescent survivors of sexual abuse; Male survivors of sexual abuse

TORRINGTON

GOSHEN COUNTY TASK FORCE ON FAMILY VIOLENCE AND SEXUAL ASSAULT
PO Box 561, Torrington, WY 82240
Crisis hotline: **(307) 532-2118 24 hrs**
Information: (307) 532-2118 8am-5pm (Mon-Fri)
Contact: Rayna L Bennett, Dir
TYPE OF AGENCY: Rape crisis center; Domestic violence program
AREAS SERVED: Goshen
YEARS IN OPERATION: 4
LANGUAGES: Spanish
ACCESSIBILITY: Wheelchair accessible
CASES SEXUAL ASSAULT/ABUSE (%): 40
DESCRIPTION: Services for survivors of sexual assault and domestic violence; Feminist martial arts/self defense program; Group therapy for batterers
CLIENTS/SERVICES: Sexual assault survivors; Marital rape/sexual abuse survivors; Child victims of sexual abuse; Adult survivors of child sexual abuse; Incest victims/survivors; Prevention program; Community education; Adolescent survivors of sexual abuse; Male survivors of sexual abuse

WHEATLAND

PROJECT SAFE
PO Box 8, Wheatland, WY 82201
Crisis hotline: **(307) 322-4794 24 hrs**
Information: (307) 322-4794 9am-5pm
Contact: Julie Minear, Vonnie Elliott, Co-Dirs
TYPE OF AGENCY: Rape crisis center; Domestic violence program
AREAS SERVED: Platte
YEARS IN OPERATION: 6
LANGUAGES: Spanish interpretor available
ACCESSIBILITY: Wheelchair accessible; Signers for the hearing impaired
CLIENTS/SERVICES: Sexual assault survivors; Marital rape/sexual abuse survivors; Adult survivors of child sexual abuse; Incest victims/survivors; Prevention program; Community education; Adolescent survivors of sexual abuse; Male survivors of sexual abuse
REQUIREMENTS: All cases involving minor children must be reported to the Department of Public Assistanc and Social Services

WORLAND

COMMUNITY CRISIS SERVICES
PO Box 872, Worland, WY 82401
Crisis hotline: **(307) 347-4991 24 hrs**
Information: (307) 347-4992 8am-5pm
Contact: Rita Jones, Dir
TYPE OF AGENCY: Rape crisis center; Domestic violence program
AREAS SERVED: Washakie, others by request and room availability
YEARS IN OPERATION: 7
CASES SEXUAL ASSAULT/ABUSE (%): 25
CLIENTS/SERVICES: Sexual assault survivors; Marital rape/sexual abuse survivors; Child victims of sexual abuse; Adult survivors of child sexual abuse; Incest victims/survivors; Community education; Adolescent survivors of sexual abuse; Male survivors of sexual abuse

APPENDIX A: STATE AGENCIES

ALABAMA

Alabama Crime Victims Compensation Commission
PO Box 1283, Montgomery, AL 36104
Information: (205) 261-4007
Executive Director: Anita A. Morgan
DESCRIPTION: Program designed to financially compensate innocent victims of violent crime.

Alabama Department of Economic and Community Affairs, Law Enforcement Planning Division
3465 Norman Bridge Rd, Montgomery, AL 36105-2399
Information: (205) 261-5891
Contact: Tom Goree, Coordinator, Law Enforcement Planning
DESCRIPTION: State funding source for victim assistance and family violence programs, among others.

Alabama Department of Human Resources
64 N Union St, Montgomery, AL 36130
Information: (205) 261-3409
Contact: Mary Carswell
DESCRIPTION: State agency responsible for child abuse reporting. Child abuse reporting procedures: During business hours, contact the County Department of Human Resources, Child Protective Services Unit. After hours, contact the local police.

Alabama Department of Public Health
307 State Office Bldg, Montgomery, AL 36130
Information: (205) 261-5081
Contact: Clyde Barganier
DESCRIPTION: State agency funding rape crisis centers.

Alabama Network of Victim Services
PO Box 1772, Montgomery, AL 36101
Information: (205) 749-7148
Contact: Ann Mitchell, President
DESCRIPTION: Organization of victim service providers throughout the state.

North Alabama Chapter, National Committee for Prevention of Child Abuse
Parents and Children Together
PO Box 119, Decatur, AL 35602
Information: (205) 355-7252
Executive Director: Naomi Griffith
DESCRIPTION: Chapter of the National Committee for Prevention of Child Abuse

Parents Anonymous of Alabama
20 E Jeff Davis, Montgomery, AL 36104
Information: (205) 265-7838
Contact: Deborah Day
DESCRIPTION: Sponsors self-help groups for abusive parents and parents at risk of child abuse; Greater Alabama Chapter of the National Committee for Prevention of Child Abuse.

VOCAL (Victims of Crime and Leniency)
PO Box 4449, Montgomery, AL 36103
Information: (800) 239-3219;
(205) 262-7197
Contact: Miriam Shehane, President
DESCRIPTION: Private non-profit corporation established to improve the quality of justice for victims of crime. An active member must be a direct victim of a crime or a member of a victim's immediate family. Associate memberships are for individuals interested in focusing attention on the problems and needs of crime victims, including agencies, organizations, and businesses.

ALASKA

Alaska Council on Domestic Violence and Sexual Assault, Department of Public Safety
PO Box N, Juneau, AK 99811
Information: (907) 465-4356
Contact: Barbara Miklos
DESCRIPTION: State agency funding rape crisis centers.

Alaska Department of Health and Social Services, Division of Family and Youth Services
PO Box H05, Juneau, AK 99811-0630
Information: (907) 465-3170
Contact: Yvonne Chase
DESCRIPTION: State agency responsible for child abuse reporting. Child abuse reporting procedures: In-state ask operator for Zenith 4444; out-of-state, add area code 907 (toll-free).

Alaska Department of Law, Criminal Division
PO Box KC, Juneau, AK 99811
Information: (907) 465-3428
Contact: Larry Weeks, Director of Criminal Prosecution
DESCRIPTION: Victim/witness assistants in each district attorney's office assist in easing the trauma associated with criminal trials and related proceedings.

Alaska Network on Domestic Violence and Sexual Assault
130 Seward St, Ste 301, Juneau, AK 99801
Information: (907) 586-3650
Contact: Cindy Smith, Coordinator
DESCRIPTION: Coalition of programs in Alaska concerned with issues of domestic violence, sexual assault and child abuse, and child sexual abuse.

Fairbanks Chapter, National Committee for Prevention of Child Abuse
c/o Resource Center for Parents and Children, 1550 Gillam Way, Fairbanks, AK 99701
Information: (907) 456-2866
Executive Director: Diane Worley
DESCRIPTION: Chapter of the National Committee for Prevention of Child Abuse.

ARIZONA

Arizona Committee for Prevention of Child Abuse
2509 E Fillmore, Phoenix, AZ 85008
Information: (602) 275-0555
Contact: Susan Jernigan, President

DESCRIPTION: Chapter of the National Committee for Prevention of Child Abuse.

Arizona Criminal Justice Commission
1700 N 7th Ave, Ste 250, Phoenix, AZ 85007
Information: (602) 255-1928
Contact: Jacqueline Gasser, Program Director, Victim Services
DESCRIPTION: Administrative agency for Crime Victim Assistance and Crime Victim Compensation programs.

Arizona Department of Economic Security
PO Box 6123, Site Code 0862, Phoenix, AZ 85005
Information: (602) 229-2736
Contact: Lynn Echrol
DESCRIPTION: State agency funding rape crisis centers.

Arizona Department of Economic Security, Child Protective Service
PO Box 6123, 1717 W Jefferson St, Phoenix, AZ 85005
Information: (602) 542-5678
DESCRIPTION: State agency responsible for child abuse reporting. Child abuse reporting procedures: Report to Department of Economic Security local offices.

Arizona Governor's Office for Children
1645 W Jefferson, Ste 420, Phoenix, AZ 85007
Information: (602) 255-3191
Contact: Sandra Sperry, Program Administrator, Child Abuse and Prevention
DESCRIPTION: Assesses and coordinates state programs affecting children. Task forces on child abuse prevention and children's justice.

ARKANSAS

Arkansas Coalition Against Violence to Women and Children
209 W Capitol, 433 Hall Bldg, Little Rock, AR 72201
Information: (501) 375-2225
DESCRIPTION: A state-wide network of organizations addressing violence against women and children.

Arkansas Committee for Prevention of Child Abuse
2915 Kavanaugh Blvd, Box 379, Little Rock, AR 72205
Information: (501) 373-1733, 666-2227
Contact: Maxine Waller
DESCRIPTION: Chapter of the National Committee for Prevention of Child Abuse.

Arkansas Department of Health
4815 W Markham St, Little Rock, AR 72205
Information: (501) 661-2000, 661-2666
Contact: Sidney Marie Tucker
DESCRIPTION: State agency funding rape crisis centers.

Arkansas Department of Human Services, Division of Children and Family Services
PO Box 1437, 7th and Main Sts, Little Rock, AR 72203
Information: (501) 682-8772
Contact: Debbie Hopkins, Administrator, Field Operations Support
DESCRIPTION: Promotes child welfare through investigations, protective services, support services, and foster care. Emphasis on training and increased services in area of child sexual abuse. Child abuse reporting procedures: call (800) 482-5964 in-state.

Arkansas Victim/Witness Program
4th and Center Sts, Tower Bldg, Ste 750, Little Rock, AR 72201
Information: (501) 682-5045
Contact: Randy Dennis, Victim/Witness Coordinator
DESCRIPTION: State funding source for victim assistance programs.

CALIFORNIA

California Commission on the Status of Women
1303 J St, Ste 400, Sacramento, CA 95814
Information: (916) 445-3173
Executive Director: Pat Towner
DESCRIPTION: Advises the governor and legislature on inequities in laws, practices, and conditions which affect women. Provides referral service. Has reference library on women's issues, including violence to women.

California Consortium of Child Abuse Councils
4024 N Durfee Ave, McLaren Hall, El Monte, CA 91732
Information: (818) 575-4362
Contact: Deanne Tilton, President
DESCRIPTION: Chapter of the National Committee for Prevention of Child Abuse.

California Consortium of Child Abuse Councils
1401 Third St, No. 13, Sacramento, CA 95814
Information: (916) 448-9135
Contact: Paul Crissey, Program Director
DESCRIPTION: State chapter of the National Committee for Prevention of Child Abuse.

California Department of Social Services, Office of Child Abuse Prevention
744 P St, Mail Station 9-100, Sacramento, CA 95814
Information: (916) 323-2888
Contact: Beth Hardesty Fife, Chief, Office of Child Abuse Prevention
DESCRIPTION: State focal point for the collection, coordination and dissemination of child abuse and neglect information. Technical assistance and consultation in the delivery of child abuse prevention. Catalyst for public policy development/implementation for child abuse prevention services. Child abuse reporting procedures: report to County Departments of Welfare and the statewide Central Registry of Child Abuse (916) 445-7586.

California Office of the Attorney General, Crime Prevention Center
1515 K St, Sacramento, CA 95814
Information: (916) 324-7863
Contact: Cynthia Katz, Child Abuse Program Manager
DESCRIPTION: Influences public policy in the field of child abuse investigations and judicial practices, influences public policy and promotes public awareness in child abuse prevention and intervention.

California Office of Criminal Justice Planning, Sexual Assault and Child Abuse Branch
1130 K St, Ste 300, Sacramento, CA 95814
Information: (916) 324-9210
Contact: Linda Bryan, Chief, Sexual Assault/Child Abuse Branch
DESCRIPTION: Funds rape crisis centers, child sexual abuse prevention and treatment programs, child sexual abuse prevention training centers, and sex offender treatment programs. Training programs and specialized prosecution units for child abuse and sexual assault are funded to improve the effectiveness of the criminal justice system and its treatment of sexual assault victims. A statewide medical protocol has been developed to standardize procedures for the examination of sexual assault victims.

California Office of Criminal Justice Planning, Victim/Witness and Domestic Violence Branch
1130 K St, Ste 300, Sacramento, CA 95814
Information: (916) 324-9100
DESCRIPTION: Funding for local victim assistance programs and domestic violence centers.

California Professional Society on the Abuse of Children (CAPSAC)
c/o 2827 Concord Blvd, Concord, CA
Contact: Eliana Gil, President
DESCRIPTION: Multidisciplinary professional organization dedicated to assuring a sensitive and effective response to child abuse.

California State Coalition of Rape Crisis Centers
1760 Clayton Rd, Concord, CA 94520
Information: (415) 798-7273 (hotline)
DESCRIPTION: State coalition/association against sexual assault.

Parents Anonymous of California
7120 Franklin Ave, Los Angeles,
CA 90046
Information: (213) 876-0933,
(800) 352-0386 in CA
Contact: Linda Levinson, Program
  Director
DESCRIPTION: Provides weekly support
  groups for parents under stress who are
  concerned about abusing their children.
  SPEAKS weekly support groups for
  adult survivors of physical and/or
  emotional abuse. Counseling
  information and referrals through
  toll-free telephone number.

Victims of Crime Resource Center
c/o McGeorge School of Law, 3200 Fifth
Ave, Sacramento, CA 95817
Information: (800) VICTIMS,
(916) 739-7049
Contact: Shane Kramer, Director
DESCRIPTION: Statewide toll-free legal
  information and referral number.
  Provides information on the California
  Victims Compensation Program,
  victims rights in the criminal justice
  system, and civil suits.

COLORADO

Colorado Association for Children of Alcoholics and Other Addictions
1701 Aspen Dr, Evergreen, CO 80439
Information: (303) 333-0340
DESCRIPTION: Organization that supports
  and serves children of all ages from
  alcoholic, as well as addictive and
  dysfunctional families. State chapter of
  the National Association for Children
  of Alcoholics.

Colorado Civil Rights Division
1525 Sherman, Rm 600C, Denver,
CO 80203
Information: (303) 866-2621
Contact: Jack Lang y Marquez,
  Compliance Director; Nancy Snow,
  Compliance Specialist
DESCRIPTION: Handles complaints of sexual
  harassment (including sexual assault) in
  employment, housing, and public
  accommodations.

Colorado Child Protection Council
2323 S Troy St, 202F, Aurora, CO 80014
Information: (303) 369-8008
Contact: Theresa Costello, President
DESCRIPTION: Chapter of the National
  Committee for Prevention of Child
  Abuse.

Colorado Child Protection Council
9725 E Hampton Ave, Denver, CO 80231
Information: (303) 695-0811
Contact: Judee Filip, Chapter Liaison
DESCRIPTION: Chapter of the National
  Committee for Prevention of Child
  Abuse.

Colorado Coalition Against Sexual Assault
PO Box 18663, Denver, CO 80218
Information: (303) 443-8500, ext 221
Contact: Vanessa Kelly, President
DESCRIPTION: State coalition/association
  against sexual assault.

Colorado Department of Education, Action Against Assault Program
201 E Colfax Ave, Denver, CO 80203
Information: (303) 866-6664
Contact: Debra Sandau-Christopher,
  Senior Consultant, Health Education
DESCRIPTION: Provides in-service training
  for school staff members for the Action
  Against Assault Program, a sexual
  assault/intervention program for youth
  from kindergarten through 12th grade.

Colorado Department of Social Services, Central Registry
1575 Sherman, Denver, CO 80203-1714
Information: (303) 866-3003
Contact: Pam Hinish
DESCRIPTION: State agency responsible for
  child abuse reporting. Child abuse
  reporting procedures: Call
  (800) 842-2288.

CONNECTICUT

Collaboration for Connecticut's Children
60 Lorraine St, Hartford, CT 06105
Information: (203) 233-4437
Executive Director: Jeanann Celli
DESCRIPTION: Chapter of the National
  Committee for Prevention of Child
  Abuse.

Connecticut Commission on Victim Services
1155 Silas Deane Hwy, Wethersfield,
CT 06109
Information: (203) 566-4156,
(800) 822-VICT in CT
Contact: John C Ford, Administrator
DESCRIPTION: Provides compensation for
  innocent victims of crime and court
  advocacy for victims who are involved
  in court trials. Also provides
  information and referrals to other
  agencies throughout the state.

Connecticut Department of Children and Youth Services, Division of Children and Protective Services
170 Sigourney St, Hartford, CT 06105
Information: (203) 566-5506
Contact: Patricia Wilson-Cokers
DESCRIPTION: State agency responsible for
  child abuse reporting. Child abuse
  reporting procedures: Call
  (800) 842-2288 in-state; (203) 344-2599
  out-of-state.

Connecticut Department of Health Services
150 Washington St, Hartford, CT 06106
Information: (203) 566-4174
DESCRIPTION: Provides funding,
  coordination and technical assistance
  for sexual assault centers in the state.

Connecticut Sexual Assault Crisis Services, Inc (CONNSACS)
763 Burnside Ave, East Hartford,
CT 06108
Information: (203) 282-9881
Executive Director: Gail Burns-Smith
DESCRIPTION: Statewide coalition of 13
  individual sexual assault crisis services
  that work to end violence.

DELAWARE

Delaware Department of Justice, Victim Witness Assistance Program
820 N French St, Carvel State Office
Bldg, 8th Fl, Wilmington, DE 19801
Information: (302) 571-2055
Contact: Doris Schnee, Social Worker,
  Rape Response Unit
DESCRIPTION: Provides advocacy and direct
  services for crime victims, including
  victims of sexual offenses and their
  families, through the Rape Response
  Unit social workers.

Delaware Department of Women's Health
PO Box 637, Dover, DE 19903
Information: (302) 736-3111
Contact: Helen Gelof
DESCRIPTION: State agency funding rape
  crisis centers.

Delaware Division of Child Protective Services
330 E 30th St, 3rd Fl, Wilmington,
DE 19802
Information: (302) 571-6417
Contact: Linda M Shannon,
  Intake/Investigation Coordinator
DESCRIPTION: Investigates complaints of
  alleged abuse, neglect, or dependency
  and provides treatment services for
  families if case is substantiated. One of
  three counties has a specialized sexual
  abuse unit which provides combined
  investigation and treatment services.
  Child abuse reporting procedures: Call
  (800) 292-9582.

Delaware Division of Public Health, Office of Medical Social Services
PO Box 637, Dover, DE 19903
Information: (302) 736-4744
Contact: Dennis L Rubino, ACSW, MPH,
  Director of Medical Social Services
DESCRIPTION: Coordinates mutual cases in
  Public Health who are active with
  Child Protective Services. Cooperates
  in the formation of treatment/care
  plans for the children and families.

Parents Anonymous of Delaware, Inc
124-D Senatorial Dr, Wilmington,
DE 19807
Information: (302) 654-1102
Contact: Joanne M Kassees
DESCRIPTION: Sponsors support groups for
  parents who abuse or are at risk of
  abusing their children. Serves as the
  state chapter of the National
  Committee for Prevention of Child
  Abuse.

FLORIDA

Florida Committee for Prevention of Child Abuse
1928 Shawnee Trail, Lakeland, FL 33803
Information: (813) 683-6504
Contact: Sheila Huffman Dailey
DESCRIPTION: Chapter of the National Committee for Prevention of Child Abuse.

Florida Council of Sexual Abuse Services, Inc
307 N Dixie, Ste 401, West Palm Beach, FL 33407
Information: (407) 355-4008
Contact: Sandy Duncan
DESCRIPTION: State coalition/association against sexual assault.

Florida Department of Health and Rehabilitative Services, Children, Youth and Families Program
1317 Winewood Blvd, Bldg 8, Rm 110, Tallahassee, FL 32399-0700
Information: (904) 488-8762
DESCRIPTION: State agency responsible for child abuse reporting. Sponsors intrafamilial child sexual abuse treatment centers and child protection teams. Program for in-home supervision of children victimized by sexual abuse. Child abuse reporting procedures: Call (800) 342-9152 in-state; (904) 487-2625 out-of-state.

Florida Health and Rehabilitative Services, Rape Awareness Program
1317 Winewood Blvd, Koger Executive Center, Lafayette Bldg, Rm 213, Tallahassee, FL 32399-0700
Information: (904) 488-2834
Contact: Jean Becher-Powell, Coordinator
DESCRIPTION: Education and training on sexual battery issues. Provides funding for some rape crisis programs and for the Interdisciplinary Rape Science Training Institute.

GEORGIA

Georgia Council on Child Abuse, Inc
1401 Peachtree St, Ste 140, Atlanta, GA 30309
Information: (404) 870-6565
Executive Director: Larry Wheeler
DESCRIPTION: Chapter of the National Committee for Prevention of Child Abuse.

Georgia Department of Human Resources, Community Health Section, Rape Crisis Program
878 Peachtree St, NE, Rm 102, Atlanta, GA 30309
Information: (404) 894-6640
Contact: Joy Hartley, Coordinator, Rape Crisis Program
DESCRIPTION: State agency funding rape crisis centers.

Georgia Department of Human Resources, Division of Family and Children's Services
878 Peachtree St, NE, Atlanta, GA 30309
Information: (404) 656-2698
Contact: Douglas Greenwell, Director
DESCRIPTION: State agency responsible for child abuse reporting. Child abuse reporting procedures: Make reports to County Departments of Family and Children Services.

Georgia Network to End Sexual Assault
c/o Joy Hartley, Georgia Rape Crisis Program, 878 Peachtree St, NE, Rm 102, Atlanta, GA 30309
Information: (404) 894-6640
Contact: Joy Hartley, Coordinator, Rape Crisis Program
DESCRIPTION: State coalition/association against sexual assault.

HAWAII

Hawaii Criminal Injuries Compensation Commission
1149 Bethel St, Rm 412, Honolulu, HI 96813
Contact: Estra Quilausing, Executive Secretary
DESCRIPTION: Provides compensation for victims of crime, including reimbursement for out-of-pocket medical expenses, loss of earnings, etc.

Hawaii Department of Human Services, Family and Adult Services Division
PO Box 339, Honolulu, HI 96809-0339
Information: (808) 548-6123
Executive Director: Winona E Rubin
Contact: Deborah Lee, Assistant Program Administrator
DESCRIPTION: Child Protective Services is mandated to investigate child abuse (including sex abuse) complaints and to provide appropriate intervention services. Child abuse reporting procedures: Call (808) 942-5877.

Hawaii State Coalition Against Sexual Assault
PO Box 1278, Wailuku, Maui, HI 96793
Information: (808) 242-4335, 244-0547
Contact: Christine Moschetti
DESCRIPTION: Coalition of sex abuse centers that provide direct services to victims of sexual assault.

Prevent Child Abuse Hawaii
PO Box 2605, Honolulu, HI 96803
Information: (808) 533-2000
Executive Director: Millie Rivera-Griffin
DESCRIPTION: Chapter of the National Committee for Prevention of Child Abuse.

IDAHO

Idaho Council on Domestic Violence
450 W State St, 9th Fl, Boise, ID 83720
Information: (208) 334-6512, 334-5580
Executive Director: Celia V Heady
DESCRIPTION: Composed of 7 governor-appointed members from throughout the state. Distributes grants to programs aiding victims of domestic violence, sexual assault, and child abuse.

Idaho Department of Health and Welfare, Division of Family and Children's Services
Statehouse Mail, 450 W State, 10th Fl, Boise, ID 83720
Information: (208) 334-5700
Contact: Ed VanDusen, Coordinator, Child Protection Programs
DESCRIPTION: Investigates complaints of alleged child sex abuse, provides shelter, foster care, and treatment services and funding for child abuse prevention. Child abuse reporting procedures: Make reports to Department of Health and Welfare regional offices.

Idaho Network for Children
PO Box 6032, Boise, ID 83707
Information: (208) 336-4780
Executive Director: Carolyn Murphy
DESCRIPTION: Chapter of the National Committee for Prevention of Child Abuse.

Idaho Network To Stop Violence Against Women, Inc
PO Box 275, Sandpoint, ID 83864
Information: (208) 263-9631
Contact: Sandi Belote, President
DESCRIPTION: Coalition of sexual assault, domestic violence, and child abuse community service centers.

ILLINOIS

Champaign County for Prevention of Child Abuse
2006 Winchester Dr, Champaign, IL 61821
Information: (217) 337-1515
Contact: Delores Evans
DESCRIPTION: Chapter of the National Committee for Prevention of Child Abuse.

Greater Chicago Council, National Committee for Prevention of Child Abuse
332 S Michigan, No 950, Chicago, IL 60604
Information: (312) 663-3520
Executive Director: John Holton
DESCRIPTION: Chapter of the National Committee for Prevention of Child Abuse.

Illinois Coalition Against Sexual Assault
123 S 7th, Springfield, IL 62701
Information: (217) 753-4117
Executive Director: Polly Poskin
DESCRIPTION: Statewide organization of 29 sexual assault centers. The availability of comprehensive services is the distinguishing feature of ICASA member centers.

Illinois Attorney General, Crime Victims Program
500 S 2nd St, Springfield, IL 62706
Information: (217) 782-1090
DESCRIPTION: Responsible for financial compensation program for crime victims.

Illinois Department of Children and Family Services
406 E Monroe, Springfield, IL 62701
Information: (217) 785-2513
Contact: Thomas E Villiger, Deputy Director, Division of Child Welfare & Protective Services
DESCRIPTION: Mandated by law to receive reports of child abuse and neglect; authorized to investigate such reports, provide a wide range of services for children and families, and report and maintain information regarding perpetrators. Child abuse reporting procedures: Call (800) 252-2873 in-state; (217) 785-4010 out-of-state.

Illinois Department of Public Health, Division of Emergency Medical Services, Sexual Assault Survivors Emergency Treatment Program
525 W Jefferson St, Springfield, IL 62703
Information: (217) 785-2080
Contact: Donna J Lederle, Program Coordinator
DESCRIPTION: State agency funding rape crisis centers.

Quad Cities Chapter, National Committee for Prevention of Child Abuse, Council on Children at Risk
525 16th St, Moline, IL 61265
Information: (309) 764-7017
Executive Director: Roy Harley
DESCRIPTION: Chapter of the National Committee for Prevention of Child Abuse.

INDIANA

Indiana Chapter, National Committee for Prevention of Child Abuse
310 N Alabama, Ste 330, Indianapolis, IN 46204
Information: (317) 634-9282
Executive Director: Peggy Eagan
DESCRIPTION: Chapter of the National Committee for Prevention of Child Abuse.

Indiana Coalition Against Sexual Assault
PO Box 10554, Fort Wayne, IN 46853
Information: (317) 742-7281
Contact: Jill Strand
DESCRIPTION: State coalition/association against sexual assault.

Indiana State Board of Health, Division of Maternal and Child Health, Sexual Assault Prevention Program
PO Box 1964, 1330 W Michigan St, Rm 232, Indianapolis, IN 46206-1964
Information: (317) 633-0625
Contact: Nancy Kennedy, Program Coordinator
DESCRIPTION: Provides funding for rape crisis centers and professional and public awareness and knowledge of the sexual assault problem, and education in sexual assault prevention methods.

Indiana State Department of Public Welfare, Child Welfare/Social Services Division
141 S Meridian St, 6th Fl, Indianapolis, IN 46225
Information: (317) 232-4420
Contact: Lynn Arthur, Program and Policy Consultant
DESCRIPTION: Provides child protection services intervention for abused/neglected children and rehabilitative services for children and their families. Child abuse reporting procedures: Call (800) 562-2407 or make reports to County Departments of Public Welfare.

Indiana Violent Crime Compensation Division, Sex Crime Victim Services Fund
601 State Office Bldg, 100 N Senate Ave, Indianapolis, IN 46204
Information: (317) 232-0157, 232-3480
Contact: Cindy J Hudnall, Assistant to the Chairman
DESCRIPTION: Provides reimbursement to Indiana hospitals for the emergency room treatment provided for sexual assault victims, as well as follow-up visits and minimal counseling.

IOWA

Iowa Coalition Against Sexual Assault
Lucas State Office Bldg, Des Moines, IA 50319
Information: (515) 242-5096
Contact: Carole Meade, Director
DESCRIPTION: Coalition of rape crisis centers in Iowa. Provides technical assistance and training, acts as a clearinghouse for information and develops prevention programming about sexual abuse. Publications: *A Resource Guide: News Coverage of Sexual Assault* and booklets for child witnesses. Video: *Acquaintance Rape: "I Thought We Were Friends."*

Iowa Coalition for Family and Children's Services
1111 9th, Ste 200, Des Moines, IA 50314
Information: (515) 244-0074
DESCRIPTION: Coalition of private and county agencies that operates residential or home-based treatment programs for children and families.

Iowa Committee for Prevention of Child Abuse Stat Team, Inc
1200 University, City View Plaza, Des Moines, IA 50317
Information: (515) 281-6327
Executive Director: Norm Ostbloom
DESCRIPTION: Chapter of the National Committee for Prevention of Child Abuse.

Iowa Crime Victim Reparation Program
Wallace State Office Bldg, Des Moines, IA 50319
Information: (515) 281-5044, (800) 373-5044
Contact: Marda Howard, Program Administrator
DESCRIPTION: Provides financial assistance either to the victim or to the provider of medical or counseling service for the victim.

Iowa Department of Human Services, Division of Social Services
Hoover State Office Bldg, 5th Fl, Des Moines, IA 50319
Information: (515) 281-5583
Contact: John Holtkamp, Social Worker, Unit Manager, Child Protective Services
DESCRIPTION: Charged with investigating allegations of child abuse and providing services for children and families. Child abuse reporting requirements: Call (800) 362-2178 in-state; (515) 281-5581 out-of-state (during business hours).

Iowa Department of Public Health, Division of Family and Community Health
Lucas State Office Bldg, Des Moines, IA 50319
Information: (515) 281-4914
Executive Director: Dr Theodore Scurlitis
DESCRIPTION: State agency funding rape crisis centers.

KANSAS

Kansas Association of Domestic Violence Programs
PO Box 633, Lawrence, KS 66044
Information: (913) 842-3265
Contact: Juliene Maska, Vice President
DESCRIPTION: Statewide domestic violence association. Many affiliated programs also serve victims of sexual assault. All programs serve children from domestic violence homes and women who have been sexually assaulted by their partners.

Kansas Child Abuse Prevention Council
112 W 6th, Ste 305, Topeka, KS 66603
Information: (913) 354-7738
Executive Director: James McHenry, PhD
DESCRIPTION: Development of 2 primary sexual abuse prevention programs, for pre-school and elementary-school children: "Happy Bear" and "Bubbylonian Encounter." State chapter of the National Committee for Prevention of Child Abuse.

Kansas Children and Youth Advisory Committee
300 SW Oakley, Smith-Wilson Bldg, Topeka, KS 66606
Information: (913) 296-4656
Executive Director: John Pierpont
DESCRIPTION: Advocates for children and families. Administers Children's Trust Fund, which funds sexual abuse and domestic violence prevention programs.

Kansas Crime Victims Reparations Board
117 W 10th St, Topeka, KS 66612
Information: (913) 296-2359
Contact: Betty A Bomar, Director
DESCRIPTION: State reparations board, assisting crime victims in the payment of medical bills, hospital expenses, counseling expenses, etc. Also provides state and federal grants for family violence and prevention centers and rape prevention and crisis intervention centers throughout the state.

Kansas Organization of Sexual Assault Centers
c/o Family Crisis Center, PO Box 1543, Great Bend, KS 67530
Information: (316) 792-3672
Contact: Lisa Hoffmann
DESCRIPTION: State coalition/association against sexual assault.

Kansas Department of Social and Rehabilitation Services, Youth Services
300 SW Oakley, Smith-Wilson Bldg, Topeka, KS 66606
Information: (913) 296-4645
Contact: Shannon Manzanares, Program Administrator, Family and Child Protection Services
DESCRIPTION: Responsible for receiving reports and investigating child abuse, neglect, sexual abuse and for the provision of family services including emergency shelters and foster care. Child abuse reporting procedures: report to Department of Social and Rehabilitation Services area offices.

KENTUCKY

Kentucky Cabinet for Human Resources, Department for Social Services
275 E Main, 6W, Frankfort, KY 40621
Information: (502) 564-2136
Contact: Nancy Rawlings, Director of Family Services
DESCRIPTION: Investigates child abuse/neglect and exploitation and adult/spouse abuse/neglect and exploitation. Also provides protective social services where needed. Child abuse reporting requirements: report to county offices in 14 state districts.

Kentucky Child Victims' Trust Fund
US 127 South Bldg, Annex No 4, Frankfort, KY 40601
Information: (502) 564-5900
Contact: Libby Marshall, Director, Victims' Advocacy Division
DESCRIPTION: Grants monies for child sexual abuse prevention programs through the Child Victims' Trust Fund across the state.

Kentucky Coalition Against Rape and Sexual Assault
c/o Louisville-Jefferson County Crime Commission, 610 Kaufman-Straus Bldg, Louisville Galleria, Louisville, KY 40202
Information: (502) 625-5088
Contact: Kim Allen
DESCRIPTION: State coalition/association against sexual assault.

Kentucky Council on Child Abuse
240 Plaza Dr, Lexington, KY 40503
Information: (606) 276-1299
Executive Director: Jill Seyfred
DESCRIPTION: Chapter of the National Committee for Prevention of Child Abuse.

Kentucky Crime Victims Compensation Board
115 Myrtle Ave, Frankfort, KY 40601
Information: (502) 564-2290
DESCRIPTION: Administers crime victim compensation funds.

Kentucky Department for Mental Health and Mental Retardation Services
275 E Main St, Frankfort, KY 40621
Information: (502) 564-4448
Contact: Carol Jordan, MS, Domestic Violence Specialist
DESCRIPTION: State and federal funding for community mental health and rape crisis centers in Kentucky. The Domestic Violence Specialist also provides training and program consultation to domestic violence shelters on sexual assault/child sexual abuse.

Kentucky Justice Cabinet, Division of Grants Management
417 High St, Commonwealth Credit Union Bldg, Frankfort, KY 40601
Information: (502) 564-3251
Contact: Paula B Freeman, VOCA Administrator
DESCRIPTION: Administers the Victims of Crime Act of 1984 funds for victim assistance projects.

Kentucky Youth Advocates
2024 Woodford Pl, Louisville, KY 40205
Information: (502) 456-2140
DESCRIPTION: Negotiates with administrative agencies, makes contacts when services are failing, makes recommendations to legislature and administrative agencies, and provides advocacy and makes referrals for individuals negotiating the system.

LOUISIANA

Louisiana Council on Child Abuse, Inc
333 Laurel St, Ste 875, Baton Rouge, LA 70801
Information: (504) 346-0222
Executive Director: Emily DiStefano
DESCRIPTION: Chapter of the National Committee for Prevention of Child Abuse.

Louisiana Department of Health and Human Resources, Division of Children Youth and Family Services
PO Box 3318, Baton Rouge, LA 70808
Information: (504) 342-4008
Contact: Walter Fahr, Program Manager, Child Protection Investigators
DESCRIPTION: State Child Protection Agency providing intake family services and foster care for child abuse victims, including children and their families involved in intrafamilial child sexual abuse. Child abuse reporting procedures: Call parish protective service units.

Louisiana Foundation Against Sexual Assault
c/o YWCA Rape Crisis Center, 601 S Jeff Davis, New Orleans, LA 70119
Information: (504) 523-3755
Contact: Sharon Collins
DESCRIPTION: State coalition/association against sexual assault.

Louisiana Law Enforcement and Administration of Criminal Justice Commission
2121 Wooddale Blvd, Baton Rouge, LA 70806
Information: (504) 925-4418
Contact: Alyce Lappin
DESCRIPTION: Funding for crime assistance and compensation programs (VOCA programs).

Louisiana Office of Public Health, Preventive Health Block Grant Coordinator
PO Box 60630, New Orleans, LA 70160
Information: (504) 568-7210
Contact: Shirley Kirkconnell, Director
DESCRIPTION: State agency funding rape crisis centers.

MAINE

Franklin County Maine Chapter, National Committee for Prevention of Child Abuse
c/o Franklin County Children's Task Force, 32 Main St, Farmington, ME 04938
Information: (207) 778-6960
Executive Director: Tony Scucci
DESCRIPTION: Chapter of the National Committee for Prevention of Child Abuse.

Greater Maine Chapter, National Committee for Prevention of Child Abuse, Maine Association of CAN Councils
PO Box 812, Brunswick, ME 04011
Information: (207) 833-2997
Contact: Sam Wright
DESCRIPTION: Chapter of the National Committee for Prevention of Child Abuse.

Maine Coalition on Rape
PO Box 5326, Augusta, ME 04330
Information: (207) 784-5272
Contact: Marty McIntyre, Chair
DESCRIPTION: Statewide organization whose primary purpose is to have an impact on the problem of sexual assault and sexual abuse. Its work involves education, coordination between rape crisis centers, seeking and dispersing funding for the centers, and working for legislative and legal reform.

Maine Department of Human Services
State House, Station II, Augusta, ME 04358
Information: (207) 289-2983; (800) 452-1999 in ME
Contact: Robert Pronovost, Supervisor
DESCRIPTION: Mandated child protective service agency for state. Child abuse reporting procedures: Call (800) 452-1999 in-state; (207) 289-2983 out-of-state.

Maine Department of Human Services, Bureau of Social Services
Station II, 221 State St, Augusta, ME 04358
Information: (207) 289-2736
Contact: Rick Jones
DESCRIPTION: State agency funding rape crisis centers.

MARYLAND

Maryland Department of Human Resources, Social Services Administration, Protective Services
311 W Saratoga St, Saratoga State Center, Baltimore, MD 21201
Information: (301) 333-0229
DESCRIPTION: State agency responsible for child abuse reporting. Child abuse reporting procedures: call County Departments of Social Services or local law enforcement agencies.

Maryland Department of Human Resources, Women's Services Program
311 W Saratoga St, Baltimore, MD 21201
Information: (301) 333-0059
Contact: Denese Maker, Program Specialist
DESCRIPTION: State agency funding rape crisis centers.

People Against Child Abuse, Inc
3 Church Cir, Annapolis, MD 21401
Information: (301) 269-7816, (800) 422-3055 in MD
Contact: Gloria Goldfaden
DESCRIPTION: Chapter of the National Committee for Prevention of Child Abuse.

MASSACHUSETTS

Massachusetts Coalition of Rape Crisis Services
1016 Main St, Worcester, MA 01603
Information: (508) 791-9546
DESCRIPTION: State coalition/association against sexual assault.

Massachusetts Committee for Children and Youth
14 Beacon St, No 706, Boston, MA 02108
Information: (617) 742-8555
Executive Director: Jetta Bernier
DESCRIPTION: Chapter of the National Committee for Prevention of Child Abuse.

Massachusetts Department of Public Health, Women's Health Unit
150 Tremont St, 3rd Fl, Boston, MA 02111
Information: (617) 727-7222
Contact: Candace Waldron, Director, Women's Health Unit
DESCRIPTION: Develops programs and policies pertaining to violence against women, reproductive health, and occupational health with particular focus on low-income women and women of color. Provides funding for rape crisis centers.

Massachusetts Department of Social Services, Protective Services
150 Causeway St, 11th Fl, Boston, MA 02114
Information: (617) 266-9298
DESCRIPTION: State agency responsible for child abuse reporting and protective services. Child abuse reporting procedures: Call (800) 792-522 or contact protective screening unit at Department of Social Services area offices.

Massachusetts Governor's Statewide Anti-Crime Council
100 Cambridge St, 21st Fl, Boston, MA 02202
Information: (617) 727-6300
Contact: Rai Kowal, Child Abuse and Sexual Assault Policy Analyst and Coordinator
DESCRIPTION: Provides the governor and members of the criminal justice system in state government with information and research on child abuse/sexual assault issues. Also chairs the Governor's Rape Working Group and Battered Women's Working Group. Provides funding for the Rape Evidence Collection Kit Program and training to hospital clinicians in use of kit. Publication of training manual and production of Rape Kit training video.

Massachusetts Office for Victim Assistance
30 Winter St, 11th Fl, Boston, MA 02108
Information: (617) 727-5200
Contact: Ted Frier, Public Affairs Coordinator
DESCRIPTION: Central administrative office for the state victim assistance program, operated through 11 district attorney offices, the Attorney General, Parole Board and Department of Corrections. Oversees child abuse units in these agencies and supplies federal grants to community agencies that deal with child abuse.

Massachusetts Society for the Prevention of Cruelty to Children
43 Mt Vernon St, Boston, MA 02108
Information: (617) 227-2280, (800) 392-6046
Executive Director: Loretta Kowal
Contact: Michelle Fagnano, Director of Training
DESCRIPTION: Statewide private protective child welfare agency, providing crisis intervention and social services for abused children and their families, prevention, advocacy, parenting programs, and a Sexual Abuse Treatment Team in community offices.

MICHIGAN

Child and Family Services of Michigan, Inc
PO Box 348, 2157 University Park Dr, Okemos, MI 48805
Information: (517) 349-6226
Executive Director: Vern C Dahlquist
Contact: Mary Egnor, Director of Program and Staff Development
DESCRIPTION: Nonprofit family service agency providing foster care, adoption, substance abuse counseling, and family services.

Michigan Committee for Prevention of Child Abuse
116 W Ottawa St, Ste 601, Lansing, MI 48933-1602
Information: (517) 485-9113
Executive Director: Maureen Miller
DESCRIPTION: Chapter of the National Committee for Prevention of Child Abuse.

Michigan Department of Social Services, Office of Children and Youth Services
PO Box 30037, 300 S Capitol Ave, Lansing, MI 48909
Information: (517) 373-0093
Contact: Linda Shirkey
DESCRIPTION: State agency responsible for child abuse reporting. Child abuse reporting procedures: report to County Departments of Social Services.

Michigan Department of Social Services, Office of Children and Youth Services, Special Projects Division
300 S Capitol Ave, Commerce Center Bldg, Ste 923, Lansing, MI 48909
Information: (517) 373-0356
Contact: Sue Allan, Director, Special Projects Division
DESCRIPTION: Distributes funds for rape crisis centers.

Michigan Office of Criminal Justice
PO Box 30026, Lansing, MI 48909
Information: (517) 373-7373
DESCRIPTION: Provides funding for victim assistance and compensation programs. Host agency for National Sexual Assault Protocol and Evidence Project.

Sexual Assault Information Network of Michigan (SAIN)
PO Box 20112, Lansing, MI 48901
Information: (517) 371-7140
Executive Director: Debbie Frederick
DESCRIPTION: Statewide organization for providers of sexual assault services and others concerned with the issue of sexual assault.

MINNESOTA

Minnesota Coalition of Sexual Assault Services
PO Box 8451, Minneapolis, MN 55408
Information: (612) 626-1300
Contact: Irene Green, Chair
DESCRIPTION: Statewide coalition of sexual assault programs.

Minnesota Committee for Prevention of Child Abuse
1821 University Ave W, Ste S-191, Saint Paul, MN 55104
Information: (612) 641-1568
Executive Director: Larry Mens
DESCRIPTION: Chapter of the National Committee for Prevention of Child Abuse.

Minnesota Crime Victim/Witness Advisory Council
1821 University Ave, N 465
Griggs-Midway Bldg, Saint Paul, MN 55104
Information: (612) 642-0395
Executive Director: Fran Sepler
DESCRIPTION: The council reviews the way victims are treated by the system, conducts research, makes recommendations concerning policies/programs and legislation, and serves as a clearinghouse of information. The Crime Victims Reparations Board offers financial assistance to victims of crime. The Office of the Crime Victim Ombudsman assists victims who believe their rights have been violated.

Minnesota Department of Corrections, Programs for Victims of Sexual Assault
450 N Syndicate St, 300 Bigelow Bldg, Saint Paul, MN 55104
Information: (612) 642-0256
Contact: Barbara Sanderson, Director
DESCRIPTION: Administers state and federal funds to local sexual assault programs, provides technical assistance, and develops professional training on sexual assault. Sponsors Task Force on Sexual Exploitation by Counselors and Psychotherapists.

Minnesota Department of Corrections, Victim Services Unit
450 N Syndicate, 300 Bigelow Bldg, Saint Paul, MN 55422
Information: (612) 642-0202
Contact: Barbara Raye, Director
DESCRIPTION: Funding for sexual assault, domestic violence and general crime victims, and for community-based programs.

Minnesota Department of Human Services
444 Lafayette Rd, Saint Paul, MN 55155-3830
Information: (612) 296-2217
Contact: Becky Montgomery, Child Protection Program Consultant
DESCRIPTION: Minnesota has a county-administered, state-supervised social services system. The state department develops policies and legislation that pertain to social services, including the assessment/investigation of child sexual abuse and the provision of services to families of sexually abused children. Child abuse reporting procedures: Make reports to County Departments of Human Services.

MISSISSIPPI

Greater Jackson Chapter, National Committee for Prevention of Child Abuse
c/o Exchange Club Parent/Child Center, 2906 N State, Ste 401, Jackson, MS 39216
Information: (601) 366-0025
Executive Director: Becky Williams
DESCRIPTION: Chapter of the National Committee for Prevention of Child Abuse.

Jones County Chapter, National Committee for Prevention of Child Abuse
c/o Pinebelt Mental Health Center, PO Box 113, Laurel, MS 39440
Information: (601) 649-7921
Contact: Barbara Davis, President
DESCRIPTION: Chapter of the National Committee for Prevention of Child Abuse.

Mississippi Attorney General, Child/Victim Advocacy
PO Box 22947, Jackson, MS 39225
Information: (601) 354-6351
Contact: Betty Daugherty, Special Projects Officer
DESCRIPTION: Legislative advocacy for children and victims. Training of judges, attorneys, and victim coordinators witness.

Mississippi Coalition Against Sexual Assault
c/o Mississippi State Department of Health, PO Box 1700, Jackson, MS 39215
Information: (601) 960-7470
Contact: Fran Baker, Special Projects Coordinator/Rape Crisis
DESCRIPTION: Funding for rape crisis centers, training and technical assistance.

Mississippi Department of Public Welfare
PO Box 352, Jackson, MS 39205
Information: (601) 354-0341
Contact: Marty Foote, Program Manager, Child Protection
DESCRIPTION: Agency mandated to investigate child physical and sexual abuse and provide protective service. Child abuse reporting procedures: call (800) 222-8000 in-state; (601) 354-0341 out-of-state (during business hours).

MISSOURI

Missouri Committee for Prevention of Child Abuse
4391 Bettyhill Dr, House Springs, MO 63051
Information: (314) 375-3460
Contact: Betty Seeley
DESCRIPTION: Chapter of the National Committee for Prevention of Child Abuse.

Missouri Department of Health, Bureau of Perinatal Healthcare
PO Box 570, 1730 E Elm, Jefferson City, MO 65102
Information: (314) 751-6001
Contact: Julie Raburn-Miller
DESCRIPTION: State agency funding rape crisis centers.

Missouri Department of Social Services, Division of Family Services
PO Box 88, Jefferson City, MO 65103
Information: (314) 751-2882
DESCRIPTION: State agency responsible for child abuse reporting and child protective services. Child abuse reporting requirements: Call (800) 392-3738 in-state; (314) 751-3448 out-of-state.

MONTANA

Montana Committee for Prevention of Child Abuse
440 Parkway Dr, Kalispell, MT 59901
Information: (406) 756-5633
Contact: Susan Sandwell, President
DESCRIPTION: Chapter of the National Committee for Prevention of Child Abuse.

Montana Department of Health and Environmental Sciences
Cogswell Bldg, Helena, MT 59620
Information: (406) 444-3472
Contact: Bob Solomon
DESCRIPTION: State agency funding rape crisis centers.

Montana Department of Justice, Crime Victims Unit
303 N Roberts, 4th Fl, Helena, MT 59601
Information: (406) 444-3653
Contact: Cheryl Bryant, Administrative Officer
DESCRIPTION: Statewide compensation program for innocent victims who are injured as a direct result of criminal acts of others; payments made for medical expenses, including mental health counseling.

Montana Department of Social and Rehabilitation Services, Department of Family Services
PO Box 8005, Helena, MT 59604
Information: (406) 444-5900
Contact: John Madsen
DESCRIPTION: State agency responsible for child abuse reporting. Child abuse reporting procedures: call (800) 332-6100 or report to County Departments of Family Services.

NEBRASKA

Nebraska Committee for Prevention of Child Abuse
The Atrium, Ste 500, Lincoln, NE 68502
Information: (402) 477-3746
Contact: Deane Finnegan
DESCRIPTION: Chapter of the National Committee for Prevention of Child Abuse.

Nebraska Department of Health
PO Box 95007, 301 Centennial Mall S, Lincoln, NE 68509
Information: (402) 471-2101
Contact: Frank Harris
DESCRIPTION: State agency funding rape crisis centers.

Nebraska Department of Social Services, Human Services Division
301 Centennial Mall S, Lincoln, NE 68509
Information: (402) 471-9273
Contact: Mona Way
DESCRIPTION: State agency responsible for child abuse reporting. Child abuse reporting procedures: Call (800) 652-1999 in-state; or report to local law enforcement agencies or local social services offices.

Violence/Sexual Assault Coalition
1630 K St, Ste H, Lincoln, NE 68508
Information: (402) 476-6256
Contact: Sarah O'Shea, State Coordinator
DESCRIPTION: State coalition for sexual assault and domestic violence programs.

NEVADA

Nevada Department of Human Resources, Family Health Services
505 E King St, Rm 205, Carson City, NV 89710
Information: (702) 885-4885
Contact: Lyndia Vold, Health Educator
DESCRIPTION: Through the health education department, educational materials on sexual assault prevention are disseminated by the public health nurses and by public and professional workshops.

Nevada Victims of Crime Program
209 E Musser St, Rm No 204, Carson City, NV 89710
Information: (702) 885-4065
Contact: Rochelle Summers, Coordinator; Kay Potter, Management Assistant
DESCRIPTION: Provides compensation for medical/psychiatric expenses for victims of certain violent crimes including sexual assault.

Nevada Welfare Division
2527 N Carson St, Carson City, NV 89710
Information: (702) 885-4770
Contact: Connie Martin
DESCRIPTION: State agency responsible for child abuse reporting. Child abuse reporting procedures: report to Division of Welfare local offices.

Northern Nevada Chapter, National Committee for Prevention of Child Abuse
c/o Child Abuse and Neglect Task Force of Northern Nevada, PO Box 6274, Reno, NV 89513
Information: (702) 328-3319
Contact: Marc Fowler, President
DESCRIPTION: Chapter of the National Committee for Prevention of Child Abuse.

Southern Nevada Chapter, National Committee for Prevention of Child Abuse
c/o We Can, Inc, 3441 W Sahara, Ste C-3, Las Vegas, NV 89102
Information: (702) 368-1533
Executive Director: Barbara Ballentine
DESCRIPTION: Chapter of the National Committee for Prevention of Child Abuse.

NEW HAMPSHIRE

New Hampshire Attorney General's Office, Office of Victim/Witness Assistance
State House Annex, Concord, NH 03033
Information: (603) 271-3671
Contact: Sandra Matheson, Director
DESCRIPTION: Provides victim/witness services in all cases prosecuted by the Attorney General's Office, which include sexual abuse/assault cases. Also works on legislation in this area.

New Hampshire Coalition Against Domestic and Sexual Violence
PO Box 353, Concord, NH 03302-0353
Information: (603) 224-8893
Contact: Barry L MacMichael, Grace S Mattern, Co-Directors
DESCRIPTION: Promotes statewide networking and resource sharing among domestic violence and sexual assault programs. Provides funds from VOCA and Preventive Health Services, and Block Grant funds.

New Hampshire Department of Health and Human Services, Division for Children and Youth Services
8 Loudon Rd, Concord, NH 03301
Information: (603) 228-1571
Contact: Effie Malley
DESCRIPTION: State agency responsible for child abuse reporting. Child abuse reporting procedures: call (800) 322-9191; or make reports to district offices.

New Hampshire Task Force on Child Abuse and Neglect
PO Box 607, Concord, NH 03301
Information: (603) 225-5441
Executive Director: Shirley Ganem
DESCRIPTION: Chapter of the National Committee for Prevention of Child Abuse.

NEW JERSEY

New Jersey Chapter for Prevention of Child Abuse
17 Academy St, Ste 709, Newark, NJ 07102
Information: (201) 643-3710
Executive Director: Mary Beth Pavelec
DESCRIPTION: Chapter of the National Committee for Prevention of Child Abuse.

New Jersey Coalition Against Sexual Assault
21 N Clinton Ave, Trenton, NJ 08609-1095
Information: (609) 396-8900
Contact: Riki Jacobs
DESCRIPTION: State coalition/association against sexual assault.

New Jersey Department of Health, Rape Care Program
Division of Epidemiology, CN 360, Trenton, NJ 08625
Information: (609) 588-7509
Contact: Mary Skidmore Taylor, Program Coordinator
DESCRIPTION: Provides funding for agencies serving sexual assault victims in New Jersey. Also provides consultation and technical assistance to rape crisis centers.

New Jersey Department of Human Services, Division of Youth and Family Services
1 S Montgomery St, CN 717, Trenton, NJ 08625
Information: (609) 292-8469
Contact: Jane Cox, Administrator, Community Education Office
DESCRIPTION: State agency for provision of child protective and child welfare services. Child abuse reporting procedures: call (800) 792-8610; or make reports to district offices.

New Jersey Department of Law and Public Safety, Violent Crimes Compensation Board
60 Park Pl, Newark, NJ 07102
Information: (201) 648-2107,
(800) 242-0804
Contact: Kenneth W Welch, Commissioner/Chairman
DESCRIPTION: Provides assistance including financial compensation, free counseling and referral services, and additional support services for innocent victims of violent crime.

New Jersey Division of Criminal Justice, Office of Victim-Witness Advocacy
25 Market St, CN 085, Trenton, NJ 08625
Information: (609) 984-4996
Contact: Pamela J Fisher, Chief, Office of Victim-Witness Advocacy
DESCRIPTION: County offices provide victim advocacy in the criminal justice system, information and referral to social services, and trial preparation and case status notification. Also provide funding for law enforcement-based victim assistance programs demonstration projects only.

New Jersey Governor's Task Force on Child Abuse and Neglect
1 S Montgomery St, CN 717, Trenton, NJ 08625
Information: (609) 292-0888
Contact: Donna M Pincavage, Director
DESCRIPTION: Makes recommendations to the governor on needed programs and services. Provides training programs and conferences.

NEW MEXICO

New Mexico Coalition of Sexual Assault Programs, Inc
4177 Montgomery Blvd NE, Ste E, Albuquerque, NM 87109
Information: (505) 883-8020
Contact: Karla J Chapman, Director
DESCRIPTION: Provides training for individuals and agencies involved with the treatment of victims/offenders of sexual assault and child sexual abuse.

New Mexico Committee for Prevention of Child Abuse
14300 Piedras NE, Albuquerque, NM 87122
Information: (505) 344-1633, 298-9579
Contact: Norma Hood, President
DESCRIPTION: Chapter of the National Committee for Prevention of Child Abuse.

New Mexico Crime Victims Reparation Commission
8100 Mountain Rd NE, Ste 106, Albuquerque, NM 87110
Information: (505) 841-9432
Contact: Kelly O'Neill, Denise M Northup, Investigators
DESCRIPTION: Provides compensation to crime victims in New Mexico.

New Mexico Department of Human Services, Behavioral Health Division
1190 St Frances Dr, Santa Fe, NM 87503
Information: (505) 827-2660
Contact: Beverly Jimmerson
DESCRIPTION: State agency funding rape crisis centers.

New Mexico Department of Human Services, Child Abuse and Neglect
PO Box 2348, Santa Fe, NM 87503-2348
Information: (505) 827-4209
Contact: Ruth Rael
DESCRIPTION: State agency responsible for child abuse reporting. Child abuse reporting requirements: call (800) 432-3456; or report to County Social Services offices.

NEW YORK

New York State Coalition Against Domestic Violence, Inc (NYSCADV)
5 Neher St, Woodstock, NY 12498
Information: (914) 679-5231,
(800) 942-6906 (hotline), (800) 942-6908 (Spanish hotline)
Executive Director: Bonnie Wagner
DESCRIPTION: Primarily serves battered women and their families and domestic violence programs in New York State. Referrals are made to local services for sexual assault/child sexual abuse when requests are received.

New York State Coalition Against Sexual Assault, Inc (NYSCASA, Inc)
PO Box 4055, Schenectady, NY 12304
Information: (518) 372-0683
Contact: Laurie Bacheldor, Coordinator
DESCRIPTION: Statewide coalition of agencies and individuals believing in the fundamental right of everyone to be free from sexual violence.

New York State Crime Victims Board
97 Central Ave, Albany, NY 12206
Information: (518) 473-9649
Contact: Catherine M Abate, Chairperson; Ann D Currier, Director of Research
DESCRIPTION: Provides financial assistance to innocent victims of crime for their eligible unreimbursed expenses; grants local assistance funds to community-based programs providing service delivery to crrime victims and their family members; and advocates for the rights, needs, and interests of crime victims in New York State.

New York State Department of Health, Rape Crisis Program
Empire State Plaza Tower, Rm 878, Albany, NY 12237
Information: (518) 474-3664
Contact: Kathi Montesano-Ostrander, Coordinator, Rape Crisis Program
DESCRIPTION: Funding source for rape crisis intervention and prevention programs. Provides training and technical assistance.

New York State Department of Social Services, Division of Family and Children's Services
40 N Pearl St, 11-D, Albany, NY 12243
Information: (518) 473-6456
Contact: Sallie Perry, Coordinator for Federal Child Abuse Programs
DESCRIPTION: Responsible for receiving CPS reports and monitoring local response in the state. Child abuse reporting procedures: call (800) 342-3720 in-state; (518) 474-9448 out-of-state.

New York State Federation on Child Abuse and Neglect
134 S Swan St, Albany, NY 12210
Information: (518) 445-1273
Executive Director: James Cameron
DESCRIPTION: Chapter of the National Committee for Prevention of Child Abuse.

NORTH CAROLINA

North Carolina Coalition on Sexual Assault
PO Box 5690, Winston-Salem, NC 27113-5690
Information: (919) 755-6661
Contact: Anna Bess Brown
DESCRIPTION: State coalition/association against sexual assault.

North Carolina Committee for Prevention of Child Abuse
PO Box 843, Garner, NC 27529
Information: (919) 779-7515
Executive Director: Faith Boozer
DESCRIPTION: Chapter of the National Committee for Prevention of Child Abuse.

North Carolina Council on the Status of Women
526 N Wilmington St, Raleigh, NC 27604-1199
Information: (919) 733-2455
Executive Director: Judith D Hanna
Contact: Joyce W Allen, Director, Sexual Assault Project
DESCRIPTION: Grants management and technical assistance for rape crisis programs funded through the state.

North Carolina Department of Crime Control and Public Safety, Victims Compensation/Rape Victim Assistance
PO Box 27826, Raleigh, NC 27611-7687
Information: (800) 826-6200,
(919) 733-7974
Contact: Antony E Queen, Assistant Director
DESCRIPTION: Provides financial compensation for medical and psychological services for eligible crime victims.

North Carolina Department of Human Resources, Care-line—Information and Referral
325 N Salisbury St, Raleigh, NC 27611
Information: (919) 733-4261
Executive Director: Susan D Crocker

DESCRIPTION: Provides information on, and makes referrals to, governmental programs, nonprofit organizations, and support groups for anyone in the state needing such information.

North Carolina Department of Human Resources, Division of Social Services, Child Protective Services Unit
325 N Salisbury St, Raleigh, NC 27611
Information: (919) 733-2580
Contact: Beth Osborne, Child Protective Services Program Manager
DESCRIPTION: Primarily responsible for statewide program development and coordination of child protective services. Child abuse reporting procedures: call (800) 662-7030.

North Carolina Fund for Children and Families
121 W Jones St, Raleigh, NC 27603
Information: (919) 733-9296
Executive Director: Pam Frazier
DESCRIPTION: Provides challenge grants for local communities which seek to offer treatment to victims of child sexual abuse.

North Carolina Guardian ad Litem Program
PO Box 2448, Raleigh, NC 27602
Information: (919) 733-7107
Contact: Virginia Weisz, Program Administrator
DESCRIPTION: Court advocacy for allegedly abused and neglected children. Volunteers perform independent investigations and make recommendations in juvenile court concerning child's best interest.

NORTH DAKOTA

Coalition Against Sexual Assault in North Dakota
418 E Rosser, No 320, Bismarck, ND 58501
Information: (701) 255-7796
Contact: Loran Hills, Coordinator
DESCRIPTION: Statewide coordination of sexual assault services, data collection, public awareness and education.

North Dakota Committee for Prevention of Child Abuse
PO Box 1912, Bismarck, ND 58502
Information: (701) 255-3692
Contact: Mark Wagner, Chapter Liaison
DESCRIPTION: Chapter of the National Committee for Prevention of Child Abuse.

North Dakota Crime Victims Reparations
4007 N State St, Hwy 83 N, Bismarck, ND 58501
Information: (701) 224-4150
Executive Director: Dean J Haas
Contact: Rebecca L George, Assistant Administrator
DESCRIPTION: Compensates and assists innocent victims of criminal acts and those who suffer bodily injury or death. Victims of sexual assault/child sexual abuse apply for assistance in paying medical charges and other expenses incurred because of the abuse.

North Dakota Department of Human Services, Division of Children and Family Services
State Capitol, Bismarck, ND 58505
Information: (701) 224-2316
DESCRIPTION: State agency responsible for child abuse reporting and child protective services. Child abuse reporting requirements: report to County Social Services offices.

North Dakota Governor's Committee on Children and Youth
ND Department of Human Services, State Capitol, Bismarck, ND 58505
Information: (701) 224-2970
Contact: Tara Lea Muhlhauser, Chairperson
DESCRIPTION: Actively involved with class advocacy issues for youth. Administers the ND Children's Trust Fund, which funds and promotes child abuse prevention services and activities.

North Dakota Health Department, Maternal and Child Health
Capitol Bldg, Bismarck, ND 58505
Information: (701) 224-2493
Contact: David Cunningham
DESCRIPTION: State agency funding rape crisis centers.

OHIO

ACTION OHIO—Coalition for Battered Women
PO Box 15673, Columbus, OH 43215
Information: (614) 221-1255
Executive Director: Dr Nancy E Smith Evans
DESCRIPTION: Promotes quality programs, services, and resources for survivors of domestic violence. Network of domestic violence programs.

League Against Child Abuse
360 S Third St, Columbus, OH 43215
Information: (614) 464-1500
Executive Director: Russell Miller
DESCRIPTION: Chapter of the National Committee for Prevention of Child Abuse.

Ohio Coalition on Sexual Assault
65 S Fourth St, Columbus, OH 43215
Information: (614) 469-0011
Contact: Debra Seltzer, Coordinator
DESCRIPTION: Network of individuals and agencies providing services for survivors of sexual assault and/or doing prevention work.

Ohio Department of Health, Women's Health Program
246 N High St, 6th Fl, Columbus, OH 43266-0588
Information: (614) 466-8960
Executive Director: Ronald Fletcher, MD
Contact: Judi Moseley, Coordinator, Women's Health Program
DESCRIPTION: Funds rape crisis centers and projects offering both prevention/education and crisis intervention services. Also cosponsors conferences addressing sexual assault, domestic violence, etc.

Ohio Department of Human Services, Bureau of Compliance and Review
30 E Broad St, 30th Fl, Columbus, OH 43266-0423
Information: (614) 466-9824
Executive Director: Jean Schafer
DESCRIPTION: State agency responsible for child abuse reporting. Child abuse reporting procedures: call (800) 282-1190; or report to County Departments of Human Services.

Ohio Department of Human Services, Office of Minority Family Preservation and Prevention Services
30 E Broad St, 30th Fl, Columbus, OH 43266-0423
Information: (614) 466-2306
Contact: Julia Arbini-Haywood, Administrator Family Violence Prevention Services
DESCRIPTION: Responsible for programs and services for victims of domestic violence and their dependents.

Ohio Victim Witness Association, Inc
41 N Perry St, Ste 315, Dayton, OH 45402
Information: (513) 225-5623
Contact: Rhonda Baner

Ohio Women's Information Center
State House, Rm 19, Columbus, OH 43215
Information: (614) 466-5580
Contact: Diane W Poulton, Director
DESCRIPTION: Provides information and referral services. Maintains up-to-date files on resources for help in areas of sexual assault/child sexual abuse, among others.

OKLAHOMA

Oklahoma Coalition Against Domestic Violence and Sexual Assault
c/o Norman Shelter for Battered Women, Box 5089, Norman, OK 73070
Information: (405) 360-0306
Contact: Joanne Smith
DESCRIPTION: State coalition/association against sexual assault.

Oklahoma Committee for Prevention of Child Abuse
c/o Arthur Andersen & Co, 20 N Broadway, Ste 1200, Oklahoma City, OK 73102
Information: (405) 236-1491
Contact: Bob Lorenz, President
DESCRIPTION: Chapter of the National Committee for Prevention of Child Abuse.

Oklahoma Crime Victims Compensation Board
2200 Classen Blvd, Ste 1800, Oklahoma City, OK 73106
Information: (405) 521-2330
Contact: Charles W Wood, Administrator
DESCRIPTION: Provides up to $125 for the sexual assault exam and compensation for out-of-pocket losses incurred as a direct result of crime involving bodily injury or death. Administers VOCA grants.

Oklahoma Department of Human Services, Child Welfare Services
PO Box 25352, Oklahoma City, OK 73125
Information: (405) 521-3778
Contact: Martha Scales
DESCRIPTION: State agency responsible for child abuse reporting. Child abuse reporting requirements: call (800) 522-3511.

Oklahoma Department of Mental Health
PO Box 53277, Capital Station, Oklahoma City, OK 73105
Information: (405) 271-7474
Contact: Ann Lowrance
DESCRIPTION: State agency funding rape crisis centers.

OREGON

Oregon Chapter, National Committee for Prevention of Child Abuse
c/o Resource Center for Child Abuse Prevention, 1912 SW Sixth Ave, Rm 120, Portland, OR 97201
Information: (503) 464-4040
Executive Director: Robert Bailey
DESCRIPTION: Chapter of the National Committee for Prevention of Child Abuse.

Oregon Children's Services Division
198 Commercial St SE, Salem, OR 97310
Information: (503) 378-4722
Contact: Connie Jacoby, Program Coordinator-Family Sex Abuse Treatment Program
DESCRIPTION: Child welfare agency within is a specialized program for which intrafamilial child sex abuse treatment, the Family Sexual Abuse Treatment Program. Child abuse reporting procedures: report to local Children's Services Division offices.

Oregon Coalition Against Domestic and Sexual Violence
2336 SE Belmont St, Portland, OR 97214
Information: (503) 239-4486
Contact: Midori Hamilton, Interim Director
DESCRIPTION: Assists programs serving victims of domestic and sexual violence. Provides technical assistance, training, and other support to member programs. Administers federal funds for rape crisis centers.

Oregon State Health Division, Preventive Health Program
1400 SW 5th Ave, Portland, OR 97201
Information: (503) 229-6390
Contact: Ruth Russell, Director
DESCRIPTION: State agency funding rape crisis centers.

PENNSYLVANIA

Greater Philadelphia Chapter, National Committee for Prevention of Child Abuse
1518 Walnut St, No 907, Philadelphia, PA 19102
Information: (215) 735-8060
Contact: Beth McDaid
DESCRIPTION: Chapter of the National Committee for Prevention of Child Abuse.

Lancaster County Chapter, National Committee for Prevention of Child Abuse
607 N Duke St, Lancaster, PA 17602
Information: (717) 299-5511
Contact: Jeffrey M Fried, President
DESCRIPTION: Chapter of the National Committee for Prevention of Child Abuse.

Parents Anonymous of Pennsylvania
2141 N Second St, Harrisburg, PA 17110
Information: (717) 238-0937,
(800) 932-0313 (Childline)
Contact: Carole A Eyler, Program Coordinator
DESCRIPTION: Statewide self-help groups for parents at risk of child abuse. Support groups also offered for adults who were sexually abused as children.

Pennsylvania Coalition Against Domestic Violence
2505 N Front St, Harrisburg, PA 17111
Information: (717) 234-7353,
(800) 932-4632, in PA
Executive Director: Susan Kelly-Dreiss
Contact: Nancy Durborow, Assistant to the Director
DESCRIPTION: State coalition of domestic violence programs.

Pennsylvania Coalition Against Rape
2200 N Third St, Harrisburg, PA 17110
Information: (717) 232-6745
Executive Director: Susan Cameron
Contact: Gail Rawlings, Information Specialist
DESCRIPTION: Statewide coalition of rape crisis programs distributing funds acting as legislative and public relations liaison, providing training, conferences, technical assistance, clearinghouse of information, quarterly newsletter, video materials on the maltreatment of children, brochures, and booklets.

Pennsylvania Department of Public Welfare
PO Box 2675, Health and Welfare Bldg, Harrisburg, PA 17105
Information: (717) 783-7477

Contact: Karen Habel
DESCRIPTION: State agency funding rape crisis centers.

Pennsylvania Department of Public Welfare, Child Line and Abuse Registry
Box 2675, Lanco Lodge, Harrisburg, PA 17105
Information: (800) 932-0313,
(800) 932-0316 TDD, (717) 783-8744 (out-of-state)
Contact: Warren Lewis, Director
DESCRIPTION: State-wide hotline for reporting child abuse.

Western Pennsylvania Committee for Prevention of Child Abuse
572 One Mellon Bank Center, Pittsburgh, PA 15258
Information: (412) 361-8848
Contact: Carmen Anderson
DESCRIPTION: Chapter of the National Committee for Prevention of Child Abuse.

RHODE ISLAND

Rhode Island Committee for Prevention of Child Abuse
c/o Legal Aide Society of Rhode Island, 76 Dorrance St, Providence, RI 02903
Information: (401) 521-0083
Contact: Pamela Messore
DESCRIPTION: Chapter of the National Committee for Prevention of Child Abuse.

Rhode Island Department of Attorney General, Victim Witness Assistance Program
72 Pine St, Providence, RI 02911
Information: (401) 274-4400
Contact: Elaine Rendine, Director
DESCRIPTION: Provides information, support, and referral services for victims of sexual assault/child sexual abuse as their cases travel through the criminal justice system.

Rhode Island Department for Children and Their Families, Child Protective Services
610 Mount Pleasant Ave, Providence, RI 02908
Information: (401) 861-6000, ext 2332
DESCRIPTION: State agency responsible for child abuse reporting. Child abuse reporting procedures: call (800) 742-4453 in-state; (401) 457-4996 out-of-state.

SOUTH CAROLINA

Low Country, South Carolina Chapter, National Committee for Prevention of Child Abuse
c/o Exchange Club Center for Prevention of Child Abuse, 5055 Lackawanna Blvd, North Charleston, SC 29406-4522
Information: (803) 747-1339
Contact: JoAnne Penman, Director

DESCRIPTION: Chapter of the National Committee for Prevention of Child Abuse.

Midlands Chapter, National Committee for Prevention of Child Abuse
c/o Council on Child Abuse and Neglect, 1800 Main St, Ste 2C, Columbia, SC 29201
Information: (803) 733-5430
Executive Director: Jules Riley
DESCRIPTION: Chapter of the National Committee for Prevention of Child Abuse.

Piedmont Chapter, National Committee for Prevention of Child Abuse
301 University Ridge, Ste 5100, Greenville, SC 29601-3671
Information: (803) 240-8590
Executive Director: Russell Smith
DESCRIPTION: Chapter of the National Committee for Prevention of Child Abuse.

South Carolina Department of Corrections, Victim/Witness Office
PO Box 21787, Columbia, SC 29221-1787
Information: (803) 737-9313
Contact: Katherine Reed, Victim/Witness Liaison
DESCRIPTION: Notifies victims/witnesses of an inmate's temporary, provisional, or final release from custody. Cases are sent to SCDC by victim advocates in the 16 judicial circuits.

South Carolina Department of Health and Environmental Control
2600 Bull St, Columbia, SC 29201
Information: (803) 737-7012
Contact: Teresa J Gjennestad, Assistant Director, Office of Primary Care
DESCRIPTION: Provides state and federal funding for organizations proiding direct services for victims of rape and rape prevention/education and community awareness.

South Carolina Department of Social Services, Child Protective and Preventive Services
PO Box 1520, Columbia, SC 29202
Information: (803) 734-5670
Contact: Barry G Dowd, Deputy Commissione; Marguerite Campbell, Social Services Program Director II
DESCRIPTION: Receives and investigates reports, identifies actual and potential occurrences, and implements ameliorative intervention in order to protect and/or prevent abuse, neglect and exploitation of children. Provides Project Halt, a diversion program for incest offenders. Publications: *The Reporter Assistance Series*, a series of booklets geared to different professional groups (clergy, educators, child care workers) on recognizing child abuse and neglect. Child abuse reporting procedures: report to County Departments of Social Services.

South Carolina Department of Youth Services, Victim Assistance Program
PO Box 192, 1701 Main St, Columbia, SC 29202
Information: (803) 253-4050
Contact: Linda J Price, Victim Assistance Coordinator
DESCRIPTION: Services and referrals for victims of juvenile crime.

South Carolina Victims Compensation Fund
PO Box 210009, Columbia, SC 29221-0009
Information: (803) 737-9465
DESCRIPTION: Administers financial compensation to eligible crime victims.

SOUTH DAKOTA

Rapid City Area Child Protection Council
PO Box 2440, Rapid City, SD 57701
Information: (605) 394-2434
Contact: Linda Andeerson, President
DESCRIPTION: Chapter of the National Committee for Prevention of Child Abuse.

South Dakota Coalition Against Domestic Violence and Sexual Assault
PO Box 375, Black Hawk, SD 57718
Information: (605) 787-4169
Contact: Carol Maicki, Coordinator
DESCRIPTION: Coalition of sexual assault and domestic violence centers.

South Dakota Department of Social Services, Child Protection Services
700 Governors Dr, Pierre, SD 57501-2291
Information: (605) 773-3227
Contact: Tim Koehn, Program Administrator
DESCRIPTION: State agency responsible for child abuse reporting. Child abuse reporting procedures: report to local social services offices.

TENNESSEE

The Tennessee Coalition Against Sexual Assault
PO Box 120831, Nashville, TN 37212
Information: (615) 259-9055
Contact: Stephanie Duncan, State Coordinator
DESCRIPTION: Network for all of the rape and sexual abuse centers throughout the state. Provides technical assistance with training, public education efforts, and conferences held throughout the year.

Tennessee Commission on Children and Youth
1510 Parkway Towers, Nashville, TN 37122
Information: (615) 741-2633
Contact: Juanita Veasy, Acting Director
DESCRIPTION: Provides information, organization and advocacy activities for service providers and advocates, and policy- and lawmakers. Has two regional committees on child sexual abuse.

Tennessee Committee for Prevention of Child Abuse
346 21st Ave N, Nashville, TN 37203
Information: (615) 327-0982, (615) 321-3181
Executive Director: Dave Morison
DESCRIPTION: Chapter of the National Committee for Prevention of Child Abuse.

Tennessee Department of Health and Environment
100 9th Ave N, Nashville, TN 37219-5405
Information: (615) 741-7308
Contact: Jeanece Seals
DESCRIPTION: State agency funding rape crisis centers.

Tennessee Department of Human Services
400 Deaderick St, Nashville, TN 37219
Information: (615) 741-5927
Contact: Patricia Overton, Child Protective Services Director
DESCRIPTION: Investigates referrals of neglect and abuse, including sexual abuse, of children and provides services to strengthen families. Sponsors State Child Sexual Abuse Task Force. Child abuse reporting procedures: report to County Departments of Human Services.

TEXAS

Parents Anonymous of Texas, Inc
1112 W Ben White, No 325, Austin, TX 78704
Information: (512) 440-8666, (800) 554-2323 (TX Heartline)
Executive Director: Deborah Phillips
Contact: Sharon Blackwell, Assistant Director
DESCRIPTION: Works with abusive and at-risk parents to prevent and/or treat child abuse, including sexual abuse. The Texas Heartline is a statewide 24-hour toll-free service, for those experiencing crisis or stress related to their relationship with their children or for victims of child abuse and/or neglect. The PAPPA Project works with those who are incarcerated for child abuse.

Texas Association Against Sexual Assault
PO Box 20512, Houston, TX 77225-0512
Contact: Sherry Abbott, President
DESCRIPTION: State organization providing assistance to local rape crisis centers in the state.

Texas Coalition for the Prevention of Child Abuse
6504 Bridgepoint Pkwy, No 306, Austin, TX 78730
Information: (512) 346-4376
Contact: Wendell Teltow, Director

DESCRIPTION: Goal is to prevent all forms of child abuse by supporting local coalitions, training volunteers, and providing programs for the public. State chapter of the National Committee for Prevention of Child Abuse.

Texas Crime Victim Compensation
105 W Riverside, Ste 220, Austin, TX 78704
Information: (512) 472-7814
Contact: Jerry Belcher
DESCRIPTION: Provides financial assistance for victims of crime, including payment for counseling.

Texas Department of Health, Sexual Assault Prevention and Crisis Services
110 W 49th St, Ste 528, Austin, TX 78756-3199
Information: (512) 458-7550
Contact: Ann J Robison, Program Administrator
DESCRIPTION: Federal and state funding to Texas sexual assault centers. Sexual assault awareness week, resource library, legislative testimony, technical assistance, and workshops on managing sexual assault centers.

Texas Department of Human Services, Child Protective Services Abuse Hotline
PO Box 2960 (530-W), Austin, TX 78769
Information: (512) 450-3360, (800) 252-5400 in TX
Contact: Janess Sheets, Director, Abuse Hotline
DESCRIPTION: 24-hour hotline number for receipt of reports alleging abuse or neglect of children, elderly, and disabled individuals.

UTAH

Utah Commission on Criminal and Juvenile Justice
101 Utah State Capitol, Salt Lake City, UT 84114
Information: (801) 538-1031
Executive Director: Mark Jones
Contact: Richard Oldroyd, Director of Research
DESCRIPTION: Administers VOCA funds for the state among other responsibilities, some of which go to rape crisis centers.

Utah Committee for Prevention of Child Abuse
40 E South Temple, No 395, Salt Lake City, UT 84111
Information: (801) 532-3404
Executive Director: Tia Davis
DESCRIPTION: Chapter of the National Committee for Prevention of Child Abuse.

Utah Division of Family Services
120 N 200 W, Salt Lake City, UT 84103
Information: (801) 538-4100
DESCRIPTION: State agency responsible for child abuse reporting. Child abuse reporting requirements: report to Division of Family Services district offices.

VERMONT

Vermont Office of the Attorney General, Child Protection Unit
109 State St, Montpelier, VT 05602
Information: (802) 828-3171
Contact: Linda Purdy, Assistant Attorney General, Henrietta Jordan, Social Services Consultant
DESCRIPTION: Investigates and prosecutes criminal cases involving child abuse with special emphasis on child sexual abuse.

Parents Anonymous of Vermont
PO Box 829, 104 Main St, Montpelier, VT 05602
Information: (802) 229-5724
Executive Director: Linda Johnson
DESCRIPTION: Support groups for parents who abuse or are at risk of abusing their children. Vermont Chapter of the National Committee for Prevention of Child Abuse.

Vermont Department of Health
1193 North Ave, Burlington, VT 05402
Information: (802) 863-7330
Contact: Shevonne Shuman, Sexual Assault Prevention Director
DESCRIPTION: Training and consultation for law enforcement, medical and social services professionals and rape crisis advocates. Development of community education written materials and PSAs and legislative advocacy.

Vermont Network Against Domestic Violence and Sexual Assault
PO Box 405, Montpelier, VT 05602
Information: (802) 223-1302
Contact: Dianne Maughan, Coordinator
DESCRIPTION: Statewide association of groups whose primary goal is working to end all violence and abuse against women and children. Facilitates cooperation, resource sharing, planning, and mutual problem-solving, and raises public awareness and promotes effective public education.

Vermont Social and Rehabilitation Services/Social Services
103 S Main St, Osgood Bldg, Waterbury, VT 05676
Information: (802) 241-2131
Contact: Ann Pugh, Chief of Community Based Treatment Services
DESCRIPTION: Handles the reports and investigation of child abuse, including but not limited to child sexual abuse. Child abuse reporting procedures: call (800) 356-6552; or report to district offices.

VIRGINIA

SCAN—Stop Child Abuse Now
2222 W Main St, Richmond, VA 23220
Information: (804) 359-0014
Executive Director: Barbara Rawn
DESCRIPTION: Chapter of the National Committee for Prevention of Child Abuse.

VAASA (Virginians Aligned Against Sexual Assault)
PO Box 87, Ivy, VA 22945
Information: (804) 979-9002
Contact: Pat Groot
DESCRIPTION: State coalition/association against sexual assault.

Virginia Department of Social Services, Bureau of Child Welfare Services
8007 Discovery Dr, Blair Bldg, Richmond, VA 23229-8699
Information: (804) 662-9081
Contact: Rita Katzman
DESCRIPTION: State agency responsible for child abuse reporting. Child abuse reporting procedures: call (800) 552-7096 in-state; (804) 281-9081 out-of-state.

Virginia Division of Health Education
109 Governor St, Rm 515, Richmond, VA 23219
Information: (804) 786-3551
Contact: Ramona Schaeffer
DESCRIPTION: State agency funding rape crisis centers.

WASHINGTON

Washington Association of Child Abuse Councils
PO Box 9602, Seattle, WA 98109
Information: (206) 624-4307
Contact: Carol Mason, Director
DESCRIPTION: Chapter of the National Committee for Prevention of Child Abuse.

Washington Coalition of Sexual Assault Programs
110 E Fifth St, Ste 214, Olympia, WA 98501
Information: (206) 754-7583
Executive Director: Beverley Emery
DESCRIPTION: Statewide network of rape crisis centers. Services provided to these programs, law enforcement agencies, hospitals, child protective services, and schools are education, training of professionals, public awareness, technical assistance, information and referral, consultation, support, advocacy, and representation of victim needs.

Washington Department of Labor and Industries, Crime Victims Section
925 Plum St, HC-720, Olympia, WA 98504-0631
Information: (206) 753-6318
Contact: Richard Ervin, Program Supervisor, CVS

DESCRIPTION: Administers the state victim compensation program. Victims of sexual assault and child sexual abuse are among those eligible for compensation.

Washington Department of Social and Health Services, Division of Children and Family Services
Mailstop OB41, State Office Bldg 2, Olympia, WA 98504
Information: (206) 753-0253
Contact: Richard Winters
DESCRIPTION: State agency responsible for child abuse reporting. Child abuse reporting procedures: call (800) 562-5624; or contact local Social and Health Services offices.

Washington Department of Social and Health Services, Victims of Sexual Assault Program
Mailstop OB41, State Office Bldg 2, Olympia, WA 98504-0095
Information: (206) 586-8254
Contact: Lois Loontjens, Program Manager
DESCRIPTION: Funding for rape crisis programs and state-wide coalition.

WEST VIRGINIA

West Virginia Coalition Against Domestic Violence
PO Box 85, Sutton, WV 26601
Information: (304) 765-2250
Contact: Sue Julian, Diane Reese, Coordinators
DESCRIPTION: Central service agency for domestic violence programs throughout the state. The central service office provides technical assistance, coordinates statewide community education and awareness, facilitates training and workshop sessions, publishes a statewide newsletter, collects statistics, and develops resources.

West Virginia Committee for Prevention of Child Abuse
PO Box 2611, Charleston, WV 25329
Information: (304) 344-5437
Executive Director: Charlotte Flanagan
DESCRIPTION: Chapter of the National Committee for Prevention of Child Abuse.

West Virginia Court of Claims, Crime Victims Compensation Fund
State Capitol Bldg, Rm 6, Charleston, WV 25305
Information: (304) 348-3471
Contact: Becky A O'Fiesh, Deputy Clerk
DESCRIPTION: Innocent victims of crime apply for compensation from the Crime Victims Fund to pay their economic losses resulting from crime: medical and dental bills, work loss, etc. (whatever expenses are NOT covered by another source, such as insurance).

West Virginia Department of Human Services
Capitol Complex, Bldg Six, Rm 850, Charleston, WV 25305
Information: (304) 348-7980
Contact: Diane Crump, Social Services Contract Consultant
DESCRIPTION: State agency administering federal and state funds for statewide programs providing services for victims of sexual assault and child sexual abuse. The Department also provides services for victims directly with social work staff. Child abuse reporting procedures: call (800) 352-6313.

West Virginia Foundation for Rape Information and Services, Inc
c/o Barbara Rice, 2803 4th St, Moundsville, WV 26041
Information: (304) 234-1783
Contact: Barbara Rice, Management Consultant
DESCRIPTION: Serves as the conduit of rape block grant funding for the state. Member agencies receive a quarterly informational newsletter, meet quarterly for networking and program sharing, and collectively serve as advocates and service providers for sexual assault victims and their families.

WISCONSIN

Wisconsin Bureau for Children, Youth and Families, Protective Services
Box 7851, Madison, WI 53707
Information: (608) 267-2245
Contact: Jan Breidel
DESCRIPTION: State agency responsible for child abuse reporting. Child abuse reporting procedures: contact County Social Services offices.

Wisconsin Coalition Against Sexual Assault
1051 Williamson St, No 202, Madison, WI 53703
Information: (608) 257-1516
Contact: Catherine Ratte, Education Coordinato, Peggy Elath, Policy Development Coordinator
DESCRIPTION: State coalition of organizations and individuals committed to ensuring competent and caring services to survivors of sexual violence, while working to end sexual violence against women and children.

Wisconsin Committee for Prevention and Treatment of Child Abuse and Neglect, Inc
1045 E Dayton St, Rm 202D, Madison, WI 53703
Information: (608) 256-3374
Contact: Sally Casper, Director
DESCRIPTION: Chapter of the National Committee for Prevention of Child Abuse.

Wisconsin Department of Health and Social Services, Division of Community Health
PO Box 309, Madison, WI 53709-0309
Information: (608) 267-5114
Contact: Mike Vaughn
DESCRIPTION: Administration of federal funds distributed to the Wisconsin Coalition Against Sexual Assault.

Wisconsin Office of Justice Assistance
30 W Mifflin St, No 330, Madison, WI 53703
Information: (608) 266-3323
Executive Director: Ted Meekma
DESCRIPTION: State planning agency. Publishes annual *Sexual Assaults in Wisconsin*, a statistical analysis of annual data.

WYOMING

Wyoming Attorney General's Office, Crime Victims Compensation
123 Capitol Bldg, Cheyenne, WY 82002
Information: (307) 777-5990
Contact: Sylvia Bagdonas, Program Manager
DESCRIPTION: Provides reimbursement of expenses for victims of crime for the following: medical, dental, hospital, counseling and therapy, childcare replacement, and earnings loss.

Wyoming Committee for Prevention of Child Abuse
942 Shoshoni, Cheyenne, WY 82009
Information: (307) 634-7242
Contact: Toni Thomson, President
DESCRIPTION: Chapter of the National Committee for Prevention of Child Abuse.

Wyoming Division of Community Programs, State Office on Family Violence and Sexual Assault
355 Hathaway Bldg, Cheyenne, WY 82002-0710
Information: (307) 777-6086
Contact: Lisa Brabo, Program Manager
DESCRIPTION: Contracts with agencies to provide direct services to victims of family violence and sexual assault.

Wyoming Division of Public Assistance and Social Services
2300 Capitol Ave, Hathaway Bldg, Cheyenne, WY 82002-0071
Information: (307) 777-6095
Contact: Julia E Robinson, Administrator, Robert T Landes, Social Service Consultant
DESCRIPTION: State agency which provides child protective services. Child abuse reporting procedures: contact County Departments of Public Assistance and Social Services.

APPENDIX B: NATIONAL ORGANIZATIONS AND RESOURCES

ADULT SURVIVORS OF INCEST/CHILD SEXUAL ABUSE

*Adults Molested as Children United (AMACU)
P.O. Box 952, San Jose, CA 95108
Information: (408) 280-5055
DESCRIPTION: Self-help groups for women and men who were sexually abused as children. Affiliated with Parents United, a nationwide support organization for incestuous families. Offers adult survivors the opportunity to directly confront and work with perpetrators.

*Echoes Network Inc
P.O. Box 86231, Portland, OR 97206
Information: (503) 293-2800
Contact: Wendy Ann Wood, MA, Director
DESCRIPTION: Nationwide networking agency which connects mental health and lay professionals with survivors of sexual abuse who are seeking guidance along the healing path.
PUBLICATIONS: *Triumph Over Darkness: Understanding and Healing the Trauma of Childhood Sexual Abuse* (by Wendy Ann Wood and Leslie Ann Hutton, $12.95).

Incest Resources, Inc
46 Pleasant St, Cambridge, MA 02139
Information: (617) 492-1818 Voice/TDD for training calls only
DESCRIPTION: Provides educational and resource materials for adult survivors of incest and professionals working with survivors; provides training and consultation by survivor-therapists.
PUBLICATIONS: A literature collection of treatment, self-help, and resource articles for survivor education and professional training ($1.50-$3.50 each); *Incest: What to Think, What to Say, What to Do*, a training/sensitivity handbook for those working with adult survivors of incest or incestuous families ($10.95); "I.R.*obics," a packet of therapeutic dance/movement materials for survivors, including a 60-minute tape of music thematically related to incest and the process of healing ($12.95); "Inside Out," a packet of therapeutic bodywork materials for survivors, including a 45-minute tape of step-by-step exercises for body recovery ($14.95); "Picture This!," a packet of rage release materials for survivors, including a written series of exercises designed to direct survivor anger where it belongs ($16.95).

Incest Survivor Information Exchange
P.O. Box 3399, New Haven, CT 06515
Contact: Angela Swanger, Vice President/Networker
DESCRIPTION: *Incest Survivor Information Exchange* (ISIE) is a national newsletter which publishes contributions from men and women who have survived incest—articles, poems, art work. Each newsletter features a theme, such as Healing, Parenting, Humor, Surviving the Holidays. Provides a forum for and recognition of the collective wisdom, voice and expertise of incest survivors.

*Incest Survivors Anonymous
P.O. Box 5613 (World Service Office), Long Beach, CA 90805-0613
Information: (213) 428-5599
Contact: Erin May, Founder/Director/Survivor
DESCRIPTION: Self-help groups for incest survivors based on the twelve-step program of Alcoholics Anonymous. Contact for information about local groups.
PUBLICATIONS: *The Nightmare of Incest* ($4); *I.S.A. Talks to Friends, Survivors, Professionals* ($4); Newcomer Packet ($4).

Incest Survivors Resource Network International (ISRNI)
P.O. Box 911, Hicksville, NY 11802
Information: (516) 935-3031
Contact: Anne-Marie Eriksson, President
DESCRIPTION: Quaker-affiliated educational resource dedicated to primary prevention; functions mainly by participation in committees and conferences of national and international organizations. Concerned with intergenerational transmission of verbal and physical violence, especially regarding overt and emotional incest. Urges the development of Parents United chapters and recognizes the importance of Adult Children twelve-step fellowships.

"Looking Up"
P.O. Box K, Augusta, ME 04330
Information: (207) 626-3402
Contact: Gayle Woodsum, Executive Director
DESCRIPTION: Provides services to victims and survivors of incest.
PUBLICATIONS: *The "Looking Up" Times*, a literary publication written entirely by survivors of incest; *The Survivor Resource Chronicle*, newsletter of practical information, news and a resource listing.

*P.L.E.A. (Prevention, Leadership, Education, Assistance)
P.O. Box 59045, Norwalk, CA 90652
Information: (213) 863-4824
Contact: Hank Estrada, Founder/Director
DESCRIPTION: Represents non-offending adult male survivors of childhood emotional, physical and sexual abuse. Developing as a national clearinghouse for resources to agencies, organizations and therapists. Provides referrals on

---

NOTE: Asterisks denote organizations that provide referrals to programs and services for victims/survivors and those which have local chapters.

request. Supports men in breaking silence to prevent/stop further emotional traumas.
PUBLICATIONS: *The Survivors*, quarterly newsletter of resources, training events, and survivor-written letters of recovery and courage ($10).

Survivors Newsletter Collective
c/o Women's Center, 46 Pleasant St, Cambridge, MA 02139
Information: (617) 354-8807
Contact: Marsha Zaharsky
DESCRIPTION: Provides a forum for women survivors of child sexual abuse to share their pain and healing journeys.
PUBLICATIONS: *For Crying Out Loud*, a newsletter by and for survivors.

*Survivors of Incest Anonymous
P.O. Box 21817, Baltimore, MD 21222-6817
Information: (301) 282-3400
DESCRIPTION: 12-step recovery program, modeled after Alcoholics Anonymous, for survivors of child sexual abuse. Incest defined very broadly; men and women in groups. Contact for information on local groups.
PUBLICATIONS: Wide variety of pamphlets and brochures; *Passing It On*, monthly newsletter.

*VOICES in Action, Inc. (Victims Of Incest Can Emerge Survivors)
P.O. Box 148309, Chicago, IL 60614
Information: (312) 327-1500
Contact: Valerie Heller, (914) 225-9413, President-Elect
DESCRIPTION: National network of adult survivors of incest and child sexual abuse. Helps adult victims of child sexual abuse become survivors. Provides referrals to self-help groups, therapists, and local programs for incest survivors; generates public awareness of the prevalance of incest and child sexual abuse; provides education about its impact and the ways in which it can be prevented or stopped. Provides survival kits for members and a bimonthly newsletter; offers Special Interest Groups; and holds annual conferences all around the United States. Special Interest Groups are for survivors who have experienced a particular type of abuse; for example, victims of multiple abusers, or survivors of child pornography, or victims of female perpetrators, or of ritualistic abuse, etc. The groups operate through letter writing; a coordinator collects and copies the letters and sends them to the other members of the group.

CHILD SEXUAL/PHYSICAL ABUSE

American Academy of Pediatrics
141 NW Point Blvd, P.O. Box 927, Elk Grove Village, IL 60009-0927
Information: (312) 228-5005
Contact: Richard Krugman, MD, Chairman, Provisional Committee on Child Abuse and Neglect
DESCRIPTION: Organization of pediatricians dedicated to the health, safety, and well-being of infants, children, and adolescents. Through its Provisional Committee on Child Abuse and Neglect, the Academy offers guidance to pediatricians and the public in the area of child physical/sexual abuse.

APSAC (American Professional Society on the Abuse of Children)
969 E 60th St, Chicago, IL 60637
Information: (312) 702-9419
Contact: Theresa Reid, Executive Director
DESCRIPTION: Multidisciplinary professional society dedicated to improving the lives of maltreated children and their families. Supports research, education, and advocacy that enhance efforts to respond to abused children, those who abuse them, and the conditions associated with their abuse. Members may participate in the development of practice guidelines. To date, three Task Forces have been formed to establish national interdisciplinary guidelines on Medical Evaluation, Evaluation of Suspected Sexual Abuse in Young Children, and the Assessment and Treatment of Perpetrators of Child Sexual Abuse.
PUBLICATIONS: *The Advisor*, quarterly newsletter for sharing conference, research, and practice information.

Believe the Children
P.O. Box 1358, Manhattan Beach, CA 90254
Information: (213) 379-3514
Contact: Leslie Floberg, President
DESCRIPTION: Provides educational information and support to professionals, parents and concerned citizens regarding sexual and ritualistic exploitation of children.
PUBLICATIONS: *Believe the Children Newsletter*, quarterly.

The Chesapeake Institute
1114 Georgia Ave, Wheaton, MD 20902
Information: (301) 949-5000
Contact: Linda Blick; Thomas Berg, Executive Directors
DESCRIPTION: The Chesapeake Institute is solely devoted to the study, treatment, research and public awareness of child sexual victimization. Provides clinical services, including evaluation and treatment for sexually abused children, adult and juvenile sex offenders, non-offending spouses, non-abused siblings and adults who were victimized as children. Has group treatment program for professionals who work in the field of sexual abuse and who were, themselves, sexually abused as children. Provides information and referral to professionals; houses the National Training Center; and maintains a resource library.

Clearinghouse on Child Abuse and Neglect Information
P.O. Box 1182, Washington, DC 20013
Information: (703) 821-2086
Contact: Anita P Cowan, Project Director
DESCRIPTION: NCCAN is responsible for conducting research; collecting, analyzing, and disseminating information; providing assistance to states and communities in developing programs and activities related to the prevention, identification, and treatment of child abuse and neglect; and coordinating Federal efforts to combat child maltreatment. The Clearinghouse was established primarily as a major resource center for professionals concerned with child maltreatment issues. Maintains a database of documents, audiovisual materials, service programs, excerpts of State statutes, and ongoing research projects concerning child abuse and neglect. The database (File 64) is directly available to the public through DIALOG Information Services, Inc.
PUBLICATIONS: Catalog of brochures, reports, directories, and bibliographies.

International Society for Prevention of Child Abuse and Neglect
1205 Oneida St, Denver, CO 80220
Information: (303) 321-3963
Contact: Kim Oates, President
DESCRIPTION: The Society was founded to prevent cruelty to children in every nation where cruelty occurs in the form of abuse, neglect or exploitation and thus to enable the children of the world to develop physically, mentally and socially in a healthy and normal manner. Its aims are to provide a forum for discussions and for sharing of knowledge and experience through holding congresses at approximately two-year intervals and through publication of *Child Abuse & Neglect: The International Journal*.

*KEEPSAFE National Network for Professionals Encountering the Abused Preschool Aged Child
1205 Oneida St, Denver, CO 80220
Information: (303) 321-3963
Contact: Lindsay R March, MA, KEEPSAFE National Network Coordinator
DESCRIPTION: Serves as a communication link for professionals encountering abused preschoolers.
PUBLICATIONS: *Kaleidoscope*, semi-annual newsletter with articles on therapeutic strategies.

Kempe National Center for the Prevention and Treatment of Child Abuse and Neglect
1205 Oneida, Denver, CO 80220
Information: (303) 321-3963
Contact: Gail Ryan, Information Specialist
DESCRIPTION: Clinically-based research and demonstration center, providing evaluation and treatment for families with physical/sexual abuse or other parent-child interaction problems;

evaluation and group treatment for preschool and latency age children who have been sexually abused by someone outside the family, therapeutic preschool for ages 2 1/2 to 6; treatment for young sex offenders, ages 10-15. Sponsors the Adolescent Perpetrator Network and the KEEPSAFE Network for those working with preschool-aged abused children. The National Child Abuse and Neglect Clinical Resource Center maintains a resource library, rents nonprint materials, sells publications, provides information searches on request for a modest fee, presents workshops and seminars on demand, provides program and case consultation, presents professional education at conferences, and sponsors the Annual Child Abuse and Neglect Symposium.
PUBLICATIONS: Distributes a wide variety of books on child physical and sexual abuse, as listed in Publications Catalog; also has Audio-Visual Catalog of nonprint media available for rent from the Kempe Center.

National Adoption Center
1218 Chestnut St, Philadelphia, PA 19107
Information: (215) 925-0200,
1-800-TO-ADOPT
Contact: Julie Rosenzweig, Project Coordinator
DESCRIPTION: Provides public information on adoption and brings together special needs children waiting for adoption with families approved for adoption. Currently involved with a new 2-year project to train adoption workers and mental health therapists about the needs of sexually abused children who are adopted.
PUBLICATIONS: *National Adoption Center Newsletter.*

*National Child Abuse Hotline/Childhelp, USA
P.O. Box 630, Hollywood, CA 90028
Information: (800) 422-4453 (hotline),
(213) 465-4016
Contact: Daniel Sexton, Hotline Director
DESCRIPTION: Childhelp, USA focuses on prevention, treatment, research, and public education on child abuse. Programs include residential treatment of physically and sexually abused children (ages 2-12) and the National Child Abuse Hotline. The toll-free national hotline is staffed by professional counselors who handle crisis situations and then offer referrals and options. The service is anonymous.

National Children's Advocacy Center
106 Lincoln St, Huntsville, AL 35801
Information: (205) 533-9546
DESCRIPTION: Provides treatment for sexually abused children and their families. Serves as a national resource and training center. Sponsors annual National Symposium on Child Sexual Abuse.

National Council on Family Relations, Family Resources Database (FRD)
1910 W County Rd B, Ste 147, St Paul, MN 55113
Information: (612) 633-6933
Contact: Dr Rocky Ralebipi, Director
DESCRIPTION: The Family Resources Database is the only internationally available core collection of literature and other resources pertaining to the family. Child sexual abuse is one of the major areas covered in the database. This information involves journal articles, research reports, books, audiovisual materials and a list of experts in the area. Also includes listings of programs and other services.
PUBLICATIONS: *Journal of Marriage and the Family*, quarterly ($50); *Family Relations*, quarterly ($45); *Inventory of Marriage and Family Literature*, annual ($66.95); various annotated bibliographies ($5.45 each).

National Resource Center on Child Abuse and Neglect
9725 E Hampden Ave, Denver, CO 80231
Information: (303) 695-0811,
(800) 2AS-KAHA (telephone referral service)
DESCRIPTION: The American Association for Protecting Children works to support effective child protective services in communities. Provides training, technical assistance, and evaluation; conducts research; legislative advocacy to protect children. National Resource Center on Child Abuse and Neglect has informational materials and a national database of official reports of child neglect and abuse.

National Resource Center on Child Sexual Abuse
11141 Georgia Ave, Ste 310, Wheaton, MD 20902
Information: (301) 949-5000,
(800) 543-7006 (for professionals)
Contact: David W Lloyd, Project Director
DESCRIPTION: Information, training, and technical assistance center for all professionals working in the field of child sexual abuse. Provides information services via toll-free number to professionals; identifies successful and newly developing treatment models, particularly child-focused multidisciplinary approaches.
PUBLICATIONS: *Roundtable*, quarterly publication with articles, information updates, research, book reviews, column on the personal side of working with child abuse cases, and a focus on the child's perspective.

*Parents Anonymous
6733 S Sepulveda Blvd #270, Los Angeles, CA 90045
Information: (213) 410-9732
DESCRIPTION: Local and state chapters nationwide provide mutual help for parents who are, or fear they may be, physically and/or emotionally abusing their children. Some chapters have groups for adults who were abused (including sexual abuse) as children. Local groups use professional sponsors. Contact headquarters for information on local groups.

*Parents United/Daughters & Sons United
P.O. Box 952, San Jose, CA 95108
Information: (408) 280-5055
Contact: Henry Giarretto, Executive Director
DESCRIPTION: Self-help groups for incestuous families—offending and non-offending parents and children's groups. Groups also available for young offenders and Adults Molested as Children United. Community-based professional therapy is available in conjunction with the self-help groups. Contact headquarters to locate local chapters nationwide. Sponsoring agency, the Institute for the Community as Extended Family, provides training for professionals in the treatment of child sexual abuse.
PUBLICATIONS: *Integrated Treatment of Child Sexual Abuse* by Henry Giarretto ($27); materials on the Child Sexual Abuse Treatment Program; booklets pertaining to Parents United, Daughters & Sons United, and Adults Molested as Children United. Videotapes on treatment approaches of the Child/Sexual Abuse Treatment Program ($75 each).

Sources for Anatomically Correct Dolls:

Eymann Products, Inc.
3645 Scarsdale Court
Sacramento, CA 95827
(916) 362-8503, (916) 365-7771

Janon Inc.
4340 W Saint Joseph Hwy
Grand Ledge, MI 48837
(517) 627-5135

KIDSRIGHTS
3700 Progress Blvd
Mount Dora, FL 32757
(800) 892-5437, (904) 483-1100

Migima Designs, Inc.
1243 1/2 Oak St.
Eugene, OR 97401
(800) 826-9579, (503) 343-3400

Uniquity
P.O. Box 6
Galt, CA 95632
(209) 745-2111

CRIMINAL JUSTICE

Boston University School of Law, Program on Law and Child Maltreatment
765 Commonwealth Ave, Boston, MA 02215
Information: (617) 353-2904
Contact: David N Sandberg, Director
DESCRIPTION: Research, policy development and preparation of articles and books on child sexual

abuse and other types of abuse and neglect. Development of seminar on children's law.

Institute for the Study of Sexual Assault
403 Ashbury St, San Francisco, CA 94116
Information: (415) 861-2048
Contact: Judith Musick, Executive Director
DESCRIPTION: Research, technical assistance, and networking assistance to attorneys who represent sexual assault victims in civil litigation. Sponsors training programs and maintains speakers bureau. Maintains national database of civil sexual assault suits and legal pleadings; resource library.
PUBLICATIONS: *Civil Sexual Assault Cases: Judgments and Settlements* (2 vols); *Institutional Liability for Sexual Assault: An Annotated Bibliography of Selected Legal Cases*; *Legal Handbook for Rape Crisis Centers*.

Juvenile Justice Clearinghouse/NCJRS
Box 6000, Rockville, MD 20850
Information: (800) 638-8736,
(301) 251-5500 in the DC metropolitan area
Contact: Cynthia Diehm, Manager
DESCRIPTION: The Clearinghouse is an information service on juvenile justice matters, including child sexual abuse and exploitation, for juvenile justice practitioners, policy-makers, and researchers. Access to the database of the National Criminal Justice Reference Service containing over 100,000 documents. Prepackaged and custom searches containing document summaries are available on a modest cost recovery basis.
PUBLICATIONS: The National Criminal Justice Reference Service produces and distributes *NIJ Reports*, a bi-monthly publication of the National Institute of Justice.

National Association of Counsel for Children
1205 Oneida St, Denver, CO 80220
Information: (303) 321-3963
Contact: Laura F Michaels, Associate Director
DESCRIPTION: Membership organization for practitioners from varied professions who work with children affected by legal proceedings. Provides resources and training on legal issues for professionals working to protect children.
PUBLICATIONS: *The Guardian*, quarterly newsletter summarizing recent court decisions concerning children; books on child advocacy available.

National Center for the Prosecution of Child Abuse
1033 N Faifax St, Ste 200, Alexandria, VA 22314
Information: (703) 739-0321
Contact: Patricia A Toth, Director
DESCRIPTION: Serves as a resource for prosecutors handling child abuse cases by providing training, technical assistance and networking for prosecutors nationwide.
PUBLICATIONS: *Investigation and Prosecution of Child Abuse* ($25).

National College of District Attorneys
University of Houston Law Center, Houston, TX 77204-6380
Information: (713) 747-6232
Contact: Lauren Wilson, Assistant Director of Training
DESCRIPTION: The National College of District Attorneys provides training programs and materials on the prosecution of sexual abuse and assault, as well as other training programs.

National Council of Juvenile and Family Court Judges
P.O. Box 8970, Reno, NV 89507
Information: (702) 784-6012
Contact: Jeffrey A Kuhn, Esq, Project Director, Abuse/Neglect Department
DESCRIPTION: Continuing education of the judiciary and court professionals on juvenile justice and family law issues; support and assistance for juvenile and family courts; publication of case decisions and scholarly articles in this area.
PUBLICATIONS: *Juvenile and Family Law Digest*, monthly ($120); *Child Sexual Abuse Training Program*, including program manual, glossary of terms and 5 videotapes (judicial response to sexual cases, videotaping child victims, intake interview, child credibility, treatment and sentencing).

National Criminal Justice Reference Service
National Institute of Justice, Washington, DC 20531
Information: (800) 851-3420
Contact: Richard S Rosenthal, Director
DESCRIPTION: Maintains database of over 100,000 criminal justice information source,s including such issues as AIDS, law enforcement, drugs and crime, courts, corrections, juvenile justice, statistics, criminology and victims. Prepackaged and custom searches containing document summaries are available for modest cost.
PUBLICATIONS: *NIJ Reports*, bimonthly magazine focusing on current issues and providing summaries of latest publications; *Crime File* videotapes, presenting panel discussions by criminal justice experts on 32 critical issues facing the public.

National Legal Resource Center for Child Advocacy and Protection
1800 M St, NW, Washington, DC 20036
Information: (202) 331-2250
Contact: Howard Davidson, Director
DESCRIPTION: Provides training, program evaluation, and agency consultation related to child physical and sexual abuse and the law. Also publishes material and does nationally-relevant legal research. Sponsors annual conferences on children and the law.
PUBLICATIONS: Catalog of books available. *ABA Juvenile and Child Welfare Law Reporter*, monthly ($145).

National Sheriffs' Association
1450 Duke St, Alexandria, VA 22314
Information: (800) 424-7827,
(703) 836-7827
Contact: Anna A Laszlo, Director, Research and Development
DESCRIPTION: Law enforcement membership organization. Provides training and technical assistance in the areas of physical and sexual abuse, including sexual abuse in out-of-home settings and ritualistic abuse.
PUBLICATIONS: *The National Sheriff*, bimonthly (with membership fee $25/annual); *Roll-Call* (newsletter); *NSA Legal Bulletin*.

DOMESTIC VIOLENCE (See also organizations listed under SEXUAL ASSAULT AND MARITAL RAPE)

Center for Policy Research
1720 Emerson St, Denver, CO 80218
Information: (303) 837-1555
Contact: Nancy Thoennes; Jessica Pearson, Co-Directors
DESCRIPTION: Conducts research in a variety of socio-legal areas, including child abuse and domestic violence. Data from prior NCCAN-funded research available on the experiences of 1000 abused/neglected children and sexual abuse allegations arising in contested custody-visitation cases.

Clearinghouse on Family Violence Information
P.O. Box 1182, Washington, DC 20013
Information: (703) 821-2086
Contact: Caroline Hughes, Project Director
DESCRIPTION: Provides information services to practitioners and researchers who are working to prevent family violence and to provide assistance to victims.
PUBLICATIONS: Offers publications and bibliographies covering topical issues such as spouse abuse, abuse of the elderly, and legislative solutions to the problems of family violence. Fact sheets listing resources and national organizations will also be available. Maintains database on family violence and accepts information requests for searches of the database.

Family Violence Prevention Project, Task Force on Families in Crisis
P.O. Box 120495, Nashville, TN 37212
Information: (615) 383-4575
Contact: Tottie Ellis, Executive Director
DESCRIPTION: Task force working on prevention, intervention and public awareness of domestic violence, primarily spouse abuse. Have established community task forces in five sites (Honolulu, HI; Seattle, WA;

Essex, VT; Bossier City, LA; and Indianapolis, IN) as model projects to encourage local citizens and community agencies to develop and implement plans for preventing spouse abuse.
PUBLICATIONS: *Directory of Private Services* (1988, $3); brochures on statistics, myth/truth, and basic information on spouse abuse (free); *Spouse Abuse Awareness: Guidelines for Religious Workers* ($3).

National Clearinghouse on Battered Women's Self-Defense
910 S 49th St, Philadelphia, PA 19143
Information: (215) 724-3270
Contact: Barbara Hart; Sue Osthoff, Directors
DESCRIPTION: Sponsors the Self-Defense Advocacy Project which provides assistance and support to battered women who have killed or assaulted their abusers while attempting to protect themselves against brutal and life-threatening violence. The project gathers, organizes, and disseminates the accumulated knowledge to assist battered women defendants and their support teams develop appropriate defense strategies. The project also provides assistance to individual battered women defendants and materials to contribute to changes in social policy affecting battered women defendants.

National Coalition Against Domestic Violence
P.O. Box 15127, Washington, DC 20003-0127
Information: (202) 293-8860; 1-800-333-7233 (24-hour hotline)
Contact: Diana Onley-Campbell, Program Coordinator
DESCRIPTION: National membership organization for battered women's programs and for concerned individuals and other concerned organizations. Provides a clearinghouse for information and technical assistance; legislative advocacy; sponsors annual conferences.
PUBLICATIONS: *The Voice*, quarterly newsletter; national directory of shelters and services for battered women and their children; *Naming the Violence: Speaking Out about Lesbian Battering*; *Manual for Economic Self-Sufficiency*.

National Council on Child Abuse and Family Violence
1155 Connecticut Ave, NW, Ste 300, Washington, DC 20036
Information: (800) 222-2000
Contact: Mary-Ellen Rood, Vice President
DESCRIPTION: Organization involved with prevention and treatment of intergenerational family violence: child, spousal and elder abuse. Provides referrals to victims of all forms of abuse and provides written materials concerning prevention, programs, technical assistance and professional development.
PUBLICATIONS: *Inforum*, newsletter, published 2-3 times a year.

National Women's Health Network
1325 6 St, NW, LLB, Washington, DC 20005
Information: (202) 347-1140
Contact: Cynthia Pearson, Program Director
DESCRIPTION: Has a committee on domestic violence, headed by Louise Armstrong. Maintains an information clearinghouse on a variety of topics pertinent for women's lifetime wellness. ($5 charge per topic).
PUBLICATIONS: *The Network News*, bimonthly ($25)

University of New Hampshire, Family Research Laboratory
128 Horton Social Science Ctr, Durham, NH 03824
Information: (603) 862-1888
Contact: David Finkelhor, Co-Director
DESCRIPTION: Research on all aspects of the family, including domestic violence, child sexual abuse, and sexual assault. Occasionally sponsors conferences.

OFFENDER TREATMENT

Association for the Behavioral Treatment of Sexual Abusers
P.O. Box 66028, Portland, OR 97266
Information: (503) 279-8144
Contact: Sharon Siebert, Executive Secretary
DESCRIPTION: Organization of professionals working with sex offenders. Provides training on the treatment of sex offenders; offers instruction on the use of the penile plethysmograph; maintains speakers bureau; provides technical assistance.
PUBLICATIONS: *ABTSA Professional Forum*, quarterly.

*Molesters Anonymous
1269 N 'E' St, San Bernardino, CA 92405
Information: (714) 355-1100
Contact: Jerry M Goffman, Ph.D., Founder/Coordinator
DESCRIPTION: Provides self-help counseling at no charge to non-family-affiliated pedophiles. Program materials available to assist in developing community-based Molesters Anonymous groups and Batterers Anonymous groups. Contact headquarters for information on local groups.
PUBLICATIONS: *Molesters Anonymous Program Package*, including manuals for the sponsor and the group leader and 50 handbooks for participants ($100)

*National Adolescent Perpetrator Network
1205 Oneida, Denver, CO 80220
Information: (303) 321-3963
Contact: Gail Ryan, Facilitator
DESCRIPTION: Network of practitioners who are working with juvenile sex offenders through the schools, the courts, law enforcement, corrections, and treatment facilities. Functions as communication and information network; sponsors annual national meetings; cosponsors national training conferences.
PUBLICATIONS: *Interchange*, semiannual newsletter; *Report of the Task Force on Juvenile Sexual Offending*, including identification, prosecution, disposition, assessment, treatment, follow-up and research (80 pages $5 from the National Council of Juvenile and Family Court Judges).

*Safer Society Program and Press
Box 24-B, Orwell, VT 05760
Information: (802) 897-7541
Contact: Fay Honey Knopp, Director
DESCRIPTION: Research/advocacy center, providing referrals for treatment for victims/survivors of sexual assault and sexual abuse and referrals for adult and juvenile offender treatment. Publishes a variety of books on adult and juvenile sex offenders (including female abusers), young male victims of sexual assault, and adults molested as children. Maintains a database and provides nationwide listings of residential treatment programs for adolescent sex offenders accepting out-of-state clients and nationwide listings for juvenile and adult sex offender treatment providers and programs.

PREVENTION

Association of Sexual Abuse Prevention Professionals (ASAP)
P.O. Box 421, Kalamazoo, MI 49005
Information: (616) 349-9072
Contact: Carol A Plummer, Coordinator
DESCRIPTION: Membership organization providing for networking among sexual abuse prevention programs in the US and Canada; planning and education about quality sexual abuse prevention programming, including setting national/international standards. Sponsors annual national "Imagine" conference, focusing entirely on child sexual abuse prevention.

Big Brothers/Big Sisters of America (BB/BSA)
230 N 13th St, Philadelphia, PA 19107
Information: (215) 567-7000
Contact: Lynda A Long, Program Assistant, Standards and Agency Services
DESCRIPTION: Development of EMPOWER, a child sexual abuse education and prevention program.

Committee for Children
172 20th Ave, Seattle, WA 98122
Information: (206) 322-5050
Contact: Joan Cole Duffell, Director of Marketing/Community Education
DESCRIPTION: Organization whose mission

is the prevention of the exploitation of children. Provides educational curricula, videos, training and broadcast media for teaching children skills to recognize, resist and report abuse. The CFC's nationally acclaimed personal safety curriculum, *Talking About Touching*, and award-winning video programs are used in tens of thousands of classrooms throughout North America and in seven foreign countries. The CFC's new skill training curriculum to prevent violent and aggressive behavior in students is entitled *Second Step*.
PUBLICATIONS: *Talking About Touching*, personal safety programs for preschool through junior high; *Yes You Can Say No* and *Choices*, film and video programs for elementary and high school; *Second Step* violence prevention programs for elementary schools; teacher training videotapes on prevention and identification of child sexual abuse; *Prevention Notes*, quarterly newsletter.

Fighting Woman News
P.O. Box 1459, Grand Central Station, New York, NY 10163
Information: (212) 228-0900
Contact: Valerie Eads, Editor
DESCRIPTION: Provides a communications medium for women in martial arts, self-defense, and combative sports. There is considerable overlap between their target group and those who provide survivor support services.
PUBLICATIONS: *Fighting Woman News*, quarterly ($10)

KIDSRIGHTS
3700 Progress Blvd, Mount Dora, FL 32757
Information: (800) 892-5437; (904) 483-1100
Contact: Stephanie Carder, Customer Service
DESCRIPTION: Comprehensive source for the purchase of education and prevention materials in the fields of child abuse, molestation, teen rape and suicide, drug abuse and related childrens' rights subjects. Distributes books for children, adolescents, parents, and professionals; curricula and workbooks; audiotapes, films and videotapes; and anatomically-correct dolls.

Migima Designs, Inc
1243 1/2 Oak St, Eugene, OR 97401
Information: (503) 343-3440; 1-800-826-9579
Contact: Marcia Morgan; Virginia Friedemann, Executive Directors
DESCRIPTION: Specialists in designing products and programs for sexual assault/abuse identification, assessment, investigation, treatment and prevention. Main products include anatomical dolls, books, tapes, audiovisual programs, puppets, Teaching Torso for AIDS education. Also provides consulting, training seminars and curriculum development.

*National Assault Prevention Center (NAPC)
P.O. Box 02005, Columbus, OH 43202
Information: (614) 291-2540
Contact: Sally Dine-Fitch, Program Director
DESCRIPTION: Mission is to prevent inter-personal violence (verbal, physical and sexual assault) through curricula development, research, evaluation, public education and training. NAPC has two divisions: CAP—The Child Assault Prevention Project with primary prevention services for: pre-school-aged children; elementary-aged children; children with mental retardation (mild and moderate levels); children with multiple handicaps; children with hearing impairments; adolescents (TeenCAP); as well as parents, teachers and professionals. APT—The Assault Prevention Training Project with primary prevention services for adult women and men with mental retardation (mild, moderate, severe); adults receiving mental health services; and older adults. The Child Assault Prevention Training Center of Northern California is located in Oakland, California. Currently, there are over 200 CAP Projects nationwide. Contact the National Assault Prevention Center for up-to-date information about CAP Projects in your locale.
PUBLICATIONS: *Strategies for Free Children: A Leader's Guide to Child Assault Prevention* (1983); *Empowerment: A Systems Approach to Preventing Assaults Against People with Mental Retardation and/or Developmental Disabilities* (322 pages, 1987, $22.95); *Preventing Assaults Against Older Adults* (8 pages, 1987); *ReCAP*, quarterly newsletter ($12).

National Committee for Prevention of Child abuse
332 S Michigan Ave, Ste 950, Chicago, IL 60604
Information: (312) 663-3520
Contact: Joy Byers
DESCRIPTION: Organization with chapters in all 50 states, with the goal of educating the public about all types of child abuse and its prevention.
PUBLICATIONS: Brochures, pamphlets and booklets for parents, children and teachers on child abuse, child sexual abuse, and parenting concerns. Spanish-language materials available.

National Women's Martial Arts Federation
c/o Ms Bobbi Snyder, 1724 Sillview Dr, Pittsburgh, PA 15243
DESCRIPTION: Organization of women martial artists whose purpose is to share skills and resources, to promote excellence in the martial arts, and to encourage the widest range of women to train in the spirit of building individual and collective strength.

SAFE (Sexual Abuse Free Environment) Institute
1225 NW Murray Rd, Ste 214, Portland, OR 97229
Information: (503) 644-6600
DESCRIPTION: Publishes *Preventing Sexual Abuse*, a quarterly newsletter ($25), featuring in-depth examinations of current issues regarding prevention; a profile of a leading person working in prevention; resource reviews of films, books, pamphlets and curricula; articles highlighting prevention programs; and information on conferences and workshops.

PROSTITUTION AND PORNOGRAPHY

Feminists Fighting Pornography
P.O. Box 6731, New York, NY 10128
Information: (212) 410-5182
Contact: Page Mellish, Executive Director
DESCRIPTION: Influences federal legislation through legislative advocacy; community education through a slide show with speaker. Maintains statistics on violence against women and information on pornography.
PUBLICATIONS: *The Backlash Times*, annual news service on pornography ($15).

National Center for Missing and Exploited Children
1835 K St NW, Ste 600, Washington, DC 20006
Information: (202) 634-9821, 1-800-843-5678 (hotline)
Contact: Carla Branch, Communications Manager
DESCRIPTION: Clearinghouse and resource center providing a hotline, technical assistance and training for law-enforcement and social services pertaining to missing children (runaways, parental kidnapping, nonfamily abductions) and victims of sexual exploitation (child pornography and child prostitution).
PUBLICATIONS: Brochures for parents and books for professionals (*Child Pornography and Prostitution; Children Traumatized in Sex Rings; Interviewing Child Victims of Sexual Exploitation*).

Organizing Against Pornography: A Resource Center for Education and Action
734 E Lake St, Minneapolis, MN 55407
Information: (612) 822-1476
Contact: Jeanne Barkey, Executive Director
DESCRIPTION: Provides training for human services professionals, community awareness/education, and youth education on the victimization of pornography to promote community response and to prevent continued victimization. Provides speakers and a slide show to community groups; maintains resource library; distributes informational materials; and conducts public relations campaigns. Currently developing a slideshow on video and

accompanying teacher/student materials to educate young people about pornography and the media, especially preventing victimization and developing skills in recognizing and evaluating messages protrayed about sexuality, responsibility, sex role stereotypes and violence.
PUBLICATIONS: *Pornography: A Practice of Inequality*, an educational package with 70 slides of explicit pornographic materials with narrative that describes the slide in a way that re-educates what the viewer sees, Facilitator's Guide and audience handouts; *Pornography and Civil Rights: A New Day for Women's Equality* by Andrea Dworkin and Catherine MacKinnon, a guidebook on pornography and the Minneapolis antipornography civil-rights ordinance ($5); *OAP News Update*, quarterly newsletter ($15).

WHISPER (Women Hurt in Systems of Prostitution Engaged in Revolt)
P.O. Box 8719, Lake Street Station, Minneapolis, MN 55408
Information: (612) 644-6301
Contact: Sarah Wynter, Director
DESCRIPTION: National organization of survivors of prostitution working in conjunction with direct service providers to provide training to sexual assault professionals and women's advocates to insure effective service provision to women/girls attempting to escape prostitution. Majority of prostitutes have been victims of child sexual abuse and are sexually abused, raped & battered routinely in prostitution.
PUBLICATIONS: *Prostitution: A Matter of Violence Against Women*, 50 minute video (documentary style) which juxtaposes mainstream media images of prostitutes with interviews of women who have survived prostitution speaking about the reality of their lives and strategies for change ($150.00 plus postage).

Women Against Pornography
358 W 47th St, New York City, NY 10036
Information: (212) 307-5055
Contact: Norma Ramos, Chair of Steering Committee
DESCRIPTION: Provides community education: slide shows for school groups (ages 10-16) and presentations for college classes, community and church groups; lecture bureau which provides speakers for lectures, public forums, conferences, and community meetings; feminist-guided tours of the Times Square Pornography District in New York City; sponsors conferences and speakouts; bibliographies and literature packets available on a wide range of topics pertaining to pornography, including advertising, child sexual abuse, sexual violence in the media, social science research, and aggression.
PUBLICATIONS: *Pornography, Sexual Abuse, and Inequality*, 45 slides and script for adults, focusing on violence in pornographic materials; *Sex Roles for Sale*, slide program for youth ages 10-16, focusing on pornographic images and ideas in mainstream advertising; *Roles in Rock*, slide show on pornographic and anti-woman images and messages in rock videos. Slide shows include scripts and lesson plans and classroom assignments for youth-oriented programs. (Purchase cost: $200 each; rental: $100 deposit each, with money returned when slides are returned). Publishes *Women Against Pornography Newsreport*, semi-annual newsletter ($15).

SEXUAL ASSAULT AND MARITAL RAPE

Antisocial and Violent Behavior Branch, National Institute of Mental Health
5600 Fishers Lane, Rm 18-105, Rockville, MD 20857
Information: (301) 433-3728
Contact: Ecford S Voit, Jr, Assistant Chief
DESCRIPTION: Provides grants for research on antisocial behavior, individual violent behavior, rape and sexual assault, and law and mental health interactions. The objectives of the program are to improve understanding of mental health issues and needs in the above areas and to assist in the development of improved strategies for evaluation, prevention, management, and treatment. The scope of the Branch's program encompasses biological science, behavioral science, psychosocial science, and empirical legal studies.

Association of American Colleges, Project on the Status and Education of Women
1818 R St NW, Washington, DC 20009
Information: (202) 387-1300
Contact: Bernice Sandler, Director of Project
DESCRIPTION: Publishes materials on sexual harassment, date/acquaintance rape and campus gang rape, as well as other issues affecting women on campus; also does speaking on these issues.
PUBLICATIONS: *In Case of Sexual Harassment* ($2); Sexual Harassment Packet ($5); *"Friends" Raping Friends* ($2); *Campus Gang Rape: Party Games?* ($5).

Center for the Prevention of Sexual and Domestic Violence
1914 N 34th St, Ste 105, Seattle, WA 98103
Information: (206) 634-1903
Contact: Marie M Fortune, Executive Director; Sandra Barone, Administrative Associate
DESCRIPTION: Educational resource for the religious community on sexual and domestic violence issues through publications, films and workshops. Trains and equips clergy and lay leadership with the knowledge and skills they need to minister to their own communities and to assist survivors with the healing process. Development of sexual abuse prevention curricula to be used in religious education for 9-to-12-year-olds and for teenagers. Provides training and publications on professional ethics for clergy to prevent sexual harassment and abuse.
PUBLICATIONS: *Working Together to Prevent Sexual and Domestic Violence*, quarterly newsletter ($12); *Sexual Violence: The Unmentionable Sin-An Ethical and Pastoral Perspective*, by Marie Fortune ($9.95); *Sexual Abuse Prevention: A Study for Teenagers*, a curriculum by Marie Fortune ($3.95); *Keeping the Faith: Questions and Answers for the Abused Woman*, by Marie Fortune ($3.00); *The Speaking Profits Us: Violence in the Lives of Women of Color* ($5.00); *A Commentary on Religious Issues in Family Violence*, Christian and Jewish perspectives ($1.00); *Clergy Ethics: Sexual Abuse Within The Pastoral Relationship*, packet of 6 articles ($10).

Feminist Alliance Against Rape
P.O. Box 21033, Washington, DC 20009
Information: (202) 686-9463
Contact: Laureen France, Production Coordinator
DESCRIPTION: Provides a forum for discussion and development of strategies to end sexual assault and other types of violence against women through the quarterly publication *Aegis: Magazine on Ending Violence Against Women* ($10.50). Publishes news, theoretical articles, law reform efforts and legal cases, and information on self-defense.

The Feminist Institute Clearinghouse
P.O. Box 30563, Bethesda, MD 20814
Information: (301) 951-9040
DESCRIPTION: The Feminist Institute promotes social change to enhance the quality of life for women, including public education and outreach on feminist issues and research and policy development that brings together feminist researchers and activists. The Clearinghouse distributes materials on sexual assault, domestic violence, sexual harassment, rape prevention, and self-defense, among other issues.
PUBLICATIONS: Publications brochure available.

Journal of Interpersonal Violence
2111 W Hillcrest Dr, Newbury Park, CA 91320
Information: (805) 499-0721
PUBLICATIONS: *Journal of Interpersonal Violence*, quarterly ($30), focuses on the study and treatment of victims and perpetrators of physical and sexual violence.

Marital Rape Collection, University of Illinois Library
1408 W Gregory, Rm 415, Urbana, IL 61801
Information: (217) 244-1024

Contact: Beth Stafford, Women's Studies/Wid Librarian
DESCRIPTION: Provides maintenance and perservation of a unique collection on marital rape; provides reference service based on the collection and distribution (sale) of reference materials from the collection.

National Clearinghouse on Marital and Date Rape
2325 Oak St, Berkeley, CA 94708
Information: (415) 548-1770
Contact: Laura X
DESCRIPTION: Provides information and referral, consultation, reference and research services on marital rape and acquaintance/date rape. Also available for speaking engagements.

National Coalition Against Sexual Assault (NCASA)
2428 Ontario Road NW, Washington, DC 20009
Information: (202) 493-7165
Contact: Nancy Fride Biele, President
DESCRIPTION: Organization of rape crisis centers, women's shelters, other groups and concerned individuals committed to ending sexual violence and promoting services for the survivors of these crimes. Caucuses for lesbians, victims/survivors, and women of color. Six Regional Representatives serve on the Board and act as liaisons to the different geographic areas of the U.S.
PUBLICATIONS: *NCASA News*, quarterly newsletter; national directory of rape crisis programs.

Response to the Victimization of Women and Children, Inc
Box 2462, Ada, OK 74820
Information: (405) 332-1250, (301) 951-0039
Contact: Jane Roberts Chapman
DESCRIPTION: Publishes *Response to the Victimization of Women and Children*, quarterly journal ($30), which includes substantive articles on sexual assault and domestic violence, research reviews, information on current books and conferences. (Formerly published by Center for Women Policy Studies.) Produces *The Response Data Base* ($30, in DOS), a database of indexes and annotated listings of *Response* journal articles, books and other sources on domestic violence and sexual assault.

*Stop Abuse by Counselors
P.O. Box 68292, Seattle, WA 98168
Information: (206) 243-2723
Contact: Shirley J Siegel, Coordinator
DESCRIPTION: Organization actively working to prevent abuse by mental health practitioners (including sexual abuse) through the promotion of community education, research projects, remedial legislation, and improved professional standards. Maintains a supportive network for people who have been abused by mental health practitioners. Provides computer printout of informational articles and other resources ($5) and an organizing kit for a group similar to STOP ABC ($10).

SUBSTANCE ABUSE

*Alcoholics Anonymous (AA)
P.O. Box 459, Grand Central Station, New York, NY 10163
Information: (212) 686-1100
DESCRIPTION: Also sponsors Al-Anon, self-help groups for children and family members of alcoholics; also adults who were raised by alcoholic parents. Use phone book or telephone information to find a group in your local area.

Children of Alcoholics Foundation, Inc
200 Park Ave, 31st Fl, New York, NY 10166
Information: (212) 351-2680
Contact: Donna Bauer, Administrator
DESCRIPTION: Educates and informs the public about the prevalence of family alcoholism and how it affects the family; develops programs to break the cycle of family alcoholism. Provides informational materials and referrals to self-help groups and programs for children of alcoholics nationwide.
PUBLICATIONS: Research and literature reviews, directory of programs, and brochures geared to children and adults. Two videotapes: *Focus: Children of Alcoholics* (8 mins., $20), which identifies needed research; *Trying to Find Normal* (17 mins., $295), interview with artist Eric Fischl, who talks about the effects of his mother's alcoholism on his art and his life.

National Association for Children of Alcoholics (NACoA)
31582 Coast Highway, Ste B, South Laguna, CA 92677
Information: (714) 499-3889
Contact: Holly Lenz, Office Manager
DESCRIPTION: Provides public and professional information, referral and training to address issues relevant to children of alcoholics. Sponsors annual conventions.
PUBLICATIONS: Variety of publications geared to children in alcoholic families, adult children from alcoholic families, and professionals working with alcoholic families; some Spanish-language materials; *The Network*, quarterly newsletter (included in membership).

National Clearinghouse for Alcohol and Drug Information
P.O. Box 2345, Rockville, MD 20852
Information: (301) 468-2600 , Mary L Millar , Outreach Services Manager
DESCRIPTION: Information component of the U.S. Office for Substance Abuse Prevention (Dept. of Health and Human Services). Distributes government documents, has resource collection, and maintains a database on alcohol and drug abuse. Database searching available to the public on request (inquire about possible cost).
PUBLICATIONS: Catalog of materials available.

THERAPY, COUNSELING AND SELF-HELP GROUPS

American Association for Marriage and Family Therapy
1717 K St, NW, #407, Washington, DC 20006
Information: (202) 429-1825
DESCRIPTION: Professional association of marriage and family therapists. Has accredited training centers throughout the U.S.
PUBLICATIONS: Quarterly journal and bimonthly newspaper.

American Association of Sex Educators, Counselors and Therapists
11 Dupont Circle, NW, Ste 220, Washington, DC 20036
Information: (202) 462-1171
DESCRIPTION: Professional association for sex educators, sex counselors, and sex therapists; provides training; sponsors research; assists in development of human relations and sex education curricula; develops parent education programs. Certification program for sex educators and sex therapists.
PUBLICATIONS: Quarterly newsletter; semiannual journal; *National Register of Certified Sex Educators and Sex Therapists*, published annually.

Family Service America
11700 W Lake Park Dr, Milwaukee, WI 53224
Information: (414) 359-2111
Contact: Geneva B Johnson, President/CEO
DESCRIPTION: Assists its membership network through assistance, information clearinghouse on family issues, research reports, and national and regional conferences and seminars. Member agencies offer counseling to individuals and families under stress and sometimes additional supportive services to victims of abuse and therapy for perpetrators.
PUBLICATIONS: Books, workshop models, videotapes and audiotapes for the family practice field; *Social Casework*, journal published 10/year ($29).

International Association for Dissociation and Multiple Personality
1653 W Congress Pkwy, Chicago, IL 60612
Information: (312) 942-5000
DESCRIPTION: Focus on treating multiple personality disorders, many of whom are survivors of ritualistic abuse.

Many Voices
P.O. Box 2639, Cincinnati, OH 45201-2639
PUBLICATIONS: *Many Voices* ($30) is a bimonthly, self-help publication for persons with multiple personality

disorder and/or dissociative disorders. Each issue features contributions by survivors, art, cartoons, book reviews, and a therapist's page—all designed to provide positive ideas, creative situations, and words of hope.

*National Self-Help Clearinghouse
33 W 42nd St, New York, NY 10036
Information: (212) 840-1259
DESCRIPTION: Facilitates access to self-help groups and increases the awareness of the importance of material support through training of community and professional groups; research; publications; and information and referral services to self-help groups and regional self-help clearinghouses.
PUBLICATIONS: *Self-Help Reporter*, quarterly ($10); publications on organizing self-help groups and clearinghouses ($5-$6).

*Re-Evaluation Counseling Community
719 2nd Ave, N, Seattle, WA 98109
Contact: Harvey Jackins, International Reference Person
DESCRIPTION: Write to find out if there is a co-counseling group in your area.

*Self-Help Clearinghouse
St Clares-Riverside Medical Center, Pocono Rd, Denville, NJ 07834
Information: (201) 625-7101
Contact: Ed Madara
DESCRIPTION: Helps people to find and form self-help groups nationwide.
PUBLICATIONS: *The Self-Help Sourcebook* (1988, $8), a national directory of self-help groups for a broad range of stressful life situations (addictions, illnesses, parenting concerns, etc.)

The Society for Traumatic Stress Studies
P.O. Box 1564, Lancaster, PA 17603-1564
Information: (717) 396-8877
Contact: Scott Sheely, Executive Director
DESCRIPTION: Membership organization of persons treating or studying victims/survivors of life-threatening experiences.
PUBLICATIONS: *Journal of Traumatic Stress*, quarterly (included in membership); *Traumatic Strees Points*, newsletter; videotapes ($25 each) and audiotapes ($10 each) of conference programs.

VICTIM ASSISTANCE

*National Association for Crime Victims Rights
P.O. Box 16161, Portland, OR 97216-0161
Information: (503) 252-9012
Contact: Raymond L Montee, Executive Director/Founder
DESCRIPTION: Computerized database and referral services for crime victims to all state Crime Victims Compensation Programs and local self-help groups.

National Organization for Victim Assistance (NOVA)
717 D St, NW, 2nd Fl, Washington, DC 20004
Information: (202) 393-6682
Contact: Michaela Cohan, Librarian
DESCRIPTION: Organization for victim and witness practitioners and programs, criminal justice professionals and agencies, mental health professionals, former victims/survivors, and others committed to victim rights. Activities include national advocacy for victim interests in state legislature and the U.S. Congress; direct services to victims of crime through telephone counselors; technical assistance and training, including annual conferences and the HORIZONS Training Institutes (four 40-hour institutes on care skills for victim assistance practitioners). Sponsors annual Victim Rights Week with support materials and posters available.
PUBLICATIONS: *NOVA Newsletter*, monthly (included in membership); books and manuals and information packets available.

*National Victim Center
307 W 7th St, Ste 1001, Fort Worth, TX 76102
Information: (817) 877-3355
Contact: Linda Barker-Lowrance, Director of Program Services
DESCRIPTION: Provides information and referral services to crime victims. Maintains a database of 5,500 organizations nationwide that serve victims of rape, sexual abuse, domestic violence, drunk driving and survivors of homicide, as well as police and prosecutors victim assistance units. Crime Victims Litigation Project serves as a resource for attorneys handling lawsuits on behalf of crime victims.
PUBLICATIONS: *Networks*, quarterly newsletter (free); *Exemplary Programs Bulletin*, semiannual (free); publications and curricula for establishing and implementing a victim assistance program.

*National Victim Center
11 Park Pl, Ste 1601, New York, NY 10007
Information: (212) 732-8662
Contact: Sherry Price, Regional Director
DESCRIPTION: Provides information and referrals to crime victims; promotes victims' rights and services. Regional office of the National Victim Center in Ft. Worth, TX.

*National Victims Resource Center
Box 6000, Rockville, MD 20850
Information: (301) 251-5525
Contact: Janet Goss; Stephanie Greenhouse, Victim Specialists
DESCRIPTION: National clearinghouse for victim information. Individuals can receive free publications and reading lists, borrow hard-to-find publications, and purchase videotapes. In addition, NVRC provides referrals; compiles federal victimization statistics; and maintains a resource library and a database of victim-related books, articles, and nonprint media. Database searches available to the public on request.
PUBLICATIONS: Catalog available on research reports, information packets, bibliographies, and videotapes.

The Spiritual Dimension in Victim Services
P.O. Box 163304, Sacramento, CA 95816
Information: (916) 446-7202
Contact: David W Delaplane, Executive Director
DESCRIPTION: Educational organization created for the specific purpose of educating clergy and the religious community on the extent and nature of victimization (including sexual abuse) in our society and methods by which congregations can respond to this need. Provides individual consultation, congregational sessions and clergy training workshops and conferences.

ALPHABETICAL LISTING OF FACILITIES IN AGENCY PROFILES

AAP (Associates in Adolescent Psychiatry) Mental Health Resources, Skokie, IL
Abate One, Newport, VT
The Abilene Rape Crisis Center, Abilene, TX
Abuse and Rape Crisis Center, Towanda, PA
Abuse and Rape Crisis Center, Grand Forks, ND
Abuse Counseling and Treatment, Inc (ACT), Fort Myers, FL
Abused Adult Resource Center, Bismarck, ND
Abused and Battered Humans, Inc, Craig, CO
Abused Deaf Women's Advocacy Services, Seattle, WA
Abused Persons Outreach Center, Valley City, ND
Abused Persons Program, Prince Frederick, MD
Abused Women's Advocacy Project, Auburn, ME
ACCESS (Assault Care Center Extending Shelter and Support), Ames, IA
ACESS-York, Inc, York, PA
Action Associates, Inc, Clinton, OK
Ada County Sheriff's Department—Victim-Witness Unit, Boise, ID
Ada County Victim/Witness Assistance Unit, Boise, ID
Adams County State's Attorney—Victim Witness Program, Quincy, IL
ADAPT, Indianapolis, IN
Addison County Women in Crisis, Bristol, VT
Adirondack Prevention Services, Inc, Glens Falls, NY
Adolescent, Children, Family and Group Counseling, Lexington, KY
Adolescent Special Offenders Program, Roseburg, OR
Adult and Child Mental Health Center, Inc, Indianapolis, IN
Adult Probation Department—Victim Services Unit, Philadelphia, PA
Advocate Program for Victims of Sexual Assault, Buffalo, NY
Advocates Against Domestic Assault, Trinidad, CO
Advocates for Children, Auburn, ME
Advocates for Peaceful Homes, Selmer, TN
Advocates for Victims of Assault, Frisco, CO
Advocates for Victims of Violence (AVV), Valdez, AK
Advocates for Victims Program/Advocates for Sexually Abused Children, Homestead, FL
Advocates for Victims Program/Advocates for Sexually Abused Children, Miami, FL
Advocates of Lake County, Inc, Leadville, CO
Affirmations: A Center for Psychotherapy and Growth, Columbus, OH
AFTER/Parents United of Sacramento, Sacramento, CA
AID Center, Sioux City, IA
Aid for Victims of Crime, Saint Louis, MO
Aid to Victims of Domestic Abuse, Houston, TX
Aid to Victims of Sexual Assault, Hickory, NC
Aid to Women in Abuse and Rape Emergencies (AWARE), Hardwick, VT
Aid to Women Victims of Violence, Cortland, NY
Aiding Women from Abuse and Rape Emergencies (AWARE), Juneau, AK
Aiken Coalition to Assist Abused Persons, Aiken, SC
Aiken County Sheriff's Department—Victim Assistance Program, Aiken, SC
Alachua County Rape and Crime Victim Advocate Program, Gainesville, FL

Alameda County District Attorney—Victim Witness Assistance Division, Oakland, CA
Alamo Area Rape Crisis Center, San Antonio, TX
Albany County Rape Crisis Center, Albany, NY
Albuquerque Counseling Cooperative, Inc, Albuquerque, NM
Albuquerque Rape Crisis Center, Albuquerque, NM
Alcoholism Center for Women—Prevention Services, Los Angeles, CA
Alexandra House, Inc, Circle Pines, MN
AlexAndria Associates, Ontario, OR
ALIVE, Inc, Steubenville, OH
Allegheny County Center for Victims of Violent Crime, Pittsburgh, PA
Alle-Kiski Area Hope Center, Pittsburgh, PA
Alliance on Family Violence, Bakersfield, CA
Alpatha Healing Center, Columbus, OH
Alpha Counseling, Bloomington, IN
Alpine Women's Center, Alpine, TX
Alternative House, Lowell, MA
Alternatives Counseling Center, Inc, Binghamton, NY
Alternatives for Abused Adults, Staunton, VA
Alternatives for Battered Women, Rochester, NY
Alternatives for Battered Women, Inc, Loveland, CO
Alternatives for People, Northridge, CA
Alternatives for Women, Honolulu, HI
Alternatives for Women/Advocacy, Resources and Education (AW/ARE), Sharon, PA
Alternatives to Domestic Violence, Hackensack, NJ
Alternatives to Fear, Seattle, WA
Alternatives to Violence, Colville, WA
Alternatives to Violence of Palouse, Inc, Moscow, ID
Ambulatory Pediatrics, Springfield, MA
American Indian Community House, New York, NY
American Red Cross Family Violence Team, Great Lakes Service Center, Great Lakes, IL
Amherst County Victim/Witness Program, Amherst, VA
AMICAE, Inc: Hotline for Rape and Battering, Fredonia, NY
Anchorage Center for Families, Anchorage, AK
Anderson Pastoral Counseling and Consultation Service, Anderson, SC
Anne Arundel County Sexual Assault Crisis Center, Annapolis, MD
The Susan B Anthony Project, Inc, Torrington, CT
The Apostles' House Parent Aide Program, Newark, NJ
ARADIA Counseling for Women, Boston, MA
Arctic Women in Crisis (AWIC), Barrow, AK
Ardsley Karate Club, Ardlsey, PA
Area Services for Battered Women, Inc, Ada, OK
Arizona Center for Psychotherapy, Prescott, AZ
Arkansas Children's Hospital/Department of Pediatrics Program for Children at Risk, Little Rock, AR
The Arlington Community Temporary Shelter, Arlington, VA
Arlington Counseling Associates, Arlington Heights, IL
Arlington Handicapped Association, Arlington, TX
Arlington Police Department—Community Services Section, Arlington, TX
The Arlington Psychological Center, Jacksonville, FL
Army Community Service, Fort Sill, OK

Army Family Advocacy Program, Fort McPherson, GA
Army Family Advocacy Program (FAP), Fort Lewis, WA
Artesia Counseling and Resource Center, Artesia, NM
Arts for Living, Minneapolis, MN
ASAAC—Center for Adults Sexually Abused as Children, New York, NY
ASAP—Advocates for Sexually Assaulted People, Bainbridge Island, WA
Asheville Police Department—Victim Assistance Program, Asheville, NC
Asian Community Mental Health Services, Oakland, CA
Asian Counseling and Referral Service, Seattle, WA
Asian Family Services, New York, NY
Asian Program, Oakland, CA
Asian-American Mental Health Services—Japanese Unit, New York, NY
Assault Crisis Center, Ann Arbor, MI
Assault Recovery Associates, Benton Harbor, MI
Assault Recovery Associates, Saint Joseph, MI
Assault Survivors Assistance Program, Wheat Ridge, CO
Assessment and Treatment Services, Bozeman, MT
Assessment and Treatment Services and Montana Psychotherapy, Helena, MT
Associated Counseling Services, Harker Heights, TX
Associated Psychotherapists, Herrin, IL
Associates for Growth, Culpeper, VA
Associates for Psychotherapy and Education, Colorado Springs, CO
Associates for Psychotherapy and Education, Pueblo, CO
Associates for Sexual Abuse Treatment, Arvada, CO
Associates in Counseling, Federal Way, WA
Associates in Mental Health, Muncie, IN
Associates in Psychotherapy, Tucson, AZ
Association House of Chicago, Chicago, IL
Assumption College Student Development Center, Worcester, MA
Athens County Prosecutor's Victim Assistance Program, Athens, OH
Athens Rape Crisis Line, Athens, GA
Atlantic Care Medical Center—Rape Crisis Services, Lynn, MA
Atlantic County Office of Victim Witness Advocacy, Mays Landing, NJ
Atlantic County Women's Center, Northfield, NJ
Au Sable Valley Community Mental Health, West Branch, MI
Augusta Area Rape Crisis Center, Augusta, ME
Aurora Community Mental Health Center, Aurora, CO
Austin Child Guidance Center, Austin, TX
Austin Police Department—Victim Services Division, Austin, TX
Austin Psychotherapy Associates, Austin, TX
Austin Rape Crisis Center, Austin, TX
AVAIL, Antigo, WI
The Avalon Center, Inc, Milton, FL
AVOW—Aid to Victims or Witnesses, Olean, NY
Awareness Counseling Services, Thiensville, WI
Baltimore County Department of Social Services—Sexual Abuse Treatment Program, Towson, MD

BANANAS, Child Care Resource and Referral and Parent Support, Oakland, CA
Barnwell County Help Line, Barnwell, SC
Barstow Victim/Witness Center, Barstow, CA
Barton County Attorney's Office—Victim/Witness Program, Great Bend, KS
Bath-Brunswick Rape Crisis Helpline, Inc, Brunswick, ME
Battered Persons' Advocacy, Roseburg, OR
Battered Persons' Crisis Center, Youngstown, OH
Battered Spouse Program of Gaston County, Gastonia, NC
Battered Spouse Project, Jackson, TN
Battered Women, Inc, Crossville, TN
Battered Women's Alternatives, Concord, CA
Battered Women's Resources, Inc, Fitchburg, MA
Battered Women's Services of Hubbard County, Park Rapids, MN
Battered Women's Task Force, Topeka, KS
Battered Women's Task Force, Inc, Colstrip, MT
Bay Area Medical Center, Marinette, WI
Bay Area Sexual Harassment Clinic, San Francisco, CA
Bay Area Women Against Rape, Fremont, CA
Bay Area Women Against Rape, Oakland, CA
Bay County Women's Center, Bay City, MI
Bay Family and Child Center, Panama City, FL
Baytown Area Women's Center, Baytown, TX
Beacon Support Group, Milwaukee, WI
Bear River Mental Health Services, Inc, Logan, UT
Bedford Hills Correctional Facility—Family Violence Program, Bedford Hills, NY
Behavior Therapy and Psychotherapy Center, Burlington, VT
Behavioral and Developmental Pediatrics, Bangor, ME
Behavioral Health Agency of Central Arizona, Casa Grande, AZ
Bellevue Community College—Women's Resource Center, Bellevue, WA
The Bellshire Psychology Group, Lynnwood, WA
Beloit Memorial Hospital, Beloit, WI
Bennington County Victim Advocate, Bennington, VT
Benton County Prosecutor's Office, Kennewick, WA
Benton-Franklin Rape Relief and Sexual Assault Program, Richland, WA
Bergen County Coalition Against Sexual Assault, Hackensack, NJ
Bergen County Prosecutor's Office—Victim/Witness Advocacy, Hackensack, NJ
Bergen County Rape Crisis Center, Hackensack, NJ
Bering Sea Women's Group, Nome, AK
Berks Women in Crisis, Reading, PA
Berrien County Mental Health, Benton Harbor, MI
Beth Israel Hospital—Rape Crisis Intervention Center, Boston, MA
Bethesda Alternative, Inc, Norman, OK
A Better Way, Muncie, IN
BIHA Women in Action, Minneapolis, MN
Billings Rape Task Force, Billings, MT
Bingham Crisis Center, Blackfoot, ID
Anna Bixby Women's Center, Harrisburg, IL
Blackfeet Indian Child Welfare Program, Browning, MT
Blackstone Valley Rape Crisis Team, Inc, Milford, MA
Bladen County Mental Health Center, Elizabethtown, NC
Blanchard and Associates, Sheridan, WY
Boise Hotline, Boise, ID
Boise Valley Chapter of Parents United, Boise, ID
Bolton Refuge House, Inc, Eau Claire, WI
Bonner County Crisis Line, Inc, Sandpoint, ID
Catherine Booth House, Seattle, WA
Dr Geraldine Boozer Rehabilitation Program for Sex Offenders, Hollywood, FL
Border Area Mental Health Services, Inc, Silver City, NM
Boston Area Rape Crisis Center, Cambridge, MA
Boston Women's Health Book Collective, Watertown, MA
Boulder County Rape Crisis Team, Boulder, CO
Boulder County Safehouse, Boulder, CO
Boulder County Sexual Abuse Team, Boulder, CO
Boulder District Attorney's Office—Victim/Witness Assistance Program, Boulder, CO
Bowen Center for Human Services, Warsaw, IN
Boys and Girls Home and Family Services, Sioux City, IA
Bradley-Angle House, Inc, Portland, OR
Braintree Psychological Associates, Braintree, MA
Branch County Coalition Against Domestic Violence, Coldwater, MI
Brandeis Rape and Sexual Assault Hotline, Waltham, MA
Brazos County Rape Crisis Center, Inc, Bryan, TX

Bresler and Dugo, Ltd, Des Plaines, IL
Brevard County Commission Against Sexual Assault, Rockledge, FL
The Bridge, Stanford, CA
The Bridge Children and Family Services, Gilroy, CA
The Bridge Over Troubled Waters, Inc, Pasadena, TX
Bridgeway Counseling Services, Inc, Saint Charles, MO
Bridgework Theater, Inc, Goshen, IN
Bristol Crisis Center, Bristol, VA
Bronx District Attorney's Office—Crime Victim Assistance Unit, Bronx, NY
Bronx Municipal Hospital Center—Jacobi Hospital Pediatric Emergency Room, Bronx, NY
Brooklyn Women's Anti-Rape Exchange, Brooklyn, NY
Rose Brooks Center, Kansas City, MO
Broward County Sexual Assault Treatment Center, Fort Lauderdale, FL
Buncombe County Rape Crisis Center, Inc, Asheville, NC
Butler County Association to Counter Abuse, El Dorado, KS
Butte County Victim Witness Program, Oroville, CA
CAARE Project, Inc, Fort Bragg, CA
Cabell County Child Protection Team, Inc, Huntington, WV
Cabrillo College Rape Prevention Program, Aptos, CA
CADA (Citizens Against Domestic Abuse and Sexual Assault), Oak Harbor, WA
Cairo Women's Shelter, Cairo, IL
Calcasieu Women's Shelter, Lake Charles, LA
Call Care, Inc, Tulsa, OK
Call Someone Concerned, Inc—Sexual Assault Program, Adrian, MI
CALM (Child Abuse Listening and Mediation), Santa Barbara, CA
Cambridge Hospital Victims of Violence Program, Cambridge, MA
Camden County Prosecutor's Office, Camden, NJ
Cameron County District Attorney's Office—Victim Assistance Program, Brownsville, TX
Campbell County Commonwealth's Attorney—Victim Assistance Program, Newport, KY
Campbell County Prosecuting Attorney's Office—Victim/Witness Coordinator, Gillette, WY
Canarsie AWARE, Inc, Brooklyn, NY
Canyon Crisis Center, Mill City, OR
CAPSEA, Inc/Citizens Against Physical Sexual and Emotional Abuse, Inc, Ridgeway, PA
Carbon County Citizens Organized to See Violence Ended (COVE), Rawlins, WY
CARE (County Abuse and Rape Emergency) Services, Chehalis, WA
CARE Rape Crisis Center, Washington, PA
Careline Survivor Advocacy, Athens, OH
Careline Survivor Advocacy, Logan, OH
Careline Survivor Advocacy, McArthur, OH
CARES, Lovell, WY
CARES (Child Abuse Response and Evaluation Services), Portland, OR
Caring House, Iron Mountain, MI
The Caring Place, Inc, Wheeler, IN
Caring Unlimited, Sanford, ME
Carlsbad Battered Families Shelter, Carlsbad, NM
Carlsbad Mental Health Association, Carlsbad, NM
Barbara Carter, MS, Psychologist, Joplin, MO
Carteret County Rape Crisis Program, Morehead City, NC
CASA (Court Appointed Special Advocate), Johnson City, TN
Casa de Esperanza, Saint Paul, MN
Casa de los Ninos, Tucson, AZ
Casa De Yuma, Yuma, AZ
CASA, Inc, Hagerstown, MD
Casa Myrna Vazquez, Inc, Boston, MA
Cass County Victim/Witness Assistance Program, Fargo, ND
Catalyst Women's Advocates, Chico, CA
Catawba Mental Health Center—Lancaster Office, Lancaster, SC
Cathedral Home for Children, Laramie, WY
Catholic Charities, Granite City, IL
Catholic Family Service—Saint Charles District Office, Saint Charles, MO
Catholic Family Services, Enfield, CT
Catholic Social Service—Domestic Violence Program, Council Bluffs, IA
Catholic Social Services, Mobile, AL
Catholic Social Services of Wayne County, Taylor, MI
CAUSES (Child Abuse Unit for Studies, Education and Services), Chicago, IL
CAVA Rape Crisis Center (Citizens Against Violent Acts, Inc), Canton, NY
CAVE—Citizens Against Violent Crime, Columbia, SC

Center Against Domestic Violence, Inc, Flagstaff, AZ
Center Against Rape and Domestic Violence, Corvallis, OR
Center Against Sexual and Domestic Abuse, Superior, WI
Center Against Sexual Assault, Phoenix, AZ
Center Against Sexual Assault (CASA), Peoria, IL
Center for Abuse and Rape Emergencies, Inc, Punta Gorda, FL
Center for Abuse Prevention and Treatment, Inc, Napoleon, OH
Center for Action Against Sexual Assault, Waco, TX
Center for Behavioral Intervention, Beaverton, OR
Center for Child Abuse Prevention Services, Tacoma, WA
Center for Counseling and Development, Summerville, SC
Center for Counseling Services, Brighton, MI
Center for Growth and Change, Brewer, ME
Center for Life Management, Orlando, FL
Center for Living, Phoenix, AZ
The Center for Preventive Psychiatry, Inc, White Plains, NY
Center for Psychological Services, Orange Park, FL
Center for Special Problems, San Francisco, CA
Center for the Pacific-Asian Family, Inc, Los Angeles, CA
Center for Treatment of Sexual Abuse, San Diego, CA
Center for Wellness, Holbrook, MA
Center for Women and Children in Crisis, Inc, Provo, UT
Center for Women in Transition, Holland, MI
Center for Women's Services, Plymouth, NH
Center of Protective Environment, Alamogordo, NM
Center on Rape and Assault (CORA), Butler, PA
Central Baptist Family Services, Elgin, IL
Central Iowa Mental Health Center, Ames, IA
Central Minnesota Sexual Assault Center, Saint Cloud, MN
Central Nebraska Task Force on Domestic Abuse and Sexual Assault Services, Broken Bow, NE
Central Oregon Battering and Rape Alliance (COBRA), Bend, OR
Centre County Victim/Witness Advocate, Bellefonte, PA
Centre County Women's Resource Center, State College, PA
Champlain Valley Victim Services, Burlington, VT
The Changing Woman Counseling and Educational Center, Calumet City, IL
Charity Hospital of Louisiana at New Orleans—Rape Crisis Center, New Orleans, LA
Charleston Area Mental Health Center, Charleston, SC
Charter Counseling Center, Los Alamos, NM
Charter Counseling Center of Beaufort, Beaufort, SC
Chautauqua Offices of Psychotherapy and Evaluation (COPE), DeFuniak Springs, FL
Chelan County Prosecuting Attorney—Victim Witness Unit, Wenatchee, WA
Chelsea Community Counseling Center, Chelsea, MA
Cherokee Counseling and Psychological Association, Woodstock, GA
Chesterfield County Sheriff's Office—Victim-Witness Assistance Program, Chesterfield, VA
Chicago Abused Women Coalition—Greenhouse Shelter, Chicago, IL
Chicago Commission on Women—Safety and Legal System Committee, Chicago, IL
Chicago Counseling and Psychotherapy Center, Chicago, IL
The Chicago Sexual Assault Services Network, Chicago, IL
Child Abuse and Neglect Council, County of Oakland, Inc, Pontiac, MI
Child Abuse and Neglect Interdisciplinary Training Project, Columbia, SC
Child Abuse Council of Sacramento, Inc, Sacramento, CA
Child Abuse Network Center, Tulsa, OK
The Child Abuse Prevention and Education Council of Story County, Ames, IA
Child Abuse Prevention Association, Beaufort, SC
Child Abuse Prevention Council, Kalispell, MT
Child Abuse Prevention Council of Contra Costa County, Inc, Pleasant Hill, CA
Child Abuse Prevention Intervention Education Program, Victorville, CA
Child Abuse Prevention Network, Juniata, NE
Child Abuse Prevention Services, Inc, Shelby, NC
Child Abuse Program, Columbus, OH
Child Abuse Treatment Program, Miami, FL
Child/Adolescent Services, Greenville, SC
Child Advocacy Center, Mobile, AL

Child Advocacy Council, Palo Alto, CA
Child Advocacy Network, Anchorage, AK
Child Advocacy Resource and Education, Inc, Greeley, CO
Child Advocates, Inc, Houston, TX
Child Advocates San Antonio, San Antonio, TX
Child and Adolescent Mental Health Program, New Orleans, LA
Child and Adolescent Psychiatric Clinic, Inc, Buffalo, NY
Child and Adolescent Sexual Abuse Resource Center, San Francisco, CA
Child and Family Advocacy Center, Canton, OH
Child and Family Associates, Jackson, MS
Child and Family Counseling Center, Glenwood Springs, CO
Child and Family Institute, Sacramento, CA
Child and Family Resource Council, Missoula, MT
Child and Family Service, Inc, Austin, TX
Child and Family Services, Portsmouth, VA
Child and Family Services of Buffalo and Erie County, Buffalo, NY
Child and Family Support Team, Lewiston, ME
Child and Family Therapy Center, Martinez, CA
Child Assault Prevention of Contra Costa County, Inc, Concord, CA
Child Assault Prevention Project (CAP), Reno, NV
The Child Assault Prevention Project of Greater Worcester, Worcester, MA
Child Assault Prevention Training Center of Northern California, Oakland, CA
Child Guidance Clinic of the Family Service Agency, Santa Barbara, CA
Child Protection Center, Cedar Rapids, IA
Child Protection Team, Bradenton, FL
Child Protection Team, Jacksonville, FL
Child Protection Team, Tallahassee, FL
Child Protection Team, Fort Myers, FL
Child Protection Team/Child Crisis Prevention Program/Sexual Assault Treatment Program, Daytona Beach, FL
Child Protection Team, Inc/Family Sexual Abuse Treatment Program, Mangonia Park, FL
Child Protection Team of Brevard County, Rockledge, FL
Child Protection Team of Broward County, Inc, Fort Lauderdale, FL
Child Protection Team of Collier County, Naples, FL
Child Safe, Fort Collins, CO
Child Sex Abuse Treatment Program, Honolulu, HI
Child Sex Abuse Treatment Program, Brooksville, FL
Child Sexual Abuse Awareness, Scottsdale, AZ
Child Sexual Abuse Institute of Ohio, Wooster, OH
Child Sexual Abuse Program, Los Angeles, CA
Child Sexual Abuse Project, Ithaca, NY
The Child Sexual Abuse Team, Raleigh, NC
Child Sexual Abuse Therapy Program/Parents United, Eureka, CA
Child Sexual Abuse Treatment and Training Center, Bolingbrook, IL
Child Sexual Abuse Treatment Center, Tempe, AZ
Child Sexual Abuse Treatment Center, Hartsdale, NY
Child Sexual Abuse Treatment Center of Yolo County, Woodland, CA
Child Sexual Abuse Treatment Program, Fremont, CA
Child Sexual Abuse Treatment Program, Hayward, CA
Child Sexual Abuse Treatment Program, San Francisco, CA
Child Sexual Abuse Treatment Program (C-SAT), Las Vegas, NV
Child Sexual Abuse Treatment Program (CSATP), Tustin, CA
Child Sexual Abuse Treatment Program (CSATP), Athens, OH
Child Sexual Abuse Treatment Program/Parents United—Mental Health Services, Inc, Gainesville, FL
Child Sexual Abuse Treatment Team, San Rafael, CA
Child/Teen Abuse Prevention Program, Cocoa, FL
Child Victim Unit, Bronx, NY
Children and Youth Services, Clarion, PA
Children First Center, Grand Prairie, TX
Children of the Night, Hollywood, CA
The Children's Alcohol Resource and Education Center, Freeport, NY
Children's Bureau of Delaware, Wilmington, DE
Children's Center, Miami, FL
Children's Center for Behavioral Development, Edgemont, IL
Children's Hospital—Sexual Abuse Treatment Team, Boston, MA
Children's Inn, Sioux Falls, SD
Children's Institute International—Family CARE Center, Los Angeles, CA

Children's Medical Care, Tampa, FL
The Children's Place, Kansas City, MO
The Children's Place, Aiken, SC
Children's Self-Help Project, San Francisco, CA
ChildSafe, Ames, IA
Chippewa County District Attorney—Victim/Witness Program, Chippewa Falls, WI
Chippewa County Prosecuting Attorney—Crime Victim's Assistance Program, Sault Sainte Marie, MI
Chisago County Attorney's Office—Victim Assistance Program, Center City, MN
Chittenden County State's Attorney's Office—Victim/Witness Program, Burlington, VT
Choice Program of Family Services Society, Corning, NY
CHOICES—Creating Healthy Options in Confronting Exploitive Sexuality, Eugene, OR
Choices for Victims of Domestic Violence, Columbus, OH
Christian Counseling Center, Gadsden, AL
Chrysalis Counseling Services for Women, Inc, Santa Rosa, CA
Chrysalis Family and Child Treatment Program/Chrysalis Mental Health Clinic, Minneapolis, MN
Chrysalis Therapy Center, Bellingham, WA
CIRCA Psychotherapy Associates for Women, Northampton, MA
Citizens Advice Bureau, Bronx, NY
Citizens' Advisory Committee on Rape Prevention, Ann Arbor, MI
Citizens Against Family Violence, Inc, Martinsville, VA
Citizens Against Physical and Sexual Abuse (CAPSA), Logan, UT
Citizens Against Rape, Beaufort, SC
Citizens Against Rape and Domestic Violence, Sioux Falls, SD
Citizens Against Rape in Evansville, Evansville, IN
Citizens Against Sexual Assault (CASA) of Harrisonburg, Rockingham County, Harrisonburg, VA
Citizens Against Spouse Abuse, Inc (CASA), Sedalia, MO
Citizens Committee on Rape, Sexual Assault, and Sexual Abuse, Inc, Buffalo, NY
Citrus County Abuse Shelter Association, Inverness, FL
City Attorney's Office—Domestic Violence Unit, Los Angeles, CA
City of Houston Department of Health and Human Services—Sexual Assault Program, Houston, TX
City of Milwaukee—Common Council Task Force on Sexual Assault and Domestic Violence, Milwaukee, WI
City of San Antonio, Department of Human Resources and Services—Children's Resources Division, San Antonio, TX
Clackamas Adolescent Intervention Services, Inc, Maryhurst, OR
Clackamas County District Attorney—Victim Assistance Division, Oregon City, OR
Clackamas Woman's Services, Milwaukie, OR
Clarion County Counseling Center, Clarion, PA
Clark County Juvenile Court Services—Victim Assistance Center, Las Vegas, NV
Clark County Prosecuting Attorney—Victim/Witness Unit, Vancouver, WA
Dr Isaiah Clark Family and Youth Clinic, Hartford, CT
Clearfield-Jefferson Community Mental Health Center, DuBois, PA
Clearwater Police Department—Victim Assistance Program, Clearwater, FL
Clermont Counseling Center, Batavia, OH
Clermont County Prosecutor's Office—Victim/Witness Assistance Program, Batavia, OH
Clermont County Youth Services Coordinating Council, Batavia, OH
Cleveland County Abuse Prevention Council, Inc, Shelby, NC
Cleveland Rape Crisis Center, Cleveland, OH
Clinic for Counseling and Psychotherapy, Inc and Northwest Passage, Inc, Salt Lake City, UT
Clinic for the Sexualities, San Diego, CA
Clinical and Forensic Consultants, Charlotte, NC
Clintonville Counseling Services, Columbus, OH
CLLB Psychotherapy, Lakewood, CO
CMS Child Protection Team, Miami, FL
Coalition Against Rape, Muncie, IN
Coalition Against Rape and Abuse (CARA), Cape May Court House, NJ
Coalition for Children and Youth, Inc, Norwalk, CT
Coastal Area Community Mental Health, Hinesville, GA

Coastal Counseling Association, Portland, ME
Coastal Empire Mental Health, Ridgeland, SC
Coastal Empire Mental Health Center, Beaufort, SC
CODE, Inc, Acton, MA
Coles County Mental Health Center, Mattoon, IL
Collin County Rape Crisis Center, McKinney, TX
Collins, Kubale, and Miles Counseling Offices, Danville, KY
Colorado Department of Corrections, Buena Vista, CO
Colorado Outward Bound School, Denver, CO
Columbia County Women's Resource Center, Saint Helens, OR
Columbia-Greene Rape Crisis Center, Hudson, NY
Columbus Area Domestic Violence/Sexual Assault Program, Columbus, NE
Columbus Rape Crisis, Inc, Columbus, GA
Commission on Victim Services, Stamford, CT
Committee for Child Abuse Prevention, Frederick, MD
Committee for Kids, Inc, Covington, KY
Committee to Aid Abused Women, Sparks, NV
Common Bond, Inc, Albuquerque, NM
Commonwealth Attorney's Office—Victim/Witness Assistance, Williamsburg, VA
Commonwealth Attorney's Office—Victim/Witness Assistance Program, Lexington, VA
Commonwealth Attorney's Office—Victim/Witness Assistance Program, Newport News, VA
Commonwealth Attorney's Office—Victim/Witness Assistance Program, Salem, VA
Commonwealth Attorney's Office—Victim/Witness Program, Roanoke, VA
Commonwealth Attorney's Victim/Witness Program, Portsmouth, VA
Commonwealth's Attorney's Office—Victim/Witness Program, Virginia Beach, Virginia Beach, VA
Community Abuse and Assault Center, Walla Walla, WA
Community Action Against Rape, Las Vegas, NV
Community Advocates, Portland, OR
Community Against Rape, Inc, Taos, NM
Community Assault Prevention Services, Jackson, OH
Community Behavioral Services, Gainesville, FL
Community Behavioral Services, Orange Park, FL
Community Counseling and Education Center, Fremont, CA
Community Counseling and Psychological Services, Bakersfield, CA
Community Counseling Services, Inc, Hot Springs, AR
Community Crisis Center, Elgin, IL
Community Crisis Services, Worland, WY
Community Help Line, Great Falls, MT
Community Mental Health Center—Rape Crisis Program, Lawrenceburg, IN
Community Program Against Sexual Assault (CPASA), Dorchester, MA
Community Referral Agency, Inc/"Welcome Home" Shelter, Balsam Lake, WI
Community Resources of Fayette County, Inc, Uniontown, PA
Community, Runaway and Youth Services (CRYS), Reno, NV
Community United Against Violence, San Francisco, CA
Community—University Health Care Center, Minneapolis, MN
Comprehensive Care Center/Graham B Dimmick Child Guidance Service, Lexington, KY
Comprehensive Child Abuse Program, Nashville, TN
Comprehensive Clinical and Consulting Services, Saint Louis, MO
Comprehensive Emergency Services, Revere, MA
Comprehensive Sexual Awareness and Treatment Team (CSATT), Fresno, CA
Compton YWCA Sexual Assault Crisis Program, Compton, CA
CONSEJO Counseling and Referral Service, Seattle, WA
Contact Ashtabula County, Inc, Ashtabula, OH
CONTACT of Burlington County, Moorestown, NJ
CONTACT Rape Crisis Counseling Team (RCCT), Huntington, WV
Continental Crown Counseling, Sandpoint, ID
Contra Costa Crisis and Suicide Intervention Service, Walnut Creek, CA
Converse County Coalition Against Family Violence, Douglas, WY
Cook County State's Attorney's Office—Victim/Witness Assistance, Chicago, IL
Cooke County Friends of the Family, Gainesville, TX
Coordinated Intervention System for Domestic Abuses (CISDA), Crete, NE
Coos County Women's Crisis Service, North Bend, OR

COPE—Ozaukee County Hotline, Cedarburg, WI
Cornerstone Sexual Assault Services, Grand Rapids, MI
Correctional Specialties, Bellevue, WA
Correctional Treatment Programs—Sex Offender Unit, Salem, OR
Coshocton County Crisis Hotline, Coshocton, OH
Council Against Domestic Assault (CADA), Lansing, MI
Council Against Rape, Montgomery, AL
Council for the Prevention of Domestic Violence, Estherville, IA
Council on Domestic Violence and Sexual Assault, Midland, MI
Council on Sexual Assault and Domestic Violence, Sioux City, IA
Council on Sexual Assault of Spartanburg, Spartanburg, SC
Counseling and Consultation Service, Columbus, OH
Counseling and Health Associates, Manhattan Beach, CA
Counseling and Readjustment Services, Columbia, SC
Counseling and Training Associates, Wiscasset, ME
Counseling Associates, Bronson, MI
Counseling Associates, Virginia Beach, VA
Counseling Associates, Grand Junction, CO
Counseling Associates, Inc, Roswell, NM
The Counseling Center, Havelock, NC
Counseling Center, Alamogordo, NM
Counseling Center of Lambertville, Lambertville, NJ
Counseling Center of Lebanon, Lebanon, NH
The Counseling Center of Milwaukee, Inc, Milwaukee, WI
The Counseling Institute, Park City, UT
Counseling Service of Addison County, Middlebury, VT
Counseling Services Center, Everett, WA
Counseling Services of Camden, Camden, SC
Counselors for Personal Growth, Westminster, CO
County of Orange Social Services Agency—Children's Services, Orange, CA
Cowlitz County Sexual Assault, Kelso, WA
Creative Counseling Services, West Hartford, CT
Crime Victim Assistance, Buffalo, NY
Crime Victim Assistance Program, Hood River, OR
Crime Victim Assistance Program, Menomonie, WI
Crime Victim Center, Reading, PA
Crime Victim Center, Los Angeles, CA
Crime Victim Center, Minneapolis, MN
Crime Victim Foundation, Phoenix, AZ
Crime Victim Services, Inc, Lima, OH
Crime Victim/Sexual Assault Program, Plattsburgh, NY
Crime Victims and Rape Counseling, Garden City, NY
Crime Victims Assistance Program, Lexington, KY
Crime Victims Assistance Program, Kingston, NY
Crime Victims Assistance Program, Chicago, IL
Crime Victims Center of Chester County, West Chester, PA
Crime Victims' Counseling Services, Inc, Brooklyn Heights, NY
Crime Victims Research and Treatment Center (CVC), Charleston, SC
Crime Victims/Witness Assistance Program, Norwich, NY
Crimes Against Women Task Force, Inc—T/A Albemarle Hopeline, Elizabeth City, NC
Criminal District Attorney's Office—Victim Witness Program, Richmond, TX
Crisis and Emergency Services (CARES), Basin, WY
Crisis and Suicide Intervention Service, Indianapolis, IN
Crisis Center, Sherman, TX
Crisis Center for South Suburia, Worth, IL
Crisis Center, Inc, Grand Island, NE
The Crisis Center, Inc, Manhattan, KS
Crisis Center of Lompoc—Rape Crisis/For Kids Sake, Lompoc, CA
The Crisis Council, Inc, Troy, NC
Crisis Hotline, Houston, TX
Crisis Hotline, Ketchum, ID
Crisis Intervention Center, Lakeview, OR
Crisis Intervention Center, Saint Maries, ID
Crisis Intervention Service, Mason City, IA
Crisis Intervention Services, Cody, WY
Crisis Intervention Services (CIS), Saginaw, MI
Crisis Line of Will County, Joliet, IL
Crisis Ministries, Anderson, SC
Crisis Services, Corpus Christi, TX
Crisis Services, Waterloo, IA
Criss-Cross, Inc, Clarksburg, WV
Crist Clinic for Women, Jacksonville, NC

Crook County Family Violence and Sexual Assault Services, Sundance, WY
Crook County Victims' Assistance Program, Prineville, OR
Cross Roads Crisis Center, Lima, OH
Crossroads Programs, Inc, Lumberton, NJ
Crossroads Safehouse for Battered Women and Their Children, Fort Collins, CO
CSP Sexual Assault Victim Services/Prevention Program, Fullerton, CA
CSP Sexual Assault Victim Services/Prevention Program, Laguna Niguel, CA
CSP Sexual Assault Victim Services/Prevention Program, Santa Ana, CA
CSP Sexual Assault Victim Services/Prevention Program, Westminster, CA
Cumberland County Guidance Center—Sexual Assault Program, Millville, NJ
Cumberland County Prosecutor's Office—Sexual Assault Unit, Bridgeton, NJ
Cumberland River Comprehensive Care Centers, Corbin, KY
Dallas County Rape Crisis and Child Sexual Abuse Center, Dallas, TX
Dane County Advocates for Battered Women, Madison, WI
Dane County District Attorney—Victim/Witness Unit, Madison, WI
Dane County Rape Crisis Center, Madison, WI
Davidson County Domestic Violence Services, Inc, Lexington, NC
Dawson County Spouse Abuse Program, Glendive, MT
Dayglo Family Treatment Program, Austin, TX
Dayton Free Clinic and Counseling Center, Dayton, OH
DC Hotline, Inc, Washington, DC
DC NOW Task Force Against Child Sexual Abuse, Washington, DC
DC Self Defense Karate Association and DC Model Mugging, Silver Spring, MD
Dearborn Crisis Center, Dearborn, MI
Edmund L Decker and Associates, Peoria Heights, IL
Delaware Opportunities, Inc—Safe Against Violence, Delhi, NY
Delaware State Police—Victim Assistance Unit, Dover, DE
Delson-Kokish Associates, Eureka, CA
Delta County Prosecutor's Office, Escanaba, MI
Deming Crisis Center, Deming, NM
Denton County Friends of the Family, Inc, Denton, TX
Denver District Attorney—Domestic Violence Unit, Denver, CO
Denver General Hospital—Sexual Assault Victim Advocate Program, Denver, CO
Department of Children and Family Services, Marion, IL
Department of Employment Services, Washington, DC
Department of Family Practice—Family Medical Center, Lexington, KY
Department of Sociology, Anthropology, and Criminal Justice Administration, Boise, ID
Department of the Prosecuting Attorney—Victim/Witness Assistance Program, Wailuku, HI
Des Moines Child and Adolescent Guidance Center, Inc, Des Moines, IA
Des Plaines Valley Community Center—Sexual Assault Program, Summit, IL
Detroit Police Department—Rape Counseling Center, Detroit, MI
Developmental and Residential Services, Clarkston, WA
Devereux and Associates, Jacksonville, FL
Diagnostic Center for Victimized Children, Stratford, NJ
Dial Help, Inc, Houghton, MI
District Attorney—Victim Assistance, Fort Worth, TX
District Attorney Victim/Witness Assistance Program, Grand Junction, CO
District Attorney Victim/Witness Program, Montgomery, AL
District Attorney Victim/Witness Program, Monterey, CA
District Attorney's Office, Moulton, AL
District Attorney's Office, Anniston, AL
District Attorney's Office—Children's Advocacy Center, Colorado Springs, CO
District Attorney's Office—Rape/Sexual Abuse Victim Services, Bolivia, NC
District Attorney's Office—Victim Assistance Center, Oklahoma City, OK
District Attorney's Office—Victim/Witness Assistance, Ketchikan, AK

District Attorney's Office—Victim/Witness Assistance, Superior, WI
District Attorney's Office—Victim/Witness Assistance, Greensboro, NC
District Attorney's Office—Victim/Witness Assistance, Golden, CO
District Attorney's Office—Victim/Witness Assistance, Hot Sulphur Springs, CO
District Attorney's Office—Victim/Witness Assistance, Leadville, CO
District Attorney's Office—Victim/Witness Assistance, Englewood, CO
District Attorney's Office—Victim/Witness Assistance Program, Machias, ME
District Attorney's Office—Victim/Witness Assistance Program, Dillingham, AK
District Attorney's Office—Victim/Witness Assistance Program, Kenai, AK
District Attorney's Office—Victim/Witness Assistance Program, Palmer, AK
District Attorney's Office—Victim/Witness Assistance Program, Fairfield, CA
District Attorney's Office—Victim/Witness Assistance Program, Green Bay, WI
District Attorney's Office—Victim/Witness Assistance Program, Rome, GA
District Attorney's Office—Victim Witness Assistance Program, El Paso, TX
District Attorney's Office—Victim/Witness Assistance Program, Victorville, CA
District Attorney's Office—Victim Witness Assistance Unit, Brighton, CO
District Attorney's Office—Victim/Witness Assistance Unit, Cortez, CO
District Attorney's Office—Victim Witness Center, Ada, OK
District Attorney's Office—Victim Witness Center, Enid, OK
District Attorney's Office—Victim/Witness Program, Woodward, OK
District Attorney's Office—Victim/Witness Program, Eufaula, AL
District Attorney's Office—Victim/Witness Program, Auburn, CA
District Attorney's Office—Victim/Witness Program, Idabel, OK
District Attorney's Office—Victim/Witness Program, Alfred, ME
District Attorney's Office—Victim/Witness Program, Belfast, ME
District Attorney's Stop Rape Crisis Center, Baton Rouge, LA
District Attorney's Victim/Witness Assistance Program, Barnstable, MA
District Attorney's Victim/Witness Program, Newkirk, OK
District Attorney's Victim-Witness Assistance Program, San Diego, CA
District VI B—Child Protection Team, Lakeland, FL
District III—Child Protection Team, Gainesville, FL
Division of Indian Work—Sexual Assault Project, Minneapolis, MN
Dodge County District Attorney—Victim/Witness Program, Juneau, WI
Domestic Abuse and Rape Crisis Center, Inc, Belvedere, NJ
Domestic Abuse Program of Samaritan Inn (DASI), Newton, NJ
Domestic Abuse Project, Minneapolis, MN
Domestic Abuse/Sexual Assault Crisis Center, Fremont, NE
Domestic Abuse/Sexual Assault Services, McCook, NE
Domestic Abuse Shelter, Inc, Marathon, FL
Domestic Abuse Women's Network (DAWN), Kent, WA
Domestic Assault/Rape Elimination Services (DARES), Port Huron, MI
Domestic Assault Shelter, Three Rivers, MI
Domestic Crisis Services of Monterey County, Salinas, CA
Domestic Harmony, Hillsdale, MI
Domestic Violence Aid Center, Inc, Sioux Center, IA
Domestic Violence and Child Abuse Bureau, White Plains, NY
Domestic Violence and Rape Crisis Center, Dickinson, ND
Domestic Violence and Sexual Assault Program of the Upper Valley, Lebanon, NH
Domestic Violence and Sexual Assault Services, Benkelman, NE
Domestic Violence Center, Ionia, MI
Domestic Violence Center, Manitowoc, WI
Domestic Violence Coalition, Grass Valley, CA

Alphabetical Listing of Facilities in Agency Profiles / 331

Domestic Violence Escape (DOVE), Inc, Ironwood, MI
Domestic Violence Intervention, Fallon, NV
Domestic Violence Intervention of Pershing County, Lovelock, NV
Domestic Violence Prevention Center, Colorado Springs, CO
Domestic Violence Prevention, Inc—Battered Women Shelter and Sexual Assault Services, Texarkana, TX
Domestic Violence Program, Murfreesboro, TN
Domestic Violence Program, Dayville, CT
Domestic Violence Program of North Central Oklahoma, Inc, Ponca City, OK
Domestic Violence Program of Walsh County, Grafton, ND
Domestic Violence Project/SAFE House, Ann Arbor, MI
Domestic Violence Services, Pendleton, OR
Domestic Violence Services Center, Jackson, MS
The Domestic Violence/Sexual Assault Program of Eastern Jefferson County, Port Townsend, WA
The Domestic Violence Shelter, Inc, Mansfield, OH
Douglas County District Attorney's Office—Victim/Witness Assistance Program, Roseburg, OR
Douglas County Prosecuting Attorney, Waterville, WA
Douglas County Rape Victim Support Service, Lawrence, KS
Douglas County Sheriff Victim Assistance, Castle Rock, CO
Dove Domestic Violence Program, Decatur, IL
DOVE, Inc (Domestic Violence Ended), Quincy, MA
DOVES (Domestic Violence Emergency Services), Scottsbluff, NE
DOVES, Inc—Rape Crisis Services, Danville, VA
Doves of Big Bear Valley, Inc, Big Bear Lake, CA
Driggs and Associates, Minneapolis, MN
Dunn House—Rape Crisis: Sexual and Domestic Violence Intervention, Medford, OR
DuPage Women Against Rape, Glen Ellyn, IL
DuPage YWCA Counseling Services, Glen Ellyn, IL
Dutchess County Crime Victims Assistance Program, Poughkeepsie, NY
Dutchess County Department of Mental Hygiene (DC/DMH), Poughkeepsie, NY
Early Childhood Development Center, Evanston, IL
East Los Angeles Rape Hotline, Inc, Los Angeles, CA
East Orange General Hospital—Crisis Intervention Unit, East Orange, NJ
East Side Center, Inc, Providence, RI
East Texas Association for Abused Families, Longview, TX
East Texas Crisis Center, Tyler, TX
Eastern Montana Mental Health Center, Glendive, MT
Eastern Upper Peninsula Domestic Violence Program, Sault Sainte Marie, MI
Eastern Wyoming Mental Health Center—Sexual Assault/Abuse Services, Lusk, WY
Eastmoreland Consulting, Portland, OR
Echoes Counseling Services, Portland, OR
Ector County District Attorney's Office—Victim Assistance, Odessa, TX
Ecumenical Women's Center, Chicago, IL
Edgefield County Rape Crisis Center, Edgefield, SC
Edmonds Community College—Women's Programs, Lynnwood, WA
Education and Support Programs for Women, Chico, CA
El Centro Human Services Corporation, Los Angeles, CA
El Paso Rape Crisis Services, El Paso, TX
Emergency Housing Service, Inc, Boise, ID
Emergency Support Shelter, Kelso, WA
Employee Counseling and Assistance, Greenville, SC
END DV Program, Elizabethtown, NY
Ending Violence Effectively, Denver, CO
Equinox Counseling Center, Albany, NY
Erie County Rape Crisis Center, Inc, Erie, PA
Erie Hotline, Erie, PA
Escondido Youth Encounter, Escondido, CA
Essex County District Attorney's Office—Victim/Witness Assistance Program, Salem, MA
Essex County Family Violence Program, Newark, NJ
ETC, Lake Charles, LA
Eugene Family Institute, Eugene, OR
Every Woman's House, Inc, Wooster, OH
Every Woman's Place Crisis Center, Muskegon, MI
Everywoman's Center Programs Against Violence Against Women, Amherst, MA
Exchange Club—Carl Perkins Center for the Prevention of Child Abuse, Jackson, TN
Exchange Club Center for the Prevention of Child Abuse of Southern Minnesota, Inc, Owatonna, MN
Exchange Club—Child Abuse Prevention Center, Memphis, TN

Exchange Club of Vicksburg—Child Abuse Prevention Center, Inc (CAP), Vicksburg, MS
Exchange Club—Parent/Child Center, Jackson, MS
Face to Face Health and Counseling, Saint Paul, MN
FACT Hotline—Families and Children in Trouble/Together, Washington, DC
Fair Harbor Emergency Shelter, Portland, ME
Fairbanks Child Sexual Abuse Task Force, Fairbanks, AK
Fairfax County Police Department—Victim/Witness Assistance Program, Fairfax, VA
Fairfax County Victim Assistance Network, Alexandria, VA
Fairfield Family Counseling, Lancaster, OH
Faith House, Inc, Prescott, AZ
Families First, Aurora, CO
Families in Crisis, Inc—Rape Crisis Center, Killeen, TX
Families in Transition Center, Milford, DE
Families Inc, West Branch, IA
Families of Crimes of Silence, Canoga Park, CA
Family Abuse Project, San Leandro, CA
Family Advocacy, White Sands Missile Range, NM
Family Advocate, Rockford, IL
Family Advocates, Inc, Platteville, WI
Family and Children Evaluation Services (FACES), Valdosta, GA
Family and Children's Center, La Crosse, WI
Family and Children's Center, Mishawaka, IN
Family and Children's Service, Minneapolis, MN
Family and Children's Services, Inc, Fort Wayne, IN
Family and Children's Services, Inc—Psychotherapy and Counseling Division, Albuquerque, NM
Family and Children's Services of Chattanooga, Tennessee, Chattanooga, TN
Family and Mental Health Services/Southwest Sexual Assault/Abuse Services, Worth, IL
Family and Personal Support Centers, Saint Louis, MO
Family and Youth Counseling Agency, Lake Charles, LA
Family Awareness Center, Adrian, MI
Family Care Council, Spartanburg, SC
The Family Center, Springfield, MO
The Family Center—Domestic Violence and Sexual Assault Prevention Program, Saint Albans, VT
The Family Center, Inc, Greenwich, CT
Family Consultants, Inc, Monroe, LA
Family Counseling Agency, Inc—Work Against Rape Program, Alexandria, LA
Family Counseling and Shelter Services, Monroe, MI
The Family Counseling Center, Savannah, GA
Family Counseling Center, Sarasota, FL
Family Counseling Center of Aurora, Aurora, IL
The Family Counseling Center of Fulton County, Gloversville, NY
Family Counseling of Greater New Haven, Inc, New Haven, CT
Family Counseling Service, Camden, NJ
Family Counseling Service of Evanston and Skokie Valley, Evanston, IL
Family Counseling Service of Northern Nevada, Reno, NV
Family Counseling Services, Tuscaloosa, AL
Family Counseling Services, Inc, Harrisonburg, VA
Family Counseling Services of Elkhart, Elkhart, IN
Family Crisis and Resource Center, Polson, MT
Family Crisis Center, Bastrop, TX
Family Crisis Center, Stevens Point, WI
Family Crisis Center, Great Bend, KS
Family Crisis Center, Inc, Keyser, WV
Family Crisis Center, Inc, Harlingen, TX
Family Crisis Center, Inc (FCCI), Farmington, NM
The Family Crisis Intervention Center, Parkersburg, WV
Family Crisis Network, Newport, WA
Family Crisis Program, Oceanside, NY
Family Crisis Resource Center, Inc, Cumberland, MD
Family Crisis Resource Center, Inc, Oakland, MD
Family Crisis Service, Northridge, CA
Family Crisis Services, Canon City, CO
Family Crisis Services, Inc, Garden City, KS
Family Crisis Shelter, Williston, ND
Family Crisis Shelter of Montgomery County, Inc, Crawfordsville, IN
Family Development Center (FDC), Austin, TX
Family Focus, Inc., Denver, CO
Family Friends, Grants Pass, OR
Family Guidance Center/Community Mental Health Center, Saint Joseph, MO
Family Haven Crisis and Resource Center, Inc, Paris, TX
Family Intervention Team, Lowell, MA

Family Learning Center—Community Mental Health Center, Winter Haven, FL
Family Life Consultants, Collinsville, IL
The Family Living Center, Tallahassee, FL
Family Mending, Asheville, NC
Family Offender Program, Grants Pass, OR
Family Outreach of San Antonio, San Antonio, TX
The Family Place, White River Junction, VT
The Family Place: A Child Abuse Treatment Agency, Louisville, KY
Family Project, Roslindale, MA
Family Psychology Institute of Dallas, Dallas, TX
Family Recovery, Albuquerque, NM
Family Refuge Center, Lewisburg, WV
Family Resource Center, Salinas, CA
Family Resource Center, Seaside, CA
Family Resource Center, Saint Louis, MO
Family Resource Center of Northwest Alabama—DAYBREAK, Jasper, AL
Family Resource Center/Sexual Assault Program, Wytheville, VA
Family Resources, Pittsburgh, PA
Family Service, Lansdale, PA
Family Service Agency, Cedar Rapids, IA
Family Service Agency, Mesa, AZ
Family Service Agency Child Abuse Treatment, San Bernardino, CA
Family Service and Child Guidance Center of the Oranges, Maplewood and Millburn, Orange, NJ
Family Service Association, Warren, OH
Family Service Association of Butte and Glenn Counties, Chico, CA
Family Service Association of Indianapolis, Martinsville, IN
Family Service Association of Middlesex County, Highland Park, NJ
Family Service Association of Riverside, Riverside, CA
Family Service Association of San Diego County, San Diego, CA
Family Service Association of Waterbury, Waterbury, CT
Family Service, Inc, Huntington, WV
Family Service of Burlington County, Mount Holly, NJ
Family Service of Champaign County, Champaign, IL
Family Service of Coachella Valley, Indio, CA
Family Service of Detroit and Wayne County, Detroit, MI
Family Service of Greater New Orleans, New Orleans, LA
Family Service of Kanawha Valley (Sexual Assault Services), Charleston, WV
Family Service of Montgomery County, Norristown, PA
Family Service of the East Bay, Oakland, CA
Family Service of the East Bay, Fremont, CA
Family Service Princeton Area, Hightstown, NJ
Family Service Princeton Area, Princeton, NJ
Family Services, Renton, WA
Family Services Center, Huntsville, AL
Family Services, Inc, Lafayette, IN
Family Services of Bergen County, Inc, Hackensack, NJ
Family Services of Central Massachusetts, Worcester, MA
Family Services of Greater St Paul, Saint Paul, MN
Family Services of Tulare County, Visalia, CA
Family Services Program, Miami, FL
Family Sex Abuse Treatment Program, San Antonio, TX
Family Sexual Abuse Treatment, Inc, Madison, WI
Family Sexual Abuse Treatment Program, Olathe, KS
Family Sexual Abuse Treatment Program (FSATP), Tulsa, OK
Family Shelter, Eugene, OR
Family Social and Psychotherapy Services, Hales Corners, WI
Family Stress Center, Chula Vista, CA
Family Stress Clinic Ltd, Libertyville, IL
Family Stress Service, Burlingame, CA
Family Support Center, Aurora, IL
Family Support Center, Presque Isle, ME
Family Support Center, Chippewa Falls, WI
Family Support Center, Salt Lake City, UT
Family Support Program, Columbus, OH
Family Support Team, Bangor, ME
Family Therapy and Recovery Center, Minnetonka, MN
Family Therapy Center of Madison, Inc, Madison, WI
Family Therapy Center of Morris County, PC, Morris Plains, NJ
Family Violence and Rape Crisis Association of Lee County, Sanford, NC

Family Violence and Rape Crisis Volunteers in Chatham County, Pittsboro, NC
Family Violence Intervention Program of Region K, Henderson, NC
Family Violence Law Center, Berkeley, CA
Family Violence Network, Lake Elmo, MN
Family Violence Program, New Rochelle, NY
Family Violence Project, Van Nuys, CA
Family Violence/Sexual Assault Network, Jamestown, NY
Faribault Victim Support Program, Faribault, MN
Fayette County Prosecutor's Office—Sexual Assault Services, Connersville, IN
Feminist Karate Union, Seattle, WA
The Feminist Therapy Center, Oak Park, MI
Feminists in Self-Defense Training (FIST), Olympia, WA
Fenway Community Health Center: Gay and Lesbian Victim Recovery Program, Boston, MA
Ferry County Community Services, Republic, WA
Finex House, Inc, Jamaica Plain, MA
First Step Domestic Violence Shelter, Fostoria, OH
First Step, Inc, Wichita Falls, TX
First Step—The Western Wayne County Project on Domestic Assault, Westland, MI
Florida Visiting Family Therapy Associates, Inc, New Port Richey, FL
Focus on Women Program, Dearborn, MI
Fond du Lac County Health Care Center, Fond du Lac, WI
Fond du Lac County Victim/Witness Assistance, Fond du Lac, WI
Foothill Family Service Agency, Pasadena, CA
Forbes House, Painesville, OH
Forensic Mental Health Associates, Webster, MA
Forensic Mental Health Associates, Albany, NY
Forensic Mental Health Services of Connecticut, Inc, New London, CT
Forest Park Center for Counseling, Forest Park, IL
Forgach House Domestic Crisis Shelter, Sierra Vista, AZ
Forks Abuse Program, Forks, WA
Formerly Abused Children Emerging in Society (FACES), Lawton, OK
Fort Bend County Women's Refuge, Inc, Richmond, TX
Fort Wayne Police Department—Victim Assistance Program, Fort Wayne, IN
Fort Worth Police Department—Crime Prevention Unit, Fort Worth, TX
Forte Foundation, Van Nuys, CA
45th Street Community Health Clinic, Seattle, WA
Franciscan Mental Health Center, Rock Island, IL
Franklin County Prosecuting Attorney—Victim/Witness Assistance, Pasco, WA
Franklin County Prosecutor's Office—Victim Witness Assistance Program, Columbus, OH
Frederick Psychiatric Resources, Frederick, MD
Fredericksburg Area Rape Crisis Program, Fredericksburg, VA
Freedom House Shelter, Inc, Princeton, IL
Free-To-Grow Counseling Center, Harwood, ND
Fremont Counseling Service, Lander, WY
Fremont County Alliance Against Domestic Violence and Sexual Assault, Riverton, WY
Fresno County Victim/Witness Assistance Center, Fresno, CA
Friend to Friend, Southern Pines, NC
Friends Aware of Violent Relationships, Fond du Lac, WI
Friends of Abused Families, West Bend, WI
Friends to Youth, Missoula, MT
Friendship Center of Helena, Inc, Helena, MT
Fulton County and Montgomery County Rape Crisis Service, Amsterdam, NY
The Galaxy Center, Garland, TX
Garland County Rape Task Force, Hot Springs, AR
Gateway Counseling Center, Madison Heights, MI
Gateways, Minot, ND
Gavilan Community College Re-Entry Program, Gilroy, CA
Gay and Lesbian Community Center of Colorado, Inc, Denver, CO
Gay and Lesbian Community Center of Orange County, Garden Grove, CA
Gay and Lesbian Peer Counseling, Philadelphia, PA
Georgia Highlands Center for Mental Health, Dalton, GA
Giant Springs Counseling Associates, Great Falls, MT
Gil and Associates, Concord, CA
Gillette Abuse Refuge Foundation, Gillette, WY
Glendale Victim Assistance, Glendale, AZ

Gloucester County Rape Assault Prevention Program, Glassboro, NJ
Goshen County Task Force on Family Violence and Sexual Assault, Torrington, WY
Grace House Sexual Abuse Resource Center, Dayton, OH
Grady Memorial Hospital—Rape Prevention Project, Delaware, OH
Graham County Attorney's Victim Witness Assistance, Safford, AZ
Grays Harbor Rape Crisis, Aberdeen, WA
Green Haven Family Advocates, Inc, Monroe, WI
Green River Comprehensive Care—Crisis and Information Line, Owensboro, KY
Green River Regional Rape Victim Services, Inc, Owensboro, KY
Greene County Mental Health Center, Cairo, NY
Greene County Prosecuting Attorney—Victim/Witness Services, Springfield, MO
Greene County Prosecutor's Office—Victim/Witness Division, Xenia, OH
A Growing Place, Cincinnati, OH
Growing Strong Sexual Assault Center, Decatur, IL
Growth Counseling Services, Spokane, WA
Guardian ad Litem, Fayetteville, NC
Guardian ad Litem, Twin Falls, ID
Guardian ad Litem Program, Jacksonville, NC
The Guidance Clinic, Inc, Eau Claire, WI
Gulf Coast Women's Center, Biloxi, MS
Gunter and Associates, Houston, TX
Hale County Rape Crisis Center, Plainview, TX
Halifax County Mental Health Center, Roanoke Rapids, NC
Hampden County District Attorney—Victim/Witness Support Program, Springfield, MA
Hancock Adolescent Sex Offender Program, Ellsworth, ME
Hancock County Council on Domestic Violence, Findlay, OH
Harbor House, Vincennes, IN
Harbor House, Inc, New Philadelphia, OH
Harbor, Inc, Smithfield, NC
Harborview Medical Center—Battered Women's Program, Seattle, WA
Harris YWCA Women's Services, Chicago, IL
The Hart Group, Houston, TX
Hartford Police Crisis Intervention Unit, Hartford, CT
Hartford Region YWCA Sexual Assault Crisis Service, Hartford, CT
HAVEN, Conway, AR
HAVEN, Pontiac, MI
HAVEN (Help for Abused Victims with Emergency Needs), Blacksville, WV
Haven House, Alcoa, TN
Haven House Family Services Center, Wayne, NE
Haven House, Inc, Pasadena, CA
HAVIN (Helping Abuse Victims In Need), Inc, Kittanning, PA
Hawaii Island YWCA—Sexual Assault Support Service, Hilo, HI
Hawaii State Judiciary—Children's Advocacy Center, Honolulu, HI
Hawthorn Children's Psychiatric Hospital, Saint Louis, MO
Hays County Women's Center, San Marcos, TX
Hays Shelter Home, Boise, ID
Haywood Pediatrics, Clyde, NC
Headrest, Lebanon, NH
Healing Through Play, Lisbon Falls, ME
Health Information Referral Service, Inc, Marlborough, MA
Heart of America Family Services, Independence, MO
Heart of America Family Services, Kansas City, MO
Heartline, Inc, Detroit, MI
Heartly House, Inc, Frederick, MD
Heartsparkle Players, Olympia, WA
Helmuth Psychological Associates, Inc, Norton, OH
Help and Emergency Response, Portsmouth, VA
Help End Abuse Today (HEAT), Winter Park, FL
Help for Abused Partners, Sterling, CO
Help for Abused Women and Their Children (HAWC), Salem, MA
HELP Hotline, New Bremen, NY
Help Hotline, Inc, Youngstown, OH
Help In Crisis, Tahlequah, OK
Help, Inc, Idaho Falls, ID
"Help Me", Niles, OH
Help Me!, Inc, East Detroit, MI
HELP of Door County, Inc, Sturgeon Bay, WI
Helping Hands of Clemson, Inc, Clemson, SC
Helpline—ASAP, Mansfield, OH
Helpline, Information and Referral, Angleton, TX
Helpmate, Lusk, WY

Hemet/San Jacinto Center Against Sexual Assault, Hemet, CA
Henderson County Rape Crisis Center, Hendersonville, NC
Hernando County Child Abuse Prevention Project, Brooksville, FL
Hernando County Rape Crisis/Spouse Abuse Center, Brooksville, FL
Lexie Hicks Counseling Center, Owensboro, KY
High Plains Mental Health Center, Hays, KS
Highland County Domestic Violence Task Force, Hillsboro, OH
The Highland Institute for Behavioral Change, Inc, Atlanta, GA
Highland Sexual Assault Center, Oakland, CA
Hill Country Crisis Council, Kerrville, TX
Hillcrest Family Center, Frederick, MD
Hillsborough County Attorney's Office—Victim/Witness Services, Manchester, NH
Hillsborough County Crisis Center, Inc/Sexual Abuse Treatment Center, Tampa, FL
Hillview Mental Health Center, Inc, Lake View Terrace, CA
Home Start, Inc, San Diego, CA
Hope, Inc Task Force on Domestic Violence, Fairmont, WV
HOPE of Manatee, Inc, Bradenton, FL
Hope of South Texas, Victoria, TX
HOPE Place, Inc, Huntsville, AL
Hope Unlimited, Inc, Iola, KS
Hopewell Victim/Witness Assistance Program, Hopewell, VA
Hopkins Project, Inc, Hopkins, MN
Horizons Mental Health Center, Hutchinson, KS
Hospitality House, San Francisco, CA
Hospitality House for Women, Inc, Rome, GA
Hot Springs County Counseling Services, Thermopolis, WY
Hot Springs Crisis Intervention Team, Hot Springs, SD
Hot Springs Crisis Line, Thermopolis, WY
Hotline, Inc, Charleston Heights, SC
House of Imagene, Washington, DC
The House of Ruth, Dothan, AL
House of Ruth, Baltimore, MD
House of Ruth, Claremont, CA
Houston Drug Action Council (HODAC)—Rape Crisis Program, Warner Robins, GA
Howard County Sexual Assault Center, Columbia, MD
Hubbard House, Inc, Jacksonville, FL
Hudson County Prosecutor's Office—Sexual Assault Victim Assistance (SAVA) Unit, Jersey City, NJ
Human Development Associates, La Crosse, WI
Human Development Center of Pasco, New Port Richey, FL
Human Effective Living Programs (HELP), Chicago, IL
Human Resource Center, Superior, WI
Human Resource Center for Rural Communities, Athol, MA
Human Response Network/Family Care Project, Weaverville, CA
Human Service Center, Webster, MA
Humboldt County District Attorney's Victim-Witness Program, Eureka, CA
Humboldt County Rape Crisis Team, Eureka, CA
Humboldt Women for Shelter, Eureka, CA
Hunterdon Medical Center—Community Mental Health Center, Flemington, NJ
Huron YWCA, Huron, SD
Illusion Theater's Prevention Programs, Minneapolis, MN
Imperial County Victim/Witness, El Centro, CA
Incest Awareness Project, Fargo, ND
Incest Recovery Association, Dallas, TX
Incest Research and Treatment Institute, Columbus, OH
Incest Survivors Anonymous (ISA), Albuquerque, NM
Incest Survivors Network, Cambridge, MA
Independence House, Hyannis, MA
Independent Child Abuse Relief Enterprise (I-CARE), Daytona Beach, FL
Indian Health Board of Minneapolis, Inc, Minneapolis, MN
Indiana University Office for Women's Affairs, Bloomington, IN
Indiana University Sexual Assault Crisis Service (SACS), Bloomington, IN
Indianapolis Police Department—Victim Assistance Unit, Indianapolis, IN
Individual and Family Counseling/Crisis Line, Grand Junction, CO
INFOLINE of the Human Services Planning Council, Schenectady, NY

Information and Referral Service, Charlotte, NC
Ingham Counseling Center, Lansing, MI
Ingham County Sexual Assault Task Force, Lansing, MI
Institute for Applied Psychology, Freehold, NJ
Institute for Human Progress, Lomita, CA
Institute for Sex Therapy, Education, and Research, Traverse City, MI
Institute for the Community as Extended Family, San Jose, CA
Intensive Services to Families Department, New York, NY
Intensive Treatment Program for Sexual Aggressives, Saint Peter, MN
Interact, Raleigh, NC
Interface: Children, Family Services—Child Abuse Intervention and Prevention Services, Camarillo, CA
Interfaith Family Counseling Services, Inc, Coeur D'Alene, ID
Interim House, Detroit, MI
Ionia County Community Mental Health, Ionia, MI
Iris Personal Renewal Center, Bemidji, MN
Ithaca Rape Crisis, Inc, Ithaca, NY
Jackson County District Attorney—Crime Victim/Witness Assistance Program, Medford, OR
Jackson County Prosecutor's Office—Sex Crimes Unit—Victim/Witness Assistance, Kansas City, MO
Jackson County State's Attorney's Office—Victim/Witness Program, Murphysboro, IL
Jackson County Victim/Witness Assistance, Black River Falls, WI
Jackson Rape Crisis Center, Jackson, MS
The Jacob Center, Inc, Fort Collins, CO
Ada James Women's Counseling Service, Madison, WI
Jasper County Prosecutor's Office—Victim Services, Joplin, MO
Jefferson City Rape and Abuse Crisis Service, Jefferson City, MO
Jefferson County Commonwealth's Attorney's Office—Victim Information Program, Louisville, KY
Jefferson County District Attorney's Office—Victim Assistance Program, Madras, OR
Jefferson County Human Services Department, Jefferson, WI
Jefferson County Women's Center, Watertown, NY
Jensen Counseling Centers, PC, Farmington Hills, MI
Jewish Board of Family and Children's Services, Bronx, NY
Jewish Community Services of Long Island, Hempstead, NY
Jewish Family and Children's Service, Phoenix, AZ
Jewish Family Service of Greater Miami, Miami, FL
Johnson County Attorney's Office—Victim/Witness Assistance Program, Iowa City, IA
Johnson County District Attorney's Victim/Witness Assistance Program, Olathe, KS
Johnson County Family Crisis Center, Cleburne, TX
Johnson County Prosecutor's Victim Assistance Program, Franklin, IN
JOURNEYS, Chicago, IL
Jubilee House Community, Statesville, NC
The Julian Center, Inc, Indianapolis, IN
Justice for Abused Children, Inc, Orange Park, FL
Justice for Sexually Abused Children, Greenville, SC
Juvenile Justice Center, Kennewick, WA
Kalamazoo County Prosecuting Attorney—Victim Assistance, Kalamazoo, MI
Kankakee County Coalition Against Domestic Violence, Inc—Harbor House, Kankakee, IL
The Karate School for Women/Karate for Kids, New York, NY
Karate Temple, Columbus, OH
Kauai Victim Witness Program, Lihue, HI
Robert Kearney and Associates, Evanston, IL
Kedish House, Ellendale, ND
Kenosha County District Attorney's Office—Victim/Witness Program, Kenosha, WI
Kent County Prosecutor's Office—Victim Witness Program, Grand Rapids, MI
Kern County Mental Health, Bakersfield, CA
Kershaw County Coalition Against Sexual Assault, Inc, Camden, SC
Kids In Distress, Inc, Fort Lauderdale, FL
Kilgore Community Crisis Center, Kilgore, TX
King County Prosecuting Attorney's Office—Victim Assistance Unit, Seattle, WA
King County Prosecutor's Office—Special Assault Unit (SAU), Seattle, WA
King County Rape Relief, Renton, WA
Kings Community Action Organization, Hanford, CA
Kingsbridge Heights Community Center, Bronx, NY
Kitsap Sexual Assault Center/Rape Response, Bremerton, WA

Kittitas Sexual Assault Unit, Ellensburg, WA
Kleberg County Family Guidance Services, Kingsville, TX
Kodiak Women's Resource and Crisis Center, Kodiak, AK
La Casa de las Madres, San Francisco, CA
La Casa, Inc, Las Cruces, NM
La Clinica de la Raza—Fruitvale Health Project, Inc, Oakland, CA
La Crosse County District Attorney's Office—Victim/Witness Assistance Program, La Crosse, WI
La Familia Counseling Service, Hayward, CA
La Frontera Center, Inc, Tucson, AZ
Lafayette House, Joplin, MO
Laguna Family Shelter Program, Laguna, NM
Lake County Council Against Sexual Assault, Waukegan, IL
Lake County Office of the District Attorney—Victim/Witness Assistance Center, Lakeport, CA
Lake Cumberland Clinical Services, Somerset, KY
Lake Shore Clinic, Milwaukee, WI
Lake Sumter Rape Crisis Center, Eustis, FL
Lancaster County Rape Crisis Center, Lancaster, SC
Lancaster Shelter for Abused Women, Lancaster, PA
Lane County Victim/Witness Services, Eugene, OR
Langdon Psychiatric Clinic, Anchorage, AK
Lao Family Community, Inc, Santa Ana, CA
Lapeer County Community Mental Health Center, Lapeer, MI
Lapeer County Crime Victim Assistance, Lapeer, MI
Laredo State Center-Mental Health Mental Retardation—Sexual Assault Center, Laredo, TX
Larimer County Advocates for Victims of Sexual Assault, Fort Collins, CO
Larimer County Child Sexual Abuse Treatment Program, Fort Collins, CO
Las Familias, Tucson, AZ
LaSalle County Youth Services Bureau, Inc, Ottawa, IL
Laurel House, Norristown, PA
Law Firm of Anderson and Howell, Jacksonville Beach, FL
The Learning and Counseling Center, Colorado Springs, CO
Lebanon County District Attorney's Office—Victim/Witness Program, Lebanon, PA
Lee County Witness Management/Victim Assistance, Fort Myers, FL
Lee-Harnett Mental Health Center, Sanford, NC
Legal Aid Services, Inc—Social Services Program, Louisville, KY
Legal Services for Children, Inc, San Francisco, CA
Lesbian Resource Center, Seattle, WA
Lesbian Switchboard, New York, NY
Lewis and Clark County Attorney—Victim/Witness Assistance, Helena, MT
Lexington County Sheriff's Dept, Lexington, SC
Lexington Rape Crisis Center, Lexington, KY
Liberal Area Rape Crisis and Domestic Violence Service, Liberal, KS
Life Crisis Center, Inc, Salisbury, MD
Life Management Center, Panama City, FL
Life Management Center of Northwest Florida, Inc, Bonifay, FL
Life Span, Des Plaines, IL
LifeGuides Counseling Services, New Britain, CT
LifeGuides Counseling Services, Bristol, CT
LifeGuides Counseling Services, Terryville, CT
LifeGuides Counseling Services, Plainville, CT
Lighthouse Counseling Associates, Racine, WI
Lincoln County Attorney's Office—Victim/Witness Assistance Unit, North Platte, NE
Lincoln County District Attorney's Office, Wiscasset, ME
Lincoln Police Department—Victim/Witness Unit, Lincoln, NE
Lincoln Shelter and Services, Inc, Lincoln City, OR
Linder, Waddell and Associates, Greenville, SC
Listening Ear Crisis Center, Alexandria, MN
Listening Ear Crisis Center—Child Sexual Abuse Treatment Program, Mount Pleasant, MI
Lives Unlimited Psychotherapy and Resource Center, Madison, WI
Long Island Women's Coalition, Inc (LIWC), Islip Terrace, NY
Los Alamos Women's Center, Los Alamos, NM
Los Angeles City Attorney—Victim Assistance Program, Los Angeles, CA
Los Angeles Commission on Assaults Against Women, Los Angeles, CA
Los Angeles County Child Sexual Abuse Crisis Center, Torrance, CA
Los Angeles County Department of Children's Services, Los Angeles, CA

Los Angeles Women's Therapy Center, Los Angeles, CA
Loudoun Abused Women's Shelter, Purcellville, VA
Loudoun County Mental Health Center, Leesburg, VA
Loup Valley Task Force on Domestic Violence and Sexual Assault, Elyria, NE
Lower Valley Crisis and Support Services, Sunnyside, WA
Lubbock County—Criminal District Attorney Victim/Witness Assistance, Lubbock, TX
Lubbock Rape Crisis Center, Inc, Lubbock, TX
Florence Luscomb Women's Center, Salem, MA
Lutheran Child and Family Service of Michigan, Bay City, MI
Lutheran Family and Children Services of Missouri, Saint Louis, MO
Lutheran Family Service, Portland, OR
Lutheran Family Service of Yamhill County, McMinnville, OR
Lutheran Social Services, Kenosha, WI
Lutheran Social Services—East Region, Lititz, PA
Lutheran Social Services of Wisconsin and Upper Michigan, Ironwood, MI
Lynchburg Commonwealth Attorney's Office—Victim/Witness Assistance Program, Lynchburg, VA
Lyon County ALIVE (Alternatives to Living In Violent Environments), Yerington, NV
Lyon-Martin Women's Health Services, San Francisco, CA
Macomb County Crisis Center, Mount Clemens, MI
Macomb Family Services, Mount Clemens, MI
Macon Rescue Mission, Macon, GA
Madison County Prosecutor's Office—Victim/Witness Division, London, OH
Magdala Foundation, Saint Louis, MO
Mahoning County Children Services, Youngstown, OH
Mahoning County Prosecutor—Victim/Witness Program, Youngstown, OH
Malcomb Grow USAF Medical Center/Family Advocacy Program, Washington, DC
Malden Police Department—Victim Assistance Program, Malden, MA
Malheur County District Attorney—Victim/Witness Assistance Program, Vale, OR
MAM (Mothers Against Molesters), Canton, MI
Manatee Rape Crisis, Bradenton, FL
Maniilaq Regional Women's Crisis Project, Kotzebue, AK
Maricopa County Attorney's Office—Victim Witness Program, Phoenix, AZ
Marin Abused Women's Services, San Rafael, CA
Marin County District Attorney's Victim Witness Service, San Rafael, CA
Marion County District Attorney—Victim/Witness Assistance Program, Salem, OR
Marion County Prosecutor's Office—Victim/Witness Program, Indianapolis, IN
Marriage and Family Treatment Center, Colorado Springs, CO
Marshall County Rape Crisis Center, Inc, Marshall, NC
Maryland Institute for Individual and Family Therapy, College Park, MD
Marjaree Mason Center/YWCA, Fresno, CA
Massachusetts/CAPP, Boston, MA
Massachusetts Society for the Prevention of Cruelty to Children, Centerville, MA
Massachusetts Society for the Prevention of Cruelty to Children, Orange, MA
Massachusetts Society for the Prevention of Cruelty to Children, Framingham, MA
Massachusetts Society for the Prevention of Cruelty to Children, Taunton, MA
Massachusetts Society for the Prevention of Cruelty to Children, Braintree, MA
Massachusetts Society for the Prevention of Cruelty to Children, Lawrence, MA
Massachusetts Society for the Prevention of Cruelty to Children, Holyoke, MA
Massachusetts Society for the Prevention of Cruelty to Children, Greenfield, MA
Massachusetts Society for the Prevention of Cruelty to Children, Springfield, MA
Massachusetts Society for the Prevention of Cruelty to Children, Brockton, MA
Massachusetts Society for the Prevention of Cruelty to Children, Worcester, MA
Massachusetts Society for the Prevention of Cruelty to Children—Berkshire District, Pittsfield, MA
Massachusetts Society for the Prevention of Cruelty to Children (MSPCC), Salem, MA
Matagorda County Women's Crisis Center, Bay City, TX

May Day, Inc, Baker, OR
McDonough County State's Attorney—Victim/Witness Assistance Program, Macomb, IL
Kevin B McGovern, PhD and Associates, Portland, OR
McKennan Hospital—Sexual Trauma Program, Sioux Falls, SD
McLean County State Attorney's Office—Victim/Witness Service, Bloomington, IL
McPherson County Council on Violence Against Persons, McPherson, KS
Medical Center of Central Georgia, Macon, GA
Medical University of South Carolina—Children's Hospital, Charleston, SC
Memphis Police Department—Child Abuse Squad, Memphis, TN
Memphis Rape Crisis Center/Child Victim Advocate Program, Memphis, TN
MEN, Inc, Juneau, AK
Mendocino County Child Sexual Abuse Treatment Project, Ukiah, CA
Mendocino County District Attorney's Victim Witness Assistance, Ukiah, CA
Menninger Foundation, Topeka, KS
Men's Caucus, Los Angeles, CA
Men's Resource Center, Portland, OR
Men's Workshops, Cold Springs, NY
Mental Health Association of Central Middlesex, Concord, MA
Mental Health Association of Dallas County, Dallas, TX
Mental Health Association of Greater Tucson, Tucson, AZ
Mental Health Center of LaSalle County, Ottawa, IL
Mental Health Resources, Inc, Clovis, NM
Mental Health Resources, Inc, Tucumcari, NM
Mental Health Services, Inc, Butte, MT
Mental Health Services, Inc (Tri-County), Trenton, FL
Mental Health Services—Mescalero Indian Health Service Hospital, Mescalero, NM
Merced County Mental Health, Merced, CA
Mercer County Prosecutor's Office—Office of Victim/Witness Advocacy, Trenton, NJ
Mercer County Rape Crisis Program, Trenton, NJ
Mercer County Women's Action and Resource Center, Beulah, ND
Mercy House, Inc, Nampa, ID
Meriden/Wallingford Chrysalis, Meriden, CT
Meta Resources, Saint Paul, MN
Metropolitan Organization to Counter Sexual Assault (MOCSA), Kansas City, MO
Metropolitan Police Department—Victim Intervention Program, Nashville, TN
Metrowest Youth Guidance Center, Framingham, MA
Miami County Prosecutor's Office—Victim Witness Program, Troy, OH
MICSAIT Program (Multidisciplinary Institute for Child Sexual Abuse Intervention and Treatment), Fort Worth, TX
Mid Valley Counseling Center, Salem, OR
Middle District Attorney's Office—Victim/Witness Assistance Program, Worcester, MA
Middle Way House Rape Crisis Center, Bloomington, IN
Middlesex County District Attorney's Office—Victim Witness Service Bureau, Cambridge, MA
Middlesex County Rape Crisis Intervention Center, Metuchen, NJ
Midland Rape Crisis Center, Midland, TX
Mid-Life Women's Crisis Support Group, New York, NY
Mid-Peninsula Support Network for Battered Women, Mountain View, CA
Mid-Peninsula YWCA Rape Crisis Center, Palo Alto, CA
Mid-Step Mid-County Interagency Sexual Abuse Treatment Program, Banning, CA
Midtown Community Mental Health Center—Family Growth Center, Indianapolis, IN
Midway Hospital Center for Domestic Abuse, Saint Paul, MN
Midwest Family Resource, Chicago, IL
Midwest Family Resource, Evergreen Park, IL
Mifflin County Abuse Network, Lewistown, PA
Military Family Abuse Shelter, Honolulu, HI
Milwaukee County Children's Court—Victim/Witness Service, Milwaukee, WI
Milwaukee Women's Center, Milwaukee, WI
Missoula County Victim's Assistance Program, Missoula, MT
Missoula County Victim's Response Unit, Missoula, MT
Missouri Shores Women's Resource Center, Pierre, SD

Monmouth County Board Social Services—Family Services Division, Neptune City, NJ
Monroe County District Attorney—Domestic Violence Bureau, Rochester, NY
Monroe County District Attorney's Office—Victim/Witness Assistance Program, Sparta, WI
Monterey Rape Crisis Center, Monterey, CA
Montgomery Area Family Violence Program (MAFVP), Montgomery, AL
Montgomery Counseling Center, Montgomery, AL
Montgomery County Protectionline, Kensington, MD
Montgomery County Sexual Assault Services, Rockville, MD
Montgomery County Sheriff's Office—Victim/Witness Assistance, Dayton, OH
Montgomery County Women's Center—Rape Crisis Program, The Woodlands, TX
Montrose Community Counseling Center, Montrose, PA
Montrose County Incest Group Treatment Program, Montrose, CO
Morgan, Morgan and Associates, Edmond, OK
Morris Campus Women's Resource Center, Morris, MN
Morris County Prosecutor's Office—Victim/Witness Assistance Unit, Morristown, NJ
Morrison County Sexual Assault Program, Little Falls, MN
Morrow County Mental Health Service, Boardman, OR
Morrow County Sexual Abuse Prevention and Education Team, Mount Gilead, OH
Mother Lode Women's Center, Sonora, CA
Mount Carmel SHARE, Columbus, OH
Mount Pleasant Correctional Facility, Mount Pleasant, IA
Mount Sinai Medical Center—Rape Crisis Intervention Program, New York, NY
Mount Vernon Community Service Center, Mount Vernon, NY
Mountain Affiliates in Psychology, Stowe, VT
MOVE (Men Overcoming Violent Expression), Anchorage, AK
Movement Arts, Inc, Lansing, MI
Mujeres Unidas/Women Together Foundation, McAllen, TX
Multidisciplinary Sexual Abuse Treatment Program, Traverse City, MI
Multnomah County District Attorney—Victim's Assistance Program, Portland, OR
Multnomah County Juvenile Justice Division, Portland, OR
Mutual Ground, Inc, Aurora, IL
My Sister's Place, Athens, OH
Nacogdoches Rape Crisis Hotline, Nacogdoches, TX
Nashville Coalition on Child Abuse, Nashville, TN
Nassau Coalition on Child Abuse and Neglect, Hempstead, NY
Natchitoches Sheriff's Office, Natchitoches, LA
National Children's Advocacy Center, Huntsville, AL
Navy Family Services Center, Norfolk, VA
Necessities/Necesidades, Northampton, MA
Neighborhood Justice Project, Watkins Glen, NY
Neighborhood Justice Project of the Southern Tier, Inc, Elmira, NY
Hannah Neil Center/Willson Family and Child Guidance Clinic, Columbus, OH
NELCWIT (New England Learning Center for Women in Transition), Greenfield, MA
NE-NAIAH-KAHA-KOK, Keshena, WI
Network of Victim Assistance (NOVA), Doylestown, PA
Neuse-Trent Rape Assistance Program, New Bern, NC
Nevada County Victim/Witness Assistance Center, Nevada City, CA
New Beginnings, Newark, OH
New Beginnings, Springfield, VT
New Beginnings Shelter for Battered Women and Their Children, Seattle, WA
New Choices, Inc, Sidney, OH
New Directions, Mount Vernon, OH
New Directions, Inc, Lawton, OK
New England Clinical Associates, West Hartford, CT
New England Forensic Associates, Arlington, MA
New England Medical Center—Division of Child Psychiatry, Boston, MA
New Haven Project for Battered Women, New Haven, CT
New Haven Sexual Harassment Support Group, New Haven, CT
New Hope for Women, Rockland, ME
New Hope, Sexual Assault Program, Attleboro, MA
New Horizons Women's Shelter, La Crosse, WI

New Mexico State University—Counseling and Student Development, Las Cruces, NM
New Women Against Violence (WAV), Worthington, MN
New York Asian Women's Center, Inc, New York, NY
New York City Gay and Lesbian Anti-Violence Project, New York, NY
New York City Self-Help Clearinghouse, Inc, Brooklyn, NY
New York City Task Force Against Sexual Assault, New York, NY
New York County District Attorney's Office—Witness Aid Services Unit, New York, NY
New York Foundling Hospital—Child Abuse Prevention Services, New York, NY
New York Women Against Rape, New York, NY
New York Women Against Rape, New York, NY
Newcastle Holistic Center, Newcastle, ME
The Next Step Counseling and Training Center, Newton Center, MA
Clarina Howard Nichols Center, Morrisville, VT
NLP (Neuro-Linguistic Programming) Institute of San Diego, San Diego, CA
Noah Project, Inc, Abilene, TX
Norfolk Commonwealth's Attorney—Victim/Witness Assistance Program, Norfolk, VA
Norfolk County District Attorney—Sexual Assault Unit, Dedham, MA
Norfolk Task Force on Domestic Violence and Sexual Assault, Norfolk, NE
North Carolina Memorial Hospital Emergency Department, Chapel Hill, NC
North Central Bronx Hospital, Bronx, NY
North Central Health Care Facilities, Wausau, WI
North Central Human Services, Gardner, MA
North Essex Helpline, Montclair, NJ
North Shore Child and Family Guidance Center, Manhasset, NY
North Shore Rape Crisis Center, Beverly, MA
North Star Mental Health Services, Malone, NY
North Suburban Counseling Associates, Mount Clemens, MI
North Worcester County Sexual Abuse Program, Gardner, MA
Northeast Guidance Center, Detroit, MI
Northeast Parent and Child Society—Sexual Abuse Treatment Program, Schenectady, NY
Northeastern Connecticut Sexual Assault Crisis Services, Inc, Willamantic, CT
Northern Nevada Child/Adolescent Services (NNCAS), Reno, NV
Northern Pines Mental Health Center, Brainerd, MN
Northern Virginia Family Service, Alexandria, VA
Northern Virginia Hotline, Arlington, VA
Northern Westchester Guidance Clinic—Child and Adolescent Sexual Abuse Project, Mount Kisco, NY
Northern Westchester Shelter Peekskill Office, Peekskill, NY
Northern Wyoming Mental Health Center, Sheridan, WY
Northfield Victim Support Program, Northfield, MN
Northland Mental Health Center—Sexual Assault Program, Grand Rapids, MN
Northside Community Counseling Center, Atwater, CA
Northwest Action Against Rape, Rolling Meadows, IL
Northwest Arkansas Rape Crisis, Inc, Fayetteville, AR
Northwest Domestic Crisis Services, Inc, Woodward, OK
Northwest Florida Comprehensive Services for Children, Inc—Impact, Pensacola, FL
Northwest General Hospital—Domestic Abuse Project, Milwaukee, WI
Northwest Iowa Mental Health Center, Spencer, IA
Northwest Kansas Family Shelter, Inc, Hays, KS
Northwest Oklahoma Pastoral Care Association, Inc, Enid, OK
Northwest Safeline, Dyersburg, TN
Northwest Treatment Associates, Seattle, WA
Northwestern Ohio Rape Crisis Intervention, Defiance, OH
Northwestern University—Women's Center, Evanston, IL
Northwoods Coalition for Battered Women, Bemidji, MN
Nova House, Houlton, ME
Nueces County District Attorney—Victim/Witness Assistance, Corpus Christi, TX
Oak Grove Psychotherapy Associates, Minneapolis, MN
Oak Specialized Counseling Program, Ione, CA
Oakland Family Services—Children Services, Pontiac, MI
Oasis Center, Inc, Nashville, TN

OASIS, Inc (Opposing Abuse With Service, Information, and Shelter), Boone, NC
Oasis Shelter Home, Gold Beach, OR
Ocean County Commission on the Status of Women, Toms River, NJ
Ocean County Office of Victim Witness Advocacy, Toms River, NJ
Oceana Community Mental Health, Hart, MI
Odessa Rape Crisis Center, Odessa, TX
Office of District Attorney—Victim/Witness Advocate Program, Skowhegan, ME
Office of District Attorney—Victim Witness Assistance Center, San Francisco, CA
Office of Solicitor—Victim Witness Assistance, Hartsville, SC
Office of Solicitor—Victim Witness Assistance, Orangeburg, SC
Office of the State Attorney—Victim/Witness Assistance Program, Key West, FL
Office of the State's Attorney for Washington County, MD—Victim/Witness Assistance, Hagerstown, MD
Ohio Women Martial Artists, Columbus, OH
Onondaga County Sheriff's Department—Abused Person's Unit, Syracuse, NY
Onslow County Women's Center, Jacksonville, NC
Open Line, Inc, Ames, IA
Option, Inc, Hobbs, NM
Options, Inc, Morganton, NC
OPTIONS: to domestic violence and sexual assault, Washington, NC
Orange County Center for Health, Inc, Anaheim, CA
Orange County Crime Victim Assistance Program, Goshen, NY
Orange County Rape Crisis Center, Chapel Hill, NC
Orange County Safe Homes Project, Inc, Newburgh, NY
Orange County Safeline, Chelsea, VT
Orange County Sexual Assault Network (OCSAN), Orange, CA
Orange County Sheriff's Office—Victim Assistance Program, Orlando, FL
M A Orcutt, PhD, and Associates, Columbus, OH
Oswego Hospital Mental Health Division, Oswego, NY
Ottawa County Prosecuting Attorney—Victim Assistance, Grand Haven, MI
Ouachita Parish Sheriff's Department, Monroe, LA
Our Kids Need to Know, Bismarck, ND
Our Town Family Center, Tucson, AZ
Outagamie County Domestic Abuse Program—"Harbor House", Appleton, WI
Outer Banks Hotline, Manteo, NC
Outreach and Advocacy Project for Battered Women, Brooklyn, NY
Oxford Crisis and Referral Center, Oxford, OH
Oxnard Police Department—Victim Services Unit, Oxnard, CA
Pacific Center for Sexual Health, Honolulu, HI
Pacific Clinics, Pasadena, CA
Pacific County Crisis Support Network, Naselle, WA
Pacific Treatment Associates, Santa Cruz, CA
Paducah McCracken County Child Watch, Inc, Paducah, KY
Page Women's Resource Center, Page, AZ
Palm Beach County Sexual Assault Program, West Palm Beach, FL
Panhandle Crisis Center, Perryton, TX
Parent Assistance Center, Santa Fe, NM
Parental Stress Center and OASIS Program, Madison, WI
Parental Stress Services, Chicago, IL
The Parenting Center, Morristown, NJ
Parenting Guidance Center, Fort Worth, TX
Parents Anonymous of Greater Milwaukee, Milwaukee, WI
Parents Assistance Center—Sexual Abuse Treatment Program, Oklahoma City, OK
Parents Center, Santa Cruz, CA
Parents/Daughters/Sons United, San Luis Rey, CA
Parents United, Fairfield, CA
Parents United, Spokane, WA
Parents United, Rifle, CO
Parents United, Albuquerque, NM
Parents United, Fairfax, VA
Parents United, Summerville, SC
Parents United, Fort Worth, TX
Parents United/Children United, Burlingame, CA
Parents United/Daughters and Sons United, Oroville, CA
Parents United/Daughters and Sons United, Omaha, NE
Parents United, Dorchester County, Charleston, SC
Parents United, Inc of Prince William County, Virginia, Manassas, VA
Parents United—Kansas City Chapter, Kansas City, MO
Parents United of Hill County, Havre, MT
Parents United of Jefferson Area, Mount Vernon, IL
Parents United of Marin, San Rafael, CA
Parents United of Mercer County, Inc, Trenton, NJ
Parents United of North Central Iowa, Inc, Mason City, IA
Parents United of Roanoke Valley, Roanoke, VA
Parents United of Stanislaus County/Stanislaus County Child Abuse Treatment Team, Modesto, CA
Parents United of Utah Valley, Provo, UT
Parents United of Virginia, Inc/Human Potentials, Norfolk, VA
Parents United of Washoe County, Inc, Reno, NV
Parents United; Sons and Daughters United; Adults Molested as Children United; Sex Addicts Anonymous, Brockton, MA
Parents United, South Santa Clara Chapter, San Martin, CA
Parents United, Turtle Mountain Counties Chapter, Rolla, ND
Parents United, Ventura County Chapter, Ventura, CA
Park Center, Fort Wayne, IN
Park Psychological Services/Park Psychosocial Resource Center, Durham, NC
Park Rapids—Walker Clinic Counseling Department, Park Rapids, MN
Parkland Memorial Hospital, Dallas, TX
Rosa Parks Sexual Assault Crisis Center, Los Angeles, CA
Parkview Psychological Services, Sioux City, IA
Pasadena YWCA Rape Crisis Center, Pasadena, CA
Pasco County SAVE (Sexual Abuse Victim Examination) Program, New Port Richey, FL
Paso Nuevo Counseling Service, Albuquerque, NM
Passages—A Program for Victims of Domestic Abuse and Sexual Assault, Richland Center, WI
Passageways Center, Oklahoma City, OK
Pastoral Counseling and Consultation Center, Inc, Louisville, KY
PATH, Inc (Prevention of Abuse in the Home), Forest City, NC
Pathfinders—Safepath Project, Milwaukee, WI
Pathways Counseling Center, San Leandro, CA
Pathways, Inc, Ashland, KY
Pathways, Inc, Owingsville, KY
Alice Paul House, Indiana, PA
PAVE (Project Against Violent Encounters), Bennington, VT
Pawnee Mental Health Services, Manhattan, KS
Peace River Center—Rape Crisis Program, Lakeland, FL
Pebble Project, Austin, TX
Pee Dee Coalition Against Domestic and Sexual Assault, Florence, SC
Pend Oreille County Prosecuting Attorney—Victim/Witness Assistance Program, Newport, WA
Peninsula Counseling, Redondo Beach, CA
Peninsula Counseling Center, Woodmere, NY
The Peninsula Parents United/Daughters and Sons United, Hampton, VA
Penn Women's Center, Philadelphia, PA
People Against a Violent Environment (PAVE), Beaver Dam, WI
People Against Rape, Staunton, VA
People Against Rape, Charleston, SC
People Against Rape, El Centro, CA
People Against Sexual Abuse, Inc (PASA), Brooklyn, NY
People Against Violent Environments, Centralia, IL
People Research, Denver, CO
Peoples' Bridge Action, Inc, Athol, MA
Permian Basin Center for Battered Women and Their Children, Midland, TX
Personal and Family Development Center, San Jose, CA
The Personal Development Center, Inc, Marshfield, WI
Personal Development Consultants, Reno, NV
Joseph J Peters Institute, Philadelphia, PA
Phenix I, Garden City, NY
Philadelphia District Attorney's Office—Child Abuse Prosecution Unit, Philadelphia, PA
Philadelphia Sexual Abuse Project, Philadelphia, PA
Phoebe's Home, Bryan, TX
Phoenix Counseling, Fall River, MA
Piedmont Center for Counseling and Psychotherapy, Oakland, CA
Piedmont Psychological Practice, Sheridan, WY
Pierce County Office of the District Attorney—Victim/Witness Assistance, Ellsworth, WI
Pierce County Rape Relief, Tacoma, WA
Pinellas County SAVE (Sexual Assault Victim Examination), Saint Petersburg, FL
Pinellas Park Police Department, Pinellas Park, FL
Piscataquis County District Attorney's Office—Victim/Witness Services, Dover-Foxcroft, ME
Pittsburgh Action Against Rape (PAAR), Pittsburgh, PA
Placer County Child Sexual Abuse Treatment Program, Auburn, CA
Placer Women's Center, Auburn, CA
Planned Parenthood Association of Idaho, Boise, ID
Planned Parenthood of Chicago, Chicago, IL
Planned Parenthood of East Central Indiana, Muncie, IN
Playing It Safe, New Hyde Park, NY
Plymouth Area Crisis Services, Plymouth, NH
Plymouth County Rape Crisis Center, Brockton, MA
Pocatello YWCA Women's Advocates, Pocatello, ID
Polk County Sheriff's Office—Crime Prevention Section, Bartow, FL
Polk County Victim Services—Rape Care Program and Intrafamily Sexual Abuse Program, Des Moines, IA
Pomonok Neighborhood Center, Flushing, NY
Porter County Sexual Assault Recovery Project, Valparaiso, IN
Portland Counseling and Psychotherapy Associates, Portland, OR
Portland Police Bureau—Sexual Assault Prevention Adult Program, Portland, OR
Portland Women's Crisis Line, Portland, OR
Post Oak Psychiatry Associates, Houston, TX
The Pottstown YWCA Parent's Support Group Program, Pottstown, PA
Preble County Counseling Center, Eaton, OH
Prehab's Autumn House, Mesa, AZ
Presbyterian Medical Services—Community Counseling Center, Farmington, NM
The Prescott House, Birmingham, AL
Prestera Center for Mental Health Services, Inc, Huntington, WV
Prestera Center—Lincoln County Office (Satellite), West Hamlin, WV
Prevail, Inc, Noblesville, IN
The Prevention Center for Child Abuse and Neglect of Central Virginia, Lynchburg, VA
Preventive Services Program, New York, NY
Prince William County Mental Health Center, Manassas, VA
Probation Offenders Program, Freehold, NJ
Professional Alliance Counseling and Consultation Center, Fort Worth, TX
Program for Aid to Victims of Sexual Assault, Inc, Duluth, MN
Programs for Children, Albuquerque, NM
Project Against Sexual Abuse of Appalachian Children, Knoxville, TN
Project Against Sexual Assault Abuse, Newton, NJ
Project for Victims of Family Violence, Fayetteville, AR
Project Help, Inc, Naples, FL
Project Promoting Alternatives to Violence through Education (PAVE), Inc, Denver, CO
Project SAFE, Wheatland, WY
Project Safe, Inc, Crookston, MN
Project Sanctuary, Ukiah, CA
Project SISTER Sexual Assault Crisis Services, Claremont, CA
Project Woman, Springfield, OH
Prosecuting Attorney's Office, Fort Smith, AR
Prosecutor's Office—Crime Victim Witness Assistance, Asotin, WA
Prosecutor's Office of Victim Witness Advocacy, New Brunswick, NJ
Prosecutor's Office—Victim/Witness Assistance Program, Hilo, HI
Prosecutor's Office—Victim/Witness Assistance Unit, Yakima, WA
Prosecutor's Victim/Witness Assistance Program, Gold Beach, OR
Prostitutes Union of Massachusetts (PUMA), Cambridge, MA
Providence Home Women's Shelter, Columbia, SC
Providence House/Willingboro Shelter, Burlington, NJ
Providence Sexual Assault Center, Everett, WA
Psychological and Consulting Services, Tucson, AZ
Psychological Associates, Peoria, IL
Psychological Associates, Inc, Newark, OH
Psychological Associates of Oxon Hill, Oxon Hill, MD
Psychological Services Center, Vermillion, SD
Psychological Services of St Augustine, Saint Augustine, FL
Psychologically and Physically Abused Persons Center, Hempstead, NY

Psychology and Education Associates, Clinton, MD
Psychotherapy Associates, Bennington, VT
Psychotherapy Resources of Norfolk (PRN), Norfolk, VA
Psychotherapy Services, Redding, CA
Pucci and Associates, Kenosha, WI
Pueblo YWCA Rape Crisis Center, Pueblo, CO
Puget Sound Legal Assistance Foundation, Olympia, WA
Putnam-North Westchester Women's Resource Center, Mahopac, NY
Quad County Coalition Against Domestic Violence, Macomb, IL
Quad County Counseling Center, Princeton, IL
Quad Unit Intervention and Treatment Program (QUIT), Payette, ID
Quakerdale Home, New Providence, IA
Quanada, Quincy, IL
Queens College Women's Center, Flushing, NY
Queens Hospital Center Rape Crisis Program, Jamaica, NY
Racine County District Attorney's Office—Victim/Witness Program, Racine, WI
Ragsdale and Associates Counseling Services, Farmington, NM
Rainbow House/Arco Iris, Chicago, IL
The Rainbow Project, Inc, Madison, WI
Rainbow Psychotherapy Associates, Oakland, CA
Rainbow Services Ltd, San Pedro, CA
Ramsey County Attorney's Office—Victim/Witness Assistance Unit, Saint Paul, MN
Ramsey County Court—Domestic Abuse Office, Saint Paul, MN
Rancho Victim/Witness Assistance Program, Rancho Cucamonga, CA
Randolph County Family Crisis Center, Asheboro, NC
The Rape Action Committee of the Women's Center, Inc, Carbondale, IL
Rape Aid and Prevention, Lancaster, PA
Rape and Abuse Crisis Center, Fargo, ND
Rape and Abuse Crisis Center, Inc, Binghamton, NY
Rape and Assault Support Services, Nashua, NH
Rape and Domestic Violence Crisis Center, Concord, NH
Rape and Domestic Violence Information Center, Morgantown, WV
Rape and Domestic Violence Services of Arlington, Arlington, VA
Rape and Sexual Abuse Care Center, Edwardsville, IL
Rape and Sexual Abuse Center of Davidson County, Nashville, TN
Rape and Sexual Abuse Center of Ventura County, Camarillo, CA
Rape and Sexual Abuse Crisis Center, Inc, Stamford, CT
Rape and Sexual Assault Center, Minneapolis, MN
Rape and Suicide Crisis of Southeast Texas, Inc, Beaumont, TX
Rape and Victim Assistance Center, York, PA
Rape/Assault Care Services, Muscatine, IA
Rape Assistance and Awareness Program, Denver, CO
Rape Awareness Program, Fort Wayne, IN
Rape Awareness Program (RAP), Tuscaloosa, AL
The Rape, Child and Family Abuse Crisis Council of Salisbury-Rowan, Inc, Salisbury, NC
Rape Companion Program, Lynchburg, VA
Rape Counseling and Prevention, Topeka, KS
Rape Counseling Service, Fresno, CA
Rape Crisis, Canton, OH
Rape Crisis, Albany, GA
Rape Crisis Alliance of Alamance County, Inc, Burlington, NC
Rape Crisis and Prevention Center, Bowling Green, KY
Rape Crisis and Sexual Abuse Center, Springfield, MO
Rape Crisis and Sexual Assault Services, Augusta, GA
Rape Crisis and Sexual Assault Services, Vicksburg, MS
Rape Crisis Assistance, Waterville, ME
Rape Crisis Center, Atlanta, GA
Rape Crisis Center, Portland, ME
The Rape Crisis Center, San Diego, CA
Rape Crisis Center, Wilmington, NC
Rape Crisis Center, Hillsboro, OR
Rape Crisis Center, Hobbs, NM
Rape Crisis Center, Newark, OH
Rape Crisis Center, Reno, NV
Rape Crisis Center, Bismarck, ND
The Rape Crisis Center, Inc, Brookville, PA
Rape Crisis Center of Berkshire County, Inc, Pittsfield, MA
Rape Crisis Center of Marin, San Rafael, CA

Rape Crisis Center of McLean County, Bloomington, IL
Rape Crisis Center of Milford, Inc, Milford, CT
Rape Crisis Center of Northwest Florida, Pensacola, FL
The Rape Crisis Center of Schuylkill County, Pottsville, PA
Rape Crisis Center of Syracuse, Inc, Syracuse, NY
Rape Crisis Center of the Coastal Empire, Inc, Savannah, GA
Rape Crisis Center of Volusia County, Inc, Daytona Beach, FL
Rape Crisis Center of West Contra Costa, San Pablo, CA
Rape Crisis—CONTACT, Milford, DE
Rape Crisis Contact, Wilmington, DE
Rape Crisis Council of Greenville, Greenville, SC
Rape Crisis Council of Greenwood, Greenwood, SC
Rape Crisis Council of Pickens County, Inc, Easley, SC
Rape Crisis Counseling of Greenville, Greenville, MS
Rape Crisis/Domestic Violence Center, Amarillo, TX
Rape Crisis for Washington County, Cambridge, NY
Rape Crisis Helpline, Yonkers, NY
Rape Crisis Helpline, New Rochelle, NY
Rape Crisis Helpline, Mount Vernon, NY
Rape Crisis Helpline, White Plains, NY
Rape Crisis Intervention, Arkadelphia, AR
Rape Crisis Intervention, Chico, CA
Rape Crisis Intervention of Harnett County, Lillington, NC
Rape Crisis Intervention Program, New York, NY
Rape Crisis Intervention Program and Social Work Department, Brooklyn, NY
Rape Crisis Intervention Service of Carroll County, Inc, Westminster, MD
Rape Crisis Network, Eugene, OR
Rape Crisis Network, Spokane, WA
Rape Crisis Network, Columbia, SC
Rape Crisis of Central Contra Costa County, Concord, CA
Rape Crisis of Durham, Durham, NC
Rape Crisis Outreach Program/Women's Advocacy Program, Richmond, VA
Rape Crisis Program, Olean, NY
Rape Crisis Program, Houston, TX
Rape Crisis Program, Fort Worth, TX
Rape Crisis Program for Rensselaer County, Troy, NY
Rape Crisis Program of Worcester, Inc, Worcester, MA
Rape Crisis Service, Fort Smith, AR
Rape Crisis Service, Newark, NY
Rape Crisis Service of Livingston County, Geneseo, NY
Rape Crisis Service of Planned Parenthood, Albion, NY
Rape Crisis Service of Planned Parenthood—Genesee County, Batavia, NY
Rape Crisis Service of San Mateo County, Burlingame, CA
Rape Crisis Service—Ontario County, Canandaigua, NY
Rape Crisis Service—Planned Parenthood of Schenectady and Affiliated Counties, Schenectady, NY
Rape Crisis Services, Danbury, CT
Rape Crisis Services, Oneonta, NY
Rape Crisis Services, Urbana, IL
Rape Crisis Services for Concho Valley, San Angelo, TX
Rape Crisis Services of Greater Lowell, Inc, Lowell, MA
Rape Crisis Services of Homesafe, Ashtabula, OH
Rape Crisis Services of Lebanon County, Lebanon, PA
Rape Crisis Services of Niagara County, Niagara Falls, NY
Rape Crisis/Spouse Abuse Center, Ocala, FL
Rape Crisis Team, Macon, GA
Rape Crisis Team, Farmington, NM
Rape Crisis Team of Trumbull County, Inc, Warren, OH
Rape Crisis/Victim Services, Big Spring, TX
Rape Crisis Volunteers of Cumberland County, Fayetteville, NC
Rape/Domestic Abuse Program of North Platte, Inc, North Platte, NE
Rape Education and Prevention Program, Columbus, OH
Rape Information and Counseling, Youngstown, OH
Rape Information and Counseling Service, Springfield, IL
Rape Intervention Program/Crime Victim Assessment Project (RIP/CVAP), New York, NY
Rape Intervention Team, Inc, Durango, CO
Rape Prevention/Crisis Intervention of Hamilton County, Indian Lake, NY

Rape Prevention Education Program, Davis, CA
Rape Prevention Education Program, Riverside, CA
Rape Prevention Education Program, Women's Resource Center, Irvine, CA
Rape Prevention Seminars, Inc, Saint Louis, MO
Rape Response, Birmingham, AL
Rape Response, Winston-Salem, NC
Rape Response, Inc, Gainesville, GA
Rape Response Program, Huntsville, AL
Rape/Sexual Assault Intervention Program, Dubuque, IA
Rape/Sexual Assault Victim Advocates, Fort Dodge, IA
Rape/Spouse Abuse Crisis Center, Lincoln, NE
Rape Survivor Advocacy Program, Goshen, NY
Rape Survivors, Inc, Portland, OR
Rape Treatment Center, Santa Monica, CA
Rape Treatment Center, Miami, FL
Rape Victim Advocacy Program, Iowa City, IA
Rape Victim Advocate Program, Fort Walton Beach, FL
Rape Victim Advocates, Chicago, IL
Rape Victim Companion Program, Alexandria, VA
Rape Victim Services Program, Prestonsburg, KY
Rape Victim Services Program, Chicago, IL
Rape Victim Support Team, Junction City, KS
Rape Victim's Advocacy Program, Great Falls, MT
Rape Victims Services Program, Elizabethtown, KY
Rapeline/Sexual Assault Program, Rochester, MN
RapeResponse Program, Orlando, FL
Rappahannock Council on Domestic Violence, Fredericksburg, VA
RAVEN (Rape and Violence End Now), Saint Louis, MO
Ravenswood Hospital Community Mental Health Center, Chicago, IL
Ravenwood Center, Chardon, OH
Isaac Ray Center, Inc, Chicago, IL
REACH, Davie, FL
REACH, Inc, Murphy, NC
REACH of Haywood County, Waynesville, NC
REACH of Jackson County, Sylva, NC
REAL Crisis Intervention, Inc, Greenville, NC
Recovery: Aid to Victims of Sexual and Domestic Abuse, Shelton, WA
Recovery Mountain, Inc, Westminster, SC
Refuge House/Rape Crisis Center, Tallahassee, FL
Region III Mental Health, Caldwell, ID
Regional Rape Crisis Service, Rochester, NY
Regional Sexual Assault Treatment Center, Eau Claire, WI
The Regional Treatment Center for Sexual Abuse, Ogden, UT
Relief After Violent Encounter, Saint Johns, MI
Resolutions, Montpelier, VT
Resolve Family Abuse Program, Charleston, WV
Resource Center for Women, Aberdeen, SD
Response, Aspen, CO
Response of Suffolk County, Inc, Stony Brook, NY
Response Program, Los Angeles, CA
Response Sexual Assault Support Services, Norfolk, VA
Response to Sexual and Domestic Violence, Berlin, NH
Resurrection Home, Inc—Family Abuse Shelter, Beattyville, KY
Retired Senior Volunteer Program, Las Vegas, NV
Rheedlen Place, New York, NY
Rhode Island Rape Crisis Center, Cranston, RI
Rice County Sexual Assault Program, Faribault, MN
Richland Memorial Hospital, Columbia, SC
Richmond City Commonwealth Attorney—Victim/Witness Services, Richmond, VA
Richstone Family Center, Hawthorne, CA
Riverside Area Rape Crisis Center, Riverside, CA
Roadhouse Crisis and Information, Fort Collins, CO
Rochester Police Department—Victim Assistance Unit, Rochester, NY
Rock County 51.42 Board, Janesville, WI
Rock County Victim/Witness Assistance Program, Janesville, WI
Rockford Sexual Assault Counseling, Inc, Rockford, IL
Rockland Family Shelter—Rape Crisis Program, Spring Valley, NY
Roosevelt County Rape Crisis Advocacy, Portales, NM
Rosebud County Attorney's Office—Victim/Witness Assistance, Forsyth, MT
Roswell Refuge for Battered Adults, Roswell, NM
RSA, Inc (Redirecting Sexual Aggression), Lakewood, CO
RTAT, Inc (Restitution Treatment and Training), Ontario, OR
Runaway and Homeless Youth Program, Valhalla, NY
Runaway Hot Line, Bellmore, NY

Runaway Youth Coordinating Council, Inc (RYCC), Hempstead, NY
Rush—Presbyterian—St Luke's Medical Center Family Violence Program, Chicago, IL
Russell Student Health Center—Mental Health Section, University, AL
Ruston Mayor's Commission for Women, Ruston, LA
Rutherford County Guidance Center/Sexual Abuse Treatment Program, Murfreesboro, TN
Rutland County Women's Network and Shelter, Rutland, VT
R-VAN (Rape Victims Assistance Network), Pittsburg, KS
Sacramento County District Attorney's Office—Victim and Witness Assistance Program, Sacramento, CA
Sacramento Rape Crisis Center, Sacramento, CA
Sacramento Youth and Family Services Center, Sacramento, CA
Sacred Heart Center/Women's Shelter, Eagle Butte, SD
SAF (Services to Aid Families), Oswego, NY
Safe Alternatives for Abused Families, Devils Lake, ND
Safe and Fear Free Environment (SAFE), Dillingham, AK
The SAFE Center, Kearney, NE
Safe Harbor—Spouse Abuse Shelter, Ashland, KY
Safe Haven, Inc, Columbus, MS
Safe House/Sexual Assault Services, Inc, Cheyenne, WY
SAFE, Inc Sexual Assault Program, Tupelo, MS
SAFE, Inc—Stop Abusive Family Environments, Welch, WV
Safe 'N' Strong, San Mateo, CA
Safe Passage, Inc, DeKalb, IL
Safe Place, Battle Creek, MI
Safe Place, Montgomery, AL
A Safe Place, Waukegan, IL
A Safe Place, Oakland, CA
Safe Place and Rape Crisis Center (SPARCC), Sarasota, FL
A Safe Place, Inc (ASP)/Nantucket Child Assault Prevention (CAPP), Nantucket, MA
SAFE Project, Laramie, WY
SAFE Shelter, Jamestown, ND
Safe Space, Newport, TN
Safe Space, Butte, MT
Safe Space Domestic Violence Program, Vero Beach, FL
Safehome, Inc, Overland Park, KS
Safehome/Sexual Assault Program, Port Angeles, WA
Safeplace, Inc, Florence, AL
Safeplace: Rape Relief/Women's Shelter Services, Olympia, WA
Safer Futures, Kent, OH
Saginaw County Sexual Assault Center, Saginaw, MI
SAIF—Survivors of Abuse in Families, Park Ridge, IL
St Anne Institute—Sex Abuse Prevention Services, Albany, NY
St Anthony Rape Treatment Center, Columbus, OH
St Elizabeth Medical Center, Granite City, IL
St Francis Center for Personal Growth, North Clarendon, VT
Saint Francis Hospital Emergency Department, Evanston, IL
St Lawrence Valley Renewal House for Victims of Family Violence, Canton, NY
St Louis Circuit Attorney's Victim Services, Saint Louis, MO
St Louis County Victim/Witness Assistance Program, Duluth, MN
St Luke Hospital Community Pediatric Clinic, Fort Thomas, KY
St Martha's Hall, Saint Louis, MO
St Mary's Boys Home, Beaverton, OR
St Mary's Mental Health Center, Hoboken, NJ
Salem County Prosecutor's Office—Victim-Witness Advocacy, Salem, NJ
Salem County Rape Crisis Center, Elmer, NJ
Salt Lake Rape Crisis Center, Salt Lake City, UT
The Salvation Army, Nashville, TN
The Salvation Army Family Haven, Saint Louis, MO
Salvation Army Family Service Division, Chicago, IL
The Salvation Army Social Service Center, Indianapolis, IN
San Bernardino District Attorney's Office—Victim/Witness Center, San Bernardino, CA
San Bernardino Sexual Assault Service, San Bernardino, CA
San Diego County Child Sexual Abuse Treatment Program, San Diego, CA
San Diego Youth and Community Services, San Diego, CA

San Fernando Valley Child Guidance Clinic, Van Nuys, CA
San Francisco Rape Treatment Center, San Francisco, CA
San Francisco Women Against Rape, San Francisco, CA
San Francisco Women's Center/The Women's Building, San Francisco, CA
San Juan County Prosecuting Attorney—Victim/Witness Program, Friday Harbor, WA
San Leandro Community Counseling, San Leandro, CA
San Luis Obispo County Rape Crisis Center, San Luis Obispo, CA
San Luis Obispo County Victim/Witness Assistance Center, San Luis Obispo, CA
San Mateo Women's Shelter, San Mateo, CA
Sanctuary, Inc, Harrison, AR
Sandhills Center for Mental Health, Mental Retardation, Substance Abuse, Pinehurst, NC
Sandusky County Department of Human Services—Children's Services Unit, Fremont, OH
SANE (Sexual Abuse Now Ended), Boise, ID
Sangre de Cristo Community Mental Health Services, Las Vegas, NM
Santa Barbara County District Attorney's Victim/Witness Assistance Program, Santa Barbara, CA
Santa Barbara Rape Crisis Center, Santa Barbara, CA
Santa Clara County Victim Witness Assistance Center, San Jose, CA
Santa Cruz Men's Alternatives to Violence, Santa Cruz, CA
Santa Cruz Victim/Witness Center, Santa Cruz, CA
Santa Fe Mountain Center, Santa Fe, NM
Santa Fe Rape Crisis Center, Inc, Santa Fe, NM
Santa Maria Valley Youth and Family Center, Santa Maria, CA
Santee-Wateree Mental Health Center, Sumter, SC
Sarah Center, Long Beach, CA
Sarah House, Washington, DC
Sarpy County Attorney's Office—Victim/Witness Unit, Papillion, NE
Satilla Community Mental Health Clinic, Waycross, GA
Sauk County Human Services, Reedsburg, WI
SAVES (Sexual Assault Victims Emergency Services), Farmington, ME
SCAN (Stop Child Abuse Now) of Northern Virginia, Alexandria, VA
SCAN Volunteer Service, Inc, Little Rock, AR
Schoharie County Mental Health Center, Schoharie, NY
Schoharie County Rape Crisis Service, Cobleskill, NY
Scioto Paint Valley Mental Health Center, Chillicothe, OH
SCIP (Sandhills Crisis Intervention Program), Ogallala, NE
Seacoast Mental Health Center, Portsmouth, NH
Seattle Counseling Services for Sexual Minorities, Seattle, WA
Seattle Institute for Sex Therapy, Education, and Research (SISTER), Seattle, WA
Seattle Police Department—Victim Assistance Section, Seattle, WA
Seattle Rape Relief, Seattle, WA
Seattle Youth and Community Services, Seattle, WA
Second Judicial Circuit Solicitor's Office, Aiken, SC
Senior Victim Services, Inc of Delaware County, Folsom, PA
Serve, Inc—Watch House, Fulton, MO
Services to Abused Families, Inc/Women's Abuse Shelter, Culpeper, VA
Services to Victims of Sexual Assault, Jersey City, NJ
Servicios de la Raza, Inc, Denver, CO
Seton Catholic Family and Community Services, Troy, NY
Sex Abuse Interventions, Inc, Wailuku, HI
Sex Abuse Treatment Center, Honolulu, HI
Sex Abuse Treatment Program, Lihue, HI
Sex and Marital Therapy Clinic, Chicago, IL
Sex Offender Program, Somers, CT
Sex Offender Treatment and Evaluation Project, Atascadero, CA
Sex Offense Services (SOS), South Bend, IN
Sexology Associates, Inc, Bethesda, MD
The Sexual Abuse and Assault Program, Brant Beach, NJ
Sexual Abuse Clinic, Portland, OR
The Sexual Abuse Clinic, Shelton Office, Shelton, WA
Sexual Abuse Investigation Network (SAIN), Malden, MA
Sexual Abuse Management Program, Saint Louis, MO
Sexual Abuse Prevention Program, Saint Joseph, MO

Sexual Abuse Resource Center, Dayton, OH
Sexual Abuse Services, Oshkosh, WI
Sexual Abuse Services Unit—Child Protective Services (SASU, CPS), Hyattsville, MD
Sexual Abuse Treatment and Support Program, La Crosse, WI
Sexual Abuse Treatment Center, El Paso, TX
Sexual Abuse Treatment Center, Westminster, MD
Sexual Abuse Treatment Program, Cedar Rapids, IA
Sexual Abuse Treatment Program, Moline, IL
The Sexual Abuse Treatment Program, Manchester, CT
Sexual Abuse Treatment Program, Fort Myers, FL
Sexual Abuse Treatment Program, Wichita, KS
Sexual Abuse Treatment Program, Baltimore, MD
Sexual Abuse Treatment Program of Sarasota, Sarasota, FL
Sexual Abuse Treatment Program (SATP), Dover, NH
Sexual Abuse Treatment Program (SATP), Spring Hill, FL
Sexual Abuse Treatment Program/Victim and Offender Services, Meriden, CT
Sexual Abuse Treatment Program/SAFE (Safety Awareness for Everyone), Winter Haven, FL
Sexual Abuse Treatment Team, Norwalk, CT
Sexual Abuse Treatment Team/Kidability, Council Bluffs, IA
Sexual and Physical Abuse Resource Center (SPARC), Gainesville, FL
Sexual Assault and Domestic Violence Center, Inc, Baltimore, MD
Sexual Assault and Family Emergencies, Vandalia, IL
Sexual Assault and Family Emergency (SAFE) Center, Clearwater, FL
Sexual Assault and Rape Analysis (SARA) Unit, Newark, NJ
Sexual Assault and Rape Relief of Bonneville County, Inc, Idaho Falls, ID
Sexual Assault Care Center, San Mateo, CA
Sexual Assault Center, Stockton, CA
Sexual Assault Center, Cheverly, MD
Sexual Assault Center, Jacksonville, FL
Sexual Assault Center—Family Service Association, Green Bay, WI
Sexual Assault Center of Harborview Medical Center, Seattle, WA
Sexual Assault Center of Lake County, Painesville, OH
Sexual Assault Center of Lancaster County, Lititz, PA
Sexual Assault Counseling, Jackson, MI
Sexual Assault Counseling and Information Service, Charleston, IL
Sexual Assault Counseling Unit, Milwaukee, WI
Sexual Assault Crisis Agency, Long Beach, CA
Sexual Assault Crisis and Safety Education Program, East Lansing, MI
Sexual Assault Crisis Center, Knoxville, TN
Sexual Assault Crisis Center, Appleton, WI
Sexual Assault Crisis Center, Auburn, ME
Sexual Assault Crisis Center, Inc, Hattiesburg, MS
Sexual Assault Crisis Counseling, Carmel, NY
Sexual Assault Crisis Service, Meriden, CT
Sexual Assault Crisis Service, Waterbury, CT
Sexual Assault Crisis Service of Middlesex County, Inc, Middletown, CT
Sexual Assault Crisis Services, Danville, IL
Sexual Assault Crisis Team of Washington County, Inc, Montpelier, VT
Sexual Assault Division, Newport News, VA
Sexual Assault Domestic Violence Center, Hutchinson, KS
Sexual Assault Help Center (Upper Ohio Valley), Wheeling, WV
Sexual Assault Helpline/Emergency Services, Presque Isle, ME
Sexual Assault Prevention/Intervention Program, Conway, SC
Sexual Assault Program for Scott County, Shakopee, MN
Sexual Assault Program of Beltrami, Cass, and Hubbard Counties, Bemidji, MN
Sexual Assault Program of North Saint Louis County, Virginia, MN
Sexual Assault Recovery Assistance (SARA), Howell, MI
Sexual Assault Recovery Center, Baltimore, MD
Sexual Assault Recovery Service, Gainesville, FL
Sexual Assault Recovery Thru Awareness and Hope—SARAH, Inc, Derry, NH
Sexual Assault Resource Agency (SARA), Charlottesville, VA
Sexual Assault Resource Service, Minneapolis, MN
Sexual Assault Response and Awareness (SARA), Roanoke, VA

Sexual Assault Response Service, Lancaster, CA
Sexual Assault Response Team (SART), Santa Barbara, CA
Sexual Assault Response Team/Sexual Assault Nurse Examiner Program, Santa Cruz, CA
Sexual Assault Safety Center, Bartlesville, OK
Sexual Assault Services, Indio, CA
Sexual Assault Services, Brainerd, MN
Sexual Assault Services, Mankato, MN
Sexual Assault Services, Oakdale, MN
Sexual Assault Services of Dakota County, Burnsville, MN
Sexual Assault Services Program/Shelter House, Willmar, MN
Sexual Assault/Spouse Abuse Resource Center, Bel Air, MD
Sexual Assault Support, Grand Junction, CO
Sexual Assault Support Service, Livingston, NJ
Sexual Assault Treatment Center, Kenosha, WI
Sexual Assault Treatment Center of Greater Milwaukee, Milwaukee, WI
Sexual Assault Treatment Program, Manitowoc, WI
Sexual Assault Treatment Program, Helena, MT
Sexual Assault Treatment Services, Inc, Albuquerque, NM
Sexual Assault Unit, Yakima, WA
Sexual Assault Victim Services, Inc, Stevens Point, WI
Sexual Assault Victim Services/Prevention Program, Santa Ana, CA
Sexual Assault Victim Services/Prevention Program, Costa Mesa, CA
Sexual Assault Victim Services/Prevention Program, Orange, CA
Sexual Assault Victims Advocacy Services (SAVAS), Manassas, VA
Sexual Assault Victim's Advocate Resource, Auburn, NY
Sexual Assault Victims Care Unit, Belleville, IL
Sexual Assault Victims Care Unit, Edgemont, IL
Sexual Assault Victims Services, Napa, CA
Sexual Assault Volunteer Effort (SAVE), Altoona, PA
Sexual Battery Committee of the Gainesville Commission on the Status of Women, Gainesville, FL
Sexual Behavior Clinic, New York, NY
Sexual Offenders Program, Los Lunas, NM
Sexual Offense Services of Ramsey County (SOS), Saint Paul, MN
The Sexual Trauma Institute, Metairie, LA
Sexual Trauma Institute, New Orleans, LA
Sexual Violence Center, Minneapolis, MN
Sexual Violence Center in Carver County, Chaska, MN
Shalom Christian Counseling Center, Medford, OR
SHARE (Sexual Harassment/Assault Advising, Resources, and Education) Program, Princeton, NJ
Sharing, Riverdale, NY
Shasta County Child Sexual Abuse Treatment Program, Redding, CA
Shasta County Mental Health Services—Outpatient Children's Program, Redding, CA
Shasta County Women's Refuge, Redding, CA
Sheboygan Memorial Medical Center—Sexual Assault Treatment Center, Sheboygan, WI
Shelter, Marinette, WI
Shelter Against Violent Environment (SAVE), Fremont, CA
The Shelter for Abused Women, Winchester, VA
Shelter for Families of Domestic Violence, Greenville, SC
Shelter for Help in Emergency, Charlottesville, VA
Shelter Home of Caldwell County, Lenoir, NC
The Shelter, Inc, Gadsden, AL
Shelter, Inc, Alpena, MI
The Shelter, Inc, Lawrenceburg, TN
Shelter Services for Women, Inc, Santa Barbara, CA
Sheltered Aid to Families in Emergency (SAFE), Inc, Wilkesboro, NC
Shenandoah Valley Sex Offender Treatment Program, Harrisonburg, VA
Shenandoah Women's Center, Martinsburg, WV
Sheriff's Office—Victim/Witness Assistance, New Orleans, LA
Shore Mental Health Center, Lakewood, NJ
Shumard Counseling PC, Livonia, MI
Barbara Sinatra Children's Center, Rancho Mirage, CA
Siskiyou Sexual Assault, Yreka, CA
Sistercare, Inc, Columbia, SC
Six County, Inc—Muskingum Counseling Center, Zanesville, OH
Sixth District Department of Corrections, Sex Offenders Treatment Program, Cedar Rapids, IA
Sixth Judicial District Department of Correctional Services, Iowa City, IA

Skagit County Prosecuting Attorney's Office—Victim/Witness Assistance Unit, Mount Vernon, WA
Skagit Rape Relief and Battered Women's Services, Mount Vernon, WA
Skamania County Council on Domestic Violence and Sexual Assault, Stevenson, WA
SMU Women's Center, North Dartmouth, MA
SOAP Box Players, Bellingham, WA
Social Advocates for Youth, Cupertino, CA
Social Work Services, Fort Campbell, KY
Society for Seamen's Children—Teen Advocacy Program Prevention Unit, Staten Island, NY
Society's League Against Molestation (SLAM), Crown Point, IN
Sojourn Services for Battered Women and Their Children, Santa Monica, CA
Sojourn Women's Center, Springfield, IL
Sojourner, Indianapolis, IN
Sojourner Center, Phoenix, AZ
Solicitor's Office—Victim/Witness Program, Hampton, SC
Somerset Coalition for Prevention and Treatment of Sexual Abuse, Bridgewater, NJ
Somerset Rape Crisis Service, Somerville, NJ
Somerville Hospital—Child and Parents Program, Somerville, MA
Sonoma County Child Abuse Council, Santa Rosa, CA
Sonoma County Victim Witness Project, Santa Rosa, CA
Sonoma County Women Against Rape, Santa Rosa, CA
Sopris Mental Health Clinic, Glenwood Springs, CO
SOS, Inc, Emporia, KS
South Bay Center for Counseling, Manhattan Beach, CA
South Bay Community Counseling Center, San Jose, CA
South Brevard Women's Center, Melbourne, FL
South Carolina Guardian ad Litem Program, Columbia, SC
South Carolina Guardian ad Litem Program, Lancaster, SC
South Carolina Volunteer Guardian ad Litem Program, Rock Hill, SC
South Central Human Relations Center, Owatonna, MN
South Peninsula Women's Services, Inc, Homer, AK
South Shore Child Guidance Center, Freeport, NY
South Shore Therapy Center, Quincy, MA
South Shore Women's Center, Plymouth, MA
South Suburban Family Service, South Saint Paul, MN
Southeastern Oklahoma Services for Abused Women, Antlers, OK
Southern Arizona Center Against Sexual Assault (SACASA), Tucson, AZ
Southern Methodist University—Human Resource Women's Center, Dallas, TX
Southern Minnesota Crisis Support Center, Fairmont, MN
Southern Ohio Task Force on Domestic Violence, Portsmouth, OH
Southwest Institute for Research and Treatment in Human Sexuality, Ltd, Tempe, AZ
Southwest Minnesota Sexual Assault Program, Marshall, MN
Southwest Women Working Together, Chicago, IL
Southwestern Alaska Council for Prevention of Child Sexual Abuse, Bethel, AK
Southwestern Indiana Mental Health Center—Rape Treatment Program, Evansville, IN
Southwestern Mental Health Center, Luverne, MN
Spartanburg County Guardian ad Litem Program, Spartanburg, SC
SPEAKS (Survivors of Physical and Emotional Abuse as Kids), Los Angeles, CA
Special Assessment and Management Clinic, Saint Louis, MO
SPIN (Special People in Need), Chicago, IL
Spokane County Prosecuting Attorney—Victim/Witness Assistance Unit, Spokane, WA
Spouse Abuse, Inc, Orlando, FL
Spouse Abuse Network, Tuscaloosa, AL
Spouse Abuse/Sexual Assault Crisis Center, Hastings, NE
Spring Branch/Memorial Family Outreach and Harris County Children's Protective Services, Houston, TX
Spring Garden Psychological Associates, Philadelphia, PA
Springfield Child Abuse Resources, Springfield, OR
Spruce Run Association, Bangor, ME
Standing Together Against Rape (STAR), Anchorage, AK

Stanislaus County District Attorney's Office—Victim/Witness Program, Modesto, CA
Stanislaus Rape Crisis Center, Modesto, CA
State Attorney's Office—Sexual Assault Assistance Program, Fort Pierce, FL
State Attorney's Office—Victim/Witness Assistance Program, Ocala, FL
State Attorney's Office—Victim/Witness Unit, Tallahassee, FL
State of Florida Guardian ad Litem Program—20th Judicial Circuit, Fort Myers, FL
State's Attorney for Montgomery County, MD, Rockville, MD
State's Attorney's Office, Deadwood, SD
State's Attorney's Office for Baltimore City—Sex Offense Unit, Baltimore, MD
Step II Psychological Services, Chico, CA
STEPS to End Family Violence, New York, NY
Stillwater Domestic Violence Services, Inc, Stillwater, OK
Elizabeth Stone House, Jamaica Plain, MA
Stop Abuse, Everett, WA
Stop Abuse For Everyone, Inc, Clarion, PA
STOP Center on Domestic Violence, Plattsburgh, NY
Stop Child Abuse and Neglect (SCAN), Dayton, OH
STOP Sexual Addictions and Disorders Treatment Program, Miami, FL
Story County Attorney's Office—Victim Witness Assistance Program, Nevada, IA
Strafford County Human Services, Dover, NH
Stress and Trauma Recovery Center, Paige, TX
Sublette County SAFV Task Force, Pinedale, WY
Suffolk County District Attorney—Victim-Witness Assistance, Boston, MA
Suffolk County District Attorney's Office—Family Crime Bureau, Hauppauge, NY
Suicide Prevention and Crisis Service, Ithaca, NY
Summit County Psychological Associates, Akron, OH
Sunrise Counseling and Wellness Center, Carroll, IA
Sunshine Center, Montgomery, AL
SUPPORT, Elkhart, IN
The Support Center, Omak, WA
Support Group for Survivors of Sexual Abuse, Kingston, NY
Support, Inc, Ely, NV
Survival Adult Abuse, Inc, Warrensburg, MO
The Survivors, Chillicothe, MO
Survivors Healing Center, Santa Cruz, CA
Survivors, Inc, Gettysburg, PA
Survivors of Incest Anonymous, Bayside, CA
Susquehanna Valley Women in Transition, Lewisburg, PA
SVOI, Inc (Silent Victims of Innocence), Portland, OR
SWAN (Stopping Women Abuse Now), Olney, IL
Sweetwater County Task Force on Sexual Assault, Rock Springs, WY
Tapestry, Inc, Cambridge, MA
Tarrant County Mental Health/Mental Retardation, Fort Worth, TX
Task Force for Battered Women and Sexual Assault Victims, Owatonna, MN
Task Force on Child Sexual Victimization, Charlottesville, VA
Task Force on Domestic Violence and Sexual Assault, La Grande, OR
Task Force on Family Violence, Houston, TX
Ben Taub General Hospital, Houston, TX
Taunton Area Mental Health Clinic, Taunton, MA
Taylor County Citizens Against Domestic Abuse, Medford, WI
Taylor County Victim Witness Assistance Program, Medford, WI
Tazewell County Office of the Commonwealth's Attorney—Victim/Witness Assistance Program, Tazewell, VA
Tecumseh Area Planned Parenthood Association, Inc, Lafayette, IN
Templum House, Cleveland, OH
Teton County Task Force on Family Violence and Sexual Assault, Jackson, WY
Texas Department of Human Services, Arlington, TX
Therapy Network, Oakland, CA
Third Level Crisis Intervention Center, Inc, Traverse City, MI
E W Throckmorton and Associates, Portsmouth, OH
Thumb Area Assault Crisis Center, Caro, MI
Thursday's Child—Teen Outreach Program, West Hills, CA
Time-Out Family Abuse Shelter, Inc, Ladysmith, WI
Tioga County Women's Coalition, Mansfield, PA
Titusville YWCA Women's Center, Titusville, PA
Townhall II, Kent, OH

Alphabetical Listing of Facilities in Agency Profiles / 339

The Training Institute—Planned Parenthood of Wisconsin, Milwaukee, WI
Tralee Crisis Center for Women, Inc, Pampa, TX
Transition House, Cambridge, MA
Travis County District Attorney's Office—Victim/Witness Program, Austin, TX
The Treatment Place, Fort Worth, TX
Tri County Citizens Against Sexual Assault (CASA), Orangeburg, SC
Tri Lakes Community Center, Inc, Saranac Lake, NY
Triangle Women's Martial Arts Center, Carrboro, NC
Tri-City Youth and Family Center, Inc, Choctaw, OK
Tri-County Council on Domestic Violence and Sexual Assault, Rhinelander, WI
Tri-County Task Force for the Prevention of Domestic Violence, Gordon, NE
Tri-County Women Strength, Peoria, IL
Tri-State Coalition Against Family Violence, Keokuk, IA
Tri-Valley Haven, Livermore, CA
Trumbull County Prosecutor's Office—Victim/Witness Division, Warren, OH
TRUST—Roanoke Valley Trouble Center, Roanoke, VA
Harriet Tubman Shelter for Battered Women, Chicago, IL
Tucson Centers for Women and Children, Tucson, AZ
Tug Valley Recovery Shelter, Williamson, WV
Tulare County Child Sexual Abuse Treatment Program, Tulare, CA
Tulsa County District Attorney—Victim/Witness Center, Tulsa, OK
Turnabout Counseling Center, Seaford, DE
Turning Point, Woodstock, IL
Turning Point, Columbus, IN
Turning Point, Greensboro, NC
Turning Point, Marion, OH
The Turning Point, Kemmerer, WY
Turning Point Family Services Program, Inc, Garden Grove, CA
Turning Point, Inc, Mount Clemens, MI
Turningpoint for Victims of Domestic Abuse, Inc, River Falls, WI
Turtle Trail Counseling Center, Mekinock, ND
The Tuscaloosa Children's Center, Inc, Tuscaloosa, AL
UC Santa Cruz Rape Prevention Education Program, Santa Cruz, CA
UCSF Rape Prevention Education Program, San Francisco, CA
Uinta County Counseling Service, Evanston, WY
Uinta County Sexual Assault—Family Violence Task Force, Evanston, WY
Umbrella Rape Crisis Team, Saint Johnsbury, VT
Underground Railroad, Saginaw, MI
Union County Rape Crisis Center, Westfield, NJ
Union County Rape Crisis Companions, Monroe, NC
The United, Madison, WI
United Action for Youth, Iowa City, IA
United Family Services Victim Assistance, Charlotte, NC
United Hospitals Medical Center and Children's Hospital of New Jersey, Newark, NJ
United States Attorney's Office, Grand Rapids, MI
United States Attorney's Office—Victim/Witness Assistance Unit, Washington, DC
The Unity Group, Inc, Eldersburg, MD
Unity House Families In Crisis, Troy, NY
University of California at Berkeley—Rape Prevention Education Program, Berkeley, CA
University of California Los Angeles—Psychology Clinic, Los Angeles, CA
University of Cincinnati—Office of Women's Programs and Services, Cincinnati, OH
University of Illinois at Urbana-Champaign—Office for Women's Resources and Services, Champaign, IL
University of Kentucky Medical Center, Department of Psychiatry, Child Abuse Clinic, Lexington, KY
University of La Verne Counseling Center, La Verne, CA
University of Maine at Presque Isle—Counseling Center, Presque Isle, ME
University of Michigan—Lesbian-Gay Male Programs Office, Ann Arbor, MI
University of Michigan—Sexual Assault Prevention and Awareness Center, Ann Arbor, MI
University of Minnesota Department of Sociology, Roseville, MN
University of Minnesota, Family Practice Department—Program in Human Sexuality, Minneapolis, MN
University of Minnesota—Sexual Violence Program, Minneapolis, MN

University of Missouri, St Louis—Community Psychological Service, Saint Louis, MO
University of Missouri, St Louis—Women's Center, Saint Louis, MO
University of New Mexico—Sex Offender Research and Treatment Program, Albuquerque, NM
University of Oklahoma Health Sciences Center—Child Study Center, Oklahoma City, OK
University of South Florida—Everywoman's Center, Tampa, FL
Uptown Mental Health Center, Minneapolis, MN
US Attorney's Office, Northern District of Florida—Victim-Witness Program, Tallahassee, FL
Valley Community Counseling Services, Inc, Stockton, CA
Valley East Counseling, Mesa, AZ
Valley Human Services, Inc, Ware, MA
Valley Oasis, Lancaster, CA
Valley Women's Martial Arts, Inc, Easthampton, MA
Vermilion County State's Attorney—Victim Assistance Program, Danville, IL
Vermont Educational Support Associates, Inc, Rutland, VT
Vermont Victim Assistance Program, Rutland, VT
Vermont Victim Assistance Program—Washington County, Barre, VT
Victim Advocate Division, La Porte, IN
Victim Advocate Office, Fort Lauderdale, FL
Victim Assistance and Advocacy Organization, Buffalo, NY
Victim Assistance Center, Inc, Houston, TX
Victim Assistance Program, Tampa, FL
Victim Assistance Program, Marion, OH
Victim Assistance/Rape Crisis, Charlotte, NC
Victim Assistance Team, Fort Collins, CO
Victim Center of San Mateo County, South San Francisco, CA
Victim Center of San Mateo County, Redwood City, CA
Victim Coordinator Services, Dixon, IL
Victim Counseling Unit, Salt Lake City, UT
Victim of Crime Assistance Program, Jefferson, OH
Victim Outreach Information, Evergreen, CO
Victim Service Council, Clayton, MO
Victim Service Office, Gadsden, AL
Victim Services, Cincinnati, OH
Victim Services Agency, Jamaica, NY
Victim Services Agency, New York, NY
Victim Services Agency, Staten Island, NY
Victim Services Agency—Child Victim Unit, Brooklyn, NY
Victim Services Agency—Family Assistance Project, Brooklyn, NY
Victim Services Center of Montgomery County, Inc, Norristown, PA
Victim Services Division, Jacksonville, FL
Victim Services, Inc, Johnstown, PA
Victim Services Program, Chicago, IL
Victim Services Project, Fremont, CA
Victim Treatment Center, New York, NY
Victim/Witness Assistance, Anderson, SC
Victim/Witness Assistance, Sheboygan, WI
Victim/Witness Assistance, Ventura, CA
Victim/Witness Assistance Center, Annapolis, MD
Victim/Witness Assistance Center, Owego, NY
Victim Witness Assistance Center, Syracuse, NY
Victim/Witness Assistance Program, Bristol, VA
Victim/Witness Assistance Program, Lynn, MA
Victim/Witness Assistance Program, New Bedford, MA
Victim Witness Assistance Program, Greenville, SC
Victim/Witness Assistance Program, Spartanburg, SC
Victim/Witness Assistance Program, Newport Beach, CA
Victim/Witness Assistance Program, Waupaca, WI
Victim/Witness Assistance Program, Chardon, OH
Victim/Witness Council, Ogden, UT
Victim Witness Office, Leesburg, VA
Victim/Witness Program, Lock Haven, PA
Victim/Witness Program, Concord, CA
Victim/Witness Program, Jackson, CA
Victim Witness Program, Placerville, CA
Victim/Witness Services, Live Oak, FL
Victim Witness Services Bureau, Woburn, MA
Victim/Witness Services for Coconino County, Flagstaff, AZ
Victim/Witness Services Program, Lancaster, PA
Victims' Assistance Program, Klamath Falls, OR
Victims Assistance Program, Rapid City, SD
Victims Compensation Coordinator, Fort Morgan, CO
Victim's Crisis Center, Albert Lea, MN
Victim's Crisis Center, Austin, MN
Victims for Victims New York Chapter, New York, NY

Victims Information Bureau of Suffolk, Hauppauge, NY
Victims Information Bureau of Suffolk, Smithtown, NY
Victims of Crime Assistance Program, Marysville, OH
Victims of Sexual Assault Program, Tazewell, VA
Victims of Violence, Oneida, NY
Victims of Violent Assault Assistance Program, New York, NY
Victims Outreach, Dallas, TX
Victims Resource Center, Tunkhannock, PA
Victims Resource Center, West Hazleton, PA
Victims Resource Center, Wilkes-Barre, PA
Victim's Rights Advocacy, Cincinnati, OH
Victims Services Agency, New York, NY
The Village Family Service Center, Fargo, ND
Violence Free Crisis Line, Kalispell, MT
Virginia Peninsula Council on Domestic Violence, Hampton, VA
VOICES of California, Inc, Tustin, CA
VOICES of Fargo-Moorhead, Fargo, ND
VOICES of Kansas City, Kansas City, MO
VOICES (Victims of Incest/Sexual Abuse Caring Educating Surviving), Detroit, MI
Volunteer Center "Helpline", Syracuse, NY
Volunteer Counseling Service of Rockland County, Inc, New City, NY
Volunteers Against Violence, Twin Falls, ID
Volunteers in Courts Rape Crisis Counseling Program, Pine Bluff, AR
Volunteers of America of Illinois, East Saint Louis, IL
Walden/Sierra, Inc, California, MD
Waldo County Child and Parent Council, Belfast, ME
Walker County Family Violence Council, Huntsville, TX
Walk-In Counseling Center, Minneapolis, MN
Wallowa County District Attorney's Office—Victim/Witness Assistance Program, Enterprise, OR
Walworth County District Attorney's Office—Victim/Witness Assistance Program, Elkhorn, WI
WAR (Women Against Rape), Collingswood, NJ
Wareham Area Counseling Service, Inc, Wareham, MA
Warren County Council on Domestic Violence, Front Royal, VA
Warren County Family Abuse Shelter, Inc, Lebanon, OH
Warren County Prosecutor's Office, Lebanon, OH
Warren Yazoo Mental Health Service, Vicksburg, MS
Wasco County District Attorney's Office—Victim/Witness Assistance, The Dalles, OR
Washburn Child Guidance Center, Minneapolis, MN
Washington County District Attorney—Victim/Witness Program, Bartlesville, OK
Washington County Prosecuting Attorney's Office—Victim Advocacy Program, Fayetteville, AR
Washington Department of Corrections—Sex Offender Treatment Program, Monroe, WA
Waukesha County District Attorney's Office—Victim/Witness Program, Waukesha, WI
Waycross Area Shelter for the Abused, Inc, Waycross, GA
Wayne County Prosecutor's Office—Victim Services, Detroit, MI
Wayne State University—Women's Resource Center and Re-Entry to Education Program, Detroit, MI
WBH/PCM Rape Victim Services, Paducah, KY
WEAVE, Inc, Sacramento, CA
Webster House, Muskegon, MI
Henrietta Weill Memorial Child Guidance Clinic, Bakersfield, CA
Weinberger, Hall, and Associates, PC, Houston, TX
Welborn Baptist Hospital—Mulberry Center Sexual Abuse Awareness Program, Evansville, IN
Weld County District Attorney's Office—Victim/Witness Program, Greeley, CO
Weld Sexual Assault Support Team, Greeley, CO
Wenatchee Rape Crisis and Domestic Violence Center, Wenatchee, WA
West Central Human Service Center, Bismarck, ND
West Houston Psychological Associates, Houston, TX
West Nassau Mental Health Center, Franklin Square, NY
West Oakland Mental Health Center—Mental Health Department, Oakland, CA
West Valley Child Crisis Center, Inc, Glendale, AZ
West Women's and Children's Shelter, Portland, OR
West Yavapai Victim Assistance Program, Prescott, AZ
Westchester Coalition of Family Violence Agencies, White Plains, NY
Westcoast Children's Center, Albany, CA
Western Kentucky Regional Mental Health/Mental Retardation Board, Inc, Paducah, KY

Western Washington University—Women's Center, Bellingham, WA
Westoaks Personal Growth Center, Westlake Village, CA
Westside Adolescent Service Network, Cleveland, OH
Whatcom County Crisis Services—Rape Relief, Bellingham, WA
Whitman County Prosecutor's Office—Victim/Witness Unit, Colfax, WA
WHO (We Help Ourselves) Program, Houston, TX
Wichita Area Sexual Assault Center, Inc, Wichita, KS
Wichita/Sedgwick County Exploited and Missing Child Unit, Wichita, KS
Wilbridge Consultation Center, Worthington, OH
Wild Iris Women's Services, Bishop, CA
Wilder Community Assistance Program, Saint Paul, MN
Williams County Victim/Witness Assistance Program, Williston, ND
Williamsburg Task Force on Battered Women/Sexual Assault, Williamsburg, VA
Williamson County Crisis Center, Round Rock, TX
Windham County State's Attorney—Victim Assistance Program, Brattleboro, VT
Windsor County Victim Assistance Program, White River Junction, VT
Wings Therapy Collective, Cambridge, MA
WINGS (Women in Need Growing Strong), Johnson City, TN
Wise Options for Women, Williamsport, PA
WISH (Women-in-Self-Help), White Plains, NY
Witness/Victim Center of Cuyahoga County, Cleveland, OH
Wo/Men's Renewal, Minneapolis, MN
Wo/men's Resource and Rape Assistance Program, Jackson, TN
WOMA (The Woman's Alliance), San Jose, CA
Woman House, Saint Cloud, MN
WOMAN, Inc, San Francisco, CA
Woman Reach, Inc, Charlotte, NC
Womancare/Aegis Association, Dover-Foxcroft, ME
WomanKind, Inc, Machias, ME
A Woman's Place, Doylestown, PA
Women Against Abuse, Philadelphia, PA
Women Against Rape, Columbus, OH
Women Against Rape (WAR), Loveland, CO
Women Against Violence, Inc, Rapid City, SD
Women Against Violence (WAV), Endicott, NY
Women and Children in Crisis, Inc, Bartlesville, OK
Women and Families' Psychotherapy Resources, Inc, Waukesha, WI
Women Aware, Inc, New Brunswick, NJ
Women Empowered, Inc, Sarasota, FL
Women Helping Battered Women, Burlington, VT
Women Helping Women, Jamaica, NY
Women Helping Women, Inc, Cincinnati, OH
Women in Crisis, Arvada, CO
Women in Crisis, Hummelstown, PA
Women in Crisis Coalition, Inc, Spearfish, SD
Women in Crisis—Counseling and Assistance (WICCA), Fairbanks, AK
Women in Dialogue, Philadelphia, PA
Women in Distress of Broward County, Inc, Fort Lauderdale, FL
Women in Need, Inc (WIN)/Victim Help Services, Chambersburg, PA
Women In Safe Homes (WISH), Ketchikan, AK
Women in Transition, Philadelphia, PA
Women of Nations, Saint Paul, MN
Women Organized Against Rape (WOAR), Philadelphia, PA
Women Together, Cleveland, OH
Womencare Shelter, Bellingham, WA
Women's Action Alliance, Inc, New York, NY
Women's Action Program—Domestic Violence Crisis Center, Minot, ND
Women's Advocacy Network, Lisbon, ND
Women's Advocates, Saint Paul, MN
Women's Aid in Crisis (WAIC), Elkins, WV
Women's Aid Service, Inc, Alma, MI
Women's Aid Service, Inc, Mount Pleasant, MI
Women's Aid Service, Inc, Harrison, MI
Women's Alternatives, Inc, Anderson, IN
Women's and Children's Shelter of Southeast Texas, Sour Lake, TX
Women's Center, Cranston, RI
Women's Center, Kalamazoo, MI
Women's Center, Marquette, MI
Women's Center, Westminster, CO
Women's Center, Mankato, MN
Women's Center, Grand Forks, ND
Women's Center, Columbia, MO
Women's Center, Fall River, MA

Women's Center, Bloomsburg, PA
Women's Center, Sheridan, WY
Women's Center and Police Department's Rape Prevention Education Program, Santa Barbara, CA
Women's Center and Shelter of Greater Pittsburgh, Pittsburgh, PA
The Women's Center, Inc, Waukesha, WI
Women's Center of Beaver County, Beaver, PA
Women's Center of Brazoria County, Angleton, TX
The Women's Center of Bridgeway Counseling Services, Saint Charles, MO
Women's Center of Central Kentucky, Inc, Lexington, KY
Women's Center of Rhode Island, Inc, Providence, RI
The Women's Center of Southeastern Connecticut, Inc, New London, CT
Women's Center/Shelter, Yankton, SD
Women's Center—University of Idaho, Moscow, ID
Women's Choice Clinic, Oakland, CA
Women's Coalition, Duluth, MN
The Women's Community, Inc—Sexual Assault Victim Service, Wausau, WI
Women's Counseling and Resource Center, Austin, TX
Women's Counseling and Therapy Center, Forest Hills, NY
Women's Counseling Center of West Virginia, Charleston, WV
Women's Counseling Clinic, Honolulu, HI
Women's Counseling Collective, Saint Louis, MO
Women's Counseling Project, Inc, New York, NY
Women's Counseling Services, Nashville, TN
Women's Crisis Center, Maysville, KY
Women's Crisis Center, Tillamook, OR
Women's Crisis Center, Newport, KY
Women's Crisis Center, Ann Arbor, MI
Women's Crisis Center, Fergus Falls, MN
Women's Crisis Center, South Norwalk, CT
Women's Crisis Center, Brattleboro, VT
Women's Crisis Center of Salinas Valley, Salinas, CA
Women's Crisis Service, Manchester, NH
Women's Crisis Services, Inc, Flemington, NJ
Women's Crisis Support, Santa Cruz, CA
Women's Crisis Support Team, Grants Pass, OR
Women's Growth and Therapy Center, Washington, DC
The Women's Gym Fitness Center, Chicago, IL
Women's Health Resources, Chicago, IL
Women's Horizons, Inc, Kenosha, WI
Women's Information Center, Seattle, WA
Women's Information Center, Syracuse, NY
Women's Information Service (WISE), Big Rapids, MI
Women's Institute for Psychotherapy, New York, NY
Women's Justice Center, Detroit, MI
Women's Law Project, Philadelphia, PA
Women's Organization and Resource Center, Burlington, VT
Women's Place, Missoula, MT
Women's Protective Services, Lubbock, TX
Women's Protective Services, Natick, MA
Women's Psychotherapy Centre of Wisconsin, Madison, WI
Women's Rape Crisis Center, Burlington, VT
Women's Referral Center, Glassboro, NJ
Women's Resource and Action Center, Duluth, MN
Women's Resource and Action Center, Iowa City, IA
Women's Resource and Crisis Center/LeeShore, Kenai, AK
Women's Resource and Crisis Center of Galveston County, Inc, Galveston, TX
Women's Resource and Survival Center, Keyport, NJ
Women's Resource Center, Wayne, PA
Women's Resource Center, San Luis Rey, CA
Women's Resource Center, Portsmouth, NH
Women's Resource Center, Howell, MI
Women's Resource Center, Beckley, WV
The Women's Resource Center, Bloomington, MN
Women's Resource Center, Winona, MN
Women's Resource Center, Racine, WI
Women's Resource Center, Clinton, IA
Women's Resource Center, Salt Lake City, UT
Women's Resource Center, Bozeman, MT
Women's Resource Center, Missoula, MT
Women's Resource Center, Scranton, PA
Women's Resource Center, Norman, OK
Women's Resource Center, Inc, Lawrence, MA
Women's Resource Center of Eagle County, Vail, CO
Women's Resource Center of Montrose, Montrose, CO
Women's Resource Center of Northern Michigan, Inc, Petoskey, MI
Women's Resource Center of South County, Wakefield, RI
Women's Resource Center of the New River Valley, Radford, VA

Women's Resource Center—Rape Prevention Education Program, Sacramento, CA
Women's Resources, Inc, Gardner, MA
Women's Resources of Monroe County, Inc, Stroudsburg, PA
Women's Self Help Center, Casper, WY
Women's Self Help Center, Inc, Saint Louis, MO
Women's Service and Family Resource Center, Chickasha, OK
Women's Services Center, Pittsfield, MA
Women's Services, Inc, Meadville, PA
Women's Services of Westmoreland County, Inc, Greensburg, PA
Women's Shelter, Inc, Rochester, MN
Women's Shelter Network, Ridgecrest, CA
Women's Shelter of East Texas, Inc, Nacogdoches, TX
Women's Shelter Program of San Luis Obispo, San Luis Obispo, CA
Women's Shelter/Rape Crisis Center, New Castle, PA
Women's Studies and Service Center, Billings, MT
Womens' Support and Resource Center, New Brunswick, NJ
Women's Support Services, Vineyard Haven, MA
Women's Supportive Services, Claremont, NH
Women's Survival Center, Pontiac, MI
The Women's Therapy Center, El Cerrito, CA
Women's Therapy Center, Philadelphia, PA
Women's Therapy Center Institute, New York, NY
Women's Transit Authority, Madison, WI
Women's Transitional Care Services, Inc, Lawrence, KS
Women's Transitional Living Center, Orange, CA
Women's Tri-County Help Center, Inc, Saint Clairsville, OH
Womenspace, Eugene, OR
Womenspace Unlimited, South Lake Tahoe, CA
Wood County District Attorney's Office—Victim/Witness Services, Wisconsin Rapids, WI
World for Women, Inc, Lynnwood, WA
Wyoming Regional Counseling Center, Gillette, WY
Wyoming State Honor Farm, Riverton, WY
Yale New Haven Hospital, New Haven, CT
Yamhill County District Attorney's Office—Crime Victim Assistance Program (CVAP), McMinnville, OR
YMCA Family Services, Bayshore, NY
Yolo County District Attorney's Office—Victim/Witness Assistance Program, Woodland, CA
Yolo County Sexual Assault and Domestic Violence Center, Woodland, CA
York County Child Abuse and Neglect Council, Inc, Biddeford, ME
York County Commonwealth's Attorney—Victim/Witness Assistance, Yorktown, VA
York County Rape Crisis Council, Inc, Rock Hill, SC
York County Solicitor's Office—Victim/Witness Assistance Program, York, SC
Young House Family Services, Inc, Burlington, IA
Your Community Connection, Ogden, UT
Youth and Family Counseling Center, Boone, IA
Youth and Family Resource Center, Austin, TX
Youth and Family Services, Kenosha, WI
The Youth Center of Family Service and Child Guidance Center of the Oranges, Maplewood and Millburn, South Orange, NJ
Youth In Need, Saint Charles, MO
Youth Line, San Francisco, CA
Youth Services Center, Inc, Merritt Island, FL
Youth/Victim Services, Colorado Springs, CO
Youth Victim/Witness Program, Houston, TX
Youthworks, Inc, Medford, OR
YW CARES (Committee Against Rape Emergency/Educational Services), Olympia Fields, IL
YW CASA, Kankakee, IL
YW Rape Crisis Center, Toledo, OH
YWCA, Lincoln, NE
YWCA, Monroe, LA
YWCA Assault Prevention and Intervention Services, San Jose, CA
YWCA Battered Woman Project, Dayton, OH
YWCA/Battered Women's Services, San Diego, CA
YWCA Battered Women's Shelter, Evansville, IN
YWCA Battered Women's Shelter, Missoula, MT
YWCA Clark County Sexual Assault Program, Vancouver, WA
YWCA/COVE (Citizens Opposing Violent Encounters), Sterling, IL
YWCA Crisis Center, Enid, OK
YWCA Domestic Assault Shelter, West Palm Beach, FL
YWCA Domestic Violence Program, Freeport, IL
YWCA Emergency Housing Program (Interfaith Rooms), Binghamton, NY
YWCA—Family Intervention Center, Kokomo, IN

YWCA Intervention Program, Lewiston, ME
YWCA Lewiston/Clarkston Crisis Services, Lewiston, ID
YWCA of Greater Des Moines, Des Moines, IA
YWCA of Greater Flint—Domestic Violence/Sexual Assault Services, Flint, MI
YWCA of Greater New Haven—Rape Crisis Services, New Haven, CT
YWCA of Greater Pittsburgh, Pittsburgh, PA
YWCA of the Sumter Area, Inc, Sumter, SC
YWCA Rape Crisis Center, Oklahoma City, OK
YWCA Rape Crisis Center, Shreveport, LA
The YWCA Rape Crisis Center, Durham, NC
YWCA Rape Crisis Center, Akron, OH
YWCA Rape Crisis Center, Saint Joseph, MO
YWCA Rape Crisis Center of Cobb County, Marietta, GA
YWCA Rape Crisis Program, New Orleans, LA
YWCA Rape Crisis Service, Utica, NY
YWCA Rape Crisis Service, New Britain, CT
YWCA Rape Crisis Services, Harrisburg, PA
YWCA Rape Prevention and Sexual Assault Programs, Slidell, LA
YWCA Rape Relief Center, Louisville, KY
YWCA Sexual Abuse Treatment Center, Grand Rapids, MI
YWCA Sexual Assault Intervention Program, Cedar Rapids, IA
YWCA Sexual Assault Program, Kalamazoo, MI
YWCA Shelter and Substance Abuse Center, Burlington, IA
YWCA Shelter for Battered Persons and Their Children, Hamilton, OH
YWCA Stepping Stones Teen Program, Pueblo, CO
YWCA Valley Rape Crisis Center (VRCC)/YWCA Child Assault Prevention (CAP) Services, San Jose, CA
YWCA—West Suburban, Lombard, IL
YWCA Women Against Violence, Omaha, NE
YWCA Women in Crisis Program, Norfolk, VA
YWCA Women in Jeopardy, Salt Lake City, UT
YWCA Women's Crisis Center—Rape Crisis Alliance, Boise, ID
YWCA Women's Resource Center, University City, MO
YWCA Women's Resource Center, Dallas, TX
YWCA Women's Resource Center, Portland, OR
YWCA Women's Services/Loop, Chicago, IL
YWCA—Women's Shelter, South Bend, IN
YWCA Women's Support Shelter, Tacoma, WA

INDEX OF SPECIALIZED SERVICES AND CLIENTELE IN AGENCY PROFILES

Local organizations listed in the Agency Profiles section that provide unique programs or provide services to specialized clientele are listed in this index. For further information about these programs or services, check the appropriate listings in the Agency Profiles section. This index **does not** provide information on local agencies which have not indicated a unique or specialized focus in their services for victims/survivors of sexual assault and/or child sexual abuse.

ADOLESCENT/JUVENILE OFFENDERS

Center for Behavioral Intervention, Beaverton, OR
Child and Family Institute, Sacramento, CA
Child Protection Team of Brevard County, Rockledge, FL
Children's Center for Behavioral Development, Edgemont, IL
Choice Program of Family Services Society, Corning, NY
Clackamas Adolescent Intervention Services, Inc, Maryhurst, OR
Comprehensive Sexual Awareness and Treatment Team (CSATT), Fresno, CA
Correctional Specialties, Bellevue, WA
The Counseling Center of Milwaukee, Inc, Milwaukee, WI
Family Violence Network, Lake Elmo, MN
Forensic Mental Health Associates, Webster, MA
Forensic Mental Health Associates, Albany, NY
Forensic Mental Health Services of Connecticut, Inc, New London, CT
Hancock Adolescent Sex Offender Program, Ellsworth, ME
The Jacob Center, Inc, Fort Collins, CO
Juvenile Justice Center, Kennewick, WA
Oak Specialized Counseling Program, Ione, CA
Probation Offenders Program, Freehold, NJ
Project Promoting Alternatives to Violence through Education (PAVE), Inc, Denver, CO
Psychological and Consulting Services, Tucson, AZ
Quakerdale Home, New Providence, IA
Resolutions, Montpelier, VT
RSA, Inc (Redirecting Sexual Aggression), Lakewood, CO
St Mary's Boys Home, Beaverton, OR
San Diego County Child Sexual Abuse Treatment Program, San Diego, CA
Sexology Associates, Inc, Bethesda, MD
Sexual Behavior Clinic, New York, NY
Shenandoah Valley Sex Offender Treatment Program, Harrisonburg, VA
Turning Point Family Services Program, Inc, Garden Grove, CA
Vermont Educational Support Associates, Inc, Rutland, VT
Youth/Victim Services, Colorado Springs, CO

ADOLESCENT SEXUAL ABUSE PREVENTION PROGRAMS

Battered Women's Alternatives, Concord, CA
Bay Area Women Against Rape, Fremont, CA
Bay Area Women Against Rape, Oakland, CA
Bridgework Theater, Inc, Goshen, IN
Center for Women in Transition, Holland, MI
The Changing Woman Counseling and Educational Center, Calumet City, IL
Child Assault Prevention of Contra Costa County, Inc, Concord, CA
Child Assault Prevention Training Center of Northern California, Oakland, CA
Child/Teen Abuse Prevention Program, Cocoa, FL
Children's Self-Help Project, San Francisco, CA
Citizens Committee on Rape, Sexual Assault, and Sexual Abuse, Inc, Buffalo, NY
The Counseling Center of Milwaukee, Inc, Milwaukee, WI
East Los Angeles Rape Hotline, Inc, Los Angeles, CA
Family Counseling Services, Tuscaloosa, AL
Family Outreach of San Antonio, San Antonio, TX
Illusion Theater's Prevention Programs, Minneapolis, MN
Mid-Peninsula YWCA Rape Crisis Center, Palo Alto, CA
New York Women Against Rape, New York, NY
Orange County Rape Crisis Center, Chapel Hill, NC
Our Town Family Center, Tucson, AZ
Rape and Abuse Crisis Center, Inc, Binghamton, NY
Rape and Sexual Abuse Center of Ventura County, Camarillo, CA
Rape Crisis and Sexual Abuse Center, Springfield, MO
Rape Crisis of Durham, Durham, NC
Rape Intervention Program/Crime Victim Assessment Project (RIP/CVAP), New York, NY
Rape Treatment Center, Santa Monica, CA
Santa Barbara Rape Crisis Center, Santa Barbara, CA
Sexual Assault Counseling and Information Service, Charleston, IL
Sexual Assault Help Center (Upper Ohio Valley), Wheeling, WV
Sonoma County Women Against Rape, Santa Rosa, CA
Tecumseh Area Planned Parenthood Association, Inc, Lafayette, IN
Tri-County Women Strength, Peoria, IL
United Action for Youth, Iowa City, IA
Unity House Families In Crisis, Troy, NY
Westside Adolescent Service Network, Cleveland, OH
YW CARES (Committee Against Rape Emergency/Educational Services), Olympia Fields, IL
YWCA Valley Rape Crisis Center (VRCC)/YWCA Child Assault Prevention (CAP) Services, San Jose, CA

ADOLESCENT SURVIVORS

Canarsie AWARE, Inc, Brooklyn, NY
Cathedral Home for Children, Laramie, WY
Center for Child Abuse Prevention Services, Tacoma, WA
Choice Program of Family Services Society, Corning, NY
Clackamas Adolescent Intervention Services, Inc, Maryhurst, OR
Community, Runaway and Youth Services (CRYS), Reno, NV
Comprehensive Sexual Awareness and Treatment Team (CSATT), Fresno, CA
The Counseling Center of Milwaukee, Inc, Milwaukee, WI
Dayglo Family Treatment Program, Austin, TX
"Help Me", Niles, OH
Hospitality House, San Francisco, CA
Human Effective Living Programs (HELP), Chicago, IL
Incest Recovery Association, Dallas, TX
The Jacob Center, Inc, Fort Collins, CO
La Familia Counseling Service, Hayward, CA
Legal Services for Children, Inc, San Francisco, CA
Northern Nevada Child/Adolescent Services (NNCAS), Reno, NV
Project Against Sexual Abuse of Appalachian Children, Knoxville, TN
Psychological Associates of Oxon Hill, Oxon Hill, MD
Quakerdale Home, New Providence, IA
Rape and Abuse Crisis Center, Fargo, ND
Runaway and Homeless Youth Program, Valhalla, NY
Sarpy County Attorney's Office—Victim/Witness Unit, Papillion, NE
Seattle Youth and Community Services, Seattle, WA
The Sexual Abuse and Assault Program, Brant Beach, NJ
Society for Seamen's Children—Teen Advocacy Program Prevention Unit, Staten Island, NY
Tecumseh Area Planned Parenthood Association, Inc, Lafayette, IN
Thursday's Child—Teen Outreach Program, West Hills, CA
Turning Point Family Services Program, Inc, Garden Grove, CA
United Action for Youth, Iowa City, IA
Walden/Sierra, Inc, California, MD
Webster House, Muskegon, MI
Welborn Baptist Hospital—Mulberry Center Sexual Abuse Awareness Program, Evansville, IN
Westside Adolescent Service Network, Cleveland, OH
Youth In Need, Saint Charles, MO
Youth Services Center, Inc, Merritt Island, FL

ADULT SURVIVORS OF CHILD SEXUAL ABUSE

ASAAC—Center for Adults Sexually Abused as Children, New York, NY
Boise Valley Chapter of Parents United, Boise, ID
Formerly Abused Children Emerging in Society (FACES), Lawton, OK
Free-To-Grow Counseling Center, Harwood, ND
"Help Me", Niles, OH
Incest Awareness Project, Fargo, ND
Incest Recovery Association, Dallas, TX
Incest Research and Treatment Institute, Columbus, OH
Incest Survivors Anonymous (ISA), Albuquerque, NM
Incest Survivors Network, Cambridge, MA
Institute for the Community as Extended Family, San Jose, CA
JOURNEYS, Chicago, IL
Metropolitan Organization to Counter Sexual Assault (MOCSA), Kansas City, MO
Newcastle Holistic Center, Newcastle, ME
The Next Step Counseling and Training Center, Newton Center, MA
Oak Grove Psychotherapy Associates, Minneapolis, MN
Parental Stress Center and OASIS Program, Madison, WI
Parents United of Stanislaus County/Stanislaus County Child Abuse Treatment Team, Modesto, CA
People Research, Denver, CO
Phenix I, Garden City, NY
Philadelphia Sexual Abuse Project, Philadelphia, PA
Psychotherapy Resources of Norfolk (PRN), Norfolk, VA

Rape and Sexual Abuse Center of Ventura County, Camarillo, CA
Ravenswood Hospital Community Mental Health Center, Chicago, IL
Sexual Assault Crisis Center, Knoxville, TN
Sexual Assault Recovery Thru Awareness and Hope—SARAH, Inc, Derry, NH
Sexual Assault Victims Care Unit, Belleville, IL
Sharing, Riverdale, NY
SPEAKS (Survivors of Physical and Emotional Abuse as Kids), Los Angeles, CA
Survivors Healing Center, Santa Cruz, CA
Survivors of Incest Anonymous, Bayside, CA
SVOI, Inc (Silent Victims of Innocence), Portland, OR
The Village Family Service Center, Fargo, ND
VOICES of California, Inc, Tustin, CA
VOICES of Fargo-Moorhead, Fargo, ND
VOICES of Kansas City, Kansas City, MO
Women In Safe Homes (WISH), Ketchikan, AK
YWCA Rape Crisis Services, Harrisburg, PA

ART THERAPY

Aid to Victims of Sexual Assault, Hickory, NC
Albuquerque Rape Crisis Center, Albuquerque, NM
Associates for Psychotherapy and Education, Colorado Springs, CO
Associates for Psychotherapy and Education, Pueblo, CO
Associates in Mental Health, Muncie, IN
Austin Psychotherapy Associates, Austin, TX
Buncombe County Rape Crisis Center, Inc, Asheville, NC
Chicago Counseling and Psychotherapy Center, Chicago, IL
Chrysalis Family and Child Treatment Program/Chrysalis Mental Health Clinic, Minneapolis, MN
Committee to Aid Abused Women, Sparks, NV
Community Against Rape, Inc, Taos, NM
Creative Counseling Services, West Hartford, CT
Domestic Violence Services, Pendleton, OR
Echoes Counseling Services, Portland, OR
Employee Counseling and Assistance, Greenville, SC
The Feminist Therapy Center, Oak Park, MI
Grace House Sexual Abuse Resource Center, Dayton, OH
Green River Regional Rape Victim Services, Inc, Owensboro, KY
Gunter and Associates, Houston, TX
Hays County Women's Center, San Marcos, TX
Henderson County Rape Crisis Center, Hendersonville, NC
Incest Research and Treatment Institute, Columbus, OH
Marshall County Rape Crisis Center, Inc, Marshall, NC
Park Rapids—Walker Clinic Counseling Department, Park Rapids, MN
Quakerdale Home, New Providence, IA
Rape Crisis Center, Hobbs, NM
Rape Crisis Center of Northwest Florida, Pensacola, FL
St Francis Center for Personal Growth, North Clarendon, VT
Santa Fe Rape Crisis Center, Inc, Santa Fe, NM
Sexual Assault and Domestic Violence Center, Inc, Baltimore, MD
Sexual Assault and Family Emergency (SAFE) Center, Clearwater, FL
Sexual Assault Crisis Center, Knoxville, TN
Sexual Assault Services, Mankato, MN
Sexual Assault Victims Care Unit, Edgemont, IL
Sexual Trauma Institute, New Orleans, LA
Sharing, Riverdale, NY
Unity House Families In Crisis, Troy, NY
University of Minnesota—Sexual Violence Program, Minneapolis, MN
Women Against Abuse, Philadelphia, PA
Women's Self Help Center, Inc, Saint Louis, MO

ASIAN AMERICANS

Asian Community Mental Health Services, Oakland, CA
Asian Family Services, New York, NY
Asian Program, Oakland, CA
Asian-American Mental Health Services—Japanese Unit, New York, NY
Center for the Pacific-Asian Family, Inc, Los Angeles, CA
Community—University Health Care Center, Minneapolis, MN
Family Crisis Services, Inc, Garden City, KS
King County Rape Relief, Renton, WA
Lao Family Community, Inc, Santa Ana, CA
Marin Abused Women's Services, San Rafael, CA
New York Asian Women's Center, Inc, New York, NY
Rapeline/Sexual Assault Program, Rochester, MN
Seattle Rape Relief, Seattle, WA

BATTERERS

Colorado Outward Bound School, Denver, CO
Community United Against Violence, San Francisco, CA
Marjaree Mason Center/YWCA, Fresno, CA
MEN, Inc, Juneau, AK
Men's Resource Center, Portland, OR
Men's Workshops, Cold Springs, NY
MOVE (Men Overcoming Violent Expression), Anchorage, AK
Phoenix Counseling, Fall River, MA
Santa Cruz Men's Alternatives to Violence, Santa Cruz, CA
University of Minnesota—Sexual Violence Program, Minneapolis, MN
WOMAN, Inc, San Francisco, CA

BISEXUALS

Affirmations: A Center for Psychotherapy and Growth, Columbus, OH

BLACKS

BIHA Women in Action, Minneapolis, MN
Harris YWCA Women's Services, Chicago, IL
Hartford Region YWCA Sexual Assault Crisis Service, Hartford, CT
Marin Abused Women's Services, San Rafael, CA
Midway Hospital Center for Domestic Abuse, Saint Paul, MN
Rape Education and Prevention Program, Columbus, OH
Safe 'N' Strong, San Mateo, CA
Seattle Rape Relief, Seattle, WA
Women's Center and Shelter of Greater Pittsburgh, Pittsburgh, PA

BLIND/VISUALLY IMPAIRED

Finex House, Inc, Jamaica Plain, MA
Los Angeles Commission on Assaults Against Women, Los Angeles, CA
Seattle Rape Relief, Seattle, WA

BODY WORK/MASSAGE

Alpatha Healing Center, Columbus, OH
Arts for Living, Minneapolis, MN
Ending Violence Effectively, Denver, CO
The Family Place, White River Junction, VT
Family Recovery, Albuquerque, NM
Incest Research and Treatment Institute, Columbus, OH
Sharing, Riverdale, NY
Women Against Abuse, Philadelphia, PA

CHILD ABUSE PREVENTION PROGRAMS

Asian Family Services, New York, NY
BANANAS, Child Care Resource and Referral and Parent Support, Oakland, CA
Child Abuse Prevention Services, Inc, Shelby, NC
Child Sexual Abuse Treatment Program (C-SAT), Las Vegas, NV
Committee for Child Abuse Prevention, Frederick, MD
Community Advocates, Portland, OR
CONSEJO Counseling and Referral Service, Seattle, WA
The Counseling Institute, Park City, UT
Exchange Club Center for the Prevention of Child Abuse of Southern Minnesota, Inc, Owatonna, MN
FACT Hotline—Families and Children in Trouble/Together, Washington, DC
Family Friends, Grants Pass, OR
The Family Place, White River Junction, VT
Family Service of Detroit and Wayne County, Detroit, MI
Independent Child Abuse Relief Enterprise (I-CARE), Daytona Beach, FL
Mahoning County Prosecutor—Victim/Witness Program, Youngstown, OH
Marjaree Mason Center/YWCA, Fresno, CA
Massachusetts Society for the Prevention of Cruelty to Children, Brockton, MA
Mental Health Association of Dallas County, Dallas, TX
Rape and Abuse Crisis Center, Fargo, ND
Safe 'N' Strong, San Mateo, CA
Safe 'N' Strong, San Mateo, CA

CHILD ABUSE SERVICES

Child Abuse and Neglect Council, County of Oakland, Inc, Pontiac, MI
Child Sexual Abuse Treatment Program (C-SAT), Las Vegas, NV
Dayglo Family Treatment Program, Austin, TX
Family Focus, Inc., Denver, CO
Heart of America Family Services, Kansas City, MO

CHILD ADVOCACY PROGRAMS

CASA (Court Appointed Special Advocate), Johnson City, TN
Child Abuse and Neglect Council, County of Oakland, Inc, Pontiac, MI
Child Abuse Prevention Association, Beaufort, SC
Child Advocacy Center, Mobile, AL
Child Advocates San Antonio, San Antonio, TX
Children's Center, Miami, FL
County of Orange Social Services Agency—Children's Services, Orange, CA
District Attorney's Office—Children's Advocacy Center, Colorado Springs, CO
Guardian ad Litem, Fayetteville, NC
Guardian ad Litem, Twin Falls, ID
Guardian ad Litem Program, Jacksonville, NC
Hampden County District Attorney—Victim/Witness Support Program, Springfield, MA
Legal Services for Children, Inc, San Francisco, CA
Mercer County Prosecutor's Office—Office of Victim/Witness Advocacy, Trenton, NJ
Paducah McCracken County Child Watch, Inc, Paducah, KY
The Prescott House, Birmingham, AL
SCAN (Stop Child Abuse Now) of Northern Virginia, Alexandria, VA
Sexual Assault Center of Lake County, Painesville, OH
South Carolina Guardian ad Litem Program, Columbia, SC
South Carolina Guardian ad Litem Program, Lancaster, SC
South Carolina Volunteer Guardian ad Litem Program, Rock Hill, SC
Spartanburg County Guardian ad Litem Program, Spartanburg, SC
The Tuscaloosa Children's Center, Inc, Tuscaloosa, AL
Youth/Victim Services, Colorado Springs, CO

CHILD PORNOGRAPHY

Children of the Night, Hollywood, CA

CHILD SEXUAL ABUSE PREVENTION PROGRAMS

The Abilene Rape Crisis Center, Abilene, TX
Anne Arundel County Sexual Assault Crisis Center, Annapolis, MD
Asian Family Services, New York, NY
BANANAS, Child Care Resource and Referral and Parent Support, Oakland, CA
Bay Area Women Against Rape, Fremont, CA
Bay Area Women Against Rape, Oakland, CA
Bridgework Theater, Inc, Goshen, IN
Buncombe County Rape Crisis Center, Inc, Asheville, NC
Center on Rape and Assault (CORA), Butler, PA
Centre County Women's Resource Center, State College, PA
Child Abuse and Neglect Interdisciplinary Training Project, Columbia, SC
Child Abuse Prevention Services, Inc, Shelby, NC
Child Assault Prevention Training Center of Northern California, Oakland, CA
Child/Teen Abuse Prevention Program, Cocoa, FL
Children's Self-Help Project, San Francisco, CA
Christian Counseling Center, Gadsden, AL
Citizens Committee on Rape, Sexual Assault, and Sexual Abuse, Inc, Buffalo, NY
Columbia-Greene Rape Crisis Center, Hudson, NY
Committee for Child Abuse Prevention, Frederick, MD
Community Advocates, Portland, OR
Community Against Rape, Inc, Taos, NM
Crime Victim/Sexual Assault Program, Plattsburgh, NY
East Los Angeles Rape Hotline, Inc, Los Angeles, CA
FACT Hotline—Families and Children in Trouble/Together, Washington, DC
Fairfax County Victim Assistance Network, Alexandria, VA
Family Consultants, Inc, Monroe, LA
Family Outreach of San Antonio, San Antonio, TX

The Family Place, White River Junction, VT
Forgach House Domestic Crisis Shelter, Sierra Vista, AZ
Greene County Prosecutor's Office—Victim/Witness Division, Xenia, OH
HAVEN, Pontiac, MI
Heartsparkle Players, Olympia, WA
Henderson County Rape Crisis Center, Hendersonville, NC
Howard County Sexual Assault Center, Columbia, MD
Illusion Theater's Prevention Programs, Minneapolis, MN
King County Rape Relief, Renton, WA
La Frontera Center, Inc, Tucson, AZ
Mahoning County Prosecutor—Victim/Witness Program, Youngstown, OH
Marshall County Rape Crisis Center, Inc, Marshall, NC
Massachusetts/CAPP, Boston, MA
Mental Health Association of Dallas County, Dallas, TX
Mental Health Association of Greater Tucson, Tucson, AZ
Midland Rape Crisis Center, Midland, TX
Mid-Peninsula YWCA Rape Crisis Center, Palo Alto, CA
Monterey Rape Crisis Center, Monterey, CA
Montgomery Area Family Violence Program (MAFVP), Montgomery, AL
Orange County Rape Crisis Center, Chapel Hill, NC
Our Kids Need to Know, Bismarck, ND
Playing It Safe, New Hyde Park, NY
Project Against Sexual Abuse of Appalachian Children, Knoxville, TN
The Rainbow Project, Inc, Madison, WI
Rape and Abuse Crisis Center, Fargo, ND
Rape and Abuse Crisis Center, Inc, Binghamton, NY
Rape Crisis and Sexual Abuse Center, Springfield, MO
Rape Crisis Center of Berkshire County, Inc, Pittsfield, MA
Rape Crisis Center of West Contra Costa, San Pablo, CA
Rape Crisis Network, Eugene, OR
Rape Crisis of Durham, Durham, NC
Rape Crisis Program, Fort Worth, TX
Rape Victim Advocacy Program, Iowa City, IA
Ravenswood Hospital Community Mental Health Center, Chicago, IL
Response Sexual Assault Support Services, Norfolk, VA
Safe 'N' Strong, San Mateo, CA
Saginaw County Sexual Assault Center, Saginaw, MI
Sexual Abuse Resource Center, Dayton, OH
Sexual Abuse Services, Oshkosh, WI
Sexual Assault Counseling and Information Service, Charleston, IL
Sexual Assault Crisis Center, Appleton, WI
Sexual Assault Program of Beltrami, Cass, and Hubbard Counties, Bemidji, MN
Sexual Assault Treatment Center, Kenosha, WI
SOAP Box Players, Bellingham, WA
Sonoma County Women Against Rape, Santa Rosa, CA
Southwestern Alaska Council for Prevention of Child Sexual Abuse, Bethel, AK
Special Assessment and Management Clinic, Saint Louis, MO
Standing Together Against Rape (STAR), Anchorage, AK
The Training Institute—Planned Parenthood of Wisconsin, Milwaukee, WI
Tri-County Women Strength, Peoria, IL
Underground Railroad, Saginaw, MI
Unity House Families In Crisis, Troy, NY
WHO (We Help Ourselves) Program, Houston, TX
Wichita Area Sexual Assault Center, Inc, Wichita, KS
Women in Crisis—Counseling and Assistance (WICCA), Fairbanks, AK
Women In Safe Homes (WISH), Ketchikan, AK
Women's Crisis Center of Salinas Valley, Salinas, CA
Women's Services, Inc, Meadville, PA
York County Child Abuse and Neglect Council, Inc, Biddeford, ME
YW CARES (Committee Against Rape Emergency/Educational Services), Olympia Fields, IL
YWCA Rape Prevention and Sexual Assault Programs, Slidell, LA
YWCA Sexual Assault Program, Kalamazoo, MI
YWCA Valley Rape Crisis Center (VRCC)/YWCA Child Assault Prevention (CAP) Services, San Jose, CA

CHILD SEXUAL ABUSE SERVICES

Child Abuse and Neglect Council, County of Oakland, Inc, Pontiac, MI
Child Sexual Abuse Institute of Ohio, Wooster, OH
Child Sexual Abuse Treatment Program (C-SAT), Las Vegas, NV
ChildSafe, Ames, IA
CHOICES—Creating Healthy Options in Confronting Exploitive Sexuality, Eugene, OR
Community Behavioral Services, Gainesville, FL
County of Orange Social Services Agency—Children's Services, Orange, CA
Crime Victims Research and Treatment Center (CVC), Charleston, SC
Dayglo Family Treatment Program, Austin, TX
Dutchess County Department of Mental Hygiene (DC/DMH), Poughkeepsie, NY
Eugene Family Institute, Eugene, OR
Family Crisis Program, Oceanside, NY
Family Mending, Asheville, NC
Family Service of Kanawha Valley (Sexual Assault Services), Charleston, WV
Heart of America Family Services, Kansas City, MO
Institute for Sex Therapy, Education, and Research, Traverse City, MI
Institute for the Community as Extended Family, San Jose, CA
Legal Aid Services, Inc—Social Services Program, Louisville, KY
Menninger Foundation, Topeka, KS
Merced County Mental Health, Merced, CA
Meta Resources, Saint Paul, MN
Metrowest Youth Guidance Center, Framingham, MA
Middlesex County District Attorney's Office—Victim Witness Service Bureau, Cambridge, MA
Nassau Coalition on Child Abuse and Neglect, Hempstead, NY
Northern Nevada Child/Adolescent Services (NNCAS), Reno, NV
Onondaga County Sheriff's Department—Abused Person's Unit, Syracuse, NY
Joseph J Peters Institute, Philadelphia, PA
Project Against Sexual Abuse of Appalachian Children, Knoxville, TN
Providence Sexual Assault Center, Everett, WA
The Rainbow Project, Inc, Madison, WI
Rape and Sexual Assault Center, Minneapolis, MN
RTAT, Inc (Restitution Treatment and Training), Ontario, OR
San Luis Obispo County Victim/Witness Assistance Center, San Luis Obispo, CA
Sarpy County Attorney's Office—Victim/Witness Unit, Papillion, NE
Sexual Abuse Services Unit—Child Protective Services (SASU, CPS), Hyattsville, MD
Sexual Assault Program of North Saint Louis County, Virginia, MN
Springfield Child Abuse Resources, Springfield, OR
Texas Department of Human Services, Arlington, TX
University of Kentucky Medical Center, Department of Psychiatry, Child Abuse Clinic, Lexington, KY
Welborn Baptist Hospital—Mulberry Center Sexual Abuse Awareness Program, Evansville, IN

CHILD VICTIM/WITNESS PROGRAMS

Campbell County Prosecuting Attorney's Office—Victim/Witness Coordinator, Gillette, WY
Child Victim Unit, Bronx, NY
Cook County State's Attorney's Office—Victim/Witness Assistance, Chicago, IL
County of Orange Social Services Agency—Children's Services, Orange, CA
Crime Victims Research and Treatment Center (CVC), Charleston, SC
District Attorney's Office—Victim/Witness Program, Alfred, ME
Humboldt County District Attorney's Victim-Witness Program, Eureka, CA
Legal Services for Children, Inc, San Francisco, CA
Middlesex County District Attorney's Office—Victim Witness Service Bureau, Cambridge, MA
Milwaukee County Children's Court—Victim/Witness Service, Milwaukee, WI
Norfolk Commonwealth's Attorney—Victim/Witness Assistance Program, Norfolk, VA
Polk County Victim Services—Rape Care Program and Intrafamily Sexual Abuse Program, Des Moines, IA
Providence Sexual Assault Center, Everett, WA
San Luis Obispo County Victim/Witness Assistance Center, San Luis Obispo, CA
State Attorney's Office—Victim/Witness Assistance Program, Ocala, FL
Victim Services Agency—Child Victim Unit, Brooklyn, NY
Victim/Witness Council, Ogden, UT
Youth Victim/Witness Program, Houston, TX

CHILDREN'S ADVOCACY PROGRAMS

Hawaii State Judiciary—Children's Advocacy Center, Honolulu, HI

CHILDREN'S HOSPITALS

Arkansas Children's Hospital/Department of Pediatrics Program for Children at Risk, Little Rock, AR
Child Abuse Program, Columbus, OH
Children's Hospital—Sexual Abuse Treatment Team, Boston, MA
Medical University of South Carolina—Children's Hospital, Charleston, SC
New York Foundling Hospital—Child Abuse Prevention Services, New York, NY
United Hospitals Medical Center and Children's Hospital of New Jersey, Newark, NJ

CHILDREN'S PROGRAMS

Aid to Women Victims of Violence, Cortland, NY
Caring Unlimited, Sanford, ME
Committee to Aid Abused Women, Sparks, NV
Domestic Abuse/Sexual Assault Crisis Center, Fremont, NE
Midway Hospital Center for Domestic Abuse, Saint Paul, MN
Underground Railroad, Saginaw, MI
Womancare/Aegis Association, Dover-Foxcroft, ME

CHILDREN'S SHELTERS

Families First, Aurora, CO
Kids In Distress, Inc, Fort Lauderdale, FL
West Valley Child Crisis Center, Inc, Glendale, AZ

CORRECTIONAL FACILITIES

Bedford Hills Correctional Facility—Family Violence Program, Bedford Hills, NY
Colorado Department of Corrections, Buena Vista, CO
Correctional Treatment Programs—Sex Offender Unit, Salem, OR
Mount Pleasant Correctional Facility, Mount Pleasant, IA
Sex Offender Program, Somers, CT
Sex Offender Treatment and Evaluation Project, Atascadero, CA
Sexual Offenders Program, Los Lunas, NM
Sixth Judicial District Department of Correctional Services, Iowa City, IA
The Survivors, Chillicothe, MO
Washington Department of Corrections—Sex Offender Treatment Program, Monroe, WA
Women's Crisis Center of Salinas Valley, Salinas, CA

CREATIVE ARTS THERAPY

Aid to Victims of Sexual Assault, Hickory, NC
Albuquerque Rape Crisis Center, Albuquerque, NM
Arts for Living, Minneapolis, MN
Associates for Psychotherapy and Education, Colorado Springs, CO
Associates for Psychotherapy and Education, Pueblo, CO
Associates in Mental Health, Muncie, IN
Austin Psychotherapy Associates, Austin, TX
Buncombe County Rape Crisis Center, Inc, Asheville, NC
CAARE Project, Inc, Fort Bragg, CA
Casa de Esperanza, Saint Paul, MN
Chicago Counseling and Psychotherapy Center, Chicago, IL
Chrysalis Family and Child Treatment Program/Chrysalis Mental Health Clinic, Minneapolis, MN
Committee to Aid Abused Women, Sparks, NV
Community Against Rape, Inc, Taos, NM
Compton YWCA Sexual Assault Crisis Program, Compton, CA
Creative Counseling Services, West Hartford, CT
Domestic Violence Services, Pendleton, OR
Echoes Counseling Services, Portland, OR
Employee Counseling and Assistance, Greenville, SC
The Feminist Therapy Center, Oak Park, MI
Grace House Sexual Abuse Resource Center, Dayton, OH
Green River Regional Rape Victim Services, Inc, Owensboro, KY
Gunter and Associates, Houston, TX
Hays County Women's Center, San Marcos, TX

Henderson County Rape Crisis Center, Hendersonville, NC
House of Ruth, Claremont, CA
Incest Awareness Project, Fargo, ND
Incest Research and Treatment Institute, Columbus, OH
Marshall County Rape Crisis Center, Inc, Marshall, NC
Park Rapids—Walker Clinic Counseling Department, Park Rapids, MN
Psychological Associates of Oxon Hill, Oxon Hill, MD
Quakerdale Home, New Providence, IA
Rape Crisis Center, Hobbs, NM
Rape Crisis Center of Northwest Florida, Pensacola, FL
St Francis Center for Personal Growth, North Clarendon, VT
Santa Fe Rape Crisis Center, Inc, Santa Fe, NM
Sexual Assault and Domestic Violence Center, Inc, Baltimore, MD
Sexual Assault and Family Emergency (SAFE) Center, Clearwater, FL
Sexual Assault Crisis Center, Knoxville, TN
Sexual Assault Services, Mankato, MN
Sexual Assault Victims Care Unit, Belleville, IL
Sexual Assault Victims Care Unit, Edgemont, IL
Sexual Trauma Institute, New Orleans, LA
Sharing, Riverdale, NY
United Action for Youth, Iowa City, IA
Unity House Families In Crisis, Troy, NY
University of Minnesota—Sexual Violence Program, Minneapolis, MN
Victim Services Program, Chicago, IL
Women Against Abuse, Philadelphia, PA
Women's Resource Center of the New River Valley, Radford, VA
Women's Self Help Center, Inc, Saint Louis, MO
YWCA, Monroe, LA

DANCE/MOVEMENT THERAPY

St Francis Center for Personal Growth, North Clarendon, VT
Sexual Assault and Domestic Violence Center, Inc, Baltimore, MD
Sexual Assault Crisis Center, Knoxville, TN
Sexual Assault Victims Care Unit, Belleville, IL
Unity House Families In Crisis, Troy, NY
Victim Services Program, Chicago, IL
Women Against Abuse, Philadelphia, PA

DATABASES

The Rape Crisis Center, San Diego, CA

DATE/ACQUAINTANCE RAPE PREVENTION PROGRAMS

Aiken Coalition to Assist Abused Persons, Aiken, SC
Alternatives to Fear, Seattle, WA
Austin Rape Crisis Center, Austin, TX
Battered Women's Alternatives, Concord, CA
Bay Area Women Against Rape, Fremont, CA
Bay Area Women Against Rape, Oakland, CA
Boulder County Rape Crisis Team, Boulder, CO
Brandeis Rape and Sexual Assault Hotline, Waltham, MA
Brazos County Rape Crisis Center, Inc, Bryan, TX
Center Against Sexual Assault, Phoenix, AZ
Center for Women in Transition, Holland, MI
Center for Women's Services, Plymouth, NH
Center on Rape and Assault (CORA), Butler, PA
Child Assault Prevention of Contra Costa County, Inc, Concord, CA
Citizens' Advisory Committee on Rape Prevention, Ann Arbor, MI
East Los Angeles Rape Hotline, Inc, Los Angeles, CA
Fairfax County Victim Assistance Network, Alexandria, VA
Family Counseling Services, Tuscaloosa, AL
Fredericksburg Area Rape Crisis Program, Fredericksburg, VA
Greene County Prosecutor's Office—Victim/Witness Division, Xenia, OH
Illusion Theater's Prevention Programs, Minneapolis, MN
King County Rape Relief, Renton, WA
Mid-Peninsula YWCA Rape Crisis Center, Palo Alto, CA
New York Women Against Rape, New York, NY
Northwestern University—Women's Center, Evanston, IL
Orange County Rape Crisis Center, Chapel Hill, NC
Orange County Sexual Assault Network (OCSAN), Orange, CA

Our Town Family Center, Tucson, AZ
People Against Rape, Charleston, SC
People Against Sexual Abuse, Inc (PASA), Brooklyn, NY
Polk County Victim Services—Rape Care Program and Intrafamily Sexual Abuse Program, Des Moines, IA
Prevail, Inc, Noblesville, IN
Project Help, Inc, Naples, FL
Project Promoting Alternatives to Violence through Education (PAVE), Inc, Denver, CO
Psychological Services Center, Vermillion, SD
Rape and Sexual Abuse Center of Ventura County, Camarillo, CA
Rape Crisis of Durham, Durham, NC
Rape Prevention Education Program, Riverside, CA
Rape Prevention Education Program, Women's Resource Center, Irvine, CA
Rape Treatment Center, Santa Monica, CA
Safehome, Inc, Overland Park, KS
Sexual Assault Recovery Center, Baltimore, MD
Sexual Assault Recovery Service, Gainesville, FL
Spouse Abuse/Sexual Assault Crisis Center, Hastings, NE
Tecumseh Area Planned Parenthood Association, Inc, Lafayette, IN
UC Santa Cruz Rape Prevention Education Program, Santa Cruz, CA
UCSF Rape Prevention Education Program, San Francisco, CA
University of California at Berkeley—Rape Prevention Education Program, Berkeley, CA
University of Cincinnati—Office of Women's Programs and Services, Cincinnati, OH
University of Illinois at Urbana-Champaign—Office for Women's Resources and Services, Champaign, IL
Victims Information Bureau of Suffolk, Smithtown, NY
Women in Crisis Coalition, Inc, Spearfish, SD
Women's Center and Police Department's Rape Prevention Education Program, Santa Barbara, CA
Women's Center and Shelter of Greater Pittsburgh, Pittsburgh, PA
Women's Center—University of Idaho, Moscow, ID
Women's Crisis Center of Salinas Valley, Salinas, CA
Women's Resource Center, Salt Lake City, UT
Women's Resource Center—Rape Prevention Education Program, Sacramento, CA
Women's Self Help Center, Inc, Saint Louis, MO
Women's Services, Inc, Meadville, PA
Women's Tri-County Help Center, Inc, Saint Clairsville, OH
YW CARES (Committee Against Rape Emergency/Educational Services), Olympia Fields, IL
YWCA of Greater New Haven—Rape Crisis Services, New Haven, CT
YWCA Rape Crisis Center, Saint Joseph, MO

DATING VIOLENCE PREVENTION PROGRAMS

Battered Women's Alternatives, Concord, CA
Boulder County Safehouse, Boulder, CO
Center for Women's Services, Plymouth, NH
Crimes Against Women Task Force, Inc—T/A Albemarle Hopeline, Elizabeth City, NC
Dane County Advocates for Battered Women, Madison, WI
Family Violence Project, Van Nuys, CA
Marin Abused Women's Services, San Rafael, CA
Marjaree Mason Center/YWCA, Fresno, CA
Midway Hospital Center for Domestic Abuse, Saint Paul, MN
Our Town Family Center, Tucson, AZ
Project Promoting Alternatives to Violence through Education (PAVE), Inc, Denver, CO
Safe 'N' Strong, San Mateo, CA
Templum House, Cleveland, OH
Transition House, Cambridge, MA
Turning Point, Columbus, IN
Unity House Families In Crisis, Troy, NY
Women in Crisis Coalition, Inc, Spearfish, SD
Women in Transition, Philadelphia, PA
Women's Self Help Center, Inc, Saint Louis, MO
Women's Shelter, Inc, Rochester, MN

DEAF/HEARING IMPAIRED

Abused Deaf Women's Advocacy Services, Seattle, WA
Finex House, Inc, Jamaica Plain, MA
Intensive Treatment Program for Sexual Aggressives, Saint Peter, MN
Los Angeles Commission on Assaults Against Women, Los Angeles, CA
Rape Crisis Network, Eugene, OR
Seattle Rape Relief, Seattle, WA

DEVELOPMENTALLY DISABLED

CHOICES—Creating Healthy Options in Confronting Exploitive Sexuality, Eugene, OR
Eugene Family Institute, Eugene, OR
Forensic Mental Health Associates, Webster, MA
Forensic Mental Health Associates, Albany, NY
Los Angeles Commission on Assaults Against Women, Los Angeles, CA
Rape and Abuse Crisis Center, Fargo, ND
Rape Crisis Network, Eugene, OR
Seattle Rape Relief, Seattle, WA
Sexology Associates, Inc, Bethesda, MD
Sexual Abuse Resource Center, Dayton, OH
Sexual Assault Crisis Center, Auburn, ME
Sexual Assault Help Center (Upper Ohio Valley), Wheeling, WV
Sexual Assault Services Program/Shelter House, Willmar, MN
The Training Institute—Planned Parenthood of Wisconsin, Milwaukee, WI
Valley Human Services, Inc, Ware, MA
YWCA Rape Prevention and Sexual Assault Programs, Slidell, LA

DISABLED

Abused Deaf Women's Advocacy Services, Seattle, WA
Alternatives to Fear, Seattle, WA
Arlington Handicapped Association, Arlington, TX
CHOICES—Creating Healthy Options in Confronting Exploitive Sexuality, Eugene, OR
Citizens' Advisory Committee on Rape Prevention, Ann Arbor, MI
Eugene Family Institute, Eugene, OR
Finex House, Inc, Jamaica Plain, MA
Forensic Mental Health Associates, Webster, MA
Forensic Mental Health Associates, Albany, NY
HAVEN, Pontiac, MI
Intensive Treatment Program for Sexual Aggressives, Saint Peter, MN
Los Angeles Commission on Assaults Against Women, Los Angeles, CA
Rape and Abuse Crisis Center, Fargo, ND
Rape Crisis Center of West Contra Costa, San Pablo, CA
Rape Crisis Network, Eugene, OR
Seattle Rape Relief, Seattle, WA
Sexology Associates, Inc, Bethesda, MD
Sexual Abuse Resource Center, Dayton, OH
Sexual Assault Counseling and Information Service, Charleston, IL
Sexual Assault Crisis Center, Auburn, ME
Sexual Assault Help Center (Upper Ohio Valley), Wheeling, WV
Sexual Assault Services Program/Shelter House, Willmar, MN
The Training Institute—Planned Parenthood of Wisconsin, Milwaukee, WI
University of California at Berkeley—Rape Prevention Education Program, Berkeley, CA
Valley Human Services, Inc, Ware, MA
Women's Counseling Clinic, Honolulu, HI
YWCA Rape Prevention and Sexual Assault Programs, Slidell, LA

DOMESTIC VIOLENCE PREVENTION PROGRAMS

Child Assault Prevention of Contra Costa County, Inc, Concord, CA
CONSEJO Counseling and Referral Service, Seattle, WA
Family Counseling Services, Tuscaloosa, AL
Illusion Theater's Prevention Programs, Minneapolis, MN
Los Angeles Commission on Assaults Against Women, Los Angeles, CA
Marin Abused Women's Services, San Rafael, CA
Marjaree Mason Center/YWCA, Fresno, CA
Midway Hospital Center for Domestic Abuse, Saint Paul, MN
Montgomery Area Family Violence Program (MAFVP), Montgomery, AL
Rape and Sexual Abuse Center of Ventura County, Camarillo, CA
Safe 'N' Strong, San Mateo, CA
Templum House, Cleveland, OH
Transition House, Cambridge, MA
Westchester Coalition of Family Violence Agencies, White Plains, NY
Women In Safe Homes (WISH), Ketchikan, AK

DOMESTIC VIOLENCE PROGRAMS

Bedford Hills Correctional Facility—Family Violence Program, Bedford Hills, NY
Community United Against Violence, San Francisco, CA
Crisis Intervention Service, Mason City, IA
Family Violence Law Center, Berkeley, CA
STEPS to End Family Violence, New York, NY
The Survivors, Chillicothe, MO
University of Minnesota Department of Sociology, Roseville, MN
WOMAN, Inc, San Francisco, CA
Women of Nations, Saint Paul, MN

DOMESTIC VIOLENCE SHELTERS

BIHA Women in Action, Minneapolis, MN
Caring Unlimited, Sanford, ME
Casa de Esperanza, Saint Paul, MN
Committee to Aid Abused Women, Sparks, NV
Finex House, Inc, Jamaica Plain, MA
Jubilee House Community, Statesville, NC
Marin Abused Women's Services, San Rafael, CA
Midway Hospital Center for Domestic Abuse, Saint Paul, MN
Outreach and Advocacy Project for Battered Women, Brooklyn, NY
Project for Victims of Family Violence, Fayetteville, AR
Relief After Violent Encounter, Saint Johns, MI
Elizabeth Stone House, Jamaica Plain, MA
Transition House, Cambridge, MA
Underground Railroad, Saginaw, MI
Unity House Families In Crisis, Troy, NY
Womancare/Aegis Association, Dover-Foxcroft, ME
Women's Center and Shelter of Greater Pittsburgh, Pittsburgh, PA
Womenspace, Eugene, OR
Yolo County Sexual Assault and Domestic Violence Center, Woodland, CA

ELDERLY

Aiding Women from Abuse and Rape Emergencies (AWARE), Juneau, AK
Allegheny County Center for Victims of Violent Crime, Pittsburgh, PA
Alternatives to Fear, Seattle, WA
Ardsley Karate Club, Ardlsey, PA
House of Ruth, Claremont, CA
Mahoning County Prosecutor—Victim/Witness Program, Youngstown, OH
Rape Crisis Service of Planned Parenthood—Genesee County, Batavia, NY
Retired Senior Volunteer Program, Las Vegas, NV
Riverside Area Rape Crisis Center, Riverside, CA
Safe 'N' Strong, San Mateo, CA
Santa Barbara Rape Crisis Center, Santa Barbara, CA
Senior Victim Services, Inc of Delaware County, Folsom, PA
Sexual Assault Services of Dakota County, Burnsville, MN
SWAN (Stopping Women Abuse Now), Olney, IL
Victim Services, Inc, Johnstown, PA
Women Organized Against Rape (WOAR), Philadelphia, PA
YWCA Sexual Assault Intervention Program, Cedar Rapids, IA

FEMALE OFFENDERS

Child Sexual Abuse Institute of Ohio, Wooster, OH
Children's Center for Behavioral Development, Edgemont, IL
Correctional Specialties, Bellevue, WA
Sexology Associates, Inc, Bethesda, MD
University of California at Berkeley—Rape Prevention Education Program, Berkeley, CA
Vermont Educational Support Associates, Inc, Rutland, VT

FOSTER PARENTS

El Centro Human Services Corporation, Los Angeles, CA
Rape and Sexual Abuse Center of Ventura County, Camarillo, CA
SOAP Box Players, Bellingham, WA

GAY MEN

Affirmations: A Center for Psychotherapy and Growth, Columbus, OH
Ardsley Karate Club, Ardlsey, PA
Brandeis Rape and Sexual Assault Hotline, Waltham, MA
The Bridge, Stanford, CA
Chicago Counseling and Psychotherapy Center, Chicago, IL
Common Bond, Inc, Albuquerque, NM
Community United Against Violence, San Francisco, CA
Fenway Community Health Center: Gay and Lesbian Victim Recovery Program, Boston, MA
Gay and Lesbian Community Center of Colorado, Inc, Denver, CO
Gay and Lesbian Peer Counseling, Philadelphia, PA
Los Angeles Women's Therapy Center, Los Angeles, CA
New York City Gay and Lesbian Anti-Violence Project, New York, NY
The Next Step Counseling and Training Center, Newton Center, MA
Phenix I, Garden City, NY
Rape Intervention Program/Crime Victim Assessment Project (RIP/CVAP), New York, NY
Seattle Counseling Services for Sexual Minorities, Seattle, WA
The United, Madison, WI
University of Michigan—Lesbian-Gay Male Programs Office, Ann Arbor, MI

HEALING

Arts for Living, Minneapolis, MN
Associates in Mental Health, Muncie, IN
Austin Psychotherapy Associates, Austin, TX
Bolton Refuge House, Inc, Eau Claire, WI
Boulder County Rape Crisis Team, Boulder, CO
CAARE Project, Inc, Fort Bragg, CA
Casa de Esperanza, Saint Paul, MN
Chicago Counseling and Psychotherapy Center, Chicago, IL
Child and Family Service, Inc, Austin, TX
CLLB Psychotherapy, Lakewood, CO
Community Against Rape, Inc, Taos, NM
Compton YWCA Sexual Assault Crisis Program, Compton, CA
Counseling Associates, Virginia Beach, VA
Creative Counseling Services, West Hartford, CT
DC Self Defense Karate Association and DC Model Mugging, Silver Spring, MD
Echoes Counseling Services, Portland, OR
Ending Violence Effectively, Denver, CO
The Family Place, White River Junction, VT
Family Recovery, Albuquerque, NM
The Feminist Therapy Center, Oak Park, MI
Free-To-Grow Counseling Center, Harwood, ND
Gateways, Minot, ND
Gay and Lesbian Community Center of Colorado, Inc, Denver, CO
Green River Regional Rape Victim Services, Inc, Owensboro, KY
A Growing Place, Cincinnati, OH
Gunter and Associates, Houston, TX
Hays County Women's Center, San Marcos, TX
Healing Through Play, Lisbon Falls, ME
Helmuth Psychological Associates, Inc, Norton, OH
House of Ruth, Claremont, CA
Incest Awareness Project, Fargo, ND
Iris Personal Renewal Center, Bemidji, MN
JOURNEYS, Chicago, IL
Los Angeles Women's Therapy Center, Los Angeles, CA
Mid-Life Women's Crisis Support Group, New York, NY
NE-NAIAH-KAHA-KOK, Keshena, WI
Newcastle Holistic Center, Newcastle, ME
Oak Grove Psychotherapy Associates, Minneapolis, MN
Outreach and Advocacy Project for Battered Women, Brooklyn, NY
Park Rapids—Walker Clinic Counseling Department, Park Rapids, MN
People Against Rape, Charleston, SC
Philadelphia Sexual Abuse Project, Philadelphia, PA
Phoenix Counseling, Fall River, MA
Pierce County Rape Relief, Tacoma, WA
Psychological Associates of Oxon Hill, Oxon Hill, MD
Psychotherapy Resources of Norfolk (PRN), Norfolk, VA
Quakerdale Home, New Providence, IA
Santa Barbara Rape Crisis Center, Santa Barbara, CA
Santa Fe Rape Crisis Center, Inc, Santa Fe, NM
Sexual Assault Crisis Center, Knoxville, TN
Sexual Assault Program of Beltrami, Cass, and Hubbard Counties, Bemidji, MN
Sexual Assault Victims Care Unit, Belleville, IL
Shalom Christian Counseling Center, Medford, OR
Sharing, Riverdale, NY
Shumard Counseling PC, Livonia, MI
South Shore Therapy Center, Quincy, MA
Stress and Trauma Recovery Center, Paige, TX
Survivors Healing Center, Santa Cruz, CA
Triangle Women's Martial Arts Center, Carrboro, NC
Turtle Trail Counseling Center, Mekinock, ND
University of Minnesota—Sexual Violence Program, Minneapolis, MN
Valley Women's Martial Arts, Inc, Easthampton, MA
Western Kentucky Regional Mental Health/Mental Retardation Board, Inc, Paducah, KY
Wo/Men's Renewal, Minneapolis, MN
Women Against Abuse, Philadelphia, PA
Women's Counseling Clinic, Honolulu, HI
Women's Crisis Center of Salinas Valley, Salinas, CA
Women's Resource Center of the New River Valley, Radford, VA
YWCA, Monroe, LA
YWCA Rape Crisis Services, Harrisburg, PA

HEALTH CARE PROVIDERS

Arkansas Children's Hospital/Department of Pediatrics Program for Children at Risk, Little Rock, AR
Beth Israel Hospital—Rape Crisis Intervention Center, Boston, MA
Child Abuse Program, Columbus, OH
Crisis Center of Lompoc—Rape Crisis/For Kids Sake, Lompoc, CA
Hillsborough County Crisis Center, Inc/Sexual Abuse Treatment Center, Tampa, FL
Joseph J Peters Institute, Philadelphia, PA
Rape Treatment Center, Santa Monica, CA
Santa Barbara Rape Crisis Center, Santa Barbara, CA
Sexual Assault Resource Service, Minneapolis, MN
Sexual Assault Response Team/Sexual Assault Nurse Examiner Program, Santa Cruz, CA
Victims of Violent Assault Assistance Program, New York, NY
Women's Center and Shelter of Greater Pittsburgh, Pittsburgh, PA

HISPANICS

Austin Police Department—Victim Services Division, Austin, TX
BANANAS, Child Care Resource and Referral and Parent Support, Oakland, CA
BIHA Women in Action, Minneapolis, MN
Bronx District Attorney's Office—Crime Victim Assistance Unit, Bronx, NY
CALM (Child Abuse Listening and Medication), Santa Barbara, CA
Casa Myrna Vazquez, Inc, Boston, MA
Center for Women in Transition, Holland, MI
Child Abuse and Neglect Council, County of Oakland, Inc, Pontiac, MI
Child Victim Unit, Bronx, NY
Clackamas Woman's Services, Milwaukie, OR
CONSEJO Counseling and Referral Service, Seattle, WA
Cumberland County Guidance Center—Sexual Assault Program, Millville, NJ
Detroit Police Department—Rape Counseling Center, Detroit, MI
East Los Angeles Rape Hotline, Inc, Los Angeles, CA
El Centro Human Services Corporation, Los Angeles, CA
Family Crisis Services, Inc, Garden City, KS
Hartford Region YWCA Sexual Assault Crisis Service, Hartford, CT
Help for Abused Women and Their Children (HAWC), Salem, MA
King County Rape Relief, Renton, WA
La Clinica de la Raza—Fruitvale Health Project, Inc, Oakland, CA
La Familia Counseling Service, Hayward, CA
Marin Abused Women's Services, San Rafael, CA
Metrowest Youth Guidance Center, Framingham, MA
Midway Hospital Center for Domestic Abuse, Saint Paul, MN
Mount Sinai Medical Center—Rape Crisis Intervention Program, New York, NY
Mujeres Unidas/Women Together Foundation, McAllen, TX
Necessities/Necesidades, Northampton, MA
New York City Gay and Lesbian Anti-Violence Project, New York, NY
New York Women Against Rape, New York, NY
Parents United/Children United, Burlingame, CA
Rape Crisis Intervention Program, New York, NY
Rape Crisis Services of Greater Lowell, Inc, Lowell, MA

Rape Treatment Center, Santa Monica, CA
Regional Rape Crisis Service, Rochester, NY
Services to Victims of Sexual Assault, Jersey City, NJ
Servicios de la Raza, Inc, Denver, CO
Sexual Assault Services Program/Shelter House, Willmar, MN
SOS, Inc, Emporia, KS
Elizabeth Stone House, Jamaica Plain, MA
Victim Services Agency, New York, NY
Victim's Crisis Center, Albert Lea, MN
Women Organized Against Rape (WOAR), Philadelphia, PA
Women's Center of Brazoria County, Angleton, TX
Women's Resource Center, Inc, Lawrence, MA
Yolo County Sexual Assault and Domestic Violence Center, Woodland, CA

HOSPITALS

Beth Israel Hospital—Rape Crisis Intervention Center, Boston, MA
Crisis Center of Lompoc—Rape Crisis/For Kids Sake, Lompoc, CA
Rape Treatment Center, Santa Monica, CA
St Anthony Rape Treatment Center, Columbus, OH
Sexual Assault Resource Service, Minneapolis, MN
Sexual Assault Response Team/Sexual Assault Nurse Examiner Program, Santa Cruz, CA
STOP Sexual Addictions and Disorders Treatment Program, Miami, FL
Victims of Violent Assault Assistance Program, New York, NY
Women's Center and Shelter of Greater Pittsburgh, Pittsburgh, PA

HYPNOSIS

CLLB Psychotherapy, Lakewood, CO
Menninger Foundation, Topeka, KS
Metrowest Youth Guidance Center, Framingham, MA
Park Rapids—Walker Clinic Counseling Department, Park Rapids, MN
Psychological Associates of Oxon Hill, Oxon Hill, MD
Sexual Assault Services Program/Shelter House, Willmar, MN

INCEST SURVIVORS

JOURNEYS, Chicago, IL
Rape Victim Advocates, Chicago, IL

INCEST SURVIVORS (ADULTS)

ASAAC—Center for Adults Sexually Abused as Children, New York, NY
Boise Valley Chapter of Parents United, Boise, ID
Child and Family Service, Inc, Austin, TX
Formerly Abused Children Emerging in Society (FACES), Lawton, OK
Free-To-Grow Counseling Center, Harwood, ND
"Help Me", Niles, OH
Incest Awareness Project, Fargo, ND
Incest Recovery Association, Dallas, TX
Incest Research and Treatment Institute, Columbus, OH
Incest Survivors Anonymous (ISA), Albuquerque, NM
Incest Survivors Network, Cambridge, MA
Institute for the Community as Extended Family, San Jose, CA
Metropolitan Organization to Counter Sexual Assault (MOCSA), Kansas City, MO
Newcastle Holistic Center, Newcastle, ME
The Next Step Counseling and Training Center, Newton Center, MA
Oak Grove Psychotherapy Associates, Minneapolis, MN
Parental Stress Center and OASIS Program, Madison, WI
Parents United of Stanislaus County/Stanislaus County Child Abuse Treatment Team, Modesto, CA
People Research, Denver, CO
Phenix I, Garden City, NY
Philadelphia Sexual Abuse Project, Philadelphia, PA
Psychotherapy Resources of Norfolk (PRN), Norfolk, VA
Rape and Sexual Abuse Center of Ventura County, Camarillo, CA
Sexual Assault Crisis Center, Knoxville, TN
Sexual Assault Recovery Thru Awareness and Hope—SARAH, Inc, Derry, NH
Sexual Assault Victims Care Unit, Belleville, IL
Sharing, Riverdale, NY
SPEAKS (Survivors of Physical and Emotional Abuse as Kids), Los Angeles, CA
Survivors Healing Center, Santa Cruz, CA
Survivors of Incest Anonymous, Bayside, CA
SVOI, Inc (Silent Victims of Innocence), Portland, OR
Victim Services Agency, New York, NY
The Village Family Service Center, Fargo, ND
VOICES of California, Inc, Tustin, CA
VOICES of Fargo-Moorhead, Fargo, ND
VOICES of Kansas City, Kansas City, MO
Women In Safe Homes (WISH), Ketchikan, AK
YWCA Rape Crisis Services, Harrisburg, PA

INFORMATION CENTERS

Boston Women's Health Book Collective, Watertown, MA
Community Program Against Sexual Assault (CPASA), Dorchester, MA
Crime Victims and Rape Counseling, Garden City, NY
FACT Hotline—Families and Children in Trouble/Together, Washington, DC
Family and Children's Services, Inc—Psychotherapy and Counseling Division, Albuquerque, NM
Institute for Sex Therapy, Education, and Research, Traverse City, MI
Mental Health Association of Greater Tucson, Tucson, AZ
Rape Intervention Program/Crime Victim Assessment Project (RIP/CVAP), New York, NY
Sexual Abuse Resource Center, Dayton, OH
Welborn Baptist Hospital—Mulberry Center Sexual Abuse Awareness Program, Evansville, IN

INTERAGENCY TEAMS/ORGANIZATIONS

Athens County Prosecutor's Victim Assistance Program, Athens, OH
Bergen County Coalition Against Sexual Assault, Hackensack, NJ
Buncombe County Rape Crisis Center, Inc, Asheville, NC
Center for Child Abuse Prevention Services, Tacoma, WA
The Chicago Sexual Assault Services Network, Chicago, IL
Child Abuse Program, Columbus, OH
Child Advocacy Center, Mobile, AL
Child Protection Team of Brevard County, Rockledge, FL
ChildSafe, Ames, IA
Clermont Counseling Center, Batavia, OH
Coalition for Children and Youth, Inc, Norwalk, CT
County of Orange Social Services Agency—Children's Services, Orange, CA
Crisis Center of Lompoc—Rape Crisis/For Kids Sake, Lompoc, CA
Dallas County Rape Crisis and Child Sexual Abuse Center, Dallas, TX
District Attorney's Office—Victim/Witness Assistance, Superior, WI
Domestic Violence Center, Ionia, MI
Dutchess County Department of Mental Hygiene (DC/DMH), Poughkeepsie, NY
Essex County District Attorney's Office—Victim/Witness Assistance Program, Salem, MA
Fairfax County Victim Assistance Network, Alexandria, VA
Family Offender Program, Grants Pass, OR
Family Support Program, Columbus, OH
Hemet/San Jacinto Center Against Sexual Assault, Hemet, CA
Henderson County Rape Crisis Center, Hendersonville, NC
Jubilee House Community, Statesville, NC
Marshall County Rape Crisis Center, Inc, Marshall, NC
Middle District Attorney's Office—Victim/Witness Assistance Program, Worcester, MA
Mid-Step Mid-County Interagency Sexual Abuse Treatment Program, Banning, CA
Multidisciplinary Sexual Abuse Treatment Program, Traverse City, MI
Nassau Coalition on Child Abuse and Neglect, Hempstead, NY
New York City Task Force Against Sexual Assault, New York, NY
Orange County Sexual Assault Network (OCSAN), Orange, CA
Parents United of Roanoke Valley, Roanoke, VA
People Against Sexual Abuse, Inc (PASA), Brooklyn, NY
RTAT, Inc (Restitution Treatment and Training), Ontario, OR
San Luis Obispo County Victim/Witness Assistance Center, San Luis Obispo, CA
Santa Clara County Victim Witness Assistance Center, San Jose, CA
Sexual Assault Center, Jacksonville, FL
Sexual Assault Response Team/Sexual Assault Nurse Examiner Program, Santa Cruz, CA
Sexual Battery Committee of the Gainesville Commission on the Status of Women, Gainesville, FL
Somerset Coalition for Prevention and Treatment of Sexual Abuse, Bridgewater, NJ
University of Kentucky Medical Center, Department of Psychiatry, Child Abuse Clinic, Lexington, KY
Victim/Witness Assistance Program, Lynn, MA
Victims Outreach, Dallas, TX
Westchester Coalition of Family Violence Agencies, White Plains, NY
Youth/Victim Services, Colorado Springs, CO
YWCA of Greater New Haven—Rape Crisis Services, New Haven, CT

JOURNAL WRITING

House of Ruth, Claremont, CA

LEGAL SERVICES

Creative Counseling Services, West Hartford, CT
Family Violence Law Center, Berkeley, CA
Law Firm of Anderson and Howell, Jacksonville Beach, FL
Legal Services for Children, Inc, San Francisco, CA
Puget Sound Legal Assistance Foundation, Olympia, WA
Seattle Rape Relief, Seattle, WA
STEPS to End Family Violence, New York, NY
Women of Nations, Saint Paul, MN
Women's Justice Center, Detroit, MI
Women's Law Project, Philadelphia, PA

LESBIANS

Ardsley Karate Club, Ardlsey, PA
Brandeis Rape and Sexual Assault Hotline, Waltham, MA
The Bridge, Stanford, CA
Chicago Counseling and Psychotherapy Center, Chicago, IL
Common Bond, Inc, Albuquerque, NM
Community United Against Violence, San Francisco, CA
Creative Counseling Services, West Hartford, CT
Fenway Community Health Center: Gay and Lesbian Victim Recovery Program, Boston, MA
Free-To-Grow Counseling Center, Harwood, ND
Gay and Lesbian Community Center of Colorado, Inc, Denver, CO
Gay and Lesbian Peer Counseling, Philadelphia, PA
Hartford Region YWCA Sexual Assault Crisis Service, Hartford, CT
Lesbian Resource Center, Seattle, WA
Lesbian Switchboard, New York, NY
Los Angeles Women's Therapy Center, Los Angeles, CA
Lyon-Martin Women's Health Services, San Francisco, CA
Marin Abused Women's Services, San Rafael, CA
New York City Gay and Lesbian Anti-Violence Project, New York, NY
Phenix I, Garden City, NY
Phoenix Counseling, Fall River, MA
Rape Intervention Program/Crime Victim Assessment Project (RIP/CVAP), New York, NY
Seattle Counseling Services for Sexual Minorities, Seattle, WA
Elizabeth Stone House, Jamaica Plain, MA
Tapestry, Inc, Cambridge, MA
UCSF Rape Prevention Education Program, San Francisco, CA
The United, Madison, WI
University of Michigan—Lesbian-Gay Male Programs Office, Ann Arbor, MI
University of Minnesota—Sexual Violence Program, Minneapolis, MN
WOMAN, Inc, San Francisco, CA
Womenspace, Eugene, OR

MALE SURVIVORS

ASAAC—Center for Adults Sexually Abused as Children, New York, NY
Beth Israel Hospital—Rape Crisis Intervention Center, Boston, MA
Child and Family Institute, Sacramento, CA
Counseling Center of Lambertville, Lambertville, NJ
Fenway Community Health Center: Gay and Lesbian Victim Recovery Program, Boston, MA

Forensic Mental Health Associates, Webster, MA
Incest Research and Treatment Institute, Columbus, OH
Incest Survivors Anonymous (ISA), Albuquerque, NM
Men's Resource Center, Portland, OR
Men's Workshops, Cold Springs, NY
Merced County Mental Health, Merced, CA
New York City Gay and Lesbian Anti-Violence Project, New York, NY
The Next Step Counseling and Training Center, Newton Center, MA
Project Against Sexual Abuse of Appalachian Children, Knoxville, TN
Rape and Sexual Abuse Center of Ventura County, Camarillo, CA
Rape and Sexual Assault Center, Minneapolis, MN
Rape Crisis Center of Berkshire County, Inc, Pittsfield, MA
St Mary's Boys Home, Beaverton, OR
Santa Cruz Men's Alternatives to Violence, Santa Cruz, CA
Services to Victims of Sexual Assault, Jersey City, NJ
Sharing, Riverdale, NY
University of California Los Angeles—Psychology Clinic, Los Angeles, CA
University of Minnesota Department of Sociology, Roseville, MN
VOICES of California, Inc, Tustin, CA

MARITAL RAPE

The Susan B Anthony Project, Inc, Torrington, CT
Citizens' Advisory Committee on Rape Prevention, Ann Arbor, MI
Puget Sound Legal Assistance Foundation, Olympia, WA
University of Minnesota Department of Sociology, Roseville, MN

MEDIA PROGRAMS

Bering Sea Women's Group, Nome, AK

MEDIA PROGRAMS (CHILD SEXUAL ABUSE)

Albany County Rape Crisis Center, Albany, NY
Arkansas Children's Hospital/Department of Pediatrics Program for Children at Risk, Little Rock, AR
Associates for Psychotherapy and Education, Colorado Springs, CO
Associates for Psychotherapy and Education, Pueblo, CO
Child Abuse Program, Columbus, OH
Child Protection Team, Inc/Family Sexual Abuse Treatment Program, Mangonia Park, FL
Child Sexual Abuse Project, Ithaca, NY
Chrysalis Family and Child Treatment Program/Chrysalis Mental Health Clinic, Minneapolis, MN
Family Sex Abuse Treatment Program, San Antonio, TX
Institute for the Community as Extended Family, San Jose, CA
Kevin B McGovern, PhD and Associates, Portland, OR
Joseph J Peters Institute, Philadelphia, PA
Rape and Sexual Assault Center, Minneapolis, MN
RTAT, Inc (Restitution Treatment and Training), Ontario, OR
Services to Abused Families, Inc/Women's Abuse Shelter, Culpeper, VA
Sexual Abuse Services, Oshkosh, WI
Society's League Against Molestation (SLAM), Crown Point, IN
University of Kentucky Medical Center, Department of Psychiatry, Child Abuse Clinic, Lexington, KY
Welborn Baptist Hospital—Mulberry Center Sexual Abuse Awareness Program, Evansville, IN
Western Kentucky Regional Mental Health/Mental Retardation Board, Inc, Paducah, KY

MEDIA PROGRAMS (CHILD SEXUAL ABUSE PREVENTION)

Asian Community Mental Health Services, Oakland, CA
Assault Recovery Associates, Saint Joseph, MI
Bridgework Theater, Inc, Goshen, IN
Columbia-Greene Rape Crisis Center, Hudson, NY
East Los Angeles Rape Hotline, Inc, Los Angeles, CA
The Family Place, White River Junction, VT
Forgach House Domestic Crisis Shelter, Sierra Vista, AZ
Heartsparkle Players, Olympia, WA
King County Rape Relief, Renton, WA
Mental Health Association of Greater Tucson, Tucson, AZ
Rape and Abuse Crisis Center, Fargo, ND
Rape Crisis Center of West Contra Costa, San Pablo, CA
SOAP Box Players, Bellingham, WA
Umbrella Rape Crisis Team, Saint Johnsbury, VT
WHO (We Help Ourselves) Program, Houston, TX

MEDIA PROGRAMS (DATE/ACQUAINTANCE RAPE PREVENTION)

Aiken Coalition to Assist Abused Persons, Aiken, SC
Austin Rape Crisis Center, Austin, TX
Battered Women's Alternatives, Concord, CA
Center Against Sexual Assault, Phoenix, AZ
Citizens' Advisory Committee on Rape Prevention, Ann Arbor, MI
Fredericksburg Area Rape Crisis Program, Fredericksburg, VA
Orange County Sexual Assault Network (OCSAN), Orange, CA
Polk County Victim Services—Rape Care Program and Intrafamily Sexual Abuse Program, Des Moines, IA
Rape and Sexual Abuse Center of Ventura County, Camarillo, CA
Sexual Assault Recovery Center, Baltimore, MD
Sexual Assault Recovery Service, Gainesville, FL
Spouse Abuse/Sexual Assault Crisis Center, Hastings, NE
University of Cincinnati—Office of Women's Programs and Services, Cincinnati, OH
Women's Tri-County Help Center, Inc, Saint Clairsville, OH
YWCA Clark County Sexual Assault Program, Vancouver, WA

MEDIA PROGRAMS (DATING VIOLENCE PREVENTION)

Marin Abused Women's Services, San Rafael, CA
Turning Point, Columbus, IN
Women's Shelter, Inc, Rochester, MN

MEDIA PROGRAMS (DISABILITIES)

Citizens' Advisory Committee on Rape Prevention, Ann Arbor, MI
Rape Crisis Center of West Contra Costa, San Pablo, CA

MEDIA PROGRAMS (DOMESTIC VIOLENCE)

BIHA Women in Action, Minneapolis, MN
Marin Abused Women's Services, San Rafael, CA
Relief After Violent Encounter, Saint Johns, MI
Elizabeth Stone House, Jamaica Plain, MA
Transition House, Cambridge, MA
Women's Center and Shelter of Greater Pittsburgh, Pittsburgh, PA
Women's Self Help Center, Inc, Saint Louis, MO

MEDIA PROGRAMS (ELDERLY)

Sexual Assault Services of Dakota County, Burnsville, MN

MEDIA PROGRAMS (HEALTH CARE)

Arkansas Children's Hospital/Department of Pediatrics Program for Children at Risk, Little Rock, AR

MEDIA PROGRAMS (HISPANICS)

Yolo County Sexual Assault and Domestic Violence Center, Woodland, CA

MEDIA PROGRAMS (INCEST SURVIVORS)

Boise Valley Chapter of Parents United, Boise, ID
Parents United of Stanislaus County/Stanislaus County Child Abuse Treatment Team, Modesto, CA
People Research, Denver, CO
Rape Victim Advocates, Chicago, IL

MEDIA PROGRAMS (MINORITIES)

BIHA Women in Action, Minneapolis, MN

MEDIA PROGRAMS (OFFENDER TREATMENT)

Assault Recovery Associates, Saint Joseph, MI
Forensic Mental Health Associates, Webster, MA
Institute for the Community as Extended Family, San Jose, CA
Kevin B McGovern, PhD and Associates, Portland, OR
Rape and Sexual Assault Center, Minneapolis, MN

MEDIA PROGRAMS (PARENT EDUCATION)

San Fernando Valley Child Guidance Clinic, Van Nuys, CA

MEDIA PROGRAMS (RAPE PREVENTION)

Citizens' Advisory Committee on Rape Prevention, Ann Arbor, MI
Rape Awareness Program (RAP), Tuscaloosa, AL
Rape Crisis Network, Spokane, WA
Seattle Rape Relief, Seattle, WA
Sexual Assault Center, Jacksonville, FL
University of Cincinnati—Office of Women's Programs and Services, Cincinnati, OH
Women's Protective Services, Natick, MA

MEDIA PROGRAMS (SELF DEFENSE)

Los Angeles Commission on Assaults Against Women, Los Angeles, CA
Rape Awareness Program, Fort Wayne, IN
Sexual Assault Crisis Center, Knoxville, TN
UCSF Rape Prevention Education Program, San Francisco, CA

MEDIA PROGRAMS (SEXUAL ASSAULT)

Albany County Rape Crisis Center, Albany, NY
Boulder County Rape Crisis Team, Boulder, CO
Careline Survivor Advocacy, Athens, OH
Careline Survivor Advocacy, Logan, OH
Careline Survivor Advocacy, McArthur, OH
Citizens' Advisory Committee on Rape Prevention, Ann Arbor, MI
Citizens Committee on Rape, Sexual Assault, and Sexual Abuse, Inc, Buffalo, NY
Metropolitan Organization to Counter Sexual Assault (MOCSA), Kansas City, MO
Neuse-Trent Rape Assistance Program, New Bern, NC
Northwest Arkansas Rape Crisis, Inc, Fayetteville, AR
Onslow County Women's Center, Jacksonville, NC
Pittsburgh Action Against Rape (PAAR), Pittsburgh, PA
Rape and Sexual Abuse Center of Ventura County, Camarillo, CA
Rape Crisis Program, Houston, TX
Rape Treatment Center, Santa Monica, CA
Rape Victim Advocates, Chicago, IL
Rape Victim Companion Program, Alexandria, VA
Regional Rape Crisis Service, Rochester, NY
Santa Barbara Rape Crisis Center, Santa Barbara, CA
University of Cincinnati—Office of Women's Programs and Services, Cincinnati, OH
Women's Protective Services, Natick, MA
Women's Self Help Center, Inc, Saint Louis, MO
YW Rape Crisis Center, Toledo, OH
YWCA Clark County Sexual Assault Program, Vancouver, WA

MEDIA PROGRAMS (VICTIM ASSISTANCE)

Allegheny County Center for Victims of Violent Crime, Pittsburgh, PA
Crime Victim Center, Reading, PA
Lincoln Police Department—Victim/Witness Unit, Lincoln, NE
Office of Solicitor—Victim Witness Assistance, Orangeburg, SC
Polk County Victim Services—Rape Care Program and Intrafamily Sexual Abuse Program, Des Moines, IA
Victim Services, Inc, Johnstown, PA

MEDICAL EXAMINATION AND TREATMENT

Arkansas Children's Hospital/Department of Pediatrics Program for Children at Risk, Little Rock, AR
Beth Israel Hospital—Rape Crisis Intervention Center, Boston, MA
Crisis Center of Lompoc—Rape Crisis/For Kids Sake, Lompoc, CA
Hillsborough County Crisis Center, Inc/Sexual Abuse Treatment Center, Tampa, FL
Orange County Sexual Assault Network (OCSAN), Orange, CA
Rape Treatment Center, Santa Monica, CA
St Anthony Rape Treatment Center, Columbus, OH
Santa Barbara Rape Crisis Center, Santa Barbara, CA
Sexual Assault Resource Service, Minneapolis, MN
Sexual Assault Response Team/Sexual Assault Nurse Examiner Program, Santa Cruz, CA
Victims of Violent Assault Assistance Program, New York, NY

MEN INVOLVED IN RAPE PREVENTION

Los Angeles Commission on Assaults Against Women, Los Angeles, CA
Men's Caucus, Los Angeles, CA
Rape Education and Prevention Program, Columbus, OH

MINORITIES

American Indian Community House, New York, NY
Asian Community Mental Health Services, Oakland, CA
Asian Family Services, New York, NY
Asian Program, Oakland, CA
Asian-American Mental Health Services—Japanese Unit, New York, NY
Austin Police Department—Victim Services Division, Austin, TX
Behavioral Health Agency of Central Arizona, Casa Grande, AZ
BIHA Women in Action, Minneapolis, MN
CALM (Child Abuse Listening and Medication), Santa Barbara, CA
Center for the Pacific-Asian Family, Inc, Los Angeles, CA
Community Program Against Sexual Assault (CPASA), Dorchester, MA
Community United Against Violence, San Francisco, CA
Community—University Health Care Center, Minneapolis, MN
Division of Indian Work—Sexual Assault Project, Minneapolis, MN
East Los Angeles Rape Hotline, Inc, Los Angeles, CA
El Centro Human Services Corporation, Los Angeles, CA
Everywoman's Center Programs Against Violence Against Women, Amherst, MA
Hartford Region YWCA Sexual Assault Crisis Service, Hartford, CT
Highland Sexual Assault Center, Oakland, CA
King County Rape Relief, Renton, WA
La Clinica de la Raza—Fruitvale Health Project, Inc, Oakland, CA
La Familia Counseling Service, Hayward, CA
Laguna Family Shelter Program, Laguna, NM
Lao Family Community, Inc, Santa Ana, CA
Marin Abused Women's Services, San Rafael, CA
Mujeres Unidas/Women Together Foundation, McAllen, TX
New York Asian Women's Center, Inc, New York, NY
Northwestern University—Women's Center, Evanston, IL
Rape Intervention Program/Crime Victim Assessment Project (RIP/CVAP), New York, NY
Rape Treatment Center, Santa Monica, CA
Rapeline/Sexual Assault Program, Rochester, MN
Safe 'N' Strong, San Mateo, CA
Seattle Rape Relief, Seattle, WA
Elizabeth Stone House, Jamaica Plain, MA
West Oakland Mental Health Center—Mental Health Department, Oakland, CA
Women Organized Against Rape (WOAR), Philadelphia, PA
Women's Center of Brazoria County, Angleton, TX

MULTIPLE PERSONALITY

Creative Counseling Services, West Hartford, CT
JOURNEYS, Chicago, IL
Oakland Family Services—Children Services, Pontiac, MI
Joseph J Peters Institute, Philadelphia, PA
Psychotherapy Resources of Norfolk (PRN), Norfolk, VA

MUSIC THERAPY

Arts for Living, Minneapolis, MN
Associates in Mental Health, Muncie, IN
Bolton Refuge House, Inc, Eau Claire, WI
Buncombe County Rape Crisis Center, Inc, Asheville, NC
Counseling Associates, Virginia Beach, VA
Grace House Sexual Abuse Resource Center, Dayton, OH
Henderson County Rape Crisis Center, Hendersonville, NC
Marshall County Rape Crisis Center, Inc, Marshall, NC

NATIVE AMERICANS

American Indian Community House, New York, NY
Behavioral Health Agency of Central Arizona, Casa Grande, AZ
BIHA Women in Action, Minneapolis, MN
Blackfeet Indian Child Welfare Program, Browning, MT
Division of Indian Work—Sexual Assault Project, Minneapolis, MN
Indian Health Board of Minneapolis, Inc, Minneapolis, MN
Laguna Family Shelter Program, Laguna, NM
Mental Health Services—Mescalero Indian Health Service Hospital, Mescalero, NM
NE-NAIAH-KAHA-KOK, Keshena, WI
Sexual Assault Services Program/Shelter House, Willmar, MN
Women of Nations, Saint Paul, MN

OFFENDER TREATMENT

The Arlington Psychological Center, Jacksonville, FL
Associates in Counseling, Federal Way, WA
Blanchard and Associates, Sheridan, WY
Dr Geraldine Boozer Rehabilitation Program for Sex Offenders, Hollywood, FL
Center for Behavioral Intervention, Beaverton, OR
Child and Family Institute, Sacramento, CA
Child Protection Team of Brevard County, Rockledge, FL
Child Sexual Abuse Institute of Ohio, Wooster, OH
Children's Center for Behavioral Development, Edgemont, IL
Choice Program of Family Services Society, Corning, NY
CHOICES—Creating Healthy Options in Confronting Exploitive Sexuality, Eugene, OR
Clackamas Adolescent Intervention Services, Inc, Maryhurst, OR
Clinic for Counseling and Psychotherapy, Inc and Northwest Passage, Inc, Salt Lake City, UT
Colorado Department of Corrections, Buena Vista, CO
Comprehensive Sexual Awareness and Treatment Team (CSATT), Fresno, CA
Correctional Specialties, Bellevue, WA
Correctional Treatment Programs—Sex Offender Unit, Salem, OR
The Counseling Center of Milwaukee, Inc, Milwaukee, WI
Crime Victims Research and Treatment Center (CVC), Charleston, SC
Eugene Family Institute, Eugene, OR
Family Services Program, Miami, FL
Family Stress Center, Chula Vista, CA
Family Violence Network, Lake Elmo, MN
Forensic Mental Health Associates, Webster, MA
Forensic Mental Health Associates, Albany, NY
Forensic Mental Health Services of Connecticut, Inc, New London, CT
Hancock Adolescent Sex Offender Program, Ellsworth, ME
The Highland Institute for Behavioral Change, Inc, Atlanta, GA
Institute for Sex Therapy, Education, and Research, Traverse City, MI
Institute for the Community as Extended Family, San Jose, CA
Intensive Treatment Program for Sexual Aggressives, Saint Peter, MN
The Jacob Center, Inc, Fort Collins, CO
Juvenile Justice Center, Kennewick, WA
Kevin B McGovern, PhD and Associates, Portland, OR
MEN, Inc, Juneau, AK
Mount Pleasant Correctional Facility, Mount Pleasant, IA
Nassau Coalition on Child Abuse and Neglect, Hempstead, NY
New England Forensic Associates, Arlington, MA
Northern Nevada Child/Adolescent Services (NNCAS), Reno, NV
Northwest Treatment Associates, Seattle, WA
Oak Specialized Counseling Program, Ione, CA
Pacific Center for Sexual Health, Honolulu, HI
Joseph J Peters Institute, Philadelphia, PA
Probation Offenders Program, Freehold, NJ
Project Promoting Alternatives to Violence through Education (PAVE), Inc, Denver, CO
Psychological and Consulting Services, Tucson, AZ
Quakerdale Home, New Providence, IA
Rape Crisis Network, Columbia, SC
Isaac Ray Center, Inc, Chicago, IL
REACH, Davie, FL
Resolutions, Montpelier, VT
RSA, Inc (Redirecting Sexual Aggression), Lakewood, CO
St Mary's Boys Home, Beaverton, OR
San Diego County Child Sexual Abuse Treatment Program, San Diego, CA
Sex Abuse Interventions, Inc, Wailuku, HI
Sex Offender Program, Somers, CT
Sex Offender Treatment and Evaluation Project, Atascadero, CA
Sexology Associates, Inc, Bethesda, MD
Sexual Behavior Clinic, New York, NY
Sexual Offenders Program, Los Lunas, NM
Shenandoah Valley Sex Offender Treatment Program, Harrisonburg, VA
Sixth District Department of Corrections, Sex Offenders Treatment Program, Cedar Rapids, IA
Sixth Judicial District Department of Correctional Services, Iowa City, IA
STOP Sexual Addictions and Disorders Treatment Program, Miami, FL
Texas Department of Human Services, Arlington, TX
The Treatment Place, Fort Worth, TX
Turning Point Family Services Program, Inc, Garden Grove, CA
University of Minnesota Department of Sociology, Roseville, MN
University of New Mexico—Sex Offender Research and Treatment Program, Albuquerque, NM
Valley Human Services, Inc, Ware, MA
Vermont Educational Support Associates, Inc, Rutland, VT
Washington Department of Corrections—Sex Offender Treatment Program, Monroe, WA
Women's Crisis Center of Salinas Valley, Salinas, CA
Youth/Victim Services, Colorado Springs, CO
YWCA Rape Relief Center, Louisville, KY

PARENT SUPPORT PROGRAMS

Anchorage Center for Families, Anchorage, AK
BANANAS, Child Care Resource and Referral and Parent Support, Oakland, CA
Behavioral Health Agency of Central Arizona, Casa Grande, AZ
Center for Child Abuse Prevention Services, Tacoma, WA
Child Abuse Prevention Services, Inc, Shelby, NC
Child Protection Team of Collier County, Naples, FL
Domestic Abuse/Sexual Assault Crisis Center, Fremont, NE
El Centro Human Services Corporation, Los Angeles, CA
Exchange Club Center for the Prevention of Child Abuse of Southern Minnesota, Inc, Owatonna, MN
FACT Hotline—Families and Children in Trouble/Together, Washington, DC
Family and Children's Services, Inc—Psychotherapy and Counseling Division, Albuquerque, NM
Family Service of Detroit and Wayne County, Detroit, MI
A Growing Place, Cincinnati, OH
Howard County Sexual Assault Center, Columbia, MD
Independent Child Abuse Relief Enterprise (I-CARE), Daytona Beach, FL
Rape and Sexual Abuse Center of Ventura County, Camarillo, CA
Rape and Sexual Assault Center, Minneapolis, MN
Safe 'N' Strong, San Mateo, CA
San Fernando Valley Child Guidance Clinic, Van Nuys, CA
The Sexual Abuse and Assault Program, Brant Beach, NJ
Victim/Witness Services for Coconino County, Flagstaff, AZ
Victims Information Bureau of Suffolk, Smithtown, NY

PLAY THERAPY

Chicago Counseling and Psychotherapy Center, Chicago, IL
Dayglo Family Treatment Program, Austin, TX
Echoes Counseling Services, Portland, OR
Gunter and Associates, Houston, TX
Healing Through Play, Lisbon Falls, ME
Park Rapids—Walker Clinic Counseling Department, Park Rapids, MN
St Francis Center for Personal Growth, North Clarendon, VT
Sexual Assault Program of North Saint Louis County, Virginia, MN
Sexual Assault Services, Mankato, MN

University of Minnesota—Sexual Violence Program, Minneapolis, MN

PORNOGRAPHY

Children of the Night, Hollywood, CA
Everywoman's Center Programs Against Violence Against Women, Amherst, MA

PRESCHOOLERS

Anchorage Center for Families, Anchorage, AK
Anne Arundel County Sexual Assault Crisis Center, Annapolis, MD
BANANAS, Child Care Resource and Referral and Parent Support, Oakland, CA
Bethesda Alternative, Inc, Norman, OK
Child Assault Prevention Training Center of Northern California, Oakland, CA
Child Protection Team of Brevard County, Rockledge, FL
The Children's Place, Kansas City, MO
The Children's Place, Aiken, SC
Children's Self-Help Project, San Francisco, CA
Columbia-Greene Rape Crisis Center, Hudson, NY
Community Advocates, Portland, OR
Crime Victim/Sexual Assault Program, Plattsburgh, NY
Dayglo Family Treatment Program, Austin, TX
Early Childhood Development Center, Evanston, IL
East Texas Crisis Center, Tyler, TX
Families First, Aurora, CO
The Family Living Center, Tallahassee, FL
Family Outreach of San Antonio, San Antonio, TX
The Family Place, White River Junction, VT
The Family Place: A Child Abuse Treatment Agency, Louisville, KY
Family Resource Center, Saint Louis, MO
Family Service Association of Waterbury, Waterbury, CT
Family Stress Clinic Ltd, Libertyville, IL
Family Support Center, Aurora, IL
Kids In Distress, Inc, Fort Lauderdale, FL
Mahoning County Prosecutor—Victim/Witness Program, Youngstown, OH
Massachusetts Society for the Prevention of Cruelty to Children, Brockton, MA
Mid-Peninsula YWCA Rape Crisis Center, Palo Alto, CA
Monterey Rape Crisis Center, Monterey, CA
Northern Nevada Child/Adolescent Services (NNCAS), Reno, NV
Orange County Rape Crisis Center, Chapel Hill, NC
The Rainbow Project, Inc, Madison, WI
Rape Victim Advocacy Program, Iowa City, IA
Saginaw County Sexual Assault Center, Saginaw, MI
San Fernando Valley Child Guidance Clinic, Van Nuys, CA
SOAP Box Players, Bellingham, WA
Sonoma County Child Abuse Council, Santa Rosa, CA
Standing Together Against Rape (STAR), Anchorage, AK
Victim Services Program, Chicago, IL
West Valley Child Crisis Center, Inc, Glendale, AZ
Women's Services, Inc, Meadville, PA
York County Child Abuse and Neglect Council, Inc, Biddeford, ME
YWCA Sexual Assault Program, Kalamazoo, MI

PRISONERS

Bedford Hills Correctional Facility—Family Violence Program, Bedford Hills, NY
Ecumenical Women's Center, Chicago, IL
Everywoman's Center Programs Against Violence Against Women, Amherst, MA
HAVEN, Pontiac, MI
Helpmate, Lusk, WY
Joseph J Peters Institute, Philadelphia, PA
Project Woman, Springfield, OH
Sex Offender Treatment and Evaluation Project, Atascadero, CA
Sexual Assault Recovery Thru Awareness and Hope—SARAH, Inc, Derry, NH
Sexual Offenders Program, Los Lunas, NM
The Survivors, Chillicothe, MO
Women's Crisis Center of Salinas Valley, Salinas, CA
Women's Crisis Service, Manchester, NH
Women's Self Help Center, Inc, Saint Louis, MO

PROSTITUTES

Austin Police Department—Victim Services Division, Austin, TX
Children of the Night, Hollywood, CA
Family and Children's Service, Minneapolis, MN
Finex House, Inc, Jamaica Plain, MA
Hospitality House, San Francisco, CA
Prostitutes Union of Massachusetts (PUMA), Cambridge, MA
Seattle Youth and Community Services, Seattle, WA
Thursday's Child—Teen Outreach Program, West Hills, CA

PUBLICATIONS (ADOLESCENT SEXUAL ABUSE PREVENTION)

Bridgework Theater, Inc, Goshen, IN
Santa Barbara Rape Crisis Center, Santa Barbara, CA
Women Organized Against Rape (WOAR), Philadelphia, PA

PUBLICATIONS (ADULT SURVIVORS OF CHILD SEXUAL ABUSE)

Institute for the Community as Extended Family, San Jose, CA
Oak Grove Psychotherapy Associates, Minneapolis, MN
Psychological Associates of Oxon Hill, Oxon Hill, MD
Rape and Sexual Assault Center, Minneapolis, MN
Survivors Healing Center, Santa Cruz, CA

PUBLICATIONS (CHILD ABUSE)

Family Focus, Inc., Denver, CO

PUBLICATIONS (CHILD ABUSE PREVENTION)

BANANAS, Child Care Resource and Referral and Parent Support, Oakland, CA
Child Guidance Clinic of the Family Service Agency, Santa Barbara, CA
FACT Hotline—Families and Children in Trouble/Together, Washington, DC
Sonoma County Child Abuse Council, Santa Rosa, CA

PUBLICATIONS (CHILD SEXUAL ABUSE)

Forensic Mental Health Associates, Webster, MA
Institute for the Community as Extended Family, San Jose, CA
Kevin B McGovern, PhD and Associates, Portland, OR
Middlesex County District Attorney's Office—Victim Witness Service Bureau, Cambridge, MA
Rape and Sexual Assault Center, Minneapolis, MN
Rape Intervention Program/Crime Victim Assessment Project (RIP/CVAP), New York, NY
Rapeline/Sexual Assault Program, Rochester, MN
Sexual Abuse Treatment and Support Program, La Crosse, WI
Umbrella Rape Crisis Team, Saint Johnsbury, VT
Valley East Counseling, Mesa, AZ
Welborn Baptist Hospital—Mulberry Center Sexual Abuse Awareness Program, Evansville, IN

PUBLICATIONS (CHILD SEXUAL ABUSE PREVENTION)

BANANAS, Child Care Resource and Referral and Parent Support, Oakland, CA
Bridgework Theater, Inc, Goshen, IN
Child Assault Prevention Training Center of Northern California, Oakland, CA
Child Guidance Clinic of the Family Service Agency, Santa Barbara, CA
Child/Teen Abuse Prevention Program, Cocoa, FL
Community Advocates, Portland, OR
Crimes Against Women Task Force, Inc—T/A Albemarle Hopeline, Elizabeth City, NC
FACT Hotline—Families and Children in Trouble/Together, Washington, DC
The Family Place, White River Junction, VT
Howard County Sexual Assault Center, Columbia, MD
Illusion Theater's Prevention Programs, Minneapolis, MN
King County Rape Relief, Renton, WA
Kevin B McGovern, PhD and Associates, Portland, OR
Mental Health Association of Greater Tucson, Tucson, AZ
Playing It Safe, New Hyde Park, NY
Rape and Abuse Crisis Center, Fargo, ND
Rape and Sexual Assault Center, Minneapolis, MN
Rape Crisis Center of Berkshire County, Inc, Pittsfield, MA
Rape Crisis Center of West Contra Costa, San Pablo, CA
Sexual Abuse Treatment and Support Program, La Crosse, WI
Sexual Assault Program of Beltrami, Cass, and Hubbard Counties, Bemidji, MN
Southwestern Alaska Council for Prevention of Child Sexual Abuse, Bethel, AK
Women in Crisis—Counseling and Assistance (WICCA), Fairbanks, AK
Women In Safe Homes (WISH), Ketchikan, AK
Women Organized Against Rape (WOAR), Philadelphia, PA
Women's Resource Center, San Luis Rey, CA

PUBLICATIONS (DATE/ACQUAINTANCE RAPE PREVENTION)

Alternatives to Fear, Seattle, WA
Illusion Theater's Prevention Programs, Minneapolis, MN
King County Rape Relief, Renton, WA
Orange County Sexual Assault Network (OCSAN), Orange, CA
Rape Treatment Center, Santa Monica, CA
Tecumseh Area Planned Parenthood Association, Inc, Lafayette, IN
Victims Information Bureau of Suffolk, Smithtown, NY

PUBLICATIONS (DATING VIOLENCE)

Boulder County Safehouse, Boulder, CO

PUBLICATIONS (DISABILITIES)

Finex House, Inc, Jamaica Plain, MA
Howard County Sexual Assault Center, Columbia, MD
Los Angeles Commission on Assaults Against Women, Los Angeles, CA
Rape Crisis Center of West Contra Costa, San Pablo, CA
Seattle Rape Relief, Seattle, WA

PUBLICATIONS (DOMESTIC VIOLENCE)

Boston Women's Health Book Collective, Watertown, MA
Committee to Aid Abused Women, Sparks, NV
Crisis Intervention Service, Mason City, IA
Finex House, Inc, Jamaica Plain, MA
Project for Victims of Family Violence, Fayetteville, AR
Elizabeth Stone House, Jamaica Plain, MA
Transition House, Cambridge, MA
Women's Center and Shelter of Greater Pittsburgh, Pittsburgh, PA

PUBLICATIONS (DOMESTIC VIOLENCE PREVENTION)

Illusion Theater's Prevention Programs, Minneapolis, MN
Women In Safe Homes (WISH), Ketchikan, AK

PUBLICATIONS (ELDER ABUSE)

House of Ruth, Claremont, CA

PUBLICATIONS (ELDERLY)

Alternatives to Fear, Seattle, WA
Women Organized Against Rape (WOAR), Philadelphia, PA

PUBLICATIONS (INCEST SURVIVORS)

Incest Awareness Project, Fargo, ND
Institute for the Community as Extended Family, San Jose, CA
Oak Grove Psychotherapy Associates, Minneapolis, MN
Phenix I, Garden City, NY
Psychological Associates of Oxon Hill, Oxon Hill, MD
Survivors Healing Center, Santa Cruz, CA
The Village Family Service Center, Fargo, ND
Women In Safe Homes (WISH), Ketchikan, AK

PUBLICATIONS (MALE SURVIVORS)

Santa Cruz Men's Alternatives to Violence, Santa Cruz, CA

PUBLICATIONS (OFFENDER TREATMENT)

Blanchard and Associates, Sheridan, WY
Forensic Mental Health Associates, Webster, MA
Institute for the Community as Extended Family, San Jose, CA
Joseph J Peters Institute, Philadelphia, PA

PUBLICATIONS (RAPE PREVENTION)
Community Advocates, Portland, OR
Jackson Rape Crisis Center, Jackson, MS
Lubbock Rape Crisis Center, Inc, Lubbock, TX
Rape Crisis Service of Planned Parenthood—Genesee County, Batavia, NY
Rape Treatment Center, Santa Monica, CA
Sexual Assault Recovery Service, Gainesville, FL
UCSF Rape Prevention Education Program, San Francisco, CA
Women Organized Against Rape (WOAR), Philadelphia, PA

PUBLICATIONS (SELF DEFENSE)
Alternatives to Fear, Seattle, WA
Community Advocates, Portland, OR
Los Angeles Commission on Assaults Against Women, Los Angeles, CA
Women Organized Against Rape (WOAR), Philadelphia, PA

PUBLICATIONS (SEXUAL ASSAULT)
Boston Women's Health Book Collective, Watertown, MA
Centre County Women's Resource Center, State College, PA
Los Angeles Commission on Assaults Against Women, Los Angeles, CA
Lubbock Rape Crisis Center, Inc, Lubbock, TX
Rape and Abuse Crisis Center, Fargo, ND
Rape and Sexual Assault Center, Minneapolis, MN
Rape Intervention Program/Crime Victim Assessment Project (RIP/CVAP), New York, NY
Seattle Institute for Sex Therapy, Education, and Research (SISTER), Seattle, WA
Umbrella Rape Crisis Team, Saint Johnsbury, VT
Valley East Counseling, Mesa, AZ
Women Organized Against Rape (WOAR), Philadelphia, PA

PUBLICATIONS (SEXUAL EXPLOITATION)
Central Minnesota Sexual Assault Center, Saint Cloud, MN
Sexual Violence Center, Minneapolis, MN
Walk-In Counseling Center, Minneapolis, MN

PUBLICATIONS (SPANISH LANGUAGE)
BANANAS, Child Care Resource and Referral and Parent Support, Oakland, CA
Bridgework Theater, Inc, Goshen, IN
Hartford Region YWCA Sexual Assault Crisis Service, Hartford, CT
King County Rape Relief, Renton, WA
New York City Gay and Lesbian Anti-Violence Project, New York, NY
Rape and Abuse Crisis Center, Fargo, ND
San Francisco Women Against Rape, San Francisco, CA
Sonoma County Child Abuse Council, Santa Rosa, CA
Sonoma County Women Against Rape, Santa Rosa, CA
Women Organized Against Rape (WOAR), Philadelphia, PA

PUBLICATIONS (VICTIM ASSISTANCE)
Campbell County Prosecuting Attorney's Office—Victim/Witness Coordinator, Gillette, WY
Crime Victims' Counseling Services, Inc, Brooklyn Heights, NY
District Attorney's Office—Victim/Witness Program, Alfred, ME
Middlesex County District Attorney's Office—Victim Witness Service Bureau, Cambridge, MA
Milwaukee County Children's Court—Victim/Witness Service, Milwaukee, WI
Norfolk Commonwealth's Attorney—Victim/Witness Assistance Program, Norfolk, VA
State Attorney's Office—Victim/Witness Assistance Program, Ocala, FL
Victim/Witness Council, Ogden, UT
Women in Dialogue, Philadelphia, PA

RAPE PREVENTION PROGRAMS
Alternatives to Fear, Seattle, WA
Cabrillo College Rape Prevention Program, Aptos, CA
Center for Women's Services, Plymouth, NH
Centre County Women's Resource Center, State College, PA
Citizens' Advisory Committee on Rape Prevention, Ann Arbor, MI
Community Advocates, Portland, OR
Department of Sociology, Anthropology, and Criminal Justice Administration, Boise, ID
Fairfax County Victim Assistance Network, Alexandria, VA
Jackson Rape Crisis Center, Jackson, MS
Los Angeles Commission on Assaults Against Women, Los Angeles, CA
Men's Caucus, Los Angeles, CA
Northwestern University—Women's Center, Evanston, IL
People Against Sexual Abuse, Inc (PASA), Brooklyn, NY
Polk County Victim Services—Rape Care Program and Intrafamily Sexual Abuse Program, Des Moines, IA
Psychological Services Center, Vermillion, SD
Rape and Sexual Abuse Center of Ventura County, Camarillo, CA
Rape Awareness Program (RAP), Tuscaloosa, AL
Rape Crisis Team of Trumbull County, Inc, Warren, OH
Rape Education and Prevention Program, Columbus, OH
Rape Prevention Education Program, Davis, CA
Rape Prevention Education Program, Riverside, CA
Rape Prevention Education Program, Women's Resource Center, Irvine, CA
Rape Prevention Seminars, Inc, Saint Louis, MO
Rape Treatment Center, Santa Monica, CA
Response Sexual Assault Support Services, Norfolk, VA
Retired Senior Volunteer Program, Las Vegas, NV
Sexual Assault Center, Jacksonville, FL
Sexual Assault Crisis and Safety Education Program, East Lansing, MI
Sexual Assault Recovery Service, Gainesville, FL
UC Santa Cruz Rape Prevention Education Program, Santa Cruz, CA
UCSF Rape Prevention Education Program, San Francisco, CA
University of California at Berkeley—Rape Prevention Education Program, Berkeley, CA
University of Cincinnati—Office of Women's Programs and Services, Cincinnati, OH
University of Illinois at Urbana-Champaign—Office for Women's Resources and Services, Champaign, IL
University of Minnesota—Sexual Violence Program, Minneapolis, MN
Women Against Rape, Columbus, OH
Women Organized Against Rape (WOAR), Philadelphia, PA
Women's Center, Mankato, MN
Women's Center and Police Department's Rape Prevention Education Program, Santa Barbara, CA
Women's Center—University of Idaho, Moscow, ID
Women's Resource Center, Salt Lake City, UT
Women's Resource Center—Rape Prevention Education Program, Sacramento, CA
Women's Studies and Service Center, Billings, MT
Women's Transit Authority, Madison, WI
YWCA of Greater New Haven—Rape Crisis Services, New Haven, CT

RELIGIOUS COMMUNITY
CARE (County Abuse and Rape Emergency) Services, Chehalis, WA
City of Milwaukee—Common Council Task Force on Sexual Assault and Domestic Violence, Milwaukee, WI
Ecumenical Women's Center, Chicago, IL
Jubilee House Community, Statesville, NC
Rape and Sexual Assault Center, Minneapolis, MN
Safe 'N' Strong, San Mateo, CA
Walk-In Counseling Center, Minneapolis, MN

RESEARCH
Crime Victims Research and Treatment Center (CVC), Charleston, SC
Project Against Sexual Abuse of Appalachian Children, Knoxville, TN
Sex Offender Treatment and Evaluation Project, Atascadero, CA
University of Minnesota Department of Sociology, Roseville, MN
University of Minnesota, Family Practice Department—Program in Human Sexuality, Minneapolis, MN
University of New Mexico—Sex Offender Research and Treatment Program, Albuquerque, NM
The Village Family Service Center, Fargo, ND

RESIDENTIAL TREATMENT PROGRAMS
Cathedral Home for Children, Laramie, WY
Clinic for Counseling and Psychotherapy, Inc and Northwest Passage, Inc, Salt Lake City, UT
Intensive Treatment Program for Sexual Aggressives, Saint Peter, MN
Northern Nevada Child/Adolescent Services (NNCAS), Reno, NV
Quakerdale Home, New Providence, IA
St Mary's Boys Home, Beaverton, OR
Springfield Child Abuse Resources, Springfield, OR
Elizabeth Stone House, Jamaica Plain, MA
Walden/Sierra, Inc, California, MD

RITUALISTIC ABUSE VICTIMS/SURVIVORS
Associates in Counseling, Federal Way, WA
Echoes Counseling Services, Portland, OR
Healing Through Play, Lisbon Falls, ME
Park Rapids—Walker Clinic Counseling Department, Park Rapids, MN
Ravenswood Hospital Community Mental Health Center, Chicago, IL
Sexual Assault Services, Brainerd, MN
University of California at Berkeley—Rape Prevention Education Program, Berkeley, CA

SELF DEFENSE TRAINING
Alternatives to Fear, Seattle, WA
Ardsley Karate Club, Ardlsey, PA
Boulder County Rape Crisis Team, Boulder, CO
Cabrillo College Rape Prevention Program, Aptos, CA
Community Advocates, Portland, OR
Community United Against Violence, San Francisco, CA
Compton YWCA Sexual Assault Crisis Program, Compton, CA
Dane County Rape Crisis Center, Madison, WI
DC Self Defense Karate Association and DC Model Mugging, Silver Spring, MD
Ending Violence Effectively, Denver, CO
Feminist Karate Union, Seattle, WA
Feminists in Self-Defense Training (FIST), Olympia, WA
Gay and Lesbian Community Center of Colorado, Inc, Denver, CO
Incest Research and Treatment Institute, Columbus, OH
The Karate School for Women/Karate for Kids, New York, NY
Karate Temple, Columbus, OH
Los Angeles Commission on Assaults Against Women, Los Angeles, CA
Movement Arts, Inc, Lansing, MI
Ohio Women Martial Artists, Columbus, OH
Rape Awareness Program, Fort Wayne, IN
Rape Crisis Team of Trumbull County, Inc, Warren, OH
Rape Education and Prevention Program, Columbus, OH
Rape Prevention Education Program, Women's Resource Center, Irvine, CA
Retired Senior Volunteer Program, Las Vegas, NV
Santa Fe Rape Crisis Center, Inc, Santa Fe, NM
Sexual Assault Crisis Center, Knoxville, TN
Triangle Women's Martial Arts Center, Carrboro, NC
UCSF Rape Prevention Education Program, San Francisco, CA
University of California at Berkeley—Rape Prevention Education Program, Berkeley, CA
Valley Women's Martial Arts, Inc, Easthampton, MA
Women Empowered, Inc, Sarasota, FL
Women Organized Against Rape (WOAR), Philadelphia, PA
The Women's Gym Fitness Center, Chicago, IL
Women's Resource Center, Salt Lake City, UT
YWCA Rape Crisis Service, New Britain, CT

SEXUAL EXPLOITATION BY THERAPISTS, DOCTORS, CLERGY
Central Minnesota Sexual Assault Center, Saint Cloud, MN
City of Milwaukee—Common Council Task Force on Sexual Assault and Domestic Violence, Milwaukee, WI
Creative Counseling Services, West Hartford, CT
Joseph J Peters Institute, Philadelphia, PA
Sexual Violence Center, Minneapolis, MN
University of Minnesota—Sexual Violence Program, Minneapolis, MN
Walk-In Counseling Center, Minneapolis, MN

SEXUAL HARASSMENT

Austin Rape Crisis Center, Austin, TX
Bay Area Sexual Harassment Clinic, San Francisco, CA
Brandeis Rape and Sexual Assault Hotline, Waltham, MA
Cabrillo College Rape Prevention Program, Aptos, CA
Center for Women's Services, Plymouth, NH
Menninger Foundation, Topeka, KS
New Haven Sexual Harassment Support Group, New Haven, CT
Rape Prevention Education Program, Riverside, CA
Sexual Violence Center, Minneapolis, MN
SHARE (Sexual Harassment/Assault Advising, Resources, and Education) Program, Princeton, NJ
UCSF Rape Prevention Education Program, San Francisco, CA
Women's Resource Center, Salt Lake City, UT

SEXUALITY

Driggs and Associates, Minneapolis, MN
Family Guidance Center/Community Mental Health Center, Saint Joseph, MO
Free-To-Grow Counseling Center, Harwood, ND
Intensive Treatment Program for Sexual Aggressives, Saint Peter, MN
Menninger Foundation, Topeka, KS
Psychotherapy Resources of Norfolk (PRN), Norfolk, VA
Rape and Sexual Assault Center, Minneapolis, MN
Seattle Institute for Sex Therapy, Education, and Research (SISTER), Seattle, WA
University of Minnesota, Family Practice Department—Program in Human Sexuality, Minneapolis, MN

SEXUALLY REACTIVE VICTIMS/OFFENDERS

Child and Family Institute, Sacramento, CA
Children's Center for Behavioral Development, Edgemont, IL
Children's Institute International—Family CARE Center, Los Angeles, CA
Foothill Family Service Agency, Pasadena, CA
Los Angeles County Child Sexual Abuse Crisis Center, Torrance, CA
Oak Specialized Counseling Program, Ione, CA
RSA, Inc (Redirecting Sexual Aggression), Lakewood, CO
San Diego County Child Sexual Abuse Treatment Program, San Diego, CA

SPIRITUAL FOCUS

Arts for Living, Minneapolis, MN
Behavioral Health Agency of Central Arizona, Casa Grande, AZ
Bolton Refuge House, Inc, Eau Claire, WI
Center for Living, Phoenix, AZ
The Changing Woman Counseling and Educational Center, Calumet City, IL
Christian Counseling Center, Gadsden, AL
Community Against Rape, Inc, Taos, NM
Creative Counseling Services, West Hartford, CT
Echoes Counseling Services, Portland, OR
Ending Violence Effectively, Denver, CO
The Feminist Therapy Center, Oak Park, MI
Free-To-Grow Counseling Center, Harwood, ND
Helmuth Psychological Associates, Inc, Norton, OH
Incest Awareness Project, Fargo, ND
Los Angeles Women's Therapy Center, Los Angeles, CA
Mid Valley Counseling Center, Salem, OR
MOVE (Men Overcoming Violent Expression), Anchorage, AK
NE-NAIAH-KAHA-KOK, Keshena, WI
Northwest Oklahoma Pastoral Care Association, Inc, Enid, OK
Shalom Christian Counseling Center, Medford, OR
Sharing, Riverdale, NY
Shumard Counseling PC, Livonia, MI
Stress and Trauma Recovery Center, Paige, TX
YWCA, Monroe, LA

THEATER GROUPS

Bridgework Theater, Inc, Goshen, IN
East Los Angeles Rape Hotline, Inc, Los Angeles, CA
Heartsparkle Players, Olympia, WA
Illusion Theater's Prevention Programs, Minneapolis, MN
New York Women Against Rape, New York, NY
Northwestern University—Women's Center, Evanston, IL
Our Town Family Center, Tucson, AZ

Safehome, Inc, Overland Park, KS
SOAP Box Players, Bellingham, WA
Templum House, Cleveland, OH
Transition House, Cambridge, MA
United Action for Youth, Iowa City, IA
YW CARES (Committee Against Rape Emergency/Educational Services), Olympia Fields, IL

THERAPEUTIC CHILD CARE

Anchorage Center for Families, Anchorage, AK
The Children's Place, Kansas City, MO
The Children's Place, Aiken, SC
Dayglo Family Treatment Program, Austin, TX
The Family Place: A Child Abuse Treatment Agency, Louisville, KY
Family Resource Center, Saint Louis, MO
Family Service Association of Waterbury, Waterbury, CT
Kids In Distress, Inc, Fort Lauderdale, FL
La Familia Counseling Service, Hayward, CA
Sonoma County Child Abuse Council, Santa Rosa, CA

TRAINING

Sexual Battery Committee of the Gainesville Commission on the Status of Women, Gainesville, FL
University of Missouri, St Louis—Community Psychological Service, Saint Louis, MO

TRAINING (BATTERERS PROGRAM)

MOVE (Men Overcoming Violent Expression), Anchorage, AK

TRAINING (CHILD SEXUAL ABUSE)

Child Abuse and Neglect Interdisciplinary Training Project, Columbia, SC
Child Abuse Program, Columbus, OH
Child Sexual Abuse Institute of Ohio, Wooster, OH
Children's Hospital—Sexual Abuse Treatment Team, Boston, MA
Children's Institute International—Family CARE Center, Los Angeles, CA
Commonwealth Attorney's Office—Victim/Witness Assistance Program, Newport News, VA
Crime Victims Research and Treatment Center (CVC), Charleston, SC
Eugene Family Institute, Eugene, OR
Family Sexual Abuse Treatment, Inc, Madison, WI
Forensic Mental Health Associates, Webster, MA
Institute for Sex Therapy, Education, and Research, Traverse City, MI
Institute for the Community as Extended Family, San Jose, CA
Legal Aid Services, Inc—Social Services Program, Louisville, KY
Kevin B McGovern, PhD and Associates, Portland, OR
Menninger Foundation, Topeka, KS
MICSAIT Program (Multidisciplinary Institute for Child Sexual Abuse Intervention and Treatment), Fort Worth, TX
Parents United of North Central Iowa, Inc, Mason City, IA
Park Psychological Services/Park Psychosocial Resource Center, Durham, NC
Joseph J Peters Institute, Philadelphia, PA
Project Against Sexual Abuse of Appalachian Children, Knoxville, TN
RTAT, Inc (Restitution Treatment and Training), Ontario, OR
San Diego County Child Sexual Abuse Treatment Program, San Diego, CA
Springfield Child Abuse Resources, Springfield, OR
STOP Sexual Addictions and Disorders Treatment Program, Miami, FL
University of Kentucky Medical Center, Department of Psychiatry, Child Abuse Clinic, Lexington, KY
Victim Treatment Center, New York, NY

TRAINING (CHILD SEXUAL ABUSE PREVENTION)

Child Assault Prevention Training Center of Northern California, Oakland, CA
Massachusetts/CAPP, Boston, MA
Rape and Abuse Crisis Center, Fargo, ND
The Training Institute—Planned Parenthood of Wisconsin, Milwaukee, WI

TRAINING (DOMESTIC VIOLENCE)

Westchester Coalition of Family Violence Agencies, White Plains, NY

TRAINING (ELDER ABUSE)

House of Ruth, Claremont, CA

TRAINING (INCEST SURVIVORS)

Incest Research and Treatment Institute, Columbus, OH
Phenix I, Garden City, NY
Survivors Healing Center, Santa Cruz, CA

TRAINING (OFFENDER TREATMENT)

Child Abuse and Neglect Interdisciplinary Training Project, Columbia, SC
Child Sexual Abuse Institute of Ohio, Wooster, OH
Correctional Specialties, Bellevue, WA
Eugene Family Institute, Eugene, OR
Forensic Mental Health Associates, Webster, MA
Institute for Sex Therapy, Education, and Research, Traverse City, MI
Kevin B McGovern, PhD and Associates, Portland, OR
New England Forensic Associates, Arlington, MA
Joseph J Peters Institute, Philadelphia, PA
Sexology Associates, Inc, Bethesda, MD

TRAINING (RAPE PREVENTION)

Rape Prevention Seminars, Inc, Saint Louis, MO

TRAINING (SEXUAL ASSAULT)

Albany County Rape Crisis Center, Albany, NY
Crime Victims and Rape Counseling, Garden City, NY
Institute for Sex Therapy, Education, and Research, Traverse City, MI
Menninger Foundation, Topeka, KS
Rape Crisis Center of West Contra Costa, San Pablo, CA
STOP Sexual Addictions and Disorders Treatment Program, Miami, FL
University of California Los Angeles—Psychology Clinic, Los Angeles, CA
Victim Treatment Center, New York, NY
The Women's Therapy Center, El Cerrito, CA

TRAINING (SEXUALITY)

University of Minnesota, Family Practice Department—Program in Human Sexuality, Minneapolis, MN

VICTIM ASSISTANCE PROGRAMS

Alameda County District Attorney—Victim Witness Assistance Division, Oakland, CA
Allegheny County Center for Victims of Violent Crime, Pittsburgh, PA
Athens County Prosecutor's Victim Assistance Program, Athens, OH
Campbell County Prosecuting Attorney's Office—Victim/Witness Coordinator, Gillette, WY
Cass County Victim/Witness Assistance Program, Fargo, ND
Child Victim Unit, Bronx, NY
Cook County State's Attorney's Office—Victim/Witness Assistance, Chicago, IL
Crime Victim Center, Reading, PA
Crime Victim Services, Inc, Lima, OH
Crime Victims' Counseling Services, Inc, Brooklyn Heights, NY
Department of Sociology, Anthropology, and Criminal Justice Administration, Boise, ID
District Attorney's Office—Victim/Witness Program, Alfred, ME
Humboldt County District Attorney's Victim-Witness Program, Eureka, CA
Legal Services for Children, Inc, San Francisco, CA
Lincoln Police Department—Victim/Witness Unit, Lincoln, NE
Middlesex County District Attorney's Office—Victim Witness Service Bureau, Cambridge, MA
Milwaukee County Children's Court—Victim/Witness Service, Milwaukee, WI
Norfolk Commonwealth's Attorney—Victim/Witness Assistance Program, Norfolk, VA
Office of Solicitor—Victim Witness Assistance, Orangeburg, SC
Office of the State Attorney—Victim/Witness Assistance Program, Key West, FL
Polk County Victim Services—Rape Care Program and Intrafamily Sexual Abuse Program, Des Moines, IA
San Luis Obispo County Victim/Witness Assistance Center, San Luis Obispo, CA
Santa Clara County Victim Witness Assistance Center, San Jose, CA

Sexual Assault Center, Jacksonville, FL
State Attorney's Office—Victim/Witness Assistance Program, Ocala, FL
Victim Services Agency—Child Victim Unit, Brooklyn, NY
Victim/Witness Council, Ogden, UT
Volunteer Center "Helpline", Syracuse, NY
Witness/Victim Center of Cuyahoga County, Cleveland, OH
Women in Dialogue, Philadelphia, PA
Youth Victim/Witness Program, Houston, TX

WILDERNESS THERAPY

Albuquerque Rape Crisis Center, Albuquerque, NM
Boulder County Rape Crisis Team, Boulder, CO
Colorado Outward Bound School, Denver, CO
Community Against Rape, Inc, Taos, NM
Ending Violence Effectively, Denver, CO
Hays County Women's Center, San Marcos, TX
Meta Resources, Saint Paul, MN
Pueblo YWCA Rape Crisis Center, Pueblo, CO
Santa Fe Mountain Center, Santa Fe, NM
Santa Fe Rape Crisis Center, Inc, Santa Fe, NM
Women in Crisis—Counseling and Assistance (WICCA), Fairbanks, AK
Women's Resource Center of the New River Valley, Radford, VA

WRITING AS HEALING

Associates in Mental Health, Muncie, IN
Buncombe County Rape Crisis Center, Inc, Asheville, NC
CAARE Project, Inc, Fort Bragg, CA
Creative Counseling Services, West Hartford, CT
Echoes Counseling Services, Portland, OR
The Feminist Therapy Center, Oak Park, MI
Hays County Women's Center, San Marcos, TX
Henderson County Rape Crisis Center, Hendersonville, NC
House of Ruth, Claremont, CA
Marshall County Rape Crisis Center, Inc, Marshall, NC
Quakerdale Home, New Providence, IA
Sexual Assault Crisis Center, Knoxville, TN
Sexual Assault Program of Beltrami, Cass, and Hubbard Counties, Bemidji, MN

YOUTH SHELTERS

The Counseling Center of Milwaukee, Inc, Milwaukee, WI
Hospitality House, San Francisco, CA
Runaway and Homeless Youth Program, Valhalla, NY
Webster House, Muskegon, MI
West Valley Child Crisis Center, Inc, Glendale, AZ
Youth In Need, Saint Charles, MO
Youth Services Center, Inc, Merritt Island, FL

LINDA WEBSTER

Linda Webster is an information specialist in the areas of education, library science and the social and health sciences. She has written and lectured extensively on women's issues, librarianship, and continuing education and is the author of *Censorship: A Guide for Successful Workshop Planning*, also published by The Oryx Press.

APR 1 7 1990